FACTS ABOUT

CHINA

Previous H.W. Wilson titles by New England Publishing Associates

Famous First Facts About the Environment
Facts About the World's Languages
Facts About the American Wars
The Wilson Calendar of World History

Other titles by H.W. Wilson

Dictionary of Military Terms, Second Edition
The Wilson Chronology of Human Rights
The International Book of Days
The American Book of Days, Fourth Edition
Famous First Facts, Fifth Edition
Famous First Facts, International Edition
Famous First Facts About Sports
Famous First Facts About American Politics
Facts About the Presidents, Seventh Edition
Facts About American Immigration
Facts About Retiring in the United States
Facts About the 20th Century
Facts About the Congress
Facts About the Supreme Court of the United States
Facts About Canada, Its Provinces and Territories
Facts About the British Prime Ministers
Facts About the Cities, Second Edition
Facts about the World's Nations

FACTS ABOUT

CHINA

Edited by Xiao-bin Ji

Contributors:

Eric Dalle
John C. Didier
Ronald J. Formica
Michael Golay
David A. Graff
Victoria Harlow
Ron Irwin
Edward Knappman
Jing Liao
Patrick P. Lin
Xiaoping Shen
Yiyi Wu
Hong Yang
Xiaohe Zhang

The H.W. Wilson Company
New York ◆ Dublin
2003

Library of Congress Cataloging-in-Publication Data

Facts about China / editor Xiao-bin Ji.
     p. cm.
    Includes bibliographical references and index.
    ISBN 0-8242-0961-3 (alk. paper)
    1. China. I. Ji, Xiao-bin, 1966–

DS706 .F25 2001
951—dc21

2001045510

Copyedited by
    Dorothy Anderson
    Barbara Jean DiMauro
    Kathleen White

Proofread by Marlene London

Printed in the United States of America

The H. W. Wilson Company

950 University Avenue

Bronx, NY 10452

Visit H.W. Wilson's Web site: www.hwwilson.com

Contents

Introduction

With about one-fifth of the world's population living in China, it is almost trite to say that China is an important country for Westerners to understand. Learning about China can be an engaging adventure, but it can also be a frustratingly confusing experience. The purpose of this book is to serve as a reference guide for readers who are just beginning to learn about China. In the specialized chapters and A–Z entries, the authors seek to provide some basic facts that will help readers to orient themselves in their studies. Since the rest of this book covers these facts in detail, this introduction will provide some general pointers to beginners in the study of China.

This introduction is divided into two parts. Part I will discuss several basic ideas about China. Part II will discuss some common difficulties for the beginner in Chinese studies, and will suggest ways to deal with such difficulties. To put it another way, Part I includes a broad interpretation of what one needs to know in order to begin to understand China. Part II presents some technical tips on how to read about China. In the broad interpretation, I have tried to remain as impartial as possible. Nevertheless, anything interpretative is inevitably colored by the author's own understanding of the issues involved. It is my hope that the readers who disagree with my general interpretive ideas will still find the technical tips in Part II of this introduction useful.

PART I. SOME GENERAL IDEAS ABOUT CHINA

Although media reporting of China has become increasingly sophisticated over the last 30 years, one can still be confused by contradictory reports about China. At one moment, an expert will tell us that China is becoming so powerful that it is bound to become the main rival of the United States in the 21st century. At another moment, other experts will argue that China has so many problems that the country might collapse very soon. While these two opinions seem mutually exclusive, there are also experts who have agreed with both opinions. To avoid being confused by such reporting, one needs to look not to the various predictions about the future of China, but to China's past and present. The predictive value of history has been much maligned by some scholars. Still, when the unexpected happens in China, those who have some knowledge of China's culture and history will be in a better position to understand it than those who do not.

In Part I of this introduction, I will present five general ideas about China. They should be useful not only for understanding the past and present of China, but also for understanding China in at least the near future. Of course, with the size and complexity of China, it is impossible for five simple ideas to explain everything about China. Nevertheless, they should be a helpful point of entry for beginners.

1) Historical Consciousness

For at least the last few thousand years, the Chinese people have been looking to their history as a source of wisdom for understanding the present and the future. While China is not the only country that takes its history seriously, history does carry a greater weight in Chinese culture than in some others. While this idea may seem trite—and coming from a historian of Chinese descent, prideful—it is nevertheless useful for students of Chinese culture to bear in mind.

Chinese people tend to have very long historical memories. Politicians, scholars, and common people alike often cite examples from history to justify their ideas. Government reforms in the 11th century continue to inspire reformers of today, while the discussion of China's wars in the 12th century may inform current discussions of patriotism. In the Chinese television industry, it is well known that historical drama remains one of the best selling genres. For example, *A Romance of Three Kingdoms* (based on the great historical novel of the same title) was one of the most successful series on Chinese TV in recent years. The story of this 84-episode series is set in the 3rd century A.D.

This historical consciousness is related to many other aspects of Chinese culture. We will discuss three here. First, many Chinese people have the tendency to look for historical situations that are analogous to the situation they face at the present. Once the analogous, past situations have been found, they then examine how earlier people dealt with such situations. Success in the past situations can be used as inspiration for the present, while past failures can serve as warnings of potential pitfalls.

Second, history is also a source of national, and local, pride. The claim that China is the world's oldest continuously surviving civilization is an important part of patriotic education in China. At the same time, local governments also emphasize the glorious history of their areas as a way to inspire local pride, to win respect from outsiders, and even to attract outside investment.

Third, the painful memory of 19th- and 20th-century history has pushed many generations of Chinese youth towards nationalism. To many Chinese, much of their modern history consists of a long string of humiliating defeats at the hands of foreign powers. From the Opium War (1839–1842) to the devastating Japanese invasion that ended in 1945, China was repeatedly attacked, humiliated, and exploited by stronger foreign powers. To a large, proud, and ancient country like China, this modern experience is particularly difficult to bear. This third point, of course, leads us to the discussion of Chinese nationalism.

2) Nationalism

The importance of history to Chinese culture is related to the modern phenomenon of Chinese nationalism. With the memory of past foreign aggression so vivid in their minds, it is difficult for Chinese nationalists to view the world as a safe place for China. (Here "nationalist" with a small "n" is distinguished from "Nationalists" with a capitalized "N," the latter meaning members of the Guomindang.) Because they remember the humiliation China suffered at the hands of foreign powers, they cannot take respect from the international community as a given. They therefore regard the strengthening of the Chinese state as one of the most important goals of the Chinese nation. There is always an outward-oriented but defensive aspect to Chinese nationalism. Chinese nationalists want to prove their country's ability to withstand foreign pressure as they try to win and keep the respect of the international community.

While nationalism remains a powerful force in modern Chinese society and politics, it is important to remember that as far as the modern Chinese culture is concerned, this nationalism is fundamentally defensive. The phrase "save the nation" is often on the lips of Chinese patriots, whereas the idea that "China conquers all" is so outlandish as to be laughable. In other words, Chinese nationalism is about saving the nation from the crisis and insecurity of the modern era, rather than about China subduing others.

Some readers may object to this characterization of Chinese nationalism by pointing to Chinese "occupation" of Tibet and China's "aggressive" posture towards Taiwan. Still, whatever one's opinion regarding such political issues, the fact is that the Chinese government gains popular support for its policies towards Tibet and Taiwan by presenting such policies as defensive. All Chinese citizens have been taught since elementary school that Tibet and Taiwan have been integral parts of China "throughout history." Thus in the eyes of the Chinese citizenry, the Chinese government is trying to defend China's territorial integrity.

3) Environmental Limitations

Because China is so large, it is difficult to think of it as resource poor. Indeed, Chinese school children are often taught to take pride in China's large land mass and abundant resources. Still, we can talk about abundance only in absolute terms. As soon as we begin to calculate China's resources on a per capita basis, we recognize the severe limits nature has placed on the economic development of China.

From my experience teaching, I find that students often have the feeling that China is many times larger than the United States. Actually, in land mass China is about the same size as the United States. China is several times larger than the United States only in population. According to the official estimate of the Chinese government, China has over 1.3 billion people. Some scholars claim that China's population is actually much larger than that, although such private estimates are not fully substantiated. In the chapter on geography, the reader will learn about the environmental challenges faced by China. But to start, the reader might imagine what the United States would be like if it had 1.3 billion, rather than less than 300 million, residents.

4) China's Status as a Developing Country

With frequent news reports on the fantastic rate of economic growth in China during recent years, it is easy for people to develop an impression that China is a wealthy place. Indeed, if one were to go to the metropolitan centers of Shanghai and Beijing, one could easily forget that one was in the middle of a developing country. Although China's economy is growing at a much faster pace than the U.S. economy, the overall size of the Chinese economy is still much smaller. The average Chinese is considerably poorer than the average American.

During recent years, the exaggeration of China's prosperity has been pushed forth by two opposing forces in the United States. First, media experts and members of the business community who are very interested in promoting trade with China emphasize China's astounding growth rate. Second, members of the media who seem intent on making China into the next great enemy of the United States emphasize China's strength. Unfortunately, perhaps because of China's eagerness to be taken seriously by the outside world, there has not been a strong Chinese effort to correct this exaggerated estimate of China's wealth. Indeed, some Chinese nationalists enjoy hearing foreign journalists talk about how strong China has become.

If one examined the arguments "proving" China's great strength, one would find that both sides often base their arguments on the unspoken assumption that the majority of the Chinese people are very poor. Some promoters of trade with China often talk about China's advantage in "low labor costs." Although low labor costs indeed constitute a kind of advantage in international trade, one must remember that from the worker's perspective "labor cost" is just another way to say "pay and benefits." In other words, the business advantage of low labor cost implies the disadvantage of very poorly paid consumers. Indeed, according to the chapter in this book on the Chinese economy, the annual income of the average Chinese city dweller was merely 5,425 yuan in 1998. In rural areas, where the vast majority of the Chinese people live, the per capita annual income was only 2,162 yuan. Given the standard exchange rate of roughly 8.3 yuan to the dollar, the average Chinese city dweller made only a bit over $653 in the whole year of 1998.

The promoters of the "China threat" theory often emphasize the lower prices in China. They say that with the same amount of money, one can buy far more goods and labor in China than in a country with a higher per capita income, such as the United States. While it is true that the cost of living is much lower in China than in the U.S., this is the case partly because what is considered a normal standard of living is much lower in China than in the United States. Although food and clothing are much cheaper in China than in the West, complicated industrial products and high tech items are not necessarily less expensive. Certainly, the average Chinese soldier is paid much less than his American counterpart, but the same Chinese soldier is also much more poorly equipped and fed.

5) Understanding the Different Meanings of Words and the Importance of Human Relationships

Although Confucius emphasized the importance of making names and realities match each other, a Western visitor may often find that names and realities often do not match in

China. Or to put it another way: The names and realities might actually match perfectly from certain local Chinese points of view, but because Western visitors define these names differently, they might not perceive this congruence. One must learn to deal with this phenomenon in order not to be misled by mismatched expectations of what certain terms mean.

For example, the Chinese government makes much of the idea of building "socialism with Chinese characteristics." Many Americans believe that socialism means everybody has lifetime job security and nationalized health care. But of course in today's China, most people enjoy neither of these. So to understand what is really happening in China, one must be willing to put aside one's own definition of certain terms, and ask what these terms mean to the Chinese. To take one step further, the same term might mean different things to different Chinese. While this process of understanding may seem very complicated, it is really not very different from the process of realizing that in the United States, the Republican Party and the Green Party understand the concept "patriotism" quite differently.

Another source of misunderstanding may come from what one may expect from looking at a person's job title. For example, Deng Xiaoping was the paramount leader of China from 1978 to his death in 1997. However, he never held the highest offices in the Chinese government and the Chinese Communist Party. In other words, he never held positions such as premier, president, chairman of the Communist Party, or general secretary of the Communist Party. The true source of his power came from the personal loyalty and respect he commanded from key military officers, civil officials, and party leaders. Thus, to understand how Chinese institutions function, one must go beyond the formal institutional structure and examine the actual human relationships.

PART II. SOME COMMON DIFFICULTIES

There are two main difficulties in learning about China: the thorny issue of Chinese names, and the issue of incomplete information.

1) Names and Romanization

Difficulties with Chinese names are often the first obstacles Americans encounter when they study China. Besides the difficulty with Chinese sounds, the beginning American student might also experience frustration with the following issues: First, Chinese names do not follow the Western pattern of first name + middle name + surname. Second, the same Chinese names can be spelled differently in different texts. In this book, we have tried to make the use of names as simple and consistent as possible. Nevertheless, since this book should serve as a launching pad for further exploration in Chinese studies, this section offers some tips on how to deal with these issues.

a) Naming Patterns and Alternative Names

The Difficulties: In general,

Chinese people say and write their names with the family name first. In other words, Mao Zedong's family name is "Mao." "Zedong" is his given name. Similarly, Wang Meng's family name is Wang. Journalists usually respect this naming pattern when they write about Chinese people. Thus President Jiang Zemin, whose family name is "Jiang," is generally referred to in the American news as "Jiang Zemin" rather than "Zemin Jiang."

In spite of the increased sophistication of Western reporters assigned to China during recent years, occasionally a few American newscasters still make the mistake of referring to "Jiang Zemin" as "President Zemin." Now that Mr. Hu Jintao has become the general secretary of the Chinese Communist Party, the reader may also begin to hear about "Mr.

Jintao." Calling Hu Jintao "Mr. Jintao," or calling Jiang Zemin "President Zemin," is as wrong as calling President George W. Bush "President George."

To complicate the matter, the "family names come first" rule usually does not apply to ethnic Chinese who live in the West. When people of Chinese descent live in the West, they often reverse their names to follow Western practice. For example, Dr. Jing Liao, the author of the chapter on the arts, has "Liao" as her family name. In China, people would call her "Liao Jing." Similarly, "Ji" is my family name, while "Xiao-bin" is my given name. In China, I would be called "Ji Xiao-bin." But in the U.S., I identify myself as "Xiao-bin Ji."

In this book, we arrange the names as the owners of these names would. In other words, for Chinese people living in China, we place their family names first. For Chinese citizens living permanently in the West, and for American citizens and citizens of other Western countries whose ethnic origin is Chinese, we place their family names last. Since this is a book about China, almost all the Chinese names in the main text belong to Chinese people who spent their lives in China. In the few cases where we mention people of Chinese descent living in the West, their status as such will be clear from the context.

With Chinese people living before the last decades of the 20th century, their names often have further levels of complexity. First, one person could have several names. For example, one famous 11th-century poet has the formal name "Su Shi," the courtesy name "Su Zizhan," and the sobriquet "Su Dongpo." When this poet was alive, "Su Shi" would be the name on his official records, "Zizhan" would be the name his friends called him, and "Dongpo" would be the name he sometimes signed on his literary compositions and art works.

To make things even more complicated, some pre-modern people actually changed their names several times during the course of their lives. The purpose of such name changes could be practical or symbolic. A person might decide to change his outlook on life, and pick a new name that was more closely identified with this new outlook. For example, a scholar who wanted to create a new identity for himself as a strategic thinker might rename himself after a great strategist in early Chinese history. Alternatively, one might change one's name because the old given name is the same as the given name of the newly enthroned emperor. Since the emperor's given name was taboo, a subject was not allowed to share his given name. At other times, a man might change his name because he did not like what the government records said about him. So by adopting a new name, he could have a chance to disassociate himself from his old paper trail.

Second, there is the phenomenon of "posthumous titles" and "reign titles." In the age of imperial dynasties, when an important person died, most likely the government would give him or her a posthumous title, which in theory was designed to be a concise description of the essential qualities of that person. Sometimes individuals would be known to history by their posthumous titles rather than by their real names. This is especially the case with emperors. For example, most historians would call the founding emperor of the Song dynasty (960–1279) "Song Taizu" or "Emperor Taizu of Song." (The Ming dynasty has its own "Taizu," so in most cases it is important to specify the dynasty unless the context already makes this clear.) Actually, "Taizu" just means "grand progenitor" and is the abbreviated posthumous title of this emperor. His full posthumous title is "Taizu qi yun li ji yingwu ruiwen shende shenggong zhiming daxiao huangdi." A rough translation of this title would be "grand progenitor, the emperor who opened up the fortune [of the dynasty] and established the utmost [i.e. reached the highest achievement humanly possible], and was heroically martial, perspicaciously cultured, divinely virtuous, sagely accomplished, perceptive to the extreme, and greatly filial." Thankfully, this full posthumous title is almost never used in texts written in English. The emperor's personal name is "Zhao Kuangyin."

Why don't historians just call Song Taizu "Zhao Kuangyin"? The reason is that in pre-modern China, it was considered extremely disrespectful to speak—or even write—the given name of the reigning emperor or the given names of all previous emperors of the dynasty under which one lived. Obviously, the family name is not taboo—only the given name. In other words, during the Song dynasty, "Kuangyin" was taboo, but "Zhao" was not. Thus, no writer during the Song dynasty would dare to refer to Song Taizu as "Zhao

Kuangyin." By the time the Song dynasty had been replaced by the next dynasty, "Zhao Kuangyin" had so fallen out of use that it had become much less recognizable to readers than "Taizu." This is why posthumous titles of emperors are so widely used in history books.

In addition to "posthumous titles," emperors of China are sometimes also identified by their "reign titles." By convention, each time a new emperor is enthroned, he would consider the first new year of his reign as "year one." How would one then tell the "first year" of one reign from the "first year" from another reign? To solve this problem, we need to refer to "reign titles," which are names the rulers gave to the periods of their rule.

Unfortunately, some emperors liked to signal "renewal" by restarting the counting of years several times. For example, when the Emperor Taizu of Song first became emperor in 960, he named his reign "Jianlong." About three years later, he decided to start over again, so 963 became the first year of the "Qiande" reign. Then about five years after that, he again decided to start over, so 968 became the first year of the "Kaibao" reign.

In cases such as Taizu of Song, historians generally do not refer to him by his reign title, because he has too many reign titles. However, in the Ming (1368–1644) and Qing (1644–1911) dynasties, almost all of the rulers had only one reign title each. As a result, sometimes historians identify the emperors by their reign titles. For example, the founding emperor of the Ming dynasty is sometimes called Emperor Taizu ("Grand Progenitor") of Ming, but sometimes also called Emperor Hongwu (Hongwu being his reign title).

Third, in high antiquity, people's names did not always follow the "family name plus given name" model. For example, the legendary doctor Bianque (5th century B.C.) is simply called Bianque.

Fourth, the names of Buddhist monks and nuns also do not follow the "family name plus given name" model. When a man becomes a monk or a woman becomes a nun, s/he simply drops his/her secular family name and given name, and adopts a completely different religious name, which usually does not include a family name. However, in some cases a monk might identify his family name as "Shi," which is the first syllable of "Shijiamouni," the Chinese transliteration of Sakyamuni, one of the names of the Buddha. (There are at least two secular family names that are spelled as "Shi" in Pinyin. They are written differently in Chinese characters, though.)

Some Solutions: In this book, we have minimized the use of multiple names. People are generally referred to by their personal names, except in the case of emperors, who are usually referred to by their most commonly used posthumous titles or reign titles. In cases where two different names of the same person are both frequently used in English language books, we have placed the alternative name (courtesy name or sobriquet) in parentheses after the formal name.

How is one to deal with all these complexities of names when reading other books on China? Perhaps the most important strategy is to be on the lookout for these complexities. If one reads about a "Su Dongpo" who sounds very much like a certain "Su Shi" one has encountered elsewhere, then it's wise to check to see whether these are in fact different names of the same man.

b) Differences in Romanization

The Difficulties: Before the 1970s, the vast majority of English language books about China used the "Wade-Giles" romanization system to spell out Chinese names in Latin alphabet. Since the 1970s, scholars and the news media have gradually switched to Pinyin, the official romanization system promoted by the Chinese government. Meanwhile, there are scholars who have continued to use the Wade-Giles system. Because of the coexistence of two popular ways to spell Chinese names, students of Chinese studies are forced to deal with alternative spellings of the same Chinese names. For example, Chairman Mao's name is spelled as "Mao Tse-tung" in Wade-Giles and "Mao Zedong" in Pinyin. The name of the paramount leader of the Chinese government from 1978 to 1997 would be "Teng Hsiao-p'ing" in Wade-Giles and "Deng Xiaoping" in Pinyin. Actually, Wade-Giles and Pinyin are not the only systems for spelling out Chinese names in Latin alphabet. Fortunately, the other systems are so rarely used that even advanced students of Chinese studies are often unfamiliar with them.

A further complication arises when we consider that even in the age when Wade-Giles was dominant, scholars did not always use Wade-Giles consistently. In fact, by scholarly convention, when one uses Wade-Giles to spell out Chinese personal names in a text, one must use the 19th-century English postal spelling for well-known Chinese place names. For example, "Peking" is the old "postal" spelling for "Beijing." The Wade-Giles spelling of "Beijing" would be "Pei-ching," but scholarly convention demands "Peking" when one adopts Wade-Giles spelling for all personal names.

Even with personal names, texts using Wade-Giles are not always consistent in the use of Wade-Giles spelling rules. For example, the name "Chiang Kai-shek" is neither Pinyin nor Wade-Giles, but a spelling based on the pronunciation of Mr. Chiang's name in his regional dialect. The spelling "Chiang Kai-shek" has become so conventional that it is usually adopted even in texts that otherwise use Pinyin for all Chinese names, although recently the standard Pinyin spelling "Jiang Jieshi" has also begun to appear in some scholarly works.

Some Solutions: Because Pinyin is becoming increasingly dominant in English language publications, we have decided to use Pinyin in this book. In cases where alternative spellings are so commonly used that they are impossible to ignore, we have included the alternative spelling in parentheses. In very rare cases where the non-standard spelling is the most commonly used (as in the case of "Chiang Kai-shek"), we have used the non-standard spelling as the main spelling, and included the Pinyin spelling (preceded by a "p.") in parentheses.

For the convenience of readers who might read books that use Wade-Giles, we are also enclosing a conversion table between Pinyin and Wade-Giles.

How is one to determine whether a book uses Pinyin or Wade-Giles? Here is a method for readers who do not know Chinese: Look at the patterns of the spelling. If many (but not necessarily all) of the Chinese names include apostrophes (e.g. Ch'eng I), then most likely the text uses Wade-Giles. On the other hand, if the Chinese names often include "x," "z," "zh," and "j," and almost never include apostrophes, then Pinyin is the sure bet. (A note of caution: Only a few apostrophes here and there would not be sufficient to identify the romanization system of a text as Wade-Giles. Sometimes a scholar using Pinyin would insert an apostrophe between two syllables to indicate where one syllable ends and another begins. However, they would insert the apostrophe only in cases where it is absolutely necessary to avoid confusion. One example would be "Yan'an.")

Some teachers might also suggest looking for hyphens as a defining feature of Wade-Giles. The reason is as follows. According to the Chinese government's current standard for Pinyin spelling, no hyphens are allowed in personal names (e.g. "Mao Zedong" rather than "Mao Ze-dong"). With Wade-Giles, when a given name contains two syllables, these syllables are invariably linked with a hyphen (e.g. "Mao Tse-tung" rather than "Mao Tsetung"). In actual usage, however, this method is not always helpful. The no-hyphen rule for Pinyin is often ignored in practice, sometimes even by branches of the Chinese government itself. Many individuals with two-syllable first names also feel the need to separate the two syllables with a hyphen. For example, when I first arrived in the United States as a teenager in the 1980s, I spelled my first name with a hyphen. It was not until the 1990s that I realized that the "official" Pinyin rules prohibited hyphens. But of course, by then all my academic records had listed my name as "Xiao-bin Ji." Given the importance of the paper trail for an academic, I can no longer afford to change the spelling of my name in a professional context.

One More Note of Caution: While Western scholarly publications and prestigious news organizations in the West are usually quite consistent in their use of Pinyin and Wade-Giles, this is not always the case with some commercially published texts or, for that matter, texts published in Asia. Some novelists and authors of martial arts manuals have chosen to spell Chinese names the way they have liked, with the result that they often end up with spellings that are consistent with neither Pinyin nor Wade-Giles.

Moreover, some institutions and even local governments in China have also chosen to continue to spell their names in ways that are not consistent with Pinyin rules. For example, while the city government of Beijing has changed the transliteration of the city's name from the old "postal" spelling of "Peking" to the standard Pinyin spelling of "Beijing," the venerable Peking University continues to identify itself as "Peking University." On the other hand, some authors, who are either unsympathetic to or unaware of the university's attachment to the old spelling, have chosen to identify this university as "Beijing University" in their articles in English. As a result, the American reader is burdened with the need to remember that "Peking University" and "Beijing University" are in fact the same institution.

Some people with Chinese names have also chosen to spell their own names in non-standard ways. Because of the weight of established usage, these non-standard spellings have become the most widely used version. Sometimes founders of organizations might also spell out the names of their organizations in a non-standard way. For example, the Tzu Chi Foundation is one of the largest charitable foundations in the Chinese-speaking world. Although "Tzu Chi" is neither standard Wade-Giles nor standard Pinyin, this is the spelling used on the foundation's own Web sites. Some scholars, however, have insisted on applying the standard Pinyin spelling to the foundation's Chinese name. As a result, I have seen at least one scholarly article on the "Ciji" Foundation.

In cases such as these, there is no pre-designed conversion table to cover all possibilities. One can only be thankful that nowadays, the major newspapers and magazines are usually consistent about using Pinyin.

2) Dealing with Dates and Uncertainties

If one studies history long enough, sooner or later one must deal with the fact that not all details can be known for certain. Although China has had a long history of careful recordkeeping, there are still facts and dates that we cannot know for sure. Readers need to keep this in mind so that they will not be confused by discrepancies between different texts and claims. Moreover, true understanding can be reached only if one acknowledges the limitation of what one can know. This section will bring the reader's attention to a few key areas of uncertainty.

Separating Legend from History

In the popular press, legends are sometimes presented as historical facts. However, legends do not become history just because some writers sound very sure of their historical knowledge. For example, some texts claim that the Chinese calendar began in 2600 B.C. under the Yellow Emperor ("Huang Di" or "Huangdi" in Chinese). There is nothing wrong with this claim as long as one realizes that it is only a legend. From the historical point of view, we have no solid evidence proving the existence of the Yellow Emperor. Moreover, even if he did exist, we would not be able to date his reign so precisely.

The Issue of Dates

If readers compared this book with other books on China, they might find different books might disagree over the dates of some early dynasties and even of some individuals. This does not necessarily mean that one or more of these books is "wrong." Rather, it often means that scholars cannot be 100% sure.

Among Chinese historians, it is generally accepted that years given as major events became accurate after 841 B.C. (although there are exceptions even after that). This means historians often cannot be certain about the dates of major events that happened before 841 B.C. Even the date of the founding of the Zhou dynasty is not completely certain. In our book, we use the date 1045 B.C. But this is only the best estimate as understood by those among our authors who are specialists in pre-modern Chinese history. Not all scholars agree this estimate is the best. In essence, dates of events that happened before 841 B.C.

tend to be working hypotheses constructed from imperfect information. And there is not always a scholarly consensus on what these working hypotheses should be.

Information on Individuals and Events

In this book, the authors have tried to provide accurate dates of individuals mentioned whenever possible. However, there are some rare cases where this is not possible. Sometimes, we can ascertain the death date but not the birth date. Sometimes history only records the events certain individuals participated in, but leaves no trace of where these individuals came from before or where they went after. Because of the necessarily incomplete nature of historical records, we must learn to live with uncertainty, even though we have tried our best to discover the vital facts and record them with precision.

To indicate the uncertain and/or imprecise information available, the authors have used a number of devices. For events that occurred more than several thousand years ago, we have sometimes opted to use B.P. ("before the present"), rather than B.C.; this indicates that we can only be sure that the event happened so many thousands of years ago, and we cannot provide the actual date with any precision. In other cases, we have used "c." (short for "circa") to indicate that the dates we provide are only very rough estimates.

Matters of Convention

The reader should also keep in mind that even when we have precise information on certain events, people, and institutions, there might still be different conventions regarding how to present this information. In such cases, the use of different dates does not necessarily represent serious disagreements over the interpretations of particular events.

For example, the dates of most of the major events surrounding the fall of the Qing dynasty are quite clear. However, there is still more than one way to date the Qing dynasty. Some scholars would write 1644–1912, while others would prefer 1644–1911.

The ending date of 1912 is valid for a simple reason: The last Qing emperor did not formally abdicate until February 12, 1912. However, the date of 1911 is also valid, because the revolution in 1911 effectively ended the imperial rule of the Qing court. Moreover, 1912 is the first year of the Republic of China, so it is only reasonable to list 1911 as the last year of the last imperial dynasty of China. In addition, at the time of the revolution, the Qing government still used the traditional Chinese calendar. By traditional Chinese calendar, February 12, 1912, is actually the 25th day of the 12th month of the third year of the Emperor Xuantong's (a.k.a. "Henry" Puyi) reign, otherwise known as the year 1911. Since 1911 and 1912 are both valid in their own ways, we have no choice but to put up with the simultaneous use of both dates to represent the end of the Qing dynasty.

Concluding Advice to the Beginning Student

Learning about China can be confusing, but it can also be great fun. As one of my favorite teachers says, sorting out contradictory information in history can be as interesting as reading a detective novel. The greater the challenge, the greater the pleasure of discovery at the end. In learning about China, as in learning about anything else, patience and wise effort can bring great rewards. Enjoy!

Xiao-bin Ji
June 2003

Part I

Geography and Climate

By Xiaoping Shen

INTRODUCTION

China is the most populated country in the world. More than 1 billion Chinese people live on a vast land—the third largest in the world after Russia and Canada. From Mount Everest (the world's tallest mountain) to Turfan (the lowest land in the world at 154 meters [505 feet] below sea level) and from the cool-temperate climate in the north to the tropical climate in the south, China includes an extraordinary variety of physical environments. As one of the world's oldest continuous civilizations, the Chinese people have created unique cultural landscapes on this great landmass. This section will introduce both the physical and cultural aspects of the geography of China.

1. LOCATION AND TERRITORY

Geography

China is an east Asian country located in the southeastern portion of the Eurasian landmass and on the western shore of the Pacific Ocean. The territory lies between latitudes 3°50'N to 53°31'N and longitudes 73°E to 135°5'E. It covers about 50 degrees of latitude and 60 degrees of longitude. China is about 5,200 kilometers (3,232 miles) from west to east, and about 5,500 kilometers (3,418 miles) from north to south.

China and the United States are both mid-latitude countries in the Northern Hemisphere. With a very similar longitudinal extent between China and the 48 contiguous U.S. states, China is considerably wider from north to south. The northernmost point of China is located in the middle of the Heilong Jiang River, which is the same latitude as Edmonton in Alberta, Canada. The southernmost point of China is in the Nansha Islands on the same latitude as Cali in Colombia. Comparing the latitudes, Miami—which is almost the southern limit in Florida—is only halfway between Shanghai and Hong Kong.

Area: China covers a land area about 9.6 million square kilometers (3.7 million square miles), including the mainland and islands. The territory of China includes Taiwan, although it is currently administered by governments other than that of the People's Republic of China.

The area of China is exceeded only by those of Russia and Canada. It is slightly larger than the area of the United States (9.4 million square kilometers, or 3.6 million square miles) and is similar to the area of all of Europe. China occupies about one-fifteenth of the total land surface on the earth and one-quarter of the area of Asia.

Seas and Islands: China has four neighboring seas on the east and southeast of the land area. From north to south, they are Bo Hai, Huang Hai (Yellow Sea), Dong Hai (East China Sea), and Nan Hai (South China Sea).

Besides the mainland territories, there are more than 5,000 islands scattered along the east and southeast coast. The largest island is Taiwan and the second largest is Hainan Island.

Time Zones: China's vast land crosses four time zones, similar to the 48 continuous states of the United States. But the difference between the two countries is that the United States uses four times in four time zones, China uses only one time, Beijing time, for the entire country. Since Beijing is located in east China, people in western China are inconvenienced by this. People in west get up "late" and go to work "late"; eight o'clock in the morning Beijing time is only five o'clock local time in the west. If Chinese people were more equally distributed over the territory, as in the United States, using one time for the entire country would be even more awkward.

Beijing time is ahead of U.S. time between 16 hours (Pacific time) to 13 hours (Eastern time). When it is daytime in the United States, it is nighttime in China. China does not have daylight savings time in the summer. Therefore, the time difference decreases one hour during daylight savings time in the United States. When people in the United States make phone calls to China, they must calculate the time difference.

Hong Kong

Hong Kong is a special administrative region under the central government of the People's Republic of China. Hong Kong is a port city located on China's southeast coast near Guangzhou city. The area of the Hong Kong administrative region is 1,072 square kilometers (414 square miles). That includes Hong Kong Island, Kowloon peninsula, nearby islands, and the New Territories north to Kowloon. Hong Kong's population was 6.67 million in 2000.

Hong Kong was a British crown colony for 155 years between 1842 and 1997. According to the Sino-British Joint Declaration signed in 1984, China resumed sovereignty over Hong Kong at midnight on June 30, 1997. The central government of China handles defense and foreign affairs, and the Hong Kong government is responsible for other governmental functions. The Chinese government has promised that Hong Kong will keep its own currency, (the Hong Kong dollar) and its capitalist market system for fifty years after its return to China.

Macao

Since the 16th century, Macao has been a Portuguese overseas territory in South China. Macao is in the delta of the Zhu Jiang River (Pearl River) and includes two small islands. The area of Macao is 17 square kilometers (6.6 square miles), comprising the Macao Peninsula and the islands of Taipa and Colôane. The population of Macao was 438,000 in 2000.

According to the Joint Declaration on the Question of Macao by the Governments of the People's Republic of China and the Republic of Portugal signed in 1987, China resumed sovereignty over Macao on December 20, 1999.

Taiwan

Taiwan is a part of China and is currently administered by the Guomindang (Nationalist Party) government. Taiwan is located to the southeast of the Chinese mainland, opposite Fujian Province and is separated from the southeast coast of China by the Taiwan Straits. To the east of Taiwan is the Pacific Ocean. Taiwan Province consists of Taiwan Island, the P'enghu (Penghu) Islands, and 80 other smaller neighboring islands and islets. The total area covers 36,000 square kilometers (13,900 square miles). Taiwan had a population of 22.28 million in 2000.

Taiwan was occupied by Japan from 1895 to 1945, and was returned to China at the end of World War II. When the Chinese Communist Party won the civil war and founded the People's Republic of China, the Guomindang authorities retreated from the mainland to Taiwan in 1949. To this day, the Guomindang government continues to refer to itself as the government of the Republic of China. The delegate from Taiwan held the seat of China in the United Nations until 1971, when the United Nations recognized that the government of the People's Republic of China was the sole legal government of China. The seat of China in the United Nations is now held by the delegate from the People's Republic of China. Working channels for nongovernmental contacts have been established across the Taiwan straits since 1992.

Chinese Place Names

Frequently Used Characters

English	Pinyin	Example
north	bei	Hebei: north of a river (*he* means river); it is a province located north of Huang He River.
south	nan	Henan: south of a river; it is a province located south of Huang He River.
east	dong	Dongbei: Northeast region.
west	xi	Shanxi: west of a mountain; it is a province located west of Taihang Shan mountain.
mountain	shan	Huang Shan: a scenic mountain in Anhui Province.
mountain	ling	Qin Ling: a mountain in Shaanxi Province.
river	he	Huang He: the second longest river in China.
river	jiang	Chang Jiang (Yangtze River): the longest and largest river in China.
river	shui	Han Shui: a river in Hubei Province.
lake	hu	Qinghai Hu: the largest lake in China.
sea	hai	Hainan: the second largest island south of the mainland.

4. LANDFORM

Geological Evolution

China lies east of the Eurasian Plate that adjoins the Indo-Australian Plate in the south and the Pacific and Philippine Plates in the east. About 1 billion years ago, the land was being formed in northern, northeastern and northwestern China. Besides those areas, much of today's China was covered by the sea. Since then, several major tectonic movements formed and reformed this vast land.

The Yan Shan Tectonic Movement:
The Yan Shan tectonic movement occurred between 100 and 150 million years ago. The name came from the uplift of Yan Shan Mountains in Beijing and Hebei Province. During this movement, most of central and southern China uplifted and became land area. Those land areas joined northern, northeastern, and northwestern land areas, and unified the present territory of China into a continuous landmass except for the Himalayas, Taiwan, and Tarim Basin.

The Yan Shan movement had great impact on the Chinese physical environment. It determined the broad geological structures and macro-geomorphological features of China. Most major mountain ranges and plateaus were formed during the movement.

The Himalayan Tectonic Movement:
The Himalayan tectonic movement started about 25 million years ago, and is still going on today. The most significant change that this movement has brought is the uplift of the Himalayan Mountains and the Qinghai-Tibet Plateau from the sea-floor to the highest mountains and plateau

in the world. Even today, the Himalayan Mountains are still growing at the speed of about 1 centimeter per year. Taiwan Island and the folding belts were also created during this movement.

The Himalayan movement was caused by collision between the Indo-Australian Plate and the Eurasian Plate. During its long geological history of more than 200 million years, the Indo-Australian Plate has moved northward and collided with the Eurasian Plate at today's Himalayas. The collision between plates is called subduction. Subduction describes when tectonic plates collide, the heavier oceanic crust is forced beneath the lighter continental material. The plates are destroyed at subduction zones, where the plates are consumed downward, back into the earth's mantle, forming deep ocean trenches. It is similar to when two cars collide: their front ends smash, and one is forced up on the other.

The continuous pushing force from the Indo-Australian Plate meets a firm resistance from the Eurasian Plate. The forces break the colliding edges of both plates and push the area upward. That movement has been the dominant force in shaping the modern Chinese physical landform and climate. It first created the highest plateau in the world, and changed China's landform to three topographic land steps. Second, the plateau blocked the moist ocean air of the Indian Ocean from reaching the central Eurasian continent, creating today's huge deserts and dry areas north of the Himalayas. Third, the plateau also blocked east and west wind movement, then reinforced monsoon climate in southeastern China.

Topographic Steps

China's topography is characterized by high to low elevation from west to east. From east to west, the elevation gets higher step by step, just like stairs. From west to east, or from the top of the stairs looking down, there are three inland topographic steps and one continental shelf step at 4,000; 1,500; 200; and –200 meters (13,120; 4,920; 656; and –656 feet) respectively.

The First Inland Step—Qinghai-Tibet Plateau: This plateau, known as the "roof of the world," is completely above 3,000 meters (9,842 feet) elevation, and most of the area is between 4,000 and 5,000 meters (13,123 and 16,404 feet)—double the height of the Colorado Plateau, at 1,300 to 2,200 meters (4,000 to 7,000 feet). The area of the plateau covers about 2.5 million square kilometers (965,000 square miles). This is about 25 percent of China's land area and is equivalent to the area of Arizona, California, Colorado, Nevada, New Mexico, Texas, and Utah combined.

The Second Inland Step—Central Mountains and Plateaus: The elevation of this step varies between 1,000 and 2,000 meters (3,280 and 6,560 feet), about the height of the Colorado Plateau. The east side of the step is bordered by the Da Hinggan Ling–Taihang Shan–Wu Shan mountain ranges, which are higher than 3,000 meters (9,840 feet). The major plateaus in this area are the Inner Mongolia Plateau, the Loess Plateau, the Yunnan-Guizhou Plateau, and the Alashan Plateau.

The Third Inland Step—Plains: The plains are located in the east coast region and northeast China. The elevation of the area is about 200 meters (656 feet). It is the major agricultural area of China. The major plains are the North China Plain, the Northeast China Plain, the Lower Chang Jiang Plain, the Lower Xi Jiang Basin, and the Southeast Hills and Basins. The largest one is the Northeast Plain, which is 350,000 square kilometers (135,193 square miles) in area.

The Continental Shelf in the Neighboring Seas: This is an extension of the inland topographic steps. The continental shelves in the neighboring seas (Bo Hai, Yellow Sea, East China Sea, and South China Sea) are very shallow and are obviously continuous parts of the continent. The shelves are generally less than 200 meters (656 feet) in depth and are petroleum-bearing.

Major Mountain Ranges

China is a mountainous country. One-third of the land area is mountain. If hills and plateaus are included, then 65 percent of the land areas are hills, mountains, and plateaus. Five major mountain systems can be identified in China. Those systems form the topographic and geomorphological structure of China.

East-West Mountain System: There are three east-west mountain ranges in China. From north to south, these three mountain ranges are quite evenly distributed about 8 latitude degrees apart. The northernmost is the Tian Shan–Yin Shan–Yan Shan mountain range system. It is located between 40°N and 43°N and extends from Tian Shan at the western border to Yan Shan in Hebei and Beijing near the east coast.

The middle range consists of the Kunlung Shan–Qin Ling–Dabie Shan mountains. They are located between 33°N and 35°N and extend from Kunlung Shan at the western border to the Dabie Shan mountains in Anhui Province.

The southern range is the Nan Ling mountains, located at 25°N to 26°N. Compared to the other two ranges, its west to east extent is very short. It is mainly in Guangxi Province.

North-South Mountain System: There is only one north to south mountain range in China. It consists of the Helan Shan–Liupan Shan–Hengduan Shan Mountains. This range is located in central China and divides the land area into two parts. Qinghai-Tibet Plateau, the roof of the world, is on its west, and medium-height and lower mountains are on its east.

Northeast Mountain System: There are three northeastern mountain ranges in China. The western range is the Da Hinggan Ling–Taihang Shan–Wu Shan Mountain range. It stretches from the northern border of the country to the Wu Shan mountains in the Chang Jiang basin of central China. This range borders the second inland topographic step and divides east and central China into plains and plateaus.

The second northeast mountain range is the Changbai Shan–Qian Shan–Wuyi Shan mountains. Changbai Shan is the border mountain range between China and North Korea. Qian Shan and Wuyi Shan are located near the east coast and stretch from Shandong to Fujian Provinces. All of the mountains in this range are low elevations at about 1,000 meters (3,280 feet).

Taiwan's mountains occupy two-thirds of the island and extend toward the northeast, the same direction as the island and the underwater folding belt. The Taiwan mountain range was created during the Himalayan movement. Therefore, it is a younger and higher mountain range than the eastern mountain ranges in mainland China. There are more than 60 peaks above 3,000 meters (9,840 feet), with the highest reaching to 3,997 meters (13,110 feet)—the highest point in eastern China.

Northwest Mountain System: The Altay (Altai) mountains and Qilian Shan mountains are both located in northwestern China. The Altay mountain range is at the northern border of the Xinjiang autonomous region with Mongolia and Russia. The Qilian Shan mountains are located mostly in Qinghai Province and stand as the northeast border of the Qinghai-Tibet Plateau.

Arc Mountain System: The Himalayas and several other mountain ranges on the Qinghai-Tibet Plateau stretch from the east of the plateau and then turn toward the northwest. These mountain ranges curve toward the south. The Himalayas range is the most typical one. The Himalayas stand 6,000 meters (19,680 feet) above sea level, and are the highest mountains in the world. Mount Everest, the world's highest peak, is 8,848 meters (29,028 ft) above sea level.

Four Major Plateaus

The four major plateaus are the Qinghai-Tibet Plateau, Inner Mongolia Plateau, Loess Plateau, and the Yunnan-Guizhou Plateau. Except for the Qinghai-Tibet Plateau, all of the other three plateaus are located on the second inland topographic step and at 1,000 to 2,000 meters (3,280 to 6,560 feet) elevation.

Inner Mongolia Plateau: The Inner Mongolia Plateau is the second largest plateau in China and well known for its huge grassland. It is located mainly in the Inner Mongolia autonomous region. The area of the plateau is about 1 million square kilometers. Precipitation drops from east to west on the plateau. Therefore, the grassland is very rich in the east, dry in the middle, and arid in the west.

Loess Plateau: Loess is a thick deposit of wind-blown dust. When it accumulates in an area, it gradually develops into a very fine, pale yellow, fertile soil-like material. It covers an extensive area in the mid-latitude area such as in the United States, central Europe, central Asia, and Argentina. The loess-covered area in China totals 600,000 square kilometers (250,000 square miles), about the size of Texas. The Loess Plateau itself covers about 400,000 square kilometers (154,402 square miles). This is the largest loess-covered area in the world. The plateau is located in northern China west to the Taihang Shan mountains and between the Inner Mongolia Plateau and the Qin Ling mountains. The depth of loess is typically 30–50 meters (98–164 feet) but goes as deep as 200 meters (656 feet).

Yunnan-Guizhou Plateau: This plateau is located in southwest China, mostly in Yunnan and Guizhou Provinces. The plateau and surrounding mountains cover about 400,000 square kilometers (154,402 square miles). Covered by limestone and located in humid south China, this plateau contains a variety of spectacular limestone landscapes (Karst topography), such as the Stone Forest in Yunnan.

Three Major Plains

The Northeast Plain, North China Plain, and Middle and Lower Chang Jiang Plain are the three major plains in China. They are all located in eastern China, with elevations between 50 and 200 meters (164 and 656 feet).

Northeast Plain: Located between the Da Hinggan and Changbai Shan mountains, the Northeast Plain covers 350,000 square kilometers (135,135 square miles) and is the largest plain in China. Covered by deep, fertile black soil, Northeast Plain is the most important grain-producing zone in China.

North China Plain: With an area of 300,000 square kilometers (115,830 square miles), the North China Plain mainly follows the lower reach of the Huang He River. Being one of the most densely popu-

lated areas in the world, this plain has a very long history of cultivation and is still the major wheat-producing area.

Middle and Lower Chang Jiang Plain: The plain stretches east to the Three Gorges and along the Chang Jiang River's so-called golden waterway. This plain can be further divided into four parts: the Lianghu Plain between southern Hubei and northern Hunan Provinces, Boyang Hu Plain around Boyang Hu Lake in northern Jiangxi and southwest Anhui Provinces, Wanzhong Plain in central Anhui Province, and Chang Jiang Delta in Jiangsu and Zhejiang Provinces and Shanghai municipality. This low and flat plain has an elevation of about 50 meters (164 feet) and a dense network of rivers and many lakes. The plain is a center of both agricultural and industrial production.

Four Major Basins

Junggar Basin and Tarim Basin: Divided by the Tian Shan mountains, the Junggar Basin in the north and the Tarim Basin in the south are both located in Xinjiang Uighur autonomous region. The larger Tarim Basin occupies 530,000 square kilometers (204,633 square miles) and contains the largest desert in China, the Takalamacan. Originating in the Tian Shan Mountains and ending in the Tarim Basin, the Tarim River is the longest inland river in China. Oases are developed along Tarim River. The Junggar Basin is also a dry basin, although 25 to 30 percent of its land is covered by plants, which is higher than in the Tarim Basin.

Qaidam Basin: The Qaidam Basin is on the Qinghai-Tibet Plateau. The bottom of the basin is about 2,500 to 3,000 meters (8,200 to 9,480 feet) above sea level. The Qaidam Basin is a dried-up salt lake; *Qaidam* is the Mongolian word for salt. When the salt lake dried up, it left behind a vast, flat, salty basin. The salt crust—15 meters (49 feet) thick—is a valuable mineral, but nothing grows on it. Temporary workers even build their homes out of salt blocks. Since reserves of oil and coal have been discovered under this basin, more workers may build "salt houses" in this region.

Sichuan Basin: The Sichuan Basin is located in Sichuan Province with an area about 180,000 square kilometers (69,500 square miles). Covered by fertile, purple-colored soils, this basin supports a population of 100 million and is the most densely populated basin of the four. The basin is known as "The Land of Plenty."

5. SURFACE WATER AND GROUNDWATER

It is estimated that China has 2,812 billion cubic meters (99,235 billion cubic feet) of surface water (including rivers, lakes, glaciers, and marshes) and 800 billion cubic meters (28,232 billion cubic feet) of shallow underground water. The distribution of China's water resources is very unbalanced. East coast regions, especially southeastern and southern regions, have abundant surface and groundwater, but the western part of China, where coal and oil are abundant, desperately needs water.

Rivers

China has approximately 5,000 rivers, with drainage areas (the area drained by a river and all its tributaries) in excess of 100 square kilometers (38.6 square miles). Among them, 1,600 rivers have drainage areas in excess of 1,000 square kilometers (386 square miles). Most rivers flow from west to east and enter the Pacific Ocean. According to the destination of discharge, those rivers can be classified into two types: oceanic rivers and inland rivers. Oceanic rivers end up at a sea or in an ocean; inland rivers end up at an inland lake or dry up in deserts.

The land area of China can be divided into two major drainage areas: the oceanic drainage area and the inland drainage area. The oceanic drainage area occupies about 64 percent of the total land area, and the inland drainage area covers the rest of the land, about 36 percent. The division of the two drainage areas is along the line of mountain ranges starting from the north on the west side of Da Hinggan Ling, turning to the west and the southwest through Yin Shan, Helan Shan, Qilian Shan, Riyue Shan, Bayan Har Shan, Nyainqentanglha Shan, and ending at the west end of Gangdise Shan at the southwest border in Tibet. This line is also generally along the line of 400 millimeters (15.7 inches) annual precipitation. The western side of the line is in the inland drainage area except for a small area near the northwestern border along the Altay Shan mountain ranges.

Oceanic Rivers: The oceanic river drainage area can be further divided into three sub-areas, according to the ocean that the rivers end up in: the Pacific Ocean, the Indian Ocean, and the Arctic Ocean. Most rivers go to the Pacific Ocean; only Ertix He goes to the Arctic Ocean, and Yarlung Zangbo Jiang and Nu Jiang enter the Indian Ocean.

Most rivers in China originate in the mountainous areas and plateaus in the west. The Qinghai-Tibet Plateau is the original place of superior rivers in China and Asia, such as Chang Jiang, Huang He, Lancang Jiang, Yarlung Zangbo Jiang, and Nu Jiang rivers. The east edge of the second topographic step, from Da Hinggan Ling to Yunnan-Guizhou Plateau, is the source of some of the major rivers in China, such as the Heilong Jiang, Liao He, Hai He, Huai He, and Xi Jiang.

The oceanic drainage area largely overlaps the monsoon climate region. Great annual variation in precipitation produces comparable variations in river discharge and water levels, which has major significance for this area. Rivers in northern China have the largest annual variation, such as Huai He, Huang He, Yongding He, and Luan He. Rivers with very large annual variations in flow create problems for navigation. This is one of the main reasons for the relatively short extent of navigable inland waterways (110,000 kilometers, 68,365 miles) in China.

Although China has 5,000 rivers, seven large rivers account for 1,500 billion cubic meters of surface runoff, or 55 percent of the national total. The basic information about those seven rivers is listed in Table 3.

Chang Jiang River: The Chang Jiang is the greatest river in China with a length of 6,300 kilometers (3,915 miles) and a fall of 6,500 meters (21,320 feet). Inland, the Chang Jiang is the longest river in Asia and the third longest river in the world after the Nile River in Africa and the Amazonas-Ucayali River in South America. It starts in the Tanggula Shan Mountains in the Qinghai-Tibet Plateau, runs eastward through Qinghai, Tibet, Yunnan, Sichuan, Hubei, Hunan, Jiangxi, Anhui, Jiangsu, and Shanghai, and enters the East China Sea at Chongming Island near Shanghai. The Chang Jiang is divided into three sections: the upper reach from source to Yichang in Hubei Province, the middle reach from Yichang to Hukou in Jiangxi Province, and the lower reach from Hukou to the mouth on the east coast near Shanghai.

Together with its tributaries (such as Ming Jiang, Tuo Jiang, Jialing Jiang, Wu Jiang, Han Jiang, Xiang Jiang, and Gan Jiang), the Chang Jiang forms a dense network of water courses in central and southern China. In its drainage area of 1.8 million square kilometers, fertile plains produce high yields of cereals and cotton, while in the lower reaches, many large and medium industrial centers, including Shanghai, are supported by year-round navigation.

The sand and silt brought by the Chang Jiang River are deposited near the mouth, where the river has created a 50,000-square-kilometer (19,305-square-mile) delta plain, mostly over the past 2,000 years. The delta is roughly bordered by Zhenjiang (Jiangsu Province) on the west, the Tongyang Canal on the north, and Hangzhou Wan bay (Zhejiang Province) on the south. The Chang Jiang Delta has been extending seaward and is still growing at an annual rate of about 40 meters (131.2 feet). This newly created delta is one of the richest agricultural regions and supports Shanghai, the largest city in China.

Huang He River: The Huang He is famous because it has nurtured the heart of Chinese civilization for thousands of years. Rising in the Bayan Har Shan Mountains in Qinghai, the Huang He flows through nine provinces and autonomous regions from Qinghai, Sichuan, Gansu, Ningxia, Inner Mongolia, Shanxi, Shaanxi, Henan, to Shandong, and finally enters the Bohai Sea. Named after its water color, Huang He has been known as the Yellow River (translation of the meaning of its Chinese name) to the world. The Huang He's water is clear at the upper reach until it passes through the Loess Plateau, where it picks up huge amounts of yellow, silty loess. The Huang He can be divided into three sections: the upper reach from its source to Hekou in Inner Mongolia, the middle reach from Hekou to Mengjin in Henan Province and the lower reach from Mengjin to the east coast at Kenli in Shandong Province.

Table 3: Major Rivers in China

River	Drainage area km^2 (mile^2)	Length km (mile)	Annual total discharge bil.m^3 (bil.ft^3)
Chang Jiang	1,808,500 (698,262)	6,300 (3,915)	933.5 (32,943)
Huang He	752,443 (290,518)	5,464 (3,396)	56.3 (1,987)
Songhua Jiang	557,180 (215,127)	2,308 (1,434)	73.3 (2,587)
Liao He	228,960 (88,401)	1,390 (864)	14.8 (522)
Hai He	263,631 (101,788)	1,090 (677)	22.8 (805)
Huai He	269,283 (103,970)	1,000 (621)	61.1 (2,156)
Zhu Jiang	453,690 (175,169)	2,214 (1,376)	336 (11,857)

Sources:

China Ministry of Water Resource and Electric Power. *Evaluation of China's Water Resources.* Beijing: China Water Resource and Electric Power Publishing House, 1987.

Zhao Songqiao. *Geography of China, Environment Resources, Population and Development.* New York: John Wiley, 1994.

Downstream from Mengjin in Henan Province, where the Huang He flows slowly across the North China Plain, the riverbed becomes very wide; and large quantities of sand and silt are deposited. Year by year, the deposition causes the riverbed to rise until in places it is 4 to 5 meters (13 to 17 feet) above the original river bed and becomes an "Above Ground River." The sandy banks and dikes are too weak to stop water overflowing or breaking through it during the flooding season. Therefore, the Huang He changes its river course frequently, somewhat like a dragon swings its tail. In the last 2,000 years, the Huang He broke the dikes in its lower reaches 1,500 times, and has had 26 major changes on the river's course. The last change in the river's course occurred in 1976. The changes in the river's course start at Mang Shan near Luoyang and Mengjin (Henan Province), and the "end of the tail" moves between Tianjin and Huaiyin (Jiangsu Province). The Huang He moves wildly on this triangular-shaped, 250,000-square-kilometer (96,525-square-mile) floodplain.

Inland Rivers: China's inland rivers are in the western region. Although these rivers carry much less water than oceanic rivers, the rivers play a vital role in these arid regions. As long as there is a river, there are towns and villages along it, even deep within deserts. The water sources of those inland rivers are mostly melting snow and ice from the nearby mountains. Most inland rivers are seasonal. Some are not even continuous rivers, disappearing for a certain distance along their courses.

The Tarim River: The Tarim River in Tarim Basin (Xinjiang) is the largest inland river in China. *Tarim* means farm or farming in the local Uighur language. The Tarim River has two major sources; one is from the Tian Shan Mountains, and the other is from the Karakorum Shan Mountains. The Tarim River is 2,179 kilometers (1,354 miles) long, with a 198,000-square-kilometer (76,448-square-mile) drainage basin. The lower reach of the river does not have a fixed course, but runs only when there is an abundant snow melt. The Tarim River terminates at the Lop Lake (Lop Nor) and the Taitima Lake, which has been completely dry since 1972.

Lakes

China has 2,300 lakes (not including seasonal lakes), with an area of more than 1 square kilometer (0.4 square mile). The total surface area of the lakes is about 71,787 square kilometers, or about 0.8 percent of China's total land area. There are both freshwater and saltwater lakes. Most freshwater lakes are in the eastern and northeastern region; the saltwater lakes are mostly in Qinghai-Tibet and northwestern regions. Table 4 lists major lakes in China. Notice that six large freshwater lakes are listed from numbers one to six in the table.

Groundwater

China's 800 billion cubic meters of shallow groundwater accounts for about 23 percent of the total water resources. Groundwater resources are mainly found in plains and basins. The Northeast Plain, North China Plain, Tarim Basin, Junggar Basin, Hexi Corridor in Gansu Province, and the Sichuan Basin have extensive groundwater resources. Limestone areas in the southern and southwestern regions also have large groundwater resources.

6. WEATHER AND CLIMATE

As a mid-latitude country with a vast land, China has a variety of climates from hot to cold and from wet to dry. Those can be grouped under three major types: monsoon climate, continental dry climate, and highland climate.

Monsoon Climate

The monsoon is a prevailing wind that changes direction seasonally, especially the winds in the Indian Ocean and Southeast Asian region. The directional change of winds is caused by the change of air

Table 4: Major Lakes in China

No.	Lake	Location	Area km^2 (mile^2)	Total volume 10^{9}m^3 (10^{9}ft^3)	Type
1	Poyang Hu	Jiangxi	3,583 (1,383)	25.9 (914)	Fresh
2	Dongting Hu	Hunan	2,740 (1,058)	17.8 (614)	Fresh
3	Tai Hu	Jiangsu	2,338 (903)	4.4 (155)	Fresh
4	Hongze Hu	Jiangsu	1,851 (715)	2.4 (85)	Fresh
5	Chao Hu	Anhui	753 (291)	1.8 (64)	Fresh
6	Nansi Hu	Shandong	1,225 (473)	1.9 (67)	Fresh
7	Qinghai Hu	Qinghai	4,200 (1,622)	74.2 (2,619)	Salt
8	Hulun Nur	Nei Monggol	2,000 (772)	11.1 (392)	Salt
9	Nam Co	Tibet	1,961 (757)	76.8 (2,710)	Salt
10	Siling Co	Tibet	1,628 (628)	49.2 (1,736)	Salt
11	Zhari Nam Co	Tibet	996 (384)	6 (212)	Salt
12	Bosten	Xinjiang	960 (371)	7.73 (273)	Salt

Sources:
China Ministry of Water Resource and Electric Power. *Evaluation of China's Water Resources.* Beijing: China Water Resource and Electric Power Publishing House, 1987.
Zhao Songqiao. *Geography of China, Environment Resources, Population and Development.* New York: John Wiley, 1994.

pressure that is related to temperature. Therefore, the temperature difference between land and water controls the wind direction, and the seasonal change of the temperature between land and water causes the seasonal change of wind direction. The land areas that are dominated by monsoon winds are monsoon climate regions. China is sandwiched between the largest continent on the west (Eurasia) and the largest ocean (the Pacific) on the east. The temperature difference between the continent and the ocean induces the seasonal winds, or monsoon, and influences the eastern part of China's land area. About 95 percent of the Chinese people reside in this eastern monsoon climate region.

Winter Monsoon: In the winter, the polar air mass (a large body of air with similar temperature and humidity) controls most of the land area. Cold and dry monsoon winds blow from the Siberia-Mongolia high-pressure ridge to the Pacific Ocean and give most of China a cold and dry winter.

Summer Monsoon: In the summer, the ocean is relatively cooler than the land area; therefore, maritime high pressure is over the Pacific and Indian Oceans. Tropical and sub-tropical maritime air mass controls the region. Warm and moist monsoon winds from the Pacific and Indian Oceans create a warm and wet summer.

Monsoon Rains: Summer monsoons bring heavy rain to the region. The location of the main rain belt is closely related to the advance and retreat of the summer monsoons. In eastern China, southeastern monsoons from the Pacific Ocean reach the southeastern region in March and advance to the central region in June, then to the north and northeast regions in July. In late August, it starts to retreat, then retreats entirely from China in September. Southwestern monsoons from the Indian Ocean make a clear distinction between dry and wet seasons in southwestern China. The wet season starts in the region in late May and then changes to the dry season in October.

Temperature

The latitude and topography of a location determine temperature. From the equator to the North Pole, temperature decreases along with the increase of latitude. The higher the elevation is, the lower the temperature falls. In addition to these two major factors, China's seasonal temperature difference is affected by the monsoons. Generally speaking, most of China has a colder winter and hotter summer than places at similar latitude locations elsewhere on the globe.

Winter Temperature: The winter temperatures change progressively according to latitude; southern China is warmer than northern China. In January, mean temperatures differ greatly between north and south. In northern Heilongjiang, the mean temperature is –30°C (–22°F), but it is above 15°C (68°F) on southern Hainan island—a difference greater than 45°C (90°F).

Summer Temperature: Temperatures are high all over China during the summer months. The influence of latitude is reduced to a minimum, and isotherms (lines connecting points having equal temperature) are arranged in a longitudinal pattern. The mean temperature in July in northern Heilongjiang is 20°C (68°F) and in southern Guangdong is 28°C (82°F). The difference in mean temperature is only 8°C (14°F) in the summer, compared with 45°C (90°F) in the winter.

Two high-temperature centers with mean temperatures in July over 30°C (86°F) are Poyang Hu lake in Hubei Province and the Turpan Basin in Xinjiang autonomous region. There are four climactic ovens that have a daily maximum above 38°C (100°F) along the Chang Jiang valley. From the upper reach to the lower reach of Chang Jiang River, those four ovens are: Chongqing municipality, Changsha in Hunan Province, Wuhan in Hubei Province, and Nanjing in Jiangsu Province.

Precipitation

Precipitation Distribution: China is open to oceans on its eastern and southeastern sides where moist air comes from. Therefore, annual precipitation decreases from the eastern and southeastern coast toward the western and northwestern interiors. The annual rainfall lines (isohyets) are parallel to the coasts.

The 500-millimeter (20-inch) annual rainfall line divides China into humid and dry climates. This line also makes distinc-

tions between the densely populated eastern region and the sparsely populated western region in China. The 750-millimeter (30-inch) annual rainfall line follows the Qin Ling Mountains–Huai He River line, dividing eastern China into the rice paddy areas in the south and the dry farmland in the north.

Variation Among Regions: The variation of annual precipitation is tremendous among regions. The highest annual precipitation can be found in Haoshaoliao in Taiwan. Its maximum annual precipitation was 8,408 millimeters (331 inches) in 1912, and its mean annual precipitation is 6,570 millimeters (259 inches). The lowest annual precipitation is recorded at 3.9 millimeters (0.15 inches) in the Eastern Tarim Basin in Xinjiang autonomous region. The Eastern Tarim Basin has a mean annual precipitation of 50 millimeters (2 inches), the lowest anywhere in China.

Variation Among Seasons: The seasonal distribution of precipitation is very uneven in all of China. Rainfall is concentrated in the summer in most areas, due to the impact of monsoons. In northern China, half of the annual precipitation is received between June and August. In southern China, spring and summer are major rain seasons, because the summer monsoon influences the region for a longer period of time than in northern China. Southwestern China has a clear distinction between dry and wet seasons. The wet season from May to October accounts for 80 to 90 percent of the rainfall in the region. Taiwan has a relatively even distribution of precipitation during the year. In northeastern Taiwan, about 30 percent of annual total precipitation occurs in winter.

Annual Variation: Large variations of precipitation occur in most areas from year to year. This is caused by the unreliability of monsoons and results in flooding or drought. In the east coast area, there is about a 20 percent variation among years, with some more extreme variations. For example, Beijing has a mean annual precipitation of 26.9 inches, but in 1958, it was 55 inches, and in 1819 it was only 6.6 inches. The annual variation is about 30–50 percent in northwestern arid areas and occasionally much greater. This has a significant impact on agricultural production in the northwest.

Wind

Wind Direction: Northwest winds dominate the whole country in the winter. These dry and cold winds from Siberia and Mongolia bring chilly temperatures. In the summer, southwestern and southeastern winds dominate and bring moist air and precipitation in from the oceans.

Wind Speed: Wind speed is highest in the winter and spring seasons and lowest in the summer all over the country, except during typhoons. Typhoons (similar to hurricanes in the Atlantic region) occur in the summer and fall, bringing the most destructive winds in the southern and southeastern region.

Some Special Weather Phenomena

Cold Waves: Cold waves occur on the average of once every seven to 10 days during late fall, winter, and spring. These cause sandstorms or snowstorms in northern and northeastern China. The cold and dry northwest winds during cold waves are so strong that people find it difficult to walk into the wind. The temperature drops sharply during a cold wave, more than 10°C (18°F) in one day in Beijing.

Cold waves also cause heavy precipitation in central China and continuous rain in southern China. The temperature also drops in those southern regions during the cold waves. Strong cold waves can even reach Hainan Island at 18°N latitude and can damage tropical crops on the island.

Plum Rains: The name of plum (*mei*) rain comes from the rain's arrival when the plum fruit is ripening. It is also a pun on the Chinese word for mold (*mei*) that spreads everywhere in the damp weather, especially during plum rain season.

Plum rains are caused by the interaction between polar and tropical air masses. During late spring and early summer (usually from mid-June to mid-July), the weakening polar air mass meets the tropical air mass over the middle and lower Chang Jiang and Huai He River Basins. Because

neither of the two air masses is significantly stronger than the other at the time, they both stagnate over the area for a month. The interaction between the two air masses causes continuous rain, moderate temperatures, low wind speeds, and high humidity in the region.

It is uncomfortable weather for human beings but very important for rice growth. A normal plum rain usually means a good harvest for rice in this important rice-producing region of China. However, if the season's plum rain begins or ends too early or too late, rice production can plummet. Unfortunately, just as with the monsoons, plum rain can start as early as May and end as late as August.

Typhoons: A typhoon is a tropical storm that originates in the western Pacific Ocean or the South China Sea and hits the east and southeast coasts of China between May and October. Typhoons bring strong winds and heavy rain. About 280 typhoons strike somewhere on the China coast each year, some with devastating results for the fishing and shipping industries.

Climate Regions

There are three major climate regions in China: the eastern monsoon climate region, the northwestern dry climate region, and the Qinghai-Tibet highland climate region.

Eastern Monsoon Climate Region: The eastern monsoon climate region includes all of eastern China from the northeastern to southern regions. The whole region has a humid or subhumid climate with an annual precipitation of more than 500 millimeters (20 inches) in most areas. From the east coast to the west in the region, the annual rainfall decreases. From the south to the north, the annual mean temperature drops. This region occupies about 46 percent of the land area in China.

According to temperature changes, this region can be further divided into four subclimate regions: northeastern China with a temperate humid and subhumid climate, northern China with a warm temperate humid and subhumid climate, central and southeastern China with a subtropical humid climate, and southern China with a tropical humid climate.

Northwestern Dry Climate Region:

This region is dry with an annual precipitation below 500 millimeters (20 inches). From the east side of the region to the interior of the Eurasian continent, the annual precipitation decreases. In the Shamo (sand desert) and Gobi (gravel desert) areas, annual precipitation is below 100 millimeters (4 inches). This region covers about 27 percent of the area of the country and, according to annual precipitation, can be further divided into two subregions: the temperate Inner Mongolia grassland and the northwest China temperate and warm-temperate desert.

Qinghai-Tibet Highland Climate Region:

This region is the largest area of highland climate in the world. Although its latitude location is between warm temperate and subtropical regions, this region is much colder and drier than its neighbors due to its average elevation of 4,000 meters (13,120 feet). This region occupies 26 percent of the area of the territory of China.

7. PLANTS AND WILD ANIMALS

China's vast land area and variety of climates have created a very diversified natural environment, which nurtures a wide range of plant and animal species. It is estimated that there are more than 32,000 species of higher plants (those with ducts for transporting water and nutrients), 7,000 species of woody plants (including 2,800 tree species), 2,000 species of edible plants, and 4,000 species of medicinal plants. About 57 percent of higher plant families in the world can be found in China.

Major Plant Types

China has a variety of forest, grassland, desert, and crop species.

Forests: Due to 8,000 years of cultivation, China's wild forests are mostly limited to the mountainous areas of the eastern monsoon climate region. Some are also found in the northwestern mountain ranges. From north to south, there are five major forest types:

1. The cool-temperate coniferous forest found in the Da Hinggan mountains in Heilongjiang Province of northeastern China. Major species include the Dahurian larch, Mongolian Scots pine, Asian white birch, Mongolian oak, and David's poplar.

2. The temperate coniferous and deciduous broad-leaved mixed forests of the Xiao Hinggan and Changbai Mountains of northeastern China. Forest coverage in this area exceeds 40 percent, and it is one of the main commercial forests in China. The main species of needle-leaved tree is the Korean pine, an excellent building timber. The major broad-leaved trees are Mongolian oak, Manchurian ash, several species of maple, and the Japanese yew. Among those trees, Manchurian ash is a hardwood tree used for making furniture. This area is also home of some well-known herbs, such as ginseng. Ginseng's root, stem, leaf, and fruit are all used in medicine for giving vigor and health to the body and relieving stress.

3. The warm-temperate deciduous broad-leaved forests in northern China. The area was once covered by dense forest, but as a result of 8,000 years of agriculture and a high population density in the region, today's forest is only sparsely distributed in mountainous areas. The main species in this area are oaks, maples, Chinese pine, Japanese red pine, Chinese chestnut, and Chinese walnut. Chinese pine is a long-lived tree and can be found near ancient temples and palaces. This area also grows peaches, apples, pears, apricots, and other fruits and nuts.

4. The subtropical evergreen broad-leaved forest in the area between the Qin Ling Mountains in the north and the Tropic of Cancer in the south. Benefiting from

warm and humid climates, very diverse plant species flourish in this area. There are 14,500 angiosperm (flowering plants with seeds enclosed in ovaries) species in the area. The main species are oaks, teas, and bamboos. The water larch, originated 100 million years ago and honored as a "living fossil," is found in Hubei Province, and attracts many visitors. Most land in the area is cultivated, with forest coverage found only in mountainous areas. A few small virgin forests are found on high mountains.

5. Tropical monsoon rain forests and tropical rain forests are located in a small area south of the Tropic of Cancer in southern China. The difference between monsoon rain forests and tropical rain forests is that monsoon rain forests have a dry season, and some leaves fall off. True tropical rain forests are found only in the warmest and wettest area near the southern border of China, such as in the southern areas of Yunnan, Guangdong, Guangxi, Tibet, and on the entire Hainan Island. Although this area only covers 3 percent of China's land area, it has more plant species than any other region. Most tropical species of southeastern Asia rain forests are found in this area.

Grassland: About 3 million square kilometers (1.2 million square miles) of grasslands are located in Inner Mongolia, in the northern part of the Loess Plateau, and the central part of the Qinghai-Tibet Plateau. The Inner Mongolia and Loess Plateau grasslands are part of the Eurasian grasslands that also cover Mongolia and southern Russia.

From east to west in the grasslands, annual rainfall gradually decreases from 400 millimeters (16 inches) to 100 millimeters (4 inches). The grasslands change along with the annual rainfall from meadow steppes in the east to typical steppes in the center to desert steppes in the west. The density and height of grass drops from east to west.

Deserts: Deserts occupy about 11 percent of the land area in China. In this huge desert area, plants are sparsely distributed at places where water is available. Woodlands and oases can be found near some rivers.

Crops: The Chinese Ministry of Agriculture estimates that China has more than 1,000 species of trees usable for timber, more than 300 fruits, 500 fiber plants, 300 starch plants, 600 oil producing plants, and more than 80 species of vegetables. Some of them were first domesticated in China, such as paddy rice, barley, Chinese apple, and tea.

Wild Animals

It is estimated that there are about 2,200 species of terrestrial vertebrates (land animals with backbones or spinal columns) in China, more than 10 percent of the world total. There are 1,189 known species of birds, nearly 500 mammal species, 320 reptiles, and 210 amphibians. Due to thousands of years of deforestation, wild animal populations are declining, with many rare species endangered, such as the giant panda, the golden-haired monkey, and red-crown crane.

Giant Pandas: The giant pandas are one of the most famous and favorite animals in the world. Unfortunately, there are only a thousand giant pandas left in the wild, and they are all in a small area in China. Pandas feed almost exclusively on bamboo, although the species belongs to the bear genus and has a carnivore's digestive tract. Pandas are comparable in size to American black bears. Although a newborn panda weighs only about 100 grams (3.5 ounces), an adult giant panda can grow up to 2 meters (6.56 feet) long and weigh up to 160 kilograms (350 pounds). Protecting the giant panda is a worldwide effort. China has established more national reserves for pandas in recent years.

8. NATURAL RESOURCES

Natural resources are defined as anything that we get from the living and non-living environment to meet human needs and wants. Compared with other countries, China has rich natural resources, but taking its huge population into consideration, many major resources are in short supply.

Energy Resources

China has a complete range of energy resources from coal, natural gas, oil, and hydropower to nuclear power. Unlike major industrialized countries such as the United States, Canada, and western European countries where oil has replaced coal since the 1950s, China still relies heavily on coal as a major energy resource and will continue to do so in the near future. This is due to a lower economic development level (especially the low level of personal automobile use) and to the structure of energy resources in China. Of proven energy resources, coal accounts for 67.3 percent, hydropower for 30.4 percent, oil and natural gas for 1.5 percent, and all others for 0.7 percent. Both energy production and consumption structures match the resource structure (Table 5).

In 1997, China's energy consumption was only 907 kilograms (2,016 pounds) per capita (oil equivalent), compared to 8,076 kilograms (17,946 pounds) in the United States and 7,930 kilograms in Canada. The low energy consumption level is an indication of low industrialization and economic development.

The distribution of energy resources is very unbalanced. Table 6 shows that energy resources are highly concentrated in the north and west regions, yet economic centers are in the eastern region. Therefore, energy resources must be transported and electricity transmitted over long distances in China.

Table 5: Energy Production and Consumption Structure in China 1980–2000 (percentages by year)

Year	Coal		Oil		Natural Gas		Hydropower	
	Prod.	Cons.	Prod.	Cons.	Prod.	Cons.	Prod.	Cons.
1980	69.4	72.2	23.8	20.7	3.0	3.1	3.8	4.0
1985	72.8	75.8	20.9	17.1	2.0	2.2	4.3	4.9
1990	74.2	76.2	19.0	16.6	2.0	2.1	4.8	5.1
1995	75.3	75.0	16.6	17.0	1.9	1.8	6.2	6.0
2000	67.2	67.0	21.4	23.6	3.4	2.5	8.0	6.9

Sources: China State Statistical Bureau. *China Statistical Yearbook, 1981, 1986, 1991, 1996, 2001.* Beijing: China Statistical Publishing House.

Table 6: Percentage of Energy Resources by Region

Energy	North	Northeast	East	Central	Southwest	Northwest
Coal	64.0	3.1	6.5	3.7	10.7	12.0
Oil & Gas	14.4	48.3	18.2	2.5	2.5	14.1
Hydro	1.8	1.8	4.4	9.5	70.0	12.5
Total *	43.9	3.8	6.0	5.6	28.6	12.1

* Percentage of standard coal

Source: Li, Wenyan, and Hang Chen. "A Preliminary Study of Energy Economic Division in China." *Acta Geographica Sinica* 38 (4), 1983.

Coal: China has the third largest proven coal reserves in the world after Russia and the United States, but measured on a per capita basis, China's reserves are lower than the world average. At the end of 1993, the coal reserves were 1,008.7 billion metric tons.

China has a complete range of coal from lignite (a soft coal) to anthracite (a hard coal). Each kind provides a reasonable share in the resources, which is beneficial for industrial and commercial purposes.

China's coal resources are highly concentrated in the northern region. In fact, up to 70 percent of the resources are in Shanxi, Shaanxi, and Inner Mongolia. Shanxi Province alone accounts for 27 percent of national reserves.

The largest coal-producing area is the Dongsheng-Shenfu-Yuheng coal basin in the border area of Shaanxi Province and Inner Mongolia autonomous region. The area of the basin is about 27,000 square kilometers (10,546 square miles), and is one of the largest in the world. In 1992, its proven coal reserves were 240 billion tons, or 25 percent of the national total. Since geologists are still exploring the southern and western edges, it is estimated that the ultimate reserves of the basin could reach 1,000 billion tons. The grade of the fuel coal is exceptionally good: Ash is below 10 percent (even better than washed coal); and sulfur is lower than 0.7 percent, which means that it is less polluting when burned.

Oil and Natural Gas: Prior to 1949, China was believed to have very small oil resources, and depended heavily on imported oil for its industry. During the 1950s, Chinese geologists developed "the theory of continental origin of oil" and used it to explore areas previously believed devoid of oil-bearing geological structures. Several major oil fields were discovered, including the Daqing oil field in 1959. As a result, China has been self-sufficient in oil since 1963.

There were 17.3 billion tons of verified crude oil reserves in 1997, and the country's total estimated onshore reserves is 70 billion tons. Again, because of its huge population, China's reserves per capita are less than half of the world's average. Nonetheless, China has exported crude oil from time to time since 1973.

Although oil resources are not evenly distributed over the country, there are some large oil fields located in the east coast region near the economic centers. Northeast China has been—and remains—the largest oil producing region since 1963. Since this is the center of heavy industry in China, the proximity of the oil fields is quite fortunate. Studies and test wells in the 1980s and 1990s on the continental shelves and northwestern deserts, especially the Qaidam Basin, point toward the exploitation of promising new oil fields. By 1997, 200 million tons of crude oil reserves had been verified in the Qaidam Basin, and it's projected that proven reserves will climb to 800 million tons in 2005.

The largest oil field in China is the Daqing oil field, located in the Songliao Basin of northwest Heilongjiang Province. It was discovered in 1959 and named Daqing ("big celebration") because the discovery coincided with the 10th anniversary of the People's Republic of China. By 1992, the proven oil reserves were more than 2 billion tons. Since 1976, Daqing's output of crude oil has been more than 50 million tons annually, between 35 to 60 percent of the national total. It is estimated that this level of annual output can continue until 2012.

China has 1,200 billion cubic meters (42,348 billion cubic feet) of proven natural gas reserves. Projections put the country's total resources at 30,000 billion cubic meters (1,058,700 billion cubic feet). Natural gas only accounts for 1.7 percent of the energy used in the country; therefore, it is less important than coal, oil, and hydropower. The resources are highly concentrated in Sichuan Province and large oil fields.

Hydropower: With 676 million kilowatts in total, China leads the world in hydropower resources. Nonetheless, hydropower kilowatts per capita are still lower than world average. Moreover, China's hydropower resources are highly concentrated on the Qinghai-Tibet Plateau where they are often inaccessible and far from population centers. China's exploitable hydro-power, 378 million kilowatts, is only a little over half the total resources.

In 1996, hydropower accounted for only 5 percent of China's energy production and consumption. To increase the share of hydropower, China will have to build dams on large rivers, which represent most of the unexploited hydropower resources. The Chang Jiang River drainage basin alone holds 40 percent of the resources, mostly in the upper reaches of the river. The Yarlung Zangbo Jiang River and other rivers in Tibet hold another 23.6 percent of the resources.

The World's Largest Hydropower Project: The Three Gorges project on the Chang Jiang River is the world's largest hydropower project. The dam is 185 meters (607 feet) high, and the reservoir will be approximately 600 kilometers (400 miles) long. It is designed to generate more than 18,000 megawatts of electricity, enough to power much of eastern and central China. It will create a huge, deep-water reservoir enabling 10,000-ton ocean-going cargo ships and passenger liners to sail 1,500 miles inland from the Pacific to Chongqing municipality. It is also designed to provide flood management for the lower Chang Jiang Basin. The costs of the project are enormous. It will submerge approximately 60,704 hectares (150,000 acres) of land, including 160 towns and cities, and reset-tle 1.3 million people. A number of archae-ological sites will be under the water. Its impact on the ecology and environment will be so significant that its construction has sparked protests from environmental-ists not only in China, but throughout the world. Despite the controversies, the first stage of the dam construction was finished and the cofferdam was demolished on May 1, 2002. The completion of the Three Gorges Dam, along with the electricity gen-eration and opening of permanent locks for navigation, is projected in 2009.

Mineral Resources

China has rich mineral resources, rank-ing third in the world in total reserves. Through 1992, geologists had confirmed 148 different minerals—some in greater quantities than are found anywhere else in the world. Yet the supplies of some major minerals, such as iron, manganese, baux-ite, and copper, cannot meet demand, either because of insufficient proven reserves or poor quality.

Iron: As of 1993, China had 47.8 billion tons of proven iron ore reserves, fifth high-est in the world after Russia, Brazil, Aus-tralia, and Canada. About 87 percent of China's iron ore resources are low grade (32 percent iron); only 4 percent of iron ore reserves has a grade over 60 percent that can be used directly by furnaces. Due to the shortage of quality iron ore resources and the high demand, China imports about 20 percent of its iron ore consumption each year.

Iron ore resources can be found in every province and autonomous region except Shanghai and Tianjin, but more than half of the resources are concentrated in the Anshan-Benxi region in Liaoning Province, the Panzhihua-Xichang region in Sichuan Province, and Beijing-Tianjin-Tangshan region mostly in Hebei Province.

Some of China's large iron ore reserves contain other minerals that are more valu-able than iron but difficult to separate and fully utilize. For example, the Baotou-Bayan Obo iron ores are poor in iron (33 percent) but contain very rich rare-earth metals (13 percent). In fact, the rare-earth metal reserves in this region alone exceed the total reserves of all other countries. The iron ores in the Panzhihua-Xichang region contain 11 percent titanium and 0.3 percent vanadium. This is the largest vanadium reserve in the world.

Nonferrous Metal: China is rich in resources of almost all types of commer-cially used nonferrous metals in the world. The proven reserves of more than 15 non-ferrous metals are ranked first in the world: These include tungsten, antimony, titanium, magnesite, and rare-earth met-als. Table 7 lists some nonferrous metals in which China's ranked in the top five (1980 data). Table 8 shows the distribution of major nonferrous metals within China.

Although China has relatively high lev-els of proven reserves, the resources per capita of most nonferrous metals are still lower than the world average. Only some top-rank metals can provide a per capita level higher than the world average.

Table 7: Selected Nonferrous Metal Reserves in the World

Metal	Reserves of top five countries with their share (%) in the world	Total share of the top five countries in the world (%)
Tungsten	China (52), Canada (10), Russia (8), United States (5), Australia (4)	80%
Antimony	China (53), Bolivia (8), South Africa (7), Russia (6), Mexico (5)	79%
Magnesite	China (30), Russia (26), Korea (18), Brazil (5), Australia (3)	82%
Tin	Indonesia (16), China (15), Malaysia (12), Russia (10.1), Bolivia (9.9)	63%
Molybdenum	United States (54), Chile (25), Russia (7), Canada (6), China (2.3)	95%
Mercury	Spain (32), Russia (11), Yugoslavia (11), China (11), United Kingdom (8)	73%

Source: Chen, Hong, and Xiwu He, eds. *Handbook of Natural Resources in China*. Beijing: Science Press, 1990.

Table 8: Regional Distribution of Nonferrous Metal Resources

Region	Proportion in China		
	More than 20%	10–20%	Less than 10%
Northeast	molybdenum	lead, zinc, silver, gold	copper, lead, zinc, nickel
North	rare-earth metals, niobium, bauxite	lead, zinc, silver gold	vanadium, titanium, copper, tin
East		copper, lead, zinc	
Central	tungsten, antimony, lead, zinc, copper, germanium, bismuth, niobium, tantalum	molybdenum, gold, bauxite	vanadium, nickel, mercury
South	tin, lead, zinc antimony	tungsten, bauxite	cadmium, indium, mercury, gold
Southwest	copper, lead, zinc, mercury, vanadium, titanium, tin	nickel, antimony, bauxite	tungsten, bismuth, beryllium, yttrium
Northwest	nickel, molybdenum, platinum group, cobalt, beryllium, niobium, tantalum	copper, antimony, lead, zinc, gold, silver	tungsten

Source: Li, Wenyan, and Dadao Lu. *Industrial Geography of China*. Beijing: Science Press, 1995.

Aluminum (bauxite): Aluminum is a relatively new metal; its history from stone to valuable metal is only one century long. Because of its lightweight strength, aluminum and aluminum alloy use has grown rapidly. Aluminum is now used for a wide variety of purposes in aviation, military weapons, transportation, construction, food packaging, and solar energy equipment. Since the 1980s, aluminum products account for about 40 percent of the world's total nonferrous metal production.

In 1992, China had about 1.6 billion tons of proven bauxite (aluminum ore) reserves, ranking fifth in the world after Guinea, Australia, Brazil, and Jamaica. There are about 280 proven deposits located in nineteen provinces. But the resources are highly concentrated in four provinces and autonomous regions: Henan, Guizhou, Shanxi, and Guangxi. Among them, Shanxi Province alone holds 30 percent, and Henan Province accounts for another 20 percent of the resources.

Copper: China has a long history of copper mining and smelting. Archaeological remains at the Tonglushan mining and smelting site in Hubei Province show that the copper industry appeared in the beginning of the Western Zhou dynasty (c. 1000 B.C.). Although China is ranked sixth in the world, the qualities of its copper resources are poor after many years of mining. In China, ore is considered rich at 1 percent copper and is mined as low as 0.2 to 0.4 percent. Ore is not considered rich in some countries below 3–4 percent copper.

Copper resources are relatively dispersed over the country, with some concentrations in Jiangxi, Hubei, Yunnan, Gansu, Shanxi, Liaoning, and Anhui Provinces. As of 1992, Jiangxi Province held 22 percent of the copper resources; the Dexing copper mine in Jiangxi is the largest copper mine in China.

Tungsten: China has the largest tungsten reserves in the world. There are more than 250 known deposits in 22 provinces and autonomous regions. The concentration of tungsten reserves are in Hunan and Jiangxi Provinces, with some large deposits in Guangxi and Fujian Provinces. The largest deposit is found in Shizhuyuan in Hunan. Four large tungsten mines in southern Jiangxi Province are: Xihua

Shan, Daji Shan, Kuimei Shan, and Pangu Shan. Those four mines are in traditional blumite–producing areas.

Land and Forest Resources

Of China's vast territory, 65 percent is hilly, mountainous, or in plateau areas. The area over 1,000 meters (3,280 feet) elevation occupies about 57 percent of the land area. This means the areas that can be cultivated are quite limited.

Farmland: In 1995, China had 95 million hectares (235 million of acres) of cultivated land, about 10 percent of the total land area. China accounts for only about 7 percent of the world total cropland, but supports 22 percent of world population. The cropland per capita in China is only one-third of the world average. On average, every hectare (2.471 acres) of cropland supports 1.8 people in developed countries and 4 people in developing countries but 8 people in China. Of the small amount of cropland, 25 percent has low productivity.

China's farmland has been intensively cultivated for thousands of years. Many peasants are more like gardeners than farmers, with only 0.28 hectares (0.69 acre) of farmland per farmer in 1992. By contrast, each U.S. farmer had an average of 54.8 hectares (135.4 acres) of farmland in 1991. The multiple cropping (the use of the same field for two or more crops, whether of the same or of different kinds, successively during a single year) rate is very high and increasing in China. The average multiple-cropping rate was 130 percent in 1952 and 157 percent in 1995.

Farmland is very unevenly distributed; 90 percent of the cultivated land is in eastern monsoon China. The huge area in the northwestern region (including Gansu, Ningxia, Xinjiang, and Shaanxi) and the Qinghai-Tibet Plateau occupies 45 percent of the country's land area but only has 12 percent of the country's farmland. Table 9 shows the distribution of farmland at the provincial level.

According to the *Statistical Yearbook* of 1996, there are 35 million hectares (86.5 million acres) of usable agricultural land. But of this land, only 3 percent has high productive potential. The rest is salty, wet, hilly, or located in dry or cold areas. Most

Table 9: Farmland in China, 1995 (figures multiplied by 1,000 Hectares [1,000 acres])

Region	Cultivated Areas	Paddy fields	Dry fields
Beijing	399.5 (987.2)	23.7 (58.6)	375.8 (928.6)
Tianjin	426.1 (1,052.9)	48.5 (119.8)	377.7 (933.3)
Hebei	6,517.3 (1,6104.2)	126.5 (312.6)	6,390.7 (15,791.4)
Shanxi	3,645.1 (9,007.0)	8.8 (21.7)	3,636.3 (8,985.3)
Inner Mongolia	5,491.4 (13,569.2)	84.3 (208.3)	5,407.1 (13,360.9)
Liaoning	3,389.7 (8,375.9)	468.6 (1,157.9)	2,921.1 (7,218.0)
Jilin	3,953.2 (9,768.4)	425.2 (1,050.7)	3,528.0 (8,717.7)
Heilongjiang	8,995.3 (22,227.4)	868.8 (2,146.8)	8,126.5 (20,080.6)
Shanghai	290 (716.6)	253.9 (627.4)	36.1 (89.2)
Jiangsu	4,448.3 (10,991.7)	2,669.7 (6,596.8)	1,778.6 (4,394.9)
Zhejiang	1,617.8 (3,997.6)	1,344.9 (3,323.2)	272.9 (674.3)
Anhui	4,291.1 (10,603.3)	1,857.6 (4,590.1)	2,433.5 (6,013.2)
Fujian	1,204.0 (2,975.1)	972.5 (2,403.0)	231.5 (572.0)
Jiangxi	2,308.4 (5,704.1)	1,946.9 (4,810.8)	361.6 (893.5)
Shandong	6,696.0 (16,545.8)	156.7 (387.2)	6,539.3 (16,158.6)
Henan	6,805.8 (16,817.1)	446.6 (1,103.5)	6,359.2 (15,713.6)
Hubei	3,358.0 (8,297.6)	1,780.4 (4,399.4)	1,577.6 (3,898.2)
Hunan	3,249.7 (8,030.0)	2,562.9 (6,332.9)	686.8 (1,697.1)
Guangdong	2,317.3 (5,726.0)	1,698.7 (4,197.5)	618.7 (1,528.8)
Guangxi	2,614.2 (6,459.7)	1,540.3 (3,806.1)	1,073.9 (2,653.6)
Hainan	429.2 (1,060.6)	248.2 (613.3)	181.0 (447.3)
Sichuan	6,189.6 (15,294.5)	3,156.0 (7,798.5)	3,033.6 (7,496.0)
Guizhou	1,840.0 (4,546.6)	768.4 (1,898.7)	1,071.6 (2,647.9)
Yunnan	2,870.6 (7,093.3)	958.8 (2,369.2)	1,911.9 (4,724.3)
Tibet	222.1 (548.8)	0.8 (2.0)	221.3 (546.8)
Shaanxi	3,393.4 (8,385.1)	176.0 (434.9)	3,217.4 (7,950.2)
Gansu	3,482.5 (8,605.3)	9.3 (23.0)	3,473.2 (8,582.3)
Qinghai	589.9 (1,457.6)	—	589.9 (1,457.6)
Ningxia	807.2 (1,994.6)	170.9 (422.3)	636.3 (1,572.3)
Xinjiang	3,128.3 (7,730.0)	76.7 (189.5)	3,051.6 (7,540.5)

Source: China State Statistical Bureau. *China Statistical Yearbook, 1996.* Beijing: China Statistical Publishing House, 1996.

of the usable land is located in the areas that are difficult to access; therefore, the cultivation of the usable land requires tremendous effort.

The annual reduction of cultivated land by construction and transportation averaged about 780,000 hectares (1,927,000 acres) from 1978 to 1995 and totaled 14 million hectares, or over 10 percent of the cropland. Most of this loss was in highly productive farmland, making it all the more significant. Therefore, protecting every inch of farmland is crucial to the country and people.

Forest and Grassland: As of 1999, China had 263 million hectares (650 million acres) of land usable for afforestation, including 63 million hectares (156 million acres) of afforested area. The total forest area, including natural and afforested, was 159 million hectares (390 million acres) in 1999, and the forest coverage rate was only 16.6 percent, or less than half of the rate in the United States and the world average.

The distribution of forest area is very uneven; 50 percent of forest area and 75 percent of forest growing stock are concentrated in the northeastern and southwestern regions. The densely populated east coast region has only 4 percent of the national total of forested area.

China has 400 million hectares (988 million acres) of grassland, but only 313 million hectares (773 million acres) of grasslands are utilizable. The grasslands are distributed in the Inner Mongolia autonomous region and huge western region. Dry climate limits the productivity of the grasslands, and overgrazing is a serious problem in most regions. On average, only 2.25 kilograms (5 pounds) of meat is produced per hectare of grassland, and total meat output in the grassland regions accounts for only 5 percent of the national total.

9. HUMAN IMPACT ON THE ENVIRONMENT

Supporting the largest population in the world for thousands of years, China's physical environment has been significantly modified by human activities: Forests have been converted to farmlands, rivers have been dammed to make reservoirs, animal species have been domesticated for human use. The human impact can be seen almost everywhere in this ancient land. The overuse, misuse, and abuse of the physical environment are very significant. Air pollution occurs in almost every large city; many rivers in the eastern region are polluted; soil erosion, deforestation, and desertification are widespread problems.

Land Degradation

Land degradation includes soil erosion, deforestation, desertification, and soil pollution. Facing the pressure of supporting the vast population, nearly every inch of farmland in China is intensively used, in many places overused and misused. Land degradation is the most serious environmental problem in China.

Soil Erosion: Soil erosion is the loss of fertile topsoil that provides nutrients to plants and crops. Soil erosion is a natural process that can be caused by water, wind, and glaciers. If soil erosion can not be balanced by soil generation, the land can not overcome problems caused by soil erosion (when generated topsoil is less than the eroded soil). Under this condition, topsoil becomes thinner, less fertile, and less productive. In some cases, when the topsoil is completely eroded and the bedrock exposed, the land is permanently lost for farming or forestation. Human activities such as agriculture, logging, and construction remove plant coverage on the land surface, expose the topsoil, and accelerate soil erosion.

Soil erosion is the most serious land problem in China and is getting worse every year. At the beginning of the 1950s, about 1.16 million square kilometers (622,000 square miles) had soil erosion problems, and that figure increased to 1.79 million square kilometers (691,000 square miles), or one-sixth of the total land area, by the end of the 1980s. About one-third of land affected by soil erosion consists of farmland. The annual loss of topsoil is more than 5 billion tons, or 8 percent of the world's total.

The worst soil erosion occurs in the Loess Plateau. The soft, fine, and deep loess is very easily carried away by water when exposed. The careless cultivation in the region, especially on the steep slopes, causes soil erosion problems on 70 percent of the land area in this region, which results in a 1.6 billion–ton topsoil loss every year. The Huang He River turns yellow after passing through this region.

Desertification: Desertification is the process in which a plant-covered area becomes a desert. It is usually caused by drought and overexploitation of grasses by people near the edge of the existing desert. China already has about 1.16 million square kilometers (448,000 square miles) of desert area, and an area of 371,000 square kilometers (143,243 square miles) undergoing desertification. Together, that accounts for about 16 percent of the nation's land area. The problem of desertification is very serious, with the affected areas expanding yearly by 1,500 to 2,100 square kilometers (579 to 810 square miles) since the 1950s. Desertification, attributable to human activity, is caused by overcultivation (45 percent), overgrazing (29 percent), and woodcutting or firewood gathering (20 percent).

Desertification areas are mainly found in eleven provinces and autonomous regions: Xinjiang, Qinghai, Ningxia, Shaanxi, Gansu, Inner Mongolia, Shanxi, Hebei, Liaoning, Jilin, and Heilongjiang. From east to west, the areas threatened by desertification stretch over 5,000 kilometers (3,107 miles), longer than the coast-to-coast length of the U.S.-Canadian border. There are about 35 million people in the threatened areas. Some 3.9 million hectares (9.6 million acres) of farmland and 4.9 million hectares (12.1 million acres) of grassland are facing desertification.

Soil Pollution: Industrialization and urbanization also pollute precious farmland. It is estimated that 21.9 million hectares (54.1 million acres) of cultivated land, or 16 percent of the total, was polluted in the 1980s, resulting in a grain production loss of more than 11.7 billion kilograms (25.8 billion pounds) a year. Agricultural chemicals polluted 16 million hectares (39.5 million acres), urban industry polluted 4 million hectares (9.9 million acres), and rural industry polluted 1.9 million hectares (4.7 million acres).

Air Pollution

China is the largest coal producer and consumer in the world. Burning coal produces more pollutants than burning oil or gas. Therefore, China faces more serious air pollution problems than the United States or Canada, especially in large cities. According to official statistics, China's discharge of air pollutants increased from 7,397 billion cubic meters (260,900 billion cubic feet) in 1985 to 8,306 billion cubic meters (293,118 billion cubic feet) in 1989.

Sulfur dioxide emission increased from 13.24 million tons in 1985 to 15.64 million tons in 1989. Although 66 percent of waste air was treated, only 18 percent was purified. Dust and ash float in the air. In some heavily industrialized cities, such as Shenyang and Taiyuan, a white shirt will become noticeably dirty during the course of a brief outdoor walk.

Millions of households in northern China still depend on individual small coal stoves for heating and cooking. The smoke from their low chimneys reduces the visibility in urban areas, especially early on winter mornings. As China's economy has grown, the numbers of motor vehicles on the roads has increased tremendously—from 1.35 million in 1978 to 10.4 million in 1995. This increase has not only caused traffic congestion, but has also aggravated air pollution problems in cities. Since 1997, China has promoted the use of no-lead gasoline and has publicly reported daily air quality in some large cities.

Water Pollution

China's waste water discharge increased from 31.5 billion tons in 1980 to 35.3 billion tons in 1989. Although the proportion of treated water increased in the 1980s, in 1989, only 20 percent of discharged water was treated, and only 58 percent of treated water actually met the discharge standard in 1989. For industrially discharged water, only 30 percent was treated and more than 70 percent was drained directly into rivers and lakes. According to official statistics, over half of the industrially discharged water did not meet the standard. This caused some lakes and sections of some rivers to become polluted. Some sections of rivers are so seriously polluted that factories, such as pulp and paper mills along the Huai He River, have had to be shut down.

10. CULTURAL LANDSCAPE

Over thousands of years, the Chinese people have created a unique cultural landscape. This section reviews the spatial aspect of human activities on the land, which include population distribution and migration, cities, industrial and agricultural distribution, and border issues.

Population Distribution

China's 1.295 billion population (2000) is highly concentrated in eastern China. A line from Heihe City in Heilongjiang to Ruili City in Yunnan divides China into eastern and western areas. The western part covers 57 percent of the territory but has only 5.8 percent of the population; 94.2 percent of Chinese people live in the eastern area with only 43 percent of the territory. In fact, 80 percent of the population is concentrated on just 17 percent of the land area, mostly in major plains, such as the North China Plain, the Middle and Lower Chang Jiang Plain, the Zhu Jiang Plain, and in the Sichuan Basin.

The most densely populated area is Shanghai. The population density in Shanghai was greater than 11,312 people per square kilometer (29,298 people per square mile) in 1990. Jiangsu is the most densely populated province; its population density was 664 people per square kilometer (1,720 people per square mile) in 1993. The most sparsely populated areas are in the northwestern regions and on the Qinghai-Tibet Plateau. The provincial-level unit with the lowest population density is Tibet. Its population density is fewer than two people per square kilometer (five people per square mile).

With 56 nationalities, China is a multiethnic country. However, the Han nationality accounts for 94 percent of the Chinese population. Most Han people live in eastern China, and most minorities live in northern, western, and southwestern autonomous regions near the borderland. Yet more than 70 percent of counties in China have more than two nationalities. Among those minorities, the Hui nationality (Muslim) is the most widely distributed. Outside the Ningxia Hui autonomous region, Hui nationality people can be found in two-thirds of the counties in China. Northern China has more Hui people than southern China.

Migration

There are two major types of migration: interregional and international.

Interregional Migration: Interregional migration includes migration between towns, counties, cities, and provinces. Given the size and complexity of China, this section can only introduce major inter-provincial migrations and note the impact on population distribution.

About 2,200 years ago, or before the Han dynasty (206 B.C.–220 B.C.), the Chinese people were concentrated in the middle and lower reaches of the Huang He River. There were some urban centers that were the capitals of the early Chinese states, such as Xi'an in Shaanxi Province and Luoyang in Henan Province.

The end of the Han dynasty stimulated major migrations. This migration period lasted about 200 years. People moved mainly from the Huang He Basin to the Chang Jiang Basin due to civil war and natural disasters in northern China. After this migration, northern China and southern China had similar populations, about 20 million people each.

During the mid-Tang and after the Tang dynasty (A.D. 618–906), civil wars occurred in northern China, and people migrated to southern China again. After this migration, southern China had a larger population (1.6 million families) than northern China (960,000 families).

After the mid-Qing dynasty (1644–1911), people moved from northern China to northeastern China. Northeastern China was a sparsely populated region compared to northern China at the time; therefore, it was attractive to people seeking good land to cultivate. The northeastern region was opened up to migrants from northern and southern China after the ruler of the Qing dynasty, who was from the northeastern region, took the throne.

During the period of the Japanese invasion between 1931 and 1945, the northeastern, northern, and eastern regions were occupied by Japanese troops. The Chinese government moved to Chongqing; and many businesses, universities, and research institutes also moved to southwestern or northwestern regions. Ordinary people in eastern China moved out of their hometowns and cities to escape the killing, raping, and sacking.

Between 1949 and 1958, economic recovery and growth brought many people from rural to urban areas: about 27.7 million in total, or an average of 2.77 million annually. From 1959 to 1965, when the failure of the Great Leap Forward caused a nationwide recession, the Chinese government required laid-off workers to go back to rural areas. The urban population dropped 2.6 million in three years, from 1961 to 1963. During the period 1949 through 1965, the government assigned high school and university graduates, technical personnel, and skilled workers to the northwest and other periphery provinces to help the economic development in those regions.

During the Cultural Revolution from 1966 to 1976, the Chinese government ordered many factories to move entirely from the eastern to the western region for "the construction of the third line of defense" in preparation for "the Third World War." (Counting from the east coast, the first, or front, line for national defense was the east coast provinces; the central region was considered as the second line; the third line was in the west, such as in Sichuan Province.)

Also during the Cultural Revolution between 1967 and 1976, approximately 17 million young people, middle and high school graduates from cities, were assigned to poor rural areas and state farms in periphery provinces. This movement was called *shangshan xiaxiang*, meaning going up to mountains and going down to villages.

After economic reforms started in 1978, rural people from the remote and poor provinces migrated to large cities and the east coast provinces seeking business and job opportunities. According to the 1990 census, 61.7 percent of people who moved in the year moved into cities. During the five-year period from 1986 through 1990, the cities had a surplus population inflow of 14.6 million. At the provincial level, people moved from interior provinces to coastal provinces. The regions with the maximum net inflow of population between 1986 and 1990 were Guangzhou (915,000), Beijing (543,000), Shanghai (507,000), and Jiangsu (251,000).

International Migration: International migration includes immigration (people moving into a country) and emigration (people moving out of a country). As the world's most populated country, China has more emigrants than immigrants. The major destinations where Chinese people have migrated to are:

- **Southeast Asian countries:** Chinese people from Zhejiang, Fujian, and Guangdong provinces moved to the Philippines, Indonesia, Singapore, Malaysia, and Thailand.

- **North America:** During the 17th, 18th, and 19th centuries, laborers were sold to North America (both Canada and the United States) to build railways. Those people were mainly from Fujian and Guangdong provinces. After 1980, a group of highly educated young Chinese went to North America for scholarly exchange and education. Some of them stayed in North America.

Development of Chinese Cities

China has more than 4,000 years of urban development. This section can give only a very brief introduction on the development and distribution of Chinese cities. If we translate *city* into Chinese, it becomes two Chinese characters: *cheng shi*. *Cheng* means an area surrounded by a wall; *shi* means a market. Those two Chinese characters tell us a city's main functions in ancient China. Today, cities function as political, administrative, and economic centers.

Walled Cities: China built its first walled city more than 4,000 years ago. From then until 1911, about 2,000 walled cities and towns were built. Those walled cities were administrative centers, but most of them were smaller than 1 square kilometer (0.386 square mile).

A typical walled city, such as Xi'an (the capital city during the Qin dynasty), was a square- or rectangular-shaped area aligned due north and south. The city walls had some battlements and some gates with gate towers. In ancient times, those gates opened every morning and closed in the late afternoon. Outside the wall, a moat protected the city. Inside the city, there was a palace quarter for the emperor's family and an administrative quarter for the emperor and government. There were always some markets and parks inside the city walls.

The Evolution of the Urban System in China: During the Qin dynasty (221–206 B.C.), cities were highly concentrated in the middle and lower reaches of the Huang He River, which is the original home of the Han Chinese. About 1,000 years later, in A.D. 1077, during the Northern Song dynasty, the capital and major cities were still concentrated in the middle and lower reaches of the Huang He River Basin. But there were also urban centers in the middle and lower reaches of the Chang Jiang Basin, Sichuan Province, and southern China. China already had developed some foreign trade by that time, and there were some port cities, such as Guangzhou, Quanzhou, and Wenzhou.

By 1953, the distribution of urban centers had changed dramatically from 1077. First, the concentration of large urban centers switched from central China to the east coast due to the development of foreign trade and foreign-owned industries since 1840, which resulted in the growth of cities such as Hong Kong, Guangzhou, Shanghai, and Tianjin. Second, the heavy industrial cities in northeast China also developed mainly during the Japanese occupation from 1931 to 1945. Such cities include Shenyang, Anshan, and Dalian, all of which produced military equipment for Japanese troops. Third, a few interior cities developed during the Anti-Japanese War. Those included Chongqing, Lanzhou, and Chengdu.

From 1949 to 1978, China had a highly centralized, planned economy, and was largely isolated from the rest of the world. The urbanization process during this period reflected the situation. First, the number of cities increased from 157 in 1953, to 300 in 1982. Second, most new cities were developed in the interior region, and the existing cities in the interior region grew faster than those on the east coast. Government policies on national defense, on balancing economic development between the eastern and western regions, and on self-reliance had significant impacts on the development of cities.

From 1978 to 1998, three major changes in government policies affected urbanization. First, the decentralization policy gave individual regions and cities more control of their own revenue and decision making, which enabled the east coast cities to take advantage of their large revenues. Second, open foreign trade policies benefited port cities. Third, the rural industrialization policy added many small urban centers to the country and also sped up suburban industrialization around large cities. The principal beneficiaries were east coast cities, which grew much faster than those in the interior during this period.

Urban Population: The proportion of China's urban population has increased greatly since cities developed thousands of years ago. Although the increase during the last 20 years (1978–1998) was much faster than previous years, the urban population in 2000 was still only 36.2 percent. Though the criteria for counting urban population differs, there is no question that China has a very low level of urbanization compared with the United States (70 percent) or even with the world average (43 percent). This indicates that China is still in the process of transferring agricultural population to manufacturing centers.

Distribution of Cities: In 1996, China had 663 cities. The distribution of the cities is listed in Table 10, which shows that most cities are concentrated on the east coast and in heavily populated provinces. The number of cities in three east coast provinces (Jiangsu, Guangdong, and Shandong) exceed the number of cities in eight provinces and autonomous regions in northwestern and southwestern regions.

Agriculture

The Chinese people have cultivated the land for more than 8,000 years. Many crops, such as rice, millet, sorghum, and soybean, originated in China. With farmers accounting for more than 50 percent of the total labor force, China is still an agricultural country. In order to support the large population, China is the largest producer in the world for most agricultural products, such as cereals, meat, cotton lint, peanut, and rapeseed. In 1995, China produced 22 percent of the world's cereals, one-fourth of its cotton lint and meat, 30 percent of its rapeseed, 36 percent of its peanuts in the shell, 37 percent of its tobacco leaves, and 43 percent of its eggs. Considering that China has 22 percent of the world's population, its per capita pro-

Table 10: Distribution of Chinese Cities, 2000

Region	Provincial and regional capital	Total cities	Prefecture- level cities	County-level cities
Beijing	Beijing			
Tianjin	Tianjin			
Hebei	Shijiazhuang	34	11	23
Shanxi	Taiyuan	22	10	12
Inner Mongolia	Hohhot	20	5	15
Liaoning	Shenyang	31	14	17
Jilin	Changchun	28	8	20
Heilongjiang	Harbin	31	12	19
Shanghai	Shanghai			
Jiangsu	Nanjing	41	13	28
Zhejiang	Hangzhou	35	11	24
Anhui	Hefei	22	17	5
Fujian	Fuzhou	23	9	14
Jiangxi	Nanchang	21	11	10
Shandong	Jinan	48	17	31
Henan	Zhengzhou	38	17	21
Hubei	Wuhan	36	12	24
Hunan	Changsha	29	13	16
Guangdong	Guangzhou	52	21	31
Guangxi	Nanning	19	9	10
Hainan	Haikou	9	2	7
Sichuan	Chengdu	32	18	14
Chongqing	Chongqing	4		4
Guizhou	Guiyang	13	4	9
Yunnan	Kunming	15	4	11
Tibet	Lhasa	2	1	1
Shaanxi	Xi'an	13	9	4
Gansu	Lanzhou	14	5	9
Qinghai	Xining	3	1	2
Ningxia	Yinchuan	5	3	2
Xinjiang	Ürümqi	19	2	17

Source: China State Statistical Bureau. *China Statistical Yearbook, 2001.* Beijing: China Statistical Publishing House, 2001.

duction of most major agricultural products has reached or exceeded the world average.

During the period from 1949 through 1996, both total output and per capita output of crops increased. Compared with the increase in total output, the increase in per capita output is much lower, due to the rapid increase of population. For example, grain products increased more than four times from 1949 to 2000, yet per capita output of grain did not even double during that period (see Table 11).

Distribution: The distribution of crop production in China corresponds to the tremendous differences in physical environment, especially in climate. From east to west, China can be divided into humid-sub-humid and dry areas by the 500-millimeter (20-inch) annual precipitation line. From north to south in the eastern monsoon climate region, China can be divided into temperate and tropical-subtropical areas along the January 0°C (32°F) mean temperature line, along the Qin Ling Mountains and the Huai He River. Between

Table 11: Major Agricultural Products, 1949–2000

Agricultural products	Total output 1,000 metric tons (1,000 U.S. short tons)		Per capita output kilogram (pound)	
	1949	2000	1949	2000
Grain	113,180 (124,785)	405,220 (446,796)	201 (443)	320 (711)
Cotton	444 (490)	4,417 (4,870)	0.7 (1.54)	3.5 (7.8)
Vegetable Oil	2,564 (2,827)	29,548 (32,580)	4.5 (10)	23.3 (51.8)

Source: China State Statistical Bureau. *China Statistical Yearbook, 2001.* Beijing: China Statistical Publishing House, 2001.

warm temperate northern China and temperate northeastern China, the division line is along the Great Wall.

In the tropical-subtropical region south of the Qin Ling and the Huai He line, paddy rice is the dominant crop. About 95 percent of China's paddy fields are in this region, which accounts for about one-fourth of the world's total paddy land and two-fifths of the world's rice production. This region is under double to triple cropping from north to south. Rice production is rotated with winter wheat, winter rapeseed, winter sweet potatoes, winter green manure crops, and summer corn. This region is also one of the major cotton-producing areas in China.

In the warm temperate region between the Qin Ling–Huai He line and the Great Wall, wheat is the dominant crop, with spring wheat in the north and winter wheat in the south of the region. This region can produce three crops (or have three harvests) in two years. Wheat is rotated mainly with summer corn, summer millet, sorghum, and summer soybean. The middle and lower portion of the Huang He Basin is also one of the main cotton-producing areas in China.

In the temperate northeast regions north of the Great Wall, there is only one crop per year due to the low temperatures. The main crops produced in this region are spring wheat, corn, sorghum, soybean, and millet. This region has very fertile black soil and has the most potential cultivatable land in China.

In the western region, a dry climate dominates. It is also cold on the Qinghai-Tibet Plateau. Spring wheat grows in basins— low slopes that are warmer and where

water is available. Highland barley grows on the Qinghai-Tibet Plateau, where it is the major grain crop.

Industry

Industrial Development Before 1949:

China developed modern industry later than western countries. Before 1840, China had only small mills and handicraft shops. The development of modern industry started after the Opium War in 1840, largely under foreign control. From 1840 to 1894, the British controlled Hong Kong as its colonial port and Shanghai as a treaty port. The British invested in shipbuilding, silk textiles, and sugar refining in those regions. At the same time, Chinese-owned industries started with small-scale military factories in Wuhan and light textile and food industries in the Chang Jiang Delta and Guangzhou. At the end of the initial period, there were about 170 enterprises and 100,000 manufacture workers.

From 1895 to 1936, China's industry had a relatively rapid development. About 70 percent of industrial output was still produced by the textile and food industries. The spatial distribution of the industry was very unbalanced: About 70 percent of industry, both foreign-owned and Chinese-owned, was concentrated in the east coast region, especially in Shanghai and the surrounding area. Small industrial enterprises developed rapidly in Tianjin, but Wuhan's industry declined during that period. Heavy industries, such as coal, iron, steel, and machinery, developed in northeastern China under Japanese control. The interior region had less than 20 percent of the industry in China.

From 1931 to 1949, the destructive Japanese invasion, World War II, and the civil war, which broke out one after the other, seriously damaged China's industries. Industrial output in 1949 was only half of the output in 1936. Shanghai and surrounding areas lost more than half of their industrial output. Japanese troops continuously developed heavy industry in northeastern China, mainly in Liaoning Province, to produce military equipment. Sichuan Province, especially the temporary capital, Chongqing, received some industrial investment due to the Japanese occupation in eastern China. Foreign-owned industries did not move out of the eastern region but did not operate normally either. Although the concession regions in Shanghai and Guangzhou were not occupied by Japanese troops, they were often attacked and their economies damaged by bombing, killing, and forced selling.

Before the end of both the Anti-Japanese War and the civil war, industrial fixed assets (such as machines and factories) were either damaged by the war or destroyed before the owner left, especially in the heavy industry sector.

In 1949, China's industry could be characterized by three 70 percent figures: 70 percent of output was produced by foreign-owned industry; more than 70 percent of the output came from light industry; and more than 70 percent of industry was concentrated in the east coast region. Shanghai alone produced 23 percent of national industrial output.

Industrial Development after 1949:
From 1949 to 1977, China had a planned economy with more than 80 percent of industry being state owned. The central government controlled industrial investment and collected all of the industrial profit. This was a period of rapid development, but sometimes growth was hampered by politically motivated movements such as the Great Leap Forward and the Cultural Revolution. During this period, the government emphasized the interior region's development, and more than 55 percent of investment was targeted at the interior region (Table 12). This policy reduced the efficiency of the national economy.

Table 12: Investment in Capital Construction by Region 1953–1980 (State-Owned Firms)

Period	Investment (billion yuan) East coast	Investment (billion yuan) Interior	Percentage (%) East coast	Percentage (%) Interior
1953–1956	21.7	27.6	44.1	55.9
1957–1962	46.3	67.6	40.6	59.4
1963–1965	14.7	24.6	37.5	62.5
1966–1970	26.3	63.1	29.4	70.6
1971–1975	62.5	95.9	39.5	60.5
1976–1980	98.8	117.2	45.8	54.2

Source: Guo, Wanqing. "The Transformation of Chinese Regional Policy." *Development Policy Review* 6.1 (1988): 29-50.

Since economic reforms started in 1978, China's economy has taken off, with industrial output increasing about 10 percent annually. The industrial ownership structure has changed from 80 percent output produced by state-owned firms in 1978 to 35 percent in 1996. Privately owned, collectively owned, and foreign-owned firms became the major producers of China's industrial products. However, the state-owned firms still have many excess employees, and their productivity is lower than in firms under private ownership. In fact, many state-owned firms lose money. Market competition is pushing state-owned firms to lay off workers and even close down completely. The Asian financial crisis, starting in 1997, made things even worse. The restructuring and layoffs in state-owned firms became nationwide problems after 1997.

The regional emphasis switched from the interior to the east coast region after 1978. Table 13 shows that the investment in the east coast region increased from 48 percent in 1981 to 62 percent in 1995. This change in policies and investment fueled the rapid growth of the national economy but widened the gap between the rich east and poor interior.

Rural Industry

Rural industry is the largest industrial sector in China. It produced 55.8 percent of the total industrial output in 1995, com-

Table 13: Investment in Capital Construction by Regions (1981–2000)

Year	Investment (billion yuan)		Percentage (%)	
	East coast	Interior	East coast	Interior
1981	20.8	22.0	48.6	51.4
1985	127.5	126.8	50.1	49.9
1988	259.2	175.7	59.6	40.4
1992	469.0	316.5	59.7	40.3
1995	1,218.8	725.7	62.7	37.3
2000	1,933.6	1,256.1	60.6	39.4

Source: China State Statistical Bureau. *China Statistical Yearbook, 1982, 1986, 1989, 1993, 1996, 2001.* Beijing: China Statistical Publishing House.

pared to 34 percent produced by state-owned industry. Rural industry employed 72.6 million rural laborers, compared to 44.6 million employees in state-owned enterprises in 1995. Rural industry has enjoyed a growth twice as fast as the rest of the economy since 1984, because it has benefited from the market-oriented reforms, the surplus labor released by the rural household responsibility system, and many favorable policies such as tax exemptions. Rural industry has surpassed state-owned industry and has become the largest industrial sector since 1993.

Definition of Rural Industry: The definition of rural industry in China is not the same as in other countries, which define rural industry by its small scale and rural location. China's rural industry is defined by the owner of the enterprises. No matter how large the scale of the enterprise is, what products it produces, and where it is located, as long as the owner of the factory is an agricultural resident, the factory is classified as a rural industry.

Obviously, the question is who is considered an agricultural resident in China? Classification as an agricultural or non-agricultural resident is determined at birth according to the regulations of the household registration system, mostly based on the mother's status. Generally, agricultural and non-agricultural residents live respectively in rural or urban areas, but this is not always true. Some non-agri-cultural residents may live in rural areas but retain the privilege of their status, such as access to government-subsidized food supplies and urban manufacturing jobs. On the other side, agricultural residents may reside in a city and work in a manufacturing firm, but their status remains agricultural. There are some ways for a person to change his or her status from agricultural to non-agricultural, such as graduation from a university, promotion to government officer, or employment by state-owned firms, but workers in rural industrial firms cannot change their status.

Rural industry consists of all industrial activities, from mining, logging, manufacturing, repairing of capital goods (machines), to electricity, gas, and tap water supply activities. "Rural enterprises" (or township and village enterprises) is another often-used term for rural non-agricultural activities. Rural enterprises include industry, construction, transportation, retail, and service firms. Rural industry is the largest sector in rural enterprises, accounting for 73 percent of the total rural enterprise output in 1995.

Rural Industrial Location Policy: China's industrial location policy constrains rural industry to rural areas. The policy allows rural industry to be built only within the community that the owner lives in or in a market town near his community, but not in a city proper. Since the late 1980s, rural entrepreneurs have been allowed to take a term manager's position in a state-owned enterprise with contracted responsibilities but are not allowed to change their rural resident status or to employ rural workers in the urban enterprise. The best expression of the policy is the government slogan "leave the land but not the countryside, enter the factory but not the city." This is a continuation of China's regional development and urbanization policies that strictly control migration from backward regions to developed regions, from small cities to large cities, and from rural to urban areas.

Regional Differences of Rural Industrial Development: The distribution of rural industry has been very unbalanced, and the gap in rural industrial output between the east and the interior has widened in both the 1980s and 1990s. The east coast region produced 72 percent of output in 1989, and the proportion increased to 74 percent in 1994. In 1995, four eastern provinces, Shandong, Jiangsu, Guangdong, and Zhejiang, produced 44 percent of the total rural industrial output. The difference in rural industrial output between the highest (Shandong: 631 billion yuan) and the lowest (Qinghai: 0.77 billion yuan) provinces was more than 800 times in 1994, compared with 380 times in 1989. Thus, the gap more than doubled during the five-year period from 1989 to1994. The inequality of rural industrial development among regions is greater than the overall regional difference. The increasing share of rural industrial output in the national total industrial output (1978: 9 percent, 1989: 28 percent, 1995: 55 percent) has aggravated overall regional disparities of national industrial output (east 1989: 62 percent, 1994: 67 percent).

Transportation

China's transportation activities started thousands of years ago with horse carts and inland waterways. China developed railways, highways, airways, and a pipeline network later than other countries. The density of the transportation networks is either lower than, or similar to, the world average. Railway density was 0.56 kilometers per 100 square kilometers (0.9 mile per 100 square miles) in 1995, a little lower than the world average of 0.95. The density of roads was 12 kilometers per 100 square kilometers (19 miles per 100 square miles), which is higher than the 10.3 world average.

Railways: Railways provide one of the most important transportation networks in China, important for both passenger and freight transport. The rail system is the largest carrier for inland freight and the most important passenger carrier for medium and long distances. The first railway was built in Shanghai in 1876. Rail lines reached 22,900 kilometers (14,232 miles) in 1952 and 56,700 kilometers (35,239 miles) in 1996.

The distribution of the railway network is very unbalanced. The northeastern region has the most railing, with 12,000

kilometers (7,458 miles) in 1994, or 22 percent of China's total. Considering the land area of the region, its railway density is much higher than other regions.

Major rail lines in China can be classified into two groups: north-south and east-west. Major north-south rail lines include Beijing-Shanghai-Fuzhou, Beijing-Wuhan-Guangzhou, Beijing-Jiulong (Hong Kong), and Baoji-Chengdu-Kunming. The major east-west rail line is Lianyungang-Zhengzhou-Xi'an-Ürümqi.

- **Beijing-Shanghai-Fuzhou:** This 1,470-kilometer (914-mile) rail line crosses the coastal plains of north and central China and the economically developed coastal belt. Large amounts of coal, lumber, and petroleum are transported southward; and grains and manufactured products go northward.

- **Beijing-Wuhan-Guangzhou:** The most important and busiest railway in China, it is 2,300 kilometers (1,429 miles) long, crosses Chang Jiang by the famous bridge at Wuhan, and links the railway network to the Chang Jiang's water transport and connects with 16 other lines.

- **Beijing-Jiulong (Hong Kong):** This railway, built in the 1990s, is 2,381 kilometers (1,480 miles) long and parallels the Beijing-Wuhan-Guangzhou line. This line connects Hong Kong directly with Beijing and Tianjin.

- **Baoji-Chengdu-Kunming:** This 1,760-kilometer- (1,094-mile) long rail line was built in 1955. It crosses the Qin Ling mountains to Chengdu, then passes through the eastern margin of the Hengduan Shan Mountains. It was very difficult to build and maintain but is very important because it makes southwest China accessible.

- **Lianyungang-Zhengzhou-Xi'an-Ürümqi:** This line parallels the ancient Silk Road. Built in 1955, it is 3,600 kilometers (2,237 miles) in length. In the 1980s and 1990s, it was extended westward to the Sino-Russian border and will become the shortest trans-Eurasian continental rail link between Europe's coastal ports on the Atlantic and China's Pacific coast.

Inland Waterways: Inland waterways have been used for transportation for seven thousand years in China. As early as in the Qin dynasty, the Chang Jiang and Zhu Jiang were connected by canals. Built in the Tang dynasty, the Grand Canal is 1,500–2,000 kilometers (932–1,243 miles) in length and connects north and south from Beijing to Hangzhou in Zhejiang Province.

The Chang Jiang River and its tributaries are the most important waterways, accounting for 70 percent of the total navigable length of inland waterways in China. The Chang Jiang is navigable year round, and is one of busiest inland waterways in the world. Steamships of 10,000 tons can reach Wuhan in Hubei Province during the high-water season, and 1,000-ton steamships can reach Chongqing. After the building of the Three Gorges Dam, 10,000-ton ocean cargo ships will be able to reach Chongqing.

Sea Waterways: With a 32,000-kilometer (19,888-mile) coast line, China has 158 seaports. From these seaports, ships link China with more than 100 countries and more than 400 seaports.

Fifteen Chinese seaports are major ports, and 14 have been designated as open cities (open to international shipping and with greater local authority over international trade and investment) since 1984. They are: Dalian, Qinhuandao, Tianjin, Qingdao, Yantai, Lianyungang, Nantong, Shanghai, Ningbo, Wenzhou, Fuzhou, Guangzhou, Zhanjiang, and Beihai.

Connecting the Chang Jiang with the East China Sea, Shanghai is the largest ocean and river port in China. It alone handles about 30 percent of China's total seaborne trade and is one of the largest seaports in the world.

Highway: China built its first highway in Hunan Province in 1913. From 1949 to 1996, paved road length increased 17 times and reached 1.2 million kilometers (0.746 million miles). Compared with the area of the country, the highway density is still very low, and the quality of the roads needs to be improved. About 60 percent have sand or stone surfaces.

Civil Aviation: China's first civil aviation company was established in 1929. Air routes increased from 45 in 1948 to 779 in 1995, including 694 domestic and 85 international air routes. Beijing and Shanghai have the busiest international airports in China.

Boundary Issues

China shares her inland border with sixteen countries and ocean boundaries with nine countries. Boundary problems have been ongoing issues in Chinese history since the first state was established. There have been many changes and disputes over thousands of years, including many armed clashes. This section will briefly survey some major issues along the Sino-Russia, Sino-India, Sino-Vietnam, and Sino-Mongolia boundaries.

National boundaries are usually defined by official treaties signed and approved by all parties involved, usually the two countries who share the border. Since one of the two countries may be much stronger than the other, the terms of such treaties are, in effect, imposed on the weaker country. China's refers to treaties signed by previous governments under such outside pressure as "unequal treaties," even though the boundaries they set are still legally recognized.

Most Chinese legal boundaries are also natural boundaries, such as mountains or rivers. Natural boundaries are easy to identify and easy to defend, but determining the actual border lines along river courses, mountain crests, or watersheds can cause disputes. China's boundary problems with her neighboring countries, such as Russia, India, Japan, Vietnam, and the Philippines, are mostly related to problems of natural boundaries.

Sino-Russian Boundary: The first treaty, the Nerchinsk Treaty, signed between Russia and China, came in 1689 when Russia's forces reached the Sea of Okhotsk. China claimed a loss of about 90,000 square miles. There were no major disputes for more than 100 years after the Nerchinsk Treaty. After the loss of the Opium War to the British in 1840, the government of the Qing dynasty was getting weaker. Taking advantage of this opportunity, Russia pushed for a renegotiation of the eastern border with China. Russia and China signed two major treaties: the Aihui

(Aigun) Treaty of 1858, under which China gave up about 485,000 square kilometers (187,000 square miles) north of the Amur River, and the Beijing Treaty of 1860, under which Russia gained an additional area of 346,000 square kilometers (133,000 square miles) east of the Ussuri River.

The Amur River and Ussuri River now serve as boundaries, but disputes remain over some 700 islands in the rivers. According to international laws, river boundaries are based on the deepest line of the main navigable channel, or the median line of the streams, but the Soviet government insisted the boundary was on the Chinese bank and claimed all the islands even though about 600 of them were closer to the Chinese side of the rivers. Russian troops even occupied Zhenbao (Chenpao) Island in the Ussuri River, triggering an armed clash in early 1969. The Russian occupation of Black Blind Bear Island is another unsettled dispute.

On the west end of the Sino-Russia boundary, treaties have moved boundary marks back and forth between China and Russia. China suffered a loss of 455,840 square kilometers (176,000 square miles) of territory under the Tacheng Treaty of 1864, a loss of 38,850 square kilometers (15,000 square miles) under the St. Petersburg Treaty of 1881, and a loss of 85,470 square kilometers (33,000 square miles) in the Pamirs under an agreement between Russia and Great Britain in 1895, which was not recognized by China.

The total loss of Chinese territory to Russia under these treaties has been over 1,683,500 square kilometers (650,000 square miles), which is about the area of California, Arizona, New Mexico, and Texas combined.

Sino-India Boundary: China and India share about 3,542 kilometers (2,200 miles) of boundary. The two countries have had many disputes and armed conflicts over border issues. There are still quite a few sections where the boundary line remains unsettled.

The first treaty was signed between Britain and China in 1842, but the actual boundary was not surveyed at the time. In the 19th century, the British drew several new boundaries toward the Chinese side to separate China from Ladakh. There are

three major parts of these new boundaries: T. Saunders line in the southern part, the J. McCartney and C. McDonald line in the middle, and W. H. Johnson and John Ardagh line in the north. Those new boundaries were not officially recognized or sanctioned by the treaty and caused disputes between the two countries. In the early 1900s, China was too weak to dispute its boundary with British India. After 1949, the Chinese government pushed India to settle the border issues, but without result. Both countries claimed a large portion of Aksai Chin, and an armed conflict occurred there in 1959. A cease-fire was declared in 1962, and Chinese forces retreated 10 kilometers (6.2 miles) and requested the Indian side to do the same; instead, India advanced in several places. This part of the boundary is still unsettled.

Sikkim and Bhutan once both belonged to China. The British took over Sikkim in 1890. Bhutan became a protectorate of British India in 1869 and has been controlled by India since 1949.

On the eastern end of the boundary, British soldiers invaded Tibet in 1904 and forced Tibet to sign the Simla Treaty in 1914. The McMahon line gave a large area to India and was used as the boundary. This line has been one of the major disputes between the two countries. First, China did not participate or sign the treaty, and the independence declared by Tibet in 1912 was never accepted by China. Therefore, China claims the Simla Treaty was illegal. On the other side, the Indian government declared in 1954 that the McMahon line was an official boundary because the treaty was signed when Tibet was independent. Second, the McMahon line only exists on paper; no actual survey was done. The Himalayan Mountains have both watershed and crest, but they are not the same. The crest is more on the Indian side, and the watershed is more on the Chinese side. The McMahon line did not address this issue at all, leaving room for conflicting interpretations by the two countries.

Sino-Mongolia Boundary: Mongolia was called Outer Mongolia and was part of China before 1912. Mongolia declared its independence in 1912, but Russia agreed that Mongolia was still part of China in

1913. With Russian support, Mongolia declared its independence again in 1921. Its independence was officially accepted by China at the Yalta Conference in 1945. The boundary between the two countries was agreed upon in 1962. However, because of thick-moving sands in the deserts, the borderline cannot be clearly identified. Consequently, some disputes have occurred.

Sino-Vietnam Boundary: Vietnam was the Nan Yueh Kingdom conquered by the Han dynasty about 100 B.C. Vietnam became independent around A.D. 939. France gained control over Vietnam in 1883 and defeated China in an 1885 border conflict. A treaty was signed in 1887 by France and China, settling the eastern boundary between China and Vietnam. The western boundary was later agreed upon between China and French Indochina. There are 285 pillars, one every two miles, along the whole boundary, but disputes still occurred between pillars. When the relationship between China and Vietnam deteriorated, it led to an armed conflict along the border in 1979. Since the collapse of the Soviet Union in the late 1980s, relations between China and Vietnam have improved.

Diaoyu Dao (Tiao-yü-t'ai) Islands Issue: The Diaoyu Dao Islands include eight mainly volcanic and coral islands. The largest, Diaoyu Dao, is about 5 square kilometers (less than 2 square miles) in area, and other islands are smaller than 1 square kilometer (0.4 square mile). China claims that Diaoyu Dao was first discovered by the Chinese and appeared in a Chinese atlas in 1403. Japan occupied Taiwan and the Diaoyu Dao Islands from 1895 to 1945. When Japan surrendered in 1945 after World War II, the Diaoyu Dao and Ryukyu Islands were under the supervision of the United States, which returned them to Japan in 1972. Both the central government in China and the Nationalist government in Taiwan claimed that the Diaoyu Dao Islands were part of the Chi-

nese territory and objected to the transfer. In 1978, China and Japan agreed to put the Diaoyu Dao Islands issue on hold. Minor clashes have occurred several times when the Japanese tried to build a lighthouse and other buildings on the islands.

The real importance of the islands lies in their rich resources, especially petroleum deposits and fishing grounds. Whoever controls the islands will have the exclusive rights to those resources.

Islands in South China Sea: There are more than 150 inlets and reefs in the South China Sea near China, Vietnam, Malaysia, Brunei, Indonesia, Singapore, and the Philippines. China claims that the Zenmu (James) Shoal is its southernmost territory, at 3°50'N. All of the islands in the South China Sea are quite small—the largest one is only 1.1 square miles—and volcanic or coral in origin. About half of the South China Sea basin is very shallow, less than 190 meters (600 feet) deep. This is a rich petroleum-bearing continental shelf. It has been estimated that the South China Sea shelf may have more than 47,000 million barrels of oil reserves. These resources have caused disputes over the small islands.

Historically and socially, the Chinese discovered or came to the islands first. The records can be traced back for more than two thousand years in the Han dynasty. Politically, China claimed all of the islands in the South China Sea before World War II. In 1931, French Indochina (Vietnam) claimed several islands and occupied some of them in 1933. During World War II, Japan occupied all the islands. After the war, Japan withdrew from the area. Disputes occurred on some islands soon afterward. Several clashes between China and Vietnam occurred in the 1950s and the 1980s. Disputes have also occurred among China, the Philippines, and Malaysia and also among the Philippines, Malaysia, and Vietnam.

KEY RESEARCH SOURCES

Cannon, Terry, and Alan Jenkins, eds. *The Geography of Contemporary China.* London: Routledge, 1990.

China State Statistical Bureau. *China Statistical Yearbook 1985–2001*. Beijing: China Statistical Publishing House, 1985–2001.

Dathorne, O. R. *Asian Voyages: Two Thousand Years of Constructing the Other*. Westport, Conn.: Bergin & Garvey, 1996.

Institute of Geography of the Chinese Academy of Sciences. *The National Economic Atlas of China*. Hong Kong: Oxford University Press, 1994.

Jen, Mei-o. *An Outline of China's Physical Geography*. Comp. Ren Mei'e, Yang Renzhang, and Bao Haosheng. Trans. Zhang Tingquan and Hu Genkang. Beijing: Foreign Language Press, 1985.

Guo, Wanqing. "The Transformation of Chinese Regional Policy." *Development Policy Review* 6.1 (1998): 29–50.

Kiang, Ying Cheng. *China's Boundaries*. Chicago: The Institute of China Studies, 1991.

Leeming, Frank. *Changing Geography of China*. Boston: Blackwell Publishers Inc., 1993.

Li, Wenyan, and Dadao Lu. *Industrial Geography of China*. Beijing: Science Press, 1995.

Pannell, Clifton W., and Laurence J. C. Ma. *China: The Geography of Development and Modernization*. London: E. Arnold, 1983.

Sivin, Nathan, et al., eds. *The Contemporary Atlas of China*. London: Weidenfeld and Nicolson, 1988.

Smith, Christopher J. *China: People and Places in the Land of One Billion*. Boulder: Westview Press, 1991.

The Institute of Geography, the Chinese Academy of Sciences, and China Pictorial Publications (Zuo Dakang and Xing Yan, chief eds.; Ru Suichu and Yang Qinye deputy chief eds.). *The Natural Features of China*. Beijing: China Pictorial Publishing House, 1992.

The Population Census Office of the State Council of the People's Republic of China and the Institute of Geography of the Chinese Academy of Sciences, comp. and ed. *The Population Atlas of China*. New York: Oxford University Press in association with China Statistics Publishing House, 1987.

Yeung, Yue-man, and Hu Xu-wei, eds. *China's Coastal Cities*. Hawaii: University of Hawaii Press, 1992.

Zhao, Ji, et al. *The Natural History of China*. London: Collins, 1990.

Zhao Songqiao (Chao, Sung-ch'iao). *Geography of China, Environment Resources, Population and Development*. New York: John Wiley, 1994.

Peoples and Languages

By Patrick P. Lin

INTRODUCTION

China is the most populous country in the world. More than one-fifth of the world's entire population is Chinese. The Chinese people created one of the world's earliest civilizations with a recorded history that dates back some 3,500 years. Within the Chinese population, approximately 92 percent are ethnic Han Chinese. The other 8 percent consist of 55 national minorities settled throughout 60 percent of China's territory. This gives the non-Han peoples of China a significance that looms larger than their percentage of the population might suggest.

The Han people speak the Chinese language, which is commonly spoken in all parts of the country as well as in distinct communities outside China. Most of China's national minorities have their own languages and dialects. The Han Chinese language comprises seven major dialect groups, some of which are mutually unintelligible. The numerous languages and dialects spoken in China make the overall language situation very complex. However, most Chinese share a common writing system, known as Chinese characters, which was invented more than 3,000 years ago. The Chinese government has promoted language reform to meet the challenges it faces in the modern communication age.

1. A BRIEF HISTORY OF THE HAN CHINESE

Millennia of development in China have produced a great variety of languages and dialects, a distinctive system of writing, and political organizations. It also bred the Han nationality through nationwide migration and national amalgamation and assimilation.

The Formation of the Han Chinese

The Legendary Emperor—Huang Di: The earliest vestiges of Chinese settlement can be traced to the Peking man of approximately 450,000 years ago, as evidenced by excavations at a site near Beijing. However, the establishment of more extensive communities did not begin until much later. Communities sprang up in the Yellow River Basin approximately 10,000 years ago. The tribes in those communities later became the subjects of folklore and myths. A legendary leader of a tribe, named Huang Di (c. 3000 B.C.), united other tribes and controlled the Great Plains of north China. This tribe later came to be considered as the ancestors of the Chinese. Han Chinese still call themselves "descendants of Huang Di."

The Prehistoric Dynasty—Xia: Xia (c. 2200–1554 B.C.) is believed to be China's first prehistoric dynasty. Since the 1970s, archaeologists have uncovered urban sites, bronze implements, and tombs that lend credence to this theory. Due to the undocumented history of the Xia era, this dynasty has been the subject of myths. Xia Yu (c. 2200 B.C.) was another legendary leader in Chinese history. One of his greatest accomplishments was controlling the flooding of the Yellow River.

The Beginning of Written History—Shang: Thousands of archaeological findings in the Yellow River Valley provide evidence about the Shang dynasty (1554–1045 B.C.). This era experienced revolutionary changes in technology, such as the development of the writing system and the first use of bronze. The earliest Chinese characters, known as Oracle Bone Script, were carved on tortoise shells and flat cattle bones. Those were the first written records in China.

The Expanding Period—Zhou: The Zhou (1045–256 B.C.) was the longest dynasty in Chinese history, with capitals at Hao (near present Xi'an) and later at Luoyang. During their reign of 800 years, Zhou rulers extended Shang culture through much of China proper by conquering neighboring barbarians. In 771 B.C., the Zhou king was killed by invading barbarians, and the capital was moved eastward. Historians regard this as the watershed between the periods of the Western Zhou (1045–771 B.C.) and the Eastern Zhou (770–256 B.C.), which is further divided into two subperiods: the Spring and Autumn period and the Warring States period. Although disunity and civil wars marked the end of the Eastern Zhou, it was an unprecedented era of cultural prosperity, known as the era of the Hundred Schools of Thought. Many of the period's great thinkers, such as Confucius (551–479 B.C.), Meng Zi (372–289 B.C.), Han Fei (d. 233 B.C.), and Li Si (d. 208 B.C.), greatly influenced Chinese people for the next two millennia.

The First Imperial Period—Qin: Lasting fewer than 20 years, the Qin dynasty (221–206 B.C.) was the shortest in Chinese history, yet it marked an important dividing line in the nation's development. Much of China proper was unified for the first time by the king of Qin, Shi Huangdi (259–210 B.C.), in 221 B.C. His legacy was the central bureaucratic system, which influenced imperial policies for the next two millennia. He standardized the forms of writing and forced people to believe in only one philosophy and religion. To fend off barbarian intrusions, Qin connected the existing fortifications to make a 5,000-kilometer-long wall. Known as the Great Wall, it would come to symbolize China's isolation 2,000 years later. The Qin legacy resulted in a unified China empire with a vast territory and a deep-rooted culture.

The Origin of the Name—Han: The Han empire (206 B.C.–A.D. 220) was known for its military prowess. The empire expanded its territory westward as far as the rim of the Tarim Basin (in the modern Xinjiang autonomous region). Han armies also annexed parts of northern Vietnam and northern Korea. Culturally, the Han dynasty was notable for the establishment of Confucian ideals in government and its flourishing literature. China's most famous historian, Sima Qian (c. 145–87 B.C.), wrote his great book, *Shiji* (The Book of History) during this period. The formation of the ethnic Han nationality was established in this period, as well as the term Han Chinese language.

Further Expansions and Developments

The High Point in Chinese Civilization—Tang: The collapse of the Han dynasty was followed by nearly four centuries of disunity caused by warlords. To escape from wars, a great number of Chinese people moved from the north to the south, bringing a strong Chinese influence to the southern minorities. China was reunified in A.D. 589 by the short-lived Sui dynasty (581–618). The Tang dynasty (618–907) soon followed the fall of the Sui. The tradition of military superiority was reestablished in the Tang, and its territory was even greater than that of the Han empire. The Tang period was also the golden age of literature and art. Classic Chinese poetry and prose reached its peak in the Tang dynasty.

The Beginning of Military Decline—Song: The Tang dynasty was terminated by northern invaders in 907 after prolonged internal rebellions. China fragmented into five northern dynasties and ten southern kingdoms. The Song dynasty (960–1279) reunified most of China in 960. Learning lessons from the warlord rebellions during the Tang dynasty, the Song rulers replaced regional military governors and their supporters with centrally appointed officials. This system of civilian rule led to a greater concentration of power in the emperor but weaker military leadership. The empire soon suffered from invasions by northern nomadic tribes. In 1127, the Song court abandoned northern China. Although the dynasty continued in the South, the Song never regained either north China or their power. Mongolian forces eventually eliminated the southern Song in 1279.

The First Alien Dynasty—Yuan: The Mongolians established the first alien dynasty to rule all China. Believing the Chinese to be inferior, the Mongols discriminated against them socially and politically. Ironically, the Mongols still sought to govern China by employing the traditional political system and Chinese bureaucrats. Consequently, a rich cultural diversity developed during the Yuan dynasty (1276–1368). The Mongols' major military achievement was the conquest of west Asia and part of Europe, which produced a fair amount of cultural exchange between China and the outside world. The major cultural achievement during the Yuan dynasty was the development of drama and the novel and the increased use of the written vernacular.

Han Chinese Regain Power—Ming:
The Mongol government was overthrown by numerous Chinese uprisings. A Han Chinese peasant and former Buddhist monk founded the Ming dynasty (1368–1644). He established the capital first at Nanjing and later moved it to Beijing. Since then, Beijing has been the political and cultural center of China. With strong military forces, the Ming dynasty expanded its territory to northern Vietnam. The famous maritime expeditions of the Ming dynasty further enhanced the contacts between China and the outside world. A Chinese fleet sailed the seas off China and far across the Indian Ocean, cruising to the east coast of Africa. From that time on, a path to the outside world was established.

The Last Imperial Dynasty—Qing: In 1644, the Manchus invaded Beijing and established the second alien dynasty to rule all China. The Qing (1644–1911) rulers retained many institutions of the Ming, including the Confucian civil service system, and employed many Chinese officials, except in high military positions. Although the Qing rulers took measures to prevent the absorption of the Manchus into the dominant Han Chinese population, such as

prohibiting intermarriage between the two groups, the national amalgamation and cultural fusion was inevitable. As a result, the Manchus lost almost all of their own traditions within 300 years. Another development of the Qing dynasty was in Chinese literature. The "four great novels" in Chinese literature were published in the Ming and Qing periods. As the last imperial dynasty, the Qing acquired extensive territory, including all of what is now considered modern China.

Emergence of Modern China

The Republican Revolution of 1911:
In the 19th century, Japan and the western powers were eager to open China's door for profits. They invaded China and forced the Qing rulers to sign unequal treaties. Facing the threat of invasion, the Qing court failed to reform its old political and economic systems. The corrupt government was unable to protect the interests of peasants or prevent the intrusion of foreign soldiers. In 1905, Sun Yat-sen (1866–1925) founded the anti-Qing organization Tongmeng Hui (United League). Under the Tongmeng Hui organization, the anti-Qing republican revolution broke out on October 10, 1911, in Wuchang, the capital of Hubei Province. The revolt quickly spread throughout the whole country. On January 1, 1912, Sun Yat-sen was inaugurated in Nanjing as the provisional president of the newly founded Republic of China. The last emperor of China, Puyi, was forced to abdicate on February 12, 1912. The last imperial dynastic tradition of China was concluded.

The Republic of China: The Republic of China lasted from 1912 to 1949. After its establishment, China fell under the control of warlords, and civil wars continued for decades. In August 1912, one of the major parties in modern China's history, the Guomindang (Nationalist Party), was founded. On May 4, 1919, a leftist political and cultural movement was founded in Beijing. Under its influence, another major party in modern China, the Chinese Communist Party, was set up in Shanghai on July 1, 1921. The union and struggles between the Guomindang and the Chinese Communist Party constituted China's modern history. In 1949, after losing the third civil war of 1945 to 1949, Chiang Kai-shek (1887–1975) and his Republican government fled to the isolated island of Taiwan. The Chinese mainland fell under the control of the Chinese Communist Party.

The People's Republic of China: On October 1, 1949 the leader of the Chinese Communist Party, Mao Zedong (1893–1976), announced the establishment of the People's Republic of China in Beijing. To reconstruct and develop China's economy, Mao launched an economic campaign in 1958 known as the Great Leap Forward. Largely because of poor planning and widely ambitious goals, this campaign ended in economic disaster, causing tens of thousands of people to die of hunger. Mao also led several political movements to consolidate the leadership of the Communist

Party in China. One of the largest movements was the Great Proletarian Cultural Revolution (1966–1976). The Cultural Revolution caused economic and social chaos and developed into the biggest political upheaval for the nation since 1949. After Mao Zedong's death in 1976, his successors gradually made changes in the party's political and economic policies. The classic party line emphasizing class struggle was officially changed to promote the Four Modernizations (modernization of industry, agriculture, national defense, and science and technology). In January 1979, full diplomatic relations were established with the United States. In the 1980s and early 1990s, the implementation of the Reform and Open Door policy successfully sparked an economic boom.

2. CHINA'S GROWING POPULATION

China has been blessed with vast fertile lands and a long history of highly centralized government. That combination naturally led to a rapid growth of population. However, social issues always reversed this trend. To fully understand China's population trends in the present, some historical background information is necessary.

China's Population in the Imperial Era

The Historical Records: The first nationwide census took place in the Western Han dynasty in 2 A.D. This was the earliest record of China's population. After the Western Han, every dynasty took its population counts at irregular intervals. The table below shows the historical data of China's population during the period from A.D. 2 to 1851.

Population Fluctuation and the Causes: The historical data in Table 1 indicates two large decreases and three rapid increases in China's population during the 1,850-year-long period.

All population decreases in Chinese history are associated with dynastic struggles, wars, and disunity. The first big decrease

Historical Population Estimates

Date	Dynasty	Persons counted	Adjusted to PRC boundaries
2	Western Han	59,594,978	N/A
88	Eastern Han	43,356,367	N/A
156	Eastern Han	56,486,856	N/A
606	Sui	46,019,956	N/A
705	Tang	37,140,000	N/A
755	Tang	52,919,309	N/A
1014	Northern Song	21,996,965	54.3
1103	Northern Song	45,981,845	123.1
1193	Southern Song	27,845,085	122.3
1290	Yuan	58,834,711	N/A
1381	Ming	59,873,305	N/A
1749	Qing	177,495,000	176.5
1851	Qing	431,896,000	429.5

Source: *China's Changing Population* (Judith Banister, 1987).

in population took place after the Western Han dynasty collapsed after a series of civil wars. The population dropped from 59.6 million to 43.4 million in a period of 86 years. The second largest decrease in

China's history took place during the era of civil wars after the collapse of the Eastern Han dynasty. In 550 years, China's population decreased from 56.5 million (A.D. 156) to 46.0 million in the Sui dynasty (A.D. 606). The short-lived Sui dynasty (37 years) did not stop the trend of decline. After numerous internal struggles, the Tang dynasty replaced the Sui and reunited China. China's population totaled only 37.1 million in A.D. 705.

All the periods of population growth in China took place at times of peace and prosperity. The first recorded instance of sustained population growth occurred under the Tang dynasty in the early eighth century. After the strong Tang empire restored peace and unity, China's population increased from 37.1 million to 52.9 million within 50 years. The second largest recorded growth came during the Northern Song period. The adjusted population increased from 54.3 million to 123.1 million in 80 years from 1014 to 1094. The most rapid population growth occurred in the middle of the 18th century during the Qing dynasty. The empire had enjoyed a long period of peace and prosperity. China's population jumped from 176.5 million in 1749 to 429.5 million in 1851, more than a doubling in a century.

Population Growth after 1949

Upon its founding in 1949, the People's Republic of China (PRC) inherited a huge population. In order to assess its manpower, the Chinese government has conducted four censuses within its borders since 1953. Compared to the historical population data mentioned above, the results from these censuses are more reliable.

Methodology of the Census: It is very difficult to conduct a nationwide census in such a vast country with such a great population. The first two censuses conducted in 1953 and 1964 were generally faulty due to inefficient technology and methods. To avoid such mistakes, foreign analysts were hired for the census project after 1982. Aside from the analysts and foreign funds, foreign contributors also provided advanced equipment and new technology. Scholars from China were sent abroad to learn new methods. A computer network

was established in each of the provinces, each linked to the Statistics Department in Beijing. The new computer network improved communication by relaying information directly to Beijing. New technology and new methods contributed greatly to the accuracy of the last two censuses.

Results from the Censuses: In order to assess the human resources available for the first Five-Year Plan of economic development, the Chinese government conducted the first census in 1953. The total population was 567,446,758. The second census, taken in 1964, counted 694,581,759 people. The 1982 census, considered more comprehensive than the previous two, revealed a population of 1,008,175,288. That was the first time China passed the billion mark. The number was widely quoted as China's official population total. In 1983, the Chinese government announced that there would be one census every ten years thereafter. The fourth census was conducted in 1990. That census reported China's total population as 1,133,682,501. The fifth census conducted in 2000 found China's population had reached 1,295,330,000 (including Hong Kong, Macao, and Taiwan).

Estimated Population in 1998: Demographers nationwide and abroad are well aware of China's growing population. Based on the latest census conducted in 1990 and the population data obtained from the State Council Population Office of China, the *World Almanac and Book of Facts* (1998) estimated the total population of China in 1998 as 1,210,004,956. That number excludes the estimated population in Taiwan (20,390,000), Hong Kong (6,400,000), and Macao (500,000). The State Family Planning Commission estimated that China's population would reach 1.4 billion in 2010.

Mortality, Life Expectancy, and Fertility: The following data show the mortality, life expectancy, fertility, and rate of natural increase in China during the period from 1953 to 1987.

Mortality: In 1949, China's crude death rate was probably higher than 30 per 1,000. After the founding of the PRC, the mortality rate steadily declined. By 1969, the crude death rate was less than 10 per

1,000. It continued to decline in the 1970s and remained relatively constant through the 1990s. In 1990, the census reported the mortality rate to be only 6.28 per 1,000. The only major fluctuation, according to a report by the United States Bureau of the Census (Judith Banister, 1987), took place during the famine years associated with the Great Leap Forward (1958–1961). The crude death rate dramatically increased to 44 per 1,000. Millions of people reportedly died during that period. However, the Chinese government did not confirm the number.

Life Expectancy: The average life expectancy in China was only 32 years in 1949. Since then, life expectancy has dramatically increased. By 1987, life expectancy was 66 years. This rate increased steadily through the 1990s. This trend was reversed once, during the famine years

Life Expectancy

Year	Crude birth rate (per thousand)	Crude death rate (per thousand)	Rate of natural increase (per thousand)	Life expectancy at birth
1953	42.24	25.77	16.47	40.25
1954	43.44	24.20	19.24	42.36
1955	43.04	22.33	20.71	44.60
1956	39.89	20.11	19.78	46.99
1957	43.25	18.12	25.13	49.54
1958	37.76	20.65	17.11	45.82
1959	28.53	22.06	6.47	42.46
1960	26.76	44.60	-17.84	24.56
1961	22.43	23.01	-0.58	38.44
1962	41.02	14.02	27.00	53.00
1963	49.79	13.81	35.98	54.91
1964	40.29	12.40	27.84	57.08
1965	38.98	11.61	27.37	57.81
1966	39.83	11.12	28.71	58.59
1967	33.91	10.47	23.44	59.41
1968	40.96	10.08	30.88	60.29
1969	36.22	9.91	26.31	60.84
1970	36.98	9.54	27.44	61.41
1971	34.87	9.24	25.63	61.98
1972	32.45	8.85	23.60	62.55
1973	29.85	8.58	21.27	62.96
1974	28.08	8.32	19.76	63.37
1975	24.79	8.07	16.72	63.79
1976	23.05	7.84	15.21	64.21
1977	21.04	7.65	13.39	64.63
1978	20.73	7.52	13.21	65.06
1979	21.37	7.61	13.76	64.98
1980	17.63	7.65	9.98	64.89
1981	21.04	7.73	13.31	64.80
1982	21.09	7.89	13.20	64.72
1983	18.66	7.93	10.73	65.05
1984	17.20	7.79	9.73	65.46
1985	17.82	7.72	10.10	65.75
1986	17.43	7.69	9.74	65.99
1987	17.38	7.65	9.73	66.24

Source: *China's Changing Population* (Judith Banister, 1987).

(1958–1961). The death of millions of people brought down life expectancy significantly.

Fertility: According to Chinese government statistics, the crude birth rate has experienced wild fluctuations in four different periods since the founding of the PRC. The first period, from 1950 to 1957, had a crude birth rate above 4 percent. During the second period, from 1958 to 1961, the crude birth rate declined sharply due to the famine. The birth rate reached as low as 2.2 percent in 1961. The crude birth rate varied widely in the third period, from 1962 to 1969, with a high of 4.9 percent and a low of 3.3 percent during the chaos of the Cultural Revolution. Starting in 1970, the fourth period has shown a steady decline in the crude birth rate following the implementation of the nationwide birth control program. In 1984, the crude birth rate was only 1.7 percent. This low birth rate trend carried through the 1990s.

3. POPULATION CHARACTERISTICS

Based on the population data provided by the four censuses, it is possible to take a closer look at different aspects of China's population, including the geographic and ethnic distribution, population density, population structure, inter-provincial migration, and urbanization.

Population Distribution

Uneven Geographic Distribution: The majority of Chinese people live in the eastern segment of the country. In the northern and western sections of China, steep mountains, vast deserts, high plateaus, and arid grasslands thwart any attempts at large-scale agriculture. Thus, these areas are incapable of supporting a dense population. By contrast, the eastern, central and southeastern parts consist of plains, river valleys, and basins. These areas are ideal for farming, and hence the bulk of the population is found here. Censuses show that the vast majority of China's population was always found in the 19 eastern provinces that have been the historical heartland of China for thousands of years.

Countryside Versus Cities: Most Chinese people are peasants living in the countryside. The 1953 census found that 86.7 percent of the population lived there. The rural population decreased to 81.6 percent in the 1964 census. The rural population further decreased to 79.2 percent and 73.8 percent in 1982 and 1990, respectively. In 1990, the rural population nevertheless still constituted the majority of China's population.

Meanwhile, China's population has become more urban since the beginning of the 1980s. The 1990 census reported China's urban population at 297 million, an increase of nearly 90 million, or 30 percent, since 1982. During the same period, Beijing's population increased by 17 percent though the natural increase was estimated at 8 percent. These statistics show the ongoing trend of migration to the cities.

Population Density

The Nation's Population Density: For the whole country, the population density increases as the population grows. In 1953, the first census revealed the country's population density to be 59 people per square kilometer. By 1964, the density had increased to 72 people per square kilometer, to 105 in 1982, and to 118 in 1990. In 1998, the population density was estimated at 126 people per square kilometer (about 327 per square mile).

The Provincial Population Density: China has very uneven terrain. Therefore, the population densities between provinces and cities are quite different, ranging from 2,174 people per square kilometer in Shanghai to 2 people per square kilometer in Tibet. The following table shows the contrast in population density between the twenty-two provinces, five autonomous regions, and three cities of municipality in the Chinese mainland in 1992.

Inter-Provincial Migration and Urbanization

The Government's Policy: The Chinese government utilizes a permanent residence system, known as the *hukou* system, binding a person to the place where the person was registered. Social benefits, including education, housing, and employment, are integrated with the hukou system. Without government approval, one cannot alter one's registered permanent residence.

Population Density

Province / City	Population in 1949	Population in 1992	Area in sq. km.	Population per sq. km. in 1992
North				
Beijing	4,140,000	11,020,000	16,807	656
Tianjin	3,990,000	9,200,000	11,305	814
Hebei	30,860,000	62,750,000	187,700	334
Shanxi	18,810,000	29,790,000	156,300	191
Inner Mongolia	5,150,000	22,070,000	1,183,000	19
Northeast				
Liaoning	18,310,000	40,160,000	145,700	276
Jilin	10,090,000	25,320,000	187,400	135
Heilongjiang	10,140,000	36,080,000	453,300	80
East				
Shanghai	5,030,000	13,450,000	6,186	2,174
Jiangsu	35,120,000	69,110,000	102,600	674
Zhejiang	20,830,000	43,360,000	101,800	426
Anhui	27,860,000	58,340,000	139,900	417
Fujian	11,880,000	31,160,000	123,100	253
Jiangxi	12,680,000	39,130,000	166,600	235
Shandong	45,490,000	86,100,000	153,300	562
Central & South				
Henan	41,740,000	88,620,000	167,000	531
Hubei	25,360,000	55,800,000	185,900	300
Hunan	29,870,000	62,670,000	204,000	307
Guangdong	30,040,000	65,250,000	212,000	362
Guangxi	18,420,000	43,800,000	236,200	185
Hainan	N/A	6,860,000	34,000	202
Southwest				
Sichuan	57,300,000	109,980,000	569,000	193
Guizhou	14,160,000	33,610,000	176,300	191
Yunnan	15,950,000	38,320,000	394,000	97
Tibet	1,150,000	2,280,000	1,228,400	2
Northwest				
Shaanxi	13,170,000	34,050,000	205,600	166
Gansu	9,680,000	23,140,000	454,000	51
Qinghai	1,480,000	4,610,000	721,500	6
Ningxia	1,200,000	4,870,000	60,000	81
Xinjiang	N/A	15,810,000	1,646,800	10
Total	519,900,000	1,166,710,000	9,629,698	121

Source: *Atlas of China.* Beijing: China Maps Publishing House, 1994.

Since the 1960s, the Chinese government has promoted inter-provincial migration to the thinly populated western provinces and autonomous regions. Thousands of People's Liberation Army soldiers, government cadres, and college graduates were assigned to work in those areas. These activities led to population increases in those areas. On the other hand, the Chinese government strictly prohibits spontaneous migration from the countryside to the city. The government also restricts residents' movement within cities. A person must have the government's approval and a guarantee of a residence and employment before moving.

Movement of the Educated Urban Youth: During the Cultural Revolution, the Chinese government launched a nationwide campaign of sending educated urban youths to the countryside for several years or permanent settlement. This was officially called the "movement of the educated urban youth settling in the rural areas." The original motive was to provide urban skills in rural areas, thereby discouraging peasant migrations to the cities. In addition, the scheme was designed to provide jobs to millions of youths and high school graduates. This movement was eliminated at the beginning of 1980s, at which time migration to the cities began to increase significantly.

Economic Reform and Urbanization: In the early 1980s, the Chinese government began to implement a new policy called "Reform and Open Door Policy." Many investors from Taiwan, Hong Kong, Macao, and abroad were attracted to China to open enterprises. A nationwide economic boom occurred. As a by-product, spontaneous migration from the underdeveloped areas to cities took place throughout the country. Millions of peasants from western and southeastern rural areas poured into the so-called "Special Economic Zones" such as Shenzhen, Zhuhai, and Xiamen along the eastern coast. Statistics show that the population of the cities in the Pearl River Delta of Guangdong almost doubled in the 1990s. About half of the workforce was from other provinces. Although many of the non-local workers were temporary residents, some of them became permanent local residents through marriage and permanent employment status.

Population Among Ethnic Groups

Most of the population in China is Han Chinese. Only a small portion of the population belongs to the 55 national minorities. The table at the bottom of this page shows the population of Han Chinese and all minorities in the four censuses conducted from 1949. Note the 1953 census included the military in its breakdown of ethnic groups. Only the ethnic composition of the civilian population was recorded in later censuses.

In 1949, the minority population in China totaled 32.9 million. By 1990, this number had increased to 91.2 million, 2.77 times the total in 1949. The annual population growth rate was as high as 2.52 percent, 0.7 percent higher than that of the Han Chinese during the past 41-year period. This increase can be attributed to the nation's population policy, which favors minorities. By the end of 2000, the minority population had increased to 106.43 million.

Population Among Sexes

The following table, based on the four censuses conducted, shows the breakdown of population by gender in the past 40 years.

Population Among Ethnic Groups

Year	Total population	Han Chinese		All Minorities	
		Population	Percentage	Population	Percentage
1953	567,446,758	547,283,057	96.45	35,320,360	6.22
1964	694,581,759	651,296,368	93.77	39,923,736	5.75
1982	1,008,175,288	936,703,824	92.91	67,233,254	6.67
1990	1,133,682,501	1,042,482,187	91.96	91,200,314	8.04

Population by Gender, 1953–1990

Year	Total population	Males	Females	Male-to-female ratio
1953	567,446,758	291,969,807	275,746,951	105:98
1964	694,581,759	356,517,011	338,064,748	105:45
1982	1,008,175,288	519,433,369	488,741,919	106:28
1990	1,133,682,501	584,949,922	548,732,579	106:60

The above data indicate that while the sex structure in the total population remained relatively stable in the past 40 years, the number of males increased more quickly than that of females. The increase of the male-to-female ratio suggests the rise of female infanticide and selective abortion, two unintended negative results of China's population control program.

4. CHINA'S POPULATION CONTROL PROGRAMS

After the founding of the People's Republic of China in 1949, China's leaders initially viewed a large population as an asset. However, the problems of a large, rapidly growing population soon became apparent. After the interval of the Great Leap Forward, Chinese leaders realized the importance of population control and began the population control programs.

Problems of the Rapid Growth Population

A Great Economic Burden: With less than 7 percent of the cultivated farmland in the world, China had to feed one-fifth of the world's population. This was a great burden for the Chinese economy in the 1960s. Indeed, there would be great political and economic implications for China if economic growth cannot equal or exceed the trend of population growth. Even if the Chinese government maintains steady economic growth, a huge population would cause high unemployment, crowded transportation, pollution, and other social problems.

Housing Shortage: Housing shortages became apparent in the 1960s as the children born after 1949 reached adulthood. Many young people of marriageable age were forced to wait for residences provided by the government. In Shanghai, Beijing, and other large cities, there was an ironic joke to describe the situation: "It is harder to find a wedding room than to find a wife." In the late 1980s, the implementation of the Reform and Open Door Policy lessened this problem by creating new residential buildings. However, housing shortages remain a problem in many urban areas.

Education Problem: The huge population caused problems in education. With a growing population of students, there were shortages in funds, universities, colleges, and schools. According to official statistics, only 5 percent of all high school graduates could enroll in a college or university. Only about half of the middle school graduates could continue their secondary education. This lack of educational resources will cause great problems for China in the future.

Administration of the Population Control

In 1964, the government created the State Family Planning Commission to administer the population control program. The commission was directly under the State Council, the highest administrative authority of the country. Within years, family planning committees were established at all administrative levels and in various collective enterprises to oversee birth control activities. However, much of the success of the family planning program was attributed to the huge number of people who carried it out. These people included numerous female cadres, barefoot doctors, midwives, and other family planning motivational workers. They actually implemented the family planning instructions handed down from higher authorities. They held meetings of the married women or couples in their unit to transmit the latest policies. They visited households regularly to promote family planning and delivered contraceptives. They were not paid by the committee, but worked voluntarily for the country's future.

The First Birth Control Campaign

The first large-scale birth control activity was the so-called *Wan, Xi, Shao* propaganda campaign during the 1970s. The Chinese words *Wan, Xi, Shao* are defined as "later marriage, longer intervals between births, and fewer children."

Late Marriage: Young people of marrying age were encouraged to marry late and give birth late. According to the propaganda, the ideal age to marry was 26 for men and 24 for women in urban areas, and 25 and 23 in rural areas. Late marriages were legislated in the new "Marriage Law" for several years in the early 1970s. In urban areas, the authorities refused to issue a marriage certificate to couples under age 24. Later, along with the continued promotion of late marriage was a new emphasis on "late birth." "Late birth" meant that no matter what the age at marriage, couples should postpone their first birth until the woman was 24 or 25. This idea was contrary to historical custom in China.

Longer Intervals Between Births: The government recommended that there should be at least a four-year interval between the first and second child. An abortion was forced on couples who disobeyed the law. Young couples were also urged to take contraceptives after their first child was born. Contraceptives were available in hospitals, clinics, and drugstores free of charge. In rural areas, female cadres and barefoot doctors (doctors

trained for working in the countryside) delivered contraceptives door to door for young couples.

Fewer Children: The Chinese government also promoted the idea that the fewer children, the better. In the mid-1970s, the maximum recommended family size was two children in cities and three in the countryside. To ensure families would have fewer children, sterilization was encouraged for parents who already had two or more children. Male sterilization, however, was not as popular as female sterilization in most parts of China, because men usually associated it with castration, which was considered a shame in Chinese society.

One-Child-Per-Family Policy

China has instituted and sustained the world's first lasting nationwide compulsory family planning program. The Chinese government was also the first in the world to attempt to popularize the ideal of a one-child family.

Goal of the One-Child Policy: Facing the pressure of a rapidly growing population, China's leaders changed their early two-child policy to a one-child-per-family policy in 1979. The government attributed this change to the fact that 65 percent of the population was less than 30 years of age and that a substantial proportion of the population will be of childbearing age for at least the next several decades. As the goal of the one-child policy, the Chinese government declared in 1982 that the nation must limit its population to 1.2 billion by the year 2000. This ambitious goal required an intensification of population control efforts. By 1988, the government recognized the goal as unattainable and revised it to 1.27 billion, and revised it again to 1.3 billion in 1998. This goal has finally been met. According to the census conducted in 2000, China's total population was successfully limited to 1.295 billion.

Special Considerations for Minorities: Initially, the population control program did not apply to minorities. Under the nationwide one-child-per-family policy, special considerations were given to the national minorities. As of 1986, the policy for national minorities was two children per couple, three in special circumstances, and no limit for ethnic groups with very small populations. Given this favorable population policy, China's minorities grew at a much faster rate than the Han Chinese.

Rewards and Penalties: The Chinese government employed a combination of propaganda, social and economic pressure, and in some cases coercion to implement the one-child policy. The one-child program rewarded those who observed the policy with benefits such as cash bonuses, longer maternity leave, better child care, and preferential housing assignments. Penalties for those who did not observe the policy included fines, loss of jobs, and social discrimination. For an extra child, parents had to pay a fine of thousands of *yuan* (the Chinese dollar) to the local government. The size of the fine varied in different areas, ranging from 2,000 to 10,000 yuan. It usually exceeded a parent's income for a whole year. In urban areas, the birth of the second child would sometimes cause the parents to lose their jobs immediately.

Mixed Results

Low Population Growth Rates: After the implementation of the one-child policy, for years the nation's population growth rates went down significantly. In 1980, the crude birth rate decreased to 17.6 per thousand from 36.9 per thousand 10 years before. Starting in 1984, the low crude birth rate of 17.5 per thousand steadily declined through the 1990s. In general, the one-child-per-family policy was very successful in urban areas. In Shanghai, the natural population growth rate has been negative since 1993. In 1997, its crude birth rate was 5.5 per thousand, and the natural population growth rate was −1.3 per thousand. In the rural areas, however, the population control program was less successful. The demand for laborers to work in the field, the lack of a retirement benefit system, and the traditional thinking "more sons, more happiness" were the main reasons peasants produced more children, especially sons.

Aging Population: The one-child-per-family policy also had negative results. One of the biggest problems was the aging population. Based on United Nations statistics and data provided by the Chinese government, it was estimated that the population of 65 years and older would reach 90 million by the year 2000, and 167 million by 2020. Compared with an elderly population of 66 million in the 1990 census, the speed of population aging is worrisome. In China, most rural elderly have no old-age pensions and must rely on their adult children for support. Since a family only has one child, when the child becomes an adult he or she may not be able to take care of his/her own parents and grandparents. This will bring social and economic problems to the country.

Quality of the New Generation: Family and social concerns are also problems. In the cities, the parents easily spoil the family's only child. On the other hand, families in the countryside usually have two or more children. Some Chinese intellectuals worry that in the future, the new generation may consist of more under-educated than well-educated people.

The Rise in Female Infanticide: Traditional Chinese people believed a boy was better than a girl. Because of the compulsory one-child-per-family policy, a traditional Chinese family might try its best to get a boy rather than a girl. Consequently, female infanticide has often been found in rural areas. This might have a negative effect on the sex structure in China's population.

5. China's Ethnic Groups

Officially, China has 56 nationalities. Among them, the Han are the dominant nationality, while the other 55 ethnic groups are referred to as the national minorities. Although the minorities constitute only 8 percent of China's population, they occupy 60 percent of the country's lands, which are mostly located along the borders and in rich resource areas. This factor weighs heavily on the Chinese government's minority policy.

China's Nationalities

Definition of Nationality: The Chinese define a nationality as a group of people of common origin living in a common area, using a common language, and having a sense of group identity in economic life, social organization, and behavior. Fifty-six ethnic groups were defined as nationalities under these characteristics.

Han as a Nationality: Over the past three centuries numerous peoples who were originally not Chinese have been assimilated into Chinese society. The Han Chinese have become an amalgamation of such peoples. All the Han, nevertheless, speak the Chinese language, use Chinese characters as a common written form, have a common origin in history, and share the cultural characteristics universally recognized as Chinese. Han ethnic unity is the result of two ancient institutions that have been central to Chinese culture. One is the written Chinese language. Although Chinese from different areas speak different dialects and may not be able to understand others, they communicate in written Chinese without any problems. Another major force contributing to Han ethnic unity has been the 3,000 years of history associated with the centralized imperial state. Being Han, even for illiterate peasants, has meant conscious identification with a glorious history and a state of immense territories. Most Han Chinese believe in ancestor worship and Confucianist social and political values. The major traditional religions of the Han people are Buddhism and Taoism.

Minority Nationalities: A minority group in China can be defined as a separate nationality if its members share a common origin, live in a common area, use a common language, and have a sense of group identity such as their special religions and customs. Minority nationalities usually live in autonomous regions, or autonomous prefectures, and autonomous counties. Most of the minority groups are distinguished from the Han Chinese by language, religion, and origin rather than by racial characteristics.

Distribution of China's Minorities

Location of the Minorities: In general, the minority nationalities are concentrated in the northwest and southwest of China. Most of the minorities live in five autonomous regions: Inner Mongolia (Nei Monggol), Xinjiang Uighur, Tibet, Guangxi Zhuangzu, and Ningxia Huizu. Autonomous prefectures have also been set up for minorities in eight provinces: Yunnan, Guizhou, Qinghai, Sichuan, Gansu, Jilin, Hunan, and Guangdong. Some minority nationalities can be found in only a single region, and other minorities may have settlements in two or more areas. In the autonomous regions of Tibet, Xinjiang, and Nei Monggol, minorities occupy large frontier areas. Minority nationalities in the Guangxi autonomous region, Guizhou, Sichuan, and Gansu are more fragmented and inhabit smaller areas.

The Major Minorities: Among the 55 minority nationalities, 18 had a population of more than 1 million as of 1990. The principal minorities are the Thai-speaking Zhuang, numbering about 15.5 million; the Man (Manchus), numbering 9.8 million; the Hui, or Chinese Muslims, about 8.6 million; the aboriginal Miao, about 7.4 million; the Turkic-speaking Uighur, about 7.2 million; the aboriginal (but largely assimilated) Yi, about 6.6 million; the Tujia, about 5.7 million; the Mongols, about 4.8 million; and the Tibetans, about 4.6 million. Other major minority groups include Bouyei (2.5 million), Dong (2.5 million), Yao (2.1 million), Koreans (1.9 million), Bai (1.6 million), Hani (1.2 million), Kazak (1.1 million), Li (1.1 million), and Dai (1.0 million).

Languages of the Minorities

Most of the minority groups have their own languages. All non-Chinese languages spoken in China can be classified into four language groups: the Altaic, the Tibeto-Burmese, the Thai, and the Miao-Yao.

The Altaic Language Group: The Altaic language group includes the Turkic languages spoken by the Uighur and Kazakhs in Xinjiang and the dialects spoken by the Mongols in the Inner Mongolia autonomous region. People who speak the Altaic languages live in a wide area encompassing Asia Minor, Central Asia, and Siberia. The inhabitants of China who speak Altaic languages represent only a small proportion of the total speakers found in the area described.

The Tibeto-Burmese Language Group: The Tibeto-Burmese language group (a branch of the Sino-Tibetan language family) includes the Tibetan, Yi, and Tujia tongues. The people who speak these languages live mainly in the west and southwest areas of China. The Tibetans, for example, inhabit a large area of China and are the most numerous ethnic group speaking Tibeto-Burmese language. The other Tibeto-Burmese speakers are hill people who live by subsistence farming in the southern area of Sichuan Province and scattered areas of Yunnan.

The Thai Language Group: The Thai language group, spoken by more than 15.5 million people of different ethnic groups living in China, is closely related to the Chinese language. The Thai language is mostly confined to the Guangxi autonomous region and the Zhuang minority. Most of these dialects possess no written form.

The Miao-Yao Language Group: The languages spoken by the Miao-Yao group belong to the Sino-Tibetan family. Originally, it was believed that these two ethnic groups spoke dialects that belonged to different language families, yet linguistic studies have brought evidence to light suggesting that they are in actuality closely related.

Complicated Language Situation

Differences Between the Distribution of Minorities and Minority Languages: Surveys of the minority languages show that the distribution of the minority nationalities and the minority languages in China are identical. Some minority nationalities have Chinese as their language, and some Han Chinese speak a minority language. For instance, the members of the Hui nationality speak dialects of Chinese, and almost all members of the Manchu nationality speak Chinese Mandarin. Conversely, the Be language and the Cun language are spoken in Hainan Province by about 520,000 and 60,000 people respectively, who are officially of Han nationality. At the same time, some different minority groups speak dialects of the same language, and some members of the same nationality speak different languages. For instance, the members of the Bouyei nationality speak a dialect of the Zhuang language, and members of the Mongolian nationality speak different languages of the Mongolian linguistic family, and some even speak Tibetan. In general, there are more non-Chinese languages than minority nationalities in China.

General Distribution of the Minority Languages: The non-Chinese languages are largely concentrated along a belt across the northern part of China and in a large area in the southwest and south. The large southwestern and southern area contains 74 percent of all the speakers of non-Chinese languages. Another major area, the very large northern part of China, contains only 25 percent of all non-Chinese speakers. The remaining 1 percent of non-Chinese speakers inhabit the remaining parts of China, in which the great majority of the speakers of Chinese dialects are concentrated.

Intertwined and Overlapping Language Areas: In many of the areas situated in the main regions of the non-Chinese languages, Chinese dialects and non-Chinese languages are located side by side. Their territories are intertwined and overlapping. For example, the Guangxi Zhuangzu autonomous region is the present homeland of China's largest minority group, Zhuang nationality. Another 11 minorities—Dong, Sui, Maonan, Mulao, Yao, Miao, Gelao, Yi, Jing, Hui, and Manchu—also live there. In this region, however, there are also a lot of Han people. Many Mandarin speakers and Yue speakers live in so-called Chinese dialect islands, which are surrounded by minority language areas. There are strong mutual influences among the Chinese language and the non-Chinese languages.

Religion and Customs: The Miao people mainly live by agriculture on mountain slopes. They prefer to live in houses on piles rather than in houses set on the ground. The space under the piles is where their animals, such as buffaloes or cows, stay at night. Miao people love to sing and have festivals of singing that may end in dating and sexual activities. One of the Miao's famous sporting activities is the dragon-boat race in the dragon-boat festival. The size of dragon boats varies. A regular one can hold about 20 men. The honor for the winning team is more valuable than the award itself.

The Miao religion features magical rites and elaborate ceremonies, sometimes involving animal sacrifice. The Miao particularly place strong emphasis on supernatural beings, and any unusual events are attributed to the spiritual world. Although not much is reported about their religion, one of their customs, making *gu-poison*, is often mentioned. The following practice is often alleged in Chinese sources: Several poisonous animals, such as snakes and scorpions, are put together in a jar. As they are not fed, they devour one another. When the last surviving animal that contains the poison of the others is dead, its pulverized body is the gu-poison. The poison was used to kill an unfaithful lover or an enemy slowly.

The Yi

Population and Distribution: The Yi are another major national minority group in southern China. The 1953 census found the Yi had a population of 3,254,269. This number increased to 3,380,960 in 1964 and to 4,850,000 in 1982. The latest census in 1990 reported the Yi had a population of 6,572,173. The Yi people mostly live in Yunnan, Sichuan, and Guizhou provinces, as well as in the Guangxi autonomous region.

A Brief History: The Yi trace their history back more than 2,000 years. However, scholars are divided on the origin of the Yi people. Most scholars agree that there is a close relationship between the ancient Qiang (Chiang) in northwestern China and the present Yi. It is believed that in 400 B.C., a great number of Qiang people moved southward into Yunnan and Guizhou areas and settled there. During the long course of history, they mixed with the southwestern natives and formed the Yi nationality.

Language and Writing System: The Yi language belongs to the Tibeto-Burmese group of the Sino-Tibetan language family. The language shares many common features with modern Chinese, such as initials, finals, tones, and certain word order. However, most finals in the Yi language include only single vowels, and most of its vocabulary has single syllables. Its word order is also different from Chinese. For example, "not happy" is said as *dzu ma di* (happy not).

The Yi also have their own writing system called *Yi wen* (Yi characters). It is ideographic and looks like Chinese characters. However, it is not derived from Chinese characters. The earliest Yi characters recently found were carved on a bronze bell in 1485. Hand-written books in Yi characters were also found. Most of them were about religion, history, and medicine. A Romanized pinyin system for the Yi characters was invented and put into use in 1975.

Customs and Religion: Agriculture is the main focus of Yi life. The Yi group used to be divided into clans, which had a social organization based on caste. The dominant caste owned all property and thereby controlled the lower caste, which was a laboring group without lands. Marriage was confined within clans and castes. This situation has changed since the establishment of the People's Republic of China. In Yi society, in order to marry a girl, the groom has to pay a high bride price, usually a certain amount of money plus goods, to the bride's family. Since the bride price is high, the family of a woman who initiates a divorce has to pay it back to the husband's family. For the same reason, men seldom initiate the divorce.

The Yi believe that all objects possess spirits and that their lives are ruled by destiny. There is a large element of magic and sorcery in their religion. The Yi wear charms to protect them throughout life. The Yi people believe they will become gods after death if they are good, or demons if bad, both of them having supernatural power. Consequently, ancestor worship has shared a very significant place with nature worship. One important Yi festival is the torch festival. On that night, men and women, with one or two torches in hand, march along mountain roads to a meeting place. This festival usually ends in dating activities.

7. Principal Minorities in the North

The other group of minorities—the people in the north and the northwest—presents a different picture from the southern minorities. To a large extent, this population was formerly nomadic and cattle breeding. The principal minorities in this group include the Manchu (the second largest but assimilated minority), the Hui, the Turkic-speaking Uighur, and the Mongols.

The Manchu

A Brief History: The Manchu are one of the most important minorities in China's history. The immediate ancestors of the Manchu were the Nüzhen (also called Jurchens), who had once established the state of Jin in the northern part of China and eliminated the Northern Song dynasty in the 12th century. The Nüzhen living in Heilongjiang united and formed the Manchu nationality at the beginning of the 17th century. In 1644, the Manchu of the northeast conquered the whole of China, establishing an enormous empire that lasted almost 300 years (1644–1912). However, as the conquerors, the Manchu were in turn assimilated by the culture of the conquered. Within a few generations, the Manchu lost their language and almost all their traditions. Those who today claim Manchu nationality are almost indistinguishable from the Han except for their lineage.

Population and Distribution: The Manchu nationality had a population of 2,418,931, making it the sixth largest minority group in China in 1953. Its population increased to 2,695,675 in 1964 and 4,299,159 in 1982. The population grew at an annual rate of 2.6 percent during the period from 1964 to 1982. The 1990 census found there were 9,821,180 Manchu people throughout the country, making the Manchu the second largest minority group in China. They live predominantly in the northeast and north of China in Liaoning, Heilongjiang, Jilin, and Hebei, as well as in the Inner Mongolia autonomous region. In addition to the above areas, the Manchu also live in big cities all over the country. This characteristic of distribution was formed when the Manchu ruled China in the Qing dynasty.

Language and Customs: The Manchu people speak and write the Chinese language. Only a small portion of the elderly Manchu in the mountainous areas in Heilongjiang can still speak their original language.

The Manchu were good at riding horses and shooting. They once had distinctive clothing, customs, and religious beliefs. However, during the 300 years of the Qing dynasty, under the strong influence of Chinese culture, the Manchu gradually lost their traditions. Nowadays, the Manchu are completely indistinguishable from the Han Chinese.

The Hui (Chinese Muslims)

A Brief History: The Hui national minority group is often referred to as Muslims. The term reveals the origin of the Hui in China. *Hui* is a short term for the *Huihui* nationality. It was formed over many centuries by the mixing together of nationalities inside and outside China. In 651, Islam was formally introduced to China under the Tang dynasty. Right after that, a considerable number of Muslim merchants moved into China from Arabia and Persia. They settled in such cities as Guangzhou, Hangzhou, and Quanzhou and intermarried with the local people. They were called Huihui people and became the ancestors of the present Hui. In the 12th century, the Mongol troops conquered central and western Asia. As a result, a great number of Muslims from different areas, forcedly or willingly, moved into China. They spread throughout northwestern and southern China. They were also called Huihui. In its long course of development as a nationality, the Huihui absorbed many attributes of the Han Chinese, the Uighurs, and the Mongols.

Population and Distribution: The Hui used to be the second largest minority group in China. The 1953 census found a total number of 3,559,350 Hui people. The number increased to 4,473,147 in 1964 and to 7,219,493 in 1982. The census in 1990 reported the Hui had a population of 8,602,978 and had become the third largest minority, next to the Zhuang and Manchu. The Hui people mainly live in the Ningxia autonomous region toward the upper reaches of the Yellow River. There are also settlements in the Xinjiang autonomous region, as well as in the provinces of Gansu, Henan, Hebei, Qinghai, Shandong, Yunnan, and Anhui.

Language and Special Custom: The Hui people speak and write the Chinese language. They are indistinguishable from the Han Chinese except for their Islamic religion. Under the strong influence of Chinese culture, the Hui have been almost completely assimilated by the Han Chinese. One of their special customs is that they do not eat pork or the blood of other animals, in keeping with their Islamic dietary rules.

The Uighurs

A Brief History: The Uighurs have a long history. According to an early Chinese history book, the ancestors of the Uighurs were called Dingling in the third century B.C. They lived northwest of Xiongnu, another minority in ancient China, which was also often mentioned in early Chinese history books. In the fifth century A.D., a great number of Uighurs moved into today's Xinjiang areas and settled there. Over the last 1,500 years, the Uighurs have been in close contact with Han Chinese. Adopting many attributes of the Han culture while maintaining its own language and customs, the Uighur nationality was gradually developed.

Population and Distribution: Other important ethnic societies in China are the Turkic groups of the Xinjiang Uighur autonomous region. The most important peoples in the group are the Uighurs, the Kazakhs, and the Kirghiz. The Uighurs live almost entirely in the Xinjiang autonomous region. The Uighurs used to be the third largest minority in China in the 1950s. The Uighurs numbered 3,640,125 in 1953 and 5,957,112 in 1982. The annual population growth rate was 1.7 percent during the period from 1953 to 1982. In the census in 1990, the Uighurs had a population of 7,214,431, making them the fifth largest minority following the Zhuang, Manchu, Hui, and Miao. The Uighurs have a strong sense of national identity and maintain relations with the rest of the Muslim world.

Language and Culture: The Uighur people speak the Uighur language, which belongs to the Turkic group in the Altaic family of languages. The Uighur language spoken in China is divided into three dialects: Central, Hotan, and Lop. The standard Uighur language, which is based on the central dialect, is most widely spoken. The Uighurs have their own writing system based on the Arabic alphabet. A new writing system based on the Latin alphabet was invented and put into use after the People's Republic of China was established in 1949. However, the new writing system was abandoned and the old Uighur writing system restored in the 1980s.

Customs and Religion: The Uighurs are Muslims. Their social customs place great emphasis upon the family. Although the Uighurs consider marriage and raising a family to be a religious obligation, their attitude toward the family unit is probably weaker than in most other Muslim communities elsewhere in the world. The Uighurs have a reputation as a fun-loving people with a fondness for feasting, music, and uninhibited sexual pleasure. Living as they do in one of the most barren parts of China and largely dependent on agriculture supported by irrigation, their livelihood relies greatly upon oases and natural springs.

The Mongols

A Brief History: Under their great leader Genghis Khan, the Mongols invaded China in the 13th century and took control of the area north of the Yellow River. They took the whole of China and established the Yuan dynasty in Beijing in 1271. This was the first non-Han dynasty to rule China in its entirety. The powerful Yuan empire, however, lasted for only 97 years. Mongol power ended in China in 1368. The Mongols were eventually expelled from China. They settled north of the Great Wall in the region now divided into Nei Monggol and the Mongolian People's Republic.

Population and Distribution: There are about 3.5 million Mongols living in China, mostly along the northern border areas in the Inner Mongolia autonomous region, Gansu Province, and Heilongjiang Province. There were only 1,462,956 Mongols in the 1953 census. This number increased to 1,965,766 in 1964 and to 3,411,657 in 1982. The natural population growth rate was as high as 3.1 percent during the period from 1964 to 1982. The census in 1990 found the number of Mongols had reached 4,806,849.

Language and Culture: Because of their common origin, the Mongols in China are closely related in culture and language to the people of the Mongolian People's Republic. However, the Mongols in China still use the traditional Mongol script, whereas those living in the Mongolian People's Republic have officially adopted the Cyrillic alphabet. About 3 million people in China speak the Mongol language. It has three different dialects: the Inner Mongolian dialect, the Oirat dialect, and the Bargu-Burial dialect. As the largest dialect group, the Inner Mongolian dialect speakers constituted about 90 percent of all the Mongolian speakers in China in 1990. In the Inner Mongolian dialect, the vowel contrasts occur in length as well as in tenseness. On the lexical level, it has a considerable number of loanwords from Chinese. In grammar, all Mongolian languages have case markings.

Special Customs and Religion: The Mongols have for centuries been nomads, dependent for their livelihood on domestic animals such as cattle, sheep, and horses. They are a proud race, possessing characteristics usually associated with nomadic existence: independence, resourcefulness, and endurance. Over the centuries, they have adopted the view that a sedentary lifestyle is inferior. For a long time, the Mongol religion has been Tibetan Buddhism, which many of the Mongols still practice today.

8. THE CHINESE LANGUAGE

The Chinese language is spoken by the Han Chinese, but it is a language for all of China. Among contemporary languages with a long history, Chinese is the only one whose history is documented in an unbroken tradition extending back to the second millennium B.C. A language spoken by so many people over such a long period is characterized by many special features.

Typological Characteristics of the Chinese Language

The Chinese language is classified in the Sino-Tibetan language family. These languages possess unique characteristics, which are absent in English and other Indo-European languages.

Tone Differentiates Meanings: Chinese is a tonal language. In languages of this type, each syllable is characterized by a fixed pitch pattern, called "tone." A tone may be level, or contoured (rising, falling, or some combination of the two). Tones are phonemic, that is, they may serve to differentiate meaning just like consonants and vowels. For example, modern standard Chinese has four tones: the first has a high-level pitch, the second is high-rising, the third low falling-rising, and the fourth high-falling. The same spellings with different tones have different meanings:

Tone 1:   mā "mother"

xiān "first"

liū "slide"

Tone 2:   má "hemp"

xián "salty"

liú "flow"

Tone 3:   mǎ "horse"

xiǎn "dangerous"

liǔ "willow"

Tone 4:   mà "to scold"

xiàn "at present"

liù "six"

Chinese dialects and the other tonal languages of Asia vary greatly in the number of tones, as well as the pitch patterns. Some have eight to nine tones, and others have only three.

Each Syllable Has a Meaning: Like many of the languages of East Asia, Chinese is a monosyllabic language—a language in which every syllable generally has a meaning. A syllable in Chinese usually contains at least a vowel and a tone. Sometimes a syllable is a word; sometimes it is the smallest meaningful part of a word, known as a morpheme. For instance, *wǒ* (I, me) has only one syllable, and *wǒmen* (we, us) has two syllables, meaning "I" with a plural suffix; *yǔhángyuán* (astronaut) has three syllables, meaning "space-traveling-person." There are exceptions, though. In some words, it takes more than a syllable to represent a minimum meaningful unit. For example, *pútao* (grapes) has two syllables; *pú* and *tao* do not mean anything individually. Other examples are *chóuchú* (hesitates) and *kāfēi* (coffee). However, these kinds of words are not common in the Chinese language. Many of them are loanwords from foreign languages.

Function Words and Word Order Versus Inflection: The Chinese language is an isolating language. This means that in Chinese the syntactic relationships are shown either by independent function words or by a certain word order rather than by inflection. For example, in English, there are different forms for plurals of nouns (dog—dogs), past-tense forms of verbs (do—did—done), and the comparative and superlative forms of adjectives (high—higher—highest). All those form changes are called inflection. In Chinese, there are no such internal changes in a word itself. Instead, the Chinese language uses different function words (particles) and certain word order like SVO (subject-verb-object) in order to indicate grammatical changes. For example, "high" is *gāo* in Chinese, "higher" is *bǐjiào gāo*, and the "highest" is *zuìgāo*; "I beat him" is *wǒ dǎ tā*, and "He beat me" is *tā dǎ wǒ*.

Evolution of the Chinese Language

Stages of the Chinese Language: The Chinese language has undergone thousands of years of evolution. Because of this long history and inadequate language sources, it is very difficult to give a scientific division for the periods of Chinese language development. In his monumental work, *Studies of the Chinese Phonology* (1915–1926), Swedish sinologist Nernhard Karlgren (1889–1978) for the first time divided the long history of Chinese phonology into five periods: Proto-Chinese, Archaic Chinese, Ancient Chinese, Middle Chinese, and Old Mandarin. Some old terms have been replaced by more conventional and convenient terms, and new periods have emerged since the 1940s. The following four stages and terms have been well received by experts in this field: Old Chinese, Middle Chinese, Near-Modern Chinese, and Modern Chinese. Because of China's regional dialect diversities, all of these terms refer to a specific or representative language.

Old Chinese: Old Chinese refers to the "archaic" and "ancient" Chinese, the language of the *Shijing* (The Book of Poetry), about 1000 B.C. It is very difficult to know exactly what Old Chinese was like because of the historical distance and limited sources. Chinese philologists in the Qing dynasty, such as Duan Yucai (1743–1796) and Qian Daxin (1728–1804), made great efforts to study Old Chinese phonology. It was not until 1915 that Karlgren introduced a modern method for Old Chinese reconstruction. In 1940, he provided the first complete reconstruction of Old Chinese, mainly based on the *Shijing* and phonetic compound characters. Although many Chinese experts in the field did not agree with Karlgren's reconstruction, they followed his research methods and continued his research in the same direction. After several decades of research work, various Old Chinese reconstructions have been proposed. There is universal agreement that Old Chinese had tones, initial consonant clusters(such as *kw-, gw-, ngw-*), but no laminals (such as *f-*). These are the distinguishing features of Old Chinese phonology.

Middle Chinese: Middle Chinese is in the "middle" between Old Chinese and Modern Chinese. The sixth-century rhyme dictionary *Qieyun*, by Lu Fayan (b. 562) was the main source. Southern dialect words are also useful in this task. Because *Qieyun* was arranged by tones and finals, the reconstruction of Middle Chinese is based on fairly solid ground. After thorough studies of rhyme dictionaries by Sinologists, the distinguishing characteristics of Middle Chinese were found. Middle Chinese had only simple consonant initials, and Old Chinese possessed cluster initials. It had voiced consonant initials parallel with the voiceless initials. In finals, Middle Chinese had -*m, -p, -t, -k* endings and Modern Chinese does not. As in the tone system, Middle Chinese had four tones: Ping, Shang, Qu, and Ru, the last one, also named entering tone, has disappeared in Modern standard Chinese.

Near-Modern Chinese: Near-Modern Chinese refers to the language of the Yuan dynasty dictionary, the *Zhongyuan Yinyun*, in the early 14th century. From the 12th to the 14th centuries, north China fell under the foreign rule of first the Jurchens and then the Mongols. These Altaic overlords established two dynasties with their capitals in the vicinity of present-day Beijing. Quite naturally, a new common spoken language arose. This was also called Old Mandarin Chinese. In the early 14th century, a Chinese scholar named Zhou Deqing (1277–1365) compiled the rhyme dictionary *Zhongyuan Yinyun* (Rhymes of the Central Plain) to represent the new vernacular. He classified almost 6,000 characters into 19 rhymes, each of them subdivided into groups of homonym characters. This rhyme dictionary made it easy to reconstruct the language spoken in that period. When viewed in the light of Chinese phonological history, the *Zhongyuan Yinyun* actually presents a very modern aspect. The voiced consonant initials of Middle Chinese had already evolved into voiceless initials. Another great change was the total loss of the entering tone category and the -*p, -t, -k* final endings. In summary, Near-Modern Chinese is very close to Modern standard Chinese.

The Modern Chinese Language: The modern Chinese language refers to the Chinese language spoken in the 20th and 21st centuries. The standard language is called *Putonghua* (common speech) in the Chinese mainland and *Guoyu* (national language) in Taiwan and abroad. The modern Chinese language has great variety over different regions. In China, every region has its own dialect, many of which are mutually intelligible.

Modern Standard Chinese and Modern Dialects

Relationships between Standard Chinese and Dialects: The *Putonghua* ("common speech," sometimes called "Mandarin" by Westerners) is the national standard language. It is taught in public schools, used in media, at conferences, and in all official situations. At this point, the common speech is above all dialects and affects the local dialects in their direction of development. However, the common speech is only a "human-made" language. People all over China speak their own dialects with their relatives and friends at home and in many private situations. While educated people can speak both Putonghua and their own dialects, many illiterate or semiliterate people can speak only their own dialects. Therefore, dialects are at least as important as standard Chinese to the Chinese people. Standard Chinese pronunciation is based on the Beijing dialect. Its vocabulary and grammatical model is also based on the northern dialect and other dialects' exemplary literary works. Therefore, common speech is also affected by all dialects. In past decades, common speech has absorbed many new words from different dialects. This mutual relationship between common and modern dialects will continue for a long period of time.

Historical Values of Modern Chinese Dialects: The Chinese language has had dialectal diversity in all its stages of development. We know very little about the Chinese dialects in ancient time because we do not have enough sources to study. However, we can obtain as much contemporary data as we want through a modern dialect survey. Since the early 20th century, many dialectologists have conducted dialect surveys and accumulated numerous materials about modern Chinese dialects. Those dialectal materials have great value not only for gaining a better understanding of the modern Chinese language, but also for studying the ancient Chinese language. Since modern dialects, especially the southern dialects, maintain various characteristics of ancient Chinese, they are very useful in reconstructing the Chinese language in different stages of its development.

Classification of Modern Chinese Dialects: Classification of modern Chinese dialects is difficult due to the lack of sources and of a common system of criteria for classification. The first scientific classification of the Chinese dialects was proposed by Li Fangkuei (1902–1987) in 1937. In Li's classification there were nine groups, but present dialectologists use them very little. Since then, many scholars have developed their own classification based on Li's scheme. In 1981, Zhan Bohui (1931–) proposed a new classification in his book, *Xiandai Hanyu Fangyan* (Modern Chinese Dialects). He divided modern Chinese dialects into the following seven groups: the Mandarin dialects, the Wu dialects, the Xiang dialects, the Gan dialects, the Kejia dialects (hakka), the Min dialects, the Yue dialects (Cantonese). In 1987, the Chinese Academy of Social Sciences proposed a new classification of ten dialect groups. The Mandarin group and Min group in Zhan's classification were promoted as "supergroups." The Jin group and the Hui group were separated from the original Mandarin group, and the Pinhua group was separated from the Yue group. In addition, a small number of dialects were temporally named as "unclassified" and "not-yet grouped." At the present time, Zhan's classification of dialects was still used by most of the dialectologists in China and abroad.

Degree of Diversity Among the Chinese Dialects: Some experts believe that the Chinese dialects are different languages because the degree of diversity among Chinese dialects is very high. Some compare the difference between the dialects of Beijing and Chaozhou with that between Italian and French and believe the Hainan Min dialects are as different from the Xi'an dialect as Spanish is from Romanian. It is definitely true that the differences among the Chinese dialects are very considerable. The greatest dialectal diversity is found in the southern zones. People from Beijing cannot understand at all the dialects spoken in Guangzhou and Fujian. Even within Fujian Province where the Min dialect is spoken, the Minnan dialect and the Minbei dialect are mutually unintelligible. However, it is important to keep in mind that the differences among the Chinese dialects are mostly in pronunciation. The grammar structure and writing system are basically the same. In the largest dialect group, the Mandarin dialects group, the degree of dialectal diversity is low. A person from Harbin in the northeast has little difficulty understanding a native of Kunming some 2,000 miles away.

9. THE MODERN STANDARD CHINESE LANGUAGE

Modern standard Chinese is a "human-made" language. That means that modern standard Chinese is not spoken naturally the way Cantonese is naturally spoken in the Guangzhou area. There is no city or area where modern standard Chinese is spoken as its native language. However, that does not mean there is no such thing as modern standard Chinese. For several centuries, the language has existed in the minds of educated people and has been spoken by them. The language was known as *Guanhua* in the 19th century. Nowadays, it is known as Putonghua on the Chinese mainland and as *Guoyu* elsewhere.

Different Terms and Definitions

In describing the formation of the modern standard Chinese language, several terms have been used that have particular historical meanings. The following are the common terms that have caused some confusion among non-Chinese readers:

Zhongwen: This term refers both to written and spoken forms of Chinese. Although the second syllable, *wen*, strictly means "written language," the whole term can also refer to spoken language in everyday usage.

Hanyu: This term literally means "the language of the Han Chinese." It is the formal term for Chinese language in all academic writing, for example, *gudai hanyu* (ancient Chinese language), *xiandai hanyu* (modern Chinese language).

Guanhua: This term refers to the old "official speech" used in a large multilingual and multidialectal empire, like Qing. This old term has been replaced by a new term, *Putonghua*. Guanhua now only refers to the name of a large dialect group, also known as Mandarin.

Guoyu: Meaning "national language" in Chinese, the term *guoyu* refers to modern standard Chinese. In the early part of this century, this term replaced *guanhua* as the name of the national language as opposed to foreign languages, minority languages in China, and non-standard Chinese dialects. The term was replaced by Putonghua

in China in 1956, but it continues to be used as the name of standard Chinese in Taiwan and abroad.

Putonghua: Meaning "common speech" literally, this term is the official name of the modern standard Chinese language in the People's Republic of China. In February 1956, the Chinese government officially called modern standard Chinese Putonghua and gave its definition as follows (Ramsey, Robert: *The Languages of China*, 1987):

The foundation for the unification of the Chinese (Han) language is already in existence. The Common Language (*Putonghua*), which has as its standard pronunciation the Peking pronunciation, as its basic dialect the Northern dialect, and as its grammatical model the exemplary literary works written in the modern colloquial.

Pronunciation

According to the above definition, the standard pronunciation of modern Chinese is based on the speech sounds of the Beijing dialect. These are represented in written form by a Romanized alphabet, the pinyin scheme.

The Syllables: Modern standard Chinese has 405 basic monosyllables in spelling. Each of the Chinese basic monosyllables is traditionally divided into two parts: an "initial" and a "final." The initial is the beginning consonant. The final is the rest of the syllable. The final part contains a tone, one or two vowels, and possibly a consonant ending. In standard Chinese, a syllable may have no initial, or no final in several special cases, but it always has a tone. The chart below depicts different types of Chinese syllables.

The Initials: There are 21 initial consonants in modern standard Chinese. These are given to the right in the usual Chinese order, with the Wade-Giles system of Romanization in brackets for comparison. One thing that should be noted is that modern Chinese has no distinctively voiced consonants. What are written in pinyin as *b*, *d*, and *g* are actually pronounced voiceless.

Chinese Syllables

Syllable	English meaning	Initial	Final	Tone
nǐ	you	n	i	third tone
hǎo	good, well	h	ao	third tone
xiào	laugh, smile	x	iao	fourth tone
shāng	injure	sh	ang	first tone
qiáng	strong	q	iang	second tone
ài	love		ai	fourth tone
ú	eh (an interjection)	n		second tone

The Finals: A final may include as many as three elements: a medial, a main vowel, and an ending. A medial is a short vowel sound (like i-, u-, ü-) that comes before the main vowel. The main vowel is the principal carrier of the syllable with a tone on it. An ending is a short vowel sound (-i, -u) or consonant (-n, -ng, -r) that comes after the main vowel. In the final -iang, for example, the medial is i-, the main vowel is -a-, and the ending -ng. A complete list of the 37 finals in standard Chinese appears below.

The Tones: "Tone" is a fixed pitch pattern that serves to differentiate meaning just like consonants and vowels. Standard Chinese has four basic tones. The first tone, *yinping*, is high and level. The second tone, *yangping*, is high and rising. The third tone, *shangsheng*, is a low falling-rising tone, and the fourth tone, *qusheng*, is high and falling. In addition to these four basic tones, standard Chinese also has a special feature known as the neutral tone. It is shorter in length and less stressed than the other tones. The table below shows some examples of these tones. The tone

Initials in pinyin	Wade-Giles
b	[p]
p	[p']
m	[m]
f	[f]
d	[t]
t	[t']
n	[n]
l	[l]
g	[k]
k	[k']
h	[x]
j	[chy]
q	[ch'y]
x	[hs]
z	[ts]
c	[ts']
s	[s]
zh	[chr]
ch	[ch'r]
sh	[shr]
r	[r]

Finals in Standard Chinese

No-medial group	Medial i- group	Medial u- group	Medial ü- group
	i	u	ü
a	ia	ua	
o		uo	
e			
ê	ie		üe
er			
ai		uai	
ei		uei	
ao	iao		
ou	iou		
an	ian	uan	üan
en	in	uen	ün
ang	iang	uang	
eng	ing	ueng	
ong	iong		

mark of a syllable is placed over the main vowel, and the neutral tone does not have a tone mark.

Tone 1:	mā "mother"
	gē "elder brother"
	jiā "family"
	shū "book"
Tone 2:	má "hemp"
	gé "leather"
	jiá "cheek"
	shú "be ripe"
Tone 3:	mǎ "horse"
	gě "boat"
	jiǎ "false"
	shǔ "mouse"
Tone 4:	mà "to scold"
	gè "each"
	jià "price"
	shù "tree"
Neutral tone:	ma "question marker"
	ge "measure word"

Tone Change and Intonation: When a syllable is pronounced in isolation, it keeps its original tone. However, when a syllable is pronounced together with other syllables, the syllable may change its original tone. This is called "tone change." For instance, a third tone may change to the second tone when it is followed by another third tone. The actual pronunciation for "Nǐ hǎoma?" is "Ní hǎoma?" since the third tone syllable "Nǐ" naturally changes to second tone "Ní" when it precedes another third tone syllable "hǎo."

Like all languages, standard Chinese has stress and intonation. With different stress and intonation, a sentence or a phrase may have different meanings or implications.

Vocabulary

Monosyllabic Morphemes and Polysyllabic Words: Syllable is a term in phonology. Morpheme is the smallest meaningful unit in lexicology. A Chinese word usually contains one or two morphemes. The monosyllabic word *diàn* (electricity, electric) contains one morpheme, and the polysyllabic word *diànhuà* (telephone) contains two morphemes: *diàn* (electric) and *huà* (speech) because both of them have meanings. The polysyllabic word *pútao* (grapes) contains only one morpheme, because *pú* and *tao* do not mean anything by themselves. Two syllables *pú* and *tao* must be put together to mean "grapes." Therefore, "pútao" is a polysyllabic morpheme. In Chinese, the vast majority of morphemes are monosyllabic. That is why Chinese is considered a monosyllabic language. In modern Chinese, there are many more polysyllabic words than in ancient Chinese. Many monosyllabic words in ancient Chinese have become polysyllabic. For example, *yā* (duck) is now called *yāzi*, *shī* (teacher) has become *lǎoshī*, and *xiōng* (elder brother) has changed to *gēge*. However, these polysyllabic words still consist of strings of monosyllabic morphemes. In other words, each syllable in these words has a meaning.

Loanwords: Research shows that a considerable number of words in modern standard Chinese are loanwords that were imported from foreign languages. The polysyllabic morphemes *pútao* (grapes) and *zhīzhū* (spider) are loanwords. In general, modern Chinese is very resistant to borrowing foreign terms outright. Most modern loanwords are purely native creations even though they were borrowed from foreign languages. For example, "telephone" is *diànhuà* (electric speech), "club" is called *jùlèbù* (all-enjoyment unit). The Chinese name for Coca-Cola is *kěkǒu-kělè*. This name not only reproduced the English sound fairly accurately, but also generated an elegant marketing phrase meaning "tasty and enjoyable." It sometimes happens that a loanword appears in Chinese first as a sound interpretation; it soon disappears when a suitable term, usually a meaningful translation or a mixture of translation and sound interpretation, is created. "Science" was first introduced to China as *sàiēnxī*, a sound interpretation. This was eventually replaced by a purely Chinese term *kēxué* (academic branch of study). Another example was "democracy," first *démókēláixī*, then *mínzhū* (people manage). Many loanwords have become so natural that few people know their origins.

Word Formation: Many words in modern Chinese are monosyllabic. These short words make up much of the basic vocabulary of the language. However, beyond this monosyllabic core, a great number of words in modern Chinese consist of two or more morphemes. These polysyllabic words can be roughly classified into three categories. The first category is compound words. This is the most important and efficient way of making up words. Some examples of compound words are *dì* (earth) and *zhèn* (shake) makes *dìzhèn* (earthquake); *kāi* (open) and *guān* (close) makes *kāiguān* (switch); *fù* (father) and *mǔ* (mother) makes *fùmǔ* (parents); *rè* (hot) and *xīn* (heart) makes *rèxīn* (enthusiastic). The second type is reduplicated words. Repeating a morpheme or word also makes a new word. For example, *yéye* (grandfather), *māma* (mother), *děngdeng* (wait a bit), and *píngpíngchángcháng* (quite usual and ordinary). The third category of polysyllabic words consists of a morpheme plus a suffix or a prefix. For instance, the prefix *dì* (ordinal number indicator) plus *yī* (one) makes *dìyī* (number 1, the first); the prefix *lǎo* (old) plus *shī* (teacher) makes *lǎoshī* (teacher); *hái* (child) plus suffix *zi* (small thing) makes *háizi* (child, children), *shàng* (above) plus the suffix *tou* (location indicator) makes *shàngtou* (above, top).

Grammar: In an inflecting language such as English, tense, mood, and case are indicated by changes in the shape of a word. In Chinese, the shape of a word remains the same regardless of its function or place in the sentence. Instead, Chinese uses different grammatical particles and certain word order to indicate the grammatical relationships between the parts of a sentence.

Topics: Most Chinese sentences can be divided into two parts: the topic and the predicate. The topic (or subject) is a word or phrase that sets the stage for the statement or question that follows. A few sentences do not have a topic, but if there is one, it is always said first. That makes the general word order in Chinese: the topic (subject)—the verb—the object. For example: *Wǒ dǎ tā.* (I beat him.) *Tā dǎ wǒ.* (He beats me.)

Predicates: There are three kinds of predicates in Chinese: verbal, adjectival, and nominal. The nominal predicate does not need a verb. This is a typical feature of Chinese. For example: *Wǒ sānshí suì.* (I thirty years, or I [am] thirty years [old].) *Zhè běn shū wǔkuài qián.* (This [measure] book five dollar money, or This book (is) five dollars.)

Modification: In English, some modifiers precede, such as "my wife's book," and other modifiers follow, such as "something important." In Chinese, a modifier always precedes what it modifies, no matter whether the word it modifies is a noun or a verb. For example: *Wǒ mǎide shū.* (I buy [particle] books, or The books that I bought.) *Tā gāoxìngde chànggē.* (He happily sings, or He sings happily.)

Grammatical Particles: In Chinese, there are many functional words, called particles. They can be roughly classified into three groups: structural particles, aspectual particles, and modal particles:

- **Structural Particles:** The main function of structural particles is to form different structures. There are three important structural particles in modern standard Chinese. All of them are pronounced as *de*, but they are used with different characters.
  Mài shū de rén. (People who sell books; *de* is attached to the noun, forming a noun modifier.) *Tā dàshēngde shuō.* (She speaks loudly; *de* is attached to the adverb, forming a verb modifier.) *Nǐ pǎode bǐ wǒ kuài yī xiē.* (You ran a little bit faster than I did; *de* is attached to the verb, forming a verb complement.)

- **Aspectual Particles:** There are no tenses in Chinese. However, there are particles to indicate an action in different stages, such as progression, continuation, or completion. These different stages of an action are called aspects (*tài*). There are three important particles to indicate aspects: *zhe, le,* and *guò.* Here are some examples: *Tā dàshēngde chàngzhe gē.* (He is singing songs loudly; *zhe* indicates an action in progress.) *Tā qùle Zhōngguó.* (He went to China; *le* indicates an action has been completed.) *Wǒ qùguò Yīngguó.*

(He has been to England; *guò* indicates past experience.)

- **Modal Practicles:** Modal particles are used to add various moods, spirit, and tones to an expression. "Mood" includes such diverse qualities as interrogation, request, command, emphasis, and exclamation. There are many mood particles in Chinese. The following are some examples: *Nín shì*

Wáng Xiǎojie ma? (Are you Miss Wang? *Ma* is a yes-or-no question marker.) *Wǒ bù xiǎng qù, nǐ ne?* (I don't want to go, how about you? *Ne* is a tag-question marker.) *Wǒmen zǒu ba.* (Let's go; *ba* is used for a suggestion.) *Duō me měilìde fēngjǐng a!* (What beautiful scenery! *A* is used for an exclamation.)

10. THE NORTHERN AND CENTRAL DIALECTS

Modern Chinese dialects can be roughly divided into three categories according to their distribution: the northern dialects or Mandarin dialects; the central dialects, including the Wu dialects, the Xiang dialects, and the Gan dialects; and the southern dialects, including the Kejia dialects (Hakka), the Min dialects, and the Yue dialects (Cantonese). The northern and central dialects constitute the major part of the modern Chinese dialects. They are comparatively close to modern standard Chinese.

The Northern Dialects

Speaking Areas and Speakers: The northern dialects are known as the Mandarin dialects. The word *Mandarin* has two meanings. In a narrow sense, Mandarin refers to the modern standard Chinese language, which is based on the Beijing dialect. In a broad sense, Mandarin also refers to a large group of dialects spoken in the northern part of China. The areas where Mandarin is spoken include all provinces to the north of the Yangtze River, except for the border regions where non-Han languages predominate. Most of the Han people, except those in the southeastern part of China, speak Mandarin dialects. There were 711 million Mandarin speakers in 1987. There is no doubt Mandarin is the largest and most important dialect group in China.

Subgroups and Diversity: Mandarin group dialects are divided into four subgroups: (1) Northern Mandarin is spoken in the cities of Beijing and Tianjin and in

the provinces of Hebei, Henan, Shandong, Heilongjiang, Jilin, Liaoning, and parts of Nei Monggol. (2) Northwestern Mandarin is spoken in the provinces of Shanxi, Shaanxi, and Gansu and parts of Qinghai, Ningxia, and Nei Monggol. (3) Southwestern Mandarin is spoken in the Han areas of Yunnan, Guizhou, and Sichuan provinces; most parts of Hubei; and northwestern Guangxi and Hunan. (4) Jiang-Huai dialects are spoken on both sides of the Yangtze River in Anhui, Jiangsu north of the Yangtze, and the region of Nanjing.

Of these subgroups, northern Mandarin is the closest to standard Chinese, and southwestern Mandarin is the most homogeneous within its subgroup. Both the northwestern Mandarin and the Jiang-Huai dialects display a very high degree of diversity. For this reason, the Chinese Academy of Social Science suggested in 1987 that two new groups, the Jin and the Hui, be separated from the northwestern and the Jiang-Huai Mandarin subgroups.

Distinctive Features: Mandarin dialects are clearly distinctive with respect to their phonology, grammar, and vocabulary. The Middle Chinese voiced initials, and the final endings *-p*, *-t*, *-k*, and *-m* have been lost in Mandarin dialects. This group also has a small number of tones, usually four tones but sometimes only three. The *ru* tone in the Middle Chinese has merged into other tones in Mandarin dialects. In the areas of vocabulary and grammar, one of the most typical features is the third person form *ta*, and the plural suffix *-men*. In other dialects, there are no such expressions.

The Wu Dialects

Speaking Areas and Speakers: The Wu dialects are spoken in Jiangsu south of the Yangtze River and most of Zhejiang Province. The Wu dialect group is roughly divided into a northern (Jiangsu) type and a southern (Zhejiang) type. The northern Wu dialects have undergone heavy influence by Mandarin, though southern Wu dialects have changed relatively little. The total number of Wu dialect speakers in China was 70.1 million as of 1987. The Shanghai dialect is considered representative of the Wu dialects.

Distinctive Features: The Wu dialects have their distinctive features. The most prominent feature is the uniform preservation of the voiced consonant initials of Middle Chinese. However, Middle Chinese final endings -*m* and -*n* tend to be lost in most Wu dialects. The entering tone (*ru*) is preserved in Wu dialects as a separate category. This is generally characterized by the presence of a final glottal stop, not a set of -*p*, -*t*, -*k* as in Middle Chinese. Consequently, the number of tones in Wu dialects is seven or eight. Unlike Mandarin, the Wu dialects display a great variety in their basic vocabulary.

The Gan Dialects

Speaking Areas and Speakers: The Gan dialects are spoken chiefly in Jiangxi Province and in the eastern part of Hunan. They are distributed mainly in the areas along the Fuhe River, the middle and lower reaches of the Ganjiang River and in the Lake Poyang region. The dialects of the northwestern corner of Fujian Province also belong to this group. Altogether, the Gan dialects are spoken in about 100 counties and cities. The total number of speakers was 31.27 million as of 1987. The Nanchang dialect is considered the typical Gan dialect.

Distinctive Features: All of the Gan dialects have voiceless aspirated stops in all tones for the Middle Chinese voiced initials. The Kejia dialects also possess this feature. That is why some linguists suggested that Gan and Kejia form a single group. However, the Gan dialects have ü group of finals and Kejia dialects do not. In vocabulary, Gan resembles Wu and Xiang more than it does Kejia. Therefore, most dialectologists want to separate Gan and Kejia. Located in the central zone, the Gan dialects are clearly of a transitional type from Mandarin to southern dialects.

The Xiang Dialects

Speaking Areas and Speakers: The Xiang dialects form the smallest group both in speaking area and number of speakers. The Xiang dialects are mainly spoken in Hunan Province; they are also called the Hunan dialects. The name itself is inaccurate, however, because the Xiang dialects are not the only dialect group spoken in Hunan Province, where Mandarin and Gan dialects are also spoken. According to a province-wide dialect survey in 1985, the Xiang dialects are spoken in only 37 of the 87 counties in Hunan Province, plus four northern counties in Guangxi. Totally, the Xiang dialects had 30.85 million speakers in 1987. The Changsha dialect is considered representative of the Xiang dialects.

Distinctive Features: The Xiang dialects commonly preserve the Middle Chinese voiced consonant initials in all tones. The number of tones is five or six. The maximum number of tones for all Xiang dialects is six. The Xiang dialects are undergoing erosion of their original non-Mandarin features. In so-called new Xiang dialects, this process is virtually complete, while in "old" Xiang dialects it is still not advanced. Under the strong influence of Mandarin, it is predicted that Xiang dialects will eventually lose their distinctive features and merge into southwestern Mandarin dialects.

11. THE SOUTHERN DIALECTS

The southern dialects include three different groups: Kejia, Min, and Yue. Although they are mutually unintelligible, they share a common historical source and have undergone a common process of formation. Compared to the northern and central dialects, the southern dialects preserve more features of Old Chinese and Middle Chinese in pronunciation, vocabulary, and grammar.

Formation of the Southeastern Dialects

In the pre-Han period of Chinese history, the present homeland of the southeastern dialects, Fujian, Guangdong, and Guangxi, was occupied by a variety of non-Han peoples. Chaos caused by war brought many waves of Han immigrants with their Old Chinese or Middle Chinese language to these areas. Isolated in the mountains and valleys of the far south, the Han immigrants' language was influenced greatly by the other languages. Different waves of Han immigration brought in Chinese language features in different stages of development, though local aboriginal languages provided them with different features. All of these factors played an important role in the formation of the southern dialects. Just as dialects in more remote and mountainous regions generally preserve their original features more faithfully, all southern dialects preserve more features of Old Chinese and Middle Chinese than Mandarin and other dialects do. The southeastern dialects have great value in the study of the Chinese language.

The Kejia Dialects (Hakka)

The Hakka People: The name *Kejia* means "guest" or "stranger." The name was given to those Han immigrants from north China settling in Yue-speaking areas. Research shows that the Kejia people originally lived in the provinces of Henan, Anhui, and Shanxi. Starting during the Western Jin dynasty (265–316), the Han people moved southward on a large scale to escape from the chaos caused by the invasion of minorities. First, they moved into southern Anhui and northern Jiangxi.

Then, some of these Han immigrants moved into their present homeland in southwestern Fujian and eastern Guangdong in the late Tang dynasty (850–907). Later, in the Song and Ming dynasties, more Kejia people moved from the north into Guangdong, Guangxi, Fujian, and Jiangxi, and some Kejia moved into Sichuan from Guangdong. Because the purpose of the immigration was to escape the chaos of war, the Kejia people usually settled in mountain areas. They are well known for their unity and preservation of their language and culture.

Speaking Areas and Number of Speakers: The Kejia dialects are mainly spoken in eastern and northern Guangdong, western Fujian, and southern Jiangxi. In addition, the Kejia dialects are found in Guangxi, Fujian, Sichuan, and Taiwan. There was a total of 35 million Kejia speakers in China in 1987.

Distinctive Features: As represented by the Meixian dialect in Guangdong, the Kejia dialects are distinctive in phonology and lexicon. The voiced consonant initials of Middle Chinese have become voiceless in all four tones. The Kejia dialects also have the V-initial, which is very rare in other dialects. Most of the Kejia dialects preserve the whole set of final endings (-m, -n, -ng, -p, -t, -k) in Middle Chinese. The Kejia dialects do not have the ü group finals. The Kejia dialects usually have six tones. One of their unique lexical features is that all Kejia dialects have the same word—*hai* for first person pronouns (I, me). For this reason, the Kejia dialects have their nickname "*-ngai* dialects."

The Min Dialects

Speaking Areas and Number of Speakers: The Min dialects are mainly spoken in the provinces of Fujian, Guangdong, and Taiwan. In Fujian, 54 counties, about three-fourths of its total territory, are Min-speaking areas. In Guangdong, about one-third of its counties and cities are Min-speaking areas. They are mainly located in the eastern part. In Taiwan, about three-fourths of the total population are Min speakers. In addition to these three provinces, Min dialects can be found in south Zhejiang and parts of Jiangxi, Jiangsu, Sichuan, and Guangxi. There were 55.07 million Min speakers in China, including Taiwan, in 1987. There are several million overseas Chinese who have a Min dialect as their native language. This population is concentrated in Indonesia, Thailand, Malaysia, and Singapore.

Subgroups and Diversity: Min dialects form the most diversified and complex group of Chinese dialects. Within the Min dialect group, there are five different subgroups. Despite a homogenous classification, members of different subgroups find it hard to communicate with one another.

1. Southern Min is spoken in the southern part of Fujian, including the three cities of Xiamen, Zhanzhou, and Quanzhou, as well as 24 counties nearby. All Min dialects spoken outside Fujian Province also belong to this subgroup. This is the largest and most influential subgroup of the Min dialects. The Xiamen dialect is the representative of this subgroup, as well as Min dialects in general.

2. Eastern Min is spoken in the eastern part of Fujian. The Fuzhou dialect is representative of this subgroup.

3. Northern Min is spoken in the northern part of Fujian, with the Jian'ou dialect as its representative.

4. Central Min is spoken in three counties located in the central part of Fujian. The Yong'an dialect is its representative.

5. Pu-Xian dialects are spoken in only two counties: Putian and Xianyou, located on the east coast of Fujian.

Distinctive Features: Despite the great differences among its subgroups, the Min dialect is one of the most distinctive groups of Chinese dialects. The Min dialects preserve many features of the Old Chinese in initials, such as no *f-* initial, *t-/t'-* initials corresponding to Modern Chinese *zh-/ch-* initials, etc. In finals, most of the Min dialects preserve the Middle Chinese final system with the *-m*, *-n*, *-ng*, and *-p*, *-t*, *-k* endings. The Min dialects usually have six to eight tones, with the most complicated tone change system among Chinese dialects. In vocabulary, the Min dialects also have a great abundance of words that

either are not found or are very rare in non-Min dialects. For example, in Xiamen dialect, "son, child" is *kia*, and "cooking vessel" is *tia*; in Mandarin, they are pronounced as *ér* and *guō* respectively.

The Yue Dialects

Speaking Areas and Number of Speakers: The Yue dialects are also called Cantonese or Guangdong dialects. The term Cantonese should be reserved for the dialect of Guangzhou (Canton) and not used as a general name for the group as a whole. The term Guangdong dialects is also inadequate for this group because Min and Kejia dialects are also spoken in Guangdong Province. The Yue dialects are mainly spoken in Guangdong, Guangxi, Hong Kong, and Macao. In Guangdong and Guangxi, Yue dialects are spoken in 79 counties by 40.2 million speakers. Cantonese is the predominant dialect among the seven million residents of Hong Kong and Macao. There are also a great number of Yue speakers among overseas Chinese in Southeast Asia, South and North America, Australia, and New Zealand. In Chinatown of San Francisco, most of the Chinese residents are Yue speakers. The total number of Yue speakers among overseas Chinese has been estimated at more than two million (O. Y. Hashimoto, 1972). Thus, the total number of Yue speakers in the world was about fifty million in 1987.

Supgroups and Diversity: The Yue dialects are relatively homogeneous; however, significant differences among Yue dialects have been found, and six different subgroups have been identified as follows:

1. Guangfu Yue is spoken in Guangzhou, the capital city of Guangdong Province, and its nearby counties in the Pearl River Delta. It is also spoken in Hong Kong, Macao, and central and northern parts of Guangdong. This is the largest and most influential subgroup among Yue dialects. Cantonese (the Guangzhou dialect) is representative of this subgroup, as well as the entire Yue dialect group. A great number of overseas Chinese speak Cantonese.

2. Siyi Yue, spoken in four counties of Taishan, Kaiping, Enping, and Xinhui.

Since *Siyi* means "four counties" in Chinese, this is the origin of the name for this subgroup. Siyi Yue is also spoken in Jiangmen City and Doumen County near *Siyi*. Siyi Yue had once been a widespread dialect among Chinese immigrants in the United States who were mostly from those four counties. The Taishan dialect is representative of this group. Other Yue speakers find it very difficult to communicate with Siyi Yue speakers.

3. Xiangshan Yue is spoken in Zhongshan City and Zhuhai City in the Pearl River Delta. Zhongshan dialect is representative of this group.

4. Guan-Bao Yue is spoken in Dongguan and Baoan counties in the Pearl River Delta. Dongguan dialect is representative of this group.

5. Gao-Yang Yue is spoken in the Gaozhou and Yangjiang areas of southeastern Guangdong.

6. Southern Guangxi Yue, spoken in 23 counties and cities in the south and southeast of Guangxi. Nanning dialect is considered the representative of this group. Because of the high degree of diversity in this subgroup, the Chinese Academy of Social Science suggested that the Pinhua group be separated from Yue dialects.

Distinctive Features: Compared to northern and central dialects, the Yue dialects have relatively simple initial systems. For example, Cantonese has only a single set of sibilant initials *ts-*, *ts'-*, *s-* corresponding to Mandarin's *j-*, *q-*, *x-*, *z-*, *c-*, *s-*, and *zh-*, *ch-*, *sh-*. The Yue dialects are the most conservative group in the preservation of the Middle Chinese final system. The *-m*, *-n*, *-ng*, and *-p*, *-t*, *-k* final endings are preserved quite faithfully, with only the merest handful of exceptions. The Yue dialects have more tones than any other dialect group. Typical Yue dialects have eight tones, some even have ten tones. The entering tone (*ru*) in Middle Chinese has split into three or even four categories conditioned by vowel length. In the lexicon, there is a long list of words that can be found only in Yue dialects. For example, "thing" is *je*, and "give" is *pei* in Cantonese; though they are said as *dongxi* and *gei* in Mandarin, respectively.

Cantonese Influence: Cantonese is considered the common speech among Yue speakers, and even among Min and Kejia speakers living in Guangdong Province. Cantonese is the predominant dialect in Hong Kong and Macao, where even the modern standard Chinese (*Putonghua*) cannot be used to communicate among local Chinese people. Cantonese has been so well developed in Hong Kong and Macao that it even has a rich written folk literature, including Cantonese songs and operas. For the purpose of writing down this literature, a large number of special Cantonese characters have been developed. A great number of local newspapers, magazines, and even novels published in Hong Kong and Macao use these Cantonese characters widely. Due to its special political position and strong economic power, Cantonese has become the most important and influential dialect among Chinese dialects. Since the implementation of the Reform and Open Door Policy, a great number of immigrants from northern China have gone to Yue-speaking areas and become Cantonese speakers. As a result, many Cantonese words have been absorbed into the modern standard Chinese (*Putonghua*, or "Mandarin"), as well as other dialects.

12. THE CHINESE WRITING SYSTEM

The written Chinese language, Chinese characters, is one of the oldest written languages in the world. Although the Chinese language is comprised of many dialects, many of which are mutually unintelligible, people speaking different dialects use the same writing system. This literary unity has contributed significantly to the national unity of the Chinese people for more than 3,000 years.

The Evolution of Chinese Characters

A Legend About the Invention of Characters: There is a legend pertaining to the invention of Chinese characters. It is said that Chinese characters were created by a mythical figure named Cang Jie (c. 3000 B.C.) who had four eyes and was born with the talent of writing. He spent years developing his wondrous writing system. After he invented the characters, grain fell from the sky and ghosts howled through the night in celebration. Although this is only a legend, it is helpful in tracing the history of characters. According to Chinese historical records, Cang Jie was an official under the reign of Huang Di, approximately 5,000 years ago. Based on archaeological finds, a primitive form of writing apparently already existed long before Cang Jie was born. His contribution seemingly was to collect the extant writing forms and organize them into a formal writing system.

The Chinese writing system has undergone the following stages in its evolution of forms:

- **Oracle Bone Inscription:** Oracle bone inscriptions were carved on tortoise shells and ox bones during the Shang dynasty. This is why they are called *Jiaguwen*, which literally means "shell-bone writing." More than 150,000 examples of oracle bone writing have been unearthed so far. They represent an archaic style of Chinese characters that appeared 3,000 years ago. Most scholars believe that the oracle bone inscriptions constitute the earliest systematic array of Chinese characters. Therefore, Chinese characters have at least over 3,000 years of history.

- **Bronze Inscription:** Bronze inscriptions represent another archaic style of characters. They were cast on bronze ware during the late Shang dynasty and throughout the Zhou dynasty. Because bronze was the most popular metal in that period, they are called *Jinwen* in Chinese, literally meaning "metal writing." Most of the bronze inscriptions found today are on bells and cauldrons.

- **Seal Script keep (c. 722–221 B.C.):** The seal script was a style of Chinese characters used in the late Zhou and Qin dynasties. Compared to their predecessors, the seal characters were simpler in structure, with characteristic curving strokes. This style is still used in seal cutting today.

- **Official Script (Lishu) (206 B.C.–220 A.D.):** Official script was a style of Chinese characters used during the Qin and Han dynasties. Although the seal characters were simpler in structure, writing their curving strokes was time-consuming. Thus, a simpler script was developed for the people to record a sea of documents. This was how it acquired its Chinese name *Lishu*, which literally meant "clerk's script." The change from the seal script to official script marks the greatest improvement in Chinese character structure.

- **Regular Script (Kaishu) (200 A.D.–present):** Regular script was a direct development of official script, which had already reformed the Chinese characters. Regular script went a step further to standardize and regularize the Chinese characters. Regular script has been in continuous use for more than 1,800 years, since the late Han dynasty. All the characters in printing materials now use regular script.

In addition to regular script, the following scripts are also in use in people's daily life:

- **Running Script (Xingshu keep):** Running script is the handwritten form of regular script. Compared to the stroke-by-stroke regular script, which may be likened to a person standing straight and still, the running script characters are more like a person strolling along in a leisurely manner. Its Chinese name *Xingshu* means "walking" or "running" characters. Although the strokes in a running-hand character are connected, the whole character is still very legible.

- **Cursive Script (Caoshu):** Cursive script is an offshoot of the regular script. Cursive script tends to link separate strokes into one wherever it is possible, thus often making the script illegible, as its Chinese name *Caoshu*, "careless characters," indicates. Cursive script has become a calligraphic art, rather than a means of transmitting information.

- **Short-form (Simplified) Characters:** Some characters of the regular script have two forms: the original form and the short form. The short-form characters have fewer strokes and simpler structures than their originals. In 1964, the Chinese government announced 2,238 simplified characters to be used in the Chinese mainland. However, for various reasons, long-form (original) characters are still used in Taiwan, Hong Kong, Macao, and in overseas Chinese communities.

The table below briefly illustrates the evolution of characters from the earliest form to present-day form.

The Construction of Chinese Characters

There are certain ways to create a character. Traditionally there are four methods of character construction. They are called *Sishu* in Chinese, meaning "four categories of characters." The following are the four categories of characters, with examples:

Pictographic Characters: Pictographic characters are simplified pictures of objects. For example, to indicate the sun, one draws a circle with a dot inside to represent the sun. To indicate a cow, one draws a cow's head with horns. This was the earliest method of character construction.

Evolution of Characters

Oracle bone (1171–1066 B.C.)	Bronze (1066–256 B.C.)	Seal (722–221 B.C.)	Official (206 B.C.–250 A.D.)	Regular (200 A.D.–Present)	English Meaning
					moon
					man
					eye
					mountain
					tiger
					above
					to pick
					step

Indicative Characters: Indicative characters are symbols of abstract ideas. For example, to express the idea "above," one draws a long curve to indicate the surface, and one dot above the curve to indicate above. To indicate the idea of "below," one simply draws a long curve and one dot below it.

Associative Characters: An associative character is formed by two or more single characters. Each single character has its own meaning, and thus the meaning of the associative compound character is determined by the association of their meanings. For example, the associative character *míng* is formed by two single characters: *rì* (the sun) and *yuè* (the moon). It means "bright" or "tomorrow."

Picto-phonetic Characters: A picto-phonetic character, as its name indicates, is formed by two parts: the meaning element and the sound element. Take *mā* (mother) as an example; it is formed by two parts (characters): *nǚ* (female) and *mǎ* (horse). The *nǚ* (female) serves as the meaning element indicating that this character is related to female, while *mǎ* (horse) is the sound element indicating the character's sound. This part, however, has no effect on the character's meaning. In modern Chinese, more than 80 percent of characters are picto-phonetic characters.

Chinese Dictionaries

Radicals: A radical is the part of a character that classifies it for placement in most character dictionaries. It also suggests the character's original meaning. For instance, all characters containing the radical *nǚ* will be put together in a character dictionary under the radical *nǚ*. Because the radical *nǚ* means "female," all characters containing this female radical have something to do with "female" in meaning, such as sisters, wife, mother, marriage, to marry a lady, etc. Traditionally, there are 214 Chinese radicals. The number of radicals varies from 189 to 226 in modern Chinese dictionaries.

Traditional Chinese Dictionaries: Most Chinese dictionaries arrange characters first under radicals, and then by stroke count. Therefore, in order to look up a character in a traditional dictionary, one has to locate the radical of the character first. Unfortunately, there are no clear-cut rules for locating the radical in a character. The left part, the right part, the top, or the bottom can be the radical. After locating the radical, the second step is to count the stroke number for the rest of the character and find the character under the radical.

Modern Chinese Dictionaries: Since the Chinese pinyin system was created in 1956, many new character dictionaries have been published. Instead of organizing characters under their radicals, modern dictionaries arrange characters by their alphabetical order. It is much easier to locate a character in a modern dictionary when one knows its pronunciation. However, the traditional method is still useful when one does not know the character's pronunciation and spelling.

The Number of Chinese Characters

How many characters are there altogether in Chinese? This is a frequently asked question that no one can answer clearly or accurately. The reasons for this are that Chinese character writing has more than 3,000 years of history and Chinese characters are widely used not only by Han Chinese but also by some minority nationalities in China, plus people in Japan, Vietnam, and Korea. It would be almost impossible to collect and count all the Chinese characters that have ever been used.

Total Number of Characters: A practical approach to the answer is to count the total number of characters collected in Chinese dictionaries. The first Chinese character dictionary, *Shuo Wen Jie Zi* (A.D. 100), recorded 9,353 characters. Almost 2,000 years later, a comprehensive character dictionary, the *Kangxi Zidian* (1716), collected 47,035 characters. In 1986, the most comprehensive Chinese character dictionary in history, *Hanyu Da Zidian*, was published in the Chinese mainland. It aimed to collect all characters ever used in dictionaries, and the total number reached around 56,000.

Frequently Used Characters: In 1987, the State Language Commission and the State Education Commission jointly conducted a research project on frequently used Chinese characters. The following year, the "List of Frequently Used Characters in Modern Chinese" was published.

The list contains 3,500 frequently used characters. The first 2,500 most frequently used characters on the list are designated to be taught in primary schools. The remaining 1,000 are to be taught at middle schools.

13. LANGUAGE REFORM

Because Chinese characters are so numerous, only a few scholars could fully master the entire set. The Chinese dialects are so diverse and complex that people of different regions could not communicate with one another. For those reasons, the Chinese government has found language reform to be necessary. In 1951, the Chinese government issued a directive that inaugurated a three-part plan for language reform: establishing a standardized common language, simplifying written characters, and introducing Romanized forms based on the Latin alphabet.

Elimination of Illiteracy

Language reform started with the elimination of illiteracy as its first step in the early 1950s. Chinese government statistics indicated that of a total population of nearly 1.1 billion in 1985, about 230 million people were illiterate or semiliterate. The illiteracy rate was even higher in the 1950s. Most of the illiterate people were adults living in the rural areas. In order to eliminate illiteracy, the Chinese government opened numerous literacy classes in the countryside, as well as in towns and cities. In literacy classes, the most frequently used characters were taught within several weeks. Spare-time education for workers and peasants and literacy classes for adults also became a part of the nation's basic education program.

The Simplification of Characters

The Chinese government believes that the difficulty of mastering Chinese characters creates a problem in increasing the literacy rate. It believes Chinese characters should be made easier to learn, which in turn would foster both literacy and linguistic unity. The Chinese writing system reform included two parts: eliminating the number of frequently used characters and reducing their strokes.

Eliminate Alternative Forms of Characters: From the government's point of view, too many characters were used in books, newspapers, and magazines. Some characters have several alternative forms with the same meaning. In 1964, the State Committee for Reforming the Chinese Written Language announced a list of alternative forms of characters to be abandoned. Those alternative forms of characters are no longer used in printing materials in China.

Reduce Strokes of Characters: The main task to simplify Chinese characters was to choose or create frequently used characters that have fewer strokes. In 1964, the State Committee for Reforming the Chinese Written Language released an official list of 2,238 simplified characters to be used in most printed material. The government claims that the simplification of characters made literacy easier, although people taught only in simplified characters were cut off from the wealth of Chinese literature written in traditional characters.

The Popularization of Putonghua (Common Speech)

Because many Chinese dialects are mutually unintelligible, it was necessary to establish a universal spoken language as the national common speech. In 1956, *Putonghua* (common speech) was introduced as the national language. The government stipulated that Putonghua was the official language of instruction in schools and in the national broadcast media. In the 1990s, the Chinese government continued to promote the universal use of Putonghua. More and more people used this common speech consciously and fluently.

The Creation and Popularization of the Pinyin System

The *Pinyin Fang'an* ("Chinese Phonetic Scheme"), the Romanized forms based on the Latin alphabet, was first approved by the National People's Congress in 1958. It was taught in the first grade in elementary schools all over the country. It was designed to facilitate the spread of Putonghua in regions where other dialects and languages was spoken, to assist people in learning the pronunciation of Chinese characters. It is also used in dictionaries, textbooks, libraries, and other situations involving alphabetic sequence, as well as in the transcription of Chinese terms for international usage. In 1983, the pinyin system was accepted by the United Nations as the official method of transcribing Chinese personal names and place names. After 40 years of promotion by the Chinese government, the pinyin system has been widely spread among intellectuals and students. However, the use of the pinyin system is not as widespread as the use of Putonghua.

Review and Prospect

A Controversy About the Simplified Characters: As early as 1957, when the Chinese government began promoting simplified characters, some Chinese people, mostly living outside the Chinese mainland, opposed the simplification of characters. They asserted that simplified characters would destroy the traditional philology and would cause unnecessary confusion among Chinese people. Some scholars are also unconvinced by the claim that the simplification of Chinese characters helped the spread of literacy. They point out that in Taiwan, where traditional, unsimplified characters are the standard, the literacy rate and average educational level are much higher than on the Chinese mainland. Until recently, most people on the Chinese mainland seem to have preferred the simplified characters. However, as a result of economic reform, more and more investors from Taiwan, Hong Kong, and abroad opened enterprises in China in the 1980s. The use of unsimplified characters has become popular in some big cities of China. Some social activists thus advocated using the unsimplified characters in printed materials and using the simplified characters only for writing. This was the so-called "learn unsimplified but write simplified movement." Although this movement was in conflict with the Chinese central government's policy on language reform, it was well received by many people, especially business people.

The Movement of the Modernization of the Chinese Language: Since the world entered the epoch of high technology and the computer era, the argument about the use of Chinese characters also entered a new stage. At the beginning of the computer age, Chinese characters were difficult to input. Even today, Chinese input methods are harder to learn than English typing. Some Chinese intellectuals came to the conclusion that the Chinese language needed to be modernized. They believed that the modernization of the Chinese language was not only a matter of linguistics but was directly related to matters in economics, politics, and education. All this would eventually affect the fate of the nation. In 1994, The Association for Chinese Language Modernization (ACLM) was established. It was an all-China cross-disciplinary non-government academic organization under the guidance of the State Language Commission. Most of its members were scholars in the fields of linguistics, computer science, and technology. As its name indicates, the aim of this organization was to promote the movement of "the modernization of the Chinese language." This association advocated a so-called "bilingualism and digraphia" language policy. "Bilingualism" means Putonghua is used in formal situations as a polyfunctional language, and dialects or ethnic languages are only used locally. "Digraphia" refers to two independent writing systems, namely the simplified characters and the normalized pinyin system. Even though the ACLM was a non-government academic organization, it had a strong influence over Chinese intellectuals.

The Future of Chinese Characters: As language reform proceeds, an increasing number of Chinese intellectuals are thinking an interesting yet serious question: Will all Chinese characters be eventually abandoned?

Since pinyin was created in 1958, some Chinese linguists had developed an idea to replace the traditional characters with a pinyin *Wenzi* (pinyin orthography) in the future. Since the dawn of the computer era, this idea has gained more supporters. However, characters have been used for thousands of years already. Moreover, several usable systems for inputting Chinese characters into computers are already in wide use. Chinese handwriting recognition programs and equipment are already on the market. Innumerable books were written with characters. Chinese characters have become a part of Chinese culture and civilization. Characters have also played an important role in the unity of the Chinese nationality. Most Chinese people feel that abandoning traditional characters will violate their heritage and culture. No matter how deep reform is adopted, one thing is certain: Chinese characters will not be abandoned in the near future.

KEY RESEARCH SOURCES

Atlas of China. Beijing: China Maps Publishing House, 1994.

Banister, Judith. *China's Changing Population*. Stanford: Stanford University Press, 1987.

Chao, Yuen Ren. *A Grammar of Spoken Chinese*. Berkeley: University of California Press, Ltd. 1968.

The Chinese Academy of Social Science & the Australian Academy of the Humanities. *Language Atlas of China*. Hong Kong: Longman Group Ltd., 1987.

DeFrancis, John. *The Chinese Language: Fact and Fantasy*. Honolulu: University of Hawaii Press, 1984.

————. *Nationalism and Language Reform in China*. Princeton: Princeton University Press, 1950.

Eberhard, Wolfram. *China's Minorities: Yesterday and Today*. Belmont, Calif.: Wadsworth Publishing Company, 1982.

Federal Research Division of the Library of Congress. *China, a Country Study*. Eds. Robert L. Worden, Andrea Matles Savada, and Ronald E. Dolan. Washington, D.C.: Federal Research Division, Library of Congress, 1988.

Information Office of the State Council of the People's Republic of China. *Family Planning in China*. Beijing: Information Office of the State Council, 1995.

Karlgren, Bernhard. *The Chinese Language: An Essay on Its Nature and History*. New York: The Ronald Press Co., 1949.

Kratochvil, Paul. *The Chinese Language Today*. London: Hutchinson University Library, 1968.

Lai, T. C. *Chinese Characters*. Hong Kong: Wing Tai Cheung Printing Co., 1980.

Li, Cheng-Jui. *A Study of China's Population*. Beijing: Foreign Languages Press, 1992.

Li, Dun J. *History*. Beijing: Foreign Languages Press, 1982.

Mackerras, Colin. *China's Minority Culture: Identities and Integration Since 1912*. New York: St. Martin's Press, 1995.

Norman, Jerry. *Chinese*. New York: Cambridge University Press, 1988.

Peng, Xizhe. *Demographic Transition: Fertility Trends in China Since 1954*. Oxford, England: Clarendon Press.

————. *Recent Trends in China's Population and Their Implications*. London: Research Program on the Chinese Economy, 1994.

Ramsey, S. Robert. *The Languages of China*. Princeton: Princeton University Press, 1987.

Seybolt, Peter J., and Gregory Kuei-ke Chiang. *Language Reform in China: Documents and Commentary*. Armonk, N.Y.: M. E. Sharpe, Inc., 1979.

Wang, Jun. "On the Modernization of the Chinese Language: Bilingalism and Digraphia in China." *Journal of the Chinese Language Teachers Association* Oct. 1996: 10–14.

Yin, Binyong, and John Rohsenow. *Modern Chinese Characters*. Beijing: Sinolingua, 1994.

Yin, Binyong, and Mary Felley. *Chinese Romanization: Pronunciation and Orthography*. Beijing: Sinolingua, 1988.

Zhan, Bohui. *Chinese Dialects and Dialect Survey*. Wuhan: Hubei Education Publishing House, 1991.

Systems of Thought and Belief

By John C. Didier

INTRODUCTION

This chapter traces developments in Chinese thought and religious beliefs and practices from the 16th century B.C. to the beginning of the third millennium A.D. Confucianism, Daoism, and Buddhism—known as the Three Teachings—are central to this history, but before, between, and within these systems other philosophies waxed and waned with social, political, and economic shifts. After approximately 100 A.D., the stimuli for change originated from both within and without the Chinese cultural systems so that subsequently Chinese thought and belief constituted a series of world amalgams that nevertheless retained a preponderance of Chinese content. This pattern of continuous adaptation and blending has never ceased, belying the once-common assumption that China was somehow "other" and unknowable.

1. THE SHANG DYNASTY

The earliest knowable Chinese religious system of was that of the Shang dynasty (1545–1045 B.C.). Also known as the Yin, this dynasty established some basic patterns of thought that persisted through later periods. The patterns include a commitment to the leader's rule by right, rather than merely might, and a belief that humans enjoyed with otherworldly beings a reciprocal relationship.

Most of our knowledge about the Shang derives from artifacts excavated primarily at and around the later Shang capital of Anyang, Henan. The most useful artifacts for the study of Shang religion are 150,000 inscribed bones excavated so far and tens of thousands of bronze vessels used in ritual performances.

Theocratic Rule

Shang religion and rulership were inseparable. The Shang king served as both chief priest and chief ruler. In this theocratic system the king, in order to make important decisions of state, sought guidance or assistance from various unseen superhuman powers. These powers were of three general types: (1) a supreme god called Di, often translated as "God"; (2) spirits of natural phenomena; and (3) spirits of former humans.

Di was unpredictable and unapproachable. In fact, it was not the exclusive god of the Shang, but at times even seems to have helped other tribes or groups of competing peoples against the Shang. Since Di was very powerful and efficacious, it was very important for the Shang to access this god's favor. This they did largely through petitions to either deceased ancestors of the ruling clan (usually former kings or queens) or nature spirits. Shang leaders hoped that these spirits would interact with Di to bring about a favorable result.

Pyromancy

The Shang contacted these powers by means of pyromancy, or divination by fire. Divination is the process of communicating with divine beings. The king's diviners drilled holes in shoulder bones (scapula) of oxen or stomach plates (plastrons) of tortoises. Shang divination is also called either "scapulimancy" or "plastrimancy." With holes pre-drilled, the diviners then engraved into the bone statements or ques-

83

tions originating with the king. These charges, or queries, usually took the form of positive and negative pairs regarding mysterious phenomena or future acts, events, or kingly decisions. Often the queries, in fact, represented the king's beseeching the spirits/gods for favors.

For instance, if the king wished to know what the weather would be like within the next 10-day period, hoping for rain, he might order the diviners to inscribe into the bone these statements: (A) "In the next moon it will rain"; (B) "In the next moon it will not rain." The diviners then inserted heated rods into the pre-drilled holes of the bone. This produced cracks that the king interpreted. For instance, he might announce, "Good fortune. It will rain." His assistants then recorded this statement on the bone. This was the king's prognostication, or prediction, regarding future events. Eventually, when actual events later either confirmed or contravened the king's prognostication, the diviners carved this result into the opposite side of the scapula or plastron.

Pyromancy and the Right to Rule

However, usually the diviners did not record a king's misinterpretations of the cracks. Therefore, most excavated bones contain only a king's accurate prognostications. The reason is that much of the king's power in the human world rested on his ability to access the gods and spirits via pyromancy. These beings provided the king with knowledge of strange phenomena and future events. If the king were commonly wrong in interpreting or predicting events, then the spirits apparently did not favor him with privileged knowledge. Thus, recording the king's mistakes would have weakened his claim to rule.

Ritual Sacrifice and Human Sacrifice

In order to persuade spirits to act on behalf of the Shang, the king and others of the royal clan performed sacrifices to their deceased ancestors. They offered them ritual food in bronze vessels. Authoritative clans associated with the ruling Shang did likewise for their own ancestors at their own ancestral temples. For all, bronzes symbolized wealth and power.

Often humans were sacrificed at major events, such as the death of a member of the royal clan or the consecration of a new building. Regular, scheduled sacrifices to dead kings also involved the ritual killing of people. While many of the sacrificial victims were slaves who had been taken as prisoners of war from competing tribes, others were servants of deceased royalty. These servants, like others of the royalty's valued possessions, such as bronzes, horses, chariots, and weapons, were buried with the deceased. In Shang belief, since the afterworld resembled the physical world and the possessions of this world could be transferred to the afterworld, then the deceased royalty continued to need such possessions.

2. THE ZHOU DYNASTY, PART I (C.1045–550 B.C.)

The Zhou were a competing tribe from modern Shanxi Province, far west of the Shang capital. In about 1045 B.C., they conquered the Shang and established a feudalistic system of governance developed on the model of the Shang system. Qualifying royal clan members, political allies, military associates, and the old Shang ruling clan were each allotted a parcel of land, similar to later European fiefs.

Tian and the Mandate to Rule

In many ways, the early Zhou continued the Shang outlook and religion, although significant differences can be detected. The Zhou believed that their high god, Tian ("sky" or "heaven"), like Di of the Shang, substantially influenced both the collective royal Zhou fortunes and individual royal clan members' lives. In fact, the Zhou belief in a "mandate of heaven" whereby heaven dispensed authority to a certain tribe to rule the world resembles Shang beliefs regarding Di. Indeed, in rituals of the early Zhou period, the Zhou king observed not only Tian but also Di, whom the Zhou often called Shangdi, or Lord on High.

Kingly Moral Power: The Zhou differed from the Shang in stressing that it was the king's moral purity that won him heaven's support. The king, therefore, concerned himself with the image that he projected to his supporting clansmen and other allies. Theoretically, the latter supported the king only if he continued to manifest in his speech and behavior a moral strength that heaven required of its ruling representative on Earth. The measure of the king's (and also his clan's) moral power was called his *de*, or "potency" (often also translated as "virtue").

Religion as Political Legitimation: In so defining a heavenly mandate centering on the king's *de*, the Zhou royal clan justified its conquering of the Shang. They claimed that heaven directed them, as morally upright leaders, to overtake and punish the Shang because the Shang leaders had become corrupt, wasteful, and cruel to their people. That is, they no longer had *de*. But the Zhou explained that they, now with *de* and the heavenly mandate, could not but obey heaven, and so vanquished the evil Shang. They explained to the Shang people that in the very same way eighteen generations earlier the Shang ancestors had had to overthrow their predecessors, the Xia (c. 2200–1545 B.C.).

According to the Zhou myth of legitimization, the final test of the Zhou right to rule lay in its ability to maintain peace and order in its vast domain. If the people believed in the Zhou and did not rebel against it, then the Zhou must possess both *de* and the heavenly mandate. The other side of this coin, of course, was as dangerous to the Zhou as it was to the Shang: Any rebel could claim that he had the most powerful *de* and that Heaven therefore had ordered him to overthrow the Zhou.

Communication with the Other World

Ancestors and Rituals: The tangible measure of one's possession of both *de* and the mandate was the king's performance of ritual at the altars to Heaven and Earth and the royal ancestors. Very similar to the Shang system, the king was deemed worthy if he performed the obligatory rituals and sacrifices correctly and opportunely.

Sacrifices to Heaven and Earth, and the Triad: Only the Zhou king could make ritual sacrifices to heaven and earth. These so-called Suburban Sacrifices, since they took place in the southern suburbs of the Zhou capital, were of paramount importance and occurred just once a year. They reaffirmed humanity's ties with the universe itself. Through them the king, acting as a conduit between the spiritual and human worlds, ensured that the spiritual powers would use their resources to benefit only him and his people. Therefore, humanity formed a triad with heaven and earth: Heaven bestows benefit from above, Earth supports from below, and humanity completes the triad by receiving and returning these gifts. This sense of human participation and the overall reciprocity of the universal system hereafter remained an essential pattern in Chinese thought.

Ancestor Worship: As the sole heir to the Zhou clan's power, only the king could propitiate the Zhou ancestors. Similarly, the heads of the great collateral lineages of the Zhou clan and other enfeoffed allied clans were privileged and responsible for making proper ritual observances of the ancestors in their own lineages. The head of a great lineage worshiped all of his own lineage's past chiefs. Heads of lesser collateral lineages could observe only four generations of past lineage heads.

In addition, each local duke, as the head of his own great lineage, sacrificed regularly to the local gods of soil and grain. These spirits oversaw agricultural productivity in the duke's domain. Identical to the Shang in relying on an agricultural economy to prosper, the Zhou particularly stressed maintaining healthy relations with agricultural gods.

Divination by Gua: Human sacrifice also continued during the Zhou, but far less commonly than during the Shang and with decreasing significance after the first few centuries. Similarly, although the Zhou employed pyromancy, they did so less as time went on. Increasingly they preferred an alternate method of divination that the later Shang rulers had begun to employ in addition to pyromancy. Using this *bugua* ("divining the graph") method, the diviner began, as did the pyromancer, with a question. Seeking an answer, he manipulated in a complex counting process several tens of stiff milfoil stalks, with the goal of producing a series of six numerical values. These values, each either a 6, 7, 8, or 9, he represented visually by drawing either a broken or a solid line.

Altogether, the six divined lines stacked vertically constituted a graph, *gua* ("hexagram"). Each of a total of 64 *gua* represented a present or future circumstance that spoke subtly and vaguely to the diviner's charge. The *gua* overall constituted all situations, events, and things in the known universe. This is because by the middle Zhou, the lines of the *gua* represented the powers of heaven (7 and 9; solid) and earth (6 and 8; broken). Heaven was the force of light, creation, dominance, might, male power, and so on. Earth was dark, warm, nurturing, acquiescing, and female. Since together heaven and earth constituted the universe, then their representations in the many combinations of lines did so as well. In the late Zhou, these ideas were combined with a separate set of values surrounding the concepts of Yin (indicated with a dark, broken line – –) and Yang (a bright, solid line ——). For the theory of Yin and Yang, see page 91.

The Sixty-Four Gua of the Changes of Zhou: The graphs and the written descriptions of their meanings were written down in several competing versions. By about the seventh century B.C., one version dominated Zhou divination: the *Changes of Zhou*, or the *Classic on Change*, which later became one of the five basic classics and a cornerstone of Chinese civilization.

The *Changes of Zhou* can best be explained with a brief example. Take, for instance, the *gua* titled *tai*, meaning "peace" (three broken lines above three solid lines [see Graph 1 below]). Symbolically, this means that earth rests above heaven. The usual interpretation of *tai* is that the pure earth's quiet, restraining, and nurturing influence (the three upper lines) controlling the wild, bright, often overly energetic—and thus destructive—force of heaven below produces peace (*tai*). If ungoverned, the energy of heaven would create havoc. However, without this energy there would be no life. Therefore, *tai* can represent an ideal situation.

In contrast is the hexagram *pi*, "stagnance." It is no coincidence that its graph is just the opposite of *tai* (three solid over three broken lines [see the graph below]). In this case, heaven's energies are ungoverned and thus wasted, resulting in stagnation. Therefore, *pi* often represents unproductivity.

"Tai": 3 broken lines above 3 solid lines.

"Pi": 3 solid lines above 3 broken lines.

Changes in the Zhou Belief System

By the eighth century B.C., Zhou power had declined considerably; the process had begun as early as the 10th century. Largely this reflected the growing distance in time from the original Zhou conquest, which by the eighth century was but a vague memory. Formerly allied peoples on the periphery of the empire rebelled, and often the Zhou failed to reconquer them. This in turn led to divisions within the central power matrix of Zhou control—that is, among the closely allied relatives and cooperative chieftains. As the system gradually decayed, the Zhou found it increasingly difficult to persuade allies of the efficacy and legitimacy of Zhou rule. In addition, according to traditional accounts, the Zhou kings began to fail to perform the rituals of power correctly and even abused them. Thereafter, the many allied dukes and lesser family heads lost faith in the Zhou's mandate to rule. Zhou politics became cynical. Consequently, after the mid-eighth century, while the Zhou remained figurehead leaders, power decentralized, falling to the dukes and great families.

As ritual lost its religious significance, so too did the bronzes around which the system centered. They became expressions more of economic than ritual power. At the same time, wealth became more widespread and an end in itself.

As a further consequence of the increasing cynicism toward the ritual power system, the rituals grew more humanized: Feudal chieftains increasingly lost their reverence for a spirit-centered, politically oriented ritual as they realized that humans, not spirits, controlled human events. Human-oriented ritual was likely more profitable politically, economically, and socially.

Always a part of the greater ritual system that included observances of spiritual beings, human ritual reflected and mimicked the spiritually directed ritual. Just as the head of a family paid respects to his ancestors, so his sons respected him and treated him with absolute deference. This pattern extended throughout the feudal society too; just as the king knelt before the Zhou ancestral rulers, so did the dukes and other heads of Zhou clan lineages pay formal respects to the Zhou king. Moreover, in each duke's domain his high ministers of state (often also Zhou relatives) treated him in turn with the same respect. Human ritual thus constituted a political and social hierarchy.

3. THE ZHOU DYNASTY, PART II: THE HUNDRED SCHOOLS AND THE WARRING STATES (C. 550–221 B.C.)

The fifth through third centuries B.C. produced the richest bed of thought that China would create. This flourishing certainly derived from the intellectual tendencies of the previous periods, but the most significant immediate stimuli were in fact social, economic, and military.

Changes in Zhou Societies

The nobility's increasingly cynical view of the Zhou's religious-political legitimation of power led eventually to the deterioration of the humanistic ritual system. By the sixth century B.C. previously exclusive privileges of the hereditary elite were opening up to all classes as wealth edged out birthright as the crucial measure of worth and power.

From this time on, as the political vacuum at the center of the system increased, the old fiefs entered a virtual free-for-all for power, land, and wealth, becoming quasi-independent states. Heads of noble families who owned these states hired experts not on the basis of their social class, but rather on how efficiently they could gather wealth and fight wars on their masters' behalf.

As economic stakes grew, warfare among the states increased in frequency and ferocity. Thinkers of all classes responded to the chaos by seeking to either patch up the old system, create a new one, or simply make the best possible life for themselves. In this intellectually flourishing period of the so-called Hundred Schools of Thought, the central question that all asked was, "What is the right way?"

Confucius's Humanistic Reaction to an Inhumane World

Confucius (551–479 B.C.) was the first of the great Chinese thinkers, although he was not very highly regarded in his own time. Only centuries later, after his disciples had promulgated and expanded on his foundation, did the comprehensive humanist system known as Ru (usually known outside China as "Confucianism," a misnomer avoided in the present chapter) begin to dominate Chinese civilization.

Confucius denounced many of the changes occurring in the Zhou social structure. One such change was a growing trend toward making laws that were announced to the public. In his time, laws replaced social etiquette in some of the states as the mechanism of social behavioral control. Confucius viewed this as but one aspect of the greater problem of society's loss of civility. He considered it a problem of leadership.

The Junzi, Humaneness, and Rites:
Confucius visited various states to try to reinvigorate rule by moral power. He promoted what seemed to be the old-fashioned ideal of the "noble man," *junzi* (literally, "son of a lord"). But he significantly altered the ideal by defining *junzi* in terms of the quality of nobility, not its inherited rank. That is, nobility was earned, not inherited.

To Confucius, any man could become a *junzi*. All he needed was to be *ren*, humane, and thus *de*, morally potent. In turn, Confucius considered the *junzi's ren* and *de* to be the fruits of his sincere faithfulness and altruism in his treatment of others. Such trustworthiness or reliability began in the home by a man acting out of absolute love and respect for his parents.

Only a *junzi* possessing these values could serve as a model on whom the rest of society could rely for behavioral guidance. With such a guide, the people themselves learned to be filial and humane by acting out the old comprehensive Zhou system of reciprocal *li*, or rites (or ritual). It was the moral power of the *junzi's de* that enabled him to so influence the people.

Within the family, *li* expressed the sincerity and filiality of one's *xin* (meaning "mind-heart"). More broadly, *li* were expressed in behavioral decorum according to which people of differing social levels interacted. On an even broader scope, religious *li,* manifested in people's ritual observances of their ancestors, demonstrated their commitment to a universal filiality that bridged generations. At each level of participation, one's interaction with the systemic *li* also inculcated the values of trustworthiness, altruism, faithfulness, filiality, and humaneness in his *xin*. *Li* was conceived as a comprehensive and self-regenerating moral system of behavioral etiquette.

Confucius expressed his ritual-based political ideals very concisely when he indicated that good and moral government rests on the simple quality of "correctness."

Correctness he defined as the proper application of ritual whereby each person knows his or her proper place and understands and acts out flawlessly the proper ritual social behavior germane to that position.

Competition from the Lower Classes: The Mohists

As several of Confucius's disciples took positions in the governments of the various states, they faced stiff competition from Mohists, clannish followers of Mozi (c. 478–392 B.C.).

Frugality and Profit: Mozi was an artisan—perhaps a carpenter—and thus also a commoner. Mohist organization and views reflected this background. Mohists argued most forcefully in favor of giving primary consideration to issues of profit and against wasteful expenditure in governance (thus they are known for their extreme frugality).

For Mohists, all other considerations must derive from those of profit. Thus, for instance, they attacked the Ru for expending so extravagantly on rites and music. While acknowledging the practical value of certain rites, the Mohists denied the value of aesthetic concerns altogether. Hence, since music largely brought no profit, then it should largely be suppressed as impractical and wasteful. However, certain religious rites performed in moderation, including accompanying music, were allowable, since such would bring recompense from spiritual beings.

Even Mohist condemnation of warfare derived from concerns over efficiency and profit: Offensive warfare was expensive, wasteful, and unproductive; therefore, it should be abandoned. To encourage leaders to do so, Mozi and the Mohists developed unusual skill in defensive warfare.

Morality and Universal Concern: The Mohists determined even morality on the basis of profit and harm. This is apparent in the Mohist ideal of "universal concern." It was impractical and unprofitable, they believed, to differentiate one's concern between those close to and distant from oneself. Therefore, one should feel as much concern for another person's sibling as for one's own.

Identification With the Superior and Unified Morality: Universal concern dovetails with the Mohist ideal of socio-governmental organization, called "identification with the superior." Mohists preached that everyone throughout society must identify with only his immediate superior. Even the most elevated person, the king, emulated his immediate superior, heaven itself.

Such a system creates two results. First, there is no room for expressing more or less concern for anyone, for to do so would upset the loyalties that in all cases must direct upward toward one's official superior. The only practical solution is to maintain universal concern, or a complete lack of favoritism or disfavoritism. Second, all ideas about goodness in human society are unified, since morality derives simply from heaven through the king's emulation of it as his superior. Heaven, of course, likes profit.

Language of Debate, Logic, and the End of Mohism: Because they constantly debated thinkers who represented other traditions, Mohists developed a specialized jargon of debate and tests of linguistic adequacy. In the fourth and third centuries B.C. these tests evolved into the true beginning of a Chinese science of logic.

Perhaps as a result of such disputative tendencies, Mohists split into three competing groups and eventually, in the violent wars that concluded the third century B.C., disappeared entirely.

Individualistic Yang Zhu

Sometimes mistakenly characterized as egoists, Yang Zhu (c. fourth century B.C.) and his disciple "Yangists" were in fact individual preservationists who sought to maximize their mortal lives. When Yang Zhu said that he would not give a hair of his to save the world, he meant that doing so would be fruitless since it would not save the world. Mencius (fl. c. 323–314 B.C.) misconstrued Yang's words to mean that he would not give up even one of his hairs to save the entire world.

Yangists promoted withdrawal from all activities that did not nourish one's person. The danger in such a philosophy is that one might thereby justify gluttony. In fact,

the Yangists taught just the opposite, advising that one should use and collect things—food, drink, valuables, and goods in general—only in moderation, only to the extent necessary to sustain one's body. By limiting reliance on external things, one maximizes his life's potential. Conversely, attaching oneself to external things places too little importance on the self, causing self-destruction.

Primitivistic Divine Agriculturists

Another competing voice in the fourth and third centuries B.C. came from a group promoting primitive lifestyles, the Divine Agriculturists. Their name derives from an ancient legendary culture hero, the Divine Agriculturist, who long had been credited with having invented agriculture and teaching it to his people. The most prominent among the Divine Agriculturists was Xu Xing (Hsü Hsing, c. 300 B.C.). The Divine Agriculturists taught that all in the world, rulers and subjects alike, each should perform all the activities that sustain him or her and family. This system left no room for the division of labor characteristic of advanced civilization. Because of this, the Divine Agriculturists are also called Primitivists.

Dialecticians

Like the later Mohists, the Dialecticians made the proper use of language their intellectual centerpiece. However, unlike the politically motivated Mohists, they did so for purely intellectual reasons. Largely they wished to identify the true realities of things so that appropriate names could be applied to them. Their activities helped stimulate Mohists to specialize in the language of debate.

Among the most famous of Dialecticians was Hui Shi (fl. ca. 320 B.C.), who loved to debate with his good friend Zhuang Zhou. Among China scholars, Zhuang Zhou is generally known as "Zhuangzi," the namesake of the philosophical text *Zhuangzi*. (See the section on the text of Zhuangzi for a discussion of the philosophy associated with Zhuang Zhou.) Hui forever attempted to trip up the clever and free-thinking Zhuangzi for the latter's seemingly wild statements. Zhuangzi considered language a very imperfect tool necessary for discourse between people; he believed little good could come from splitting hairs over the meanings or uses of words. Still, Zhuangzi was perhaps the cleverest wordsmith of all, for he was always able to outwit Hui and prove the inadequacy of language.

Hui Shi developed twenty-one paradoxes that demonstrated the inadequacies of contemporary language and practices of naming. One of his paradoxes is the statement: "The eye does not see." Hui apparently meant that the mind interprets the information that the eye provides.

Perhaps the most famous paradox of the Dialecticians is the difficult "A white horse is not a horse." Through complicated arguments, Gongsun Long (third century B.C.) "proved" that a "white horse" is not the same as a "horse" because *horse* refers to the thing's shape and *white* refers to its color. To allow the color to define the shape (that is, to allow that "white horse" belongs to the category of things "horse") thoroughly confounds any rational basis for the use of language.

Mencius's Refinement of Ru Teachings

Mencius is among the most important of Chinese thinkers. He strengthened Ru teachings by both expanding and refining Confucius's message. In this way, the itinerant lecturer believed, he could compete successfully against the thousands of other traveling speakers of the day and persuade the ruler of a state to enact his program of humane rule.

Humaneness, Rightness, and the Five Relationships: Confucius's humaneness formed the basis of Mencius's thought, but Mencius developed it further by promoting the concept of rightness. The latter referred to a state of affairs in which each person attained and maintained conditions and circumstances appropriate to himself or herself. Much like Confucius, Mencius saw decorum as the only ethically correct means of achieving such appropriateness. He further defined the social relationships that, on the one hand, social decorum created and sustained and, on the other,

constituted the basis for attaining appropriateness and, therefore, the ethically correct society. Mencius' Five Relationships, including those between (1) father and son, (2) ruler and minister, (3) husband and wife, (4) the old and the young, and (5) friend and friend.

A Model for the World: As did Confucius, Mencius taught that the transformation of the world must begin with a model for the people to follow. He believed that the ruler must refine his mind of compassion such that it fills with fatherly concern for the people and thereby enriches them. The people would gladly work diligently for such a ruler, and others would wish to immigrate to become his subjects, thus enriching his state.

The Goodness of Human Nature: Mencius saw humanity's problems as stemming from an internal struggle between two natures, the human and the animal (or major and minor). Without proper training, the human/major nature remains undeveloped and obscured by the selfish, destructive animal/minor nature. Mencius hoped ultimately to defeat the selfish animal nature by nourishing the good human nature.

The human nature in each person consists in Four Seeds: feelings of (1) commiseration, (2) shame and dislike, (3) deference and compliance, and (4) right and wrong. With correct training, each leads respectively to the four mature, ideal human qualities of humaneness (*ren*), rightness (*yi*), decorum (*li*), and wisdom (*zhi*).

Teachings of the Sages: In order to bring out these qualities in his subjects, the ruler and his ministers must first have attained an intimate connection with the purely good heaven by developing fully their own humane and right natures (attaining *de*). And such execution of the Way, Mencius insisted, can be achieved only through arduous study of and meditation on the wisdom and doings of the ancient sages.

The Ru developed the myth of a pristine past that included a series of cultural heroes, particularly the legendary Yao and Shun, who supposedly had performed great deeds on behalf of humanity. Repositories of sagely wisdom included the *Book of Odes (Shi), Book of History (Shu)*, and various records of rites. These later would become a substantial portion of China's classical canon.

The Jixia Academy

During the fourth century B.C., several leaders of the warring states extended their mutual competition to encompass the world of thought. They patronized leading thinkers lavishly, in return for which these guests debated in the leaders' courts the most pressing issues of the day. They discussed the origins and structure of the universe, the role of a moral or amoral heaven in the natural and human worlds, ethical principles and human conduct, and the meaning of individual and collective human life.

The most famous and productive of these academies was the Jixia in the powerful northeastern state of Qi, operating first from c. 319 to 301 B.C. and again early in the third century B.C. Likely Mencius visited here and met many of the greatest minds of his day.

Zou Yan and the Theories of Yin/Yang and the Five Processes: Among the more interesting of the Jixia scholars was Zou Yan (Tsou Yen, c. 300 B.C.). He combined and then introduced into mainstream thinking two old cosmological theories, yin-yang phasing and Five Processes (sometimes translated as "Five Elements" or "Five Phases") cycling. Zou's manipulation of these theories deeply influenced all of Chinese thinking thereafter. At the bottom of Zou Yan's understanding of the universe was his belief that, in all of their activities, humans were connected intimately with natural processes.

Yin and Yang: Yin-yang theory purported that the universe is constructed and operates according to these two contrasting principles of existence and interaction. Originally the character yin referred to what is shaded, and yang denoted the unshaded or brightly lit. The theory thus centers on the presence or absence of sunlight. But the moon was associated with yin, as well, most likely because of its normal appearance during the shaded night.

According to Zou's mature yin-yang theory, all things, events, and time fall into one or the other category: Yang things are associated with daylight, energy, sharpness, leadership, aggressiveness, heat, hardness, dryness, and the male principle; yin things are dark, submissive, quiet, following, receptive, moist, soft, nurturing, and associated with the female principle. Later, yang was identified with the dynamic and life-giving heaven, and yin became associated with the supportive and life-nurturing earth below. Between them, they created and sustained all living things.

The Five Processes: Thus yin and yang had both temporal (sun and moon phasing day and night) and spatial (heaven and earth) aspects. The theory of the Five Processes (including earth, wood, metal, fire, and water) likewise involved identifying complementary elements of things in terms of time, but more long term.

Whereas yin and yang explained daily cycles, the Five Processes described natural cycles of 500 or so years that manifested themselves in the human political world. The fortunes of each historical political dynasty were identified according to the dynasty's association with one of the Five Processes. The rise and fall of a dynasty could be both explained and predicted according to the sequence of the succeeding ascendancies of each of the Five Processes. The earliest legendary dynasty, that of the legendary Yellow Emperor (c. 2700 B.C.), was associated with the earth process; the next, the Xia, with wood; the succeeding Shang, with metal; and the subsequent Zhou with fire.

Zou Yan's theory has been highly influential. In the second century B.C., it contributed a central component to the new imperial Han government's self-legitimation. Moreover, developments from Zou's basic theory are ubiquitous in later Chinese religion, philosophy, medicine, culture, and cyclical theories of history.

Looking Inward to Cultivate the Mind-Heart: Many of those associated with the Jixia Academy betrayed a common concern with individual attainment of extraordinary power. This they usually identified as *de*, the very power that had legitimized early Zhou kings' possession of the heavenly mandate to rule. Cultivating the human mind-heart was the key to achieving *de*.

In general, the theorists on power split into two groups, depending on their understanding of human nature and the nature of human society. One group, the Ru, considered *de* a moral power that society's mores brought to fruition in both the individual and, by extension, the world. The other group, who did not form a cohesive school of thought, generally disparaged society's role. They argued that human nature was complete and perfect at birth and only through socialization degenerated, losing its original perfection. To such thinkers, achieving *de* amounted to returning to the unthinking, intuitive mind of the infant.

Early "Daoism"

Daoism never existed as a school of thought in the Zhou period, but later historians imposed this unity on several thinkers whose ideas shared some essential elements. Some of the thinkers' positions apparently evolved from those of the individualistic Yangists and non-conforming, non-participating Divine Agriculturists, among others. Most representative of the early "Daoists" are the works *Laozi* and *Zhuangzi*.

Laozi or Daode jing: The first mention of *Laozi* occurs in a mid-third century B.C. text, but sections of the work may precede this by centuries. It supposedly was written by Li Er (Li Erh, sobriquet Dan, sixth century B.C.), also known as Laozi ("Master Venerable"), but the existence of such a person is unproved.

Theory of Universal Construct: Dao and De: *Laozi* concerns two overriding themes, *dao*, the Way, and *de*, power. Here *de* clearly denotes an organic power that is both universal life source and individual font of renewed personal and political vigor. *De* in turn has its source in the primordial *dao*.

According to *Laozi*, the universe consists in both non-material and material factors, or "vacuity" and "solidity." Similar are the terms *nothingness*, and *thingness*. In nothingness there are no things; in thingness things exist. The combined states of nothingness and thingness create and sustain the universe, both seen and unseen.

However, since thingness is the most apparent of realms, people normally cognate it only. The danger in neglecting nothingness is this: Since nothingness, as the source and power of thingness, always accompanies thingness, then losing its contact and stimulation causes a person, who is a thing also powered by nothingness, to gradually deplete his store of this life-giving power. One's unnurtured nothingness then exhausts itself powering his interactions with the daily world of thingness.

Rejuvenation of the Self: One rejuvenates oneself by recommuning with nothingness, thereby rebuilding one's inborn store of *de* power. The key to success is losing all desires for any sort of gain in thingness. One must detach from all things and use only what is absolutely necessary to sustain oneself. This one does by quieting the mind and concentrating it on the existence of vacuity, or nothingness, disregarding everything learned relative to thingness, including human culture. One discards standards of behavior, pleasure, measurement, identification, naming, differentiation among things, and expectations. One resides the mind only in quiet vacuity, experiencing no emotions, thoughts, desires, or expectations. Eventually, *Laozi* claims, a person achieves a oneness with nothingness, suffused with the vacuous power *de*. One then becomes as vacuity itself while remaining physically in the realm of thingness.

Wuwei: Nonrulership of the Human World: One who has fully realized his *de* does not seek to rule, though he is the only one qualified to do so. His rulership is nonactive, *wuwei* ("no-doing"). Though other Hundred Schools thinkers, including Confucius, promoted *wuwei* rulership, *Laozi's* was most hands-off: Rulership is best, the *Laozi* advises, if the people have only vaguely heard of the ruler and neither ever see him nor consider his rulership; the ruler with *de* rules through *de*, which allows him to connect with the *de* inherent in all things, at a mystical level of understanding far more potent than the realm of words and policies. Under such rulership, the people rejuvenate themselves without knowing so and live out undisturbed the full potentials of their lives.

Zhuangzi: This long and complex text contains the work of many distinct authors. Consequently, some sections resemble the work of Divine Agriculturists; others, the personal and political thinking represented in *Laozi*; and still others, the syncretic political philosophies of Huang-Lao that gained popularity in the late third and early second centuries B.C.

The dominant philosophy of the book, however, is that of the man Zhuang Zhou (Chuang Chou, c. 320 B.C.) and his followers. Most scholars refer to Zhuang Zhou as Zhuangzi, which simply means "Master Zhuang." Like *Laozi*, these writings postulate the existence of a perfect ancient past in which sages dwelled in a mental quietude that maintained them in the state of vacuity and nothingness. Since for them things did not exist, then things could not exhaust their inborn power of *de*. Zhuang Zhou claimed that his contemporaries were the victims of a gradual historic loss of this pure and perfect state of being and, because of that, lived a miserable life in which they continuously differentiated things. Doing so, Zhuang Zhou argued, allows things to use people up as, for instance, fire does wood. He maintained that, as soon as people determine for themselves which things are better and which are worse, then they have created an unmanageable desire for the "better" thing. Occurring hundreds of times a day, such desires make people exert efforts on things' behalf. In the end, these efforts drain a person's *de*, leading to premature death.

Zhuang advocated that people not divorce themselves from things but instead live mentally in the vacuous state that intersects all things. Conducting oneself in this way allows one's *de* to guide the person effortlessly to float unimpeded through the world of things, leaving *de* undiminished. This is an individual application of *Laozi's wuwei*. And, as in *Laozi*, the person who conducts his life accordingly then lives out his or her full natural life span.

The process of coming to understand this universally intersecting *dao* is merely a matter of mentally/spiritually concentrat-

ing on the vacuous. To Zhuang Zhou and his followers, doing anything more, including attempting to rule over people's lives in any capacity, causes one to sacrifice the life force of *de* and thus also his or her life. This is because governing people is to treat them as things; this leads to either exhaustion or a more immediate and violent demise. In thus promoting absolute non-participation in rulership, *Zhuangzi* differs substantially from the otherwise similar *Laozi*.

The Ru Respond: Xunzi's Revolving World

The innovative Xun Kuang (Hsün K'uang, a.k.a. Xunzi [Master Xun], c. 310–230 B.C.), whose collected essays in *Xunzi* must be categorized among the Ru writings, nevertheless borrowed substantially from outside the Ru tradition to transform Ru thinking. Unlike Confucius and Mencius, Xun served in a relatively authoritative position in the government of one of the seven Warring States (403–221 B.C.). This clearly influenced his understanding of government.

Empiricism and the Steady Cosmos: Xun attempted to debunk people's common fear that the world operated according to unknowable forces, including a willful heaven and potentially harmful ghosts and spirits. Xun endeavored to demonstrate that natural anomalies, a source of the people's fear, occur only randomly and as natural by-products of the regular, predictable revolving of a rational system of cosmological order. He pointed out that humanity, not nature, causes humanity's troubles. Xun argued that humanity must fulfill its duty to itself and its creator, heaven and earth, by ordering its affairs on a rational basis and thereby completing the natural triad of heaven, earth, and humanity. This trinity Xun called *can*, a character that means both "three" and "participation."

A Problem of Human Nature: Unlike Mencius, Xun argued that people's nature is to be greedy and self-serving. He reasoned that, since people always desire what they do not possess and they all desire to be good, then goodness must not be part of inborn human nature.

Human Nature and Culture: To Xun, inborn human covetousness leads to all human social degeneracy, political corruption, and wars. Xun sought to dissolve covetousness through a program of cultural development on the basis of the sagely values and principles found particularly in the *Book of Changes*, *Book of Odes*, and the various works on rites. Through these works, he envisioned a society bound by clearly defined social etiquette and high standards of human understanding.

Cultivation and Moral Leadership: Like Mencius and Confucius, Xun taught that the would-be ruler's self-cultivation constitutes the beginning of cultural rectification. However, Xun's program of quiet, meditational self-perfection clearly reflects the discussions at the Jixia Academy, where he spent time on a stipend in the early third century B.C. This is apparent in his understanding of *de*, which for him was a power both cultural (the human element) and natural (from heaven and earth). Such understanding also reflects and is reflected in his thesis of *can*.

Transformed by culture, the ruler of *de* in turn cultivates his subjects with this powerful human-natural humane force such that each attains what is appropriate, or right, for itself in the human and natural worlds. Xun stressed particularly the need to establish a system of consistent names of things, governmental offices, and events on the basis of rational differentiation of their unique and shared characteristics. He intended with this "rectification of names" to create an unequivocal universal basis of human understanding and action. This develops on Confucius' own thesis of *zheng*.

However, contrary to his Ru tradition, Xun warned that culture alone sometimes could not achieve order. He thus advised establishing a secondary system of control consisting of rewards and punishments. Therefore, Xun allowed for a legal code.

Xun's Legacy: Xun was highly influential in his own time and in the subsequent two or three centuries. His system was fully capable of being put into practice, and indeed his universalism influenced significantly the Han dynasty thought on rulership. In addition, two of Xun's students were instrumental in bringing about among the greatest revolutions in Chinese and world history. These students were Han Fei (d. 233 B.C.) and Li Si (Li Ssu, d. 208 B.C.).

Legalism (Fajia)

Legalism is, like Daoism, a term applied after the fact to categorize thinkers whose ideas share certain similar trends. In this case, the major thinkers and politically practicing developers of these ideas include Gongsun Yang (Kungsun Yang, or Lord Shang or Shang Yang, d. 338 B.C.), Shen Buhai (Shen Pu-hai d. 337 B.C.), Shen Dao (Shen Tao, fl. c. 310 B.C.), Han Fei, and Li Si. Their ideas concerning statecraft, law, taxation, social engineering, and economics began in the northwestern state of Qin with Lord Shang in the 350s B.C. Lord Shang's innovative practices in rulership eventually changed the face of the world. They resulted in the great synthesis of Legalist ideas by Han Fei in the third century B.C.

Han Fei: Han Fei entirely disavowed the foundering Zhou feudal order. Unlike most of his contemporaries, he dismissed the past as outdated and incapable of providing lessons for the contemporary late-Warring States world.

Han Fei proposed a highly centralized state power structure centering on the king. A professional bureaucracy of experts, appointed by the king and his ministers (themselves appointees) on the basis only of their abilities to perform specific tasks, were to operate the machinery of the state. Good government, he said, depends not on morality but on the correct functioning of solidly conceived and developed political, economic, and military institutions.

Han Fei's overall purpose was to increase the power and might of the state. This depended in turn on the wealth of the state. All people, therefore, were to serve this purpose of enriching the state. Individual lives meant little, if anything, in this system. However, Han argued, eventually the system would benefit all who lived in the enriched state.

Statecraft: At the center of Han's system was the king who, like the proposed rulers of the Confucians and Daoists, practiced *wuwei* rulership. In Han Fei, however, *wuwei* assumes that the institutions of the state, being set up and staffed optimally, carry out the myriad busy activities of government, leaving the ruler to do nothing but remain mysteriously hidden in the palace, secretive and awe inspiring.

The best of rulers is the worst of rulers, Han argued, because in the properly functioning system, the ruler should do nothing; a "good" ruler is a busybody engaging in *wei*, or "active," and thus disastrous, government.

Once established, the ruler's only task is to avoid intimacy with his highest advisers and, in fact, foment distrust among them so that they will not conspire to overthrow him. This is *shu*, or statecraft.

Law and Human Nature: Other than the barely perceivable ruler and his personal statecraft of smoke and mirrors, the institutional centerpiece of Han Fei's system was a comprehensive and objective system of laws. Even the ruler had to abide by it.

A collateral system of extravagant rewards and severe punishments enforced the law. Han and the other Legalists thus sought to control people via external means, not internal cultivation. Han Fei reasoned that people have neither good nor bad tendencies in their natures but respond only to external stimuli; that is, they seek to earn rewards and avoid punishments. Issues of morality are irrelevant, for people are driven only by pleasure, pain, and material gain.

4. EARLY IMPERIAL ERA: QIN, HAN, AND WEI/JIN PERIODS (221 B.C.–417 A.D.)

Qin (221–206 B.C.)

The founding emperor of the Qin dynasty, Shi Huangdi (r. 221–211 B.C.), employed Han Fei's synthesis in establishing the institutional, political, social, cultural, and ideological framework of his centralized state.

Shi Huangdi's Eclectic Interests and Change of Heart: Late in his reign Shi Huangdi suppressed Ru and most of the other Hundred Schools as competitors against the dynasty's rulership. Earlier he had attempted to portray himself as an ideal Ru king in his speeches, oozing beneficence for the people even as he imposed draconian rule.

Simultaneously at his court in Xianyang (near present-day Xi'an) he lavished rewards on the *fangshi* (roughly, "magicians") from the old Qi culture in northeastern China. The *fangshi* promised to provide the emperor with the secrets of immortality. Shi Huangdi, in fact, sent two expeditions headed by *fangshi* into the Eastern Sea to seek fairy isles of lore.

Despite his personal broad intellectual interests, in 213 B.C. Shi Huangdi manifested his intolerance for ideologies potentially threatening to his absolute rule. In

that year, he ordered that most of the books in the empire outside of the collections of the imperial library be confiscated and burned. Only works of agriculture, medicine, and divination were spared. Another manifestation of Shi Huangdi's increasing insecurity and intolerance occurred the following year when, feeling betrayed by some of his advisers, he ordered them investigated. Subsequently, he executed more than 460 people, including *fangshi* and Ru scholars in his service.

Shi Huangdi as Universal Emperor: Shi Huangdi established some of the essential institutional and ideological patterns that remained virtually standard through the subsequent 2,200 years of Chinese imperial history. For instance, in 219 B.C., he initiated imperial sacrifices to heaven and earth, called the Feng and Shan sacrifices. According to the lore of the time, seventy-two world-ruling kings had performed these during the legendary period (pre-Shang and pre-Xia). Their significance for Shi Huangdi's pretense to universal rulership was thus great. The Feng he performed on top of sacred Mt. Tai in Shandong Province and directed toward heaven, and the Shan he carried out below the northern slope of the mountain, on a foothill named Liangfu, to consecrate earth. In this way, Shi Huangdi attempted to legitimize his rulership by establishing a unique relationship between himself and heaven and earth. This reflects Xun's concept of *can*; it remained a central concern of later emperors.

Shi Huangdi also attempted to systematize all major religious cults by centering their activities in the capital. Thus, in Xianyang he had altars built for the Lords of the Four Directions, the Gods of the Four Seas, the Lord of Rain, the Lord of the Wind, and other universalistic deities recognized across the empire. Later empires continued to monopolize significant cults.

While sacrifices to such superhuman agencies legitimized Shi Huangdi as universal emperor, during his many personal tours of his empire he also took care to co-opt the power of local cults by making sacrifices to local deities of mountains, rivers, and other natural phenomena. In this way, he attempted to center all of the people's religious activity on himself. Again, later emperors imitated his practices.

Han (206 B.C.–220 A.D.)

The Han succeeded the Qin both institutionally and ideologically. For 15 years after the founding of the Han to 191 B.C., the new dynasty maintained the Qin proscription against most written works. However, in the meantime, the Han employed non-Legalist approaches to statecraft, as well as non-Legalist-thinking statesmen and bureaucrats. Inheritors of the Ru intellectual traditions of the various Warring States became valued participants at the Han court in Chang'an (near present-day Xi'an). Thus, Ru political ideology soon made its mark on the Han.

The New Vision of Huang-Lao: During the second century B.C., another ideology gained ground at court, especially among the imperial family. It owed more to Shi Huangdi's magicians than it did to Ru-inspired statesmanship. Termed generally "Huang-Lao," this amorphous ideology made use of magicians' theories of achieving immortality in the context of a cosmol-

ogy developed partially from Xun's naturalistic universe that required full human participation.

Huang-Lao was also Daoist in its veneration of the legendary Yellow Emperor, now supreme immortal of heaven, and the now-apotheosized Laozi, master political theorist. But Huang-Lao further maintained a certain Legalistic trend in its reliance on law. In fact, by combining elements drawn from numerous sources—Ru, Legalist, Daoist, yin-yang/Five Processes, immortalist, and so on—it produced an entirely new universal view.

Huang-Lao Cosmology: Huang-Lao theorists envisioned a world created from vacuity and nothingness. The immaterial stuff of nothingness, called *yuanqi* ("incipient pure energy"), split into two to create yin and yang: Yang rose to form heaven and yin sank to form Earth. Residual yin and yang energies recombined and then split yet again, creating the Five Processes and their parallel phenomena. These included five spatial *qi*, "energies," of the five directions (including center) and the everlasting temporal sequence of the five seasons (including a month-long fifth season, called *tuyong*, correlating with the "center" spatial direction and sandwiched between summer and autumn).

The two sets of defining qualities of *qi*, yin and yang and the Five Processes, created all things in the world. Since all things, therefore, correlated according to their combinations of the *qi* of Yin/Yang and the Five Processes, they resonated *ganying*: things of like *qi* type responded to one another. For example, two massive yin things, the moon above and water on earth, were thought to create the oceanic tides through *ganying*.

Cosmology and the Laws of Nature and Humanity: According to Huang-Lao tenets, all things, including humans, were produced or born according to a natural law. Huang-Lao theorists reasoned that, since the principles of universal production were known and understood to be constant, then it followed naturally that humans, also being products of this system, should model their organizational patterns (bureaucracy, family, etc.) on the larger cosmological patterns. Consequently, the purpose of government was to ensure that this occurred.

Thus, Huang-Lao theorists believed that the imperial Han bureaucracy should be organized on the basis of natural law such that all names or titles of official positions (*ming*) accorded with the duties assigned to, or the reality of (*shi*), that position. This system of human order was often called *mingshi*, or "names and reality."

In this system, the emperor's role mirrored on earth that of the Yellow Emperor in heaven: He remained the unmoving center who assured that his system did not warp its reflection of the universal order. Obviously, this reapplies old *wuwei* theory.

Imperial Cults and Rituals: Part of the emperor's ability to accomplish his task of ensuring accordance with universal patterns rested on his employment of magical charms, talismans, and techniques popularized at the early Han court by magicians akin to those who had served Shi Huangdi. Similarly, imperial rituals enhanced the emperor's public prestige and legitimacy.

Especially Liu Che, posthumously known as the Martial Emperor (Wudi, r. 142–87 B.C.), stressed grand state ritual centering on the emperor's role as the center of the human world and thus the human tether between Heaven and Earth. Of particular importance were the Martial Emperor's reenactment—twice, in 110 and 106 B.C.— of the Feng and Shan sacrifices initiated by Shi Huangdi in 219 B.C.

Without a standard to follow, Liu Che modeled the sacrifices on those already made to the god Great One (Taiyi) at the capital's southern suburban altar. This chief god of heaven, represented visibly in the sky by the Pole Star, had originated with the southern Chu culture in the middle reaches of the Yangtze River Valley.

Liu Che found the Great One attractive and useful as well for his ability to identify with the god. Like the Great One/Pole Star, the emperor sat at the center of all activity: Positioning himself on his throne in the north and facing south, the world turned about his axis just as the heavens revolved around the Pole Star. In this again is the old ideal of *wuwei*.

Han Ru: New Universalism: Even more importantly, beginning in the 130s B.C. the Martial Emperor sought an ideology to justify magnifying his power far beyond that of his predecessors. For this he turned to a new Ru system being developed at that time largely on the basis of Huang-Lao cosmology.

Han Ru thinkers inserted into the borrowed Huang-Lao universe the typical Ru concern for ethics and moralism. To Gongsun Hong (Kung-Sun Hung, d. 121 B.C.) and his disciple Dong Zhongshu (Tung Chung-shu, c. 179–104 B.C.) the emperor's responsibility was thoroughly moral: He was to complete the trinity with heaven and earth by ordering humanity according to those great creative entities' universal moral principles. If he failed, he would display a lack of both moral fortitude and political legitimacy. The emperor's moral shortcomings would become apparent via heaven's omens—earthquakes, droughts, violent storms, shooting stars, comets, and other natural anomalies either destructive or frightening. The Martial and subsequent emperors utilized the positive, centralizing aspects of this new ideology to focus attention on and enhance imperial power.

At its core, this new universalistic Ru was a sophisticated reincarnation of the crude early Zhou theory of a heavenly mandate that relied on advances made in Huang-Lao ideology. Huang-Lao in turn syncretized various developments achieved by Warring States thinkers.

The Establishment of the Five Ru Classics: The two pillars of the Martial Emperor's strengthened imperial rule, namely Ru state cosmic ritual and the Ru universalistic ideology, themselves were rooted largely in the ancient cultural classical texts that now became explicitly "Ru." Thus, in 136 B.C., on the foundation of a curriculum centered on these texts, the Martial Emperor established both an imperial university and five erudites (*boshi*) to staff it. In this (as in many other ways) the Martial Emperor imitated Shi Huangdi: The latter had established a college of 70 erudites a century earlier. In 124 B.C., 50 students were assigned to study with the erudites. By the second century A.D., the number had increased to 30,000.

Each of the five erudites was an expert in one of the ancient classics, including *Chunqiu* (Spring and Autumn Annals), *Zhouyi* (Changes of Zhou), *Shi* (Book of Songs), *Shu jing* (Book of Documents), and *Li* (Rites), including *Liji* (Book of Rites), *Yili* (Ceremonial Etiquette), and *Zhouli* (Rites of Zhou).

Schools of Interpretation and Competition for Favor: The selection of each erudite and his text represented an ideological choice on the part of the Martial Emperor because there were several versions of each of the ancient texts that competed for ideological dominance to be considered officially Ru classics, and each version had its own champion.

In the Western Han period (206 B.C.–A.D. 8) the most influential of the interpretive schools was the Gongyang. This highly moralistic group of scholars specialized in *Gongyang Zhuan*, or the *Gongyang Commentary* to the classic *Spring and Autumn Annals*. Through the *Gongyang Commentary* and related works, these scholars claimed that Confucius, purported author of the *Spring and Autumn Annals*, had chosen every word of that classic very carefully in order to demonstrate very subtly his support or criticism of historical people and events.

Dong Zhongshu, mentioned above, was a Gongyang scholar. His *Chunqiu fanlu* (Luxuriant Gems of the Spring and Autumn Annals) was among the major works of Han dynasty Ru thought.

Competition for imperial favor naturally created dissension among Ru scholars as they vied for coveted erudite positions. Twice during the Han, in 51 B.C. and A.D. 79, the imperial court convened a capital conference to attempt to determine the correct interpretations of the classics by selecting which commentaries—each of which represented a different interpretive tradition—would be taught by which erudite in the imperial university. Since the differences proved unreconcilable, gradually the court increased the number of erudite positions. Thus, originally there were five, in the first century B.C., there were twelve, and by the first century A.D., the number had reached fourteen.

New Texts and Old Texts: Complicating the debates was a fundamental division into "New Text" and "Old Text" interpretive schools. During the Han, "New Text" classics generally were considered the standard versions. They were thus called because they were written in the "new script" that had been imposed by Shi Huangdi in the late third century B.C. to standardize the writing system. During the early Han, books that had been lost to the Qin proscriptions and the violent wars and library burnings of the second half of the third century B.C. were recorded in the standardized new script on the basis of scholars' recitations from memory. Others likely were merely copied into the new script from extant old-script versions.

"Old Texts" were those purported to have been passed down secretly through the disruptions of the third century B.C. or unearthed from secret caches since the fall of the Qin. Since they were written in the old scripts and therefore represented the old writings directly, their champions claimed that they were more authoritative than the indirectly descended New Texts. This controversy was so divisive that to this day scholars continue to debate what are the "correct" versions of the classics.

Decline of Han Ru and the New Synthesis of the Learning of the Abstruse (Xuanxue): By the end of the Han, the universal Ru system had run its course. The dynasty was failing, and intellectuals turned their service from empire to the provincial estates of aristocratic clans. Thinkers and writers rebelled against the constrictions of the Han Ru system and sought to express themselves freely, pursuing individual interests. The aristocratic clans supported their iconoclasm. At gatherings removed from the court, intellectuals engaged in "pure conversation" (*qingtan*) formalized debate aimed at the attainment of sundry intellectual truths.

Learning of the Abstruse: The intellectual movement within which *qingtan* developed, known as the Learning of the Abstruse (*Xuanxue*), dominated elite Chinese intellectual activity between roughly A.D. 200 and 400. Centering on *Laozi*, *Zhuangzi*, and the *Changes of Zhou*, men such as He Yan (Ho Yen, d. 249), Wang Bi (Wang Pi, 226–249), Pei Wei (P'ei Wei,

267–300), Xiang Xiu (Hsiang Hsiu, c. 223–300), and Guo Xiang (Kuo Hsiang, d. 312) wrote either commentaries to these texts or independent essays expounding ideas originating in them. In their writings, they expressed individualistic tendencies, both rebelling against the Han Ru system's excessive social constriction of the individual and simultaneously seeking to reconcile the demands of a social life with the satisfaction of the individual's needs.

Substance and Function in Nothingness and Somethingness: Xuanxue focused on the Warring States–paired concepts of nothingness (*wu*)/somethingness and vacuity (*xu*)/solidity (*shi*). *Xuanxue* thinkers related these to new expressions, such as the pair "substance" (*ti*) and "function" (*yong*) that attempted to establish an ontological hierarchy.

For instance, Wang Bi posited that nothingness/vacuity is the origin and substance of existence and represents the individual's pure inborn nature. By contrast, somethingness/solidity (the world of solid things) is secondary, born from nothingness/vacuity and therefore the function of that prior state. To *Xuanxue* thinkers, somethingness/solidity represented not only physical solidity but also the accompanying human social life. In this way most found some form of compromise between social and individual demands.

5. POPULAR BELIEFS AND RELIGIOUS ACTIVITY

In addition to the elite and state-controlled intellectual realms, an undercurrent of folk religion existed at all levels of society. During and after the Han period, the elite, state, and popular levels of thought and belief interacted dynamically, providing both continuity and differentiation between those strata. Popular beliefs thus changed over time: Many gods have come and gone as the religious pantheon evolved. On the other hand, the core of religious faith in China remained virtually identical across social levels and time. Change occurred largely in its outward expression.

Ghosts, Spirits, and Gods

During the Han and later, belief in gods, ghosts, and spirits resembled those of the earlier Shang cults. If change had occurred by the time of the Han, it was that the number of such beings had increased in both number and variety.

At all times, these beings formed part of the world of the living, differing from living human beings only by being immortal. Their requirements paralleled the needs of the living, but, unable to satisfy such needs by themselves, they depended on the living to do so through sacrifices. The spiritual beings reciprocated by either bestowing good fortune on or diverting bad fortune from humans. When a spirit responded to human entreaty, then the spirit continued to receive rewards. In this way certain cults spread and even were absorbed into the state cult. However, when a spirit proved unresponsive, people reasoned that its power had waned, and thus it could be forgotten.

Hun, Po, Gui, and Shen

A person's soul was thought to have two parts, called *hun* and *po*. In late Zhou and Han elite traditions, and in later times in popular belief, these were, respectively, yang/heavenly and yin/earthly. At one's death, people believed, the *hun* resided both in a tablet placed on the family altar and also everywhere diffuse above the cold earth. It was to this *hun* that people made ritual sacrifices, and indeed the *hun*'s survival depended on them. When sacrifices ceased, then the *hun* became a "hungry ghost," a type of spiritual entity that plagued the living in search of food and security. In the process, when free to roam the world of the living during the seventh lunar month (appropriately known as "ghost month," the seventh was the month for reunion of the living and dead), loose *hun* could cause every sort of illness and misfortune. Therefore, as part of popular religious practice, during ghost month people set out at their back doors food and goods to feed and divert the ghosts. Later, Buddhism and Daoism accommodated themselves to the hungry ghost festival, calling it, respectively, the Yulanpen Festival and the Zhongyuan Festival (centering on the fifteenth day, when the moon was full).

As a yin thing, the *po* was thought to reside after death in the earth in an underworld called Yellow Springs. Often Yellow Springs in fact denoted the tomb. In some cases it was believed that death came when the *po* departed the body. In others the *po* was identified with the corpse itself.

In the late Zhou elite intellectual traditions, and especially among the Ru and Daoists, ghosts usually were identified as *gui*, and the term *shen* denoted both a spirit and a god and the power of such a being. The *gui* were associated with yin/earth and were usually troublesome ghosts or demons, and the *shen* were yang/heavenly and usually potentially beneficial.

Many identified the *gui* ghosts with the *po* and the *shen* spirits/gods with the *hun*. Early on, however, such was not universal. At the popular level, in fact throughout the Han, there often was no difference between a *gui* and a *shen*: either could be beneficial or nefarious. Later the popular tradition absorbed the elite differentiation of *gui/po/*yin and *shen/hun*/yang. Then people considered *gui* ghosts to be harmful, dark influences created when people died violent or particularly unhappy deaths. They also were *hun* transformed for lack of ritual respect and comestibles. In some way, then, *gui* were "hungry," either for food or retribution.

The Spiritual Pantheon and Human Communication with the Gods

The gods existed in a hierarchy very similar to the socio-political structure in which humans lived. In fact, by the early Han, a pantheon was developing that mirrored the imperial bureaucratic structure. Government officials had their counterparts in the spiritual realm, and officials participated in communications with and sacrifices to the various local gods. Indeed, the

officials' religious roles bolstered their administrative roles, for their involvement with the folk religion enhanced their legitimacy among the people.

The makeup of the pantheon continued to change over time, but by the late Han among the most important local gods was the Lord of the *She* Altar, which was a distinct god in each locale. The *she* had since the Zhou period served specifically as the altar to the god of soil, but now it became the center of community religious activity as the government established a *she* in each county. Even some villages were allowed to establish minor *she* to house their own local gods. In its role as communal altar, the *she* thus did not confine itself to the ritual sacrifice to the Lord of the *She* Altar but included shrines to other local gods as well. Later, the Lord of the *She* Altar became known as the Lord of the Earth (Tudi Gong). Like his predecessor, he was a distinct god in each region, only parallel in name and function. The Tudi Gong's power over local human activities surpassed that which the Lord of the *She* Altar had enjoyed previously, so much so that eventually an image of the local Tudi Gong appeared in most every home's family shrine.

Community and family religious expression formed the core of Chinese folk belief. Aside from such communal gods as the Lord of the Earth and the familial ancestral gods/spirits, other important local gods populated local shrines, *she* altars, and family shrines. Along with the family ancestors and Lord of the Earth, a family shrine typically included the God of the Stove (Zao Jun), perhaps the most important of local and accessible gods. Similar to Tudi Gong, Zao Jun was a distinct god in each representation.

In the Han, Zao Jun's protective role combined with that of another god inherited from the Warring States period, the Director of Fates (Siming Shen). As a result, people believed that every year, on the 15th day of the 12th lunar month, corresponding roughly to the winter solstice in the solar calendar, Zao Jun, in his role as Siming, ascended to Heaven to report to the emperor of heaven, the Jade Emperor (Yuhuang Shangdi), on the family members' behavior that year. Siming's report would influence the family's fortune in the imminent new year. Therefore, the family attempted to bribe him by smearing honey (or another sugary substance) on his likeness, which resided above the stove in every home, in order to sweeten the words of his report. The thick honey also prevented Zao Jun from speaking profusely, thus further ensuring that he did not make an unfavorable report on the family.

Shamanism: People used primarily divination to communicate with gods. For this they commonly relied on shamans, both male and female. Shamans communed with and exorcised spirits, performed ritual offerings and rain dances to gods, spoke in tongues, and so on.

In hiring shamans, people sought mostly to know the propitious days and times to perform certain daily tasks. For instance, they wished to know good days for traveling, making new clothes, marrying, and giving birth. Shamans accessed the ancestral spirits and other gods that could provide this information. While traveling, people also hired shamans to perform ritual sacrifices to local gods of mountains, directions, trees, lakes, rivers, etc., hoping to secure a safe journey.

During the Warring States and Qin periods, the shamans were attached to the communal *she* altar. By the Han, however, due to an inadequate number of shamans, ordinary people often performed divination procedures themselves.

Beginning in the early Han, government reforms of popular cults curtailed many of the shamans' practices. Still, through the early Song dynasty (960–1279), various emperors summoned shamans to court, seeking their services. The Song dynasty administration proscribed shamanism in the early 11th century, labeling it an aspect of "excessive cults," yet shamans have continued into the present to serve Chinese communities across the world.

Life after Life: Longevity and Immortality

Most people, of course, wished to avoid death. Toward that end, many, including Shi Huangdi of Qin and the Martial Emperor of Han, beseeched the patron god of immortality, the Yellow Emperor, to guide them to immortality. Interest in immortality had in fact begun as early as the seventh century B.C. In the pre-Han and Han periods belief in immortality grew and, with it, also techniques for achieving it.

Shamans and *fangshi* offered their expertise in attaining either longevity or immortality. Techniques included dietary regimens, ingestion of herbs and special potions, alchemy, gymnastic exercises, practices imitative of long-lived animals and plants, and, as with Shi Huangdi and the Martial Emperor, the search for fairy isles either physically or psycho-spiritually.

During the Qin, the land of immortals was thought to be in the East; during the Han, there evolved a legend of a goddess in the western Kunlun Mountains, known as Queen Mother of the West (Xiwangmu), who granted immortality to true believers. Her cult continued to thrive throughout imperial Chinese history alongside an ever-developing general cult of immortality. Part of this development was the common folks' establishment through and after the Han of numerous shrines to the Immortals throughout the empire, some of which gained official recognition and support. At such shrines common people sought assistance in their own quests to achieve immortality.

6. CHINESE BUDDHISM

Buddhist Doctrine

Sakyamuni Gautama Siddhartha (c. 563–483 B.C.), a prince of a kingdom in present-day Nepal, attained enlighten-ment while sitting in meditation under the *bodhi* tree (tree of enlightenment) and thus became the Buddha (meaning "Enlightened One"). After his death (or the end of his earthly existence), many sects developed in India from the cadre of disciples that had surrounded the Buddha. Buddhism originally tended to be intellectual and somewhat exclusive but grew into a religion of popular faith whose cosmology included a tremendous pantheon of Buddhas, gods, and demons that populated both the heavens and the 10 hells of final judgment.

Two major divisions of Buddhist teachings developed worldwide. The earlier among them, Theravada, has also been known as the Hinayana ("Lesser Vehicle") by those adhering to the later teaching, Mahayana ("Greater Vehicle"). Though the differences between them are complex, they rest largely on the fact that the Mahayana teaches universal salvation, whereas the Theravada instructs that only monks and nuns, as part of the *sangha* (regimented Buddhist community), may achieve full enlightenment. Mahayana is known as the Buddhism of compassion in that it postulates the existence of bodhisattvas, enlightened ones who postpone their Buddhahood to remain on earth to help the unenlightened achieve salvation. Such beings compassionately transfer their merit to postulants in order to help the myriad creatures attain bliss.

Enlightenment is the essence of both divisions of Buddhism. All Buddhists begin with the idea that all beings are reincarnated through countless lifetimes via the mechanisms of *karma*. Karma, or "deed," refers to the moral weight of one's thoughts and actions. By doing good to other living things, one's karma improves to help one be born into a better life. If one does harm, then one's circumstances in the next life will decline. All such determinations are made in hell, where the worst karmic cases spend aeons rising through the ranks of the tortures of hell's 10 levels. When one qualifies to return to the world of the living via the karma earned in either a previous life or in successively lesser (i.e. higher) levels of hell, then he or she reincarnates as a creature on earth (either non-human or human) or, with yet greater merit, a god. The earthly and godly realms exist between the two extremes of Buddhahood (and bodhisattvahood) and the 10 levels of hell.

All Buddhists believe further that one can cause this apparently endless cycle of life and death, *samsara*, to cease. Achieving this, then one attains enlightenment, or *nirvana* ("blowing out of a flame"). Buddhists believe one reaches nirvana by ceasing all belief in the reality of the self. According to Buddhism, the self, like all other phenomena in the world, is nothing but a transient aggregate of various properties. Through the deception of believing in the reality of the self and other phenomena, one suffers, because the self never will attain enough things to satisfy its desires. Despite these lofty philosophical tenets, as the religion developed at the popular level, people began to believe in a core entity, a pseudo-soul, in each person that does indeed transmigrate from life to life.

The Buddha summarized these teachings on self, suffering, and release in the simple formula of the Four Noble Truths. These are: (1) all life is suffering, (2) desire causes this suffering, (3) suffering can be extinguished, and (4) suffering's cessation is in following the Eight-Fold Noble Path. In other words, achieving loss of self—and thus suffering—requires that one, following the regimen of the Eight-Fold Path: observe right (1) views, (2) thought, (3) speech, (4) conduct, (5) livelihood, (6) effort, (7) mindfulness, and (8) concentration. In Theravada Buddhism, a member of the *sangha* following the Eight-Fold Path might exit *samsara*, achieving nirvana. In Mahayana doctrine, anyone may achieve enlightenment, either within or without the *sangha*.

Buddhism Develops in China

Buddhism arrived in China from Southwest Asia by around A.D. 150. By 166 foreign monks were making the first translations of Sanskrit-language Buddhist scriptures into Chinese. Those early translations focused narrowly on meditative practices, but in the third century, Mahayana scriptures began to be translated. Thereafter Mahayana doctrine dominated Chinese Buddhist thought.

Prior to China's north-south political division in 316, Buddhism gained a foothold almost exclusively among the elite. Largely these were *Xuanxue* discussants, who believed Buddhism derived from Laozi Daoism. Consequently, they accepted its meditative practices and emptiness-centered enlightening wisdom as welcome additions to and variations on the indigenous Daoist pursuits of individual attainment.

After 316, China divided north and south. Until the Sui unified China again in 589, various erstwhile nomadic peoples from Central Asia ruled the north. The intellectual milieu that had produced *Xuanxue* continued in the series of native Chinese southern dynasties that followed the division, and there Buddhism consequently remained restricted largely to the elite intellectual class.

Conversely, in the north Buddhism became a powerful devotional religion at all social levels. Northern foreign emperors viewed Buddhism as another form of shamanism whose magic could assist their rule. Furthermore, as a foreign religion, Buddhism constituted a welcome counterweight to the often stuffy Ru traditions that continued among many of the Chinese elite. In some cases the emperors even claimed to be incarnations of Buddha on earth. Therefore, in the North, Buddhism was not only a religion of the people but also a political tool.

By the fifth century, monastic Buddhism had been firmly established, with more than 80,000 members in the *sangha* and 1,700 monasteries in the north. All levels of society participated in devotion to the religion and support of the monastic community. Though the monasteries' fortunes fluctuated with official governmental policy toward Buddhism (the religion was persecuted from 452 to 466 and 574 to 578 as a result of rivalries at court with Ru and Daoist faithful), lay participation never faltered, but continued to increase dramatically through the Tang period (618–907).

Through these centuries and beyond, new Buddhist scriptures entered China with knowledgeable foreign Buddhist monks. These monks began teaching there, and the Chinese themselves graduated beyond conceiving of Buddhism as being Daoist-derived. Part of this involved the convergence of Buddhist activities north and south, especially through the travels and preaching of the monk Huiyuan (334–

416). In the early fifth century, Huiyuan combined both elite philosophical and popular devotional Buddhism in his establishment of Pure Land Buddhist teachings in China—though his teachings were by no means restricted to this specific doctrine.

Another monk, Kumarajiva (344–413), helped Buddhism mature in China by supervising a massive effort that made many more Buddhist scriptures available to the Chinese in superior-quality translations. In this way, Kumarajiva introduced into China Madhyamika Buddhist teachings, which laid the foundation for the later development of the very important Chan and Tiantai teachings during the Tang period. Through the efforts of Huiyuan, Kumarajiva, and countless other monks and lay believers, Chinese Buddhism grew in sophistication and in the process became truly Chinese.

Doctrinal Foundations of Chinese Buddhism

Madhyamika or Three Treatise Buddhism: Madhyamika (Doctrine of the Middle Path) originated in India with the monk Nagarjuna (c. A.D. 100–200). It was one of the major Mahayana sects. After Kumarajiva, in China it developed as the Three Treatise School (Sanlun) under Sengzhao (c. 374–414) and others.

Three Treatise theorists denied the reality of both the phenomenal world (that is, Being) and the world of Nonbeing that many Buddhists contrasted with it to denote reality. They argued that only the understanding that everything (Being, Nonbeing, and thoughts about them) is Emptiness (*sunyata*) is real, which realization is nirvana. Still, even one's logical or rational understanding of Emptiness as reality is unreal, dependent on thought that in turn is based on the illusion that Being and Nonbeing exist. One achieves *sunyata* only through intuition gained during a long process of meditation (*dhyana*), usually in a community of monks.

Though it expired as a transmitted lineage by approximately 650, the Three Treatise doctrine influenced all important later doctrinal developments in China, including Tiantai, Chan, and Huayan. After Sengzhao the most important figure in the Three Treatise School was Jizang (Chi-tsang, 549–623), who largely organized the doctrines of the school.

Ideation or Consciousness-Only: The other pillar of Mahayana teachings in China was Consciousness-Only (Weishi) Buddhism, also called the Ideation (or Projection; *Shelun* in Chinese) or Dharma-character (Dharmalakshana) school. Known in India as the Yogacara school, this Shelun or Ideation school in China was obscure until the seventh century Chinese monk Xuanzang (Hsüan-tsang, 599–664) traveled to India to study and collect Buddhist scriptures. On his return in 645, he oversaw the greatest translation project since Kumarajiva's fifth-century work. Through Xuanzang's efforts, the doctrines of the Consciousness-Only tradition became popular among China's intellectual elite.

Like the Madhyamika, Consciousness-Only doctrine holds that all is illusion, including the thought that all is illusion. However, its theories of psychology and enlightenment are far more complex than the tenets of its Mahayana cousin. In this school's teachings, the mind plays the central role, with its consciousness divided into eight levels. The first five involve sensory perception; the sixth is responsible for processing or understanding the data received; the seventh, called *manas*, is the conscious mind that creates a sense of ego via thought and self-perception; and the eighth, the *alaya*, is the consciousness that most closely resembles a soul. The *alaya* is the sole repository of seeds of consciousness collected from lifetimes and ages past that project their residual elements into the *manas*. The *manas* in turn creates the world around it so that the first five levels of consciousness then perceive these phenomena created or projected from within. This is the "ideation" or "projection" of the school's name.

The received data then "scent" the *alaya*, or seed repository, creating new residues or seeds. These seeds then once again influence the *manas*, which on their basis continues to create the external phenomenal world. Enlightenment occurs when one reduces, through right thought and patient long-term meditation, the seeds in the *alaya* to nothing. At this point one's perfect wisdom (*prajna*) is complete, and one achieves *tathata*, or genuine thusness. *Thatata* transcends all levels of consciousness, combining all contrasts between projectioner and projected, and is the one pure constant in the otherwise impure and fluxing universe.

While the Consciousness-Only teachings for a time enjoyed favor at court, they proved far too complex for most Buddhist faithful to appreciate. Furthermore, the Consciousness-Only teaching that only a select few could expect to achieve *thatata* doomed it to failure as a popular faith. However, in the late 19th and early 20th centuries, long after Buddhism had otherwise ceased to contribute vitally to China's intellectual climate, ironically Consciousness-Only teachings enjoyed a brief revival.

Foundations of Devotional Chinese Buddhism: Pure Land

Called Sukhavati in Sanskrit and Jingtu in Chinese (which can be translated as "pure land," "blessed realm," or "land of bliss"), Pure Land Buddhism in China centers on devotion to the Buddha Amitabha and the bodhisattva Guanyin (Avalokitesvara). Because its teachings are simple, Pure Land became the most popular form of Buddhism in China.

Its simplicity developed from adherents' belief that the world had entered a degenerate age (*mappo*, the fourth and final stage of degeneration from the pure age in which the Buddha had lived on earth) in which the destruction and re-creation of the world was near, and that, due to people's particular ignorance in so degenerate an era, then only the simplest of teachings could reach and save them.

Devotion to Amitabha derives from when, as the monk Dharmakara, this Buddha-to-be vowed to abstain from entering nirvana until all creatures that devoted themselves to him and his Pure Land (Sukhavati) had achieved the enlightened state of the bodhisattva. Therefore, for Pure Land devotees, enlightenment occurs not as the result of one's accumulation of merit through ascetic concentration on one's nonexistence or kindness toward living creatures. Rather, one achieves that blissful state through her or his faith in the great merit of Dharmakara-turned-Amitabha, who transfers his enormous merit to the faithful. Simple sincere devotion to Amitabha and his paradisiac Western Pure Land are the only requirements for personal salvation. In fifth- and sixth-century China, this revolutionized Buddhist teachings and practices by making salvation accessible to the common people.

To help common people attain salvation, from Pure Land's beginnings in China in the fifth century, spiritual leaders organized devotional assemblies where the faithful concentrated in meditation on the goodness of Amitabha and recited his name (a practice called *samatha*), visualized one's rebirth in the Pure Land and cohabitation with Amitabha and other Buddhas (a practice called *vipasyana*), chanted scriptures (*sutras*, especially the *Sukhavati-vyuha Sutra*, occurring in both a short and long version), confessed sins, and met personally with the abbot or other spiritual leader.

Under leaders such as Daochuo (Tao-ch'o, 562–645) and his disciple Shandao (Shan-tao, 613–681) Pure Land developed through the Tang period independently of the major monastic centers and the state-sponsored Buddhist church. This buffered it from political persecution. It was also the only Buddhist sect in China to consistently appeal to the masses. For those reasons it thrived long after other sects had failed.

Apogee of Chinese Buddhism, c. 600–845

In the reunified China of the Sui (581–618) and Tang periods, doctrinal, devotional, and monastic Buddhism all reached their zenith. Other than the Consciousness-Only doctrine and the Pure Land sect, significant schools included the Tiantai, Huayan, and Chan (in Sanskrit, *dhyana*; in Japanese, Zen).

Tiantai: Developed on Mount Tiantai, Zhejiang, this school's highest teachings were expressed in the *Saddharmapundarika Sutra* (*Lotus Sutra*). Borrowing significantly from the Madhyamika, Tiantai in turn influenced the Chan sect considerably. It is famous for its classifica-

tion of Buddhist doctrines into five periods of the Buddha's teaching, with the *Lotus Sutra* occupying the highest position as the Buddha's final and most pristine doctrine. This justification helped all Buddhists to understand and minimize the divisive effect of the many contradictions in the teachings expounded by the hundreds of Buddhist sutras.

Tiantai was systematized by the monk Zhiyi (Chih-i, 538–597). Zhiyi's fifth-generation disciple and leader of Tiantai, Zhanran (Chan-jan,711–782), also contributed significantly to the school's teachings.

Though drawing largely from Madhyamika and Consciousness-Only traditions, Tiantai was eclectic, evolving through time. For instance, during the Tang period it absorbed elements of both Chan and Pure Land Buddhism. In turn, it also influenced each of these great movements.

The essence of Tiantai teaching is the interpenetration of all existence. Tiantai postulates that all existence coexists in three thousand realms. These include all states, moments, and positions of all existence. Each realm can be found fully in every other realm. Therefore, the absolute origin and purity of existence, *tathagata garbha*, is in all things. *Tathagata garbha* is the universal shared Buddha-nature or Buddha-mind; it is nirvana; it is *sunyata*. Therefore, all people are already Buddhas possessing the Buddha-nature but only remain ignorant of this. Even insentient beings possess the Buddha-nature. Tiantai, thus, is very inclusive.

Huayan: Huayan (in Sanskrit, Avatamsaka), meaning Flower Garland, takes its name from the sutra that forms the core of this school's teaching. The school's popularity soared in the Sui and Tang periods due partly to its receiving sporadic imperial favor. Empress Wu Zetian (r. 684–705) strongly supported Huayan, for it in turn supported her rule.

Huayan's founder in China was Fashun (Fa-shun, a.k.a. Dushun [Tu-shun], 557–640). Its systematizer was Fazang (Fa-tsang, 643–712). Later the eclectic monk Zongmi (Tsung-mi, 780–841), a master in both Huayan and Chan traditions, classified and resystematized Huayan teachings in relation to other Buddhist doctrine. In the Huayan classification, the teachings of the *Flower Garland Sutra* represent the Buddha's highest teaching, paralleling the similar development in Tiantai teachings.

Huayan doctrine further resembles Tiantai teachings in its interpenetration of all realms and things. It postulates the existence of principle (*li*) and things (*shi*) that interpenetrate to create all existence. The *Flower Garland Sutra* employs a metaphor called Indra's Net to demonstrate the interpenetration of all discrete entities.

Indra's Net consists of several jewels (principles), each reflecting through the others all images (things) passing through any of them. All the jewels, then, are one jewel, despite the fact that they remain distinct. Thus, all principles are one unifying principle, each one distinct while fully representing the one complete and universal principle. On the other hand, the images reflected—that is, things, are unreal. With this postulation Huayan differs from phenomenon-affirming Tiantai.

At the center and origin of this limitless universe is the Tower of Vairocana (Great Sun Buddha), representing the universal principle. Vairocana's realm, akin to the Western Pure Land of Amitabha Buddha, itself resembles Indra's Net for, upon entering it, one encounters thousands of identical towers that are each independent of and one with every other. Though in the intellectual Huayan tradition this understanding constitutes the ultimate perfect wisdom (*prajna*), in popular faith Vairocana became a creator deity.

Chan: Like the other significant Chinese Buddhist schools, the Chan (*dhyana*), or Meditation, School retroactively created a pre-Chinese lineage of transmission through 28 Indian patriarchs ultimately traced back to Siddhartha Gautama. The legends then tell that the Indian monk and Twenty-Eighth Patriarch, Bodhidharma (c. 420–520), transmitted the teachings to China.

However, the historicity of Bodhidharma as patriarch cannot be confirmed, and certainly the 28 Indian patriarchs were created by early-ninth–century Chan adepts attempting to legitimize their faith. In fact, Chan origins are often traced in part to ancient Daoist thought found in the *Zhuangzi* and *Laozi*.

The early Chinese Chan lineage established retroactively during the Song dynasty professes that five Chinese patriarchs transmitted Bodhidharma's teachings. Then, according to contemporary accounts of the eighth and ninth centuries, following the death of the Sixth Patriarch, Shenxiu (Shen-hsiu, d. 706), a controversy developed over whom the Fifth Patriarch, Hongren (Hung-jen, 601–674), had designated to succeed him. Only posthumously, the challenger, Huineng (Hui-neng, 638–713) of Guangdong, won legitimacy as the Sixth Patriarch through the aggressive efforts of his disciple, Shenhui (Shen-hui, 670–762), the latter having been named the Seventh Patriarch posthumously in 796.

Therefore, after the mid-eighth–century Huineng's lineage, the Southern School dethroned Shenxiu's lineage, the so-called Northern School (it called itself the Dongshan School; "Northern" was Shenhui's pejorative name for it, used for political reasons to distinguish his Southern teachings) as the orthodox Chan teaching inherited from Bodhidharma. Later Chinese Chan developments all have traced their origins to Huineng's teachings, represented in *The Platform Sutra of the Sixth Patriarch*, which Huineng's ninth-century disciples edited.

From its very beginnings in *dhyana* practices combined with Madhyamika doctrine, Chan, while eclectic, established a monastic community separate from the mainstream and politically oriented Buddhist system of monasteries. Its purpose was to reform Buddhist teachings by promoting the achievability of enlightenment through the mentally calming exercises of individual and communal meditation, worship of Buddha images, and recitation of the Buddha's name, all within a highly disciplined and independent monastic community.

The first to establish new monastic rules governing these communities were the fourth and fifth patriarchs, Daoxin (Tao-hsin, 580–651) and Hongren. Daoxin had studied with the Tiantai systematizer Zhiyi. Chan adepts of the Song period claimed that later the monk Baizhang Huaihai (Pai-chang Huai-hai, 720–814) of the Southern School codified Chan monastic discipline in the form followed ever since. Though perhaps based on and/or including parts of Baizhang Huaihai's code, surviving Chan monastic codes actually date only to the 11th and 12th centuries and differed little from codes followed in non-Chan monasteries of the period.

Huineng's teachings wrought significant changes in the Chan doctrine. Most importantly, Huineng increased Chan reliance on intuition rather than intellect in the quest for enlightenment. Through intuitive personal knowledge of the self, one could attain enlightenment suddenly by dismissing the rational mind.

Although the monk Daosheng (Taosheng, d. A.D. 434), a Madhyamika disciple of Kumarajiva, had been the first to preach the doctrine of sudden enlightenment, it did not become influential until Huineng advanced his revolutionary approach. This involved an iconoclastic turn away from the outer forms of the Buddhist faith, including images, scriptures, and the idea of Buddha himself. Huineng and his followers insisted that enlightenment's only precondition is simply self-knowledge of the Buddha-nature within each individual. Once this is achieved, then without conscious mind one discovers that the pure (ultimate Buddha-nature) and profane (life on earth) are one and the same.

Partially for this reason, Chan monastic discipline emphasized the importance of performing physical labor, particularly in agricultural pursuits. Another reason for Chan's stress on agriculture was its need for self-sufficiency in food production. A self-sufficient monastery did not need to compromise itself or its doctrines to meet external supporters' demands.

By the Song period, two methods of enlightening adepts predominated in the Huineng-derived Chan teachings. Each found a home in one of the two Chan sects that persisted into the Ming period (1368–1644). In the Linji sect, founded by Yixuan (I-hsüan, d. 867) of Linji, abbots administered hard whacks to adepts to shock them from their habitual, rational mentality. The Linji also relied on nonsensical, rationally irrelevant (but, according to them, intuitively penetrating) statements, questions, and riddles to similarly shock students' minds into sudden enlightenment to the truth within.

The other lasting sect was the Caodong, founded by Benji (Pen-chi, 840–901) of Caoshan and Liangjie (Liang-chieh, 807–869) of Dongshan. This sect promoted mental quiescence in meditation as the means of attaining the introspection that leads to enlightenment.

During and after the Song period, the Linji and Caodong struggled over their differences in doctrine. By the Ming, the Linji had absorbed the Caodong and thus became the sole heir to the teachings of Huineng.

The Huichang Persecution, 841–846

Non-Chan and non–Pure Land forms of Buddhism were persecuted by Tang Emperor Wuzong Wu-tsung, (r. 840–846) during the Huichang reign period (841–846). In an age of increasing xenophobia, the foreign origin of Buddhism worked against it. In this atmosphere, Daoist masters at Wuzong's court, natural competitors of the Buddhists, seized the opportunity, fanning the flames of anti-Buddhist rhetoric. More importantly, however, the wealth of the Buddhist establishment invited Wuzong's envy. Not only had Buddhist monasteries and temples accumulated vast territories of untaxed land, they had also amassed enormous tax-free wealth in particularly precious metals. The Tang government, in the ninth century chronically impoverished and short of precious metals, coveted this great wealth and finally confiscated it. The government also suspected the sincerity of many self-proclaimed monastic disciples, who often entered the *sangha* only to evade taxation.

Wuzong ordered 4,600 monasteries and 40,000 temples and shrines destroyed. He also forcibly returned 260,500 monks and nuns and 150,000 temple slaves (who included former tenants of temple lands, orphans, dispossessed and unemployed farmers and laborers, and freed criminals assigned to temples) to lay life, where they once again paid taxes. Though economically the church recovered in the Song period, Buddhism never again regained the intellectual vigor that it had enjoyed during the Tang.

The Chan and Pure Land, mostly because they existed outside the politically involved Buddhist church, and, in the case of Pure Land, existed only in small local societies, escaped much of the persecution.

Buddhism in the Song and Later Periods

Chan: Under the Song, Chan became the central Buddhist monastic organization. It also increased its political activity and established a close connection with the elite. In addition, Chan enjoyed imperial favor in northern China for a time (1242–1257) under the Mongols, prior to the Mongol conquest of the Southern Song (1127–1279) and establishment of the Yuan dynasty (1276–1368).

Syncretic Trends: By the 12th century, Chan was intellectually stagnant, its most important contributions thereafter being its stimulation of various neo-Confucian (that is, Ru) and Daoist syncretisms during the Song, Yuan, and Ming periods. The most famous syncretist was the Ru thinker Lin Zhaoen (Lin Chao-en, 1517–1598). By absorbing elements from both Buddhism and Daoism, Lin attempted to turn Ru into a faith-based religion.

Pure Land and Secret Societies: Pure Land teachings, never a unified state-wide movement, continued as before, undiminished at the local level as a popular religion among the peasants. Local lay societies embracing these teachings multiplied during the Song. Some such teachings contributed to the development of secret sects and societies that often challenged the government's authority. Indeed, Zhu Yuanzhang (Chu Yüan-chang, i.e. Ming emperor Taizu [T'ai-tsu], r. 1368–1399), overthrower of the Mongols and Ming founder, developed his political and military movement as part of one such secret religious society, the rebellious Red Turbans. This group commingled with the millenarian White Lotus and Maitreya (after the Buddha who would appear on earth and transform it into paradise) societies. In fact Zhu, a novice Buddhist monk attached to the Huangjue temple in present-day Anhui Province, became associated with the Red Turbans only due to his Buddhist associations.

The White Lotus, supposedly influenced by Manichaeism, had originated largely as a form of localized Pure Land practice. It commingled with the Maitreya Society and also later absorbed Daoist alchemical/immortalist teachings as it spread through the South. After his establishment of the new Ming dynasty in 1368, Zhu Yuanzhang tried unsuccessfully to suppress the White Lotus and other secret millenarian societies. Instead, as Ming Taizu, he promoted the positive social contributions of Buddhism, Ru, and Daoism.

Tibetan Buddhism: Earlier, another form of Buddhism, Tibetan Tantrism, had become the official religion of the Mongol regime after 1260. Later, during the Qing period (1644–1911) the foreign Manchu emperors also favored Tibetan Buddhism (often misnamed Lamaism), although they embraced as well the state-supporting Ru socio-political ideology which underlay the foundations of all imperial governments. But as foreign rulers who had been nomads from the northern steppe, just as the Mongols had, the early Qing emperors found in Tibetan Buddhism both a foreign support mechanism and a source of useful shamanic ritual magic.

7. DAOISM OF THE IMPERIAL ERA, SECOND THROUGH NINETEENTH CENTURIES

Messianic and Millenarian Movements, Second and Third Centuries

Way of the Celestial Masters (Tianshi Dao): In the first century, the memory of the venerable Laozi was transformed from sage to immortal and god. Legend says that in the year 142 this messianic Lord Lao, as he was now known, revealed himself and a new religious teaching to Zhang Daoling (Chang Tao-ling). On the basis of this revelation, Zhang established the first organized religious Daoist movement, called both the Way of the Celestial Masters and the Way of Five Pecks of Rice (after the tax imposed on the faithful). Lord Lao had revealed these teachings in order to establish moral religious governance and thereby save humanity. The "historical" Laozi was not forgotten, however, since the *Laozi* text supposedly written by him was used—in a new interpretation—to teach the revealed religion to the common people.

Organization: The new church originated and prospered in what is now Sichuan Province. It organized itself on the model of the failing Han administration and, in fact, in the regions under its control, replaced the government as both an administrative and a religious institution.

The church leader was the Celestial Master, representative on earth, Lord Lao. The first Celestial Master was Zhang Daoling. Under the Celestial Master were twenty-four libationers, one for each parish. Libationers were responsible for both political and religious functions of government. A libationer's most important function was to perform rituals of purification for the people. Usually this meant causing converts to confess their sins—or those of their forebears—and repent their evil ways. As sickness was seen to result from immorality and the demons such bad behavior welcomed into one's being, then the libationer ceremonially called forth protective deities to drive the demons out. Thereafter, the healed wore a register of such deities as a sign of their protective guardianship.

Community Ritual: Most of the sect's rites originated as modified versions of folk religious ceremony. Otherwise, in its emphasis on talismanic magic and the attainment of long life and immortality, its borrowings from shamanic and immortalistic traditions are apparent.

Community rituals and festivals were important. Some revolved around shared feasts, which helped to reaffirm both the community's cohesiveness and its connection with Lord Lao and his celestial realms. In addition, libationers led their flocks in communal recitation of the *Laozi*

text. Other rites included communal sexual ceremonies called Blending of Energies.

Messianic Millenarian Revolt: In 184, under Zhang Daoling's son Zhang Heng (Chang Heng), the community of the Way of the Celestial Masters revolted against the Han. The year of the revolt coincided with the turnover of sexagenary cycles, which are celestially based Chinese equivalents of Western millennia. Since it sought to overthrow the old regime at the turn of such a "millennium," the sect therefore is called a millenarian movement. It was messianic in that the Celestial Masters hoped to establish the messiah Lord Lao's teachings on morality as the way to salvation for humanity.

Surrendering in 215 under Zhang Daoling's grandson Zhang Lu, the sect gained official recognition and even patronage under the succeeding Wei (220–265) and Western Jin (265–316) kingdoms in northern China. In return, it conferred on the regime the divine right to rule. The Way of Celestial Masters thereafter exerted considerable influence on northern aristocratic families and their local cults.

The Way of Great Peace (Taiping Dao): In 184 in Shandong Province, another new Daoist religious organization revolted. This Way of Great Peace, also called the Yellow Turbans for the color of apparel that the rebels wore, shared many traits with the Celestial Masters sect. Like the Celestial Masters, this sect was both millenarian and messianic. Further, its concerns also included talismanic magic and confession of sins for the sake of achieving moral living, long life, and immortality.

The prophetic and instructional text used by the Yellow Turbans was a book originating in the first century B.C. and presented to several Han emperors, *Taiping jing* (Scripture of Great Peace). Their organization was virtually destroyed in 184 in wars with Han generals. During the Wei and Western Jin periods, when the Way of the Celestial Masters established itself in the northern capital Loyang, it absorbed elements of the Way of Great Peace still lingering in the northeast.

Conflation of Northern and Southern Daoism, Fourth and Fifth Centuries

When in 316 the Western Jin could no longer forestall foreign invasion by northern nomadic tribes, the court and many of its attendant aristocratic families moved south of the Yangtze River to the old southern region of the Wu. As societies mixed and the southern aristocrats took a backseat to the newcomers from the north, their religions also commingled.

Ge Hong: During the third and early fourth centuries, the south had developed its own esoteric Daoist traditions derived mostly from the immortalist and alchemical teachings of the Han. These had developed to the point that Ge Hong (Ko Hung, 283–343), an eminent Daoist author of the day, could compile a rich compendium of herbal, chemical, and exercise recipes for attaining long life and immortality. This was the book *Baopuzi* (Master Who Embraces Simplicity). Otherwise, in the south, old aristocratic immortalist cults continued, as did the cultic ritual performances of the common people.

Highest Purity (Mao Shan) Daoism: Between 364 and 370 Yang Xi (Yang Hsi, 330–c. 386) responded to the mingling of the religious cultures when he experienced a revelation delivered to him by perfected beings (*zhenren*) from the most exalted heaven, the Highest Purity Heaven. This Highest Purity sect, also known as the Mao Shan sect after its headquarters (Mount Mao, Jiangsu), was messianic. Geared toward the southern aristocracy, it predicted that a millenarian and messianic revolution would occur between 384 and 392, when the ancient legendary sage-king Yao would return to rule the earth.

The Highest Purity sect also reformed the Celestial Masters teachings. In particular, it removed sexual rites from ceremonies and established a series of taboos against, for instance, stealing, being unclean, becoming drunk, and doing harm to sentient beings.

In their positive practices, adepts devoted themselves especially to meditative and intellectualized techniques of individually attaining longevity and immortality. These included visualizing cosmic powers and deities within one's own being, where they purified one's internal organs with pristine, regenerative cosmic energy (*yuanqi*). The Highest Purity teachings also further refined alchemical practices.

Yang Xi wrote down the scriptures that the perfected beings revealed to him. He then gave them to his patrons, Xu Mi (Hsü Mi, 303–373), an official at the Eastern Jin court, and Xu's nephew Xu Hui (Hsü Hui, 344–c. 370). Xu Mi and his family retired to Mount Mao, where they further developed the new practices and scriptural corpus. Among the most significant texts of the sect are *Ziwen* (Purple Texts) and *Huangting jing* (Scripture of the Yellow Court).

Later a great alchemical theorist in his own right, Tao Hongjing (T'ao Hung-ching, 456–536), collected the various Highest Purity scriptures, edited them, and published their quintessence in his *Zhen'gao* (*Declarations of the Perfected*). Since then the Highest Purity has been among the most influential sects of Daoism.

Lingbao Daoism: Emerging slightly later than the Highest Purity sect, Lingbao (Spiritual Treasure) Daoists similarly revised the rituals and customs of the Celestial Masters. And while borrowing from the Highest Purity sect, they differed in their particular pursuit of communal— not mere individual—salvation through collective ritual performances led by priests. In their concern with universal salvation, they borrowed from the Buddhists, even as they attacked that religion as foreign.

The Lingbao Corpus and the Formation of the Daoist Canon: The Lingbao developed their own body of ritual scriptures, the most important text being *Lingbao jing* (Scripture of the Spiritual Treasure). Another seminal text is *Lingbao duren jing* (Scripture on the Salvation of Humanity). Lu Xiujing (Lu Hsiu-ching, 406–477) collected these texts to form the Lingbao corpus.

Lu also collected texts of the Celestial Masters and Highest Purity sects and organized them into three sections, or "caverns" (*dong*). The Daoists had long believed that forty-six massive cavern-heavens (*dongtian*) exist beneath major terrestrial mountain ranges and formed the collective earthly center of a universal spiritual network connecting heaven, earth, and humanity. Within the *dongtian* supposedly lived thousands of immortal beings. Some two hundred interconnected lesser caverns within the earth formed a supportive sub-system of spiritual potency; Daoists have believed that the caverns and their inhabitants possessed the secrets to immortality and salvation.

The Three Caverns (*Sandong*) remain the basic structure of the Daoist Canon (*Daozang*) to the present. They are the Dongzhen (Highest Purity), Dongxuan (Lingbao), and Dongshen (Heavenly Masters) scriptures. Later, Four Supplements were added to accommodate the burgeoning number of scriptures. Roughly a thousand years later, after successive compilations and printings, the Ming government formulated and printed the extant Daoist Canon in 1444–1446. In 1607, the Ming authorized a supplement, *Xu Daozang* (Continued Daoist Canon). Since then many "unauthorized" privately printed scriptural collections have appeared.

Eclecticism During and After the Tang

Tang Daoists were highly eclectic, drawing from not only previous and contemporary Daoist but also Buddhist and Ru traditions. They developed especially the meditative arts during the Tang, borrowing heavily from the Buddhists. As a result, Tang Daoists often became experts and sometimes even masters in systems of Buddhist thought.

Many of these eclectic thinkers were also well versed in the Ru classics. In cities, temples, and especially at fast-growing mountain communities throughout China, scholars, thinkers, and ritual experts of all traditions met to teach and learn. Blendings of the Three Teachings (Ru, Buddhism, and Daoism) were common, even though at times the thinkers themselves were unaware of their own borrowings from traditions of thought outside their own.

Significant Daoist Thinkers of the Tang

Prominent Daoist thinkers and writers of the period include the semi-legendary Sun Simiao (fl. sixth–seventh centuries), a great physician and alchemical theorist; Cheng Xuanying (Ch'eng Hsüan-ying, fl. c. 631–655), a prolific commentator on Daoist classics who borrowed significantly from Buddhism; and Sima Chengzhen (Ssu-ma Ch'eng-chen, 647–735), perhaps the most important Daoist thinker of the Tang and leader of the Mao Shan sect. Sima wrote the very significant *Zuowang lun* (Treatise on Sitting and Forgetting), which established both the methodology and cosmology important for the subsequent development of Daoist meditative and alchemical theory and practice. There was also Wu Yun (Wu Yün, d. 778), a famous poet and cosmologist. His works include *Xuan'gang lun* (Treatise on the Abstruse Web) and *Shenxian kexue lun* (Treatise on the Learnability of Becoming Immortal).

Alchemy

Alchemy began in China by the third century B.C. This appears to make it the oldest alchemical tradition in world history. Ge Hong was the most famous early alchemist.

After approximately 700, among the arts of attaining longevity and immortality, alchemy in particular developed and flourished. First operative or chemical alchemy—that is, the mixing of chemical and herbal potions to achieve elixirs—was popular, but after about 850, mystical or psycho-physiological alchemy gained ascendancy.

Neidan: Internal Alchemy: From about 850 on, a new direction in alchemy and meditation developed. Essentially, thinkers combined these two approaches to immortality. The result was "internal alchemy" (*neidan*, literally "internal cinnabar").

Neidan meditative alchemists created their new system over centuries by borrowing the terminology and interactive systems (of constitutive elements) of the old chemical alchemists, the immortalist rituals and methodologies of the Mao Shan practitioners, and the Buddhists' complex understandings of metaphysics and human psychology. In addition, they supplemented such regimens by practicing age-old traditions of gymnastics, dietary restrictions, and ingestion of herbs.

Internal alchemists viewed the body as a crucible in which they could either build a new and immortal body or transform the physical body into vacuous or original creative energy (*yuanqi*), or primordial nothingness. They theorized that people (and all living things) passing normal lives exhausted their store of *yuanqi* by interacting with the confusing, tantalizing, and demanding human and physical world. They taught that a person needed to maintain and replenish his or her cache of *yuanqi*, the source of all creation, before it had been exhausted and one thus died.

Therefore, the alchemists, adapting pre-Tang methods, visualized and thereby welcomed astral gods within their internal organs. These cosmic powers renewed the *qi* that in healthy, youthful organs abounds. By continuously circulating *qi* through one's organs, eventually one could combine them to recreate *yuanqi*.

Jindan Nanzong: During the Song, there grew a particularly important form of internal alchemy, Golden Elixir Alchemy (*Jindan*, literally "Golden Cinnabar"). During the Southern Song the Southern Sect (Nanzong) of Golden Elixir developed its methods most successfully.

Zhang Boduan (Chang Po-tuan, 987–1082) has been credited with having originated the Nanzong teachings. Allegedly he wrote the important *Wuzhen pian* (Article on Awakening to Perfection) and *Jindan sibaizi* (Golden Elixir Alchemy in Four Hundred Characters), later collected in the Daoist Canon.

Another significant Nanzong thinker was Bo Yuchan (Po Yü-ch'an, 1194–1229), who syncretized Daoist, Chan Buddhist, and Ru ideas on meditation, salvation, and ritual. Many works attributed to him are contained in the central *Xiuzhen shishu* (Ten Books on Cultivating Perfection).

Mention should be made of Li Daochun (Li Tao-chun, fl. 1288–1290) and Chen Zhixu (Chen Chih-hsü, 1289–?), as well. Li wrote the influential *Zhonghe ji* (Collected Works of Centrality and Harmony), and

Chen gained fame for his *Jindan dayao* (Great Encyclopaedia of Golden Elixir Alchemy). Li and Chen contributed to an early Yuan (1279–1368) movement among Nanzong adepts to combine with the politically more successful Quanzhen (Complete Perfection) Daoist sect. Consequently, after the Yuan, Nanzong and Quanzhen formed one unified but internally diverse tradition.

Daoism under the Song and Alien Dynasties, 960–1368

Daoism flourished during this period. New sects developed, and old ones reinvigorated. Imperial support, particularly by the Song emperors Zhenzong (r. 998–1022) and Huizong (r. 1101–1125), encouraged this growth.

Zhengyi Daoism: Zhengyi, or Correct Way, Daoism constituted the reestablishment of the old Way of the Celestial Masters. Zhenzong officially recognized the sect, whereafter it shared priestly ordination and other ceremonial duties with the still-active Highest Purity and Lingbao sects.

The Celestial Masters still believed themselves to have descended from Zhang Daoling (Celestial Master priests married, their offspring inheriting their priesthoods). These priests carried out communal and state rituals in temples officially established and administered in each province. During the Ming, the Zhengyi tradition, though no longer an official religion of the state, again gained especially strong imperial support. It remains influential today on Taiwan.

Tianxin Zhengfa Daoism: The Tianxin Zhengfa (Correct Doctrine of the Center of Heaven) began in southeastern coastal China in the 10th century. This shamanic tradition, its methodologies deriving in part from the Zhengyi sect, employed talismans and other magic to call down spirits from the heavens to exorcise demonic spirits possessing the ill or causing havoc in the empire. The emperor Huizong recognized the sect in 1116 when adepts presented him with texts outlining Tianxin Zhengfa techniques. Its traditions continue today.

Shenxiao Daoism: Shenxiao (Divine Empyrean) Daoism shares roots in the tenth century with the Tianxin Zhengfa. Its founder was the shaman Lin Lingsu (Lin Ling-su, fl. 1116–1119). Huizong made Shenxiao the official state cult in 1116. Lin Lingsu oversaw religious affairs on his behalf. Huizong so believed in the power of Shenxiao rituals that in 1125 he relied on them—with disastrous results—to defend the state militarily against the invading alien Jin (1115–1234) armies. A year later the Northern Song collapsed.

Quanzhen Daoism: The Quanzhen (Complete Perfection) sect was among the most important of Daoist developments in the years after the fall of the Tang. Quanzhen teachings are very intellectual and center once again on individual attainment of perfection, in the tradition of Highest Purity Daoism.

Since its inception, Quanzhen has always been the monastic tradition in Daoism; in this it reflects its significant and direct borrowings from Chan. Throughout its history Quanzhen has consciously promoted syncretism of the Three Teachings. For instance, it adopted *Xiao jing* (Classic of Filial Piety), a venerable Ru classic from the Western Han period, as one of its essential texts for study.

Quanzhen began in Shandong Province during the twelfth century, when Wang Zhe (Wang Che, 1113–1170) experienced a revelation. After Wang's death, seven of his disciples transmitted his teachings.

These disciples successfully built the religion and gained imperial attention and support under both the Jin and, after 1234, the Mongols. Indeed, one among these seven disciples, Qiu Chuji (Ch'iu Ch'u-chi, 1148–1227), in 1219 summoned the Mongol conqueror Genghis Khan (c. 1162–1227) to south-central Asia to meet him. There, in 1222–1223, Qiu advised the great khan on matters of lifestyle and immortality, entreating him to refrain from engaging in profligate sexual activity and the killing of people.

The Mongols favored Quanzhen into the 1240s until displaced by the competing Chan Buddhists. In 1260 these monks themselves were replaced at court by Tibetan Tantric Buddhists. The latter abused the privilege of supreme religious authority, thus helping to undermine support among Chinese for the Mongol Yuan regime. In 1281, having failed in debates with the Buddhists at court, Daoism was proscribed with ferocity, its books burned and priesthoods revoked.

Quanzhen survived this holocaust. After Quanzhen and Nanzong merged during the early Yuan, the unified tradition continued to develop new sub-sects, such as the Dragon Gate (Longmen pai), and scriptures that refined Golden Elixir alchemical theories and methodologies. Through the turn of the third millennium, Quanzhen continued Daoism's monastic tradition and maintained Daoist sectarian ordination and other communal ceremonial duties.

8. RU, THIRD THROUGH NINETEENTH CENTURIES

Between the third and eleventh centuries, Ru lacked creative vigor, though it remained the foundation and legitimacy of imperial ideology and its social values of filial piety, harmony, reciprocity, etc., remained behavioral ideals of the imperial bureaucracy. In addition, Ru social values increasingly were reinforced in folk society by both local governmental administration and de facto gentry or aristocratic directing of society.

Ru thought did continue to evolve, if only through elaboration on old values found in the classical texts. Commentaries on the classics thus multiplied to the point that, by the mid-Tang, they threatened to obscure the meanings of the classics themselves. At this point began a Ru intellectual revival that, arguably, never fully lost its vigor until the Republican period (1912–1949).

Mid-Tang Ru Revival

In the late eighth century, a Ru revival began when moralists objected to the Buddhification of Chinese classical culture. They claimed that the "amoral" foreign religion had caused the disintegration of personal, social, and imperial values inherent in the Way of Confucius and Mencius. Only the Ru classics, they insisted, contained the principles of correct behavior and governance that would lead the dynasty to full and unified recovery.

Men such as Han Yu (768–824) scoured the classics for quintessential value-laden texts. They found them particularly in two chapters of *Liji* (Book of Rites), the *Great Learning* and *Doctrine of the Mean*. These texts later would form the core of the Song Ru revival.

Second Wave of Reform in the Early Song (960–1279)

In the 11th century, Song literati revived interest in Han Yu and his Ru reform. The new reformers hoped to define proper Ru education in order to recreate a moral Ru society. They included Hu Yuan (Hu Yüan, 993–1059), Sun Fu (992–1057), Fan Zhongyan (Fan Chung-yen, 989–1052), Ouyang Xiu (Ou-Yang Hsiu), Sima Guang (Ssu-Ma Kuang, 1019–1086), and Wang Anshi (Wang An-shih, 1021–1086).

Song Ru Revival: Daoxue ("Neo-Confucianism") Develops

From approximately 1050 to 1200, two trends in Ru philosophy developed under the general rubric Learning of the Way (*Daoxue*). These have been known as the schools of the Learning of Principle (*Lixue*) and Learning of the Mind (*Xinxue*). Both traditions, together known in English as neo-Confucianism, flourished and diversified through the early 17th century.

Five figures stand out as initiators of the Ru philosophical revival within *Daoxue*. These include the cosmologist Zhou Dunyi (Chou Tun-i, 1017–1073), the numerologist Shao Yong (Shao Yung, 1011–1077), the metaphysician Zhang Zai (Chang Tsai, 1020–1077), and two ethicist brothers, Cheng Yi (Ch'eng I, 1033–1108) and Cheng Hao (Ch'eng Hao, 1032–1085).

Their ideas culminated in Zhu Xi's (Chu Hsi, 1130–1200) grand universal synthesis of the mid- to late-12th century. Zhu called his learning *Lixue*. Rivaling Zhu's fully developed system of the human, ethical, and metaphysical Ru Way was Lu Jiuyuan's (Lu Chiu-yüan, a.k.a. Lu Xiangshan/Lu Hsiang-shan, 1139–1193) philosophy of mind, called *Xinxue*. The interactions between thinkers of these distinct but related systems of thought stimulated continuous evolution of Ru ideas through the early 17th century. In the process, the Ru borrowed freely from both Daoist and especially Chan Buddhist meditative theories and practices.

Zhu Xi and Lixue: Zhu Xi's branch of neo-Confucianism is usually known as the Learning of Principle (*Lixue*) because he stressed the universality of moral principle (*li*) and its presence and accessibility in all things as their creative and moral force. Zhu equated *li* with *dao*, the Way. Humans share *li* in their mind-hearts (*xin*) but normally cannot access it due to incarnation's inherent pollutive effect. Only by investigating the principles in things can one know *li* in those things and thus understand one's own morality in *li*. Zhu therefore stressed the importance of the "investigation of things." To Zhu, "things" denoted the Ru classics and human affairs.

Zhu Xi, Ru Education, Examinations, and Bureaucracy: Zhu Xi codified the educational foundation of his system in his collection of the *Four Books*, including the *Analects* of Confucius, the *Mencius*, the *Great Learning*, and the *Doctrine of the Mean*. Zhu rearranged and/or commented on these texts, offering iconoclastic interpretations of key terms and ideas. Because of its usefulness to the state, from 1313 to 1905 his program of Ru learning (the *Four Books*, with his commentary/interpretations) served as the outline for preparation for the imperial examinations. It therefore also constituted the basis of education.

Zhu Xi and Buddhism: Ironically Zhu borrowed from Tiantai and Huayan Buddhism their concepts of the *tathagata-garbha* and principle (*li*), respectively. Especially obvious is Zhu's appropriation of the idea that the universal principle is absolutely complete in each of its manifestations, that is, in all things, including the human mind.

Origins and Development of Xinxue:
Unlike Zhu Xi, Lu Jiuyuan turned inward
for the ultimate source of the moral principle of creation. Stressing the value of meditation, he equated the mind-heart (*xin*)
with the Way and claimed that the entire
universe is contained in and depends for
existence on the principle in one's mind.
Thus his teachings have come to be known
as *Xinxue*, or Learning of the Mind. Like
Zhu Xi, Lu obviously borrowed extensively
from Buddhism.

*Wang Shouren (Wang Yangming,
1472–1529) and "Idealism":* In the
Ming, Wang Shouren (1472–1529) continued to develop Lu's theory, but he especially advanced Ru elements by stressing
self-completion through action: Although
meditation provides intuitive knowledge,
in order to fully understand the universal
moral principle *li/dao* in one's *xin*, one
must act out *li/dao* in human society. This
completes one's knowledge of both self and
universal principle. In its stress on participation ("Knowledge and action are one,"
Wang claimed), his program is very Ru.

*Chan Buddhist Tendencies in Wang
Yangming Idealism:* Many of Wang's
disciples stressed Chan Buddhist tendencies in his thought. Though some, such as
Wang Ji (1498–1583), promoted a mystical
escapism through the universality of the
principle of the mind, others such as Wang
Gen (1483–1541) and Li Zhi (1527–1602)
stressed all people's universal and complete possession of the one universal mind.
Popularizing Wang's thought, increasingly
they promoted conduct while deemphasiz-
ing learning, arguing that all people are
complete sages in potential. Not surprisingly, as its popularity spread through the
early 17th century the movement became
ever more religious and missionary.

Qing Dynasty (1644–1911)
Learning of Verifications

After the foreign Manchus conquered
China in 1644–1646, Ru scholars turned
against what they called the "idealism" of
Song-Ming *Daoxue*. Men such as Huang
Zongxi (1610–1695), Wang Fuzhi (1619–
1692), and especially Gu Yanwu (1613–
1682) experienced the fall of the Ming.
Embittered by it, they largely blamed the
unrealistic idealism of *Daoxue*. They
argued that their Ru forebears had inter-
polated Buddhist idealism into the classics.
Consequently, they had divorced themselves from the physical world such that
they had not understood humanity in relation to its actual surroundings.

In the 17th century, Wang Fuzhi sought
to remedy humanity's disjunction with its
context by postulating that human society
and government evolve due to nature's primary transformative force. Wang arrived
at his theory after recording and considering his extensive empirical observations of
human-nature interactions.

Other scholars similarly stressed in their
studies the collection and objective analysis of empirical data. In the 18th century,
this trend became known as the Learning
of Verifications (*Kaozheng xue*, often translated as "Evidential Learning"), or Han
(dynasty) Learning (*Han xue*). *Kaozheng
xue* scholars, highly scientific in orientation, studied and wrote expertly on mathematics, geography, economics, phonetics,
history, and, most importantly, philology.

Critical Views of the Classics: One of
the most useful fruits of their labors came
in philology, as they used this science to
debunk numerous classics. For instance,
Yan Ruoju (Yen Jo-chü, 1636–1704) helped
to prove that the usually venerated Old
Text version of *Shangshu* (Book of Documents) was in fact a forgery of the early
centuries A.D. Another scholar, Yuan Mei
(Yüan Mei, 1716–1798), discovered that
much of the revered highbrow Ru classic
Shijing (Book of Odes) consisted of common folk songs.

*The End of the Learning of Verifica-
tions:* Significant among *Kaozheng xue*
scholars were Dai Zhen (Tai Chen, 1723–
1777) and Zhang Xuecheng (Chang Hsüeh-
cheng, 1736–1801). Dai Zhen's mind was
among the most scientific in Chinese intellectual history. He began as a philologist
but developed a monistic alternative philosophy to neo-Confucian dualism.

Instead of splitting the Way (*dao*) from
the stuff of matter (*qi*) as did Zhu Xi, Dai
maintained that all is *dao* because *qi* and
the things it produces, including all human
psychological states, are manifestations of
the universal cosmological *dao*. Therefore,
there is no need, as in Buddhism, Daoism,

and Ru *Daoxue*, to deny emotions their place in the complete person. Rather, he argued, the expression of emotion is an important element of human survival and growth. Ironically, despite Dai's "modernism," his argument resembles the thesis of the classical *Doctrine of the Mean*, a text central to the *Daoxue* theories that Dai criticized.

Zhang Xuecheng was a historian who expanded the Chinese understanding of history. He moved history center stage by arguing that Chinese history texts are fully the equal of the cultural and philosophical classics. The key to understanding and producing appropriate and useful history, he argued, is in carefully collecting and verifying facts and creating a living, personal interpretation of those facts. No differently from the classics, such "personal" history expresses the Way. Ironically, this demonstrates Zhang's subtle return to the subjectivism or idealism that *Kaozheng xue* had attacked and from which it had originally recoiled.

9. NON-BUDDHIST FOREIGN RELIGIONS, SEVENTH THROUGH EIGHTEENTH CENTURIES

Since the seventh century, several originally southwest Asian religions have existed sporadically in China. They include Christianity, Zoroastrianism, Manichaeism, Judaism, and Islam.

Judaism

Judaism was first practiced in China no later than the ninth and tenth centuries, although it likely had reached current Xinjiang Province about a century earlier. Apparently by 879, a large population of Jews had settled in Guangzhou on the southeast coast, for there in that year the rebel Huang Chao slaughtered approximately 120,000 Jews, Muslims, and Christians. Jews also settled in Kaifeng, Henan, between about 1000 and 1126. This community's continuous presence ever since has been attested by Mongol decrees in the 14th century, Jesuit interviews with community leaders in the 16th century, and even by scholars who interviewed some descendants at the end of the 20th century. However, though some people in Kaifeng can still trace their ancestry to the Jewish community there, ethnically and culturally they have all been absorbed into the greater Chinese population. The last known reading of the Torah in Hebrew occurred in Kaifeng during the years 1721–1723.

By 1850, when the Kaifeng community had already lost its active Jewish culture and identity, other Jews, from Russia in particular, were immigrating to Chinese cities. This continued into the 20th century, especially after the Russian Bolshevik Revolution of 1917–1918. Later, during World War II, Jewish refugees once again immigrated to China. Most, however, later emigrated.

Christianity

Christianity entered China in four waves: with Nestorian Christian missionaries; Franciscan friars; Jesuit, Franciscan, and Dominican missionaries; and finally, both Protestant and renewed Catholic missions.

Nestorian Christianity: Nestorianism began with Nestorius (fl. c. 410–451), the Christian Patriarch of Constantinople, whom the Christian Council of Ephesus declared heretical in 431 because of his insistence on the dual–divine and human–nature of Christ. A Nestorian mission from Persia entered China by 635, when it visited Tang emperor Taizong's (r. 627–649) court.

Known in China as the Teaching of Light (Jing jiao), Nestorianism flourished largely among foreigners in Changan, the Tang capital. As a foreign religion, it was proscribed along with Buddhism in the Huichang Suppression of the 840s. It survived, however, and enjoyed a brief revival during the Yuan period. Although thereafter it largely disappeared from China, in the early 20th century some Mongols in northern China were known to be Nestorian Christians.

The Franciscan Catholic Mission:
During the Yuan, a mission of Franciscans established themselves briefly in the Mongol capital, Khanbaliq (Beijing). Rome had sent them to attempt to convert the Mongols to Christianity. The mission failed and disappeared after approximately 60 years (c. 1350).

The Catholic Society of Jesus (Jesuits), Dominicans, and Franciscans:
After 1550 Catholic missionaries again attempted to gain a foothold among the Chinese population. Finally in 1599–1601 the Jesuit Matteo Ricci (1552–1610) succeeded in establishing permanent missions in Nanjing and Beijing. Thereafter throughout much of the 17th century, missionaries, especially Jesuits, won favor at both the Ming and Qing courts. The Jesuits succeeded in part because they adopted the garb of Chinese scholar officials. Once accepted, their expertise in astronomy, mathematics, mechanics, and military technology won them great respect. The clocks they made and the defensive artillery they manufactured particularly fascinated and pleased their hosts.

After 1625, missionaries of other Catholic orders established themselves in China. By the end of the 18th century, the Catholic missionaries could count approximately 300,000 Christians in China. Many of these were among the highest elite. The most famous convert was Xu Guangqi (Hsü Kuang-ch'i, 1562–1633), or Paul Hsü, who served the Ming court in the preeminent position of grand secretary.

Most of the Catholics' proselytizing success came from the efforts of the Jesuits. However, conflicts among the orders limited the overall effectiveness of Catholic missionary efforts. Their arguments among themselves eventually drew the suspicion of the Manchu Qing court, the scholar bureaucrats, and the common people alike.

Rites Controversy:
Dominicans and Franciscans felt that the Jesuits had accommodated themselves too much to Chinese ways. Thus, when the Jesuits argued in favor of accepting the worship of Confucius and clan ancestors as expressions of reverence for cultural and familial icons rather than religious devotion to gods, the Dominicans and Franciscans disagreed. These rivals tried conversely to convince potential Chinese converts to abandon their worship of ancestors and Confucius. They pointed out that Christ was the only godhead and to worship false idols was sacrilege. Catholic missionaries, they demanded, must remain true to their faith, for to do otherwise is to lead people not to salvation but rather damnation for their idolatry.

The papacy in Rome considered this conundrum until 1704, when Pope Clement XI ordered that no (Catholic) Christians could perform rites devoted to Confucius or ancestors. Reinforced in 1715 and 1742, this decision essentially doomed this wave of Catholic missionary efforts in China. Only in 1939 did Pope Pius XII reverse the papacy's position. Although the Jesuit mission continued in China, the papacy suppressed this order in 1773 (to be restored in 1814). Thereafter in the 19th century, the various orders of Catholicism, as well as many Protestant denominations, renewed Christian proselytizing efforts in China. In the meantime, the Qing government had officially proscribed Christianity in 1724.

Zoroastrianism

Known in China as the Teaching of Fire Worship (Baihuo jiao), Zoroastrianism began in Persia with the man Zarathustra, more commonly known as Zoroaster, sometime between 1100 and 600 B.C. Its central dualistic teaching is that the universal epic struggle between good and evil will end in victory by the forces of good, embodied in the god Ahuramazda, over those of evil, represented by the vicious spirit Ahriman. At that time, Ahuramazda will judge each person's eternal fate according to his or her life's preponderance toward good or evil.

Zoroastrianism arrived in China around 640 with imperial and other elite refugees from the Arab conquest of the Sassanids (224–651) of Persia. Establishing themselves originally in the capital Changan, they spread through the next two centuries to other major Chinese cities. As a foreign religion, they were proscribed in the Huichang Suppression of 843–845. Much later, in the 19th and early 20th centuries, Indian Zoroastrians settled in coastal Chinese cities. None of their communities lasted beyond the mid-20th century.

Manichaeism

This gnostic religion began with the Persian Mani (216–c. 277). In Manichaeism, one achieves salvation with the realization that one's own soul is pure light and shares its purity with transcendent God. In China, therefore, it has been known as the Teaching of Lucidity (Ming Jiao).

Manichaeism arrived in China by the late seventh century and came to be practiced largely by the Turkic Uighur, a Central Asian tribe that converted to Manichaeism in the early eighth century. Until the 840s, the Uighur, Chinese allies whose military forces helped quell the An Lushan rebellion in 762, were welcome to practice their new faith in temples erected in major Chinese cities. However, the Tang court proscribed Manichaeism during the Huichang Suppression, 843–845. While Manichaeism survived until the Ming in the southeastern coastal province of Fujian, it never again flourished in China.

Islam

Islam (Hui Jiao) first entered China in 756 with troops sent by the Arab Muslim Abbasid Caliph to assist the Tang in their fight against the An Lushan rebels. Many of the Muslim soldiers settled in China.

Shortly after this, for centuries Islam also entered coastal Chinese cities along with Arab merchants and sailors, who dominated the coastal Asian–Persian Gulf sea trade. Guangzhou and Quanzhou (Fujian) became coastal Muslim centers. A third major influx of Muslims occurred during the Yuan, since the Mongols employed mostly foreigners to govern their new Chinese territories, and Muslims often possessed desired technical skills.

Though Muslims spread throughout China, they usually remained a semi-autonomous community. Still, through intermarriage with Chinese, Muslims have become physically indistinguishable. At the end of the 20th century, Muslims were especially numerous in the western regions of the People's Republic.

10. THOUGHT AND RELIGION, NINETEENTH AND TWENTIETH CENTURIES

Christianity

Rebellion and Christian Persecution: Generally, previous patterns of thought and belief continued during the early 19th century. A massive rebellion by the resurgent White Lotus Society occurred in 1796–1804. In part a peasant reaction to the government's inability to relieve rural poverty and peasant famine, this millenarian movement preaching the coming of the messianic Maitreya Buddha also represented a reaction against Western—and especially Christian—influences. Unfortunately for Christians, the government confused their secret rites with those of the rebels and therefore officially persecuted them in 1805. Such official persecutions continued through the early 1840s, while private persecutions, occasionally rejoined by government-inspired attacks, continued throughout the 19th and 20th centuries.

Protestant Christianity: By 1800 there were an estimated 150,000 Christians in all of China, about half the number of a century before, all of whom were Catholic. In 1807, Protestant missionaries arrived. The first, Robert Morrison, with his companion John Milne completed his translation of the Bible into Chinese in 1819.

Both Protestant and Catholic missions of virtually all major denominations and sects developed throughout China during the 19th century. This was so especially after the Western powers forced treaties on the Chinese government in the 1840s, 1858, and 1860 that ensured that the missionaries could spread into the Chinese interior. The French secured edicts of toleration of Catholicism in 1844 and 1866.

The Heavenly Kingdom of Great Peace: However, Christianity's greatest effect on China was neither positive nor purely religious but rather negative and political. After the White Lotus Rebellion at the beginning of the century, twice more before 1900 large Christian-inspired rebellions broke out.

The first, the Taiping Rebellion (1851–1864), was a full-blown civil war begun and led by Hong Xiuquan (Hung Hsiu-ch'üan, 1814–1864). Fundamentalist Protestant pamphlets inspired the impressionable Hong to believe that he was the younger brother of Jesus Christ and destined to establish the millenarian Heavenly Kingdom of Great Peace (Taiping tianguo) on earth. For 11 years, from its capital at Nanjing, this anti-Manchu, anti-Ru rebellion ruled a vast expanse of territory in central-southeast China. Utopian and reformist, the Taiping forced their citizens to gender-segregate, collectivize wealth and production, and follow a strict social reform law that mimicked the principles of the Old Testament's Ten Commandments. With some foreign assistance, Qing troops wiped out the Taiping in 1864.

The Boxer Rebellion: The other Christian-related rebellion was the Boxer (*Yihequan*) Rebellion of 1899–1900. In an age of increasing revolutionary fervor, the Boxers were both pro-dynastic and anti-Western. The latter aspect focused largely on the perceived decadent teachings of Christianity. Supported by the Qing central government, which in fact declared war on the foreign powers in China in June 1900, the Boxer "rebels" killed more than 200 foreigners, mostly Christian missionaries, as well as Chinese Christians. During the summer of 1900, the Boxers laid siege to the foreign communities in the northern cities Tianjin and Beijing. While foreign troops quickly put down the "rebellion," the Boxer movement and its widespread support both in the central Chinese government and populace in fact betrayed the deep-seated and long-festering resentment of Westerners that most Chinese shared.

Main Intellectual Currents, to 1949

New Text Learning: In the centuries after the Han, most of the works adopted as the correct versions of the classics were the Old Texts. During the 19th century some scholars revived the New Text–Old Text debate. Their point of departure was Yan Ruoju's 17th-century demonstration of the forgery of the Old Text *Book of Documents*. They scoured the other classics for further evidence of forgery.

Kang Youwei: In the 1890s, the revived New Text school found its intellectual focus in the person of Kang Youwei (K'ang Yu-wei, 1858–1927). Kang is especially famous for his central involvement in the failed Hundred Days of Reform in the summer of 1898, when a pro-modernization faction at the Qing court (including the emperor Guangxu) attempted to engage China in an aggressive program of political and economic reform.

Kang's principle of reform originated in his theory of historical progression that derived in turn from his support of New Text classics and theory. Claiming the Old Texts forgeries, Kang argued boldly that Confucius had in fact written the classics and that in his choice of words Kang could discern the ancient sage's prophecy that human history would develop through three evolutionary ages: Disorder, Approaching Peace and Tranquility, and Great Peace and Unity. Kang theorized that he, a reformist sage like Confucius, could lead China—and the world—out of the Age of Disorder to evolve into the Age of Approaching Peace and Tranquility. When opponents at court ended his reform program after approximately a hundred days, Kang fled to Japan to avoid the execution that six of his fellow reformers, including his younger brother, suffered.

Social Darwinism: Kang Youwei was influenced by Darwinism, the biological theory that postulates that species evolve through a process of natural selection. Still, in *On the Origin of Species* (1859), Charles Darwin had written of only biological, not social or political, evolution. The sources of Kang's social evolutionary twist of Darwin's theory were Herbert Spencer and Thomas Huxley. In his *The Study of*

Sociology (1873), Spencer explicitly applied the Darwinist theory of natural selection to human societies. He called this "survival of the fittest," arguing that societies compete to survive and only the most competitive and adaptable endure and evolve. Later, scientist-philosopher Thomas Huxley, in his *Evolution and Ethics* (1893), argued against Spencer and in the process enunciated the very tenets of Social Darwinism that he opposed. Yan Fu (Yen Fu, 1853–1921), among the first significant translators of English works into Chinese, translated Huxley's work into Chinese (1896).

Social Darwinism dominated sociological speculation worldwide during the more than half century (c. 1875–1945) that China struggled against the aggressions of imperialist powers to maintain the integrity of its land and people. In China, Social Darwinism inspired both hope that Chinese society would evolve and survive to rival the aggressive imperialist powers and despair over China's seeming inability at the turn of the 20th century to do just that.

These trends are apparent in the Chinese response to the events of 1898. Following the failure of the Hundred Days of Reform in that year, while some such as Kang Youwei remained loyal to the Qing Manchu regime and attempted to establish a constitutional monarchy, many more over the next two decades viewed a sweeping revolution as the only means of ensuring China's competitive survival in a brutal world.

Nationalism: The Boxer Rebellion and Kang and others' attempts in 1898 to reform the Qing government were expressions of nationalistic sentiments. They attempted to return control of China from foreign (here, "Western") to domestic powers. However, Kang eventually lost support for his program, in large part because his nationalism in fact supported what revolutionaries of the time considered to be not Chinese but foreign, that is, Manchu, rule. In the early years of the 20th century, an increasing body of revolution-minded Chinese demanded a purely Han Chinese rulership of China. Though later not conceived so restrictively to include only Han Chinese, Chinese nationalism continued to constitute a significant element in

most reform movements—including those instituted by the Communists—throughout the 20th and into the 21st centuries.

Zou Rong and The Revolutionary Army: A significant contribution to Chinese nationalistic ideology came from the young writer Zou Rong (Tsou Jung, 1886–1905), who in 1903 published his influential *The Revolutionary Army*. Zou harangued his fellow Chinese for allowing the Manchu overlords to oppress and murder them. He demanded the people unite to violently overthrow the increasingly hated Qing.

Sun Yat-sen and the Revolutionary Alliance: Most famous among Nationalist movements was Sun Yat-sen's (*p.* Sun Yixian/Sun Yi-hsien; sobriquet of Sun Wen, 1866–1925) Revolutionary Alliance (Tongmeng Hui), founded in 1905. This group, with its roots in both domestic secret societies and growing revolutionary fervor among overseas Chinese in the late 19th century, was primarily responsible for eventually overthrowing the Qing in 1911–1912.

Sun Yat-sen contributed greatly to the Chinese Revolution of 1911 through activism, singular leadership, and significant fund-raising. Sun appealed to other revolutionaries due to both his revolutionary zeal (from 1895 he led several anti-Qing armed insurrections) and his development of a concrete ideological blueprint for Chinese self-governance. His Three People's Principles (San min zhuyi), including nationalism, democracy, and the people's livelihood, provided a believable adaptation of Western political ideals to Chinese socio-political realities.

The Nationalist Party: Eventually, the Revolutionary Alliance was transformed into the National People's Party, or the Nationalists (Guomindang or GMD; Kuomin-tang or KMT). With its leadership seized by Chiang Kai-shek (*p.* Jiang Jieshi, 1887–1975) in the years after Sun Yat-sen's death, this party controlled the government of the Republic of China (ROC)—whatever regions of China this government could claim to govern at any given time—sporadically from the mid-1920s through 1949. After 1949 and through the remainder of the 20th century, the Guomindang, through 1988 dominated by Chiang and his son, Chiang Ching-kuo (*p.* Jiang Jingguo, 1909–1988), controlled the government of Taiwan. In May 2000, after losing the popular presidential election two months before, the Guomindang on Taiwan relinquished control of the presidency of the ROC for the first time, to Ch'en Shui-bian (*p.* Chen Shuibian, 1952–). Chen was the candidate of the once-banned opposition Democratic Progressive Party (Minjindang).

May 4, 1919, and the May Fourth/New Culture Movement: On May 4, 1919, between 3,000 and 5,000 students from 13 Beijing universities gathered to protest the post-World War I Versailles Convention's disregard for China's rights of self-determination when it formally assigned erstwhile German rights in Shandong to the Japanese. Marching through Beijing, students clashed with police in several violent episodes. Police arrested only 10 students, but in subsequent days, all Beijing area university and college students staged a general strike. Quickly, students and workers in major cities across China joined them.

By July the students had won a landmark victory. Not only had the arrested students been released (May 7), but in June the cabinet of the Beijing government of China resigned, the government dismissed three officials known to have acquiesced to Japanese demands in the past, and on June 28 the Chinese delegation at the Versailles Conference refused to attend the signing ceremony of the Versailles Treaty.

The significance of the students' achievement was in their uniting Chinese people across class lines and thus strengthening Chinese national identity. These events catalyzed Chinese intellectuals in their search for new ways to release China from the bondage of its traditionalistic (Ru) past and foreign domination. Consequently, the May Fourth demonstrations are viewed as the central and unifying events of an ideological revolution that developed in China from about 1915 through the 1920s.

This complex revolution is called variably the New Culture Movement or May Fourth Movement. It involved radical rethinking of culture in all facets and at all levels, leading eventually, among other things, to the establishment of socialist sentiments among intellectuals, the Chinese Communist Party, and the vernacular language as the basic medium of written expression. At the time, the latter was perhaps the most significant change, for by displacing the ancient written language as the basic mode of elite and governmental communication, the use of the vernacular in print opened up education to the commoner, who now could participate fully in a literate culture. Through this culture, new social and political ideas and ideals could spread.

Communism: Communism, ultimately the most significant intellectual movement in 20th-century China, developed in opposition to the Nationalists but also within and alongside the Nationalist movement. The Chinese Communist Party (CCP) held its first plenary meeting in July 1921 in Shanghai. Important founding members included Mao Zedong (Mao Tse-tung, 1893–1976), Li Dazhao (Li Ta-chao, 1888–1927), Chen Duxiu (Ch'en Tu-hsiu, 1879–1942), Zhou Enlai (Chou En-lai, 1898–1976), and Deng Xiaoping (Teng Hsiao-p'ing, 1904–1997). Though Li and Chen early invigorated the CCP, Mao, Zhou, and Deng later played crucial long-term leadership roles in the party and China.

In the 1920s, the CCP developed most strongly in the cities. At the time a number of regional warlords ruled a China still unable to break from its politically autocratic and socially Ru past. The CCP sought to overturn this system by creating a revolutionary army among mostly the poor and oppressed workers in the cities. Facing serious setbacks from 1927 in the cities, however, the communists increasingly concentrated on fomenting revolution in the countryside. This strategy led them to complete victory in 1949.

Mao Zedong and His Total Revolution, 1935–1949: The most influential Chinese communist theorist and leader was Mao Zedong. Originally a revolutionary with vague Social Darwinist and anarchist ideals, Mao increasingly gravitated to the pragmatism and extremism of communist revolutionary ideology between 1910 and 1920. Involved in the organizing and founding of the CCP, Mao played a crucial role in developing and spreading the new doctrine in the countryside. In January

1935, during the CCP's Long March to Yan'an (Yenan) in northwestern China (1934–1935), Mao emerged as the new party leader.

More than any other developing CCP or Chinese leader, Mao created a total revolution, one that encompassed not only military insurrection, but sweeping economic, social, institutional, and ideological changes as well. When the CCP and its Red Army succeeded in defeating Guomindang forces in 1949, Mao and his associates were prepared to spread their rural-based total revolution to every corner of China. Indeed, through their land, social, economic, and ideological reforms of the 1930s through 1950s, they completely remade China. Only in this way did they accomplish the goal of which other revolutionaries during the preceding 60 years had only dreamed—reunification under Chinese rule. The human costs, however, were tremendous.

Thought and Belief in the People's Republic of China (PRC), 1949–

Chinese Communism: Since 1949 Chinese communism has repeatedly undergone dramatic changes. While in the early 1950s, the CCP and its new government concentrated on consolidating their victory through agricultural and industrial development, in the later 1950s Mao led the country into a period of radical thought reform. In subsequent decades, Mao and others took the CCP and all of China through dizzying reversals in ideological orthodoxy. This created a China that at the turn of the 21st century remained uncertain of its direction and, outside the major urban, trade, and manufacturing areas, largely poor.

Until his death in 1976, Mao and his revolutionary faction in the CCP/PRC leadership continuously struggled against ideological moderates such as Liu Shaoqi (LIU Shao-ch'i, 1898–1969), Deng Xiaoping, and Peng Dehuai (P'ENG Te-huai, 1899–1974). The latter group, often associated with so-called "technocrats," normally supported planned economic development that relied on careful, rational assessment of the state and the economy in world and regional markets. They understood that China needed to rely on foreign, more technologically advanced nations to modernize its agricultural and industrial sectors.

In the 1950s and 1960s, moderates achieved success in rebuilding these sectors. Each time, Mao and his supporters worried that the communist revolution was losing ground to "revisionists," "feudalists," "bureaucratists," and "capitalist roaders." His insecurity and revolutionary fervor led to several purges of intellectuals, CCP cadre, and PRC bureaucrats (Hundred Flowers Movement, 1956–1957, and the Anti-Rightist Campaign, 1957; Great Proletarian Cultural Revolution, 1966–1976).

Through such purges China lost virtually two entire generations of its most capable, educated people to revolutionary bickering among party elite. As a result, despite insistence by Deng Xiaoping and Jiang Zemin (1926–) since 1978 on developing China economically and technologically, at the turn of the new millennium the nation was only beginning to catch up with the industrialized world.

In the meantime, after 1978 Deng, Jiang, and other moderate leaders fudged the question of the meaning of communism and its revolution. Both of these economically capitalist-oriented leaders insisted that China evolve according to "Marxist-Leninist-Mao Zedong thought" and operate according to the indistinct formula of "socialism with Chinese characteristics."

Though vague, this really meant that China would continue to devote itself to socialist ideals in the political and social realms and the central government would remain highly authoritarian, but economically China would enrich itself and its people by following a capitalist, free-market model of development.

That this constituted a great irony of modern history—the development into capitalists of the anti-capitalist proletariat of the last great proto-Communist Marxist state—seemed to matter less to the Chinese and the world than the fact that China was indeed beginning to both catch up and open up.

Religion in Contemporary China

Despite PRC constitutional guarantees of freedom in religious practice, religions in China were closely controlled and actively suppressed. After all, communism's atheistic theory of "scientific materialism" discounts faiths other than the firm belief in the evolution of human societies on the basis of changes in economic technologies.

Officially Sanctioned Religions: On the other hand, most major world religions continued to exist in China throughout the post-revolutionary period. Still, by and large they were centrally controlled by the state Religious Affairs Bureau, and only five religions were officially recognized: Protestant and Catholic Christianity, Islam, Buddhism, and Daoism. Each religion was organized into a national association that the Bureau oversaw.

However, these "world religions" remained largely isolated from world religious life and theological discussions. Nearly all foreign missionaries were expelled in the 1950s; and, in 1957, when the Roman papacy recognized Taiwan (Republic of China) as the official government of China, the PRC severed the connection between the officially sanctioned Chinese Catholic Church and the papacy. Consequently, two Catholic churches existed in China in the year 2000, one underground, which secretly recognized the Holy See, and the other official, which elected its own bishops.

Until 1966, most religions, whether officially sanctioned or not, continued to thrive on a limited basis. From 1966 through 1978, religions were more or less thoroughly suppressed, attacked during the Cultural Revolution as "spiritual pollution" and a feudalistic manifestation of Mao's hated "four olds": old ideas, habits, culture, and customs. Both people (priests, nuns, monks, ministers, and lay believers) and institutions (temples, mosques, and churches) representing the sundry religions of China were physically and spiritually attacked.

However, during China's general intellectual liberalization under Deng Xiaoping (after 1978), the CCP acknowledged a limited positive role that religion could play in promoting an orderly and stable society. Thereafter, religion appeared to flourish once again in China.

While unreliable, estimates of numbers of adherents suggest healthy growth rates through the end of the 20th century, particularly for Protestant Christianity. In 1949, an estimated 930,000 Protestants and 3.3 million Catholics practiced their Christian faith in China. In the late 1990s, Protestants were estimated at between 12 and 65 million, and the number of Catholic faithful had grown to between 5 and 12 million. For comparison, an estimated 17 to 25 million Muslims lived in China in the year 2000.

For Buddhism and Daoism there existed no concrete estimates of the numbers of faithful. Still, in each case in the year 2000 followers likely numbered in the tens of millions. One problem in generating estimates lay in defining the boundaries of Buddhist and Daoist faiths and practices.

Popular Religion: In the late 20th century, even popular religious traditions reemerged and thrived, especially among rural people. Considered "superstitions" and thus specifically outlawed by the Chinese constitution for their "pernicious" influences, expressions of local traditional "popular" beliefs (such as geomancy, physiognomy, divination, sacrifices to deities, horoscope readings, shamanism, and so on) were actively suppressed whenever possible. The state/party's fear of local cults reflected its understanding of their influential role historically in toppling unpopular regimes (the Yuan and Qing). Often, however, local CCP authorities lacked either the will or the resources to suppress these expressions of the people's beliefs.

Suppression of Dangerous Cults: The Falun Dafa: An exception was the Falun Dafa (Great Method of the Wheel of the Law, a.k.a. Falun Gong), which the government attempted concertedly to suppress in and after 1999. Claiming a following of 100 million in China and abroad, the Falun Dafa converged in Beijing in April 1999 to protest peacefully the arrests of its members and the PRC's continuing refusal to recognize the cult as a legitimate religion.

The Falun Dafa combine traditional Daoist and Buddhist mystical faith and meditation with gymnastic exercises, teaching a total lifestyle of faith that centers on the ages-old tradition of cultivating *qi*.

The sect's founder, Li Hongzhi (1951–), who established the faith in 1992 and in 1997 moved to New York, claimed that his teachings healed the faithful. He argued that, worldwide, people generally suffer from degenerative moral and physical illnesses in an increasingly dark and evil world where moral values have been overtaken by harmful modern technologies and their derivative cultures (such as rock-and-roll, MTV, drugs).

The sect's sudden and secretly convened demonstration in Beijing in 1999 alarmed PRC and CCP authorities, who already were frightened by the sect for its having attracted many high governmental, party, and military officials to its fold. Furthermore, Li claimed to possess spiritual authority beyond that of all other religious icons, past and present. He also asserted that he had been sent to earth to save humanity from its modern corrupt societies.

Finding Li and the cult's direct challenges to its authority intolerable, the PRC/CCP actively suppressed the cult in April 1999 and in July outlawed it. Suppression of the Falun Dafa continued thereafter. In early 2000, the government also began suppressing another *qigong* sect, Zhong Gong, which claimed some 20 million members.

The Exile of the Dalai Lama and Control of Tibetan Buddhism: The most infamous example of religious oppression in the PRC was the forced escape of the Tibetan Dalai Lama to India in 1959. The PRC considered the Dalai Lama, both the spiritual and political leader of Tibet, threatening to Chinese rule there.

Significantly, in early 2000 the 17-year-old Karmapa Lama absconded to the Dalai Lama's center of government in exile, Dharamsala, India. This move complicated the PRC's attempt to co-opt Tibetan Buddhist leadership from the Dalai Lama. Now two of the three highest Tibetan spiritual leaders are together in exile and control as well the legitimate succession to the second-highest position of spiritual and political authority in Tibetan culture, that of the Panchen Lama (all of the Dalai, Panchen, and Karmapa Lamas are considered reincarnations of their predecessors).

Taiwan

Under the GMD/ROC government the Taiwanese enjoyed an atmosphere of relative religious tolerance since 1949. Still, like the PRC, the ROC retained the power to restrict "pernicious" organizations and cults, despite constitutional guarantee of freedom of religious observance.

Virtually all world religious groups are represented on the island. Aside from Hong Kong (returned by the British to PRC sovereignty in 1997) and Singapore, it is in Taiwan that one can find manifestations of traditional popular religion that differ little in substance from the religions practiced by Chinese for a thousand years.

KEY RESEARCH SOURCES

General Intellectual

Barrett, Timothy. "Postscript." *Cambridge History of China*. Vol. 1, *The Ch'in and Han Empires*. Eds. Denis Twitchett and Michael Loewe. Cambridge: Cambridge University Press, 1986. 873–878.

Chan, Hok-lam, and William Theodore de Bary, eds. *Yüan Thought: Chinese Thought and Religion under the Mongols*. New York: Columbia University Press, 1982.

Chan, Wing-tsit. *A Source Book in Chinese Philosophy*. Princeton: Princeton University Press, 1963.

de Bary, William Theodore, et al., eds. *Sources of Chinese Tradition*. 2 vols. New York: Columbia University Press, 1960–1964.

Demiéville, Paul. "Philosophy and Religion from Han to Sui." *Cambridge History of China*. Vol. 1. Trans. Francesca Bray. Ed. Denis Twitchett and Michael Loewe. Cambridge: Cambridge University Press, 1986. 808–872.

Fung, Yu-lan. *A History of Chinese Philosophy*. 2d ed. Trans. Derk Bodde. Princeton: Princeton University Press, 1952–1953.

Graham, A. C. *Disputers of the Tao*. La Salle, Ill.: Open Court, 1989.

Hsiao, Kung-ch'üan. *A History of Chinese Political Thought*. Vol. 1, *From the Beginnings to the Sixth Century A.D.* Trans. Frederick W. Mote. Princeton: Princeton University Press, 1979.

Knoblock, John. *Xunzi: A Translation and Study of the Complete Works*. Stanford: Stanford University Press, 1988–1994.

Mather, Richard. "The Controversy over Conformity and Naturalness during the Six Dynasties Period." *History of Religions* 9 (1969–1970): 160–179.

Mote, Frederick W. *Intellectual Foundations of China*. 2d ed. New York: McGraw-Hill, 1989.

Needham, Joseph, et al., eds. *Science and Civilisation in China*. Cambridge: Cambridge University Press, 1956.

Schwartz, Benjamin. *The World of Thought in Ancient China*. Cambridge, Mass.: Belknap Press of Harvard University Press, 1985.

Wilhelm, Richard, trans. (from Chinese to German) and ed. *The I Ching or Book of Changes*. 3d ed. Trans. (from German) Cary F. Baynes. Princeton: Princeton University Press, 1967.

Yü, Ying-shih. "Individualism and the Neo-Taoist Movement in Wei-Chin China." *Individualism and Holism: Studies in Confucian and Taoist Values*. Ed. Donald Munro. Ann Arbor: Center for Chinese Studies, University of Michigan, 1985.

———. "'Oh Soul, Come Back!': A Study of the Changing Conception of the Soul and Afterlife in Pre-Buddhist China." *Harvard Journal of Asiatic Studies* 47.2 (1987): 363–395.

Religions—General

Bodde, Derk. "Myths of Ancient China." *Mythologies of the Ancient World*. Ed. Samuel N. Kramer. Garden City, N.J.: Doubleday & Co., 1961. 367–408.

———. *Festivals in Classical China: New Year and Other Annual Observances During the Han Dynasty, 206 B.C.–A.D. 220*. Princeton: Princeton University Press, 1975.

Chang, K. C. *Art, Myth, and Ritual: The Path to Political Authority in Ancient China*. Cambridge, Mass.: Harvard University Press, 1983.

Ching, Julia. *Chinese Religions*. London: Macmillan Press, 1993.

Ebrey, Patricia Buckley, and Peter N. Gregory, eds. *Religion and Society in T'ang and Sung China*. Honolulu: University of Hawaii Press, 1993.

Keightley, David N. "The Religious Commitment: Shang Theology and the Genesis of Chinese Political Culture." *History of Religions* 17 (1978): 211–255.

Lopez, Donald S., Jr. *Religions of China in Practice*. Princeton: Princeton University Press, 1996.

MacInnis, Donald E. *Religion in China Today: Policy and Practice*. Maryknoll, N.Y.: Orbis Books, 1989.

McDermot, Jospeh P. *State and Court Ritual in China*. Cambridge: Cambridge University Press, 1999.

Overmyer, Daniel L. *Religions of China: The World as a Living System*. Rev. ed. San Francisco: Harper & Row, 1992.

Thompson, Laurence G. *Chinese Religion, an Introduction*. 5th ed. Belmont, Calif.: Wadsworth Publishing Co., 1996.

Thompson, Laurence G., comp., and Gary Seaman, ed. *Chinese Religions: Publications in Western Languages*. Vol. 3, 1991–1995. Ann Arbor: Association for Asian Studies; Los Angeles: Produced by Ethnographics Press, Center for Visual Anthropology, University of Southern California, 1998.

———. *Chinese Religions: Publications in Western Languages, 1981 Through 1990*. Ann Arbor: Association for Asian Studies; Los Angeles: Produced by Ethnographics Press, Center for Visual Anthropology, University of Southern California, 1993.

———. *Chinese Religion in Western Languages: A Comprehensive and Classified Bibliography of Publications in English, French, and German Through 1980*. Tucson: Published for the Association for Asian Studies by the University of Arizona Press, 1985.

Ware, James R. *Alchemy, Medicine, Religion, in the China of A.D. 230: The Nei P'ien of Ko Hung (Pao-p'u-tzu)*. Cambridge, Mass.: M.I.T. Press, 1966.

Yang, C. K. *Religion in Chinese Society; the First Comprehensive Sociological Analysis of Chinese Relgious Behavior*. Berkeley: University of California Press, 1970.

Popular Religion

Dean, Kenneth. *Taoist Ritual and Popular Cults of Southeast China*. Princeton: Princeton University Press, 1993.

de Groot, Jan J. M. *The Religious System of China*. 6 vols. 1892–1910. Reprint. Taipei: Ch'eng-wen, 1972.

Hansen, Valerie. *Changing Gods in Medieval China, 1127–1276*. Princeton: Princeton University Press, 1990.

Harper, Donald. "A Chinese Demonography of the Third Century B.C." *Harvard Journal of Asiatic Studies* 45.2 (1985): 459–498.

Johnson, David. "The City God Cults of T'ang and Sung China." *Harvard Journal of Asiatic Studies* 45 (1985): 363–457.

Johnson, David, Andrew J. Nathan, and Evelyn S. Rawski, eds. *Popular Culture in Late Imperial China*. Berkeley: University of California Press, 1985.

Jordan, David K. *Gods, Ghosts, and Ancestors: The Folk Religion of a Taiwanese Village*. Berkeley: University of California Press, 1972.

Jordan, David K., and Daniel L. Overmyer. *The Flying Phoenix: Aspects of Chinese Sectarianism in Taiwan*. Princeton: Princeton University Press, 1986.

Shahar, Meir, and Peter Weller, eds. *Unruly Gods: Divinity and Society in China*. Honolulu: University of Hawaii Press, 1996.

Poo, Mu-chou. *In Search of Personal Welfare: A View of Ancient Chinese Religion*. Albany: State University of New York Press, 1998.

Weller, Robert P. *Unities and Diversities in Chinese Religion*. Seattle: University of Washington Press, 1987.

Wolf, Arthur P. *Studies in Chinese Society*. Stanford: Stanford University Press, 1978.

Ru (Confucianism)

Bol, Peter K. *"This Culture of Ours": Intellectual Transitions in T'ang and Sung China.* Stanford: Stanford University Press, 1992.

Chan, Wing-tsit. *Chu Hsi and Neo-Confucianism.* Honolulu: University of Hawaii Press, 1986.

———. *Chu Hsi: New Studies.* Honolulu: University of Hawaii Press, 1989.

de Bary, William Theodore, ed. *Self and Society in Ming Thought.* New York: Columbia University Press, 1970.

Elman, Benjamin. *From Philology to Philosophy: Intellectual and Social Aspects of Change in Late Imperial China.* Cambridge, Mass.: Council on East Asian Studies, Harvard University/Harvard University Press, 1984.

Gardner, Daniel K. *Chu Hsi and the Ta-hsueh: Neo-Confucian Reflection on the Confucian Canon.* Cambridge, Mass.: Council on East Asian Studies, Harvard University/Harvard University Press, 1986.

Graham, A. C. *Two Chinese Philosophers: The Metaphysics of the Brothers Ch'eng.* Reprint. La Salle, Ill.: Open Court, 1992.

Lau, D. C. *Confucius, the Analects.* London: Penguin, 1979.

———. *Mencius.* London: Penguin, 1970.

Loewe, Michael. *Crisis and Conflict in Han China, 104 B.C. to A.D. 9.* London: George Allen and Unwin, 1974.

McMullen, David. *State and Scholars in T'ang China.* Cambridge: Cambridge University Press, 1988.

Taylor, Rodney L. *The Religious Dimensions of Confucianism.* Albany: State University of New York Press, 1990.

Wechsler, Howard J. *Offerings of Jade and Silk: Ritual and Symbol in the Legitimation of the T'ang Dynasty.* New Haven: Yale University Press, 1985.

Wilhelm, Hellmut. "Trends of Thought in the Early Nineteenth Century." *Asia Major* 3.2 (1990): 3–23.

Daoism, Pre-Han

Graham, A. C., trans. *Chuang-Tzu: The Inner Chapters.* London: Unwin Hyman Ltd., 1981.

Henricks, Robert G., trans. *Lao-tzu: Te-Tao Ching: A New Translation Based on the Recently Discovered Ma-wang-tui Texts.* New York: Ballantine Books, 1989.

Lao-tzu. *The Classic of the Way and Virtue: A New Translation of the Tao-te ching of Laozi as Interpreted by Wang Bi.* Trans. Richard John Lynn. New York: Columbia University Press, 1999.

———. *Tao te Ching.* Trans. D. C. Lau. Baltimore: Penguin, 1963.

Roth, Harold D. *Original Tao: Inward Training and the Foundations of Taoist Mysticism.* New York: Columbia University Press, 1999.

Waley, Arthur. *The Way and Its Power: A Study of the Tao Te Ching and Its Place in Chinese Thought.* New York: Grove/Atlantic, 1988.

Watson, Burton. *The Complete Works of Chuang-tzu.* New York: Columbia University Press, 1968.

Daoism, Han and Later

Barrett, Timothy. *Taoism under the T'ang*. London: Wellsweep, 1996.

Bokenkamp, Stephen R. *Early Daoist Scriptures*. Berkeley: University of California Press, 1997.

Boltz, Judith. *A Survey of Taoist Literature, Tenth to Seventeenth Centuries*. Berkeley: University of California Press, 1987.

Kohn, Livia. *The Taoist Experience: An Anthology*. New York: State University of New York Press, 1993.

———. *Taoist Meditation and Longevity Techniques*. Ann Arbor: Center for Chinese Studies, the University of Michigan, 1989.

Lagerway, John. *Taoist Ritual in Chinese Society and History*. New York: Macmillan Publishing Co., 1987.

Maspero, Henri. *Taoism and Chinese Religion*. Trans. Frank A. Kierman, Jr. Amherst: University of Massachusetts Press, 1981.

Robinet, Isabelle. *Taoism: Growth of a Religion*. Trans. Phyllis Brooks. Stanford: Stanford University Press, 1997.

———. *Taoist Meditation: The Mao Shan Tradition of Great Purity*. Trans. Julian F. Pas and Norman J. Girardot. Albany: State University of New York Press, 1993.

Schafer, Edward H. *Mao Shan in T'ang Times*. 2d ed. Boulder, Colo.: Society for the Study of Chinese Religions, 1989.

Seidel, Anna. "Chronicle of Taoist Studies in the West, 1950–1990." *Cahiers d'Extrême-Asie* 5 (1989–1990): 223–347.

Sivin, Nathan. "Chinese Alchemy and the Manipulation of Time." *Isis* 67.239 (1976): 513–526.

———. *Chinese Alchemy, Preliminary Studies*. Cambridge, Mass.: Harvard University Press, 1968.

Schipper, Kristofer. *The Taoist Body*. Trans. Karen C. Duval. Berkeley: University of California Press, 1993.

Welch, Holmes, and Anna Seidel, eds. *Facets of Taoism*. New Haven: Yale University Press, 1979.

Non-Buddhist Foreign Religions

Bays, Daniel H. *Christianity in China from the Eighteenth Century to the Present*. Stanford: Stanford University Press, 1996.

Dunne, George H. *Generation of Giants: The Story of the Jesuits in China in the Last Decades of the Ming Dynasty*. Notre Dame, Ind.: Notre Dame University Press, 1962.

Gernet, Jacques. *China and the Christian Impact*. Trans. Janet Lloyd. Cambridge: Cambridge University Press, 1985.

Goldstein, Jonathan. *The Jews of China*. Armonk, N.Y.: M. E. Sharpe, 1998.

Israeli, Raphael. *Islam in China: A Critical Bibliography*. Westport, Conn.: Greenwood Press, 1994.

———. *Muslims in China: A Study in Cultural Confrontation*. Atlantic Highlands, N.J.: Humanities Press, 1980.

Latourette, Kenneth. *A History of Christian Missions in China*. New York: Macmillan, 1929.

Lieu, Samuel N. C. *Manichaeism in the Later Roman Empire and Medieval China: A Historical Survey*. Manchester, England: Manchester University Press, 1985.

Spence, Jonathan. *God's Chinese Son: The Taiping Heavenly Kingdom of Hong Xiuquan*. New York: Norton, 1996.

Buddhism

Ch'en, Kenneth. *Buddhism in China, a Historical Survey*. Princeton: Princeton University Press, 1964.

———. *The Chinese Transformation of Buddhism*. Princeton: Princeton University Press, 1973.

Dumoulin, Heinrich. *Zen Buddhism: A History*. Vol. 1, *India and China*. Trans. James W. Heisig and Paul Knitter. New York: Macmillan, 1988.

Faure, Bernard. *Chan Insights and Oversights: An Epistemological Critique of the Chan Tradition*. Princeton: Princeton University Press, 1993.

———. *The Rhetoric of Immediacy: A Cultural Critique of Chan/Zen Buddhism*. Princeton: Princeton University Press, 1991.

———. *The Will to Orthodoxy: A Critical Genealogy of Northern Chan Buddhism*. Stanford: Stanford University Press, 1997.

Gregory, Peter N. *Tsung-mi and the Sinification of Buddhism*. Princeton: Princeton University Press, 1991.

McRae, John. *The Northern School and the Formation of Early Chan Buddhism*. Honolulu: University of Hawaii Press, 1986.

Overmyer, Daniel L. *Folk Buddhist Religion: Dissenting Sects in Late Traditional China*. Cambridge, Mass.: Harvard University Press, 1976.

Teiser, Stephen F. *The Ghost Festival in Medieval China*. Princeton: Princeton University Press, 1988.

Weinstein, Stanley. *Buddhism under the T'ang*. Cambridge: Cambridge University Press, 1987.

Welch, Holmes. *The Buddhist Revival in China*. Cambridge, Mass.: Harvard University Press, 1968.

———. *The Practice of Chinese Buddhism: 1910–1950*. Cambridge, Mass.: Harvard University Press, 1967.

Wright, Arthur F. *Buddhism in Chinese History*. Stanford: Stanford University Press, 1959.

Yampolsky, Philip B. *The Platform Sutra of the Sixth Patriarch*. New York: Columbia University Press, 1967.

Zürcher, Erik. *The Buddhist Conquest of China: The Spread and Adaptation of Buddhism in Early Medieval China*. Leiden, Netherlands: E. J. Brill, 1959 (repr. 1979).

Political and Cultural Thought of the 19th and 20th Centuries

Chow, Tse-tsung. *The May Fourth Movement: Intellectual Revolution in Modern China*. Cambridge, Mass.: Harvard University Press, 1960.

Clubb, Edmund O. *20th-Century China*. New York: Columbia University Press, 1964.

Cohen, Paul A. *History in Three Keys: The Boxers as Event, Experience, and Myth*. New York: Columbia University Press, 1997.

Goldman, Merle, with Timothy Cheek and Carol Hamrin. *China's Intellectuals and the State: In Search of a New Relationship*. Cambridge, Mass.: Harvard University Press, 1987.

Hsiao, Kung-ch'üan. *A Modern China and a New World: K'ang Yu-wei, Reformer and Utopian*. Seattle: University of Washington Press, 1975.

Levenson, Joseph. *Confucian China and Its Modern Fate*. Berkeley: University of California Press, 1971.

Liang, Ch'i-ch'ao. *Intellectual Trends in the Ch'ing Period*. Trans. Immanuel C. Y. Hsü. Cambridge, Mass.: Harvard University Press, 1959.

Lin, Yü-sheng. *The Crisis of Chinese Consciousness: Radical Antitraditionalism in the May Fourth Era*. Madison: University of Wisconsin Press, 1979.

MacFarquhar, Roderick. *The Origins of the Cultural Revolution*. New York: Columbia University Press, 1974–1983.

Wakeman, Frederic E., Jr. *History and Will: Philosophical Perspectives of Mao Tse-tung's Thought*. Berkeley: University of California Press, 1973.

Wang, Y. C. *Chinese Intellectuals and the West, 1872–1949*. Chapel Hill: University of North Carolina Press, 1966.

Health and Medicine

By Yiyi Wu

1. THE ANCIENT PERIOD

The Beginning: The practice of medicine began to take shape in China around 2200 B.C. In the beginning, medical practitioners were not much different from shamans. Both dealt with evil spirits or ghosts responsible for bad luck and illnesses.

The Earliest Medical Records: Among the inscriptions on bones and tortoise shells of the mid-Shang period (about the 14th to 13th centuries B.C.), modern scholars have found more than 500 records about illnesses and healing in China. Those records include discussions on disorders of different parts of the human body. A set of technical vocabulary was used to describe different categories of illnesses. Illnesses that were believed to be caused by pernicious weather were called *wind-diseases*. Those believed to be caused by parasites were called *gu*, the symbol for which in the early Chinese pictographic writing system shows venomous insects in human bowels. A description of a decayed tooth inscribed on a piece of bone is believed to be the earliest extant dental record in China.

Medicines and Remedies: The discovery of various herbal and mineral medicines is said to be the major contribution of Shen Nong (sometimes translated as "Divine Peasant"), a demigod emperor in early Chinese legends. According to the legends, Shen Nong experimented with hundreds of species of herbs by ingesting them. When he ingested a poisonous herb, he saved himself by taking an antidote, the most prominent of which was tea leaves. Shen is credited with the authorship of the classic medical text *Shen Nong Bencao* (Shen Nong's Materia Medica), which appeared in the second century B.C., some 10 centuries later than when it is believed he practiced his art of healing. This book is, however, the first Chinese medical text

to give a careful and systematic discussion of the geographic origins, properties, collection methods, and therapeutic value of a great variety of herbs.

After Shen Nong, a group of 10 doctors, led by Peng, is said to have gained, through communications with the supernatural, mastery in the use of various medicinal substances that "helped people fight against death." According to some accounts, this group used more than 120 kinds of medicinal potions of herbal, animal, and mineral origins.

From approximately the 13th to the 12th centuries B.C., decoction became the primary method of administering herbal medicines. The prescribed herbs were boiled in water for a certain length of time, usually 15 to 30 minutes, although the herbs could be boiled for as long as an hour or more for some cases. The boiling process allowed the active components to dissolve in the water. Sustained boiling allowed the dissolved components to react with one another chemically to form a more potent medicinal compound.

Hygiene in the Mid-Shang Period: In the mid-Shang period, about the 12th century B.C., people already knew that bathing and washing one's hair regularly helped one stay healthy. In an excavation site at a Shang village, archeologists found many pieces of pottery pipe and well-like structures believed to be traces of water pipes and a drainage system.

Doctors Working in Specialized Fields: About the 10th century B.C., according to the Confucian classic *Zhou li* (Rituals of Zhou), some doctors began to specialize in fields such as nutrition, internal medicine, surgery, and veterinary medicine. A government office supervised those doctors. At the end of each year, the doctors were required to take examinations to determine their ranks and salaries for the coming year. If a doctor misdiagnosed four cases out of 10, he was labeled *substandard*. Although this picture presented in the *Zhou li* is probably more idealized than real, the account gives a sense of how some early Chinese thought the medical profession should be regulated.

Early Theories on the Causes of Diseases:

In 541 B.C., the Marquis of Jin became ill. Doctors were called in, and their discussion on the cause of his illness was recorded in the early Confucian text *Zuo zhuan*. Taking a firm stand against shamanism, court officials and doctors claimed that the Marquis' disorders had nothing to do with evil spirits or ghosts of mountains and rivers. Instead, said the officials and doctors, the Marquis' promiscuous lifestyle and unbalanced diet were the major causes for his illness. One of the doctors participating in the discussion, Yi He, also specified six harmful weather conditions, including excessive humidity and extreme heat, that might have led to the Marquis' illness.

Bianque:

One of the legendary doctors of early China was a man named Bianque, believed to have lived in the fifth century B.C. According to legend, Bianque's skills were so great that he cured several patients other doctors had declared dead. He is said to be the inventor of "pulse feeling," a technique for diagnosis and prognosis based on feeling a patient's pulse pattern. The remedies and therapies Bianque prescribed included decoction, acupuncture, moxibustion, massage, and breathing exercises. Consistent with Yi He's tradition, Bianque claimed that doctors should never work under the same roof as shamans. Magic or sorcery would not, he emphasized, help to determine if a patient was curable. Instead, careful analysis of the patient's physical condition alone should be the basis for diagnosis.

Bianque is also credited with authoring *Nanjing*, or *The Classic on Difficulties [in Curing Patients]*. But most historians of medicine believe Bianque was not an actual person, but an idealized image that personified the best characteristics of doctors active in the fifth to fourth centuries B.C.

The First Monographs on Medicine:

Unearthed in 1973 in a Han tomb, *Wushier bingfang*, or *The 52 Disorders and the Prescriptions Thereof*, is generally regarded as one of the earliest monographs on medicine. More than 100 diseases are categorized into 52 groups, for which about 300 prescriptions are recommended. Archaeologists date the book as having been compiled in the fourth or third century B.C. About the same time, two other books on acupuncture appeared, with descriptions of 11 "meridians" of acupoints. (*Acupoints* are sensitive spots on the human body that are used in acupuncture.)

Huangdi Neijing, The Yellow Emperor's Classic of Internal Medicine, or The Canon of Medicine:

A comprehensive medical book compiled in this period, *Huangdi Neijing*, remained authoritative for all branches of Chinese medicine, theoretical and practical, until the mid-19th century, when Western medicine was introduced in China. Today, *Huangdi Neijing* remains an essential text for practitioners of traditional Chinese medicine.

The Canon, 18 chapters in total, consists of two parts—one dealing with regular medicine and one with acupuncture. The concepts of yin and yang are employed as a theoretical basis for understanding the functions of the human body and physiological and/or pathological phenomena. Conditions of the human body are analyzed and explained in terms of a balance between these two opposites. When yin and yang are out of balance, a person becomes ill. Although causes of the illness might vary, the illness is in essence no more than an imbalance between these forces. Therefore, the physician's role is to help the patient restore the balance between yin and yang.

According to *The Canon*, food and drink are first digested in the stomach. Then the "lighter elements extracted from food and water" go to the liver, and the "heavier elements" are distributed to all other parts of the body by the blood. The terms for visceral organs and the vascular system designated in *The Canon* are, however, more diagnostic than anatomical. The term *stomach*, for instance, might or might not be the stomach referred to in present-day anatomy; and *qi*, sometimes rendered as "vital energy," hardly finds its equivalent in modern science. This feature of *The Canon* made Chinese understanding of the human body and diseases very different from modern Western understanding.

More than 300 diseases are enumerated in *The Canon* in 44 categories. Malaria, asthma, icteric hepatitis, diabetes, mumps, and hematuria, among many others, are discussed in depth. *The Canon* also recommends tested prescriptions for various illnesses.

The Canon places a great emphasis on preventive care. According to this book, preventing illness is far better than curing illness. In one chapter, a detailed description of abdominal paracentesis for patients with ascites suggests that this technique was actually in use some 2,300 years ago.

2. THE FORMATION OF THE SYSTEM

Chunyu Yi: Most historians believe that Chunyu Yi (also know as Cang Gong, which was his official title and was used by his biographer) was born in 215 or 216 B.C. He was a student first of Yangqing and later of Gongsun Guang, two famous doctors of his time. Yangqing was more than 70 years old when Chunyu Yi became his pupil. Yangqing first introduced Chunyu Yi to Bianque's books and to *The Canon* and taught him the techniques of pulse feeling. A few years later, Yangqing gave Chunyu his notebook of prescriptions, a secret usually shared with only the most trusted disciple. Sometime between 176 and 167 B.C., Chunyu Yi was entangled in a criminal case and was brought to the capital Luoyang for trial. His youngest daughter followed him to the capital and wrote letters to the emperor to plead his case. The emperor, moved by the daughter's filial devotion, pardoned Chunyu Yi.

Chunyu Yi seems to have been extremely successful in his practice. After pardoning him, the emperor sent him an edict commanding him to give an account of his specialty and the cases he treated. In response to the emperor's command, Chunyu reported on his diagnosis of 25 patients in great detail. The cases he reported on involved cirrhosis of the liver, traumatic lumbago, and febricity caused by various reasons, as well as many other disorders. The discussion of each case stated the name of the patient and his or her complaints, then the diagnosis and treatment, and concluded with an analysis of the symptoms, usually supported by citations from the medical canons. These records are the earliest examples of medical case studies.

Zhang Zhongjing: Zhang Zhongjing (c. A.D. 150–211) lived in a time of war and depression. Epidemics swept through China every two or three years. There were outbreaks of epidemics in A.D. 169, 171, 173, 179, 182–185, and 196. According to a report by Zhang, only one-third of his family survived the epidemic of 196. Zhang Zhongjing's training was based on the teachings of Bianque and Chunyu Yi. *The Canon* and *Nanjing* are frequently cited in his writing. Zhang was known as a careful doctor. He achieved the reputation of sage-doctor with his book *Shanghan lun*, or *Treatise on Cold Damage* (sometimes translated as *Treatise on Febrile and Other Diseases*).

Compiled early in the third century A.D., the *Treatise* was edited and amended repeatedly until the Song dynasty (960–1279), when it finally took the shape of two almost independent books: *Treatise on Cold Damage* and *Jingui Yaolue*, or *The Metal Box Collection of Prescriptions*. Historians of medicine agree that the appearance of this esteemed classic in the third century marked the mature systematization of the Chinese art of healing.

The *Treatise* proposes a four-step diagnostic procedure: visual examination, auscultating, inquiring, and pulse feeling. This procedure became the standard in China for some 20 centuries. As for diseases themselves, the *Treatise* categorizes acute fevers into six major groups according to their symptoms. It describes the typical symptoms of each group and uses them as criteria for classification. Then the principles of treatments are summarized into "eight therapies," each of which is designed for a specific clinical condition, such as acute infection, comprehensive weakness, or sluggish digestion. The *Treatise* emphasizes the importance of monitoring the development of a patient's symptoms and suggests different treatments for different stages of the illness. It also discusses mistakes a doctor might make and the probable consequences of those mistakes.

The *Treatise* also discusses 375 prescriptions in which 384 plants, minerals, and even animal parts can be used for therapeutic purposes.

Hua Tuo: A contemporary of Zhang Zhongjing, Hua Tuo (c. A.D. 141–203) was known for his extraordinary surgical skill. He is credited with the invention of mafeisan, an effervescing powder used as an anesthetic. Modern scholars cannot be sure of the precise ingredients of mafeisan, but some historians of medicine believe that marijuana and the flower of datura were most likely the main active components.

The historian Fan Ye (A.D. 398–445) described Hua Tuo's surgery as follows: "[The patient was first served with mafeisan.] When [the patient was] intoxicated and unconscious, he [Hua] opened his [the patient's] body cavity. If the disorder was in the stomach and the intestines, he [Hua] would cut off the bad and dirty parts and clean the rest. After this, he would stitch [the muscles and skin] together, and then apply marvelous ointment [on the surgical area]." After the surgery, the patient usually recovered within a month. According to Fan Ye, Hua Tuo conducted at least two abdominal operations and one orthopedic operation. But some scholars find this type of description of events difficult to accept because they have not found any evidence of adequate surgical instruments from this period.

Hua Tuo believed in the importance of physical exercise for maintaining a healthy body. He invented Games of Five Animals, an exercise that imitates the activities of the tiger, the deer, the crane, the bear, and the monkey to improve physical fitness.

Hua Tuo is also known as a practitioner of acupuncture and moxibustion (burning a cone treated with moxa or mugwort near certain points on the skin). He is credited with discovering a series of acupoints.

Hua Tuo was imprisoned by a warlord because he refused to serve as the warlord's personal physician. Hua is said to have written books about his experiences in medicine, but none have been found.

Materia Medica: Legend has it that Shen Nong was the first Chinese scholar to systematically study plants for their medical use. Historians of medicine know for certain that *Book of Odes* and *Shan hai jing*, or *Classic of Mountains and Seas*, contain information about the uses of 120 plants, minerals, and animal parts in curing and preventing diseases. The compilation of those texts can be dated to as early as the fourth and third centuries B.C. By the end of the second century B.C., *Bencao Jing*, or *Materia Medica*, appeared. This book is believed to be the earliest book on the study of pharmacology.

A comprehensive summary of the knowledge accumulated over centuries, the *Materia Medica* enumerates 365 drugs, presumably matching the number of days in a year. Each of the drugs is described, with its geographic origin, its therapeutic value, and the proper ways of collecting and preserving it. Among the 365 drugs, 252 are of herbal origin, 67 are animal parts or organs, and 46 are minerals.

The *Materia Medica* was apparently designed for clinical use. Diseases and symptoms are discussed, and proper drugs are recommended. Some prescriptions, such as ephedra for cough and asthma, dichroa root for malaria, and seaweed for goiter, have been deemed clearly effective by modern medical standards.

Not all the drugs listed in the book are designated for the treatment of diseases; some supposedly could help people attain Daoist immortality. The drugs are thus graded into three classes: The first class of 120 drugs consists of mainly tonics that were thought to help humans become immortal. The second class, also including 120 drugs, consists of drugs used to improve a person's health in order to prevent disease. The third class consists of medicines used to treat various diseases.

The introduction to *Materia Medica* advocates a sophisticated theory on the combination of drugs. The roles the principal components and their auxiliary parts play in a prescription are analyzed, and the interaction of the drugs when combined are carefully discussed.

The *Materia Medica* was revised in the sixth century A.D. by Tao Hongjing (456–536). The new enlarged and amended version of the book was published in 502 with the new title *Commentaries on Materia Medica*. In this version, 730 medicines, twice as many as in the original, are discussed.

Pharmacological Theory: Early Chinese pharmacologists developed a unique theory to explain the nature of medicines, mainly medicinal herbs. First, they were grouped by "taste:" sour, salty, sweet, bitter, and pungent. Second, they were explained in terms of the four *qi*, described in terms of temperature—cool, cold, warm, and hot. The cold medicines were used to fight against the "hotness" of the body, presumably a fever; and the warm medicines, usually tonics, were used to warm the body when it was weak and when the patient experienced an uncomfortable chilly feeling.

Decoction, pills, and powder were the most common methods to administer medicines to a patient. Alternative methods, such as soaking in, or washing with, hot water or wine or vinegar, are also mentioned from time to time in the medical classics.

Drugs were supposed to be used in combination so that their therapeutic function could be promoted and toxicity restrained. A compound prescription might incorporate more than a dozen different items.

Pulse-Feeling Diagnosis: Viewing the human body as a whole, traditional Chinese medicine believes that illness in one part of the body affects the appearance and function of other parts. For example, coating on the tongue, the texture of the nails, and certain sensitive spots on the skin are all of diagnostic significance. Among the various external manifestations of a person's health, the pulse pattern is considered the most important.

Bianque, the medical scholar of the fifth century B.C., had already singled out the pulse as an important indicator of a person's physical condition. From Bianque's time on, doctors such as Chunyu Yi and Zhang Zhongjing made great effort to improve the technique of pulse feeling. Notes on what they experienced and learned in practice can be found throughout their books. Based on this accumulated knowledge, the first monograph on the technique of pulse feeling and its application in diagnosis came in the second century B.C.

The authorship of *Mai jing*, or *Classic on Pulse*, was at first attributed to Wang Shuhe (c. A.D. 180–270). But modern philologists have shown that a considerable part of the book is a summary of the writings of other pioneer doctors, especially Zhang Zhongjing, who might have taught Wang. In any case, Wang was an erudite scholar and an experienced doctor. His compilation represents the systematization of the theory of pulse-feeling diagnostics.

In the practice of pulse-feeling diagnosis, the doctor would gently press his fingers on the pulse on a patient's wrist and deduce the patient's condition based on the strength and pattern of the pulse. *Mai jing* defines 24 different conditions of the pulse and their corresponding diagnostic significance. For instance, a "floating" pulse is defined as follows: The pulse is easily felt when the doctor places his fingers lightly on the patient's wrist, but weakens notably when the wrist is pressed harder. This kind of pulse points to an "external" disease, or a disease caused by some external pathological factors. It may also suggest that the disease is "cold" in nature and that the patient's vital energy is declining.

The patterns of the patient's pulse vary according to the patient's age, sex, general physical condition, the weather, and the season. Needless to say, pulse-feeling diagnosis depended greatly on the practitioner's personal experience and was to some measure subjective. Modern research, however, has shown that pulse-feeling diagnosis, when used by a competent practitioner, can be an effective diagnostic technique.

Acupuncture: *Acupuncture* is a therapeutic treatment unique to traditional Chinese medicine. The word comes from the

Latin prefix *acu*, "needle," and *puncture*. The basic idea of acupuncture is to change a patient's physical condition by sticking extremely thin and fine needles into one or more selected points on the body. These points are called *acupoints*.

When and by whom acupuncture was invented is not known. Historical documents suggest that as early as the eighth century B.C. some practitioners were using metal needles for therapeutic purposes. The advantage of acupuncture is that it costs little and usually has no side effects. The disadvantage is that the effectiveness depends heavily on the mastery and experience of the practitioner. When the practitioner is skillful, the cure may be prompt. In untrained hands, however, the needles can often be ineffective and even dangerous.

By the second century B.C., acupuncture had already become one of the major procedures of Chinese medicine. In the third century A.D., Huangfu Mi (215–282) composed *Jiayi jing*, or *Classic of Acupuncture*, in which he systematically summarized previous knowledge on this healing art and offered his opinions on the procedure.

Huangfu led an adventurous life in his teens and early twenties. Believing in the miraculous quality of a certain mineral drug for strengthening the body, he took an overdose and was almost paralyzed. This episode is said to be the direct reason for his decision to study medicine. After studying several major works on medicine, he found there was a need for a comprehensive treatise on acupuncture. He therefore compiled one. In 256, the book, *Jiayi jing*, was completed and has been the classic in this field ever since.

Jiayi jing deals with the diagnosis and acupuncture treatment of illnesses. The book includes 118 articles which are grouped into 12 volumes, according to types of diseases. The major contribution of this book is that, based on the experience accumulated in previous centuries, it defines and describes 349 acupoints. Among these points, 49 are "single points," acupoints near or along the spine; 300 are "double points," acupoints located symmetrically on the body and the four limbs. *Jiayi jing* also discusses the relationship between regular diagnostic theory and the theory of acupuncture. In addition, *Jiayi jing* provides information on technical details of the manipulation of the needle, such as the depth of puncture at a certain acupoint and the length of time the needle should be left at the acupoint to attain maximum effectiveness. The indications and contraindications are also discussed.

Moxibustion: A treatment developed along with acupuncture is moxibustion, which calls for igniting a cone or a stick prepared with moxa or mugwort (*Artemisia vulgaris L.*) near certain sensitive points on the skin. Moxibustion and acupuncture share the same theory of vital energy. According to this theory, the human body has a system of "meridians," through which *qi* circulates. Stimulating particular points on these meridians can affect the energy balance of the human body. Along with acupuncture, moxibustion has been employed by medical practitioners in China for more than 20 centuries. Although moxibustion has proved effective, its effectiveness, like that of acupuncture, remains unexplained by modern science.

3. THE DAOIST CONTRIBUTION

The Daoist Tradition: Although claiming allegiance to classic Daoist philosophy, followers of religious Daoism developed ideas that were quite foreign to classic philosophers. One of the key concerns of religious Daoists was the search for immortality. For this purpose, some religious Daoists developed various forms of alchemy, not for gold but for an elixir, a miracle drug that would help a human become immortal.

Ge Hong: One of the most prominent scholars in religious Daoist alchemy was Ge Hong (A.D. 281–340). Ge was born in poverty, so he worked as a woodcutter and traded in stationery to support his studies. He devoted himself to reading the classics and sometimes traveled thousands of miles to consult a learned scholar. Ge became known as an erudite scholar in pharmacology and alchemy.

Ge's book *Baopuzi*, or *The Master Who Embraced Simplicity*, advocates two routes to longevity, the *daoyin*, a method that helps regulate the *qi* of the body, and the fushi, the systematic ingesting of food and drugs. Ge regarded the study of medicine as the preliminary stage in the long process of enabling human beings to become immortal. To Ge Hong, *fushi* was the best way to achieve immortality.

Ge Hong is often credited as the first person to describe smallpox, phthisis, hepatitis, acute lymphangitis, and the incubation period for rabies. His *Yuhan Fang*, a collection of medical recipes, was lost except for the preface and 86 recipes from volume 93, which was later titled *Zhouhou jiuzu fang*, or *Recipes for Emergency*. One of Ge's main concerns was to help the poor and those living in remote areas. The recipes he recommended, therefore, consisted of only inexpensive and easy-to-find drugs. *Recipes* was edited and enlarged by Tao Hongjing. It is known to modern students of medicine as *Zhouhou Beiji Fang*, or *Handy Recipes for Emergencies*.

Tao Hongjing: Tao Hongjing (452–536) was born at a time when Buddhism was at its peak of influence in China. He is the acknowledged successor of Ge Hong. Tao dreamed of becoming immortal, just as Ge Hong had. In 492, Tao went to Mountain Mao and began his study of medicine. He also studied Confucian classics for some forty years. When he died, Tao was a master of Daoism. His claim to fame, however, is as the editor of Ge Hong's *Handy Recipes* and as the annotator of *Materia Medica*.

Tao Hongjing's *Bencao jing jizhu*, or *The Annotation of Materia Medica*, is a pharmacopoeia based on the *Materia Medica*, the ancestor of all monographs on medical herbs and minerals. In addition to the 365 drugs listed in the original *Materia Medica*, the *Annotation* discusses 365 more drugs. The 730 drugs are categorized into seven groups, some of which are minerals, herbs, fruits and berries, crops and grains. For each drug entry, the original text of the *Materia Medica* is copied in red ink, followed by Tao's annotations in black ink. For a drug not mentioned in the *Materia Medica*, the entire entry is in black ink. Following the practice of *Materia Medica*, the *Annotation* includes a discussion of the place of origin of the drug, its method of collection, its morphology, and an appraisal of its medical usefulness. In annotating the *Materia Medica*, Tao employed many collections of medical recipes, such as Ge's *Recipes* and Wang's *Recipes*. Tao also interviewed drug collectors and double-checked the descriptions he found in classics by personally examining each drug described. This meticulous effort made the *Annotation* a valuable and reliable reference for later doctors and a model for authors of later works on medical herbs and minerals.

Mineral Medicines: The final goal of Daoist alchemy was to find the elixir, the miracle drug that would help human beings attain longevity and, in its ultimate form, help humans become celestial immortals. At first the Daoist adepts favored certain herbs and fungi. But as time passed, the Daoists became increasingly attracted to *jinshi yao*, or "metal and stone agents," hoping that the durability and immortality of stone and metal could be transmitted to human bodies. The Reign of Emperor Wu of the Han dynasty saw the first records of "mineral drugs." By the third century B.C., Ge Hong had spent more than half his *Baopuzi* discussing the preparation of the elixir in which mineral drugs played the primary role. He started with realgar, chalcanthite, saltpeter, mica, loadstone, iron, table salt, tin, and arsenic. (To modern pharmacologists, some of those would be the last things to include in a recipe for longevity.) Ge also used, as European alchemists would 10 centuries later, sulfate acid, quicksilver, and sulfur. He failed to attain longevity, but he did find a number of "minerals," or inorganic compounds, that proved medically useful. Examples of such compounds included arsenic oxide for malaria, mercurous chloride for certain skin diseases, and mercury chloride, used as a germicide. Such medical uses of inorganic compounds were to develop further during the Tang dynasty (618–907).

In search of the elixir, Ge Hong and other Daoist alchemists came to know how to distill, to melt, to sublime, to crystallize. They also developed a set of chemical apparatus for drug processing and preparation.

Hanshi san: One of the most popular mineral drugs used during the late third century through the early fourth century was *Hanshi san*, or "Pulvis of Eating Things Cold." Pulvis is so named because the body of the person taking pulvis became so "heated" that the person had to counteract the heat by eating only cold foods. Pulvis was ground from a hard solid drug. If the pulvis was to be used in decoction, the hard solid drug was milled into coarse granules. If the pulvis was to be swallowed with water, the hard solid drug was ground into a fine powder. These methods seemed to be the only ways to make pulvis edible.

Hanshi san, the major ingredients of which were stalactite, amethyst, and sulfur, was said to be helpful in strengthening the body. The real effect of *Hanshi san* was never clear to doctors, although many medical notes from its heyday reported that it helped patients, especially those with a lavish lifestyle. Ironically for most later users of *Hanshi san* looking for longevity, this drug often resulted in poisoning and sometimes sudden death. Huangfu Mi, the author of the first systematic study of acupuncture, for example, suffered so much from poisoning that he once tried to kill himself. In addition, a number of Tang emperors were known to have died of *Hanshi san* poisoning.

The misfortunes of *Hanshi san* users did not lead the Daoist adepts to abandon its use immediately. Instead, they embarked on an occult study of how to use this drug properly. Daoist adepts and their believers were convinced the users, not the drug, were at fault. The later part of the third century A.D. saw a flood of books discussing the drug, many of which developed recipes for antidotes. Some historians of medicine consider the discussion helpful in understanding drug preparation and human physiology and pathology.

4. THE SUI-TANG PERIOD

The Causes and Symptoms of Diseases: By A.D. 581, the Sui empire (581–618) had reunified China after a long period of division. The energetic new dynasty sponsored the compilation of an encyclopedia of symptoms of diseases and their causes. Chao Yuanfang, the imperial physician at the court, supervised the project. The resulting book became known to later students of medicine as *Zhubing yuanhou lun*, or *Causes and Symptoms of Diseases*.

Zhubing yuanhou lun was completed in 610. It is divided into 67 parts, each of which focuses on one or two major causes of diseases. The first part, for example, discusses "wind dizziness," which in the terminology of Chinese traditional medicine stood for the symptoms caused by hypertension and related diseases. During the time of Chao Yuanfang, the "ill-wind" was drawing serious attention among medical researchers and practitioners, as seen in monographs such as *Fengxuan Fang*, or *Recipes for Wind Dizziness*, written by Xu Cibo.

Among the 1,726 articles on symptomatology and etiology in *Causes and Symptoms of Diseases*, many were of great significance for clinical diagnosis and the theoretical study of diseases. The causes of infectious diseases are identified as "external," which could therefore be avoided by proper preventive measures. As for parasites, the book first records the symptom of the whitish segments of taenia in human waste and then speculates that the cause might be "eating beef not well cooked." It also describes itch-mite, and points out correctly that this skin disease is caused by a "small insect." Allergies are related to the nature of the individual body: "When the nature of the body could not stand lacquer, the individual would be poisoned; . . . while for those tolerant to lacquer, they would not be hurt even when dealing with lacquer day after day." Common diseases, such as apoplexy, facial neuralgia, lymphnoditis, pneumonic plague, amoebic and bacillary dysentery, and tuberculosis, are described correctly. Diabetes is sometimes confused with other disorders, but the major symptoms are singled out precisely, especially the unbearable thirstiness and emaciation, symptoms which caused diabetes to be known as "disease of emaciation and thirstiness."

The Causes and Symptoms of Diseases became the standard textbook at institutes of medicine in China soon after it appeared and remained one of the main sources for descriptions of diseases that many later works cited.

The New Pharmacopoeia: About 50 years after the appearance of *Causes and Symptoms of Diseases*, an encyclopedia of medical herbs and other agents was edited under the sponsorship of the Tang government. Twenty-two learned scholars and experienced doctors, led by Su Jing, worked for two years on the first government-sponsored pharmacopoeia in Chinese history, the *Xinxiu Bencao*, or *New Pharmacopoeia*, which was completed in 659.

The descriptions of medicinal herbs in *New Pharmacopoeia* are based on the study of life specimens. "Life specimens" are specimens that are still alive, as opposed to specimens that are already dead. The significance of this is that the doctors studying these herbs are getting their hands dirty and get as close to the real plants as possible, instead of relying on dried-out plants provided by medicine shops. The Tang emperor ordered all local governments to send samples of drugs to the capital to be studied by the editors of the book. Sketches of these samples were attached to their descriptions. Amendments and corrections were made on philological studies of medical classics. Materials were added from information received from thousands of local medical practitioners. In addition to traditional drugs, more than 20 nontraditional drugs, opium for instance, are included. "Silver paste," or an amalgam of one portion of mercury, about half a portion of silver, and nine portions of tin, is for the first time mentioned as a caulk-like mixture for filling cavities in teeth.

The *New Pharmacopoeia* is divided into three parts: 20 volumes of basic description, 25 volumes of illustrations, and 7 volumes of explanations and discussions. Some 850 herbal drugs are included. Among these, 114 are first recorded here.

This voluminous encyclopedia was, unfortunately, too bulky to copy and too difficult to publish. After the civil war and social upheaval that lasted one-and-a-half centuries during the later part of the Tang period, only parts of the volumes of "basic description" survived.

Internal Diseases: Chinese doctors in the seventh and eighth centuries developed precise knowledge of tuberculosis, leprosy, diabetes, and rabies. Medical notes and historical records of the time mention doctors with expertise in treating particular diseases. For example, Liu De specialized in asthenia; Shi Tuo, in jaundice; and Gong Tai, in respiratory disorders.

Tuberculosis was identified as a consumptive disease. Doctors generally identified emaciation, cough, hemoptysis, and night sweating as typical symptoms of this illness. Su You's monograph on tuberculosis, which he called "corpse infectious disease," was regarded as a direct response to the epidemic of the deadly disease from 618 to 626. And Chen Chuan clearly pointed out excessive urination and excessive thirst as key symptoms of diabetes.

Beriberi was first mentioned by Zhang Zhongjing, who also noted that dietary treatments were generally helpful. Although Zhang had no concept of vitamin deficiency, he recommended foods rich in vitamins. In the seventh century, monographs on beriberi enhanced the reputations of Xu Shuxiang, Xu Wenbo, Tang Lin, and Su Jing, contributors to the *New Pharmacopoeia*.

Surgery: As reported in *The Causes and Symptoms of Diseases*, the anastomosis of ruptured intestines and surgical repairs of harelip were performed during the Tang dynasty. Books such as *Secret Healing of Wounds, Fractures, and Dislocations*, dated 841, systematically described how to wash wounds, apply skeletal traction, use splints, and administer an ointment made of glutinous rehmannia and other drugs. The idea of sterilization appears occasionally in the book. The use of a bamboo curtain as a splint is recommended for wound healing because the curtain leaves the wound exposed to fresh air, thus helping to prevent the wound from festering.

Gynecology, Obstetrics, and Pediatrics: *The Causes and Symptoms of Diseases* spends eight volumes discussing female diseases, such as continuous uterine bleeding. The major attention of the doctors, however, focused on *zhengjia*, or tumors in female organs. Xu Wenbo, who once served as court physician, is said to have cured a maid in the imperial palace of tumors of this kind. He later wrote *The Cure of a Female "Jia,"* which is believed the first treatise in the field of gynecology.

Xu Zhicai, another court physician during the Beiqi dynasty (550–577), wrote on obstetrics. Appearing in A.D. 847, Jiu Ying's treatise on pregnancy, labor, and the care of newborns is the first monograph in the field of obstetrics. He emphasized that a quiet and clean environment is important for lying-in women and discussed how emergencies during labor should be handled. Xu also wrote *Pediatric Prescriptions*, although his reputation in pediatrics did not match his reputation in obstetrics.

Slightly later than Xu's work, came *Lucong Jing*, or *Classic of Cranial Bones and Fontanel*, by an unknown author. This book discusses infantile convulsion, epilepsy, dysentery, and erysipelas, all common childhood diseases. The book recommends tortoiseshell for rickets. Since the 19th century, Western scientists have known that tortoiseshell is particularly rich in vitamin D, which is essential for curing rickets.

Sun Simiao and Wang Tao: Along with the encyclopedias sponsored by the government, individual scholars and doctors edited voluminous works on medical knowledge during the Sui-Tang period. Among those scholars and doctors, Sun Simiao and Wang Tao are the most prominent.

Sun Simiao (c. 581–682) practiced medicine in his native town Huayuan, not far from Chang'an (modern Xi'an), the capital of the Tang empire. He was known as a hard-working student and a solicitous doctor. Throughout his life, he diligently read the classics on medicine. He also traveled thousands of miles to consult with other doctors. He was under the influence of Daoism and was interested in the quest for immortality. Although he obviously did not achieve immortality, he did live to the age of 101. And he achieved lasting fame with his book *Qian jin fang*, or *Invaluable Prescriptions*, and its supplement, which were completed in 652 and 682, respectively, when he was probably 70 and 100 years old, respectively.

Invaluable Prescriptions: The title of this book was based on the belief that human life is invaluable, and so the prescriptions that help save or prolong it are also invaluable. According to Sun Simiao, medical knowledge was meaningful because this skill enabled the emperor and his subjects to be cured of their diseases, might save the poor and the lowly from their difficulties, and enabled the medical man himself to enjoy longevity. The moral principle for medical practitioners was summarized in Sun's slogan, "No pursuit after material award; no regret before professional dignity." This standard of morality became the first principle for later students of medicine.

The main body of the *Invaluable Prescriptions* is a vast collection of tested prescriptions, many of which were selected from the *Canon*, the *Febrile*, and journals of well-known doctors such as Wang Shuhe (c. third century A.D.) and Chen Yanzhi (dates unknown).

Invaluable Prescriptions also incorporates many prescriptions not listed in the classics. Those include: areca for taeniasis, the root of Chinese pulsatilla and the rhizome of Chinese goldthread for dysentery, and henbane for cough, all of which Sun presumably learned about from local medical practitioners who had tried many kinds of herbs to cure illness. The medical effects of common foods is another topic first addressed in this book. Delicacies are not necessarily good food, Sun preached. Instead, he said, the best food should be what the body needs. Some 150 diets are recommended in *Invaluable Prescriptions*: Animal livers for night blindness, grains for beriberi, for example. Sun's pupil Meng Xian (621–714) developed Sun's study of nutrition into a book, which is the first monograph on nutrition in the history of medicine.

The Supplement: By the time he was 100 years old, Sun had finished his second book, which was modestly named a "supplement" to the first. The main body of this supplement is a pharmacopoeia of more than 800 drugs, of which 200 are described with details on collecting and processing. The discussion on cold-damage diseases, apoplexy, and boils and carbuncles are original and became classic text soon after the publication of the supplement.

Philological Studies on Medical Books: Wang Tao (675–755) was born into a family who for generations was in the civil service. He suffered from a severe illness in his boyhood. In his teens, he was distraught when he found that he did not have enough medical knowledge to help his sick mother. Those experiences made reading medical classics a lifelong interest for him. Taking advantage of his access to the royal library, a privilege limited to court scholars, Wang read and copied "several thousand volumes of medical manuscripts, dating from ancient times down to the Tang dynasty. This intensive study resulted in a compendium of 40 volumes.

Waitai miyao, or *Medical Secrets Held by an Official*, written by Wang, is, as its title indicates, a classic written by a medical amateur. Consisting of 1,104 articles, this book reviews "all diseases known to physicians of our time" and more than 6,000 prescriptions. Each entry starts with a citation from *Causes and Symptoms*, then enumerates the related prescriptions, and concludes with Wang's comments and amendments. Wang is the first author of medical books to make the titles and volume numbers of every citation available to his readers. When most of the books Wang cited were lost in the upheaval that broke out four years after the publication of *Medical Secrets Held by an Official*, Wang's compendium, finished in 752, became in many cases the only access for later doctors and scholars to the lost classics.

Medical Administration: Medical administration had been in part a government responsibility since at least as early as the Han dynasty in the second century B.C. The extant documents of the Jin dynasty (265–419) showed that a complicated bureaucracy for medical administration had been established in the second or third century A.D. The department in charge of medical administration was headed by the *Taiyi Ling* (the imperial physician in chief), who supervised the medical service for the royal family, the preparation of drugs, the publication of medical books, and the training and testing of physicians. By the Sui dynasty, this department had more than 200 employees; and by the Tang dynasty, the number had reached as high as 340. In 624, the Tang Bureau of Medicine established a botanical garden for medicinal herbs, where the central school of medicine was also built.

Tang emperors decreed repeatedly that medicine be stored in temples and other public buildings in preparation for epidemics and natural catastrophes and that hospitals be built for those who could not care for themselves. Laws regulating medical practitioners were enacted in 653. Medical malpractice could bring a physician about two-and-a-half years' imprisonment. An intentional alteration of a prescription that caused the death of the patient was deemed the equivalent of premeditated murder.

Medical Education: Medical education was from its very beginning a government enterprise. The first medical school was founded in 443 but lasted only 10 years. In 469, the court heard a petition for reforming medical education and administration because "many doctors were incompetent, and the people were so disappointed that they went to witches instead." Not until 629 during the prosperity of the Tang dynasty, however, did the government finally consider a national system of medical education. After a century's effort, in 723, a nationwide system of medical education was established. Even in the most remote province a medical school was, as documents indicate, to be established "at a separate section of the county school compound."

The central medical school in the capital Chang'an was a well-organized institute. Students started with a common program on the basics of medicine. The *Canon*, the *Materia Medica*, the *Classic of Acupuncture*, and the *Classic of Pulse-feeling Diag-*

nosis were required reading. After an examination, those qualified were selected for advanced studies in specialties. There were four departments in the school: clinical medicine, acupuncture, traumatology and orthopedics, and supplication, or the skill of averting diseases by praying. The forty physicians in the department of clinical medicine were further divided into five specialized groups. Doctors in the first group, internal medicine, required seven years of study. Those in the other four groups, pediatrics, external medicine, ENT (the field of specialization in ear, nose and throat), dentistry, and physical therapy,

each underwent a five-year course of study. The 20 students in acupuncture studied Huangfu Mi's book. The students in traumatology learned skills in physical exercises and therapeutic massage in addition to how to deal with wounds and fractured bones.

Students were tested each month to measure their progress. Those who failed twice in the finals were expelled. Those who graduated with good grades were appointed to key positions in the government for medical administration or to teaching positions in local medical schools.

5. A Period of Great Progress

The Song Versions of Pharmacopoeia:
In 973, the Song government commissioned Liu Han (*fl.* c. 954–973) and eight other scholars to compile a new edition of the *Materia Medica*. The basis of the work was the *New Pharmacopoeia* of the Tang and the *Shu Bencao*, a micropedia of drugs finished under the auspices of the Shu (in the area now known as Sichuan) government during 938–965. The book was finished in a year. A revised edition appeared in the next year and proved much better. The book, titled *Kaibao Pharmacopoeia* after the name of the emperor's reign (*Kaibao*), enumerates 983 drugs, some 140 more than its Tang predecessor. In the late 1050s, the Song government ordered all local governments to send in samples of drugs used or produced within their jurisdictions, which inspired a still newer edition of the pharmacopoeia, *Jiayou Pharmacopoeia*, which discusses 1,082 drugs in 20 volumes. A collection of illustrations of the drugs came out the following year, facilitating the recognition and collection of the drugs discussed in the *Jiayou Pharmacopoeia*.

The nationwide collection for medical herbs encouraged many doctors to contribute their expertise to the enterprise of "exhausting all the herbs that help" in the treatment of illnesses. Tang Shenwei (*fl.* c 1102), a renowned doctor in Sichuan, revised the existing *Pharmacopoeia* and compiled a new book titled *Zhenlei Phar-*

macopoeia, which includes 1,558 drugs and more than 3,000 prescriptions. For each drug included, there are citations from medical classics, discussions for contraindications and incompatibilities, instructions for preparing and processing the drug, and illustrations to help in identifying the drug. This book was soon adopted by the government and published in 1108. The second revised edition of this book, dated 1157, which incorporates 1,748 drugs, remained the major reference book in the field of pharmacology until 1578, when Li Shizhen's *Bencao gangmu* was published.

The Administration and Education:
In 987, the Song emperor issued a decree summoning all "celebrated doctors" to the capital Kaifeng for consultation. In 992, the emperor added to the bureaucracy established under the Tang government two more departments for medical administration, namely the Department of Drug Sales and the Department of Drug Preparation. The purpose of these departments was to enable commoners to obtain medicine safely and conveniently. Those departments supervised the prices and quality of medicines sold to the public. During epidemics, the departments offered free medicine to those who could not afford to buy needed medicines.

The Song government also established institutions of medical education. At the Bureau of Imperial Doctors, located in the capital, at any point in time some 300 students studied medical theories. Their progress in understanding the classics was tested annually. When students were ready to help patients, they practiced by assisting senior doctors at clinics affiliated with the bureau. Following the traditional definition of the art of healing, teaching was divided into nine specialties that included internal medicine, pediatrics, ulceration and abscess, ophthalmology, obstetrics, and acupuncture. The prestige of the bureau was such that the tests it used were often discussed in writings of leading doctors of that period. The bureau's Bronze Figures, a pair of bronze statues with all the acupoints marked to facilitate students' learning the positions of the acupoints, marked a monumental achievement in the teaching of acupuncture, as well as in the systematization of previous knowledge in acupoints. The figures were so well known that the Jurchens, the northerners who sacked the Northern Song capital of Kaifeng in 1126, demanded to have them as a condition for their armistice with the Song empire in 1128.

The Publication of Medical Books: In 1026, by order of the emperor the Song government commissioned scholars to direct a project of collecting, editing, and amending medical books submitted by all local governments. This project became the function of an official department (*Jiaozheng yishu ju*, or "The Bureau for Editing Medical Books") in 1057. A great number of medical classics, which had been copied by hand and pigeonholed in the imperial library, were published with the newly developed technology of printing. The *Canon*, the *Cold Damage*, *The Causes and Symptoms*, the *Classics of Acupuncture*, and the *Invaluable Prescriptions*, among many others, became affordable references on desks of almost all doctors.

The Collection of Prescriptions: Another Song governmental project was the collection of prescriptions. As early as 992, a gigantic collection of prescriptions was completed under the auspices of the emperor. In 1,670 volumes, the *Taiping shenghui fang*, or *Taiping Collection of Prescriptions*, incorporated 16,834 prescriptions that had been proved effective through clinical tests. The structure of the book is traditional in that each chapter starts with citations from *The Causes and Symptoms*, followed by comments and pathological studies, and ends with a complete set of related prescriptions. The prescriptions were either recommended by celebrated doctors in their books or were proved effective in practice. This compilation was revised from 1111 to 1117. The revised work, bearing the new title *Shenji zonglu*, contains more than 20,000 prescriptions, which are discussed in detail.

A concise version of the original compilation, *Heji jufang*, or *Officially Approved Medical Formulas for People's Welfare*, appeared in 1110. Intended to be a guidebook for the Department of Pharmacies, the book became one of the most influential in Chinese medical history. This useful handbook had 297 prescriptions, grouped in 21 categories for the user's convenience. Often referred to as *Jufang*, or "official [officially approved] prescriptions," the book recommends prescriptions that were so competent and effective that, unexpectedly and ironically, doctors tended to use them as set formulas and did little investigation of their own. As a result, medical practice became more and more a dogmatic routine and involved fewer and fewer thoughtful investigations into the causes of illnesses.

Pediatrics: In the 11th century, pediatrics became a branch of medical practice clearly separated from other specialties. As reported by one of his pupils, Qian Yi (1032–1113) had developed a comprehensive guideline for treating children and infants. The major physiological feature of children and infants, Qian said, was that their bodies and organs had not reached full growth. Accordingly, the yin-yang balance of their bodies could be easily disturbed by illness. This instability often resulted in a changeable pattern of excess and deficiency syndromes. Qian advised doctors to use mild and small doses of prescriptions when treating children. Qian processed and prepared counterweighted medicines. One such medicine was *Liuwei dihuang wan*, or rehmannia pills, which became a classic formula for later pharmacists soon after it came into use. Qian paid great attention to the most common childhood diseases, such as chicken pox, scarlet fever, and smallpox, but he was not impeccable in differentiating them.

In the winter of 1092, an epidemic of smallpox in Shandong triggered an intensive study of the disease. Many theories were proposed. Some doctors recommended purgation; others suggested antidotes. The following year, Dong Ji's monograph *On Prescriptions for Reddish or Purplish Patches* appeared. It incorporated a detailed discussion on smallpox.

During the 1150s, comprehensive treatises on obstetrics appeared. New methods of caring for mothers and newborns were introduced. To prevent tetanus, for example, doctors advised that the knife for cutting the umbilical cord should be heated until it turned red—in other words, sterilized.

Internal Medicine: The traditional discussion on fevers caused by "cold damage" developed into a new phase of medicine in 1181, when Guo Yong (1109–1187) refined the general theory of cold damage to analyze latent pathogens, new infections, and acute cold-damage diseases. Pestilence came to doctors' attention during the Song empire when the Chinese economic center moved from the north to the south, where warm and humid weather aggravated epidemics. Beriberi, a syndrome caused by deficiency of vitamin B1, had been recorded during the Tang dynasty, yet the first systematic study of beriberi appeared only in 1039, when Dong Ji published his monograph discussing the cause of beriberi, its symptoms, and its remedies.

The 12th century first saw the appearance of the word *ai* (which means "cancer") in Chinese medical terminology. The clear description of the tumor was found in the medical text *Renzhai yifang lun*, published in 1264. *Ai*, as suggested by the pictographic character, was said to be like a piece of rock, hard and rough to the touch.

Anatomy: The earliest mention of dissecting a human body was in *The Canon*. A more refined record was made in the first century A.D. when the usurper Wang Mang had the bodies of his opponents dissected. However, medical drawings of human organs extracted by doctors were first made in the 11th century. In the 1040s,

after putting down a rebellion, local officials called in medical doctors and artists to study the rebels' corpses. In two days, the professionals dissected 56 bodies. They carefully recorded the shape and location of various organs in pictures and in words. In the early 1100s, a similar study was made when a criminal was executed. The chest, abdomen, digestive system, urinary tract, and reproductive organs were all depicted in a record of the dissection. The illustrations were supported with written descriptions, and pathological changes were occasionally noted.

Forensic Medicine: Song Ci (1186–1249) was the first Chinese medical scholar to devote all his talent to forensic science. Serving a long time as a high-ranking officer in criminal court, Song Ci assisted coroners with autopsies and read many books and articles dealing with criminal investigation. In 1247, his encyclopedic manual on forensic medicine came out in five volumes. The title of this book is *Xiyuan lu*, or *The Washing Away of Wrongs*. The first volume deals with laws and regulations regarding crime. The remaining volumes discuss anatomy, autopsy, fieldwork at a crime scene, determination of the cause of death, and the differences that denote suicide and homicide. The study of toxicology, first aid, and emergency management are other topics discussed in Song's *The Washing Away of Wrongs*.

Shen Gua on Pharmacopoeia: In addition to his great contribution to the recording and studying of natural phenomena, Shen Gua (also pronounced "Shen Kuo"), a leading scholar in the Song empire, corrected many mistakes from previous pharmacopoeias. During his study of medicinal herbs, he found that the same drug had been given different names by different authors. He also discovered that in some cases earlier writers had mistaken different species for the same kind of plant. In 1075, along with Su Song, another leading scholar in the Song empire, Shen published a collection of prescriptions titled *Su Shen liangfang*, or *Su and Shen's Good Prescriptions*. In the preface to this book, Shen declared proudly, "I witnessed with my own eyes the effectiveness of all the prescriptions incorporated in this book; information based on hearsay alone [has been] excluded."

The preparation of "autumn stone" (extracts from urine) has attracted serious attention of historians of medicine. As reported by Shen since the 11th century A.D., the Chinese had been able to derive sex hormones from human urine by sublimation. From that time on, Chinese scholars recorded at least 10 different methods of obtaining sex hormones and pituitary hormones from urine.

One of the striking features in the development of Chinese medicine is that the contributors were often scholars, not professional practitioners with clinical experience. No evidence suggests that Shen or Su had ever established a full-time practice, but their expertise in medicine has never been questioned.

Medical Science in the Jin and the Yuan: By the end of the Song dynasty, the Chinese government was no longer able to organize statewide research and publication projects as it had some two centuries earlier. As time passed, the authorized explanations of the medical classics and the old "official prescriptions" promoted by the government were questioned with increasing frequency. Along with this trend, doctors developed their own theories and remedies for diseases. Schools of medical thought were formed, of which four were exceptionally influential. (Note that *school* here means "school of thought," not an actual institution of learning.)

Liu Wansu and "Cold and Cool School": Liu Wansu (c. A.D. 1120–1200) was the first to found a distinctive school of medical thought. Liu Wansu was born during the Jin, the Jurchen dynasty that ruled much of north China from A.D. 1127 to 1279. Liu was deeply involved in the practice of Daoism. Legend has it that Liu was helped by a celestial being in a dream when he was working on the *Canon.* The dream illuminated medical theories so clearly and caused Liu's mind and eyesight to become acute. Liu advocated the building up of the *qi*, or inner energy of the splenetic system through the use of mainly cooling medicines. That was in direct contradiction to the traditional treatment prescribed by "official prescriptions," which

called for heating medicines. Liu assumed that the cause of the splenetic disorder was an agent that had the nature of fire; he therefore sought medicine that would help dampen the "fire." This strategy was reportedly successful in clinical practice and made his reputation as a distinguished doctor. Because of his unique theory, this school of thought is generally called the "Cold and Cool School."

Zhang Congzheng (1156–1228), who was one of Liu Wansu's disciples, combined Liu's doctrine with his (Zhang's) experience in practice and founded a new school of medical thought known as the "Purging School." Zhang agreed with Liu's theory that the cause of disorder was "fire." According to Zhang, the best way to attack this "ill-fire" was to purge it. Purging relieved stagnation, which eliminated the pathogenic heat. The elimination of pathogenic heat drove out the bad *qi* and excreted accumulated water through perspiration and vomiting. Zhang became so well known that the emperor invited him to be a court physician. However, not long after becoming a court physician, he resigned because he was "unable to tolerate the ritual formalities."

Unlike Liu Wansu, Zhang Congzheng was under Confucian influence. He believed that medical knowledge was a necessary tool for fulfilling the filial duty required by Confucianism. Zhang made medical knowledge one of the prerequisites for becoming a Confucian scholar. Partly through Zhang's efforts, the social value of medicine became better recognized in China.

While Zhang Congzheng was concentrating on counterattacking the ill-fire, Li Gao (1180–1251) was elaborating on the need to strengthen the body's defense against illness. Li believed that since the intake of food provided the only source of energy for the body, digestion was of primary importance for health. Instead of using purgation, which he regarded as harmful to the stomach and, therefore, for digestion, Li Gao claimed that the main goal of clinical treatment was to help the patient through the use of tonics to build up a healthy and strong yang, or vital fire. The main focus of Li's medical theory was that the digestive organs, namely the spleen and the stomach, should be nourished so that the vital fire would be nourished. For this reason, his school of thought was called the "Spleen-Nourishing School."

Zhu Zhenheng (1281–1358), the founder of the fourth and perhaps the most influential school of medical theory, was first trained as a Confucian scholar. When he failed the civil service examination, his interest turned to medicine. After many years of study, Zhu decided that the best ways to help people were to be either a good official or a good doctor. After reading Liu's books and some collections of Li Gao's prescriptions, Zhu came to the conclusion that Zhang Congzheng's method of treating patients was too reckless. He then worked with Luo Zhidi (dates unknown), a famous Daoist doctor. Zhu first tried his medical knowledge on his Confucian teacher and cured him of a disease that had persisted for years. That success led to a long and distinguished career. According to Liu Wansu, disorders were always caused by the fire factor; thus, the remedy should be an attack against the fire. Zhu developed Liu's theory by taking into account the other side of the problem—insufficiencies in the "yin" side of the body's energy. In addition to advocating attacking the excessive yang "fire" that caused illness, Zhu advocated replenishing the body's yin, which is the complement to the yang. By cultivating the yin, the balance of the body could be restored.

In his book *Jufang fahui*, or *On the Official Prescriptions*, Zhu Zhenheng criticized his contemporaries for following the "official prescriptions" without giving them any thought. He argued that the old prescriptions were not suitable for diseases of the time and called for more active study in medical science.

Families of Doctors: During the Yuan dynasty, medicine became a more respectable profession. And medical practice became a tradition in some families. Historical records from that time mention many cases in which families produced generations of doctors. The Ge family, natives of Changzhou in the lower Yangtze River Valley, was known for producing at least four generations of doctors. Ge Yinglei (1264–1323) was a famous doctor whose father, grandfather, and uncles were all doctors. Ge studied books such as the *Canon* and the *Classics of Acupuncture*. His reputation spread from his hometown to neighboring provinces. His son, Ge Qiansun (1305–1353), also became a doctor and was known for his unusual treatment techniques.

In addition to regularly examining his patients, Ge paid close attention to the environments in which they lived. By doing so, he often discovered hidden causes of his patients' disorders in their surroundings. Once a woman was introduced to him with the complaint of being weak and limp all the time. By looking over her bedroom, Ge found that the woman was allergic to her cosmetics. After the cosmetics were removed on Ge's order, the woman recovered.

An unfortunate drawback of generations of doctors in families was that they tended not to share their expertise and experience with outsiders. Ge Qiansun's monograph on tuberculosis, for example, was published in 1857, some 500 years after it was finished and circulated among family members. This, of course, hindered development of medical science.

6. THE MING AND QING PERIODS

History of Medicine: Long before modern ideas of the history of medicine took shape, there was a tradition of collecting and collating biographical data about prominent doctors. The fame of Bianque and Hua Tuo was recorded by their biographers in general historical writings. By the Song period, there appeared collections consisting exclusively of biographies of doctors. Examples of such collections include Chen Yi's *Biographies of Celebrated Doctors* and Xu Mengshen's *Collected Biographies of Doctors*.

The writing of medical history flourished in the Yuan dynasty and reached its heyday in the Ming dynasty. Song Lian (1310–

1381), known for his lucid prose style, recorded the stories of a number of doctors, focusing on the origins of their expertise, their successes in curing patients, and the benevolence they had demonstrated. Wang Lu (1332–?), one of the famous doctors of his time, compiled *A History of Medicine*, which comprised one hundred volumes. Li Lian's *Yishi*, or *History of Medicine*, published in 1513, was the most comprehensive of his time. Less than 50 years later, Li's book was superseded by *Gujin yitong*, or *The Encyclopedia of Medicine*, in 560 volumes, completed by Xu Chunfu in 1556.

Li Shizhen: After the publication of Tang Shenwei's *Zhenlei Pharmacopoiea*, some four centuries passed in which only mediocre works on pharmaceutical studies were produced. Doctors were still using reference books compiled centuries before. To make the situation worse, many doctors did not have access to Tang's *Pharmacopoiea* and had to use the much-simplified versions of the *Pharmacopoiea*, such as the *Zhenzhu nang*.

Li Shizhen (1518–1593) was born into a family of doctors in Hubei Province in central China. He learned the art of medicine from his father. From 1523 to 1530, several epidemics claimed thousands of lives. While in his early twenties, Li assisted in his father's practice. He soon earned a reputation as an excellent doctor and was summoned by the emperor to the Bureau of Medicine as a court physician. One of the privileges of this position was access to the royal library, and Li read prodigiously. In 1552, he started writing the *Bencao Gangmu*, or *Compendium of Materia Medica*. After three revisions and numerous discussions with his colleagues and friends, Li Shizhen finally completed the book (in 52 volumes) in 1578. The importance of this work was evident as soon as it was published. In the two centuries after its publication, *Compendium of Materia Medica* was translated into Japanese, Korean, German, French, English, Latin, and Russian. Charles Darwin employed this book as a source in writing his *The Descent of Man*.

In *Compendium of Materia Medica*, the medical functions of herbs, minerals, and animal parts are listed in 16 categories, which are further divided into 62 groups.

Through a careful selection based on his research, Li Shizhen eliminated about a hundred items from the original *Materia Medica* because their clinical effects were uncertain. Li also added 374 new items that he found useful in his practice. *Compendium of Materia Medica* examines 1,892 drugs in total. Many historians of pharmacology believe that the *Compendium of Materia Medica* might well have exhausted all the drugs known up to the 16th century.

In the *Compendium of Materia Medica*, the name of the drug is followed by citations from classics that present the drug's background and history. This is followed by a geographical study of the places where the drug was produced, a morphological description of the drug, the proper ways of collecting and preparing it. The entry concludes with comments on pharmacology. Tested prescriptions, 11,096 in total, are found, with the discussion of drugs; and 1,160 illustrations help identify the drugs in their natural forms.

In addition to listing and discussing drugs and their clinical uses, *Compendium of Materia Medica* offers an encyclopedic study of many related topics. The history of drugs and dietetic therapies are discussed extensively. A number of new drugs, especially those that were widely used by local practitioners, are registered and recommended. Li Shizhen denounced categorically the curative, or nourishing, effects of "Pulvis of Eating Things Cold" and other mineral drugs popular at the time. Some evolutionary relations between species are observed, and the fact that some living creatures changed "from inferior to superior" is noted. The skills in chemical or alchemic processing, such as distillation, vaporization, sublimation, and precipitation, are also introduced.

The *Compendium of Materia Medica* was amended by later scholars, notably by Zhao Xuemin (c. the 18th century) and Wu Qirui (1789–1846).

The Cold Damage Disease: Since the earliest time, acute infectious diseases had existed in both the north and the south of China. In the Han dynasty, Zhang Zhongjing's *Treatise on Cold Damage* defined the first criteria for the treatment of such diseases. At the time, however, the diseases were indiscriminately called *cold damage*, after the heat syndromes seen in all cases. Doctors knew that outbreaks of the diseases tended to be seasonal: Wind fever tended to occur in spring, and cold damage occurred more frequently in winter. The pathogens were, therefore, assumed to be the weather. According to *The Causes and Diseases*, written in the Sui period, cold-damage diseases could be further divided into four groups: *shanghan*, or "cold damage," seasonal flu, heat diseases, and *wenbing*, or "lukewarm illnesses." All the classics failed to give a clear definition of the term *wenbing*.

In the 16th century, epidemics ravaged China repeatedly. In the spring of 1534, an epidemic reportedly claimed "nine out of ten lives" in certain provinces. Again in 1544 and 1554, similar disasters occurred. In the early summer of 1559, an epidemic devastated the northern part of the lower Yangtze valley. A doctor in that region wrote in his journal that "the symptoms and the [way of] infecting were all the same." Throughout the 276 years of the Ming dynasty, 64 serious epidemics were recorded. It became imperative for doctors to deal with the problem.

The pamphlet *Wenyi lun*, or *On Infectious Diseases*, was published in 1642 to answer the challenge of those serious epidemics. Wu Youxing (1592–1672), the author, was a doctor who was experienced in treating victims of the epidemic in many provinces. Believing that "many died of malpractice instead of the epidemic itself," Wu wrote his essay to differentiate the wenbing from what had been called shanghan, or cold damage. He assumed an ill *qi* was the external pathogen responsible for the disease. Noticing that an epidemic of a disease among pigs or chickens would not likely infect human beings, Wu came to the hypothesis that there was a great variety of ill *qi*, each of which could cause one kind of disease. He affirmed further that external disorders such as lesions, carbuncles, and erysipelas were caused by an ill *qi*. The ill *qi* entered the body through the mouth and nose or through the skin and caused disorders when the body was already weak.

Later Developments: Influenced by Wu's theory, Ye Gui (1667–1746) further pointed out that the ill *qi* would attack the lungs first and then the heart. He divided the course of the disorder into four phases. He also recommended principles of treatment for each phase. Following this line of thinking, Wu Tang (1736–1820) wrote two books on wenbing, or infectious diseases, which marked the maturation of the study in the field.

"External" Medicine: In traditional Chinese medicine, "external" medicine refers to the specialization in disorders that have predominantly external manifestations and/or call for external treatment. That includes what modern Western medicine calls dermatology, surgery, and orthopedics.

Wang Ji's (1463–1539) *Waike lili*, or *Theories and Case Studies of External Disorders*, published in 1531, advocated the widely accepted belief that any external disease must have its roots inside the body. Xue Ji (c. 1488–1558) discussed in his case records cellulitis, a kind of suppurative inflammation of subcutaneous tissue, and cancers in various parts of the human body. Wang Kentang (1549–1613) finished the first specialized work on orthopedics in 1608, describing the structure of the human skeleton and the total number of human bones and their forms. Chen Shigong (1555–1636) summarized his experience, based on his 40-year practice, in *Authentic Treatment in External Medicine* in 1617. Deviating from the traditional point of view, Chen did not confine himself to finding the inside roots of external disorders but emphasized surgical treatment of those disorders. He depicted amputation, tracheotomy, removing objects in the larynx and nasal polyps, and the treatment of hemorrhoids by surgery.

Internal Medicine: Many new developments in internal medicine occurred in the Ming and Qing periods. Wang Lü (1332–1391), a disciple of Zhu Zhenheng, pointed out the limitations of Zhang Zhongjing's *Treatise on Cold Damage*. According to Wang Lu, Zhang's methods were fine for some illnesses caused by external pathogens but were not adequate for wenbing.

The field of gynecology also developed. Many books on this subject came out in the 1600s. One prominent example of such works was Wang Kentang's *Nüke zhengzhi zhunsheng*, or *The Principles of Female Diseases*.

The invention of a vaccine for smallpox was perhaps the most important development in Chinese medicine in this period. The vaccine was processed from either the puss or scab of the pox of a human patient. The doctor would then administer the vaccine by placing it into the nose of a healthy child. Medical texts from the 18th century attribute this invention to an anonymous practitioner in the period between 1567 and 1572.

Acupuncture: The Ming dynasty saw the publication of some important books on acupuncture, especially the encyclopedic compilation *Zhenjiu dacheng*, or *The Complete Book of Acupuncture and Moxabustion*, published in 1601 by Yang Jizhou. Yang (*fl. c.* 1522–1619) studied literature and classics in his youth, but before long he developed an ardor for the healing arts, which had been the profession of his family for generations. Yang traveled widely in the north and in the Yangtze valley, where he recognized the shortage of medical treatment in rural areas. His books on acupuncture and on first aid were intended to improve the health of the common people. In his books, Yang described different methods of treatment in rhymed prose so rural doctors, who usually had limited schooling, could easily memorize the basic principles.

Zhao Xuemin, an expert on the *Compendium of Materia Medica*, wrote a book in 1759 titled *Chuanya*, or *The Elegance of Being a Bell-Ringing Doctor*. Zhao's book speaks highly of local practitioners who walked from village to village ringing a bell as an identification of their profession. The book includes more than 4,000 prescriptions used by the bell-ringing doctors. It also records first-aid methods used by those doctors. As the book notes, those prescriptions and other therapies, though not mentioned in standard medical books, used inexpensive treatments, were convenient for those living in remote areas, and were quite effective. Therefore, no doctors should belittle or ignore them.

Anatomy: After examining 30 dead bodies, Wang Qingren (1768–1831) wrote a book on human anatomy. He found that the body cavity was divided by a membrane, the diaphragm, and described the trachea, the bronchus, and the lobes of the lungs. He also checked the brain and the spinal cord and concluded incorrectly that wisdom must reside in the heart instead of the brain. The idea of anatomy had no place in Chinese scholarship and to dissect the human body was regarded as a crime against humanity. Wang argued bravely for the significance of anatomy. "When doctors diagnose without knowing the inner organs of the body," his book states, "this is no different from a blind man walking in the darkness of night." His ideas were rejected by traditional doctors of his time. His book found no successors until the Western science of anatomy was introduced to China about a century later.

7. THE ARRIVAL OF WESTERN MEDICINE

Foreign Drugs as Tribute: According to Song government documents, drugs, among many other novelties from remote countries, were often brought to the court as tribute. In the 30 years after A.D. 984, as recorded in Chinese texts, the Persians went to China at least four times with drugs from their country. Litharge (or yellow lead), frankincense, myrrh, agalloch eaglewood, opium, and bezoar repeatedly caught the attention of Song government officials. Hawksbill turtle shells, round cardamom, aniseed and fennel oil, and areca nut, among many other tropical products, arrived from Vietnam and neighboring countries. For an envoy to bring drugs as part of the tribute paid to the Chinese emperor was common. During the 318 years since the founding of the Song dynasty, as official records indicate, 98 of 633 foreign envoys to the court presented drugs from their countries to the emperor.

There is no indication in Song records that the drugs were ever tested on patients. In 1262, however, a decree of the Yuan emperor gave evidence of the clinical use of foreign drugs. The Yuan emperor ordered the Vietnamese envoy to deliver drugs not readily available in China, such as cinnabar and liquidambar spirit, an oil-like fragrant liquid given to patients who suffered from stroke or epileptic convulsions. In the early Ming dynasty, a number of Japanese doctors went to China to study medicine. In 1433, the king of Ceylon sent an envoy to China with drugs. The first significant transmission of Western medical knowledge and practice was introduced to China in 1601, when the Italian Jesuit Matteo Ricci (1552–1610) arrived in Beijing, the capital, with medical books. Father Ricci had spent twenty years in the port city of Macao and was proficient in the Chinese language. To the surprise of Chinese doctors, their Western colleagues did not check a patient's pulse but paid more attention to the color of the patient's urine and complexion. In a matter of two decades, many Western medical books were translated into Chinese by Niccolo Longobardi (1559–1654), Julio Aleni (1582–1649), Johann Adam Schall von Bell (1591–1666), and their Chinese partners, such as Bi Gongchen (d. 1644). Almost at the same time, Giacomo Rho and Jean Terrenz (1576–1630) finished translating *Illustrated Treatise of Human Body* and *Introduction to Human Body*, respectively. And in 1723, Dominique Parrenin (1665–1741) wrote *Human Anatomy* in Manchu. Emperor Kangxi was apparently pleased and gave his endorsement by crowning the title of the book with the phrase "the emperor's version." At least two copies of the book have survived: One is in the Paris Museum of Natural History; the other, in the Capital Hospital in Beijing.

The basic Western and Chinese concepts of the human body and diseases, as well as the philosophy of medicine, were not even comparable, much less compatible. Western scholarship introduced by missionaries in the late 17th and 18th centuries received little professional attention.

The Early 1800s: In 1805, the Chinese first heard from Englishman Alexander Pearson (1780–1874) about a smallpox vaccine that was similar to what had been used in China for about a century. That fact strongly suggested to the watchful Chinese that Westerners and Chinese were physically similar enough to benefit from the same therapy. That Europeans and Chinese were anatomically identical came as a revelation to many Chinese. In 1820, R. Morrison (1782–1834) and T. Livingston began practicing medicine in Macao. They were followed by Thomas Colledge (1797–1879), a doctor of the British East India Company and a pupil of Sir Astley Cooper. Colledge first set up a clinic in 1827, then expanded it into a hospital. In 1834, the American Methodist Church sent Dr. Peter Parker (1804–1888) to China. Parker founded a hospital of ophthalmology in Guangzhou. Scholars believe this hospital was the first fully equipped hospital in mainland China. By 1876, doctors from Europe and North America had established 26 clinics and 16 fully equipped hospitals in China. Most of those clinics and hospitals were located in port cities, such as Guangzhou and Shanghai. In those hospitals, surgeries such as amputation, embryotomy, female lithotomy, and ovariotomy were performed. The successes of Western style surgery helped promote Chinese interest and understanding of Western medicine. Wang Tao (1828–1897), one of the first Chinese savants to open his mind to Western scholarship, developed a friendly attitude toward foreigners when a foreign doctor cured him of beriberi, from which he had suffered for more than a decade.

The Tianjin Case: For most unschooled Chinese and conservatives in the Chinese government, however, the doctors who had come to China with opium were objects of suspicion. Christian doctrines, which the missionary doctors preached to their patients at every possible occasion were suspect.

The churches of the missionaries, with their high steeples and narrow windows, looked strange to the Chinese. The work of Western doctors was even more incomprehensible. Rumors that eyeballs from dead bodies were collected for medicine spread. And the fact that women had to take off their underwear during medical examination was offensive to Chinese sensibilities.

In 1869, bodies of dead infants were found in a graveyard not far from a church in Tianjin. For many Chinese, this confirmed their suspicions that Western doctors, under the guise of medical practice, had kidnapped Chinese babies and performed evil magic on them in the church. Angry mobs rushed to the church, killed all foreigners, and burned the church to the ground. Zeng Guofan, (1811–1872) the principal official appointed by the Qing government to deal with this case, made a strenuous effort to explain to the emperor and the mobs that Western medicine was not what they believed. "Using human parts for medicine is inconceivable for even savages, not to say for the Englishmen and Frenchmen, who came from reputable countries." Unfortunately, he convinced neither the imperial court nor the people. Introducing the Chinese to Western medicine was not an easy task.

Medical Schools: One tool for introducing the Chinese to Western medicine was the establishment of Western-style medical schools in China. In 1854, Dr. John Glasgow Kerr, from the United States, founded the first such school in Guangdong. The second medical school, which was affiliated with the hospital Dr. Peter Parker had started some 30 years before, opened in 1866. The British opened the Hong Kong College of Medicine in 1887. In 1902, Germans founded the Tongji Medical College in Shanghai.

In 1906, the Union Medical College was founded in Beijing. The main sponsors of that college were the North China Educational Union, the American Board of Commissioners for Foreign Missions, and the American Presbyterian Mission. Baptist minister Frederick Gates had proposed building that school in 1892. Gates had a close connection with the Rockefeller Foundation. In the century to come, that institute would play a leading role in China in the fields of medical research, medical education, and, through its affiliated hospital, clinical services.

By 1906, missionary organizations had set up 166 hospitals and 241 clinics throughout China; more than three hundred physicians from abroad were working in those hospitals and clinics. While working in China, those doctors introduced to their Chinese colleagues a number of medical books. Many of those books were later either translated or adapted into Chinese. For example, in the mid-1850s Benjamin Hobson compiled the *New Treatises of Human Body*, providing the Chinese with the newest information on anatomy. The American medical missionary J. (John Glasgow) Kerr (1824–1901) finished translating some 20 Western medical books into Chinese during the period from 1859 through 1886. Most of those books were used in medical schools.

Medical Periodicals: Periodicals were also a fast and convenient channel for disseminating up-to-date medical knowledge to both professionals and nonprofessionals alike. Outstanding examples of such journals include the *Guangzhou xinbao* (later renamed *Xiyi xinbao*), or *Newsletter of Western Medicine*, founded in Guangzhou in 1866, and *Boyi huibao*, or *Reports on General Medicine*, founded in Shanghai in 1888.

Traditional Scholarship: Although Western medical scholarship and practice were spreading in China in the late 19th century, a number of Chinese doctors still followed the traditional way of understanding the human body and diseases. Inspired by the examples set by the great philological studies of the 18th century, medical experts of the traditional school became more and more involved in textual research and emendation of classics. Ding Songsheng edited 12 titles of medical classics in 1878. In 1891, Zhou Xuehai compiled a collection of important medical books. In 1929, He Lianchen published *Quanguo mingyi yan'an leibian*, or *Categorized Cases of Famous Doctors*, which enumerated 370 cases dealt with by more than 80 celebrated doctors during the late 19th and early 20th centuries.

The New Trend: After witnessing China's repeated humiliation by Western imperialist powers during the 19th century, many Chinese scholars were forced to face the reality of Western superiority in science and technology.

Tang Haizong (1851–1908), a medical writer and a physician trained in traditional Chinese medicine, advocated combining Chinese traditional knowledge and Western knowledge in a way that he described as "balancing both the classic and the modern, considering both the Chinese and the foreign." What Tang actually suggested, however, was finding supporting evidence for Chinese traditional theories in Western medicine.

Yun Tiejiao (1875–1935), a physician and writer, believed that Western and Chinese medicine were not mutually exclusive. Rather, he claimed, they were "different roads leading to the same destination."

Zhang Xichun (1860–1933) was probably the first physician to combine Chinese medicine and Western medicine in practice. His book, written in 1909, recorded his experiments using Western drugs and Chinese herbal medicine at the same time. He also tried, with little success, combining the two systems to found a new unified system of medicine.

"Ban Traditional Medicine": In the first two decades of the 20th century, the ideas of science and democracy, along with calls for modernization, proved extremely enticing to a new generation of Chinese intellectuals. Despite a distinguished history of clinical successes, traditional Chinese medicine could not explain itself in modern scientific terms. In 1914, an act was proposed in the Chinese legislature to ban traditional medicine. Then in 1924, the Ministry of Education refused to charter schools of traditional medicine. The law against traditional medicine was finally passed in 1929. The law called for closing schools of traditional medicine, requiring mandatory government registration and supervision of traditional doctors, banning promotion of traditional medicine in the news media, and, eventually, outlawing the practice of traditional medicine.

The Nationalist government did not, however, enforce the law it had enacted. Traditional medicine still met a crucial need in Chinese society, especially in rural and remote provinces where Western medicine was unavailable or unaffordable. In big cities, such as Shanghai and Tianjin, Western-trained doctors gradually replaced traditional practitioners.

Pulse-Feeling Diagnosis: Abu-Ali al-Husayn ibn-Sina, or Avicenna, (980–1037) was the first to mention the technique of pulse-feeling diagnosis in a medical text

outside of East Asia. The Chinese book *Classic on Pulse* was mentioned in Avicenna's medical encyclopedia *Al-Qanun*, the Latin translation of which appeared in 1473.

The 17th century saw the introduction of a number of Chinese medical books in the West. In 1659, the Jesuit Michael P. Boym (1612–1659), who had visited China, translated a part of the *Compendium of Materia Medica* into Latin. This is the earliest known work on Chinese medical herbs in a Western language. Boym's illustrated 144-page book titled *Andreas Cleyerus*, or *Clavis medica ad Chinarum doctrinam de pulsibus*, was published in 1686 in Nuremberg, Germany. Boym also wrote *Flora sinensis, frucuts floresque*, published in 1656 in Vienna. In 1676, Hermann Busschof, a Dutchman, wrote a book titled *Erste Abhandlunguber die Moxibustion in Europa*, which discussed acupuncture and moxibustion. The book was later translated into English. These two pioneer books were followed by Williamten Rhyne's book on arthritis in 1686.

John Floyer (1649–1734) did research on pulse diagnosis which, according to some Chinese historians of medicine, was based on his knowledge of Chinese traditional medicine. Floyer's essay, *The Physician's Pulse-Watch*, published in 1707, recorded his invention of an instrument for measuring a patient's pulse.

About the time those books were published, the Chinese smallpox vaccine, called *dou*, was introduced into Europe. In 1688, Russian doctors went to Beijing and brought back the dou vaccine. The use of the dou vaccine spread to Turkish doctors, then to doctors of other European countries. Madame W. Montague, the wife of an English diplomat, learned of this preventive treatment for smallpox in Turkey in 1717. The dou vaccine was used until E. Jenner (1749–1823) introduced smallpox inoculations in 1796.

The Epidemics: The first half of the 20th century was a miserable period for the people of China. The collapse of the Qing empire in 1911 ushered in a period of civil war, which was hardly interrupted by the Japanese invasion from 1931 to 1945 which created millions of war refugees. By the time the Communists came to power in 1949, the Chinese people were thoroughly exhausted by war, famine, and pestilence.

From 1900 to 1950, epidemics repeatedly devastated China. In Shanghai, the largest city in China, epidemics of cholera broke out 12 times. From 1937 to 1945, about a quarter of a million people in Shanghai were infected with cholera. In Manchuria, the pneumonic plague claimed more than 10,000 lives in 1910, 1917, and 1947. In 1936 and 1937, epidemics of cholera broke out in the entire Yangtze valley and in other southeastern regions. In the 11 years from 1937 to 1949, the death toll from the cholera plague reached 20,000 in that area. From 1937 through 1946, an estimated 1 million people were infected with cholera; 115,000 died.

In the first half of the century, schistosomiasis, or blood fluke, an endemic infection transmuted by polluted water, was out of control in 324 counties of 12 provinces in the lower Yangtze valley and in southern China, endangering more than 100 million people. Other endemic diseases were filariosis, malaria, and tuberculosis. Filariosis, a disease caused by a parasitic nematode worm that infested vertebrates, was rife in 14 provinces. In the early 1930s, malaria prevailed in the southern part of China, where some two of three people were affected.

Public Health: An estimate of the death rate in 1943 was 25 deaths per 1,000 population. The infant mortality rate was about 200 deaths per 1,000 live births. This meant that one of every five babies died in the first year of life. The infant mortality rate for the United States in 1900 was 140 deaths per 1,000 live births. A Western observer described the distressful situation: "Everywhere I went, I found scurvy-headed children, lice-ridden children, children with inflamed red eyes, children with bleeding gums, children with distended stomachs and spindly arms and legs, children covered with horrible sores on which flies feasted, children having a bowel movement which, after much straining, would eject only tapeworms."

Hospitals and Schools: The poor state of public health was aggravated by the lack of physicians and hospitals. In 1947, China had about 2,000 hospitals, with a total of about 90,000 beds. Estimates of the number of doctors and technicians trained in Western medicine practicing in China in 1947 was around 23,000. In a country with a population of 450 million, the shortage of health care was immense. By contrast, in the United States in 1949, there was one doctor for every 750 persons. To match this ratio, China would have needed 600,000 additional doctors to care for its people.

Unfortunately, China did not have enough medical schools to train all the doctors it needed. In 1949, there were only 38 medical schools, 12 departments of pharmacy in various colleges and universities, and six dental schools. During the 20 years from 1928 through 1947, only about 9,000 students graduated from those schools.

8. HEALTH CARE IN THE PEOPLE'S REPUBLIC OF CHINA

The Establishment of Government Goals: Shortly after its founding in 1949, the central government of the People's Republic of China established the Ministry of Public Health and put it in charge of health care and medical services. Local government branches with similar responsibility were also set up in all administrative regions within the jurisdiction of the People's Republic of China. In 1950 and 1952, the Ministry of Public Health called two national conferences. At those conferences, the ministry set the basic goals for medical care: serving the common people, giving priority to preventive medicine over curative medicine, fostering the unity between Western medicine and traditional medicine, and involving the vast majority of people in promoting public health. Known as the "Four-Point Principle," that doctrine has been the guideline for Chinese medical work since the early 1950s, with only minor revisions in 1979 and 1982.

Hospitals and Medical Facilities: One of the primary goals set by the Ministry of Public Health was reached in 1952, when China announced that, except for a few minor regions, every county had clinics and at least one hospital. By 1982, there were 55,496 clinics, or "commune hospitals," with 753,232 beds, providing basic medical services in some 5,000 counties in rural China. The total number of medical facilities and organizations increased from 3,670 in 1949 to 193,438 in 1982. And the number of hospital beds increased from an estimated 80,000 in 1949 to 2,017,088 in 1981.

In December 1978, the State Council approved *The Principles for Organization and Establishment of General Hospitals.* According to that document, at a hospital with 500 or more beds, the medical staff must consist of 70 percent to 72 percent of the total personnel. Among the medical staff, a quarter should be physicians; half, nurses; 8 percent, dispensers of medicine and supplies; 11 percent, lab and radioactive radiology technicians; and 8 percent, other technical support staff. A hospital of 500 or more beds should be organized in specialized departments, including a general medical department; a surgical department; and departments of obstetrics, gynecology, and pediatrics, as well as units for traditional medicine and preventive medicine. The principles also call for specialized departments in infectious diseases; stomatological diseases; ear, nose, and throat and ophthalmologic disorders; and dermatologic diseases. Hospitals of this size are also required to have offices for case records, statistics, and family planning guidance.

Laws and Regulations: As of 1982, the government of the People's Republic of China had created 191 laws and regulations concerning medical services and public health. Among those laws and regulations, 78 concern the prevention and control of epidemics, 42 concern medical and pharmaceutical administration, and 26 concern pharmacological education and research. The most influential include *The Proclamation Banning Opium,* enacted in 1950; *The Rules for Controlling Infectious Diseases,* enacted in 1955 and revised in 1978; and *The Regulations on Food Hygiene,* enacted in the early 1960s, which became a law in 1982. To explain the laws and regulations, the Ministry of Public Health dispatched more than 800 circulars, official papers, and notes between 1949 and 1982. Those circulars answered questions and gave instructions on how the laws and regulations were to be implemented.

Medical Fees: Since 1950, three major measures have been designated to deal with medical costs in China. The Labor Insurance system, adopted in February 1951, covers 100 percent of medical costs for about 80 million workers and staff members in government-owned factories and mines. The workers are also entitled to 69 percent to 70 percent of their regular wages if absent from their position for fewer than six months due to illnesses. Free Medical Service was instituted at the beginning of 1952 and covers about 18 million government employees, disabled veterans, and staff and students in higher education institutions and research facilities. Medical costs are fully covered if the patient receives treatment at a designated clinic or hospital.

Cooperative Medical Services was first tried in 1959 in rural areas on the basis of voluntary participation and mutual assistance. For a service unit, which could be a village, a local district, or a township, medical facilities have been set up to provide health care. The "commune hospitals," or clinics of this kind, often provide a lower standard of care compared to medical services in developed counties, but they provide basic and efficient help in dealing with common ailments and in controlling infectious diseases. Funding for local cooperative medical services comes mainly from fees paid by patients, and in some cases, funding is supplemented by government or other outside help. In 1982, about half the villages in mainland China had adopted the Cooperative Medical Services; that is, more than 400 million people were covered by the service.

Since the late 1980s, fee-for-service medical care offered by individual practitioners, private clinics, and public hospitals in certain selected areas has grown considerably. A copayment, or surcharge, is applied within the systems of Labor Insurance and Free Medical Service. The government hopes that the fees charged will help to reduce the huge deficits the system faces, thanks to excessive administrative costs and overtreatment of patients.

The Bureaucratic System: The Ministry of Public Health has always regarded the control of epidemics and infectious diseases as its highest priority. A special group of about 400 medical professionals, known as the Antiepidemic Corps, works in various localities. A watching-and-reporting network was set up in the 1950s in four levels that are parallel to administrative divisions. A province, for example, has a regional and/or municipal antiepidemic station, county substations that are affiliated with a commune hospital, and paraprofessionals who have rudimentary training at the township or village level. The network's goal is to establish sanitation and antiepidemic measures, disseminate medical information, provide inoculations, and report on epidemics.

Infectious Diseases: The *Rules for Controlling Infectious Diseases* enacted in 1955 singles out 18 infectious diseases as the most dangerous. Those diseases are further divided into two categories. Diseases in Category A (which include, for example, the pneumonic plague) are to be reported to the higher level of the network within 12 hours in urban areas and within 24 hours in rural areas. For diseases in Category B (such as encephalitis B, relapsing fever, and dysentery), the time limit is 24 hours for urban areas and three days for rural areas. In 1978, the regulation added seven diseases, including flu and hepatitis, for the network to monitor.

Reports in 1982 showed that the incidences per 100,000 population were 0.65 for diphtheria, 268.14 for dysentery, and 44.94 for measles. As of 1983, no cases of smallpox, the plague, cholera, and kala-azar had been reported since 1960.

Patriotic Health and Sanitation Campaign: The 1958 mass campaign of eliminating the "four pests"—namely rats, bedbugs, flies, and mosquitoes—was an effort to improve public hygiene and sanitation. That campaign was successful in that living conditions, especially in urban areas, were significantly improved. On the other hand, some measures, such as the rushed campaign to improve personal hygiene and

sanitation, were criticized as extreme or poorly conceived. Critics argued that education would have made personal hygiene and sanitation a day-to-day habitual activity. But the achievements were quite visible. Some 35 million tons of garbage were removed; 280,000 kilometers (or approximately 174,000 miles) of ditches and sewers were dredged; and about five million public toilets were built. Millions of people received instructions that improved their knowledge of their bodies, diseases, and the environment. The incidence of infectious diseases and the death rate was reduced.

Parasitic Diseases: Until recently, schistosomiasis had been a major scourge in China. A 1957 survey showed that 346 counties were infested and that the victim toll was as high as 10 million, of whom 60 percent were in incubation. In the winter of 1955, 197 centers for prevention and treatment, with 1,282 active units, together with 42 research institutes, were set up to fight the endemic. By 1982, the disease had been controlled in 250 counties and had been eradicated in thirty-eight counties.

About 30 million cases of malaria were reported annually in 1,800 counties in the 1930s. In the 1950s, 34 centers staffed by 900 specialists using synthetic preparations such as atabrine and chloroquine were set up to combat malaria. By 1982, the number of malaria cases had been reduced to about 2 million annually. To reinforce the fight against malaria, 1,780 test stations were set up in 1980 to monitor the disease in infected areas.

Tuberculosis: One of the 10 leading causes of death in China, tuberculosis claimed more than 300,000 lives per year in the mid-1970s. A 1979 census showed that the rate of tuberculosis was 717 per 100,000 and that the number of new cases was 187 per 100,000. In some urban areas, such as Shanghai, the mortality rate dropped from 208.61 per 100,000 in 1951 to 10.25 in 1979. The Anti-Tuberculosis Association of China has been the major organization dealing with the disease. First founded in 1933, the association had branches in 28 provinces and municipalities by the end of 1979.

Leading Causes of Death: The mortality rate in China dropped steadily from 1949 to 1982, from 20 per 1,000 to 6.6 per 1,000. According to a survey by the World Bank in 1984, China's pattern in the leading causes of death fell in between that of most industrialized countries and that of the developing world. In urban areas, cerebrovascular diseases were the leading cause of death, causing 135.35 deaths per 100,000 in 17 cities. In rural areas, a survey of 38 counties showed that heart disease was responsible for 170.57 per 100,000, or 25.84 percent of the total deaths. In the cities, heart disease and malignant tumors were the two leading causes of death following cerebrovascular diseases.

Hypertension: A higher incidence of cigarette smoking and a richer diet have contributed to the high incidence of hypertension, or high blood pressure. If heart disease, kidney disease, and stroke caused by high blood pressure were added to this category, hypertension might be China's single highest risk factor for mortality. Studies indicate that by 2010, China might have more than 110 million cases of hypertension. Efforts to disseminate basic knowledge of preventing hypertension by reducing salt and fat intake and the dangers of smoking have had limited success.

Malignant Tumors: From 1973 through 1975, China conducted a national cancer mortality survey. The results indicated that for both males and females stomach cancer was the leading cause of cancer mortality. Cancers in digestive organs— the stomach, the esophagus, and the liver—were responsible for 47.4 percent of cancer deaths for females and 68.7 percent for males. The prevalence of cancer varied from region to region. For example, nasopharyngeal cancer had the highest incidence in Guangdong, a southern province, and liver cancer was concentrated in the southeast coastal region of China.

The incidence of lung cancer has gone up sharply since the 1970s. Smoking is blamed as the major contributing factor. Statistics show that 24 percent of boys in the suburbs of Beijing smoked before the age of 18 and that 56 percent of male adults in Henan Province smoked. In 1980, China consumed 760 billion cigarettes,

about 700 per capita. In addition, the tar level in Chinese cigarettes is more than twice as high as that in most U.S. cigarettes. Although since the early 1980s smoking has been banned in public buildings, such as cinemas and libraries, and numerous education projects to persuade people to quit smoking have been conducted, the antismoking campaign is far from successful.

The major difficulty in dealing with cancer has been a lack of funds and personnel to improve treatment facilities and to carry out extensive epidemiological surveys. Both epidemeology and oncology were still fairly new subjects in the medical school curricula in the 1970s. Early diagnosis and early treatment are crucial for certain cancers, but most county hospitals cannot afford the necessary equipment and training.

The government strategy has been to give priority to prevention. Led by the Institute of Cancer of the Chinese Academy of Medical Science, a three-tier network of education, identification, and registration has been set up in all counties and cities. A comprehensive survey in high-incidence areas was conducted in 1975. During that survey, physicians, epidemiologists, microbiologists, environmental chemists, geologists, and experts in related fields worked together for the first time to study the disease from different perspectives. Surgical treatments for liver and esophageal cancers and the use of traditional medicines to improve a patient's general health have achieved positive results.

Laws and Regulation for Maternity and Child Care: Female workers are barred by law from jobs that require heavy physical work, such as loading and unloading articles weighing more than 25 kilograms. They are also exempted from nightshift work beginning in their seventh month of pregnancy and lasting for four months after giving birth, a time of nursing. Women workers are entitled to free prenatal care and free hospitalization for delivery. Maternity leave is 56 days for normal cases and seventy days for difficult cases. A nursing mother is allowed two 20-minute breaks each workday for breastfeeding her baby. In the late 1980s, some businesses extended maternity leave up to one year.

Health Care: Like the network to combat epidemics, the maternity care and child care network has three or four tiers, from the province hospitals of gynecology and obstetrics to the village clinic. By 1982, there were 182 such hospitals and 2,645 clinics employing 42,982 gynecologists/obstetricians, 31,991 pediatricians, and 73,305 midwives.

The establishment of "woman health rooms" in factories, the increase in the number of women using midwives and seeing their gynecologists for regular checkups, and the dissemination of information on women's health and child care have resulted in general improvement in the health of women and children. According to statistics for 1977, the mortality rate for women giving birth had dropped from 1,500 per 100,000 in 1950 to 54 per 100,000 in 1977, and the infant mortality rate had dropped from 200 per 1,000 to 13.85 per 1,000 and 37.53 per 1,000 in urban and rural areas, respectively.

The Growth of Population: In 1911, China's population was estimated at around 380 million. Forty years later in 1950, China's population was believed to be 552 million. The first national census in 1953 registered 602 million, the second in 1964 confirmed an increase of about 100 million, with the total population reaching 695 million. The third national census in 1982 showed the population was 1,031,882,551. A comparison between the third national census and the second national census indicates that China's population had gained a net increase of 313,593,529 people, or 45.1 percent over the 18 years from 1964 to 1982, or 2.1 percent annually. Those figures sent a clear alarm. China cannot afford to allow its population to grow by the equivalent of the entire U.S. population every 10 years. Family planning became a vital national priority.

In March 1981, the National People's Congress set up the State Family Planning Commission to supervise the implementation of population control. Thirteen government departments and social organizations—including the Civil Affairs Min-

istry, the Finance Ministry, the All-China Federation of Trade Unions, the Communist Youth League, and the All-China Women's Federation—joined the State Family Planning Commission. The State Science and Technology Commission was asked to organize national family planning research projects. The Ministry of Public Health was responsible for promoting late marriage, late birth, and having fewer and healthier babies. It was also responsible for technical guidance and services for birth control. The Ministry of the Chemical Industry was designated to develop and produce better contraceptive pills. Family planning guidance stations in provincial areas and education centers in big cities were also set up.

By 1996, China officially estimated it had gained an increase of 300 million people in the 14 years since the census of 1982. For urban areas and people with higher education, the necessity of family planning has been well understood. In the vast majority of rural areas, many people still fail to see the catastrophic consequence of unlimited and uncontrolled growth in population.

The Structure of Medical Education: Medical education in the People's Republic of China has been designed in a three-tier structure. The medical education system consisted of 116 universities and colleges in 1982, in which 162,725 students were enrolled. That represented some 12 percent of the total number of the students enrolled in institutions of higher education. In those institutions, there were 30,606 teaching staff members, of which 727 were professors and 3,006 were associate professors. The learning period of the students, usually six to eight years, was divided into three major parts: theoretical courses on general science and medicine, medical courses on selected specialties with clinical practice, and in-hospital internships. For all medical students, excluding the time spent in hospital internships, the total time required for medical education was set at no fewer than 5,000 hours.

Secondary medical education was given a high priority among the three tiers because that type of education was believed the most efficient and affordable way to provide basic medical services to China's large population. During the 30-year period between 1950 and 1981, 947,580 professionals graduated from 526 intermediate medical schools in all the provinces of mainland China. In 1982, 164,038 students were enrolled in the four-year course for paramedics or in the three-year course for parapharmacists.

The serious shortage of medical professionals has dictated the demand for millions of people with rudimentary knowledge in medicine to provide basic services for their peer groups in the workplace, especially in the countryside. Training is usually sponsored by the local health administration and sometimes by employers. In the training sessions, which usually last three to twelve months, trainees attend basic anatomical and physiological classes and infectious disease prevention classes. They also learn basic first aid, antiepidemic measures, drinking-water control, how to assist a woman in labor, maternity care and childcare, and birth control. After graduation, these part-time health workers return to their factories, farms, and villages. These paraprofessionals are sometimes called "barefoot doctors" because they do not wear leather shoes the way most doctors do.

Medical Research: By 1982, there were 292 medical and health research institutions in China, each with a standing staff, fixed equipment, and independent financial accounting.

The Academy: Founded in 1956, the Chinese Academy of Medical Science embraces 10 branch institutes—such as the Institute of Medical Biology and the Institute of Antibiotics—an information center, the Union Hospital, and several specialized departments. Concentrating on theoretical research, the academy has played a leading role in the development of medical science in China. In one recent year, of the academy's 10,313 employees, 12 were members of the Chinese Academy of Sciences, and 388 held advanced degrees. They were supported by 1,445 assistant research fellows and 2,373 mechanics and technicians. In 1982, the library associated with the academy had a collection of about 360,000 volumes and 2,000 journals; the two affiliated hospitals each had 1,720 beds.

Preventive Medicine Center: The National Center for Preventive Medicine was founded in August 1983 to engage in prevention research, disease surveillance, and public health supervision. The research topics emphasize clinical practice and environment control. Five institutes, which include the Institute of Virology, the Institute of Epidemiology and Microbiology, and the Institute of Parasitic Diseases, are clinically oriented research units. The Station of Environmental Hygiene Monitoring and the Institute of Food Hygiene Supervision and Inspection function as advisers and assistants to corresponding government departments.

Recent Policies toward Traditional Medicine: Traditional medicine has been controversial since Western medicine proved its effectiveness in China in the early 1900s. At that time, there seemed no conceivable way to incorporate one into the other, nor to unite the two on any basis of common understanding. By the 1950s, the issue had been dealt with in a more balanced and rational way. A national conference in 1950 affirmed that medical services in the newly founded republic should be delivered by both Western and traditional medicine. In 1955, the Ministry of Public Health set up the Academy of Traditional Medicine, which became the center of research and education in the field of public health. In the same year, the government asserted that the progress of medical science in China should develop along three lines: the Western, the traditional, and a combination of the two. The next year, 1956, six colleges specializing in traditional medicine were founded in Beijing, Shanghai, Guangzhou, and other cities. Projects to help Western-style doctors learn traditional theories and therapies were funded by various government sources. At the same time, seminars and symposia on traditional medicine were encouraged. By the end of 1957, there were 43 institutes focusing on herbal drugs and related remedies.

Academy of Traditional Medicine: Founded at the end of 1955, the Academy of Traditional Medicine incorporated the Chinese Pharmaceutical Institute, the Experimental Institute of Acupuncture and Moxibustion, the School of Traditional

Medicine, and the North China Hospital. In 1982, the academy was reorganized into seven institutes: Clinical Medicine, Acupuncture, Orthopedics and Traumatology, Materia Medica, and Medical History. The academy now has a publishing house, a library, and a medical school. According to academy records, in 1981 there were 133 senior research fellows and 350 research assistants at the academy, and its affiliated hospital had about 500 beds and treated some 700,000 outpatients. The Academy of Traditional Medicine published three quarterly journals: *The Journal of Chinese Acupuncture*, *Bulletin of Traditional Chinese Medicine*, and *Chinese Journal of Integrated Medicine*. As of the early 1980s, the library, or the Information Center as it was once called, possessed 80,000 books on Chinese medicine written before the 20th century.

Research in Traditional Medicine:
In the 1950s, promoting the mutual understanding of traditional and Western medicine was the major concern of health officials. In the late 1970s, after a 10-year interruption caused by the Cultural Revolution, research results were reported in all branches of traditional medicine, especially in acupuncture.

As early as 1958, some doctors had tried to use acupuncture as an anesthesia. By the late 1970s, an estimated 2 million operations had been performed using acupuncture as an anesthesia, which was safe and economical. When a patient's body was too weak to tolerate the disruption caused by anesthesia, acupuncture anesthesia served as an alternative. In 1979, 149 scholars and doctors from 32 countries attended the National Symposium on Acupuncture Anesthesia. During the 1980s, some 300 diseases were treated using the acupuncture technique. Acupuncture was reported effective in treating about one-third of the diseases. The physiological, pathological, and anatomical basis of the technique, however, remained more or less mysterious.

The study of the classics of Chinese medicine continues at the Institute of Medical History as well as at universities and colleges in China. In 1981, a nationwide conference on medical classics was held for the first time in the People's Republic of China. In 1983, the academy's affiliated publisher published 450 books, with a total of 17 million copies. And most of the major works in traditional medicine have been edited, collated, and republished.

KEY RESEARCH SOURCES

Bowers, John Z., and Elizabeth F. Purcell, ed. *Medicine and Society in China*. New York: Josiah P. Macy Jr. Foundation, 1974.

Bowers, John Z., William Hess, and Nathan Sivin, eds. *Science and Medicine in Twentieth-Century China: Research and Education*. Ann Arbor: Center for Chinese Studies, University of Michigan Press, 1988.

Eisenberg, David, and Thomas Lee Wright. *Encounters with Qi: Exploring Chinese Medicine*. New York: Norton, 1995.

Furth, Charlotte. *A Flourishing Yin: Gender in China's Medical History: 960–1665*. Berkeley: University of California Press, 1998.

Ho, Peng Yoke, and F. P. Lisowski. *A Brief History of Chinese Medicine*. River Edge, N.J.: World Scientific, 1998.

Ho, Peng Yoke. *Concepts of Chinese Science and Traditional Healing Arts: A Historical Review*. River Edge, NJ: World Scientific, 1993.

Hoizey, Dominique, and Marie-Joseph. *A History of Chinese Medicine*. Trans. Paul Bailey: Vancouver: UBC Press, 1993.

Huard, Pierre, and Ming Wong. *Chinese Medicine*. Trans. Bernard Fielding. New York: McGraw-Hill, 1968.

Jamison, Dean T., ed. *China, the Health Sector.* Washington D.C.: The World Bank, 1984.

Liu, Yanchi, et al. *Essential Book of Traditional Chinese Medicine.* 2 vols. New York: Columbia University Press, 1988 and 1995.

Quinn, Joseph R., ed. *Medicine and Public Health in the People's Republic of China.* Bethesda, MD: U.S. Department of Health, Education and Welfare and National Institute of Health, 1972.

Shen, Tzu-yin, and Chen Zelin. *The Basis of Traditional Chinese Medicine.* Boston, Mass.: Shambhala Publications, 1996.

Shi, Jizong, and Chu Feng Zhu. *The ABC of Traditional Chinese Medicine.* Trans. Shi Jiaxin. Hong Kong: Hai Feng, 1985.

Sivin, Nathan. *Medicine, Philosophy and Religion in Ancient China: Researches and Reflections.* Brookfields, VT: Variorum, 1995.

Sivin, Nathan. *Traditional Medicine in Contemporary China.* Ann Arbor: Center for Chinese Studies, University of Michigan, 1987.

Strickman, Michel, and Bernard Faure, eds. *Chinese Magical Medicine.* Stanford: Stanford University Press, 2002.

Temple, Robert. *The Genius of China: 3,000 Years of Science, Discovery and Invention.* New York: Simon and Schuster, 1986.

Unschuld, Paul Ulrich. *Medicine in China: A History of Ideas.* Berkeley: University of California Press, 1985.

Unschuld, Paul Ulrich. *Medicine in China: A History of Pharmaceutics.* Berkeley: University of California Press, 1986.

Wu Heguang, ed. *Modern Chinese Medicine: A Comprehensive Review of Medicine in the People's Republic of China.* Vols. 1–3. Lancaster: MTP Press Lit., 1984.

Wu Yiyi. "A Line of Many Masters: A Prosopographical Study of Liu Wansu and His Disciples from the Jin to the Early Ming." *Chinese Science* (UCLA) 11 (1994): 36–65.

The Arts, Entertainment, and Sports

By Jing Liao

1. PREHISTORY

The Dawn of Civilization

The picture we have of Chinese civilization emerges from the discoveries of numerous sites of prehistorical human settlement. Judging by unearthed human remains and artifacts, Chinese civilization began around the Lower Paleolithic Age, represented by the Yuanmou Man in Yunnan, Lantian Man in Shaanxi, and Peking Man in Zhoukoudian near Beijing. In addition to human fossils, archaeologists excavated from these three major sites a large quantity of stone tools, very primitive and yet created with hammers.

With the advent of the Middle Paleolithic, the ancestors of the modern Chinese people developed skills for refining stone tools. Choppers and chopping tools have been unearthed at the sites of Dingcun Man in Shanxi, Maba Man in Guangdong, and Changyang Man in Hubei. In 1933 in Zhoukoudian, on a hill atop the site of the Peking Man, the site of the Upper Cave Man was excavated. (This dates from much later in the Upper Paleolithic Age.) There, archaeologists unearthed a wide range of tools and beads made from small pebbles, animal bones, and teeth. Those objects, whether for practical or decorative purposes, were all carefully shaped, smoothly polished, drilled with holes, and dyed with hematite. This red iron coloring was also used to dye cloth and, in powder form, spread around the dead. Besides those major archaeological relics, other sites of the earliest Chinese civilization include Hetao Man in Inner Mongolia; Xiaonaihai culture in Henan Province; Liujiang Man in Guangxi Province; and Ziyang Man in Sichuan Province.

Yangshao Culture: At the beginning of the Neolithic era, a form of human society developed along the Yellow River. With the emergence of urban life came a shift from hunting and fishing to farming and the manufacture of pottery. One of the milestones of this revolution was the Yangshao culture, widely known for its painted pottery. The first site of Yangshao culture was discovered by the Swedish geologist J. Gunnar Andersson, who initiated the excavation in 1921 at a village called Yangshao, located at Yingchi in Henan Province. In 1953, archaeologists found another site of Yangshao culture at Banpo in Shaanxi with similar clay wares.

Judging by other related locations, such as Miaodigou in Henan, and Caojiazui and Majiawan in Gansu, Yangshao culture probably began in Henan Province around 5000 B.C., then expanded westward to Shaanxi and Gansu Provinces and existed for 3,000 years in the middle and upper Yellow River areas. The painted pottery consists mainly of utensils, urns, bowls, vases, and basins, displaying various shapes and patterns. The background is either red or gray, and elegant black patterns are decorated on the upper part of the clay wares. The patterns represent a rich variety of geometric forms—squares, diamonds, crosses, waves, triangles, and spirals. Other patterns depict abstract animals, human faces and figures, human faces on fish or frog bodies, and totemic figures with half-human bodies. These geometric and symbolic patterns exhibit the rich imagination of the potters, but their meanings are still a mystery to us.

Longshan Culture: Around 2500 B.C., there emerged a different culture called Longshan culture, known for its black pottery. Whether Longshan culture superseded or overlapped with Yangshao culture is still unclear. Longshan culture originated in Shandong Province and essentially remained in the eastern part of China. The major Longshan culture locations include Longshan at Zhangqiu in Shandong, discovered in 1928; Dawenkou at Ningyang in Shandong, found in 1959; Miaodigou (the second stage) in Henan; Hougang at Anyang in Henan, found in 1971; and Qijia Ping at Guanghe in Gansu, found in 1971. Longshan pottery is characterized by its black substance, extreme fragility, burnished surfaces, and complicated angular contours. Most of these pieces indicate the use of rapid spinning wheels and high baking temperatures. The shapes of Longshan pottery are their most dramatic and spectacular features. Drinking vessels are made with a curved stem, a wide base, and tulip-shaped cup. A wine-cup has a long spinal stem and a plate-shaped top. Cooking tripods are shaped either with an extended mouth for pouring water or with a long handle on the shoulder for carrying. Some of the tripods exhibit the embryonic forms of Li, Yu, and Ding—three kinds of bronze vessels made during the Shang (c. 1554–1045 B.C.) and Zhou (c. 1045–221 B.C.) dynasties.

2. BRONZE VESSELS

The Shang Dynasty: The oldest bronze ware (an alloy of copper, lead, and tin), representing the earliest Bronze Age civilization, was found in Erlitou in Henan. Since Erlitou, archaeologists have discovered hundreds of sites with buried Shang bronze vessels, made for sacrificial and ceremonial purposes. There are about 30 types of ritual vessels. The sizes vary from very delicate drinking cups only a few inches in height, to gigantic cooking vessels more than 1 meter (about 4 feet) high and weighing about 800 kilograms (1,764 pounds). The color of the vessels may be green, yellowish green, or red, depending upon the components and the time of oxidization. Most patterns are zoomorphic, profiling dragons, cicadas, or birds. The dominating silhouette is called *Taotie*, an auspicious animal head with bulging eyes. Each *Taotie*, configured into a single silhouette, is repeated, covering the whole surface of the vessel or forming a frieze on the neck or bottom of the item. Although *Taotie* dominated bronze decoration throughout the Shang dynasty, it appeared in five distinctive styles, reflecting the progress in casting techniques, as well as a change in aesthetic sensibility. Style I shows the motif in shallow relief in very fine lines; Style II reveals some calligraphic shapes with rough and raised strips; Style III eliminates the clear individual register, burying the motif into very fine and curly lines; Style IV constitutes the opposite of Style III, raising the motif to form an independent unit against a background; Style V poses the motif in convex relief with broader and bolder stripes set against a plain background.

The Zhou Dynasty: The Zhou dynasty is divided into Western Zhou (c. 1045–771 B.C.), and Eastern Zhou (770–256 or 221 B.C.), which is further divided into the Spring and Autumn (770–476 B.C.) and the Warring States (475–221 B.C.) periods. The traditions of the ritual bronzes were carried over from the Shang but considerably adjusted to suit the Zhou rulers' tastes. The shapes became more fluid and somewhat over-elaborate: extravagant forms replaced simple and smooth contours; *Taotie* motifs dissolved into very elaborate backgrounds; bird motifs accounted for a large proportion of decorations, some with recognizable features, some mixed with quills in the background. The dragon was another major design motif, usually appearing in an interlaced format.

Other changes mirror the Zhou's improved casting techniques. Very complicated flanges, shaped into three-dimensional animals or other motifs, were attached to vessels. In some bronze vessels, archaeologists have found the first text inscriptions, which describe the function of the object or pay homage to ancestors. In Eastern Zhou, more advanced casting techniques enabled coopers to make very complicated tripod sets with intricate ornaments. Dragons, tigers, and birds were cast in shallow relief or on openwork and decorative bodies, flanges, and lids of vessels. The vividness of the decorations transforms practical utensils into works of art.

In addition to vessels, bronze sculptures and other objects were made during the Zhou dynasty. Archaeological discoveries include a bronze imaginary winged beast inlaid with silver, bronze oil lamps held by human figure statues, and weapons, all demonstrating the advanced bronze technology well before the time of Christ. In 1978, archaeologists found the tomb of the Marquis Yi of Zeng of the late Eastern Zhou at Leigudun, Sui county in Hubei Province. Among the remarkable objects found in the tomb is a set of musical instruments containing sixty-five bells encompassing five octaves. The bells are arranged in groups on a three-tiered wooden frame supported by a bronze figure on each corner. The largest bell is 96.3 centimeters (3 feet) in height and 79.5 kilograms (175 pounds) in weight; the smallest only 36.8 centimeters (14 inches) in height and 6.75 kilograms (15 pounds) in weight. Unearthed with the set of bells were 36 stone chimes, a bronze drum, and wooden zithers and pipes.

The Han Dynasty (206 B.C.–A.D. 220): After the fall of the Zhou dynasty, craftsmen made fewer bronze vessels for ceremonial and sacrificial purposes and concentrated on creating more utilitarian and decorative items. Vessels were simplified in shape but inlaid with gold and silver with great complexity. Besides bronze vessels, craftsmen invented other kinds of bronze objects for use in daily life. *Boshan hu* was an incense burner consisting of two parts: a lid shaped into mountains of immortals and a base covered with a sea of immortals. Small animals, human figures, and trees in relief dot the mountains. Other extraordinary bronze articles vary from drums, drum-shaped containers with cowry shells, and weapons to money-holding trees, oil lamps with holders, and mirrors.

The Tang, Song, Ming, and Qing Dynasties: In the Tang dynasty (618–907), large, high-quality bronze mirrors were made with shiny surfaces; and the backs were decorated with flowers, animals (especially birds), or other symbols of good fortune. After the Tang, metal-working techniques declined. Song dynasty (960–1279) scholars revered the ancient traditions and put forth great effort to record and analyze the shapes, decorations, and inscriptions of earlier bronze vessels. Foundries were set up to reproduce several types of bronze vessels in modified forms. In the Ming (1368–1644) and Qing (1644–1911) dynasties, bronze products were limited to two categories: large items mainly for ceremonial purposes and small items of purely decorative value.

3. SCULPTURE

The Shang and Zhou Dynasties

In 1986, archaeologists excavated a Shang sacrificial pit dated around 1200 B.C. at Sanxingdui in Guanghan, Sichuan Province. It is the most remarkable Shang site, containing 300 artifacts, such as a bronze figural statue, 41 bronze human heads, and several large masks, as well as many jades and a large quantity of elephant tusks. Perhaps the most unique item is the 172-centimeter (5.7 feet) high bronze figure, wearing a crown and a long robe decorated with elaborate patterns. His facial features are rather angular, and his large hands form a holding gesture. The figure stands on a 90-centimeter base supported by four elephants' heads, their trunks curled up, each facing a cardinal direction. The 41 human heads typically have long necks; slanted eyes; heavy, rough brows; and wide mouths with thin lips. They vary in headgear and hairstyles, and two have applied gold leaf on their faces. Three masks have similar facial features, but they are much larger and are characterized by protruding pupils and long, upright posts rising from the noses. The Sanxingdui site provides an unparalleled resource for the study of China's earliest bronze sculptures.

The Tomb of the First Emperor Qin

The discovery in the 1970s of the tomb of the first Qin emperor astounded the world. Containing a huge army of terra-cotta soldiers, the tomb was built for the emperor who, by conquering other states of the Zhou, established the Qin dynasty (221–206 B.C.). During his reign, the emperor expressed great enthusiasm for building vast palaces. Though none of these has survived, the famous tomb pits found in 1970 at Lintong in Shaanxi Province give us some idea of the grandeur of the palace buildings of the time. The vast tomb, with 15,000 square feet of space and 38 columns of soldiers and horses, was modeled on an actual palace. An artificial pyramid on the ground floor was the main hall for receiving court officials; two thick walls surround the underground structure and divide the tomb into outer and inner sections. Many of the individual units are connected by corridors and form a very cohesive but colossal complex. The tomb site consists of four pits. In Pit 1, 6,000 figures are aligned in battle formation, some kneeling, most standing; Pit 2 has another 1,400 figures; Pit 3 holds a small group of generals and officials, and Pit 4 is empty. The sculptors regularized the heights of the figures; all are 1.8 meters (5.9 feet) tall. But their faces are personalized, and their ranks can be identified by different hair and mustache styles. Thus, these tremendous groups form a uniform appearance, yet retain a high degree of individuality. All the soldiers wear uniforms and carry bronze weapons, some with swords, and most with daggers. Standing at the front of the army are archers and horse-drawn chariots made of bronze. They seem ready to fight or to undergo inspection by the emperor. As the tomb has not been fully excavated, we cannot be sure what remains to be discovered.

Han Sculptures

Sculpture continued to develop in the Han dynasty in both round and relief formats. Animals, warriors, soldiers, entertainers, and architectural motifs were fashioned in bronze, stone, wood, clay, and ceramics. The Han sculpture blended a realistic style with romantic imagination. A notable example is a piece of bronze sculpture called *Galloping Horse*. With its three soaring hoofs and tail, the horse rests the remaining hoof on the back of a swallow. This posture suggests that the horse is "lighter than a swallow," a Chinese idiom describing speed and agility. In a contrast to this elegant horse, tomb guards cast in animal forms give the impression of clumsiness.

Besides round sculptures, relief was also employed during the Han dynasty on vessels, stones, and bricks with motifs ranging from depictions of daily life to religious and historical themes. The upper part of a piece of tile relief found at Guanghan in Sichuan Province depicts people hunting on a lake shore, and the lower part shows farmers harvesting a rice field. The best-known reliefs are those from stone slabs in the tomb shrine at Wuliang, Jiaxiang in Shandong Province. Some of those slabs illustrate Confucian ideas; some are about Daoist mythology, historical events, and legends from folklore. Relief is also applied to architectural tiles, showing images of the four gods of direction: Green Dragon, Zhuque (the vermilion bird), Xuanwu (variously depicted as a turtle or the union of a turtle and a snake), and White Tiger.

Stone Reliefs During the Age of Division

Stone relief remained common during the Age of Division (222–589), but the style changed dramatically, as illustrated by a sarcophagus at the Nelson-Atkins Museum in Kansas City. The reliefs on the sarcophagus depict stories of filial duty, a theme similar to that in the Wuliang Shrine. The treatments, however, are very different. In the Wuliang Shrine, stories are arranged in rows without a center figure. But on the panels of the later sarcophagus, each story centers on a human figure who is surrounded by landscape scenery carved three dimensionally. In the Wuliang Shrine, figures are chiseled in broad strokes; on the sarcophagus, every detail is carved in extremely fine lines, each figure carefully drawn with contour, drapery, and distinctive features. This style of fine line depiction was also adopted in a literary relief, *The Seven Sages of the Bamboo Grove*, which describes seven famous neo-Daoist figures sitting under trees and indulging in wine—a deliberate act of defiance against Confucian morality.

Buddhist Sculpture

The introduction of Buddhism to China during the Han dynasty brought a new form of art with it. Huge quantities of Buddhist sculptures were made in temples, pagodas, and stone caves. Among many famous sites, the most outstanding are Dunhuang, Maijishan, Yungang, and Longmen. The construction of Maijishan in Tianshui county, Gansu Province, began around the fourth century. Its 194 caves house more than seven thousand statues. Yungang is in the Wuzhou Mountains of Shanxi Province. The major caves there were built between A.D. 460 and 494. Longmen is in the Longmen and Xiangshan Mountains in Henan Province. Among its 1,375 caves and 785 niches, the first cave was opened between A.D. 477 and 499, and the rest were built over the next 400 years.

Yungang Buddhist Grottoes

Yungang is located outside of Datong in Shanxi Province. From the soft rock cliffs, 53 caves have been hewn to house more than 51,000 images of Buddha, bodhisattvas, and other attendants in varying sizes, the tallest one 17 meters (56 feet). The main caves were dedicated to the emperor and other important rulers. In Cave No. XX, the major grotto in Yungang, a colossal 15-meter (48 feet) tall Buddha sits in a meditative posture, with two bodhisattvas standing nearby, hands held in a blessing gesture. This image, typical of China's Buddhist figures, represents a mixture of Indian and Chinese characteristics, the straight nose from India, and the narrow long eyes and elongated ears from China.

The broad chest and shoulders imply the vigorous power and infinite wisdom of the divine, and the rigid expression on the statue's round face serves to reinforce this impression. The body is wrapped in a robe carved with thin, dense lines. The U-shaped pattern is reminiscent of the earliest Buddha statue done almost 100 years before. With the major caves housing the giant Buddha statues, walls of the lesser caves are literally covered with reliefs of smaller Buddha images (including scenes depicting Buddha's life), bodhisattvas, and many attendants.

The Longmen Buddhist Grottoes

The passion for Buddhism continued and led to another famous group of grottoes in Longmen, Henan Province. The limestone cliffs there provided softer surfaces for sculptors to work. In Longmen, 1,353 grottoes, and 785 niches shelter more than 97,000 statues. The four major caves and two stone cave temples (Guyang, Binyang, Lianhua [Lotus], and Fengxian) reveal what some experts describe as the most marvelous work of the Age of Division. The entire Guyang Cave is covered with reliefs in a free arrangement. The Lianhua Cave is famous for its round lotus surrounded by celestial beings, and the Binyang Cave holds a notable group of statues: Buddha and bodhisattva stand on a lotus against flame mandalas. Above and around this group, smaller statues cover every inch of available space. The bodies and faces are elongated; the drapery is folded and angular. The style of these features, together with the lotus and flame mandala decoration, reached full maturity and dominated later Buddhist sculpture. Although some traits from Central Asia remained, the overall arrangement and style became increasingly more Chinese, particularly after the mid-sixth century. Artists were now consulting the tastes and desires of Chinese authorities, as, for example, in the Binyang Cave, where two relief panels were reserved for the emperor and empress, depicted in an attitude of worship.

The Vairocana Statues in Longmen

After Buddhism survived the first persecution by the imperial court in the middle of the sixth century, Buddhism regained imperial patronage in the Tang dynasty. After a considerable hiatus, work at Longmen was resumed. However, sinicized Buddhism brought dramatic changes to Buddhist sculptures, as sculptors established new aesthetic standards in accordance with the expectations and tastes of the emperors. The monumental Vairocana statue group, located in a Fengxian cave temple and completed by 675, displays such adjustments and reveals a very different style from that of the Yungang statuary. The colossal Vairocana Buddha, embodiment of wisdom and absolute purity, is joined by bodhisattvas, monks, and heavenly kings. It stands even larger, at 17.12 meters (about 56 feet), than the statues in the Buddha of Cave No. XX at Yungang. The most remarkable changes took place in the depiction of facial features. The rigid seriousness of Yungang's statue gave way to a more natural style. The Vairocana Buddha's long narrow eyes, straight nose, and delicate mouth exhibit a femininity that suggests its features might have been modeled after Empress Wu of the Tang period (624–705). The Buddha's expression seems to exude a benevolence sufficient to bless all the world under his merciful power. This fine and careful portrait technique is extended to the images accompanying the Vairocana. Scaled and arranged to indicate different ranks, the bodhisattvas exemplify compassion, the regal power of the heavenly kings, and the sincere piety of the monks.

Realistic Style in and after the Tang Dynasty

Thousands of miles from central China, the realistic style was also employed on Buddhist sculptures in Dunhuang, a splendid Buddhist site on the ancient Silk Road between central Asia and inland China. Sculptors there endowed their human forms with great verisimilitude, in both body proportions and facial features. Of course, this realism is not limited to Buddhist sculptures: Other subjects, such as stone reliefs, tomb guards, and decorative works impress viewers with their inexhaustible natural beauties. After the Tang dynasty, sculpture declined somewhat, due in part to the development of painting and calligraphy and in part to the decline of Buddhist influence in Chinese society. Nonetheless, some sculptures made in the Liao and Jin dynasties (916–1234) still warrant our interest. One of them is a set of Luohan (Arhat) made in three-colored glazed pottery. The dignified facial expressions and realistic physical details illustrate not only specific personalities, but also the different states of the artists' religious enlightenment. Another notable example is a group of Buddhist sculptures completed around A.D. 1038 in the Huayan Temple at Datong, Shanxi Province. The complicated garment details matched by the long and broad ribbons winding and curling over the figures' shoulders and arms beautifully represent the lavish and spectacular style that was employed in Chinese sculpture until the Song dynasty. Beginning with the Ming, sculptors shifted their attentions from Buddhist subjects to secular, architectural decoration.

4. ARCHITECTURE

The Earliest Residential Sites

The history of Chinese architecture can be traced back to the Neolithic period. Unfortunately, except for some sacrificial pits and a few shrines, no actual buildings have survived to our times. Based on their archaeological findings, scholars argue that the earliest villagers built their huts in pure "organic" style. This ancient style stands in sharp contrast to the "artificial" style represented by the palace of the first Qin emperor. According to historical records, the wooden structure built for the emperor had an upper floor that could seat

10,000 people, a huge open space on the lower floor, and long balconies on all sides. All the important architectural evidence from the Han dynasty lies in its tombs. They are categorized according to their structures—octagonal columns characterize one type, capitals attached with two S-curve arms characterize another, and rafter-supported roofs and eaves characterize a third. From the many clay house models also discovered in these tombs, scholars conclude that multi-storied mansions and modest houses existed as two of the major types of residential housing during the Han dynasty.

Earliest Buddhist Architecture

Buddhist architecture consists mainly of three forms: the temple, the pagoda, and the stone cave. According to historical records, more than 30,000 Buddhist buildings existed during the Northern Wei period (386–534). In Luoyang alone, the capital of the Northern Wei empire, 1,300 temples and pagodas once stood. Unfortunately, none of these has survived. The oldest Buddhist pagoda today is the Songyu Pagoda of Kaifeng (Henan Province), built in approximately A.D. 520. This type of Buddhist tower originated in India as a tomb for Buddha's relics and other sacred Buddhist objects. Chinese pilgrims to India brought this idea, along with Buddhist doctrine, back to their own architects, thus enabling them to blend foreign inspirations with China's indigenous traditions. The Songyu Pagoda is a good example of the blending. The main brick body of the pagoda was modeled after the Han timber tower, but its decorative details are borrowed from Indian and central Asian traditions, particularly the lotus bud capitals. The interior is an empty cylinder, which at one time might have held a wooden structure. This kind of brick structure, with its high base, 15 eaves, and 12 sides, constitutes the unique design of the earliest Buddhist pagodas.

Buddhist Temples and Pagodas of the Sui and Tang Dynasties

Temples: Buddhist worship requires temples as well as pagodas, and the Sui (581–618) and Tang dynasties produced a large number of temples. Liang Sicheng (1901–1972) a prominent architect and architectural historian, describes the history of China's traditional timber frame buildings as a three-staged process: the Period of Vigor, from the ninth to the 11th centuries; the Period of Elegance, from the 11th to the 14th centuries; and the Period of Rigidity, between the 15th and the 19th centuries. The oldest wooden structure of the Vigor style is the Fogang temple built in 857 in the sacred Wutai Mountains. This single-story temple is divided into seven bays under the hip roof, which is supported by hypostyle columns and architrave girders, corbel brackets, long slanted lever arms, and tie beams. The complexity of the wooden structure itself reflects exquisite workmanship, and inside, sculpture, murals, and calligraphy combine to form a splendid effect. A two-story, hexagonal pagoda, built around 600, stands nearby. On the lower story of the pagoda, lotus petals are arranged in three tiers entirely covering the cornices. The upper story rests on a balcony supported by a high base with decorated moldings, a special feature of the pagodas during the sixth and seventh centuries. The columns between the two stories are carved with lotus blossom patterns. A flame-shaped mandala caps the arched doorway. Inside, the mural painting on the dark red wall imitates earlier Buddhist sculptural styles.

Pagodas: Two examples of pagodas from the Period of Vigor survive in the Wild Goose Pagoda (the current structure was rebuilt between 701 and 704), and the Xuanzang Pagoda (built in 681 to house the ashes of the famous Buddhist master of Xuanzang 602–664). Although architects continued to model their pagodas on the timber tower of the Han dynasty, they dramatically simplified the building structure. The earlier 12-sided structure was reduced to four sides. Simple arched side gates replaced the gaudy decorations. As the tower rises, each story shrinks slightly in height and width. The final sloped roof supports a small pagoda in the style of central Asia.

Buddhist Architecture in the Song and Yuan Dynasties

Chinese architecture enters what Liang Sicheng called the Period of Elegance in the Song dynasty. The Elegant style is marked by the significant development of the bracket set (a joint section of timber bearing blocks and arms placed either on top of a column or on a beam connecting to the top of a column. For detailed explanations, please see *Grove's Dictionary of Art*). The long, slanted lever arms with extended tails were cleverly used to support either the weight of the beam or the purling above. Inside, the height of columns varied with the contours of the roof—some were elevated higher in order to support the beams directly. Whenever a column was joined to a horizontal structure, a set of brackets was employed to share the supportive functions. With the improved brackets, the shape of the slanted arms changed from a simple rectangular cross to a scooped and pulvinated cross, providing new "spaces" for artistic ingenuity. Fabulous sculptures, fresco paintings, and other decorations impressed Buddhist worshippers. In the main hall of Jingtu Temple (built in 1124), Ying County, Shanxi Province, for example, architects hollowed out the ceiling into a myriad of recessed square, hexagonal, and octagonal boxes, which artists then filled with painted images of worshippers, holy figures, sculpted dragons, and phoenixes. Other surviving examples can be found at the Saintly Mother Hall (built from 1023–1031) of the Jinci religious building complex, and the Huayan Temples (built in 1038 and 1140), all in the Taiyuan area in Shanxi. The oldest and the tallest timber pagoda was built around 1056 at Ying County in Shanxi Province. With a total height of 118 meters (387 feet), the pagoda consists of 10 levels, each of which is a self-contained structure. Other pagodas were built in stone or brick, even glazed brick. The best example of that kind of architecture is a 13-story pagoda called Youguo

Temple (built in 1044) in Kaifeng, Henan Province. The whole structure is made of iron-red brick. The projected eaves on each story curve slightly upward at the point where two sections join.

In 1271, the Mongols conquered China and established a dynasty under the title of *Yuan*, meaning "original." Under the new Yuan regime (1276–1368), Buddhist temples and pagodas continued to be built, but some of them revealed the strong foreign tastes of the Mongols. The White Pagoda at the Miaoyan Temple in Beijing, dated 1279, is a typical example. The pagoda was designed by a Nepalese and modeled after Nepal's popular pagoda style. On a square base, a lotus seat with 24 petals supports the round, very white main body of the pagoda, which is further topped by a 13-tiered cone symbolizing the Buddha-truth. A canopy, decorated with six bronze tassels for hanging bells, crowns the cone-shaped structure. Another site located outside of Beijing is the Cloud Terrace of the Juyong Pass stronghold on the Great Wall. The rectangular tower, white marble interior, and the Buddhist doctrine carved on the wall in six languages, including Chinese, Mongolian, and Sanskrit, all attest to the influence of Mongol rulers. One can also find temples built by other religions during this period. In Fujian Province, the Qingjiang Temple represents Islamic styles with its arched ceiling, windows, and the arabesque inscriptions.

Temples of the Ming and Qing Dynasties

Islam was very active during the Ming dynasty, and Muslim mosques were built throughout the country. These mosques are characterized by their large worship halls (essential for the daily worship of the faithful), which always face westward, the direction of Mecca.

Although Islam spread to all parts of China during the Ming dynasty, Daoism remained the official religion. Hundreds of Daoist temples were built or rebuilt as traditional Chinese wooden structures. The Ming imperial court even ordered 300,000 laborers to rebuild an important group of Daoist temples in the Wudang Mountains, Hubei Province, a seven-year enterprise. But Daoism slowly declined with the collapse of the Ming regime. The new Manchu ruling class preferred to patronize Tibetan Buddhism, which they found more compatible with their own shamanism. Thus, many temples built during this regime reflect the strong influence of Tibetan Buddhism. At the beginning of the 18th century, the Qing emperor built a summer palace in Chengde, Hebei Province. Around the palace, roughly 20 groups of temples were built in the styles of Tibetan Buddhism, Chinese Buddhism, or a mixture of the two branches. The greatest Tibetan Buddhist temple in Beijing is the famous Yonghe Temple. The compound was originally Yongzheng's (r. 1722–1735) private residence before he became the emperor. After Yongzheng's death, his son, Emperor Qianlong (1711–1799) had the residence transformed into the Yonghe Temple as a gesture to show his devotion to Tibetan Buddhism. This temple has five courtyards and five major halls, all with splendid mural paintings and sculptures. The most astonishing object is a standing statue of the 18-meter (57 feet) tall Future Buddha, made from the trunk of a single, enormous tree.

Imperial Architecture in Beijing

Compared to the Yuan rulers, the Ming and Qing emperors preferred an architectural style that expressed or even flaunted their power. Thus the Elegant manner of the Yuan gave way to the austere and powerful style visible in the imperial tombs of Ming, the Forbidden City, and the Summer Palaces.

Imperial Tombs: The most famous tomb site of the Ming dynasty is the Thirteen Mausoleums, with its long path lined with stone statues of animals and human figures on either side. The entrance to the tomb consists of a stone memorial archway with five gates and a watchtower with red walls and a yellow roof. The tomb itself is actually an underground palace, including a huge hall roofed with yellow, glazed tiles and supported by towering columns made of whole tree trunks, and a tomb with polished marble vaults and walls. To allow

imperial family members to pay tribute to their ancestors, architects built temples on the side of the tomb.

The Forbidden City: The most splendid architectural achievement in Beijing is the Forbidden City, the palace for 24 emperors of the Ming and Qing dynasties. The principle behind its "city within a city" plan dates back to palace traditions since the Qin dynasty. The Forbidden City's front gate is called the Gate of Heavenly Peace (Tiananmen) and consists of a tower connected to the open square in front by five elaborately carved stone bridges. Beyond the gate tower, the palace divides into inner and outer courts along a north-south axis, containing a total of 9,000 individual rooms and halls over an area of 73 hectares (180 acres). All the individual units were thoughtfully placed and connected by hallways, bridges, and open courtyards. The outer court, occupying the south side, consists of three main halls known as the Hall of Supreme Harmony, Hall of Middle Harmony, and Hall of Protecting Harmony and were used primarily for state events and ceremonies. Behind those three halls, on the northern side, are groups of buildings used for private living quarters, offices, workshops, entertainment theaters, and gardens. The stairways and railings are made of white marble and carved with dragons, contrasting beautifully with the painted columns and yellow-glazed roofs. Marble and bronze sculptures, wood carvings, tiling, paintings, lacquering, enameling, jade, stone and shell inlaying, and silk mounting—all applied perfectly and lavishly to the very diverse building surfaces such a vast enclosure affords—make the "city" one of China's great art museums.

The Summer Palaces: Historically, there have been two summer palaces on the outskirts of Beijing. The new Summer Palace is the better known to modern tourists. It was built in the late 19th century about 94 miles northwest of Beijing. Occupying a total of 290 hectares (717 acres), the palace grounds encompass both a mountain and a large lake which cover more than three-quarters of the total area. Yet there are still more than 3,000 halls, temples, pavilions, and gardens in this Summer Palace.

The older Summer Palace was built in the 17th century and expanded in the 18th century. Occupying more than 425 hectares (1063 acres) northwest of Beijing, it contained gardens, courtyards, and buildings of diverse architectural styles. For example, gardens built in the Suzhou style (see below) and European-style buildings could both be found in the palace. The Summer Palace was looted and burned by the Anglo-French expeditionary forces during the Arrow War in 1860. Parts of its ruins, however, are still available for tourists to visit. Ironically, the most notable part of its ruins is the site where several European-style columns still stand.

The Great Wall

As the most famous symbol of China, the Great Wall stretches along the top of Yan Mountain, originating in southwest China and ending in the northeast of the country, totaling 4,000 miles. To be a defense against the nomadic tribes from the north, the monolithic project was initiated by the first emperor of the Qin dynasty, continued by different dynasties, and finally completed and connected as a whole in the Ming dynasty. The entire wall, its watchtowers, and its ramps were all built with huge stones, chosen and placed with astonishing precision to conform to the varying slope (some 45 degrees) of the mountains. Today, the part of the Great Wall outside Beijing is restored and has become a major tourist attraction.

Suzhou Gardens

Contrasting with the giant palace in Beijing are the very delicate and exquisite gardens in Suzhou. Around the 11th century, Suzhou and its adjacent areas formed the cultural center of China, attracting both intellectuals and wealthy merchants drawn to its rich culture and beautiful scenery. The wealthy created their own luxurious facilities, building houses with beautiful interiors and filling them with paintings and elaborate furniture. But the outstanding feature was the setting— nature, as appreciated and cultivated by early landscape architects. The main elements of the gardens—water, rocks, pavilions, halls, houses, flowers, and trees—

were set off against one another, then integrated into an organic whole. The layout usually began with a gate that led visitors through a narrow, winding corridor or small courtyard into a large and bright space, the main scenery of the garden. The crucial component of such a garden was water, shaped into a pond for goldfish and lotuses or water lilies, or formed into a curving brook or creek running through the whole garden. Rocks, often taken from Lake Tai (a large lake in Jiangsu Province), formed a pleasing contrast with water when arranged on the shores of a pond or piled up in the center of the water. Rocks were also used to create artificial hillocks or peaks in front of a building and on top of a hill. The central part of a garden included various halls, lounges with windows, guest houses, multi-storied houses, pavilions, waterside pavilions, and land boats. The size and placement of buildings, linked by meandering corridors and bridges, involved careful design so that they could function as part of the landscape together with water, rocks, flowers, and trees. The architectural details obeyed the principles of openness and good air circulation. Open corridors, hollowed windows, tracery windows, and transparent screens all brought external nature into the living space and created a more pleasant atmosphere for the interior.

The most famous gardens in the city are Zhuozheng Garden, Liu Garden, Shizilin Canglang Pavilion, and Wangshi Garden. Zhuozheng Garden is characterized by water surrounded by trees, flower gardens, bamboo groves, pavilions, and halls and houses connected by winding corridors. Liu Garden, though it is known for the harmony between hillocks and pools, and courtyards and buildings, also has two artificial hills built with lake stones. The larger hill sits in front of the garden's other focal points, including several courtyards, a large and luxurious hall, a study, and accessory buildings. The smaller hill is a whole piece of rock, standing on the shore of a pool facing nearby pavilions. Shizilin, created for a Buddhist hermit monk, is famous for its stone peaks, formed of rocks with many cavities and holes. Doors in full-moon and half-moon shapes lead to different settings with rocks, pools decorated with lotus and willows, and pavilions or houses with hollowed railings. Canglang Pavilion has a central mound and a long winding corridor forming its layout. Wangshi Garden was actually built for a high official. The luxurious living quarters are circled by water, hills, bamboo groves, gardens, and rocks. The distinctive features of this garden are the exquisite buildings with petite and transparent characters.

Residential Houses

The garden houses in Suzhou represented one kind of residence, but houses for civilians also had special features that varied by geographic and climatic conditions and reflected the local traditions and customs. Houses in cities were grouped into different districts, arranged by orderly streets or avenues. In the countryside, houses were placed along fields or roads, their exact positions determined by Feng Shui. (Chinese people believe that the natural environment of a particular location can influence the fortune of its inhabitants and descendants. It also reflects the concepts of *yin and yang* and five elements that constitute all reality.) Cave dwellings were very popular in mountainous areas in northwestern China. Many fishermen of south China used their fishing boats and ships as their living quarters.

Nevertheless, one feature dominated the traditional layout of Chinese homes and can be seen everywhere in the country: the whole plan almost always centered on a courtyard or a hall with rooms arranged symmetrically on the four sides. A typical example is the old Beijing quadrangles; one of these had a courtyard in the middle, a main section on the north, other subordinated sections on the east and west sides, and the front gate on the south side. In southern China, because of the hot and humid climate, houses usually had a high-ceiling front hall facing a small courtyard to increase air circulation.

5. PAINTINGS

The Chinese painting tradition differs from that of the West in tools, media, and formats. For Chinese painters, the most important tools are brushes, inks, and pigments. Artists have to control the brush movements skillfully in order to produce lines, dots, and strokes in varied ink tonalities. Before paper was invented, most paintings were done on hard surfaces such as stone, wood, and bamboo slips. Once paper was available, around A.D. 121, artists preferred it along with silk because of its ability to absorb ink. Painting formats vary from hand scrolls and hanging scrolls to albums and fans. Seals made from high-quality stones carved with the artist's name are used on paintings to identify the artist and sometimes the ownership.

Early Works

Painting has always been an important part of Chinese art. At different archaeological sites, scholars have found paintings on pottery, bronze, lacquer, and silk. In 1973, archaeologists discovered the tomb of Lady Dai, dated around A.D. 168, at Mawangdui, near Changsha in Hunan Province. In the tomb, they unearthed a silk banner and two beautifully painted coffins. The upper part of the silk banner is filled with mythological symbols to accompany the soul of the deceased in heaven. A watchtower, with two guards sitting inside to secure the heavenly gate, divides the upper world from the lower, occupied by the deceased lady accompanied by her servants and a creature with the power to bring the dead back to life. The paintings on the coffins repeat the theme. On a black background, cloud patterns in gold and other bright colors set off tiny figures and creatures believed to protect the soul of the dead and drive the demons away. On the panels of the inner coffin, geometric patterns form a frame in which mountains, dwellings of immortals, curling dragons, soaring unicorns, flying phoenixes, and dancing guardians suggest a wonderful world for the afterlife.

Narrative Paintings of the Age of Division

Narrative paintings developed in conjunction with achievements in literature. The earliest work of this type is attributed to Gu Kaizhi (c. 345–406) titled *The Nymph of the Luo River*. The painting presents a story from a poem about the love between the poet Cao Zhi (192–232) and a river nymph. The figures are repeated several times and end in a farewell scene: the nymph returns to the river, and the poet, accompanied by several attendants, watches her sadly from the shore. The elegant ink lines and the rich colors of this painting won a reputation for the artist. Even more important was the artist's use of landscape as a setting for the plot, ushering in a new era of landscape painting. Gu Kaizhi also produced two other famous works, *The Admonitions of the Instructress to the Palace Ladies* and the *Record of Eminent Women*. The former portrays emperors as arrogant and powerful characters in contrast to their concubines' slender features and delicate gestures. The latter illustrates biographical stories that served as models for women.

Tang Dynasty

The Masters of Figure Painting: The tradition of figure painting was continued during the Tang dynasty in the form of pure line drawings. The best works were done by Wu Daozi (689–758), who painted his subjects with three-dimensional quality, allowing viewers to study them from all directions. Under Wu's brushes, figures acquired a vividness and energy as if able to walk out of the painting at any moment. No works by Wu survived to our time, but his influence was crucial for three court painters: Yan Liben (600–673), Zhang Xuan (active 713–42), and the Zhou Fang (740–800). Yan Liben did a long hand scroll with the images of 13 emperors accompanied by high-ranking officials and attendants. They are dressed in loose, flowing robes depicted in thick but smooth brush lines, which, together with some shading, create an impression of dimension. Yan's talent was further applauded after the discovery of a wall painting in the tomb of Princess Yongtai. Experts believe

his students painted it. The wall painting, showing a group of elegantly dressed court ladies in different postures but all wearing long skirts, was painted with free, vivacious, and yet controlled brush strokes. Zhang Xuan and Zhou Fang specialized in describing court ladies' activities. The hand scroll *Ladies Preparing Newly Woven Silk*, attributed to Zhang Xuan, shows three groups of ladies making silk. The same subject of court ladies performing daily activities was adopted by Zhou Fang in his painting *Court Ladies Adorning Their Hair with Flower*. The artist captured the moment when a noble woman was loitering in a garden, surrounded by servants, a puppy, and a crane. The treatments in these two hand scrolls are very similar, exhibiting little personal style, but following the beauty standards of the Tang dynasty: round face, long and narrow eyes, straight nose, and small mouth. The luxurious dresses decorated with embroidery not only indicate the status of the ladies but also suggest elegant movements through the lines of swinging drapery. The colors used by these two court painters were very bright, though Zhou Fang was more cautious in using vermilion, purple, crimson, and pink, and Zhang Xuan boldly attempted to harmonize red, green, yellow, and white.

Landscape Painting: Since the birth of landscape painting with Gu Kaizhi's *Nymph of the Luo River*, this genre has occupied a prominent place in Chinese art. In the Tang dynasty, landscape painting appeared in the "blue-and-green colors" style, as, for example, in *The Emperor Minghuang's Journey to Shu*. The work alludes to the rebellion in 756 that drove Emperor Minghuang from the capital into the treacherous mountains of Shu (another name for the Sichuan area). The anonymous artist successfully depicted the precipitous nature of the place through an inaccessible narrow road, steep cliffs, and the visibly exhausted human figures. In contrast with this chaotic theme is a peaceful and simple snow-scene painting called *Riverside Under Snow* done by the highly esteemed poet and painter Wang Wei (699–759). It was Wang who developed the "broken ink" and "texture stroke" techniques, thus becoming an essential pioneer of Chinese ink painting. His use of ink in different tones against a white background allowed him to vividly express the softness and pure tranquillity of the snowscape.

Dunhuang Caves: The Dunhuang caves in Gansu Province were opened around the fourth century by Buddhist pilgrims from central Asia to China, with construction of caves reaching a peak during the Tang dynasty and falling to disuse after the 13th century. Today there exist roughly 486 caves, with 2,415 statues and 393,000 square feet of mural paintings. Dunhuang sculptures executed in a realistic style certainly reached a level of perfection in Buddhist art. The most remarkable achievements of Dunhuang art, however, lie in the paintings. The evolution of the painting style in Dunhuang mirrors the progress of Buddhism in China. Beginning with purely Indian or central Asian styles, Dunhuang painters gradually incorporated Chinese styles until their art form was dominated by Chinese taste. In the last period of Dunhuang painting, the artwork also showed influence from Tibetan Buddhist elements. Colors of Dunhuang paintings ranged from dark brown and green to rich and splendid mixtures. Subjects centered on Buddhist sutras and legends, but there were also images of imperial members and famous donors. The most popular themes were Amitabha, the symbol of Mercy and Wisdom, with scenery of his Western Paradise, and stories of the Buddha in his various incarnations. Those legends advocated self-sacrifice, one of the main principles in Buddhism and a means for Buddhists to accumulate merit to gain a better rebirth in their future lives. Although the glories of these great paintings have diminished somewhat with the faded details and colors, they testify to the towering achievements of Chinese Buddhist art.

The Northern Song Dynasty

The intense and varied interests of the emperors of the Northern Song made it a fruitful period for Chinese paintings of all kinds. Emperor Huizong (1082–1135) was perhaps the most instrumental in fostering the development of Chinese painting

toward excellence. He built a solid foundation for the Painters' Academy and demanded that all painters focus on accurate, realistic depiction, study the traditions, and strive for the attainment of a poetic ideal. The emperor himself was a competent painter, calligrapher, and poet, and he sought to bring these three art forms together. At his command, an imperial collection catalog was created. The text declared Li Cheng (919–967) the master of landscape painting, Li Gonglin (c. 1041–1106) the master of figure painting, and Xu Xi (d. before 975) the primary painter of birds and flowers. The catalog is of great value to scholars of art history.

The Monumental Landscape Paintings: Li Cheng initiated the style of monumental landscape paintings in the Northern Song with his wintry mountain scenery. The realistic detail in his paintings reflected typical geographical characters of gigantic mountains in northern China. He introduced a new density of details in his compositions, yet managed to convey a sense of orderly arrangement. Li's works generally contained three sections: water or open space in the foreground; lively hills embellished with trees, small houses, temples, and human figures in the middle ground; and huge mountain peaks emerging from the background, dominating more than half the composition, as seen in *A Solitary Temple amid Clearing Peaks.* Artists did not use perspective, but they established a sense of depth and distance through modulation of ink tonalities and brush strokes. Li Cheng deeply inspired his followers, among whom ranked Fan Kuan (active c. 1023–1031), Yan Wengui (active 980–1010), Xu Daoning (c. 970–1051–52), and Guo Xi (c. 1001–1090). One invaluable work by Fan Kuan is the silk hanging scroll titled *Traveling Among Streams and Mountains.* In the painting, huge mountains are treated in "raindrop strokes," and boldly outlined shapes occupy almost the entire space, leaving room for only a thin waterfall line from the top of a tall cliff dropping down to the foreground, where several travelers hurry between dense wood and a small stream. Guo Xi's masterpiece *The Early Spring* is a signed silk hanging scroll dated 1072, depicting a lively spring scene in the mountains. His painting is a fine example of the monumental style called Li-Guo (from Li Cheng to Guo Xi). Forming a parallel to these northern masters are two southerners, Dong Yuan (c. 900–962) and Juran (active c. 960–985). Dong Yuan inherited many traditions from Wang Wei and thoroughly mastered the techniques of wet ink and the "hemp fiber stroke" applied mainly in depiction of mountains and rocks. The hanging scroll attributed to him, *Wintry Groves and Layered Banks*, presents uninterrupted landscape scenery treated in wet ink and light colors. Juran learned from Dong Yuan but also diverged from his style somewhat. In his painting *Seeking the Dao in the Autumn Mountains*, Juran assembled a group of steep and convex slopes in the center, but left a small space on the front for a stream and a winding road leading to a hut at the foot of the mountain. Together with his master, Juran brought their style, which is known as the Dong-Ju style, to maturity.

Figure Painting: Figure paintings in this period depicted all kinds of people: from emperors, aristocracy, and high officials to scholars and ordinary civilians, as well as literary characters and religious images. When painting portraits of emperors and other authorities, artists sought to express their subjects' dignity and power. Such artistic concern can be seen in the portrait of the first Song emperor, shown sitting on a red lacquered throne in a three-quarter view, wearing the Song court hat with two long stiff flaps and a white silk dragon robe. Artists of other figure paintings conformed to principles of realism. The pure line drawing master Li Gonglin (1049–1106) clearly illustrated his specialty in his *Five Tribute Horses*. Gu Hongzhong (active 10th century), the artist of *The Night Revels of Han Xizai*, recorded in a hand scroll a luxurious night event taking place in the house of the high scholar-official Han Xizai. Religious paintings, such as the long hand scroll *Eighty-seven Immortals*, depicted all immortal figures as humanized and drawn in beautiful, dense, free-flowing lines. Zhang Zeduan (active early 12th century) in his long hand scroll *Peace Reigns over the River* (done between 1111 and 1126) vividly unfolded the civilians' life in the capital of Kaifeng. Zhang

Zeduan's long scroll is filled with intricate details, beginning with a village scene and developing along the river's shore to the tall Rainbow Bridge, on top of which crowds of people watch in excitement and anxiety as a large boat is pulled across the bridge. The artist then led viewers through a city gate tower and into the center of the town, full of shops, entertainment venues, crowds, and all kinds of activities.

Miscellaneous Subjects: Paintings of animals, birds, flowers, fishes, and architecture all achieved great triumphs simultaneously in the Northern Song. The emperor favored horses and water buffaloes because they symbolized imperial power. Li Gonglin copied Tang painter Wei Yan's (d. 800) work *Pasturing Horses*, in which the painter projected a spectacular scene with more than a thousand horses and hundreds of horsemen. The same panoramic view appears in *Pasturing Water Buffalo*, attributed to Qi Xu (active late 10th and early 11th centuries), whose observation of numerous water buffaloes lent great accuracy to this attempt at revealing a typical scene in the Jiangnan area (south of the Yangtze River).

Though horses and water buffaloes suggested imperial power and dignity, birds and flowers signified peace and happiness and became another favored subject among artists. Emperor Huizong painted *The Five-Colored Parakeet* and accompanied the art with elegant calligraphy in an elongated style written on the right half of the scroll. Another well-known bird-and-flower painting, *Magpies and Hare* dated 1061, was by Cui Bo (c. 10th century), who used two magpies as the symbol of happiness and good fortune. Similar to the birds and flowers, fish also symbolized wealth and good fortune, inspiring Song artists to change their images from static still life to images of lively animals swimming around lotuses and watercress.

Architecture became another popular subject to display the Song's flourishing economy. Artists by this time had matured in their mastery of ink line drawing, enabling them to paint architectural objects accurately, as if they were using a ruler to draw each line. Most houses, bridges, temples (including the small temple in Li Cheng's landscape work), and even boats were painted precisely with all structural details. The master of this style was Zhang Zeduan, who presented colorful and joyful urban life along with realistic architecture in accurate detail. Another master, Guo Zhongshu (c. 910–977), exhibited these skills in *Traveling on the River in Clearing Snow*, a hand scroll describing two heavily loaded boats with sophisticated detail in faultless ink lines.

The Literati Paintings: Reacting against this realistic style was a small group of scholars led by the great poet and statesman Su Shi (1036–1101). Included in the group were the famous bamboo painter Wen Tong (c. 1019–1079), painter and calligrapher Mi Fu (1051–1105), and the poet and calligrapher Huang Tingjian (1045–1107). In their minds, an artist should focus on expressing ideas and emotions through mountains, rocks, trees, and bamboo, rather than pursuing accurate likenesses. They used only paper and ink, and viewed silk and colors as vulgar, seductive components. Although this kind of practice was forbidden at court, several important court artists who significantly influenced Emperor Huizong's artistic interests and achievements accepted the techniques invented by this group of scholars.

The Southern Song Dynasty

The Landscape Paintings: After the fall of the Northern Song and the establishment of the Southern Song court in Hangzhou in 1127, the monumental landscape painting style was brought to the south. However, the style was soon modified into a more refined style by Li Tang (c. 1050–after 1130). In his long hanging scroll *Wind Through the Pine Valleys* (dated 1124), modeled after Fan Kuan's *Traveling Among Streams and Mountains*, Li abandoned the simplified manner of his predecessor and adapted an "ax-cut stroke" to create the varied formations of rocks. Li Tang established a standard painting vogue for later artists with his tall and jagged rocks and cliffs, twisting trees, and ax-cut stroke. Another leading figure was Zhao Boju (d. c. 1162), who adapted the

Tang blue-and-green manner in his *Autumn Colors over Streams and Mountains*, dated 1160.

The Southern Song Academy: The Painting Academy was an art institution that gathered the empire's most outstanding artists to serve the court. There is no clear record of the origins of the institution. After the collapse of the Northern Song regime, the academy moved to Hangzhou, together with the Southern Song court. The academy employed outstanding artists to serve the needs of the imperial family and members of the court. Probably affected by the delicate and exquisite scenery around the capital, the empress and many high-ranking officials began to demand paintings in a portable format so they could carry them around. Thus, artists created small fan and album paintings to delight their masters. One of the finest examples is an anonymous fan-shaped album leaf called *The Han Palace*, which reproduces ancient palace life in minute detail. Besides fan painting, academy members continually produced landscape subjects on a large scale by order of the emperors. The most prominent court painters were Ma Yuan (c. 1189–1225) and Xia Gui (active 1200–1230), the two founders of the Ma-Xia School, which produced the most significant accomplishments of the Song Painting Academy. Their paintings embodied the quintessence of the former masters: varied totality from Fan Kuan, twisting trees from Li Cheng, and ax-cut strokes from Li Tang. But the composition of their paintings is easily distinguished from that of their forerunners. Later painters added more empty space to each piece of work, especially the paintings done by Ma Yuan, who pushed all elements to a corner or to one side of the composition, leaving the rest for colophons or emperors' inscriptions. His elegant painting *On a Mountain Path in Spring*, an album leaf, evidences such a style. Ma Yuan's son, Ma Lin, inherited his father's specialties and joined them to his ability to catch a touching moment in nature. In the hanging scroll *Sunset Landscape*, Ma Lin painted several swallows flying across a lake toward distant mountains, which almost merge with the setting sun. A couplet from Wang Wei's poem was written by the emperor on the upper half of the scroll.

Similarly, Xia Gui showed his skills and qualities in simplified and purified form. His hand scroll *Pure and Remote View of Hills and Streams* illustrated his particular talent—dark trees and solid rocks in ax-cut strokes form a contrast with the soft, even-blurring rivers winding in front of mountains, which are elevated in mist in the background. Small houses, boats, and human figures all find a place in this painting. Xia Gui was highly praised by later painters and became the model of the Zhe School in the Ming dynasty.

The Chan (Zen) Paintings: Chan Buddhism, first developed in China, is better known in the West by its Japanese name, Zen. The last chapter of the Southern Song painting history was written by a group of Chan painters, led by a retired official, Liang Kai, and two monks, Muqi (d. 1239), and Yujian (c. 13th century). Their paintings, rooted in Buddhist and Daoist thought, clearly reflected the tendency to ignore realistic likenesses in order to concentrate on exploring one's own inner world. Liang Kai's portrait *Li Taibo* exemplified those principles. In this hanging scroll, Liang sketched the famous poet Li Bo with a few very bold and vigorous strokes: two ink dots suggested the feet, a dot with a tail formed an eye, and a small triangle represented the nose. And yet the aura of the man shone vividly through the slightly raised head, tilted mustache, and sharp expression of the eye. The portrait left no doubt that the poet was walking, thinking, and ready to compose another unforgettable poem.

Muqi followed closely in Liang Kai's footsteps. His important work, *Six Persimmons*, illustrated abstract fruit forms endowed with inner power and spiritual values. An excellent painting by Muqi is the triptych *The White Robed Guanyin, Crane, and Gibbons*. The work was an icon of the late Song Buddhist practice: at the center, the bodhisattva Guanyin is meditating on a rock by a stream; on the right, a gibbon in a tree holds her baby tightly as if facing some danger; and on the left is a crane running out from a bamboo grove toward Guanyin for help. Every detail in the work carried a definite meaning: Guanyin was the savior of the universe, the gibbons and crane were symbols of longevity. Together they delivered a clear Buddhist message: Guanyin was ready to help everyone escape misery and achieve immortality in the Buddhist paradise. It is not always easy to understand the esoteric meanings in the Chan paintings, but their approaches to exploring the inner, spiritual world was developed by the literati painters of the Yuan dynasty.

The Yuan Dynasty

Landscape Paintings: After the Mongols established the Yuan regime, the new rulers mixed their own artistic tastes with Saracenic, Buddhist, and Chinese traditions, a mixture clearly exhibited in their imperial portraits. But in landscape painting, artists clung to Chinese traditions as an expression of national loyalty and nostalgia for the old empire. Thus, landscape painting reached a new era of development, led by Qian Xuan (c. 1235–1301), a retired official who had retreated from the government after the Mongol takeover. The other leaders were Zhao Mengfu (1254–1322) and Gao Kegong (1248–1310), who served at the court, but privately remained loyal to the old Chinese regime. Qian Xuan carefully selected his themes and styles from the remote past to express his nostalgia. The hand scrolls *Wang Xizhi Gazing at Geese* and *Returning Home* represent Qian's painting style. Both of these paintings are in Tang blue-and-green style. The former depicted the supreme Jin dynasty calligrapher Wang Xizhi watching swimming geese and trying to catch the graceful lines of the "sinuous necks" in his cursive script; the latter portrayed the well-known poet Tao Yuanming retiring from his political life and returning to his home village. Qian Xuan's student Zhao Mengfu was a descendant of a Song emperor and played an important political role in bridging the gap between Chinese culture and foreign customs. Meanwhile, he continued to explore the history and inner nature of painting and calligraphy, rediscovering the merits of the long-neglected Northern Song Dong-Ju style and combining them with his own direct and spontaneous expressions. One of the most well-known paintings by Zhao Mengfu is a hand scroll called *The Autumn Colors on the Que and Hua Mountains*. The artist evoked the methods of drawing hills and clouds of Dong Yuan, but put them into his own symmetrical arrangement. He also used simple brush strokes to depict details of trees, houses, and boats, as seen in the work of Zhao Lingrang (active c. 1080–1100). The calligraphic treatments, especially of the tree leaves, heralded a new approach: painting and calligraphy could no longer be separated. The most important evolution in this painting is that the artist executed the work according to the mountains in his mind. In reality, Mt. Que and Mt. Hua are located far apart, but the artist moved them together and created this masterpiece to express the picture in his heart. Gao Kegong was another official artist, who freely combined in his landscape the terrain from Dong-Ju with the mist from Mi Fu (1052–1107). These three artists—Qian Xuan, Zhao Mengfu, and Gao Kegong—heralded a new era, emphasizing the significance of self-expression in an artistic composition. Their theories had great influence on their followers, especially the literati painters of the Yuan dynasty.

The Literati Paintings: Under Mongol rule, many high officials preferred to resign their posts and live as hermits in the south, in an area once the center of cultural activities. There, they formed the literati circles famous for producing paintings in the traditions of Qian Xuan and Zhao Mengfu. The most well-remembered are the Four Great Masters: Huang Gongwang (1269–1354), Wu Zhen (1280–1354), Ni Zan (1301–1374), and Wang Meng (1308–1385). Huang Gongwang spent the last part of his life composing the long hand scroll *Dwelling In the Fuchun Mountains*, which presented his whole painting theory: to produce a piece of work from the mind rather than from nature. The front of the long scroll opens with a river, dotted with small fishing boats and bridges, trees, and lowlands on either side; the background is occupied by hills and slopes decorated with more trees, and small houses. The whole piece gives the impression of grace and clarity, as if the artist himself were walking in a dream full of a pure freshness that does not exist in the real world.

Huang's contemporary Wu Zhen painted many pictures of his own favorite theme—a fisherman much less interested in catching fish than in communicating with nature and meditating on poetry, typical of the ideal life of many scholars. The composition of Wu's paintings is rather simple: in the front there is a small boat or boats carrying a lonely fisherman, then an open space implying a vast expanse of water extending to the horizon where a few blurred mountains are painted in wet ink. There are no extra silhouettes, and every element contributes to the calm and harmonic atmosphere.

Ni Zan followed these two masters. As a well-educated scholar, he could not accept an office from the court without also stating his mood of protest through his painting. A cottage empty of human life, trees without roots, bare hills in the distance—all executed in dry, almost icy brush strokes—hinted at his feelings of loss and loneliness living in his own country under foreign domination.

Wang Meng was a grandson of Zhao Mengfu. He benefited a great deal from both his grandfather and grandmother Guan Daosheng (1261–1319), who was also a gifted artist. Unlike his grandparents, Wang created many mountain scenes. He did not leave any empty space in his works, but filled every available square inch with ebullient and rich motifs arranged in a logical and smooth rhythm.

Bamboo and Plum Paintings: Landscape was a favorite subject for the Yuan masters. But artists also adored the bamboo and plum trees because they symbolized noble scholarly characteristics. Zhao Mengfu's wife, Guan Daosheng, was well known for her bamboo paintings, and Wu Zhen and Li Kan (1245–1320) produced manuals of bamboo painting. Tang Di (c. 1286–1354), another well-established landscape painter, also left some ink traces in the bamboo genre. The most famous ink plum painter is Wang Mian (1287–1359), who used plum blossoms as a metaphor for scholars under Mongol rule, particularly their ability to survive in freezing weather and retain their purity and courage.

The Ming Dynasty

The Court Painters: In 1368 the Mongols were expelled from China, and the Ming dynasty began. The reinstatement of Chinese authority brought back the Southern Song Academy traditions. Emperor Xuanzong (r. 1427–1435), an amateur artist himself, imitated what Emperor Huizong of the Northern Song had done in many respects, including the establishment of a painters' organization similar to the Song Painters Academy, and gathering many famous scholar artists around the court. Most notable among the court painters were Bian Wenjin (c. 1400–1440) and Lu Ji (1477–1521). Bian was probably inspired by the stimulating development of full-color prints at that time and specialized in full-colored bird and flower paintings in a very carefully outlined, decorative style. Lu mainly concentrated on landscape subjects, but he abandoned the Yuan self-expressive manner and aimed instead at decorative results. His paintings are powerfully and vigorously executed, exhibiting a skillfully cultivated sculptural quality using refined techniques.

The Zhe School of Landscape Paintings: The Zhe School was established by Dai Jin (1388–1462) and Wu Wei (1459–1508). Dai was a dismissed official who returned to his hometown in the lower Yangtze valley where, due to his extraordinary capacity for painting, he founded the Zhe School, thereby reviving the Southern Song Ma-Xia styles. Dai Jin did many paintings with these styles, varying from careful, conservative interpretations to freer and bolder schemes. The hanging scroll *Returning Late from a Spring Outing* is reminiscent of works by Ma Yuan and other Southern Song painters, though his hand scroll *Fishermen on the River* obviously owes more to Wu Zhen, who inspired Dai Jin's imagination in his treatment of fishermen, boats, and bamboo. Dai Jin's follower Wu Wei was a famous figure and landscape painter, who served at the Ming court. He is often described as a drunken painter, and his works closely resemble Liang Kai's in the Song dynasty, usually expressing the images with a few free brush strokes. He is more like Dai Jin in his landscape paintings, but his manner is more flamboyant and his ink line rougher and wilder, especially in the hand scroll *The Pleasures of the Fishing Village*.

Literati Painting—The Wu School: The Wu School was formed near Suzhou by a group of scholar-painters who gradually learned the traditions from the Four Great Masters of Yuan. One of its founders was Shen Zhou (1427–1509), a wealthy literati painter, who was very active among scholars. He imitated the Four Great Masters of the Yuan dynasty but absorbed their techniques into his own unique style in a way that was more casual, lyrical, and lucid. His hanging scroll *Walking with a Staff*, incorporates some motifs and techniques from Ni Zan, but the dynamic terrain, the axial arrangement of the stream, the tall trees, and the monumental scale, are his own innovations. In the hand scroll *Watching the Mid-Autumn Moon*, he blended his literary ideas with the techniques of the Yuan master Wu Zhen. Shen used smooth lines, wet ink, and light colors in composing his image of three scholars sitting in a simple hut, drinking wine, and looking at the full moon.

Wen Zhengming (1470–1559) was another important figure in the Wu School. As a pupil of Shen Zhou, Wen was committed to painting and calligraphy after retiring from the court and produced many works in a variety of styles. The most profound expression of his own personality can be found in his pine trees and cypresses with their twisting, complicated branches, symbolizing the scholar as well as presenting the artist's emotions at that particular moment. Even in many of his landscape paintings, Wen Zhengming allowed trees to dominate the scenery, such as in the *Old Trees by a Cold Waterfall*. His son Wen Jia (1501–1583) was active during the last period of the Wu School. His paintings are characterized by a symmetrical format and patterned motifs, effects intended to show the innocence of his imagination.

The other two important followers of the Wu School were the famous scholars Lu Zhi (1496–1576) and Chen Shun (1483–1544). Lu Zhi illuminated Ni Zan's simple and pure style and transferred them into his own slow rhythm in appropriate ink tones and light colors. Chen Shun followed

Mi Fu and Mi Youren and used wet ink combined with small, dark, hooked strokes in his landscape paintings.

Landscape Paintings by Zhou Chen, Tang Yin, and QiuYing: A new trio was formed by Zhou Chen (c. 1450–1535), Tang Yin (1470–1523), and Qiu Ying (c. 1494–1552), who considered themselves disciples of the Northern Song master Li Tang. The three were also a bridge between the Zhe School (faithful to the principles of the Southern Song Academy) and the Wu School (which promoted the tradition of Northern Song and Yuan literati painters). Some scholars group Shen Zhou, Wen Zhengming, Tang Yin, and Qiu Ying together and, in a gesture that seems to crowd them, label them the Four Great Masters of the Ming.

Zhou Chen was the teacher of Tang and Qiu. His paintings adopted the shapes of trees and rocks of Li Tang. But the warm and poetic feeling, the tonal contrast, and the combination of powerful and free brush techniques, which are apparent in his hand scrolls *The Northern Sea* and *Dreaming of Immortality in a Thatched Cottage*, had never been seen before. Tang Yin was a student of Zhou Chen, and friend of Shen Zhou and Wen Zhengming. Because of those relationships, Tang Yin produced his paintings bearing certain intellectual qualities from his master and friends, as well as professional ax-cut and "squeezed" brush strokes from the old masters. But the elaborate, consistent, and dense format was his own. Tang Yin's figure paintings also gained high admiration for their beautiful colors and elegant images. Like Tang, Qiu Ying achieved great success in paintings of court ladies modeled after the Tang painters Zhang Xuan and Zhou Fang. The Tang blue-and-green style also influenced Qiu Ying's landscape paintings, establishing him as the last great painter of the blue-and-green style. Finally Qiu Ying explored a variety of techniques, modulating strong colors into lighter tones that were then harmonized with wet ink and dry brush strokes—all in the service of his exquisite forms and perfect drawing.

Dong Qichang: Dong Qichang (1555–1636) played a very significant role in the later Ming dynasty as a scholar-painter, official, calligrapher, and art critic. He was the first to conduct serious studies of the long history of Chinese landscape painting and the first to divide painters into the Northern and Southern Schools. Dong eulogized the literati tradition and depreciated academy painting, arguing that only literati painters could produce truly great work because they understood the moral law of nature. He listed all his favorites of the Northern School: Wang Wei from the Tang; Dong Yuan, Juran, Li Cheng, Fan Kuan, and Mi Fu from the Song; the Four Great Masters from the Yuan; and Shen Zhou and Wen Zhengming from his own time. The Southern School pantheon contained Li Sixun (651–716, a court painter well known for the blue-and-green style) in the Tang; and Li Tang, Ma Yuan, and Xia Gui in the Song. In composing his own paintings, Dong selected from different masters only those elements that satisfied him, then freely reworked them, always with more interest in powerful forms than in concepts.

Portraits, Figures, and Other Subjects: Portraiture reached its last stage of development in the Ming, slowly declining in the Qing. The first Ming emperor requested in his portraits the Yuan tradition's frontal pose and the Song's natural style. Later portraits gradually returned to the Southern Song Academy tradition with its three-quarter position, sometimes also revealing features of Mongol ancestry, such as curly mustaches and plaited beards. Various facial features and cloth details were used to identify the subject's social status. Unlike the imperial portraits that were constrained by the emperors' tastes and demands, figure paintings and those of other subjects granted free reign to Ming artists' imaginations.

The most outstanding figure painters were Chen Hongshou (1599–1652) and Cui Zizhong (d. 1644). Cui, a Northern painter, specialized in historical and supernatural themes; his style derived from the manner and techniques of the professional tradition. Chen Hongshou, resident of the South, excelled in historical and religious figure paintings with awkward features and strong personalities. His paintings recall those of the Jin painter Gu Kaizhi, but the elongated faces, slim bodies, and curving, smooth, uninterrupted lines indicated a mannerism very much Chen's own. Besides those two, other outstanding painters of the period include Wu Bin (active 1573–1620), who specialized in Buddhist images, birds and flowers, and small landscapes; Xu Wei (1521–1593), who concentrated on plants, vegetables, flowers, and bamboo; Zhang Feng (c. 1645–1673), who executed landscapes with rough and bold brush strokes in calligraphic looseness; and Sun Kehong (1532–1610), who adapted color wood prints to landscape paintings.

Women Artists: For a thousand years, the accomplishments of women artists were concealed. Only at the end of the Ming dynasty, when their numbers increased, did they begin to receive recognition. By some scholars' accounting, out of 216 famous women artists from ancient times to 1820, half were active in the Ming. The most prominent was Wen Shu (1595–1634), a great-granddaughter of Wen Zhengming, who specialized in flowers, plants, and insects depicted in a realistic and elegant manner. Ma Shouzhen (1548–1604) was a cultured courtesan, who was skilled in using long double outlines for orchid leaves. Xue Susu (c. 1564–1637), also a courtesan, mastered calligraphy and painted orchids, narcissus, and bamboo in smooth brush strokes and varied ink tones. Lin Yin (c. 1616–1685) as well left some works of flowers and birds, drawn with dark ink in a very mature and skillful style.

The Qing Dynasty

It is more difficult to divide the Qing artists by subject matter because they grouped themselves together naturally by region and interests. Many artists of this period used painting as a weapon against the Manchu rulers to express their spiritual loneliness or to preserve the great cultural traditions. They admired the literati painters, viewing them as the most prestigious representatives of quintessence of Chinese culture. Among the most notable groups of Qing artists are the Four Great Monks, the Orthodox School, the Eight Masters of Jinling, and the Eight Eccentrics of Yangzhou.

Landscape by the Four Great Monks: The Four Great Monks included Hongren (1610–1644), Kuncan (1612–1673), Zhu Ta (also known as Baida Shanren 1626–1705), and Shitao (1642–1718). Hongren took Ni Zan as his model, and his landscape paintings represent the peaceful world of the past. He preferred to arrange mountains and streams in a smooth rhythm, using very fine brush strokes with a kind of dream-like quality. Kuncan differed from Hongren by choosing the best elements from the Yuan Four Great Masters and the Ming masters Shen Zhou, Wen Zhengming, and Dong Qichang, and blending them into a very compelling and exuberant style. His brush strokes were free and forceful, sometimes even disordered. He added calligraphy to his paintings, which allowed him to state his happiness in forgetting himself in the beauty of nature. Zhu Ta was a descendant of the Ming imperial family and devoted himself to the pursuit of Buddhist enlightenment. He gave himself the name Bada Shanren, meaning "Dweller of the Eight Great Mountains," and signed it on his works in the shape of the character of "cry" or "laugh" to imply his conflicted spirits. He mingled painting, poetry, and calligraphy into one. He created many ink paintings with a distinct style—birds and fish with their eyes turned upward, looking at the world contemptuously, lotuses and flowers growing lonely and isolated in nature, stunted trees beside bamboo, signifying the scholars, with its noble character. The last great Monk painter was Shitao, another descendant of the Ming imperial family. He became a great painter of landscape after becoming a Chan monk. Shitao believed that each stroke should originate from the artist's personality. He himself traveled to many places and executed his landscape paintings based not on a single scene, but on the images in his mind, accumulated through his travel experiences. His landscapes have a very unique style, displaying an unusual technique of well-controlled brush strokes in varied tones, sweeping brush lines, and different kinds of ink dots. The power and subtlety of Shitao's vision of nature is evident in the long hanging scroll *The Waterfall on Mount Lu*, in which he captured the spirit of the scene and adapted it to his own language.

Landscape and Bird and Flowers by the Orthodox School: The practice of using landscape to express one's spiritual being was also adopted by the Orthodox School, led by the four Wangs, Wu Li (1632–1718), and Yun Shouping (1633–1690). The four Wangs were Wang Shimin (1592–1680), Wang Jian (1598–1677), and their pupils Wang Hui (1632–1717) and Wang Yuanqi (1642–1715). It was called the Orthodox School because the artists all conformed to the consolidated theories of Dong Qichang. Wang Shimin learned from Huang Kongwang and painted landscapes in slow and lyric brush movements alternated by dry and wet ink. He painted a hanging scroll *Pavilions on the Mountains of Immortals*, in which he juxtaposed elegance with vigor, and hardness with delicacy. Wang Jian highly regarded Wang Meng and applied different well-controlled brush strokes to different elements. His paintings were usually done with dark ink, sharply contrasting with the blank areas of the paper, which suggest water or air, as can be observed in his famous hanging scroll *Dreamland*. Wang Hui was a student of Wang Shimin and Wang Jian. Though following his masters and showing great esteem for the Four Great Masters of Yuan, he picked up earlier styles and elements from different dynasties according to his needs. Wang Yuanqi was a grandson of Wang Shimin and was strongly influenced by his grandfather, who was an admirer of Huang Gongwang. However, Wang Yuanqi went beyond the confines of his grandfather's style when he merged ink tones with appropriate colors, creating rich shades and new layers in his paintings. Wu Li also admired the Four Great Masters of the Yuan, but refused to simply imitate them. He poured his feelings into the objects of his paintings and gave expression to his own personality through his use of brush and ink. As a result, mountains and other objects were often unnaturally shaped, but he was able to cover all awkwardness with beautiful ink dots, brush lines, and light colors. Yun Shouping did some landscapes too, but his best-known works are his flower paintings. He tried to replace what he felt were the rigidities of the old paintings with fresh and natural images, without outlines but with delicate colors, as if aiming to bring the fragrance of the flowers out from the paper.

Landscape and Bird and Flowers by The Eight Masters of Jinling: The Eight Masters of Jinling (today's Nanjing) were Gong Xian (1618–1689), Fan Qi (1616–after 1694), Zou Zhe (1636–1708), Wu Hong (active c. 1670–1680), Hu Zao (active c. 1670–1720), Gao Cen (active c. 1679), Ye Xin (fl. 1647–1679), and Xie Sun (c. late 17th century). They were called Jinling Masters because they expressed their loyalty to the former regime through paintings of the scenery around Jinling, the capital of the Ming dynasty. The most accomplished artist in this group was Gong Xian. He was opposed to a rigid imitation of the old masters and instead advocated that artists learn from them, while carefully observing mountains and rivers for themselves and drawing inspiration directly from nature. In his *Thousand Peaks and Myriad Ravines*, Gong Xian demonstrates his unique style: somber and dark tones accumulated by several light ink layers; a monumental aura built up by stiff and precipitous mountains; and soft, luminous clouds suggested by white spaces around the dark peaks. Fan Qi tried to imitate Gong Xian, but his paintings, especially those of flowers and butterflies, are very decorative and ornamented. Gao Cen used outline and colors with dry brush for his casual album leaves. Wu Hong executed his works in a very lyrical yet realistic style with free brush strokes. Zou Zhe liked to place pine trees and rocks together and sometimes included small buildings and human figures in his works.

Bamboo and Rock, Flower and Insects by the Eight Eccentrics of Yangzhou: The Eight Eccentrics of Yangzhou were Li Shan (c. 1688–1757), Wang Shishen (active c. 1730–1750), Jin Nong (1687–1764), Huang Shen (1687–after 1768), Li Fangying (1695–1755), Zheng Xie (also known as Zheng Banqiao, 1693–1766), Gao Xiang (1688–c. 1753), and Luo Pin (1733–1799). This group centered their activities in Yangzhou and concentrated on painting birds, flowers, bamboo, and rocks. Their subjects were fully developed to represent their own personalities. Li Shan was influenced by Xu Wei and composed his work with very defined brush strokes in a free and natural style. Jin Nong showed special talents in drawing full-blown and charming plum blossoms, banana trees, and orchids. Li Fangying did not stay in Yangzhou very long, but he shared the interests of the others and produced paintings of bamboo, orchids, plums, pines, and rocks in a very elegant and simple style. Zheng Xie seemed to comfort his lonely heart through his paintings—his deep attachment to bamboo and orchids inspired his most successful paintings in which he applied the rhythm of the calligraphy brush. Gao Xiang also created a beautiful escape from the troubles of the real world. In the *Tanzhi Pavilion*, he arranged a very elegant Buddhist temple in an almost visibly quiet environment, totally separated from the outside world. Luo Pin took a different approach to condemning the Manchu rulers. Besides painting bamboo and plum blossoms, he won his reputation painting ghosts, hinting through ugly images at high-ranking officials known for their corruption and immoral behaviors.

Interaction Between Eastern and Western Artists: Jesuit missionaries began arriving in China during the 16th century, and with them came Western artists and traditions. Emperor Kangxi (r. 1662–1723) set up a studio in the Forbidden City to foster interaction between Western artists and Chinese court painters. The latter noticed the perspective accuracy and three-dimensional quality in the Western paintings and began to develop interest in light, shade, and perspective. For their part, Western artists were deeply impressed by the Chinese paintings. An Italian missionary painter, Giuseppe Castiglione, with the Chinese name of Lang Shining (1688–1768), synthesized Western naturalism with Chinese media and techniques and produced many works in this mixed style,

including the hanging scroll *Auspicious Objects*, done in celebration of the emperor's birthday.

The Last Stage of the Pre-Modern Paintings: Artists of the period from mid to late Qing were diversified in their specialties. Among the artists, Hua Yan (1682–1756) achieved fame as a professional scholarly painter. Yuan Jiang (active c. 1680–1730) and Yuan Yao (active c. 1739–1788) specialized in meticulous depictions of palaces and other architecture. Shen Quan (1682–1765) devoted himself to the bird and flower genre. Gai Qi (1773–1828) concentrated on painting beautiful women. And two important schools, the Jingjiang School and the Shanghai School, appealed to artists in different subjects. The Jingjiang (today's Zhenjiang in Jiangsu Province) School was guided by Zhang Yin (1761–1829), a master of pines, and Gu Heqing (1766–after 1830), a master of willows. Painters in the school carried on the traditions of the Jinling masters and painted from nature. The Shanghai School was formed in the 19th century when the city became an open commercial port after the Opium War (1839–1842). Artists in this school followed the aesthetic change of the city dwellers and expanded their interests to include different genres. Xugu (1824–1896) liked to paint flowers, birds, vegetables, and fruits with the dry-brush and broken-stroke methods. Ren Xiong (1820–1857) demonstrated his style in his *Self Portrait*, showing a tall figure staring forward with a very serious expression. Ren Bonian (1840–1895) achieved prominence in portraits, as well as in flowers and birds. This last period of the pre-modern Chinese painting flourished with many famous artists and paved the way for the new era of modern art.

6. CALLIGRAPHY

Chinese characters bear sounds and meanings individually. Strokes are organized from top to bottom, left to right. The earliest Chinese characters appeared around 1300 B.C. in pictographs and ideo-

graphs inscribed on tortoise shells and cattle bones. During the Shang and Zhou dynasties, inscriptions were carved on bronze vessels, often conveying sacred meanings. Bamboo was another material used for writing purposes—archaeological discoveries contain, for example, a neat inscription of *The Book of Ritual* carved on bamboo strips linked with a cord for rolling up.

Two important innovations helped to propel calligraphy as an art form. The first occurred during the Qin dynasty when the government unified the writing system. The other took place with the invention of paper (conventionally attributed to Cai Lun, d. 121), which multiplied the space available for the development of calligraphy. Used together with paper and silk are six essential writing tools: different-sized brushes made from animal hairs, ink sticks, ink stones, water pots for moistening the ink stones, basins for washing brushes, and seals made from stones. Through a long history of innovations in the writing system, the basic strokes for the standard ("Regular") script are condensed to eight, all of which are well exemplified in the character *Yong* (see the illustration on the following page).

The Six Major Scripts

Chinese characters can be written in six different types of scripts: Seal script, Clerical script, Regular script, Running script, Cursive script (or "Draft"), and Wild cursive script. These scripts form the foundations for the styles of individual calligraphers. Seal script refers to both large and small seal scripts. Large seal script varies the size and shape of each character according to the nature of pictographic elements. Small seal script treats each character equally in square structures. Clerical script in abbreviated manner is derived from seal script with features of waved strokes known as "silkworm head and goose tail." Regular script requires an equal distribution of force in every stroke and the formation of characters with regular rhythm. Running script constructs characters with very smooth and coherent movements, while keeping each character separated. Cursive script shows dynamic and emotional brush movements that connect some characters without upsetting the balances. Wild cursive allows calligraphers the maximum freedom to express their ideas and emotions and shows characters dancing on paper, some solo, some in unison.

The Seal Script and the Clerical Script in the Qin and Han

The Shang and Zhou bronze inscriptions were mostly cast in large seal scripts. During the Qin dynasty, small seal script was invented and soon employed for official stone inscriptions, as, for example, in the *Stone Drum Inscription*, a piece of stele (stone tablet with inscription) recording imperial hunting activity. Clerical script later replaced the small seal script and was used in government documents and correspondence.

Three Great Pioneers

Inscriptions on stone steles reached their peak during the Eastern Han Dynasty (25–220) and the subsequent Age of Division. Hundreds of steles were left whose contents were composed by famous historians and then carved by well-known calligraphers. Among more than 150 famous calligraphers, the most prominent were Zhong You (150–230), Wang Xizhi (307–365), and his son Wang Xianzhi (344–386). Zhong You was a master of small seal script, clerical script, and regular script. His calligraphy is characterized by squared and neat-looking words with forceful strokes at the beginnings and ends of each character. Wang Xizhi and his son Wang Xianzhi were obviously influenced by Zhong You but made greater contributions to the development of this special art form.

Many scholars regard Wang Xizhi as the father of calligraphy. He mastered six calligraphy styles, as well as the important technique called "flying white," a skill of leaving some blank space in a brush stroke, as if the brush had not absorbed enough ink. The best examples by Wang Xizhi are his *Preface to the Orchid Pavilion* and *Preface of Sangluan Album*, both in running script. Wang Xizhi had many followers, including his gifted son Wang Xianzhi, who inherited the great techniques from his father and established his own reputation in the cursive style with his elegant strokes. Wang Xianzhi's best

The Character "Yong"

The eight strokes of Yong:

1) dot

2) horizontal stroke

3) vertical stroke

4) hook

5) short rightward stroke

6) downward stroke to the left

7) short downward stroke to the left

8) long downward stroke to the right

Source: Ren Zheng and Quian Zhongyun, *Kaishu jichu zhishi* (Shanghai: Shanghai shu hua chubanshe, 1987), 58–60.

surviving works are his *Ode to the Nymph of the Luo River*, done in regular script, and *Yatouwan Album*, done in cursive script.

Achievements in the Tang Dynasty

Wang Xizhi and Wang Xianzhi astonished scholars, high officials, even the emperors in the Tang dynasty who then spent a fortune collecting the Wangs' works and demanded court calligraphers to copy them. Three leading figures among the court calligraphers were Ouyang Xun (557–641), Yu Shinan (558–638), and Chu Suiliang (596–638). They inherited the style of classical regular script from Wang Xizhi, but they mastered the skills even better than their pioneer. They demonstrated absolute balance between horizontal and vertical, curved and straight strokes and between square and rectangular forms. Because of their outstanding achievements, these three masters were appointed as the calligraphy teachers to imperial princes, calligraphy advisors to emperor, and editors of catalogues of imperial collections. The new development made by them provided an opportunity for Yan Zhenqing (709–785), a Middle Tang regular script master, to work out a new model for regular script in broader and squarer formation. Yan Zhenqing's calligraphy reflects his full understanding of the traditional regular and cursive scripts, and the fine points of his brush strokes are powerfully expressive. In the subsequent century, a regular script master Liu Gongquan (778–865), returned to an earlier style of writing characters with narrower strokes. But Liu's careful attention to every brush stroke reveals the distinct influence of Yan Zhenqing. Even today, those regular script masters are highly admired, and stele rubbings of their works are still widely used as models for calligraphy exercises.

Two master calligraphers of the Wild cursive script, Zhang Xu (658–748) and Huai Su (735–c. 800), gained remarkable victories in configuring the cursive script to the Wild cursive script. In his *Autobiography*, dated 777, Huai Su astonished future generations with a combination of quick swing-brush movements and still very accurate and well-balanced strokes. One story maintains that Zhang Xu was inspired while watching a court lady perform a sword dance and attempted to imitate her rapid movements in his calligraphy. Both Zhang Xu's and Huai Su's works have been used as models of the Wild cursive script for many generations.

The Four Masters of the Song Dynasty

The four great calligraphers of the Song are Cai Xiang (1012–1067), Su Shi (1036–1101), Huang Tingjian (1045–1105), and Mi Fu (1051–1107). Cai and Mi belonged to an orthodox school, and Su and Huang were scholar-calligraphers. Cai Xiang modeled himself after different masters: Yan Zhenqing in regular script, and Wang Xizhi in running and cursive scripts. Although Cai's approaches differed greatly from Su Shi's, the latter admired and praised Cai as "the best in the realm." Su Shi regarded Wang Xizhi and others as great masters but never followed their technique precisely as he believed that a calligrapher should emphasize his feelings rather than techniques.

Huang Tingjian, a master of several scripts, adhered to the same philosophy. He did not respect Wang Xizhi or his followers, criticizing their work for its lack of spiritual components and arguing that elegance in calligraphy must be based on spiritual harmony. Huang liked to write calligraphy with a pliant goat hair brush and in an inebriated state. He demonstrated his excellence in the beautiful poem scroll *Li Taibo's Recalling Past Wandering*. He once joked with Su Shi, saying that Su's calligraphy was like a crab crawling along, to which Su replied, "yours is like a snake wrapped around a tree."

Mi Fu conducted a very thorough study of the different traditions in an effort to assimilate all the finest elements. His best works reveal a unique style, with stable and firm brush movements and alternating ink tones, reminiscent of the techniques he used in his paintings.

Three Masters of the Yuan Dynasty

Achievements made by the Song masters in painting and calligraphy strongly influenced artists of the Yuan. Among them were Yelü Chucai (1190–1244), Xianyu Shu (1257–1302), and Zhao Mengfu (1254–1322). Yelü was of Mongol origin and an official of the Yuan court. From this position, he initiated the Mongol rulers into Chinese culture, while he himself excelled in learning Chinese calligraphy traditions. His achievements can be seen in his work *Poem of Farewell to Liu Man*, in which he followed the principles of Yan Zhenqing but merged them with his own style, involving heavy brush strokes and thick ink. Xianyu Shu was also from a minority tribe and made his way to court, bringing with him a stubbornness and arrogance that affected his style in calligraphy. Nonetheless, his cursive script surpassed that of his contemporaries and so aroused the jealousy of Zhao Mengfu that Zhao is said to have traded three of his own works for one of Xianyu's, only to burn it with hatred. This strange behavior of Zhao Mengfu is all the more difficult to explain when considering his prominence as a calligrapher and the range of his reputation, extending as far as India, Japan, and Korea, where many were enthusiastic about his compositions. Zhao Mengfu reached the peak of his development by mastering different kinds of scripts and assimilating the best of each kind into his own style. As a result, Zhao moved his brushes freely and fluidly, as if he directed the movement completely by heart rather than by hand. Moreover, he endeavored to apply calligraphy techniques to his painting, thereby combining poetry, calligraphy, and painting.

The Literati Movement

Zhao Mengfu continued to enjoy great fame throughout the early period of the Ming dynasty. Then some calligraphers and artists, active between 1488 and 1566, became interested in the works of the Song literati Su Shi and Huang Tingjian. They incorporated the techniques of the literary works and calligraphy of these masters into their own works. In this group were three literati: Zhu Yunming (1460–1526), Wen Zhengming, and Dong Qichang. Zhu Yunming in his earliest works stuck to ancient traditions but later acquired fame for his accomplishments in Wild cursive with his free and graceful stroke movements. Wen Zhengming, famous for his painting, calligraphy, and poems, revealed his talents in *Twelve Verses from Tao Yuanming's Drinking Poem*, a beautiful work combining running and cursive scripts. Because he insisted on creating his works by relying on his feelings, *Twelve Verses* radiates a kind of purity and clarity that perfectly mirrors his inner world. Dong Qichang, an extremely influential art critic, also achieved great success in painting, calligraphy, and poems. In evaluating the history of achievements in calligraphy, he concluded that the masters of calligraphy in Jin emphasized grace; those in Tang, technique; and those in Song, self-expression. He himself most valued self-enlightenment—for him the only means to perfect calligraphy. This allowed him to use different scripts in a single composition according to his mood at a particular moment.

The Revival of Traditions

Calligraphers in the later part of the Qing did not initiate any extraordinary improvements in calligraphy but held instead to old traditions. Although different artists and calligraphers chose individual styles, they can basically be divided into two large groups: those who copied from copybooks and those who imitated styles found in rubbings from their research of ancient steles. Calligraphers in the first group concentrated on practicing cursive script with strenuous brush strokes like those of Wang Duo (1592–1652) and Fu Shan (1607–1684); or they followed Zhao Mengfu and Dong Qichang and gradually traced styles back to Su Shi, Huang Tingjian, and Mi Fu of the Song, then further to Zhong Yao and the two Wangs of ancient times. Outstanding among those historian-calligraphers are Jin Nong, who had a strong belief in classical revivals, and Zheng Xie, who based his innovations on Huang Tingjian's style. The Qing Manchu rulers, fearful of provoking anti-government feelings among scholars, pressured them instead to cultivate their pride in Chinese culture. For that reason, the other major group of calligraphers turned their interests into conducting scholarly research on the history of ancient steles. They imitated different styles found in the steles and produced many astonishing copies of the old reversions.

7. DECORATIVE ARTS

Jade

Liangzhu culture is a term used to describe the civilization located in the Hangzhou area in southeastern China. Just as Yangshao culture and Longshan culture are symbolized by different types of pottery, Liangzhu culture is represented by outstanding jade carvings during the Neolithic period. In 1986, archaeologists unearthed a site in Fanshan, Yuhang county, in Zhejiang Province. There they discovered many jade articles, including ornaments, ceremonial weapons, and ritual carvings. The objects were done with very fine workmanship, perfectly shaped and highly polished. Some items were decorated with mystical human masks carved in thick and thin slices of jade, evidence of the mastery of complex jade carving techniques in the Neolithic period. In the Shang dynasty, jade was valued both because of its attractive colors, and more importantly, because advanced carving techniques enabled people to process a piece of stone into a desired object. The major products were ceremonial weapons (knives and axes), tools, and cloth pendants and ornaments (disks and plaques in beautiful animal shapes.) In the tomb of Fuhao at Anyang in Henan Province, jade tigers, elephants, and birds were found. Another item is a kneeling lady with her hands on her knees and her head bending slightly forward—the gesture matches exactly with the ancient Chinese character for "woman." In 1968, an archaeological discovery in the tomb of Prince Liu Sheng at Mancheng in Hebei Province astonished the world with an extravagant jade suit made around 100 B.C. The suit consists of 2,498 small, grayish-green, bowenite plaques pierced at the four corners and sewn together with gold thread and knots. Jade body plugs were applied. The upper part of the suit rests on a jade headrest wrapped in gilt bronze. Two dragon heads in beautiful openwork are attached to the two sides of the headrest.

Jade carving has been an important Chinese art form since this early beginning. Different from other materials used in decorative arts, jade provides natural forms and colors, inviting craftsmen to give full play to their imagination and skill. Before the Qing dynasty, jade was widely used for a variety of purposes; besides ornaments and decorations, it was carved into different kinds of utensils, bowls, vases, cups, washbasins, ewers, and dishes. All exhibited natural beauty as well as elegant and delicate decorations carved according to their forms and colors.

Lacquer

In 1978, in the same tomb of the Marquis Yi of Zeng (d. around 433 B.C.) where a set of bronze bells was discovered, archaeologists also found some beautiful lacquer artifacts. They included five clothes chests and a duck-shaped box. The interior of the chests was painted red, and the exterior was black with red-painted motifs. Hooks and mushroom-shaped motifs dominated the lid decoration, and hunting scenes were painted on the two opposite ends. All the details in the scenes were dramatically stylized: a pair of trees with eye-shaped leaves, two birds and two tigers in the trees. A line of intertwined serpents, symbolic of the oldest mythological figure, occupied one side of the lid. The duck-shaped box also had a black background, painted with red patterns. On the front and top of the box were several feather-like silhouettes. On the sides, two scenes of entertainment were depicted—one comprising two bells, held by the mouths of two ducks, while the other embodied very abstract dancers and drummers, seeming to move to the rhythmic sound.

Prior to the discovery of the tomb of Marquis Yi of Zeng, another site found in 1975 at Fenghuangshan, Jiangling county, in Hubei Province, revealed more than a hundred pieces of lacquered items made during the third century A.D. The items included a group of seven servant figures and a large dish decorated with a black circle on which cloud and phoenix patterns were painted in red. In another site at the same location, about 160 pieces of lacquer ware were discovered. In addition to a large wine container and an oval-shaped dish with fish decorations, the most extraordinary item was a set of ten oval-shaped bowls in a box, with cloud and phoenix and other motifs painted in red. Gradually, lacquer items became more ornate, some inlaid with mother-of-pearl. Today, lacquer is still employed for painting, sculpture, and furniture.

Ceramics

The earliest form of ceramics appeared in the Neolithic era as painted pottery. In A.D. 200, craftsmen could already make fine porcelain coated with a glaze. Although the design of most utensils imitated those of the Bronze Age, they nonetheless allowed expression for the rich imagination and artistic talents of the craftsmen. In Henan Province, archaeologists found a ceramic oil lamp in the form of a tree. The tree trunk is the oil container; its branches stretch out to support flowers and birds; and at the ends, bowls are inserted with flame-like rosettes. The tree grows on a mound, which is the lamp base. The mound is shaped to represent a mountain where immortals live. On the mound, two human figures sit under the tree, with various animals playing around them.

This oil lamp is just one of many burial items illustrating the fine and elaborate workmanship during the Han dynasty. Other objects include painted ceramic houses, towers, models of wells, dancers, acrobats, farmers, soldiers—all executed with vivid and captivating workmanship. Only later were glazed colors introduced. The Tang dynasty was known for its glazed ceramic items, the famous *Tang San Cai*, meaning the three glazed colors of blue, green, and brown. These colors were splashed on white figures, animals, and

Buddhist images, and form very natural patterns. In addition to these polychrome objects, another kind of porcelain, known as Yue ware, attracted users with its pure white or light olive-green colors and its decorative flower and plant shapes.

The ceramics during the Song dynasty varied from one kiln to another, but they all reflected the tastes of that time. Artists used different colors: creamy white, black, iron-red, light blue, celadon, or yellow. Some ceramics were painted with decorative floras under a transparent glaze, and others were made with cracks on the surface, signifying natural beauty. One type of porcelain, known as Cizhou ware, includes the Meiping vase (plum vase), which was decorated with black spiral flowers on a white background and further distinguished by its short neck, wide shoulders, and narrow bottom. The robustness of the earlier ceramic ware gave way to finesse in modeling and decoration of the later products. The achievements made during the Song dynasty provided a solid foundation for the Yuan pottery industry and enabled Mongol rulers to order products made to their taste yet still within the style of Chinese traditions. Examples of this appropriation might be seen in their blue-glazed, pear-shaped vases and the colorful flasks of Near Eastern design decorated with Chinese dragons, lotuses, or chrysanthemums.

The technology of ceramic production reached its peak of refinement during the Ming dynasty, particularly in the manufacture of blue-and-white porcelain ware. That durable porcelain was characterized by very delicate decorations of lotus scrolls, vines, and chrysanthemums painted in a blue glaze underneath a white coating. Besides bowls, dishes, flasks, jars, and stem cups, articles for calligraphy, such as brush rests, boxes, and lamp bases, were made in this elegant style. Another type of monochrome porcelain was produced in kilns located in Jingde county in Jiangxi Province. Those pieces are famous for their finely made, paper-thin bodies and scarcely visible patterns, which can be seen only against light. Finally, there is the porcelain decorated with figures, flowers, and animals painted with five colors of enamel, which were not only widely used by the Chinese but also exported around the world.

Both the quality and quantity of ceramics suffered a decline at the end of the Ming dynasty. At that time, the most appreciated items, by Chinese and foreigners alike, were utensils glazed with a very rare reddish color that dripped down along the contours of the pieces, creating unusual effects. Small items such as rice bowls painted in polychrome decorations and vases painted with enamels were also popular. Trade with European countries had an obvious impact on the designing of patterns. Some kilns in China were even put under the supervision of European agents and began producing articles depicting Western scenes in a very realistic style. That practice, however, died out as Europeans opened their own ceramics industry.

Textiles

Marks left by woven textiles were found on ceramic segments in Banpo, indicating that weaving activities already existed in the Neolithic period. In 1982, a tomb unearthed at Mashan, Jiangling county in Hubei Province shed light on the very advanced textile skills in both weaving and embroidery of that early time. It contained fragments of woven silk with geometric patterns, as well as silk gauze embroidered in chain stitches, displaying colorful motifs of dragons, tigers, and phoenix against a floral background. For generations, silk embroidery has been valued in China. Emperors wore robes with embroidered dragons to symbolize the power of the throne, and civilians have used embroidery for a variety of purposes.

In many places throughout China, skilled men and women produced exquisite works, from whole portraits, landscapes, and animal paintings to designs of flowers, butterflies, and luck symbols on clothes and other decorative items. Patterns and techniques were passed down from generation to generation, but styles and techniques often varied by region. The four major schools were Xiang embroidery in Hunan, Shu embroidery in Sichuan, Guang embroidery in Guangdong, and Su embroidery in Suzhou. The style of Xiang embroidery was enchanting; Shu focused on very rigorous technique; Guang charmed with its bright and contrasting colors; and Su embroiderers excelled in exquisite and accurate depictions, made possible by extremely thin silk thread, sometimes as thin as one-sixteenth the size of normal silk thread. Beyond those four main styles, other embroidery works reveal strong regional styles and the rich imagination of women amateurs, whose beautiful patterns often surpass the work of designers who have undergone special training.

Masterpieces of Gold and Silver

As early as in the Zhou dynasty, Chinese craftsmen employed gold for decoration. During the Han dynasty, craftsmen had already inlaid gold and silver into bronze vessels to highlight patterns. A great triumph was achieved during the Tang dynasty when very fine techniques were developed to use these materials on vessels and other decorative items. In 1987, archaeologists unearthed an underground chamber at the foundation of Famen Temple (a temple containing Buddha's finger relic) in Shanxi Province. This discovery provides excellent information on the tastes of the Tang period, particularly in Buddhist sculptures based on Central and Near Eastern models. The excellent workmanship exemplified here in the silver and gold articles was not equaled for generations. One of the most delicate items was a basket made from gold and silver filigree for warming teacakes.

Other fine treasures included a gilt silver box and tea grinder, a silver brazier, and a salt container. In 1986, archaeologists discovered another important 10th-century site with unusual silver and gold artifacts. A joint tomb for the Princess Chen, granddaughter of the Emperor Jingzong (r. 969–982), and her husband contained items rougher in workmanship than those at Famen Temple, but they were no less exquisite in their own way. The items included two gold masks, gilt silver crowns hollowed in openwork, gold belt plaques, and two pairs of silver boots inlaid with gold.

8. FOLK ART

Prints

The earliest forms of printing can be traced back to the inscriptions on bronze vessels of the Zhou, the stone carvings of the Western Han, and the block-printed motifs on textiles of the Eastern Han. Although there is no accurate date for the first piece of printed work, scholars believe that printing in China might have taken place in the late seventh century. During the eighth and ninth centuries, printing was already quite popular, used mainly to produce Buddhist documents. At Dunhuang in 1907, numerous wood-block printed Buddhist sutras with hand-stamped Buddhist images were found by Aurel Stein and in 1908 by Paul Pelliot. Among them there is the world's oldest book with a frontispiece, the *Diamond Sutra*, published by Wang Jie in 868. In addition to Buddhist texts, few secular printed works survived from the Song and Yuan dynasties. Most of them are Confucian texts, government records, and simple illustrations for poems.

Chinese printing reached its peak of development in the late 16th century and early 17th century. During that period, beautiful book illustrations and woodcuts were produced for popular literature, drama, and artistic manuals. The most famous works were made in Anhui Province in the Huizhou style, characterizing for its linear refinement. When China entered the modern period, wood printing, as with other art forms, was strongly influenced by Western realism. Lu Xun (1881–1936), a famous writer, organized several exhibitions during the 1930s and encouraged young artists to blend the Chinese traditions with elements of wood prints from Russia, Germany, and other European countries. Graphic artists during this time focused on subjects of social inequities and war. The representative works were done by Li Hua (b. 1907), well known for his realistic and powerful style.

Chinese New Year Prints: The Chinese New Year Print (*Nienhua*) is one specialized type of print. Even now, before each Chinese New Year, peasants and some city dwellers will hang up one or two hand-painted or mass-produced colorful prints. The history of the New Year Print can be traced back to the fifth century in the form of inexpensive motif prints, with the art form reaching its peak of development in the early 19th century. The subjects vary from well-known historical stories and folk legends to Buddhist and Taoist themes, all somewhat simplified for this form of popular consumption. The Chinese God of the Stove, for example, is commonly seen because he and his wife are thought to bring a family peace and happiness. Another favorite motif depicts a fish carrying a lovely child on its back—because "fish" in Chinese sounds like "surplus"; it symbolizes good fortune for the coming year, and the chubby child represents the family's hope for healthy children. The pictures are bordered by fortune couplets and sometimes accompanied by a Chinese calendar. The colors of these prints are all very bright and flashy, but the style remains artistic, either very vigorous or delicate depending upon the traditions of the region where they are produced.

Paper Cutouts

The earliest paper cutout appeared between A.D. 386 and 581, but the art was popularized only in the 12th century. From then on, cutouts were collected by members of imperial households as well as used for decoration and gifts among the population at large. Both professionals and amateurs, chiefly women, from all over the country made the paper cutouts. Subjects ranged from religious themes and literary and folk stories to images of daily activities, figures, landscapes, flowers, insects, and birds. Styles were very dynamic with energetic lines or were hair-thin and had extremely delicate lines. People like them not only because of their aesthetic value, but also because they are inexpensive and can be used for many different kinds of decorations. In northern China, cutouts are still used to decorate windows and doors, and in the south, they are adopted as models for embroidery works. In the countryside, farmers attach paper cutouts to gift wrappings. Before electricity, people pasted them on gauze lanterns and let the candlelight inside project the patterns onto the gauze covering.

Puppets

Paper cutouts were the inspiration for shadow puppet theater. Taking their subjects from literature and folk stories, craftsmen formed human figures from carefully perforated leather, then articulated them with joints. Performers hold puppets by attached sticks and project them onto white paper or gauze, delighting audiences with the shadows dancing and acting on the screen. As early as 200 B.C., shadow puppet theater existed, though it did not become popular until the 10th century.

Kites

The idea of the kite is thought to have come from observing the flying eagle. Over the years, the role of kites has changed from signaling in military actions (around A.D. 200) to being used today in games and physical exercises. Sometime in the 10th century, members of the imperial family tied a bamboo flute to the head of a kite. When it flew in the sky, winds played the bamboo flute, sending out lovely melodies from the air. Thus, kites gained the name *Fengzheng*, meaning a zither played by the wind. The most beautiful and delicate kites were made during the Qing dynasty in the shapes of eagles, swallows, butterflies, flying dragons, the Monkey King, celestials, and flower baskets. Today, Weifang in Shandong Province is well known for its kite manufacture (where it remains a cottage industry) and hosts an international kite festival every year.

Toys

Toys hold an important position in folk art history because they express the rich imagination of their creators. For generations, children and collectors have cherished toy animals and dolls for their beautiful designs and rich colors. Traditional Chinese toys were made of clay or cloth and sometimes ceramics which, because of their fragility, were meant more for appreciation than play.

9. ART OF THE 20TH CENTURY

Architecture

As exchanges between East and West became more common, Chinese architects increasingly assimilated foreign elements into their designs—especially in the case of churches, sometimes built almost exactly in the style of the West. Liang Sicheng, known for his red brick buildings with glazed green roof tiles and curved, projecting eaves, was the most influential Chinese architect in the first half of the 20th century. He and Henry K. Murphy successfully combined Western and Chinese styles in imposing and yet graceful university buildings in Beijing, Nanjing, and Shanghai. Unfortunately, most of them were destroyed during World War II and the subsequent civil wars. Today, one extraordinary example of sinicized Western buildings is the National Palace Museum in Taipei, characterized by the traditional curved roof and exotic post-and-frame structures.

Since 1949, architecture has been erected to meet political and social necessities principally in the form of government buildings and public structures. The most obvious change occurred at Tiananmen Square in Beijing with the Great Hall of the People, the Military Museum of the Chinese People's Revolution, the History Museum, and later, the Mao Zedong (1893–1976) Memorial Hall. Built in 1959, the Great Hall of the People consists of an immense assembly hall with 10,000 seats, surrounded by large reception halls, one for each province as well as one for Hong Kong. Its conservative style and gigantic scale modeled after the ancient Greek temples tend to overwhelm.

Since China re-opened its door to the world, it has experienced a rapidly growing economy, spurring the construction of skyscrapers for commercial as well as residential use in large cities throughout the country. Shanghai World Financial Center, designed by Kohn Pedersen Fox Associates, which will be 460 meters in height, is now under construction in Shanghai.

Sculpture

At the center of Tiananmen Square is the Monument to the People's Heroes, 37.94 meters tall. The stone base is divided into two levels carved with floral wreaths and inlayed with 10 pieces of white marble reliefs, showing more than 170 figures of heroes who participated in key events of Chinese history since the Opium War. This piece of work indicates the trends of Chinese sculpture from 1949 to 1976. For almost 30 years, sculptures served mainly the purpose of political propaganda. One such work is the life-sized group sculpture *Rent Collection Courtyard*, depicting the oppression of poor peasants by their landlord. This kind of political theme, expressed in a realistic style, was repeated again and again. Until the Cultural Revolution, few other works were produced— only statues of Mao Zedong, from miniatures, busts, and life-sized statues to the standing figure several times larger than Mao himself.

Today, human figures cast in realistic styles still dominate the field of sculpture, but the political themes have disappeared. Abstract works too are beginning to emerge from the studios of sculptors as they gain more freedom to express their individuality.

Painting

The late Qing rulers, afraid of being displaced by Han culture, did not give full support to painters, except a few outstanding ones. Ren Bonian (1840–1895) survived the hardship and achieved nationwide fame with his figure painting, done in the narrative manner, and flower-and-bird paintings in rich colors. Ren also influenced the prolific Wu Changshuo (1844–1927), whose figures and bamboo-and-rock and flower paintings were deeply appreciated by scholars for their recondite meanings, presented in an unrestrained manner.

East Meets With West: During the 20th century, a new era in Chinese painting was ushered in, with the merging of old and new, Sinitic and foreign ideas. The May Fourth Movement in 1919 challenged the old Chinese traditions and advocated democracy and science. Along with scholars in other fields, Chinese painters, facing the challenge of Western civilization, now had to reconsider their directions. In Guangdong Province, artists of the Lingnan School, led by Gao Jianfu (1879–1951), Gao Qifeng (1889–1933), and Chen Shuren (1884–1948), committed themselves to reform. Learning drawing from a French missionary and later studying in Japan, the Gao brothers tried to initiate a realistic style, but their results remained firmly within the Chinese tradition. However, their "boneless" wash technique applied to animals, flowers, figures, and landscapes were very unusual and met with wide appreciation. (Usually, traditional Chinese artists would use ink to outline the shape of a figure, animal, or object first before filling the colors. With the "boneless" technique, however, the artist would apply the colors directly without going through the step of outlining.) Chen Shuren also created his own influential style with its fresh and tranquil atmosphere.

The two pioneers who successfully combined Western and Chinese paintings together were Xu Beihong (1895–1953) and Lin Fengmian (1900–1991). Beginning with traditional Chinese training, Xu Beihong later studied in Japan and Paris. His foreign training enabled him to understand Western traditions much better than any of his contemporaries. He advocated nothing but realism. In his own paintings, he integrated line drawings with light and shadows. Even in his ink drawings, he endeavored to achieve a three-dimensional quality and perspective accuracy. In teaching, Xu Beihong insisted on strict sketching techniques, forbidding any careless haste. His major works, *Tian Heng and His Five Hundred Followers* and *Galloping Horse*, illustrate his styles well.

Xu Beihong had many students and followers, such as Wu Zuoren (1908–1997), a master in painting pandas and camels, and Jiang Zhaohe (1904–1986), who shared Xu's commitment to realism in art but also carefully attended to reality in life. It is said that in order to compose the painting *Refugees*, a long scroll depicting the suffering of Chinese people under Japanese invasion, Jiang Zhaohe traveled widely to find appropriate models for his work. The painting is remarkably effective in revealing the misery caused by war. Another master was Lin Fengmian, who began his career in Paris. After studying works by Matisse, Picasso, Modigliani, and other Western painters, Lin returned to Chinese ink and colors. His paintings clearly exhibit influences from Matisse, as well as traditional Chinese ink and wash. His unique success lies in the creative and skillful blending of these styles without any sign of mechanical strain. Lin Fengmian painted in several genres, but his favorite subjects were small birds, mandarin ducks, and cranes.

Traditions with a New Appearance:
Some painters achieved new developments after thorough study of the old traditions. Qi Baishi (1864–1957), a farmer's son who made his way through hard work, showed no interest in reformers or politics or even social change. He concentrated instead on using the old techniques to compose images in his mind and from life. Remembering the country scenes of his childhood, he vividly conveyed them to paper, filling his paintings with animated depictions of shrimp, fish, crabs, and frogs. Qi Baishi's achievements were recognized worldwide. He won the International Peace Award in 1955 and was honored as one of the Ten Giants of the World in 1962.

Another prominent artist of the 20th century is Zhang Daqian (1899–1983), known in the West as Chang Dai-chien. Zhang established his name through imitation of the famous ancient works, including the Dunhuang cave murals. Thorough study enabled Zhang to master the styles of different subject matter by employing very meticulous and bold, vigorous approaches. In his late years, Zhang's work reached new heights, establishing a precedent in Chinese painting. He now ignored realistic

forms in a style very similar to that of Western abstract painting, but he executed it with splashes of Chinese colors and ink.

Painting and Politics: After 1949, China for a long period closed its door to the world except for the former Soviet Union and some Eastern European countries. Even though China and the former Soviet Union discontinued their relationship in the 1960s, the realistic style borrowed from Russia still dominated artwork in China. The government endorsed the style because it met its political needs. Artists felt safe to adopt this style because they were required to create heroic images of the working class in a pseudo-realistic style. Even traditional Chinese painters had to adapt to this political reality. They could choose their own styles, but they were obliged to limit their subject matter to what was considered politically correct. The most famous Chinese painters of the period include Fu Baoshi (1904–1965), Pan Tianshou (1898–1971), Shi Lu (1919–1982), Guan Shanyue (1912–1986), Li Keran (1907–1989), and Cheng Shifa (1921–).

From 1966 to 1976, the Cultural Revolution significantly disrupted the development of culture. Famous painters suffered from rough treatment, and many of them were forbidden to touch their brushes and colors. The kind of paintings encouraged by the government consisted mostly of Mao Zedong's portraits and images of workers, peasants, and soldiers—the so-called masters of the country. The style was consistently very realistic.

East Meets West Again: The painters' difficulties ended in 1976. Once more, they had opportunities to explore the world and adopt new styles in a free way, some very traditional, others very Western. Wu Guanzhong (1919–) is a leading contemporary artist, expressing his "abstract beauties" through the combined media of oil, ink, and Chinese colors. His hand scroll *The Banyan Tree* is reminiscent of the work of Jackson Pollock. Modernism from the West finds a receptive audience in China, especially among young artists enjoying the freedom to extend their activities in all directions. These days the works of Chinese painters cannot be distinguished from those done in the West because the styles and techniques are so similar. Political propaganda has given way to self-expression, as can be seen, for example, in the work of the artist Zhang Xiaogang (1958–), who expresses his understanding of the relationships within a contemporary Chinese family in his 1993 oil painting *Bloodline: Family Portrait*.

10. MUSIC, DANCE, AND DRAMA

Music in the Shang and Zhou Dynasties

Folk songs were an important source for musical compositions during the Shang and Zhou dynasties. Even music played at royal banquets and ceremonies was usually derived from folk songs. According to the scripts on oracle bones, music and dance in the Shang were usually related to ancestral, military, and ritual activities. Many ritual dances, especially the rain dance, were conducted by shamans who were thought to have magical powers to prevent all natural disasters and keep peace on earth. Bronze instruments were gradually developed to meet the needs of the performances. As indicated by the oracle bone inscriptions and other archaeological discoveries, six kinds of instruments were produced in the Shang dynasty: mouth organ, flute, panpipes, zither, stone chime, and drum.

Around the 11th century B.C., after the Zhou had overthrown the Shang, several significant changes occurred in the field of music. According to traditional accounts, first, a ruler ordered scholars to collect songs and dances and had them formalized and organized for court performances. Second, he helped establish a music institute and required all children of the royal family to learn music. Third, he laid down rules for the usage of music. Officials and nobles had the sizes of their orchestras and the numbers of their dancers restricted according to their rank. The higher the rank, the more musicians and dancers one could have. The types of music and dance an official could perform were also restricted according to rank. For example, it was a great offense for a nobleman to have certain kinds of dance, reserved for the king, performed in his own house. The most frequently performed dance was the Six Dances, or Grand Dances. The whole program consisted of six sections, each of which paid tribute to a god and was accompanied by increasingly advanced instruments.

In 1978, a set of 65 bronze bells and 41 stone chimes were excavated from the Tomb of Marquis Yi of Zeng. The set consists of 19 bells for tuning and 45 for performing. The lower portion of each bell has two striking positions and each produces a different pitch. Thus, the set's 90 pitches allowed the musicians to play any five, six, or seven-tone compositions.

Besides the formal requirements of the court, numerous other folk songs were composed by civilians to address love or war or to coordinate the rhythm of heavy work. These songs were sung by groups or by a shaman, who occupied the central role in ritual or sacrificial ceremonies. Scholars have collected many of these folk songs in the *Book of Songs*, the earliest anthology of Chinese poetry. The well-known poems *Nine Songs*, written by the famous poet Qu Yuan (c. 339–278 B.C.), were based on folk songs telling stories about different kinds of shamans. Unfortunately, the music to accompany these songs has long been lost. Only the lyrics have survived.

Music and Dance of the Han Dynasty

In 206 B.C., Liu Bang (256–195 B.C.) defeated the Qin and established the Han empire. He founded the Music Bureau, which made great contributions to the development of Chinese music. The Music Bureau assembled the empire's most outstanding musicians (such as Li Yannian, d. 87 B.C.), musicologists, composers, dancers, and instrument makers. Bureau members arranged musical performances for the court, collected and categorized old folk and country songs, and wrote new compositions for the court. The basis for these compositions again came from old melodies, but they were now combined with some new elements brought back from the music of central Asia by Zhang Qian (d. 114 B.C.), a Han envoy to that region. Band music, played by percussion and wind instruments for military processions, was a new genre representing such a combination. Zhang Qian also brought back some samples of central Asian musical instruments. Thus, a court orchestra was formed with such traditional instruments as the zither, panpipe, bells, and lithophones and some new ones, including an oblong-bridged zither called *Zheng*, the side-blown flute *Di*, and the stringed instrument *Pipa*.

The well-organized musical activities of the court also boosted the popularity of music among commoners, as indicated by the birth of urban music and the appearance of mixed shows (*Baixi*). The urban music was initiated by wealthy merchants and gentry who had settled in the cities and sought to enjoy life by inviting musicians and dancers to perform for them, sometimes themselves joining in the performance. The main form of urban music was called "harmonized song" (*Xianghege*) because the singer harmonized his singing with a wooden clapper or drum or arranged for some wind instruments to accompany him. Gradually, singers, dancers, and musicians all played together and created a music form called the Grand Harmonized Song and Dance (*Xianghe daqu*), which served as the model for the later mixed shows (*Baixi*). Mixed shows, incorporating acrobatics, martial arts, and comedy into music and dance, were welcomed in all kinds of city activities: entertaining, banquets, weddings, and even funerals.

Music and Dance in the Sui and Tang Dynasties

Performers continued to receive favor from the imperial court as well as from the populace in the Sui dynasty. They assembled in the capital every year, set up stages stretching along ten miles, and performed music, dances, acrobatics, and magic shows. After the fall of the Sui in 618, Emperor Gaozu (566–635) established the Tang dynasty. During his regime, a stable social situation and a flourishing economy provided favorable conditions for great developments in the performing arts. The Music Bureau was expanded to arrange performances for court ceremonies and banquets. The Academy of Performing Arts was founded, and 10,000 performers were gathered for the court. The best were chosen by the emperor himself and trained to cater to his tastes and served him exclusively. An organization known as the Pear Garden (*Liyuan*) assembled very high-quality performers. About 300 musicians formed an orchestra and a choir, which practiced and performed in the royal palace's Pear Garden (giving the organization its name). Even now, the name Pear Garden is still used to refer to theatrical circles. Meanwhile, local governments also established their own performing arts institutes to fulfill the public's craving for music and dance.

Banquet Music: The earliest form of banquet music appeared in the Zhou dynasty for ritual ceremonies. In the Han, musicians refined it. But not until the Sui and Tang did this genre occupy the central position of court music. The earliest Tang banquet music consisted of ten forms, seven taken from central and southeastern Asia and three from native sources. When the emperor Xuanzong (685–762) came to power, he ordered that music should be Sinicized and all banquet music should be simplified into two forms. The "standing form" was to be played outdoors by either 60 or 180 musicians and dancers, while the "sitting form" was for indoor performances of 3 to 12 musicians. Repertoires included some new titles, such as "Long Live the Emperor."

Short Songs: The most popular musical form among Tang scholars and civilians was the "short song" (*quzi*). Its origins lay in collected folk songs and dances. These songs were sung in time to the dancers' steps and were thus also called step songs. Many already-existing melodies were adapted to the new repertoires with newly written lyrics. Famous poems by some of the greatest poets were favored sources for short songs because of their well-known lyrics and regulated meters. In 1907, some 8,000 short song lyrics were found in Dunhuang, indicating the great achievement of this genre during the Tang dynasty.

Transformation Texts: The chanting song (*Bianwen*) was another type of music that experienced great development in the Tang dynasty. It was the earliest form of Chinese narrative music in the cantata style. The singers chanted long stories accompanied by the rhythm of clappers. The content of these stories derived from Buddhist or historical sources or from folk legends. The chanted text section was written in four lines with five or seven Chinese characters to each line. Buddhist monks often employed this musical form for their sermons so their audiences could easily absorb the message from the rhythmic speeches.

Dances: Dancers shared in the success of musicians during the Tang dynasty. They entertained the imperial court with traditional pieces from the Han and Sui dynasties, especially with those containing good omens or glorifying the emperors. Gradually, dances from central Asia and from minority tribes in China were integrated with traditional styles, and new styles of dance resulted. One highly appreciated example was the Whirlwind Dance (*Huxuan wu*), in which performers raised their arms following the rhythm of strings and drums, whirled left and right, and spun more and more quickly for seemingly endless turns. In contrast to this energetic and fast choreography were soft and elegant pieces, such as the Dance of Rainbow-Colored Feather Gown (*Nishang yuyi wu*). Dancers dressed in colorful silk costumes with long hanging sleeves, came onstage to the beat of a drum, and swung and bent their bodies rhythmically while the gold bells on their heads tinkled along with their graceful movements. Other well-known dances in the Tang included the *Qinwang pozhen yuë* (Music of the prince of Qin breaking through enemy ranks), which praised the military exploits of Emperor Taizong (599–649), and the Lion Dance, which symbolized the power and authority of the ruler.

Music, Drama, and Dance in the Song and Yuan Dynasties

Music and Drama: The literati class made an important contribution to the development of the performing arts in the Song and Yuan dynasties. Many of them mastered the skills of writing not only new lyrics, but also new melodies for the musicians. The lyrics were usually composed of lines of irregular length. The melodies were based on a seven-tone modal structure. The most influential poet-musicians were Liu Yong (c. late 10th century), Zhou Bangyan (1056–1121), and Jiang Kuei (c. 1155–1221). In their writings, they projected their inner feelings and thoughts about various objects in nature. Many of these lyric songs were adapted to popular music and widely appreciated by civilians.

Urbanization was also an important factor contributing to the development of popular music. As city populations grew, so did the need for entertainment among their middle and upper classes. This spurred the migration of many musicians and other performers to the cities. They organized troupes, held fairs, and provided all kinds of entertainment for the urban audience. In the Northern Song's capital of Kaifeng, about 50 theaters were built, some of which could seat up to a thousand people. Besides the various programs performed daily in the theaters, a fair was held on a large scale every month that attracted huge audiences. In the Southern Song, when the capital was moved to Hangzhou, many musicians also relocated, organizing more troupes (some with as many as 300 performers) and bringing with them different kinds of music and dance. The major musical form was vocal, accompanied by flute, wooden clapper alone, or wooden clapper and drum. With the vocal music came songs written in various melodies. This type of song was similar to the narrative songs popularized in the Tang dynasty. The singers tended to combine singing with chanting to tell historical or romantic stories as seen, for example, in the *Tale of the Western Chamber*, a story of romantic love between a young scholar and a beautiful lady. Dong Jieyuan (active 1190–1208) wrote the piece, and it contains

444 labeled tunes based on 14 modes. This kind of vocal music was integrated with a stage performance and created the earliest drama, called "mixed drama (zaju)."

By the Yuan dynasty, drama had reached its maturity. A play had four acts: a comic prologue in act I, the main parts of the story in acts II and III, and a conclusion in act IV. Usually there were five characters: a lead singer, a supporting role, a comic role, an official, and a musician who played the drum and flute. The scripts were written by such famous playwrights as Guan Hanqing (c. 1220–1300), who wrote sixty plays in his lifetime. The most famous one was *The Injustice to the Young Woman Dou*, about a young widow who was wrongfully convicted of murder and was executed. When her father, a judicial intendant, returned home, he cleared her name and had her ghost released from the underworld. Mixed drama was played mainly in northern China; in the south, people preferred another dramatic style called Southern drama. When compared to mixed drama, Southern drama was thought more elegant and refined. The leading role was taken in turns by the different characters in the play or sometimes even by the chorus.

Dance: Dance in the Song and Yuan was distinguished by three features. The first was brought about by the flourishing of drama. In traditional dances, dancers would not sing nor dance in the course of performance. But in a play, singers integrated dance with singing in order to achieve the maximum dramatic effect. Thus, there was no longer any boundary between dancer and singer. The second feature was the birth of narrative dance drama. Before the Song, dance did not contain any narratives but focused exclusively on choreography. The breakdown of the boundary between singing and dancing must have inspired choreographers, who designed beautiful choreography to present famous historical events and romantic myths. The third feature was the popularized folk dances, boosted by the monthly fairs in the capital, among which the most popular were the Big Head Dance and the Flower Drums Dances. The Big Head Dance originated from a folk dance performed in the streets during the Lantern Festival, the 15th day of the lunar calendar. Dancers wore large heads painted with happy faces and imitated movements of animals or children to entertain the audience. The Flower Drums Dance was actually a conglomeration of the flower drum performances of Shandong, Shanxi, and Anhui Provinces. The dancers beat drums and cymbals and danced vigorously following the beats and rhythm. In the Yuan dynasty, Chinese folk dance absorbed some elements from the dances of Mongolia.

Music and Dance in the Ming and Qing Dynasties

Music: The maturation of drama in the Song and Yuan laid a solid foundation for the development of Chinese opera in the Ming and Qing dynasties. The most popular style of Chinese traditional opera in the Ming dynasty was the Kun Opera, originating in Kunshan, Jiangsu Province. This form of stage art consisted mainly of arias with a few choral parts, recitative speech, dance, and melodic and percussive instrumental music. Famous scholars such as Tang Xianzu (1550–1616) provided scripts. Tang's most well-known piece, *The Peony Pavilion*, is a very touching love story and is still performed today. The melodies in the Kun Opera were slow yet exuberant. Players combined their singing with acting, supported by an orchestra, including a drum, castanets, bamboo flute, pipe flageolet, pipa, reed organ, two-stringed fiddle, chiming gongs, and small kettle drum.

The Kun Opera declined somewhat in the Qing dynasty, but it provided the basic style for the later Beijing Opera. Beijing Opera was a combination of literature, music, recitation, dance, martial arts, and acrobatics. Usually four major characters appeared in a play: a male role, a female role (in the Ming and Qing, since women were forbidden to perform publicly with men, this role was played by a male), a painted-face role impersonating a man of firm or rude character, and a clown. Three general types of meters were used (single 1/4, double 2/4, and 4/4) and free meter. The major melodic structure was based on 10 styles. Just as in western opera, vocal parts contained solos, duets, and choruses. The instruments used were the same as in

Kun Opera, but the particular composition of the orchestra might have varied depending on the style of the play. Beijing Opera is even now performed all over the country. Scholars who conducted serious research and studies in music theory also enriched the accomplishments of Chinese traditional operas. The scholars wrote large quantities of music literature, including anthologies and encyclopedic books, and their efforts facilitated the development of music in the last two dynasties before the modern period. Nowadays, operas recorded by the past great masters such as Mei Lanfang (1894–1961), Cheng Yanqiu (1904–1958), Shang Xiaoyuan (1899–1976), Xun Huisheng (1899–1968), Ma Lianliang (1901–1966), and Tan Xinpei (1847–1917) are still widely enjoyed. In addition, regional operas are performed in local dialects in different parts of the country.

Dance: In contrast to the rapid development of traditional opera during the Ming and Qing dynasties, dance lost its independent position in the performing arts, dissolving into opera. Opera singers were required to undergo comprehensive training both in singing and dancing. *The Peony Pavilion*, for example, contained a passage in which a young lady, dreaming of love and happiness, expressed her desire through a series of very graceful dance movements. An opera about a hero named Lin Chong, a famous character from the well-known masterpiece *The Outlaws of the Marsh*, also merges singing with vigorous choreography. Another dance that merged into opera (and became a favorite with audiences) was the graceful and ravishing sword dance in the *Xiang Yü Bidding Farewell to His Concubine*.

Though dance had disappeared from stage as a separate art during the Ming and Qing dynasties, folk dancers were still very active. Various programs remained popular, such as the *Lion Dance, Big Head Dance, Flower Drum Dance, Dry Boat Dance, Bamboo Horses Dance, Dragon Dance,* and *Yangge. Yangge* was one of the most dominant styles of folk dance in the Qing dynasty. It was performed in the streets, in theaters, and at court. The style emanated from agricultural work—*yang* means "rice seedling," *ge* means "singing." In the spring, farmers would line up side by side in the paddy fields to plant rice seedlings. As they rhythmically moved forward and backward, an old man beat a drum to accompany and guide their movements. Gradually, the repeated rhythmic movements developed into a form of dance. Performers wearing colorful costumes and carrying drums fastened to their waists sang songs and danced to the beats of the drums. Today, *Yangge* is performed in many celebrations, as well as on stage for entertainment.

Music, Dance, and Drama in the 20th Century

Music: Beijing Opera and various local operas are deeply rooted in Chinese culture. But during the Cultural Revolution, operas with the old stories were suspended and replaced by operas with new scripts containing explicit political content. Only after the Cultural Revolution did this great national cultural treasure resume its fame, style, and popularity. However, as a whole, the influence of the West on 20th-century Chinese music has been intense. Exchanges began in the late 17th century between Chinese court musicians and Western missionaries, with the latter introducing keyboard instruments and teaching Chinese musicians how to play them. In 1872, China's first book of hymns was published in Shanghai. In 1918, the first musical score of *The Marching Band* was published. After the May Fourth Movement in 1919, musicians were increasingly attracted to Western music and sailed abroad to get a Western education. Many famous composers, such as Li Shutong (1880–1942), Xian Xinghai (1905–1945), Xiao Youmei (1884–1940), and Huang Zi (1904–1938) completed their studies abroad and then returned to China with new ideas. In 1927, Xiao Youmei graduated from the University of Leipzig with a Ph.D. and established the first Westernized music education institute, the Shanghai National Conservatory of Music, where emphasis was placed on Western music theory and training, with only a limited introduction to Chinese traditional music. Yet, except for the educated class, most people could not easily appreciate Western music. That forced the Chinese composers to turn their attention to native traditions and re-educate themselves with Chinese folk songs. In 1939, during the War of Resistance against Japan, Xian Xinghai composed the *Yellow River Cantata*, which consists of four movements: "The Song of the Yellow River Boatman," "Ode to the Yellow River," "Yellow River Ditty," and "Defend the Yellow River." He borrowed melodies from folk songs while also incorporating many elements from Western symphonies. The practice of combining Eastern and Western components has now been in existence for more than half a century. Contemporary Chinese music includes folk songs, a mixture of Chinese and Western traditional music, and rock and roll. In addition, interest in China's traditional music has been revived, and orchestras performing national scores on Chinese instruments have been very active, giving concerts both at home and abroad.

Dance: As mentioned above, *Yangge* arose from folk dance and was popularized throughout China during the Qing dynasty. This style of folk dance was then promoted to a higher position in the 20th century, becoming a regular part of celebrations and stage performances as well as an exercise for general health. Folk dances still form the main current in dance performances, and though the *Yangge* is most often performed among the Han ethnic group, many minority groups have their own beautiful dances with strong, vernacular styles. Many of these dances are appreciated not only by their own people but also by people of other ethnic groups. Examples include the *Peacock Dance* of the Dai, the *Piggyback for the Bride* of the Yi, the *Drum Dance* of the Manchu, the *Furnace Burns Brighter* of the Miao, the *Long Drum Dance* of the Koreans (some ethnic Koreans live in northeastern China), the *Straw Hat Dance* of the Li, and the *Armor Dance* of the Qiang.

11. OTHER FORMS OF ENTERTAINMENT

Music, dance, and traditional opera are forms of entertainment as well as works of art, but there are many other forms of folk art that have long entertained Chinese people. Some popular forms include ballad singing, storytelling, comic dialects, recitations accompanied by drum and clapper, and comic shows. Audiences can enjoy these performances in theaters, at gatherings in the open, or in teahouses.

Film

One form of entertainment in China strongly influenced by the West is films. On August 11, 1896, a Spaniard named Galen Bocca showed the first movie to a Chinese audience at Xuyuan, an entertainment center in Shanghai. In July 1897, an American brought several short films to Shanghai: *The Tsar's Visit to Paris*, *The Serpent Dance in Florida*, *The City of Madrid*, *The Spanish Dance*, *The Exhausted Mule*, and *The Boxer*. The first Chinese film, *Conquering Jun Mountain*, adapted from a Peking opera, was pro-

duced in 1905 by Ren Fengtai (1850–1932). In 1913, the first feature film, *The Difficult Couple*, was shot by the Asia Film Company.

The emerging film business attracted some foreign filmmakers. In 1917, an American went to China and invested all his capital, $100,000, in filmmaking, but two years later, he met with a setback and had to sell all the equipment to the Commercial Press. With this equipment, the Commercial Press established a motion picture department, which greatly stimulated the film production business. By the mid-1920s, 176 studios were set up in the country. However, facing intense competition, many of these studios closed down within a year.

The remaining companies merged into three big companies. The oldest among them was the Mingxing Film Company, founded in 1922 by Zhang Shichuan (1893–1953), Zhou Jianyun (1893–1967), and Zheng Zhengqiu (1888–1935) and later joined by Xia Yan (1900–1996), Zheng Boqi (1895–1979), A Ying (1900–1977), and

Hong Shen (1894–1955). The company was well known for producing films with social aspects. The second company was the Lianhua Film Company, founded in 1930 by Luo Mingyou (1900–1967). The company employed a group of highly educated people, including Cai Chusheng (1906–1968) and Sun Yu (1900–1990), who brought to the company many "progressive" Western ideas. The third company was the Tianyi Company, founded in 1925 by the Shao brothers, who advocated producing "authentic" Chinese films. In 1931, Tianyi was one of the earliest companies to produce a sound film in China.

The development of the film industry kindled the interests of audiences. In 1920, to meet the demands of audiences, moviemakers developed three long feature films—*Yan Ruisheng*, *Sea Oath*, and *The Vampire*. The blooming filmmaking business also elevated the social status of male and female actors. The first famous group who established their fame between the 1920s and 1930s included Zheng Zhengqiu (1888–1935), the "founding father of Chinese cinema"; Hu Die (1907–1989) and Ruan Lingyu (1910–1935), the leading actresses; and Jin Yan (1910–1983), a leading actor.

After the Nationalist government was set up, political and social issues began to interfere with the film industry. Some "leftist" filmmakers, represented by Tian Han (1898–1968), Xia Yan, Situ Huimin (1910–1987), and Yang Hansheng (1902–1993), explored in their works the dark sides of the government and society. When the Sino-Japanese war broke out, films, especially those made in the unoccupied areas, became a propaganda machine to call for anti-Japanese resistance. Documentary and cartoon films carrying propaganda messages constituted a large proportion of film outputs. After the war, films continued to depict social realities, as shown in *Eight Thousand Miles of Cloud and Moon* (1947), directed by Shi Dongshan (1902–1955), and *The Spring River Flows East* (1947–1948), directed by Cai Chusheng and Zheng Junli (1911–1969). Meanwhile, a group of film artists, led by Liu Na'ou (1900–1940), Mu Shiying (1912–1940), and Huang Tianshi (1900–1983), believed that films should focus on entertainment. They produced films with romantic themes taken from literature, particularly from the Mandarin Duck and Butterfly School (The term refers to popular urban fiction, often love stories, which were very popular in the 1910s and 1920s). This kind of film was very popular among youths and urban citizens.

With the establishment of the People's Republic of China in 1949, the direction of film production was reset. State or local governments now owned studios. Four major national studios were founded: Northeast Film Studio, Beijing Film Studio, Shanghai Film Studio, and August First Film Studio affiliated with the People's Liberation Army. Among the major studios owned by local governments were Xi'an Film Studio in Shanxi, Pearl River Film Studio in Guangdong, Emei Film Studio in Sichuan, Tianshan Film Studio in Xinjiang, and Inner Mongolian Film Studio in Nei Monggol. Although political and social issues were still the main themes, audiences had the chance to appreciate refined art embedded in the style of "socialist realism."

Some popular films included *The Song of Youth* (1959), directed by Cui Wei (1912–1979); *Legend of the Red Banner* (1960), directed by Ling Zifeng (1917–); *Red Detachment of Women* (1961), directed by Xie Jin (1923–); *Lin Zexu* (1958), directed by Zheng Junli and Cen Fan (1926–); and *Early Spring in February* (1963), directed by Xie Tieli (1925–). Although these films aimed at revolutionary education, comedies, such as *The Youth People of Our Village* (1959), directed by Su Li (1919–), and filmed theatrical performances, such as *Dream of the Red Chamber* (1962), directed by Cen Fan, were still shown to entertain people.

During the Cultural Revolution, the film industry on the mainland almost stopped producing any films except documentaries with clear political purposes. In 1971, eight "model films" adapted from revolutionary operas and ballets were made. Between 1971 and 1976, a small number of feature films appeared, and they were full of political jargon. But in Taiwan, the film industry at this time prospered. A large number of feature films were produced in 1966. The total output helped rank the Taiwan film industry third in Asia, only after Japan and India. At the same time, martial art films in Hong Kong were widely acclaimed. Bruce Lee (1940–1973), Michael Hui, Sam Hui, and, later, Jackie Chan all became worldwide stars.

The end of the Cultural Revolution signaled a new era in the history of Chinese cinema. Some film artists focused on making films to reveal political repression, as seen in director Xie Jin's *The Legend of Tianyun Mountain* (1980), and others explored the reasons for the political tragedies in the country. A group of middle-aged directors, the so-called Fourth Generation, demonstrated new approaches in their works: *In the Wild Mountain* (1985), directed by Yan Xueshu (1940–); *The Horse Theft* (1986), directed by Tian Zhuangzhuang (1952–); *Sacrificed Youth* (1985), directed by Zhang Nuanxin (1940–); *Old Well* (1987), directed by Wu Tianming (1939–). Soon another group of directors, the Fifth Generation, went even further in exploring traditional Chinese culture and society. Remarkable developments have been achieved by this group of young directors, represented by Chen Kaige (1952–), the director of *Yellow Earth* (1984) and *Farewell My Concubine* (1993), and Zhang Yimou (1950–), the director of *The Red Sorghum* (1987) and *Raise the Red Lantern* (1991). In the 1990s, the Sixth Generation emerged and injected new energy into the Chinese film industry. Now Chinese films have attracted worldwide attention and have won numerous awards at some important international film festivals in Berlin, Cannes, Locarno, Montreal, Nantes, Persaro, Rotterdam, Tokyo, Toronto, Turin, and Venice.

Radio and Television

Radio and television are popular entertainment media in China. The first radio station was set up in Shanghai in 1923 by an American, E. G. Osborn, but was soon closed down by the Nationalist government. In October 1926, the Harbin Radio Station, owned by the Nationalist government, went on the air. By 1949, there were about 49 stations with a transmitting power of 78 kilowatts, which broadcast news, religious preachers, and entertainment programs.

With the establishment of the People's Republic of China, the central government took over radio stations. Broadcasting, both domestic and international, was put under the supervision of the Ministry of Radio, Film, and Television. Local governments of the provinces and counties, however, manage their own stations. Altogether there are now more than 200 provincial and municipal broadcasting stations in the country. These stations broadcast programs both in Mandarin and in regional dialects. Of the domestic service, the Central People's Broadcasting Station is the largest. It operates through six channels: two in Mandarin, two in Minnan dialect, one in Hakka dialect, and one in Mongolian, Tibetan, Uighur, Kazak, and Korean. Segments include domestic and international news, educational lectures, and entertainment. There are also some service-orientated channels that broadcast weather reports, listeners' requests, time announcements, advertisements, and mailboxes for the audience.

The station catering to receivers abroad is Radio Beijing, which has programs on the air every day in 43 foreign languages, including Albanian, Arabic, Bengali, Bulgarian, Burmese, Czech, English, Esperanto, French, German, Hausa, Kindi, Hungarian, Indonesian, Italian, Japanese, Kampuchean, Korean, Lao, Mongolian, Nepalese, Spanish, Turkish, and Vietnamese. In addition to news, the station provides programs about various aspects of Chinese culture, literature, music, and arts, as well as Beijing operas. Broadcasts are also received from many foreign countries, such as the United Kingdom, the United States, Japan, France, Germany, Russia, Australia, and Canada.

Television has almost taken the place of radio as the most popular form of media. The first television station, Beijing Television, started showing black-and-white programs on May 1, 1958. Soon after that, a television station was established in Shanghai, followed by those in other provinces. In 1973, color TV programs were introduced to audiences through Beijing, Shanghai, and Tianjin television stations. As of 1999, China Central Television (CCTV), the largest in the country, had eight channels. Channel 1 broadcasts news and other programs dealing with important issues of the day. Channel 2 is concerned with economic and social educational programs. Channel 3 is mainly an entertainment channel. Channel 4 is an international one which broadcasts to dozens of foreign countries both news and entertainment programs, mainly in English. Channel 5 is a sports channel. Channel 6 is devoted mostly to films made in China. Channel 7 caters mainly to the military. Channel 8 presents mostly films from abroad dubbed in Chinese. Television has been developing rapidly in China. It has reached remote areas, such as the mountainous peaks in Tibet and some inland villages with only a few households.

In 1979, the Ministry of Education and Central Broadcasting Administration founded the Central Radio-Television University. Lectures are given through television and thus made available to people of all ages and vocations as long as they pass a preliminary admission examination. In 20 years, more than a half million students have graduated from the program. Now educational programs and various entertainment programs greatly enrich the lives of people. Feature films, live broadcasting from theaters and concert halls, video recordings of theatrical performances, and foreign movies are all welcomed by audiences. Important world affairs and international sporting events draw people to the screen no matter what time of day they are broadcast. Besides the CCTV, 26 provincial-level stations produce numerous programs to meet the demands of the audiences. Various radio-television review magazines help to promote the making of programs. In 1996, Oriental Pearl Television Center in Shanghai was set up, which broadcasts widely acclaimed programs to the whole country and Asia.

12. SPORTS

Sports Before the 20th Century

Ancient Chinese sports can be roughly divided into two categories. One is related to military activities, such as archery, chariot driving, horseback riding, and martial arts. The other includes activities for health and entertainment, such as qigong, equestrian sports, ice sports, skating, swimming, rowing, ancient football, swing board, shuttlecock, Go, and Chinese chess.

Archery and Martial Arts: Archery and swordcraft are the two earliest sports derived from hunting and war. Throughout the entire pre-modern period, all soldiers, whether infantry or equestrian, had to undergo archery and weapons training. In times of war, archery and swordcraft were means of violence; in times of peace, they became sports. Archery was even listed as one of the six arts practiced by Confucians in the Zhou dynasty. To promote the development of archery and swordcraft, the government organized different competitions. For archery, men vied in shooting animals, flower baskets, a piece of silk, or a lighted joss stick. For swordcraft, they chose from a variety of weapons and competed in the styles and movements of the thrusts.

Bare-hand fighting has been a part of military training since the Zhou dynasty. Though soldiers and some martial artists still practice these techniques for the purpose of fighting, some forms of wrestling and sparring have clearly evolved into sports.

Today in China, martial arts are generally referred to under the term *wushu* (martial techniques). In the West, Chinese martial arts have taken on the term "kung fu." Over the long history of Chinese martial arts, different styles or "schools" developed, with their distinctive systems of bare-hand and weapons fighting techniques. For the purpose of performance and practice, fighting techniques have been strung together into routines known as "forms." Because of the generally pacific nature of modern society, some modern practitioners have taken to practicing forms that have no fighting applications. However, in both China and abroad, there are still many martial artists who are keeping the traditional fighting skills alive.

There are literally hundreds, if not thousands, of styles of martial arts in China. People in the martial arts community have devised different ways of categorizing the numerous styles. One way is by region, with northern styles typically excelling in kicks and southern styles excelling in upper body techniques. Another is by the emphasis on practice. In general, all Chinese martial arts advocate the strengthening of tendons, bones, and skin externally and the cultivation of qi (vital life energy) internally. (It is worth noting that few Chinese martial artists would encourage the kind of muscle building practiced by bodybuilders.) Styles can be classified as "external" and "internal" styles, depending on which aspects they emphasize. Since the internal aspect of martial arts is generally considered more sophisticated, the internal stylists wear this designation as a badge of honor. On the other hand, the schools not known as internal often reject the description external, contending that they in fact emphasize both the internal and external aspects.

The best-known internal styles are tai chi, Bagua, and Xingyi. The famous Shaolin school is sometimes referred to as external, although Shaolin practitioners often resent the designation. Because of the fame of the martial arts monks of the Shaolin Temple, many styles call themselves "Shaolin," even though their relationship to the temple is difficult to prove. This situation is further complicated by the fact that Shaolin monks, being great martial arts enthusiasts, have often been on the lookout for new techniques that can strengthen their existing repertoire. As a result, many martial arts systems originally developed outside of the temple have been learned and modified by Shaolin monks.

Tai chi, Qigong, Go, Chess, and Other Ancient Sports: Although tai chi (also known as "Taiji," "Taijiquan," etc.) was originally practiced as a martial art, today the vast majority of its practitioners learn it exclusively as a form of health exercise. Because of its slow, gentle movements and its emphasis on balance and smooth trans-

fer of weight between the legs, tai chi has been especially favored by the elderly. Through the active promotion of the Chinese government and tai chi enthusiasts, groups of elderly practicing tai chi in public parks have become a common sight in China. Indeed, tai chi has become so well known that foreign reporters have often misidentified people practicing other slow-moving exercises as "tai chi practitioners."

The cultivation of qi (sometimes translated as "internal energy") has been an important part of traditional martial arts and some forms of religious practice. There have also been many centuries-old qi-cultivation exercises for health. In the 20th century, the cultivation of qi has become known as qigong (sometimes spelled Qi Gong, Ch'i-kung, or Ch'i Kung). Today, most qigong practitioners practice for health.

Unlike sports that emphasize body movements, chess is essentially a mental exercise. The two kinds of chess played in China are Go and Chinese chess. Go, invented approximately 2,000 years ago, involves a chess board with 19 lines painted both horizontally and vertically, forming 361 crossed points. Each player has to follow set rules and try to place his or her own 180 white or 181 black pieces to surround an opponent's pieces as well as occupying more cross points on the board. Chinese chess is also played by two people but on a chessboard with 10 horizontal lines and 9 vertical lines. Each player has 16 chess pieces, including a general. As in Western chess with its king, the object is to take the opponent's general.

The dragon boat race was originally held to commemorate the death of the great poet Qu Yuan, who drowned himself in a river in Hunan Province in protest against the corrupt government. Now, on each anniversary of his death (the fifth day of the fifth month in the lunar calendar), a festival is held. People in the South row dragon boats along rivers and throw rice cakes into them to enable the ghost of the poet to rest more peacefully in the underworld. Today, dragon boat racing is a very popular sport in southern China as well as in many Southeast Asian countries. The boats are made in the shape of dragons and painted with dragon motifs. At the bow sits a conductor and at the stern a drummer, with rowers dressed in colorful national costumes rowing at both sides to the beat of the drum. However artful, the boat that reaches the finish line first is still the winner. The annual races of the Dragon Boat Festival are a truly spectacular event, attracting thousands of people.

Sports in the 20th Century

Sports in the 20th century are highlighted by the achievements of many Chinese athletes. Basketball was brought to China by Christians in 1896. In 1910, the first basketball championship was held at the National Sports Meet. In 1924, the men's team won the championship in the Far Eastern Sports Meet. In 1936, China's basketball team participated in the Olympics (in Berlin) for the first time. In addition to basketball, volleyball, soccer, table tennis, badminton, tennis, gymnastics, and track and field are very popular in China. Volleyball was brought to Guangzhou in the early 20th century and then gradually spread to the rest of the country. In 1911, men's volleyball teams held their first competition, and in 1924, the women's volleyball teams gave a performance at the National Sports Meet.

After half a century, Chinese athletes began winning many international championships. The women's volleyball team, for example, has won five gold medals in international games, including the gold medal at the 1984 Summer Olympic Games.

Soccer was first introduced in Hong Kong in the early 20th century. From 1904 to 1908, college soccer championships were held among colleges in Hong Kong, Guangzhou, Beijing, and Shanghai. This sport is one of the most popular sports throughout the country. In 1931, China joined the International Soccer Association. In 1936, a Chinese soccer team participated in the Summer Olympic Games.

Table tennis was ushered into China from Japan in 1904, and it also has become a popular national sport, especially among young students. Chinese teams participate in many international tournaments. Rong Guotuan (1937–1968) won the first gold medal in 1959 at the World Table Tennis Championship. (He was the first Chinese world champion in any international sports competition.) Since then Chinese competitors have been very successful in this sport. In 1993, at the World Table Tennis Championships, they won the gold medals in the singles, in men's and women's doubles, and in mixed doubles. Chinese athletes have also distinguished themselves by winning gold medals in other sports such as badminton, gymnastics, swimming, diving, weightlifting, and the marathon.

Final Medal Standings in the Summer Olympic Games: China participated in the Summer Olympic Games held between the 1930s and the 1950s. After 28 years of absence, China rejoined the Summer Olympic Games in 1984. Xu Haifeng won the first gold medal for China in the air pistol-shooting event. Since then the medal standings for China are as follows: 1984: 15 gold, 8 silver, 9 bronze, 32 total; 1988: 5 gold, 11 silver, 12 bronze, 28 total; 1992: 16 gold, 22 silver, 16 bronze, 54 total; 1996: 16 gold, 22 silver, 12 bronze, 50 total; 2000: 28 gold, 16 silver, 15 bronze, 59 total.

Final Medal Standings in the Winter Olympic Games: China participated in the Winter Olympic Games in 1980. Yang Yang won the first gold medal during the competition of short track speed skating in 2002. The medal standings for China are as follows: 1992: 3 silver, 3 total; 1994: 1 silver, 2 bronze, 3 total; 1998: 6 silver, 2 bronze, 8 total; 2002: 2 gold, 2 silver, 4 bronze, 8 total.

KEY RESEARCH SOURCES

Barnhart, Richard M., et. al. *Three Thousand Years of Chinese Painting*. New Haven: Yale University Press, 1997.

Cahill, James. *Chinese Painting*. New York: Rizzoli International Publications, Inc., 1985.

Chinese Academy of Architecture, comp. *Ancient Chinese Architecture*. Beijing: China Building Industry Press, 1982.

Fong, Wen C. "Imperial Portraiture in the Song, Yuan, and Ming Periods." *Ars Orientalis* 25 (1995): 47–60.

Li, Zehou. *The Path of Beauty: A Study of Chinese Aesthetics*. Trans. Gong Lizeng. Beijing: Morning Glory Publishers, 1988.

Liang, Mingyue. *Music of the Billion: An Introduction to Chinese Musical Culture*. No. 8 of *Paperbacks on Musicology*. Ed. Andrew D. McCredie. New York: Heinrichshofen, 1985.

Liang, Sicheng. *A Pictorial History of Chinese Architecture: A Study of the Development of Its Structural System and the Evolution of Its Types*. Ed. Wilma Fairbank. Cambridge: The MIT Press, 1984.

Liu Dunzhen. *Chinese Classical Gardens of Suzhou*. Trans. Chen Lixian. New York: McGraw-Hill, 1993.

Murck, Alfreda, and Wen C. Fong, eds. *Words and Images: Chinese Poetry, Calligraphy, and Painting*. New York: The Metropolitan Museum of Art, 1991.

Nakata, Yujiro, ed. *Chinese Calligraphy. A History of the Art of China*. New York: Weatherhill, 1982.

Rawson, Jessica, ed. *Mysteries of Ancient China: New Discoveries from the Early Dynasties*. New York: George Braziller, 1996.

Sullivan, Michael. *The Arts of China*. 3d ed. Berkeley: University of California Press, 1984.

Tregear, Mary. *Chinese Art*. Rev. ed. London: Thames and Hudson, 1997.

Wang, Kefen. *The History of Chinese Dance: Traditional Chinese Arts and Culture*. Beijing: Foreign Languages Press, 1985.

Literature

By Jing Liao and Eric Dalle

INTRODUCTION

Traditional Chinese literature spans a period of about 3,000 years. In this brief sketch of its long history, we will introduce the representative genres of the various time periods and comment on the great works of the outstanding exponents of those genres.

1. THE ZHOU DYNASTY (1122–256 B.C.)

The two most important literary works produced during the Zhou dynasty were *Shi jing* (The book of poetry) and *Chu ci* (The songs of the chu). These two works are generally considered to be the twin fountainheads of Chinese poetry, to which later poetic themes, modes, styles, and diction are frequently traced.

The Book of Poetry is a collection of 305 poems composed between the 12th and seventh centuries B.C. It consists of three major sections: *feng* (folk songs collected from different states of Zhou), *ya* (odes used for court banquets and feasts), and *song* (ritual hymns to dynastic founders). It exhibits three distinct modes of poetic expression: *fu* (narrative mode), *bi* (analogical mode), and *xing* (associational mode). Tradition has it that Confucius selected and edited the 305 poems from a huge corpus of 3,000, but most modern scholars doubt, if not dismiss outright, the long-held belief of Confucius's involvement. Nonetheless, Confucius did speak highly of the usefulness of this anthology, and he made frequent references to it, as did many of his contemporaries. The anthology itself later became one of the Five Classics, along with *Yi jing* (The book of changes), *Shang shu* (The book of documents), *Li ji* (The record of rites), and *Chunqiu* (Spring and Autumn Annals).

The Songs of Chu is an anthology of poetic texts from the southern state of Chu. The main bulk of the collection has been attributed, with a varying degree of certainty, to Qu Yuan (c. 340–278 B.C.), but some texts are believed to have been composed later, during the Han dynasty (206 B.C.–A.D. 220). Of those texts, the most famous is "Li sao" ("Encountering sorrow"), a long allegorical poem of 187 couplets written by Qu Yuan. The poem tells how the hero, vilified by his political enemies and banished by his muddle-headed lord, continued to adorn himself with fragrant flowers and grass (moral virtues) and undertook a mystical journey through the sky to look for a virtuous lord (the "fair one"). The poem contains dramatic monologues, lamentations over the ills of the human world, shamanistic invocations, as well as accounts of the hero's failures to find the "fair one" through either matchmakers or his own initiatives. In depicting this journey, Qu Yuan gives free reign to his imagination and strong feelings and makes countless allusions to myths and legends. Because of the many notable parallels to the poet's own life, the poem is considered by many to be autobiographical in some measure and a genuine expression of the poet's intense emotions. Qu Yuan is also believed to have written "Tianwen" ("Questioning heaven"), "Jiu zhang" ("Nine chapters"), and "Jiu ge" ("Nine songs"). The distinguishing features of the *Chu ci* poems are the abundant use of the sound particle *xi* within or between lines and the tangible influence of shaman rituals in themes, imagery, diction, and rhythms.

A number of historical texts written during the Zhou are avidly read for their literary qualities. Particularly worthy of mention are *Zuo zhuan* (the Zuo commentary to *Spring and Autumn Annals*), known for its captivating depictions of events and human characters, and *Zhuangzi*, a Daoist classic popular for its pointed wit, charming style, vivid imagination, and rich vocabulary

2. THE HAN AND SUI DYNASTIES (206 B.C.–A.D. 618)

The Han dynasty (206 B.C.–A.D. 220) was one of the greatest and most prosperous periods of Chinese history. During this period, folk songs were collected and recorded by the Music Bureau (Yuefu) and therefore became known as *yuefu* poems. The subject matter of these folk songs varies. Some tell about the horror of war and the hardships people suffered, and others tell stories of love and courtship. Some of the famous love stories are "The Peacock Flew South-eastward" and "Gathering Wild Herbs upon the Mountain." Meanwhile, *fu*, a form of rhymed prose sometimes translated as "rhapsody," developed and became very popular among all the literati of the time. Among the numerous *fu* writers, the most notable ones were Sima Xiangru (179–117 B.C.), Yang Xiong (53 B.C.–A.D. 18), and Zhang Heng (A.D. 78–139). Those writers had lofty purposes in writing, and the words they used were ornate, obscure, and exaggerated. Much of the writing is often hard to understand. Sima Xiangru was the poet whose style and format was most often imitated by other Han writers.

The writing of five-character *shi* poetry began with Eastern Han writers like Zhang Heng and Cai Yong (133–192). It reached the stage of full development in the collection known as the "Nineteen Old Poems." The poems usually expressed the feelings of people away from home, of friends long departed, and of human experience, such as births and deaths. In the Wei-Jin period (220–420), a form of poetry calling for five characters (syllables) per line reached the peak of its evolution. Cao Zhi (192–232) is considered one of the best practitioners of this poetic form. His works were intensely lyrical, polished, stylish in diction, and brimming with talent and wit. Unfortunately for Cao Zhi, his older brother, Cao Pi (187–226), who was also emperor for much of this time, was very hostile to him because of long-standing jealousy. According to a legend, the emperor once maliciously challenged Cao Zhi to complete a poem within the time it takes to walk seven steps. Cao took up the challenge and promptly composed the following poem, which has been handed down to this day:

> Boiling beans to make a stew—
> Juicing them to make soup.
> Under the pot the bean stalks
> burn,
> Inside the pot the beans weep:
> "We were born of the same roots,
> Why hurry to boil us?"

Another famous poet of the period was Tao Qian (c. 372–427). He left behind about 150 poems, the most famous of which were his poems of gardens and fields. The great poet Su Shi (1036–1101) noted that these poems appear to be plain, but convey a great variety of moods and are very profound in meaning. Tao Qian's poetry was largely ignored in his own time, but it gained appreciation in the Tang dynasty (618–907). The fame of Tao has been on the rise ever since, and nowadays he is revered as one of the preeminent Chinese poets and a great cultural hero.

The Han witnessed the appearance of *Shi ji* (Records of the historian), China's first comprehensive history, by Sima Qian (c. 145–86 B.C.). It took Sima Qian 18 years to complete this gigantic work, which covers more than 25 centuries of Chinese history, from the earliest ages to about 100 B.C. His mastery of the art of prose writing, his lucid and gripping narration, and his vivid, true-to-life descriptions of prominent historical figures make the book not only a series of precious biographies but also a literary masterpiece. Later prose writers learned a great deal from his writing techniques and styles. His writings exerted an enormous influence on the popular novels and dramas of the Ming and Qing dynasties (1368–1911).

With the unprecedented development of literature, the field of literary criticism saw the production of two authoritative works, *Wenxin diaolong* (Literary Mind and the Carving of Dragons), by Lu Xie (465–22), and *Shi pin* (Grading of Poets), by Zhong Rong (479–501). The works of these two great literary critics have immeasurable theoretical value and are still important topics of literary research today.

3. THE TANG AND THE FIVE DYNASTIES (618–960)

During the nearly 300 years of the Tang dynasty (618–907), about 50,000 poems of considerable importance were produced and preserved. There were about 50 or 60 distinguished poets, each writing with his own particular style. In high Tang, a group of gifted and prominent poets was led by Wang Changling (698–757) and Cen Shen (715–770). Many of these poets were fond of writing poems about war and the frontier life. Cen was one of the few poets in Chinese history who wrote poems in praise of war. The poetic form of choice during this period was the seven-characters-per-line meter, which poets used with great gusto and displays of passion.

High Tang poetry was dominated by three towering figures: Wang Wei (699–759), Li Bo (701–762), and Du Fu (712-770). Wang is known as "the Buddha of poetry" for his Buddhist beliefs and his evocation of the Buddhist sensibility in landscape poetry. Li is known as "the immortal of poetry" for his embrace of Daoist ideals and his rich imagination. Du is remembered as "the sage of poetry" for his commitment to Confucian moral ideals.

Together with his close friend, Meng Haoran (689–740), Wang Wei produced many landscape poems, mainly in the five-characters-per-line form, that were restrained and tender in tone and noted for their superb descriptive techniques. Li Bo and Du Fu are generally regarded as the greatest of Chinese poets. Li Bo was a poetic genius of extraordinary imagination comparable to that of Qu Yuan. About 900 of his poems are still read and valued today for their romantic abandon and artistic restraint. His control of the "cut-off verse" (*jueju*) is considered perfect. (*Jueju* is a form of poetry that requires four lines per poem, with either five or seven characters per line. There are also strict rules regarding the tones of the syllables.) He produced the best of his poems while he was drunk. Li Bo and Du Fu were friends but differed in temperament, experience, and personality. As their views on life and the world were different, there is a conspicuous difference in the contents and styles of their poems. Li Bo gave free rein to his imagination, paying little attention to form and tones. His poems scale the height of the development of romanticism, as they evoke endless associations in the mind of the reader. Du Fu was principally a poet of realism. His poems, however, are interspersed with flashes of romanticism. He excelled in "regulated verse" (*lüshi*) and produced many poems in this complex form that are rich in social content. (*Lüshi* normally requires eight or more lines per poem. A *lüshi* usually has either five or seven syllables per line. As in the case of *jueju*, there are also strict rules regarding the tones of the syllables.) In these poems, Du reflected on the changing fortunes of the Tang and realistically depicted the sufferings of the common people. He was an indisputable master of poetic craft, taking care of every word he wrote and always aiming at perfection of form. He also wrote biographies, letters, allegories, and literary criticism, all in the form of poetry.

Among the well-known poets of the middle and late Tang, Bo Juyi (772–846) was the most prolific and is today best known for his two narrative poems, "The Song of Everlasting Regret" and "The Lute." Li He (790–816) is now widely admired for his eccentric imagination that sometimes borders on the grotesque. Du Mu (803–853) is today generally praised for the lyrical intensity and descriptive flair in his "cut-off verse," and his contemporary Li Shangyin (813–858) is today admired for his masterful use of rich, deliberately opaque allusions.

During the mid-Tang, the Classical Prose Movement began under the leadership of Han Yu (768–824) and Liu Zongyuan (773–819), and was further developed by Ouyang Xiu (1007–1072). The movement aimed at shedding the influence of parallel prose, a highly artificial and ornate form of writing that tended to impede the flow of thought. It advocated a clear, unadorned prose style modeled on the ancient classics. Thanks to the success of this movement, the classical prose style was firmly established as the standard model for prose writing for the next nine centuries until the Revolution of 1919, when it was replaced by spoken or vernacular Chinese as the primary medium of writing.

Short stories developed from brief, outline-like tales of previous periods into full-length works during the Tang. The most popular theme of this new genre was love. "The Story of Cui Yingying" by Yuan Zhen (779–831) was the most famous short story of the period. The story tells of an intensely romantic love affair between a young scholar, Zhang Sheng, and a beautiful young lady, Yingying. Such stories written by Tang authors provided the base for many of the dramatic works of later dynasties. Some Tang stories exhibited a strong Buddhist influence, though others vividly captured the liberal behavior and temperament of the Tang men of letters.

4. The Song Dynasty (960–1279)

If the *shi* poetry was the representative form of Tang poetry, the *ci* poetry, often translated as lyric songs, was most representative of Song poetry. *Ci* poetry originated as lyrics for various musical tunes. Each of these tunes called for a particular *ci* format, with its own rules for rhyming, line length, tonal pattern, and the total number of characters per poem. *Ci* remained closely bound to music for a long time until Su Shi and other literary writers began to write *ci* for purposes other than musical performance. But even after the rise of such purely literary *ci*, many *ci* writers continued to produce *ci* to be performed as well as read.

Su Shi brought the art of *ci* to maturity even though he also excelled in the writing of seven-character *shi* poetry. In his *ci* works, Su broke away from the then-popular theme of love and broadened it to include history, reminiscence, travels, and other themes, thus freeing *ci* from the restrictions of music performance and making it the prized vehicle of lyrical expression for the Song literati. His bold, unconstrained style and lofty sentiment imbue his *ci* works with vitality and dazzle the reader with his emotional and descriptive power. This is exemplified in "East Flows the Great River." Su's *ci*, full of verve and gusto, free and easy, forms a sharp contrast to the *ci* of Liu Yong (990–1050), which was delicate, melancholy, and restrained. Besides *ci*, Su was also accomplished in painting, calligraphy, and prose.

Huang Tingjian (1045–1105), Lu You (1125–1210), and Xin Qiji (1140–1205) were all distinguished writers of *ci*. Besides them, particular mention should be made of the poet Li Qingzhao (1084–1155). She was an accomplished woman writer of *shi* and *ci* poetry, as well as prose. But today she is most fondly remembered for her superb *ci* works. In a time when women were discouraged from giving free expression to their feelings, Li was bold enough to pour forth her emotions in lucid, unadorned, and powerfully rhythmical language.

5. THE YUAN DYNASTY (1276–1368)

The predominant literary genres of the Yuan were *qu* (arias or dramatic songs) and *zaju* (drama) of which the performance of *qu* was an integral part. The emergence of the two genres was made possible by a number of important literary developments since the Tang. The spread of *bian-wen*, or transformation texts, a type of storytelling with pictures brought in from central Asia, and the craze for traditional legendary stories, anecdotes of famous literary figures, and the trendy appreciation of foreign songs and music all helped set the stage for the large-scale production of *qu* and *zaju* during the Yuan. There are about 80 Yuan playwrights whose names are on record, with around 500 extant plays from Yuan times. *Zaju* is composed of arias, dialogues, and monologues. Playwrights enjoyed a great deal of freedom in expressing themselves, especially through the arias.

Guan Hanqing (c. 1210–1298) is perhaps the most famous Yuan playwright. He was learned, witty, and unconventional and had a sharp sense of humor. More than 60 of his dramas remain, including tragedies, comedies, and satires on a wide range of subjects. He also wrote lyric songs that were descriptive and full of gusto. *Dou E yuan* (The injustice suffered by Dou E) is considered the best of his tragedies and is regarded as a model for later playwrights. The play tells the story of the young widow Dou E, who was framed in a charge of murder. She is found guilty and is executed in June. Before her execution, Dou E makes three wishes: that her blood should stain a flag 7 feet from the ground; that it should snow; and that there should be a three-year drought. All three wishes come true, and Dou E is finally declared an innocent victim. The story has been adapted to the Beijing Opera and is still performed on the stage today as *June Snow*. Guan Hanqing is known for his readiness in learning from the vernacular and making masterful use of its rich vocabulary and ingenious grammatical variations.

Another successful drama of realism of the Yuan is *The Story of the West Chamber*, by Wang Shifu (fl. 1295–1307), based on the Tang short story "The Story of Miss Cui Yingying." Although the drama was often criticized and even banned in ensuing dynasties for being too audacious and obscene in the description of some romantic scenes, it nonetheless had plenty of supporters. Today it is rated as a work of genius.

6. THE MING DYNASTY (1368–1644)

In the Ming dynasty, drama and short stories continued to flourish, though the period did not produce as many illustrious writers as earlier dynasties. The writing of novels, however, entered a golden age of development, especially toward the end of the Ming.

Buddhist sutras, both in prose and verse, had direct influence on the growth of fiction as a literary form. To make the obscure content of the sutras understandable, Buddhist missionaries used illustrations to tell anecdotes and stories. So storytelling became a flourishing trade. Co-existing with these stories were historical, romantic, and comic stories.

The Ming also ushered in a new phase of development in drama, marked by radical changes in form, content, and musical tunes. Many restrictions laid down for drama in earlier periods were now lifted. Instead of producing plays with any contemporary social significance, many playwrights wrote about the lives of the literati of former periods. As a result, many scripts became unfit for stage performance, and some of them became just lyrical poems.

Tang Xianzu (1550–1616) was the most prominent playwright of the Ming. His *Peony Pavilion* was his masterpiece, rich in romantic spirit and enchanting in scenery and lyrical expression. Du Liniang, the daughter of an official family, dreams that she had an affair with a poor scholar, whom she has never met before. She pines away with love and dies, leaving behind a self-portrait. It happens that Liu Mengmei, the poor scholar on his way to the national examination, passes the temple where the girl and her portrait are interred. Mengmei sees the portrait and falls in love with it. On being told that the girl is buried there, he has the tomb opened, and thereupon Liniang is resurrected and the two are married. In writing his plays, Tang ignored the rules of rhyming. Tang also did not like to have any part of his play changed to conform to set rules. Owing to his brilliant talent, this "erratic" play has been preserved and is still fervently acclaimed as a work of genius.

As a recognized form of literature, the novel blossomed in the Yuan dynasty, but its real development began in the Ming. A considerable number of novels were produced, but except for a few, the names of the authors are lost. Of Ming novels, four great masterworks enjoy universal popularity. They are *The Three Kingdoms*, *Journey to the West*, *Outlaws of the Marsh*, and *The Plum in the Golden Vase*.

The Three Kingdoms was written by Luo Guanzhong (1330–1400). Luo was the first novelist to reach a substantial public through the novel form. He spent most of his life writing novels. This novel is a historical story based on real events between 187 and 280. It describes the contradictions and conflicts among more than 400 historical characters and the warfare waged among them. The characters are vividly presented, each with his own distinctive qualities and personality. The language used is half-classical and half-vernacular.

Outlaws of the Marsh was written by Shi Nai'an (c.1290–1365). It is a novel of adventure, consisting of a series of thrilling episodes involving 108 heroes who are forced by circumstances to become outlaws but press on the fight for a just cause. It is the first novel written entirely in vernacular language.

Journey to the West was written by Wu Chengen (c. 1500–1582). It is probably the best-known novel in China, consisting of a series of action-packed episodes centering on a monkey with special magical powers. The author had an extensive knowledge of allegories and legends, and in writing the book, he gave full reign to his imagination and sense of humor. The novel describes the journey of San Zang, a monk, and his disciples, the Monkey, the Pigsy, and Sandy, to the West in search of Buddhist sutras. Again and again, they encounter monsters endowed with magic powers, but they surmount the difficulties through the loyal, ingenious, mischievous and humorous Monkey until their journey is finally crowned with success. This fantastic novel, with its gripping scenes and interesting and lovable characters, continues to fascinate both young and old.

An exposé novel of the time was *The Plum in the Golden Vase*. It is the only novel of its kind that has been handed down to us. The name of the author is unknown. It reflects the decadent social conditions of the late Ming through the description of one family whose master is a newly rich and despicable scoundrel. The book was regarded as pornographic for a long time because of its bold and detailed descriptions of sexual scenes. However, modern scholars generally consider it as representing a great advance in novel writing, as it is the first book that realistically describes the life of the common people.

7. THE PROSE OF MING AND QING DYNASTIES (1368–1911)

During the Ming (1368–1644) and Qing (1644–1911) dynasties, a special style of classical prose, *baguwen* (eight-legged prose), which had reached its height of development in the Song, still prevailed in the civil service exam system. The style was required for national examinations, and thus scholars spent their lives learning and perfecting this technique. However, many Ming and Qing scholars objected to putting too much emphasis on this imitative style of writing. There emerged two schools, the Gong'an School and the Jingling School. The former tended to overemphasize individuality, the use of simple language, and originality. The latter school, in accord with the Gong'an School on most points, advocated a more reserved and studied style. With the work of the two schools, a new trail was blazed that eventually led to the emergence of *xiaopinwen*, a genre of familiar and personal writing.

8. FICTION WRITING OF THE QING DYNASTY

Literature received much attention during the Qing dynasty, and many works in poetry and prose were produced. With philological research actively encouraged by the Qing court, gigantic literary projects of lasting value were compiled. The ones that are still treasured today are the *Kang Xi Dictionary*, the great standard dictionary of the Chinese language; the *Gujin tushu jicheng*, a profusely illustrated encyclopedia in 1,628 volumes of about 200 pages each; and the *Siku quanshu*, the great 18th-century collection that included virtually all books that the government could find and approve.

In the development of different genres of literature during the Qing, fiction stands out most prominently. The works mentioned below are the most famous.

Liao Zai zhiyi (Strange stories from the scholar's studio), by Pu Songling (1640–1715), is a series of highly fascinating short stories written in succinct and lively classical Chinese. It is acclaimed for its purity and beauty of style.

Rulin wai shi (The scholars) is a novel of social satire by Wu Jingzi (1701–1754), the first novel written in a modern vernacular based on the Mandarin dialect. The popularity of the work can be attributed to the warm and humorous style of the author and to its language, which was familiar to the common people of the time. The novel pokes fun at scholars, a privileged and respected class that held sway over society.

Hong lou meng (Dream of the red chamber) is a love romance, the first great Chinese tragedy of unfulfilled triangular love, written by Cao Xueqin (1719–1763). The book represents the highest point of development in the Chinese novel to that time.

The story unfolds on a vast canvas with nearly 400 characters, each distinctly presented as a typical personality. The book is almost exhaustive in the depiction of characters representing different temperaments. The characterization is done mostly through the way a character speaks. This novel is so popular and its achievement in literature so remarkable that a "Redology," namely scholarly research devoted solely to this novel, has existed for decades in China.

Another novel worth mentioning is *Jing hua yuan* (Flowers in the mirror), a novel of ideas by Li Ruzhen (c.1763–1830). The author was an authority on poetry, classical prose, painting, mathematics, medicine, gardening, and other fields. He spent 10 years writing the novel. The book describes a journey through various countries where the characters meet with strange people. The structure of the novel is loose enough for the author to express his ideas on different subjects, social, artistic, philosophical, and otherwise. The ideas presented in the book conjure up a perfect society, and therefore the novel may be said to belong to the category of utopian literature.

The history of traditional Chinese literature covers more than 3,000 years, from the Zhou through the Qing. During those three millennia, innumerable authors ceaselessly and indefatigably replenished the treasure house of literature with brilliant works of lasting value. Of such a vast accumulation of literary classics, we have mentioned only the most representative genres of each major period and the most prominent authors and works of those genres.

9. 20TH-CENTURY LITERATURE

The May Fourth Movement

When several thousand university students flocked to Tiananmen Square on May 4, 1919, to protest the allotment of German-held concessions to other foreign powers (most notably Japan), they also called for a modernization of Chinese culture. Though the movement called for resistance against foreign imperialism, it also promoted a revision of traditional Chinese culture based on the modern, Western concepts of democracy and science. The sentiment of the May Fourth Movement can be felt in the literature of that period.

The publication of the short story "Diary of a Madman" (also translated as "A Madman's Diary"), by Lu Xun, is hailed as the seminal event of modern Chinese literature. Lu Xun, the pen name of Zhou Shuren (1881–1936), was a student in Japan from 1902 to 1909. He began studying medicine but changed his interest to literature after reaching the conclusion that China needed spiritual growth more than a physical cure for maladies.

Lu Xun wrote "Diary of a Madman" in the vernacular instead of the traditional literary language, and the work challenges traditional Chinese culture. From reading Chinese history in depth, the writer of the diary discovers a two-word message hidden between the lines of the books: "eat people." He then sees those around him as cannibals, even perceiving close family members as conspirators in a scheme to consume him. "Diary of a Madman" is Lu Xun's criticism of traditional Chinese culture which he sees as the history of the powerful and wealthy feeding on the lesser. Hence Lu Xun's assertion that traditional Chinese culture is cannibalistic. Lu Xun's work proved influential in giving intellectuals and students the energy to challenge two perceived enemies of a modern China: foreign influence and traditional Chinese culture.

Also influential in the formation of modern Chinese literature, Hu Shi (1891–1962) led the fight for the use of the vernacular in poetry. After leaving China in 1910 to study in the United States at Cornell University and Columbia University, Hu developed ideas about the possibility of creating a national Chinese literature. In an essay in *New Youth* in 1917, he proposes "eight proscriptions" for the creation of modern Chinese literature. His proposals include directives such as "Don't imitate the ancients" and "Don't use stilted language." Hu's advocacy of a new and accessible vernacular literature proved to be one of the most influential components of his work. He also enjoyed recognition from publishing a collection of vernacular poetry titled *Experiments* (1920).

Societies and Journals: The May Fourth Movement allowed Chinese writers to use the vernacular in their writing and explore new areas that had not yet been touched. The majority of Chinese writers were political leftists. The new freedom of Chinese writers led to the creation of many literary journals and societies. By the mid-1920s there were more than 100 literary journals throughout China.

The Literary Research Association was one of the first influential literary societies born out of the May Fourth Movement. The society was officially established in January of 1921 in Beijing and gained control over the literary journal *Short Story Monthly*, rallying behind the motto "literature for life's sake." The slogan of the Literary Research Association marked the purpose of realism in literature and the advancement of political ideology.

Mao Dun (1896–1981) was the most prominent and influential founding member of the Literary Research Association. In late 1920, he was appointed editor of the *Short Story Monthly*. Driven by his left-wing politics, Mao steered the revolutionary political orientation of the journal until he resigned in 1923. Like many Chinese writers of this period, Mao Dun was known for his short stories, but he also wrote novels recounting social realities of the time. His works include the short stories "The Lin Family Shop" (1932) and "Spring Silkworms" (1932) and the novel *Midnight* (1933).

The Literary Research Association had the goal of popularizing poetry written in the vernacular. It published a magazine in 1922 titled *Poetry*. It was originally the only journal dedicated to the advancement of vernacular poetry. The group also published an anthology *A Snowy Morning* (1922). Well-known members of the Literary Research Association include Kang Baiqing (1896–1945), Zhu Ziqing (1898–1948), and Yu Pingbo (1900–1990).

In the early part of the 20th century, many Chinese students pursued higher education in Japan. Some of them formed an influential literary group called the Creation Society. Unlike the realist motto and purpose of the Literary Research Association, the Creation Society promoted "literature for art's sake." It moved to China in 1921. There were two main journals under the auspices of the Creation Society: *Creation Quarterly* and *The Deluge*.

Guo Moruo (1892–1978), one of the founding members of the Creation Society, went to Japan in 1914 to study medicine and German. While in Japan, he began writing vernacular poetry and eventually decided upon a career as a poet. His most prominent poems can be found in his collection *Goddess* (1921), which proved influential during the 1920s and 1930s. Guo was an intrinsically political writer. He converted to Marxism in 1924 and remained politically active throughout his career.

Yu Dafu (1896–1945) was another founding member of the Creation Society. He studied medicine, law, and economics in Tokyo, where he lived before he moved to Shanghai in 1923. One of his first pieces of fiction, *Sinking* (1921), retells the isolation and sexual frustration of a lonely Chinese student living in Japan. The protagonist experiences a frustration that analogizes the broader Chinese national humiliation at the beginning of the 20th century. The subjectivity and self-reflective qualities of the piece exemplify Yu's exposure to confessional Japanese literature. After moving to Shanghai, he published two popular short stories: "Nights of Spring Fever" and "A Humble Sacrifice."

Tian Han (1898–1968), one of the great masters of modern Chinese drama, met Guo Moro in 1920 while studying in Tokyo. Also a founding member of the Creation Society, Tian focused on drama—specifically short one-act pieces. He was also directly involved in the production of his work. The early pieces of Tian's include "One Night in a Café" (1922), "The Night the Tiger Was Captured" (1922), "A West Lake Tragedy" (also translated as "A Lakeside Tragedy") (1928), and "Return to the South" (1929).

New Movements: The May Fourth Movement led to the creation of many other new movements and ideas in Chinese literature. With newfound literary freedom forging the way for young Chinese literary pioneers, writers sought interesting and fulfilling themes within their work.

Shen Congwen (1902–1988) relied upon his life experience in the countryside and his Miao ethnic minority background for inspiration in his work. Instead of using his home town area of western Hunan as a backdrop for his stories, he made it the main feature. The use of an actual location fictionalized as the central theme of writing exemplifies his involvement in the Native Soil Movement. He describes in detail the settings and includes local aspects to the stories, such as folk songs. Shen was a prolific writer, producing more than 200 short stories and 10 novels. Two popular works are the short story "Xiaoxiao" (1924) and the novella *The Border Town* (also translated as *Frontier City*) (1934).

Because of the fall of the Qing dynasty, Lao She was conscious of his Manchu background. Lao She is the pen name of Shu Qingchun (1899–1966). After graduating from Beijing Normal School and teaching for several years, Lao accepted a post in the School of Oriental Studies at the University of London, where exposure to British literature greatly influenced his works. His novel *The Philosophy of Lao Zhang*, for example, is based on Charles Dickens' *Nicholas Nickleby*. Lao She returned to China in 1930 and wrote the satiric novel *Cat Country* (1930) that voices his concern for the social situation at that time. Lao She's most famous work and social commentary is *Camel Xiangzi* (1936). The novel tells the story of a lowly Beijing rickshaw driver Xiangzi and his travails in working and living in the big city. Lao She's research produced an extremely detailed account of the social levels of rickshaw drivers in Beijing in the 1930s. The novel was published in the United States in 1945 with the title *Rickshaw Boy* and a different, happier ending. The novel was later modified by the Chinese Communist government, which deleted the ending altogether.

Some writers began writing about the liberation of women from traditional roles. Ding Ling, the pen name of Jiang Bingzhi (1904–1986), was born in Hunan and attended schools in Changsha, Shanghai, and Beijing where she heard lectures by Lu Xun. She took the young leftist poet Hu Yepin as her lover, and the two of them once shared a house with Shen Congwen. Ding's early works explored the liberation of women from traditional familial and social institutions. Her most famous short story, "Miss Sophie's Diary" (1928), solidified her reputation as the foremost writer on women's issues. Ding Ling's writing became increasingly political, and she wrote her first proletariat novel *The Flood* in 1932. She joined the Communist Party in 1932 and began serializing the semi-biographical novel of her mother's life. Her novel *Mother* (1933) details the evolution of a traditional woman into a liberated new woman of modern China. Ding Ling would later be active as a writer and critic for the Communist Party with works such as "When I was in a Xia Village" (1941).

Ba Jin, the pen-name of Li Feigan (1904–), was born into an upper class family in Chengdu. As a student at the Chengdu Foreign Languages School, he became acquainted with the journals and writings of the May Fourth Movement. In 1927, he went to France where he studied for more than a year. Ba Jin was a prolific writer until the liberation in 1949, producing 20 novels and 70 short stories. His most famous novel, *The Family* (1933), proved to be an inspirational and emotional work for young readers of the day. Ba Jin was persecuted during the Cultural Revolution but survived to regain popularity in the 1980s with works such as *Cold Nights* and his semi-autobiographical work *Pleasure Garden*.

Eileen Chang (known as Zhang Ailing in Chinese, 1921–1995) first gained popularity with her novella *The Golden Cangue* (1944). The story tells of a woman's problems in a troubled relationship over a 30-year period. Chang continued to publish after the establishment of the People's Republic of China. Her work *Eighteen Springs* was published in 1951. This novel explores the role of women in harmful relationships. Chang moved to Hong Kong in 1952 and then to the United States in 1955, where she remained for the rest of her life. In the United States, she published two works criticizing the Communist government of China: *Love in Redland*, which was translated under the title *Naked Earth*, and *The Rice-Sprout Song*. Both garnered interest in the United States for their critical stance against Communism.

Yan'an Forum on Literature

In the late 1930s and early 1940s, with the full-scale invasion of the Japanese army against Chinese territories, many left-wing writers were forced to flee from the larger metropolitan centers like Shanghai that had housed them and their audiences for the previous decades. While some went to territories that were still under the control of the Nationalist government of China, others went to Yan'an, then the main base area of the Communist insurgency.

Although initially attracted to Yan'an by the perceived idealism of the Communist rebels, many intellectuals began to criticize injustices they perceived in Yan'an. Ding Ling, for example, published her story "When I was in a Xia Village," which recounts a kind of ambivalence toward women who had made great sacrifices for the war effort. She and other writers at this time began publishing essays expounding upon subjects such as women's issues, social practices, and artistic autonomy.

The disenchantment of the intellectuals reflected a larger unease among many people of Yan'an. The stress and difficulty of living in an isolated area lead to ideological bickering among various groups within the Communist headquarters. The Communist leader Mao Zedong (also spelled "Mao Tsetung" in earlier publications, 1893–1976) responded in February 1942 by launching a Rectification Campaign in order to strengthen and unify a potentially disillusioned and fractured populace. To further his control over creative works, Mao called for the Yan'an Forum on Literature in May of the same year.

The forum lasted 23 days and was attended by more than 200 intellectuals who participated in workshops and discussions. Mao Zedong gave the opening and closing remarks at the conference. The opening remarks broached subjects of discussion such as the relationship between the writer and the audience. It had been assumed among the participants that the conference should focus upon how intellectuals could efficiently steer the masses. Mao's concluding remarks conversely switched the relationship between writer and audience. He asserted his conviction that all works were inherently political. No writer or artist could escape the inborn political nature of creative works; therefore, the work must further the cause of the revolution. Works of art and literature were to "serve" the masses by lauding the masses while condemning any force that opposes them.

A year after the forum, the document "Talk at the Yan'an Forum of Literature and Arts" was published and became the official policy for the Chinese Communist Party. The policy of the forum had a dramatic effect upon literature. The self-absorbed individualism and disillusionment of the May Fourth Movement needed to be replaced by the emphasis on total resolution in the plot. The most favorable resolution in a work of fiction, it was felt, was one that stems directly from the moral guidance of the Communist Party.

After the end of World War II, Communist forces quickly defeated the forces of the Nationalist government. Except Taiwan and some other nearby islands, the Communists controlled almost all of China by the end of 1949. In 1953, *Selected Works of Mao Tze-Tung* was published in four volumes to show the Chinese people (including the writers) the correct ideological path. (After Mao's death in 1976, the Communist Party decided to publish an additional volume of the *Selected Works*. Volume 5 of the *Selected Works* was published in 1977.) "Talk at the Yan'an Forum of Literature and Arts" remained an important political document of the People's

Republic of China and was used to threaten and incriminate writers even after the Cultural Revolution (1966–1976).

After the founding of the People's Republic of China, writers took different paths within their lives and creative works. Shen Congwen ceased writing literature but later published an extensive work on the history of Chinese clothing. Other writers worked within the Communist Party. Mao Dun was made minister of culture but quit writing. Guo Moruo was appointed director of the Cultural and Educational Commission and continued to write under the literature guidelines of the party. Ding Ling gained the favor of Mao Zedong and Zhou Enlai (1898–1976). During the Anti-Rightist Campaign (1957), however, she was sent to northern Chinese labor camps where she remained until the end of the Cultural Revolution.

Taiwan

After the Nationalists fled to Taiwan in 1949, the government's first concern focused on survival and security. The situation resulted in little attention to the literary field. The majority of writers associated with the May Fourth Movement remained on the mainland, and their literary works were unavailable in Taiwan. Classical Chinese and Western works similarly had very little effect upon Taiwan during this period.

One of the first writers to emerge from the initial literary inactivity of Taiwan was Jiang Gui. Jiang Gui is the pen name of Wang Lintu (1908–1980). He was born in mainland China and moved to Taiwan in 1949. Jiang is mostly known for his novels. Most of his works are set in mainland China in the 1930s and 1940s, and he concentrates his themes on political and economic corruption under the Nationalists and the warlords. He believed this situation aided the eventual success of the Communists in the mainland. *The Whirlwind*, his first novel, was published in 1952. His other works include *The Rival Suns*, *The Green Sea and the Blue Sky: A Nocturne*, *The White Horse*, and *Mount Copper Cyprus*.

Bai Xianyong (often known to his Western readers as Pai Hsien-yung, 1937–) is also considered one of the leading figures of modern Taiwanese literature. He was born in the mainland but moved to Taiwan in 1949. He later moved to the United States and published works of fiction in *Taipei Residents* (or *Taipei People*) in 1971. He also published a volume of short stories titled *The Lonely Seventeenth Year* in 1977. Bai's fiction deals with the life of the exile in Taiwan and the United States. His well-known short story "Winter Nights" recounts the feelings, jealousies, and melancholia between two professors: one living in Taiwan and one in America. Another piece of fiction, "Li T'ung: A Chinese Girl in New York," tells the story of a Chinese girl who is stranded in the United States when her parents die fleeing to Taiwan as the Communist army overruns the mainland. In 1990, Bai published the novel *Crystal Boys*, making him the foremost writer of Chinese gay literature.

As Taiwan's literary scene progressed past the first phase of development, some of the most prominent writers included Huang Chunming (1939–), Wang Wenxing (1939–), and Wang Zhenhe (1940–1990).

As newer generations of writers approached the literary scene, more and more were native-born Taiwanese. Unlike Bai Xianyong, who emigrated to Taiwan and later to the United States, writers like Zhu Tianwen (1956–) began writing about experiences of individuals in modern Taiwan and the big city of Taipei. She became one of the leading fiction writers of Taiwan of the late 20th century; her most famous novel is *Notes of a Desolate Man* (1999).

Bo Yang (1920–) declared that his real birthday was the day of his arrest on March 4, 1967, after which he spent almost 10 years as a political prisoner for a cartoon spoof he translated in the *China News Daily* that angered the government of Chiang Kai-Shek (1887–1975). Bo spent much of the 1960s writing satirical essays about Chinese culture. His most famous work, *The Ugly Chinaman* (1985), is a collection of essays and pieces of non-fiction examining the experience of China and its people set against the background of politics and Westernization.

Li Ao was another writer and essayist who met with opposition from Taiwan's government before the democratization of Taiwan in the 1980s and '90s. Li gained international recognition by being nominated for the Nobel Prize in Literature in 2000 (the award was given to another Chinese writer—Gao Xingjian). Li advocates the "one-China, two-systems" concept, which is the mainland's theoretical justification for the acquisition of territories that had non-Communist systems, such as Hong Kong. Li believes that the one-China, two-systems concept would eventually allow Taiwan to reunite with the mainland.

Hong Kong

Hong Kong has not been traditionally known as an area of intense literary production. In fact, the works that come from Hong Kong have often been associated with the entertainment industry. Jin Yong (1925–) is considered the leading fiction writer in the martial arts genre. Jin Yong moved to Hong Kong in 1948 and produced many of his works in the 1950s and 1960s. He was a prolific writer, and many of his books have been enjoyed throughout the Chinese reading world.

Xi Xi is considered the foremost writer in the Hong Kong literary scene. Xi Xi, whose name is Zhang Yin (1938–), was born in Shanghai but moved to Hong Kong in 1950. She worked in Hong Kong as a primary school teacher and gained her reputation from her poetry, fiction, film scripts, and criticism in the 1960s. Her work became especially noted in Taiwan in the 1980s. Her collections of short stories include *A Girl Like Me and Other Stories* (1986) and *Marvels of a Floating City and Other Stories* (1987). Other works include *My City: A Hong Kong Story* (1993) and *Flying Carpet: A Tale of Fertilla* (2000).

Resurgence of Literature

The Cultural Revolution marked a time of severe dismemberment of an already frail literary scene in the People's Republic of China. As the Cultural Revolution began in the 1960s, many writers, artists, and actors were humiliated, sent off for re-education, or forced to write confessions. Drama and film became virtually nonexistent. A few Beijing operas, such as *The Red Lantern* and *Taking Tiger Mountain by Strategy*, as well as the ballet *The White-Haired Girl*, remained standard pieces of the Cultural Revolution. The Beijing opera of the Cultural Revolution mixed the traditions of stylized singing, dancing, costumes, and acrobatics with an infusion of revolutionary themes. The pieces were overt political propaganda, adhering to Mao Zedong's idea of art serving the masses for the cause of the revolution. Mao's wife, Jiang Qing, a former actress in Shanghai, was the ultimate judge over the Cultural Revolution canon.

The first literature to materialize following the end of the Cultural Revolution was termed "scar literature," or "wound literature," which analyzed the emotional and intellectual damage of the previous decade. The political climate at this time sought to condemn the "Gang of Four" for the horrors committed during the Cultural Revolution. Similarly the works created between 1977 and 1979 pointed to injustices and lauded the intellectuals who had been persecuted in the past decade. Works of scar literature proved to be a catharsis that led to the resurgence of literature after the period of literary drought.

Deng Xiaoping (1904–1997) held the first post-Mao conference on literature and the arts. The Fourth Congress of Writers and Artists was held in Beijing between October and November 1979. Several thousand prominent writers, artists, and intellectuals, including Ding Ling and Mao Dun, attended the conference. Deng Xiaoping called for the modernization of literature specifically by learning from the foreign writers whose influence had been excluded from Chinese literature for decades. The translation of foreign literature into Chinese greatly influenced Chinese writers as they progressed into the 1980s.

Literature after the Cultural Revolution

During the early 1970s, there existed a powerful underground literary movement. The first publication to spring from this underground was the anthology *Revelations that Move the Earth to Tears* (1974). Underground poetry became a powerful expression of the growing rebelliousness toward the government after Premier Zhou Enlai's death on January 8, 1976. The protests in Tiananmen in 1976, the April Fifth

Movement, demonstrated the relationship between poetry and politics as poems flourished commemorating Zhou Enlai.

In November of 1978, a wall at an intersection in Beijing became the focal point of protest demanding democracy as one of the new modernizations of China. The "Democracy Wall" heavily influenced the production of literature. A literary magazine called *Today* emerged and became the center of a school of avant-garde poetry dubbed "obscure poetry" or "misty poetry."

Bei Dao, one of the editors of *Today*, earned international recognition. Bei Dao, which is the pen name of Zhao Zhenkai (1949–), was a Red Guard at the beginning of the Cultural Revolution but was later sent to work construction around Beijing. While working, he began to compose secretly. His main collection of works translated into English include *The August Sleepwalker* (1988) and *Old Snow* (1991).

Duo Duo is another poet who worked on *Today*. Duo Duo is the pen name of Li Shizheng (1951–). He left China the day after the Chinese government's crackdown on the democracy movement in 1989 and has lived abroad since. His main collection of work available in English is *Looking Out from Death* (1989).

As China made attempts to modernize, the influence of foreign works and the ability for Chinese students to study abroad inevitably affected the evolution of Chinese literature during the final decades of the 20th century. Writers began to explore new territories and create works that would soon be read among international circles. The ability for writers to live abroad (often due to self-imposed exile) brought Chinese literature to the world's attention.

Many writers whose intellectual activity had been suppressed for political reasons in the People's Republic of China began to win literary recognition. Wang Meng (1934–) was born in Beijing. He joined the Communist Party in 1948 and began his writings by criticizing the party. His story "The Young Newcomer in the Organization Department" (1956) exposed the bureaucratic tendencies and closed-mindedness that had become common among many Communist officials. This widely read story had Wang labeled as a "rightist" during the Anti-Rightist Campaign of 1957. He was sent to the countryside to be re-educated but returned in 1961. He was later sent to the remote Xinjiang Uighur Autonomous Region in 1963, where he remained until 1979. After emerging from his "re-education," Wang proved to be a progressive writer using a non-linear style associated with stream of consciousness. His work *The Man with Movable Parts* (1987) focuses on the social complexities experienced in life.

Shen Rong (1934–) wrote her first piece of fiction, *Everlasting Youth*, in the early 1970s. Published in 1975, *Everlasting Youth* exemplifies a typical Cultural Revolution work of fiction by pitting peasants against the contrary force of "privatization." Shen's most famous work, *At Middle Age* (1980), solidified her reputation as a writer who emerged after the Cultural Revolution. The novella expounds upon the difficulty faced by professionals (especially women) after the end of the Cultural Revolution.

Ah Cheng, which is the pen name of Zhong Acheng (1949–), was born in Beijing. He was sent to the remote areas of Inner Mongolia and Yunnan Province during the Cultural Revolution. He did not begin writing until the 1980s, when he created his "king" stories: "King of Chess" (1984), "King of Trees" (1985), and "King of Children" (1985). His writing uses traditional storytelling technique which introduces influences from Buddhism and Daoism. Ah Cheng moved to the United States in 1986.

Wang Anyi (1954–) was born in Nanjing and began writing while traveling the country in the Xuzhou Art Workers' Troupe. Wang writes about young women in search of love, sexual fulfillment, and happiness. Her most famous work is a trilogy which includes the books *Love on a Barren Mountain* (1986), *Love in a Small Town* (1986), and *Brocade Valley* (1987).

Mo Yan is the pen name of Guan Moye (1956–). He was born in Gaomi, Shandong, and sets many of his plots around his hometown. Mo was especially prolific in the mid-1980s. In 1986, he published his most famous work, *Red Sorghum*, which was later turned into an internationally known film of the same name by director Zhang Yimou.

Su Tong (1963–) also gained international recognition with a film version of one of his works. Su Tong writes about the bizarre and horrific aspects of Chinese culture as exemplified in his novella *Nineteen Thirty-four Escapes* (1987). His other famous work *Wives and Concubines* (1987) was made into a film by Zhang Yimou with the title *Raise the Red Lantern* (1992).

Gao Xingjian (1940–) studied French at Beijing University. He first came to be known for his dramas, including "Warning Signal" (1982), "The Bus Stop" (1983), and "The Wild Man" (1985). Because of the politically controversial nature of his work, Gao settled in France after making a trip to Europe in 1987. He acquired French citizenship and produced works in French as well as Chinese. His work *Soul Mountain* gained him such international recognition that he was awarded the Nobel Prize for Literature in 2000. With that award, Gao represented the international acceptance of Chinese literature as a powerful and innovative force in the late 20th century.

KEY RESEARCH SOURCES

Bei, Dao. *The August Sleepwalker*. Trans. Bonnie S. McDougall. New York: New Directions, 1988.

———. *Old Snow*. Trans. Bonnie S. McDougall. New York: New Directions, 1991.

Birch, Cyril, ed. *Anthology of Chinese Literature: From Early Times to the Fourteenth Century*. New York: Grove Press, 1965.

Bo, Yang. *A Farewell: A Collection of Short Stories*. Trans. Robert Renyolds. Hong Kong: Joint Publishing Co. 1980.

———. *The Ugly Chinaman and the Crisis of Chinese Culture*. Don Jing and Jing Ching. St. Leonards, New South Wales: Allen and Unwin, 1992.

Cai, Zongqi, ed. *A Chinese Literary Mind: Culture, Creativity and Rhetoric in Wenxin Diaolong*. Stanford: Stanford University Press, 2001.

Cao, Xueqin. *The Story of the Stone*. Trans. David Hawkes. Bloomington: Indiana University Press. 1979.

Chang, Eileen. *The Rice Sprout Song*. Berkeley: The University of California Press, 1998.

———. *The Rouge of the North*. Berkeley: The University of California Press, 1998.

Chaves, Jonathan. *The Columbia Book of Later Chinese Poetry: Yuan, Ming, and Qing Dynasties*. New York: Columbia University Press, 1986.

Cheung, Martha, ed. *Hong Kong Collage: Contemporary Stories and Writing*. Hong Kong: Oxford University Press, 1998.

Chu, T'ien-wen. *Notes of a Desolate Man*. Trans. Howard Goldblatt and Sylvia Li-chun. New York: Columbia University Press, 1999.

Confucius. *The Analects of Confucius*. Trans. Arthur Waley. London: Allen and Unwin, 1938.

Ding, Ling. *I Myself Am a Woman: Selected Writings of Ding Ling*. Ed., trans. Tari Barlow. Boston: Beacon Press, 1989.

Duo, Duo. *Looking out from Death: From the Cultural Revolution to Tiananmen Square*. Trans. Gregory Lee and John Cayley. London: Bloomsburg Pub. Ltd., 1989.

Gao, Xingjian. *The Other Shore: Plays by Gao Xingjian*. Trans. C. F. Fong. Hong Kong: Chinese University Press. 1999.

———. *Soul Mountain*. Trans. Mabel Lee. New York: Harper Collins, 1999.

Giles, Herbert Allen. *A History of Chinese Literature*. New York: D. Appleton and Company, 1901.

Goldblatt, Howard, ed. *Chairman Mao Would Not Be Amused*. New York: Grove Press, 1995.

Goldman, Merle, ed. *Modern Chinese Literature in the May Fourth Era*. Cambridge: Harvard University Press, 1977

Guo, Moruo. *Selected Poems from the Goddess*. Trans. John Lester and A. C. Barnes. Beijing: Foreign Language Press, 1978.

Haddon, Rosemary, trans. *Oxcart: Nativist Stories from Taiwan, 1934–1977*. Dortmund, Germany: Projekt Verlag, 1996.

Hart, Henry Hersch. *Poems of the Hundred Names: A Short Introduction to Chinese Poetry Together with 208 Original Translations*. Stanford: Stanford University Press, 1954.

Hawkes, David. *Chu Ci: The Songs of the South, an Ancient Chinese Anthology*. Oxford, Clarendon Press, 1959.

Hsia, Chih-tsing. *The Classic Chinese Novel: A Critical Introduction*. New York: Columbia University Press, 1968.

Hsia, C. T. *A History of Modern Chinese Fiction*. New Haven, Conn.: Yale University Press, 1961.

Hsu, Kai-yu, ed. *Literature of the People's Republic of China*. Bloomington: Indiana University Press, 1980.

Huters, Theodore, ed. *Reading the Modern Chinese Short Story*. Armonk, New York: M. E. Sharpe, 1990.

Idema, W. L. *A Guide to Chinese Literature*. Ann Arbor: Center for Chinese Studies, University of Michigan, 1997.

Jiang, Gui. *The Whirlwind*. Trans. Timothy Ross. San Francisco: Chinese Materials Center, 1977.

Jin Yong. *The Deer and the Cauldron: A Martial Arts Novel*. Trans. John Minford. New York: Columbia University Press, 1997.

Kao, Yu-kung, and Mei Tsu-lin. "Syntax, Diction, and Imagery in Tang Poetry." *Harvard Journal of Asiatic Studies* 31 (1971): 49–136.

Knechtges, David. *Wen Xuan or Selections of Refined Literature*. Princeton: Princeton University Press, 1982.

Lai, Ming. *A History of Chinese Literature*. New York: Capricorn Books, 1964.

Lao, She. *Blades of Grass*. Trans. William Lyell. Honolulu: University of Hawaii, 1999.

———. *Rickshaw: The Novel of Lo-to Hsiang Tzu*. Trans. Jean M. James. Honolulu: University of Hawaii Press, 1979.

Larson, Wendy. *Women and Writing in Modern China*. Stanford: Stanford University Press, 1998.

Lau, Joseph S. M., and Howard Goldblatt, eds. *The Columbia Anthology of Modern Chinese Literature*. New York: Columbia University Press, 1995.

Legge, James, trans. *Book of Change*. Seaucus, N.J.: Citadel Press, 1964.

———. *Book of History*. London: Allen and Unwin, 1972.

———. *The Book of Poetry*. New York: Paragon Book Reprint Corp., 1967.

———. *Book of Rites: An Encyclopedia of Ancient Ceremonial Usage, Religious Creeds, and Social Institutions*. New Hyde Park, N.Y.: University Books, 1967.

———. *The Chinese Classics*. Oxford, Clarendon Press, 1893.

———. *The Four Books: Confucian Analects, The Great Learning, The Doctrine of the Mean, and the Works of Mencius*. Shanghai: The Chinese Book Company, 1930.

Lévy, André. *Chinese Literature, Ancient and Classical*. Bloomington: Indiana University Press, 2000.

Liu, James J. Y. *The Art of Chinese Poetry*. Chicago: University of Chicago Press, 1962.

———. *The Interlingual Critic: Interpreting Chinese Poetry*. Bloomington: Indiana University Press. 1982.

Lu, Xun. *Diary of a Madman and Other Stories*. Trans. William Lyell. Honolulu: University of Hawaii Press, 1990.

Luo, Guanzhong. *Three Kingdoms: A Historical Novel*. Trans. Roberts Moss. Beijing: Foreign Languages Press, 1999.

Mair, Victor H., ed. *The Columbia Anthology of Traditional Chinese Literature*. New York: Columbia University Press, 1994.

Mao, Dun. *Midnight*. Beijing: Foreign Language Press, 1979.

Mao, Zedong. *Selected Works of Mao Tse-tung*. 5 vols. Beijing: Foreign Language Press, 1965.

———. *Talks at the Yan'an Conference on Literature and Art: A Translation of the 1943 Text with Commentary*. Ann Arbor: University of Michigan Center for Chinese Studies, 1980.

McDougall, Bonnie S., and Kam Louie. *The Literature of China in the Twentieth Century*. New York: Columbia University Press, 1997.

Minford, John, and Joseph S. M. Lau, eds. *Classical Chinese Literature*. New York: Columbia University Press, 2000.

Mo, Yan. *Red Sorghum*. Trans. Howard Goldblatt. New York: Penguin, 1994.

Owen, Stephen. *Traditional Chinese Poetry and Poetics: Omen of the World*. Madison: University of Wisconsin Press, 1985.

Pai Hsien-yung. *Crystal Boys*. Trans. Howard Goldblatt. San Francisco: Gay Sunshine Press, 1990.

———. *Taipei People*. Hong Kong: Chinese University Press, 2000.

Plaks, Andrew H. *Archetype and Allegory in the Dream of the Red Chamber*. Princeton: Princeton University Press, 1976.

———. *The Four Masterworks of the Ming Novel: Si Da Qi Shu*. Princeton: Princeton University Press, 1987.

Rickett, Adele Austin, ed. *Chinese Approaches to Literature from Confucius to Liang Qichao*. Princeton: Princeton University Press, 1977.

Shen, Congwen. *Imperfect Paradise*. Trans. Peter Li. Ed. Jeffrey Kinkley. Honolulu: University of Hawaii Press, 1995.

Shi, Nai'an and Luo Guanzhong. *Outlaws of the Marsh*. Trans. Sidney Shapiro. Beijing: Foreign Language Press, 1988.

Shi, Zhongwen. *Injustice to Tou O: A Study and Translation*. Cambridge: Cambridge University Press, 1972.

Su, Tong. *Raise the Red Lantern*. Trans. Michael Duke. New York: William Morrow, 1993.

Tang, Xianzu. *The Peony Pavilion*. Trans. Cyril Birch. Bloomington: Indiana University Press, 1980.

Tian, Han. "The Night the Tiger was Captured." Trans. Randy Barbara Kaplan. *Asian Theatre Journal* 11.1 (1994): 1–34.

Waley, Arthur, trans. *The Book of Songs*. New York: Grove Press, 1996.

Wang, Anyi. *Brocade Valley*. Trans. Bonnie S. McDougall and Chen Maiping. New York: New Directions, 1992.

———. *Love in a Small Town*. Trans. Eva Hung. Hong Kong: Renditions Paperbacks, 1988.

———. *Love on a Barren Mountain*. Trans. Eva Hung. Hong Kong: Renditions Paperbacks, 1991.

Wang, David Der-wei. *Fictional Realism in Twentieth Century China: Mao Dun, Lao She, Shen Congwen*. New York: Colombia University Press, 1992.

Wang, David Der-wei, and Jeanne Tai, eds. *Running Wild: New Chinese Writers*. New York: Columbia University Press, 1994.

Watson, Burton. *Chinese Lyricism: Shi Poetry From the Second to the Twelfth Century*. New York, Columbia University Press, 1971.

———. *Columbia Book of Chinese Poetry: From Early Times to the Thirteenth Century*. New York, Columbia University Press, 1984.

———. *Early Chinese Literature*. New York: Columbia University Press, 1962.

Widmer, Ellen, and David Der-wei Wang, eds. *From May Fourth to June Fourth: Fiction and Film in Twentieth Century China*. Cambridge: Harvard University Press, 1993.

Widmer, Ellen, and Kang-i Sun Chang, eds. *Writing Women in Late Imperial China*. Stanford: Stanford University Press, 1997.

Wu, Jingzi. *The Scholars*. Trans. Yang Hsien-yi and Gladys Yang. New York: Grosset and Dunlap, 1972.

Xi, Xi. *Flying Carpet: A Tale of Fertilla*. Trans. Diana Yue. Hong Kong: Hong Kong University Press, 2000.

————. *A Girl Like Me and Other Stories*. Trans. Eva Hung. Hong Kong: Renditions Paperbacks, 1986.

————. *Marvels of a Floating City and Other Stories*. Trans. Eva Hung. Hong Kong: Renditions Paperbacks, 1997.

————. *My City: A Hong Kong Story*. Trans. Eva Hung. Hong Kong: Renditions Paperbacks, 1993.

Xiaoxiaosheng. *The Plum in the Golden Vase*. Trans. David Tod Roy. Princeton: Princeton University Press, 1993.

Yang, Winston, and Nathan Mao. *Modern Chinese Fiction: A Guide to Its Study and Appreciation*. Boston: G. K. Hall & Co., 1981.

Yeh, Michelle, ed. *Anthology of Modern Chinese Poetry*. New Haven, Conn.: Yale University Press, 1994.

Yip, Wai-lim. *Chinese Poetry: Major Modes and Genres*. Berkeley: University of California Press, 1972.

Yu, Dafu. *Nights of Spring Fever and Other Writings*. Beijing: Panda Books, 1984.

Yu, Pauline. *The Reading of Imagery in the Chinese Poetic Tradition*. Princeton: Princeton University Press. 1987.

Zuoqiu, Ming. *The Zuo Zuan: Selections from China's Oldest Narrative History*. Trans. Burton Watson. New York: Columbia University Press, 1989.

Science and Technology

By Yiyi Wu

1. INTRODUCTION

Basic Features of the Development of Science and Technology in China

Science and technology in China developed quite differently from comparable processes in many other civilizations. In the 3,000 years until the beginning of the 20th century, the knowledge of nature had always been considered secondary to that of human society. During much of the imperial period, specialists in science and technology ranked low in the social hierarchy, humbly inferior to officials, Confucian scholars, and local gentry. Shadowed by the politically and morally oriented Confucianism, the investigation of nature was always relegated to technicians who played a marginal, if not heretical, role in society. Their scholarship was never independent from moral philosophy and was subordinate to it in much the same way European science was ruled by the church during the Middle Ages.

The dominance of political concerns over scientific ones was especially evident in the peculiar approach of the Chinese study of astronomy. Until sometime in the late 19th century, the studies of stars and heavenly phenomena, with which most ancient civilizations started their investigation of nature, had been strictly restricted to those assigned by the authorities. The belief that heavenly phenomena were somehow related to the fates of the emperor and the empire made its study politically sensitive. Those who observed and recorded the phenomena were allowed no more than access to technical details; those who analyzed and explained the phenomena were engaged exclusively in the worldly consequences the phenomena might engender.

Studies in areas other than astrology and astronomy were generally practical. The effectiveness of utilizing natural resources and power was often the major concern. The understanding of nature, for which Aristotle, Thomas Aquinas, the Renaissance thinkers, and other Western scholars strove through the centuries, never became the central topic for Chinese scholars prior to the 20th century. A great part of their knowledge about nature was really what we would call technology today.

During the half century following the 1860s, the approaches to nature in China shifted: The traditional view of nature was replaced by that of the modern science developed in Europe in the scientific revolution of the 17th and 18th centuries. This shift was so radical that it is difficult to analyze the developments of Chinese science before and after the shift in similar terms. Still, certain features, such as the accentuation of practical value of the knowledge and the great importance of government planning, can be seen as common to the history of Chinese science both before and after the shift.

2. THE ANCIENT TIMES

The Early Records of Heavenly Phenomena

No one knows when the earliest sky observations started in China. In the Shang dynasty (c. 1554–1045 B.C.), there were at least five recorded solar eclipses. One record reads, "There was a solar eclipse at the sunset, is it ominous?"

Solar Eclipses: The earliest record of a solar eclipse was inscribed on a tortoiseshell from approximately the 14th century B.C. For the ancient Chinese, as for many other ancient civilizations, solar eclipses were very important events. The interpretations of the awesome phenomena pointed to the fate of the emperors who, accordingly, gave the highest priority to their observation. During the 238 years between 720 B.C. and 482 B.C., for instance, Chinese documents recorded 37 solar eclipses, of which 33 have been confirmed by the calculation of modern astronomy.

Comets and Supernova: The *Spring and Autumn Annals*, a chronicle attributed to Confucius, recorded the appearance in the Great Dipper of a comet in the seventh month of 613 B.C. This comet was identified later by astronomers as Halley's comet, the one Isaac Newton and E. Halley studied in the 17th century. Among the numerous reports of comets throughout the 26 centuries since that first record, Chinese astronomers recorded 31 visits of Halley's comet, many with detailed descriptions of where and when the comet was seen.

Nova were called "new stars" in ancient Chinese literature because they appeared in the sky as if from nowhere and were bright, as if they were "brand new." The term *new stars* was later replaced by *guest stars*, when their patterns of coming in and out were more clearly recognized by careful observers. The earliest record of a nova was found in a tortoiseshell inscription of the 16th century B.C., followed by about 100 records in later Chinese documents.

Star Catalog and Star Maps: As the data of observation accumulated, the ancient Chinese sorted out their knowledge about the sky in catalogs and maps. The earliest catalog was attributed to Shi Shen (*fl. c.* fourth century B.C.). According to *Kaiyuan zhan jing*, a book on astrology and astronomy of the eighth century A.D., Shi Shen gave a list of 115 stars in his classic *Tianwen*, or *Sky Patterns*.

Early in 1957, it was reported that a star map with 55 stars was unearthed from a Han dynasty (206 B.C.–A.D. 220) tomb dat-

ing from the first century B.C. The stars on this map, however, were not grouped into constellations, nor were their positions recorded with much accuracy. The earliest star map for astronomers appeared in the Jin dynasty (A.D. 265–420). *Jin shu* (The history of the Jin, completed in A.D. 644–646) has it that Chen Zhuo (*fl. c.* third–fourth century) completed a map with 1,464 stars, presumably based upon Shi Shen's and others' books. Unfortunately, *The History of the Jin* does not copy the map, and all the details of the map remain unknown to modern scholars. Among the manuscripts Aurel Stein smuggled out of China after a controversial exploration in 1910, there was a star map dated about A.D. 940. This map consists of 13 regional maps: 12 for stars around the celestial equator and one for stars around the polestar. This is believed to be the oldest surviving star map in the world.

Pottery: Pottery items and shards are the most common objects found in Neolithic relics. In 1921, archaeologists unearthed a Neolithic site in Henan Province, central China, not far from the Yellow River. The site was named Yangshao village. Vivid colors and unique artistic features marked much of the pottery found. One of the most amazing articles found in Yangshao was *qiqi*, a water pot with a pointed bottom. The clay ears on both sides of the pot suggested that it might have been hung on a pole when in use. If half filled, it would keep upright and prevent the water from spilling out. The late Neolithic site of Longshan village, unearthed in 1928 in Shandong Province, offered refined "egg-shell pottery." The black body of this pottery was extremely hard and surprisingly thin, in most cases less than one tenth of an inch.

In the relics of the Shang (1766–1122 B.C.) and Zhou (1122–256 B.C.) dynasties, a great variety of pottery utensils was found. Vessels for wine, bowls, and jars were the most common finds. Progress in pottery-making techniques was far more advanced by this time. Many vessels were made on wheels instead of being molded by hand as the Neolithic objects had been; many were covered with glaze. A closer study also showed evidence of an improved pottery kiln, which reached a temperature of more than 1,000°C.

The Mohist Canon: The Mohist School flourished in the fifth and fourth centuries B.C. The founder of this school was Mo Di (c. 478–392 B.C.). Among many other contributions to ancient scholarship, the Mohist school proved to be one of the most important schools for its studies of nature. The *Mohist Canon*, the classics attributed to this school, recorded observations on optics and mechanics.

In the book, the Mohists recognized clearly that light traveled in straight lines. Taking this as a starting point, the Mohists were able to explain various optical phenomena. One of their best-known experiments was with "inverse shadows." When light came into a dark room through a pinhole, it would form a shadow on the opposite wall of a person who was standing outside facing the hole. The striking fact was that the shadow was an inverse one, namely, the person would be seen upside-down. This was not incomprehensible, however, to the Mohists. "The light travels like arrows in straight lines. The light from the lower parts of the man goes [through the pinhole] to the higher parts of the shadow, and vice versa."

For mirror reflections, Mohists knew that a convex mirror would always form one and only one upright image, but a concave mirror would have an inverse image that was smaller than the original object. The context of the *Mohist Canon* also showed a clear distinction between the focus and the sphere center.

In the *Mohist Canon*, force was defined with the experience of human muscle stress. Buoyancy was described with the observation of boats: a big boat would submerge less than a small one (given that they had the same loads). As for levers, the Mohists knew that the force needed depended not only on the load but also on the length of the arm.

"Kaogong ji" or "The Artificer's Record": This encyclopedic handbook, probably written in the fifth century B.C., groups crafts and technical skills into thirty categories, including woodcrafts, metal processing, leather tanning, coloring, and painting. Within each category, the craftsmanship is further divided into specialties. For instance, "vehicle making" is discussed in separate chapters for "wheel making," "wagon making," and "shaft making." In each of such subdivisions, there are detailed instructions for workers and their supervisors. For example, the section on wheel making raises 10 major points that should be honored in the process of making a good wheel and other important points of checkups for quality control. The alignment and the balance of wheels, the shape of the rim, and the symmetry of the spokes are all singled out as essential for durability.

Weapon making is another important part of the book. The book pointed out that, if an arrow fails to fly in a straight line, it must have been imperfectly made. "When too much feather is attached to the tail of an arrow, the arrow will not fly far; if not enough feather is applied, the arrow will lose its stability in flight."

The *Artificer's Record* also contains detailed discussions on making musical instruments, with clear definitions of the tones, pitches, and intensity of the instruments. In 1978, archaeologists unearthed eight sets of musical instruments in a tomb dated 433 B.C. The objects confirmed the descriptions in the book and became important samples for the study of ancient technology.

Bronze, Cast Iron, and Steel: The use of bronze reached its peak during the Shang and early Zhou periods. Bronze was an alloy of copper, tin, and lead. When mixed in a proper portion, the melting point of the alloy would be lower than 1,100°C. By the Shang time, the army had been armed with bronze weapons. In 1939, a bronze vessel of the late Shang was unearthed. It was named *Simuwu ding* after the inscription found inside the vessel. Weighing more than 1,930 pounds, *Simuwu ding* remains the largest ancient bronze vessel ever discovered. Unearthed articles have shown that bronze tools in agriculture and craftsmanship were popular early in the Western Zhou period.

The *Artificer's Record* shows that Chinese craftsmen of the Spring and Autumn period (722–481 B.C.) recognized that bronze had six alloys, each of which was good for a specific use. The book states that proper proportion of different metals was essential for metallurgy. If, for example, copper was mixed with tin at a six-to-one proportion, the alloy would be good for making bells and chimes; at a five-to-one proportion, it would be good for axes and daggers; a five-to-two proportion made the alloy good for making arrowheads, and so on.

Based upon the skills and experience in bronze metallurgy, the technology of cast iron was developed during the Spring and Autumn period. Cast iron needed a temperature of more than 1,200°C, which might cost much in terms of fuel consumption and furnace building. But cast iron was harder than bronze. The earliest documented product of cast iron can be dated to 513 B.C., when the state of Jin cast its penal code on an iron vessel for lasting reference.

Almost immediately after the invention of cast iron, a new method of smelting was developed during the Warring States period (480–222 B.C.). Archaeologists' analysis of a sample excavated in Luoyang, central China, revealed that the main constituent of this malleable cast iron was ferrite with flakes of annealed graphite.

By the end of the Warring States period, Chinese technology had reached the point where steel with .5–.6 percent carbon was used for swords and other tools. This was obtained by decarbonization of cast iron. The product was similar to modern steel in terms of crystalline structure.

Water-Control Projects: Since agriculture came to be the major source of food for humans, irrigation and flood control became important during the ancient period. According to legend, Yü, the founder of the Xia dynasty, became emperor partly because of his success in fighting the great flood of his time. Less legendary was the project of Dujiangyan, completed between 306 B.C. and 251 B.C. in Sichuan. The project consisted of three components: the primary division head that divided the mainstream of the Min River into two, the flying sands spillway that functioned as an overflow in case of a flood, and the cornucopia channel that led water into an irritation system. More than half a million acres of planting field benefited from this colossal system, which was still functioning in the 1950s. The credit

for planning and designing the project was attributed to Li Bing, the governor of Sichuan.

Other projects, such as the Zhengguo Canal, did not survive to the present. According to historical records, it was built in 246 B.C. The major waterway was about 100 miles long and provided irrigation for some 40,000 acres of fields.

Buildings in the 16th Century B.C.: As shown by archaeological excavations in the 1970s, houses with rammed foundations appeared in China as early as the 21st to 16th centuries B.C. In two sites, remnants were found of city walls built as early as the 16th century B.C. The main material for the wall was rammed earth. The procedure of construction was as follows. First, the builders set up two parallel walls with wooden boards. They then filled the space in between with earth, which they rammed until it became solid. They then put in more earth, which they also proceeded to ram solid. Layer by layer, they repeated the same procedure, until the desired height was reached.

Palace complexes began to be built no later than the early Shang dynasty. The layout of the palaces was very elaborate. In one complex, each of the buildings served different functions: the gateways, the main halls, the front landing room, and the side rooms. The palace buildings were usually set up with wooden framework on terraces of rammed earth. The facets could be more than 100 feet wide and 30 feet deep. Underground drainage pipes made of pottery were found in many places.

In 1975, archaeologists discovered a building complex dated to about 1180 B.C. The complex consisted of three parts: the front quad, the main hall, and the back part of gardens and houses for private life. The main hall, about 55 feet wide and 20 feet in depth, was built on a terrace more than 4 feet high. The hall had a wooden-frame structure and a rammed-earth wall. At some parts of the hall, the wall was more than 3 feet thick. Underground drains were also used for the whole complex.

The Great Wall: Over the course of many centuries, the Great Wall, China's most famous human-made landmark, was built. Building began during the Warring

States period, but over the years, construction of the Great Wall was interrupted for various reasons. The heyday of its construction was in the Qin dynasty (221–206 B.C.), 200 years after the first part of the wall had been erected.

The main purpose of the Great Wall was for defense against northern nomads. What is today considered the Great Wall starts from the city of Shanghai on the Pacific coast and winds westward, running through mountains, plateaus, and desert plains until finally reaching the Fort of Jiayü. Today, the wall is about 4,000 miles in length.

The Great Wall was built with rammed earth in the Qin and was reinforced in later dynasties with bricks and stone blocks. On average, the base of the wall is typically 10 to 11 feet in width, while at the top it is about 4 feet wide. Some parts of the wall, however, are considerably thicker or thinner.

At the height of its military use, the Great Wall was more than just a "wall." It was actually a complex with many defensive facilities. About every two miles, the wall was punctuated by a beacon tower, and a platform rose every five miles. The beacon tower could be 75–80 feet high, square at the base, measuring 50 feet by 50 feet on each side. These structures functioned as outposts for watching the maneuvers of the nomads and for setting signal fires when an ambush or invasion was likely. Every 10 miles of the wall had a fortress, and a stronghold marked every 30 miles. Often at those spots, garrisons, military headquarters, and supplies were stationed.

3. The Qin-Han Period and the Age of Division

Papermaking

In ancient times, tortoiseshells were used for writing. Thousands of pieces of such tortoiseshells with inscriptions were found in an archaeological site dated between the 16th and 11th centuries B.C. Later, wooden or bamboo slips were used for writing. Early in the Han dynasty, about the second century B.C., silk fabric was also used as writing material. The problems with these forms were obvious: wooden or bamboo slips were too bulky and heavy, no matter how fine they were made; silk fabrics were generally too expensive for most people to afford.

Some scholars speculate that the idea of making paper with "waste fiber" came from the silk-textile industry. The outermost layer of silkworm cocoons could not be used for spinning or weaving. There were some early types of "paper" made from various kinds of fabric early in the Western Han dynasty (202 B.C.–A.D. 8). The invention of "real paper" is conventionally attributed to Cai Lun, a eunuch at the imperial court of the Han. In A.D. 105, he tried to make writing material with fabrics such as rope ends, tree bark, and worn pieces of rag. He mixed up the fabric pieces with grass-stalk ash, which served as an agent of alkaline, and then stowed the mixture and removed the impurities like lignin or other small solid pieces. This was equivalent to the "alkaline treatment" in modern papermaking. He pounded the mixture to make a liquid pulp. When spread out and dried, the pulp became paper.

We now know that the actual invention of real paper predated Cai Lun. Segments of hemp paper, dated to the first century B.C., have been unearthed in Gansu. In Inner Mongolia, archeological excavations brought to light specimens of paper with writing dating to the second century B.C. This is the earliest "writing paper" found to date.

The techniques of papermaking spread rapidly. By the fourth century, paper had become virtually the only writing material in practical use.

Calendars

In the late Spring and Autumn period (about the fifth century B.C.), the Chinese had the knowledge that a tropical year had 365.25 days, and a lunar month of 29 days. They also knew that no simple multiples of a lunar month could make a tropical year.

In order to adjust the accumulating inaccuracy, seven months were inserted for every 19 years. This calendar, sometimes referred to as the *Ancient Quarter Calendar*, was used for more than four centuries.

In A.D. 92, it was found that there were fluctuations in the motion of the moon. This phenomenon was explained by the recognition that the moon moved in a path not always in the same distance to the earth. Taking into account this anomaly, Liu Hong created the Qianxiang Calendar in A.D. 206. Based on observations and calculations, he affirmed the length of an anomalistic month to be 27.5533590 days, only about 100 seconds shorter than the "true value" given by the most sophisticated calculation in the 20th century.

As the observation data accumulated, the calculation of the length of a tropical year reached greater accuracy. In the fifth century, Zu Chongzhi was able to obtain a better value of 365.2428148 days for the length of a tropical year, differing by only 46 seconds from the "true value" known to modern scientists. The intercalation was accordingly allotted to 144 leap months for 391 years.

Observations of Sky Phenomena

The Han dynasty saw the flourishing of astronomical studies, especially in the abundance of records for various sky phenomena.

In 134 B.C., a Chinese sky watcher wrote, "In the sixth month of the year, a guest star appeared in the Fang." *Fang* was the Chinese name of the celestial area for Scorpio. The term *guest star* described the main feature of stars that came in and out just like a guest. The records of these stars, known to modern astronomy as novas, have helped modern scientists to study the structure and origin of our universe. During the 19 centuries after this Han record, Chinese documents contained more than 90 records of such phenomena. In most of the records, Chinese observers carefully put down when and where the star was seen, as well as how it looked.

In the daytime, Chinese observers watched the sun. One record dated 28 B.C. read, "The sun looks yellowish at sunrise. A patch of black fume, about the size of a coin, stayed at the center of the sun." This is believed to be one of the earliest records of sunspots in history.

On a sheet of silk unearthed from a tomb at Mawangdui, 29 drawings exemplified various comets observed by Han scholars. The tails of the comets were shown in different sizes and shapes, some long and tapering off to a point, some short and curving. The heads of the comets were represented sometimes by a circle, sometimes by a solid dot, and sometimes both a circle and a dot. These pictures prove that the Han observers, as early as the second century B.C., had been aware that comet heads had two parts, namely the comet hair and the nucleus.

As for the regular motion of the planets and the moon, the Han scholars were equipped with more precise instruments and paid close attention to measuring and calculating the paths of the heavenly bodies. The data obtained were used for creating or amending calendars.

Theories About the Structure of the Universe: There were three schools competing in the discussion of the heavens in the Han period: the Gaitian School, the Xuanye School, and the Huntian School.

The Gaitian theory was presented in *Zhoubi suanjing*, or *The Arithmetical Classic of the Gnomon and the Circular Paths*, one of the most important books in the history of Chinese mathematics. According to this book, heaven was a hemispherical dome covering the earth, which in turn was a flat or, from later versions of this theory, a somewhat convex solid base for both the sky and the mundane world. This theory, however, was contrary to both common sense and observation data. "Where do the moon and the stars go in the daytime?" and "What would be the conjunction between the heaven and the earth?" were among many questions that the Gaitian model found extremely difficult to answer. By the end of the first century B.C., most of the leading scholars were converted to the Huntian School.

The earliest description of the Huntian model was found in an essay of Zhang Heng (78–129), *Commentary on the Armillary Sphere*: "The heaven is like an egg and the body of the heaven is spherical as a crossbow bullet; the earth is like the yolk of the egg, and lies alone in the center. Heaven is large and the earth small. Inside [the sphere of] the heavens there is water. The heaven and the earth are [in their positions by the] support of *qi* and float on the waters." Zhang had been in charge of the Imperial Observatory for 14 years. In order to demonstrate his theory of the heavens-earth structure, Zhang made a model to show how the sphere of the heaven moved. This sphere was powered by running water and adjusted by a complicated system of gears to imitate the real motion of the stars in the sky.

From the Han dynasty on, the Huntian School prevailed until Copernican theory was introduced to Chinese astronomers late in the 17th century.

Unlike the Huntian and Gaitian theories, the Xuanye School had no comprehensive description. The major arguments of the theory were found in quotations cited by its contemporary authors. The Xuanye School believed that the heavens had no tangible body and were unlimited. The sun, the moon, and the stars were moving in an empty space with the help of *qi*.

Early Mathematics

Symbols standing for numbers were found on oracle-bone inscriptions dated as early as the Shang dynasty. The largest number alluded to was 30,000. On the wall of a metal vessel dated a little later, archeologists were able to decipher a sentence about a business involving 659 men.

The oldest extant book of arithmetic was *Jiuzhang suanshu* (Nine chapters on the mathematical art), which appeared in the first century B.C. The main body of the book was 246 questions, grouped into nine chapters, each of which discussed a practical problem in daily life. The chapter on "Problems Regarding the Exchange Between Millet and Rice" incorporated 46 questions, more than any other chapter. The chapter on measuring fields was next in length, in which formulas were given for various shapes such as a square, a rectangle, a triangle, and a circle. More advanced questions such as finding the square and cubic roots were also discussed. In the two chapters concluding the book, 18 questions demonstrated the skills of problem solv-

ing—equivalent to using simultaneous equations and the Pythagorean theorem in modern math.

The calculation of the circumference or the area of a circle was of special interest to ancient scholars. The key to an accurate calculation was to find the proper value of π, or the ratio of the circumference to the diameter of a circle. Zhang Heng was able to obtain an estimation of π as 730/232, or 3.1466; on another occasion, though, he used the rougher approximation of 3.1622. In A.D. 263, Liu Hui developed a new method to determine segment areas of a circle by using inscribed regular polygons. As a result, he found with a 192-sided polygon a better estimation of π: 3.141024. When the number of the sides of the polygon increased to 3,072, he got 3.1416 for π. One and a half centuries later, Zu Chongzhi (429–500) affirmed that the true value of π would be no smaller than 3.1415926 and no larger than 3.1415927, equivalent in accuracy to the values given by al-Kashi in 1427 and François Viete in 1571. The study of the history of mathematics has also shown that it is plausible that there was Chinese influence on al-Kashi's work.

Agriculture

Chinese civilization was built upon agriculture. In the Warring States period, there were books with comprehensive discussions about crop cultivation, gardening, animal husbandry, and sericulture. Four chapters of the *Lüshi Chunqiu*, or *The Annals of Lü Buwei*, were dedicated to agriculture. Special emphasis was placed on field production, as well as the different ways of farming on different kinds of soil. Fertilization, water preservation, and common mistakes in farming were also discussed. In one of these chapters, the author wrote about the timing of sowing and harvesting for six specific crops, such as millet, rice, wheat, and setaria. The book also recorded the use of the crop rotation system, in which farmers allowed a field to lie fallow for a season to let the soil recuperate.

The earliest monograph on agriculture known to modern scholars was *Fan Shengzhi shu*, a book attributed to Fan Shengzhi during the first century B.C. Based on farming practices in northern China, the book presented detailed instructions for making fields, selecting seeds, and cultivating a great variety of crops. The crops discussed included rice, glutinous millet, wheat, soya, and common perilla. Two special measures in treatment of seed, namely urination (the soaking of seeds in natural fertilizers such as urine) and shallow-pit cultivation, were discussed for the first time in a book on agriculture. Unfortunately, only fragments of *Fan Shengzhi shu* have survived to modern times.

By the first century B.C., the use of iron had been so common that it had become the standard metal for all agricultural tools. Usually three farmers and two oxen made up a plowing team. With sharp plowshares and powerful oxen, the farmers could work on hard soil and make better farming strips. In the second century A.D., a V-shaped plowshare was introduced and soon gained widespread use in north China. At that same time, more than 30 farming tools were used for various tasks.

Qimin Yaoshu: Completed between 533 and 534, *Qimin Yaoshu*, or *Essential Skills for the Common People*, was the earliest known monograph in agronomy in Chinese history. In 92 essays and 10 parts, the book covered farming, animal husbandry, field treatment, and water conservation.

The weather in north China was often windy and dry. For maintaining soil moisture, *Qimin Yaoshu* gave detailed instructions on farming techniques, such as how to choose proper hewing time and what tools to use.

Letting fields lie fallow was one of the ways Chinese farmers restored soil richness. However, rotation was more economical. *Qimin Yaoshu* recommended the proper sequences of rotation for various crops. For instance, in the case of beans, it said, "To improve the soil, the best way is to have mung beans, then lesser beans, and then sesame." More than 80 varieties of spiked millet were described, their characteristics compared, and the principles of choosing the proper strain advised.

The First Emperor's Terra-Cotta Army

In 221 B.C., Qin Shi Huangdi, known as the "First Emperor" to many Westerners, established a unified empire after defeating the other Chinese states. We can still get a sense of what his army was like by looking at the army of terra-cotta figures guarding his tomb.

Excavated in 1974, the site consisted of three major pits, one of which was converted into a museum a few years later. In the 16-foot-deep pit, 6,000 terra-cotta figures lined up in 36 columns were found covering a total area of 755 feet by 203 feet. This was an army in full battle gear with personnel of all ranks: generals, military officers, archers, infantrymen, and chariot drivers. Six war chariots and 24 pottery horses were also found in the battle formation. The terra-cotta warriors are 5 to 6 feet tall, armed with swords, bows, spears, and crossbows. No two of the figures are identical. In some minor sites nearby and on top of this pit, archaeologists found real bronze armaments, such as curved-blade swords and bows with arrows. Archaeological studies of the site suggested that around the second century B.C. China had reached a high level of development in pottery making, bronze metallurgy, and war techniques.

4. THE HEYDAY: FROM THE TANG TO THE MING

Printing with Incised Tablets

The use of seals, or small pieces of stone with carved characters for personal names or official titles, can be traced back to the Warring States period. When more and more characters were involved in the con-

tent, seals became larger and larger. Incised stone tablets appeared. The texts on the tablets could be copied by rubbing. A printing master rubbed gently on a sheet of thin and strong paper placed on top of a pre-inked tablet; the paper would be darkened except for where the engraved characters were. Then the paper would be peeled carefully from the stone tablet, and a copy that was all black with white characters would be ready.

Wood blocks were first tried in the place of stone tablets early in the seventh century. According to *Sui shu* (The book of [or the history of] the Sui dynasty, 581–618), wood from date or pear trees was ideal for making printing plates. The engraving of the wood blocks was different from that of the stone tablets. The text was carved on the plate in relief, with the left and right sides of the text reversed. When a plate had been carved, it would be inked, and a piece of paper would be pressed against it to make a print. Using this method, hundreds of copies could be printed cheaply and quickly.

At first, religious materials were the main items printed. Less than a century later, however, wood-block printing came to be used in the publication of almanacs, phonetic dictionaries, and medical handbooks. In 865, a Japanese monk returned home with books printed with wood plates; at least two of the books were voluminous anthologies. Today, the oldest extant printed leaves are of a Buddhist sacred text, the *Diamond Sutra*. These leaves are dated 868.

The Invention of Movable-Type Printing: Although wood-block printing had great advantages over hand copying, problems still existed. Once a book was done, the wood block had to be carefully stored for a possible reprint. Saving wood blocks cost money and took up space. In the first half of the 11th century, a craftsman named Bi Sheng invented movable-type printing. Bi Sheng tried clay type, with one separate piece for each character used. The pieces were arranged to form text on a wax-covered iron plate. The pieces were held in place by first heating and melting the wax and then letting it cool. After the printing was done, Bi Sheng could melt the wax again and rearrange the pieces to form a different text. The type could be used repeatedly. The copies made were less expensive. Still, this technique required advanced skills in order to level every type and to align every line for the whole page. In addition, the printing quality was often inferior to that of the wood-block prints.

Shen Gua (1031–1095)

In his teens, Shen Gua (sometimes pronounced Shen Kuo) traveled from Sichuan to Amoy with his father, who was then an official in the government. This long journey gave him a chance to see the country: the mountains and rivers, the different crops cultivated in different areas of the vast country, and people of all professions. His curiosity for nature and how people dealt with it developed and lasted until the last days of his life.

Like many scholars in his time, Shen started his career as a local official. In 1061, he conducted a project of land reclamation. After passing the civil service examinations, he was posted to Yangzhou, where he studied astronomy. His mastery of star observation and calendar making led to an appointment in 1072 as director of the Astronomical Bureau, a branch of the imperial government in charge of "heavenly affairs." He supervised the observation of the movement of planets, comets, and meteors. All were to be continuously observed, carefully recorded, and reported to the emperor if necessary.

In 1075, he was sent as one of the major negotiators to the Khitan state of Liao, the powerful northern neighbor of the Song state. While on this journey, Shen used every opportunity to investigate the biological and geographical features of the northern region. The trip was a success, but he was soon impeached due to factional struggles in the government. Later, he was sent to the northwestern prefecture of Yenzhou as its commissioner for civil and military affairs. He showed his mastery of the art of warfare in the defense against the Tangut attack in 1081. But the victory did not help him survive the political struggle, and he was finally put into a fixed probationary residence, deprived of all the credit he deserved.

He retired to an estate, which he named "Dream Brook." Living in isolation, he began to write his great book. He called what he wrote *Mengxi bitan* (Brush talks from Dream Brook), which became one of the most important works from medieval China. After seven years' seclusion, Shen died a sick and lonely man.

Mengxi bitan was published in 1095. The book was a collection of jottings, a popular way for scholars in Shen's time to put down their thoughts and observations. *Mengxi bitan* is noted for its abundance of entries on science and technology. The book is grouped into 17 chapters, seven of which contain valuable materials about observations on natural phenomena, descriptions of craftsmanship, and solutions to mathematical problems.

Mengxi bitan recorded Shen's discovery that the polestar did not coincide with the true pole in location but had a deviation of about 3 degrees. He stated that the moon had no light of its own, but only reflected the light from the sun. He was able to explain the phases of the moon with a small ball, half whitened with paint: "when you see it at an angle, it appears to be a crescent, while you face [the whitened part of] it, it is a full moon." He recorded his observations of magnetic needles and asserted that "they are always displaced slightly east rather than pointing due south." For concave mirrors, he tried to explain why an inverted image was formed. He introduced the concept of an obstruction and used two cones apex to apex, to demonstrate that the second cone would constitute an inverted image. He described the geological strata he had investigated in some regions of China, noticing that "bivalve shells and ovoid rocks run horizontally through a cliff like a belt" and speculating correctly that "this was once a seashore, although the sea is now hundreds of miles east."

Mengxi bitan is not a book of science in the modern sense. It does not contain a systematic description or a structural explanation of nature and natural phenomena. In terms of the range and depth of the records it contains, however, it proves to be one of the most remarkable documents of early science and technology.

Su Song and His Armillary Sphere

Su Song was born in 1020. During his lifetime, the Song dynasty was at the peak of its prosperity, which made it possible for Su to carry out his great project of the astronomical observatory and to finish his book that covered all the astronomical knowledge known in China at the time.

The astronomical clock observatory was designed and planned by Su Song early in 1086. Two years later, a group of scholars and sky watchers under Su's leadership built a working prototype on a reduced scale. Su and his colleagues went on to build a full-sized tower. The observatory had two levels. The top part was a platform on which an armillary sphere was installed. The ground floor housed a machine that was powered by water and controlled by a clock-like escapement mechanism. This complicated machine was designed to drive the armillary sphere in such a way that it would synchronize with the motion of the sky.

Modern scholars have estimated the inaccuracy of this clock-like machine to be about 2 degrees per 24 hours. But it was still practical and was used for some years.

In 1092, Su Song dedicated his invention to the emperor. In his report, *Xin yinxiang fayao*, or *New Design for an Armillary Sphere*, Su Song used verbal descriptions and diagrams to explain how the observatory worked. This mechanized armillary sphere, according to Su Song, "would help us to observe the stars, record their paths, and calculate their positions, all in a great accuracy, both in the daytime and at night."

Following the descriptions and instructions Su Song presented in his book, historians of science in 1956 reconstructed a model of the observatory. The model is displayed at the Museum of Chinese History in Beijing.

Sailing and the Compass

Early in the fourth century, a Chinese sailor jotted down his experience in the vast ocean: "We found ourselves in the midst of boundless waters. . . . We advanced by observing the sun, the moon and the stars." The first record of employing a compass in maritime navigation came from *Pingzhou ketan*, a book dated 1119. The magnetic compass was used as an auxiliary or alternative means for finding directions when the weather was cloudy. When the weather was fair, the sailors were more likely to rely on the sun and the stars.

Shen Gua discussed the installation of a compass. He described four ways to keep the magnet needle free from any interference so as to obtain a better reading. In the Song time, the magnet was usually set afloat on water with a piece of wax. Shen pointed out that, since it was difficult to keep the water still in a sailing boat, the floating installation was not practical in use. The method he recommended was to hang the needle with a thin silk string. Many other books confirmed the use of magnet compass in the 12th century on Chinese ships.

Zhaozhou Bridge

One of the oldest standing arch bridges in the world is the Zhaozhou Bridge, named after the county in which it is located. The bridge was built in the Sui dynasty (581–618), presumably during the period 605–616, under the instruction of Li Chun.

Modern scholars have been drawn to research many features of the bridge. The bridge is 167 feet long and crosses the river with a single arch with piers on sedimentary strands. The arch spans about 122.5 feet. The rise from the chord line, the horizontal level of the bottom of the bridge, is 23 feet 9 inches. This makes a ratio of 1:5 between the height and span (length) of the arch. In bridge building of this kind, the flatter the arch, the harder it is to construct. The fact that the Chinese builders could build an arch this flat demonstrates the high level of technical sophistication they mastered. The bridge on top of the main arch was built with an even gentler slope, a feature that benefits pedestrians and vehicles. Two more side arches were built in each of the spandrels, or the space between the main arch and the deck. The employment of the side arches reduced the weight of the bridge and therefore reduced the load for the piers. This design is especially desirable for bridges built on sedimentary strands. The side arches also alleviated the water pressure against the piers in flood seasons by providing additional openings for water to pass through when water level was high.

Gunpowder

Saltpeter and sulfur, the two major components of gunpowder, were first recorded in the Han period as external medicine. Later in the ninth century, the mixture of the two along with charcoal was recognized as an explosive. *Wujing zongyao* (The encyclopedia of military arts, compiled in 1040–1044), includes three possible recipes for gunpowder. In addition to saltpeter, sulfur, and charcoal, other chemical agents such as realgar and asphalt were used as additives for various purposes, such as poisoning or making smoke screens or signal flares. The correct proportion of saltpeter to other ingredients was essential for maximizing the power of the explosion.

During the 12th and 13th centuries, the war against the Khitans made the research and production of gunpowder a high priority in the Song. The government established a department to take special charge of the munitions industry, supervising 11 workshops with 40,000 workers. The workshops yielded 17,000 arrows with gunpowder pouches attached and 23,000 gunpowder packages a day.

Maps and Gazetteers

Unearthed in 1973 in a Han tomb, three maps on silk fabric specified the administrative and military dispositions and topographical features of the territory of the Marquis of Changsha. These maps confirm that in the second century B.C. the techniques were available for making maps for various purposes.

Travelers' journals also contributed to the knowledge of geography. The famous monk Xuanzang, on his pilgrimage to India, visited some 100 states and cities. When he returned in 654, the emperor ordered him to write down what he had seen and heard.

Maps with detailed verbal descriptions first appeared in the period between the sixth and eighth centuries. In 801, after an effort of 17 years, Jia Dan (730–805) submitted to the emperor a map covering both the Tang empire and the "barbarian neighbors." His descriptions filled 40 volumes.

In the Northern Song period (960–1127), geographical studies focused more and more on local conditions and customs. The

Huanyü ji, or *The Encyclopedia of the World*, compiled between 976 and 984, reflected this tendency of the scholarly interests by incorporating biographies of local gentry, citations of books related to the area, and descriptions of regional events in history. Following the example of *Huanyü ji*, more than 100 gazetteers were compiled in the Song dynasty, of which some 20 have survived. The Yuan dynasty (1276–1368) saw the continuation of the Song effort in the compilation of *Dayuan yitong Zhi*, an even more comprehensive and ambitious geographical encyclopedia of 1,300 chapters.

Works of Agronomy

Rice was the principal food in southern China, where the warm weather and rainfall were favorable for its growth. Early works of agronomy, such as the sixth-century text *Qimin yaoshu* (Essential skills for commoners), were generally based on agricultural practice in northern China, dealing with such crops as millet and wheat. By Song times, the center of gravity of the Chinese economy had shifted to the southeast. With the increased importance of the South came the demand for agronomy books that suited southern conditions. In 1149, Chen Fu's book on farming in the south, *Nong shu* (Book of agriculture) was written. The book consisted of three parts discussing the cultivation of rice, the husbandry of water buffalo, and sericulture. The precision of the technical details suggest that the book was a record of Chen Fu's own field experience.

Wang Zhen's book, also with the title *Nong shu* (c. 1295–1300), covered the agriculture of both the north and the south. In addition to the discussion of traditional subjects, such as the cultivation of crops, vegetables, and fruits, Wang Zhen's book contained 306 drawings depicting the tools and mechanical devises used for farming throughout China. For centuries, these drawings served as blueprints for making agricultural machinery.

Astronomy in the Song and the Yuan

In 1907, Aurel Stein found a map of 1,350 stars in a cave in the Gobi desert of northwest China. Presumably finished in the early Tang dynasty (618–907), this map consisted of a planisphere (a hemisherical map with the northern polestar at the center) for the circumpolar stars and a set of 12 crosswise charts for those along the celestial equator.

In the 11th century, the Song government organized five systematic efforts to observe the stars. Each effort distinguished itself from the previous one with some new features. Beginning with the installation of a new armillary sphere in 1010, the first observation used a system based on the winter solstice point. The next two observations, carried out in 1034 and about 1050, accurately recorded the locations of 345 stars.

The fourth observation lasted eight years, from 1078 to 1086. The major outcome of this project, a planisphere of 1,430 stars with its explanatory text, was not committed to stone until 1247. In a planisphere, the locations of all other stars were measured with their distances and angles related to the polar star. This map also showed the curving course of the Milky Way, the celestial equator, and the southern limit of the sky visible for observers in northern China.

The fifth observation of 1102 reached a higher accuracy in measuring the locations of stars. For stars near the celestial equator, the absolute errors were often smaller than one-sixth of a degree.

Two centuries later, sponsored by the Yuan government, 27 observatories were set up under the instruction of the great scientist Guo Shoujing (1231–1316). The observatories were scattered over a wide geographical area from the southernmost island of the Xisha Archipelago (15° N) to as far north as near the Arctic circle (65° N). In 1276, one of Guo's projects recorded 2,500 stars, which meant that almost all the stars visible to the naked eye in northern China had been recorded in the 13th century.

Nova and Supernova: In 1006, the appearance of a guest star was reported. The Bureau of Astronomy carried out continuous observation on it throughout the period of its appearance. In the same manner, in 1054, when a supernova exploded near Tauri, the Chinese observers followed its course for more than two years until it became entirely invisible. Well-kept records made it possible for modern scholars to determine that the star described by the Chinese in the 11th century was the origin of the Crab Nebula, a nebula in Taurus.

The Perception of Anomalies in the Sky: The observations did not, however, lead to a comprehensive theory of the universe, as they did in the cases of Tycho Brahe and Johannes Kepler some five centuries later in Europe. For 11th-century Chinese scholars, the sky phenomena were reflections of Heaven's judgment over the imperial administration on earth.

5. Encounters with the Outside World

Shipbuilding in the Song and the Yuan

The typical vessel for inland waters during the Song was the flat-bottom boat, sometimes later called Sha-boat, named after the island where it was first built. The loading capacity of the Sha-boat was estimated at between 250 and 800 tons. By the late 13th century, when coastal waters became the major path for the Yuan government to transport its revenue from the south to the north, the capacity of the ships increased rapidly. By 1314, the capacity of the largest boats exceeded 1,200 tons.

The Sha-boat was originally designed for inland waters. For sailing far off the coast or into distant waters, improvements were needed. During the 150 years between the late Song to the early 15th century, new techniques and equipment were adopted, improving the boat's stability in harsh waters. Some of the improvements included subsidiary rudders on both sides of the boat and supporting beams on the bottom.

Zheng He and His Voyage

By 1405, when Zheng He, the imperial envoy of the Ming emperor for collecting tributes from "all barbarian states," departed for the "western seas," he commanded a fleet of 62 ships equipped with crews totaling more than 27,000 men. Most of these ships were equipped with magnetic compasses and sextants.

The largest boats in the fleet were called "treasure boats," each of which was more than 400 feet long. With the flat-bottom design and relatively shallow water draught, the boats were fairly safe when the wind blew against the tide. The sails on the three or four masts provided flexibility for wind directions and enough push for the boats to keep an average speed of 7 knots.

During the seven voyages in the period 1405–1433, Zheng visited 30 countries in Asia and Africa. In 1419, he landed on an island in the Maldives; in later voyages, he reached the entrances of the Red Sea and the Persian Gulf and might have explored the island of Madagascar.

The scholars aboard jotted down what they discovered at "the end of the earth." Three of those journals are still extant. On the return trips, the fleet brought back exotic animals and objects that stunned the Chinese. A giraffe, for instance, was almost immediately identified as *Qilin* (sometimes translated as the Chinese "unicorn"), a semi-divine creature they had heard of only from legendary stories.

Zheng He's voyages were impressive undertakings but had no lasting impact. The voyages were very costly for the emperor. Moreover, they brought little direct benefit to the common people. Confucian scholar-officials were also concerned that the people's loyalty to tradition might be weakened by the overseas ventures. In 1433, the year Zheng died, the emperor banned seagoing adventures. Zheng He's records were burned and his boats abandoned in the mud of the Yangtze River. His voyages were lost to history until his boats were unearthed in the 1950s. About 60 years after Zheng's death, from the direction opposite to Zheng He's voyage, Vasco da Gama successfully sailed from Portugal to India, marking the beginning of a new era for the Europeans.

Craftsmanship

One of the most important works on craftsmanship, *Tiangong kaiwu* (The creations of nature and man), was finished in 1637 by Song Yingxing (1587–?), a man greatly interested in how the "smiths" worked, which had been a topic too trifling for traditional scholars.

The book addressed nearly all the products and skills culled in daily life: sugar and salt, wines and liquors, limestone and metallurgy, vehicles and boats, textiles and sericulture, and so on. The step-by-step instructions were clear. In most cases, drawings with technical details made the instructions even easier to follow. Papermaking, for instance, was explained step by step. For making porcelain, the book described how Gaolin clay was treated in advance, how the kiln worked, and how the wares were glazed and colored.

Early Encounters with the West

In the last quarter of the 16th century, China saw non-Asian foreigners after more than a century of seclusion. They were not envoys coming with their tribute to the emperor, nor captives from tribes in the Gobi. They looked fairly civilized and claimed to be in China on a mission from God. They were missionaries from the Roman Catholic Church, hoping to convert the Chinese.

Matteo Ricci (1552–1610) was among the earliest when he entered China in 1582. In 1601, he finally obtained permission to visit Beijing, the capital of the Ming, where he presented a clock to the emperor as his gift. It was not an easy job to convert the Chinese. Both learned scholars and unschooled peasants were confident in the superiority of Chinese culture.

Ricci needed something new to convince the Chinese that there were valuable things beyond their world. He showed world maps in which China was only one country among many. He demonstrated the Tychonic system of the universe with which a better calendar was to be created later. He hoped that the new knowledge would arouse enthusiasm for his teachings among Chinese scholars.

Xu Guangqi was one of the first Chinese scholars converted to Ricci. Born in 1562 into an affluent family, Xu had been a typical scholar-official until he converted to Christianity in 1604. Converted by Ricci, he acknowledged that the Western scholarship in science and technology was no heresy, but an alternative at least as good as, if not better than, Confucianism. Together with Ricci, Xu translated the first half of Euclid's *Geometry* and a handful of other books on water conservancy and field survey into Chinese. With the help of his knowledge of astronomy that he learned from Ricci, he made the reform of the calendar a great success in 1633.

In addition to his study of astronomy and Christianity, Xu compiled a voluminous book on agronomy, the field of knowledge that he believed to benefit the people the most. Xu's *Nongzheng quanshu* (The complete treatise on agriculture) covered in 60 volumes 12 main topics from farm management and administration, land reclamation, and water conservancy to crops and foodstuff processing. Some of the topics, such as military colonies and preparation for natural disasters, had never been discussed by other authors on agriculture. This book was not finished at his death in 1633 and was published posthumously years later.

More Missionaries Come to China:
Following the suggestions of Matteo Ricci, a number of Catholic missionaries came to China with books on astronomy and mathematics, hoping that the new knowledge would help open Chinese minds and help open up the country, which had been secluded for a century. These missionaries included Nicolaus Longobardi (1559–1654) in 1597, Sabbathinus de Ursis (1575–1620) in 1606, Julius Aleni (1582–1649) in 1613, and Jean Adam Schall von Bell (1591–1666) in 1622. Together with their Chinese

partners, they translated and compiled more than a dozen books on astronomy and its application in calendar making.

In December 1610, Chinese astronomers failed in the calculation of the solar eclipses. This failure brought serious criticism against the traditional method that had been used since the late 14th century by the Imperial Bureau of Heavens, the department in charge of heavenly phenomena. The calls for new methods and new systems were heard in the court. Since the old Chinese way of calculation was not working well, the idea of help from Westerners was no longer heretical, at least to some of the officials.

The reform with the participation of the Westerners resulted in a new calendar based on the Tychonic model, the *Chongzhen Calendar*. Before the calendar was decreed for the more than 100 million Chinese to use, the Ming dynasty fell. Schall von Bell, surviving the chaos of the change of dynasties and winning imperial favor again from the emperor of the newly installed Qing dynasty (1644–1911), finally persuaded the court to accept the new calendar. He himself was appointed the director of the Bureau of Heavens—a very unusual occurrence in the Chinese government since he was a foreigner.

With his unique skills both in astronomy and court politics, Schall von Bell held the position until his death. In the century to come, Ferdinandus Verbiest (1623–1688), Ignatius Kogler (1680–1746), and Michael Benoist (1715–1774) were appointed to similar positions in the bureau. They wrote and translated books, built and installed new instruments, and introduced to the Chinese the Copernican theory and modern astronomy based on it.

The Reaction to the New Calendar

The new cosmology was thought to be absurd when the Chinese first heard it in the last years of the Ming. But the accuracy of the related calendar was convincing. Seeing some similarities between the Western and the Huntian theories, the Qing scholars found that the Tychonic model was not terribly inconceivable; some

even speculated that the "new system" was nothing new but a copy of what had once been taught by the ancient Chinese.

The Translation of Foreign Texts in the 19th Century

Parallel to the government's effort to introduce western scholarship into China, a group of Chinese scholars took private initiatives to cooperate with missionaries to translate books of science and technology. Through the process of translating the foreign books, the Chinese scholars also trained themselves in mathematics, chemistry, and engineering.

Li Shanlan (1811–1882) and Alexander Wylie (1815–1887) started to translate the second half of Euclid's *Geometry* in 1852. Xu Guangqi and Matteo Ricci had translated the first part some two hundred years before. Over the next seven years, six other books made their way into Chinese under the pens of Li and Wylie. Among them were Elias Loomis's *Elements of Analytical Geometry and Differential and Integral Calculus*, from which the Chinese first learned of calculus and parabola. Li, with Joseph Edkins (1823–1905), also translated the major part of W. Whewell's *An Elementary Treatise on Mechanics*, which became the first systematic explanation of Newtonian mechanics in Chinese. There is evidence to suggest that Li tried to translate Newton's *Principia*, but for an unknown reason, the project was aborted. Hua Hengfang (1833–1902), together with Daniel MacGowan (1814–1893), translated five books on geology and navigation.

Starting in 1871, Xu Shou (1818–1884) and his partner John Fryer (1839–1928) translated eight bulky books on chemistry, covering all the major branches of the subject, such as inorganic and organic chemistry and quantitative and qualitative analysis. Most of the translations were based on books that had been published in Europe less than a decade before, conveying the latest developments in the field. Xu cautiously and conscientiously made his translations faithful to the original, yet acceptable to Chinese scholars at the same time. Many of the scientific terms created by him in the translation of these books are still used in China today. In fewer than 15 years, Xu Shou translated 13 books, published in more than 120 volumes.

Organized Translation: In addition to Xu Shou and others, Jiangnan Arsenal, one of the major arsenals in the 1870s, set up a branch bureau for translating books on engineering and technology. John Fryer, A. Wylie, Daniel MacGowan, and many Chinese scholars worked together. In the 1870s, 103 books were translated, including C. Lyell's *Principles of Geology*. Mathematics, navigation/astronomy, and turbine engineering and other fields of technology were of the highest priority; among the 77 books published by 1880, 52 were in these fields.

In the 1870s and the 1880s, translations were usually made according to the following procedure. Missionaries chose the books to translate and explained the contents orally in Chinese to their Chinese partners. The Chinese partners took notes in Chinese. Since the missionaries' proficiency in Chinese was often limited, their Chinese assistants had to figure out what they really meant and decipher the notes themselves. Better translations did not come about until Western-educated Chinese students took over the task of introducing modern science and technology to their fellow countrymen in the first decade of the 20th century.

Tongwen Guan

Being repeatedly defeated by the British and other European countries in the 1840s and 1850s, the Chinese felt that the "barbarians" were stronger and more advanced than China's "celestial dynasty," especially in science and technology. By the mid-19th century, there was a general agreement among the members of the ruling group that China must learn from the West and that this learning should start with translating.

The imperial court decided in 1861 to set up a new type of school, in which the students were to study foreign languages and subjects such as astronomy and mathematics. Tongwen Guan, or "School for Unified Languages," received strong support from a group of reformers in the imperial court. However, many middle-ranking officials and the conservative gentry strongly opposed the school. Many gentry families refused to send their sons to this school because they thought the goal of the school was to train servants for "foreign devils." For the Confucian scholars, the subjects taught in the school were mere foreign novelties which were neither relevant to true Confucian learning nor useful to the preparation for civil service exams.

Students Learning in the United States

The conservative opponents contributed nothing more than destructive criticism, which could not help China cope with strong and aggressive foreign countries. Thus, the emperor had to rely on the reformers and finally accepted an even more audacious proposal backed by a group of princes and generals. According to this proposal, for the first time China, in 1872, sent 120 students, 12 through 15 years of age, to the United States, under the guidance of Rong Hong (generally known as Yung Wing in the West, 1828–1912), a graduate of Yale University (class of 1854).

According to the original proposal, the children were to live with selected American families to learn the language and culture. In a few years, when they were ready for schooling in the United States, they would be sent to high schools, and then colleges and universities until they finally became experts both in the English language and in their areas of specialization. Unfortunately, this plan was terminated in less than a decade when the imperial supervisor found that the students had been "excessively" influenced by American culture. In 1881, all the students were recalled to China.

Still, China needed to learn from developed countries if it was to survive. Students and scholars still went abroad after the program was halted. The tasks assigned to them, however, became more specialized and technical, such as learning to operate a steam engine. They were no longer assigned the task of understanding Western culture.

European countries first accepted Chinese students in the mid-1870s. Over the next 10 years, more than 80 Chinese students were trained in shipbuilding, dockyard construction, and navigation in France and Germany. In the 1890s, there was a new rush for Chinese students to go to Japan, which was emerging as a new power in the world. Between 1900 and

1906, more than 10,000 Chinese—men and women, students and scholars, princes and officials—visited Japan, hoping to find out how this small island country had succeeded and what China had to do to succeed in the coming century.

6. THE FIRST HALF OF THE 20TH CENTURY

Working with Westerners

Suffering from political and social turmoil, China provided no foundation for the growth of science and technology in the first quarter of the 20th century. Many Chinese students in mathematics and physics stayed in the foreign countries in which they were educated and continued their research.

In 1918, Hu Mingfu published a math paper in the United States, which is believed to be the first paper on modern math published by a Chinese scholar. In 1921, "Some Laws Concerning the Unlimited Series," by Chen Jiangong (1891–1971), known in the United States as K. K. Chen, came out in Japan and received a great deal of attention from mathematicians at the time.

In the studies of experimental physics, Ye Qisun (1898–1977), with W. Duane and H. H. Palmer, obtained in 1921 a new measurement of Planck's constant, which was employed by American and European physicists for the next 16 years.

The Compton effect, or the increases of the wavelength of X-rays when penetrating certain matter, was first reported in 1923 in the United States. Working at the University of Chicago with A. H. Compton, Wu Youxun (1897–1977), known as Y. K. Woo in the United States, conducted a series of experiments on the energy distribution of incident X-rays and had his findings published in issues of *Physical Review* in 1924–1926. His experimental data were cited in 19 places by A. H. Compton in his book *X-Rays in Theories and Experiments* (1926) and provided some of the most important evidence for the Compton effect.

The existence of neutrinos had been puzzling to physicists since the theory of β-decay first developed. A neutrino was diffi-

cult to detect because of its electrical neutrality and extreme lightness. Wang Ganchang (1907–1998) designed an experimental setting for tracing this particle. With the help of Wang's design, Allen Stuart succeeded in recording this particle in 1942.

In the 1940s, Qian Sanqiang (1913–1992) obtained the fine structure of an α-ray when he worked in Paris at the National Laboratory, directed by F. Joliot-Curie. In 1946–1947, at the Nuclear Chemistry Lab of the College of France, he confirmed experimentally the tri-split of a nucleus and developed an explanatory theory for this phenomenon in the next year.

As was the case with physicists and mathematicians, Chinese astronomers were mainly working abroad in the early days of the 20th century. In the United States, Zhang Yuzhe was observing a minor planet closely with a 60-centimeter reflecting telescope and finally collected enough data for calculating its orbit. He named this minor planet "Zhonghua," or "China," in honor of his homeland.

Organizations: When more Chinese were trained to be scientists and experts in technology, special organizations were founded for sharing information in the field and for science education in China. The Chinese Science Society, founded in 1914 in the United States, claimed as its objectives the dissemination of the knowledge of science, the promotion of the use of the scientific method, and the encouragement of the "scientific spirit" called for in the May Fourth Movement. By "scientific spirit," the scientists meant the new philosophy and worldview prevailing in Europe and the United States since the Scientific Revolution. In 1915, the society enrolled more than 70 members in physics, mathematics, chemistry, biology, agricultural engineering, mechanical engineering, electric engineering, civil engineering, and metallurgy. During the four years leading up to 1919, the society held four meetings, attended by 604 members, including 48 economists.

With the founding of this society, two journals were published. *Science*, a monthly, was the major vehicle to disseminate the newest academic proceedings of research in all the fields. *Science Pictorial*, with a target audience of non-specialists, assumed the task of promoting the understanding of science among laymen by introducing basic knowledge of science and the latest scientific achievements.

The society and the affiliated journals returned to China in 1918, when many of its founders decided the environment for scientific research was more hospitable there.

The Main Achievements, 1925–1949: Mathematics was the first field in which Chinese scholars had opportunities to demonstrate their talent. In 1930, having earned his reputation with other papers on mathematical analysis, Chen Jiangong published *On Trigonometric Functions*, the first monograph on this subject. His work won worldwide recognition. Chen was followed by a group of Chinese mathematicians, working both in China and abroad, in the studies of Fourier functions, differential equations, and variational method. In the field of topology, Jiang Zehan, a Harvard-educated mathematician, achieved important progress on Green Functions in 1932. In 1936, Hua Luogeng (1910–1985), known in the United States as Loo-Keng Hua, published papers on the Warling problem and the Tarry problem, two acclaimed problems in numbers theory. Hua had learned mathematics almost entirely on his own.

Chemical Engineering: As early as 1921 and 1922, Hou Debang (1890–1974), known in the United States as Te-pang Hou, and his colleagues started researching new methods in manufacturing certain alkali, and soon they were able to apply their findings in mass production. Hou's monograph *The Manufacture of Soda* (1932) remains one of the standard references in the field. His method, adopted by many other countries, was named Hou's Method to honor his contribution to the chemical industry.

Geology: Chinese geologists had to start their work by making geological maps for China, which was an essential precondition for almost all further field studies in the vast country. Between 1924 and 1929, three regional maps were finished, covering a small portion of the total territory of 3.7 million square miles. This work was interrupted by the war of 1937, when the Japanese army invaded and occupied a great part of eastern and northeastern China. Theoretical studies in geology were focusing on developing a comprehensive model for Chinese topographic and geological features, represented by Li Siguang's books in 1926 and 1936.

Paleoanthropology: In December 1929, at an excavation site near Beijing, Pei Wenzhong and J. G. Anderson found a skull that was later proved to be from *Homo erectus*, a species believed to be one of the most immediate ancestors of modern humans. Found with the skull were stone tools and wood ashes, suggesting that a group of highly developed proto-humans was living in this area some 1.5 million years ago. Seven years later, in November 1936, Jia Lanpo (1908–2001) found three more skulls and other articles in a nearby site, which confirmed the existence of Peking man, named after the nearby city (Peking is the old transliteration of the name of the city, which is now called Beijing). Many Chinese anthropologists claimed that Peking man was the remote ancestor of the modern Chinese people.

Astronomy: In 1904, a group of Christian missionaries near the city of Shanghai built Sheshan Observatory, the first observatory of modern astronomy in China. Astronomers at Sheshan Observatory concentrated on observing sunspots through the late 1950s. At Xujiahui, a sister observatory of Sheshan, time signals were given twice a day, beginning in 1914, with an accuracy of one-hundredth of a second. Directed by Zhang Yuzhe (1902–1986), who had discovered the minor planet *Zhonghua*, the Chinese astronomers obtained essential data for about 160 minor planets by 1941.

Organizations: Associations of scientists and engineers played a significant role in the development of science and technology during the second quarter of the 20th century, when the Chinese government at the time could not come up with its own policy on science and technology.

The Chinese Physical Society: In the winter of 1931, Paul Langevin (1872–1946), sent by the League of Nations, went to China to survey the status of science and education. In accordance with his suggestion, the Chinese Physical Society was founded in August 1932 at Qinghua (Tsinghua) University in Beijing. Nineteen physicists met at the preliminary conference. The next year about 80 more physicists were accepted as members, including Langevin, the first foreign member of this society. In its first annual meeting, 10 papers were presented, among which were studies of X-rays and spectra by Wu Youxun and others. The meeting set three subcommittees for the objectives it was to commit to, namely the publication of an academic journal in physics, the normalization and unification of terminology, and the promotion of physics education in universities and colleges.

The Chinese Physical Society had held 16 annual meetings by the time the Communists came to power in 1949. The journal of the society, known as the *Chinese Journal of Physics*, in English, French, and German with abstracts of each article in Chinese, was published between 1933 and 1950. Its publication was sporadic, often interrupted by war.

The Chinese terminology used in physics and in other branches of science and technology as well, came to be a major problem for three reasons. First, modern science and engineering could hardly find counterparts in Chinese traditional scholarship. Often the terms were not actually "translated" into Chinese. Instead, the scientists and translators had to create new Chinese terms for objects and concepts that were unknown to the Chinese. Second, when physics was for the first time introduced to the Chinese, it was used by Chinese scholars with little knowledge of science and by the missionaries with limited training in Chinese and physics. Naturally, the translations of the texts were not always

authentic or adequate. The terms were often awkward or even arbitrary. Third, the first generations of Chinese physicists were educated abroad in Europe and the United States. When they returned to China, their knowledge of the terminology was in different languages. With the coordination of the Chinese Physical Society, the normalization of terms was slowly completed. In 1934, the first list of more than 5,000 terms was published in 42 volumes.

Physics Education at Universities: Recognizing how the knowledge of modern science, especially physics, was needed for the new generations of Chinese students, the Chinese Physical Society took education as one of its major objectives. Many of the students in the 1920s and 1930s were educated at the leading universities in the United States and Europe. In addition to receiving training in physics, they had the experience of an entirely new pedagogy. Upon their return to China, they created departments of physics in many universities, using textbooks they had brought back and conducting demonstrations they had seen in foreign classrooms. By the late 1930s, all leading Chinese universities had built their own physics departments. Among the students from this period, three were to win Nobel Prizes in the 1950s and 1970s. Many more worked in China and, in the 1950s and 1960s, became the leaders in China's nuclear missile projects.

Associations for Chemists: In 1922, a group of Chinese graduate students in chemistry at the University of Chicago proposed an organization for Chinese chemists living in the United States. Supported avidly by Chinese students at the University of Michigan, the University of Illinois, and the University of Wisconsin, the Chinese Chemical Society was founded in September 1922 in Chicago. A Chinese Association of Chemistry had been formed in 1908 in Paris, organized by seven Chinese students studying in France, England, and Belgium. This earlier association, however, disappeared a few years after its founding when the members graduated and lost touch with one another.

In 1932, a nationwide union was founded in Nanjing, China, at a meeting of 45 chemists, including some of the members of the Chinese Chemical Society from Chicago. The new union, named the Chinese Association of Chemistry, was to play a central role among Chinese chemists during the next 17 years until 1950 and would be reestablished in the mid-1950s in the People's Republic of China. This association had two journals: the *Journal of the Chinese Association of Chemistry*, devoted to academic research, was published in English and other European languages; *Chemistry*, the popular magazine, mainly reported new developments in chemistry achieved abroad, the pedagogy of chemistry at the universities, and news about the domestic chemical industry.

Other Associations: The Chinese Association of Geology was founded in 1922 with 26 members. One of the earliest unions of scientists in China, it remained active for 35 years. Two periodicals, *Journal of the Chinese Association of Geology* and *Geological Review,* were published continuously until 1952. This association was extremely strong in international cooperation. In the beginning, it had three foreign members, including J. G. Anderson, the Swedish geologist and archaeologist who took part in the excavation at the site of Peking man. By 1947, the heyday of this association, there had been 28 international correspondence members from eight countries, including C. D. (Charles Doolittle) Walcott (1850–1927) and H. G. Osborn of the United States, M. Boule (1861–c. 1930s) of France, and V. Loczy of Austria.

7. The People's Republic: The First 30 Years

The First Steps

After more than a century of social and political turmoil, the first half of the 1950s saw a new China where programs of land reform and rapid industrialization were undertaken. The first steps of the Communist government regarding the development of science and technology sought to recover and reorganize. On October 19, 1949, fewer than three weeks after the founding of the People's Republic, the central government appointed Guo Moruo (1892–1978), a paleophilologist and historian, to preside over the Chinese Academy of Science. Reorganized from parts of the old Academia Sinica and the Beiping Research Academy, the Chinese Academy consisted of 14 research institutes, one observatory, and a lab for industrial research, with about 200 research fellows at its founding in November 1949.

Starting in April 1952, the government carried out a program to restructure the science departments in colleges and universities in order to meet the needs of the nation's development. Existing departments were sometimes redivided and recombined, while some new departments were also founded.

At the same time, research institutes and laboratories were set up in various industrial enterprises, and governmental departments were established to deal with more specific topics and problems in their fields.

In order to enforce its function in organizing and conducting research in different fields, the Chinese Academy of Science established four separate departments in June 1956. They were the Departments of Physical Sciences, Bio and Geo Sciences, Technology, and Social Sciences. Two hundred and thirty-three scientists and scholars were elected to the academy, representing the elite group of Chinese science.

By 1955, the Chinese Academy of Science had under its jurisdiction 44 research institutes with 2,485 research specialists in all fields. At the same time, a teaching staff of 42,000 was working at 194 universities and colleges. More than 260,000 students were enrolled by 1955, twice as many as in 1949.

Soviet Assistance: From February 28 through June 17, 1953, a Chinese science delegation headed by Qian Sanqiang visited the Soviet Union at the invitation of the Soviet Academy of Science. Twenty-six Chinese scientists, specializing in 19 fields, discussed with their Soviet colleagues the possibility of establishing close cooperation between the two countries. This visit resulted in programs that sent scholars and graduate students to the Soviet Union, shared information in science and technology, and used Soviet consultants for Chinese projects. Eight hundred Soviet professors and associate professors taught in Chinese universities.

Achievements: Within five years, a preliminary system of higher education in science was taking shape. Research institutes and laboratories had also obtained better equipment and more up-to-date information. The major concern of the academy was to "serve the socialist construction" or, in other words, to solve the problems encountered in industrial and agricultural development for the region.

The 10,000-kilowatt hydraulic generator, the steam turbine, and the steel plants at Wuhan and Baotou incorporated many research projects in both theoretical and applied science. Geographical surveys in many provinces were finished and geographical maps completed.

The Tasks Set for the Academy in 1955: In June 1955, the academy held a meeting of all its members to discuss the principles for its future work. At this meeting, it was decided that the academy was to concentrate on basic scientific research and to solve "problems essential to the national economy." Ten topics were given the highest priority. Peaceful utilization of atomic energy, construction of large steel enterprises, liquid fuel development, earthquake research, unified planning and comprehensive utilization of the major river valleys, a biological and geographical survey in southern China, and the development of antibiotics were some of the areas where considerable progress was achieved during the late 1950s.

In January 1956, the Communist Party called a meeting for making policies concerning intellectuals (including scientists) and the development of science and technology. Zhou Enlai, premier of the State Council, and Mao Zedong, chairman of the People's Republic and the Communist Party, delivered speeches emphasizing the indispensable role that science and technology were to play in the industrialization and modernization of the country. They assured the intellectuals that criticism and suggestions would be welcome, and that the Communists would learn from experts.

In May 1956, Mao Zedong affirmed that debate and competition in scientific research and other academic activities were beneficial for the advancement of knowledge and that it was counterproductive to label one school, one opinion, or one style as heresy. The issues and disagreements, he said, should be solved through free discussion and academic practice. "Let a hundred flowers blossom and a hundred schools of thought contend," was the slogan.

The Twelve-Year Program: In order to reinforce scientific research and cooperation, in June 1956 the State Council set up the Science and Technology Planning Commission. The council had also authorized Chen Yi and two other high-ranking officials in January 1956 to form a working group to create a general plan for development in science and technology. More than 600 scholars took part in the drafting of the work; thousands were consulted for their suggestions. The first long-term plan, known as the *Long-Range Program for Scientific and Technological Development: 1956–1967*, or the "Twelve-Year Program," was finished and adopted by the State Council by the end of 1956. This program listed atomic energy, jet engineering, computers, semiconductors, electronics, and automated controls as main areas for development.

In March 1956, the State Council set up the State Technology Commission to supervise the Twelve-Year Program. The main purpose of the commission was to make long-term and annual national plans, to budget the national funds for scientific research, and to coordinate the planning of key projects.

In November 1958, the State Technology Commission merged with the State Science and Technology Planning Commission to form the State Science and Technology Commission, which became the central department of the government in charge of research and other activities in science and technology. Its mission included advising the central government, regulating and planning the nation's research work, coordinating and organizing major projects, and maintaining the use of scientific information, equipment, and personnel.

The Interruptions: From the winter of 1956 through the end of May 1957, the Communist Party officially invited criticisms and suggestions. Many intellectuals, especially some leading scientists, complained about the imposition of the party's authority upon scientific research and academic activities. Perhaps expecting only minor, friendly criticism, the Communist Party was shocked by this challenge to its leadership role. The outspoken critics were denounced as "rightists," and most of them were soon dismissed from their positions, assigned to non-professional jobs, or even exiled to provincial camps for forced labor. Thousands of scientists and experts in related fields were stunned by the harsh punishments, which in effect broke the cooperative relationship between the party and the intellectuals. Having effectively silenced the voices of criticism, the party in turn made it very difficult for its leaders to receive honest advice from experts.

An immediate consequence was the Great Leap Forward movement in 1958. The pragmatism and rationalism seen in the Twelve-Year Program were no longer honored. The anxiety to become a world power "in fifteen years," as the party had called for, could be seen everywhere. Proper procedures for research and production yielded to political needs, and experts were overruled by zealous mobs. Politically important dates, such as July 1 (the party's birthday), became the deadlines for presenting research results.

In order to reach steel production comparable to developed countries, small rudimentary furnaces were built in backyards all over the country. Most of these furnaces used scrap metal in the place of ores and consumed charcoal processed from wood as fuel. Unfortunately, most of the pig iron produced by these furnaces was of such low quality that it was of little industrial use.

By late 1959, the catastrophic consequences of the Great Leap Forward had become too apparent to ignore. Recognizing the mistakes, the party put forth a series of policies of correction. Rational measures replaced some of the extreme measures of

1957–1958, and the rehabilitation of many of the so-called rightists was quietly carried out.

The official announcement of the *Fourteen Points Proposal on the Present Work of Research Institutions of Natural Sciences* and Nie Rongzhen's interpretation of this document in July 1961 marked a deviation from the policies of the Anti-Rightist Movement and the Great Leap Forward. Nie, the highest party official in charge of the nation's research in science and technology, emphasized that it was wrong to label a scientist "anti-socialist" or "counter-revolutionary" based on his academic preferences or his views on certain scientific theories, such as the discredited Soviet theory of genetics. He criticized some research institutes for spending too much time on political activities. According to him, the research fellows should devote 85 percent of their time to their academic work.

In the next year, Nie presided over the National Conference on Science and Technology. Zhou Enlai, the premier, and Chen Yi, the vice premier of the State Council, attended the meeting and delivered important speeches. Both leaders affirmed before their audience of more than 300 scientists that the majority of Chinese intellectuals were patriotic and that they were no longer bourgeoisie but part of the working class. In other words, at least in theory, the intellectuals were no longer to be discriminated against politically but should be welcomed into the vanguard of the revolution. The policies in the next few years up to 1966, when the Cultural Revolution started, were mainly based on this understanding.

A Review of the Twelve-Year Program in 1962: By the end of 1962, the State Science and Technology Commission reviewed the progress of the Twelve-Year Program. The review showed that 46 out of 54 major projects had been completed.

The comprehensive geological survey of natural resources, carried out by 11 exploration teams, was completed in five major regions, covering about half of the territory of the country. One hundred and thirty minerals were mapped and listed. With the newly discovered Daqing oil field in production by the early 1960s, the nation's oil shortage was effectively ended.

Between 1956 and 1962, China had begun to reap some fruit from its emphasis on the development of heavy industry. The successful production of a hydraulic press with a capacity of 12,000 tons, a generator with an inner water-cooled stator and rotor, ships of 5,000-ton displacement, and 135-ton electric locomotives all demonstrated China's increasing industrial strength. Although such products were not very impressive by American standards, in the context of China's industrialization they represented unprecedented achievements.

Although applied technology that would be more significant to the nation's economy was always given higher priority, Chinese scientists also achieved significant progress in several fields of high-tech and theoretical science. The first nuclear reactor was put into operation in late 1958, followed almost immediately by a cyclotron, a special scientific apparatus for producing beams of electrically charged particles with very high energy levels. A computer center was set up in Beijing in 1959, only some 10 years later than in developed countries. In February 1960, a sounding rocket was launched successfully, marking the beginning of a "space era" for China.

By 1962, according to the official statistics, China had 1,296 scientific institutes with nearly 70,000 research workers, representing an increase of about 300 percent since 1956, when the Twelve-Year Program started. But China's pace in science and technology still lagged behind other countries. The nation's industry could provide less than one-tenth of the machinery needed for China's agriculture and forestry industries. Metallurgy was still far behind in both lab research and large-scale production of most alloys and high-quality steel. By 1962, China had only 10 large computers in operation. Moreover, these computers were significantly slower than their U.S. and Soviet counterparts.

At the same time, the Sino-Soviet alliance broke down. About 2,000 Russian consultants and other experts left China, jeopardizing hundreds of research projects. As a result of the U.S. policy of containment during the 1950s, European countries and the United States limited exchanges in scientific information and personnel with China. To a large degree, China was isolated from the international scientific community. Chinese scientists had few opportunities to learn what their colleagues in other countries were doing and what had been achieved abroad.

The Formation of the New Program for 1963-1972: The review of 1962 showed that most of the major objectives of the Twelve-Year Program had been fulfilled or nearly fulfilled five years ahead of schedule. Inspired by what had been achieved, the State Science and Technology Commission started to make a new program for the next 10 years. Taking into account the suggestions and advice from nearly 10,000 scientists and experts in engineering, social science, and macro planning, the design of the program was finished by December 1963. It was later known as the Ten-Year Program.

The difficulties of facing hostility from the superpowers—the United States and the Soviet Union—and the widespread famine that had claimed millions of lives in 1960 and 1961 left visible marks on the new program. The program focused on two main areas: high technology to help strengthen the nation's defense and agricultural research to help feed the nation.

The Objectives of the New Program: The new program for 1963–1972 had established as its objectives 32 major projects. In agriculture, 10 central labs were set up for studies in agricultural meteorology, water conservancy, improvement of salinized soil, forestry, and grassland protection. In industry and technology, 13 projects were implemented to strengthen the nation's modernization. Petroleum chemistry and chemical engineering, research and production of high-strength and high-temperature materials, steel metallurgy, high-precision industrial meters, and transistors were given highest priority. For theoretical research, six main directions were identified as having the "potential for bringing about fundamental changes in industry and defense," including laser technology and molecular biology.

In addition to those projects, standardization and normalization of measurement units and measurement apparatus were recognized as a must, and scientific information and patent regulation also received attention. By the end of 1963, the new Ten-

Year Program was approved by the Central Committee of the Chinese Communist Party and the State Council. About 2,000 institutes, 1,000 universities, and numerous labs and research units in industry and agricultural communes were employed in helping modernize China.

The First Three Years: During the period 1963–1966, research in electronics led to the development of such high-tech equipment as an electronic microscope, a radio telescope, a high-speed camera, the NH4-molecule clock, and a 300,000-kilowatt (kW) water-cooling generator. At the same time, computers were used more and more extensively in scientific research and industry. A number of comprehensive industrial centers were set up in central and southwest China, where natural resources were abundant but industry had been previously absent. By situating the factories and mills right next to the natural resources they exploited, the government hoped to increase the efficiency of industrial production.

In June 1964, China launched a carrier rocket. Four months later, on October 16, 1964, the explosion of the atomic bomb made China the fifth nation with nuclear capabilities. Immediately after the explosion, China declared that it would use nuclear weapons only in retaliation against a nuclear strike. As a result of China's membership in the "nuclear club," China became a significant force in international politics.

The synthesis of materials closely connected with life functions was essential for theoretical studies in molecular biology and had invaluable potential for medical applications. Bovine insulin was the only protein of a structure known to scientists in the early 1960s. Since 1958, the topnotch experts in biochemistry, organic chemistry, biology, and cytology had been working together to create a replica of insulin. In early 1966, the experts successfully produced synthetic crystalline bovine insulin that proved to be a precise replica of natural insulin. This success momentarily placed China on the forefront of the development of biochemistry in the world.

The Cultural Revolution: Parallel to the development in science and technology, calls for devotion to communism grew in intensity. Mao Zedong and some other leaders of the Communist Party were deeply concerned that the government and people's "overemphasis" of material progress might lead to the dissipation of revolutionary fervor. This concern was directly reflected in Mao's policies towards the scientists during the Cultural Revolution (1966–1976). During the fanatic first years of the Cultural Revolution, many scientists were persecuted by radicals who understood little science. Many scientists were charged with disloyalty to the party; more were sent to the countryside so that their ideological outlook could be reformed through hard labor. Except for a few projects immediately connected with the nation's defense, developments in science and technology were severely retarded.

Any progress achieved during the Cultural Revolution was either defense-related or the continuation of projects begun earlier. On June 17, 1969, fewer than five years after the first explosion of the atomic bomb, a thermonuclear bomb (a "hydrogen bomb") was tested in the desert in west China. On April 24, 1970, a satellite, named *Dongfanghong* (named after "The East Is Red," a song in praise of Chairman Mao), weighing 383 pounds was launched into an orbit with a perigee at 275 miles, marking the start of Chinese space exploration. With the launch of *Experiment I* on March 3, 1971, Chinese space technology demonstrated its maturity in satellite making, launching, tracking, and control.

8. THE PEOPLE'S REPUBLIC: 1978–1985

After the Cultural Revolution: The Cultural Revolution ended in late 1976. It was recognized as a disaster which had brought chaos to the country even before its dramatic ending following the death of Mao Zedong. Shortly after a transitional period, Deng Xiaoping came to power. Deng realized that China could not match developed countries in almost any aspect of economic development. He also knew that the nation's prosperity and dignity were essentially relying on the development of science and technology. He therefore took the reform of the academic research system as one of his first projects. Under Deng, the Chinese government began to improve basic working conditions for intellectuals, including the scientists. The intellectuals were again counted as members of the working class—that was to say, their political status would be no lower than that of the workers and peasants. Their research was again appreciated, and their contribution to the nation acclaimed.

In the fall of 1977, the Chinese Academy of Science, at the direction of the State Council and the Central Committee of the party, conducted a meeting to draft a program for the nation's science and technology in the coming decade. More than a thousand experts and scholars attended the meeting, while another 20,000 were consulted for suggestions and criticism. In January 1978, the *Draft Outline Program for National Scientific and Technological Development, 1978–1985* (commonly known as the Eight-Year Program) was finished. This Eight-Year Program explicitly stated that science and technology were the keys to the modernization of the nation and that the "new features of modern science" should be fully recognized in conducting the nation's development.

The program divided the nation's economy into 27 categories such as agriculture, industry, national defense, transportation, environment, and medical/clinic science, to which 108 projects were assigned as objectives for research workers over the coming years. Among the 108 projects, 17 involved research in agriculture, 7 in environmental science, 25 in industrial research and development, 14 in high technology, and 27 in theoretical research. Agriculture, energy, material, electronics, laser, space technology, high-energy physics, and genetic engineering were singled out as vital or potentially vital fields for the development of the nation in the future.

In contrast to the Twelve-Year Program of 1956 and the Ten-Year Program of 1963, the Eight-Year Program gave more attention to theoretical research and high-tech development. An electronic accelerator of 4 trillion electron volts (eV), an observatory for modern astrophysics, cytology and photosynthesis, catalysis theory, agricultural genetics, engineering thermophysics, high-speed fluid dynamics, electronics, artificial intelligence, cybernetics and system control, optimizing theory, and history of science were among the topics given priority.

In April 1979 and December 1980, the Eight-Year Program was revised. According to the official report, by 1985 the main objectives of the plan were fulfilled. Hybrid rice, offshore oil-drilling platforms, vanadium-titanium enrichment techniques, a polyester plant with an annual yield of 15,000 tons, and a hydraulic power station at Gezhouba on the Yangtze were a few of the 37,722 items recorded for their "major significance" to the nation's economy during the 1980–1985 period. The multiple independently targeted re-entry vehicle launched in September 1981, the long-range missile launched by a nuclear-powered submarine from under water in October 1982, and a computer with a speed of 100 million operations per second exemplified the achievements in high-tech, reflecting the developments in all branches of science and industry.

National Labs: From 1980 to 1985, the state established 120 national labs, some of which were remodeled and upgraded from existing labs and some of which were reorganized to meet new requirements.

The Molecular Biology and Enzyme Lab carried on the study of bovine insulin, which had been one of the major achievements of Chinese biochemists in the mid-1960s. The Organic Geochemistry Lab, the Genetic Engineering Lab, the Micro-circulation Lab, and the Organic Chemistry and Rare Elements Lab were all pioneering in their fields. The testing centers, such as Chinese Ship Center and Railroad Center, provided large-scale and high-precision equipment and well-trained operating staffs. As a result, many complicated tests needed for scientific research and industrial application became possible and affordable.

In theoretical studies, the Hefei National Synchrotron Radiation Lab was founded in 1984 and, by 1989, had been finished with an electron accelerator of 200 million electron volts (MeV), a storage circle of 800

MeV, and laboratories. Five lab stations could work simultaneously on two beams of soft X-rays and three beams of Vacuum Ultra-Violet (VUV) Light generated by the accelerator.

International Exchange and Scientific Information: In the 1950s, the People's Republic of China received Soviet assistance in all aspects of science and technology. Of the 13,656 items listed in various agreements between the two governments, 10,819 were completed by 1960. A long period of seclusion followed 1960, brought about by ideological differences with most Soviet-bloc countries and by the U.S. policy of containment. Starting in 1979, Deng Xiaoping inaugurated a policy of reform and openness to the outside world, which led to cooperation and exchanges in science and technology with 106 countries, including 53 that had formal governmental agreements on cooperation and exchange with China.

Japan was among the first to have governmental cooperation in science with China. During the period 1980–1986, the Cooperation Committee in Science and Technology held four meetings, resulting in 34 cooperative projects in 10 fields, including an agreement on the peaceful utilization of nuclear energy. By 1985, 1,236 Chinese scholars and interns had been accepted by Japanese enterprises to learn business management and administration, and about 2,000 Japanese specialists visited China to work with their Chinese colleagues on joint projects.

In the matter of scientific cooperation and exchange, China's relationship with France was considerably better than with most other developed countries. In 1978, the two governments signed a cooperation agreement that started the exchange between the two countries and soon led to 382 joint projects. At the same time, 25 Chinese university departments in science and technology established partnerships with French counterparts. In 1979 alone, 597 Chinese scientists visited France. In return, various Chinese institutes hosted 473 French scholars in the same year.

Other examples of early cooperation included Antarctic exploration assisted by the New Zealand and Australian governments. In 1984, China and Australia signed a memorandum on Antarctic exploration.

From 1978 to 1985, 535 groups of Chinese scientists visited Germany, and 514 German groups went to China. In 1984, the two governments signed a number of agreements on scientific cooperation, including one on nuclear energy.

Cooperation with the United States started with an agreement signed by President Jimmy Carter and Deng Xiaoping in January 1979. By 1985, the two governments had agreements on more than 400 joint projects. After six meetings on nuclear cooperation, the United States and China reached an agreement on cooperation in the peaceful use of nuclear energy in 1985, followed by a new round of talks on space cooperation.

Establishing the Information Network: By 1985, the Chinese Scientific Information System had recorded 16,000 periodicals in all the major European languages and 6,500 journals in Chinese, which embraced about 24 million items of information. After 1981, the Department of Petroleum Chemistry and the Department of Conventional Weapons connected with the databases of DIALOG. Two years later, the Chinese Institute of Scientific Information, the central controller of Chinese network, developed the CCITT system, which was compatible with ESA-IRS and EURONET of European countries and with TELENET, TYMNET, and DIALOG of the United States.

9. THE PEOPLE'S REPUBLIC SINCE 1985

Experimental High Energy Physics: Nuclear accelerators are necessary for advanced research in many fields. Beginning in 1985, China paid great attention to the research and construction of all kinds of nuclear accelerators.

A heavy ion cyclotron with a 12-meter acceleration radius was installed in the Institute of Modern Physics in Lanzhou in January 1987. Later in the same year, a linear electron accelerator, affiliated with the Beijing Electron-Positron Collider (BEPC) Project, was put to work, followed by the cyclotron electron storage. The collider, aiming at detecting quarks, was an apparatus for both theoretical study and industrial research in applied surface physics, material development, Hyper LIC design and manufacture, and medical research.

The BEPC became operational in October 1988, marking a new phase of Chinese research in high-energy physics. The first electronic-induced linear accelerator was put to use at the Institute of Physical Engineering in late May of 1989. The functional energy of BEPC—that is, the amount of energy that can be used during an experiment—was 5.6 giga electron-volts (GeV), which averaged around the same energy level of the similarly designed colliders installed in the 1970s in Europe, the United States, and the Soviet Union.

Parallel with research in elementary particle physics, China also made great strides in the study of controlled fusion. It was reported in January 1987 that the first magnetic bounding plasma apparatus, HT-6M, for high-power microwave heating and plasma experiments was installed in the Hefei Plasma Institute of the Chinese Academy of Science. This apparatus was believed to be part of an ambitious plan for controlled fusion. In November 1989, a laser-irritated fusion facility in Shanghai recorded a power output of 2 billion kW, comparable with the Shiva or Argus facilities of the United States.

Space Technology: China's first synchronous satellite—one that appears to be "fixed" at a point in the sky when observed from the ground—with an effective load of 3,100 pounds was launched on April 8, 1984. The second was launched on February 1, 1986, with a CZ-3 carrier rocket. Three weeks later, that satellite entered the designed orbit and started to transmit TV programs. Another improved version was launched on March 7, 1987, less than a year from the previous launching. On December 23, 1988, a fourth one was launched from Xichang Space Center with a CZ-3 rocket. U.S., French, German, Iranian, and Australian scientists and officials were invited to observe the launching. With those satellites, it was reported in February 1989 that a satellite communication network was complete, covering the entire Chinese territory.

The late 1980s also saw a series of experimental satellite launchings. On September 18, 1987, after spending eight days in orbit, a satellite was recovered in the province of Sichuan. Launched by a CZ-2 rocket, this satellite carried more than 70 samples of plant seeds, tissues, and fungi for research in agriculture, cytology, genetics, and microbiology. An institute specializing in the research of near-zero gravity was established at Harbin Polytech University soon after the recovery. A year later, on August 6, 1988, a second recoverable satellite was launched. Eight days later, this spacecraft reentered the atmosphere and landed in a pre-determined area. On September 7, 1988, a solar synchronous satellite was launched for meteorological research from Taiyuan Space Center with a CZ-4 rocket.

The rapid development in high-tech industries also benefited China's military. In September 1988, a Chinese nuclear submarine launched an intercontinental missile from under water. The missile later landed in a pre-set target area. China remains years behind the United States and Russia in missile and submarine technology, but that launch was considered an example of a successful application of Chinese rocket technology.

The Antarctic and Ocean Explorations: In the late 1980s, China sent three teams to the Antarctic area and carried out large-scale studies in geology, meteorology, oceanography, marine biology, and mineralogy.

Early in July 1984, China and Australia signed an agreement on Antarctic exploration. Shortly after the first visit to Antarctica on November 20, 1985, the second team arrived at the Great Wall Station, the first Chinese Antarctic research station, on King George Island, near the Shetland Islands, to join scientists from more than 10 nations. During their four-month-long stay, 40 scientists worked on 76 projects concerning Antarctic geography, atmospheric physics, glaciers, and communication in polar areas. In August 1986, the Chinese exploration ship *Poles* took a third team of 88 scientists to the Great Wall Station. That team completed the construction of the station by building labs, a medical and support center, an oil depot, and a power station for year-round stay. From that time on, Antarctic exploration became a part of the regular geophysical and oceanographic survey for Chinese scientists. In February 1989, the second research station, the Zhongshan, was completed on the mainland of Antarctica.

In addition to polar exploration, China carried out a series of ocean surveys. From November 1986 to March 1987, the Chinese exploration ship *Xiangyanghong 5* took part in a joint survey with U.S. and Australian ships. *Xiangyanghong 5* studied tropical weather in the west Pacific and monsoons in the Gulf of Carpentaria, Australia. At the same time, a branch of the third Antarctic exploration team was sailing in the Atlantic and the Indian Oceans, collecting samples and data in a voyage of 17,000 miles. From May through November 1988, the Chinese exploration ship *Xiangyanghong 16* completed a survey of ocean-bottom mineralogy in the eastern Pacific.

Hybrid Rice: Feeding China's large population has always been a source of research for Chinese scientists. In 1973, Yuan Longping, a research worker at the Hunan Institute of Agriculture, began to grow several varieties of hybrid rice which demonstrated a strong resistance to diseases and pests, while reaching a 20 percent increase in yield. In 1987, hybrid rice was planted in 10.9 million hectares of fields, with an average 6,615 kilograms-per-hectare yield. That meant that hybrid rice accounted for 42 percent of the total rice production of China. Yuan was awarded special recognition by the United Nations Educational, Scientific, and Cultural Organization (UNESCO).

Awards System: Early in December 1978, the State Council revised The Regulations on Awards for Inventions, first enacted in 1963 but never enforced because of objections from "leftist" officials. The officials argued that the glory for any accomplishment should "belong to the people and the party." To implement the regulation, an independent committee for appraisal and registration was set up in April 1979. The independent committee consisted of 32 experts and senior engineers, with a consulting and assisting staff of 258 specialists in 12 fields. From 1978 through 1990, about 1,700 National Invention Awards were made. Among them were 30 Rank A awards for achievements such as developing techniques for separating titanium from iron in a blast furnace, steel making, and the breeding of a new hybrid strain of cotton.

For achievements in science, the Interim Regulations of the Chinese Academy of Science on Science Cash Awards were implemented in 1980. Among those receiving Rank A awards were researchers in studies of the synthesis of bovine insulin and the geological research for the Daqing oil field. In 1984, the award was replaced with the National Awards for Science and Technology Progress, which were established distinctly and exclusively for items that were "highly advanced in science, effectively beneficial for furthering the progress of science and technology, and extremely profitable to the nation's economy and the society."

Since the mid-1980s, many organizations and institutions of scientific research started to establish secondary awards, usually named after celebrated Chinese scientists in their fields. The Chinese Physics Society, for instance, issued a set of awards for researches in experimental physics (Hu Awards), optics (Yao Awards), solid state physics (Ye Awards), and atomic physics (Wu Awards). The Geology Society set up the Zhu Award in its field.

The Principles of Reform: Until the early 1980s, the development of science and technology was generally planned, organized, funded, and supervised by the state. The results of scientific research or inventions in technology belonged, accordingly, to the state as a whole rather than to any individual person or institution. Sharing information and inventions was considered "Communist cooperation." In December 1980, the National Conference of Science and Technology listed a number of problems in the administration of science and technology to be solved in the coming decade, among which the management of scientific achievements was prominent.

Since the implementation of economic reform and the open-door policy in the late 1970s, the old system did not fit the marketization of the national economy. In April 1981, the State Commission put forth, though cautiously, a proposal discussing the possibility of "paid transfers" of inventions, scientific information, and other scientific achievements.

On April 1, 1984, after a five-year study of patent laws in 29 nations, the Chinese Patent Law came into effect. By the end of 1985, the Patent Bureau had processed 14,372 applications, including 4,961 from abroad. On September 10, 1985, the bureau issued the first 150 certificates for inventions and merchandise designs. The affiliated library, with a collection of 20 million patent documents from 14 nations and two international organizations, was opened to the public at the same time and offered service to more than 10 million patrons in its first year.

By December 31, 1991, the Chinese Patent Bureau had received 217,383 applications, of which 86,253 were approved.

Research Funds: The National Science Fund, formerly the Academy of Science Fund, was the major fund among the 22 available for research in science and technology. In 1986, 3,432 projects were funded by the National Science Fund. The secondary funds included the Young Scientist Fund and the Spark Fund, established in 1987.

Government grants and business contributions were the two major sources of funds for most research projects. In 1991, the total budget for scientific research and technology development was 47.427 billion yuan (approximately $5.714 billion U.S.), among which 15.623 billion, or 33 percent, came from governmental funds.

The total research and development expenditure in 1991 was 14.23 billion yuan, which constituted 4.1 percent of the government's annual budget. The share of research and development in the total gross national product was 0.72 percent, considerably lower than that of developed countries/regions, such as 2.69 percent in

the United States. Of the funds spent on research in 1991, 80.26 percent was used on industrial research and development, 6.78 percent on theoretical and comprehensive scientific research, and 5.56 percent on agriculture, with the remainder spent on smaller fields.

Governmental Programs in the Late 1980s: Six major programs were at work in the late 1980s, each with a well-defined and specific purpose. The National Science and Technology Program (NSTP) and the National Industrial Development Program (NIDP) were most closely connected to the mainstream of the nation's economic development. During its first phase of implementation in 1988, the NSTP made an investment of 6.75 billion yuan for 76 projects, which generated 4,696 business contracts. The second phase started in 1991, when 170 projects were identified. The NIDP was more closely connected with plants and manufacturers. It set up a number of "models," both large-scale production centers and industrial assembly lines, to demonstrate and popularize new technology and new designs.

The High-Tech Program (also known as the 863 Program, because it was first put forth by a group of scientists in the third month of 1986) identified seven categories, including bio-engineering, space technology, and information science, as the leading areas on which Chinese scientists should focus in order to achieve a balance with developed nations. In 1991, 11,165 personnel with a 186-million yuan budget were involved in research work in this program. Government resources funded all the projects implemented by this program.

Based on the High-Tech Program, the Torch Program was enacted in 1988 to bring high-tech achievements into profitable application through marketing and merchandising. By 1991, 878 sites, including 27 industrial zones, were set up for this purpose.

For agriculture, the Spark Program performed a role similar to that of the High-Tech Program in industry. Proposed in 1986, the budget of this program kept increasing and reached 5.96 billion yuan in 1991, of which less than 0.4 percent, or 20 million, was funded by the government.

Programs in the 1990s: In the early 1990s, two national programs were proposed for strengthening basic and theoretical research in science. The National Lab Program was an outgrowth of the existing Key-Lab project. By 1991, 74 national labs were installed: 34 in universities, 25 under the Chinese Academy of Science, and the remaining 15 under government branches, including the Agriculture Department, the Department of Public Health and Medicine, and the Commission of Family Planning. The national labs were open to domestic research workers.

The Climb Program was set up in 1992 with 30 projects in 10 categories. The program focused on theoretical research in major scientific questions.

Higher Education: In the 1991–1992 academic year, there were 1,075 universities and colleges, of which 286 were polytech universities or industrial colleges, 257 were normal universities or teachers' colleges, and 122 were medical schools. The proportions reflected the main concerns of the country and its most urgent problems: industry, education, and public health. A closer examination of the specialties of the schools showed an even more visible inclination to industry: nearly 44 percent specialized in industry and engineering, and only about 9 percent was devoted to humanities and social sciences.

In 1991, 36.6 percent of the 2.04 million Chinese registered as full-time students majored in engineering or industry-related fields, whereas only 4.61 percent majored in humanities or social sciences.

With strenuous efforts, China also lowered the illiteracy rate from 23.67 percent in 1982 to 18.16 percent in 1990.

Public Science Literacy: The Chinese Society of Science and Technology, sponsored by the State Commission of Science and Technology, conducted a poll to investigate public science literacy in late 1991. The analysis of the 4,219 responses showed, for scientific terms such as *molecule, software,* and *mercury thermometer,* only 2.5 percent, 1 percent, and 21.4 percent of the sample group, respectively, responded with correct answers, though 30 percent, 13.1 percent, and 41 percent of the individuals claimed understanding of the concepts. To the question "What field is DNA related to?" 22.3 percent of the people responded correctly, though 37.7 percent answered that they had never heard of the word DNA. Two-thirds knew that hot air moves upward, cold air downward, but 41.6 percent thought that table salt was carbonized calcium (a fake compound created by the investigators). For more philosophical questions, such as "What are scientific methods?" only 0.3 percent gave a correct answer.

Some health publicity campaigns were apparently effective in disseminating scientific knowledge: 74.6 percent of the adults, for instance, knew that smoking causes cancer, but just 14 percent of them knew that antibiotics would not kill a virus.

Generally speaking, according to the poll, the Chinese public was not sufficiently interested in science and its development. More than two-thirds of the respondents said that they were not interested in new discoveries in science, new technology, medical research, and space exploration. The Chinese Society of Science and Technology decided to conduct similar polls every two years to collect basic information of public literacy and attitude. The State Commission planned to consult the poll results for establishing policies on development of science and science education.

KEY RESEARCH SOURCES

Bodde, Derk. *Chinese Thought, Society, and Science: The Intellectual and Social Background of Science and Technology in Pre-Modern China.* Honolulu: University of Hawaii Press, 1991.

Bowers, John Z., William Hess, and Nathan Sivin, eds. *Science and Medicine in Twentieth-Century China: Research and Education*. Ann Arbor: Center for Chinese Studies, University of Michigan Press, 1988.

Bray, Francesca. *The Rice Economies: Technology and Development in Asian Societies*. Berkeley: University of California Press, 1994.

———. *Technology and Gender: Fabrics of Power in Late Imperial China*. Berkeley: University of California Press, 1997.

———. *Technology and Society in Ming China, 1368–1644*. Washington, D.C.: American Historical Association, 1999.

Chen Cheng-Yih. *Early Chinese Work in Natural Science: A Re-examination of the Physics of Motion, Acoustics, Astronomy and Scientific Thoughts*. Hong Kong: Hong Kong University Press, 1996.

Chen Cheng-Yih, and Roger Cliff. *Science and Technology in Chinese Civilization*. Philadelphia: World Scientific, 1987.

Ho, Peng Yoke. *Li, Qi and Shu: An Introduction to Science and Civilization in China*. Hong Kong: Hong Kong University Press, 1985.

The Institute of the History of Natural Science, Chinese Academy of Science. *Ancient China's Technology and Science*. Beijing: Foreign Language Press, 1983.

Nakayama, Shigeru, and Nathan Sivin eds. *Chinese Science: Explorations of an Ancient Tradition*. Cambridge: MIT Press, 1973.

Needham, Joseph. *Heavenly Clockwork: the Great Astronomical Clocks of Medieval China*. 2nd ed. Cambridge: Cambridge University Press, 1986.

———. *Science and Civilization in China*. Multiple vols. Cambridge: Cambridge University Press, 1954– .

———. *Science in Traditional China*. Hong Kong: Chinese University of Hong Kong Press, 1981.

Ronan, Colin A. *The Shorter Science and Civilization in China: An Abridgement of Joseph Needham's Original Text*. Multiple vols. Cambridge: Cambridge University Press, 1978– .

Simon, Denis Fred, and Merle Goldman, eds. *Science and Technology in Post-Mao China*. Cambridge, Mass.: Council on East Asian Studies, 1989.

Sivin, Nathan. *Chinese Alchemy: Preliminary Studies*. Cambridge, Mass.: Harvard University Press, 1968.

———. "Ruminations on the Tao and Its Disputers." *Philosophy East & West* 42 (1992): 21–29.

———. *Science in Ancient China: Researches and Reflections*. Brookfield, VT: Variorum, 1995.

———. *Science and Technology in East Asia*. New York: Science History Publications, 1977.

———. "Why the Scientific Revolution Did Not Take Place in China—or Didn't It?" *Transformation and Tradition in the Sciences: Essays in Honor of I. Bernard Cohen*. Ed. Everett Mendelsohn. Cambridge: Cambridge University Press, 1984.

Temple, Robert. *The Genius of China: 3,000 Years of Science, Discovery and Invention*. New York: Simon and Schuster, 1986.

Tsien Tsuen-hsuin. *Written on Bamboo and Silk: The Beginnings of Chinese Books and Inscriptions*. Chicago: University of Chicago Press, 1962.

Wright, David. *Translating Science: The Transmission of Western Chemistry into Late Imperial China, 1840–1900*. Leiden, Boston: Brill, 2000.

Wu Yiyi. "Chinese Technology in Van Braam's Journal." *Gest Library Journal* (Princeton) 6 (1993): 31–54.

Yao Shuping. "Chinese Intellectuals and Science: A History of the Chinese Academy of Science." *Science Context* 3 (1989): 447–473.

Economy and Trade

By Hong Yang and Xiaohe Zhang

INTRODUCTION

China has a long history of civilization. In many ways, Chinese civilization before the 19th century was more advanced than that of the West. However, during the 19th and 20th centuries, China fell far behind. China's economic development was stunted by dynastic changes, rebellions, foreign invasions, civil wars, and several policy blunders by successive governments. In the post-Mao era, China's economic development is accelerating as it adopts market-oriented reforms. Nonetheless, China still has the extraordinary task of feeding, housing, and providing a livelihood for the largest population in the world. Whether China will ever be able to catch up with the developed world remains to be seen. This chapter discusses China's economy and its trade policies with the outside world from imperial times to the present.

1. THE ECONOMY AND TRADE ROUTES IN EARLY IMPERIAL CHINA

Agricultural Fundamentalism and Anti-mercantilism

All of the rulers in early imperial China regarded agriculture as the basic economic activity and a "fundamental profession." The idea of protecting agriculture was crystallized in *nongben*—meaning physiocracy, or agricultural fundamentalism. The physiocratic ideology was derived partly from the Confucian tradition, which looked down upon commerce and merchants, and from the rulers' desire to prevent farmers from changing to the "nonproductive" occupation of merchant. In theory, if not always in practice, the peasantry was recognized as higher than other working classes, and the merchant class was placed at the bottom of the class ranking. An immediate consequence of the agricultural fundamentalism was discrimination against merchant activity. Commerce was restricted to closely regulated official markets, in which the local authorities controlled the prices of commodities and all activities of merchants. The travel

of merchants was also restricted, and they were subjected to constant inspections and tolls. Commerce in some goods was limited and even forbidden. The salt trade, for example, was controlled by government monopolies during most of the imperial period. Control over commerce gradually relaxed with the increase in urbanization and decline in central power after the Han dynasty (206 B.C.–A.D. 220). By the late eighth and ninth centuries, the merchant class saw a burgeoning prosperity. Nevertheless, the traditional emphasis on agriculture as the foundation of China's economy remained unaltered for the successive imperial dynasties. Accordingly, the mercantile class never gained a high status in imperial Chinese society.

"Jingtian" Farm System: According to traditional accounts, a *jingtian*, or "well-field," farm system was developed under the Zhou dynasty (1045–221 B.C.) as the basis of conscription, government, and taxation. The well-field system derived its name from the fact that the land was supposed to be divided into square units, with each unit divided into nine equal squares.

The inner boundary lines resembled the shape of the Chinese character *jing*, meaning "well." The eight outer squares were cultivated by eight individual families, who jointly cultivated the central, or "public" square. The produce of this square was submitted to the feudal lord as taxes. Although it is not clear to what extent this idealized form of land division was actually implemented in practice, the ideal of the *jingtian* system influenced the designers and managers of the land distribution system in the successive dynasties.

"Juntian" Farm System: The *juntian*, or equal land allocation, was first enacted in the North Wei period (386–535) and inherited with modifications by the Sui (581–618) and Tang (618–907) dynasties. The aim was to maximize the use of land and achieve the highest level of productivity. Under this system, land was allocated to the individual male for his productive adult lifetime, and in return he paid taxes and performed labor services for the state. Although land was granted to the peasants, excessive accumulation of property in individual hands was restricted. Large land holdings were limited to certain groups, such as the state and imperial clans or the families of the nobility and of high-ranking officials. With the continuous weakening of central authority and the consequent decentralization and localization of power in the late Tang dynasty, the *juntian* system was gradually replaced by a system of private ownership under which tenant cultivators flourished. This system continued throughout the remainder of the imperial period and the Republican period (1911–1949), until the land reform schemes were carried out under the Communist regime in 1949 and 1950.

Innovations in Farming Techniques and Agricultural Treatises

Before the Spring and Autumn period (722–481 B.C.), agricultural implements were made of either stone or wood. As a result, cultivation was largely restricted to land that could be worked by a primitive plow employing human labor. During the Warring States period (480–222 B.C.), iron implements and animal power were introduced in agriculture. Flood control and irrigation works were also developed. The introduction of the iron plow and the use of oxen as draft animals made it possible to work a much greater area in a shorter time and also made much deeper cultivation possible. Cultivation was extended to previously untouched land. Flood control dikes built by the local rulers in the Yellow River Valley made it possible to bring the vast alluvial flood plain into cultivation. As a consequence of the application of new techniques and the expansion of areas under cultivation, the rigid control of the process of cultivation previously exercised by the clans and village communities started to break down. Individual families rapidly became the basic unit for agrarian production in lands newly reclaimed.

In ancient times, farmers judged the changing seasons by closely observing natural phenomena that occurred periodically, such as hibernation, migration, and blossoming. They also noted periodic changes in the weather and celestial phenomena. These observations were collected and written down in early agricultural treatises. From the Han dynasty (206 B.C.–A.D. 220), comprehensive agricultural treatises on all aspects of agriculture, including specialized works on everything from crop systems to pest controls, pigeon raising to horse breeding, irrigation to tea cultivation, gradually became an established genre. Some of these treatises were officially sponsored with the goal of popularizing a new crop or technique. Many were written by private authors based on experience and observation and discussed the agriculture of a single county, locality or estate. Most of the comprehensive agricultural treatises contained chapters on the general principles of agriculture, crop types, farming seasons, tools, and side occupations. The agricultural treatises are an important source for the history of Chinese agriculture and agricultural techniques.

Early Imperial Trade Routes

The Silk Road: The Silk Road was a network of trade routes from northwest China through the oases of central Asia and northern Persia to the ports of the Black Sea and the Mediterranean Sea. The silk trade emerged at least as early as the Han dynasty, with silk being exchanged by China for special kinds of wood, precious metals, and glass. The Silk Road was not only a commercial route but also a major channel of ideas, culture, and technology between the two great civilizations of Rome and China. China received Christianity and Buddhism (from India) via the road. After the Yuan dynasty (1276–1368), trade and travel along the Silk Road declined as a result of increasing danger on the route and the rise of maritime trade.

Maritime Trade: As early as the 10th century, Chinese merchant ships began to trade at ports along the peninsula of Southeast Asia. The 13th and 14th centuries saw a great advance in Chinese shipbuilding and nautical technology. This led to an increase in maritime trade to Japan and southeastern and southern Asia. Chinese merchants shipped exported silk, porcelain, and copper coins. By the early 15th century, Chinese trade goods were finding markets all across southeastern and southern Asia and as far as the east coast of Africa. The rulers of the Ming dynasty (1368–1644), however, severely restricted

Chinese overseas commerce between the mid-15th and mid-16th centuries. Many scholar-officials, influenced by the conservative inclinations of Confucianism, opposed trade and foreign contact in principle. This anti-commercialism hampered China's economic development for centuries.

The Grand Canal: The Grand Canal was a series of waterways linking Hangzhou in the south of the Yangtze River with Beijing. The Grand Canal was first built during the Sui dynasty. The aim was to enable the regime to transport surplus grain from the Yangtze and Huai River Valleys to feed the capital cities and large standing armies in the north. The Grand Canal was not one long canal but consisted of short stretches of canals that linked existing waterways. It relied wherever possible on the natural flow of the rivers it linked. As most of the course of the Grand Canal traversed flat ground, canal building was relatively easy. Still, construction and maintenance were essential to ensure the minimum depth needed for the shallow-draft barges to clear the bottom. During the successive imperial dynasties, the Grand Canal underwent several extensions and repairs.

2. THE ECONOMY IN LATE IMPERIAL CHINA (1600–1911)

Improvement in Land Productivity

During the late imperial period, technological advances took place in several forms. One was the introduction from the south of earlier-ripening varieties of rice, which made double cropping possible. New crops such as corn (maize), sweet potatoes, peanuts, and tobacco were introduced from the Americas. Irrigation, water storage and control, and grain storage facilities were extended or improved. There was a shift to crops that produced higher yields and at the same time required more labor for their cultivation. As a result, the sown acreage of corn and sweet potatoes increased, whereas the acreage of barley, sorghum, and millet declined. Despite the

progressive growth in food production, the late imperial era saw declining productivity in agriculture. That was partly because of the continuous worsening of the person-to-land ratio resulting from population growth. The labor surplus also constrained progress in the innovations and applications of machines that aimed to save labor in farming. Iron plow and draft animal power, already widespread in the Han dynasty, had continued to be the major agricultural means for the next millennium. The shortage of available land had led to a steady encroachment on China's lakes as early as the Ming period. The "reclamation" of land from lakes, however, reduced the catchment basin for floodwaters, exacerbating the flood problem.

Handicrafts

The most important household handicraft in the late imperial era was spun and woven cotton. Although cotton cultivation was fairly widespread, the principal producing areas were in the Yangtze Valley provinces, particularly Jiangxi, Jiangsu, and Hunan. Substantial quantities of hand-woven cotton cloth were exported to England and the United States. From the early 1890s onward, however, cotton output in China stagnated. Handicraft weavers turned to imported machine-spun yarn.

Tea processing was another important handicraft activity in the late imperial era. Tea exports peaked in the mid-1880s before declining sharply. This decline resulted largely from the competition of teas from colonial India and Ceylon (present-day Sri Lanka). In contrast to Chinese exporters, the exporters in those British colonies had sufficient control over production to maintain quality standards.

Silk weaving, oil pressing, rice milling, and mining by native methods were also important household handicraft activities. Oil pressing in handicraft workshops, however, expanded rapidly after the 1890s in response to the demand for soybean oil by European soap manufacturers and for bean, beancake, and oil in Japan.

Emergence of Modern Industry

Until the late Qing dynasty (1644–1911), the overall prospects for a modern manufacturing industry in China were limited. By 1895, there were only about 100 foreign-owned industrial enterprises, and most of them were located in Shanghai. Between 1895 and 1913, about 549 Chinese-owned private and semi-official modern industrial enterprises were established. They concentrated on coal mining, metal smelting and minting, silk reeling, flour milling, oil pressing, match manufacturing, and cotton spinning and weaving. Both the foreign and the Chinese-owned firms were differentiated from handicraft industries only by the fact that they employed some power-driven machinery. Unlike their foreign counterparts, the Chinese-owned modern industries did little exporting. The cities of Shanghai, Wuhan, Tianjin, and Canton were the most important manufacturing centers during the late Qing dynasty.

Land Taxation and Land Measurement Unit

Land taxes constituted, by far, the largest source of state revenue during the entire imperial period. The land tax, in principle, was imposed at a fixed rate. The unit of land measurement was the *mu*, which was equivalent to approximately 1/15 hectare. Nevertheless, per *mu* productivity varied widely in China. The richest rice paddy field often yielded 10 times more than the poorest dry land of equivalent size. During the Qing dynasty, most districts solved the problem of how to set taxes on land of different quality by using the so-called fiscal *mu* conversion. In general, each *mu* of standard measure that had an average or above-average yield was assessed as a fiscal *mu*. Less productive land was converted into fiscal *mu* by counting one and a half, two, three, or even more *mu* as one fiscal *mu*. *Mu* as a measurement unit of land has been in use since antiquity and continues in present-day China. The various conversion rates in different areas, however, have caused much confusion in the estimation of China's cultivated land areas. For example, the estimate of cultivated land based on recent satellite imagery exceeded the figure reported in the Chinese official statistics by 30 to 40 percent.

Salt Monopoly

Up to the end of the Qing dynasty, the transport and sale of salt for human consumption was usually monopolized by the government and specially authorized merchants. The idea behind this practice was that salt was a daily necessity for the people but was produced only in certain areas. Were salt marketed by merchants, farmers would be subjected to extortionate prices. Moreover, because no one could live without salt, the salt monopoly guaranteed a steady source of revenue for the government. Salt laws were changed many times throughout the imperial days but always returned to the principle of government monopoly. During the Qing dynasty, each salt-producing region had its designated sales area. In other words, salt designated for area A could not be sold in area B and vice versa. Carrying salt across the boundaries of a designated sales area was a felony. The effectiveness of the monopoly was ensured by the control on the labor force that produced the salt. Families of officially registered salt merchants often retained this status in perpetuity. The merchant families were rewarded according to the amount of salt they produced.

Market and Commerce

Traditional Chinese farm households produced all or much of their own food. Nevertheless, grains, cash crops, local agricultural specialties, and the products of household handicraft were regularly sold throughout the entire imperial period at a large number of local markets. Constrained by the means of transportation, each local market was roughly defined by a radius equal to the distance that a peasant buyer or seller and his products might cover round trip on foot in one day. The markets were normally periodic rather than continuous, occurring every few days according to the scheduling systems that were characteristic of different regions.

Markets at a national level emerged in China during the Song dynasty (960–1279) and developed rapidly in the mid-1600s,

after the Ming dynasty. The trade along the Yangtze River was the most important. The Grand Canal was also a major artery along which grain and cotton cloth were transported to the north, and raw cotton produced north of the Yangtze River was transported to the south for cloth production. In terms of both volume and value, grain was the most important commodity traded in the market. Since trade in salt was under government control, cotton was the second-most important traded item. A third major commodity was silk. Jiangsu and Sichuan were two major silk-producing areas.

Guilds: In the late 18th century, trade guilds, particularly native-place guilds, proliferated. Guilds were associations in various provincial centers to accommodate merchants and others who shared the same place of origin. The guilds served traders from a distance in the interregional trade. They provided them not only with the amenities of a meeting place but often warehouse spaces, living quarters, shrines to the patron deity of the guilds, and schools for examination candidates. With the establishment of staple trades, guilds became an important social element in the late Qing dynasty and the Republican period.

3. FOREIGN TRADE AND INVESTMENT IN LATE IMPERIAL CHINA

Opium Trade

By about the mid-18th century, China and Great Britain developed a stable trade. China exported tea, silk, and porcelain to Great Britain and imported silver, woolen textiles, and opium from India, then a British colony. By the early 19th century, the opium trade was leading to a serious outflow of silver from the Chinese economy. Meanwhile, opium smoking became a social curse for both individual smokers and their families. This tremendous social evil was sparked by the lust for profits among the British Indian government, the

foreigners who took opium to China, and the corrupt Chinese distributors. The Qing government attempted to ban the sale of opium. In 1839, Lin Zexu (1785–1850), an imperial commissioner, was sent to Canton to compel the foreign traders to stop bringing opium to China. Lin was met with a fierce military reaction by the British government. Great Britain's gunboats won the Opium War (1839–1842) and secured the opium trade. The Qing government was forced to sign the Treaty of Nanjing in August 1842. In addition, Hong Kong, then a barren island, was ceded to Great Britain.

Treaty Ports

Treaty ports were ports opened to foreign trade and residence under treaties. Toward the end of the 19th century, the Western countries demanded more and more concessions from China. The number of treaty ports increased steadily from the original five (Guangzhou, Xiamen, Fuzhou, Ningbo, and Shanghai) named in the Treaty of Nanjing at the end of the Opium War to 48 in 1913. Foreigners enjoyed rights of extraterritoriality, the restriction of Chinese customs duties, and the provision of the right for foreigners to establish manufacturing facilities in the treaty ports. They were under the control of their own consuls and were not subject to the laws of China. An independent legal, judicial, police, and taxation system was applied in each of the treaty ports. Compradors (foreign-hired local business managers) managed affairs beneath the overlordship of the foreign *taipans* (firm managers). Shanghai was the most important treaty port, accounting for almost two-thirds of China's foreign trade in 1870 and almost half of direct foreign investment in 1931.

Foreign Investment and Trade

After the Opium War, foreign investment started to come into China. Most of the investment was located in the treaty ports. One-half of the total amount of foreign investment was directly related to the business activities and living accommodations of foreign traders in treaty ports. A quarter of the total amount was transportation-related, mainly involving the financing and operation of railroad lines, notably the Chinese Eastern Railway (Russian) and the South Manchurian Railroad (Japanese). Although the railroads were intended to serve the interests of their foreign owners, they also provided the necessary transport facilities for Manchuria's industries to enter foreign trade. Until the end of the Qing period, the manufacturing sector accounted for a small percentage of total foreign investment.

Structure of Foreign Trade: Opium imports increased rapidly after the Opium War. In 1880, opium accounted for about 40 percent of total imports. Its share declined thereafter to some 15 percent in 1900 and 7 percent in 1913, due partly to the diversity of imported items. At the turn of the century, opium, cereal, and cotton products together composed more than half of China's imports. Until the end of the 19th century, tea and silk dominated China's exports. Tea exports declined rapidly in the beginning of the 20th century due to the competition of teas from India and Ceylon. Tea exports were replaced by exports of a variety of agricultural goods, such as beans and bean cake, seed oils, cotton, and hides. Such a pattern of trade had little stimulative effect on either user or supplier industries, and was thus of negligible significance for China's industrialization. Tables 1 and 2 provide a statistical history of China's import/export industry from 1870 to 1910.

Table 1: Percentage Distribution of China's Principal Imports, 1870–1910

Year	Opium	Cotton cloth & cotton yarn	Cereals & flour	Others
1870	43.0	31.0	0.0	25.96
1880	39.3	29.5	0.1	31.10
1890	19.5	35.5	9.6	35.40
1900	14.8	35.8	7.0	42.40
1910	12.0	28.3	7.7	52.00

Source: Feuerwerker, 1969, p. 52.

Table 2: Percentage Distribution of China's Principal Exports, 1870–1910

Year	Tea	Silk	Seed oil & beans	Others
1870	49.9	38.8	2.4	8.9
1880	45.9	38.0	0.3	15.8
1890	30.6	33.9	1.0	34.5
1900	16.0	30.4	4.4	49.2
1910	9.4	25.4	14.0	51.2

Source: Feuerwerker, 1969, p. 53.

4. BANKING AND MONETARY SYSTEM IN LATE IMPERIAL CHINA

Silver Standard Monetary System

From the late imperial period until the end of the 1930s, China's currency was based on silver. Gold was used for jewelry and as a means for conserving wealth, rather than for economic exchange. Tael was the unit of silver in the monetary system. A tael was an ounce of silver. Silver provided the medium of exchange for large-scale trade and the unit of account for business and government. China's silver money was cast in the form of "shoes," with the weight and fineness stamped on each shoe. Minted copper cash was, however, commonly used to settle retail transactions. A typical Chinese bronze coin was round in shape with a square hole in the middle, with the weight cast on the surface. Following the rise of European trade in the 17th century, coined silver was imported from Europe and the Americas. Chinese traders welcomed the coined silver because it fulfilled the long-standing need for convenient, easily negotiable, low-risk monetary instruments. Throughout the late imperial period, small quantities of paper money were issued intermittently.

Financial Institutions and Banks

Pawnshops: Pawnshops were the earliest credit institutions. Pawnshops first appeared in Buddhist monasteries about the fifth century. In the Ming and Qing periods, pawnshops developed rapidly. As a protection against fire and robbery, a solid, high brick wall generally surrounded a pawnshop. Outside the shop, usually a huge character, *dang* (or "pawnshop"), was displayed and could be seen from a considerable distance. Pawnbroking was one of the most profitable businesses in the Qing period. By the 18th and the first half of the 19th centuries, pawnshops were seen all over the empire. They functioned as commercial banks and made loans on such commodities as grain, silk, and cotton. From the second half of the 19th century and especially after the Taiping Rebellion

(1851–1864), pawnshops began to decline. The decline resulted from the unsteady political situation in China, but more so from the strong competition in loan making that came from traditional and modern banks.

Qianzhuang ("Money Shops"): The *qianzhuang* were important financial institutions during the late imperial time. They were local institutions (native banks) linked mainly by correspondent relationships with banks in commercial centers, although some maintained small networks of branches. The *qianzhuang* were owned by individuals, partnerships, or small groups of stockholders who bore unlimited liability for the discharge of bank obligations. The *qianzhuang* specialized in short-term loans to merchants. They also provided services such as deposits, direct investments in business ventures, interregional transfers, and exchange bills. Personal reputation and credit, rather than collateral, served as the cornerstones of banking operations. The *qianzhuang* were generally free of government supervision but were subject to self-regulation through their own guilds.

The Shanxi Banks: The Shanxi banks, named for their province of origin, specialized in interregional transfers. The Shanxi banks were one of the most important economic institutions in Chinese traditional society during the late Qing dynasty. The trade of Manchuria and Mongolia with China proper contributed partly to the development of Shanxi banks. The Shanxi banks operated branches in important cities all over the country, although their greatest strength was concentrated north of the Yangtze River. Much of their business involved government funds. The Qing government relied heavily on their services in transmitting revenues and expenditures. The banks also derived income from loans and deposits. After 1900, Chinese revenues began to be deposited in foreign banks, and the Shanxi banks lost their monopoly of government business. Most of them failed to survive the Republican revolution of 1911 and quickly faded into obscurity.

Foreign Banks: Foreign penetration into China's financial system began with the introduction of western coined silver to coastal trading regions in the 19th century. The expansion of foreign trade after the Opium War created fresh demands for credit and transfer facilities. This encouraged the creation of foreign banking outlets in the treaty ports. The first foreign firm, the (British) Oriental Bank, was opened in 1848. The Hong Kong and Shanghai Bank was formed in 1865 to serve the express purpose of entering the Chinese financial market. Other institutions from Germany, Japan, Russia, France, and the United States began to appear by the 1890s. By the mid-1930s, the number of foreign banks in China, including subsidiaries of banks with overseas headquarters, had risen to 53 firms with more than 150 offices.

The Emergence of Chinese Modern Banks: Modern-style banks are known in Chinese by the name *yinhang*, literally "silver guild" or "silver market." The first Chinese modern bank, the Chung-Kuo T'ung-Shang Yinhang (known before 1911 as the "Imperial Bank of China"), was established in 1896. Between 1896 and 1911, 16 modern-style Chinese banks were opened (of which only seven survived into the 1930s), including the Hu-pu Bank, which evolved into the Bank of China in the Republican period. Their main offices and branches were located exclusively in large cities. They maintained only small and indirect connections with the trade of the interior in the form of short-term advances to inland *qianzhuang*. Modern commercial banking did not begin to penetrate the traditional marketing system until the 1920s.

5. THE ECONOMY DURING THE REPUBLICAN PERIOD (1912–1949)

Small-Scale Farming and Land Parcelization

During the Republican period, China remained an agrarian society. Until the late 1940s, about 85 percent of Chinese people lived in the countryside, the great majority of them farmers. Of all land under cultivation, 90 percent was devoted to crops and only 1.1 percent to pasture for animals (as compared with U.S. figures of 42 percent and 47 percent, respectively, in the same period). Farm households normally ranged from cultivating 1.3–2 hectares in north China and .8–1 hectare in the south. More than 70 percent of farms were less than 1 hectare. Very large estates were uncommon. The median landholding of elite families was only around 6–10 hectares (in contrast to the roughly 50 hectares that constituted an average farm in the United States at that time). Tenancy was common. Many farm families cultivated their own land and at the same time rented additional land from larger landowners.

About 7.6 percent of land was not in productive use. To some extent, that was due to the high density of China's rural population and its housing requirements. It was also related to the need of private landowners to demarcate their land from that of others and have access to it via paths between parcels. The death of a household head was often followed by a division of the household's land among his sons. Free commerce in land further encouraged fragmentation of the land. During the Republican period, a typical family's landholding was divided into several parcels scattered at different locations. Consequently, much land was used for boundaries and paths rather than for growing crops. Moreover, during the busy season, much labor time was spent transporting farmers, equipment, and draft animals from field to field. Irrigation and drainage were both rendered difficult by fragmentation, which often led to endless disputes over ownership and access.

Industry

In the early 20th century, China's modern industry experienced a relatively rapid growth. However, this was confined to the treaty ports and had only limited influence

Table 3: Regional Distribution and Nationality of Manufacturing Output in 1933 (million yuan in current prices)

Region	Chinese firms	Foreign firms	Total	% shares of total
China proper	1,771.4	497.4	2,268.8	85.8
Shanghai	727.7	323.3	1,051.0	39.7
Jiangsu	225.7	5.2	230.9	8.7
Other	818.0	168.9	986.9	37.3
Manchuria	154.8	221.9	375.7	14.2
National total	1,926.2	719.3	2,645.5	—
Percentage share	72.8	27.2	—	100

Source: Rawski, 1989, p. 74.

on the rest of the economy. In 1933, the output of manufacturing accounted for 2.1 percent of the gross domestic product, and factory employment accounted for only 0.4 percent of the labor force. This pattern of dualism—a small modern sector growing alongside a large, unchanging agricultural and handicraft sector—persisted until 1949. To avoid competition with foreign firms, Chinese native firms concentrated on textiles and other products that did not require complex technology or massive fixed investment. The role of the Republican government in industrialization was small and fragmented. The public sector concentrated mainly in the repair works of the national railways, a small number of arsenals, and the construction and cement industries. Available statistical data, however, suggest that economic development in pre-Communist China peaked in 1936, the year before Japan's full-scale invasion of China. The Republican government prepared ambitious and detailed plans for the construction of state-owned factories in metallurgy, construction, and other industries. Japan's invasion of China in 1937 disrupted the implementation of those new efforts to industrialize.

Regional Disparities

Until the end of the Republican period, industrialization in China had been primarily a regional phenomenon. The Yangtze River Delta (including Shanghai and Jiangsu) and the Manchurian regions produced nearly two-thirds of China's industrial output. Industrialization in Jiangsu and Shanghai was largely linked with investment from western countries, notably Great Britain, the United States, and Germany. Industrialization in Manchuria involved considerable participation of Japan, which became a major investor in transport, metallurgy, engineering, and other activities. (Japan had considerable colonial interests in Manchuria in the early part of the 20th century and fully occupied Manchuria from 1931 to 1945.) A breakdown of Chinese manufacturing output can be found in Table 3.

Shanghai

Shanghai is located at the mouth of the Yangtze River. This has provided it with a unique advantage in access to materials, product markets, and ancillary services. The superior location quickly helped the metropolis to become an industrial leader in pre-war China, closely resembling New York's status in the 19th-century American economy. In both cases, superior access to information and transport routes attracted businesses and industries, which enlarged its initial advantage as the effects of scale stimulated the proliferation of such ancillary services as finance, insurance, communication, repair, and storage.

Starting from the 1850s, the value of Shanghai's imports and exports increased rapidly, and the city replaced Guangdong as the national center for foreign trade. By the 1930s Shanghai had become the biggest comprehensive seaport in China and one of the 10 biggest ports in the world. The city was also a pioneer in introducing to China modern technology, such as railways, highways, telegraphs, and telephones.

The concentration of foreign trade commodities in Shanghai stimulated the development of its trade with its hinterland; and in the early 20th century, Shanghai became the financial center of China. Both foreign and Chinese modern banks were based here. Foreign trade also stimulated the development of modern industry. In 1933, Shanghai accounted for 34 percent of Chinese factories, 40 percent of its industrial capital, 43 percent of its industrial workers, and 50 percent of its industrial output.

The Economy During the Anti-Japanese War (1937–1945)

In 1937, Japan invaded China proper. From 1938 to 1940, many factories and technicians moved inland along with the retreating Nationalist government and armies. In contrast to the pre-war industry focus on consumer goods, about half of the wartime industry in unoccupied areas manufactured military-related and producers' goods. The state-owned enterprises played a major role in the wartime industry. The relocation of industries from the coastal areas to inland provinces, particularly Sichuan, ignited the process of industrialization there. Nevertheless, industrial output in occupied China proper stagnated or declined from 1937 to 1947.

Before the mid-1930s Manchuria's economic growth was based mainly on the extension of the agricultural frontier. From 1936 to 1941, industry expanded rapidly under Japanese control. The principal modern industries were a network of Japanese-controlled enterprises designed to fur-

nish raw and semi-finished materials to the Japanese economy. The Anshan and Benxi ironworks and the Fushun coal mine, large vertically integrated installations, were the most prominent among those units.

Civil War and the End of Nationalist Rule (1946–1949)

The Japanese surrender in 1945 was accompanied by a partial paralysis of industry throughout China. In the formerly occupied areas, Japanese technicians and managers were withdrawn, and production came to a standstill. Manchuria suffered a large-scale looting of its industrial plant by the Soviets who occupied the region for a short period of time after Japan's defeat. In the interior, the wartime industry was left to wither. As a result, post-Japanese war manufacturing output was below the peak 1936 level. Later the economy declined further under the impact of full-scale civil war between 1947 and 1949.

Between 1937 and 1948, the price index increased from 100 to 287,700,000 under the Guomindang Nationalist government. The runaway inflation was principally caused by the Japanese seizure of China's richest provinces during the eight years of war and then the civil war. However, much of the blame could be placed on the Nationalist government, which did little to stem inflation. Runaway inflation led to a complete collapse of the financial system and contributed to the end of Nationalist rule in the mainland part of China in 1949. The Nationalist government retreated to Taiwan and continued its rule on the island until voted out of office in 2000.

6. ECONOMIC PLANNING (1949–1978)

Nationalization

The People's Republic of China was established on October 1, 1949. All of the former Nationalist "state treasures," including factories, public facilities, banks,

and other economic agencies, were confiscated and nationalized by the Communist government. By 1952, state-owned factories were producing more than half of China's gross industrial output. A similar degree of state dominance was in wholesale trade, and a lesser but rapidly growing one was in retail trade. Beginning in 1956, all economic activities in China were undergoing socialist reorganization. In industry, the target of this activity was the formation of joint state-private enterprises. The former owners/managers of private enterprises became state wage-earning employees while receiving interest payments on the value of their shares in the enterprises. The interest payments were fixed, usually equal to 5 percent of the assessed value of their shares, regardless of the profitability of the enterprises. After the reorganization, private enterprises virtually disappeared in pre-reform Communist China. The interest payments were ceased in September 1966 with the start of the Cultural Revolution.

Planned Economy

The Chinese planned economy was copied from that used in the Soviet Union. Economic activities, from material goods production through final distribution, were undertaken according to the plan. There was little use of price incentives to encourage output growth since output targets were presumed to be attainable through direct commands to production units. In 1952, the State Planning Commission was set up. Its mandate was to construct annual and five-year economic plans embodying decisions about the allocation of national resources.

In the industrial sector, the plan stipulated the amount of raw materials to be extracted and processed, the amount of energy to be generated, the amount of manufactured goods to be produced, the prices at which producer goods and products would be exchanged, the allocation and wages of the labor required to achieve those goals, and the amount and destination of investments. In the agricultural sector, production planning was characterized by the imposition of detailed sown area and output targets and specific cropping patterns by higher-level authorities on production units.

Economic Plans: The Chinese economy has been directed under long-, medium-, and short-term plans. Long-term plans embody thinking and aspirations about the general shape and size of the future economy. The five-year plan is the principal medium-term plan (see Table 4). For practical purposes, there are also annual and short-term plans. In most enterprises, there are also half-yearly, quarterly, and monthly plans.

Population Registration (Hukou)

Population registration, or *hukou*, was introduced in the late 1950s. *Hukou* status divided Chinese citizens into two fundamentally distinguished groups: agricultural population and nonagricultural population. The latter roughly describes urban residents, though a small number reside in rural areas. Until the mid-1980s, urban residents received food, housing, employment, and other social services such as health care and education. Rural residents, in contrast, had to be self-sufficient and received none of the above benefits. Under the *hukou* system, population movement was vigilantly monitored by the government through the Ministry of Public Security and local administrative networks, such as street and district neighborhood committees. Rural-urban migration was prohibited. The move from city to city and from village to village was also restricted. The control was highly effective because it was accompanied by a simultaneous ban of a free market for grain and other necessities of life. An individual could purchase grain, cooking oil, and cotton cloth only with coupons in the place where his or her *hukou* was registered. As *hukou* was linked with the source of necessities, it was very difficult, if not impossible, for an individual to survive outside his or her *hukou* registered place.

The Great Leap Forward (1958) and the Three-Year Disaster (1959–1961)

The Great Leap Forward was a campaign launched by the Chinese Communist government in 1958 for the purpose of mobilizing the vast labor resources of China to overcome shortages of capital in both industry and agriculture. Through the campaign, it was hoped that the country

Table 4: Growth Rates of National Income by Five-Year Plan Period (annual percentage rate)

Five-year plan period	Real rate of growth of national income	Agriculture	Industry	Construction	Transportation	Commerce
1953–1957 First Five-Year Plan	8.9	3.7	19.6	19.4	12.0	8.0
1958–1962 Second Five-Year Plan	–3.1	–5.9	1.8	–7.8	–0.5	–4.3
1963–1965 Readjustment period	14.7	11.5	21.3	20.9	15.1	2.8
1966–1970 Third Five-Year Plan	8.3	2.6	12.6	8.0	5.6	9.2
1971–1975 Fourth Five-Year Plan	5.5	3.0	8.5	5.2	5.3	2.1
1976–1980 Fifth Five-Year Plan	6.1	0.7	9.2	6.9	5.6	7.6
1981–1985 Sixth Five-Year Plan	10.0	8.5	10.2	11.6	11.9	13.2
1986–1990 Seventh Five-Year Plan	7.9	4.8	13.2	14.6	9.4	3.3
1991–1995 Eighth Five-Year Plan	11.6	7.4	22.2	37.3	—	10.7
1991–1998	10.5	7.4	18.8	27.7	—	10.7

Sources: 1952–1985 data: Yabuki, 1995, p. 27; 1986–1998 data: China State Statistical Bureau, 1999, pp. 21–24.

could bypass the slow, more typical process of industrialization through gradual capital accumulation. Ambitious targets were set for all sectors, and both traditional and modern methods were applied to achieve the goal of "more, faster, better and more economical results."

In the countryside, a major step of the Great Leap Forward was the establishment of people's communes. It was hoped that such large-scale organization would help raise investment, production, and savings to accelerate industrialization. Other policies of the Great Leap Forward included the construction and development of "backyard steel plants," deep plowing practices, water conservation projects, and rural industries. In some places, people melted household implements and even iron woks to make steel by primitive methods in their backyards. Agricultural production was severely damaged by this chaotic campaign, which totally ignored the fundamental principles of economics. The Great Leap Forward was abandoned in late 1960 following its disastrous consequences.

The turmoil of the Great Leap Forward, combined with bad weather, resulted in three consecutive years of disastrous harvests from 1959 to 1961. Livestock were slaughtered, and agricultural output fell drastically. The level of nutrition approached starvation in many areas. Between 1959 and 1961, 20–30 million people died of malnutrition and starvation. As the collapse of the Great Leap Forward led to economic crisis, the Five-Year Plan was disrupted, and the Chinese economy was forced to readjust itself between 1963 and 1965. In the countryside, the backyard factories and construction work on industrial projects were halted and agricultural production was re-emphasized.

7. RURAL INSTITUTIONS AND RURAL ECONOMY UNDER CENTRAL PLANNING (1949–1978)

Land Reform

Prior to the Communist takeover, small-scale, self-sufficient household farming was typical of Chinese agricultural production. Land distribution, however, was uneven. A substantial amount of land was concentrated in a small minority of landlords and rich peasants, with most households owning some land and renting additional land from this minority group. In 1949, at the time of the establishment of the People's Republic of China, the government launched the land reform program in the rural areas. Land formerly owned by landlords and rich peasants was confiscated and distributed equally among poor villagers.

The land reform stimulated enthusiasm among poor peasants to expand agricultural production. The land reform also redeemed the principle of "land to the tiller" that the Chinese Communist Party had promised poor peasants during its struggle for power. It helped the newly established Communist government win support from the mass of peasants. Nevertheless, the land redistribution program left some unsolved problems in the countryside. Landholdings were still too small to enable poor peasant households to produce a marketable surplus under the technological conditions of the time. The shortage of the means of production was another problem. Poor peasants had few draft animals, plows, or other production tools. The newly established state was unable to provide credit facilities to meet the critical need for farm capital.

Agricultural Collectivization: The prevailing orthodoxy under Mao Zedong regarded agricultural surpluses as a source of funds for industrialization. As a consequence, resources were taken away from agriculture. One way that was done was by bringing rural households together to share capital equipment. That process led to the formation of Mutual Aid Teams (1951–1953), which originally grouped between three and five households together. Land and other production means remained privately owned, and peasants were free to join or withdraw their membership. Between 1954 and 1956, lower-level agricultural producers cooperatives formed, in which farmers pooled their land and equipment and got a return in proportion to them. Forming cooperatives kept the rich peasant community from fighting back because its position was not destroyed. But soon came the third stage of collectivization (1956–1957), which moved from the lower level of agricultural producers cooperatives to a higher level of collective. In the higher-level cooperatives, all peasants worked for wages regardless of their input of property, tools, animals, and land. A cooperative at the higher level was usually part or all of a village.

People's Commune: The structure of agricultural collectivization was capped in 1958 by the establishment of people's communes. Each commune was generally comparable in size to an old standard market community. The communes were multipurpose organizations for the direction of local government and the management of all economic and social activities, including agriculture, local industry, marketing, administration, schooling, and local security. At the early stage of their establishment, communes owned private plots, houses and their sites, most domestic animals, trees, and fishponds.

After the disastrous harvests between 1959 and 1961, there was a decentralization of commune management. The average size was reduced, and a three-tier structure was established. Under the communes were brigades, each of which was roughly the size of a village typically comprising about 220 households numbering almost 1,000 persons. Beneath the brigades were production teams, each of about 33 households or 145 persons. The production team was the basic unit of collective ownership. About 5 percent of arable land was distributed among team households as private plots. Individual households were able to grow vegetables and raise animals upon them. This institutional structure remained unchanged until the late 1970s, when the household responsibility system was introduced. The people's commune system was abolished in the mid-1980s. The township has since taken the place of the commune as the lowest level of government administration.

Work Points: Work points were the means of remunerating farmers' work under the people's commune system. Work points were assigned based on the difficulty of the task, the capability of the worker, and the amount of time spent at work. Men, who were considered more capable than women at working, routinely received more work points for performing the same task for the same period of time. A healthy male could usually earn 10 points for a full day's work. Those who could do less work earned fewer points. Those with a "bad class background," such as former landlords and rich peasants, or the "wrong political viewpoints" also received fewer points. After the harvest, work points were totaled. The team's net income, after deducting state taxes, the grain for basic allocation, and compulsory contributions to the commune welfare fund, was divided by the total number of work points earned by all the team members. That fixed the value of the work point. Team members then received compensation based on the points they earned.

In theory, work points were an incentive to do more work. In practice, however, because of the difficulties involved in measuring the quality of work carried out and the differences between jobs, work points were often allocated on the basis of the number of days worked. Under such a system the incentive to work hard and effectively was small. The basic allocation of grain to households according to family size and age structure further reduced the incentive. In some areas, 70 percent of grain was allocated according to this egalitarian principle. Thus, even when a farmer was far more productive than his peers, his income would still be barely above average.

Grain Production

Grain in China is defined to include all the major crops, such as rice, wheat, corn, millet, and sorghum. It also includes beans, peas, and potatoes. Grains are measured on an unmilled basis, and potatoes are converted to a "grain equivalent" by dividing their weight by a factor of five.

Grain production is the most important activity in the rural economy. During the mid-1960s to mid-1970s, grain self-sufficiency strategy was prevalent. All regions or even localities were required to achieve self-sufficiency in the supply of basic cereals, regardless of whether that coincided with the region's natural comparative advantage. When local grain self-sufficiency was a policy objective, many production teams were forced to move away from non-grain crops. The gross grain output grew at a compound rate of about 2.3 percent per year between 1957 and 1978. However, over the same period China's population grew at about 2.2 percent per year, which meant that output per person hardly increased. The situation did not improve until the economic reform started in 1978. As a result of those economic reforms, grain production and per capita output increased significantly in the early 1980s (see Table 5).

State Grain Procurement: In late 1953, compulsory grain sales were introduced by the central government. This was spurred by the declining ability of the state to obtain low-price grain through the market at a time when the first five-year plan required substantial increments in state acquisition of grain. In 1952, the state purchased 72 percent of the marketable surplus. In the following year, as high demand drove up the market price, sales to the state dropped to just 55 percent. Consequently, the urban grain supply barely kept up with the growth of population, and grain rationing was introduced in the cities. The government imposed a unified purchase system for grain in November 1953. Grain quotas were set for each pro-

Table 5: Grain Output and Per Capita Grain Output, 1952–1998

Year	Grain output (million tons)	Population (million persons)	Per capita output (kg/person)
1952	163.92	574.82	285.17
1953	166.83	587.96	283.74
1954	169.52	602.66	281.29
1955	183.94	614.65	299.26
1956	192.75	628.28	306.79
1957	195.05	646.53	301.69
1958	200.00	659.94	303.06
1959	170.00	672.07	252.95
1960	143.50	662.07	216.74
1961	147.50	658.59	223.96
1962	160.00	672.95	237.76
1963	170.00	691.72	245.76
1964	187.50	704.99	265.96
1965	194.53	725.38	268.18
1966	214.00	745.42	287.09
1967	217.82	763.68	285.22
1968	209.06	785.34	266.20
1969	210.97	806.71	261.52
1970	239.96	829.92	289.14
1971	250.14	852.29	293.49
1972	240.48	871.77	275.85
1973	264.94	892.11	296.98
1974	275.27	908.59	302.96
1975	284.52	924.20	307.86
1976	286.31	937.17	305.50
1977	282.73	949.74	297.69
1978	304.77	962.59	316.61
1979	332.12	975.42	340.49
1980	320.56	987.05	324.77
1981	325.02	1,000.72	324.79
1982	354.50	1,015.41	349.12
1983	387.28	1,024.95	377.85
1984	407.31	1,043.57	390.30
1985	379.11	1,058.51	358.15
1986	391.51	1,075.07	364.17
1987	402.98	1,093.00	368.69
1988	394.08	1,110.26	354.94
1989	407.55	1,127.04	361.61
1990	446.24	1,143.33	390.30
1991	435.29	1,158.23	375.82
1992	442.66	1,171.71	377.79
1993	456.49	1,185.17	385.17
1994	445.10	1,198.50	371.38
1995	466.62	1,211.21	385.25
1996	504.54	1,223.89	412.24
1997	494.17	1,236.26	399.73
1998	512.30	1,248.10	410.46

Source: China Statistical Bureau, 1984, pp. 81, 141; 1999, pp. 111, 395.

duction unit with regard to output, surplus, and sale of grain. After 1961, grain quotas were assigned to production teams. The quota grain sales were compulsory, and production teams had to fulfill their quotas before they could sell grain in markets or distribute it among households. The prices that the state paid for quota grain were lower than the market prices. In part to encourage higher production, the state fixed grain taxes and quotas for each production unit for a period of years. The compulsory grain sales system was in effect until the mid-1990s. Relying upon this system, the government assured the basic supply of grain to urban residents.

Rural Small Industries

Rural small industries emerged alongside the "backyard steel furnaces" during the Great Leap Forward. Workshops and small factories were set up in rural China. The period of readjustment after the failure of the Great Leap Forward saw a decline in rural small factories. The development of commune and brigade enterprises resumed during the late part of the Cultural Revolution (1966–1976). A major effort was launched to open small rural factories and to make rural areas as self-sufficient as possible. Some of the factories belonged to the state sector, often owned and managed by county governments, but most were owned and managed by communes and brigades. By the mid-1970s rural small-scale industry was producing about 10 percent of China's total industrial output. In certain lines, such as chemical fertilizer and cement, the small-scale rural factories accounted for more than half of the nation's total production.

8. PLANNED INDUSTRIALIZATION

Heavy Industry Development Strategy

In accordance with the Soviet Union's practice and Marxist theory, China's industrial strategy aimed to lay the foundations for a comprehensive heavy industrial structure. It was believed that heavy industry would provide the basis for light industry, which required machines, steel, chemicals, and means of transport. It was also believed that agriculture would benefit from heavy industry since it needed the chemicals, fertilizers, tractors, and implements that only heavy industry could provide. The emphasis placed on heavy industrial development was reflected in the investment made in capital construction. During the period prior to 1978, heavy industry received about half of the total capital investment, compared with less than 7 percent to light industry and less than 12 percent to agriculture. Table 6 provides a breakdown of investment from 1953 to 1978.

Heavy Industry: Heavy industry refers to industry that produces capital goods and provides various sectors of the national economy with materials and a basic infrastructure. It consists of the following three branches:

1. Mining and felling industry: extracts natural resources, including petroleum, coal, metal, and nonmetal ores and timber.

2. Raw materials industry: provides various sectors of the national economy with raw materials, fuel, and power. That includes the smelting and processing of metals; coke making and coke chemistry; manufacture of chemical materials and building materials, such as cement, plywood, and power petroleum; and coal processing.

3. Manufacturing industry: processes raw materials. It includes machine-tool industry, metal fabrication and cement works, agricultural equipment manufacture, and chemical fertilizer and pesticide production.

Light Industry: Light industry refers to industry that produces consumer goods and hand tools. It consists of two categories, depending on the materials used:

Table 6: Sectoral Allocation of Investment, 1953–1978 (percentage)

Year	Agricultural	Heavy	Light
1953–1957	7.1	36.1	6.4
1958–1962	11.3	54.0	6.4
1963–1965	17.7	45.9	3.9
1966–1970	10.7	51.1	4.4
1971–1975	9.8	49.6	5.8
1976–1978	10.5	45.9	6.7
1953–1978	12.0	54.2	5.4

Source: Lardy, 1983, p.130. Note: The investment figures in the table are for only agriculture and heavy and light industries. Other sectors, such as service, transport, construction, etc., are not included. That is why the percentage in each year does not add up to 100.

1. Industries using farm products as raw materials. Those are branches of industry that directly or indirectly use farm products as basic raw materials. Industries in this category include the manufacture of food and beverages; tobacco processing; textile, clothing, fur, and leather manufacturing; paper making; printing; etc.

2. Industries using nonfarm products as raw materials. These are branches of industry that use manufactured goods as raw materials. Industries in this category include the manufacture of cultural, educational and sports articles, chemicals, synthetic fibers, glass and metal products for daily use, hand tools, medical apparatus and instruments, and the manufacture of cultural and office machinery.

The Third-Front Construction

The Third-Front Construction strategy was stipulated in the mid-1960s. The fear that the country might be invaded along the eastern seaboard and disputes with the Soviet Union led to the concept of the "third-front" or "third-line" strategy. According to the strategic location, the coastal and northeastern regions were called the first front; the interior areas of the southwest and northwest (except Tibet and Xinjiang) were the third front; the areas between the two were the second front. The aim of the third-front strategy was to create self-sufficient bases for defense in remote mountainous areas. In line with this strategy, beginning in the mid 1960s, the focus of investment shifted to the third-front regions far from the coastal zone and away from existing cities. During the next decade, nearly 2,000 large and medium-size plants were built, many of them to make military equipment, heavy machinery, and electronic components. The third-front provinces absorbed about two-fifths of all state investment when the strategy was in effect. Most enterprises in the third-front regions were directly controlled by central ministries and operated in areas having underdeveloped economies and poor infrastructures. Their production efficiency lagged far behind that of their longer-established counterparts in the coastal zone.

In 1972, in the wake of the visit of U.S. President Richard M. Nixon to China, the international situation surrounding China relaxed. The urgency felt about preparing for war diminished, and the large-scale construction in the third-front entered a lull in the mid-1970s.

State-Owned Enterprises

China's industry before the 1980s was dominated by the public sector. There were two basic kinds of business: those owned by the Chinese people as a whole, termed state-owned enterprises (SOEs), and those owned by a group of people, termed collectives. SOEs were usually large- and medium-sized companies, many of them in heavy industry. Most small handicraft businesses were absorbed into the collective sector. SOEs were by far the dominant force, accounting for nearly 80 percent of the value of industrial output in the late 1970s.

Prior to the 1980s, the residual income of state-owned enterprises; that is, the amount of revenue left after recovering the costs of production, went straight into the budget of the central government. As such, there was no distinction between taxation of company profits and dividends paid to the "owners" of the firm. Property rights in SOEs were inalienable. The enterprises could not be bought and sold in the marketplace. Neither could they be leased out. As a consequence, "State property belonged to all and to none."

Normally, decisions about what an enterprise produced were made by the central bureaucracy under its relevant ministry, based upon the national plan. The ministry also determined production quantities. The means of achieving those production targets, such as the required amounts of raw materials, semi-finished products, capital, and even the labor force, were all allocated by the bureaucracy. The most important target for an enterprise to achieve was its output volume, not its quality or profit. As for workers in SOEs, they had de facto job tenure for life, a situation that was often referred to as the "iron rice bowl."

Soft Budget Constraint: The economic inefficiencies of SOEs were associated with their bureaucratic management and operation. This often caused SOEs to operate at a loss. However, under the planned economy, loss-making SOEs could continue their operation. That was largely helped by the "soft budget constraint." SOEs operating at a loss had four options: Their losses could be directly covered by the state; they could negotiate a reduction in their rate of "corporate taxation"; they could renegotiate their prices for outputs; or they could be given access to cheap credit. Managers of SOEs knew that if they made losses, it would not lead to the closure of their factories and/or the loss of their jobs. As a result, SOE managers had little incentive to minimize their costs of production, so inefficiency became a pervasive and persistent problem in SOEs.

Pre-Reform Foreign Trade System

China's pre-reform foreign trade was tightly controlled by the state. The Ministry of Foreign Trade, created in 1952, was the executive department responsible for China's foreign trade and economic relations, including technical cooperation with other countries. The Ministry exercised control of foreign trade through a number of corporations that specialized in trade in specific product areas. Foreign trade corporations were responsible for implementing the state's foreign trade plan. The annual foreign trade plan was an integral part of the economic planning process. The purpose of importing was to lay the foundation for China's industrial independence, so that in the future China could produce all of the goods it needed without having to rely on imports from other countries.

Under the pre-reform foreign trade regime, producing firms were forbidden from having direct contact with the outside world. They could not engage directly in foreign trade and had to conduct trade through the appropriate foreign trade corporations. The latter exported and imported goods at world market prices and bought and sold them in China at domestic prices. Domestic prices often bore no relation to world prices. As a result of China's limited contact with the rest of the world, trade value (imports plus exports) was only a small percentage of the GDP prior to reform, amounting to less than 10 percent in 1978.

9. ECONOMIC REFORMS SINCE 1978

Background of the Economic Reform

When Mao Zedong died in September 1976, Deng Xiaoping (1904–1997) and his allies increased their influence. A new economic goal was proclaimed in 1977, when the Eleventh Congress of the Chinese Communist Party approved the Four Modernizations—agriculture, industry, science and technology, and national defense—and wrote them into the constitution.

After 20 years of central planning, several consequences had become apparent by the late 1970s: a high urban unemployment rate of up to 9.5 percent, stagnating food consumption, deteriorating urban housing conditions, falling real wages in the urban sector, and widespread rural poverty. Despite the heavy investment in the 1960s and 1970s, the living standard was not qualitatively higher than that of the mid-1950s. In the crucial category of grain consumption, average per capita food-grain availability in 1977 was similar to the 1955 level. The general freeze of wages and the entry of new workers into the lowest rungs of the wage ladder in the urban sector caused the average wage in real terms to actually fall by 17 percent between 1957 and 1977. Approximately 100 million peasants had yearly per capita grain consumption of less than 150 kg, an amount that would supply a daily intake of only 1,500 calories. Productivity growth was sluggish. Most of China's industrial growth came from increases in fixed capital, and very little was due to more efficient use of inputs. The growth of labor productivity was achieved principally by increases in the amounts of physical capital per worker. All of these consequences called for a reform in the conventional socialist economic regime.

Rural Institutional Reform: Household-Responsibility System

The rural institutional reform, represented by the household-responsibility system, first emerged in some poor areas of China in the late 1970s. Land and production equipment and supplies were assigned to individual households according to contracts that stipulated the amount of grain to be produced on the plot. Households could dispose of everything produced on the plot over the contractual amount as they wished—sold to the state, sold on the free market, or consumed by the families. The household-responsibility system was officially approved at the Third Plenum of the Eleventh Central Committee of the Chinese Communist Party in December 1978. The system rapidly spread throughout the country in the following years. Contracts were extended to all crops, animal husbandry, forestry, and fisheries. By the end of 1982, the system became nearly universal in China's countryside. The combined political and economic unit of people's communes was replaced by a solely administrative local government

structure—the township government. In 1984, the people's commune system officially came to an end.

Under the household-responsibility system, farmland was distributed to households primarily on the basis of household size, that is, the number of people in the household. As a general practice, each household got its share of fertile land, exhausted land, land close to home, land far from home, grain fields, cotton fields, seedling fields, etc. This method of distribution increased the fragmentation of land management. Land ownership was separated from usage rights. The collective retained the ownership of land but allowed individuals to use the land on a leasehold basis (the length of the leases has since been extended to at least 20 years to encourage farmers to make long-term investment in their land). Although farmers do not own the land, they are allowed to transfer or release their land to other farmers. Farmers are also allowed to own their draught animals, tractors, and other agricultural equipment.

Reforms in State-Owned Enterprises

Before 1978, China's state-owned enterprises were subject to state control. There were mandatory production targets for each enterprise. Material inputs were allocated by administrative fiat, product prices were set by the government administration, wages and salaries were determined by national pay scales and unrelated to productivity, all profits were remitted to the state, and losses were met from the state budget. Under the state-owned enterprises, reforms since the early 1980s include the following:

• Enterprises have been given more freedom through decentralization and the simplification of administration. At the beginning of the reform, enterprises were allowed to retain a proportion of their profits. In the mid-1980s, a profit tax was introduced. State-owned enterprises were allowed to retain the after-tax profits. A personal-responsibility system for employees of enterprises was introduced in the early 1980s and quickly evolved into a contracting system. By 1988, about 90 percent of medium- and large-scale state-owned enterprises had signed management contracts. Leasing arrangements were generally used for small enterprises in the service sector. A new national bankruptcy law was enacted in 1986 and came into effect in June 1988.

- The lifetime employment of state workers was officially replaced by a contract labor system in 1986. Under the new system, all new workers in state-owned enterprises, with few exceptions, were hired on a contractual basis, usually for a period of three to five years. In 1993, contracted workers accounted for 20 percent of total workers in state-owned enterprises. In 1986, unemployment insurance schemes were established to protect both contract and permanent workers of enterprises that might be closed under the implementation of the bankruptcy law. Dismissal of unqualified workers became legally permitted, although there were only a few cases of dismissals in the 1980s.

- Since the 1990s, the key issue of enterprise reform has been to clarify property rights and to establish a modern enterprise regime. Large and medium state-owned enterprises are gradually being transformed into exclusive proprietary corporations, limited-liability companies, or limited joint stock companies, though public ownership is still stressed. Small state-owned enterprises are evolving into cooperative shareholding companies or private firms by contracting, leasing, and auctioning.

Reforms in Marketing and Pricing

Prior to the 1980s, virtually all prices of agricultural and industrial goods were directly controlled by the state. The marketing reform of the early 1980s produced a progressive relaxation of such control. By the mid-1980s, there was a large growth in the role of free markets. In 1985, a "dual-track" price system was implemented. By and large, the dual track means different prices for the same product in parallel state-controlled and free markets. Farmers and enterprises deliver the contractual quantity of products to the state at the price set by the state and sell the rest at free markets. Pricing and marketing reforms in recent years have led to a continuous decline in the proportion of state-controlled products and an increasing role for the free market.

In the reformed agricultural sector, state purchases of farm products were made on a contractual basis. Farmers could sell their produce in the free market after they fulfilled the contractual sum. To encourage farmers to sell their produce to the state, grain quota purchase prices increased by more than 20 percent in 1979 and continued to rise through the 1980s and 1990s. Purchase prices of cotton, oil-bearing crops, sugar, and other farm and sideline products were also raised. Meanwhile, the quantities and varieties of products under state control were gradually reduced. By the mid-1990s, most non-grain agricultural products had become free of state control. As a result, both the wholesale markets and the retail markets for agricultural goods mushroomed.

In the industrial sector, the dual-track system enabled enterprises to acquire inputs from two sources—a quota allocation at low (that is, government-fixed) prices and additional amounts at higher market prices. After fulfilling their plan quota, enterprises were allowed to sell their products at higher market prices. The number of products that were allocated through the state plan declined from about 250 items in the early 1980s to approximately 20 items in 1988. A large proportion of output was sold in the free market. Despite the reduced scope of planning controls, the bulk of production of important intermediate products, including steel, coal, petroleum, and electricity, was still subject to a relatively high degree of central- and local-government control until the 1990s.

Reforms in the Taxation System

The taxation system in China was highly centralized before the reforms. The central government controlled all income and expenditures of local governments, ministerial governments, and enterprises. This system frustrated the initiatives of local governments and enterprises.

Tax reform is an important component of China's overall economic reform effort because taxation raises government revenue and influences enterprise decisions. Starting from 1980, the taxation regime was decentralized by a *huafen shouzhi* (division of revenue and expenditure) between central and local governments. Fixed revenue was divided into two parts: the central government collected about 80 percent and local governments about 20 percent. Expenditures were also divided into two parts. Current expenditures of enterprises and government institutions were paid by the government in charge of those enterprises and institutions. The central government funded some big economic programs.

In the mid-1980s, state enterprises began paying industrial and commercial taxes instead of remitting all profits to the state. A radical reform in the fiscal system was implemented in the beginning of 1994. There were three aspects of the reform: (1) Fiscal contracts were replaced by a tax assignment system on the basis of a division of power between central and local authorities; (2) a uniform income tax was applied to domestic and foreign enterprises; and (3) the original industrial and business taxes were replaced by a system of turnover taxes (for example, taxes charged on the total value of business transactions), a form of value-added taxes.

The Open-Door Policy

China had been closed to the outside world before the 1970s due to both an internal socialist dogma of self-sufficiency and an external embargo by the United States and its Western allies. The general improvement in China's international position, particularly the improvement of the Sino-U.S. relationship during the 1970s, gave rise to a change in its view of foreign economic relations. When Deng Xiaoping took power in 1978, China's trade and foreign direct investment policies changed dramatically. Having examined the success of the "Four Little Dragons" (Singapore, Taiwan, Korea, and Hong Kong), China's reform-minded leaders concluded that becoming involved in foreign trade and encouraging foreign firms to invest in Chinese enterprises were vital for improving enterprise efficiency and stimulating economic growth. The policy was referred to as an open-door policy.

In accordance with the open-door policy, four special economic zones were established in 1979: Shenzhen north of Hong Kong, Zhuhai across the Pearl River estuary, Shantou in north-eastern Guangdong, and Xiamen in Fujian opposite Taiwan. In 1984, 14 additional coastal cities were opened to foreign investors. Hainan province was also opened as the largest special economic zone in 1988. The initial purpose of the zones was to act as centers for the introduction of modern techniques to the nation. In reality, they have been used to process imported materials for export. Foreign firms were encouraged to establish factories and processing plants under conditions more preferable than those available elsewhere. Throughout the 1980s, in line with a coastal area development strategy, increasing numbers of coastal cities were identified as open areas for foreign investment. Numerous economic development zones, high-tech development zones, and tariff-free export processing zones were established in the 1990s in coastal cities and areas surrounding them.

10. TYPES OF BUSINESS OWNERSHIP IN THE POST-REFORM ERA

China's Enterprise System

State-Owned Enterprises: The economic reform started in the late 1970s has seen a substantial decline in the role of state-owned enterprises in the national economy. In the late 1970s, state-owned enterprises contributed nearly 80 percent of the gross value of industrial production. By 1990, their contribution had declined to around 50 percent, and in 1998, the contribution had dropped to only 28 percent.

Since the reforms, the overall financial performance of state-owned enterprises has been weak. Losses at state-owned enterprises have continued at a very high level. It was estimated that in 1994 about one-half of state-owned enterprises were incurring losses. Another problem facing state-owned enterprises has been the so-called triangle debt. That term refers to a chain of enterprises that cannot pay their debts to banks, general creditors, and suppliers, including other companies in the chain, because they cannot collect their money from one another.

Urban Collective Enterprises: Urban collective enterprises fall into three categories with different historical backgrounds and somewhat different characteristics. The largest category was formed during the 1950s through the forced participation of handicraft workers. Those enterprises are called "big collectives" because local authorities own them. The second category consists of collectives created by neighborhood committees during the period of the Great Leap Forward (1958–1962) that are called "street industries." They are usually small in size, and their employees are mostly women and middle school graduates. The third category consists of collective firms established and managed by large state-owned enterprises. They are primarily established to provide employment for dependents of state workers. The second and third categories are also called "small collectives," not only because they are usually small in size but also because they are responsible for their profits and losses.

Township and Village Enterprises: China's rural collective enterprises, commonly known as township and village enterprises, are economic units established in the countryside by local governments or by the peasants themselves. Township and village enterprises operate outside the state plan and are subject to "hard-budget constraints" in that the owners (the peasants or the townships) do not have any guaranteed fiscal support from above. They buy inputs and sell outputs in free

markets and do not have to fulfill plan obligations to the state. Despite that market orientation, however, the enterprises' origins in the collective system mean that they commonly have a strong linkage with local governments and are an important source of local government revenue. As a result, local governments are generally keen to promote their growth.

Since the economic reform, township and village enterprises have experienced an unprecedented phase of rapid development. The total number of enterprises increased to more than 20 million in 1998, more than a three-fold increase over 1984. Their total labor force by the end of 1998 was more than 125 million, compared to a total rural labor force of 493 million, a total urban labor force of 207 million, and total employment of 91 million in state-owned enterprises.

Private and Individual Enterprises: In China, private and individual enterprises consist of two statistical categories. The difference between the two is the number of people employed. A private enterprise is defined as an independent legal entity that hires eight or more employees and is run by individuals, partnerships, or shareholders. An individual enterprise is an independent legal entity in which eight or fewer workers are hired, run by individuals or households. Small private enterprises initially developed quietly in the early 1980s, and the larger ones were only formally recognized and regulated after 1988. Since the 1990s, the difference between the two entities has become obscure.

Foreign-Funded Enterprises: Foreign-funded enterprises are those owned wholly or partially by foreigners. They can be classified into three categories: wholly foreign-owned, equity joint ventures, and cooperative joint ventures. The last two categories include joint operations between foreigners and domestic enterprises and are often referred to as joint venture enterprises.

A wholly foreign-owned enterprise is an independent legal entity entirely owned by the foreign investor. Wholly foreign-owned ventures were rare until 1988. They had been restricted to "advanced technology" and "export oriented" projects, and until 1986 they were found only in the special economic zones. However, the number of those enterprises increased rapidly in the 1990s, totaling 9,673 by 1998.

According to joint venture law, an equity joint venture takes the form of a limited liability company. Each party (investor) in an equity joint venture is jointly responsible for investment and management and shares risks, gains and losses. Equity joint ventures increased greatly over the years, rising from a mere 112 in 1983 to 8,107 in 1998.

A cooperative joint venture is formed by a contract in which both parties agree upon (1) the conditions for investment or cooperation, (2) the distribution of earnings or products, (3) the share of risks and losses, (4) the methods of operation and management, and (5) the ownership of the assets at the termination of the joint venture. It is a flexible form of cooperative operation that was popular in the early 1980s. However, that form of venture has tended to be replaced gradually by wholly foreign-owned ventures since the 1990s. Cooperative joint ventures accounted for 32 percent of total foreign investment projects in 1990 but dropped to a mere 10 percent in 1998.

Joint Ownership Enterprises: Joint ownership is any combination among those domestic firms, including shareholding units, joint-owned units, limited liability corporations, and shareholding corporations. Joint ownership emerged in the 1990s when cross ownership and cross-sector integration were encouraged. However,

except for investment in fixed assets, shares of joint ownership in both production and employment were still small by 1998.

Changes in Enterprise Employment Structure

Since the economic reform begun in the late 1970s, the ownership structure of enterprises has changed substantially. State-owned enterprises have declined steadily in their share of total employment. In 1980, state-owned enterprises accounted for more than 60 percent of all non-agricultural employment. The share fell to 24 percent in 1998.

The share of urban collective enterprises in total employment has also undergone a decline, from 18 percent in 1980 to only about 5 percent in 1998. The share of rural collective enterprises in total employment has experienced uneven growth. There was a rapid expansion of employment until the mid-1990s, but employment fell substantially thereafter.

The expansion of nonpublic enterprises, that is, private and individual enterprises, and foreign-funded enterprises was rapid in the 1990s. In 1998, one-fifth of the labor force was employed in private and individual enterprises. Wholly foreign-owned and joint venture enterprises grew from virtually zero in the early 1980s to more than 4 percent in 1998 (see Table 7).

11. ECONOMIC GROWTH AND STRUCTURAL CHANGES

Economic Growth

Despite the failures of economic development in many aspects during the Maoist period, the Chinese economy did achieve some important accomplishments. From 1952 to 1975, China's gross domestic product grew at an average annual rate of 6.7 percent, and the industrial sector (the so-called secondary sector; see Table 8) increased its share of gross domestic product from 20.9 to 45.7 percent. Economic growth in China accelerated in the 1980s

and 1990s. The annual growth rate of gross domestic product was about 10.2 percent during the 1980s and 11.9 percent between 1990 and 1997. This growth exceeded the growth record of almost all other countries in the world during the same period. In the early 1980s, a goal was set by Deng Xiaoping to quadruple China's gross national product by the year 2000. That goal was attained five years ahead of schedule when the Chinese gross national product reached 5,760 billion yuan in 1995.

Table 7: Structure of the Total Nonagricultural Employment by Ownership, 1980–1998 (million persons)

Year	Total	State-owned enterprises	Urban collective enterprises	Rural enterprises	Foreign-funded enterprises	Private and individual enterprises	Joint ownership
1980	132.39	80.19	24.25	30.00	—	—	—
1985	187.43	89.90	33.24	69.79	—	—	0.38
1990	297.92	103.46	35.49	92.65	0.66	22.93	0.96
1991	300.04	106.64	36.28	96.09	1.65	24.92	0.49
1992	307.59	108.89	36.21	106.25	2.21	27.00	0.56
1993	324.07	109.20	33.93	123.45	2.88	33.13	2.30
1994	298.43	112.14	32.85	120.17	4.06	44.33	3.53
1995	349.29	112.61	31.47	128.62	5.13	55.88	3.81
1996	359.40	112.44	30.16	135.08	5.40	61.97	4.21
1997	373.79	110.44	28.83	130.50	5.81	67.91	5.12
1998	378.07	90.58	19.63	125.37	5.87	78.21	10.78
Shares percent							
1980	100	60.57	18.32	22.66	—	—	—
1985	100	47.96	17.73	37.24	—	—	0.20
1990	100	34.73	11.91	31.10	0.22	7.70	0.32
1991	100	35.54	12.09	32.03	0.55	8.31	0.16
1992	100	35.40	11.77	34.54	0.72	8.78	0.18
1993	100	33.70	10.47	38.09	0.89	10.22	0.71
1994	100	37.58	11.01	40.27	1.36	14.85	1.18
1995	100	32.24	9.01	36.82	1.47	16.00	1.09
1996	100	31.29	8.39	37.58	1.50	17.24	1.17
1997	100	29.55	7.71	34.91	1.55	18.17	1.37
1998	100	23.96	5.19	33.16	1.55	20.69	2.85

Sources: China Statistical Bureau, 1991, p. 391; 1995, pp.377–381; 1996, p.389; 1997, pp. 413–416; 1999, pp.139–156.

Changes in the Industrial Structure

In China, the three sectors in the national economy are defined as follows. The primary sector refers to agriculture, including farming, forestry, animal husbandry, and fisheries. The secondary sector refers to mining and quarrying, construction, manufacturing, and production and supply of electricity, water, and gas. The tertiary sector covers all economic activities not included in the primary or secondary sectors.

Before the 1950s, China was overwhelmingly rural and dominated by the primary sector. In 1952, the shares of the gross domestic product of primary, secondary, and tertiary sectors were 50.5 percent, 20.9 percent, and 28.6 percent, respectively. The second half of the 20th century saw a decline in the share of primary sector and an increase in secondary and tertiary sectors. By the end of the 1990s, China had turned itself from an agrarian economy to an industrial one. In 1998, the primary sector accounted for about 18 percent of the total industrial gross output, and the shares of secondary and tertiary sectors were 48.8 and 32.9 percent, respectively. Despite the substantial increase in the shares of secondary and tertiary sectors, a large proportion of the labor force was still employed in agriculture. In 1998, about 50 percent of the total labor force in China remained in the primary sector. (See Table 9 for a breakdown of employment by sector.)

Table 8: Gross Domestic Product by Sector, 1952–1998 (current prices)

| | Figures in billions of yuan | | | | Percent | | |
Year	Total gross domestic product	Primary	Secondary	Tertiary	Primary	Secondary	Tertiary
1952	68	34	14	19	50.50	20.88	28.62
1957	107	43	32	32	40.26	29.68	30.06
1962	115	45	36	34	39.42	31.26	29.31
1965	172	65	60	46	37.94	35.09	26.97
1970	225	79	91	55	35.22	40.49	24.29
1975	300	97	137	66	32.40	45.72	21.88
1978	362	102	175	86	28.10	48.16	23.74
1980	452	136	219	97	30.09	48.52	21.39
1985	896	254	387	256	28.35	43.13	28.52
1986	1,020	276	449	295	27.09	44.04	28.87
1987	1,196	320	525	351	26.79	43.90	29.31
1988	1,493	383	659	451	25.66	44.13	30.21
1989	1,691	423	728	540	25.00	43.04	31.95
1990	1,855	502	772	581	27.05	41.61	31.34
1991	2,162	529	910	723	24.46	42.11	33.43
1992	2,664	580	1,170	914	21.77	43.92	34.31
1993	3,463	688	1,643	1,132	19.87	47.43	32.70
1994	4,676	946	2,237	1,493	20.23	47.85	31.93
1995	5,848	1,199	2,854	1,795	20.51	48.80	30.69
1996	6,788	1,384	3,361	2,043	20.39	49.51	30.09
1997	7,446	1,421	3,722	2,303	19.09	49.99	30.93
1998	7,940	1,460	3,869	2,610	18.39	48.73	32.88

Source: China Statistical Bureau, 1999, p. 55.

Growth of Agriculture Production

Before the reforms, agriculture grew slowly partly due to the policy bias favoring industrialization and the consequent extraction of resources from the agricultural sector and partly due to the inefficient management of people's communes. Between 1958 and 1978, the growth rate of agriculture was less than 2 percent. After the household-responsibility system was introduced in the late 1970s, agriculture experienced vigorous development. From 1978 to 1984, the growth rate of agricultural output averaged nearly 8 percent annually. However, after 1985 agricultural performance weakened. The annual growth rate in the gross value of agricultural output fell to 3 to 4 percent, substan-

tially lower than that achieved in the early 1980s. Production of grain and other crops dropped in absolute terms in 1985 and stagnated in the following years. In the 1990s, agriculture showed a renewed dynamism.

In 1978, when the economic reform program was launched in rural areas, farming output contributed to 80 percent of the total gross output value in the agricultural sector; and forestry, animal husbandry, and fishery sectors contributed 3.4 percent, 15 percent, and 1.6 percent, respectively. The share of farming declined to 58 percent in 1998, while the shares of output of animal husbandry and fisheries grew significantly, leaving the share of forestry almost unchanged. Table 10 contains a summary of China's agricultural industry from 1978–1998.

Table 9: Employment by Sector, 1952–1998

Year	Numbers of persons (x 10,000)				Percent		
	Total	Primary	Secondary	Tertiary	Primary	Secondary	Tertiary
1952	20,729	17,316	1,528	1,885	83.54	7.37	9.09
1957	23,771	19,300	2,115	2,356	81.19	8.90	9.91
1962	25,910	21,259	2,033	2,618	82.05	7.85	10.10
1965	28,670	23,372	2,376	1,922	81.52	8.29	6.70
1970	34,432	27,786	3,479	3,167	80.70	10.10	9.20
1975	38,168	29,415	5,075	3,678	77.07	13.30	9.64
1978	40,152	28,318	6,945	4,890	70.53	17.30	12.18
1980	42,361	29,122	7,707	5,532	68.75	18.19	13.06
1985	49,873	31,130	10,384	8,359	62.42	20.82	16.76
1986	51,282	31,254	11,216	8,811	60.95	21.87	17.18
1987	52,783	31,663	11,726	9,395	59.99	22.22	17.80
1988	54,334	32,349	12,152	9,936	59.54	22.37	18.29
1989	55,329	33,225	11,976	10,129	60.05	21.65	18.31
1990	63,909	38,428	13,654	11,828	60.13	21.36	18.51
1991	64,799	38,685	13,867	12,247	59.70	21.40	18.90
1992	65,554	38,349	14,226	12,979	58.50	21.70	19.80
1993	66,373	37,434	14,868	14,071	56.40	22.40	21.20
1994	67,199	36,489	15,254	15,456	54.30	22.70	23.00
1995	67,947	35,468	15,628	16,851	52.20	23.00	24.80
1996	68,850	34,769	16,180	17,901	50.50	23.50	26.00
1997	69,600	34,730	16,495	18,375	49.90	23.70	26.40
1998	69,957	34,838	16,440	18,679	49.80	23.50	26.70

Source: China Statistical Bureau, 1999, p. 134.

Manufacturing

Since the 1950s, China has established a relatively comprehensive industrial structure. Gross output value of manufacturing grew rapidly from 34.9 billion yuan in 1952 to 1,190 billion yuan in 1998, a more than 341-fold augmentation during this period (measured by current price levels). The annual growth rate averaged 12.5 percent. Among the various branches of manufacturing, the metallurgical and machine tool industries received the highest priority. Those two branches alone accounted for about one-third of the total gross value of industrial output in the 1990s. Much of the country's steel output comes from a small number of producing centers, the largest being Anshan in Liaoning province.

The principal products of the chemical industry are chemical fertilizers, plastics, and synthetic fibers. China is among the world's leading producers of nitrogenous fertilizers. In the consumer goods sector, the main emphasis is on textiles and clothing, which also are an important part of China's exports. Textiles accounted for about 15 percent of the gross industrial output in the late 1990s. Although the textile industry is scattered throughout the country, there are a number of important textile centers, including Shanghai, Guangdong, and Harbin.

Energy Industry

After the United States and Russia, China is the world's third-largest consumer of commercial energy. Until 1992, China produced more energy than it consumed. After 1992, China's total consumption exceeded total production. Production and consumption in 1998 were 1,240 million tons of coal equivalent and 1,360 million tons of coal equivalent, respectively. The consumption of coal equivalent per

Table 10: Gross Value of Agriculture, 1978–1998

Year	Total Agriculture	Farming	Forestry	Animal Husbandry	Fisheries
	Yuan (in millions)				
1978	13,970	11,175	481	2,093	221
1980	19,226	14,541	814	3,542	329
1985	36,195	25,064	1,887	7,983	1,261
1990	76,621	49,543	3,303	19,670	4,106
1991	81,857	51,464	3,679	21,592	4,835
1992	90,847	55,880	4,225	24,605	6,136
1993	109,955	66,051	4,940	30,144	8,820
1994	157,505	91,692	6,111	46,720	12,982
1995	203,409	118,846	7,099	60,450	17,013
1996	223,582	135,398	7,781	60,200	20,204
1997	237,640	138,525	8,178	68,110	22,827
1998	245,167	142,419	8,513	70,007	24,229
	Percent				
1978	100	79.99	3.44	14.98	1.58
1980	100	75.63	4.23	18.42	1.71
1985	100	69.25	5.21	22.06	3.48
1990	100	64.66	4.31	25.67	5.36
1991	100	62.87	4.49	26.38	5.91
1992	100	61.51	4.65	27.08	6.75
1993	100	60.07	4.49	27.41	8.02
1994	100	58.22	3.88	29.66	8.24
1995	100	58.43	3.49	29.72	8.36
1996	100	60.56	3.48	26.93	9.04
1997	100	58.29	3.44	28.66	9.61
1998	100	58.09	3.47	28.55	9.88

Source: China Statistical Bureau, 1999, p. 382.

capita was 993 kg in 1998, roughly half of the world average. A shortage of energy is one of the principal constraints on the Chinese economy.

The strategic importance of energy has kept this sector more closely under government control. During the reform period, energy industries failed to enjoy the boom that deregulation generated in many other sectors of the economy. Government fears of inflation kept prices of coal, oil, gas, and electricity artificially low. As a result, industries had few incentives to conserve, and energy utilization in China was highly inefficient by the world standards.

Coal provides about 70 percent of China's energy consumption. The distribution of coal resources is highly concentrated north of the Yangtze River. Inner Mongolia, Shanxi, and Shaanxi are the largest coal-producing provinces in China. The regional imbalance is the root of the problems in coal transportation that have long plagued the economy. About half of rail transport in China is used for the transport of coal. Petroleum production, which began growing rapidly from an extremely low base in the early 1960s, has basically remained at the same level since the late 1970s. There are large petroleum reserves in the northwest and potentially significant offshore petroleum deposits, but the bulk of the country's oil production still comes from the eastern part, notably Daqing in the northeast, which produces about half the country's oil output. Since the 1990s, economic policy has stressed sustaining investment flows, increasing efficiency, rationalizing prices, promoting exploration, stressing conservation, and improving the financial situation in the energy sector.

Rural Enterprises

Rural enterprises are spread across all sectors of the national economy. Nevertheless, rural industries are, by far, the dominant component of rural enterprises. In 1998, industrial output accounted for 70 percent of total value added of rural enterprises. Other activities are in the service sector, and a small proportion (2 percent) is classified as agriculture, but this is usually intensive agricultural activities such as meat production and grain processing. As early as 1988, the total output value of rural enterprises had surpassed the agricultural output value to become dominant in the rural economy. In 1998, gross domestic product (value added) of rural industries accounted for 30 percent of the national total. Total business income of rural enterprises reached 383 billion yuan, becoming the largest source of rural income, as compared to gross output value of farming (142 billion yuan), forestry (85 billion yuan), animal husbandry (70 billion yuan), and fisheries (24 billion yuan).

The Tertiary Sector

The tertiary sector is made up of mainly commerce, catering, transportation, and services. The development of China's tertiary sector was dampened by a Marxist theoretical dogma of dividing the primary, secondary, and tertiary sectors into "productive" and "nonproductive" categories. Agriculture and manufacturing, according to this theory, were productive, whereas services, especially intangible services, were considered nonproductive. As a result, the share of employment in the tertiary sector in the 1970s was below 10 percent, nearly the same level as it was in the 1950s. During the reform period, the tertiary sector rapidly grew. Its share increased to 18.5 percent in 1990 and 26.7 percent in 1998.

Transportation

Despite a great emphasis on the development of transport during the reform period, China's domestic transport system continues to constitute a major constraint on economic growth as well as the efficient movement of goods and people. Railroads provide the major means for freight haulage, but their capacity cannot meet demand, especially for the shipment of coal. Inadequate transport capacity has often been identified (along with energy) as a "key bottleneck" or a "prominent weak link" in China's economy.

Railways: Between 1952 and 1979, China's railway network grew by an average of 1,000 kilometers a year. The main focus of expansion, however, was on new routes, especially in the frontier regions of the northwest and southwest, where population is sparse and the terrain extremely inhospitable to railways. During the 1980s and 1990s, the tons-per-kilometer carried by rail increased at a rate of 6 percent a year. During that period, the passengers-per-kilometer carried by rail increased at a rate of nearly 10 percent a year. That performance, however, was mainly achieved by an intensive utilization of equipment and track that were already heavily utilized. Inevitably, there were some adverse consequences, including poor service, overloading, and increased crashes. Though railway charges were increased in steps, overcrowding continued to be a serious problem at the outset of the 21st century. Only four cities—Beijing, Shanghai, Tianjin, and Guangzhou—had metro railways by 2000.

Highways: In many respects, the phases of development of China's highway network paralleled the pattern for railways. China's highway system expanded from 127,000 kilometers in 1952 to 515,000 kilometers in 1965, an average annual growth rate of nearly 11 percent. Between 1965 and 1978, the expansion of the highway network increased about 4 percent a year. In the 1980s, the expansion of the highway network slowed even further, to a mere 1 percent a year. This decrease was a result of shifting the concentration from expanding highways to upgrading existing routes in heavy-traffic regions. The expansion of highways accelerated to about 3 percent after 1994.

Water Transport: Broadly speaking, China's large navigable rivers are grouped in three basins: the Heilongjiang system in the northeast, the Yangtze system in central China, and the Pearl River system in the south. The Yellow River, which drains the north China plain, is plagued by heavy silting. Its navigational use is quite limited.

In 1961, China established the Ocean Shipping Company. Since then, China has invested heavily in port construction. In addition to new construction, older ports have been rebuilt and expanded. Shanghai was the largest port before Hong Kong was returned to China's sovereignty in 1997.

Aviation: Chinese civil aviation was carried out solely by the Civil Aviation Administration of China from 1949 until the mid-1980s. Since then, regional airlines have been established in competition with the airlines operated by the national administration. The number of air routes grew markedly in the 1990s. Beijing, Shanghai, Guangzhou, and Ürümqi in Xinjiang autonomous region became major centers of air transport by 2000.

12. Banking and Monetary System

Banking System

The People's Bank of China is the country's central bank. The bank has the power to issue currency, formulate and implement monetary policies, and exercise strict surveillance over financial institutions to ensure a safe and effective operation of the banking system. The Bank of China is a subsidiary of the People's Bank. The role of the Bank of China is the management of foreign exchange and international payments. The Bank of China implements exchange controls and manages operations in relation to foreign currencies.

Domestic banking arrangements are carried out predominantly by "specialized banks." The Industrial and Commercial Bank of China conducts ordinary commercial transactions and acts as a savings bank for the public. The Agricultural Bank of China serves the agricultural sector. The People's Construction Bank of China is responsible for capitalizing a portion of overall investment and for providing capital funds for certain industrial and construction enterprises. In addition to these, the Investment Bank, begun in 1981, handles foreign investments; the Transportation Bank was restored in 1986; and the China Trust (Zhongxin) was established in 1987. Since the 1990s, some regional banks have been established. A number of foreign banks have also been permitted to set up their offices and conduct banking business in China's large cities and special economic zones.

Renminbi (People's Money): Renminbi (RMB), literally meaning "people's money," is the Chinese currency used on the mainland. Before the reforms, China did not permit market forces to determine foreign exchange rates, but allocated it administratively. China devalued its domestic currency several times over the post-reform era, from 1.57 yuan per U.S. dollar in 1979 to 5.73 yuan per U.S. dollar in 1992, and 8.61 yuan per U.S. dollar in 1994. The depreciation of RMB has helped the rapid growth of China's international trade, especially the growth of exports in the post-reform era.

The official exchange rate and the actual rate used in the foreign exchange centers in China were merged in 1994. Foreign exchange can be purchased from the Bank of China upon government approval. The RMB is convertible among foreign trade corporations on the condition that either the foreign exchange required is less than 50 percent of the foreign exchange earned by the enterprise, or it is sponsored by the government due to necessity. This change has encouraged enterprises to export more to raise the possibility of earning more foreign exchange. However, the RMB is still not a fully convertible currency.

Security Markets: Security markets include bond and share (stock) markets. Bonds are contracts between an issuer and a purchaser; in return for a specified sum of money advanced by the purchaser, the issuer agrees to make payments (usually of interest and principal) to the purchaser at specified dates. Bonds in China are seen as a means to finance the government deficit in a non-inflationary way and to reduce the amount of idle money in the hands of local governments, bureaucratic departments, and enterprises, as well as individuals. Beginning in 1985, the People's Bank extended the power to issue bonds to other banks and enterprises.

Like bonds, shares are seen as a useful supplement to the financial system in China. In 1990 and 1991, Shanghai Securities Market and Shenzhen Securities Market were established, respectively. Since then, China's stock markets have grown rapidly. Two types of shares denominated in different currencies are traded in the stock markets. Shares sold in yuan are called A-shares, and shares sold in U.S. dollars are called B-shares. A-shares are available to domestic investors only, and B-shares were available only to foreigners until February 19, 2001. After that date, B-shares became available to both foreign and domestic investors with foreign currencies.

13 INTERNATIONAL TRADE AND FOREIGN INVESTMENT

Growth of International Trade

Prior to the 1980s, the foreign trade corporations made all decisions about foreign trade. After the reform, local/municipal governments gained greater authority to allow them to engage in foreign trade transactions. Corporations, enterprises, and factories were also encouraged to make contact with foreign firms directly. International trade grew dramatically and made the country the largest exporter of manufactured goods in the developing world. Between 1979 and 1998, China's international trade (imports plus exports) grew at an average rate of 13 percent per year, compared to the average growth rate of 8 percent between 1952 and 1978. The trade-dependence ratio, defined as the total trade value to gross national product, increased from 5.8 percent in 1978 to 34.4 percent in 1998. The increasing presence of China on the world trade scene signified that the Chinese economy had turned from being a closed to an open one. In 1978, China was placed as the world's 32nd largest exporting country. It became the world's 11th largest in 1992 and the ninth largest in 1998.

Export Pattern: China's export pattern experienced a dramatic change between 1985 and 1998. Primary exports declined sharply and manufacturing exports increased dramatically; after the 1986 oil price drop, the importance of mineral exports declined. The share of manufacturing exports reached 88.8 percent in 1998.

China started to import agricultural goods in the early 1960s, although the quantities of the imports were small, considering the size of the domestic market. The limited land resources and increasing demand for food have continued to push up the prices of China's agricultural products in relation to world prices. By the 1990s, domestic market prices of major agricultural outputs had been close to or even higher than international prices. It has become economically rational for China to import agricultural goods from the international market. However, since the imports of agricultural goods are sensitive to political and national security considerations, the domestic agricultural market has not been completely open, and imports of grain remained largely under government control.

Sources of Export Growth: Foreign-funded enterprises and rural township and village enterprises were the main source of export growth in China during the 1980s and 1990s. The share of exports of foreign-funded enterprises in total national exports was below 1 percent in 1985, but increased to 13 percent in 1990 and 41 percent in 1996. The share of rural manufacturing exports in total exports increased from about 5 percent in 1985 to 43 percent in 1995. With China's foreign trade sector moving toward a more liberalized stage, foreign-funded enterprises and township and village enterprises began overtaking the state sector to play an increasingly important role in exporting manufacturing goods. See Table 11 below.

Foreign Investment

Foreign investment in the mainland part of China increased dramatically in the 1980s and early 1990s. In 1992, foreign direct investment exceeded the total amount of foreign loans. Following the 1985 and 1988 highs of foreign capital investment, the third wave of foreign investment emerged in the 1990s. In 1992 alone, the number of newly registered foreign-funded enterprises came to 1.29 times the total in the period between 1979 and 1991. The contract growth in 1993 was even more impressive, with a rate of 71

percent over 1992. The growth of new contracts began to fall thereafter, resulting in a substantial decline in actually utilized foreign capital during the rest of the 1990s.

Foreign investments were very unevenly spread and concentrated mostly in a small number of coastal provinces. Guangdong province had the largest share of foreign capital. In 1991, Guangdong had 22.37 percent of total contracted foreign capital and 41.74 percent of realized foreign capital. In terms of the value of contracts, Guangdong accounted for an overwhelming 44.7 percent of all investment received in the whole country in 1991. This dominance diminished marginally by the late 1990s.

The five largest sources of "foreign" direct investment in China were Hong Kong and Macao, Taiwan, the United States, Japan, and South Korea. At the end of 1998, the cumulative value of Hong Kong's realized direct investment in the mainland was estimated at $139 billion, about 52 percent of total foreign capital investment. Hong Kong continued to be the

Table 11: Exports Growth by Township and Village Enterprises and Foreign-Funded Enterprises, 1980–1998

Year	Total exports (millions of U.S. $)	Exports of township and village enterprises		Exports of foreign-funded enterprises		Exchange rate
		Millions of U.S. $	Percent of total exports	Millions of U.S. $	Percent of total exports	RMB/U.S. $
1980	10,627	1,328	4.82	8	0.05	1.7050
1985	27,545	2,881	9.19	297	0.37	2.9367
1986	31,340	4,351	11.02	582	0.54	3.4528
1987	39,494	8,025	16.91	1,220	3.09	3.7221
1988	47,465	9,863	18.99	2,460	5.18	3.7221
1989	51,940	9,664	15.48	4,920	9.47	3.7659
1990	62,415	18,014	25.05	7,810	12.51	4.7838
1991	71,901	21,628	25.51	12,050	16.76	5.3227
1992	84,794	38,060	41.50	17,357	20.47	5.5149
1993	91,720	39,429	32.61	25,237	27.52	5.7619
1994	120,921	64,605	43.33	34,713	28.71	8.6187
1995	149,101			46,876	31.44	8.3507
1996	151,264			61,506	40.66	8.3142
1997	182,790			74,900	40.98	8.2898
1998	183,810			80,962	44.05	8.2791

Sources: China Statistical Bureau, 1992, p. 627; 1995, p. 537; 1997, p. 543; 2000, p.588 and p.603. Ministry of Agriculture, 1990, p. 174; 1993, p. 148; 1994, p. 202; 1995, p. 100.

largest source of external direct investment in the mainland at the beginning of the 21st century. In 1992, Taiwan was recorded as China's second largest investor. Most of the foreign capital to China comes from ethnic Chinese living outside mainland China: from Hong Kong, Taiwan, Southeast Asia, and other countries in the world, particularly the United States, Canada and Australia.

14. Population, Labor Force, and Income Differentiation

Population Growth

China's population was estimated at 574.82 million in 1952. During the following three decades, population growth in China was rapid, largely due to the improvement of sanitation and medical care, as well as the control of epidemics. According to the census in 1982, the Chinese population passed one billion. Since then, the government has sought to restrain childbearing to reduce the population growth. In 1982, the policy of one child per family was formally established, with rewards in money and preference for those who followed the policy and penalties, such as fines and public criticism, for those who refused to accept restrictions. The policy was implemented because production of food grains per head had increased only 10 percent between 1952 and 1978. From the beginning of Communist rule to the mid-1960s, the natural growth rate of population was more than 2 percent. During the late 1970s and early 1980s, it dropped to 1.5 percent. The rate declined significantly to around 1 percent by the late 1990s. Nevertheless, due to the extremely large base population of China, the absolute growth of the population is still enormous, more than 10 million a year. The population of China by the end of 1998 was 1.25 billion.

Rural-Urban Migration: In 1957, rural population accounted for 83 percent of the total population of China. This share remained almost unchanged during the following two decades. In 1987, the share was still more than 80 percent. Nonetheless, economic reforms made living necessities available on the free market, and the rationing system no longer worked as a means of controlling the migration of rural residents to cities. In the late 1980s and 1990s, rural laborers flooded cities in search of more lucrative employment. Most employment available to rural laborers in cities was short-term, without job security or benefits. Since they did not have urban registration status, they were not officially city residents and had no claim for public services. Most of them did not have regular housing in cities and lived in squatter settlements in the suburbs. These rural migrants were also called "floaters" by urban dwellers. There were reports of a substantial floating population in Chinese cities totaling 80 million in the late 1980s. The floaters bought food and other consumer goods from the private retail shops that emerged in the 1980s but at relatively high prices. The floaters were not allowed to stay in the urban areas permanently unless they had permanent jobs. Because the floaters could not put their children in public schools, many of the young and educated rural migrants came to cities alone.

Income Inequality

Despite its socialist egalitarian ideology, China is far from an equal society in income distribution. Income inequality has increased since the 1980s, with increased emphasis on family farming in rural areas and privatization of state-owned enterprises in the urban sector. Using the well-known measurement of Gini coefficient (an index between 0 and 1, a larger Gini coefficient implies more inequality in income distribution), the overall income inequality increased from 0.28 in 1979 to 0.38 in 1988 and to 0.45 in 1995. At those levels, inequality in China was significantly higher than in India, Indonesia, Pakistan, and Taiwan in the 1990s.

Rural-urban income inequality is substantial in China. From the mid-1950s forward, the gap in income and benefits grew significantly in favor of the city over the countryside. State workers won the eight-hour day, secure employment, pensions, and heavily subsidized housing and food. Collectivized rural producers, dependent on self-financed village welfare programs, enjoyed none of those benefits and labored for a fraction of the income of state-sector workers. The long-term trend was a considerable widening of urban-rural income and welfare differentials. The situation has continued during the period of the economic reform despite the temporary narrowing of income gaps in the first half of the 1980s. See Table 12.

Poverty Alleviation

Despite the rapid economic growth during the 1980s and 1990s, poverty remains a serious problem in China. In 1977, 515 out of China's some 2,300 counties (about 90 million people) had per capita collective distributed incomes below 50 yuan per year (about $6 U.S.), the officially designed poverty line at the time. In 1986, there were still 271 counties with 45 million people under the poverty line of between 200 and 300 yuan. Applying the World Bank's

Table 12: Urban and Rural Average Income Per Capita, 1978–1998 current yuan*

Year	Rural	Urban	Urban-rural ratio
1978	134	343	2.57
1980	191	478	2.50
1985	398	739	1.86
1990	686	1,510	2.20
1995	1,578	4,283	2.71
1998	2,162	5,425	2.51

Source: China Statistical Bureau, 1999, p. 318.
* Current yuan corresponds to the year. For example, the figure for 1970 is the value of the yuan in 1970; the figure for 1998 is the value of the yuan in 1998.

poverty line standard—$1 U.S. a day per person—11.5 percent of the Chinese rural population lived in poverty in 1990. The majority of the people lived in the mountainous northwest and southwest areas. Although the number of households living below the poverty line was greatly reduced during the 1990s, poverty alleviation remains a tremendous task for the Chinese government.

15. ECONOMY AND TRADE IN TAIWAN

Taiwan is an island located about 100 miles (161 kilometers) off the southeast coast of China's mainland. The population of Taiwan was 21.74 million in 1998, about one-sixtieth the population of mainland China. Its land area is about 36,000 square kilometers, less than one-half of one percent of mainland China. Its gross domestic product per capita was $13,198 U.S. in 1997, 18 times higher than that of mainland China.

History

Although settled by a small number of mainland Chinese immigrants, Taiwan was not incorporated into the united Chinese empire until the late 16th century during the Ming dynasty. Early pioneers arrived from Fujian province. Under the East India Company, the Dutch governed Taiwan between 1624 and 1662. They were expelled under the leadership of Zheng Chenggong (1624–1662) who, with his son, ruled the island as a Chinese Nationalist until 1683, when the Manchu government restored the island to imperial rule. Following its defeat in the Sino-Japanese War, China ceded the island to Japan in 1895, but reacquired it in 1945 at the conclusion of World War II. When Chiang Kai-shek (1887–1975) arrived in Taipei from the mainland on December 10, 1949, Taiwan had a largely agrarian economy, with more than half the population engaged in primary production and 44 percent of the total income contributed by that sector.

Land Reform

Before 1949, land was unequally owned in Taiwan. Thirty-six percent of all farm families were owners; 39 percent were tenants; and 25 percent were part owners. About one-tenth of the farm population owned 60 percent of the land, and some two-fifths possessed a mere 5 percent. A land reform program was undertaken in 1949 with three steps. It started from the rent reduction program that resulted in a reduction of farm rent from an effective 50 percent in most fertile areas to a maximum after-rent return of 37.5 percent of the annual yield of the major crops. The second step involved the sale of public land to cultivators and tenants at below-market prices. The third step was the Land-to-the-Tiller Program, which limited land ownership to a maximum of about 7.4 acres. As a result of the reforms, 60 percent of all farm families owned their land, and the proportion of purely tenant farmers fell by more than half to 17 percent. Within a decade, Taiwan was transformed into an island of family-owned farms.

Economic Planning and Economic Growth

In 1953, the government of Taiwan announced a four-year plan to promote the growth of industry. The plan was launched largely as a means of making effective use of U.S. economic aid, which accounted for more than 30 percent of total domestic investment in the island during the 1950s. In contrast to mainland China, Taiwan concentrated on light industries. The first four-year plan was successful. The following plans maintained and increased the speed of development. By the mid-1960s, the gross national product of Taiwan was more than $3 billion U.S., three times that of the early 1950s.

As light industry progressed, an expansion of heavy industry and mining followed. Almost equally impressive was the rise in rice production from less than 1.6 million tons to more than 2.5 million tons, more than keeping pace with the population growth and providing the highest calorie consumption in Asia. After 1961, export expansion increased rapidly and made an increasingly large contribution to the economy in general and the manufacturing sector in particular. Real gross national product grew at 9.2 percent from the 1950s through the 1970s. Though the pace of growth eventually slowed in the 1980s and 1990s, Taiwan has one of the most rapidly growing economies in the world. See Table 13 for a summary of Taiwan's economic growth.

Export Promotion

Beginning in 1958, leaders in Taiwan switched their development strategy from an import-substitution policy for a limited domestic market to the development of labor intensive, manufactured goods for exports to world markets (principally the United States). The value of Taiwan's total trade volume reached $237 billion U.S. in 1997, placing Taiwan in 14th place in the world.

Table 13: Economic Growth in Taiwan, 1966–1997

Year	Gross national product at 1991 prices (millions U.S. $)	Per capita gross national product at 1991 prices (millions U.S. $)
1966	3,148	237
1976	18,492	1,132
1986	77,299	3,993
1990	164,076	8,111
1996	275,144	12,872
1997	285,100	13,198
1998	268,600	12,333

Sources: Clancy, 1998, p. 12; China Statistical Bureau, 2000, p.854.

In 1960, primary and processed agricultural products constituted 68 percent of exports, and industrial goods made up 32 percent. By 1985, agriculture's contribution to exports fell to 6 percent and industry's rose to 94 percent. In less than one generation, Taiwan was transformed from a largely agricultural economy to an industrial one. In 1997, Taiwan's industrial products accounted for 98 percent of total exports. Exports as a share of gross national product stood at 8.6 percent in 1952 but rose sharply to surpass 50 percent in 1984. Employment in agriculture decreased from 51.4 percent of total employment in 1952 to less than 9.6 percent in 1997. Employment in the industrial sector increased from 20.4 to a peak of 41.8 percent between 1952 and 1979 and then fell back to 38 percent in 1997. The gap was accounted for by the tertiary (largely service) sector.

Income Distribution

The Taiwan model of economic development was characterized by rapid economic growth and export expansion, low inflation, and relatively fair income distribution. In 1950, per capita gross domestic product in Taiwan was about $196 U.S., but it increased rapidly to $2,280 U.S. in 1980, and $13,000 U.S. in 1997. From the early 1950s, the proportion of national income accruing to the benefit of the wealthiest in the community steadily declined, and opportunities for improvement of those in the lowest reaches of society consistently increased. The Gini coefficient decreased from 0.3208 in 1964 to 0.2887 in 1978. Life expectancy rose from 58.6 in 1952 to 72.7 in 1983 and to 73.9 in 1997.

Government Policy

Though committed to a free-enterprise system, Taiwan has not dismantled the network of government-owned corporations and monopolies that still control or retain influence in many sectors of the economy. The government also played a positive and moderate role in accelerating economic success and in providing the infrastructure, substantial incentive, some level of partnership, and supervision to aid smaller private investors and individual entrepreneurs. A multiple foreign exchange rate system was carefully and successfully transformed into a unitary exchange system in 1961, and U.S. aid was efficiently utilized. From the 1950s on, export promotion was emphasized. Various export promotion schemes were implemented, including trade, investment, tax refund, loans, and government expenditures on education.

16. Economy and Trade in Hong Kong

Hong Kong lies inside the tropics on the southeast coast of China, adjoining the province of Guangdong. It consists of a small part of the Chinese mainland and a scattering of offshore islands, the most important of which is the island of Hong Kong. The total land area was 1,097 square kilometers in 1998. On June 30, 1997, Great Britain officially returned Hong Kong to the People's Republic of China. At the time of the handover, there were 6.5 million people living in Hong Kong with a per capita gross domestic product of $26,701 U.S.

History

The British government acquired Hong Kong in three transactions. Hong Kong Island was ceded to Great Britain in 1842. The southern part of the Kowloon Peninsula was ceded in 1886, and the New Territories were leased for 99 years from 1898 to 1997. After the Korean War in the early 1950s, as refugees poured across from China, the population of Hong Kong soared. In 1953, the colonial government closed the border and restricted further immigration. Gradually, many major projects such as the development of reservoirs, the extension of Kai Tak airport, and the enlargement of the harbor foreshore were carried out. During the 1960s, Hong Kong gained economic benefit from the Vietnam War as a manufacturing source for basic items of equipment, a staging post to the region, and a convenient center for the rest and recreation of American and allied service personnel. The opening of China in the late 1970s and the continued economic reforms throughout the 1980s and 1990s brought enormous prosperity to Hong Kong.

Economic Growth

Hong Kong's economic growth has been spectacular. A war-devastated region in 1946, Hong Kong had attained a per capita income by 1985 that rivaled Great Britain's own living standard. Between 1961 and 1980, total gross domestic product in Hong Kong grew at an average rate of about 10 percent. The growth was sustained through the 1980s. Between 1978 and 1997, stimulated and incorporated by the successes of economic reforms in the mainland, the Hong Kong economy more than tripled. Gross domestic product in Hong Kong grew at an average annual rate of about 6 percent in real terms during the 1980s and 1990s to $789 billion in 1998. This growth was twice as fast as for the world economy and outperformed the Organization for Economic Cooperation and Development economies (OECD). Per capita gross domestic product in Hong Kong was more than doubled in real terms, equivalent to an average annual real growth rate of about 4 percent during the same period. In 1998 it reached $24,900 U.S., among the highest in Asia, next only to Japan. However, in late 1997, economic growth was severely hit by the financial turmoil in eastern Asia. In 1998, the economy contracted by 5.1 percent and unemployment rose to a record 6.3 percent in the first few months of 1999. In late 1999 and the first half of 2000, however, the economy saw a strong recovery.

International Trade

International trade is the engine of Hong Kong's sustained economic growth. For 150 years, the territory's population lived and prospered on keen trading wits. Hong Kong is the ninth largest trading entity in the world. Trade in goods expanded by about 11 times and services by four times between 1978 and 1997. Reflecting the externally oriented nature of the Hong Kong economy, the total value of visible trade (comprising re-exports, domestic exports, and imports) amounted to $356 billion U.S. in 1998. Hong Kong is one of the world's leading exporters of textiles, clothing, toys, and timepieces. About 80 percent of Hong Kong's manufactured products are for export. The total value of domestic exports in 1998 was $188.45 billion, and its major export markets were the Chinese mainland (29.8 percent), the United States (29.1 percent), the United Kingdom (5.3 percent) and Germany (5.2 percent).

Economic Structure

The relative importance of the various economic sectors is reflected in their contributions to the gross domestic product and to total employment. In the absence of natural resources, the contribution of primary production (agriculture and fishing, mining, and quarrying) to gross domestic product and employment is negligible in Hong Kong. Within secondary production (comprising manufacturing; construction; and supply of electricity, gas, and water), the contribution of the manufacturing sector to gross domestic product declined significantly, from 24 percent in 1980 to 18 percent in 1990 and to 7 percent in 1997. That was mainly as a result of the continued development of the service sector in Hong Kong as well as the ongoing relocation of the more labor-intensive manufacturing processes across the Hong Kong–mainland border since the mid-1980s.

The open-door policy and economic reforms in the mainland have not only provided a huge production hinterland and market outlet for local manufacturers but have also created an abundance of business opportunities for a wide range of service activities in Hong Kong. Since the mid-1980s, the Hong Kong economy has become increasingly oriented toward services. Among the service industries, the growth and development of finance and business services, including banking, insurance, real estate, and a wide range of other professional services have been particularly rapid. The share of the tertiary services sector in gross domestic product rose steadily, from around 67 percent in 1980 to 74 percent in 1990 and to 85 percent in 1997.

Financial Service

Hong Kong is the world's eighth largest banking center in terms of external transactions. Its stock exchange is the world's 10th largest by market value. Hong Kong is also a regional center for portfolio management activity and a major capital-raising center for mainland China. The favorable business environment in Hong Kong continues to attract financial investments from around the world since the handover in 1997. Hong Kong attracts substantial investments from the United Kingdom, Japan, mainland China, and the United States. The value of external investment in Hong Kong totaled $223.6 billion U.S. at the end of 1998. Hong Kong is also the host of 2,490 regional headquarters and offices established by overseas companies.

Manufacturing

Although the manufacturing industry has diminished as an important sector of Hong Kong's economy, accounting for mere 6.5 percent of the 1997 gross domestic product, it is still the fourth largest employer. There were 23,631 manufacturing establishments in Hong Kong in September 1998, of which 23,297 were small and medium enterprises employing fewer than a hundred people, among them 21,317 with fewer than 20 employees. Mechanization, automation, and the relocation of labor-intensive and lower value-added manufacturing processes to the mainland contributed to the decline in manufacturing employment in the 1990s, which in turn facilitated Hong Kong's development of more knowledge-based and higher value-added manufacturing.

The local manufacturing sector became increasingly diversified in the 1990s. Apart from the toys and electronics industries, the textiles and clothing industries remained prominent, notwithstanding their decline in relative importance. Other important industries included printing and publishing, machinery and equipment, fabricated metal products, plastic products, watches and clocks, and jewelry. Manufacturing operations that stayed in Hong Kong were generally more knowledge-based, with a higher value-added content and wider application of computer-aided technologies in the production process. Coupled with increasing capital intensity in production, labor productivity in the manufacturing sector was able to improve significantly over the years. During the 10 years from 1989 to 1998, labor productivity in the local manufacturing sector, as measured by the ratio of the industrial production index to the manufacturing employment index, increased by an average of 11 percent a year.

Hong Kong: Mainland Connection

After mainland China adopted economic reform and an open-door policy in 1978, economic links between Hong Kong and the mainland grew from strength to strength. Specifically, visible trade between Hong Kong and the mainland grew strongly from 1978, at an average annual rate of 26 percent in value terms. The mainland was Hong Kong's largest trading partner in 1998, accounting for 38 percent of Hong Kong's total trade. In addition, 90 percent of Hong Kong's re-export trade was attributable to the mainland, making it both the largest market for, and the most significant source of, Hong Kong's re-exports. Reciprocally, Hong Kong was the mainland's third largest trading partner (just behind Japan and the United States), accounting for 14 percent of the mainland's total trade in 1998.

By the end of the 20th century, Hong Kong was a major service center for the mainland, and southern China in particular. Hong Kong provided a wide range of financial and business support services, such as banking and finance, insurance, accounting, transport, and warehousing. In addition to a continuous growth of direct investment in the mainland, there was a notable shift in the composition of Hong Kong's investment in the 1990s, from industrial processing to a wider spectrum of business ventures, such as hotels and tourist-related facilities, real estate, and infrastructure development. Relative to other places on the mainland, Hong Kong had much more intimate economic links with Guangdong. At the end of 1998, the cumulative value of Hong Kong's realized direct investment in Guangdong was estimated at $63 billion U.S., accounting for about 77 percent of the total for the province. More than five million Chinese workers were employed in Guangdong by industrial ventures with Hong Kong interests in the late 1990s. That was more than 18 times the size of Hong Kong's own manufacturing work force.

Hong Kong also became a major funding center for the mainland during the late 1990s. Apart from being a direct source of funds, Hong Kong served as a window through which foreign funds could be channeled into the mainland for financing various development projects there. The ongoing restructuring of the mainland's financial sector into a more rational and market-oriented system, in parallel with its continuing economic liberalization on a wider front, began to help attract more foreign investment. In the opposite direction, there was a sizable flow of investment capital from the mainland to Hong Kong. By the end of 1997, the mainland had invested a total of $18 billion U.S. in the territory.

17. Economy and Trade in Macao

Macao is located at the entrance of the Pearl River delta, 90 miles (144 kilometers) southeast of Guangzhou and 40 miles (64 kilometers) southwest of Hong Kong. It covers a total area of 9.11 square miles (23.6 square kilometers), consisting of a mainland peninsula and two islands, Taipa and Colôane, linked by two modern bridges and a causeway. Macao's population stood at 430,539 in 1998, of which over 96 percent were Chinese-speaking and 2 percent spoke Portuguese. English is Macao's third language and is generally used in trade, tourism, and commerce.

History

As the oldest European trading post in China, Macao was first settled by the Portuguese in the 1550s and for several centuries was an important gateway for overseas trade and contact between the east and west. In 1987, the Sino-Portuguese Joint Declaration on the future of Macao was signed by the People's Republic of China and the Portuguese government. According to the document's provisions, China resumed sovereignty over Macao on December 20, 1999. As the second special administrative region after Hong Kong, Macao enjoys a high degree of autonomy.

Economy

Macao is a free port and has a completely open market. It offers a highly attractive fiscal system with a very low level of taxation. Taxes levied on corporate profits don't exceed 15 percent. Despite its small size, Macao's economy grew rapidly during the 1980s and 1990s. Gross domestic product was approximately $6,844.2 million U.S. in 1998 and increased at a rate of 7.2 percent between 1990 and 1998. Gross domestic output per capita was approximately $14,000 U.S. in 1998.

Its strategic position in the Pearl River delta puts Macao in close proximity to China's special economic zone of Zhuhai, and that provides an important entrance to China for the international business community. Because of its close proximity to both the Chinese mainland and the financial center of Hong Kong, Macao offers a unique opportunity for investors and business people. In addition, Macao offers such special advantages as low taxation on company profits, the total absence of import duties, and a number of other concessions and exemptions.

Tourism is an extremely important factor in the economy. Gambling contributes more than two-fifths of Macao's gross domestic production.

Macao's economy is characterized by the following features:

- As a duty-free port, Macao levies no import duties. Raw materials and capital equipment are not liable to any taxation, nor are there any quantitative restraints on imports.

- There is free access for all goods and services and no restrictions on the importation or repatriation of capital or profits.

- All foreign currencies can be taken in or out of the territory in unlimited amounts.

- Major export markets are the European Union (France, Germany, United Kingdom, etc.) and the United States. Other markets include mainland China, Japan, Hong Kong, and Australia.

- Major import markets are Hong Kong and mainland China. Others include the United States and Japan.

KEY RESEARCH SOURCES

Adshead, S. A. M. *China in World History*. New York: St. Martin's Press, 1988.

Ash, Robert, ed. *Agricultural Development in China, 1949–1989. The Collected Papers of Kenneth R. Walker (1931–1989)*. Oxford: Oxford University Press, 1988.

Ash, Robert, and Y. Y. Kueh, eds. *The Chinese Economy Under Deng Xiaoping*. Oxford: Clarendon Press, 1996.

Bowles, Paul, and Corden White. "The Dilemmas of Market Socialism: Capital Market Reform in China." *The Journal of Development Studies* 28.3 (1992): 363–85; 28:4 (1992): 575–94.

Bristow, Roger. *Land-use Planning in Hong Kong*. Hong Kong: Oxford University Press, 1987.

Brown, Judith, and Rosemary Foot, eds. *Hong Kong's Transitions, 1842–1997*. Basingstoke, England: Macmillan, 1997.

Brugger, Bill, and Stephen Reglar. *Politics, Economy and Society in Contemporary China*. London: Macmillan Press LTD, 1994.

Buck, Lossing. *Land Utilization in China*. New York: Paragon Book Reprint Corp, 1964.

Byrd, William, and Qingsong Lin, eds. *China's Rural Industry: Structure, Development, and Reform*. Oxford: Oxford University Press, Published for the World Bank, 1990.

Chang, John. *Industrial Development in Pre-Communist China: A Quantitative Analysis*. Chicago: Aldine, 1969.

Chen, Nairuenn, and Walter Galenson. *The Chinese Economy Under Communism*. Chicago: Aldine Publishing Company, 1969.

Chiang Kai-shek. *China's Destiny and Chinese Economic Theory*. New York: Roy Publishers, 1979.

China Statistical Bureau. *China Statistical Yearbook*. Beijing: China Statistical Publishing House, 1984.

———. *China Statistical Yearbook*. Beijing: China Statistical Publishing House, 1991.

———. *China Statistical Yearbook*. Beijing: China Statistical Publishing House, 1992.

———. *China Statistical Yearbook*. Beijing: China Statistical Publishing House, 1995.

———. *China Statistical Yearbook*. Beijing: China Statistical Publishing House, 1996.

———. *China Statistical Yearbook*. Beijing: China Statistical Publishing House, 1997.

———. *China Statistical Yearbook*. Beijing: China Statistical Publishing House, 1999.

————. *China Statistical Yearbook*. Beijing: China Statistical Publishing House, 2000.

Chow, Gregory. *The Chinese Economy*. New York: Harper and Row, 1984.

Clancy, Michael. *The Business Guide to Taiwan*. Singapore: Butterworth-Heinemann Asia, 1998.

Clark, Cal. *Taiwan's Development: Implications for Contending Political Economy Paradigms*. New York: Greenwood Press, 1989.

DeCrespingy, Rafe. *China This Century*. Hong Kong: Oxford University Press, 1992.

Derenberger, Robert, F. "The Role of the Foreigner in China's Economic Development." *China's Modern Economy in Historical Perspective*. Ed. Dwight Perkins. California: Stanford University Press, 1975.

————. "The People's Republic of China at 50: The Economy." *China Quarterly* 159 (1999): 606–15.

Fairbank, John, ed. *The Cambridge History of China*. Vol. 10, *Late Qing, 1800–1911, Part I*. Cambridge: Cambridge University Press, 1978.

————. *The Cambridge History of China*. Vol. 12, *Republican China, 1912–1949, Part I*. Cambridge: Cambridge University Press, 1983.

Fairbank, John, and Merle Goldman. *China: A New History*. Cambridge: The Belknap Press of Harvard University Press, 1998.

Faure, David. *The Rural Economy of Pre-Liberation China: Trade, Expansion, and Peasant Livelihood in Jiangsu and Guangdong, 1870–1937*. New York: Oxford University Press, 1989.

Feuerwerker, Albert. *The Chinese Economy, 1870–1911*. Ann Arbor: The University of Michigan, Center for Chinese Studies, 1969.

————. *The Chinese Economy, 1912–1949*. Ann Arbor: The University of Michigan, Center for Chinese Studies, 1968.

Goodman, David, and Gerald Segal, eds. *China Deconstructs: Politics, Trade and Regionalism*. London: Routledge, 1996.

Harvie, Charles, ed. *Contemporary Development and Issues in China's Economic Transition*. New York: Macmillian Press, 2000.

Hou, Chi-ming, and Tzong-shian Yu. *Modern Chinese Economic History*. Taipei: The Institute of Economics, Academia Sinica, 1977.

Howe, Christopher. *China's Economy: A Basic Guide*. London: Paul Elek, 1978.

Lardy, Nicholas. *Agriculture in China's Modern Economic Development*. Cambridge: Cambridge University Press, 1983.

————. *Foreign Trade and Economic Reform in China, 1978–1990*. Cambridge: Cambridge University Press, 1992.

Lichtenstein, Peter. *China at the Brink: The Political Economy of Reform and Retrenchment in the Post-Mao Era*. New York: Praeger, 1991.

Lin, C. S. George. *Red Capitalism in South China, Growth and Development of the Pearl River Delta*. Vancouver: UBC Press, 1997.

Linge, G. J. R., and D. K. Forbes, eds. *China's Spatial Economy: Recent Developments and Reforms*. Hong Kong: Oxford University Press, 1990.

Liu, James, and Wei-ming Tu. *Traditional China*. Englewood Cliffs, N.J.: Prentice-Hall, Inc, 1970.

Lo, C. P. *Hong Kong*. London: Belhaven Press, 1992.

Maguire, Keith. *The Rise of Modern Taiwan*. Aldershot, England: Ashgate, 1998.

Mastel, Greg. *The Rise of the Chinese Economy: The Middle Kingdom Emerges*. Armonk, N.Y.: M. E. Sharpe, 1997.

Ministry of Agriculture. *Yearbook of China's Rural Enterprises*. Beijing: Agricultural Publishing House, 1990.

———. *Yearbook of China's Rural Enterprises*. Beijing: Agricultural Publishing House, 1993.

———. *Yearbook of China's Rural Enterprises*. Beijing: Agricultural Publishing House, 1994.

———. *Yearbook of China's Rural Enterprises*. Beijing: Agricultural Publishing House, 1995.

Ministry of Foreign Trade. *A Statistical Encyclopedia of Chinese Foreign Economy*. Beijing: Foreign Economy Press. Various issues.

Perkins, Dwight, ed. *China's Modern Economy in Historical Perspective*. Stanford, Calif.: Stanford University Press, 1975.

Perry, Phillip. *Business Directory: A Practical Guide to Trading with the People's Republic of China*. Epping, England: Bowker Publishing Company, 1980.

Powell, Simon. *Agricultural Reform in China: From Communes to Commodity Economy 1978–1990*. Manchester: Manchester University Press, 1992.

Prybyla, Jan. *The Chinese Economy: Problems and Policies*. 2nd ed. Columbia: University of South Carolina Press, 1981.

Pyle, David. *China's Economy: From Revolution to Reform*. London: Macmillan Press Ltd, 1997.

Rabushka, Alvin. *The New China: Comparative Economic Development in Mainland China, Taiwan, and Hong Kong*. San Francisco: Westview Press, 1987.

Rawski, Thomas. *Economic Growth in Prewar China*. Berkeley: University of California Press, 1989.

Riskin, Carl. *China's Political Economy*. Oxford: Oxford University Press, 1987.

Selden, Mark. *The Political Economy of Chinese Development*. Armonk, N.Y.: M. E. Sharpe, 1993.

Shih, Chih-yu. *State and Society in China's Political Economy: The Cultural Dynamics of Socialist Reform*. Boulder, Co.: Lynne Rienner Publishers, 1995.

Starr, J. Bryan. *Understanding China*. New York: Hill and Wang, 1997.

Tian, Xiaowen. *Dynamics of Development in an Opening Economy: China Since 1978*. New York: Nova Science Publishers, 1998.

Twitchett, Denis, ed. *The Cambridge History of China*. Vol. 3, *Sui & Tang China, 589–906, Part 1*. Cambridge: Cambridge University Press, 1979.

Twitchett, Denis, and John Fairbank, eds. *The Cambridge History of China*. Vol. 10, *The Late Ch'ing, 1800–1911, Part 1*. Cambridge: Cambridge University Press, 1978.

Twitchett, Denis, and Frederick Mote, eds. *The Cambridge History of China*. Vol. 8, *The Ming Dynasty, 1368–1644, Part 2*. Cambridge: Cambridge University Press, 1998.

Vines, Stephen. *Hong Kong: China's New Colony*. London: Aurum, 1998.

Wilkinson, Endymion. *Chinese History: A Manual*. Cambridge, Mass.: Harvard University Press, 1998.

Wright, Tim, ed. *The Chinese Economy in the Early Twentieth Century: Recent Chinese Studies*. New York: St. Martin's Press, 1992.

Yang, Hong. "A Comparative Analysis of China's Permanent and Temporary Migration During the Reform Period." *International Journal of Social Economics* 27.3 (2000): 172–193.

————. "Growth of China's Grain Production 1978–1997: A Disaggregate Analysis." *World Development* 27.12 (1999): 2137–2154.

————. "Trends in China's Regional Grain Production and Their Implications." *Agricultural Economics* 19.3 (1998): 309–325.

Yang, Lien-sheng. *Money and Credit in China: A Short History.* Cambridge, Mass.: Harvard University Press, 1971.

Yubuki, Susumu. *China's New Political Economy: The Giant Awakes.* Trans. Stephen Harner. Boulder, Colo.: Westview Press, 1995.

Zhang, Xiaohe. "Growth of China's Rural Enterprises: Impacts on Urban-Rural Relations." *The Journal of Development Studies* 31.4 (1995): 567–84.

————. "Growth of Township and Village Enterprises and Change in China's Export Pattern." *Advances in Chinese Industrial Studies* 6 (1998): 89–100.

————. "Urban-Rural Isolation and Its Impact on China's Production and Trade Pattern." *China Economic Review* 3.1 (1992): 85–105.

Institutions Governing Chinese Society

By David A. Graff

INTRODUCTION

In the broad sense of the term, institutions can be defined as "a cluster of social usages" that serve to "fix the confines of and impose form upon the activities of human beings" (Walton H. Hamilton). Therefore, the institutions covered in this chapter include not only government agencies and administrative practices but also extra-governmental social organizations—of which the family is by far the most basic and the most important. In addition, the chapter includes the laws and customs that have given order to government, society, and human interactions in China. Since institutions have changed over time, the first half of this chapter will trace the development of social and political organization from antiquity to the heyday of the Qing dynasty (1644–1911). Later sections will deal with the major changes in Chinese institutions that took place as a result of Western influence in the first half of the 20th century, the organization of Chinese society under Communist rule after 1949, and the institutional aspects of the reforms that have been carried out in China since 1978. Some attention will also be given to the social and political organization of Taiwan and Hong Kong since 1949.

1. THE EVOLUTION OF RULERSHIP IN EARLY CHINA

Shang Political Authority

The first Chinese polity to leave written records of any sort was the Shang dynasty (c.1554–1045 B.C.). Neither Shang nor its still shadowy predecessor, the Xia (Hsia) (c.2200–1554 B.C.) dynasty, was a centralized imperial state. Political authority in what is now northern China was divided among hundreds of local clans, each with its own walled town and ruling lineage (a kinship group tracing descent from a common ancestor). The Shang rulers, based in the eastern part of the Yellow River valley, were the leaders of the most powerful of the clans and had succeeded in imposing their hegemony on most of the other communities. Political authority rested not only on armed force but also on religious rituals, wealth, and kinship ties (with the senior lineages receiving allegiance from settlements established by their junior branches). Rulers based their claim to power in part on their role as shamans who could communicate with the deified spirits of their royal ancestors and placate them with sacrifices. The performance of these rituals required collections of costly bronze vessels that were the exclusive possessions of the ruling lineages and served as symbols of their sovereignty. Communication with ancestors took the form of scapulimancy (divination by means of animal bones); bones were heated and the resulting patterns of cracks were interpreted to yield an answer to the diviner's question. The questions that were put to ancestors concerned not only ritual observances and the well-being of the royal family, but also such practical matters of government as, for example, the number of men to be sent on a military expedition.

The Mandate of Heaven

Some time around 1045 B.C. (the date remains uncertain), the Shang hegemony was overthrown by the Zhou people, whose homeland was in the Wei River valley in today's province of Shaanxi. The Zhou had long been subordinate members of the Shang political structure and shared many of the cultural and political characteristics of their more powerful neighbors. The Zhou rising against Shang was planned by King Wen and carried out by his son and successor King Wu. After the Zhou leaders defeated the Shang in battle and extended their own hegemony over the former Shang territories, they sought to strengthen their control by persuading their new subjects that the Zhou victory had occurred as a consequence of the villainy of the last Shang king. They claimed that heaven had withdrawn its support from Shang. The idea that the "mandate of heaven" could be forfeited by an oppressive or immoral ruler and claimed by the more virtuous founder of a new dynasty became a key element in Chinese political thought. Virtue was understood not only as a matter of personal morality but also as a required concern for the welfare of the common people. Suffering or rebellion among the people could be interpreted as a sign that heaven had withdrawn its mandate.

The Early Zhou Period

The decentralized system of rule established by the Zhou conquerors has sometimes been described as "feudal," reflecting some superficial similarities with the political structure of medieval Europe. The early Zhou rulers sent their close relatives and the leaders of allied clans to exercise hereditary control over portions of the conquered Shang territory. The state of Lu, for example, was granted to a nephew of King Wu and remained in the hands of his descendants. According to *Xunzi*, a philosophical text of the third century B.C., 71 new states were founded at the beginning of the Zhou dynasty, of which 53 were given to members of the royal family. The rulers of these states received symbols of authority (such as flags, drums, and chariots) from the king and were expected to provide tribute and perform military ser-

vice. Some of them also held important posts at the royal court. They and their followers lived in walled towns and were at first quite distinct from the local population. As time passed, however, the blood relationships between the "feudal lords" and the Zhou kings became more and more distant, and strong local identities developed. After a major rebellion greatly weakened the monarchy in 771 B.C., local rulers paid little more than lip service to royal authority.

The Spring and Autumn Period

During the Spring and Autumn period (722–481 B.C.), several dozen states formed shifting alliances and engaged in almost constant warfare with one another, with the larger ones gradually annexing the smaller. Especially menacing was the southern state of Chu in the Yangtze valley, which lay on the periphery of the Zhou political and cultural zone. The more powerful of the northern state rulers organized successive coalitions to uphold the nominal authority of the Zhou royal court and resist the inroads of Chu and other outside forces. The first of these so-called hegemons was Duke Huan of Qi, who reigned from 685 to 643 B.C. Within the individual states, lordship was normally inherited by the eldest son of the ruler by his principal wife. Junior branches of the ruling lineage filled the top offices of the state, often claiming these posts by hereditary right. Lower-level government posts were filled by the class known as *shi* (knights or gentlemen), who also formed the backbone of the state's armed forces. Ritual and war were the principal concerns of the nobility, whose behavior was governed by an elaborate code of conduct.

The Rise of the Centralized State

The decentralized, ritual-oriented state structure of the Spring and Autumn period broke down during the fifth century B.C. as the great noble families competed for power and usurped the prerogatives of the rulers. In 453 B.C., the large state of Jin was partitioned by several of its leading families. Armed conflicts between the states became more intense and desperate. By the third century B.C., only seven major states remained: Qin, Qi, Zhao, Han, Wei, Yan, and Chu. Their rulers appropriated the title of king, and the vestigial territory of the last Zhou king was absorbed by Qin in 256 B.C. This violently competitive environment was conducive to radical reform as the new state rulers sought to maximize their power. They selected men for office on the basis of ability rather than birth and extended military service to the peasantry to form huge new armies of conscripts. The rulers of the "Warring States" were especially receptive to the ideas of Legalist thinkers who sought to exalt the position of the ruler and increase the power of the state. They established strict legal codes and used rewards and punishments to promote obedience, hard work, and bravery on the battlefield. Legalist ideas received their most thorough application in the western state of Qin, where the reformer Shang Yang (c. 390–338 B.C.) abolished aristocratic privileges and replaced the old estates and fiefs with commanderies and counties administered by royal appointees.

The First Empire

In 221 B.C., King Zheng of Qin (259–210 B.C.) conquered the last of the other kingdoms and extended his system of autocracy, harsh laws, and centralized administration to the whole of China. In keeping with his new status as the ruler of a unified empire, he adopted the more elaborate title of Qin Shi Huangdi, "first emperor of Qin." The Qin empire was brought down by a series of rebellions that began soon after the first emperor's death, but there was to be no lasting restoration of the multi-state system that had existed before the Qin conquest. One of the rebel leaders, Liu Bang (256–195 B.C.), vanquished his rivals and restored imperial unity as the first emperor of the Western Han dynasty (202 B.C.–A.D. 8). Liu, who had been a minor local official under Qin, retained the institutional structure and

administrative procedures of the Qin dynasty. Under the Han emperors, however, the Legalist harshness of the Qin regime was tempered by the more humane values of Confucianism. The synthesis of Legalist and Confucian elements would remain characteristic of China's imperial system until its end in 1912.

Ritual, Portents, and Legitimacy

Chinese emperors of Han times and later were not simply political leaders but also performed important ritual and symbolic roles. The ancestral sacrifices of earlier times were not abandoned by the new imperial house, but other deities and powers now became the focus of their attention. From 31 B.C. until 1912, imperial religious ritual focused mainly on the worship of heaven. In Han cosmological thought, the emperor was responsible for maintaining harmony between Heaven, earth, and man through virtuous behavior and performance of the appropriate rituals. Many of the imperial rites were linked to the passage of the seasons and intended for the benefit of agriculture. Calamitous or unusual happenings in the natural world—such as comets, floods, or sightings of bizarre animals—were interpreted as signs that the emperor was somehow remiss or lacking in virtue, and portended the possible loss of heaven's mandate should he fail to mend his ways. Auspicious omens, such as the discovery of numinous stones or the descent of "sweet dew," were reported as evidence of heaven's blessing and were eagerly seized upon by ambitious claimants to the imperial throne and would-be dynastic founders. The first to manipulate auspicious omens in this way was Wang Mang (45 B.C.–A.D. 23), a high-ranking Han official who deposed a child emperor and set himself up as the first and only emperor of the short-lived Xin (Hsin) dynasty from A.D. 9 to 23.

2. THE STRUCTURE OF IMPERIAL GOVERNMENT

The Imperial Bureaucracy

From Qin and Han times onward, China was administered by a large and complex bureaucracy of literate, educated officials. By 5 B.C., near the end of the Western Han dynasty, this bureaucracy included more than 120,000 men. Officials were ranked according to a regular, hierarchical scale similar to the "government service (GS)" ranks of the United States government, with salaries, status, and privileges clearly tied to rank. The Han dynasty used a 21-rank scale, and later dynasties such as the Tang had as many as 30 ranks. There was often a sharp distinction drawn between regular officials and local clerical personnel. Within the hierarchical structure there were regular procedures for evaluation, promotion, and transfer; and it was possible for a man in the course of his official career to rise from a low-ranking, entry-level position to one of the highest offices in the realm. The bureaucracy was divided into a large number of offices and agencies, including secretarial and advisory bodies in the capital, functionally specialized executive departments, and local and regional administrations. Usually (if not always) educated in the classic texts of Confucianism, officials shared basic values and a commitment to precedent and regular administrative procedures; the bureaucracy as a whole worked to restrain the authority of the emperor within the bounds of custom and tradition.

Chancellors and Grand Secretaries:

The highest-ranking government officials served as leaders of the bureaucracy and spokesmen for its collective interests. As such, they represented an obvious threat to the untrammeled authority of the emperors. Tensions often arose, and emperors in many dynasties took measures to weaken the top officials or circumvent the regular bureaucracy. In Qin and Han, the highest officials were the chancellor and the imperial secretary. A third position, the military office of grand commandant, was not regularly filled. Han emperors experimented with division of the post of chancellor between two incumbents (designated as "left" and "right" chancellors) in order to further diffuse the power of the office. During the Song dynasty (960–1279), the government administration was usually headed by two grand councillors and several vice grand councillors. These men composed the Council of State, the highest decision-making body of the civil administration, but military matters were controlled by an entirely separate body, the Bureau of Military Affairs. The founder of the Ming dynasty (1368–1644), Zhu Yuanzhang (1328–1398), was especially suspicious of senior officials. Not only did he eliminate the position of the prime minister, but he also abolished the secretariat that he had inherited from earlier dynasties, giving its function to relatively low-ranking scholars from the Hanlin Academy (a body responsible for drafting and editing imperial pronouncements), who were easier to control.

Inner and Outer Courts:

Emperors often tried to bypass the regular bureaucracy by entrusting authority to outsiders. At various times these included palace eunuchs and male relatives of the empresses, as well as imperial favorites. Such strategies sometimes backfired, as weaker emperors came to be dominated by their in-laws (a common pattern in Han) or by the eunuchs. Another device was to employ a corps of private secretaries within the palace to deal with administrative paperwork that had been the responsibility of the regular bureaucracy. But with the passage of time, such groups tended to become bureaucratized themselves. The three major branches of the Tang dynasty central administration, the Department of State Affairs (an executive agency), the Secretariat (which issued imperial orders), and the Chancellery (which reviewed the orders from the Secretariat), all had their origin in the private secretaries and palace advisers of Han times. A similar process occurred during the Ming dynasty, when the lowly academicians employed by the Ming founder evolved into the powerful grand secretaries of the late Ming, some of whom were prime ministers in all but name.

The Central Departments

All of China's imperial regimes had a group of central departments with specific functional responsibilities, though both their number and the nature of their duties changed over time. Under the Han dynasty there were nine ministers (*jiu qing*), several of whom were more concerned with the management of the imperial household than the governance of the empire. The superintendent of the imperial household (*langzhongling*) was responsible for the security of the palace, the director of the imperial clan (*zongzheng*) kept an eye on the emperor's relatives, and the privy treasurer (*shaofu*) served as chief administrator of the imperial household. By the time of the Tang dynasty, the real work of government administration had been taken over by the Six Boards (*liu bu*) under the Department of State Affairs; these were War, Civil Office (responsible for personnel management of the bureaucracy), Rites, Revenue, Public Works, and Justice. The imperial household functions that had been performed by the Nine Ministers in Han were carried on by the Nine Courts (*jiu si*) in Tang. Real administrative authority gravitated to a number of ad hoc agencies during late Tang and early Song, but an important reform of the late 11th century restored the power of the old boards. The six-board system was retained until the Qing dynasty, which created a seventh board, the Court of Colonial Affairs (*lifan yuan*), to handle relations with the Mongols and Tibetans.

The Censorate

In imperial China, there was a special category of officials responsible for policing the bureaucracy and bringing charges against administrators who were suspected of corruption or malfeasance. Some of these "censors" (*yushi*) were based in the capital, and others toured the provinces to inspect government administration at the regional and local levels. In Han times, the second-ranking official in the capital, the imperial secretary (*yushi dafu*), was responsible for making sure that government officials did not abuse their authority. By Tang times, the Censorate (*yushi tai*) had emerged as an organized branch of the imperial administration staffed by the elite of the civil service, and relatively low-ranking censors had the authority to investigate and impeach much higher-ranking officials. Closely related to the censors in function were the remonstrance officials, whose duty was to criticize the emperor himself whenever they believed that he was violating Confucian ethical principles or dynastic precedents. This could be a dangerous job since they enjoyed no immunity from the emperor's wrath. In Tang times the remonstrance officials served under the Secretariat and the Chancellery, but in Ming and Qing they became regular members of the Censorate.

Local Government

The basic unit of local administration in imperial China was the county (*xian*), originally a walled town and its surrounding countryside. The number of counties remained roughly the same—about 1,200 to 1,600—after Han times, but as a result of increases in population, the average late Qing county had a population of more than 300,000, though the average Tang county had had only 30,000. A magistrate governed the county and was a regular civil official appointed by the center for a fixed term in office. The magistrate was responsible for the full range of government business, including tax collection, justice, water conservancy, education, and the maintenance of law and order. In performing his many functions, the magistrate was assisted by a small staff of regular officials and a somewhat larger group of local sub-officials, including both clerks and "runners" who served as policemen and messengers. Since officials were not normally permitted to serve as magistrates in their home counties, they often had to rely very heavily on their local staff who were familiar with local conditions, customs, and precedents. And because of the small size of his staff relative to the population of the county, the magistrate was also dependent on the cooperation of local elites (such as the leaders of prominent families and lineages) in order to govern effectively.

Commanderies and Prefectures:
Under the Qin and Han dynasties, the next level of territorial administration above

the county was the commandery (*jun*). Qin initially established 36 commanderies after the unification of China in 221 B.C., and the number continued to increase thereafter. By the end of the Eastern Han, there were approximately a hundred commanderies. A Han commandery was governed by an administrator (*shou*), a military commandant (*wei*), and an assistant administrator. In 106 B.C., the empire was first divided into 13 regions (*bu*, later *zhou*) of 5 to 10 commanderies each. These regions were initially supervised by travelling censors bearing the title of inspector (*cishi*), but by the latter half of the second century A.D., the men appointed to regional leadership had become powerful regional governors (*zhou mu*). During the centuries of division between the fall of Eastern Han and the reunification of China by the Sui dynasty (581–618) in 589, the number of regions increased dramatically while the size of each individual region declined. The result was unnecessary and wasteful duplication in territorial administration, and the first Sui emperor eventually abolished the commanderies in 586. The zhou (now better translated as "prefecture" rather than region) remained as the largest regular unit of local government. Under the Tang dynasty there were some 328 prefectures with an average population of approximately 145,000.

Regional Administration

A perennial problem confronting China's imperial regimes was that of supervising the large number of local administrative units. It was not efficient to have all 300 or more prefectures report directly to the center, but the creation of permanent provincial or regional administrations as an intermediate level in the command hierarchy raised the specter of concentrations of power large enough to challenge the imperial court. Various solutions were attempted by different dynasties. The Han government eventually appointed strong regional governors (*zhou mu*), who acquired extensive military power and de facto autonomy during the great peasant rebellion of the Yellow Turbans after A.D. 184. A similar process occurred in the second half of the Tang dynasty when provincial military governors (*jiedushi*)

controlling as many as a dozen prefectures were able to defy the imperial court, appoint their own officials, and withhold tax revenues from the center. The Song dynasty found an effective solution to the problem of regional administration by grouping the prefectures into circuits (*dao*) and assigning commissioners to handle specific functional areas such as financial, judicial, and military affairs. This division of authority along functional lines made it impossible for strong regional leaders to emerge to challenge the center. China's modern provinces took shape during the Ming dynasty, but functional divisions were retained at the provincial level in both Ming and Qing. The Qing government did appoint provincial governors in place of the Ming "coordinators," but they were provided with minimal staffs, since most of the work of provincial administration was still handled by the various commissioners.

The Eunuchs

Eunuchs were a presence in the palaces of China's rulers from very early times; and at several points in Chinese history, they became powerful enough to dominate the government of the empire. Their original function was as servants in the women's quarters of the imperial palace. Since there might be as many as several thousand palace women, the number of eunuchs could also be quite large—perhaps 20,000 in the late 16th century. Dependent on the ruler and with no power base in society, eunuchs were often assigned important responsibilities by emperors who wished to enhance their autocratic power at the expense of the bureaucracy. At different times they were employed as palace secretaries, imperial envoys, and even military commanders, and they often were able to dominate the court when weak emperors were on the throne. Eunuchs were especially influential in the late Eastern Han (second century A.D.), the late Tang (ninth century), and the Ming. Basing their power on control of the formidable imperial palace armies, the Tang eunuchs were able to select the emperor on more than one occasion. Scholar-officials deeply resented the power of the eunuchs, and strong protest movements arose in both the Eastern Han and the Ming. In the

Han case, the conflict ended with the massacre of some 2,000 eunuchs in A.D. 189. In the Ming, however, the eunuchs who controlled the imperial secret police agencies retained the upper hand and carried out a bloody persecution of their leading critics in 1625–1627.

3. Official Recruitment in Imperial China

The Recommendation System

The principle that appointment to government office should be on the basis of merit rather than aristocratic birth was first established during the Warring States period (480–222 B.C.). Under the Han dynasty, men were selected for government office primarily through a system of recommendation. Commandery administrators and senior officials in the capital were required to recommend promising men for appointment to office and then stood as guarantors of the competence and good behavior of their protégés. The system was regularized in 130 B.C. when it was decreed that each commandery should recommend two men every year. Those recommended were designated as "Filially Pious and Incorrupt" (*xiaolian*). They were sometimes given written tests when they arrived in the capital and were expected to serve for a time in the emperor's bodyguard before being assigned to posts in the bureaucracy. Another path to office was through the Imperial Academy, an institution set up in 124 B.C. Originally of very modest size, it had grown to include 30,000 students by the middle of the second century A.D. Students of the Imperial Academy might be appointed to low-ranking offices after passing written examinations. Other men entered government service through direct appointment, since senior officials were allowed considerable latitude to choose their own subordinates. And emperors were always able to appoint favorites and members of consort families to high positions without reference to the recommendation system.

The Nine-Rank System

During the Eastern Han period, powerful local families began to monopolize appointment to the central bureaucracy through the recommendation system. Their influence was institutionalized in the office of rectifier (*zhongzheng*) created by the Wei dynasty in 220 A.D. Rectifiers were appointed for each unit of territorial administration to judge the suitability of local men for government office. They evaluated families according to a system of nine status ranks, often reserving the best ranks for their own friends and relations. Assessments soon came to be based on the elite standing of the family rather than the qualifications of the individual. The result was that for more than three centuries, government offices tended to be dominated by a small group of aristocratic families. It was only with the advent of the Sui dynasty that the nine-rank system was abolished and written tests were revived as a means of judging candidates for office.

The Birth of the Examination System

It was during the Tang dynasty that a significant portion of the imperial civil service came to be selected by means of competitive written examinations. Unlike later dynasties, the Tang did not have a hierarchy of examinations to be taken in sequence. Qualified candidates might choose among several tests, of which the most prestigious was the "presented scholar" (*jinshi*) examination stressing literary talent and skill at composition. Only a small percentage of Tang officials entered the civil service through examination success, but they represented an intellectual elite within the bureaucracy. They were on the fast track for promotion and tended to rise to the highest posts. Many other Tang officials entered the bureaucracy on the basis of hereditary privilege because their fathers or grandfathers had been high-ranking officials, and still more were promoted from the clerical service. It was only during the Song dynasty, with the vast expansion of the educated elite, that written examinations became the principal path to government office. It was also during the Song that the examinations began to take on the shape that they would retain until the beginning of the 20th century, with all candidates pursuing the same examination path from the prefectures to the capital.

The Mature Examination System:

Under the Ming and Qing dynasties, the examination process began at the local level where men aspiring to government office had to pass one test at the county level and two more administered at the prefecture. The prefectural examinations were held two years out of three, and those who passed received the title of licentiate (*shengyuan*) but were popularly known as "flourishing talents" (*xiucai*). This degree did not in itself open the door to office, but it conferred elite status on its holders who were no longer subject to corporal punishment or *corvée* labor. The next step in the process, the provincial examination, was held in the provincial capitals once every three years. There were more than 10,000 exam takers in the average province, and the pass rate was only about 1 percent. The fortunate few received the title of "recommended man" (*juren*) and became eligible for appointment to low-ranking official positions at the county and prefectural levels. Most preferred to proceed to the next level, the metropolitan examination, held in the capital in the year following the administration of the provincial examination. The pass rate in the capital was closer to 2.5 percent, and those who passed the metropolitan examination and the last step, the palace examination, received the "presented scholar" (*jinshi*) degree. However, even this crowning achievement did not necessarily lead directly to appoint-

ment to office; the new *jinshi* often had to wait until vacancies occurred in the civil service.

Social Effects of the Examinations:

The imperial civil service examinations emphasized skill at literary composition and knowledge of the Confucian classics. The demands of the examinations made for a uniform school curriculum throughout the empire and guaranteed that all of the men who emerged from the process shared a similar outlook and approach to government. The system was designed to produce generalists rather than technical specialists (the latter did exist in such fields as law and calendar making, but they were limited to subordinate positions). There has been some disagreement among scholars regarding the implications of the examination system for social mobility. In theory, the examinations were open to all males save those whose families were engaged in certain occupations that were considered demeaning, and it was possible for men from poor families to rise to important positions. For example, the Ming grand secretary Xu Guo (1527–1596) came from a family of poor urban tradesmen. In practice, however, the examination system was not an entirely level playing field, since wealthy families could always provide their sons with better educations.

Other Paths to Office

Examination success was not the only route to government office, even in Ming and Qing. The sons and grandsons of senior officials could still enter the bureaucracy through hereditary privilege (*yin*). It was also possible for wealthy men to purchase examination degrees. This practice became especially widespread at times when the government was under pressure to raise new revenues, as was the case during and after the Taiping Rebellion (1851–1864). Of course, such men did not enjoy the same respect as officials who had earned their degrees through the regular examination process.

4. Law in Imperial China

The Nature of Chinese Law

The Chinese tradition of written law dates back at least as far as 536 B.C., when the state of Jin inscribed its laws on a bronze vessel. Legalist thinkers such as Shang Yang and Han Fei Zi (d. 233 B.C.) emphasized the utility of clear legal codes, backed by rewards and punishments, for controlling the people and molding their behavior. Heavily influenced by Legalism, the Qin state had developed a very large corpus of written law by the middle of the third century B.C. The Qin laws and later Chinese legal codes were basically sets of detailed administrative regulations and penal statutes. The primary concern of the law was the smooth functioning of the imperial administration and the prevention and punishment of crime; no rights were conceded to the people. Each dynasty established a legal code (lü) derived largely from the code in effect under the preceding dynasty. Hence there was remarkable continuity from the 500-article Tang code of 737 to the legal code of the Qing dynasty, which was still in effect as late as 1911. In all dynasties, the code was supplemented, amended, and clarified by various sets of administrative rules, regulations, and ordinances, and judicial decisions were often based on these rather than on the code itself.

Characteristic Features of Traditional Chinese Law

Traditional Chinese law did not seek to judge individuals impartially and without regard to their particular place in society. The legal codes were crafted to support the family system and reinforce the social hierarchy and the authority of the state. The severity of punishment prescribed by law often depended upon the relative status of the offender and the victim. A father could strike his son with impunity, whereas a son who struck his father was subject to death by decapitation. High-status individuals, such as members of the imperial family and senior officials, were treated more leniently than ordinary people, but low-status groups (such as slaves) were treated much more harshly. Rebellion was by far the most serious offense; high-status individuals found guilty of this charge were stripped of all of their usual immunities, and collective punishments could be imposed on the families of rebels even when individual family members had not been involved in the rebellion.

Law and the Family: The traditional family system received considerable support from the penal codes. Failure to observe mourning for deceased elders—and especially parents—was a criminal offense. Family heads were allowed considerable discretion in dealing with offenses that occurred within the confines of the family. When the interests of state and family came into conflict, the law sometimes put the family first. Family members were not required to testify against one another, and young people were positively prohibited from bearing witness against their senior relatives—except when the senior relatives were implicated in a rebellion.

The Judicial Process

Most cases were initiated with the submission of a written complaint to the county (xian) magistrate, whose office (or yamen) served as the court of first instance. The defendant was then required to submit a written statement and was expected to appear in court on the day chosen for the trial. Through questioning in court and other investigative means, the magistrate was responsible for determining the guilt or innocence of the accused. If the defendant was found guilty, the magistrate simply had to determine which statute had been violated and apply the prescribed penalty, since the laws left very little room for judicial discretion. Defendants were allowed to appeal decisions to higher administrative levels, and serious cases involving heavy penalties were automatically subject to review. (Death sentences had to be approved by the emperor himself.) In the event that the defendant was found to be innocent, the accuser was made to suffer the same penalty that the defendant would have faced had he been found guilty.

Mediation and Extra-Official Justice:
Most of the disputes that arose in traditional China never reached the magistrate's yamen, but were resolved within the local community through the mediation of village elders, degree holders, and other local notables. A cultural tradition emphasizing the value of harmony and compromise—together with the high likelihood that litigation would expose both plaintiff and defendant alike to extortion and abuse from corrupt clerks and yamen runners—tended to discourage people from bringing cases before the officials. Outside the scope of the state's written law, there was considerable space for the operation of extra-official judicial institutions that handled many cases of a civil or commercial nature. Many lineages (extended kinship groups) had their own rules and punished violators with fines, corporal punishment, and expulsion from the lineage; they might also prohibit their members from bringing intra-lineage disputes before the magistrate's court. In similar fashion, merchant and craft guilds established regulations regarding working conditions and the price and quality of their products, imposed penalties on violators, and established tribunals to resolve conflicts between guild members.

State Control Over the Economy

During the thousand years from Han to Tang, the imperial government often attempted to impose tight controls over the people of the empire and key areas of economic activity. Beginning in 119 B.C., the Han court established state monopolies over the production and distribution of salt and iron. The policy aroused considerable opposition from Confucian scholars, who argued that the state should not compete with the people for profit, and was later abandoned. Some dynasties also sought to regulate market activity in general. During the first half of the Tang dynasty, for example, the government designated the times and places where markets could operate, and the markets were closely supervised by officials who enforced the official prices. The Tang and its predecessors also employed the "equal-field" (*juntian*) system, a legacy from the Northern Wei dynasty (386–535), under which the state assigned land allotments to peasant families according to their size and redistributed the land on a regular basis. The equal-field system and state control of markets were abandoned after the middle of the Tang period, when the An Lushan Rebellion (755–763) inaugurated a precipitous decline of central authority. The salt monopoly, however, was revived in the middle of the eighth century and remained an important source of revenue for the Ming and Qing dynasties.

5. MILITARY INSTITUTIONS OF IMPERIAL CHINA

Recruitment and Military Service

During the Spring and Autumn period, warfare was primarily the responsibility of noble charioteers who went into battle accompanied by relatively small numbers of foot soldiers. After about 500 B.C., however, the demands of inter-state competition drove the principalities to introduce conscription of the farming population in order to increase the size of their military forces. The system of universal and obliga-

tory military service that existed in the early years of the Han dynasty was the result of this process. Able-bodied males entered military service at the age of twenty-three, spent one year training in their home commandery, and then were sent to serve for another year guarding the capital or the frontier. The men received periodic retraining after they returned home and were available for local militia service until age 56. The ideal of the farmer-soldier remained strong throughout the history of imperial China and into the

20th century, and successive dynasties did not hesitate to conscript men for military service when the need arose. However, beginning already in Western Han, there was a tendency to place the real burden of military service on long-serving regular troops. Professional troops formed the backbone of Eastern Han armies, and during the chaotic centuries of division that followed the Han collapse, battlefields were often dominated by troops who were private retainers (or tribal followers) of their commanders. Military status often became hereditary. When China was reunified, the Sui and Tang dynasties were able to combine the advantages of militia and professional service in the *fubing* system: Military service was not a universal obligation, nor was it hereditary. Men who were selected for service did periodic tours of duty until retirement; when not on active duty, they lived at home, farmed the land, and supported themselves at no cost to the state. About the middle of the eighth century, this system was replaced by a more flexible (and expensive) system of long-service mercenary troops, an arrangement that survived until the end of the Song dynasty. The Ming dynasty relied heavily on troops drawn from hereditary military households; when these men became demoralized and ineffective, the late Ming rulers also turned to mercenary troops. The pattern of hereditary service was restored under the Qing dynasty, whose elite Manchu, Mongol, and Chinese Banner troops were members of a hereditary military caste. The other major component of the Qing military, the Green Standard Army, consisted of long-service Chinese troops who were recruited from families that produced soldiers generation after generation.

Supporting the Military

The strong ideological preference for militia-type forces in imperial China had much to do with the high cost of maintaining large forces of regulars. In the early ninth century, for example, the Tang empire was supporting approximately one million mercenary soldiers, and the military was by far the single largest item of government expenditure. The Song and Ming dynasties later maintained even larger forces, with the Ming armies growing from 1.1 million men at the beginning of the dynasty to as many as 4 million in late Ming. Regular forces garrisoning the frontier were often expected to engage in farming to offset part of the burden on the state treasury and to ease the logistical problems of transporting supplies to distant frontier regions. The military agricultural colony (*tuntian*) was a staple of Chinese frontier policy from Han times onward.

Controlling the Military

The principle of subordination of the military to civilian political authorities (namely the imperial bureaucracy in the capital) was established very early in the history of imperial China. Different devices were employed by different dynasties to ensure that military commanders remained firmly under control. The Han and Tang dynasties employed a system of tallies in two parts (these were tiger-shaped in Han and fish-shaped in Tang). One half of the tally was kept with the military unit, the other was held by the central government in the capital. Military commanders were only allowed to move when the two halves had been matched. A commander who moved his forces without authorization might face the death penalty. In some dynasties, such as the Song, the command structure was divided and checks and balances created within the military so that none of the empire's military forces would be able to threaten the throne. Other dynasties, such as the Tang, made use of eunuchs as army supervisors. Assigned to the headquarters of military commanders, they kept the court informed of conditions in the army. Another aspect of civilian control was the assignment of senior civil officials to direct military campaigns, a fairly common practice under both the Song and Ming dynasties. Military men seldom enjoyed comparable authority over the civilian bureaucracy.

6. TRADITIONAL FOREIGN RELATIONS

The Tributary System

As the source and center of East Asian civilization and by far the largest polity in the region, imperial China did not view itself as one among a number of sovereign states. The Chinese emperor was in theory a universal ruler, the ritual intermediary between heaven and all of humanity. China, the center of the civilized world, was ruled by the emperor directly. Outlying territories were ruled indirectly through native kings and chieftains who recognized the superior authority of the Chinese emperor. In general, the farther away a people were from China, the less civilized they were seen to be and the less worthy of China's attention. This worldview found institutional expression in a pattern of foreign relations that modern scholars have labeled the "tributary system." Though some elements were already present in the Han dynasty, this pattern was not fully articulated until the Ming and Qing dynasties. Foreign rulers were expected to acknowledge China's superiority by sending tribute missions to the imperial court on a regular basis.

Tribute Missions: Tributary relations were supervised by the Board of Rites, whose officials met tribute missions at the frontier, coached their members in court etiquette, and conducted them to the capital. There they would be granted a brief audience with the emperor, in whose presence they were required to perform the ritual obeisance (kowtow; *ketou*) of three kneelings and nine prostrations. They presented their tribute, usually rare and valuable items from their home country, and received gifts from the emperor in return. In addition, members of the mission might be allowed to trade in the capital for a few days before being sent home. The rulers of tributary states had their authority confirmed by the Chinese emperor, received seals of office from China, and were expected to follow China's lead in policy matters.

The Reality of Foreign Relations

In contrast to the conventional, idealized picture of the tributary system, the reality was much more complicated. The tributary relationship functioned best in the case of sedentary, agricultural societies such as Vietnam and Korea that had borrowed much of their high culture from China and organized their governments along Chinese lines. Korea, a model tributary state, sent tribute missions three or four times a year in Ming and Qing times, used the Chinese calendar, and sought China's approval in such internal matters as the selection of the heir to the throne. Tribute relations worked less smoothly with peoples who were farther away from China's borders or deviated significantly from Chinese cultural norms. Relations with the nomadic peoples of the steppes directly north of China were especially problematic; these peoples were often militarily powerful, and conflict was a frequent occurrence. The nomads engaged in tributary relations largely because this was a prerequisite for trade with China. When strong states arose around China's periphery—or during periods when China itself was divided—dealings between states tended to be on a more equal footing, though Chinese records often covered up unpleasant realities by portraying foreigners as subservient. After the Treaty of Shanyuan in 1004, the Song court actually accepted inferior status vis-à-vis the Khitan Liao and sent regular payments in order to preserve the peace.

The Range of Frontier Policies

Since frontier realities did not always conform to the tributary ideal, successive Chinese dynasties found it necessary to employ a considerable range of practical policies to safeguard the borders. The problem was especially acute on the empire's northern and western frontiers, where China was at various times faced with such warlike neighbors as the Xiongnu, Turks, Mongols, Khitan, Jurchen, and

Manchu. One approach adopted by relatively strong Chinese rulers such as Han Wudi (156–87 B.C.) and Tang Taizong (600–649) was to launch major offensive expeditions in order to subjugate the nomads. Less ambitious policies might include limited punitive expeditions or the defense of frontier fortifications. When China was relatively weak, its rulers might pursue the policy of "harmonious kinship" (*heqin*), which involved the payment of substantial gifts (effectively tribute) to foreign leaders who might also be provided with wives from the imperial family. The establishment of commercial relations and frontier markets might also placate the nomads, who craved Chinese grain, silk, and luxury goods. When the nomads were powerful, the terms of trade could be extremely disadvantageous for the Chinese—as in the latter half of the Tang dynasty when the Uighurs compelled the Chinese to exchange large quantities of silk for horses of very poor quality.

The "Loose Rein" System

Foreign peoples that accepted Chinese authority and tribal groups within the Chinese border were often incorporated into the Chinese imperial order by means of the "loose rein" (*jimi*) system: Their leaders were granted seals of office and titles (as prefects or governors) within the Chinese bureaucratic framework, but continued to rule their own people according to local tradition and precedent and were permitted to pass on their offices to their descendants. This approach to rule over non-Chinese was first employed in Han times. Its basic outline was still evident under the Qing dynasty, especially in the southwest where the institution of indirect rule through native chieftains was called the *tusi* system.

Qing Foreign Relations

A conquest dynasty established by Manchu invaders, the Qing introduced some new features into China's foreign relations and management of non-Han peoples within the empire. Though most of China's tributary relations were still handled by the Board of Rites, the Qing created the Court of Colonial Affairs to manage relations with peoples on China's land frontiers in inner Asia. These included Mongols (Manchu allies in the conquest of China in 1644), Tibetans, the Muslim communities of Xinjiang, and even the Russians who were spreading across Siberia. Another noteworthy feature of Qing foreign relations was the effort to limit foreign trade to specific points on the frontier. Russians were allowed to trade with Chinese merchants at Kiakhta, and after 1759 European traders arriving by sea could only do business with China at Guangzhou (Canton)—where they were not allowed within the city walls and could stay for only part of the year. The Western traders at Guangzhou could deal only with an officially recognized guild of Chinese merchants called the Cohong, watched over by an official superintendent of trade. The capital, Beijing, was off limits to most Westerners unless they were travelling as tribute bearers.

7. THE TRADITIONAL FAMILY

Family Structure and Organization

Whenever wealth and circumstances allowed, the traditional Chinese family displayed a strong tendency to expand beyond the nuclear family, consisting of a husband, a wife, and their unmarried children. The typical pattern was for one or more sons to remain in the parental home after marriage and to raise their own children as part of an extended household; the ideal—rarely achieved in practice—was to have five generations under one roof, sharing the same kitchen and holding the family's property in common. The traditional family was an authoritarian and hierarchical structure in which elders had authority over younger members and women were subordinated to men. The highest authority normally rested with the eldest male in the most senior generation. Descent was traced along the male line. A man inherited his father's surname and was expected to observe kinship obligations toward many more relatives on his father's side than on his mother's side. Though brides received dowries in Song times and later, daughters did not normally inherit property except in cases where there were no male heirs. A man brought his wife into his own family's home, but a woman had to leave her birth family at the time of her marriage to enter a strange new household. Marriages were arranged by elders, and neither bride nor groom had much say in the choice of partner. New wives ranked at the bottom of the family hierarchy and were subject to the authority of the mother-in-law, in particular. Confucian teachings held that women were to observe the "three obediences": They were to obey their father before marriage, their husband after marriage, and their eldest son after the husband's death. In reality, however, increasing age tended to bring a woman more seniority and authority within the family, of which she might even become the de facto head.

Social Function of the Family

In exchange for their obedience, members of a traditional family were offered economic security and a safe haven in a society that was not friendly to the isolated individual. The traditional Chinese family differed from the modern nuclear family, in that it did not end with the departure of grown children to found families of their own. It was instead conceived as a sort of family business to be passed on from generation to generation. The younger generation provided support and security for elders no longer able to work in the fields, and descendants were expected to offer sacrifices to the spirits of departed ancestors so that they would not become hungry ghosts in the afterlife. Given these concerns, the production of male offspring to continue the family line was an important responsibility. Married men were allowed to take as many concubines as they wished (or could afford), though the original wife retained her superior status and could not

be set aside in favor of a concubine. When all else failed, it was always possible to adopt an heir—preferably a male relative such as a nephew or cousin—to carry on the family line.

Mourning

One extremely important kinship obligation was the observance of mourning for deceased relatives. This obligation extended well beyond one's immediate household. On his father's side, a man was expected to observe mourning for relatives as distant as third cousins. The intensity and duration of the observance depended greatly on the closeness of the relationship. For his most distant relatives, a man remained in mourning for only three months. If his father died, however, he was supposed to wear coarse hemp clothing and abstain from rich food and entertainment for "three years" (though in actual mourning practice, 27 months were considered long enough to be called "three years"). And if he was a government official, he was expected to resign his post and return to his native place for the duration of the mourning period.

Mourning obligations for an unmarried woman were the same as for her brothers. After a woman married, however, she assumed mourning obligations toward many members of her husband's family. At the same time, her obligations toward her natal family were scaled back. For example, an unmarried woman was expected to mourn her mother for three years, but after marriage she would owe her one year of mourning (as opposed to three years for her *husband's* mother). The husband, in contrast, was not expected to observe mourning for any of his wife's relatives other than her parents (in which case the mourning period was a mere three months).

The Lineage

The lineage was a special form of Chinese kinship organization that went far beyond the extended family residing in a single household. Lineage-type organizations had existed in antiquity, but the modern lineage was a development of the Song period and was most frequently encountered in South China. It consisted of a group of males who traced descent from a common ancestor, along with their wives and unmarried daughters. Members of the lineage maintained separate households but held some property in common and joined together for purposes of ancestral worship, mutual aid, and defense against outsiders. Lineages could grow to include as many as several thousand people, and there were many single-lineage villages in South China. In the lineage, as in the family, leadership normally fell to the eldest male of the most senior generation. But real power was usually held by the wealthiest, best-educated, and best-connected members of the lineage, who were best equipped to advance the group's interests in the wider society. The lineage was usually organized around a bequest of property (most often farmland) that the founder had left to be owned and managed by all of his descendants collectively. The proceeds from this property were often used for charitable purposes, such as providing assistance to indigent members of the lineage or supporting a school where the sons of the lineage might be educated in the Confucian classics in preparation for the imperial civil service examinations.

Fictive Kinship: So central was the role of the family in Chinese social organization that people who were not related to one another sometimes invented or pretended to kinship ties. Wishing to pool their resources or maximize their political influence, a group of unrelated lineages sharing the same surname might fabricate a common genealogy as the basis (or justification) for setting up a clan organization. Members of secret societies, espousing anti-government ideologies and engaged in criminal activities, swore oaths of blood

brotherhood. Fictive kinship ties were of special importance for individuals who were not able to participate in the Chinese family system and could not expect to produce descendants who would observe the ancestral rites. Palace eunuchs, for example, often adopted younger eunuchs as their "sons," and Buddhist monks and nuns were known to offer sacrifices to those of their fellows who had passed away.

Changes in the Traditional Family

The basic structure and organizing principles of the Chinese family remained largely stable from the time of the Han dynasty, when partible inheritance (division of property among all the male heirs) became firmly established, until the breakup of the traditional family system in the 20th century under the twin onslaught of foreign ideas and political upheaval. Some changes may be discerned, however, especially regarding the status and treatment of upper-class women. It was common for the groom's family to pay a bride price in Tang times, but from Song onward, dowries became prevalent. Upper-class women of Tang times and earlier enjoyed considerably more freedom to move about outside the home than women of Song times and later. Foot binding was imposed on increasing numbers of women beginning in the Song dynasty, and young widows were increasingly discouraged from remarrying. It has been suggested that many of these developments were related to the strict new rules for virtuous conduct and family management that were formulated by Song neo-Confucian thinkers.

8. REFORM AND WESTERNIZATION

The Treaty Ports and the Structure of Western Privilege

The characteristic institutions of imperial China remained in place until the beginning of the 20th century. Pressures

for change had begun to build much earlier, however, as a consequence of the growing presence of the Western powers and their merchants, missionaries, and gunboat-backed diplomats on the China coast. The inability of the Qing dynasty to offer effective resistance on the basis of the existing institutions also led to change. The system of restricted foreign trade at Guangzhou (commonly known as the "Canton system") was swept away by Britain's victory in the Opium War (1839–1842). The Treaty of Nanjing (August 29, 1842) abolished the monopoly of the Chinese Cohong merchants and opened the five ports of Guangzhou, Xiamen, Fuzhou, Ningbo, and Shanghai to British trade and residence. Subsequent treaties with Britain, France, and the United States established additional foreign privileges. Privileges included extraterritoriality (the right of foreigners who committed crimes in China to be tried by their own consuls rather than by the Chinese authorities) and most-favored-nation treatment. That meant that all of the foreign powers were able to enjoy any new privileges that might be extracted from China by any one of them. Additional treaty ports were opened as a result of the Anglo-French victory over China in the Arrow War (1856–1860), from which Christian missionaries also won the right to proselytize in the interior of China. In the treaty ports, the foreign powers leased land from the Qing authorities and set up their own municipal governments in foreign enclaves outside of Chinese jurisdiction, such as the French Concession and the (Anglo-American) International Settlement at Shanghai. In the last years of the 19th century, some of these ports became the nuclei of larger concession areas as foreign powers and their business interests developed mines, factories, and railroads in the hinterland. The number of treaty ports eventually rose to more than eighty, and the major Western powers did not renounce their treaty privileges in China until 1943.

The New Pattern of Foreign Relations

As a result of its defeats in the Opium War and the Arrow War, the Qing government was compelled to abandon the pretense of tributary relations and deal with the Western powers on the basis of formal equality. This necessitated institutional changes. In 1861, after Britain and France had extracted the right to establish legations in Beijing, the Qing court established a new agency to handle the empire's rela-

tions with the Western powers. This "Office of General Management" (*Zongli Yamen*) was something less than a full-fledged foreign ministry. It was headed by a Manchu prince who was assisted by several associate ministers, high-ranking officials who held other important posts concurrently. The Zongli Yamen reported to the Qing Grand Council, which usually followed its foreign policy recommendations. In order to provide interpreters for the Zongli Yamen, an Interpreters' College (*tongwen guan*) was established in 1862. In addition to teaching English, French, and Russian, the school was later expanded to offer courses in astronomy, mathematics, physics, chemistry, and international law. In the 1870s, China began to send diplomatic representatives to reside in foreign capitals; the first minister to Britain, Guo Songtao (1818–1891), took up his post in 1877.

The Maritime Customs Service

One of the new institutions spawned by the foreign presence in China was the Maritime Customs Service. In 1854, after a rebel group had seized control of Shanghai and driven out the Qing Customs officials, the foreign consuls undertook to collect tariff duties from their businessmen on behalf of the Qing government. This system proved so successful that the Qing court soon set up a permanent agency, the Maritime Customs Service, staffed by Westerners. Foreign customs inspectors, eventually numbering more than 400, were stationed in all of the treaty ports. In 1863, the Qing court appointed a British subject, Robert Hart (1835–1911), to head the Maritime Customs Service. Hart continued to serve in this position until 1908.

The Institutional Products of Self-Strengthening

In response to the military challenges posed by the Western powers and by domestic rebels such as the Taipings, Qing regional military commanders made serious efforts, beginning in the 1860s, to acquire Western technology and equip their forces with modern weapons. Zeng Guofan (1811–1872) established the Jiangnan arsenal at Shanghai in 1865 to produce artillery, ships, and small arms. Zeng's associate Zuo Zongtang (1812–1885) established a naval shipyard at Fuzhou the following year. And in 1867, another regional commander, Li Hongzhang (1823–1901), established an arsenal at Nanjing. Their operations were supervised by Western technicians and soon had schools and translation offices attached to them. Li Hongzhang went on to establish full-fledged naval and military academies at Tianjin, in 1880 and 1885 respectively. Li and other "self-strengtheners" also sought to lay the foundations of a modern transportation and communications infrastructure that would be under Chinese rather than foreign control. Borrowing an old formula for cooperation between government officials and merchants that had been used in the Qing salt monopoly, they set up a number of government-sponsored commercial ventures, such as the China Merchants Steamship Navigation Company (1872) and the Kaiping Coal Mines (1877).

Late Qing Institutional Reforms

As imperialist pressures on China intensified in the 1890s—and especially after China's defeat at the hands of Japan in 1895—growing numbers of intellectuals began to call for far-reaching institutional reforms. The brief period during the summer of 1898 when the reformist scholar Kang Youwei (1858–1927) enjoyed the backing of the Guangxu emperor (1871–1908) saw the issuance of a stream of decrees that promised sweeping changes. Archaic, outmoded offices such as the Court of State Ceremonial were to be abolished, for example, and an imperial university was to be established in Beijing and a modern school system in the provinces. Before these decrees could be implemented, the "hundred days" of reform were brought to an abrupt halt by the conservative Empress Dowager Cixi (1835–1908). After the suppression of the Boxer Uprising (1900) and the occupation of Beijing by the forces of eight foreign powers, however, even the conservatives had to concede that institutional restructuring along Western lines had become a necessity. The reforms implemented under the aegis of the

empress dowager between 1901 and 1906 went even further than those proposed by Kang Youwei in 1898. In 1906, the old Six Boards were reorganized into eleven Western-style ministries, with the Zongli Yamen becoming the Ministry of Foreign Affairs. New armies were formed in the provinces, trained, equipped, and organized according to the European model and manned mainly by natives of the provinces in which they were stationed. Traditional government schools were to be reorganized as a network of colleges, middle schools, and elementary schools with a modernized curriculum. And the imperial civil service examinations, linchpin of the old political, social, and intellectual order, were abolished in August 1905.

The Assemblies

In August 1906 the Qing court announced that constitutional government would be introduced gradually over the next nine years. After the death of the empress dowager in November 1908, the court moved forward with the first phase of the transition, the creation of provincial assemblies. Elections were held in the spring of 1909 with an electorate amounting to only about one-half of one percent of the population. (The franchise was limited to men who were degree holders under the old examination system, graduates of modern schools, government officials, or wealthy businessmen.) Voting, moreover, was indirect, with voters in each province selecting an electoral college which then chose the assemblymen. A provisional national assembly was inaugurated on October 3, 1910. The provincial assemblies elected half of its 200 members; the remainder were appointed by the Qing court. The provincial assemblies had some jurisdiction over local matters, but the National Assembly was an advisory body with no real legislative power. Members of both the national and provincial assemblies lost no time in pressing for the creation of a real parliament.

The Assemblies and the 1911 Revolution: The new institutions that emerged from the late Qing reforms played a major role in the fall of the dynasty in 1911–1912. The revolt of New Army units at Wuchang on October 10, 1911, was followed within six weeks by declarations of independence from 15 provinces, a clear vote of no confidence in the Qing leadership. The provincial assemblies sent delegates to Nanjing, where they elected the revolutionary leader Sun Yat-sen (1866–1925) provisional president of the Republic of China on December 29, 1911. The Qing government's principal military commander, Yuan Shikai (1859–1916), opened negotiations with the revolutionaries, and the last Manchu ruler, six-year-old Puyi (1906–1967), abdicated on February 12, 1912. Yuan, then the most powerful man in the country, had been offered the presidency of the republic in order to secure his support for the new government in Nanjing. Before stepping down in favor of Yuan at the beginning of April, Sun Yat-sen promulgated a provisional constitution for the Chinese republic. Under the terms of the provisional constitution, new provincial assemblies and a bicameral national parliament were elected in December 1912. Due to a significant relaxation of the education and property requirements for voting, the potential electorate expanded to include approximately 10 percent of the population, with about half of those eligible actually registering to vote. The new legislators assembled in Beijing in April 1913.

9. The Republic of China from 1912 to 1949

The Beijing Government

The provisional constitution of 1912, which remained in effect for most of the period until 1923, located sovereignty in the people and provided for popular election of a national parliament, which in turn had the power to choose the president. The president named the prime minister from among the parliamentary leaders, and the prime minister assembled the cabinet. In practice, however, the military leaders who controlled the capital and the presidency dominated the parliament and the government. The pattern was established in November 1913, when Yuan Shikai dissolved the strongest of the new parliamentary parties that had emerged from the 1912 elections, the Guomindang, and expelled its members from the parliament. The parties that remained in Beijing were for the most part the personal followings of individual politicians, held together by personal connections and corruption and largely innocent of ideological or policy commitments. When new parliamentary elections were held, as in the spring and early summer of 1918, they were marked by vote buying, fraud, and intimidation on a very large scale. After the death of Yuan Shikai in 1916, the fortunes of the Beijing government soon became hostage to the machinations and conflicts of rival military factions, with no fewer than seven presidents and 24 different cabinets holding office between 1916 and 1928.

Warlordism

Beginning with the 1911 revolution, real power in a number of provinces fell into the hands of local military commanders such as Yan Xishan (1881–1960), who ran Shanxi province as an all but independent state for more than 25 years. The devolution of power to provincial military leaders accelerated after the death of Yuan Shikai in 1916, since his successors in Beijing were no longer able to command such widespread respect within the military establishment. By 1920, almost all of China had been divided between these provincial militarists or "warlords" (*junfa*). Those who controlled whole provinces held the title of military governor (*dujun*). A few provinces, such as Sichuan and Guangdong, were divided among a number of rival militarists, in some cases down to the county level. Although the warlord forces remained components of the national army in name, their leaders were essentially autonomous potentates who taxed the territories under their control to support their armies and dominated their civilian counterparts at all levels. The most powerful militarists put together multi-province coalitions and struggled with one another for control of the Beijing government. Dominating the struggle were Duan Qirui (1865–1936) from 1916 to 1920, Wu Peifu (1874–1939) from 1920 to 1924, and Zhang Zuolin (1873–1928) from 1924 to 1928. During that period, the authority of the Beijing government extended only as far as the military power of the warlord who controlled it. As a result of the incessant fighting, the total number of soldiers in the country grew from about half a million in 1916 to more than 2 million in 1928.

The Reorganization of the Guomindang

After Yuan Shikai expelled the Guomindang from the Beijing parliament in 1914, its leader, the veteran anti-Manchu revolutionary Sun Yat-sen, was able to hold a territorial base at Guangzhou with the support of local warlords. At the time, the organization and discipline of the Guomindang were extremely weak, as had been the case with the earlier revolutionary group founded by Sun in 1894 and renamed the Alliance Party (or Revolutionary Alliance) in 1905. In 1923, however, Sun negotiated an alliance of convenience with the Soviet Union and accepted the plan of Russian advisers to reorganize the Guomindang after the model of the Russian Communist (Bolshevik) Party created by V. I. Lenin (1870–1924).

The New Structure of the Guomindang: The party branches at the local level were to report to district executive committees, which were responsible to county committees, which in turn reported to provincial committees. At the top of this hierarchy was the Central Executive Committee (CEC), whose members were to be elected by a National Congress held every two years. When the CEC of several dozen members was not in session, day-to-day leadership authority rested with a much smaller standing committee. The CEC would be assisted by a Secretariat, an Organizational Bureau to deal with personnel matters, and eight functional bureaus for such matters as propaganda, military affairs, and the mobilization of groups such as workers, farmers, women, and youth. The reorganized party would observe the Leninist principle of "democratic centralism": free debate was permitted in party meetings, but once the vote had been taken and the decision made, no dissent or disobedience would be tolerated. In theory, power flowed from the bottom up, and ultimate authority rested with the party's National Congress. In practice, however, real power was lodged with the CEC, its standing committee, and Sun Yatsen himself. Sun was given the title of director (*zongli*) and the authority to veto even the decisions of the National Congress. The First National Congress of the Guomindang, which met in Guangzhou in January 1924, formally adopted the new organizational scheme.

The Whampoa Academy and the National Revolutionary Army

Since Sun Yat-sen's plan was to defeat the northern warlords and reunify the country by force, Russian advisers also helped him to create a party army for the Guomindang. The initial step was the establishment of a military academy at Whampoa (*p.* Huangpu) near Guangzhou in May 1924, with Chiang Kai-shek (*p.* Jiang Jieshi, 1887–1975) as commandant. Between 1924 and 1926 the academy turned out five thousand new officers who had received political indoctrination as well as military training. These men formed the core of the new Guomindang army and would continue to dominate the Nationalist officer corps thereafter. The Guomindang followed the Soviet model by placing party representatives (that is, political commissars) in all of their major military units. Belonging to a separate chain of command parallel to the regular military hierarchy, they were responsible for the political education of the troops and also kept tabs on the unit commanders—whose orders were not valid without the commissar's endorsement. The Guomindang forces, designated as the "National Revolutionary Army," were 65,000 strong when the party launched its Northern Expedition against the warlords in 1926.

The Nationalist Government in Nanjing

After the success of the Northern Expedition, the Guomindang leadership moved the national capital to Nanjing and announced the beginning of the period of "tutelage" envisioned by Sun Yat-sen, during which the Guomindang would exercise sovereign power and prepare the Chinese people for the eventual introduction of democracy and constitutional government. On October 8, 1928, the party's Central Executive Committee (CEC) promulgated the Organic Law of the National Government, which was formally inaugurated two days later. In accordance with Sun's blueprint, the new government was organized in five branches (*yuan*). In addition to the Executive, Legislative, and Judicial Yuan, there were also two branches of government inspired by the institutions of imperial China. The Examination Yuan administered tests for would-be civil servants, and the Control Yuan inherited the investigative responsibilities of the Censorate. The Executive Yuan included most of the administrative ministries. Members of the Legislative Yuan were appointed rather than elected. The Central Political Council, a subcommittee of the Guomindang's CEC, supervised the government on behalf of the party, formulating major policies and selecting the top officials. Chiang Kai-shek, who had emerged as the dominant figure in the Guomindang after Sun Yat-sen's death in 1925, was also placed at the head of the government structure, serving concurrently as chairman (head of state), president of the Executive Yuan,

and chairman of the National Military Council. He did not, however, hold the party office of zongli (which had been abolished soon after Sun's death), nor did he wield dictatorial powers.

Weaknesses of the Nationalist Party and Government

Guomindang membership had grown from 23,360 in 1924 to more than 630,000 in 1929. However, most of the new recruits were either opportunists or low-ranking functionaries who entered the party as a condition of employment (more than half were soldiers who were enrolled en masse). The result was a loss of enthusiasm and a weakening of party organization at the lower levels. At the higher levels, the party was divided into squabbling factions such as the "CC clique" headed by the brothers Chen Guofu (1892–1951) and Chen Lifu (1900–2001), which was based in the Organization Department, and the "Whampoa clique" of army officers loyal to Chiang Kai-shek. Military influence in both party and government was pronounced; in 1935, for example, 43 percent of the members of the Guomindang's Central Executive Committee were military officers. The Nanjing government exercised full and direct control over little more than the lower Yangtze provinces. In most of China's provinces, the old warlords, now nominal members of the Guomindang and leaders of its "branch political councils," remained in effective control.

10. THE CHINESE COMMUNIST PARTY

Origins of the Chinese Communist Party

The Chinese Communist Party (CCP) was formally established in July 1921, when a dozen delegates representing scattered socialist study groups gathered in Shanghai. In alliance with the Guomindang from 1924 to 1927, the party grew rapidly and had perhaps 20,000 members by

the end of 1925. Driven from the cities by Guomindang repression after 1927, the CCP turned to the countryside to establish revolutionary base areas and build up its armed forces. After 1936, the party's headquarters was located at Yan'an in northwest China. The CCP was able to extend its area of control during the anti-Japanese war of 1937–1945 and governed a population of approximately 100 million when the civil war with the Nationalists resumed in 1946. During the time that the party was based at Yan'an, Mao Zedong (1893–1976) emerged as its unquestioned leader; the party constitution adopted in 1945 specifically identified not just Marxism-Leninism but also Mao Zedong Thought as the guiding ideology of the CCP.

The Yan'an Legacy: The experience of mass mobilization and revolutionary war in the countryside had a powerful influence on the attitudes and practices of the CCP after it took control of all of China in 1949. The great majority of party members were poorly educated peasants, and at the highest levels of the CCP there was no clear distinction between the civilian and military leadership. Important devices that the Communists would use to transform China after 1949 were pioneered and developed during the Yan'an period. These included "campaigns" (*yundong*—sometimes also translated as "movements"), periods of intense mass mobilization to achieve goals selected by the party leaders, the use of small study groups, confessions, and self-criticism to reform the thinking of party members, and the "mass line"—which meant that the party was supposed to pay attention to the concerns of the masses in formulating its policies and involve them actively in the process of implementation.

The Party Structure at the Center: The CCP, like the Guomindang, took the organizational structure of the Russian Communist Party as its model, but Leninist rules of party discipline were much more strictly enforced. In theory, the highest organ of the CCP was the Party Congress. Congresses could have 2,000 or more delegates and were held only briefly and at intervals of several years. (Beginning in 1977, congresses were held every five years; before that time intervals between congresses were highly irregular and could be as long as 17 years.) The chief duties of the Congress were to announce the main tasks of the party and elect a new Central Committee. This body typically had about 100 members in the early years of the People's Republic of China (PRC) but had grown to more than 300 (including alternates) by the late 1990s. The full Central Committee might hold meetings (called plenums) several times a year. When the Central Committee was not in session, its powers were delegated to a subcommittee made up of its most powerful members. This group, called the Politburo, met much more frequently and consisted of anywhere from 12 to 24 members. The Politburo, in turn, elected a standing committee of five to nine of its members. Although authority in theory flowed upward, with the individuals at each level elected by the level below, the reality was exactly the opposite. The smaller the group and the more frequent its meetings, the more power it held, and the top leadership of the party was always able to draw up the slates of candidates who would be duly confirmed by the lower-level organs. Members of the Central Committee and Politburo normally held important substantive offices in the party, government, or military structures concurrently with their membership in these bodies.

The Secretariat: The Central Committee and its Politburo were supported by an administrative staff called the Secretariat, headed by the party's general secretary. The Secretariat supervised a number of Central Committee departments responsible for specific functional areas of the party's work. After 1949, the most important of these departments were Organization (responsible for personnel management and appointments), Propaganda (supervising education and the media), International Liaison (handling relations with foreign Communist parties), and United Front (handling relations with noncommunist groups within China).

Party Organization at the Provincial and Local Levels

The Central Committee of the CCP stood at the apex of a hierarchy of territorial party committees reaching down to the local level. These included the 30 provincial party committees (including those for the autonomous regions and province-level municipalities), more than 2,000 county-level party committees, and tens of thousands of committees for rural communes (later townships) and urban work units (*danwei*). At each level of the hierarchy, the structure of the central party organization was duplicated in miniature. For example, the provincial party committee was elected by the provincial party congress (which also chose delegates for the National Party Congress) and was served by functional offices analogous to the Central Committee departments. Territorial party committees at the provincial, county, and local levels were headed by first secretaries, who bore primary responsibility for implementing central directives and were, without question, the most powerful political authorities within their jurisdictions. Each party committee was directly subordinate to the committee at the next level up and had to obey its orders, while functional departments were primarily responsible to the party committee at their own level rather than to the corresponding departments at higher levels. The lowest level, or "basic level," party committees were found in factories, communes (or townships), schools, government offices, army regiments, and other such workplace or residence units. If these units included more than a hundred party members, there might be a further subdivision into party branches and small groups.

The Top Leadership

The Politburo named Mao Zedong chairman of the CCP in March 1943, and he held the post until his death in 1976. The office was subsequently held by Hua Guofeng (1921–) and then Hu Yaobang (1915–1989). It was abolished by the Twelfth Party Congress in 1982, at which time the general secretary became the highest-ranking officer of the CCP. The office of chairman carried few clear powers and duties, but it served to designate Mao's superior position relative to the rest of the party leadership. Although forms of collective leadership were usually observed, other Politburo members seldom challenged Mao over important matters of politics or ideology. A rare exception was Marshal Peng Dehuai (1898–1974), then minister of defense, who criticized Mao's Great Leap Forward (see below) at the Lushan plenum in August 1959—and was promptly purged. No one has wielded the same power in the post-Mao era; after 1978, the position of Deng Xiaoping (1904–1997) in relation to his senior colleagues

was more that of first among equals. Significantly, many of the senior leaders of the party in the 1980s and 1990s retained their power even after they had given up all or most of their formal offices; Deng himself continued to be recognized as China's "paramount leader" after he resigned his last official position, the chairmanship of the CCP Central Military Commission, in 1991. To a considerable extent, power at the top belonged to individuals— thanks to networks of personal loyalties and patron-client ties—rather than to offices.

Party Control of Government

Although the CCP and the Chinese government are separate organizations, the government has been very tightly controlled by the party. After the first few years of the PRC, almost all senior government officials were CCP members subject to party discipline, and all government offices had party committees that received orders from higher-level party organs. Each government office also had a party "core" consisting of a handful of top-ranking CCP members in the organization who would meet as a group to discuss important issues and problems. In the hierarchy of territorial administration, provincial and county party committees exercised authority over the corresponding governmental structures. Another important tool of control was the *nomenklatura* system, imported from the Soviet Union, which gave each party committee the right to fill a list of positions in government offices and other work units. According to one estimate, the total number of positions under the nomenklatura system in the late 1980s was more than eight million. But since unit personnel offices were closely linked to the organization departments of local party committees, the party's control of appointments was by no means limited to the nomenklatura lists.

Party Membership and Recruitment

The Chinese Communist Party had 4.5 million members when it came to power in 1949 and had grown to include approximately 58 million members by the late 1990s. Almost all "cadres"—that is, those individuals holding formal leadership positions in government and other organizations—were party members, but the majority of party members were not cadres. Party membership was almost a prerequisite for the ambitious and upwardly mobile, and even the rank-and-file enjoyed considerable prestige and certain concrete privileges. Under Mao, those who aspired to party membership were expected to demonstrate that they were "activists" by working selflessly for the community and showing off their ideological purity and revolutionary fervor. A candidate's class background was also taken into consideration. The Communist Youth League (CYL) represented a stepping-stone to party membership, accepting young activists between the ages of 15 and 25. The CYL had its own large bureaucracy and hierarchy of committees and congresses paralleling the structure of the party itself. Before the Cultural Revolution, it had more members than the CCP—in 1959, 25 million, organized into 1 million branch units—and was by far the largest source of new party members.

11. THE GOVERNMENT OF THE PEOPLE'S REPUBLIC OF CHINA

The State Council

The chief administrative body of the Chinese government is the State Council, which superseded the Government Administrative Council, an interim structure, in 1954. The State Council is headed by the premier (*zongli*), and there are also several vice premiers with specific functional areas of responsibility. Zhou Enlai (1899–1976) served as premier from 1949 until his death; in the post-Mao era, premiers have included Zhao Ziyang (1919–) from 1980 to 1988, Li Peng (1928–) from 1988 to 1997, and Zhu Rongji (1928–). Zhu is expected to step down from the premiership in 2003. The State Council includes the ministers of all of China's central government ministries, which have ranged in number from about 20 to 60 as a result of frequent mergers, divisions, and other reorganizations. It also includes the heads of several commissions (such as the State Planning Commission and State Education Commission), which are of higher bureaucratic rank than the ministries, and a few other agencies such as the People's Bank of China. As of 2002, there were 29 ministries, commissions, and other agencies under the State Council.

The National People's Congress

The National People's Congress (NPC) serves as China's legislature. It has the authority to pass legislation, approve the budget, elect the president of the PRC, confirm the president's nominee as premier, and confirm the premier's nominees to head ministries and commissions. In addition, it elects the president of the Supreme Court and the head of the Supreme People's Procuratorate. And it has the authority to adopt a new constitution, as happened in 1954, 1975, 1978, and 1982. (Of course, the NPC also has the power to amend the constitution, and two articles of the 1982 constitution were revised in 1988 to provide a stronger legal basis for economic reforms.) The NPC had 1,226 members before 1965 and has averaged about 3,000 thereafter. Members have been chosen by local People's Congresses rather than directly elected by the people. They serve for a term of five years, but meet only once each year in a session of several weeks' duration. When the NPC is not in session, its powers are delegated to a standing committee of 200 members. In the 1980s and 1990s, some two-thirds of NPC members were also members of the Chinese Communist Party, and the NPC has never failed to do the party's bidding.

The Chinese People's Political Consultative Conference

The Chinese People's Political Consultative Conference (CPPCC) is a legacy of the CCP's "united front" efforts to win allies during its conflict with the Guomindang and its concern to gain the support of liberals and the urban middle class for economic reconstruction in the early days of the PRC. The CPPCC included representatives of eight non-Communist political parties—the Revolutionary Committee of the Chinese Nationalist Party, the China Democratic League, the China Democratic National Construction Association, the China Association for Promoting Democracy, the Chinese Peasants' and Workers' Democratic Party, the China Zhi Gong Dang, the September Third Society, and the Taiwan Democratic Self-Government League. It met for the first time in September 1949, when it voted to establish the People's Republic of China. CPPCC national committees met again in 1954, 1959, 1965, 1978, 1983, and 1988; the national committees formed in the 1980s had about 2,000 members. The CPPCC has always accepted the leadership of the Chinese Communist Party.

The Head of State

China's head of state is the president of the PRC, elected by the National People's Congress to serve for a five-year term. Presidents have included Mao Zedong (to 1959); Liu Shaoqi (1898–1969), who succeeded Mao in 1959 and in theory served until 1968 (although in reality his function as the president ended in 1966); Li Xiannian (1909–1992), elected in 1983, Yang Shangkun (1907–1997), elected in 1988, and Jiang Zemin (1926–), elected in 1993. The office was abolished during the Cultural Revolution and restored in the 1982 constitution. The presidency—in and of itself—has been largely a ceremonial office, with the real power of the incumbent deriving more from personal ties and other offices held concurrently.

Provinces and Counties

The most important levels of territorial administration are the provinces and counties. For most of the period after 1949, China had 29 province-level units (not counting Taiwan). Those included 21 provinces, five autonomous regions with substantial minority populations, and three municipalities directly under the central government. The three municipalities were Beijing, Shanghai, and Tianjin; the autonomous regions were Tibet, Inner Mongolia, Xinjiang, Guangxi, and Ningxia. A new province, Hainan, was carved from Guangdong province in 1986, and the city of Chongqing was later separated from Sichuan province as a province-level municipality to bring the total number of provincial units to 31 by the late 1990s. Beneath the provinces are approximately 2,150 county-level units—mostly counties (*xian*) but also including more than 400 county-level municipalities and some 175 autonomous counties and "banners" (*qi*) inhabited by national minorities. In some areas an intermediate level of administration can be found between the province and the county, such as a district (*diqu*), an autonomous prefecture, or a district-level municipality. At the end of 1997, China had 110 districts and 222 district-level municipalities. Government at each of these levels duplicated the structure of the central government in Beijing, with each province and county having its own People's Congress (complete with standing committee) and a government divided into 40 or more departments, most of which corresponded to the ministries of the State Council. Lines of control were extremely complex since departments at the provincial and county levels reported not only to their respective governments, but also to the corresponding functional departments at the next higher level of administration. In order to resolve the confusion created by multiple chains of command, the Chinese government has distinguished between a "leadership relationship" (*lingdao guanxi*), which carries the power to issue orders, and a lower-priority "professional relationship" (*yewu guanxi*).

The Xitongs

An important means of policy coordination in China's highly complicated bureaucracy was the structure of *xitongs*. A xitong, literally a "system," is a loose grouping of government and party agencies responsible for dealing with a particular issue area. Each xitong is directed by a "leadership small group" under the Politburo member with special responsibility for that issue area. Among the most important of them have been the following:

Organization Affairs: This system is responsible for personnel management and includes the Ministry of Labor, personnel departments in all work units and government agencies, and organization departments at all levels of the party structure. Personnel departments have been closely controlled by the party's Organization departments.

Finance and Economics: This xitong is concerned primarily with management of the urban industrial economy. It has included the State Planning Commission, the Ministry of Finance, the People's Bank of China, and a large number of ministries responsible for the direction of specific industries.

Propaganda and Education: This xitong includes not only the Ministry of Culture and the party propaganda departments at various levels, but also newspapers, magazines, radio and television stations, and almost all schools and universities. It has also included hospitals and research institutes.

Military Affairs: This includes both the People's Liberation Army (to be described in a separate section) and China's defense industries.

Political and Legal Affairs: This powerful xitong includes not only the Ministry of Public Security and the Public Security bureaus (police departments) at the various levels of territorial administration, but also the courts, the procuratorates (prosecutors' offices), and the prisons and labor camps.

State Control of the Economy

Within a few years after taking power in 1949, the CCP began to move China toward a Soviet-style planned economy based on state ownership. The first Five-Year Plan was launched in 1953, and by the end of 1956, virtually the whole of the urban industrial economy had been brought under government control. Some factories and enterprises were directly controlled by the center, others by the provinces, counties, and municipalities. The State Planning Commission, under the State Council, was responsible for drawing up annual plans for industrial expansion. In accordance with the plan, individual enterprises were assigned output quotas and allocated the material inputs and other resources needed to attain those goals; prices were set administratively rather than by the operation of market forces. Since all enterprises were part of the state budget, they were not held responsible for profits and losses. The emphasis was on growth rather than profitability. State control of the urban industrial economy did not begin to relax until the 1980s.

The Legal System

The key institutions of the Chinese legal system are the courts, the procuratorates, and the Public Security Bureaus—a triad found at all levels of the territorial hierarchy down to the county and municipality. The Public Security Bureaus are the police departments. Before the beginning of the reform era in the late 1970s, they were responsible not only for maintaining order and apprehending criminals, but also for supervising the "five bad elements" (landlords, rich peasants, counterrevolutionaries, rightists, and others), controlling travel between different counties and provinces, and preventing unauthorized changes of residence. The procuratorates prosecute cases for the state and are responsible for issuing arrest warrants and indictments. The People's Courts try cases, pass judgment, and hand down sentences.

Judicial Process and Punishments:
The Public Security Bureau is by far the most powerful of the three agencies, and there has always been a strong presumption of the guilt of the accused. Defendants are seldom acquitted and have often come under intense pressure to confess in order to receive more lenient treatment. Punishments have ranged from the death penalty (often carried out in public at mass rallies) to imprisonment and "supervision." Imprisonment is usually combined with reeducation and some form of manual labor. "Reform through labor" (*lao gai*) is a penal sentence that requires conviction by a court, but the less severe "education through labor" (*lao jiao*) was an administrative penalty that could be imposed by Public Security without reference to the judiciary. Individuals under "supervision" were subject to very close surveillance by either the police or their own work units. The idea of an independent judiciary was never really accepted by the Communist Party, and party committees at all levels have usually had tremendous influence over verdicts and sentences. The traditional preference for mediation over law has also survived in the PRC, and a great many minor disputes are resolved by mediators in work units without ever reaching the courts. Prior to the 1980s, the PRC was without penal, civil, and commercial codes, and the total number of lawyers in the entire country rarely exceeded 3,000.

Party Members and the Law: In contrast to the situation in the Soviet Union under Joseph Stalin (1879–1953), China's police were not supposed to have jurisdiction over the party. The investigation and disciplining of party members was instead the responsibility of Discipline Inspection Commissions elected by Party Congresses at the various levels of the organizational hierarchy. Individual party members were usually not handed over to Public Security until one of the commissions had stripped them of party membership, though this was a matter of usage rather than written law.

12. THE PEOPLE'S LIBERATION ARMY

The Party and the Military

The third major governing institution in China, alongside the CCP and the government of the PRC, is the country's military establishment, the People's Liberation Army (PLA). Although nominally subject to government authority, the PLA has actually been controlled very tightly by the top leadership of the party. At the very top of the military chain of command stands the Central Military Commission (CMC) of the CCP, which has almost always been headed by the most powerful of the party leaders. Mao Zedong was the chairman of the CMC from 1935 until his death in 1976, and the 1975 constitution of the PRC actually stipulated that the chairman of the CCP would also serve as chairman of the CMC. In 1991, Deng Xiaoping arranged for his designated successor, Jiang Zemin, to replace him as head of the CMC. The minister of National Defense (normally a senior general) has usually been the first vice chairman of the CMC, responsible for handling its routine business. Other important members of the CMC are the heads of the service branches and departments of the PLA. Many of these individuals have also been members of the Politburo. The pattern of overlapping leadership in party and army dates from the years of revolutionary warfare before 1949, and quite a few party leaders of the Long March generation (such as Deng Xiaoping) were comfortable in both military and civilian leadership roles.

The Political Work System in the Military

The General Political Department (GPD) is one of three PLA general departments directly under the CMC. The GPD is responsible for running the party organization within the PLA. Every military headquarters down to the regimental level has a party committee, and party branches extend down to the company level. In each unit at each command level there is a political commissar who chairs the party committee and countersigns the orders of the unit commander. CCP directives are passed down from the CMC through the hierarchy of committees and commissars. The political commissars have also been responsible for political indoctrination of the troops, for maintaining unit morale, and for counterespionage work and psychological warfare. They are assisted in these tasks by political departments, which are present down to the regimental level.

Organizational Structure of the PLA

In addition to the General Political Department, there are three other general departments reporting directly to the CMC. Military orders from the CMC are routed through the General Staff Department, which has a number of specialized offices dealing with military training, intelligence, mobilization, and other matters related to military preparedness and operational planning. The General Logistics Department (GLD) is responsible for keeping the PLA supplied with munitions, fuel, and all manner of equipment; it runs the military transport system and the medical system. A fourth department, the General Armament Department (GAD), was created in 1998. Beneath the level of the general departments, the PLA can be divided into five separate forces: the main ground forces, the regional forces, the navy (PLAN), the air force (PLAAF), and the "Second Artillery" (China's strategic nuclear force, which was formed after China exploded its first atomic bomb in 1964). The total strength of the PLA at the time of Mao's death in 1976 was about 4 million, of which about 3 million were ground troops. The main ground forces consisted of between 35 and 40 group armies, most of which had a paper strength of 43,000 men. These were the backbone of the PLA, and each group army received operational orders directly from the General Staff Department. The regional forces were considerably inferior to the main forces in quality; they generally lacked armor and artillery and were distributed in smaller units (divisions, regiments, and battalions) to play more of an internal security role. The regional forces were subordinated to 11 (later seven) military regions, and beneath the military regions were military districts corresponding to China's provinces. For most of the history of the PRC, it was customary for the first secretary of the provincial party committee to serve concurrently as political commissar of the corresponding military district.

Recruitment and Promotion

In theory, the PRC has had a system of military service based on conscription. In practice, however, there was no shortage of eager volunteers. Before the economic reforms began in the late 1970s, military service was the principal path of upward mobility open to young peasants. It increased their chances of being admitted to party membership, which might open the way to further advancement; at the very least, they could expect to become respected and influential members of their communities after finishing their military service. Under these circumstances, all recruiting officers had to do was select the cream of the crop by rejecting volunteers with bad class backgrounds or less than perfect eyesight. New recruits never amounted to more than 10 percent of the eligible males. Between 1 and 2 percent of openings were reserved for women. Young people were selected for military service between the ages of 17 and 21 and served a minimum term of three to five years, depending on the branch of service. Officers were usually selected from the ranks and then received some training in military schools.

The Militia

Up until the military reforms of the 1980s, the PLA was supplemented by large militia forces; in the event of war, these part-time troops were supposed to join the regulars in resisting an invader as part of Mao Zedong's favored defensive strategy of "people's war." Militia units were organized around the workplace and were open to male and female volunteers between the ages of 16 and 50. They were administered by local People's Armed Departments, which were controlled by local party committees rather than the high command of the PLA. The militia included three different types. The common militia, numbering perhaps 100 million, received no training and was little more than a manpower pool that the military could draw on as needed. The basic militia, probably between 15 and 20 million strong, received a few days of military training each year. The armed militia of 7 to 9 million received several weeks of military training and were often issued arms and used to reinforce PLA patrols in coastal and border regions.

Military Reforms

Efforts to reform and reorganize the PLA began in earnest after China's border war with Vietnam in 1979. The efforts focused on streamlining the PLA and converting it into a better equipped and more technologically proficient military force. Substantial funds were allocated to acquire advanced weapons systems and military technology, and higher education became an extremely important consideration in the selection and promotion of military officers; by the early 1990s it was reported that more than half of PLA officers had received at least some higher education. In accordance with the new emphasis on quality over quantity, the PLA underwent a significant reduction in size—from about 4 million in 1976 to 2.5 million as of 2002. Much of this reduction

was accomplished by transferring peripheral units of the PLA, such as the Railroad Corps and the Capital Construction Corps, to civilian control. The People's Armed Police (PAP), a paramilitary internal security force that was approximately 1 million strong in 2002, has also been carved from the PLA regional forces. These reorganizations freed the remainder of the army to concentrate on the primary mission of national defense. The main ground forces were reduced to 26 group armies of about 50,000 men each, but these formations were better trained and equipped than before. In the 1980s, the militia was reduced to 4.3 million, and here too there was an emphasis on improving quality. Demobilized PLA troops entered the reserves and were supposed to receive periodic retraining. The economic reforms pursued since 1978 have provided the funds for upgrading PLA equipment but may well have had a deleterious effect on the military in other ways. Not only have new economic opportunities made the military a less attractive career option, but they have also drawn PLA units into the world of business. By 1998, the PLA controlled at least 15,000 enterprises ranging from factories to hotels to ice cream parlors. In June of that year, after a series of corruption scandals involving military units and personnel, President Jiang Zemin ordered the PLA to give up its business operations.

13. THE STRUCTURE OF LOCAL AUTHORITY IN THE PEOPLE'S REPUBLIC OF CHINA

Organization of Chinese Society by the Communist State

During the 1950s, the CCP organized the Chinese people into units that could be firmly controlled by the party-state. The "socialist transformation of industry and commerce," largely completed by the end of 1956, brought the factories and other business enterprises of the urban economy under government control and management. City dwellers who were not

employed by major enterprises were grouped into neighborhood-based "residents' committees," each of which included several hundred households. Peasants were organized into Agricultural Producers' Cooperatives of 200 or 300 households in 1955–1956 and the much larger People's Communes in 1958 during the Great Leap Forward. The communes were reduced in size after the collapse of the Great Leap but survived until the early 1980s as the basic unit of local government and economic organization in the Chinese countryside. All of these organizations functioned as grassroots agencies of state control, performed an important police role, and had an almost all-encompassing influence over the lives of their members. State control of job assignments and a strict system of household registration introduced in the wake of the Great Leap Forward made it extremely difficult for individuals to move from one organizational compartment to another. Peasants in particular were prohibited from migrating to urban areas, and residents of smaller cities were discouraged from moving to major metropolitan centers such as Beijing and Shanghai.

The Urban Work Unit

Work units (*danwei*) were the basic building blocks of social organization in China's cities. Factories, schools, hospitals, and government ministries are all examples of danwei. Urban Chinese were assigned to units by the state personnel bureaucracy upon completion of their schooling, and could normally expect to spend the whole of their working lives in the same unit. Units were not simply workplaces; the larger ones often provided housing, dining halls, schools, and clinics for their employees and came close to being self-contained communities. It was quite common for people to marry within their danwei. The work units had pervasive authority over the lives of their employees, who could not change jobs or even get married without the approval of the danwei's leaders. The personnel department of the work unit, which was in close contact with the organization department of the local CCP committee, kept secret dossiers on all employees. Although it was highly unusual for a person to be fired, a black mark in one's file could put an end to hopes of promotion, party membership, or transfer to another job. Each danwei belonged to a functional-administrative hierarchy and also had a basic-level party committee linking it to the CCP structure. Since the late 1970s, the relaxation of social controls and the growth of private enterprises and foreign involvement in the Chinese economy have greatly reduced the power of the work units.

The People's Communes

From 1958 up until the mid-1980s, the People's Communes were both the lowest level of local government administration and the highest level of collective agricultural organization in the Chinese countryside. There were more than 50,000 communes in the early 1980s, with an average size of 15,000 people (or about 3,000 families). Communes were run by management committees, which were closely supervised by the commune party committees, and they also elected their own local People's Congresses, the lowest level of a hierarchy of congresses reaching up to the NPC. The communes provided local government services (such as schools, clinics, and police) and also ran small industrial and commercial enterprises such as retail shops, repair facilities, and cement and fertilizer factories.

Brigades and Teams: Communes were subdivided into production brigades and production teams. The average commune had 15 brigades of about a thousand people (or about 200 families) each, and each brigade was further divided into between 5 and 20 teams. Brigades and teams had their own management committees and specialized personnel (such as the brigade accountant and the local medic or "barefoot doctor"); the brigade had a party branch and might run a primary school and some very small non-agricultural enterprises. Except for a few short periods of radical experimentation during the Great Leap Forward and the Cultural Revolution, the production team was the basic unit of accounting. In other words, the agricultural output from the team's collective labor was divided among team members (instead of being pooled at the brigade or commune level). Income was not divided equally among the team members but was based on a system of "work points," with more points going to those who performed more strenuous or highly skilled labor. The production teams elected their own leaders and had considerable leeway in determining how their work would be done, though cropping patterns and output targets were dictated by the state. One of the major functions of management at the commune level was to plan and direct large capital-

improvement projects (such as land reclamation or construction of irrigation systems) that required more labor than could
be mobilized at the team or brigade levels.

Class Status and Labels

Since the ideology of the CCP was based
on the concept of class struggle, considerable effort was devoted to analyzing and
identifying the classes that made up Chinese society. Mao Zedong distinguished
five classes in rural China: (1) Landlords,
who lived off the rent paid by tenant farmers; (2) rich peasants, who worked their
own land but could not farm all of it themselves and therefore either rented some of
it out or hired laborers to help them; (3)
middle peasants, who owned and worked
their own land and were basically self-sufficient; (4) poor peasants, who had to rent
all or most of the land they farmed; and (5)
landless laborers. The class composition of
the cities was even more complex, with
proletarians (industrial workers), petty
bourgeois (such as shopkeepers), and several different varieties of big capitalists.
Even after the private property that had
formed the basis for this categorization
was abolished in the early 1950s, the
authorities continued to classify individuals on the basis of their pre-1949 class status—a practice that continued until 1979
and the advent of the reform era. Those
with "bad" class backgrounds (such as
former landlords and rich peasants) were
usually barred from leadership positions
and party membership and faced various
forms of discrimination and harassment.
And class status was in effect hereditary.
To these unfortunates were added others
who had had "labels" pinned to them on
account of various misdeeds; petty criminals, for example, became "bad elements,"
and those who criticized the CCP became

"rightists." All of these pariah groups
became targets of criticism and attack
whenever the party chose to launch a campaign emphasizing class struggle. On the
other hand, a relatively small number of
"patriotic capitalists," Guomindang defec-
tors, former warlords, and other "democratic personages" (*minzhu renshi*) who
supported the party through the CPPCC
and other united front forums continued to
enjoy certain privileges and higher-than-
average living standards.

Campaigns

Between 1949 and 1976, the normal
rhythms and patterns of organizational life
were frequently disrupted by "campaigns."
These involved mass mobilization of the
populace in order to transform some aspect
of social, political, or economic life in accordance with the ideological goals of Chairman Mao and the CCP leadership.
Different campaigns had different aims.
The Three-Anti and Five-Anti Campaigns
in 1951–1952 targeted corruption in government and business and brought much
of the urban economy under state control.
The Great Leap Forward (1958–1960), in
contrast, aimed to increase industrial and
agricultural production while transforming
the basis of economic organization. Campaigns were usually run by the party organization and promoted by the party-
controlled media. Normal work routines
might come to a standstill as coworkers
were formed into small groups to study and
discuss campaign-related directives and
criticize both one another and themselves.
Specific individuals—often those with bad
class backgrounds or people who had been
targeted in previous campaigns—might be
subjected to severe criticism and even formal punishment (such as reform through
labor) in the final phase of the campaign.

14. THE FAMILY IN 20TH-CENTURY CHINA

Social Change and Legal Reform in Republican China

In the second decade of the 20th century,

young Western-influenced intellectuals
began to blame traditional Confucian values and the old-fashioned patriarchal family for China's economic backwardness and
political weakness vis-à-vis the West. They

argued that individuals—especially young people and women—should no longer have to conform to the wishes of family elders. From this time on, more and more of China's educated urban youth began to choose their own marriage partners. These trends were reflected in the new Civil Code introduced by the Guomindang government in 1931, which marked the end of state support for the traditional extended family. Marriage now required the consent of both partners, and women as well as men could initiate divorce. Concubinage was officially abolished, monogamy became the legal norm, and minimum ages were established for marriage. Due to the persistence of old attitudes and the limited reach of the Nationalist government, however, the new laws were hardly enforced outside of the major cities. In the countryside, marriage practices and family organization were little different from the days of the Qing dynasty. Sweeping social reforms covering the entire country and reaching to the grassroots did not occur until the Communist Party came to power in 1949.

The Marriage Law of 1950 and the Family in Communist China

The land reform carried out by the CCP in the late 1940s and early 1950s destroyed the economic underpinnings of the great lineages, and the Marriage Law adopted by the PRC government in the spring of 1950 struck directly at the traditional structure of familial authority. Its provisions were much the same as those adopted by the Guomindang. It outlawed bigamy and concubinage, banned child betrothal, and established minimum ages for marriage (20 for men and 18 for women). Marriages could not occur without the consent of both partners. Husband and wife were to have equal status in the home, free choice of occupation, and equal right to the possession and management of family property. Unlike the Guomindang, the CCP had the power to enforce its social legislation. The extended patriarchal family disappeared, as stem families (husband, wife, and children sharing a home with the husband's parents) and nuclear families became the norm. Male authority continued to be dom-

inant within the family, however. The state made little serious effort to eradicate deeply rooted social customs such as patrilineal inheritance of surnames and patrilocal residence (with married couples sharing a household with the husband's parents). In the countryside in particular, the family continued to be the basis of social organization. A production team consisted of a group of families, with work points being paid to family heads rather than individuals. Team membership was inherited from one's father, and when a woman married, she was transferred from her father's production team to that of her husband.

Population Control and the Effects of Economic Reform

China did not make serious and sustained efforts to limit the growth of its population until the 1970s, when it became apparent that a continued high rate of increase would cancel out the gains in living standards that might be expected from economic growth. In 1980, Premier Hua Guofeng announced a policy of limiting families to only a single child. This policy was implemented and enforced by family planning committees established at all levels of the government administrative hierarchy. Material and financial incentives (such as better housing) were used to induce compliance, and monetary fines and other penalties were used to punish violators. Implementation was most successful in the cities. In the countryside, however, it was not uncommon for couples to have two children, especially if the first child was a girl. This reflected a traditional preference for sons, who would remain at home to provide for the parents in their old age—an important consideration given that China did not have a system of pensions for the rural population. The economic reforms introduced after 1979, and especially the decollectivization of agriculture, also enhanced the value of male offspring, whose labor might lead to a direct increase in family income. And increased family income under the reforms gave farm families the wherewithal to pay the fines levied for over-quota births. The government has sought to address some of these concerns by holding daughters as well as sons responsible for the support of their parents.

15. INSTITUTIONAL CHANGES SINCE THE DEATH OF MAO

The Cultural Revolution and Its Institutional Legacy

In the spring of 1966, Mao Zedong unleashed the greatest of his mass campaigns, the Great Proletarian Cultural Revolution. Instead of running this campaign, the Communist Party organization now found itself the target. One of Mao's main reasons for launching the Cultural Revolution was to reverse the processes of bureaucratization and routinization that he believed were turning CCP cadres into a privileged caste and a conservative social force. To spearhead the campaign, he used his unrivalled prestige and control of the propaganda apparatus to encourage millions of students to organize Red Guard groups and attack party and state cadres. The Red Guards ousted much of the existing leadership at all levels of the administrative hierarchy but failed to provide a viable alternative, as different groups became involved in sometimes violent factional conflicts. Eventually, Mao called on the PLA to step in and restore order. In 1967 and 1968, party committees and local governments were supplanted by "revolutionary committees," which were supposed to include the more radical cadres, members of mass organizations (such as the Red Guards), and representatives of the PLA. In fact, these organizations were dominated by the military, which emerged as the most powerful institution in the country and was only gradually returned to the barracks during the 1970s. (After the provincial party committees were rebuilt in 1970–1971, the revolutionary committees continued in a more limited role as local governments and were written into the 1975 constitution of the PRC.) Although the state had managed to put the Red Guards under control by 1968, with some six million young people having been sent into rural exile by 1970, radical Maoists remained in control of many work units, and the egalitarian policies favored by Mao were pursued well into the 1970s. For example, it was not until 1977 that examinations replaced class background and revolutionary fervor as the basis for university admissions. A longer-term legacy of the Cultural Revolution was the backlash against these policies on the part of surviving cadres, many of whom had been persecuted by the Red Guards and later rehabilitated.

The Third Plenum and the Beginning of Reform

The decisive break with Mao's radical legacy occurred at the end of 1978. At the Third Plenum of the CCP's Eleventh Central Committee held from December 18 to 22, the rehabilitated vice premier Deng Xiaoping gained ascendancy over Mao's designated successor, CCP chairman Hua Guofeng. In addition, he inaugurated a series of economic and institutional reforms that would greatly loosen the controls that the party-state had exercised over both the economy and the lives of the people since the 1950s. The plenum made it clear that henceforth the overriding goal of the regime would be economic growth rather than revolutionary transformation, and it rejected egalitarianism and pointed to material incentives and institutional reforms as the means of attaining this objective. The party leadership agreed to raise the procurement price that peasants were paid for their grain and called for measures to decentralize the control of industry. Those steps foreshadowed the much more dramatic reform measures that would follow over the next decade. And early in 1979, the new CCP leadership signaled its abandonment of class struggle by removing the labels that had condemned individuals such as former landlords and their families to inferior status and persecution during the period of Mao's rule.

Institutional Reform in the Countryside

Between 1979 and 1984, Chinese agriculture was effectively decollectivized as China's peasants returned to family farming. Initially arising from the initiatives of local cadres, decollectivization was imposed nationwide by central directives in 1982–1983. Collective farming was replaced by various forms of the "household responsibility system," which typically involved a farm family contracting with the production team to cultivate a particular tract of land. After handing over a specified amount of its produce to meet its obligations to the collective, the family was permitted to keep or sell the remainder. The same system was also applied to other collectively owned assets, as the management of small factories that had been operated by communes and production brigades was contracted out to rural entrepreneurs (who were often cadres or former cadres). Although land remained collectively owned, by the early 1990s the state was allowing leases of 50 years or more. Leases could be inherited, and they could also be bought and sold. Moreover, it had also become possible for farmers to hire additional labor.

Local Government: The early 1980s also saw profound changes in rural administration. The communes were stripped of their responsibility for economic management and converted into townships (*xiang*), basic-level units of state administration responsible for providing services such as policing, public health, and education. In 1986, China had 71,521 townships, with an average of 11,886 persons. The production brigades, meanwhile, were converted into villages (*cun*), of which there were 847,894 in 1986. Unlike the townships, villages were not formally part of the state administration but were defined as "non-governmental institutions" and "primary mass organizations of self-government." In 1987, the NPC passed the Organic Law of Villagers' Committees, providing for the direct election of village leaders by secret ballot.

By the late 1980s, the production teams had largely disappeared, leaving the village government as the key intermediary between peasants and the state and the agency with which farm families contracted for their land rights.

Institutional Reform of the Urban Economy

The first measures to reform China's urban economy were adopted soon after the Third Plenum at the end of 1978. However, the urban economic reforms have been a much more protracted process than the decollectivization of the countryside. At the beginning of the 21st century, a substantial portion of the economy was still under state ownership and the system of work units (*danwei*) providing a range of benefits to permanent employees was not yet a thing of the past. What had changed was that the more flexible non-state sector of the economy had expanded enormously. And as market reforms and incentives came to replace the old system of central planning, even state-owned enterprises—and government agencies—began to behave in capitalist fashion. The declining importance of the state-owned enterprises in China's overall economic picture was a major long-term trend that, as of 2002, showed no sign of abating.

Reform of the State Sector: One of the decisions of the Third Plenum was to allow greater authority and autonomy to managers of state-owned enterprises, which were gradually separated from the state budget and made responsible for their own profits and losses. From the mid-1980s, it became common practice for enterprises to sign contracts with the state to hand over a portion of their profits; any profits above that amount could be retained by the firm for reinvestment or distribution as bonuses. State enterprises that consistently lost money faced the possibility of dissolution after 1987, when the NPC passed PRC's first bankruptcy law. The role of central planning was gradually reduced as plans became broadly indicative, with the details left for local governments and enterprises to fill in. The number of commodities covered by the plan declined from more than 600 in 1978 to only about 25 in the early

1990s. By the summer of 2001, only 13 commodities were still subject to central price controls. The first steps toward decontrol of prices involved a two-tier price structure: Enterprises were required to sell their output under the plan at the prices fixed by the state, but any above-quota output could be sold at the higher market price. Among the last items to be subject to administrative pricing were petroleum products and metallurgical products. In the mid-1980s the state ceased the practice of assigning new workers to state enterprises. Older employees continued to enjoy the "iron rice bowl" of lifetime employment, but new workers were hired on short-term contracts so that the labor force could be readily adjusted to meet the changing needs of the enterprise. By the beginning of the 21st century, even older employees in many state enterprises have lost their former iron-clad job security. No longer dependent on the state plan for capital allocations, enterprises funded expansion with bank loans, retained profits, bonds, and stock issues. Shares held by individuals could be publicly traded on stock exchanges opened in Shanghai in 1990 and Shenzhen in 1991.

Rise of the Non-State Sector: China's non-state sector embraces many different types of enterprises, including collectively owned township and village enterprises, joint ventures set up with an infusion of foreign capital, and businesses that are privately owned. Distinctions between these various forms of organization have become increasingly blurred as management of collective enterprises is contracted to private entrepreneurs, businessmen register formerly private firms as collectives, and government agencies, enterprises of all sorts, and domestic and foreign investors join in creating new businesses through partnerships and joint ventures. In 1985, the non-state sector accounted for 35 percent of China's industrial output; by 1997, this figure had risen to 74.5 percent. Private enterprise, especially in retail and service trades, was permitted and encouraged from the early days of the economic reforms to counter unemployment, and private entrepreneurs soon expanded into

light industry and the production of consumer goods. The non-state sector did not offer guaranteed lifetime employment, but provided short-term contract work for tens of millions of migrants from the countryside who were freed to travel by the rural reforms and the abolition of the grain rationing system in urban areas.

Foreign Investment: China's economic reformers have actively courted investment by foreigners and overseas Chinese. The country's first law regulating foreign joint ventures was introduced in 1979, and between 1979 and 1981 four southeast coastal cities—Shenzhen, Zhuhai, Shantou, and Xiamen—were designated as "special economic zones" (SEZ) where foreign investors in new export-oriented businesses would receive tax breaks and other preferential treatment. Fourteen new SEZs were later added in or near other coastal cities. By the early 1990s, additional SEZs and other areas open to foreign investment covered most of the Yangtze valley and included interior cities such as Chongqing in Sichuan. As time passed, legal restrictions on foreign investment were greatly relaxed. Whereas the original Joint Venture Law had held the foreign share of ownership to less than 50 percent, subsequent legislation eventually permitted full ownership by foreigners.

Impact of WTO Membership: In the negotiation that preceded its entry into the World Trade Organization (WTO) in December 2001, China agreed to open many hitherto protected sectors of its economy to participation by foreign firms. Foreign banks, for example, were to be given full access to the Chinese market within five years. Bringing both increased foreign competition and pressure to adhere to international norms, WTO membership is likely to hasten the disappearance of the old-style work unit (*danwei*), the emergence of more open labor markets, and the introduction of systems of health insurance, unemployment and retirement benefits similar to those found in most Western societies. It is also likely to create pressure for greater transparency in China's legal system.

Reform of the Legal System

One of the goals of China's reform leadership in the late 1970s was to restore the legal system and orderly legal procedures that had been demolished during the Cultural Revolution. Moreover, as the economic reforms proceeded, it became apparent that a great deal of new legislation would be needed to regulate the burgeoning market economy and reassure foreign investors. The new Criminal Law and Code of Criminal Procedure were adopted in 1979. They were followed by a revised Marriage Law in 1980, an Economic Contract Law in 1981, a Civil Procedure Law and a Trademark Law in 1982, a Patent Law in 1984, an Inheritance Law in 1985, and a Bankruptcy Law in 1986. The Ministry of Justice was reestablished in 1979, and the courts and procuratorates were restored about the same time. Serious efforts were made to train more judges and legal personnel; between 1982 and 1993, the number of lawyers in China increased from 5,500 to 50,000. At the beginning of the 21st century, however, China's refurbished legal system fell far short of Western ideals of judicial independence and the rule of law. The courts lacked the power to enforce their judgments in civil cases. The police retained the authority to hold certain categories of offenders for long periods (up to four years) without judicial process. Most lawyers worked in legal service offices under the authority of the Ministry of Justice (or its local counterparts). And judges at all levels remained sensitive to the wishes of the party committees that had selected them for appointment and had the power to remove them from the bench.

Political Reform

China's political reforms have lagged far behind the economic reforms. The post-Mao leadership moved quickly to restore the institutional structures that had existed before the Cultural Revolution, putting an end to the Maoist technique of mass campaigns and placing new emphasis on procedural regularity in government and party administration. Structural changes included the abolition of the office of CCP chairman in 1982, the revival of the party's Discipline Inspection Commissions, and the creation in 1982 of a new Central Advisory Commission as a means of easing elderly cadres into partial retirement. In the early 1980s, the party leadership devoted much attention to placing younger and better-educated cadres in positions of authority, and it achieved some success in this regard. For example, the average age of ministers and vice ministers fell from 64 to 58 between 1982 and 1984; over the same period, the percentage who were college-educated rose from 38 percent to 59 percent. Having served its purpose, the Central Advisory Commission was abolished by the Fourteenth Congress of the CCP in 1992.

Congresses and Elections: One of the more significant aspects of political reform has been the strengthening of the People's Congresses and their standing committees, which in the 1990s could no longer be counted upon for automatic approval of all of the legislative proposals of the party leadership. A certain amount of popular participation and input has been allowed at the bottom of this system, since direct and competitive elections have been held for township and county-level People's Congresses after 1980 (and later for village and neighborhood committees as well). However, the CCP has continued to maintain a monopoly of political power by refusing to permit the formation of new political parties. As of the late 1990s, there was no evidence of a retreat from the cardinal principle of CCP political dominance enunciated by Deng Xiaoping at the very beginning of the reform era.

16. TAIWAN

Taiwan and China

The island of Taiwan (or Formosa) had been receiving Chinese settlers for several centuries before it was brought firmly under China's control by the Manchu Qing dynasty in 1683. Taiwan was governed as part of Fujian Province until 1886, when it was made a province in its own right. The island was seized by Japan in 1895 and was ruled as a Japanese colony until 1945, when it was returned to China (represented by the Nationalist government of Chiang Kai-shek). When the Communists defeated Chiang in 1949, he retreated to Taiwan with approximately 1.5 million followers from the Chinese mainland. His regime continued to identify itself as the Republic of China (ROC) and claimed sovereignty over the Communist-ruled mainland, which it vowed to recover. The Communists for their part considered the Nationalist regime illegitimate and regarded Taiwan as an integral part of China's territory. In the late 1950s, the Nationalist leadership shifted its priority from recovery of the mainland to promotion of economic development on Taiwan, although its rhetoric remained highly bellicose. It was not until 1991 that Taiwan announced the end of its state of war with the PRC and renounced the use of force to recover the mainland.

Contacts Between Taiwan and the PRC: In 1987, the ROC authorities had begun allowing their citizens to travel to the PRC by indirect routes, and Taiwanese direct investment in the PRC had grown to an estimated $3.7 billion U.S. in 1993, when some 2,700 Taiwanese firms were believed to be operating on the mainland. Taiwan created an unofficial body, the Straits Exchange Foundation, to handle its dealings with the PRC, and in 1993, this group for the first time held face-to-face talks (in Singapore) with unofficial representatives of Beijing. In this and subsequent meetings, the two parties were unable to find a mutually acceptable formula for reunification, and Taiwan continued to resist direct transportation and communications links.

Defense: Beijing did not rule out the use of force against Taiwan, which earmarked the largest portion of its budget for defense and maintained large military forces. During the 1970s, the ROC had approximately 600,000 men under arms. By 2002 the figure was about 380,000 (out of a population of 22.2 million). To maintain such large forces, Taiwan had a system of universal conscription, with males normally required to serve two years in the military beginning at the age of 18 and to enter the reserves after completing their period of military service.

The Institutional Structure of Guomindang Rule

The institutional structure of the Nationalist government was transplanted from the Chinese mainland to Taiwan in 1949. It was based on the constitution of 1947, but because of the civil war with the Communists, it was modified in 1948 by the adoption of the "Temporary Provisions Effective During the Period of National Mobilization for the Suppression of the Communist Rebellion." The Temporary Provisions, which were not rescinded until 1991, gave sweeping powers to the president, who was permitted to serve for more than the constitutionally specified limit of two terms and was given the power to make appointments to elective offices. The government also imposed martial law in 1949; martial law provisions included strict censorship and restrictions on the formation of new political parties. Chiang Kai-shek served as president of the ROC and leader of the Guomindang until his death in 1975. His son Chiang Ching-kuo (*p.* Jiang Jingguo, 1909–1988) immediately took over as chairman of the Guomindang and became president of the republic in 1978. And when the younger Chiang died in January 1988, he was succeeded as president and party leader by his vice president, Lee Teng-hui (*p.* Li Denghui, 1929–). The president was chosen at six-year intervals by the National Assembly, a body with approximately 2,600 members whose other main duty was to vote on constitutional amendments. The members of both the National Assembly and the Legislative Yuan had been chosen in nationwide elections held in 1947 and continued to "represent" their mainland constituencies even after the retreat to Taiwan. When vacancies occurred, the president filled them by appointment. Supplemental elections to increase Taiwanese representation in these bodies were not held until 1969.

The Five-Power Government: On Taiwan after 1949, as in Nanjing in the 1930s, the Nationalist government was divided into five branches (yuan). The Executive Yuan was headed by a premier who was appointed by the president and included eight ministries (Interior, Foreign Affairs, Defense, Finance, Education, Justice, Economic Affairs, and Transportation and Communications) whose leaders were also presidential appointees. The Legislative Yuan confirmed the president's choice of premier, voted on the budget, and enacted new laws. The Judicial Yuan consisted of a Council of Grand Justices responsible for deciding constitutional issues, a Supreme Court (serving as the highest court of appeals), high courts, and district courts. Justices were presidential appointees serving six-year terms. The Control Yuan, responsible for supervising the bureaucracy and impeaching corrupt officials, consisted of 29 members who were indirectly elected by provincial and municipal councils. The Examination Yuan administered civil service examinations; its ranking officials were appointed by the president.

Local Government and Elections: Beneath the central government of the ROC there was only one fully active provincial government, that of Taiwan province. A Fujian provincial government existed for the offshore islands of Quemoy (*p.* Jinmen) and Matsu (*p.* Mazu), but most of its functions were delegated to its two constituent counties. In 1967, the city of Taipei (*p.* Taibei), the seat of the central government, was separated from Taiwan Province and made a provincial-level municipality; the southern industrial city of Kaohsiung (*p.* Gaoxiong) received the same treatment in 1979. Taiwan Province

is divided into 16 counties and 5 cities, and below the county level there are town and village governments. The governor of Taiwan and the mayors of Taipei and Kaohsiung were for many years appointed by the center, but competitive elections for other local officials (including mayors, county magistrates, and city council members) were held as early as 1950. The first island-wide elections for the Taiwan Provincial Assembly were held in December 1951.

The Role of the Guomindang: Taiwan was essentially a one-party state before 1986. Members of the Guomindang, most of whom had come from the mainland with Chiang Kai-shek in 1949, filled almost all of the important offices in the national government, and the posts of president of the republic and chairman of the Guomindang were normally held by the same person. The Guomindang in Taiwan retained its hierarchical, Leninist structure of organization (see above), and the party's Central Standing Committee (the equivalent of the CCP Politburo) often decided important matters of national policy. Individuals who were not members of the Guomindang were allowed to run for office, but they were not permitted to form new political organizations that might challenge the ruling party.

The Government and the Economy: Taiwan has had a capitalist, free-market system throughout the period of Guomindang rule. Nevertheless, the government has played a very important role in guiding economic development. Beginning in 1953, the government set broad goals for economic growth in a series of four-year plans, and it adjusted its laws and policies to favor particular industries that were targeted for expansion. In the late 1950s, for example, the government adopted an export-led growth strategy, emphasizing light industrial products such as textiles; it devalued the currency, revised regulations to facilitate the import of raw materials, and made low-interest loans available to businesses in the target sector. In the 1980s, the government took steps to encourage the growth of Taiwan's computer industry.

Political Reform and the Transition to Democracy

President Chiang Ching-kuo began Taiwan's transition to democracy in the 1980s. In 1986, opposition politicians were permitted to organize a new political party, the Democratic Progressive Party (DPP), which drew most of its support from native Taiwanese (that is, descendants of the early Chinese settlers as opposed to the post-1949 arrivals). Martial law was lifted in 1987. Lee Teng-hui's succession to the presidency in 1988 marked an important watershed, since he was the first Taiwanese to serve as head of state and leader of the Guomindang. His rise was also indicative of the extent to which the party's membership had come to reflect the population of the island (which was roughly 84 percent Taiwanese and 14.5 percent mainlander or of post-1949 mainland descent, with aboriginal groups accounting for the remainder). Lee's administration introduced sweeping constitutional reforms. In 1991, the National Assembly abolished the highly authoritarian Temporary Provisions. In the same year, it also adopted constitutional amendments that put an end to the representation of mainland constituencies in the National Assembly and the Legislative Yuan. The voters of Taiwan would henceforth elect these bodies, and new national elections were held on that basis at the end of 1991. Subsequent constitutional amendments provided for the direct election of the president and the mayors of Taipei and Kaohsiung. The president would now serve a four-year term. Taiwan's first direct presidential election, held in the spring of 1996, resulted in the re-election of Lee Teng-hui. The next presidential election, held on March 18, 2000, resulted in the victory of the DPP candidate Chen Shui-bian (1951–) in a closely contested three-way race. As of 2002 neither the DPP nor the Guomindang, weakened by the defection of disgruntled mainlanders who have formed two new political parties since 1993, held a majority in the Legislative Yuan. The authoritarian stability of Guomindang rule has been replaced by the uncertainty of divided government and competition between several major parties.

17. HONG KONG

Institutions of British Colonial Rule

The island of Hong Kong was occupied by British forces during the Opium War and ceded to Britain in perpetuity under the terms of the Treaty of Nanjing, signed in 1842. The Kowloon peninsula, across the harbor from Hong Kong island, was surrendered by China after the conclusion of another unequal treaty in 1860, and Britain secured a 99-year leasehold on the New Territories north of the Kowloon peninsula in 1898. There was little change in the basic structure of government from the early days of British rule up until the 1980s. The principal authority in the crown colony rested with the British governor, who was usually a career colonial administrator. The governor was selected by the Colonial Office in London, which had the authority to send the governor binding directives on all matters except for defense and foreign policy. Within the colony itself, the civil service reported directly to the governor. He was advised by a small Executive Council (Exco), which consisted of nine members after 1920. The members included the British military commander and five senior civil servants who were ex officio members of the council, plus three unofficial members chosen by the colonial administration. The first Chinese member was appointed to Exco in 1926.

The Legislative Council: Legislation for the colony was the responsibility of the Legislative Council (Legco). After 1929, this body consisted of the governor, nine official members, and eight unofficial members. The unofficial members were prominent professionals and businessmen and included both Europeans and Chinese. Some of them were appointed by the governor, others by groups such as the Hong

Kong General Chamber of Commerce. This structure was dominated by the governor, who introduced all the bills considered by Legco and controlled the votes of its official members. The Colonial Office in London reserved the right to disallow laws passed by the Hong Kong government.

Sino-British Negotiations and the Beginning of the Transition

The approach of 1997, the end date of Britain's leasehold on the New Territories, prompted the British government in 1983 to open negotiations with China over the future of Hong Kong. The negotiations concluded in the Sino-British Joint Agreement signed on December 19, 1984. Britain agreed to return Hong Kong to China on July 1, 1997. Under the general formula of "one country, two systems," China promised that Hong Kong would be permitted a very high degree of autonomy for at least fifty years after its retrocession. China would assume responsibility for defense and foreign relations, but the territory would retain its capitalist economic system and its British-style legal and judicial system as a Special Administrative Region (SAR) of the People's Republic of China. The Joint Agreement also contained vague language calling for an elected legislature and an executive branch that would be responsible to the legislature. In 1985, China's National People's Congress formed a special committee to draft the Basic Law that would serve as the constitution of the Hong Kong SAR. The final version of the Basic Law was ratified by the NPC in April 1990.

British Reform of Legco and the Electoral System

Britain began to take cautious steps toward greater public participation in the government of Hong Kong in 1985, when twelve new members were elected to the Legislative Council from small "functional constituencies" made up of business and professional groups and three more new legislators were chosen by the members of elected neighborhood councils. In 1991, eighteen more seats were added to Legco

and filled by direct elections. Hong Kong's first political party, the United Democrats, won these elections. This party drew its support from the middle class and sought to promote political participation and protect civil liberties. The last British governor of Hong Kong, Christopher Patten (1944–), proposed a new package of electoral reforms within a few months of taking office in the summer of 1992. These included the creation of nine broad new functional constituencies for Legco elections that would give a vote to almost everyone employed in the territory and the end of the practice of appointing members to Legco and local district boards. Most of the proposed reforms were adopted by 1994 and shaped the Legislative Council elected in 1995. This consisted of 60 members: 30 chosen by functional constituencies, 20 by direct election from geographical constituencies, and 10 by an election committee composed of the 346 elected members of the district boards. It was intended that the new Legco would serve for four years, continuing in office for two years after Hong Kong's return to China.

China's Response and the Birth of the Hong Kong SAR

The Chinese government strongly opposed Patten's reforms on the grounds that they violated the terms of the Basic Law. At the end of 1995, the Standing Committee of China's NPC established a 150-member Preparatory Committee. This group then appointed the members of a 400-seat Selection Committee composed of businessmen, professionals, political figures, and representatives of grassroots constituencies. On December 11, 1996, the Selection Committee chose the shipping magnate Tung Chee-hwa (p. Dong Jianhua, 1937–) to become the first chief executive of the Hong Kong SAR. And early in 1997, the Selection Committee named a 60-member shadow legislature; when Hong Kong was restored to China on July 1, 1997, this body immediately replaced the Legislative Council that had been elected in 1995. The existing civil service, judiciary, and police force remained in place, however, and a new Legislative Council was elected in the summer of 1998 in accordance with the terms of the Basic Law. The new Legco included members of both the Democratic Party (descended from the United Democrats) and parties representing business interests and pro-Beijing constituencies.

Institutional Structure of the Hong Kong SAR

Beginning from July 1, 1997, China's Hong Kong Special Administrative Region has been headed by a chief executive chosen by a selection committee of Hong Kong residents named by the Chinese government. The chief executive appointed the Executive Council, whose members are responsible for broad policy areas as a sort of cabinet. The Legislative Council consists of 60 members. After 1998, 30 of its members represented narrow functional constituencies, while 20 (later 30) were directly elected from geographical constituencies. At the local level, district boards include both elected and appointed members. Real power rests with the chief executive, who has been given the authority to dissolve an uncooperative Legco.

KEY RESEARCH SOURCES

Baker, Hugh D. R. *Chinese Family and Kinship.* New York: Columbia University Press, 1979.

Barnett, A. Doak. *Cadres, Bureaucracy, and Political Power in Communist China.* New York: Columbia University Press, 1967.

Bartlett, Beatrice S. *Monarch and Ministers: The Grand Council in Mid-Ch'ing China, 1723–1820.* Berkeley: University of California Press, 1991.

Baum, Richard. *Burying Mao: Chinese Politics in the Age of Deng Xiaoping.* Princeton: Princeton University Press, 1994.

Bennett, Gordon A. *Yundong: Mass Campaigns in Chinese Communist Leadership.* Berkeley: Center for Chinese Studies, University of California, 1976.

Bielenstein, Hans. *The Bureaucracy of Han Times.* Cambridge: Cambridge University Press, 1980.

Bodde, Derk. "The State and Empire of Ch'in." *The Cambridge History of China.* Vol. 1, *The Ch'in and Han Empires, 221 B.C.–A.D. 220.* Eds. Denis Twitchett and Michael Loewe. Cambridge: Cambridge University Press, 1986. 21–102.

Brady, James P. *Justice and Politics in People's China: Legal Order or Continuing Revolution?* London: Academic Press, 1982.

Burns, John P. *Political Participation in Rural China.* Berkeley: University of California Press, 1988.

Chan, Wellington K. K. "Government, Merchants and Industry to 1911." *The Cambridge History of China.* Vol. 10, *Late Ch'ing, 1800–1911, Part 2.* Eds. John K. Fairbank and Kwang-ching Liu. Cambridge: Cambridge University Press, 1980. 416–462.

Chang, K. C. *Art, Myth, and Ritual: The Path to Political Authority in Ancient China.* Cambridge: Harvard University Press, 1983.

Ch'i, Hsi-cheng. *Warlord Politics in China, 1916–1928.* Stanford: Stanford University Press, 1976.

Ch'ien, Tuan-sheng. *The Government and Politics of China.* Cambridge: Harvard University Press, 1950.

Clarke, Donald C. "The Creation of a Legal Structure for Market Institutions in China." *Reforming Asian Socialism: The Growth of Market Institutions.* Eds. John McMillan and Barry Naughton. Ann Arbor: University of Michigan Press, 1996. 39–59.

Clarke, Donald C., and James V. Feinerman. "Antagonistic Contradictions: Criminal Law and Human Rights in China." *The China Quarterly* March 1995: 135–154.

Copper, John F. *Taiwan: Nation-State or Province?* 2d ed. Boulder, Colo.: Westview Press, 1996.

Creel, Herrlee G. *The Origins of Statecraft in China.* Vol. 1, *The Western Chou Empire.* Chicago: University of Chicago Press, 1970.

Dittmer, Lowell, and Lu Xiaobo. "Personal Politics in the Chinese *Danwei* under Reform." *Asian Survey* March 1996: 246–267.

Dreyer, June Teufel. *China's Forty Millions: Minority Nationalities and National Integration in the People's Republic of China.* Cambridge: Harvard University Press, 1976.

Eberhard, Wolfram. "The Political Function of Astronomy and Astronomers in Han China." *Chinese Thought and Institutions.* Ed. John K. Fairbank. Chicago: University of Chicago Press, 1957. 33–70.

Ebrey, Patricia Buckley. *The Inner Quarters: Marriage and the Lives of Chinese Women in the Sung Period.* Berkeley: University of California Press, 1993.

Fairbank, John K. "The Creation of the Treaty System." *The Cambridge History of China.* Vol. 10, *Late Ch'ing, 1800–1911, Part 1.* Ed. John K. Fairbank. Cambridge: Cambridge University Press, 1978. 213–263.

Greenhalgh, Susan. "The Evolution of the One-Child Policy in Shaanxi, 1979–88." *The China Quarterly* June 1990: 191–229.

Heberer, Thomas. *China and Its National Minorities: Autonomy or Assimilation?* Trans. Michael Vale. Armonk, N.Y.: M. E. Sharpe, 1989.

Herman, John E. "Empire in the Southwest: Early Qing Reforms to the Native Chieftain System." *Journal of Asian Studies* February 1997: 47–74.

Hevia, James L. *Cherishing Men from Afar: Qing Guest Ritual and the Macartney Embassy of 1793.* Durham, N.C.: Duke University Press, 1995.

Ho, Ping-ti. *The Ladder of Success in Imperial China: Aspects of Social Mobility, 1368–1911.* New York: Columbia University Press, 1962.

Hsiao, Kung-ch'uan. *A History of Chinese Political Thought.* Vol. 1, *From the Beginnings to the Sixth Century A.D.* Tran. F. W. Mote. Princeton: Princeton University Press, 1979.

Hsu, Cho-yun. *Ancient China in Transition: An Analysis of Social Mobility, 722–222 B.C.* Stanford: Stanford University Press, 1965.

Hsu, Francis L. K. *Under the Ancestors' Shadow: Chinese Culture and Personality.* New York: Columbia University Press, 1948.

Hsü, Immanuel C. Y. *China's Entrance into the Family of Nations: The Diplomatic Phase, 1858–1880.* Cambridge, Mass.: Harvard University Press, 1960.

Huang, Ray. *1587, a Year of No Significance: The Ming Dynasty in Decline.* New Haven: Yale University Press, 1981.

Hucker, Charles O. *The Censorial System of Ming China.* Stanford: Stanford University Press, 1966.

———. *A Dictionary of Official Titles in Imperial China.* Stanford: Stanford University Press, 1985.

Hulsewé, A. F. P. "Ch'in and Han Law." *The Cambridge History of China.* Vol. 1, *The Ch'in and Han Empires, 221 B.C.–A.D. 220.* Eds. Denis Twitchett and Michael Loewe. Cambridge: Cambridge University Press, 1986. 520–544.

Jencks, Harlan W. *From Muskets to Missiles: Politics and Professionalism in the Chinese Army, 1945–1981*. Boulder, Colo.: Westview Press, 1982.

Joffe, Ellis. *The Chinese Army after Mao*. Cambridge, Mass.: Harvard University Press, 1987.

Johnson, Kay Ann. *Women, the Family, and Peasant Revolution in China*. Chicago: University of Chicago Press, 1983.

Karmel, Solomon M. "Emerging Securities Markets in China: Capitalism with Chinese Characteristics." *The China Quarterly* December 1994: 1105–1120.

Kracke, E. A. Jr. *Civil Service in Early Sung China, 960–1067*. Cambridge, Mass.: Harvard University Press, 1953.

Kuhn, Philip A. *Rebellion and Its Enemies in Late Imperial China: Militarization and the Social Structure, 1796–1864*. Cambridge, Mass.: Harvard University Press, 1970.

Lardy, Nicholas R. *China's Unfinished Economic Revolution*. Washington, D.C.: Brookings Institution Press, 1998.

Lewis, Mark Edward. *Sanctioned Violence in Early China*. Albany: State University of New York Press, 1990.

Li, Linda Chelan. *Centre and Provinces, China 1978–1993: Power as Non-Zero-Sum*. Oxford: Clarendon Press, 1998.

Lieberthal, Kenneth. *Governing China: From Revolution Through Reform*. New York: W. W. Norton, 1995.

Lieberthal, Kenneth, and Michel Oksenberg. *Policy Making in China: Leaders, Structures, and Processes*. Princeton: Princeton University Press, 1988.

Liu, Shuyong. "Hong Kong: A Survey of Political and Economic Development over the Past 150 Years." *The China Quarterly* September 1997: 583–592.

Lo, Winston W. *An Introduction to the Civil Service of Sung China*. Honolulu: University of Hawaii Press, 1987.

Manion, Melanie. "Politics and Policy in Post-Mao Cadre Retirement." *The China Quarterly* March 1992: 1–25.

McCormick, Barrett L. *Political Reform in Post-Mao China: Democracy and Bureaucracy in a Leninist State*. Berkeley: University of California Press, 1990.

Miners, Norman. *Hong Kong under Imperial Rule, 1912–1941*. Hong Kong: Oxford University Press, 1987.

Miyazaki, Ichisada. *China's Examination Hell: The Civil Service Examinations of Imperial China*. Trans. Conrad Schirokauer. New Haven: Yale University Press, 1981.

Nathan, Andrew J. *Peking Politics, 1918–1923: Factionalism and the Failure of Constitutionalism*. Berkeley: University of California Press, 1976.

Nelsen, Harvey W. *The Chinese Military System: An Organizational Study of the Chinese People's Liberation Army*. 2d ed. Boulder, Colo.: Westview Press, 1981.

O'Brien, Kevin J. *Reform Without Liberalization: China's National People's Congress and the Politics of Institutional Change*. Cambridge: Cambridge University Press, 1990.

Oi, Jean C. *State and Peasant in Contemporary China: The Political Economy of Village Government*. Berkeley: University of California Press, 1989.

Palmer, Michael. "The Re-emergence of Family Law in Post-Mao China: Marriage, Divorce, and Reproduction." *The China Quarterly* March 1995: 110–134.

Pepper, Suzanne. "Hong Kong in 1994: Democracy, Human Rights, and the Post-Colonial Political Order." *Asian Survey* January 1995: 48–60.

Perkins, Dwight H. *Market Control and Planning in Communist China.* Cambridge: Harvard University Press, 1966.

Potter, Pittman B. "Foreign Investment Law in the People's Republic of China: Dilemmas of State Control." *The China Quarterly* March 1995: 155–185.

Powell, Simon. *Agricultural Reform in China: From Communes to Commodity Economy, 1978–1990.* Manchester: Manchester University Press, 1992.

Pulleyblank, Edwin G. *The Background of the Rebellion of An Lu-shan.* London: Oxford University Press, 1955.

Putterman, Louis. "The Role of Ownership and Property Rights in China's Economic Transition." *The China Quarterly* December 1995: 1047–1064.

Riskin, Carl. *China's Political Economy: The Quest for Development Since 1949.* New York: Oxford University Press, 1987.

Schurmann, Franz. *Ideology and Organization in Communist China.* 2d ed. Berkeley: University of California Press, 1967.

Stacey, Judith. *Patriarchy and Socialist Revolution in China.* Berkeley: University of California Press, 1983.

Tanner, Murray Scot. "The Erosion of Communist Party Control over Lawmaking in China." *The China Quarterly* June 1994: 381–403.

T'ien, Hung-mao. *Government and Politics in Kuomintang China, 1927–1937.* Stanford: Stanford University Press, 1972.

Townsend, James R. *Politics in China.* 2nd ed. Boston: Little, Brown and Company, 1980.

Tung, William L. *The Political Institutions of Modern China.* The Hague: Martinus Nijhoff, 1964.

Twitchett, D. C. *Financial Administration Under the T'ang Dynasty.* 2d ed. Cambridge: Cambridge University Press, 1970.

Unger, Jonathan. *Education Under Mao: Class and Competition in Canton Schools, 1960–1980.* New York: Columbia University Press, 1982.

Van der Sprenkel, Sybille. *Legal Institutions in Manchu China.* London: The Athlone Press, University of London, 1962.

Walder, Andrew G. *Communist Neo-Traditionalism: Work and Authority in Chinese Industry.* Berkeley: University of California Press, 1986.

Watt, John R. *The District Magistrate in Late Imperial China.* New York: Columbia University Press, 1972.

Wechsler, Howard J. *Offerings of Jade and Silk: Ritual and Symbol in the Legitimation of the T'ang Dynasty.* New Haven: Yale University Press, 1985.

Whyte, Martin King. *Small Groups and Political Rituals in China.* Berkeley: University of California Press, 1974.

———. "The Social Roots of China's Economic Development." *The China Quarterly* December 1995: 999–1019.

Wolf, Margery. *The House of Lim: A Study of a Chinese Farm Family.* Englewood Cliffs, N.J.: Prentice-Hall, 1968.

Yü, Ying-shih. "Han Foreign Relations." *The Cambridge History of China.* Vol. 1, *The Ch'in and Han Empires, 221 B.C.–A.D. 220.* Eds. Denis Twitchett and Michael Loewe. Cambridge: Cambridge University Press, 1986. 377–462.

Yüan, Ts'ai. *Family and Property in Sung China: Yüan Ts'ai's Precepts for Social Life.* Trans. Patricia Buckley Ebrey. Princeton: Princeton University Press, 1984.

Zhu, Fang. *Gun Barrel Politics: Party-Army Relations in Mao's China.* Boulder, Colo.: Westview Press, 1998.

Part II

Chronology

By Michael Golay and Ronald J. Formica

INTRODUCTION

Chronologies covering a vast amount of time can present several problems. In the case of a China chronology, further complications arise by the differences in Eastern and Western calendars, as well as disputes in pinpointing exact dates for events, especially for events that occurred 100,000 to 10,000 years ago. This chronology uses the Western calendar for its dates. That said, there are still contradictions among scholars and reference books as to the exact dates for some events and for the time periods for the Chinese dynasties. This chronology uses the most consistently agreed upon dates employed in the major Chinese reference works.

You may notice that some of the dynasty dates overlap, with two dynasties seeming to exist at the same time. For example, the Sui dynasty began in A.D. 581, yet the Six Dynasties began prior to the Sui and lasted until A.D. 589. Keep in mind that China is a vast country, and while one part of China was being ruled by a new dynasty, another part of China may have still been under the rule of another dynasty. In this case, the Sui dynasty was firmly entrenched in North China by 581. yet it wasn't until 589 that South China fell to the Sui, thus placing all of China under the Sui dynasty. Likewise, the Yuan and Southern Song dynasties overlap as well, with the end of the Southern Song coming in 1279 but the beginnings of the Yuan happening earlier in parts of China in 1276. The reason for this is explained in the introductions to both dynasties in the chronology.

Another anomaly with dates occurs with the Qin dynasty and the Han period. The Qin dynasty ends, according to our dates, in 206 B.C. Liu Bang (Liu Pang) was also installed as the Han leader in 206 B.C. Thus, many historians regard 206 B.C. as the beginning of the Han dynasty. However, it took four years of fierce civil war before the Han firmly established their rule in China. Thus, some other historians would rather point to 202 B.C. as the real beginning date of the Han Dynasty.

1. PRE-SHANG CHINA

(400,000 B.P.–1766 B.C.)

Homo erectus walked the north China plain four hundred thousand years ago—some scholars believe it might have been at least 690,000 years ago. These early people were small people, around five feet tall, with thick skulls and receding chins. They hunted and gathered for sustenance. They used fire for warmth and for cooking. They lived in caves—most notably the series of caverns southwest of present-day Beijing, excavated beginning in the 1920s, that gave *Homo erectus* of China the name Peking man. Peking man was not the first known *Homo erectus* in China. Yuanno man and Liantian man predated Peking man.

Much of China's legendary or pre-history is based on material that was passed down orally and embellished from generation to generation. This legendary history opened around 3000 B.C. with the appearance of a series of heroes who taught the nomadic tribes the sedentary arts of civilization. By the time of the Yellow Emperor (c. 2700 B.C.), the first of the Five Premier Emperors, the Chinese had developed a system of writing and a calendar. The Yellow Emperor created a unified nation by means of force, and his successors consolidated and extended his nation-building achievement.

Again, the record of these early reigns is in part legendary because it is based on oral histories and a spare written record. With modern carbon dating, some scholars can see a rough fit between legend and history. For instance, while the semi-legendary Emperor Yu (c. 2200–1750 B.C.) is believed to have established the Xia, the first of China's three ancient dynasties, historians still dispute the Xia's existence.

400,000 B.P.	Tribes of *Homo erectus* appeared on the north China plain. They subsisted on edible leaves, nuts, and berries and used stone tools to kill deer, antelope, sheep, and other large mammals.
200,000 B.P.	Communities of *Homo erectus* were well dispersed in northern China.
200,000–50,000 B.P.	Middle Paleolithic early *Homo sapiens* inhabited China.
50,000–12,000 B.P.	Late Paleolithic *Homo sapiens* were established in half a dozen centers in China.
8000 B.C.	Scattered agricultural communities developed on the northern China plain. These Neolithic people lived in villages, farmed, used polished stone tools, and made pottery.
c. 5000 B.C.	Inscriptions were scored into Neolithic pottery by this date. Some scholars suggest that the inscriptions were an early form of Chinese writing.
4000 B.C.	In farming areas below the south bend of the Yellow River, village people lived on a millet diet with supplements of game and fish. They hunted with bows and arrows, kept domestic animals such as dogs and pigs, wove hemp, and decorated their painted pottery jars with animal and plant designs.
4000 B.C.	Settled communities developed along the southeastern coast and on the island of Taiwan. Rice cultivation began in the lower reaches of the Yangtze River.
c. 4000 B.C.	In northern China, Neolithic tribes produced the distinctive Yangshao painted pottery that was reddish with bold, black geometric designs.
c. 3000 B.C.	A household industry of silk production, using silkworms fed on mulberry leaves to produce raw silk thread, began to develop in communities of northern China.
3000–2200 B.C.	Neolithic farming culture expanded in northern China, the Yangtze Valley, and along the southeastern coast. Pottery appeared in new shapes, such as cooking tripods.

c. 2800–2300 B.C.	The Longshan culture, with its thin, black, shiny pottery, flourished at several sites in present-day Hunan, Shandong, Anhui, and Jiangsu provinces. The Neolithic Longshan people practiced a settled agriculture, including the cultivation of rice.
2698–2599 B.C.	Xuanyuan Gongsun (Hsüan-Yüan Kung Sun), the chieftain of a tribe in present-day central Henan, reigned as the semi-legendary Yellow Emperor, the first of the Five Premier Emperors. Legend credited his record-keeper, Cangxie (Cang Hsieh), with inventing the written Chinese language.
c. 2600 B.C.	By archeological evidence, domesticated worms were feeding on the leaves of mulberry trees to produce raw silk.
2514–2437 B.C.	By tradition, Zhuanxu (Chuan Hsu) reigned as second of the Five Premier Emperors. He put down an uprising of the Jiuli tribes to the south and claimed dominion south of the Yangtze.
2436–2367 B.C.	By tradition, Ku reigned in an era of general peace and plenty.
2357–2258 B.C.	By tradition, the great sage and king Yao reigned.
2300–2200 B.C.	By tradition, scholars prepared the *Yaodian*, or *Canon of Yao*. This outline of principal events of the 23rd century is the earliest authenticated written Chinese document.
c. 2258 B.C.	Near the end of Yao's long reign, a legendary Great Flood inundated the valleys of the Yellow and Yangtze Rivers. Widespread famine and political upheaval followed.
2255–2208 B.C.	By tradition, Shun rose from poor peasant origins to become emperor. His chief minister, Yu, kept back the flood by digging canals, dredging river channels, and creating reservoirs. The outlines of the ancient system of feudal land tenure began to emerge. Shun reorganized the bureaucracy, establishing government departments for agriculture, justice, education, and public works. Before his death, he appointed Yu as his successor.
2208 B.C.	By tradition, Yu succeeded Shun; he was honored as the founder of the Xia, by tradition the first dynasty of ancient China. By legend, Yu descended from the Yellow Emperor.
c. 2208–2195 B.C.	By tradition, Yu reigned for a peaceful and prosperous 13 years. Sixteen kings succeeded him in a dynasty that survived for nearly 500 years.
c. 2100–1800 B.C.	The Erlitou culture, successor to the Longshan, flourished in present-day-day northwestern Henan and southern Shanxi. Excavations of large palaces at Erlitou (in the present-day city of Yanshi) suggest it might have been a capital of the Xia dynasty.

c. 2000 B.C.	Humans were buried under the foundations of important buildings on the northern China plain—evidence, according to modern archeological sources, of human sacrifice, probably of war captives.
c. 2000 B.C.	Ceramic copies of wrought metal vessels were in use at settled sites in the Yellow and Wei River valleys.
c. 1800 B.C.	The Xia dynasty ends with the reign of a degenerate king. Often in China's history, chroniclers will present the last ruler of a dynasty as corrupt or incompetent or both.

KEY RESEARCH SOURCES

Chang, Kwang-chih. *The Archaeology of China.* New Haven, Conn.: Yale University Press, 1977.

Fairbank, John King. *China: A New History.* Cambridge, Mass.: The Belknap Press of Harvard University Press, 1992.

Keightley, David M., ed. *The Origins of Chinese Civilization.* Berkeley: University of California Press, 1983.

Treistman, Judith M. *The Prehistory of China.* Garden City, N.Y.: Doubleday & Company, 1972.

2. SHANG DYNASTY

(1766–1122 OR 1027 B.C.)

The Bronze Age Shang, the first of the historic dynasties, ruled a comparatively small area—parts of present Henan, Anhui, Shandong, Hebei, and Shanxi provinces—but Shang culture gradually spread throughout northern China and today's Sichuan. This second of China's three ancient dynasties, the first with an established historical record, was a theocratic state, with a stratified society of aristocratic landowner-warriors ruling an underclass of peasants and slaves.

Shang rulers established two capitals, the first on the Yellow River near present-day Zhengzhou and the second near Anyang, north of the great river. Labor levies built royal palaces in the capitals. A complex agricultural society developed. A written language emerged, and the first Chinese calendar came into use. Shang artisans practiced advanced metalworking and pottery techniques.

The dates below should be regarded as approximate.

1766 B.C.	Tang, the virtuous first of the Shang high kings, came to the throne. By tradition, his ascension marked the beginning of the dynasty.
1766 B.C.	Tang inaugurated his reign with a promise and a warning. He would not repeat the crimes of his deposed Xia predecessor, and the people would obey Shang law on pain of death and the deaths of their children.
1750 B.C.	Tang initially ruled a small area of eastern Henan. By tradition, he rapidly extended the Shang domain with 11 successive conquests.
1700 B.C.	A rectangular stamped-earth wall 4 miles around and up to 27 feet high protected the Shang capital at Zhengzhou.
1700 B.C.	Walled towns were the main administrative units of Shang China. They fell under the direct control of the Shang high kings.
1700 B.C.	Shang traders used strings of cowrie shells as money.
1700–1600 B.C.	The first Shang bronze vessels appeared. Their possession suggested wealth, and they were frequently used in sacrifices and burials.
1600 B.C.	Shang civilization expanded along the plains of the Yellow River, a marshy and heavily forested region, warmer and wetter than it is today.
1600 B.C.	Bronze making developed as an important Shang industry. Copper and tin ores, which together produce bronze, were mined in the present northern China provinces of Henan, Shandong, and Shanxi.

1600 B.C.	Shang Chinese exploited a diverse mammal population: wild boar, bear, badger, tiger, leopard, fox, rhinoceros, and elephant. They used dogs, water buffalo, cattle, horses, and pigs as draft animals and for meat, hide and bone, and ritual purposes.
1550 B.C.	The Yellow River valley climate permitted two annual harvests of millet and rice.
1550 B.C.	Shang peasants worked with tools of wood, stone, bone, and shell. A two-pronged stick known as a *lei* served a plow's function as the basic implement for turning the soil.
1401–1374 B.C.	Pangeng (Pan Keng) reigned as Shang king.
1400 B.C.	Shang buried prominent men with elaborate ceremony. In one grave chamber near Anyang, archeologists found 1,600 objects, including bronzes, jade items, bone and stone artifacts, ivory carvings, and pottery, along with 7,000 cowrie shells.
1384–1111 B.C.	The Shang used "oracle bones" (inscribed cattle shoulder bones and turtle shells) for divination. Some 100,000 bones were excavated at the Anyang archeological site between 1927 and 1938. They revealed the earliest-known written form of the Chinese language, with some 1,500 characters deciphered.
1330 B.C.	The Shang king moved the seat of dynastic power from Zhengzhou to Anyang. It remained the capital to the end of the dynasty.
1320–1261 B.C.	Wu Ding (Wu Ting) reigned as Shang king.
1200 B.C.	Shang warriors used two-horse war chariots, with crews of three men: driver, bowman, swordsman. Shang's hunter-warrior kings fielded armies as large as 3,000–5,000 men. Infantry were armed with spears with bronze blades, wooden bows, and halberds (wooden poles with blades affixed to the tip of the shaft).
1200–1100 B.C.	According to tradition, the last kings of Shang led the dynasty into decline. According to traditional accounts, they knew nothing of hard work, sought nothing but pleasure, and had brief reigns and short lives.
1122 B.C.	Tradition has it that a Zhou military alliance of several hundred towns or small states deposed the Shang dynasty. Modern scholars believe the Zhou triumph occurred somewhat later, between 1050 and 1025, when Zhou invaders from the Wei River Valley overpowered the Shang. The Zhou established a new capital at present-day Xi'an.

KEY RESEARCH SOURCES

Chang, Kwang-chih. *Shang Civilization*. New Haven, Conn.: Yale University Press, 1980.

Keightly, David, ed. *Origins of Chinese Civilization*. Berkeley: University of California Press, 1983.

Maspero, Henri. *China in Antiquity*. Trans. Frank A. Kierman Jr. 1965. Amherst, Mass.: University of Massachusetts Press, 1978.

Wills, John E., Jr. *Mountain of Fame: Portraits in Chinese History*. Princeton: Princeton University Press, 1994.

3. ZHOU DYNASTY

(C. 1122–221 B.C.)

Zhou culture, similar at its origins to Shang, evolved in forms the Shang princes would never have recognized. Written laws and a money economy developed. Iron implements and ox-drawn plows came into use. At its zenith, Zhou extended as far north as Mongolia and south below the Yangtze Valley. An estimated 200 small domains claimed some form of autonomy, though most recognized the Zhou king as feudal overlord.

Political disorder and turbulence characterized the later Zhou. Society developed steadily from the feudal form with a hereditary warrior nobility, in the direction of a central state with armies drawn from a landed peasantry, a unification process that reached fulfillment in the dominant state of Qin.

Zhou China is traditionally subdivided into the Western Zhou (to 771 B.C.) and the Eastern Zhou (to 221 B.C.); it is further subdivided into the Spring and Autumn (722–481 B.C.) and Warring States (403–221 B.C.) periods. The Spring and Autumn and Warring States periods were the classical age of Chinese philosophy. Such major schools of Chinese philosophy as Confucianism and Taoism took their shape in these periods.

WESTERN ZHOU

1000s B.C.	King Wu reigned, establishing the Zhou dynasty, with its capital at Hao on the Wei River.
c. 1000 B.C.	The first-known Chinese poetry appeared. Poems from the *Book of Songs* (*Shijing*) were sung at important Zhou court ceremonial events.
800s B.C.	The powerful and ambitious King Mu reigned. He extended the Zhou empire and reformed the judicial system.
897 B.C.	By tradition, the chieftain Feizu (FEI-TZU) founded the northern China state of Qin, with its capital on the Wei River near modern Xian.
c. 878–841 B.C.	Li reigned as Zhou king.
841 B.C.	An uprising drove King Li from the Zhou throne.
841 B.C.	Rebels controlled the Zhou state (841 is regarded as the first certain date in China's history). The Zhou was without a king until the death of Li around 828 B.C.
827–782 B.C.	Xuan (Hsuan) reigned as Zhou king. A bureaucratic system of government developed, with a prime minister and cabinet-level departments of agriculture, war, and public works.
822 B.C.	"Barbarian" Quan Rong tribes plundered the Zhou capital of Hao near present Xian.

c. 800–700 B.C.	Jars made from an early form of porcelain were in use.
781 B.C.	You ascended the Zhou throne.
771 B.C.	The Nomadic Quan Rong again sacked the Zhou capital at Hao. This brought the Western Zhou sub period to a close. From this point, Zhou royal power was nominal; Zhou kings reigned as figureheads.

EASTERN ZHOU

Spring and Autumn Period

770 B.C.	The weakened House of Zhou moved its seat east to Luoyang, inaugurating the Eastern Zhou.
770 B.C.	Qin became a full principality.
753 B.C.	Qin established its first corps of Annalists to record state events.
722–481 B.C.	As many as 170 small states co-existed under nominal Zhou rule. Some states were absorbed by others through alliances and wars.
600s B.C.	Qin began to gain prominence among the many Zhou states.
688 B.C.	Mention of the county as an administrative unit made its first appearance in Qin records.
685–643 B.C.	Duke Huan reigned in Qi, on the eastern edge of the northern China plain in Shandong Province. Qi cast coins, regulated the economy, and led a powerful alliance of smaller states in resisting the expansion of the semi-barbarian state of Chu to the south.
677 B.C.	Qin built a new capital at Yong.
676 B.C.	Qin adopted the summer sacrifice and festival of Fu.
659–621 B.C.	Duke Mu reigned in Qin.
656 B.C.	A Qi-led attack forced Chu to pay tribute to the Zhou king.
645 B.C.	Through armed conquest, Qin extended its boundaries west of the Yellow River.
643 B.C.	With the death of Duke Huan of Qi, vassal states fought one another for supremacy.

641 B.C.	Qin conquered the small state of Liang in modern Shaanxi Province.
636–628 B.C.	Duke Wen reigned in Jin.
632 B.C.	Duke Wen decisively defeated forces of the states of Song, Qi, and Qin at Chengpu in present-day Shandong. Jin became the leader of the states nominally in vassalage to Zhou.
627 B.C.	Jin defeated Qin's eastward expanded expedition against Zheng.
623 B.C.	Qin defeated the Rong "barbarians" of the north and west. In response, the Zhou king recognized Qin as sovereign over the western Rong.
500s B.C.	By tradition, the *Dao De Jing* (also known as *Classic of the Way and Its Power*) appeared. Attributed to the possibly legendary Laozi (Lao Tzu), it is regarded as the founding document of Taoism. Little is known of Laozi's life. The philosophical system accredited to him, with its emphasis on personal spiritual freedom, offered a complete contrast to Confucianism. Many modern scholars believe the book more likely was compiled in the early third century B.C.
598 B.C.	Chu adopted the county administrative organization.
597 B.C.	Chu, defeating Jin, took its turn as the most powerful overlord of the vassal states.
594 B.C.	The small state of Lu in Shandong Province implemented a new land tax system that lightened the burden on the peasantry. At the same time, peasants lost some landlord protections. While prosperous peasants were able to acquire landholdings, the poor were often reduced to landless laborer status.
588 B.C.	In an indication that a substantial artisan class had developed, the state of Lu sent 100 mechanics, 100 embroiderers, and 100 weavers as hostages to Chu.
551–479 B.C.	Life span of Confucius. He became China's first moral philosopher and established an enduring form of Chinese cultural thought. He taught that *ren* (humaneness or benevolence) is the leading principle of conduct, and that *yi* (righteousness, duty and justice) and *li* (propriety or ritual) are other cardinal virtues. According to Confucius, government ought to be based on ethics, not just practical politics. Humans are perfectible, he taught, and morally educable.
	The *Analects* of Confucius are reconstructed conversations of the master with his disciples, recorded after his death.

546 B.C.	A peace conference temporarily ended war and rivalry among the small states of the Yellow River Valley. Around this time, two aggressive states, Wu and Yue, became powerful in the south.
536 B.C.	The first certain written laws were in force in the state of Cheng. Punishments were inscribed on the sides of bronze vessels.
529 B.C.	Qin, with the largest army of the vassal states, maintained a force of 4,000 war chariots, but Qin commanders already had used infantry in place of chariots in mountain campaigns. Infantry and cavalry gradually displaced chariots on the battlefield. In the same year, Jin sent out 4,000 chariots in a single demonstration of force.
519 B.C.	Chu built a new capital at Yingcheng.
513 B.C.	Contemporary sources mentioned the smelting and casting of iron for the first time.
506 B.C.	Wu forces captured the Chu capital.
c. 500 B.C.	Iron farm tools were in use in northern China. Oxen and horses were used for plowing.
c. 500 B.C.	Although money circulated, it was not yet widespread and salaries were still usually paid in grain.
400s B.C.	The crossbow, more accurate and powerful than the compound bow, was introduced.
494 B.C.	Wu defeated Yue, reducing it to a dependency.
486 B.C.	A canal, built for military purposes, linked the Yangtze and Huai Rivers.
473 B.C.	Resurgent Yue attacked Wu and seized its capital, ending Wu's existence.
468–376 B.C.	Approximate life span of Mo Zi (MO-TZU). A "utilitarian" philosopher and founder of the Mohist school of philosophy, Mo focused on practical economic matters. He criticized sumptuous funeral practices and other elaborate rituals of his time. Decrying war as wasteful, he favored peaceful relations between competing Chinese states. To deter military aggression, however, Mo and his followers perfected the art of defensive warfare and volunteered their services to states under attack.
453 B.C.	Once-powerful Jin divided into three states: Han, Zhao, and Wei.

430 B.C.	Qin repulsed an attack of the "barbarian" Rong. It was the last recorded Rong challenge to Qin.
c. 410 B.C.	As the Zhou all but disappeared as a political force, a number of powerful consolidated states emerged in China.
408 B.C.	Documents mentioned the taxation of grain for the first time in Qin.
403 B.C.	The Zhou king recognized the three Jin states: Han, Zhao, and Wei.

Warring States Period

403–221 B.C.	Seven major rivals, Han, Zhao, Wei, Qin, Yan, Chu, and Qi, vied for supremacy during the Warring States period. Regional lords began calling themselves kings and refused to acknowledge the Zhou dynasty. Rival states organized along military lines. Agricultural production rose, in part because of more-widespread irrigation and draining. Population growth and urbanization characterized the period, although the vast majority of the Chinese people remained agricultural.
400 B.C.	Animal-drawn plows began to replace hand-hoe methods of cultivation. Iron was in general use for hoes, sickles, and other agricultural tools. Iron was costly, however, and stone and wooden tools were still to be found.
400 B.C.	Documents mentioned the commandery political unit for the first time in the state of Wei, although the commandery was mentioned as early as 651 B.C. in Qin. This large administrative unit replaced the feudal fiefs of the Zhou. Counties eventually became subordinate to commanderies; by the end of Zhou, 10 or 12 counties made up a commandery.
387 B.C.	Wu Qi (Wu Ch'i) became chief minister of Chu. His reforms offended the nobles, who arranged for his death in 381.
384 B.C.	Qin prohibited the practice of human sacrifice.
c. 370–300 B.C.	Life span of Mencius. Mencius was the first important successor to Confucius in the same tradition and studied with the master's grandson. The "Second Sage" extended the Confucian notion that righteousness and a sense of duty are the mark of the true ruler. He argued further that the ruler who neglects his responsibilities forfeits the loyalty of his people and that the people thus have a right to revolution. Mencius believed that human nature is inherently good, and the core of moral education should be for people to recover their lost original goodness. Like the *Analects*, the *Mencius* is a later record of the philosopher's conversations.
367 B.C.	The Zhou territory was divided in two.

361 B.C.	Gongsun Yang arrived in Qin. He was the supposed author of a surviving treatise of the Legalist school of government. Legalism used the power of government to punish and reward, in contrast to the Confucian emphasis on ritual and the virtue of rulers.
359–338 B.C.	Shang Yang became the first minister of Qin and pushed through a series of reforms that made Qin the chief power among the rival seven. His measures favored farming over commerce, clearly delineated the social hierarchy, and set up a stern system of justice.
356 B.C.	King Wei ascended the throne of Qi. His rule strengthened the state against its six rivals.
354–253 B.C.	Wei attacked Zhao, who pleaded for assistance. Qi forces, under the great strategist Sun Bin, attacked Wei instead of going directly to Zhao's aid. The Wei army, rushing back to save its own homeland, ran into a pre-planned ambush by the Qi army.
c. 350 B.C.	Shang Yang imposed a state tax on land, the first in Qin history.
342 B.C.	Wei attacked Han.
341 B.C.	Qi helped Han to repulse the Wei army.
340 B.C.	Qin attacked Wei and forced its rival to cede territory west of the Yellow River. This allowed Qin to use the river as a defensive barrier.
338 B.C.	The Qin ruler who supported Shang Yang died. Shang Yang was falsely accused of treason and executed.
336 B.C.	Qin issued currency for the first time.
334 B.C.	Chu subdued the small state of Yue.
326 B.C.	The Qin court adopted the winter festival of La. (Some historians place this event in 333 or 306.)
315 B.C.	Expanding Qin captured 25 Rong walled towns.
314 B.C.	Qi captured the Yan capital.
312 B.C.	An uprising expelled Qi forces from Yan.
311–308 B.C.	King Wu reigned in Qin. His ruled ended when, by report, he died in a sporting event after trying to lift a tripod beyond his strength.

310–220 B.C.	Approximate life span of Xunzi (Hsun-Tzu). Xunzi was an important Confucian philosopher. His *Xunzi* is a set of essays on moral philosophy and government. Unlike Mencius, Xunzi regarded human nature as evil and thought humans needed education in order to learn to be good.
c. 310 B.C.	The *Zhuangzi*, the second of the two founding tracts of Daoism, circulated. Its author might have been the philosopher Zhuang Zi (Chuang-Tzu, 369–286). His philosophy emphasized the spiritual freedom of the individual; he was drawn to the limitless possibilities of the Dao, as opposed to the limited potential of humans.
307 B.C.	In the state of Zhao, mounted archers were used for the first time, an idea taken from the nomadic tribes. The increasing use of cavalry brought about an important change in dress, from flowing robes to trousers and tunics.
302 B.C.	Qin and its allies Qi, Han, and Wei, launched an attack against the southern state of Chu.
299 B.C.	Qin tricked King Huai of Chu into making a visit to Qin, where Huai was held hostage. His son became the new king of Chu.
285 B.C.	Yan forces crossed the Yellow River, defeated a Qi army, and occupied much of Qi's territory.
c. 280–233 B.C.	Life span of Han Fei (Han Fei-Tzu). A member of the Han ruling family, Han was a leading Legalist theoretician. See "China A to Z" entry on Han Fei, page 565.
279 B.C.	A Qi counterattack drove out Yan occupying forces and regained most of the lost ground. The struggle left both states too weak to resist the growing power of Qin.
278 B.C.	Qin seized the Chu capital, Ying.
260 B.C.	Qin routed a Zhao army in modern Shanxi Province. According to a traditional Chinese account, 400,000 Zhao soldiers surrendered to Qin. The Qin commander had most of them buried alive, allowing only 240 young and weak soldiers to go home.
259 B.C.	Ying Zheng (Ying Cheng), who will become the first Qin emperor, was born.
256 B.C.	Qin moved to end the long-decayed, now powerless Zhou dynasty.
250 B.C.	Lu Buwei, a rich merchant, ruled as chancellor of Qin.
249 B.C.	Chu conquered Confucius's home state of Lu in present-day Shandong.
249 B.C.	Qin dismantled the last of the Zhou royal estate.

246 B.C.	Ying Zheng ascended to the throne of Qin.
246 B.C.	Work began on the Zheng Guo Canal in southwest Qin; it eventually irrigated 465,000 acres of former wasteland.
238 B.C.	Ying Zheng reached his majority and began to exercise power.
237 B.C.	Ying Zheng deposed Lü Buwei as chancellor.
235 B.C.	Lü killed himself with poison.
c. 235 B.C.	The Legalist minister Li Si (Li Ssu) began his ascent to power.
230 B.C.	Qin conquered Han.
228 B.C.	Zhao fell to Qin.
227 B.C.	An envoy from the rival state of Yan failed in an attempt to assassinate Ying Zheng.
225 B.C.	Qin subdued Wei.
223 B.C.	Chu fell to Qin.
222 B.C.	Qin conquered the remnant of the Yan state.
221 B.C.	Qi fell to Qin.
221 B.C.	With the defeat of Qi, the last of the Warring States, Qin unified China. Ying Zheng assumed the title of Qin Shi Huangdi— First Emperor of Qin.

KEY RESEARCH SOURCES

Hsu, Cho-Yun. *Ancient China in Transition*. Stanford: Stanford University Press, 1965.

Hsu, Cho-Yun, and Katheryn M. Lindruff. *Western Chou Civilization*. New Haven: Yale University Press, 1988.

Keightly, David, ed. *Origins of Chinese Civilization*. Berkeley: University of California Press, 1983.

Lewis, Mark. *Sanctioned Violence in Early China*. Albany: State University of New York, 1990.

Li, Xuegin. *Eastern Zhou and Qin Civilizations*. New Haven: Yale University Press, 1985.

Maspero, Henri. *China in Antiquity*. Trans. Frank A. Kierman Jr. 1965. Amherst: University of Massachusetts Press, 1978.

Wills, John E., Jr. *Mountain of Fame: Portraits in Chinese History*. Princeton: Princeton University Press, 1994.

4. QIN DYNASTY

(221–206 B.C.)

Qin conquered the last of the rival Warring States during the latter decades of the third century B.C. and forcibly unified China. The short-lived, powerful Qin dynasty established the basis of an imperial system that would last until 1911.

Qin bureaucrats standardized weights and measures, currency and, above all, the written Chinese language. They constructed roads, irrigation systems, and a network of waterways. Joining and strengthening earlier defensive systems, they created the Great Wall of China, which, in its final form, would stretch 3,750 miles.

Qin rulers followed the strict Legalist school of Shang Yang and Han Fei. Shang's system of rewards and punishments regulated Qin society. Law tablets unearthed in the 20th century suggested that Qin laws were harsh, though perhaps not extremely so for the period. There was also a rough equality before the law.

Qin emphasized obedience to the state even over loyalty to the family. For this and other reasons, successor dynasties viewed the Qin as tyrannical and culturally backward, even barbaric.

200s B.C.	Qin emerged as the most powerful of the Warring States. Qin military leaders were innovators—they deployed infantry in hill country where war chariots could not follow, and they promoted the use of iron weapons. Iron tools fostered the development of Qin agriculture.
221–210 B.C.	The First Emperor divided the empire into 36 commanderies, each subdivided into counties, and imposed centralized bureaucratic rule. He standardized the Qin law code for all the empire. Capital punishments included beheading, boiling in a cauldron, and cutting in two at the waist. Imperial weights and measures were standardized. Qin authorities tore down city walls throughout the empire and collected and destroyed stockpiles of weapons.
221 B.C.	Qin set a standard wheel gauge of around 5 feet for vehicles, so that carts could run in ruts worn into roads throughout the empire.
220 B.C.	Work commenced on an expanded system of imperial highways.
220 B.C.	In his first imperial progress, the emperor toured the western reaches of his domain. He toured other parts of China in 219, 218, and 215.
220–210 B.C.	Under Meng Tian, Qin forces extended China's borders north and northwest into modern Mongolia.
c. 219 B.C.	Li Si became chancellor of the left, the senior governmental post in Qin. He supervised simplification of ideographs and made the written language uniform throughout the empire.

c. 219 B.C.	Qin established an academy of 70 leading scholars.
219–210 B.C.	Qin pushed the empire's borders south into fertile, well-watered, and semi-tropical Guangdong and Guangxi Provinces.
216 B.C.	People were ordered to report to the government the amount of land they owned.
214 B.C.	Meng Tian (Meng T'ien), a leading Qin general, employed 300,000 laborers to build a defense line of packed earth walls along the northern frontier. Much of the work involved linking existing defensive walls built by various states of the Warring States period. With later additions, this became the Great Wall of China.
214 B.C.	In an instance of the Qin policy of favoring agriculture over trade, the government deported a large number of merchants to colonize newly conquered territories in China's far south.
213 B.C.	The First Emperor directed Li Si to carry out a widespread Burning of the Books, including the histories of conquered Warring States. He hoped to enforce a monopoly of learning for the imperial court; such material as survived was available only to court academicians. Books on "useful" subjects, such as agriculture and medicine, were exempt from burning.
212 B.C.	Using forced labor, perhaps as many as 700,000 men, the First Emperor began a new palace and a tomb for himself in the Qin capital near modern Xi'an. Artists and craftspeople created a very large number of life-size terra-cotta warriors to guard the burial site. (The excavation is not complete, so we cannot be sure of the total number, although it exceeds 7,500.)
212 B.C.	Construction commenced on a major highway running north from the Qin capital across the Ordos Desert into modern Inner Mongolia—a distance of more than 500 miles. By this date, the Qin highway network exceeded 4,000 miles.
212 B.C.	The First Emperor decreed the execution of 460 scholars who criticized him or his policies. He was alleged to have buried the scholars alive. Some modern authorities believe they were executed before burial.
211 B.C.	Qin sent 30,000 families northwest to colonize the Ordos Desert.
210 B.C.	Four to six new commanderies were formed out of newly conquered areas.
210 B.C.	When the First Emperor died, his heir apparent, a capable and humane young man, was stationed with a large army on the northern frontier. The eunuch Zhao Gao and the chancellor Li Si conspired to forge the First Emperor's order for the heir

apparent to commit suicide. After the death of the heir apparent, they put the First Emperor's far less competent second son on the throne. He was known as the Second Emperor.

July–August 210 B.C. The First Emperor died at age 49 while on his fifth imperial progress, a trip to eastern China, allegedly in search of an elixir of immortality from Daoist magicians. Many of his concubines and those who had worked on his tomb were buried with him in what is believed to be one of the last recorded instances of human sacrifice in China. Also buried were the terra-cotta soldiers. Ancient historians portrayed the First Emperor as a ruthless tyrant.

210–206 B.C. The First Emperor's lavish funeral, public works, and military projects left the imperial treasury depleted. With his passing, the empire began to break apart.

209 B.C. A gang of laborers, late for their assignment, decided to rebel in the state of Chu. This incident is generally called the Chen Sheng/Wu Guang Rebellion, after the names of its leader. The direct cause of the rebellion was that according to Qin law, the punishment for lateness was death. Thus, the laborers had nothing to lose by rebelling. The rebellion triggered a series of other rebellions all over China.

208 B.C. Zhao Gao, trying to monopolize all power in government, had Li Si executed.

207 B.C. Zhao Gao killed the Second Emperor. Ziying, the emperor who succeeded the Second Emperor, ambushed Zhao Gao in the palace and killed him.

206 B.C. Liu Bang (Liu Pang) ascended as the king of Han.

January 206 B.C. Insurgents advancing from the south sacked the Qin capital, burned palaces, and put the last Qin ruler to death after a reign of only 46 days.

202 B.C. Four years of civil war ended with the establishment of the Han dynasty on the ruins of the Qin empire.

KEY RESEARCH SOURCES

Bodde, Derk. *China's First Unifier*. 1938. Hong Kong: Hong Kong University Press, 1967.

Ebrey, Patricia. *Cambridge Illustrated History of China*. New York: Cambridge University Press, 1996.

Twitchett, Denis, and Michael Loewe, eds. *The Cambridge History of China*. Vol. 1, *The Ch'in and Han Empires*. New York: Cambridge University Press, 1986.

5. THE HAN PERIOD (INCLUDING THE FORMER HAN, XIN, AND LATER HAN DYNASTIES)

(206 B.C.–A.D. 220)

Long-enduring patterns of Chinese culture were established during the Han period. The imperial court expanded the bureaucracy. The government operated manufacturing and mining monopolies. Landed estates grew in size, and the gap between the rich and the poor grew. An upper class emerged as the dominant social group. Trade increased. The Han military extended China's borders.

Early Han rulers adopted a modified Confucianism, a mix of Qin Legalism and the ideas of Confucius, as the state ideology. The controlling idea was that the emperor's conduct and his performance of ceremony were to maintain the harmony of Heaven, Earth, and humankind—a balance of the cosmic forces of *yin* and *yang*. Han emperors emphasized, too, the special relationship between the ruler and his ancestors.

Dynastic instability and a gradual weakening of state power led to the collapse of the Former Han (also called Western Han) in the second decade of the first century A.D. After a brief period of civil war and usurper rule, a distant relative of the Han imperial family restored the dynasty. Buddhism made its appearance toward the midpoint of the first century. Mass population shifts occurred during the last two centuries of Han rule, with migrants moving from the north and west to the fertile river valleys of the south. The dynasty collapsed in 220.

WESTERN HAN (206 B.C.–A.D. 9)

c. 209 B.C.	Liu Bang, who rose from peasant origins, formed his own band of rebels after leading an uprising against Qin.
Eighth month, 207 B.C.	Liu Bang's forces advanced into the Qin heartland.
Tenth month, 206 B.C.	Liu seized the Qin imperial capital.
Twelfth month, 206 B.C.	Liu Bang's former ally Xiang Yu (Hsiang Yu), the king of Chu, entered the Qin capital and ransacked the palaces there. Now styled king of Han, Liu attacked and defeated three of Xiang Yu's sub-kings but could not match Xiang Yu's overwhelming military strength.
Fourth month, 204 B.C.	Xiang Yu defeated Liu Bang's army at the Han capital of Xiangyang on the Yellow River.
203 B.C.	Regaining his strength, Liu negotiated an agreement with Xiang Yu to divide China between them.

202 B.C.	Breaking the agreement, Liu Bang attacked and defeated Xiang Yu at Gaixia in modern Anhui. With Xiang's death by suicide, Liu became China's undisputed ruler and took the title of emperor, reigning as Gaodi (Kao-Ti, also known as Gaozu) until his death in 195.
202 B.C.	Gaodi declared a general amnesty and moved to restore order throughout his dominions. He shifted the capital from Luoyang to Chang'an near modern Xian. Over the next decade or so, he consolidated Han power. At the beginning of the Han, some of Gazou's leading generals were enfiefed as princes. As time passed, Gazou gradually eliminated the princedoms and declared that only members of the imperial family with his surname could be enfiefed as princes.
195 B.C.	The government established shrines for the worship of Han emperors' ancestors.
195–188 B.C.	Gaodi's son succeeded as emperor. He reigned as Huidi.
190 B.C.	After five years of work, Han military engineers finished a defensive line around the capital, Chang'an. Thirteen miles of 50-foot-wide walls enclosed the city.
189 B.C.	The Western Market opened in the capital, Chang'an. A center for merchants and artisans, it also became a site for divination and for public executions.
188–180 B.C.	Empress Lü, Gaodi's widow, ruled. After her death, members of the imperial family and generals loyal to him crushed her family's bid for continued power.
180–157 B.C.	Wendi reigned. He became the first Han emperor to rule for longer than a decade.
177 B.C.	Han mobilized to check the incursion of the Xiongnu (Hsiung-Nu) from their steppe empire in the Ordos region (modern Mongolia) on China's northern frontier. Diplomats arranged a temporary peace.
c. 179–104 B.C.	Life span of the Confucian philosopher Dong Zhongshu (Tung Chung-shu). See "China A to Z" entry on Dong Zhongshu, page 558.
c. 168 B.C.	The government reduced the agricultural tax in an effort to ease the burden on the peasantry.
166 B.C.	Xiongnu raiders threatened the capital, Chang'an.
157–141 B.C.	Wendi's son succeeded to the throne and reigned as Jingdi (Ching-ti).

154 B.C.	The king of Wu (eastern China) rebelled and induced six other subordinate kings to join him. Imperial forces crushed the insurgency after several months of fighting.
143 B.C.	Han China, a highly organized bureaucratic state, was made up of 40 commanderies and 25 small kingdoms, half of them ruled by the emperor's sons.
141–87 B.C.	Wudi occupied the throne in one of the longest reigns of imperial Chinese history. By the year of his accession, Han had consolidated and expanded its central authority and established an effective tax collecting system. Wudi, whose title means "the Martial Emperor," thus inherited an empire on a solid financial footing.
138 B.C.	Zhang Qian (Chang Chi'en) set out on his first journey of exploration and diplomacy in central Asia.
136 B.C.	The government created official posts for academicians specializing in the five works regarded as basic texts for the education of state officials: the *Book of Changes*, the *Book of Songs*, the *Book of Documents*, the *Book of Rites,* and the *Spring and Autumn Annals*. This established the Confucian canon as the basis for training government officials.
135–119 B.C.	Han forces repelled a succession of Xiongnu raids along the northwestern frontier in what is today Mongolia. The invaders were driven from the borders after important victories in 121 and 119.
128 B.C.	Han failed in a campaign to subdue the Korean peninsula, but imperial forces established a commandery in Manchuria.
122 B.C.	Imperial forces crushed a rebellion in the Han kingdom of Huainan.
122 B.C.	Liu An, an emperor's grandson and the patron of scholars who compiled the Daoist *Huainanzi*, died. The *Huainanzi*, a collection of essays that attempted a synthesis of earlier Chinese thought, became an influential philosophical work of the Western Han.
c. 120 B.C.	Han merchants traveled the Silk Road into central Asia, exchanging Chinese silk for livestock, fleece, and jade.
c. 120 B.C.	Foreign words and ideas began to enter the Chinese written language, the result of increased contact with central Asians and Indians.
119 B.C.	Han pushed the Xiongnu north beyond the Gobi Desert. Wars and rebellions left the Han treasury empty. To pay for Wudi's initiatives, the government introduced state monopolies of salt

and iron, brought private mining operations under state control, and levied new taxes on market transactions, vehicles and property.

115 B.C.   The government created an agency to monitor and regulate prices.

115 B.C.   Zhang Qian embarked on his second exploration of central Asia, ranging as far as Ferghana and Sogdiana.

113 B.C.   Han established controls on the minting of coin, standardizing the 5-shu copper piece of 3 grams weight.

111 B.C.   Han forces conquered Guangzhou (Canton) and the provinces of Guangdong and Guangxi in southeast China, occupied northern Vietnam, and established commanderies in the modern provinces of Yunnan and Sichuan to the southwest.

c. 110 B.C.   The Confucian scholar-statesman Dong Zhongshu urged the emperor to slow the growth of landed estates and the concentration of wealth in fewer hands.

110 B.C.   A newly created government board and an important new office, the superintendent of waterways and parks, took charge of transport matters.

110 B.C.   The Wudi emperor journeyed to Mount Tai to perform the Feng and Shan ceremonies. The rites were generally regarded as the highest rites, which were to be performed only when the empire had achieved the peak of peace and prosperity.

109 B.C.   The government undertook major dike repairs to prevent flooding in the Yellow River Valley.

108 B.C.   The Han resumed the effort to conquer Korea. Two military campaigns brought much of the peninsula under Chinese control. Divided into 80 commanderies and 18 kingdoms, the empire reached its greatest extent of the entire Han period.

104 B.C.   Zhang Qian's journeys concluded with the Han annexation of Ferghana. The region's famous horses became a symbol of status in imperial China.

c. 100 B.C.   Water clocks were in use for keeping time.

100 B.C.   Han strengthened its hold on the provinces and frontiers, virtually freeing northern China from cross-border raids. The government established control over what is now modern Guangxi Province in the south.

c. 99–85 B.C.   Sima Qian completed his history of China, *Records of the Historian*, to the reign of Wudi, beginning in 140 B.C. It contained a year-by-year chronicle, imperial genealogies, biographical studies, and essays on the economy and other subjects. For

	defending the family of a general who had surrendered to the Xiongnu after a heroic and hopeless campaign, Sima Qian was imprisoned and castrated.
98 B.C.	The government established a liquor monopoly.
91–90 B.C.	The heir apparent, falsely accused of trying to harm Wudi through witchcraft, rebelled out of desperation. The rebellion was quickly put down, and the heir apparent committed suicide. With no formally nominated successor to the throne, Han experienced a dynastic crisis.
88 B.C.	An attempt to assassinate the aging Wudi failed.
27 March 87 B.C.	The court nominated an eight-year-old son of Wudi as heir to the throne.
29 March 87 B.C.	Zhaodi (Chao-ti) succeeded as Han emperor. He reigned until 74 b.c., though real power lay with the powerful general Huo Guang.
86 B.C.	An uprising rocked the new Han commanderies of the southwest.
82 B.C.	A renewed insurgency in southwestern China ended with the slaughter of more than 50,000 rebels.
82 B.C.	Under a retrenchment policy, China began to withdraw from Korea.
81 B.C.	An imperial inquiry into the causes of hardship among the people evolved into an important conference that debated the issue of public versus private enterprise. Confucian scholars attacked the state monopolies as burdensome; finance officers from Wudi's reign regarded them as essential to raise revenue for the state. Records of the sessions were published some years later in a document titled *Discourse on Salt and Iron.*
74 B.C.	Xuandi (Hsuan-ti), 18 years old, ascended as emperor, succeeding Zhaodi, who died at 22.
66–64 B.C.	In response to hard times, the government lowered the price of salt, cut taxes, and instituted other measures to ease the burden on the poor.
c. 60 B.C.	The government established the office of protector-general of the western regions to supervise colonization.
51 B.C.	Xiongnu, by now divided into several factions and weakened by civil war, had started to pay tribute to Han.

49–33 B.C.	Yuandi reigned. In this and the following reign, officials with Confucian inclination became more influential. Hallmarks of his reign were economy in government and military retrenchment. The government failed, however, to restrict the concentration of landholdings and halt the decline of the peasantry.
47–44 B.C.	The government implemented measures to reduce spending on the imperial household.
46 B.C.	China withdrew from the island of Hainan.
c. 45 B.C.	At least three large textile factories, each employing several thousand workers, were operating in east China. Most Chinese textiles were woven from hemp and silk.
44 B.C.	The state monopolies were abolished.
41 B.C.	Revenue losses forced the government to restore the monopolies.
40 B.C.	For reasons of economy, the government reduced the number of religious shrines, elaborate institutions that employed thousands of priests and functionaries.
34 B.C.	The government moved to simplify judicial procedures.
33–7 B.C.	Chengdi reigned as emperor. Frivolous and selfish by repute, he died without producing a male heir.
c. 30 B.C.	A new round of economy measures for the imperial household included cuts in the budget for palace maintenance and reductions in palace guard arms and equipment.
30 B.C.	Widespread flooding devastated much of China. The government responded with dike building and other flood-control projects.
26 B.C.	The emperor ordered copies of literary works from the entire realm sent to the capital. The intent was to compare texts and prepare standard editions for the imperial library.
7 B.C.	The government again moved to cut costs by reducing the number of religious shrines, including those dedicated to the Heaven and Earth cults.
7 B.C.	Aidi, a half-nephew of Chengdi, ascended the Han throne.
c. 5 B.C.	A Han ship model, discovered by archeologists near Guangzhou, had a centered sternpost rudder, a major technological innovation that would not reach Europe for another thousand years.
5 B.C.	More than 120,000 officials were employed in the Han civil service.

3 B.C.	The popular Cult of the Queen Mother of the West spread throughout China, probably in response to the political upheavals of the concluding years of the Western Han.
1 B.C.	Aidi died without an heir. Wang Mang, a relative of the empress dowager, took control of government administration.
1 B.C.	Pingdi, nine years old, ascended the throne. The regent Wang Mang exercised real authority. Wang looked to the early Zhou for a model of social order. He attempted to redistribute land, abolish slavery, and encourage respect for the teachings of the classics.
A.D. 1–2	More than 50 iron foundries were in operation in northern China. A workforce of 100,000 mined China's copper and iron deposits. Workshops manufactured farm tools, weapons, and domestic utensils such as lamps, pots, and cooking stoves.
September–October 2	The world's earliest preserved census put the population of the Han empire at 57,671,400. The heaviest population concentrations, 44 million of the total, were in the Yellow and Huai River valleys in the north. Chengdu in modern Sichuan was China's largest city, with a population of 282,147. The capitals, Chang'an and Luoyang, counted 246,200 and 195,504 inhabitants respectively.
c. 3–5	Major floods caused great loss of life, destroyed crops, and altered the course of the Yellow River. The disasters triggered a major southward migration.
3	Wang Mang implemented a reform program for the schools.
5	Wang Mang ordered restoration of the cults of Heaven and Earth. A scholarly conference on the classical texts convened in the capital under his auspices.
5	A new government road linked the Wei River Valley to Sichuan in the south.
6	With the death of Pingdi, the last direct descendant of Yandi, the Han faced a succession crisis. Wang Mang chose an infant, Liu Yang, as heir apparent. Wang suggested that the boy would lose the Mandate and thus be the last emperor of the Early Han dynasty. Soon after that, Wang Mang declared himself acting emperor. Chinese historians regard him as a usurper.
7	Wang Mang's forces quelled an uprising touched off by a provincial official who accused Wang of the murder of Pingdi.
8–9	Wang Mang moved to consolidate his power. He concocted a series of omens suggesting that he should become emperor.

| 9 | Precise bronze footrules were in widespread use in China's building trades. |

XIN AND GENGSHI (A.D. 9–25)

9	Declaring the Han dynasty ended, Wang Mang proclaimed himself emperor.
9	Wang Mang ordered a bureaucratic reorganization. He also banned the private buying and selling of slaves.
9	Wang Mang's government introduced a new range of coins. As many as 20 denominations were minted from gold, silver, tortoiseshell, cowries, and copper.
9–11	Wang Mang downgraded the title of the Xiongnu chief, who was normally a Han vassal. Consequently, the Xiongnu launched new raids along the northern borders.
10	The government re-established state monopolies on liquor, salt, and iron tools and levied a 10 percent income tax on hunters, fishers, artisans, and merchants.
11	Heavy flooding in parts of the empire took many lives. The subsequent famine undermined Wang Mang's regime and touched off widespread peasant unrest.
12	Under political pressure, Wang Mang revoked measures barring the buying and selling of slaves.
14	Wang changed place names and official titles according to his understanding of the classics. Changing his mind frequently, he sometimes renamed a place five times.
16	Wang Mang ordered an executed criminal dissected for scientific research.
18	A man fixed feathers to his arms and flew several hundred paces before falling to the ground. This was perhaps the first recorded experiment in human flight in the world.
22	Insurgent Red Eyebrows, peasant soldiers who painted their foreheads red to distinguish themselves from government troops, defeated an imperial army in Shandong.
22	Imperial forces blunted the rebel offensive.
22	The Red Eyebrows advanced south into the rich region of Nanyang in present-day Hunan. Rebels there joined the Red Eyebrows uprising against Wang Mang.

Early 23	After a lull, the insurgents resumed the campaign against imperial forces.
Summer 23	The rebels inflicted a decisive defeat on Wang Mang's army at Kunyang.
Late 23	Insurgents occupied and sacked the imperial capital of Chang'an. Two days later, they captured and beheaded Wang Mang.
23–25	The insurgent Liu Xiu (Liu Hsiu), head of a Han restoration faction, raised an independent army and formed an alliance with the Red Eyebrows.

EASTERN HAN (A.D. 25–220)

25	The restoration government discarded Wang Mang's coinage system and restored the 5-shu piece as standard.
Summer 25	Han restoration forces entered Chang'an. Liu Xiu, 30 years old, proclaimed himself "Son of Heaven" and mounted the throne as first emperor of the Eastern Han.
25–29	The first emperor reigned as Guangwu.
Winter 25	Guangwu entered Luoyang and made it his capital.
26–30	Han campaigns subdued the Shandong Peninsula. Guangwu's hold on power remained shaky for some years, however.
March 15, 27	Imperial troops trapped the Red Eyebrow army and forced its surrender.
29	Imperial forces subdued the lower Han River Valley of east-central China.
30	With large-scale migration from northern China, the government abolished 30 counties in the north and contracted the government bureaucracy there.
33–44	Intermittent Xiongnu raids forced the withdrawal of Chinese farming communities from northern frontier regions.
34	Han pacified northwestern China after a hard-fought campaign.
35	Han forces moved against the last imperial rival, Gongsun Shu (Kung-sun Shu), in the Sichuan basin.
36	A Han army attacked Gongsun Shu's capital, Chengdu. Gongsun died of wounds, and the city surrendered the next day.

37	Guangwu abolished all but three of the 20 or so subordinate kingdoms. He gradually restored them, installing his sons and other near-relatives as kings—a process that slowed the concentration of imperial power.
40	Chinese colonization touched off a revolt of the aboriginal inhabitants of the Red River Valley of Vietnam. The uprising formed part of a pattern—at least 53 outbreaks against China between A.D. 1 and 200—on Han's southern frontier.
43	A Chinese expeditionary force put down the Red River uprising.
48	A violent outbreak spread through northwestern Hunan. The government bloodily suppressed it in a campaign lasting several months.
48–119 or 120	Life span of the writer and scholar Ban Zhao (Pan Chao). Ban's *Admonitions to Women* summarized the Confucian ideal of womanhood. She completed her brother Ban Gu's (Pan Ku) *History of Han*.
57	The Mingdi emperor ascended the Han throne, succeeding Guangwu. He ruled until his death in 75, an era regarded as oppressive.
c. 65	Tradition has it that a suspension bridge opened for traffic over the Mekong River, spurring trade along the mountain road connecting China and Myanmar.
65	About this time, a new religious force entered China by way of the Silk Road: Buddhism. The emperor's half-brother adopted Buddhist practices, the first record of Buddhism in China. A cult of the Buddha was said to have been active in the capital, Luoyang.
69	Hundreds of thousands of conscript workers built or repaired dikes and carried out other flood control projects.
73	China formed an alliance with the southern Xiongnu against the rival northern federation of Xiongnu.
75	Zhangdi (Chang-ti) succeeded his father on the Han throne.
76	Cattle epidemics ravaged China's herds; a shortage of draft animals led to serious food shortages.
78–139	Life span of mathematician Zhang Heng (Chang Heng). Zhang figured pi at 3.1622—the most accurate approximation to that time. He also invented a seismograph.

79	The Zhangdi emperor sponsored a conference on correct texts and interpretations of Confucian classics. The historian Ban Gu edited the conference report, *Comprehensive Discussions in the White Tiger Hall*, a landmark of Confucian scholarship.
April 9, 88	Hedi ascended as emperor. He was underage; Dou Xian (Tou Hsien), a leading general and a member of the powerful Dou family, was regent.
89	Han forces and their southern Xiongnu allies defeated the northern Xiongnu. The southern Xiongnu settled permanently in northern China.
c. 90	Buddhist monks established a monastery at Luoyang.
92	The emperor's allies accused the regent Dou Xian of plotting his murder; Dou killed himself in prison, and a number of his supporters were executed. Among the victims was Ban Gu, the historian of Han, implicated through friendship with the Dou family.
92–93	Drought and locust plagues caused large-scale crop failures. The government waived the tax on land and straw to ease peasant hardships.
92–102	Ban Chao (Pan Ch'ao), brother of the historian Ban Gu, served as protector-general of the western regions guarding the Silk Road to Persia. Reasserting China's control over the insurgent west, he led an army westward to the edge of the Caspian Sea 3,800 miles distant from Luoyang. He returned to China with information about Rome, the great empire of the West.
93	New trouble broke out with the Xiongnu in the north. Periodic armed clashes marked Chinese-Xiongnu relations for the next century.
100	A translation of the Indian Buddhist text *Sutra in Forty-two Articles* circulated in Luoyang.
100	China's first dictionary contained 9,000 characters.
101	In response to crop failures, Han authorities waived food and seed debts of distressed peasants.
101–120	The power and influence of consorts' families and eunuchs steadily expanded at the Han court.
105	This is the traditional date when paper was invented. Silk cloth and slips made of wood and bamboo remained the most commonly used writing materials for another century.
106	The government cut back on imperial palace expenses, including banquets, ballets, music, and fodder for the palace horses.

106	The infant Shangdi reigned for several months before dying. His death touched off a brief dynastic crisis, after which Andi ascended the Han throne. Ruling until 125, he is regarded as the least capable of all the Han emperors.
108–111	Tibetan raiders advanced down the Wei River Valley to the approaches of the Great Plain, accelerating the migration of Chinese farmers south into Sichuan and Yunnan.
125–144	Shundi reigned.
133	A powerful earthquake damaged Luoyang. Some saw the temblor as an omen critical of the regime for the favoritism shown relations, court cliques, and the eunuchs.
135	The palace eunuchs won the right to adopt sons. They thus were able to pass on acquired wealth and power to heirs.
137	Government forces quelled an outbreak in Jinan in northeastern China.
140	A census documented the enormous population shifts which floods, drought, famine, and war had caused since the census of 2. China's recorded population fell by around 9 million during the period, to 48 million. Xiongnu and Tibetan raids forced 6.5 million Chinese to leave the northwest permanently—a loss of 70 percent of the population recorded in the census of 2.
144–145	Chongdi (Ch'ung-ti) reigned.
144–145	Rebellions broke out in southeastern China.
145–146	The child emperor Zhidi (Chih-ti) reigned briefly; he died under murky circumstances after accusing General Liang Ji of dominating his Court. Liang Ji's control of the court became even greater.
146	Huandi ascended the Han throne.
c. 150	The imperial harem numbered 6,000 women. They arrived as virgins aged 13 to 20 and were chosen for their beauty, carriage, and manners.
c. 150	China's control of the western regions slipped. Political instability disrupted trade along the Silk Road.
153	Yellow River floods and locust infestations forced hundreds of thousands of peasants onto the roads in search of food. Provincial officials reported widespread starvation over a two-year period.
156	Government forces crushed a rebellion in Shandong.

156–157	Savants and soothsayers interpreted natural phenomena such as an earthquake in Luoyang, a solar eclipse, and a plague of locusts as signs that Heaven had become displeased with the emperor and that reforms in economic policy were in order.
160	Thirty thousand students were enrolled in the Imperial Academy, the training school for government employees.
166	Disaffected officials charged the dynasty with favoritism and extravagance. Interpretations of astronomical phenomena placed the blame for misconduct on the emperor and the palace eunuchs.
166	Roman merchants, claiming to have been sent by the Roman emperor Marcus Aurelius Antoninus, visited China.
166	The imperial court at Luoyang formally introduced worship of the Buddha.
167	Government aid for victims of a tidal wave along the east coast totaled 2,000 copper coins for each victim age seven or older.
168	Early in the year, Huandi's death touched off a political crisis and a campaign against eunuch power. The regent Dou Wu (Tou Wu) and a group of high bureaucratic allies plotted to kill the leading eunuchs, but the eunuchs forestalled the plot toward the end of the year. Dou Wu killed himself, and the eunuchs were secure for another generation.
168–189	Lingdi reigned. The throne's prestige declined during his rule, and the power of the eunuchs became almost absolute. Many bad omens were reported: A horse gave birth to a human child, a virgin delivered a two-headed baby, and earthquakes, hailstorms, and caterpillar infestations caused widespread destruction.
169–184	Conflict between the eunuchs and the bureaucracy gave rise to what became known as the era of the Great Proscription. The eunuchs won the struggle and executed 100 of their most powerful rivals, whose families were perpetually banned from government service.
175–183	Authorized texts of the Five Classics and the *Analects* were carved in stone outside the gate of the imperial university. Fragments of the total, some 40–50 tablets, survive today.
184–185	The Yellow Turbans Rebellion erupted to the south, east, and northeast of Luoyang. Several hundred thousand peasants rose in response to omens and visions of the end of the Han dynasty. The eunuch-dominated court, too weak to react, sought the aid of provincial warlords.
February 185	Imperial forces quelled the Yellow Turbans outbreak.

May 189	The rebel warlord Dong Zhuo (Tung Cho) advanced to within 80 miles of Luoyang.
May–September 189	Shaodi reigned.
September 189	Imperial troops massacred the 2,000 palace eunuchs in Luoyang. Dong Zhuo's army looted the capital, deposed Shaodi, and put his half-brother on the throne. With Han split into as many as eight warring factions, the reign of the new emperor was nominal.
189–220	Xiandi (Hsien-ti) reigned as the Han emperor.
Spring 190	Dong Zhuo's army burned Luoyang to the ground and moved the imperial court to the old capital of Chang'an. The Han archives and the imperial library were destroyed in the fire.
Spring 191	Under pressure from the warlords Yuan Shao and Cao Cao (Ts'ao Ts'ao), Dong Zhuo fell back to Chang'an where the nominal emperor kept up the Han court. Dong Zhou would die within a year.
193	Communities of Buddhist converts prospered in eastern China. One group built a large temple in the Chu capital of Pengcheng. Later in the year, Cao Cao sacked Pengcheng, driving 10,000 Buddhists south to the Yangtze; these refugees introduced Buddhism to the Yangtze Valley.
August 196	The emperor returned to a partially rebuilt Luoyang. Warlords and rebels contested for control of the provinces.
c. 200	In response to civil war, religious-political groups grew in numbers and influence. Daoism, with its aim of immortality, became, with Buddhism, one of China's two great salvationist religions. Daoist utopian movements flourished during the troubled times of Later Han. Daoist groups formed protective societies in troubled areas; the Five Pecks of Rice sect in Shanxi and Sichuan established alms and other aid programs and ruled for four decades.
200	Cao Cao defeated his rival Yuan Shao at Guandu in Henan. He gradually established control over most of northeastern China.
208	Cao Cao advanced southward. The allied armies of Sun Quan (Sun Ch'uan) and Liu Bei (Liu Pei) defeated him at Red Cliff on the Yangtze. Sun Quan retained control of the lower Yangtze Valley. Liu Bei advanced upriver to seize the rich region of Shu (modern Sichuan).
208–220	Cao Cao extended his power north and northwest. His resettlement of farmers on former Yellow Turban lands helped bring about an economic recovery after the devastation of the civil wars. The Han court remained his captive.

216	Cao Cao took the title of king of Wei and held it until his death in May 220.
December 220	The Han emperor abdicated in favor of Cao Cao's son, Cao Pi (Ts'ao P'i), ending the 400-year dynasty. China divided into three warring kingdoms: Cao's Wei, Liu Bei's Sho Han, and Sun Quan's Wu. They contested for supremacy over the next century.

KEY RESEARCH SOURCES

Ebrey, Patricia. *Cambridge Illustrated History of China*. New York: Cambridge University Press, 1996.

Loewe, Michael. *Crisis and Conflict in Han China, 104 B.C. to A.D. 9*. London: Allen and Unwin, 1974.

———. *Everyday Life in Early Imperial China During the Han Period, 202 B.C.–A.D. 220*. New York: Putnam, 1986.

Twitchett, Denis, and Michael Loewe, eds. *The Cambridge History of China*. Vol. 1, *The Ch'in and Han Empires*. New York: Cambridge University Press, 1986.

Wills, John E., Jr. *Mountain of Fame: Portraits in Chinese History*. Princeton: Princeton University Press, 1994.

6. THREE KINGDOMS (220–265), WESTERN JIN (265–317), AND SIX DYNASTIES (317–589)

This tumultuous era, the longest period of disunion in China's history, corresponds roughly to the decline and fall of the Roman Empire in the West. With the collapse of the Eastern Han dynasty, power shifted from the imperial court to large provincial landowners, who had their own courts and private armies. Three rival kingdoms, Wei, Wu, and Shu Han, temporarily survived the wreck of Han. The successor to Wei, the Western Jin, briefly reunified the country. Internal disorders and the invasion of nomadic non-Chinese doomed the Jin, however. Smaller kingdoms and dynasties co-existed until the Sui reunification toward the close of the sixth century.

Tibetan invaders in northwestern China intermarried with the Chinese, adopted Chinese ways, and ruled in partnership with established aristocratic families. Late in the fourth century, the Toba Turks founded the Northern Wei dynasty with their capital at Luoyang and held northern China together for a century and a half. Their institutions built a framework for the eventual restoration of the empire.

In the north, Chinese society and politics were strongly aristocratic in flavor. In the south, regional dynasties succeeded one after another. In both the north and the south, great families claimed high offices and high status, generation after generation. Agriculture and trade flourished. From the lower Yangtze, the dynastic states pushed southward and colonized the aboriginal peoples in their path.

A distinct north-south split developed. Southern styles differed in religious observance, manners, and dress. Women were more likely to be in seclusion and concubinage in the south. Northern women had more responsibility. Southerners cultivated rice and used sea fish; northerners tended flocks and herds and raised millet and wheat. Southerners regarded themselves as true heirs of Han civilization and scorned the martial northerners as barbarians. Northerners repaid their disdain in kind.

THREE KINGDOMS

220	With the passing of Cao Cao, his son Cao Pi overthrew the last Han emperor and claimed the "mandate of heaven" for the Wei dynasty. Rivals to the south challenged the claim. In Shu in present-day Sichuan, Liu Bei (Liu Pei), a distant relative of the Han imperial family, claimed to be the legitimate Han successor. The heroic Zhuge Liang (Chu-ko Liang) became Liu Bei's chief minister. On the Yangtze, Sun Quan (Sun Ch'uan), once allied with Liu Bei, made himself emperor of the third of the three kingdoms, Wu. The rival kingdoms engaged in intermittent conflict with each other.
May 221	Liu Bei, already in firm control of Sichuan, declared himself emperor and called his dynasty Han.
222	Shu forces attacked a Wu army in Hubei but were routed and forced to withdraw.
223	On Liu Bei's death, his son succeeded him as Han claimant in Shu.
226–239	Cao Rui reigned as the Mingdi emperor of Wei.

226–249	Wang Bi, a great scholar and commentator on the *Book of Changes*, was active.
229	Sun Quan ascended as first emperor of the Wu dynasty, giving China three emperors.
230–233	Sun Quan sent large fleets on missions to Taiwan and northeastern China.
234	Zhuge Liang died campaigning with Shu Han forces in the Wei River Valley. The passing of this brilliant strategist effectively ended the Shu Han threat to the other two kingdoms.
c. 260	The acupuncturist Huangfu Mi prepared the *Classic of Acupuncture and Moxibustion*, the earliest known treatise in the field.
263	The Shu Han kingdom fell to Wei.
280	The Wu kingdom fell to Jin.
c. 290	The *San Guo zhi* (Record of the Three Kingdoms), a dynastic history of the Three Kingdoms era, appeared.

WESTERN JIN

265	The Western Jin dethroned the Wei emperor and ruled northern China from Luoyang.
266–290	Wudi reigned as the Western Jin emperor.
280	The Jin conquered Wu in the southeast.
280–304	The Jin ruled a temporarily reunified empire.
290–306	Huidi reigned as Jin emperor.
291–306	Succession dispute led to civil wars among members of the imperial family.
300s	Constant warfare claimed tens of thousands of lives in the north, touched off a mass southward migration, and left the agricultural and trade economy in ruins. In the south, the Chinese pushed into the wilderness hinterlands from the lower Yangtze Valley.
	In troubled times, Buddhism spread throughout China; Confucian ideas continued to influence the elite's attitudes on politics, society, ethics, and etiquette. Buddhism's appeal lay in its offering of consolations and magical powers and in its power to comfort commoners in times of upheaval. Foreign invaders who

settled permanently in China accepted Buddhism along with other Chinese ways. See "China A to Z" entry on Buddhism, page 550.

Early 300s
Waves of nomads swept into China from the north and northwest, founding a series of short-lived dynasties.

304
The Xiongnu king Liu Yuan proclaimed a new Han dynasty in northern China.

306–313
Huaidi ruled as Jin emperor.

c. 310
Paper, an invention of the Later Han, was in general use. The first authenticated surviving pieces of paper were dated to 310 and 312.

311
Luoyang, the ancient capital of China, fell to the Xiongnu Han.

313–316
Mindi reigned as Jin emperor.

316
The Xiongnu Han seized China's alternate capital, Chang'an.

317
This date traditionally marks the beginning of a confused 250-year era. The Six Dynasties in southern China and the Sixteen Kingdoms in northern China jostled for power and regional primacy throughout the period.

317–322
Yuandi reigned as Eastern Jin emperor.

317–420
The Eastern Jin dynasty ruled in northern China.

322–325
Mingdi ruled the Eastern Jin.

325–342
Chengdi reigned as emperor of the Eastern Jin.

342–361
Kangdi (to 344) and Mudi reigned as Eastern Jin emperors.

361–365
Aidi ruled the Eastern Jin.

365–371
The Duke of Haixi ruled the Eastern Jin.

372–396
Xiao Wudi (HSIAO WU-TI) ruled as emperor of the Eastern Jin.

386
The Toba Turks established the Northern Wei dynasty, bringing order to northern China. The foreigners were allied with powerful Chinese families that had roots in the Han upper class. China's great families found security in the arrangement. The alien rulers exploited the governing skills of the Chinese.

386–409
Daowudi reigned as Northern Wei emperor.

396–418	Andi reigned as Eastern Jin emperor.
398	Northern Wei rulers built a Chinese-style capital at the Toba settlement in northern Shanxi. Rectangular and walled on all four sides, it contained the traditional ancestral hall and great earth mound.
399–412	The Buddhist Faxian (FA-HSIEN) made a long pilgrimage to India, returning with Buddhist works that he translated into Chinese.
Early 400s	With political power fractured, Daoist popular sects remained influential in the countryside, particularly the descendants of the Yellow Turban and Five Pecks of Rice groups that rebelled during the last decades of the Later Han dynasty. At the same time, religious Daoism, with its emphasis on immortality, gained among the elites of southern China.
409–423	Mingdi reigned as Northern Wei emperor.
420	The Song (also known as the Lin Song) dynasty conquered Jin.
420–479	The Song ruled in southern China.
423–451	Taiwudi ruled as emperor of the Northern Wei.
424–453	Wendi reigned as emperor of the Song.
471–499	Xiaowendi (HSIAO-WEN-TI) reigned as emperor of the Northern Wei. He pursued an aggressive sinicization policy, barring non-Chinese languages at court and instructing people of nomadic background to adopt Chinese surnames. Xiaowendi adopted the Chinese military organization and land allotment procedure known as the equal-field system, which formed the basis for the eventual revival of the imperial state.
479–502	The Southern Qi dynasty succeeded the Liu Song.
482–494	Wudi reigned as the Qi emperor.
495	Xiaowendi shifted the capital from northern Shanxi to the Yellow River Valley.
499–513	Xuanwudi reigned as Northern Wei emperor.
Early 500s	According to later tradition, the Indian sage Bodidharma introduced Chan Buddhism (in Japanese, Zen) to China. Chan—the word derives from the Sanskrit for meditation—was distinctively Chinese in style, imparted from a teacher-student process that appealed to China's Confucian tradition of thinker and disciples. Bodhidharma entered a monastery near Luoyang and spent years in silent meditation, his face turned to the wall. In Chan, the goal of meditation is enlightenment, in which all illusions are cleared away.

502–549	Wudi reigned as the Liang emperor.
502–557	The Liang dynasty ruled in southern China.
524	The Revolt of the Garrisons, a reaction of the steppe peoples to forced sinicization, spread to the populous northern China plain. Rebels ravaged the countryside and attacked Luoyang, where more than 1,000 Chinese court functionaries were massacred.
534–535	Rebellion and internal division split the Northern Wei dynasty into two parts. The more productive, stable, densely settled, and "Chinese" half, the Eastern Wei, established its capital at Ye in Henan. The Western Wei, still committed to the horse-and-warrior culture of the steppes, ruled from the old imperial capital, Chang'an.
534–550	Xiaojingdi reigned as emperor of the Eastern Wei.
535–551	Wendi reigned as Western Wei emperor.
542	Tan Luan, born in 476, patriarch of the Buddhist Pure Land sect, died. Pure Land scripture held that anyone who meditated on the Buddha Amita or called upon his name would be reborn into his paradise. This emerged as one of the most important Chinese traditions of Buddhism.
543	Eastern Wei forces defeated a Western Wei army, inflicting 60,000 casualties.
548	The Hou Jing (HOU CHING) rebellion ravaged the Yangtze provinces. Hou Jing occupied Jiankang, the Liang dynasty capital.
550	The usurper Gao Yang forced Xiaojingdi of the Eastern Wei to abdicate and found the Northern Qi. Gao Yang became known as Emperor Wenxuandi to historians.
550–560	Nomadic Turkish tribes were sovereign in an inner Asia empire stretching from Manchuria in the east to the Persian frontier in the west.
552	Liang forces crushed Hou Jing's rebellion.
554	A Western Wei army attacked the temporary Liang capital at Jiangling on the central Yangtze, captured the city's elite, and established a dependent state in the region.
556	The powerful Yuwen family forced the last Western Wei emperor to step down and founded the Northern Zhou dynasty. Northern Zhou rulers, descendants of the military elite of the Revolt of the Garrisons of 524, restored traditional Chinese

	forms of government. The two former Wei states, Northern Zhou and Northern Qi, engaged in a bitter rivalry for ascendancy.
557–560	Mingdi reigned as emperor of the Northern Zhou. Wudi succeeded him.
557–589	The Chen dynasty succeeded the Liang along the lower Yangtze River.
574	The Wudi emperor sought to suppress Buddhist and Daoist religious practices in favor of Confucian ritual. Temples, scriptures, and images were destroyed in the Northern Zhou, and clergy were forced to return to lay life.
575	Northern Zhou and Chen forces agreed to an alliance for an attack on the Northern Qi. The Chen rulers were to be given control of the rich region between the Huai and Yangtze Rivers.
577	Northern Zhou conquered Northern Qi and established control of all of northern China, including the heartland from the Great Wall to the Huai River Valley. The Zhou then turned on their former Chen allies, destroyed the Chen forces, and tightened their grip on the provinces of the central Yangtze and Sichuan to the west.
578	With the Wudi emperor's passing, the government relaxed the proscription of Buddhism.
581	A scion of the part-nomad Yang family, descendants of the Six Garrisons rebels, whose home base was the region between the ancient capitals of Luoyang and Chang'an, overthrew the Northern Zhou and pressed a claim to rule northern China. Yang Jian (YANG CHIEN) eventually ascended the throne as the first emperor of the Sui dynasty.

KEY RESEARCH SOURCES

Dien, Albert, ed. *State and Society in Early Medieval China*. Stanford: Stanford University Press, 1991.

Ebrey, Patricia. *Cambridge Illustrated History of China*. New York: Cambridge University Press, 1996.

Wills, John E., Jr. *Mountain of Fame: Portraits in Chinese History*. Princeton: Princeton University Press, 1994.

7. SUI DYNASTY

(581–618)

The Sui dynasty restored the unity of China. From his northern China base, the founding emperor completed the reunification with the conquest of territory south of the Yangtze. The first Sui emperor promulgated a new legal code, reformed local government, unified the bureaucracy, reorganized the military, and replenished the state treasury. He extended China's borders and built a canal system that formed a basis for Tang dynasty prosperity.

Yang Jian toppled the Northern Zhou dynasty, claimed control over northern China, and assumed the title of emperor. Holding a dawn audience, he declared an amnesty and proclaimed the dynasty of Sui. He ruled as Wendi. Among his first acts were the full restoration of rights to Buddhists and the rehabilitation of the Buddhist clergy. He also ended the suppression of Daoism. Born in 541 in a Buddhist temple, Wendi proved an authoritarian, capable, and successful ruler.

Late Summer 581	Wendi and his henchmen murdered the last of 59 rival Northern Zhou princes.
Late 581	The first Sui emperor promulgated a new code of laws and ordinances containing 1,735 articles. It lessened the severe punishments of earlier codes—the severed heads of criminals were no longer to be displayed in public view, for example. Despite the liberal tendency of his laws, the Wendi emperor often acted with severity, ordering capital punishments for comparatively minor offenses.
582	The Eastern Turks carried out large-scale raids into modern Gansu and Shanxi.
582	Wendi ordered a vast new capital built on a site southeast of ancient Chang'an.
582	The Wendi emperor sought nominations of "the worthy and the good" for government offices. He proclaimed a set of ordinances that allowed for a periodic distribution of land to the peasantry, as well as to nobles and others of high rank—a Northern Wei innovation the Sui extended. Later in the year, the Sui adopted new civil statutes regulating bureaucratic procedures, land use, taxation, and other administrative matters.
583	The first Sui emperor abolished all of the 500-plus commanderies in northern China. (He dismantled the southern commanderies with full reunification in 589.) These and other measures streamlined local government, reduced the number of local officials, and brought all officials under central government control.
	Wendi simplified the Sui legal code, reducing the number of laws to around 500. This version, a synthesis of northern and southern legal practice and tradition, helped prepare the way

for reunification. The revised code contained four types of punishment: the death penalty, deportation with forced labor, forced labor only, and the bastinado (beating with a stick).

583   The Sui court moved into the partially built new capital.

584–589   Wendi ordered the construction of a canal from Chang'an to the confluence of the Wei and Yellow Rivers. The 100-mile-long canal sped the shipment of grain into the capital region.

585   The government proposed a network of famine relief granaries in which peasant families were to deposit an average 0.7 bushels of grain a year.

586   In an overture to Daoists, the Wendi emperor ordered an inscribed monument to be set up at Laozi's supposed birthplace in Anhui. Religious Daoists venerated him as their spiritual ancestor. At the same time, the emperor remained alert to the Daoist potential for political trouble, suppressing alleged black magic and other dangerous practices. By the first decade of the seventh century, there were 120 Buddhist establishments in the capital and 10 Daoist temples.

587   To bring new people into government, Wendi directed each prefecture to send three men to Chang'an annually for possible civil service appointments. The numbers reached 900 candidates a year.

587   The Sui dynasty abolished the Liang puppet state along the central Yangtze and assumed direct control of the region.

588   The first Sui emperor prepared to advance southward on the Chen state.

589   Sui naval forces defeated a Chen fleet on the Yangtze. Land forces seized the capital, Jiankang, and captured the Chen ruler. The hinterland—practically all of eastern China south of the Yangtze—quickly fell to the Sui, making China whole again for the first time in three centuries.

589–591   With a view to rapid consolidation, the triumphant Sui imposed an easy peace on southern China. Some Chen officials retained their posts, and the emperor remitted all taxes in former Chen domains for 10 years.

590   Sui forces crushed brief rebellions that erupted in various locales south of the Yangtze.

592   Grain and textile shortages prompted a Sui effort to equalize landholdings and put more land into cultivation.

595	Contemporary documents mentioned a civil service examination system. The refined version of the exam system is today regarded as a forerunner of the Tang and Song imperial selection system that survived until 1905.
595	Sui rulers pressed the effort to pacify China after generations of warfare. Wendi ordered the confiscation of all weapons and banned the private manufacture of arms.
596	The government expanded the granary system for famine emergencies.
c. 600	The block-printing technique was perfected.
Late 600	Wendi deposed his eldest son as heir apparent in favor of a younger son, Yang Guang (YANG KUANG).
601	Wendi initiated a campaign to distribute Buddhist holy relics to shrines and reliquaries throughout the empire.
Summer 604	The first Sui emperor died after an illness. His death was probably sped by his heir. Yang Guang ascended the throne as Yangdi, the second Sui emperor. By later tradition, Yangdi was licentious and imprudent, but his reign produced a greatly expanded canal system and extended China's frontiers.
Late 604	The second Sui emperor announced he would sponsor a revival of traditional Confucian learning.
604–607	Yangdi established an eastern capital at Luoyang, rebuilding the ancient city and restocking it with "several tens of thousands" of rich merchant and trader families.
605	The second Sui emperor pursued his father's reform trend, putting into place new controls over the military.
605	Yangdi ordered the construction of the Tongji Canal to link Luoyang with Chuzhou on the Huai River. As many as 1 million workers were mobilized for the job.
605	Khitan invaders penetrated south as far as Hebei before an Eastern Turk force under Chinese generalship defeated them and drove them away.
606	Financial reforms and a more efficient registration system increased the empire's taxable population to 8.9 million households from only 4 million in 589.
607	Tightening his grip on power, Yangdi ordered the execution of three of his most persistent critics in government.
607	The second Sui emperor deployed 1 million workers for a new north-south section of the Great Wall from the Ordos region to modern Shanxi Province.

607	The Japanese sent their first full post-unification embassy to China. In return, Yangdi dispatched an embassy to Japan. It led to a massive export of Chinese culture to Japan.
608	Work began on the largest of the Sui dynasty canals, the Yongji, which ran northeast from near Luoyang to the vicinity of modern Beijing. More than 1 million laborers were involved in the project.
608	Sui forces defeated Eastern Turk tribes in their Kokonor grazing lands and annexed a large chunk of their territory to the empire.
610	The second Sui emperor imposed a special war tax in preparation for an expedition into the Korean kingdom of Koguryo.
611	Floods in the Yellow River Valley caused widespread distress and political unrest. Labor levies for canal building and conscription for the Koguryo campaign fed popular discontent.
612	The Sui assembled an army of 1 million near modern Beijing for the Koguryo invasion. Chinese forces crossed the Liao but were forced to retreat with heavy losses.
Early 613	A series of peasant rebellions erupted in Shandong. A rebel army advanced on Luoyang, the eastern capital.
Early Summer 613	The Yangdi emperor led a second offensive into Koguryo. When word of rebellion at home reached him, he detached forces to lift the Luoyang siege, bringing the Koguryo invasion to a halt.
614	Yangdi launched a third effort to subdue Koguryo. Sui armies advanced to the outskirts of Pyongyang, the capital. When the Koguryo king offered to submit, Chinese forces withdrew. The vassal failed, however, to deliver on his promises, and the emperor prepared for a fourth campaign. A spreading insurgency in China made a renewed offensive impossible.
614	The Yangdi emperor returned from the field, first to Luoyang, the eastern capital, and then to Chang'an.
Early 615	Imperial forces deployed to quell a dozen simultaneous rebellions.
Autumn 616	The Yangdi emperor set out by canal barge for an extended visit to his Yangtze capital, Jiangdu, which replaced the demolished Jiankang. He never returned to the northern China seat of the empire.
617	Rival rebel factions deposed the absent second Sui emperor and enthroned his grandson Gongdi. Li Yuan, a powerful Sui general, rebelled and seized the capital.

618   A son of one of his generals murdered Yangdi in his bathhouse.
                               A period of civil war followed the second Sui emperor's death.

KEY RESEARCH SOURCES

Dien, Albert, ed. *State and Society in Early Medieval China*. Stanford: Stanford University Press, 1991.

Fairbank, John King. *China: A New History*. Cambridge, Mass.: The Belknap Press of Harvard University Press, 1992.

Twitchett, Denis, ed. *The Cambridge History of China*. Vol. 3, *Sui and T'ang China, Part 1*. New York: Cambridge University Press, 1979.

Wright, Arthur. *The Sui Dynasty*. New York: Knopf, 1978.

8. Tang Dynasty

(618–907)

Building on the Sui achievement, the Tang dynasty consolidated and expanded the imperial Chinese state. Military expeditions into Korea, northern Vietnam, Mongolia, Tibet, and central Asia extended China's power. A long process commenced in which authority gradually shifted from hereditary aristocratic families to a developing class of classically educated gentlemen. Tang produced the skilled and ruthless Empress Wu, the only woman sovereign in Chinese history.

A renewal of Confucianism accompanied the rise of the civil service. The arts flourished; Tang poetry became a model for later eras. Population and economic changes continued to alter the north-south balance. An increase in rice cultivation made substantial population growth in the lower Yangtze Valley possible.

With the military over extended and strength-sapping rivalries at court, a decline set in during the latter half of the eighth century. The Tang ultimately quelled the destructive An Lushan rebellion, but the dynasty never fully recovered, and imperial authority eroded steadily over the last century and a half of the dynasty's life.

600–700	China's scribes began using inked seals.
c. 615–620	Tibetan tribes, driven off by the Chinese in the first decade of the century, gradually reoccupied their homelands around Kokonor Lake in the far northwest.
617	The Sui general Li Yuan's army and its Turkish allies overran Chang'an and installed the last Sui emperor's grandson as a puppet ruler.
618	Deposing the puppet, Li Yuan ascended the throne and proclaimed himself the first emperor of a new dynasty, the Tang. He reigned as Gaozu.
619	The new dynasty re-established the equal-field system of land tenure and allocation. It promised a fixed amount of land for every adult taxpayer and sought, with exceptions for the very powerful or well connected, to cap the total amount any one landowner could acquire. The equal-field system was accomplished by a direct tax on each household, payable in grain; in silk, hemp fiber, or cloth; or in 20 days' annual *corvée* (compulsory labor service).
622	Most of the Sui Imperial Library was lost in a river accident en route from Luoyang to Chang'an. Only 14,000 titles survived.
624	Gaozu subdued the last of his rivals for power.
624	The court astrologer Fu Yi attacked Buddhism as foreign and unwholesome and called upon the emperor to suppress it and return tens of thousands of monks and nuns to lay life.

624	A new waterworks system opened wasteland to cultivation in Shanxi. The government planned a transport canal to carry grain to the capital, Chang'an.
624	The Tang government issued a set of codified statutes based on the first Sui emperor's revised New Code.
626	Gaozu restricted the number of Buddhist and Daoist temples in the capital to one per faith in each prefecture. The order was not really carried out.
Mid-626	The emperor's son seized power in the coup known as the Incident at Xuanwu Gate. He killed two of his brothers, one of them the heir apparent, and took effective control. Gaozu abdicated before the end of the year. The second emperor ruled as Taizong. The Chinese regarded his reign, which lasted until 649, as a golden era. Although a warrior with an unruly temper, Taizong fostered honest government, listened to principled opposition, patronized classical scholarship, and eased religious restrictions. Opposition to his military adventures, particularly the Korea campaigns, mounted during the second half of his reign.
627	The new emperor moved to reduce the bureaucracy, cutting the number of civil and military posts at Chang'an.
627	The court established a Directorate of the State University to supervise the schools. Educational reform and improvement drew scholars and students from the provinces to Chang'an.
628	The government set up a network of relief granaries for famine times.
628–632	Schools of calligraphy and law were founded in the capital.
629	Taizong decreed execution as the punishment for the illegal ordination of Buddhist monks. Tax evasion was the usual motive for most illegal ordinations.
629–630	Eastern Turk invaders approached the outskirts of Chang'an. Chinese forces counterattacked and won a decisive victory, obliging the Eastern Turks to swear allegiance to the Tang.
629–645	The Buddhist monk Xuanzang made a pilgrimage to India. He returned to translate Buddhist texts into Chinese. His *Record of the Western Regions* chronicled his travel experiences.
632–635	The dynasty asserted dominion over the central Asian oasis kingdoms to the northwest, giving China control of the trade routes leading to the West.
633–727	Life span of the monk-astronomer Yi Xing. Yi was the first to work out a scientific study of the meridian.

634	The Tibetan king sent a request for a Tang princess to marry him.
635	The Persian Olopan (Alopan) introduced Nestorian Christianity to China.
637	Putting his stamp on the provincial bureaucracy, Taizong personally chose the candidates for appointment as prefects.
637	An imperial decree gave Daoist monks and nuns precedence over Buddhist clergy in Tang court ceremonials.
638	The first Nestorian Christian temple opened in Chang'an.
638–713	Life span of the Huineng, the Buddhist Sixth Patriarch of Chan. He founded the Southern School, with its belief in the possibility of sudden enlightenment. The Northern School saw a slow progress toward enlightenment through the discipline of meditation.
639	The government established grain-price regulation offices in major cities.
641	Moving to secure the northwestern frontier, China concluded a marriage alliance with the Tibetan king.
Autumn 644	Against his chief ministers' advice, Taizong prepared a military expedition into the Korean kingdom of Koguryo.
Spring 645	Chinese forces invaded Koguryo. The offensive sputtered, however, and with the onset of winter, Taizong withdrew. Thousands of his troops perished in the retreat.
646	After an investigation, thousands of local administrators were punished for corruption and other misdeeds; seven of the worst offenders were executed.
Early 647	China renewed the attack on Koguryo, with an inconclusive result.
649	With the death of Taizong, his heir ascended the throne and reigned until 683 as Gaozong.
651	An Arab mission introduced Islam to China.
c. 652	*The Invaluable Prescriptions* and *Supplement to Invaluable Prescriptions* of pharmacologist Sun Simiao were influential. They covered diagnosis, treatment, and prevention of disease and contained formulas for 800 drugs.
652	Wu Zhao (WU CHAO), the emperor's young concubine, began her rise to power.

653	A woman peasant, Chen Shuozhen (CH'EN SHUO-CHEN), led an uprising on the east coast of Zhejiang Province.
Winter 655–656	Gaozong deposed the Empress Wang and elevated Wu in her place.
657	Fewer than 14,000 Tang officials of the regular bureaucracy ruled a population of 45 million. A much larger bureaucracy handled local administration.
657	The Chinese and their Uighur allies divided the Western Turk empire. China's control of the northern-northwestern frontier region secured the lucrative trade routes leading to western Asia.
660	The first of a series of strokes incapacitated Gaozong, leaving him unfit to rule for long stretches. In his place, the Empress Wu ruled effectively, overcoming a powerful Chinese cultural bias against women in power.
668	With assistance from the Korean kingdom of Silla, China subdued Koguryo.
668–670	A succession of famines and other disasters caused widespread distress. Grain became so scarce in some areas that the government barred the making of wine.
669	The Tang adopted new regulations meant to limit the influence of family connections on the outcome of civil service examinations. Over the long run, however, the framers' good intentions were not fulfilled.
669–759	Life span of the Tang poet and landscape painter Wang Wei.
670s	Empress Wu turned increasingly for advice to the North Gate Scholars, a group of sages that assisted her with matters of state.
674	The empress presented the reformist Twelve Point Memorial to Gaozong. It called for the promotion of agriculture, a reduction in government expenses, and promotion through the bureaucracy by talent.
675	Li Hong, the heir apparent, died in unexplained circumstances. His mother the empress was said to have ordered him poisoned.
680	Because of poor harvests, the price of grain climbed to record levels.
680	The Empress Wu charged the new heir apparent, Li Xian, with plotting rebellion. She had him banished; he eventually killed himself.

680–750	Buddhist texts were printed from wood blocks.
681	The government toughened the civil service examinations, requiring candidates to discuss political and moral problems in detail and to demonstrate their mastery of formal styles of prose and poetry. The Ministry of Rites administered exams in politics, literature, mathematics, law, and calligraphy. There were two main degrees: Ming Jing, which emphasized memorization of the Confucian classics, and Jin Shi, which emphasized poetic composition. Jin Shi became the preferred degree. Successful candidates advanced to a second series of exams that determined a candidate's placement in the bureaucracy.
682	The chronic shortage of officially minted coins prompted the government to impose the death penalty for counterfeiting.
Late 683	The emperor Gaozong died, and the heir apparent ascended the throne as Zhongzong.
Early 684	The empress, protecting her power, forced Zhongzong from the throne and into prison. Another of her sons ascended as Ruizong (JUI-TSUNG). She allowed him no say in affairs.
Winter 684	Nobles opposed to Wu began to scheme against her. Insurgents seized Yangzhou on the Yangtze River and issued an anti-Wu proclamation. Troops were dispatched from the capital to quell the Yangzhou rebellion.
Autumn 688	Builders completed the Bright Hall in the capital. Intended to link the Empress Wu with the imagined perfection of the early Zhou dynasty, the hall rose more than 250 feet high, topped with a large figure of a phoenix, Wu's symbol.
688–690	The princes of the Tang imperial house pursued their conspiracy against the empress. She broke up their cabal and, over a period of 18 months, virtually destroyed the Li imperial family.
689	Empress Wu appeared for the first time in imperial robes and carrying the jade scepter.
Late 690	Wu's high ministers recommended that she seize full imperial powers. Her son Ruizong, the captive emperor, volunteered to abdicate in her favor. She took title as sage and divine emperor, called her new dynasty Zhou, and appointed Ruizong her successor. Empress Wu ruled through terror. Police spies infiltrated the opposition. She had hundreds of rivals murdered. Through the worst of the palace excesses, though, the Tang bureaucracy functioned competently as the day-to-day governmental authority.
694	Manichaeism appeared in China. Its adherents were called Light Worshippers.

695–697	Non-Chinese nomadic Khitan, miserable in a famine year, rose in rebellion northeast of modern Beijing. The revolt, weakened by internal dissension, eventually collapsed.
698	Resurgent Western Turks launched raids into China from the northwest, seeking Chinese support with promises to overthrow the empress and restore Tang rule.
698	Empress Wu ordered the execution of Lai Junchen, the minister who had carried out the reign of terror on her behalf. People in the capital celebrated by tearing his corpse to pieces.
c. 700	Chang'an, China's capital, was the world's largest, richest, and grandest city. It was a religious as well as political and economic center, with Buddhist and Daoist religious sites together with a mosque and even a small Syrian Christian church. There were poor districts, but Chang'an was, for the most part, a prosperous city.
c. 700	Japanese embassies in China exported Chinese calligraphy, Buddhist and Confucian thought, and governmental systems eastward to Japan.
700–800	Tang manufacturers produced fine paper with bast fibers; mulberry, rattan, and bamboo bark; and rice or wheat stalks.
700–800	Chinese merchant ships plied regularly between Guangzhou and the Persian Gulf.
700–800	Porcelain workshops in Zhejiang, Jiangxi, Anhui, Hunan, and other provinces produced everyday articles as well as objets d'art.
705	China's strengthened frontier defenses brought large-scale raiding by the Eastern Turks to a temporary end.
705	Floodwaters covered large areas of Hebei and the Wei River Valley.
February 22, 705	Tang loyalists forced Empress Wu, who was seriously ill, to abdicate in favor of Zhongzong, the son she had forced from the throne in 684. She was well treated until her death later in the year.
706–707	A drought brought famine conditions to Hebei and Henan.
710	Zhongzong died; the evidence suggested his wife had poisoned him. Ruizong succeeded Zhongzong. He turned out to be an ineffectual ruler.
710	Liu Zhiji (LIU CHIH-CHI) completed his *Understanding of History*, the first important theoretical study of historical writing in China.

711	Some 30,000 Buddhist monks and nuns were ordered returned to lay life to increase the number of taxpayers. The clergy was exempt from taxes.
711	With China facing drought and famine, the emperor replaced his four chief ministers. They proved no more efficient than their predecessors had.
Mid-712	The appearance of an inauspicious comet led to the abdication of the reluctant Ruizong. His successor, reigning as Xuanzong, reasserted imperial control. The competence and honesty of his rule assured a long period of prosperity.
712–713	Severe famine struck the Chang'an capital region.
712–755	Xuanzong reigned, the longest tenure of any Tang monarch. Known as the "Enlightened Emperor," he was a poet, musician, calligrapher, and patron of the arts and of Daoism. Population growth and general prosperity were hallmarks of his era. However, political mistakes and overextension during the last years of his reign nearly destroyed the dynasty. In the arts, Xuanzong's reign was known for the form of lyric poetry called *shi*. Among the best-known shi poets were Li Bo, Wang Wei, and Gao Shi.
714	After years of intermittent warfare, the Tibetans negotiated a peace treaty with China. They violated it almost at once, however, attacking Chinese positions around Lanzhou. The fighting ended in a Tibetan defeat later in the year.
714–719	As a famine control measure, the government extended the price-regulation granary system throughout China. Within 15 years, it produced large grain stocks for famine relief.
721–722	A Chinese army helped the forces of Gilgut repel a Tibetan invasion of the strategically important Pamir region of central Asia. War with Tibet was intermittent for the rest of the century.
722	China maintained an army of more than 600,000 men.
Late 725	Xuanzong performed the most significant of all state rites, the Feng and Shan sacrifices on the holy mountain of Tai in Shandong.
726–729	New hostilities flared along China's border with Tibet.
730	Chinese military pressure forced Tibet to seek peace. The Tibetan king signed a treaty that recognized suzerainty (overlordship) of China.

730–734	Natural disasters and intermittent famine marred an otherwise tranquil period. Grain shortages forced the imperial court to move temporarily to Luoyang because Chang'an could not be adequately fed.
732	The government, showing partiality to Daoism, ordered every prefecture to set up a temple to honor Laozi.
733–804	Life span of Lu You, author of *Book of Tea*. The volume provided details of tea bush cultivation and tea processing.
734	The Tang government established large farming colonies in Henan for the cultivation of paddy rice. The experiment proved unsuccessful.
736	The Khitan rose in revolt in northeastern China. An Lushan, a professional soldier, led a failed punitive expedition against the Khitan and received a death sentence for his failure. He was later pardoned.
736–750	Tibet renewed its attack on Gilgut. Fighting was more or less continuous for the next 15 years.
Autumn 737	The emperor promulgated a new legal code, dropping 1,300 irrelevant articles and amending another 2,180. It was the last systematic overhaul of the law during the Tang dynasty; the code itself served until the 14th century.
742	The population of China was 48,990,880, up from 45,431,265 in 732.
742	The empire maintained a force of 490,000 frontier troops with more than 80,000 cavalry horses. The overall military establishment probably exceeded 600,000. Most of the frontier army was made up of long-service professional soldiers rather than conscripts.
742–752	An Lushan won appointment to a succession of important military commands.
745	The Uighur from modern Mongolia won a decisive victory over the Eastern Turks and established their own empire. It would last until 840. Their political and economic relations with China were good for most of the Tang period.
751	Arab forces defeated a Chinese expeditionary army at the Battle of the Talas near Samarkand in central Asia. This represented the high tide of China's westward expansion.
753	Chinese forces defeated a Tibetan army and regained control of the strategic upper reaches of the Yellow River.

755	An Lushan, the adopted son of Xuanzong's favorite concubine, Yang Guifei, and said to be her lover, led a rebellion against Tang authority.
755	Unrest forced the government to abandon its attempts to control land allocation via the equal-field system. The consequences were larger landed estates, tax inequities, and a widening gap between rich and poor.
Late 755–early 756	An Lushan, with a force of 150,000, swept through Hebei Province and seized Luoyang. He there proclaimed himself Emperor of the Great Yan.
756	An Lushan's forces captured Chang'an. The emperor fled; on the retreat, his entourage forced him to acquiesce in the murder of Yang Guifei. In the midst of the rebellion, the heir apparent usurped the throne, designating the aged Xuanzong as "retired emperor." He reigned until 762 as Suzong.
757	An Lushan's son murdered him and declared himself emperor.
759	Tang imperial forces recaptured Chang'an and Luoyang.
762–779	Daizong reigned as Tang emperor.
763	With the collapse of the An Lushan rebellion, the dynasty restored a tenuous rule. Central authority extended only as far as the capital province, the northwest frontier zone, the lower Yangtze, and the Grand Canal corridor. An Lushan's uprising foreshadowed the rise of independent warlords and mercenary armies.
Autumn 763	Tibetan raiders struck deep into China and temporarily occupied Chang'an, forcing Taizong's court to flee. After two weeks, the raiders plundered and burned parts of the city and withdrew, carrying off thousands of prized Tang stud horses and other booty.
764–777	From bases in western Shaanxi, Tibetan cavalry carried out periodic raids deep in Chinese territory, usually in the autumn of the year.
768	The government granted the Manichaean sect permission to build a temple in Chang'an.
779–805	Dezong reigned. He moved vigorously to cut government waste and extravagance and abolished the alcohol tax. He also attempted to curb the power of the eunuchs, but their influence continued to grow, especially later in his reign.
780	The government introduced a two-tax system, a combination of land and household assessments collected in the summer and autumn. The new system marked a major shift from per capita-based taxation to property-based taxation.

781	Nestorian Christians put up a stele in Chang'an describing their faith.
781–786	Renewed uprisings in Hebei, which spread to much of northern China, weakened the Tang's central control.
783	A new treaty and a redrawn border led to an uneasy peace with Tibet. Both sides soon violated the truce.
791	The Tibetans dealt Chinese forces a decisive defeat in the area of modern Xinjiang. Only a small part of that area remained loyal to the Tang.
c. 800	Tea was in widespread use as a beverage.
805	Shunzong ascended the throne; a coup soon ended his reign.
805–820	Xianzong (HSIEN-TSUNG) reigned as Tang emperor. He attempted to restore Tang power and was regarded as the most effective ruler of the late Tang era.
c. 810	Exchange notes, a forerunner of banknotes, were in circulation. Traders called these negotiable certificates "flying notes."
815–817	Government forces subdued a military uprising in Henan. This victory marked the renewed strength of the central authority.
Early 820	The Emperor Xianzong was found dead. For generations, he was thought to be the murder victim of a palace eunuch. He might, however, have died from mercury poisoning caused by alchemists' potions intended to produce longevity.
820–824	Muzong (MU-TSUNG) reigned. Finding the treasury depleted, he followed a policy of military retrenchment. China maintained a military force approaching 1 million men in the early 820s.
821–822	China and Tibet negotiated yet another peace treaty. With this agreement, peace prevailed for most of the succeeding 20 years.
824–826	Jingzong (CHING-TSUNG) reigned briefly before palace eunuchs dethroned him.
824–840	Wenzong (WEN-TSUNG) reigned.
830	A war party of the Southern Zhao tribe attacked Chengdu in Sichuan and took thousands of hostages.
835	Printing was first mentioned in literature.
835	In the so-called Sweet Dew conspiracy, Wenzong attempted to destroy the palace eunuchs. They learned of the conspiracy in time, however, and military forces loyal to the eunuchs slaugh-

tered 1,000 courtiers in reprisal. The bloodletting continued into early 836, when the eunuchs finally proclaimed an amnesty.

840–846	Wuzong (WU-TSUNG) reigned. His chief minister, Li Deyu, carried out the suppression of Buddhist, Daoist, Nestorian, Zoroastrian, and Manichaean temples and monasteries.
843	The government acted to suppress the Manichaean sect.
845	Tang rulers intensified the crackdown on Buddhism. Monks and nuns were persecuted and the power and wealth of the monasteries curbed; many of the largest monasteries were shut down. As many as 250,000 priests and nuns were forced to return to lay life. Though the strictures were gradually lifted, little of the confiscated wealth was ever returned.
845	River piracy was out of hand on the Yangtze. A government report detailed how bands of pirates cruised the river, plundering villages and market centers.
846–859	Xuanzong (HSUAN-TSUNG) reigned. (This is a different Xuanzong from the one who reigned in the years 712–755.)
846	The new emperor relaxed the proscriptions on Buddhism, though he retained some curbs on temple building and ordination.
858	Floods submerged vast areas of the northern China plain. Many thousands drowned along the Grand Canal.
859	The Emperor Xuanzong died at age 49. The emperor probably died of "elixirs for immortality," which had a high mercury content. Yizong (I-TSUNG) succeeded him.
859–873	Yizong reigned. Intermittent peasant uprisings and bitter rivalries between imperial courtiers and palace eunuchs marked the era.
Early 860	A peasant uprising in modern Zhejiang Province exploded into a major revolt. Tang forces quelled it after six months of fighting.
861	Nanzhao forces sacked Yongzhou in southwestern China.
868	The earliest extant printed book, the *Diamond Sutra,* came off a press at Dunhuang.
868–869	With peasant support, dissident army officers mutinied in Guangxi. Government forces needed 14 months to put the insurgency down.

873	A catastrophic harvest triggered a popular outbreak. In some areas, only half the crop was gathered and mass starvation threatened.
873–88	Xizong (HSI-TSUNG) reigned. The protege of two eunuch generals, he ascended at age 12. His rule was regarded as harsh and capricious.
874	Rebellious peasants in Shandong defeated government forces and invaded Henan, capturing many cities and towns.
875	China's population reached 80 million.
878–884	The powerful army of bandit Huang Chao (HUANG CH'AO) ravaged Guangdong, Guangxi, and Hunan en route north toward the capital, Chang'an.
881	Huang Chao sacked Chang'an, forcing the imperial court to move to Luoyang.
881–84	Reorganized imperial forces cut off the rebels in Chang'an.
883	Zhu Wen (CHU WEN), one of Huang Chao's bandit commanders, surrendered to imperial forces and won a provincial military governorship as a reward.
884	Huang Chao, his retreating army cornered near Mount Taishan, killed himself.
885	Emperor Xizong returned to ruined Chang'an.
888	Xixong died of an illness at age 27 after a deeply troubled reign of 15 years.
888–904	Zhaozong (CHAO-TSUNG) reigned, a nominal rule confined to Chang'an and its hinterland. Powerful independent military governors controlled central and eastern China, Henan, Shandong, and Anhui. Nomads from the north occupied much of north-central and northeastern China, including Shanxi and Hebei. To the south, in the middle and lower reaches of the Yangtze Valley, small, independent states emerged.
890–907	Zhu Wen established control over a large area of northern China.
903	Zhu Wen's massacre of eunuchs in Shanxi Province and in Chang'an made him the effective ruler of the capital.
904	Zhu Wen murdered the emperor Zhaozong; Aizong ascended as the last Tang emperor.

907   Zhu Wen deposed Aizong and proclaimed himself emperor of the Later Liang dynasty, the first of the short-lived Five Dynasties in a new era of disunion. With the end of the Tang, non-Chinese Khitan occupied the far north of China, with warlords in control elsewhere.

KEY RESEARCH SOURCES

Ebrey, Patricia. *Cambridge Illustrated History of China.* New York: Cambridge University Press, 1996.

Pulleyblank, Edwin G. *The Background of the Rebellion of An Lushan.* New York: Oxford University Press, 1955.

Twitchett, Denis, ed. *The Cambridge History of China.* Vol. 3, *Sui and T'ang China, Part 1.* New York: Cambridge University Press, 1979.

9. FIVE DYNASTIES AND TEN KINGDOMS

(907–960)

This attenuated era bridged the breakup of the Tang and China's reunification under the first emperors of the Song dynasty. Five successive brief dynasties ruled the northern China plain. The Ten Kingdoms included nine in the south and one in the north. The one in the north, the Northern Han, fell to the Song in 979. The nine kingdoms in the south are actually seven kingdoms; two were counted twice because each went through two dynasties in this period.

In the north, palace coups, power struggles, rebellions, raids from beyond the frontiers, and economic dislocation marked these decades. By contrast, southern China experienced long stretches of comparative tranquillity. In fact, in the south, disunion might have stimulated economic development.

907	The rebel leader Zhu Wen (CHU WEN) proclaimed the Later Liang dynasty in the northern China plain, with its capital at Kaifeng.
907	The chieftain Abaogi (A-PAO-CHI) emerged as the leader of the Khitan federation, whose home territory lay along the northeastern frontier of China between the Manchurian forests to the east and the dry grasslands to the west. The Khitan were semi-nomadic, but they were turning increasingly to settled farming, weaving, and salt and iron production.
907–923	The Later Liang emperors ruled all or part of present-day Henan, Shaanxi, Shandong, Hubei, Hebei, Shanxi, Gansu, and Anhui provinces.
907–925	The Former Shu kingdom controlled modern Sichuan and parts of Gansu, Shaanxi, and Hubei provinces in west-central China.
907–936	The Khitan people launched intermittent raids from Mongolia across China's northeastern frontier. They gradually consolidated their hold over Chinese territory.
907–951	The kingdom of Chu ruled in Hunan and part of Guangxi in southern China.
907–971	The Southern Han kingdom controlled parts of present-day Guangdong and Guangxi in southern China.
907–978	The kingdom of Wuyue ruled parts of modern Zhejiang and Jiangsu on the east coast of China.
909	A Khitan army invaded Hebei, defeating Chinese forces near the present-day city of Tianjin.
909–945	The kingdom of Min ruled modern Fujian Province on the southern China coast.

912–913	Zhu Wen was murdered by one of his sons; brothers and half-brothers struggled for the throne of the Later Liang dynasty.
Second month, 913	Zhu Youzhen (CHU YU-CHEN), a son of Zhu Wen, ascended the Later Liang throne. He reigned until 923 as Modi. Like his father, however, he failed to subdue the border provinces and draw them into the empire.
916	Abaogi proclaimed himself emperor, founded the Liao dynasty, and declared himself the equal of China's rulers. He reigned until 926. The Venetian traveler Marco Polo's name for northern China, Cathay, was probably a corrupted form of Khitan. From their southern capital at Yanjing near modern Beijing, the Khitan eventually ruled an empire that encompassed a strip of northern China, Manchuria, and Mongolia. They governed their China holdings with Chinese help and in the Chinese manner.
916	Abaogi established the first Confucian temple in the Liao empire.
920	Later Liang forces crushed a large peasant uprising in present-day Henan Province. The effort seriously weakened the regime.
920–937	The kingdom of Wu ruled in parts of present-day Jiangsu, Anhui, Jiangxi, and Hubei.
922	The Tang loyalist Li Cunxu (LI TS'UN-HSU) cleared Hebei of enemies and prepared to advance on the Later Liang capital, Kaifeng.
923	The Later Liang armies surrendered to Li Cunxu's army before the gates of Kaifeng. He declared himself emperor of the Later Tang and ruled as Zhuangzong (CHUANG-TSUNG) until 926 from the ancient capital of Luoyang.
924–963	The kingdom of Jingnan controlled a small part of modern Hubei.
925	The Former Shu kingdom, ruling Sichuan and territory to the north, fell to the Later Tang.
926–947	Taizong (TAI-TSUNG) reigned as Liao emperor.
926	Li Siyuan ascended the Later Tang throne as the Emperor Mingzong. Reigning until 933, he strove with limited success to restore imperial authority.
928	An independent Tangut state, the forerunner of the Xia dynasty, came into existence in northwestern China.
934	Meng Zhixiang, Later Tang's commander in Sichuan, declared himself emperor of Later Shu, which controlled the territories of former Shu.

934–965	The Later Shu kingdom ruled Sichuan and parts of Gansu, Shaanxi, and Hubei.
936	Shi Jingtang (SHIH CHING-TANG) overturned the Later Tang and established the Later Jin dynasty, essentially a puppet state of the Khitan Liao. The Jin shifted the capital back to Kaifeng.
937–975	General Xu Zhiago of the Kingdom of Wu usurped the throne in 937. He changed his surname to Li and called his kingdom Tang, which historians generally call Southern Tang. Southern Tang ruled parts of Jiangsu, Anhui, Jiangxi, Hunan, and Hubei in the Han and Yangtze River valleys.
945–947	A large-scale Khitan invasion ravaged northern China.
Early 947	The Khitan occupied Kaifeng, toppled the Jin dynasty, and renamed their empire the Greater Liao.
947	The Liao empire formally split in two for administrative purposes: the Northern, or Khitan, Division, and the Southern, or Chinese, Division. Harassed by Chinese insurgents, Liao forces pulled out of Kaifeng, carrying massive amounts of loot as they withdrew.
947–950	With Khitan support, the Later Han dynasty briefly succeeded the Jin. It was the shortest-lived of the Five Dynasties.
947–951	Shizong (SHIH-TSUNG) reigned as the Liao emperor.
950	The regional state of Northern Han emerged from the wreck of the Later Han.
951	Guo Wei founded the Later Zhou dynasty, ruling northern China from Kaifeng as Taizu.
951–969	Muzong (MU-TSUNG) reigned as emperor of the Liao. In allusion to his indolence and heavy drinking, his Chinese subjects called him "the Sleeping Prince."
951–979	The Northern Han kingdom controlled parts of Shanxi, Shaanxi, and Hebei in northern China.
954	Zhou rulers carried out some reforms, including rent and tax cuts. Criminal penalties were lightened and corrupt government officials exposed and punished.
960	The Later Zhou dynasty mobilized to meet a Khitan invasion. Troops loyal to the Later Zhou commander Zhao Kuangyin (CHAO KUANG-YIN) declared him emperor. With his brother, Zhao Guangyi (CHAO KUANG-YI), he founded the Song dynasty.

KEY RESEARCH SOURCES

Franke, Herbert, and Denis Twitchett, eds. *The Cambridge History of China.* Vol. 6, *Alien Regimes and Border States, 907–1368*. New York: Cambridge University Press, 1994.

Wang Gungwu. *The Structure of Power in North China During the Five Dynasties.* Stanford: Stanford University Press, 1967.

10. NORTHERN SONG (960–1126)

WITH THE LIAO AND XIA EMPIRES

During the three centuries of the Song dynasty, China led the world in technical innovation, political theory, culture, and the arts. Concurrently, invaders from Inner Asia slowly gained political authority over large areas of the country.

Rapid economic growth, both in agriculture and industry, marked the early Song period. The pace of southward migration increased, and the Yangtze Valley overtook the Yellow River Valley in the north as a center of Chinese life. The Northern Song capital of Kaifeng developed as a major trading center. Coal from northern China fueled the expanding iron smelting industry in Shandong. The mariner's compass for navigation was an important Song invention.

Confucian ideas were reinvigorated during the Song. With the availability of the printed book came an expansion of education. The early Song emperors extended the examination system for the governing bureaucracy. Confucian reformers were increasingly influential, with their call for the imperial court and the civil service to reach the highest Confucian ideals.

A powerful upper class of scholar-officials, the product of the expanded civil service examination system, dominated Chinese life. This gentry, drawn from the landowner and degree-holder classes, formed a local elite—the governing link between peasantry below and the court and high bureaucracy above. The gentry produced the archetypal scholar-gentleman who carried on Chinese cultural traditions: classical learning, literature, calligraphy, landscape painting, and philosophical thought.

Song weakness was in the area of national defense. Song rulers turned away from the aristocratic and military traditions of the steppes. They regarded soldiers less highly even than merchants, preferring to use expensive, often unreliable mercenary troops to guard the fluid, shifting frontier zones.

During the dynasty, Inner Asian tribal peoples conquered large sections of China. The Khitan Liao dynasty (907–1125), penetrating China from the grasslands to the north, inaugurated five centuries of foreign rule of at least parts of China. Later, the Tangut Xia, generally known in history texts as Xixia (1032–1227), from the northwest and then the Jurchen Jin (1125–1234), from eastern Manchuria, annexed Chinese territory. These dynasties adopted Chinese political traditions and used Chinese bureaucrats to help them rule.

The collapse of the Northern Song in 1126 led to a new division of China. The vigorous Jin dynasty ruled in the north as an equal (and rival) to China's Southern Song, sovereign in the Huai River Valley and southward.

959–960	Later Zhou forces in northern China repulsed the Khitan invaders. In a military coup, Zhao Kuangyin toppled the last Zhou emperor, a six-month-old boy, ascended as emperor, and proclaimed the Song dynasty. Reigning until 976 as Taizu, he dismantled the independent regional armies, reorganized the imperial forces, restored central rule, and extended imperial authority through most of China.
960–975	The Song conquered and absorbed the states of Jingnan, Later Shu, Southern Han, and Southern Tang.
963	Song forces attacked the Northern Han in Shanxi. With Khitan help, the Han army repulsed the invasion.

969–983	Jingzong (CHING-TSUNG) reigned as emperor of the Liao dynasty.
974	Song diplomats sought a treaty with the Liao that would ensure the latter's neutrality in a Song military move on the Northern Han state.
976	Zhao Guangyi succeeded his brother as emperor of the Song. Zhao Guangyi is known to history as Taizong (TAI-TSUNG). Later, he was suspected of killing Taizu to gain his throne.
976–977	Song forces launched abortive attacks on the Northern Han. The Liao army moved to Han's aid.
977	As part of its diplomatic offensive, the Song government assigned five border marshals to regulate trade with the Liao state.
978	Wuyue fell to the Song.
Spring 979	Song renewed its offensive against the Northern Han, the last independent Chinese state, and inflicted a defeat on Han's Liao allies.
Sixth month, 979	The last Han forces surrendered to the Song. Imperial forces advanced northward toward the Khitan capital at Yanjing near modern Beijing.
Seventh month, 979	A Song army marched into Hebei, seeking to recover territory the Khitan had occupied a half-century earlier. Khitan forces routed the Song columns southwest of Yanjing. The Emperor Taizong fled in a donkey cart.
979–986	Liao forces in Hebei and Shanxi repulsed recurring Song efforts to recover the Khitan-occupied area south of the Great Wall.
982	An independent Tangut state, to be known as Xia, came into existence in the Ordos Desert–Gansu region along China's northern and northwestern frontier. The Tangut, a commingling of Tibetan and Tangut tribes, had moved slowly westward from their original homelands in the Kokonor Lake region along the Tibetan frontier.
983–1031	Shengzong (SHENG-TSUNG) reigned as the Liao emperor.
990	The Liao emperor recognized a "king of Xia."
990–1030	These were the productive years of the Song China painter Fan Kuan, creator of the landscape masterpiece *Travelers Amid Mountains and Streams.*
993	In a peasant uprising in present-day Sichuan, insurgents demanded a redistribution of wealth from the rich to the poor.

994	The Liao dynasty produced its first calendar, a major legitimizing element for Liao rulers.
994	Sichuan rebels captured Chengdu, gained control of its hinterland, and declared a rebel regime called the Great Shu.
995	Song forces quelled the Sichuan peasant uprising.
997	The Northern Song mint was turning out 800 million coins annually.
997–1022	Zhenzong (CHEN-TSUNG) reigned as the Song emperor.
997–1067	During this middle period of Northern Song, the size of the Song army and bureaucracy continued to grow, causing enormous strain on state finances. In the north and northwest, the Liao and the growing power of the Xixia state threatened the dynasty.
Summer 999	The Liao emperor, Shengzong, prepared a military expedition against the Northern Song. A Khitan army advanced into Hebei, but Song forces checked the offensive, forcing Shengzong to recall the army.
1000s	Upward-curving roofs became the standard in Song China for government buildings and homes of officials with high stations.
1001–1003	The Liao dynasty carried on intermittent warfare against the Song.
1004	A large Liao invasion force advanced to the Yellow River, fewer than 70 miles from the Song capital at Kaifeng. There, Song resistance stiffened, causing a military stalemate. The two sides agreed to peace talks.
1004	Song and Liao diplomats negotiated the Treaty of Chanyuan, in which China agreed to an annual tribute of 100,000 ounces of silver and 200,000 bolts of silk in return for peace and a secure border. Except for minor outbreaks, the treaty held for most of the 11th century.
c. 1010	Approximately 30,000 candidates sat for the civil service examination annually.
1016–1073	Life span of Zhou Dunyi (CHOU TUN-yi), a leading Neo-Confucian thinker.
1020	The Song government promoted the expansion of schools with grants of land and books. By century's end, the state school system supported 200,000 students.
1021	The population of Kaifeng, the Song capital, reached 500,000.

1022–1063	Renzong (JEN-TSUNG) reigned as the Northern Song emperor.
1029	A Song decree reserved the use of red lacquer beds for the emperor alone.
1031–1055	Xingzong (HSING-TSUNG) reigned as the Liao emperor, ascending the throne at age 15.
1031–1095	Life span of the scholar-official Shen Kuo. An expert in state finances, he also headed the Bureau of Astronomy, overseeing improvements to observatory instruments that made more accurate calendars possible.
1038	The Xixia ruler formally proclaimed a dynasty and dispatched an embassy to the Northern Song capital with the announcement. He reigned until 1048 as Jingzong (CHING-TSUNG), ruling a multi-ethnic state of 3 million people that included, along with its Tangut core, Chinese, Tibetan, Uighur, Khitan, and other peoples.
1039–1044	Song and Xixia forces clashed in northwest China. Song forces experienced a series of defeats; the war ended in a partial victory for the Xixia, who asserted control of large areas of China's north and northwest, including the Ordos Desert region, Gansu, and Qinghai.
1040	*The Comprehensive Essentials of the Military Classics*, a Song military manual, appeared. It contained the first recorded formula for gunpowder.
1041	Song China supported an army of 1.25 million. Military spending accounted for three-quarters of imperial revenues.
1042	With Song China distracted by the fighting with Xixia, the Liao state issued demands for new territorial cessions.
1043	Chinese living in the Southern Division of the Liao empire were forbidden to possess bows and arrows.
1043–1045	The scholar-official Fan Zhongyan (FAN CHUNG-YEN) was a powerful figure at the Song imperial court. He moved to reform the civil service and local administration and alter the examination system to emphasize the application of Confucian ideas to practical political problems. Fan also reduced labor service levies, reorganized the armed forces, and implemented measures to improve agricultural production. Within a year or so, however, he was driven from power.
1044	Xixia forces repulsed a Liao punitive expedition.

1044	China ratified a revised treaty with Liao, agreeing to increase its tribute payment of silver and silk in exchange for peace and the withdrawal of Khitan territorial demands. At the same time, Song diplomats negotiated a treaty with Xixia that called for tribute payments to this rival.
1048	Yizong (I-TSUNG) ascended the Xixia throne as an infant.
c. 1050	Northern Song China was the world's first widespread user of the printed book. Artisans produced paper from plant fibers; printers struck off their copies from wooden blocks.
1051–1107	Life span of Mi Fei, a Northern Song painter.
1055	The Song emperor granted the title Holy Duke to descendants of Confucius, another aspect of the Confucian revival.
1055–1101	Daozong (TAO-TSUNG) reigned as the Liao emperor. He continued the sinicization of the Liao state, ordering, among other things, ritual observances honoring the Confucian sages. A backlash eventually led to anti-Chinese discrimination in Liao territory.
1056–1057	Poet and essayist Su Shi (often known as Su Dongpo [SU TUNG-PO], 1037–1101) joined the bureaucracy and entered Song China's literary world. He would be a leading opponent in the 1070s of the New Laws of reformer Wang Anshi.
1057	Ouyang Xiu (OU-YANG HSIU) directed a brief new round of reform in Northern Song China. He revised the examination system to tilt even further in favor of classical over literary learning.
1063–1067	Yingzong (YING-TSUNG) reigned as the Northern Song emperor.
1067	Shenzong (SHEN-TSUNG) ascended as the Song emperor.
1068	Shenzong supported Wang Anshi (1021–1086). Wang called for greater state intervention in the economy, partly to increase state revenues and partly to check what he regarded as abuses of power deriving from great wealth. He eventually established his interpretation of the classics as the standard for civil service examination.
1068–1086	Huizong (HUI-TSUNG) reigned as the Xia emperor. During the early years of his reign, his mother, the empress dowager, influenced him heavily.
1069–1075	Wang Anshi implemented his so-called New Policies. While some seemed to trigger social unrest in Song China, others were successful. Wang Anshi established the agricultural loan program known as the Green Sprouts Act, enabling poor farm-

ers to borrow seed grain in the spring against the expected harvest in the autumn. He also imposed price controls and extended credit to small merchants and manufacturers.

1070   The leading Confucian anti-reformer Sima Guang (SSU-MA KUANG), a chief opponent of Wang Anshi, left government service and gradually slipped into retirement.

1070   Chinese in the Liao state were forbidden to hunt because the Khitan rulers regarded hunting as a form of military training. A new law code attempted to protect Khitan customs but was soon abandoned.

1070s   A series of locust plagues damaged northern China croplands, leading to widespread distress in the countryside.

1076   Wang Anshi, his reforms attracting increasing opposition, resigned his post as chief councilor and became a local official.

1076   A medical school was founded in Kaifeng, the Northern Song capital.

1077   The Lü family proposed an early form of the civic organization eventually known as the Community Compact, which came to prominence during the Ming dynasty. The idea was to regulate public behavior through mutual exhortation and discipline.

1078   Northern China's pig iron production reached 125,000 tons a year.

1080   The Xixia emperor Huizong discarded Tangut court ritual in favor of Chinese forms, part of the continuing rivalry between the emperor's supporters and the empress dowager's clique.

1081   Song forces attacked Xixia and captured the Lanzhou.

1081–1083   Song China waged intermittent warfare on the Xixia state. Increasing losses led the Song to agree to discuss peace with the Tangut, but the discussions went nowhere.

1082–1083   Large numbers of horses and livestock perished in a bitter northern China winter with heavy snow. Some estimates pegged livestock losses at 70 percent of the total.

1085   With the death of Shenzong, the reform party lost influence, and the Wang Anshi era of reform of Song China came to an end.

1085   Song China minted 6 billion coins a year.

1085–1100   Zhezong (CHE-TSUNG) reigned as the Northern Song emperor.

1086	The historian Sima Guang (SSU-MA KUANG), a conservative opponent of Wang Anshi, served briefly as chief minister. He moved rapidly to overturn most of Wang Anshi's policies.
1086–1139	Chongzong (CH'UNG-TSUNG) reigned as the Xixia emperor.
1090	A visitor to the Khitan court reported that Liao law weighed no more heavily on Chinese subjects than on the Khitan themselves. He also noted a high level of court corruption.
1091–1093	More border conflicts occurred between Xixia and Song. Imperial forces seized Xixia lands but were unable to hold onto their gains.
c. 1095	The number of candidates for the civil service examinations reached 80,000 a year.
1096–1099	Xixia attacks provoked a massive military response from the Song. In 1099, the exhausted Xixia begged for peace, which the Song granted.
1100–1125	Huizong (HUI-TSUNG) reigned as the next-to-last emperor of the Northern Song. A patron of the arts and of Daoism, and a great artist in his own right, he was the most cultured of the Song sovereigns. The imperial gallery contained 6,000 works of art. Huizong was, however, regarded as a weak and indifferent ruler.
1101–1125	Tianzuo (T'IEN-TSO) reigned as the Liao emperor.
1102	Jurchen tribes—farmers, herders, and hunters originally from the mountain forests of eastern Manchuria—launched raids on the frontiers of the Khitan Liao state.
1103–1104	The Xixia emperor Chongzong consolidated his authority by stripping the leading military clan, the Jen-to, of its power.
1111–1117	Song imperial decrees authorized a crackdown on male homosexual prostitution in Kaifeng, stipulating a punishment of 100 strokes with a rod.
Autumn 1114	Jurchen forces won two major frontier-area battles, increasing the pressure on the beleaguered Liao state.
1115	The Jurchen chief proclaimed himself the first emperor of the Jin dynasty. He reigned until 1123 as Taizu (TAI-TSU).
1119	Song China negotiated a treaty with the Xixia empire, ending four years of costly warfare.
1119	The first mention of the compass appeared in Chinese sources; the instrument might have been in use since the last quarter of the previous century.

1120	The Song sent a large punitive expedition in response to a violent uprising in modern Zhejiang Province in southeastern China.
1120	Song imperial collectors collected 18 million ounces of silver in taxes.
1120	The prosperous southern coastal city of Quanzhou supported a population of more than 500,000, including the hinterland.
1120s	Song China began issuing paper money as a means of simplifying trade and financial transactions.
1121	Song forces captured and executed the leader of the Zhejiang uprising, Fang La. The revolt swiftly collapsed.
Spring 1122	In alliance with the Jurchen, Song forces advanced on the Liao capital of Yanjing but failed to capture it. A Jurchen-Jin army eventually seized the city.
1123	Jin diplomats negotiated a treaty with Song China, receiving annual tribute of 200,000 ounces of silver and 300,000 bolts of silk. China's economy continued to prosper despite such tribute payments and nearly constant warfare on the frontiers.
1123–1135	Taizong (T'AI-TSUNG) reigned as emperor of the Jin dynasty.
1125	The Jin dynasty of northern China declared a government monopoly on wine and banned private winemaking.
1125	The Jurchen captured Tianzuo, the last Liao emperor, bringing down the dynasty.
Autumn 1125	The Jurchen-Jin dynasty launched a full-scale war against Song China. Jin forces advanced into Shanxi and Hebei on the northern China plain.
1126	A Jin edict required Chinese subjects to adopt Jurchen dress and hairstyle. It was widely disregarded.
January 1126 (last month of 1125 by Chinese calendar)	Huizong abdicated in favor of his son.
Early 1126	The Jurchen crossed the Yellow River, threatening the Northern Song capital at Kaifeng.
Winter 1126	The Jurchen lifted the siege of Kaifeng after Song negotiators agreed to cede substantial territory in the north and increase annual tribute payments.
1126–1127	Qinzong (CH'IN-TSUNG) reigned as the last emperor of the Northern Song.

Winter 1127	After renewed warfare, the Jurchen entered Kaifeng, pillaged the capital, and forced the Song dynasty to abandon all of northern China. With help from his military commanders, Prince Kang of the Song imperial family escaped and established a new capital in the south, first at modern Nanjing, later at Hangzhou. He ascended as Gaozong (KAO-TSUNG), the first emperor of the Southern Song.
Spring 1127	Jurchen forces led two former Song emperors away into captivity in Jin territory to the north.

KEY RESEARCH SOURCES

Ebrey, Patricia. *Cambridge Illustrated History of China*. New York: Cambridge University Press, 1996.

Fairbank, John King. *China: A New History*. Cambridge, Mass.: The Belknap Press of Harvard University Press, 1992.

Franke, Herbert, and Denis Twitchett, eds. *Cambridge History of China*. Vol. 6. New York: Cambridge University Press, 1994.

Hymes, Robert P., and Conrad Shirokauer, eds. *Ordering the World: Approaches to State and Society in Sung Dynasty China*. Berkeley: University of California Press, 1993.

Liu, James T. C. *Reform in Sung China*. Cambridge: Harvard University Press, 1959.

11. SOUTHERN SONG (1127–1279)

WITH THE XIA AND JIN DYNASTIES

The Song imperial entourage disengaged from the triumphant Jurchen, withdrew to the south, and established a new court and capital at Hangzhou on the East China Sea. China was again split, but the Song emperors still ruled a vast country—700,000 square miles, with a population of 60 million. The dynasty's cultural, artistic, and technological achievement continued in spite of recurrent warfare with the Xixia and Jin states. Books took on increasing importance: practical guides to farming, childbirth, pharmacology, Buddhism and Daoism, history, Confucian classics and their contemporaries, as well as artistic and literary works.

The Southern Song developed a sophisticated economy, with paper money, credit instruments, and foreign trade. Though they were rivals, the Song and Jin empires maintained close commercial ties. The Song merchant class grew in size, wealth, and influence. China emerged as the world's leading maritime trader; Chinese merchant sailors plied the sea routes to India, Arabia, and Africa.

With new strains of seed, marsh drainage, and other advances, rice culture flourished in Southern Song China. Urban life developed. Southern Song factories produced paper, ceramics, lacquerware, and metal products. Inventors and artisans developed new gunpowder armaments and advanced shipbuilding methods. China's seagoing junks, with a carrying capacity of a thousand men, were the most powerful vessels afloat.

The Southern Song dynasty's decline coincided with the rise of Mongol penetration into China. While the Southern Song dynasty lasted to 1279, Mongol dominance of China was virtually achieved by 1276, when the Songs gave the seal of their dynasty to the Mongols. Some loyal Songs continued to resist the Mongols until 1279.

1126–1138	Refugees from the north poured into the Yangtze Valley ahead of the advancing Jurchen.
1127–1130	Northern China's Jurchen rulers adopted a Chinese bureaucratic system, staffed largely with Chinese; in the beginning, it governed only the Jin empire's Chinese population. At the same time, the Jin rulers imposed compulsory military service and raised taxes.
1127–1162	Gaozong (KAO-TSUNG) reigned as the emperor of the Southern Song. He gradually consolidated imperial power in the Yangtze Valley.
1129	Gaozong quashed an attempted coup by generals who tried to replace him with his two-year-old son. The child died soon afterward.
c. 1130	The Chan and Pure Land Buddhist sects flourished in the Jin state as well as in the Southern Song. Jin rulers strictly regulated religious life, however; monks could not be ordained, for example, without government permission.
1130	Chinese inventors experimented with gunpowder as a propellant. The Song navy armed its war junks with explosives-hurling catapults.

1130–1135	Song China and the Jurchen Jin engaged in intermittent warfare. Song forces under Yue Fei recovered several provinces from the Jin. The emperor reined in the general, however, deciding instead to buy peace with tribute.
1130–1200	Life span of the scholar Zhu Xi (CHU HSI), an influential Neo-Confucian. Zhu wrote commentaries on the essence of Confucianism, called the Four Books. They were the *Analects of Confucius;* the *Book of Mencius,* a leading Confucian successor; the *Doctrine of the Mean*; and the *Great Learning*, chapters from one of the ancient ritual texts. The Four Books became the official standard for China's civil service examinations in the Yuan and later dynasties.
Early 1132	Canals and the Western Lake froze over in semi-tropical Hangzhou, the Southern Song metropolis.
Mid–1132	Fire destroyed 13,000 homes in Hangzhou. Fire disasters were all too frequent in Hangzhou, a crowded city built mainly of bamboo and wood.
1135	The former Northern Song emperor Huizong died in captivity in northern China.
1135	Yue Fei commanded an expeditionary force sent to subdue the bandit army of Dongting Lake. He successfully pacified the middle Yangtze region for the Southern Song.
1138	Song officials re-established the late Emperor Huizong's Academy of Painting on the Western Lake in Hangzhou.
1138	Southern Song authorities outlawed the practice of infant abandonment and ordered the building of foundling hospitals.
1138	Song imperial forces controlled most of China south of the Huai River. They established their permanent capital at Hangzhou, a city of some 200,000, known for its lake and attractive environs.
1138–1150	Xizong (HSI-TSUNG) reigned as emperor of the Jin dynasty.
1139–1193	Renzong (JEN-TSUNG) reigned as Xixia emperor.
1139	Ignoring the advice of Yue Fei, Southern Song negotiators concluded a preliminary treaty with the Jin dynasty. Yue Fei favored leading an army to conquer northern China and reunify the country.
1139	The Jin empire introduced a new Jurchen script. For a time, three official written languages coexisted in northern China—Jurchen, Khitan, and Chinese.

1140	The Jin emperor Xizong, who reintroduced Confucian state rituals and participated in some himself, conferred a dukedom on a 49th-generation descendant of Confucius.
1140	Breaching the agreement of 1139, the Jin attacked Southern Song China on several fronts. Song armies under Yue Fei counterattacked and recaptured some territory in Henan before the emperor ordered a withdrawal.
Summer 1140	Song armies formed a defensive front along the original Huai River frontier.
1141	Jin rulers established the price of freedom for a male slave at three bolts of textiles. Women and children could buy their freedom for two bolts.
Early 1141	A Jin army renewed the advance into Song territory. Qin Gui (CH'IN KUEI), an important adviser of the Emperor Gaozong, argued hard for peace talks. He kept Yue Fei, the Song's best field commander, idle in the capital, had him arrested, and finally arranged his murder in prison.
Autumn 1141	Song and Jin diplomats negotiated a new treaty that recognized the division of China and, at least in formal terms, made the Song a vassal of the Jin.
1142	The National University opened in Kaifeng; the school shortly moved to Hangzhou.
Autumn 1142	With the arrival of a Jin envoy at the Southern Song court, Qin Gui's peace accord was ratified. By terms of the treaty, the Southern Song ceded northern China to the Huai River and agreed to pay an annual tribute of silver and silk to the Jin. Some 6 million Jurchen thus ruled a northern China population approaching 50 million.
1142–1143	Famine and earthquake brought hardship and social unrest to the Xia domains. Southern Song forces helped Xixia pacify the rebels.
1144–1147	The Xixia emperor introduced Confucian institutions and encouraged a cult of Confucius. Schools, a training college for civil servants, and an examination system were established in the Xia state.
1149	Chen Fu's book *Agriculture* offered a detailed description of paddy rice culture.
c. 1150	Song traders and sailors made China the world's most advanced maritime power.
January 1150 (last month of 1149 by Chinese calendar)	Conspirators at court murdered the violent and mentally unstable Jin emperor Xizong.

1150–1161	Hailing, the leading figure in the Xizong murder conspiracy, reigned as the Jin emperor. Chinese and Jurchen sources portrayed him as cruel and murderous. All the same, he was an admirer of things Chinese, adopting such Song customs as tea drinking and Go-playing.
1152	Hailing ordered Yanjing (near modern Beijing) rebuilt, shifted his residence there, and dubbed the city the Central Capital.
1157	Emperor Hailing decreed Kaifeng the southern capital of the Jin dynasty.
1157	Jin rulers barred the export of antiquities.
1159–1160	Jin forces mobilized for renewed warfare with the Southern Song. The Jin army contained 120,000 Jurchen and 150,000 Chinese conscripts; some 560,000 horses were requisitioned for the campaign.
1161	Song forces fired explosive grenades from catapults in battle against the Jurchen Jin.
1161	Monks led a rebellion in Hebei.
Autumn 1161	The Jin army crossed the Huai River and advanced south toward the Yangtze, but Song defenders repulsed the Jin army in its attempt to cross the Yangtze and penetrate the Southern Song heartland.
Late 1161	Members of an officers' cabal murdered Hailing in camp near the Yangtze River. Shizong (SHIH-TSUNG) ascended the Jin throne.
1161–1189	Reforms in education, the economy, and administration were hallmarks of the long reign of the Jin emperor Shizong.
Early 1162	Shizong withdrew the Jin armies from the line of the Yangtze River and sent a peace emissary to the Southern Song court. Border clashes continued, however.
1162	Gaozong abdicated as the Southern Song emperor. His son succeeded him.
1162–1189	Xiaozong (HSIAO-TSUNG) reigned as emperor of the Southern Song.
1163	Jews reaching China via the caravan routes from Persia founded a synagogue in Jin Kaifeng.
1165	Song China concluded a new peace treaty with the Jin empire, agreeing to raise the annual tribute payment by 50,000 ounces of silver and 50,000 bolts of silk.

c. 1170	The Jin emperor Shizong prohibited his Jurchen subjects from dressing in the Chinese manner or taking Chinese names.
1170s	Drought and famine caused great hardship in northern China.
1187	The Jin empire's population totaled 44,705,086.
1188	Jin banned the heterodox Buddhist Dhuta sect. It had gained many adherents in the merchant and artisan classes.
1189–1191	Guangzong (KUANG-TSUNG) reigned as the Southern Song emperor.
1189–1208	Zhangzong (CHANG-TSUNG) reigned as the Jin emperor. An accomplished calligrapher, he was a patron of the arts.
c. 1190–1224	Life span of the Southern Song landscape painter Ma Yuan, an associate of the Academy of Painting in Hangzhou.
1191	The Jin government approved legal marriage between the empire's Jurchen and Chinese subjects
1191–1192	The Jin government formally abolished the Khitan script, a remnant from the Liao era.
1192	A Jin army prepared fortifications on the northwestern frontier to check the growing power of the Mongols.
1193–1206	Huanzong (HUAN-TSUNG) reigned as emperor of the Xixia dynasty.
1194	Massive flooding devastated the Yellow River Valley in Hebei and Shandong in northern China.
1194–1224	Ningzong (NING-TSUNG) reigned as the Southern Song emperor.
1200s	By a contemporary calculation, the Chinese consumed two pounds of rice a day per person.
1202	The Jin empire formally adopted the legal code of China's Tang dynasty.
1205	The Mongols, the rising power on the steppes, launched their first major raids into Xia territory. The raiders plundered fortified frontier towns and carried off livestock.
1206	Temujin ascended as the great khan of the Mongols—Genghis Khan.

Summer 1206	Southern Song China declared war on the Jin empire. The declaration claimed that the Jin emperor had lost the "mandate of heaven" and thus his right to rule. It also called for a rising of Chinese people within Jin borders.
Autumn 1206	Jin forces repulsed the Song invasion, crossed the Huai River, and occupied Song strongpoints in southern Shaanxi. Fighting continued intermittently into the next year.
1206–1208	Mongol raids prompted the Xixia state to seek an alliance with the Jin empire. The Jurchen declined, on the theory that warfare between the Mongols and Xixia would help them.
1206–1211	Xiangzong (HSIANG-TSUNG) reigned as the Xixia emperor.
1207	The Jin state's population totaled 53,532,151. The population of China as a whole approached 110,000,000–120,000,000.
Spring 1208	A fire destroyed 58,000 homes and killed at least 59 people in Hangzhou; others perished in panicked efforts to escape the city.
Summer 1208	The Jin empire declared a victory and an end to the war with Song China. Meeting a Jin demand, the Song sent the head of the chief minister who had started the war.
Autumn 1208	A new peace treaty with the Jin state increased Song China's annual tribute by 50,000 ounces of silver and 50,000 bolts of silk.
Autumn 1209	The Mongols launched a major invasion of the Xixia empire.
1209–1213	Wei Shao ruled the Jin but was not granted the title of emperor.
1210	After a series of defeats, Xixia submitted to the invading Mongols, who then turned their attention to the Jin empire to the east.
1211	The Red Jacket bandit-guerrilla uprising spread in Shandong in northeastern China. It flared intermittently until 1227, when the rebels swore allegiance to the Mongols.
Spring 1211	Two Mongol armies massed on the borders of the Jin empire. Mongol forces cleared the mountain pass that protected Yanjing, plundered the capital region, and withdrew before the onset of winter.
1211–1223	Shenzong (SHEN-TSUNG) reigned as the Xia emperor.
1212	The Yong Le (Permanent Joy) Daoist temple, famous for its design, opened in Shanxi Province.

Spring 1213	The Mongols resumed their raiding, pouring into Hebei, Shandong, and Shanxi provinces.
Summer 1213	A failed Jurchen general led a conspiracy that resulted in the murder of the Jin ruler Wei Shao.
1213–1224	Xuanzong (HSUAN-TSUNG) reigned as the Jin emperor.
Spring 1214	With the increase of Mongol military pressure, the Jurchen moved their capital south from Yanjing to Kaifeng.
Spring 1215	Yanjing surrendered to the Mongols.
1217	Renewed Yellow River flooding submerged parts of Shandong in northeastern China.
1220–1222	Jin diplomatic missions sought peace with the Mongols. Their efforts were rebuffed.
1223–1226	Xianzong (HSIEN-TSUNG) reigned as emperor of the Xixia state.
1224–1234	Aizong (AI-TSUNG)—known as the "pitiable ancestor"—reigned as emperor of the Jin dynasty.
1224–1264	Lizong (LI-TSUNG) reigned as the Southern Song emperor.
1225	Mongol invasion columns penetrated Shandong in northeastern China.
Spring 1226	Mongols launched a new invasion of Xixia, overrunning most of its territory. The Xixia emperor, Xianzong, was said to have died of fright as the Mongol columns approached his capital.
1226–1227	Xian (HSIEN) reigned as the last Xixia emperor.
Summer 1227	The Mongols besieged the Xixia capital, forced its surrender, captured the emperor, and executed him on the spot.
August 1227	Genghis Khan, the great Mongol ruler, died.
1230	Red Jacket insurgents advanced from their strongholds in Shandong into Southern Song territory as far as the Yangtze River.
1230–1231	The Mongols mounted a new invasion of Jin territory.
Winter 1231	The Red Jacket leader fell in battle with Southern Song forces; the insurgent movement soon collapsed.
Spring 1232	The Mongol legions pushed up to the walls of Kaifeng. Jin forces used Chinese gunpowder and a weapon known as a "fire lance," probably a primitive shotgun, against the attackers.

Summer 1232	Famine and disease struck besieged Kaifeng. What some scholars now believe was bubonic plague claimed as many as 1 million people in a matter of a few weeks.
Winter 1233	Aizong escaped Kaifeng and made his way south toward Song territory.
Spring 1233	Kaifeng capitulated to the Mongols.
1234	Aizong killed himself. Modi succeeded him as the last emperor of the Jin dynasty. He fell in battle against the Mongols, bringing about the collapse of the Jin state.
1237	As the Mongol threat grew, the Southern Song river and coastal defense navy mobilized a fleet of 22 squadrons—52,000 sailors.
1241	Declaring that the late scholar Zhu Xi had "illuminated the Way," the Song emperor ordered students at the government academy to study Zhu's commentaries, the Four Books.
1260s	Song reformers sought to curb corruption among eunuchs, bureaucrats, and imperial kin, causing deep divisions in the Song court on the eve of the Mongol invasion.
1260–1261	Mongol rulers of northern China dispatched emissaries to the Song imperial court; they were rebuffed.
1264	Khubilai, the grandson of Genghis Khan, ascended the throne of the great khan of the Mongols. He shifted his capital from Karakorum in Mongolia to Yanjing and prepared for an invasion of Song China.
1264–1274	Duzong (TU-TSUNG) reigned as emperor of the Southern Song.
1265	Mongol and Song forces clashed in the western region of Sichuan.
1268	Full-scale war erupted between the Mongols and the Southern Song. The Mongol army besieged the Han River fortress of Xiangyang, the key to control of the Yangtze Valley.
1270	The National University in Song Hangzhou enrolled more than 1,700 students.
1271	Khubilai settled upon a Chinese name, Yuan, for his dynasty and adopted Chinese court rituals. The word *yuan* means "prime" or "original."
March 1273	Under attack from Mongol batteries hurling rocks that weighed up to 100 pounds apiece, Song forces surrendered the fortress of Xiangyang after a five-year siege.

Summer 1274	The young Song Emperor Duzong died suddenly. His four-year-old son succeeded him.
1274–1276	The child Gongdi (KUNG-TI) reigned as the last emperor of the Song dynasty.
Winter 1275	Mongol forces crossed the Yangtze River on the heels of the retreating Song army. The Empress Dowager Xie (HSIEH), acting for the underage emperor, called for a mass uprising against the barbarians.
Late 1275	Xie sent to the Mongols for peace terms, fearing a slaughter should the Mongols take Hangzhou, the world's largest (1.1 million people), richest, and most cosmopolitan city, by force. Bayan, the Mongol commander, ordered unconditional surrender.
Late 1270s	China used bronze and iron mortar tubes in battle against the Mongols.
Early 1276	The Mongols received the seal of the Song dynasty and entered Hangzhou. A Mongol escort led the imperial family north to the court of Khubilai Khan at Yanjing.
1276–1278	Mongol columns resumed the southward march and continued their conquest of China, defeating bands of increasingly demoralized Song loyalists as they encountered them.
March 1279	Mongol forces defeated the last of the Song loyalists in a naval battle off the Guangdong coast. China was now wholly under foreign occupation for the first time in its long history.

KEY RESEARCH SOURCES

Ebrey, Patricia. *Cambridge Illustrated History of China*. New York: Cambridge University Press, 1996.

Fairbank, John King. *China: A New History*. Cambridge, Mass.: The Belknap Press of Harvard University Press, 1992.

12. YUAN DYNASTY

(1276–1368)

China became a division of the Mongol empire by 1276, when the Mongols received the seal of the Song dynasty and entered Hangzhou. By 1279 the Mongols defeated the last of the Song loyalists. For the first time, China was entirely under foreign domination. Many Chinese, especially southern Chinese, despised their conquerors, even as they moved gradually to adopt some Mongol ways.

Though the new rulers refrained from forcing alien customs on the Chinese, they were oppressive in other ways. The Mongols prohibited their subjects from trading in bamboo, for it could be used to make bows and arrows. They forbade intermarriage. Taxes were heavy, there were confiscations of land, and some Chinese were forced to resettle. The economy was badly dislocated, especially in much-fought-over northern China.

Even when the Yuan rulers welcomed them into the government, some Chinese scholars were disinclined to serve the new regime. As the number of educated men entering the bureaucracy declined, the arts flowered. Some 160 complete plays survive from the Yuan era. The Chinese novel developed during this period as well.

The Mongols were less adept at governing than in seizing territory, but they could claim some achievements. Agriculture and education advanced. Trade expanded. Khubilai Khan extended the Grand Canal to the Yuan capital on the site of present-day Beijing.

In the long term, the Mongols failed to keep what they took by force. The first half of the 14th century brought a succession of severe winters, floods, famine, and plagues. Thousands perished or were uprooted. Social dislocation led to political insurgency. During the closing decades of the dynasty, civil government became increasingly ineffective. The Yuan dynasty survived for less than a century.

1253–1254	The Mongols under Khubilai, a grandson of Genghis Khan, subdued Yunnan in southwest China.
1261	The Mongols established the Office for the Stimulation of Agriculture to assist the recovery of China's peasants from wartime devastation.
May 1261	Khubilai, now great khan of the Mongols, sought proposals for governing the conquered domains of China.
1262–1282	The Muslim Ahmad directed the Yuan state financial administration. He introduced a regular system of land taxation and increased the revenue stream from China's merchants.
1266	Khubilai Khan ordered construction of a new capital on the site of modern Beijing, with avenues wide enough for Mongol cavalry to ride nine abreast.
1267	The leading Confucian scholar Xu Heng (HSU HENG, 1209–1281) won appointment as chancellor of the Imperial College.
1269	Khubilai pressed for the adoption of a new Mongolian script, based on Tibetan and consisting of a 41-letter alphabet. Though it was an efficient script, it did not displace the Uighur script then in general use.

1270	China's Mongol rulers endorsed the peasant village organization *she*, which promoted farming, land reclamation, and education.
1271	Khubilai Khan proclaimed himself emperor of China, adopted the reign name of Shizu, called his dynasty Yuan (meaning original or prime), and established an imperial court in the Chinese style.
1271	The Yuan emperor Shizu (Khubilai Khan) adopted a new legal code, with some Mongol elements. The code was comparatively lenient; capital crimes totaled 135, fewer than half the number in the Song code (though Song capital sentences were reduced). He founded the Institute for Muslim Astronomy to recruit Persian and Arab astronomers to China, restored traditional Confucian court rituals, promoted the translation of the Confucian classics into Mongolian, and reached out to Buddhist and Daoist religious groups.
1271–1279	Khubilai—now Shizu—extended his rule to encompass all of China.
1273	The treatise *Fundamentals of Agriculture and Sericulture*, with details on growing cotton, was influential.
1274	Using the captured Song navy, the Mongols launched an invasion of Japan. Typhoons forced the fleet to return to China.
1274	Khubilai appointed a Muslim as governor of the province of Yunnan in the southwest. In consequence, Muslim colonization of Yunnan surged.
Early 1274	Khubilai held his first imperial court in the new capital.
1275–1279	The Mongols finished the legal classification of Chinese society with the addition of a fourth class—the newly conquered southern Chinese. The three earlier classifications, in descending order, were the Mongols, Western and Central Asians, and Chinese.
1275–1292	According to his own account, the Venetian traveler Marco Polo lived in China. His *Travels* introduced educated Europe to advanced Chinese civilization.
1276	The Yuan government imposed a state monopoly on copper tools. Earlier, the government monopolized tea, liquor, vinegar, gold, and silver.
1278–1284	Huang Hua led an intermittent rebellion against the Yuan.
1279–1280	Recognizing the growth of Muslim power and Chinese resentment of it, the Yuan government issued a series of edicts restricting Muslim religious and secular practices.

1280–1354	Life span of the scholar-painter Zhu Wen (CHU WEN). He chose not to serve in government under the Mongols and supported himself instead by telling fortunes.
1281	The Yuan repressed the Daoists, ordering all Daoist texts except for the *Laozi* destroyed.
1281	Imperial forces crushed a rebellion south of the Yangtze; Khubilai's troops were said to have beheaded 20,000 insurgents.
1281	The city's Muslims built a mosque in Hangzhou. Despite some restrictions, the Muslim community flourished there into the 1320s.
1281	The Yuan adopted the calendar of astronomer Guo Shoujing, then the world's most accurate calendar. Guo calculated that 365.2425 days made up a year.
Spring 1281	A Yuan invasion force of 100,000 soldiers, 15,000 sailors, and 900 vessels reached Japan.
Summer 1281	A typhoon hit Japan, scattering the Yuan invasion force, sinking many vessels, and giving Khubilai no choice but to call off the campaign and return to China. The Japanese named the fortuitous storm *kamikaze*, "divine wind."
April 1282	Dissident Chinese ambushed and killed the imperial finance minister, the Muslim Ahmad. Chinese historical sources memorialized Ahmad as the first of the three "villainous ministers."
c. 1285	An estimated 400,000 artisans worked in government shops and factories.
1285	Sangha authorized the restoration of Buddhist temples and monasteries.
May 1285	Ahmad's successor, Lu Shirong (LU SHIH-JUNG), the second of the "villainous ministers," was arrested and eventually executed. His successor was a Tibetan, Sangha.
1286	Khubilai Khan sought the services of the Song scholar Zhao Mengfu (CHAO MENG-FU, 1254–1322), who reluctantly agreed to leave Hangzhou for the north. Zhao became a leading supporter of Confucian values at the Yuan court.
1286–1287	A Yuan army campaigned in Annam (modern northern Vietnam). Though the fighting ended in a draw, Annam and neighboring Champa (present-day southern Vietnam) agreed to send tribute to the Yuan court.
1289	The Yuan court established a national school for the study of Arabic.

February 1289	A 135-mile extension linking the Grand Canal to Beijing opened.
1290	A government census put China's registered population at 58,834,711. The actual population doubtless was higher, though the figure still represented a sharp decrease, especially in the north, largely in consequence of the Mongol invasion, war, famine, and plague.
1291	With the Buddhist resurgence, more than 200,000 monks were in service at 42,318 Buddhist temples in China.
August 1291	Sangha, the last of the three "villainous ministers," was stripped of office and executed.
1292	The Italian Christian missionary Giovanni Montecorvino sought to spread Christianity in China.
February 1294	Khubilai Khan died of natural causes in his palace.
May 1294	Temur, a grandson of Khubilai, ascended the Yuan throne and took the name of Chengzong (CHENG-TSUNG). He issued an edict calling for the veneration of Confucius.
1295	China moved its mail through a postal network with 1,400 stations 15 to 40 miles apart. In special circumstances, delivery riders could cover 250 miles a day.
1295–1300	Wang Zhen (WANG CHEN) compiled a handbook, *On Agriculture,* that covered farming, forestry, animal husbandry, spinning, and weaving.
1298	Chengzong rejected his military advisers' recommendation for renewed effort—it would have been the third—to invade Japan.
1299	The Yuan emperor sent a peace mission to Japan.
Spring 1303	An investigation of government corruption ended with more than 18,000 officials and clerks found guilty and punished.
1307–1311	Wuzong (WU-TSUNG) reigned as Yuan emperor. Wasteful spending and unnecessary growth of the bureaucracy marked his reign.
1309	The neo-Confucian scholar Wu Cheng (WU CH'ENG, 1249-1333) accepted an appointment to the National Academy. Over time, he introduced a four-part curriculum: classical studies, the practice of Confucian teachings, the literary arts, and administration.
April 1311	Wuzong's younger brother ascended the Yuan throne, reigning as Renzong (JEN-TSUNG). He set about curbing expenses and reducing the bureaucracy.

1314–1315	In an effort to increase revenue, the government re-established the state monopoly on foreign trade and pursued more-aggressive tax collection policies.
1315	China's Mongol rulers revised the examination system, establishing quotas ensuring that half the degrees went to Mongolians and other non-Chinese candidates.
1316	Facing widespread resistance, the Yuan government abandoned its new tax collection system.
April 1320	Yingzong (YING-TSUNG) succeeded his father as Yuan emperor.
1323	The Yuan dynasty promulgated a new legal code that incorporated laws and regulations introduced since the beginning of the dynasty.
September 1323	Rebellious Mongolian princes staged a palace coup, overthrowing Yingzong. The rebels murdered the emperor and his chief minister.
October 1323	The Mongolian prince Yesun Temur, one of the coup participants, ascended the Yuan throne, taking the reign name of Taiding (T'AI-TING). He surrounded himself with Muslim advisers, leaving Chinese officials with little influence on his reign.
1328	A rival faction deposed Tianshun and placed the Mongol prince Tugtemur briefly on the throne. He abdicated in favor of his older brother, who ruled briefly as Mingzong (MING-TSUNG) before he died of poison, allegedly administered at Tugtemur's order.
August 1328	The death of Taiding touched off the bloodiest succession struggle of the Yuan era.
October 1328	Taiding's son succeeded him, reigning as Tianshun (TIEN-SHUN); with word of the succession, civil war erupted.
1329–1332	Tugtemur regained the imperial seal and reigned as Wenzong (WEN-TSUNG). In the confusion, powerful ministers such as Bayan came to dominate the Yuan court.
Spring 1329	Wenzong established the Academy of the Pavilion of the Star of Literature to introduce Chinese high culture to the Mongolian imperial court. Among other things, the academy served as a training school for the sons of high-ranking Mongols.
May 1330	Scholars of the Academy of the Pavilion began work on the *Grand Canon for Governing the World*, a compilation of all major documents and laws from the founding of the Yuan dynasty; it took 13 months to prepare.

1331–1354	A bubonic plague epidemic spread through China. According to some modern scholars, the Mongols might have carried it to Europe, where it caused the terrible Black Death of 1348 and 1349.
September 1332	Wenzong died without having settled the question of his successor.
October 1332	A child emperor ascended as Ningzong (NING-TSUNG); he died after only 53 days on the throne. A court faction prepared the way for the ascension of his older brother.
1333	Bayan, a powerful conservative, won appointment as chancellor of the right, the top post in Yuan China. He led a bureaucracy of 33,000 officials, two-thirds of them Chinese.
July 1333	Shundi, 13 years old, came to the throne as 10th (and last) emperor of the Yuan dynasty in ceremonies at Shangdu, the summer capital in Inner Mongolia, 200 miles north of Beijing.
1333–1334	Yellow River floods caused widespread loss of life and property.
1335	Chancellor Bayan moved to reduce palace expenditures and salt monopoly quotas and strove for a strict separation of Mongols and Chinese. He reserved most leading government positions for non-Chinese, barred Chinese subjects from owning weapons or horses, and canceled the Confucian examination system.
1340s	The Yuan rebuilt sections of the Grand Canal damaged by floodwaters.
March 1340	A coup removed the unpopular Bayan from office. He died in April on the way to his exile in the far south. His successor as chancellor of the right, Toghto, reversed many of Bayan's policies, reopened high positions to Chinese candidates, and reestablished the exam system.
Summer 1344	The Yellow River shifted its course, breaking through dikes and submerging large areas. The change also brought drought to the Huai Valley region of northern Henan, Anhui, and Jiangsu.
June 1344	Toghto resigned as chancellor of the right. Over the next several years, the dynasty's troubles mounted. Revenue shortages, floods and famine, outbreaks of piracy, and rebellions threatened China's stability.
October 1344	Zhu Yuanzhang (CHU YUAN-CHANG), 16 years old, from a poor tenant farmer family in Anhui, entered a Buddhist monastery as a menial laborer after the death of his parents in an epidemic. He would rise from these humble origins to found the Ming dynasty.

1345–1347	Zhu Yuanzhang wandered through the Huai River Valley as a mendicant monk.
August 1349	The emperor recalled Toghto, hoping he could save the tottering dynasty.
April 1351	The government began a project to re-channel the flood-prone Yellow River, mobilizing 170,000 troops and laborers. Thousands of peasants assembled for the river project joined the insurgent militias.
Summer 1351	Popular uprisings erupted in the Huai River Valley and spread rapidly throughout China. One important rebel group was known as the Red Turbans.
April 1352	Zhu Yuanzhang joined a rebel group and rose swiftly to become a trusted adviser of the rebel leader Guo Zixing.
1353	The Yuan government, reacting to chronic grain shortages, established state farms for cultivating rice in northern China.
January 1355	The emperor dismissed Toghto just as his counteroffensive appeared close to victory over the rebels in northern China. His removal gave the insurgents renewed life.
1355	The rebel Liu Futong enthroned Han Lin'er as King Xiaomingwang of Song (Junior King of Brightness), who became the nominal leader of all rebel forces.
July 1355	Zhu Yuanzhang led a rebel army across the Yangtze River toward Nanjing.
Ninth month, 1355	Guo Zixing died. Zhu Yuanzhang took over his army.
1356	Paper money ceased to circulate in Yuan China. Toghto's inflationary policies made it worthless after he printed vast amounts of paper currency to fund state projects and quell the rebellion.
April 1356	Zhu Yuanzhang entered Nanjing.
June 1358	Insurgents under Liu Futong captured Kaifeng.
January 1359	Rebels destroyed the Yuan summer capital at Shangdu.
September 1359	Yuan loyalist forces recaptured Kaifeng.
1363	Various rebel leaders vied for control of the Yangtze Valley. Liu Futong died in battle.
September 30–October 1, 1363	In a great battle on the Yangtze River, Zhu's fleets destroyed one of his leading rivals for supremacy in the region, taking 50,000 prisoners.

1366	Zhu ordered the rebuilding of Nanjing into an imperial capital.
First month, 1366	Zhu's forces "invited" Xiaomingwang to join Zhu, only to drown Xiaomingwang while crossing the Yangtze.
October 1, 1367	After a 10-month siege, Zhu's army entered Suchou, confirming his control over the middle and lower Yangtze regions. As the surviving warlord of the civil wars of the 1360s, he prepared to lead his army north through Shandong, Henan, and Hebei to the seat of Yuan power.
November 1367	Zhu ordered the invasion of the northern China plain.
January 23, 1368	With an offering of sacrifices to heaven and Earth, supporters proclaimed Zhu Yuanzhang the first emperor of the Ming dynasty. Ascending as Taizu, he became the first commoner to reign in China in 1,500 years.
March–April 1368	Ming forces gained control of Shandong.
April 1368	A Ming column occupied Kaifeng.
May 1368	Ming columns pacified Henan Province.
August 1368	Ming forces advanced on Beijing.
September 1368	The Yuan court fled Beijing just ahead of the Ming entry into the Mongol capital.
1370	Shundi, the last Yuan emperor, died in Mongolia.

KEY RESEARCH SOURCES

Dardess, John. *Confucians and Conquerors: Aspects of Political Change in Late Yuan China*. New York: Columbia University Press, 1973.

Franke, Herbert, and Denis Twitchett, eds. *Cambridge History of China*. Vol. 6. New York: Cambridge University Press, 1994.

Langlois, John D., Jr., ed. *China under Mongol Rule*. Princeton: Princeton University Press, 1981.

Rossabi, Morris. *Khubilai Khan: His Life and Times*. Berkeley: University of California Press, 1988.

13. MING DYNASTY

(1368–1644)

The first Ming emperor established an authoritarian tone for the new dynasty. The commoner who seized the throne and reigned as Taizu put a stamp of violence on the Ming. His limited vision—an aspect of Confucianism that regarded agriculture as the source of the nation's strength and stigmatized trade and wealth as parasitic—contributed to China's growing economic and technological stagnation.

All the same, China prospered for much of the 277-year Ming era. The population doubled during the course of the dynasty, to around 160 million. Literacy rates rose. Trade flourished, especially over the last two-thirds of the dynasty. Foreign trade brought in vast quantities of silver. Chinese silks and porcelain were in demand everywhere. A high degree of regional economic specialization evolved: The Yangtze River delta became a center for cotton and silk production; Fujian in the southeast grew tobacco and sugar cane; and neighboring Jiangxi manufactured the best Chinese porcelain.

Literature, philosophy, education, and the arts flourished. More books circulated in Ming China than in all the rest of the world. China turned inward during the Ming, though, which had long-term consequences. Just as the Europeans were setting out on their voyages of discovery, China, obsessed with frontier security, dismantled its great seagoing fleets. New laws restricted overseas trade. The Great Wall as it stands today was a product of the Ming period. Its purpose was to keep the Mongols out—an apt symbol for a dynasty that sought to keep the world at arm's length.

1368	The first emperor of the Ming (Brilliant) dynasty razed the Yuan palaces of Beijing. Taizu retained Nanjing as his capital and ordered the construction of a 30-mile network of walls to enclose the city.
	The emperor acted swiftly to implement traditional Confucian policies. He reduced government spending. In an attempt to make the army pay its way, he revived the old soldier-farmer system, under which the troops were responsible for their own subsistence. He lightened the tax burden on the peasantry and increased it for the commercial and scholarly classes. He pursued land reclamation and transportation projects.
1368	The first Ming emperor founded the Imperial Academy, drawing students from the sons and relatives of imperial officials. Local schools referred worthy sons of commoners to the academy.
1369	Taizu brought eleven Muslim astronomers to the capital to prepare an improved Chinese calendar.
June 1370	The emperor re-instituted civil service recruitment examinations.
Summer 1370	Taizu ordered grain stocks distributed in drought-stricken areas of the Yellow River Valley.

1371	Unhappy with the quality of the candidates, Taizu ignored the outcome of the recruitment exams and suspended the examination system for 10 years.
January 1371	Taizu sent a military expedition into the small surviving Xixia state in Sichuan.
August 1371	Ming forces reached the Xia capital of Chongqing and continued on to Chengdu. The empire then absorbed the Xixia remnant.
1372	The Mongols halted Ming expansion north of the Great Wall.
1376	The scholar-official Ye Boju (YEH BO-CHU) submitted a memorial criticizing the emperor for harsh punishments of civil servants for minor offenses. Imprisoned for his pains, he died of starvation.
1378–1385	Ming armies campaigned in Sichuan, suppressing a series of revolts of aboriginal peoples, including a long-running insurgency of the Tong tribe in the Huguang area.
1380	Taizu charged his chief minister, Hu Weiyong (HU WEI-YUNG), with conspiring against him and ordered Hu and his allies put to death. An estimated 15,000 perished in the purges. During Taizu's 30-year reign, an estimated 100,000 functionaries were put to death. With Hu's death, Taizu abolished the office of chief minister, making the six boards—Civil Office, Revenue, Rites, War, Justice, and Works—the top level of Ming government. Each agency head reported directly to the emperor.
1381	Taizu ordered the reorganization of the peasantry into registered groups of 110 households, with individual households responsible on a rotating basis for collecting taxes and labor services.
1381–1382	The Ming invaded, conquered, and absorbed the provinces of Yunnan and Guizhou in southwestern China.
1382	The emperor formed a unit of personal troops known as the Embroidered-Uniform Guard. It had an eventual strength of 75,000 men.
1382	In response to accusations that he favored Buddhist teachings, Taizu ordered sacrifices to Confucius throughout China. He believed that the three great systems, Confucianism, Buddhism, and Daoism, could be blended into one doctrine.
September 1382	Taizu re-established the civil service examination system.
May 1388	A 150,000-strong Chinese army traversed the Gobi Desert and routed the Mongols 500 miles north of Beijing, seizing 80,000 captives and 150,000 head of livestock.

1393	A government census put China's registered population at 60,543,812—an undercount of as many as 20 million.
1397	Scholars compiled the final version of the Great Ming Law Code.
June 24, 1398	Taizu died after an illness.
June 30, 1398	The late emperor's 16-year-old grandson ascended the throne as Huidi (HUI-TI). He moved to soften the harsher elements of the first emperor's legal code and reduced tax rates in some parts of China. The new ruler began to deprive his uncles of military power, sentencing some of them to death.
August 5, 1399	To protect his position, the Prince of Yan rebelled against Huidi, touching off a three-year civil war.
1400	Some 200,000 Chinese military colonists were resettled among the indigenous tribes of Yunnan and Guizhou.
Mid-January 1400	The Prince of Yan advanced from his bases around Beijing southwest into Shanxi.
May 18, 1400	The Prince of Yan defeated the imperial forces in a battle in which 600,000 men were said to have fought.
Summer 1401	The Prince of Yan's forces raided the Grand Canal route that supplied the imperial army.
January 1402	The Prince of Yan advanced south toward the imperial capital at Nanjing.
July 3, 1402	The Prince of Yan's army crossed the Yangtze River and pushed up to the walls of Nanjing.
July 13, 1402	Nanjing fell to the Prince of Yan, who claimed Emperor Huidi and his wife had died in a palace fire; others suggested that Huidi fled in the disguise of a Buddhist monk.
July 17, 1402	The Prince of Yan ascended the Ming throne; he was best known by his reign title, Yongle (YUNG-LO). His purges claimed tens of thousands of the second Ming emperor's loyalists. The Yongle emperor made plans to transfer the imperial capital to Beijing, mobilizing hundreds of thousands of workers to build the Forbidden City—the complex of imperial palaces in the heart of the city. He reigned until 1424.
1403–1419	The Nanjing shipyards launched 2,000 vessels, including 100 ships of 370 to 440 feet in length.
July 1405	The Muslim eunuch Zheng He (CHENG HO, 1371–1433) sailed on the first of his seven voyages into the "Western Oceans." The fleet, with 300 ships and 27,000 men, made port at

Champa, Java, Sumatra, Malacca, Ceylon, and South India. The ship's holds carried silks, embroidery, and other luxury goods as gifts for local rulers.

The first three of Zheng's voyages were to India, the fourth reached Hormuz on the Persian Gulf, and the last three touched on the coast of eastern Africa. China failed, however, to exploit the technical gains of Zheng's long-distance voyages, and no successor built on his maritime achievements.

1406	China sent an army to Annam (northern Vietnam) to support the weak Tran dynasty there.
Autumn 1406	A Chinese punitive expedition captured important towns in the Red River delta of Annam.
1407	Two thousand scholars completed a massive work that attempted to incorporate the full range of classical Chinese learning. The Great Literary Repository of the Yongle Reign contained classical texts, historical accounts, ritual, law, military affairs, philosophy, religion, natural history, medicine, geography, and literature.
1407	Zheng He's fleet engaged the notorious Chinese pirate Zhen Zu (CHEN TSU) off the coast of Sumatra and sent Zhen's fleet to the bottom of the sea. Zhen was taken prisoner, transported to Nanjing, and executed.
June 1407	Chinese forces seized key Annamite leaders and bore them in triumph to Nanjing. Rebellions against the occupying Chinese erupted at once, however.
1408	Construction of the new palace complex eventually to be known as the Forbidden City began at Beijing.
1410	The emperor began the practice of using eunuchs to supervise generals commanding troops on expeditions.
1410–1424	China carried out five campaigns intended to disperse the Mongol tribes raiding along the northern frontier. In the first campaign, the Yongle emperor led an army of 300,000 from Beijing north to Ulan-Bator in Mongolia.
July 1411	The Ming government began rebuilding the northern section of the Grand Canal. Three hundred thousand laborers cleared 130 miles of the canal and reconstructed or repaired 38 locks to speed grain shipments to the new Ming capital at Beijing.
July 1415	Ming engineers and laborers completed the southern section of the Grand Canal linking the Yellow River to the Yangtze River.

1417	The Great Compendium of the Philosophy of Human Nature appeared, containing selections from orthodox Confucian texts. With the Great Compendium of the Five Classics and Four Books (1415), it became the official standard of Ming learning.
c. 1420	As many as 100,000 artisans and other skilled workers served the imperial household in Beijing.
October 1420	The Ming formally designated Beijing as China's principal capital.
1422–1424	Ming forces launched new campaigns against the steppe tribes of the north.
August 12, 1424	Yongle died of an illness during the fifth and last of the inconclusive Mongol campaigns.
September 7, 1424	Yongle's son ascended the throne. Like his father and like his successors, he was known commonly by the reign name—in his case, Hongxi (HUNG-HSI).
May 29, 1425	The Hongxi emperor died at age 47.
June 27, 1425	Xuande (HSUAN-TE) succeeded his father as emperor of the Ming.
1427	China withdrew from Annam, giving up its 20-year effort to subdue the territory. Annam agreed to nominal tributary status in return for China's recognition of its independence.
1427	The Xuande emperor ordered the establishment of a foundry for fine bronze and copper vessels. Among other items, the foundry produced the famous Ming incense burners.
1428	Xuande compiled a guide for emperors, drawn from Confucian principles. He called it Imperial Injunctions.
1431–1433	Zheng He's seventh and last maritime expedition touched at Champa, Java, Sumatra, Malacca, the Indian Malabar Coast, and Hormuz on the Persian Gulf.
January 31, 1435	Xuande died of natural causes. His son, eight years old, ascended as Zhengtong (CHENG-T'UNG). Eunuchs rose to great power in this reign.
1436	*The Newly Compiled Four Character Glossary*, a primer, appeared in print.
1439	Grand Canal and Yellow River flooding caused massive loss of life.
1443–1445	Oirat Mongol tribes imposed effective control of the Chinese frontier from Manchuria in the east to Hami at the base of the Altai Mountains in the west.

1445	A famine in Shanxi forced thousands of peasants onto the roads in search of food.
1447–1449	Silver miners rose in rebellion in Zhejiang Province.
1448	Locusts and drought devastated northern China farmlands.
March 1448	Tenant farmers along the Fujian-Jiangxi border rebelled.
February 1449	Government forces captured the Fujian peasant leaders, carried them to Beijing, and put them to death.
July 1449	The Mongol chieftain Esen led a large-scale raid into China. The emperor opted to personally command a hastily mobilized army of 500,000.
September 1, 1449	The Mongols defeated the Chinese army at Tumu and made the emperor a prisoner.
September 1449	Rather than ransom the emperor, the Ming court enthroned his half-brother as his replacement and prepared to defend Beijing. He ascended as Jingtai (CHING- T'AI). The one courtier foolhardy enough to protest the arrangement was put to death.
October–November 1449	Beijing withstood a brief siege before the Mongol army pulled out and withdrew to the north.
1450–1457	Ming artisans created cloisonné vessels that had peony, lotus, and chrysanthemum designs in blue, turquoise, and green.
1453–1454	Tens of thousands perished in bitter winter weather; in some places, snow covered the ground for 40 days. Harsh weather as far south as Hunan took a heavy toll of livestock.
Early 1457	The former emperor won release from his Mongol captors. A coup restored him to the throne with the reign name of Tianshun (T'IEN-SHUN).
March 14, 1457	The deposed emperor died; he might have been the victim of the palace eunuchs.
1464	The Miao and Yao tribes revolted. From its beginnings in Guangxi Province, the rebellion spread to Hunan, Guizhou, Jiangxi, and the prosperous urban centers of Guangdong.
February 23, 1464	Chenghua (CH'ENG-HUA) ascended the Ming throne. He proved a dissolute man. A worsening financial situation and further growth in the eunuch bureaucracy blighted his reign.
Late Summer 1465	A 200,000-man Ming punitive expedition suppressed the Miao and Yao insurgents in a bloody campaign.

December 1465–January 1466	Imperial forces stormed the main rebel bastions in Big Rattan Gorge. The Yao leader and 800 of his men were captured, taken to Beijing, and beheaded.
1465–1476	The Qing-Xiang uprising in the refugee-choked middle Yangtze region sapped imperial resources. Government troops recorded initial successes, but the rebellion re-ignited as famine and epidemic increased the refugee influx. Imperial officials at last recommended a social solution, and the region grew quiet.
1472–1529	Life span of the scholar-official Wang Shouren (also known as Wang Yangming). His new form of neo-Confucianism became influential in Ming China. A capable soldier and administrator, he stressed tapping the moral force that he believed exists within all men. His teachings provoked an outbreak of factionalism in the Ming civil service. See "China A to Z" entry on Wang Yangming (a.k.a. Wang Shouren) on page 597.
1475–1476	The Miao tribe again rose in rebellion. Imperial forces crushed it, killing thousands.
1476	Buddhism and Daoism were vigorous in China, with 100,000 monks ordained in this year alone.
1485	Ten thousand eunuchs were employed in the imperial service.
Late 1480s	Chronic breaching of the Yellow River dikes in Shandong caused intermittent flooding that cost many lives and halted traffic on the Grand Canal.
September 9, 1487	The Chenghua emperor died.
September 17, 1487	Chenghua's son ascended the throne as Hongzhi (HUNG-CHIH).
1493–1495	The Ming government mobilized 120,000 laborers to shift the main channel of the Yellow River to the southeast, an effort that relieved chronic flooding. The Ming-era works held until the 19th century.
c. 1500	The king of Portugal began collecting Ming porcelain.
June 19, 1505	Zhengde (CHENG-TE) ascended the Ming throne. He paid slight attention to affairs of state.
October 1511	Bandit gangs burned 1,000 imperial grain barges on the Grand Canal.
February 10, 1514	During a lantern festival in the Forbidden City, an open flame reached gunpowder stores and touched off an explosion and fire that destroyed the residential palaces. The emperor assembled 30,000 troops to rebuild the palaces.

1517	The first Portuguese ships dropped anchor in the Pearl River estuary below Guangzhou.
January 1521	The Portuguese ambassador reached Beijing, the first European envoy at the imperial court. He found the emperor ill, however, and failed to obtain an audience.
April 19, 1521	The Zhengde emperor died.
May 27, 1521	A young cousin succeeded the late emperor, taking the reign name Jiajing (CHIA-CHING). He ruled until 1567. The 11th emperor set up Daoist altars in his palace and became addicted to Daoist aphrodisiac and fertility potions. Recurrent revenue crises marked the reign, and the court and bureaucracy were chronically short of resources.
c. 1522	The Ming government sought to introduce the "single whip" tax reform in an effort to stimulate revenue. The reform, carried out in different places at different times, simplified tax rates and categories of payment. Separate taxes were often combined on a single bill, payable in silver.
1524	Hundreds of scholars gathered to protest at the palace gates in Beijing. The emperor ordered a crackdown. The protesters were beaten and 134 were imprisoned; 16 died of their injuries.
1527–1602	Life span of the philosopher Li Zhi (LI CHIH), author of *Book Burning*, *Book Holding* and other works. Li drew the ire of Ming officialdom and died in prison at age 75. See "China A to Z" entry on Li Zhi, page 573.
July–August 1542	The Mongol leader Altan Khan led raids into Shanxi, capturing or killing 200,000 Chinese, seizing a million head of livestock, and burning thousands of dwellings.
1545	The first Japanese merchant fleets called at Chinese pirate anchorages off the Zhejiang coast. Trade developed in defiance of government controls of foreign contacts.
April 1545	After a long drought, dust storms ruined the winter wheat and barley crops in northern China.
July–November 1547	The imperial Censorate reported piracy out of control in Zhejiang and Fujian provinces along China's southeastern coast. The official charged with suppressing piracy recommended strict enforcement of the ban against overseas trading.
January 1550	Local officials in Zhejiang petitioned the imperial court to lift the ban on foreign trading.
Autumn 1550	Altan Khan besieged Beijing and looted the suburbs but withdrew without attempting to capture the city.

April 1551	The Mongols agreed to halt their raiding in return for a guarantee of two fairs a year at which they could trade horses for tea and other goods.
Autumn 1551	China refused a Mongol request to trade cattle for beans and grain; in reprisal, the Mongols resumed their border raids.
1552	Francis Xavier, the founder of the Roman Catholic Jesuit religious order, died on an island off the Guangdong coast before he could reach the mainland.
1553	The Outer City rose on a site south of the Imperial City of Beijing.
Early 1555	Pirates attacked the rich Hangzhou region, killing thousands in the city's environs. The government mobilized a new piracy suppression campaign over the next four years and gradually regained control of the southeastern coast.
January 1556	An earthquake struck Shanxi and Shaanxi provinces. An estimated 800,000 people died in the Wei River Valley alone.
May 1557	A fire consumed the audience halls and southern ceremonial gates of the Forbidden City in Beijing.
1559	Drought in the Yangtze River delta reduced stocks of rice and pushed up grain prices.
March 1560	The Nanjing garrison rose in protest against cuts in rations. Rampaging soldiers killed the vice minister for revenue and hanged his unclad body from an arch. Fearing worse trouble, the government did not attempt to punish the mutineers.
1567	The Ming government repealed the ban on maritime trade and allowed Portugal to set up a trading center at Macao, on the southern coast.
January 23, 1567	The Jiajing emperor died.
1567–1572	Longqing (LUNG-CH'ING) reigned.
1570	China negotiated a peace treaty with the Mongol chief Altan Khan that promised to end the incessant raiding along the northern frontier.
1573	With the lifting of the ban on trade, Chinese merchants established relations with Spanish colonists in the Philippines. Trade soon flourished, with Chinese silks and porcelains exchanged for silver flowing from the New World to Manila.
1573–1620	The Wanli emperor reigned. During the early years of his era, capable ministers restored the empire's finances. Later, stalemate ensued between the emperor and the bureaucracy. Infighting among the powerful corps of 70,000 eunuchs and the

professional civil service so disgusted Wanli that he withdrew from affairs, declining for many years to see his ministers or make necessary government appointments.

1574   The Ming government erected a barrier wall at Macao to isolate the Portuguese colonists there.

1577   With imperial demand for high-quality porcelain at its height, the Jingdezhen kilns in Jiangxi produced nearly 100,000 small pieces, 56,600 large pieces, and 21,600 pieces for sacrificial ceremonies.

1577   The head of the Jesuit missions in East Asia, Alessandro Valignano, directed China-bound missionaries to learn Chinese manners and customs before they began work.

1578   China granted permission to Portuguese merchants to push up the Pearl River to trade at Guangzhou.

1581   The Ming government renewed the tax reform effort, mandating a single tax to be paid in silver.

1583   Nurhaci, born in 1552, rose to become chieftain of the fisher-hunter-farmer tribes of Jurchen stock that inhabited the hills and forests of central Manchuria—present-day Heilongjiang and Jilin provinces. Nurhaci organized the entire population into military units called banners, after the colored pennants that identified individual commands. He eventually assembled eight banners, as well as eight banners each of Chinese and Mongol subjects. Over a period of three decades, Nurhaci built a powerful state on the Chinese model. After 1635, his people were known to the world as the Manchu.

1583   The Italian Jesuit missionary Matteo Ricci landed at Macao in southern China.

1587   The Buddhist White Lotus sect rebelled in Shandong.

May 1592   Japan, under Toyotomi Hideyoshi, invaded Korea with 150,000 soldiers. China mobilized to expel the Japanese.

1593   *The Pictorial Reference Compendium*, a manual covering agriculture, medicine, cooking, and other subjects, appeared in print.

January 1593   A Chinese expeditionary force crossed the Yalu River and advanced into Korea. The Japanese routed the Chinese army north of Seoul; an armed truce followed.

1593–1657   Life span of Tan Qian (TAN CH'IAN). His National Deliberations presented a history of the Ming dynasty in annals form.

1595   The Jesuit Matteo Ricci based his mission in Nanjing.

1597–1598	Chinese and Japanese forces in Korea resumed hostilities. Muskets were used extensively in these battles. The Japanese forces lost their momentum after Hideyoshi's death in mid-1598. By the end of 1598, joint Chinese and Korean forces destroyed the Japanese fleet, forcing the complete withdrawal of the Japanese army.
1598	Dramatist-satirist Tang Xianzu (T'ANG HSIEN-TSU, 1550–1616) finished the *Peony Pavilion*. That work, *Purple Hairpin*, *The Dream of Han Tan*, and *Southern Tributary State* are known together as the *Four Dreams of Linchuan*. Linchuan was the name of Tang's home county in Jiangxi.
1599	Merchants in Lingqing in Shandong Province struck in protest of high taxes, burning the Ming tax collector's office to emphasize their point.
c. 1600	After decades of steady growth, China's population reached 150–175 million, according to modern estimates.
1600	More than 700,000 Chinese colonists were settled in Yunnan and Guizhou.
1601	Ten thousand porcelain workers rioted to protest Ming demands for increased production.
1601–1609	Matteo Ricci shifted his mission to Beijing. He noted, in contrast with his native Italy, the large number of books in circulation in China's capital and their low cost. Ricci was welcomed at the imperial court, but he made few converts and those few only among the educated elite.
1602	Dutch traders began exporting large quantities of Chinese porcelain. Over the next 80 years, the Dutch East India Company shipped 12 million pieces to Europe.
October 1603	Spanish forces massacred 20,000 Chinese colonists on Luzon in the Philippines.
1604	The Donglin Academy near Wuxi in Jiangsu Province became a center for scholar-officials critical of the direction of the Ming.
1604	The emperor was in full retreat from the business of government. The magistracies of half the empire were vacant, as were many other offices.
1609	The Jia Canal, 110 miles long, opened for traffic.
1610	The Ming faced bankruptcy, its treasury emptied by military campaigns and the burden of paying stipends to more than 20,000 imperial clansmen.

1613–1682	Life span of Gu Yanwu (KU YEN-WU), essayist on government, ethics, economics, and social relations. His work influenced the Kaozheng movement of the 18th century.
1614	Jesuit missionaries were active in nine of China's 15 provinces. By mid-century, there were an estimated 150,000 Chinese Christians.
1616	Nurhaci proclaimed himself khan of the Great Jin (often known as Later Jin by historians), successor state to the Jurchen enemy of Song China and the forerunner of the Manchu dynasty. The Great Jin succeeded the Mongols of the steppes as the main threat to China's security. As a sign of submission, all men in Mongol dominions were forced to adopt the Manchu hairstyle—a shaved forehead with the rest of the hair braided in a long plait.
1616–1705	Life span of the painter and Ming imperial clansman Zhu Da (CHU TA). He refused to collaborate with the Manchu, preferring his expressionistic paintings of birds, fish, and scenes from nature to the artistic tastes of the Qing court.
March 1619	The Ming launched a punitive campaign against Nurhaci's Great Jin state. Within a few weeks, the Manchu won a series of battles and threatened Beijing.
April 1620	The government increased land taxes for a third time since the outbreak of war with the Great Jin.
August 18, 1620	The Wanli emperor died, ending a 48-year reign. Taichang ascended the throne.
September 1620	The new emperor fell ill and swallowed a large dose of a suspect medication called red pills.
September 26, 1620	The Taichang emperor died.
October 1, 1620	Tianqi (T'IEN-C'HI) ascended as the 15th emperor of the Ming. Historians presented him as weak and dull, and his reign was regarded as a disaster, largely because of his reliance on the corrupt eunuch Wei Zhongxian (WEI CHUNG-HSIEN).
1621	The Manchu occupied Shenyang in southeastern Manchuria.
1621–27	Fires swept Beijing, Hangzhou, and other large cities, consuming tens of thousands of homes and businesses.
1622	Chinese subjects in Manchu-ruled Liaodong rose in rebellion. The Manchu savagely put down the uprising.
June 1622	White Lotus Buddhists revolted in Shandong. Their forces blocked the Grand Canal, captured 50 imperial grain barges, and temporarily severed the supply line to Beijing and the imperial forces fighting in the northeast.

July 1624	Wei Zhongxian replied to accusations of corruption from Donglin reformers by launching a savage repression.
1624–1627	At Wei Zhonxian's order, Donglin leaders were arrested, tortured, and executed or driven to suicide; hundreds of others were stripped of public office.
1625	The philosopher Li Zhi remained so influential 20 years after his death that the emperor ordered the censors to collect and burn the wooden printing blocks of his works.
1625	A new Chinese insurgency broke out in Liaodong. Manchu rulers suppressed the rebellion and executed members of the literati suspected of stirring unrest.
1625	Nurhaci made Shenyang the Manchu capital.
Spring 1626	Ming forces turned back a Great Jin offensive; Nurhaci died of wounds during the campaign. His eighth son Huang Taiji (HUANG T'AI-CHI, 1592–1643) succeeded him.
1626–1643	Huang Taiji ruled as chieftain of the Manchu. He extended Chinese governmental institutions and imported Chinese officials to staff his bureaucracy.
September 30, 1627	The Tianqi emperor died.
October 1627	The emperor demoted the powerful eunuch Wei Zhongxian and assigned him an unimportant post in the provinces.
October 2, 1627	Tianqi's younger brother ascended, taking the reign name Chongzhen (CH'UNG-CHEN). He ruled as the last emperor of the Ming dynasty.
December 1627	Expecting and fearing arrest, Wei Zhongxian hanged himself.
1627–1628	Severe famine caused widespread distress in northern Shaanxi. The famine was a consequence of a "little" ice age in much of China during the first decades of the 17th century. Army deserters and others formed gangs that plundered the Shaanxi, Shanxi, Hebei, Henan, and Anhui countrysides. The Ming government seemed powerless to quell the bandit gangs.
December 1629	Manchu forces swept over the Great Wall defenses and threatened Beijing.
1630s	China's trade with the Spanish Philippines and Japan rose sharply. An estimated 2 million silver pesos a year flowed into China from Manila, the Philippine capital.
January 1630	The Manchu invaders defeated a Ming army only 30 miles from Beijing. They withdrew without attacking the capital, however.

1630–1638	Peasant uprisings spread through China's heartland. Rebel groups expanded their operations from Shaanxi northeast into Shanxi, east into Henan, southwest into Sichuan, and southeast as far as Jiangxi.
1636	The insurgent leader Li Zicheng became paramount in northern China. Bandit chieftain Zhang Xianzhong (CHANG HSIEN-CHUNG, 1605–1647) asserted control of most of the region between the Yellow and Yangtze Rivers.
1636	Hong Taiji of the Later Jin proclaimed a new dynasty, the Qing (pure) and took the title of emperor.
1638	Chen Zilong (CH'EN TZU-LUNG) and others published *A Collection of Essays on National Affairs During the Ming Dynasty*, a book of source materials on dynastic history and politics.
1638	The Qing Manchu forced Korea to give up its tributary relationship with Ming and became a Qing vassal state.
1639	Famine, disease, insurgency, and banditry caused widespread distress in China; imperial forces were increasingly helpless in the face of such calamities.
Summer 1639	Japan barred the century-old trade between Nagasaki and Macao. Around the same time, Spain restricted the silver flow into China. The resulting silver shortage led to deflation, tax defaults, rent riots, grain hoarding, and other signs of social dislocation.
1642	Rebels breached the Yellow River dikes; several hundred thousand people died in the floods and subsequent famine.
April 1642	The Ming defense line along the Great Wall crumbled under Manchu pressure. Manchu columns pressed their offensive in northeast China, taking 360,000 prisoners and enormous amounts of plunder.
May–October 1642	Li Zicheng's bandit army laid siege to Kaifeng. Several hundred thousand people died in the city, many from starvation and disease.
1643	Zhang Xianzhong declared himself Emperor of the Great West in Chengdu, Sichuan.
1643	First and second places in the now hopelessly corrupt imperial examination system went to the highest bidders.
Summer 1643	Li Zicheng prepared to attack Beijing.
Autumn 1643	Hong Taiji died; his third son, Fulin, ascended the throne. Fulin is generally referred to as Emperor Shunzhi in historical records.

Early 1644	Li Zicheng proclaimed himself King of the Great Shun.
April 25, 1644	With Zicheng's forces about to breach the Ming defense at Beijing, the last Ming emperor hanged himself in the Forbidden City palace compound. Li Zicheng's army entered the city later in the day. General Wu Sangui, commander of the Ming forces at the strategic Shanhaiguan Pass of the Great Wall, invited the Qing forces in to attack the rebels.
June 4, 1644	With the approach of the Manchu, Li Zicheng retreated from Beijing.
June 5, 1644	The Manchu prince Dorgon entered Beijing, marking the start of Manchu rule in China.

KEY RESEARCH SOURCES

Ebrey, Patricia. *Cambridge Illustrated History of China*. New York: Cambridge University Press, 1996.

Farmer, Edward. *Early Ming Government: The Evolution of Dual Capitals*. Cambridge, Mass.: Harvard University Press, 1976.

Huang, Ray. *1587, a Year of No Significance: The Ming Dynasty in Decline*. New Haven: Yale University Press, 1981.

Twitchett, Denis, and Frederick W. Mote, eds. *The Cambridge History of China*. Vol. 8, *The Ming Dynasty, 1368–1644, Parts 1 and 2*. New York: Cambridge University Press, 1998.

14. QING DYNASTY

(1644–1912)

The Qing dynasty dates from 1644, but nearly a generation would pass before the Manchu overwhelmed the last of the Ming claimants and were sovereign over all of China. The Manchu ruled with the aid of Chinese collaborators and the passive acceptance of most of the population of China.

The enforced act of submission—the Manchu-style tonsure with the pleated braid—was humiliating for the Chinese. The Manchu preserved many of China's traditional beliefs and social structures, however, and followed Confucian rituals at court. They governed in the Chinese way, with a dual Manchu-Chinese bureaucracy. First restoring and then maintaining order in the countryside, they won over the Chinese gentry.

The nation was stable for the first century and a half of the Qing. China expanded beyond its present boundaries, annexing Taiwan, Chinese Turkestan, and Mongolia and claiming suzerainty over Tibet. Three capable emperors ruled for a span of more than 130 years. The first confirmed Manchu rule but courted the Chinese literati and landowning gentry. The second reformed the tax system. The third, one of the most cultured of all China's emperors, reigned for nearly 60 years, presiding over what many scholars regard as the high point of traditional Chinese civilization.

By the late 18th century, though, the golden era had begun to fade. Qing institutions became weak and ineffective. Factionalism and corruption spread through the bureaucracy. The army lacked discipline. Granaries were empty and famine relief inadequate. The Grand Canal silted up. The West caught and overtook China in power, prosperity, and technological innovation. In rural areas, a rapidly rising population led to frequent social disturbances. Deforestation and soil erosion degraded the environment.

The explosion of the Taiping Rebellion and two concurrent insurgencies in the mid-19th century nearly destroyed the dynasty. Some 20 million Chinese died in the Taiping outbreak. During the last decades of the century, the Qing tried to adapt Western technology and economic practices to China's needs, building railroads, telegraph lines, steamships, heavy industrial plants, and specialized schools. Concurrently, the encroachments of the foreign powers further undermined the Qing, which was increasingly incapable of defending itself.

By 1900, despite the material gains of the Self-Strengthening Movement that sought to modernize China, the dynasty barely stood. China's venerable institutions seemed incapable of meeting the challenges of modern life. Because of diplomacy and force, China granted long-term territorial leases to foreign powers. Foreign missionaries had free run of the country. Foreign businesses opened factories in China.

External pressures and internal rebellion brought about the final collapse. With no clear successor to the fallen dynasty, a long, disturbed interregnum followed the Qing: warlord rule, ideological conflict, invasion, world war, civil war, and revolution.

June 6, 1644	A son of Hong Taiji ascended the throne as the boy emperor of the Qing; he ascended as Shunzhi (SHUN-CHIH), with Prince Dorgon as regent. The new rulers chased the eunuchs from the court, established day-to-day government authority, confiscated vast areas of northern China farmland to support their armies, and ordered Chinese men to sever their forelocks and start a queue.

Summer 1644	The Prince of Fu, a grandson of the Ming Emperor Wanli, ascended as emperor. He and his supporters sought to rally resistance to the Manchu conquerors.
December 1644	The rebel leader Zhang Xianzhong (CHANG HSIEN-CHUNG) proclaimed the Great Western Kingdom in Sichuan. He ruled from Chengdu.
Early 1645	Manchu forces pushed south down the line of the Grand Canal.
Spring 1645	Manchu columns pursued the Great Shun Army of Li Zicheng (LI TZU-CH'ENG) into the mountains of frontier Jiangxi; Li died (or was murdered) there during the summer.
May 1645	After a short siege, the Manchu seized and thoroughly ransacked the rich commercial city of Yangzhou.
June 1645	Nanjing surrendered to the Manchu. The invaders captured the Prince of Fu and led him away to Beijing, where he died in 1646.
July 1645	A Manchu decree threatened execution for any Chinese man who failed to cut his hair and start a queue within 10 days.
1646	The Manchu restored the national civil service examination system. As in the Ming, the system rested on memorization and analysis of orthodox Confucian texts and on a few approved commentaries, namely Zhu Xi's, on the Confucian canon.
January 1647	Manchu forces tracked down and killed Zhang Xianzhong in Sichuan.
January 20, 1647	Guangzhou fell to the Manchu. The victors captured and publicly executed two Ming pretenders in the city.
1648	Chinese troops composed three-quarters of the Manchu banner military units. Mongols accounted for 8 percent of the total, the Manchu 16 percent.
1648	An uprising forced the Manchu to withdraw from Guangzhou.
1650	Qing forces recaptured Guangzhou and carried out a great slaughter of the Ming defenders.
1650	With the death of the regent Dorgon, Emperor Shunzhi (SHUN-CHIH, born 1638) began to rule in his own right. He learned the Chinese language and became an admirer of Chinese high culture. He formed a close friendship with the Jesuit missionary Johann Schall von Bell, whom he appointed to head the Imperial Bureau of Astronomy, an important imperial post because it oversaw the calendar, a matter of first interest to China's emperors.

1653–1659	The last known surviving grandson of the Wanli emperor, the Prince of Gui (1623–1662), held out as the last Ming claimant. From his base in the south, he retreated westward from Guangxi to Guizhou, Yunnan and, finally, Myanmar.
1659	The pirate and trader Zheng Chenggong (CHENG CH'ENG-KUNG), known to the West as Koxinga, led a failed attack on Manchu Nanjing. When Qing forces chased him to his stronghold of Xiamen (Amoy), he took his pirate army across the Strait of Formosa and attacked the Dutch on Taiwan.
March 1659	Remnants of the Prince of Gui's court and army crossed the frontier into Myanmar.
1660s	The Manchu imposed indirect control on southern China, leaving the region to the semi-autonomous rule of the Three Feudatories—Wu Sangui (WU SAN-KUEI), Shang Kexi (SHANG K'O-HSI), and Geng Jimao (KENG CHI-MAO). They were the Chinese commanders who subdued most of the region for the Qing in the 1650s. Wu ruled Yunnan, Guizhou, and parts of Hunan and Sichuan; Shang controlled Guangdong and part of Guangxi; and Geng governed Fujian.
1661	Shunzhi died, most likely of smallpox. After a regency, his eight-year-old son succeeded him as the Kangxi (K'ANG-HSI) emperor.
December 1661	Wu Sangui led a Qing column into Myanmar in pursuit of the last Ming claimant.
January 1662	Myanmar authorities turned over the Prince of Gui and his entourage to Wu Sangui.
February 1662	The Dutch on Taiwan surrendered to Zheng Chenggong. Though the pirate chieftain died later in the year, his successors built a powerful trading empire on the island. By the early 1680s, 100,000 Chinese had resettled in Taiwan.
May 1662	The Prince of Gui and his adolescent son were put to death in Yunnan.
1669	Kangxi, 15 years old, ascended as second emperor of the Qing. He ruled until 1722. A patron of the Chinese literati, Kangxi was also greatly interested in the Jesuits, especially because of their knowledge of Western science.
1670	The Kangxi emperor issued the Sacred Edict, a compilation of Confucian maxims on morality, manners, and social relations.
December 1673	The Chinese general Wu Sangui, heretofore an important ally of the Manchu, led an uprising against the Qing. Two other so-called feudatories followed him in rebellion. Wu proclaimed a new dynasty, the Zhou, and advanced northeast into Hunan.

1674	Geng Jingzhong (KENG CHING-CHUNG), who succeeded his father as ruler of Fujian, led a rebel army northward into Zhejiang.
Late 1670s	Zunghar Western Mongol tribes seized Kashgar, Hami, and Turfan in present Outer Mongolia and Qinghai along the Tibetan frontier.
1676	Geng Jingzhing surrendered to the Qing and was executed.
1676	The third of the feudatories, Shang Zhixin (SHANG CHIH-HSIN, son of Shang Kexi) marched north into Jiangxi at the head of an insurgent column; his army collapsed under the weight of a Qing counterattack.
1677	Shang Zhixin surrendered and was put to death.
1678	Wu proclaimed himself emperor of the Zhou but died of dysentery later in the year. Qing loyalists advanced on his followers, pushing them steadily westward.
c. 1680	After decades of civil war, banditry, general unrest, famine, and other disasters, China's population was roughly 100 million, a decrease of 50 million or more from the estimated population at the beginning of the century.
1681	Zhou resistance collapsed in Yunnan; Qing authorities executed many Zhou leaders. Emperor Kangxi punished the leading rebels mercilessly but showed compassion for ordinary people caught up in events. With the crushing of the feudatories' rebellion, Qing confirmed its control over all of China.
July 1683	A Qing naval expedition of 300 warships destroyed the forces of Zheng Chenggong's descendants in the Pescadores.
October 1683	Taiwan fell to the Qing in October and was absorbed into the empire.
1688	Dramatist Hong Zheng (HUNG SHENG, 1645–1704) completed *The Palace of Eternal Youth,* a play set during the An Lushan Rebellion of the Tang dynasty.
1689	After a series of frontier confrontations, Chinese and Russian envoys negotiated a border agreement. The treaty of Nerchinsk fixed what remains the boundary between the two countries.
1692	The Kangxi emperor issued an edict extending religious tolerance to Christian converts who continued to perform ancestral rites. When a Vatican envoy barred Christians from performing the rites, the emperor rescinded the edict.
1696	A Qing army under the Kangxi emperor defeated the Zunghar at Jao Modo beyond the Gobi Desert northwest of Beijing.

1699	Kong Shangren (K'UNG SHANG-JEN, 1648–1718) completed his popular drama *The Peach Blossom Fan*. Set in the court of the Prince of Fu, the Ming pretender, it presents a Ming-era love story against a backdrop of imperial court intrigue.
1712	Kangxi emperor issued an edict freezing China's land tax. An effort to encourage land registration and accurate population counts, it had the longer-term effect of keeping the tax revenues of the empire depressed.
1717	Zunghar Mongols invaded Tibet. Qing responded with a counter-invasion of the mountain kingdom.
1720	China exported 400,000 pounds of tea to England annually. Chinese merchants in Guangzhou formed the trade association known as Cohong—combined merchant companies.
1720s	Qing authorities launched a crackdown on the opium trade. Dealers were banished to frontier military garrisons. The punishment for opium smoking: 100 strokes of the rod.
Autumn 1720	Chinese armies occupied Lhasa in Tibet, installed a new Dalai Lama loyal to the Qing, and established a permanent garrison in Lhasa.
December 1722	Kangxi died of old age at his Beijing palace. His son Yongzheng (YUNG-CHENG), 45 years old, ascended. He had a reputation as a diligent worker, a devoted Buddhist, and an adherent of conservative Confucian values.
1723	Eight thousand silk and cotton workers (known as calenderers) struck unsuccessfully for higher wages.
1724	Yongzheng banned Christianity, though the prohibition was not strictly enforced. Jesuits were permitted in Beijing only.
1726	The 800,000-page *Complete Collection of Illustrations and Writings from Earliest Times*, an encyclopedia, appeared in print.
1728	A Russian-Chinese commercial treaty allowed one Russian trading caravan to travel to Beijing every three years.
1729	Yongzheng established a secret office of finance to handle important state issues. Europeans dubbed this small group of senior officials the Grand Council.
1729	English exports of opium into China reached 200 chests. Europeans pursued the opium trade as a means of righting the balance of trade with China.
1736–1795	Qianlong (CH'IEN-LUNG), the fourth son of Yongzheng, ascended at age 25 as the fourth emperor of the Qing dynasty. His would be the longest reign in China's history and one of

sustained population growth and general prosperity. Qianlong increased the collections of the imperial galleries, patronized Jesuit painters at court, and wrote and published 42,000 poems. Using European architects and painters, he built a magnificent Summer Palace, the Yuan Ming Yuan, on a lake on the outskirts of Beijing.

Signs of decay were becoming apparent, however. Population growth put increasing pressure on the land. Conflict with Europeans began to build. For all the glory of his reign, Qianlong postponed making hard, unpopular decisions.

c. 1750   Cotton and tobacco farming were widespread in northeastern China. Western Hemisphere crops such as the sweet potato, the Irish potato, and maize were spreading elsewhere in China, diversifying and improving the Chinese diet.

1750s   Qing absorbed the Muslim region of modern Xinjiang Province.

1751–1784   Qianlong completed six costly tours of the southern domains. The trips in 1751, 1757, 1762, 1765, 1780, and 1784 were said to have cost more than 20 million ounces of silver.

1754   The government declared the Cohong merchants liable for the behavior of ships' crews ashore in Guangzhou.

1759   A Qing army under the Manchu bannerman Zhaohui (CHAO HUI) captured the Zhungar strongholds of Kashgar and Yarkand on the far western frontier. The Manchu prohibited Chinese colonization of the region, however, and they exempted Muslim men from shaving their heads and growing queues.

1759   The Qing government restricted all foreign trade to the southern China city of Guangzhou. Foreign merchants were not allowed to leave their quarter of the city and could be in residence only during the October to March trading season.

1759   James Flint, a British East India Company official, petitioned the Qing court to lift trading restrictions in Guangzhou. The authorities arrested Flint and held him in prison for three years for making improper appeals to the throne.

c. 1765   Kaozheng scholars were widely influential. They used close textual study of the Confucian classics to determine which parts were the master's and which were added later. A leading kaozheng scholar was Dai Zhen (TAI CHEN, 1723–1777). In his later work, Dai relaxed his methodological rigor to speculate about human motivations and the meaning of moral action.

1768   The *Unofficial History of the Scholars,* a fictional account of the lives of the underemployed educated elite of the 18th century, appeared in print. It became an important Qing literary work.

1772–1782	On Qianlong's orders, thousands of books were examined for critical references to the Manchu. Some 2,000 titles were destroyed. At the same time, the emperor ordered scholars to undertake a massive compilation of the Chinese classics known as the Four Treasuries. This anthology filled 36,000 volumes.
1773	When a Portuguese court in the trading colony of Macao found a British subject innocent of murdering a Chinese, Qing officials seized the Briton, tried him in a Chinese court, and put him to death. This and other disputes led to Western demands that China waive jurisdiction over Europeans in the country.
1774	An herbal healer named Wang Lun led a White Lotus–inspired outbreak in Shandong. The insurgents seized several towns before powerful Qing forces gained the upper hand.
1784	The first merchant ships of the newly sovereign United States reached China.
1784–1785	The Qing government engaged in a general persecution of the small Catholic community of China. (There were an estimated 200,000 to 250,000 Chinese Catholics in 1800.)
1786	Triad secret societies mounted an uprising in Taiwan. The triads—bandits and racketeers with an anti-Manchu political platform—soon spread to the mainland in southern China.
December 1788	A Chinese army, intervening in a Vietnamese dynastic conflict, entered Hanoi.
January 1789	A Vietnamese counterattack chased Chinese forces back over the frontier into Guangxi. This was the last Chinese military campaign in Vietnam until the 1970s.
1790s	The scholar-official Hong Liangji (HUNG LIANG-CHI) composed a series of critical essays on China's problems—particularly population growth, which was outstripping the country's production capacity.
1792	Qing forces repulsed invading Nepalese Gurkhas in Tibet. Nepal agreed to send tribute to Beijing every five years and made the payments until 1908.
1792	The *Dream of the Red Chamber,* China's greatest novel, was published; it was incomplete when the author, Cao Xueqin, died in 1763. The novel follows the fortunes of the wealthy Jia family through their decline and fall.
1792	Detailed demographic records showed the average life span of villagers of Daoyi in southern Manchuria was 32 years. This was mainly because of the high rate of infant mortality, but few in Daoyi lived longer than 65 years.

June 1793	The British lord George Macartney's trade mission reached Guangzhou. Macartney's flotilla, a 66-gun warship with two escorting vessels, won permission to sail north to Tianjin, the port of entry for Beijing.
September 1793	Lord Macartney petitioned the Qing court for European-style relations between the two countries. He asked for the lifting of trade restrictions and for a British resident in Beijing. The emperor denied Macartney an audience at first, for the Briton refused to perform the submissive bow known as the *kowtow*. When they met finally, Qianlong rebuffed Macartney. The emperor showed no outward interest in the products of English industry offered him as gifts—scientific instruments, knives, and woolen goods.
1794–1856	Life span of the scholar Wei Yuan, whose Collected Writings analyzed Chinese government theory and practice.
1796	Qianlong officially retired but continued to control his government.
1796–1805	White Lotus rebellions exploded in Hubei, Sichuan, and Shaanxi Provinces. By 1805, Qing punitive campaigns reduced the White Lotus army, once 100,000 strong, to remnants.
1799	Qianlong died. His favorite, the corrupt and powerful Heshen (HO-SHEN), who dominated court life for the last 20 years of the reign, was arrested and forced to commit suicide.
1799–1820	Jiaqing (CHIA-CH'ING), who ascended the throne in 1796, finally took control of his government. He attacked corruption, reduced government expenses, and attempted to enact administrative reforms. His era saw a temporary lessening of tensions with Europe, then preoccupied with the Napoleonic Wars.
1800	The skyrocketing population of China passed 300 million. The lower Yangtze provinces were the most seriously overcrowded. The population of England reached 11 million.
1800	Needing cash to buy Chinese tea for the home market, the British East India Company stepped up its exports of opium into China, leading the Qing government to ban the import and domestic production of the addictive drug. China's annual tea exports to England totaled 23 million pounds, worth $3.6 billion. Imports of opium from British India reached 4,000 chests a year.
1803	Heavy floods silted up the Grand Canal. The resulting interruption of grain shipments to Beijing rekindled debate over proposals for a reliable sea route for grain transport—a recurring policy question in China since the Song dynasty.

1807	Robert Morrison of the London Missionary Society established a Protestant mission in China.
1810–1820	Li Ruzhen (LI JU-CHEN) wrote China's best-known satirical novel, *Flowers in the Mirror*. Li reversed gender roles in parts of the novel, subjecting men to the pain and humiliation many Chinese women suffered.
1813	China outlawed opium smoking.
1813	One hundred thousand followers of the millenarian Buddhist Eight Trigrams cult rose near Beijing and seized several towns. A rebel column reached one of the gates of Beijing before being turned back. The outbreak claimed 70,000 lives before imperial forces snuffed it out.
1815–1850	A steady outflow of silver, mainly the result of the booming illicit trade in opium, caused a long cycle of deflation, falling prices, and economic recession in Qing China.
1816	The British lord Amherst, William Pitt, led a trade and diplomatic mission to Beijing. On reaching the capital, he was turned away and ordered out of the country.
1819	The British missionary Robert Morrison and a collaborator translated the Old and New Testaments into Chinese.
1820s	The Xuehai Tang (Sea of Learning Hall) opened in Guangzhou. It evolved into an important center of scholarship in southern China.
1820s	There were an estimated 1 million opium addicts in China.
1820s	The triad secret societies spread north from Guangdong and Fujian to the Yangtze River provinces. The triads were racketeers, bandits, and sometime insurgents.
1821–1850	Daoguang (TAO-KUANG, born 1782) reigned as Qing emperor.
1826	Qing established a coastal patrol to cut down on opium smuggling. However, widespread bribery of Qing naval officers allowed the trade to continue.
1827	The scholar He Changling (HO CH'ANG-LING) published a compendium of documents and commentary on Qing statecraft. It covered the bureaucracy, taxes, banditry, famine relief, flood control, religion and other matters.
1827	With a spreading cult of widowhood, the government ordered that only collective arches could be built in honor of faithful widows.
1835	The medical missionary Dr. Peter Parker opened a hospital in Guangzhou.

1836	An imperial edict sought suppression of the British-controlled opium trade.
June 15, 1836	The British government appointed Charles Elliot, a former naval officer, trade commissioner for China.
January 1837	Officials supervising the opium crackdown in Guangzhou reported 2,000 dealers under arrest and traffic at a standstill. British traders vigorously resisted efforts to shut down the business.
1838	The British exported 40,000 chests of opium to China, with a value of $18 million. The exports fed the habits of an estimated 12.5 million Chinese opium smokers.
July 10, 1838	In a memorial to the Qing court, the scholar-official Lin Zexu (LIN TSE-HSU) recommended harsh punishments for opium smokers and the establishment of state sanatoriums to treat addicts. At the same time, he called for a renewed campaign against opium traders.
December 31, 1838	The government named Lin Zexu commissioner for suppression of the opium trade.
January–October 1839	In London, the British opium merchant William Jardine lobbied British officials for government protection of the Guangzhou merchants. He sought a blockade of China's ports, a new commercial treaty, and the opening of additional ports to Western trade.
March 18, 1839	Lin Zexu gave the Cohong merchants of Guangzhou, partners with the British in the opium trade, three days to persuade foreign traders to surrender their opium stocks. Western houses agreed to hand over a token 1,000 chests. (Opium was legal in Britain at this period and was widely used in the form of laudanum.)
March 24, 1839	Lin Zexu halted all foreign trade in Guangzhou after the foreign merchants refused to hand over leading British opium dealer Lancelot Dent. Lin's troops blockaded some 350 foreigners in their Guangzhou factories.
March 27, 1839	To break the deadlock, Charles Elliot, the British commissioner, ordered the merchants to surrender their opium stocks, estimated at $9 million.
Mid-May, 1839	Lin Zexu's crackdown produced 1,600 arrests and 35,000 pounds of opium. He eventually confiscated and destroyed 3 million pounds of raw opium.
July 4, 1839	Fearing arrest, the entire British community in Guangzhou withdrew to Portuguese Macao. Commissioner Elliot sent a plea to London for assistance in the dispute.

August 24, 1839	Under Chinese pressure, the Portuguese expelled British merchants from Macao. They established an outpost on sparsely populated Hong Kong Island.
September 4, 1839	British warships destroyed a Chinese naval squadron at Kowloon.
November 4, 1839	British warships opened fire on Chinese war junks in the Bogue, sinking four junks and scattering the rest. The Bogue is the mouth of the Pearl River at Guangzhou; *Bogue* is an English corruption of the Portuguese *boca tigre,* or "tiger's mouth."
1840s	Triad secret society networks spread among the peasantry of the Pearl River delta at Guangdong. Armed triad bands attacked southern China cities, briefly threatening Guangzhou.
February 20, 1840	The British government appointed Admiral George Elliot to command the naval task force bound for China.
June 21, 1840	A British force of 16 warships with 540 guns and 4,000 troops in 28 transports assembled off Macao. Admiral Elliot (Charles Elliot's cousin), left four ships to blockade Guangzhou and sailed north with the rest of the fleet.
July 5, 1840	The British bombarded Zhoushan, occupied the port, and clapped a blockade on neighboring Ningbo on mainland Zhejiang.
August 30, 1840	A British fleet standing off the Dagu forts at Tianjin compelled the Chinese to negotiate.
January 20, 1841	The Chinese envoy Qishan (CH'I-SHAN) and British negotiators reached an agreement that gave Great Britain the island of Hong Kong. China agreed to pay the cost of the British naval expedition (6 million Mexican silver dollars) and allow direct British-Chinese contacts. Both sides repudiated the tentative agreement. The Daoguang emperor, outraged, ordered Qishan put to death.
August 10, 1841	A new British plenipotentiary, Sir Henry Pottinger, arrived in Hong Kong.
June–July 1842	Reinforced from India, the British captured Shanghai and Zhenjiang, halting commercial traffic on the lower Yangtze River and the Grand Canal.
August 5, 1842	A British column pushed up to the walls of Nanjing.
August 11, 1842	China again asked Britain for peace.

August 29, 1842	British and Chinese envoys signed the Treaty of Nanjing aboard H.M.S. *Cornwallis* in the Yangtze River. The treaty awarded an additional indemnity of 21 million ounces of silver and opened five new treaty ports: Guangzhou, Xiamen, Fuzhou, Ningbo, and Shanghai. It placed a 5 percent tariff on imports, gave Hong Kong to Great Britain, and stipulated that British subjects would answer only to British law, even in disputes with Chinese. The treaty was a humiliation for China, long accustomed to making its own decisions about the status of foreigners in the country. It set the tone for a series of unequal treaties between China and European powers later in the century.
1844	A Presbyterian mission school opened in the treaty port of Ningbo with an enrollment of 30 Chinese boys. A separate mission school for girls also opened.
Spring 1844	American and Chinese diplomats negotiated the Treaty of Wanghia, which gave the United States rights in China similar to Great Britain's. The treaty also opened new opportunities for American Protestant missionaries.
October 1844	France negotiated a commercial treaty with China similar to the British and American agreements.
1845	More than 60 Catholic missionaries were working in China.
1850–1900	Outward migration increased as labor contractors recruited Chinese workers for Cuba, Peru, Hawaii, and Sumatra. Chinese workers were known as coolies, from the Chinese *kuli,* meaning "bitter labor."
1850	The population of China reached 425 million.
1850	A full translation of the Bible and a Manchu version of the New Testament circulated in China.
1850–1864	The Taiping Rebellion, the greatest peasant revolt of the 19th century, swept China under the leadership of the charismatic Hong Xiuquan (HUNG HSIU-CH'UAN, born 1814). He was a member of the ethnic Chinese minority Hakka and a failed examination candidate who believed himself to be the younger brother of Jesus. From his base in Guangxi, Hong directed his paramilitary followers to wreck temples and idols, give up alcohol and opium, and abandon the custom of binding the feet of women.
December 1850	Hong Xiuquan's militia routed an imperial force at Thistle Mountain.
1851	Nian insurgents rose in east-central China, north of the Huai River. Unlike Hong Xiuquan's rebels, the Nian had no direct religious affiliation or political program. Most were poor, landless single men.

1851–1861	Xianfeng (HSEIN-FENG) reigned as Qing emperor.
January 11, 1851	Hong Xiuquan declared himself monarch of the Heavenly Kingdom of Great Peace (Taiping). His insurgent forces advanced east and north, gaining adherents and weapons as they went.
1852	The first Chinese laborers reached Hawaii.
July–December 1852	The Qing loyalist Zeng Guofan (TSENG KUO-FAN, 1811–1872) raised a local militia, the Xiang Army, to defend his home province of Hunan from the Taiping. He rose to become the most effective imperial commander in the rebellion.
September 1852	The Taiping captured Changsha in Hunan.
December 1852	A Taiping army seized Yuezhou on Dongting Lake and captured a large stockpile of arms and ammunition.
January 1853	Taiping insurgents reached Wuchang, on the Yangtze River, then advanced on Nanjing.
March 19, 1853	Nanjing fell to the Taiping rebels. They slaughtered all the Manchu survivors of the battle, including women and children. The rebels ruled Nanjing for 11 years. They set up a government in Nanjing, called for land equalization (but failed to carry it out), and proposed equality between men and women. The Taiping based their system of civil service examinations on Hong Xiuquan's teachings and a Chinese translation of the Bible.
May 1853–May 1855	A Taiping expeditionary force moved north in an ill-advised campaign. After wintering near Tianjin in 1854 and 1855, Taiping columns began a slow, costly retreat southward. Qing loyalists wiped out the last remnants of the insurgent expedition in the spring of 1855.
1854	Yung Wing (1828–1912) graduated from Yale University, the first Chinese to take a degree from an American university.
1854	The Qing government established an Inspectorate of Customs staffed with foreigners. The agency collected maritime customs that sent a steady stream of revenue into the imperial treasury.
Mid-1850s	The annual value of the Shanghai silk trade reached $20 million.
1855	Heavy flooding of the Yellow River and a subsequent famine swelled the ranks of the Nian rebels north of the Huai River.
1855	Muslims rebelled in Yunnan in the southwest. Insurgent columns captured the city of Dali and advanced on the provincial capital of Kunming.

1856	Zhang Luoxing (CHANG LO-HSING) became Lord of the Alliance of Nian rebel groups. The Nian insurgents raided throughout east-central China from a series of strongholds north of the Huai River.
August 1856	To forestall a suspected coup, Hong Xiuquan ordered the execution of Taiping leader and chief military adviser Yang Xiuqing (YANG HSIU-CH'ING); 20,000 of Yang's followers were killed.
December 1856	Qing loyalists recaptured Wuchang from the Taiping rebels. By year's end, the loyalist Xiang army had regained most of Jiangxi.
December 28, 1857–January 4, 1858	Rebuffed in their effort to renegotiate the Treaty of Nanjing of 1842, the British seized Guangzhou.
May 1858	A British expedition captured the Dagu forts covering Tianjin, opening the way to Beijing.
July 3, 1858	British military pressure forced China to accept the Treaty of Tianjin. The new agreement protected Christianity, opened interior China to foreign travelers, extended trade up the Yangtze River as far as Hankou, and established 10 new treaty ports. The treaty also stipulated that the Chinese character for *barbarian*, used officially to describe the British, be dropped from Chinese documents.
September 1858	The resurgent Taiping defeated the Xiang (Hunan) army in northern Anhui.
June 1859	Attempting to enforce the Tianjin treaty, the British again attacked the Dagu forts. They were repulsed with a loss of 432 men killed and wounded and four gunboats sunk.
1860	The scholar Feng Guifen (FENG KUEI-FEN) published a series of essays on government and society that helped inaugurate the late Qing Self-Strengthening movement. He called for the teaching of foreign languages, mathematics, and science to bring China on a par with the Western powers. In response, the Qing established arsenals, shipyards, and schools that specialized in foreign languages and technological subjects.
1860	The Mongol general Senggelinqin led a Qing army against the Nian rebels. The Nian leader Zhang Luoxing was killed in the fighting.
June 1860	Taiping forces seized Suzhou and advanced east toward the rich cities of the lower Yangtze Valley.
August 25, 1860	British and French forces stormed the Dagu forts and entered Tianjin.

September 1860	Qing authorities intercepted British and French envoys en route to Beijing; 25 Europeans were executed. Lord Elgin, Britain's chief negotiator, ordered a reinforced British-French column to march on Beijing.
October 18, 1860	The Anglo-French punitive column occupied Beijing. On Lord Elgin's orders, European troops burned Qianlong's elegant Summer Palace but spared the Forbidden City. The Qing agreed to affirm the 1858 treaty and, in addition, to cede to Britain part of the Kowloon Peninsula on the mainland opposite Hong Kong. In effect, the treaty legalized the opium trade.
1861–1875	Tongzhi (T'UNG-CHI) ascended as Qing emperor at age five. The real rulers of China were his mother, Dowager Empress Cixi (TZ'U-HSI, 1835–1908), and an uncle, Prince Gong (KUNG). Together with a small group of important senior officials, they implemented administrative and economic reforms in an attempt to save the threatened dynasty.
November 11, 1861	Qing established the Zongli Yamen (Office for the Management of the Business of All Foreign Countries)—forerunner of a ministry of foreign affairs. The bureau managed continuing crises with Western powers and also set up foreign language schools, sponsored analyses of international law and of Western government forms and institutions, and oversaw all legal cases involving Chinese Christians.
1862	A Muslim uprising shook Shaanxi and Gansu in northwestern China.
1862	The Qing government opened an interpreters' school in Beijing. Other language schools opened in Shanghai, Guangzhou, and Fuzhou.
1862	Zeng Guofan established the Anqing Arsenal to produce modern weaponry for China.
January–May 1862	With the Taiping threatening Shanghai, the Western community rallied to the city's defense. Along with Zeng Guofan's Hunan columns, Qing deployed a large mercenary force, the Ever Victorious Army, which had a heavy complement of foreign officers. Its first commander was American adventurer Frederick Townsend Ward.
June 1862	With British and French assistance, Qing loyalists beat back a renewed Taiping attack on Shanghai.
June 1, 1864	Hong Xiuquan died in the Taiping capital of Nanjing.
July 19, 1864	Zeng Guofan and his 120,000-man Xiang Army recaptured Nanjing, ending the Taiping Rebellion.
1865	A translation of Euclid's *Elements of Geometry* appeared with an introduction by Zeng Guofan.

1865–1866	Resurgent Nian rebels defeated imperial forces in Hubei, Anhui, and Shandong; the Mongol general Senggelinqin was killed during the campaign.
February 1867	The Beijing interpreters' school reopened as a college offering mathematics, chemistry, geology, mechanics, and international law, as well as languages.
January–August 1868	Qing forces trapped and destroyed Nian insurgent forces along the Grand Canal, then suppressed the last of Nian resistance in Shandong.
August 1868	Using machinery bought in the West, China launched its first steamship, the *Tianqi* (Auspicious), at the Shanghai arsenal.
June 1870	Anti-foreign resentment escalated into violence at Tianjin. In what Westerners dubbed the Tianjin Massacre, mobs killed 16 French missionaries and consular officials. Qing authorities tried and executed 16 Chinese for the murders.
1872	Li Hongzhang (LI HUNG-CHANG), a reforming official, helped establish the China Merchants Steamship Navigation Company, becoming a major stockholder. Li favored an all-steamship fleet and called for an end to building war junks.
1872	The Shenbao business newspaper in Shanghai reached a circulation of 15,000.
1873	An imperial army recaptured Dali from Muslim insurgents, ending the Yunnan Rebellion.
1873	Half a million Chinese were settled in Singapore.
1873	China acquired American-manufactured Gatling rapid-fire guns for the Tianjin arsenal.
November 1873	A Qing column retook Suzhou in northwestern Gansu, ending the Muslim rebellion in the northwest.
1874	Western missionaries founded a society for the suppression of foot binding in the port city of Xiamen (Amoy).
1875	One hundred thousand Chinese were working in Peru.
January 1875	The Tongzhi emperor died. His mother, the dowager empress Cixi, named her three-year-old nephew Guangxu (KUANG-HSU) as successor and continued to rule as regent.
1876	China's first railroad opened near Shanghai. Chinese traditionalists regarded railroads as unharmonious.
1877	The government sponsored a major expansion of the Kaiping Coal Mines in northern China.

1879	Zuo Zongtang (TSO TSUNG-T'ANG) led a Qing expedition against a renewed Muslim outbreak in Xinjiang on the northwestern frontier.
1879	The American Episcopal Mission founded St. John's College in Shanghai.
1880	China maintained diplomatic legations in London, Paris, Berlin, Madrid, Washington, Tokyo, and St. Petersburg.
1880	The first permanent railroad line began operations, connecting the Kaipeng mines and the port of Tianjin. (The short Shanghai line was torn up on orders from a provincial governor the year after it opened.)
1880	One hundred and three thousand Chinese were settled in the western United States, all but 3,000 of them men. Clashes with white Americans were common and often violent.
1880s	China developed a national system of telegraph and cable communications.
1882	The United States imposed restrictions on Chinese immigration.
1884	Xinjiang (New Territory) became a regular province of China.
August 22, 1884	French warships attacked a Chinese fleet in Fuzhou harbor after negotiations collapsed over France's colonial expansion into Vietnam. Within an hour every Chinese ship—all but two built of wood—was sunk or afire; more than 500 Chinese perished.
1885	Taiwan became a full province of China.
1890	Protestant missionaries were working in 15 of China's 16 provinces.
1890	The Hanyang iron works opened at Wuhan.
1890s	More than 10,000 laborers were employed in modern factories in the mid-Yangtze city of Hankou. Conditions were harsh and wages low for most working people.
1893	The population of China's cities totaled 23.5 million, 6 percent of the total population.
1894	The reformer Sun Yat-sen (1866–1925), educated in mission schools in Hawaii, offered his services to the senior scholar-official Li Hongzhang. When Li turned him down, Sun formed the Revive China Society in Hawaii and pledged to overthrow the Manchu.

1894	With the outbreak of rebellion in Korea, China and Japan sent expeditionary forces to the peninsula.
July 21, 1894	Japanese troops seized the Korean royal palace in Seoul and installed a puppet regent. At sea, a Japanese warship sent a Chinese troopship to the bottom, drowning 1,000 Korea-bound soldiers.
Late July 1894	The Japanese defeated China's armies in a series of battles around Seoul and Pyongyang.
September 1894	Japanese naval forces attacked a Chinese fleet of two battleships and 10 cruisers off the mouth of the Yalu River. The Chinese admiral retreated to the fortified port of Weihaiwei.
October 1894	Japanese forces crossed the Yalu River into Chinese territory.
January 1895	A Japanese column marched overland and stormed the Weihaiwei forts from the landward side. The Japanese then turned the fort's guns on the Chinese fleet, sinking one of the battleships and four cruisers.
April 1895	The Treaty of Shimonoseki obliged China to recognize the "independence" of Korea; Japan took effective control of the country. China also had to pay an indemnity of 200 million ounces of silver; cede Taiwan, the Pescadores, and Liaodong in southern Manchuria; open four new treaty ports; and allow Japan to open factories in China.
	European protests forced the Japanese to return Liaodong. Then the Europeans grabbed Chinese territory for themselves. The Germans took Jiaozhou in Shandong; the Russians occupied part of Liaodong; the British helped themselves to Weihaiwei and the New Territories opposite Hong Kong; and the French claimed Guangzhou Bay.
1895–1898	Kang Youwei (K'ANG YOU-WEI, 1858–1927) and other young reformers protested the treaty with Japan and pressured the Qing government for change. They sought to extend the Self-Strengthening movement through educational, economic, and administrative reforms. Kang attempted to blend traditional Confucian thought and modern development, arguing that Confucius had not been an opponent of social and economic change. He published *A Study of Confucius as a Reformer* in 1898.
1896	China's railroad network totaled 300 miles. By comparison, Japan had 2,300 miles of railroad, while the United States had 182,000 miles of track.
1896	The reformer Liang Qichao (LIANG C'HI-CH'AO, 1873–1929) founded the journal *Chinese Progress* in Shanghai. He published essays that exhorted China to adopt Western political thought and institutions, as well as technology.

1896	Two graduates of Chinese mission schools, given the European names of Ida Kahn and Mary Stone, returned to China with medical degrees from the University of Michigan and opened medical practices in their homeland.
1896	The Qing government founded Nanyang College in Shanghai.
1897	Germany occupied Jiaozhou Bay and Qingdao island off the Shandong Peninsula. The Germans established a brewery there that makes Qingdao beer today.
1898–1899	The United States launched its Open Door policy for China, which sought to arrest the Great Powers' division of the country into "spheres of influence." It had limited success.
1898	The secret society of the Harmonious Fists rose in northwestern Shandong. The Boxers, as they were known to Westerners, blamed all China's ills on foreigners. Mostly young, male, and poor, they formed alliances with such women's groups as the Red Lanterns Shining.
March 1898	The Qing court gave Russia 25-year leases of the ports of Dailan and Lüshun (Port Arthur) on the Liadong Peninsula.
June–September 1898	The Guangxu emperor launched the Hundred Days Reform of government, education, commerce, and the armed forces. He ordered a modernization of the exam system; the upgrade of Beijing College, which included adding a medical school; and the foundation of mining and railroad institutes.
September 21, 1898	The dowager Cixi issued an edict announcing that the emperor had asked her to resume power. Guangxu was put under palace arrest, six leading reformers were executed without trial, and most of the reforms were canceled. Kang Youwei and Liang Qichao managed to escape abroad.
Early 1899	The Boxers intensified their attacks on Chinese Christian converts along the Shandong-Hebei border. Foreign missionaries called on imperial forces to quell the outbreaks.
1900	By estimate, 10 percent of all Chinese smoked opium and 15 million people were said to be addicts.
1900	Around 500 Protestant mission stations were established in China. There were around 100,000 Protestants in the country, compared to 700,000 Chinese Catholics.
1900	Chinese immigrants who settled in the U.S. possession of Hawaii totaled 25,000. More than 500,000 Chinese were living in the Dutch East Indies (modern Indonesia).

June 1900	Armed Boxer groups appeared in Beijing and Tianjin. Several foreign missionaries and engineers were killed. The Western powers sent a contingent of 400 troops to protect foreigners in the capital.
June 17, 1900	Western troops seized the Dagu forts in preparation for the landing of a punitive expedition at Tianjin.
June 19, 1900	The Boxers besieged the legation quarter in Beijing.
June 21, 1900	The dowager Cixi issued a decree condemning the Western powers. The Boxers responded with stepped-up attacks on the missions and other foreigners. In the provincial city of Taiyuan southwest of Beijing, Qing officials with Boxer sympathies rounded up and put to death 44 missionary men, women, and children.
August 1900	The reformer Kang Youwei launched an uprising in Hubei and Anhui. He hoped to restore the Guangxu emperor as a constitutional monarch. Qing forces subdued the brief insurgency.
August 4, 1900	A multinational force of 20,000 troops representing Japan, Russia, Britain, the United States, and France marched from Tianjin toward Beijing.
August 14, 1900	Western troops entered Beijing, lifted the legation siege, and looted the city. The dowager and the emperor established a temporary capital at Xi'an in the Wei River Valley.
October 1900	Imperial forces suppressed Sun Yat-sen's small republican insurgency near Guangzhou.
January 1901	The dowager empress Cixi in Xi'an issued a call for reforms similar to those of 1898. In one major change, the Qing moved to reorganize the semi-autonomous provincial armed forces and the traditional Manchu banner formations into a New Army of 450,000 men modeled along Western lines.
September 1901	With no choice in the matter, China signed the treaty known as the Boxer Protocol. It assessed an indemnity of $330 million, called for the execution of leading Boxers, and permitted foreign troops to garrison the legation quarter of Beijing.
1902–1907	Liang Qichao edited the reform journal *New People's Miscellany* from his exile in Japan.
June 1902	Cixi and the Guangxu emperor returned to Beijing.
1903	The Japanese-educated political activist Zou Rong (TSUO JUNG) published his anti-Manchu treatise *The Revolutionary Army*. He challenged China to overthrow the Manchu and end foreign domination of the country. Zou also called for elected legislatures, the equality of women, and freedom of press and assembly.

1903	Merchants founded the Shanghai Chamber of Commerce. It quickly became an important force in the economy of China.
1903	The Qing government set up a Ministry of Commercial Affairs to spur economic growth.
1905	Sun Yat-sen brought several radical groups together in a new Revolutionary Alliance. It followed a republican and generally socialist political line.
1905	After a decade of foreign-sponsored construction, China's railroad network totaled 4,000 miles. A north-south line linked Beijing and the industrial region of Wuhan.
1905	The revolutionary writer Zuo Rong died in a Shanghai prison.
1905	The Qing government abolished the Confucian examination system, the basis of traditional Chinese education.
June–September 1905	As a protest of U.S. policies that excluded the Chinese, merchants in Guangzhou, Shanghai, Xiamen, and Tianjin carried out a successful three-month boycott of American products.
1906	Qing established a Ministry of Posts and Communications. Among the new bureau's responsibility was management of China's growing railroad network.
1906	A summary and partial translation of Karl Marx's *Communist Manifesto* circulated in China.
1906	Two hundred fifty Protestant mission hospitals treated 2 million Chinese patients a year. Fifty-eight thousand Chinese students were enrolled in Protestant mission schools.
September 1906	The dowager Cixi appointed a constitutional commission to tour Japan, the United States, Great Britain, France, Germany, Italy, and Russia and observe their governmental institutions. Upon its return, the committee recommended imperial-parliamentary Japan as a model for China.
November 1906	An edict from Cixi promised a constitution for China eventually and reform of imperial administration.
1907	Yuan Shikai (YUAN SHIH-K'AI, 1859–1916), the reforming governor of Tianjin, authorized elections for a local governing council.
1907	The Beijing Chamber of Commerce was composed of 4,500 of the capital's 25,000 commercial enterprises.
1907	The Qing government established a national system for the education of girls.

July 1907	The Zhejiang schoolteacher Qiu Jin (CH'IU CHIN) led an anti-Qing rising. Captured and executed after a short trial, she became a revolutionary martyr.
1908	The United States reserved half its Boxer indemnity, approximately $12 million, to educate Chinese students in America.
1908	The Qing announced a plan to introduce constitutional government in China over a nine-year period.
November 1908	The Guangxu emperor and the dowager Cixi died within one day of each another. The infant Puyi (1905–1967) ascended as the 10th and last emperor of the Qing.
October 1909	China's first provincial assemblies, the product of the Qing's late-hour reforms, convened.
1910	China's 40,000 girls' schools enrolled 1.6 million students.
October 1910	Under the auspices of the Qing, a provisional national assembly gathered in Beijing.
November 1910	The Qing court agreed to accelerate the constitutional process. The government announced it would permit a fully elected national parliament to meet in November 1913.
1910–1911	Floods in the Yangtze and Huai Valleys claimed hundreds of thousands of lives and sent millions of refugees onto the roads in search of food.
October 9, 1911	An accidental explosion in a revolutionary bomb factory exposed a revolutionary cell in the mid-Yangtze industrial city of Hankou. Qing police raided the headquarters and summarily executed three revolutionary leaders.
October 10, 1911	A New Army unit sympathetic to the revolutionaries mutinied in Wuchang. Within hours, other units rallied to its support. The next day, the revolutionary societies touched off a rising in the third of the Wuhan cities, Hanyang.
October 12, 1911	The Hankou garrison mutinied.
October 22, 1911	New Army units mutinied in Shaanxi and Hunan. Many imperial officials were killed. By the end of October, Shanxi, Jiangxi, and Yunnan provinces were in revolt.
October 30, 1911	The Qing court authorized the National Assembly to draft a constitution.
November 1911	Jiang Kanghu (CHIANG K'ANG-HU) founded the first Socialist Party in China.
November–December 1911	Jiangsu, Sichuan, and Shandong provincial assemblies declared for the Revolutionary Alliance.

November 8, 1911	The Beijing provisional national assembly chose the Qing reformer Yuan Shikai to be premier of China.
November 11, 1911	The Qing court ratified the national assembly's appointment of Yuan Shikai and ordered him to form a cabinet.
Early December 1911	New Army revolutionaries occupied Nanjing.
December 25, 1911	The Revolutionary Alliance leader Sun Yat-sen arrived in Shanghai from France.
December 29, 1911	Delegates from 16 provincial assemblies elected Sun Yat-sen president of the provisional Republic of China.
January 1, 1912	Sun Yat-sen assumed office in Nanjing. The provisional government announced that China henceforth would replace the traditional 28- to 30-day day lunar calendar and 10-day week with the Western seven-day week. Sun Yat-sen agreed to give up the presidency to Yuan Shikai, the last Qing premier.
January 28, 1912	Provincial delegates of the Revolutionary Alliance, meeting in Nanjing, chose a national council.
February 12, 1912	The Qing court announced the abdication of the last emperor, six-year-old Puyi. This brought to a close more than 2,000 years of the imperial history of China.
February 13, 1912	Sun Yat-sen resigned as provisional president of the Republic of China and recommended Yuan Shikai as his successor.

KEY RESEARCH SOURCES

Esherick, Joseph. *The Origins of the Boxer Uprising*. Berkeley: University of California Press, 1987.

Fairbank, John King. *Trade and Diplomacy on the China Coast*. Cambridge, Mass.: Harvard University Pres, 1953.

Naquin, Susan, and Evelyn Rawski. *China in the Eighteenth Century*. New Haven: Yale University Press, 1987.

Spence, Jonathan D. *The Search for Modern China*. New York: W.W. Norton, 1990

Wakeman, Frederic, Jr. *The Fall of Imperial China*. New York: Free Press, 1975.

15. THE REPUBLIC

(1912–1949)

China fragmented politically with the fall of the Qing dynasty. After the dictator Yuan Shikai's death in 1916, the warlords were in the ascendant, and the Western powers extended their influence. Military commanders, provincial governors, and even bandits held power in regional strongholds. Mongolia and Tibet declared their independence. Foreign products, ideas, and manners flooded China during the first decades of the 20th century. Political confusion and upheaval accompanied social change: failed efforts to revive the empire, the spread of warlord rule in the countryside, widespread nationalist and anti-foreign agitation, and expanded foreign presence in the treaty cities.

The New Culture Movement sought to overthrow conservative Confucian thought. Periodicals such as *New Youth* rejected traditional ways of thinking. Newspapers found wide audiences in the urban areas. Writers abandoned classical literary Chinese for the vernacular. Political unrest produced the nationalist May Fourth Movement of 1919, student-launched but with broad support from all classes in the cities. The two main national powers, the Nationalist Guomindang and the Chinese Communist Party, established mass political organizations and raised their own armies. Sometimes the two parties cooperated in opposing the"twin evils"of warlordism and imperialism. They remained deadly rivals, however. The Nationalists nominally unified China in 1928 under Chiang Kai-shek. They purged their Communist partners, obtained international recognition, and took control of Customs, the revenue-producing salt monopoly, and the post office.

German advisers worked with the Nationalists to upgrade the army and train elite units to attack the Communists in their interior strongholds. Western advisers helped reform the banking, currency, taxation, transportation, and communications systems. Industrial production increased, though workers endured low wages and long hours; child labor was common. A professional class of scientists, engineers, economists, and lawyers gained influence. Women's roles were rapidly changing. The custom of binding women's feet became rare, women's education expanded, and growing numbers of women entered the workplace.

Change came more slowly in the countryside. Most country people continued to live much as their ancestors had lived. Existence was precarious. Local authorities were tyrannical and often corrupt. Farming methods were primitive, with crops sown and harvested by hand and carried rather than shipped to market. Population growth outpaced the productive capacity of China and put intolerable pressure on the land.

The Japanese invasion of 1937 fragmented China again. China resisted the Japanese aggressor; Nationalists and Communists, after a short period of cooperation, fought each other. As World War II engulfed China, the Nationalists became increasingly corrupt and ineffective. The Communists under Mao Zedong gained control of the northern China countryside, which was out of range of the Japanese. They introduced land redistribution and other reforms and emphasized political indoctrination.

Civil war broke out full-scale with the end of the war in the Pacific. From their bases in the north, the Communists launched a drive for control of all China. Nationalist forces, worn down by eight years of war, melted away. Inflation and wartime damage left the economy of China in ruins. The Communists took control of the mainland in 1949, forcing the Nationalists to withdraw to the island of Taiwan, their last bastion.

1912	The government reorganized Beijing University. It succeeded Metropolitan University of the late Qing, founded in 1898. The new institution's first president was Yan Fu (YEN FU, 1854–1921), translator of Darwin, Huxley, Spencer, and Adam Smith.

February 14, 1912	Parliament formally elected Yuan Shikai (YUAN SHIH-KA'I) provisional president of the Republic of China.
March 1912	Yuan Shikai's Beijing-based government put down mutinies and outbreaks in Beijing, Tianjin, and Baoding.
March 11, 1912	The National Council in Nanjing produced a draft constitution that guaranteed equality and protection of persons before the law, freedom of worship, and freedom of assembly. It called for the election of a full national parliament by the end of the year.
April 5, 1912	Parliament declared Beijing the national capital.
August 1912	Chinese political factions prepared for the country's first national elections. The leading group, Sun Yat-sen's Revolutionary Alliance, reorganized as the Guomindang (National People's Party).
August 12, 1912	The provisional government adopted election regulations and decided on a bicameral parliament.
December 1912	Some 40 million Chinese, males with some property and an elementary school graduation certificate, were eligible for the first national balloting.
January 13, 1913	Election results showed the Guomindang a clear winner, with a near majority of 269 of 596 seats in the House of Representatives and 123 of 274 in the appointive Senate.
March 20, 1913	Agents of Yuan Shikai mortally wounded the Guomindang parliamentary leader Song Jiaoren (SUNG CHIAO-JEN), 30 years old, in an attack at the Shanghai railroad station.
March 22, 1913	Guomindang leader Song Jiaoren died of wounds inflicted by Yuan Shikai's assassins.
April 1913	Parliament convened.
May 1913	The United States extended full diplomatic recognition to the government of Yuan Shikai.
May 1913	With the Guomindang plotting his overthrow in a Second Revolution, Yuan dismissed the leading Guomindang military governors.
July 1913	Military governors of several provinces declared independence from the Beijing government as the Second Revolution spread.
July–September 1913	Troops loyal to Yuan took the offensive and routed Guomindang military forces.
September 1913	Yuan's army occupied Nanjing.

October 6, 1913	Yuan bullied parliament into electing him to a five-year term as president.
October 7, 1913	Under British pressure, Yuan declared autonomy for Tibet. Great Britain extended diplomatic recognition to Yuan's regime the same day. Japan and Russia shortly followed.
October 10, 1913	Yuan was formally inaugurated as permanent president of the republic.
October 31, 1913	Parliament approved a cabinet system of executive rule in an effort to curb Yuan's powers.
November 4, 1913	Yuan dissolved the Guomindang, declaring it a seditious organization, and expelled its members from parliament.
December 1913–January 1914	The bandit leader White Wolf swept through Henan and Anhui, drawing thousands of peasant recruits to his standard. Sun Yat-sen's organization attempted to negotiate an alliance with White Wolf.
1914	U.S.-trained Chinese scientists founded the Science Society.
1914	Foreign investment in China reached $1.61 billion, most of it concentrated in Shanghai and southern Manchuria. Great Britain was the leading investor, with a third of the total, followed by Russia, Germany, and Japan.
January 1914	Yuan formally dissolved China's parliament. In February, he ordered the dissolution of provincial assemblies and local government bodies and tightened controls on the press.
May 1, 1914	Yuan promulgated a "constitutional compact" that made him virtual dictator, with unlimited power over war, foreign policy, and finance.
July 8, 1914	From exile in Japan, Sun Yat-sen founded the Revolutionary Party (Gemingdang), a radical spin-off of the Guomindang.
August 1914	Government forces hunted down the remnants of White Wolf's bandit gang and killed White Wolf.
1915	An American chamber of commerce opened in Shanghai with 32 members.
1915	The U.S.-based Rockefeller Foundation aided in the founding of the Beijing Union Medical College. It would become China's leading center for medical research and teaching.
1915	Chen Duxiu (CH'EN TU-HSIU, 1879–1942) of Beijing University founded the periodical *New Youth,* which criticized traditional Chinese thought. The magazine abandoned classical Chinese and published reviews, essays, and other works in the vernacular.

January 1915	Japan issued the Twenty-One Demands on China. The Japanese sought extended economic rights in Manchuria and Inner Mongolia, new rights in Fujian, and joint Japanese-Chinese administration of a major coal and iron complex in central China. China's decision to yield triggered anti-Japanese protests, often led by young people returned from study abroad.
December 12, 1915	Yuan Shikai announced that he would assume the title of emperor on January 1, 1916. Yuan had moved earlier to re-establish Confucianism as the state religion, and he carried out Confucian rituals at the Qing Temple of Heaven.
Mid-December 1915	A National Protection Army organized in Yunnan Province to challenge Yuan Shikai's government. Yunnan, Guizhou, Guangxi, and other provinces proclaimed their independence from the central government.
December 23, 1915	Republicans gave Yuan an ultimatum to cancel his plan to restore the monarchy.
1916	The government established the Geological Survey of China. The survey sponsored paleontological research and other projects.
March 22, 1916	Yuan Shikai rescinded his decree promoting himself to emperor in a restored monarchy.
April–May 1916	Several provinces, including Sichuan and Shanxi, declared independence from the Yuan government.
June 6, 1916	Yuan Shikai died.
June 7, 1916	Li Yuanhong (LI YUAN-HUNG) succeeded Yuan Shikai as president. He proved ineffectual, and central authority continued to deteriorate.
1917–1926	Cai Yuanpei (TS'AI YUAN-P'EI, 1868–1948) carried out educational reforms as president of the National University of Beijing, upgrading the faculty and improving the curriculum.
June–July 1917	Zhang Xun (CHANG HSUN), one of Yuan Shikai's generals, occupied Beijing.
July 1, 1917	Zhang Xun restored the boy emperor Puyi, now eleven, to China's throne.
July 12, 1917	Rival military commanders stormed the Forbidden City in Beijing, chased Zhang into the Dutch Legation, and deposed Puyi for a second time, inaugurating a new era of warlord rule.
August 14, 1917	The Beijing government declared war on Germany, joining Great Britain, France, and their allies in World War I. China sent no troops, but 100,000 Chinese were shipped to France as laborers.

August 25, 1917	Sun Yat-sen proclaimed a military government for areas under his control in Guangzhou.
1919	Four and a half million Chinese girls were enrolled in 130,000 schools.
May 1, 1919	Beijing University librarian Li Dazhao (LI TA-CHAO, 1889–1927) published an introduction to Marxist theory in the magazine *New Youth*.
May 4, 1919	Thousands of Beijing University students rallied at Tiananmen Square to protest the Versailles peace accord's award of German treaty rights in Shandong to Japan. The rally touched off a wave of demonstrations around the country; student strikes closed schools in 200 cities. The protest inaugurated the anti-imperial May Fourth Movement, which took up a range of political and cultural issues—foreign domination, arranged marriages, education, labor, and the arts.
May 7, 1919	Beijing police released students arrested in the May Fourth demonstration.
October 1919	Sun Yat-sen dissolved the Revolutionary Party and formally re-established the Guomindang. His Three Principles—nationalism, democracy, and the people's livelihood—were the core of Guomindang ideology. Sun, based in Shanghai, had limited political authority, however.
1920	Beijing University admitted the first women students.
1920	Chinese-owned industrial concerns totaled 1,700 and employed 500,000 workers.
1920	China's modest railroad network reached 7,000 miles; the Chinese national railway system, with 3,800 miles of track, employed 73,000 workers.
1920	The Nanyang Tobacco Company of Guangzhou sold 4 billion cigarettes a year.
1920s	Satirist Lu Xun (LU HSUN), whose tales and stories skewered contemporary Chinese manners, was China's leading writer. He wrote in the baihua vernacular, to make his work available to ordinary people. Lu Xun's political views veered to the left in the later 1920s, but he remained a literary independent.
1920s	Sixty thousand rickshaw pullers worked in Beijing.
1920–1921	Severe drought caused a terrible famine in northern China. At least 500,000 people perished and nearly 20 million were destitute in Hebei, Shandong, Henan, Shanxi, and Shaanxi. Some villagers ate straw and leaves for sustenance.
1921	Chinese industrial workers staged 51 major strikes.

1921	Li Dazhao organized a Marxist study group at Beijing University. Mao Zedong, a student from rural Henan, attended.
July 21, 1921	Revolutionaries founded the Communist Party in Shanghai. The party broke with other radical groups and organized as a secret, power-seeking revolutionary group. Mao Zedong (MAO TSE-TUNG, 1893–1976) represented Hunan at the founding party conference. The son of a rich and educated peasant father and an illiterate mother, he graduated from the Changsha teachers college, worked as a librarian at Beijing University, and participated in the May Fourth Movement.
1922	Forty-nine new cotton mills opened in China. The cigarette and paper industries flourished in the Guangzhou area; northern China collieries employed 50,000 miners.
1922	Industrial unrest continued to mount, with 91 major strikes in China, nearly double the number in the previous year.
1922	Women made up 2.5 percent of the total enrollment of 35,000 in China's college's and universities.
1922	The YMCA counted 54,000 members in 36 Chinese cities.
January–March 1922	A strike of 120,000 seamen and dock workers in Hong Kong and Guangzhou yielded pay raises and recognition of the strikers' union.
February 1922	The Nine-Power Treaty negotiated in Washington, D.C., condemned "spheres of influence" in China and proclaimed China's "sovereignty, the independence, and the territorial and administrative integrity."
September 1922	With advice from the Soviet Comintern, the republican leader Sun Yat-sen formed an uneasy anti-warlord alliance with the Communists. He reorganized the Guomindang along Soviet lines. The Communists, now around 200 strong, set four priorities for China: reunification, organization of the urban working class, a war on poverty in the countryside, and the expulsion of foreign forces.
February 1923	Sun Yat-sen declared himself grand marshal of a Guomindang military government that asserted authority over southern China.
February 7, 1923	Troops of the warlord Wu Peifu (1874–1939) attacked striking railway workers in the Wuhan region, killing 35. Wu's soldiers beheaded one union leader and displayed the severed head at a railroad station.
February 9, 1923	Beleaguered railway strikers in Wuhan returned to work.
September 1923	In a party reorganization, Guomindang leaders approved an alliance with the Communists.

1924	Chiang Kai-shek (Jiang Jieshi, 1888–1975), born into a merchant-gentry family from the Ningbo area, won appointment as commandant of the new Whampoa Military Academy at Guangzhou. The Communist Zhou Enlai was the academy's political director.
September 1924	Civil war broke out among the northern China warlords.
Mid-1920s	Japan maintained an army in the Chinese province of Manchuria to protect railroad and other economic interests. The Japanese military pressed for a full occupation of the province.
1925	The Comintern supported 1,000 Russian military advisers in China. Comintern organizer Michael Borodin and the others assisted the Nationalists in party-building and military training.
February–April 1925	Guomindang forces under Chiang Kai-shek defeated the Guangdong warlord Chen Jiongming (CH'EN CHIUNG-MING) in the series of battles known as the First Eastern Expedition.
March 12, 1925	Sun Yat-sen died of liver cancer in Beijing at age 59. His death set off a struggle for succession in the Guomindang.
May 30, 1925	British police in the International Settlement of Shanghai fired on anti-foreign Chinese demonstrators, killing 11. The demonstrators responded with strikes and boycotts.
June 6–12, 1925	A Guomindang army defeated warlord forces near Guangzhou, taking 17,000 prisoners and 16,000 weapons. Chiang Kai-shek commanded the Nationalist garrison in the city.
June 10–11, 1925	British and Japanese troops fired into Nationalist crowds in Hankou, killing 14 and wounding 100.
June 23, 1925	The British fired on demonstrators in Guangzhou, killing 52 and wounding another 117. The Chinese retaliated with strikes and a successful boycott of British Hong Kong.
July 1, 1925	The Guomindang proclaimed a national government from its base in Guangzhou.
June 25, 1926	Guomindang leaders named Chiang Kai-shek to command the main party army, now dubbed the National Revolutionary Army.
July 11, 1926	Nationalists entered the important Hunan city of Changsha.
July 27, 1926	A Nationalist army under Chiang Kai-shek launched the Northern Expedition with Communist assistance and Russian arms and advisers.

August 17–22, 1926	Nationalists besieged the three-city Wuhan region of the mid-Yangtze, trapping warlord Wu Peifu's forces there.
September 6–7, 1926	Nationalists captured the Wuhan cities of Hanyang and Hankou.
October 10, 1926	Wuchang, the third of the Wuhan cities, fell to the Nationalists after a 40-day siege. The Guomindang decided to shift its capital from Guangzhou to Wuhan.
November 1926	Nationalists occupied Nanchang.
December 18, 1926	Nationalist forces advancing up the east coast occupied Fuzhou in Fujian, giving the Nationalists control of seven southern China provinces with a total population of 170 million.
1927	Shanghai's population reached 2.7 million.
January 1, 1927	Nationalists established their capital at Wuhan.
February 1927	The General Labor Union in Shanghai called a general strike in support of Nationalist columns approaching the city. Warlord forces crushed the strike after two days, beheading 20 strikers.
March 21, 1927	The General Labor Union called a second general strike in Shanghai. Some 600,000 workers left their jobs, power and telephone lines were cut, and heavy fighting broke out around the city. More than 20,000 foreign troops and police and 42 warships guarded the International Settlement.
March 22, 1927	Nationalist forces entered Shanghai.
March 23, 1927	The first Nationalist troops entered Nanjing.
March 24, 1927	Nationalist troops ran amok in Nanjing, looting the British, Japanese, and American consulates. Six foreigners were killed. American and British warships covering the evacuation of 50 foreign nationals fired into the city, killing as many as 39 Chinese. (The figures are disputed.)
April 12, 1927	Chiang Kai-shek ordered the Green Gang racketeering organization to attack union headquarters in Shanghai, the start of a wholesale purge of leftists in the Guomindang. Hundreds of union leaders and other leftists were murdered over the next several weeks.
April 17, 1927	The Wuhan government dismissed Chiang Kai-shek as commander-in-chief of the Nationalist army.
April 18, 1927	In defiance of Guomindang leaders in Wuhan, Chiang Kai-shek formed a new Nationalist government with himself at the head. He established his capital at Nanjing. The "Left" Guomindang remained in control in Wuhan.

April 28, 1927	The warlord regime in Beijing executed Communist leader Li Dazhao.
August 1, 1927	Communists within the Nationalist army started an armed rebellion in Nanchang. The Chinese Communists regard this date as the official birthday of their armed forces.
September 1927	Communists attempted a counterattack against right-wing Nationalists with the Autumn Harvest Uprising, a series of assaults on several Hunan towns led by Mao Zedong. They were unsuccessful. Chiang Kai-shek's Nationalists retaliated with a China-wide campaign against the Communists.
October 1927	Mao Zedong led 1,000 survivors of the Nationalist purges and Autumn Uprising defeats into the Jinggang Mountains along the Hunan-Jiangxi border.
December 1927	The feminist Ding Ling (TING LING) published "The Diary of Miss Sophie," a bleak fictional study of social, cultural, and sexual emancipation in Republican China. The story created a sensation and established its author's fame.
December 10, 1927	With the Communists purged, rival Nationalist factions settled their differences; Chiang Kai-shek was reappointed army commander-in-chief.
December 11, 1927	On orders from Soviet dictator Joseph Stalin, the Communist Qu Qiubai (CH'Ü CH'IU-PAI, 1889–1935) led an uprising in Guangzhou. Guomindang and warlord troops crushed the so-called Canton Commune after two days.
1928	Chiang Kai-shek founded the Guomindang Central Political Institute in Beijing for political leaders and government administrators. Courses were nationalist and anti-foreign, with a Confucian emphasis on order, harmony, discipline, and hierarchy.
1928	Chiang Kai-shek ally (and brother-in-law) T. V. Soong took charge of the newly established Central Bank of China. He introduced reforms meant to stabilize China's finances.
1928	The government established a Ministry of Railways.
March 1928	The first number of the Crescent Moon literary society's magazine appeared. Crescent Moon authors took a Western and non-political view of art, in opposition to the left-wing commitment to "proletarian" literature.
March 1928	Chiang Kai-shek's forces resumed the Northern Expedition. The Nationalists financed the campaign chiefly by levying extortionate fees on Chinese industrialists in Shanghai.
April 1928	Nationalist columns campaigned in Shandong.

May 3–11, 1928	Nationalist Chinese and Japanese forces clashed in the Yellow River city of Jinan. The Japanese, protecting their concessions in Jinan, expelled Nationalist troops from the city after heavy fighting.
June 2, 1928	Zhang Zuolin (CHANG TSO-LIN), the most powerful of the northern warlords, retreated from Beijing.
June 4, 1928	A bomb explosion wrecked Zhang Zuolin's northbound train, killing Zhang. Japanese army officers were responsible for the assassination.
June 8, 1928	Nationalists occupied Beijing.
June 9, 1928	The Nationalist government established the Academia Sinica. The academy sponsored research institutes and the National Science Council.
June 12, 1928	Nationalist forces entered Tianjin.
Late 1928	Nationalist pressure forced Mao Zedong's Communist band to flee the Jinggang Mountains. He and his followers resettled in a mountainous district along the Jiangxi-Fujian border and established the Jiangxi Soviet there, with Mao's main base in the town of Riujin. Separate soviets operated in remote regions of Anhui, Hubei, Hunan, Zhejiang, and Guangxi.
December 29, 1928	Zhang Xuelin (CHANG HSUEH-LIANG), succeeding his murdered father as Manchurian warlord, proclaimed his loyalty to the Nationalists, completing China's nominal unification. (Only four provinces, Jiangsu, Zhejiang, Anhui and Jiangxi, were under Nationalist control.) The Nationalists declared Nanjing the official capital of China.
1928–1935	Military expenditures consumed 40 percent of the national budget. Debt service accounted for an additional 25 percent.
1929	Researchers working under the auspices of the Geological Survey of China discovered Peking man.
January 1929	The National Reorganization and Demobilization Conference agreed to reduce China's armies to 800,000 men and cap military spending at 41 percent of the total budget.
March–May 1929	Chiang Kai-shek suppressed military uprisings in Guangxi and Shandong, consolidating his power.
October–December 1929	Nationalists put down an insurrection led by generals loyal to the "retired" warlord Feng Yuxiang (FENG YU-HSIANG).

1929–1937	The Academia Sinica excavated the Shang dynasty capital at Anyang, north of the Yellow River in Henan Province. Archeologists unearthed the foundations of 53 buildings, Shang bronzes, and the famous "oracle bones" before war interrupted their work.
1930	The Nationalists promulgated a civil law code that gave women the right to choose their husbands and inherit family property. The new code had slight immediate impact outside the cities.
1930	Cotton mills and other factories in Shanghai employed 170,000 women, but 50,000 women worked as prostitutes in the city.
1930	The Nationalist legislature adopted a land law that fixed the maximum rent at 37.5 percent of the harvest and allowed tenants of absentee landlords to buy farms they had worked for at least 10 years. The government never enforced the law, and rents remained at the 50 to 75 percent level.
1930	Chinese and American investors organized the China National Aviation Corporation and introduced air service from Shanghai to Chengdu and Shanghai to Beijing and other routes.
March 2, 1930	Lu Xun (LU HSUN) and others founded the mostly Communist League of Left-Wing Writers in Shanghai.
July–September 1930	A bloody civil war raged between the Nanjing government and the anti-Chiang Kai-shek Northern Coalition. Chiang's forces won at a terrible cost of 250,000 casualties on both sides.
October 1930	Chiang Kai-shek was baptized a Christian. Through his new faith and with the help of his wife, Soong Meiling, a graduate of Wellesley College in Massachusetts, Chiang made politically important connections with influential Americans.
December 19, 1930– January 3, 1931	Chiang Kai-shek launched the first of five anti-Communist campaigns of encirclement and extermination. It ended in failure.
1930–1939	With major world economies in depression, China grew modestly. Electrical power output doubled, post and telegraph systems expanded, regular air routes were established, and 2,300 miles of railroad were built.
1931	The Nankai Institute of Economics was founded.
1931	A new labor law mandated equal pay for women doing the same work as men.
1931	Yangtze River floods created 14 million refugees; 50,000 square miles were under water.

1931	Pearl S. Buck, daughter of American missionaries in China, published *The Good Earth*, a novel of Chinese life set in the present. The novel won a Pulitzer Prize, sold 1.5 million copies, and greatly influenced American views of China.
May 31, 1931	The Nationalists' two-month second campaign against the Communists ended in failure.
June 24, 1931	The Nationalist government executed the captured Communist Party secretary-general Xiang Zhongfa (HSIANG CHUNG-FA).
July–September 1931	The third campaign against the Communists recorded initial successes. Chiang Kai-shek called it off after the Japanese invasion of Manchuria.
September 18, 1931	Japanese provocateurs sabotaged the Southern Manchurian Railroad near Shenyang and used the incident as a pretext to seize the city. China appealed to the League of Nations. The league acknowledged China's claim but declined to sanction Japan for the so-called Mukden Incident.
October 25, 1931	The League of Nations called on Japan to withdraw from Manchuria. The Japanese ignored the resolution.
November 7, 1931	Mao Zedong established the Jiangxi Soviet.
December 31, 1931	With the withdrawal of all Nationalist forces south of the Great Wall, the Japanese exercised full control of Manchuria.
1931–1935	Falling farm prices caused widespread economic hardship. Floods, droughts, and hailstorms devastated the countryside.
1932	Mao Dun (MAO TUN) published *Midnight,* his novel of capitalist exploitation in Shanghai. Mao (1896–1982) was a member of the League of Left-Wing Writers and a committed Communist.
1932	A five-year grant from the U.S. Rockefeller Foundation spurred the early growth of the Nankai Institute.
1932	Artist Gao Jianfu (KAO CHIEN-FU) painted *Flying in the Rain,* showing seven biplanes flying over a typical Chinese landscape of water, trees, and mountains.
January 1932	Chiang Kai-shek resumed the office of president after a temporary "retirement" from public life following the Mukden Incident. He also held the titles of chief of the General Staff and chairman of the National Military Council.
January 29, 1932	After an exchange of fire with Nationalist troops, Japanese forces attacked Shanghai. A Japanese aerial bombardment of the working class district of Chapei killed many non-combatants.

March 1932	The Japanese named the deposed emperor Puyi, 25, chief executive of the puppet state in Manchuria dubbed *Manchukuo*—Chinese for "Manchurian nation."
March 1932	Japanese forces occupied Shanghai.
May 5, 1932	Japan agreed to an armistice that ended three months of fighting around Shanghai.
September 1932	The International Commission of Inquiry released a report condemning Japanese aggression in Manchuria.
1933	Ba Jin (PA CHIN), China's most popular novelist in the 1930s, published *Family,* a tale of the "new youth" whose leading characters, three brothers, represented types of May Fourth Movement activists.
January 1, 1933	Chiang Kai-Shek opened the fourth suppression campaign against the Communists.
January–April 1933	Japanese forces advanced into Rehe Province in northeastern China. After weeks of heavy fighting, they took control of the province.
February 1933	The League of Nations rejected an independent existence for Manchuria. The Japanese responded by quitting the international organization.
April 4, 1933	The government abolished the tael currency and replaced it with the yuan silver dollar.
April 29, 1933	The Nationalists called off the failed fourth Communist suppression campaign.
May 1933	Japanese troops advanced into Hebei Province south of the Great Wall. At month's end, China sued for peace. The truce negotiated at Tanggu declared northeastern Hebei a demilitarized zone; the Japanese pulled back to the Great Wall.
May 1933	Chiang Kai-shek enlisted the German general Hans von Seeckt as a military adviser.
October 1933	The Nationalists launched their fifth military campaign against the Communists with 500,000 troops, threatening Mao Zedong's Jiangxi Soviet. The Nationalists introduced the 37 program—an anti-Communist campaign that was three parts military and seven parts political. The political component included local government reform, rent reduction, and food, seed, tools, and other aid to peasants.
November 1933	Nationalist generals in Fujian rose against the Nanjing government, calling for war against Japan and cooperation with the Communists.

1934	Chiang Kai-shek introduced the Fascist-inspired New Life Movement. The Chinese were exhorted to be "willing to sacrifice for the nation at all times." Young military academy graduates known as the Blueshirts (founded in 1932) acted as a Nationalist secret police, spying on political opponents and carrying out assassinations and lesser acts of intimidation.
1934	Farm prices were 58 percent below 1931 levels. The year's rice harvest fell 34 percent below the 1931 crop.
1934	The Nationalist government banned labor unions in Henan, Hubei, Anhui, Jiangxi, and Fujian provinces.
January 1934	The Nanjing government suppressed the Fujian insurrection.
March 1, 1934	The Japanese enthroned Puyi as puppet emperor of Manchukuo.
August 1934	Germany and China signed a secret military and economic accord. Modern German arms and industrial capacity were to be exchanged for strategic raw materials from China.
August–September 1934	Under pressure from Nationalist blockades and encirclement (the fifth suppression campaign), Communist military leaders planned a breakout from the Jiangxi Soviet.
October 16, 1934	Eighty thousand Communist troops and 15,000 party officials broke through the Nationalist encirclement and embarked on the famous Long March, the epic of China's Communist Party. Some 20,000 wounded and many women and children were left behind to await Nationalist occupation.
1935	Schooling for women remained rare in the countryside. Only 2 percent of women in rural China were literate, compared to 30 percent of men.
1935	Nine hundred newspapers circulated in China, with a readership of 20 to 30 million.
1935	Five million Chinese were officially unemployed.
1935	Nationalist government surveys showed that nearly half of all rural householders owned their own land and supported their families by farming. Another quarter supplemented their farm income with work for wages. The rest were laborer-tenants who relied entirely on wage incomes.
January 7, 1935	Communists reached Zunyi in Guizhou Province, where they replenished their stores from large stocks of food and clothing.
January 15–18, 1935	Communist leaders analyzed the Jiangxi failure at the Zunyi Conference. The party raised Mao Zedong to full politburo membership, an important step on his climb to complete control of the Chinese Communist Party.

May–June 1935	The Communists marched north into Sichuan and across the rugged Great Snow Mountains. They reached Mougong on June 12 with around 40,000 men—half their strength at the beginning of the Long March.
August–September 1935	Communist columns advanced slowly through marshlands along the Qinghai-Gansu border. Exhaustion, illness, and exposure claimed thousands of Long Marchers.
October 1935	Japan proposed a peace settlement based on Chinese recognition of Manchukuo, joint Chinese-Japanese development of northern China, and joint defense against the Communists. China rejected the overture.
October 20, 1935	The Red Army, bled down to around 8,000 men, linked up with Communist guerrillas in remote northern Shaanxi and established a new base at Yan'an. The year-long, 6,000-mile Long March was over. Mao Zedong formulated his theory of the peasantry rather than the proletariat as the vanguard of revolution in Yan'an. He also won a power struggle for control of the Communist Party, eliminating one rival after another.
November 1935	After two consecutive poor harvests, Fuzhou peasants rose against their absentee landlords. Thousands protested the arrest of tenants who had refused to pay rents. Clashes continued intermittently into the winter.
November 3, 1935	The Nationalist government issued the *fabi yuan* unit of paper currency.
December 1935	The Communists formally established their capital at Yan'an.
December 9, 1935	Thousands of students rallied in Beijing to protest Japanese aggression. The protests spread to Nanjing, Wuhan, Shanghai, Hangzhou, and Guangzhou.
1936	A Nationalist government census totaled China's population at 479,084,651.
1936	China imposed an income tax. Heavy taxes hindered the economic growth of China. The once-prosperous Nanyang Tobacco Company paid 39 percent of its total income to the government in taxes.
1936	China's highway network totaled 70,000 miles.
1936	Severe drought led to famine in Sichuan. Food riots erupted in the cities, and in Chongqing, the desperately hungry stripped the bark from ornamental trees.
1936	Japan and Germany signed the Anti-Comintern Pact declaring their mutual hostility to communism.

July 1936	Breaking a Guomindang news blockade, U.S. journalist Edgar Snow entered Communist territory in northern China. His broadly sympathetic *Red Star over China* (1938) would be influential in shaping American views of Mao Zedong's movement.
October–November 1936	Chinese defenders repulsed an invasion of Japanese puppet forces along the northern frontier.
December 12, 1936	Chinese troops loyal to the Manchurian warlord Zhang Xuelin seized Chiang Kai-shek in Xi'an. The insurgents demanded an end to the civil war with the Communists and a united front against Japan, a coalition government, and the release of all political prisoners.
December 25, 1936	The insurgents freed Chiang Kai-shek after he agreed to ease military pressure on the Communists and negotiate a united front. Chiang ended the Nationalists' latest anti-Communist campaign.
1937–1939	Soviet military aid to China totaled $250 million. The Soviets sent 1,000 aircraft, 2,000 pilots, and 500 military advisers to assist China in the war against Japan.
1937–1945	Communist land policies yielded increased farm production despite wartime dislocation. The amount of cultivated land in selected northern China districts under Communist control doubled during the period.
1937	The popular author Lao She published *Rickshaw Boy,* a novel of underclass life in Beijing.
1937	Two thousand middle schools, 1,200 normal schools, and 370 professional schools enrolled 545,000 students.
July 7, 1937	Chinese troops fired on a Japanese unit near the strategic Marco Polo Bridge west of Beijing. Japan responded with an attack on the rail junction of Wanping.
July 8, 1937	Japanese forces occupied Wanping.
July 17, 1937	Chiang Kai-shek announced that China would resist renewed Japanese aggression and offered to negotiate a peace settlement on the basis of China's full sovereignty and territorial integrity.
July 27–31, 1937	Renewed fighting erupted around the Marco Polo Bridge. Japanese forces seized control of the entire Beijing-Tianjin area.
July 28, 1937	Chinese forces evacuated Beijing.
July 30, 1937	Japanese troops occupied Tianjin.
August 1937	Germany and the Soviet Union signed a non-aggression pact.

August 13, 1937	Japan launched an attack on Shanghai.
August 14, 1937	A Chinese Nationalist air force raid targeted Japanese warships anchored off Shanghai. The Nationalists missed their aim and hit the city instead, killing hundreds of civilians.
August–October 1937	In a series of hard-fought battles around Shanghai, the Nationalists suffered 250,000 casualties—knocking more than half of Chiang Kai-shek's best troops out of action.
September 1937	As part of a united front agreement, negotiators renamed the Red Army the Eighth Route Army and put it under nominal Nationalist command.
October 29, 1937	Japan established a puppet government in Mongolia.
November 11, 1937	The Nationalists began their retreat west from Shanghai.
December 1937	Communist troops south of the Yangtze River organized as the New Fourth Army.
December 12, 1937	Japanese warplanes attacked and sank the U.S. gunboat *Panay* during an evacuation of American nationals from Nanjing.
December 12–13, 1937	Japanese forces entered Nanjing.
December 1937–February 1938	In a savage terror campaign, rampaging Japanese troops in Nanjing raped at least 20,000 women and put 30,000 defeated Chinese soldiers and as many as 100,000 (or 300,000, according to some estimates) civilians to death. Japanese looting and arson left much of the city in ruins. Westerners called the seven-week rampage the Rape of Nanking.
December 14, 1937	Japan established a puppet "provisional" government in Beijing.
1938	The Japanese advance forced the relocation of China's universities. Nankai, National Beijing, and other institutions combined as the National Southwest Associated University in Nationalist-held Kunming in Yunnan.
1938	The Nationalist government authorized a second Communist army, dubbed the New Fourth Army.
Early 1938	Nationalist armies withdrew westward up the Yangtze River. As the Japanese advanced, they established puppet regimes to rule their conquests, leaving Chinese collaborators in nominal authority.
March 28, 1938	Japan established a third puppet government, this one in Nanjing.

May 1938	With Japanese forces nearing the ancient city of Kaifeng, Chiang Kai-shek ordered the Yellow River dikes blown up. The demolition flooded 4,000 villages, killed many peasants, and delayed the Japanese advance by four months.
July 7–15, 1938	The all-party People's Political Council met in Wuhan to pledge China's commitment to the defeat of Japan and the expulsion of all Japanese forces from the country.
August–October 1938	Chinese and Japanese forces fought a series of battles around Wuhan.
October 21, 1938	Japanese amphibious forces seized Guangzhou.
October 25, 1938	Japanese forces captured Wuhan, extending their control to most of eastern China from Beijing south to Guangzhou.
December 2, 1938	The mountainous, 715-mile-long Burma Road, the Nationalists' sole reliable supply route, officially opened. The first shipments from Rangoon reached Kunming, the Yunnan capital, late in the month.
December 8, 1938	Chiang Kai-shek reached Chongqing in Sichuan 1,000 miles up the Yangtze River and established the Nationalist capital there.
December 18, 1838	Nationalist politician Wang Jingwei (WANG CHING-WEI) announced a peace movement and the opening of negotiations with Japan. Chiang Kai-shek ordered Wang expelled from the Guomindang.
March 1939	The Communists created the Shaanxi-Gansu-Ningxia Border Government. Despite the united front, Communist forces frequently clashed with Nationalist units.
May 1939	The Japanese air force launched a systematic bombing campaign against Chongqing.
September–October 1939	With the signing of the Nazi-Soviet pact, the Soviet Union severed military aid to China.
1940	The Communists intensified recruitment efforts in their northern China strongholds. Party membership climbed to 800,000 as the Communists steadily widened their base of support among the peasantry.
1940	Enrollment in the National Southwest Associated University in Yunnan reached 3,000.
1940	The United States agreed to ship one hundred P-40 fighter aircraft to the Nationalists. The American Claire L. Chennault, an adviser to Chiang Kai-shek, began recruiting U.S. pilots for service in the Flying Tigers squadron.

March 1940	Collaborationist Wang Jingwei established a new puppet government in Nanjing. No Western powers recognized the new regime.
June–July 1940	Under Japanese pressure, France shut down railway service from Vietnam to Yunnan, and Britain closed the Burma Road, isolating the Nationalists from the outside world.
August 20, 1940	Communist forces initiated a series of attacks, known as the Hundred Regiments Offensive, against the Japanese in northern China.
September–October 1940	Counterattacking Japanese inflicted 100,000 casualties on the Communists, devastating the region of northern China through which they passed.
1941	Mao Dun published *Putrefaction,* a novel of the New Fourth Army Incident that details Guomindang secret police abuses.
January 7–13, 1941	Nationalists attacked Communist New Fourth Army units south of the Yangtze River, bringing to a virtual end the Nationalist-Communist united front against Japan. Chiang Kai-shek established an economic blockade in an effort to restrict the flow of food and weapons to Communist forces.
January 17, 1941	The Nationalists ordered the New Fourth Army disbanded. The Communists withdrew north of the Yangtze River to regroup and expand.
March 1941	The United States made the Lend-Lease military assistance program available to China.
August 1941	The U.S. volunteer Flying Tigers squadron formed.
August–October 1941	Japanese troops, in a northern China pacification campaign, killed 4,500 villagers, burned 150,000 dwellings, and shipped 17,000 Chinese to Manchuria as forced laborers.
December 1941	British Hong Kong fell to the Japanese, and the Japanese attacked the United States at Pearl Harbor, bringing the U.S. into World War II.
January 5, 1942	The Allies during World War II established the China-Myanmar-India war theater, with Chiang Kai-shek in command in China. The United States named General Joseph Stilwell as Chiang's chief of staff.
February 1, 1942	Communists at Yan'an opened a Rectification Campaign of ideological purification. Continuing into 1942, it featured readings of Mao's texts, public confessions, and public humiliation of Mao's rivals, such as party theorist Wang Ming. Mao's line became unchallengeable; any deviation was attacked as subjective, liberal, and petty bourgeois.

April 1942	Japanese forces occupied the Burmese town of Lashio, blocking the vital Burma Road supply line into China.
May 2, 1942	Mao Zedong convened the Yan'an Forum on Literature and Art, part of the Communists' ideological rectification campaign. The forum laid down the party line on literature. Mao disdained high art, whether Chinese or foreign, and urged China's writers and artists to draw their inspiration from the struggle of the masses.
1942–1945	U.S. credits to China totaled $500 million; Lend-Lease aid reached $1.3 billion.
1943	The Nationalists drafted 1.67 million men for military service. An estimated 44 percent died or deserted before they joined their units.
1943	The Communist Party's cultural commissars politicized the popular Peking Opera form with a work titled *Driven to Join the Liangshan Rebels.* The producers drew the story line from a favorite novel of Mao's, *The Water Margin,* a tale of proto-revolutionary outlaws.
January 11, 1943	The Allies agreed to abolish the system of extraterritoriality and all the unequal treaties that denied China full control of its own affairs for a century.
March 1943	Japanese troops rounded up the foreign community of Beijing, around 1,500 adults and children, for transfer to an internment camp in Shandong.
March 1943	Nationalists and Communist negotiators met in Chongqing to renew talks on a united front against Japan. Their talks were inconclusive.
December 1, 1943	Meeting in Cairo, Egypt, President Franklin D. Roosevelt and Chiang Kai-shek issued the Cairo Declaration demanding unconditional Japanese surrender and the return to China of all territory lost to Japan.
Late 1943	A U.S. Joint Chiefs of Staff analysis of China's military power estimated that only one-fifth of the Nationalist forces were capable of sustained defensive operations against the Japanese.
January 15, 1944	The U.S. political adviser John P. Davies recommended a military mission to the Communists at Yen'an. Chiang Kai-shek opposed the mission.
Spring 1944	Tens of thousands died of starvation in famine-racked Henan. As Japanese forces advanced, hungry survivors attacked retreating Nationalist units, who had continued to collect taxes during the worst part of the crisis.

April–November 1944	Japanese forces launched a drive south through Hunan along the Xiang River to Changsha and then onto Henyang and Guilin in Guangxi. The Japanese sought to open a north-south overland communications corridor stretching from Korea to Vietnam and to knock out U.S. airfields in China. Operation Ichigo, as the Japanese named it, exposed the weaknesses of Chiang Kai-shek's Nationalist forces, which acknowledged taking 300,000 casualties.
May 4, 1944	New talks on a united front opened in Xi'an. The Nationalists rejected Communist demands for an expanded Red Army, recognition of Communist border governments, and negotiations for a national coalition government.
June 1944	U.S. heavy bombers opened a bombing campaign from Chinese airfields against Japanese targets.
June 15, 1944	American warplanes bombed Japan from China for the first time, attacking a steel plant on the southern island of Kyushu.
June 23, 1944	Chiang Kai-shek reluctantly agreed to the U.S. proposal to send a military mission to the Communists.
July 22–August 7, 1944	The American observer team called the Dixie Mission reached Mao Zedong's capital at Yan'an. The Americans wanted to discuss providing assistance to Mao's forces.
October 19, 1944	At Chiang Kai-shek's urging, the United States recalled Gen. Joseph Stilwell, the American liaison with the Nationalists. Stilwell had become a harsh critic of the Chinese generalissimo.
November 7–10, 1944	U.S. envoy Patrick Hurley met with Mao Zedong in Yan'an to discuss political reconciliation. The talks produced a draft agreement calling for legal status for the Communist Party, a coalition government, and unification of the armed forces. Chiang Kai-shek rejected the agreement.
1945	The Communist Yan'an government controlled 600,000 square miles of territory that had a population of more than 100 million.
February 1945	Meeting at Yalta, the United States, the United Kingdom, and the Soviet Union reached agreement on the terms of Soviet entry into the war against Japan. Soviet dictator Joseph Stalin promised to withdraw his forces from Manchurian territory three months after the end of the fighting.
February 27, 1945	Writers and artists in Nationalist Chongqing published a manifesto demanding an end to censorship, police abuses, and war profiteering. The government responded with arrests.

March 3, 1945	The Nationalists announced they would convene the 1936 National Assembly in November to adopt a new constitution for China. Mao Zedong refused to recognize the nine-year-old assembly.
April 1945	Communist Party membership in northern China reached 1.2 million. The Eighth Route and New Fourth Armies, the main armies of the Communists, fielded 900,000 men.
April 1945	The U.S. State Department advised President Harry S. Truman to continue to support Chiang Kai-shek as the best hope for unification of China.
August 8, 1945	Russian armed forces launched an offensive against the Japanese in Manchuria.
August 9, 1945	With Japan's collapse imminent, Mao Zedong ordered a Communist general offensive.
August 10, 1945	Chiang Kai-shek ordered Japanese forces and puppet governments to surrender only to the Nationalists.
August 14, 1945	After two U.S. atomic attacks on Japanese cities, Japan surrendered, bringing World War II to a close. China's military casualties in eight years of war exceeded 3.2 million, including 1.3 million dead.
August–September 1945	Under an agreement with the Nationalists, U.S. forces occupied four key Chinese ports—Shanghai, Tianjin, Qingdao, and Guangzhou—and sent U.S. Marine contingents to Beijing and Tianjin. A U.S. airlift moved 110,000 Nationalist troops to important cities. At the same time, the 100,000-strong Communist Eighth Route Army under Lin Biao (LIN PIAO) moved into Manchuria, occupying the province's key cities. Soviet forces in Manchuria gave Lin Biao's command access to stockpiles of Japanese arms and ammunition.
August 28, 1945	Mao Zedong flew to Chongqing to open negotiations on postwar issues with Chiang Kai-shek.
September 1945	The Nationalists allowed Japanese puppet government officials to retain their positions in many places, with a view to blocking Communist expansion. Some collaborators were given senior rank in the Nationalist army.
September 1945– February 1947	Wholesale prices in Shanghai increased by 30 times.
October 1945	Soviet occupation authorities refused to allow sea-borne Nationalist troops to land at the Manchurian port of Darien.

October 10, 1945	U.S.-sponsored negotiations between Chiang's Nationalists and Mao's Communists yielded a joint statement on political democracy, a unified military force, and equal legal status for all political organizations. There were, however, no mechanisms for enforcing the agreement.
November 15, 1945	Nationalist forces attacked Communist forces in Manchuria.
November 26, 1945	After long delays, Nationalist troops occupied Jinzhou in Manchuria.
November 27, 1945	The U.S. ambassador to China, Patrick Hurley, abruptly resigned. He accused American foreign service officers of favoring the Communists and undermining U.S. efforts to stabilize the Chiang Kai-shek regime.
December 23, 1945	U.S. special envoy General George C. Marshall arrived in China.
1945–1948	With galloping inflation, prices rose an average of 30 percent a month.
1946	More than 1,700 strikes disrupted life and work in Shanghai.
January 1946	Workers struck the Shanghai Power Company.
January 5, 1946	Nationalist troops entered the Manchurian city of Zhengzhou.
January 10, 1946	U.S. envoy George Marshall persuaded the Nationalists and the Communists to agree to a cease-fire and a Political Consultative Conference.
January 11–31, 1946	Representatives of the Communists, the Guomindang, and other political parties met in Nanjing for the Political Consultative Conference. They reached an accord on constitutional government, a unified military, and a national assembly. However, both sides continually violated the truce, and military clashes were frequent. The Nationalists breached the Nanjing political agreement by reserving the presidency for Chiang Kai-shek and moving to limit the power of the Communists in the proposed new State Council.
January 13, 1946	A cease-fire negotiated by the Marshall Mission went into effect.
January 26, 1946	Nationalist forces entered Shenyang in Manchuria.
Early February 1946	Forty local unions joined the strike against the Shanghai Power Company, forcing the company to settle.
February 25, 1946	The Nationalists and Communists agreed to troop reductions and the eventual integration of both armed forces into a national army.

February 25, 1946	President Harry Truman announced the establishment of a U.S. military mission to train and equip the Chinese army.
April 1946	Both sides repeatedly violated the truce in Manchuria. Communist forces resisted Nationalist efforts to occupy Manchurian cities but were gradually forced to retreat to the north.
April 18, 1946	Communists captured the strategically important city of Zhengzhou in Manchuria.
May 1946	The May 4th Directive ordered land redistribution in areas of northern China under Communist control—a prelude to a widespread expropriation of landlord property, including dwellings.
May 1946	The last Soviet forces withdrew from Manchuria, leaving most of the countryside under control of the Communists.
May 1946	The Nationalists recaptured Zhengzhou.
June 7, 1946	The U.S. envoy Marshall negotiated a two-week cease-fire in Manchuria. He later extended the truce to the end of the month, but the Nationalists and Communists were unable to reach an agreement.
July 1946	The Nationalists renewed the military offensive in the northeast, formally opening the Chinese Civil War of 1946–1949. The Communists reorganized their forces as the People's Liberation Army.
July 1946	Communist units attacked a U.S. supply convoy en route from Tianjin to Beijing. Three Americans were killed, a fourth was mortally wounded, and a dozen others were injured.
July 1946–June 1947	The Nationalist offensive captured 165 towns and more than 100,000 square miles of territory in northeastern China. Nationalist forces crossed the Yellow River, advanced into southern Shanxi, and recorded gains elsewhere. In Manchuria, the Nationalists forced the Eighth Route Army to withdraw beyond the Sungari River to the stronghold of Harbin.
July 4, 1946	The Nationalists announced that they would unilaterally convene the National Assembly in November in disregard of the Political Consultative Conference accords. The Communists said they would boycott the session.
Late July 1946	The United States placed an embargo on shipments of war matériel to China.
October 1946	General Marshall recommended the recall of his diplomatic mission, charging the Nationalists were using negotiations as a cover for military operations against the Communists.

October 1946	The United States partially lifted the embargo on war goods to China.
October 10, 1946	Nationalist troops expelled the Communists from Kalgan in northern China.
November 1946	Communist troops under Lin Biao crossed the frozen Sungari River, attacked the Nationalists in their winter camps, then withdrew.
November 15, 1946	Acting on its own, the Guomindang convened the National Assembly without the participation of the Communists and other political parties.
December 25, 1946	The National Assembly adopted a new constitution for the Republic of China.
Late 1946	Unemployment stood at 30 percent in Nanjing, the Nationalist capital, and at 20 percent in Guangzhou.
1947	The popular writer Ba Jin published *Cold Nights,* a novel set in wartime Chongqing.
1947	The Communist land redistribution proceeded in northern China. The expropriations were often violent, especially in northern Jiangsu, Hebei, Shandong, and Shaanxi.
1947	Bubonic plague swept the Manchurian industrial center of Harbin, claiming 30,000 lives. Epidemiologists traced the outbreak to an earlier Japanese army release of flea-infested rats used in germ warfare research.
January–March 1947	Lin Biao returned to his hit-and-run operations of November, inflicting casualties, capturing weapons stocks, and disrupting Nationalist preparations for an offensive.
January 6, 1947	The United States recalled Special Envoy George Marshall, ending the Marshall Mission.
January 31, 1947	The United States dissolved the last of the Marshall Mission negotiating teams.
February 1947	The Nationalist government attempted to impose wage and price ceilings.
March 18, 1947	The Communists evacuated Yan'an ahead of advancing Nationalists.
May 1947	Nationalist victories left the Communists with control of only around 120,00 square miles and 18 million people, but Chiang Kai-shek had begun to lose momentum. The 400,000-strong Communist army of Lin Biao launched a counteroffensive

against Nationalist-held cities in Manchuria, isolating the garrisons by cutting the cities' railroad links. Apathy and defeatism gradually spread through the Nationalist ranks.

May 1947	Nationalists scrapped wage and price ceilings as unworkable.
May 1947	The United States lifted the last restrictions on shipments of war matériel to China.
June 1947	The resurgent Communist army reached 1.95 million men.
June 1947	The U.S. State Department recommended against direct American involvement in China's civil war.
July 1947	A fact-finding mission headed by U.S. general Albert Wedemeyer recommended prompt economic and military assistance to the faltering Nationalists.
July–December 1947	Separate Communist armies crossed the Yellow River and advanced into Henan, Hebei, and Anhui.
October 1947	The United States granted the Nationalist government $27.7 million in economic aid and established the Army Advisory Group to counsel Chiang Kai-shek.
November 1947	Voters in Nationalist-controlled areas elected a National Assembly.
February 18, 1948	President Truman proposed a $570 million economic aid package to avert a Nationalist collapse. Congress eventually approved $400 million.
March 29, 1948	The National Assembly chosen under the new constitution convened.
April 1948	The Communists recaptured their old Shaanxi stronghold of Yan'an.
April 1948	Luoyang fell to the Communists.
April 19, 1948	The National Assembly elected Chiang Kai-shek to the presidency.
May 1948	A Communist army surrounded Shenyang, trapping 200,000 Nationalist troops.
June 1948	The U.S. Republican presidential candidate, Thomas Dewey, pledged massive financial and military assistance to China.
July 1948	Five thousand Manchurian students in Beijing rallied in protest of Nationalist policies; police fired into the crowd, killing 14 and wounding more than 100.

July 1948	The Nationalist government dropped the inflated *fabi yuan* currency for a new currency, the gold *yuan*. Three million *fabi* bought one new *yuan* at the official rate.
July 30, 1948	Communist leader Mao Zedong predicted the speedy collapse of the Nationalist regime.
August 1948	A standard 171-pound bag of rice sold for 63 million yuan, a sign of hyper-inflation.
August 19, 1948	Chiang Kai-shek imposed a series of financial and economic emergency measures in an effort to avoid economic collapse. The measures limited inflation-inducing printing of banknotes, froze wages and prices, banned strikes and demonstrations, and raised taxes on commodities.
September 1948	Communist forces pacified the province of Shandong.
September–November 1948	Communist forces under Lin Biao scored a series of major victories in Manchuria, costing Chiang Kai-shek nearly 500,000 of his best troops.
October 1948	A Communist army, 600,000 strong, massed for an attack at the railroad junction of Xuzhou in central China.
October 1948–January 1949	Nationalist and Communist forces clashed in the giant battle of Huai-Hai near Nanjing. Nationalist losses approached 200,000.
October 14, 1948	Lin Biao's army occupied the Manchurian city of Jinzhou.
October 18, 1948	Zhangzhun in Manchuria fell to the Communists.
November 1948	President Truman won re-election; he turned down a Nationalist request for an increase in military and economic aid.
November 2, 1948	Lin Biao's army occupied Shenyang in Manchuria.
December 15, 1948	Xuzhou fell to the Communists.
December 29, 1948	Chiang Kai-shek appointed a trusted ally, Chen Cheng, as governor of the island province of Taiwan.
1949	China's industrial production stood at 70–75 percent of prewar levels.
1949	Floods affected 30–40 percent of arable land in China.
Early 1949	The Nationalists prepared Taiwan as a final retreat; 300,000 troops loyal to Chiang Kai-shek massed there.
January 1949	Nationalist battle casualties since the September 1948 totaled more than 1 million.

January 14–15, 1949	The Nationalist garrison of Tianjin surrendered to the Communists.
January 21, 1949	Chiang Kai-shek resigned as president of Nationalist China but maintained control of the Guomindang and the armed forces.
January 22, 1949	The Nationalist commander at Beijing agreed to withdraw from the city.
January 31, 1949	Communist forces entered Beijing.
March 1949	The Communist newspaper *People's Daily* moved to Beijing.
April 1949	The Communists gave Nationalist President Li Zongren (LI TSUNG-JEN) a surrender ultimatum; he refused to capitulate.
April 23, 1949	Nanjing fell to the Communists without a fight.
May 1949	The Communists introduced a new "people's currency," the *renminbi* (informally, the *yuan*), banned the circulation of foreign currencies, and took other measures to bring rampant inflation under control.
May 27, 1949	Communists seized Shanghai against token Nationalist resistance.
July 1949	The first National Conference of Literature and Arts Workers convened in Beijing.
August 1949	Communist columns advanced westward, taking Xi'an and Lanzhou.
September 1949	Beijing again became the capital of China.
September 12, 1949	Mao Zedong convened a People's Consultative Conference to form a new national government. Among other actions, the delegates adopted a new national flag, red with a large yellow star and four smaller stars in the upper left corner.
October 1, 1949	Mao Zedong announced the founding of the People's Republic of China. He spoke from a reviewing stand atop the Gate of Heavenly Peace, the main entrance to the imperial palace at Beijing.
October 2, 1949	The Soviet Union recognized the People's Republic of China.
October 4, 1949	The United States reaffirmed its recognition of the Nationalist government as the legal government of China.
October 13, 1949	The Nationalist government fled from Guangzhou to Chongqing.

October 15, 1949	Communist troops occupied Guangzhou.
December 8, 1949	The Nationalist government withdrew to the island of Taiwan.

KEY RESEARCH SOURCES

Fairbank, John King, and Albert Feuerwerker, eds. *The Cambridge History of China.* Vol. 13, *Republican China 1912–1949, Parts 1 and 2.* New York: Cambridge University Press, 1986.

Hsu, Immanuel C. Y. *The Rise of Modern China.* 2d ed. New York: Oxford University Press, 1975.

Sheridan, James. *China in Disintegration: The Republican Era in Chinese History, 1912–1949.* New York: Free Press, 1975.

Snow, Edgar. *Red Star over China.* New York: Grove Press, 1973.

Spence, Jonathan. *The Search for Modern China.* 2d ed. New York: W.W. Norton, 1999.

16. THE PEOPLE'S REPUBLIC OF CHINA

(1949–)

With the triumph of the Communists, China was again united and free of foreign occupation. Swiftly consolidating their power, the new rulers moved to implement a radical vision of a socialist and egalitarian society. The Communists limited the power of capitalists and landowners and inaugurated a massive redistribution of wealth. They restricted foreign influences and curbed the press, publishers, and intellectuals. Nearly every aspect of Chinese life came under government supervision and control.

Within a year, the new government brought China's rampant inflation under control. With Russian technical assistance, roads, railroads, bridges, electric power complexes, factories, schools, and hospitals were built. In the countryside, the Communists seized land from the landlords and parceled it out among the peasantry, then brought it under state control in a vast system of collectivized agriculture.

The Korean conflict drew China into the cold war. North Korean Communists invaded South Korea in 1950. When the United States, fighting under the United Nations flag, drove the invaders back to the Yalu River, Chinese "volunteers" crossed the Yalu and attacked the Americans. Though the fighting ended in a stalemate, there were long-term consequences. China and the United States became enemies, and the United States extended military protection to Nationalist Taiwan.

Mao Zedong was China's undisputed paramount leader. In the late 1950s, he launched the terribly mismanaged and immensely destructive Great Leap Forward, a mass redeployment of the peasantry for industrial and public works projects. The result, euphemistically labeled the Three Hard Years, was widespread famine. Estimates of the death toll ranged as high as 30 million.

Several years later, Mao's revolutionary whim touched off the devastating Cultural Revolution. Tens of thousands of radical students formed Red Guards, who terrorized China at all levels. Senior government officials were taken from their homes or offices, beaten, subjected to public trials and humiliations, and sometimes killed. When Mao finally reversed course, millions of Red Guards were "rusticated"—sent into the countryside for re-education.

China entered a new phase on Mao's death in 1976. New leadership under the pragmatic Deng Xiaoping eased government restrictions on economic life and courted foreign investment. Deng reversed the collectivist agricultural policy and encouraged farmers to grow for profit. Small private businesses sprang up in the cities and the countryside. His relaxed economic policies ushered in a period of rapid economic expansion.

Economic advance brought new problems: serious ecological damage, widespread corruption, worker exploitation, unwanted foreign cultural influences and—far worse from the leadership's perspective—an explosive demand for the loosening of political controls. The democracy movement's challenge ended in the 1989 massacre at Tiananmen Square that horrified the world.

China pursued economic reform into the 1990s. The constitution was rewritten to describe China's economic system as a "socialist market economy." There were no privately owned cars in the People's Republic in 1978. By 1993, there were 1 million. Through it all, China's Communist leadership enforced a rigid separation between economic reforms, which it consistently pursued, and political liberalization, which it ruthlessly suppressed.

September 12–25, 1949	The People's Political Consultative Conference drafted a constitution for the new Communist state. Rights of freedom of speech, assembly, thought, and religion were guaranteed—except for "political reactionaries."

October 1949	Communist party membership approached 4.5 million. Mao Zedong was party chairman, the most powerful position in the new China. The Central Committee and the smaller politburo coordinated government policy; real power lay with the politburo's five-member standing committee: Mao, Liu Shaoqi (LIU SHAO-CH'I), Zhou Enlai (CHOU EN-LAI), Zhu De (CHU TEH), and Chen Yun (CH'EN YUN).
Late 1949	The Communists banned the private practice of law in China.
December 16, 1949	Mao Zedong reached Moscow, the first foreign journey of his life, for secret negotiations with the Soviet dictator Joseph Stalin. Talks began only after Stalin ignored Mao for several days.
December 17, 1949	Myanmar became the first non-Communist country to recognize the People's Republic of China.
December 30, 1949	India recognized the People's Republic of China.
1950	The Soviets agreed to send 10,000 technical advisers to help build 156 heavy industrial plants in China.
1950	The Communist government established the Institute of Archeology with permanent field stations at Anyang, Xi'an, and Luoyang.
1950	Novelist and playwright Lao She (1899–1966, author of *Rickshaw*, 1937) returned to China from exile in the United States.
January 5, 1950	President Harry S. Truman said the United States would not provide military aid to the Nationalists on Taiwan.
January 6, 1950	The United Kingdom recognized the People's Republic of China. China rejected the gesture in protest of Great Britain's diplomatic ties with Taiwan.
January 13, 1950	The United Nations Security Council rejected a Soviet resolution for the removal of the Nationalist delegation.
January 14, 1950	Communist authorities seized the U.S., French, and Dutch compounds in Beijing.
February 14, 1950	After eight weeks of negotiation, China and the Soviet Union concluded a friendship treaty that contained security guarantees, $300 million in Soviet credits to China, and eventual Soviet withdrawal from Lüshun (Port Arthur).
February 24, 1950	The government approved a directive banning the smoking of opium.
March 1, 1950	Chiang Kai-shek resumed the post of president of the Republic of China on the island of Taiwan.
April 4, 1950	The Communists seized the British compound in Beijing.

April 23, 1950	Communist troops under Lin Biao occupied Hainan Island off the southern China coast.
May 1, 1950	A marriage reform law gave women the right to choose their husbands, initiate divorce, and inherit property. It banned arranged marriages, the sale of children, concubinage, and polygamy. The women of China ended several million marriages during the law's first five years.
June 14–23, 1950	The Communist Party's Political Consultative Conference approved an agrarian reform law that provided for land redistribution.
June 16, 1950	Work commenced on the Chengdu-Chongqing railway.
June 25, 1950	Communist North Korean columns crossed the 38th parallel into South Korea.
June 27, 1950	President Harry Truman announced that the U.S. Seventh Fleet would defend Taiwan in case of an attack from mainland China.
June–October 1950	After initial setbacks, U.S. forces in Korea, operating under the auspices of the United Nations, drove the North Koreans back across the 38th parallel and advanced north toward the Yalu River.
July 6, 1950	The United States announced that it would tighten an oil embargo on Communist China.
August 17, 1950	Communist shore batteries opened fire on the destroyer HMS *Concord* approaching British Hong Kong. The warship was not damaged.
September 19, 1950	The U.N. General Assembly refused to allow the Chinese Communists to take China's seat.
October 19, 1950	U.S. troops occupied the North Korean capital, Pyongyang.
October 24, 1950	China ordered the army to invade Tibet and "liberate" the country from imperialists.
October 25, 1950	The first of an estimated 250,000 Chinese "volunteers" under Peng Dehuai (P'ENG TE-HUAI) crossed the Yalu River into North Korea.
November–December 1950	Advancing Chinese columns pushed U.N. forces back to the 38th parallel.
December 16, 1950	President Harry Truman froze all Chinese Communist assets under U.S. jurisdiction.
December 29, 1950	The government expropriated all U.S. property in China.

1950–1952	The Communists carried out land redistribution and collectivization in southern China. Around 40 percent of all cultivable land was seized and redistributed. Allotments were small, given the high rate of population to arable land; a family of five was fortunate to receive 1 or 2 acres. The campaign frequently turned violent. As many as 1 million landlords were put to death.
January 1951	Communist Chinese troops briefly occupied Seoul.
January 2, 1951	A government decree banned all secret societies in China.
January 8, 1951	The United States confirmed it had resumed arms shipments to the Nationalists.
January 30, 1951	A U.N. General Assembly resolution branded China an aggressor in Korea.
April 29, 1951	The government expropriated all property in China of the Asiatic Petroleum Company, a Shell Oil Company subsidiary.
May 18, 1951	The U.N. General Assembly approved a resolution calling for a ban on shipping strategic materials to China.
May 23, 1951	China formally absorbed Tibet.
June 1951	The sale on easy terms of 430,000 acres of public land on Taiwan allowed nearly 140,000 small farmers to become landowners.
Summer 1951	The Communists moved against ex-Nationalists and other "subversives" who stayed behind in China after the "liberation." Estimates of executions ranged into the hundreds of thousands; as many former Nationalists were sent to labor camps. The campaign in Guangdong Province claimed to net 52,000 bandits and 89,000 other criminals; 500,000 rifles were collected. More than 28,000 people were executed.
July 10, 1951	Korean armistice talks opened at Kaesong.
August 1, 1951	The government launched the Three Antis campaign—anti-corruption, anti-waste, and anti-bureaucracy in government—in northeastern China.
October 12, 1951	Volume 1 of the projected four-volume *Selected Works of Mao Zedong* was published in Beijing.
October 25, 1951	Korean cease-fire talks, broken off in late August, resumed at Panmunjom.
1951–1953	China paid $1.35 billion for Soviet military equipment used in the Korean War.

1952	China's industrial production pulled level with the prewar peak.
January 1, 1952	The government extended the Three Antis Campaign to the entire country. The targets were Communist party members, bureaucrats, and factory and business managers.
January 19, 1952	In an encyclical, pope Pius XII denied that Roman Catholic missionaries in China were anti-Communist spies.
February–June 1952	The government's Five-Anti Campaign targeted capitalists suspected of bribery, tax evasion, theft, cheating on government contracts, and theft of economic information from the state. Business leaders were forced into group criticism sessions and made to confess past wrongdoing.
February 4, 1952	The Vatican claimed that 133 of 1,764 Roman Catholic ecclesiastics in China were in prison; most of the others were under house arrest.
March 7, 1952	The British Hong Kong and Shanghai Banking Corporation announced it had closed its offices in Beijing, Tianjin, and other cities.
April 1952	People's committees in Shanghai investigated and "criticized" 70,000 Shanghai businessmen. On confession, they were forced to pay restitution. In practice, this meant turning over their assets to the state. The campaign tightened the Communist Party's control of business and the labor movement.
April 28, 1952	Japan signed a peace treaty with the Nationalists on Taiwan rather than with the People's Republic of China.
May 19, 1952	British trading companies announced they would cease operations in the People's Republic of China.
June 20, 1952	A massive flood diversion project on the Yangtze River in Hubei Province was completed by 300,000 laborers.
July 1, 1952	The Chengdu-Chongqing Railway opened to traffic.
July 25–30, 1952	A series of border clashes erupted between Chinese and Portuguese troops at Macao.
September 29, 1952	China opened the Longhai railway linking Jiangsun with Lanzhou in Gansu.
1953	The government announced a Five-Year Plan calling for quadrupling China's steel output and doubling production of electric power and cement.

1953	The government reorganized the nation's workplaces as *danwei* (units). The *danwei*, replacing companies or employers, often provided housing and social services as well as employment.
1953	Communist party membership totaled 6.1 million.
1953	Communist mass organizations claimed 76 million members of the All-China Democratic Women's Federation; the All-China Federation of Democratic Youth claimed 18 million; and the Democratic Youth League claimed 12 million.
1953	A census put China's population at 582.6 million.
1953	Life expectancy was 40 years.
February 13, 1953	The Communist Party Central Committee announced the completion of the land redistribution program. Roughly 120 million acres were transferred to 300 million peasants. The committee called for the implementation of large-scale collectivization of farms.
May 9, 1953	A memorial program in Beijing for the Soviet dictator Joseph Stalin, who had died on March 6, was attended by 600,000 Chinese.
June 3, 1953	The government established a Chinese Buddhist Association in Beijing.
June 13, 1953	China and Japan signed a $150 million trade agreement.
July 15, 1953	Construction began on China's first automobile factory.
July 27, 1953	An armistice ended the Korean War after two years of stalemate. China's casualties were estimated at 700,000–900,000, including a son of Mao Zedong. The war deeply damaged China-U.S. relations, which would take a generation to recover.
November 2, 1953	The government expropriated the last remaining French companies in Shanghai.
1954	The government administered China through 21 provinces, five autonomous regions, and two municipalities (Beijing and Shanghai). Approximately 2,200 county governments supervised 1 million Communist party branches in towns, villages, factories, schools, and army units.
January 31, 1954	China and the Soviet Union opened the first direct passenger rail service between Beijing and Moscow. The trains ran twice a week each way.
February 1954	Upward of 400,000 Russian advisers and technicians were working in China's industrial enterprises.

April 26, 1954	A Conference on Far Eastern Problems convened at Geneva to take up Korea, Indochina, and other questions. Premier Zhou Enlai represented China.
June 9, 1954	At Geneva, Zhou Enlai accused the United States of building up Indochina as a military base from which to attack China.
July 9, 1954	A Chinese trade mission reached agreement with British interests for an annual two-way trade up to the value of 100 million pounds sterling.
July 23, 1954	Chinese warplanes shot down a British passenger aircraft over the Sea of Hainan; 10 of the 18 people aboard the British plane perished.
July 26, 1954	China apologized for bringing down the British passenger plane and offered to pay reparations.
September 3–6, 1954	Communist artillery shelled the Nationalist islands of Quemoy and Little Quemoy.
September 7, 1954	The Nationalists retaliated with air strikes on mainland targets.
September 8, 1954	The United States and several Asian nations signed the Southeast Asia Treaty Organization protocol in Manila, the Philippines. The West regarded SEATO as a bulwark against Communist expansion.
September 15–28, 1954	A National People's Congress adopted a new constitution that enhanced the powers of the top leadership position, chairman of the republic (Mao Zedong).
November 1, 1954	A census counted 601,938,035 Chinese. For political purposes, the count included 12 million overseas Chinese and 7 million Taiwanese.
December 2, 1954	China completed a 1,400-mile motor road linking Chongqing and Lhasa, Tibet.
December 2, 1954	The United States and Taiwan signed a mutual defense treaty.
1955	The government's population registration system made free movement difficult. Most peasants were bound to their native villages. Registration categories were hereditary, passing through the male line. A child of a peasant had peasant registration and so did his children.
1955	China formally abolished all wholly-private business enterprises.
January 10, 1955	The Peking Opera Company was founded.

January 19, 1955	Communist forces attacked the Nationalist-held Dachen Islands in the Taiwan Straits.
January 31, 1955	A Committee for Reforming the Chinese Written Language announced a plan to simplify Chinese characters.
February 1955	The government put the long-delayed Five-Year Plan of 1953 into operation. Most of the plan's targets would be reached or exceeded.
February 13, 1955	China claimed to have liberated the Dachen Islands.
April 18–24, 1955	Under Foreign Minister Zhou Enlai, China assumed a leading role in the Bandung Conference in Indonesia with a call for "peaceful coexistence" and African-Asian solidarity. Zhou also announced that the People's Republic would "strive for the liberation of Taiwan by peaceful means so far as it is possible."
May 25, 1955	The government dismissed the writer Hu Feng from the writer's union and other posts for "bourgeois and idealist thinking." His crime: resisting the primacy of Marxist theory in artistic criticism.
July 1955	The authorities arrested the writer Hu Feng, tried him in secret, and sentenced him to a long prison term.
Late 1950s	The government demolished the ancient walls of Beijing to improve the flow of traffic. The area to the south of the Imperial Palace was cleared for the expansion of Tiananmen Square. A massive Soviet-style Great Hall of the People rose on one side of the square; a 100-foot-tall Monument to the Martyrs of the People glorified China's revolutionary heroes.
1956	Deng Xiaoping (1904–1997) became general secretary of the Communist Party.
January 4, 1956	The Trans-Mongolian Railway linking China and the Soviet Union officially opened, providing through rail service from Beijing to Moscow via Ulan Bator.
January 10–20, 1956	All private enterprises in Beijing, Tianjin, Shanghai, Guangzhou, Wuhan, and other major cities completed the transition to joint state/private management.
March 30, 1956	The State Council said it would eliminate illiteracy in China within five to seven years.
May 2, 1956	At a closed party session, Mao Zedong proposed a Hundred Flowers Campaign that would seek criticism of the Communist Party.
May 11, 1956	Daily train service opened between Guangzhou and Shanghai.

May 29, 1956	The first passenger aircraft landed in Lhasa in Tibet after an eleven-hour flight from Beijing.
July 13, 1956	The Baoji-Chengdu Railway opened, linking northwestern China with the southwest.
July 13, 1956	The first 10 trucks manufactured in China rolled off the assembly line at a plant in Zhangzhun.
August 19, 1956	China and the Soviet Union agreed on joint development of hydroelectric power along the Amur River, the boundary between Manchuria and Siberia.
September 1956	The Communist Party National Congress approved resolutions for a collective leadership and de-emphasis of the "cult of Mao."
September 30–October 14, 1956	Indonesian President Sukharno visited China, the first non-Communist head of state to enter the People's Republic.
February 27, 1957	Mao repeated his call for a Hundred Flowers Campaign at a meeting of skeptical senior Communist Party officials. Mao said discussion rather than coercion should settle ideological and artistic controversies.
April 23, 1957	The United States announced it would allow a pool of American journalists to report from the People's Republic of China.
Late April 1957	Mao Zedong finally overrode the hard-liners' opposition and launched the Hundred Flowers Campaign.
May 1957	The United States announced that missiles capable of delivering atomic warheads on Chinese targets were being stationed on Nationalist Taiwan.
May 1957	Breaking with U.S. policy, Great Britain announced it would ease its embargo on trade with China.
May 1957	The impeccably Communist Ding Ling (1904–1985), author of "The Diary of Miss Sophie" and a Stalin Prize–winning "proletarian" work titled *The Sun Shines over the Sanggan River*, called for the lifting of government controls on literature.
May 1–June 7, 1957	The Hundred Flowers criticism proved more than Mao had bargained for. Student protests erupted in Beijing and many other cities. Thoroughly alarmed, Mao canceled the campaign.
June–December 1957	In the Communist Party's Anti-Rightist Campaign that followed the abortive Hundred Flowers, 300,000 people were branded as rightists and subjected to various forms of persecution, including exile to hard labor in the countryside and jail. The author Ding Ling was stripped of her party posts and exiled to farm labor on the Siberian frontier.

August 3, 1957	China promulgated a law establishing special farms and factories where counter-revolutionaries, vagrants, misfits, and other undesirables could be put to work.
September 25, 1957	The passage of a train carrying 1,000 travelers inaugurated the mile-long bridge over the Yangtze River at Wuhan.
October–November 1957	China and the Soviet Union negotiated a treaty on new technology and national defense that obligated the Soviets to help China develop atomic weaponry.
November 2–7, 1957	Mao Zedong led a Chinese delegation to the Soviet Union, his second and last visit there. The Soviets promised the Chinese a prototype atomic bomb and assistance in making their own.
December 1957	Liang Bin published his novel *Keep the Red Flag Flying*.
Late 1957	The Anti-Rightist Campaign targeted writer Liu Binyan (born 1925), who introduced the form of investigative journalism the Chinese called "reporting literature."
Late 1957	At Mao Zedong's direction, the Communist Party prepared to launch the Great Leap Forward. It would open with a new round of agricultural collectivization—the merging of large collectives into giant communes.
February 1958	The National People's Congress announced the Great Leap Forward, a second Five-Year Plan for economic growth that called for a 50-percent increase in national income.
February 1–24, 1958	An estimated 700,000 people saw the 22,000 items on display at the Japanese Commodity Exhibition in Guangzhou.
March 4, 1958	The first number of the weekly English-language *Peking Review* appeared.
April–August 1958	The government launched a new collectivization drive, part of the Great Leap Forward. More private farms were abolished, and rural collectives were merged into larger and larger communes.
May 12, 1958	The first East Wind model automobile was manufactured in China.
August 1958	The model Red Flag Commune of Zhengzhou in northern China contained 18,729 people centered on a spinning and weaving machinery factory. The commune included public dining halls, child care centers, schools, hospitals, banks, farms, and stores.
August 23–October 6, 1958	Chinese forces bombarded the Nationalist-held islands of Quemoy and Matsu.

September 1, 1958	The United States reinforced Air Force units on Taiwan and with the Seventh Fleet in the Taiwan Straits.
September 2, 1958	Beijing Television began broadcasting.
September 4, 1958	The United States said it would use armed force to defend Quemoy and Matsu.
September 27, 1958	The first research nuclear reactor went into service near Beijing.
Autumn 1958	With millions of farm laborers re-deployed for Yellow River flood control and other large public works projects, crops were neglected, and much of the 1958 harvest rotted in the fields.
November 1958	An estimated 98 percent of China's farm population consisted of 26,000 communes.
November 2, 1958	The Communists ended their intermittent shelling of Quemoy and Matsu.
November 27, 1958	The People's Republic of China launched its first ocean-going freighter, the 22,100-ton *Leap Forward*.
December 1958	The Communist Party Central Committee reported the merger of 740,000 cooperatives into 26,000 communes with 120 million households. The government issued inflated figures for the harvest, reporting 375 million tons of grain when the total reached only 215 million tons.
December 10, 1958	With the encouragement of Liu Shaoqi and Deng Xiaoping, Mao Zedong "retired" as chairman of the republic. He retained the title of chief of the Communist Party, however, and remained the most powerful and prestigious of China's leaders.
December 26, 1958	China announced it had built or expanded 1,300 miles of railroad during the year.
1959	China rejected Soviet requests for a naval communications station on Chinese soil and to fuel and repair warships in Chinese ports.
1959	The government abolished the Ministry of Justice.
February 7, 1959	The 360-mile-long Guangxi railroad opened for traffic.
February 7, 1959	China and the Soviet Union signed a $1.25 billion technical aid agreement for construction of heavy industrial plants.
March 10–23, 1959	Tibetans rose in rebellion. China quelled the outbreak, but an underground insurgency continued with U.S. support.
March 17, 1959	The Dalai Lama fled the Tibetan capital of Lhasa with members of his family and cabinet.

March 24, 1959	A Hong Kong newspaper reported that Mao Zedong had swum the Yalu River seven times the previous September to dispel reports his health had failed.
March 31, 1959	Having eluded Chinese pursuit, the Tibetan Dalai Lama arrived in India and sought asylum.
April 15, 1959	China accused India of interference in its internal affairs; the Indians, the Chinese claimed, had abducted the Dalai Lama and were holding him under duress.
Spring 1959	Liu Shaoqi (1898–1969), the author of *How to Be a Good Communist,* succeeded Mao as head of the Chinese state.
May 31, 1959	The United Nations estimated China's population at 640 million.
June 1959	The Soviet Union unilaterally canceled the New Technology and National Defense Treaty with China. The Soviets withdrew the offer of an atomic bomb and restricted the flow of scientific information.
June 20, 1959	The Dalai Lama charged that Chinese Communists had killed 65,000 Tibetan civilians since 1956, deported thousands to China, and destroyed 1,000 monasteries.
July–August 1959	Drought damaged as much as 30 percent of all arable land in China. Nine provinces and as many as 300 million people were affected.
August 1959	In a private letter to Mao Zedong, Defense Minister Peng Dehuai sharply criticized Great Leap Forward policies. Mao made the letter public, denounced Peng, and stripped him of his offices. Though he supported Mao over Peng, Deng Xiaoping also questioned the Great Leap Forward.
August 1959	The government admitted that Great Leap Forward production fell well below target figures. Inspectors pronounced 3 million of 11 million tons of steel produced during the Great Leap Forward drive of 1958 unfit for industrial use. Much of the inferior steel had been made in "backyard" furnaces.
September 17, 1959	Lin Biao (1907–1971) succeeded Peng Dehuai as defense minister.
October 21, 1959	Chinese and Indian forces clashed in the border region of Ladakh. Chinese troops killed 10 Indian frontier police and captured nine others.
November 1, 1959	China opened its first tractor factory, in Luoyang.

December 4, 1959	The Supreme People's Court granted an amnesty to Puyi, the last emperor. He had been held as a war criminal. The Communists assigned the "remolded" Puyi a job in a machine repair shop at a botanical garden in Beijing.
1959–1962	A series of poor harvests, mostly the result of mismanagement of the Great Leap Forward (1958–1961), led to widespread famine. As many as 30 million persons perished in what the government euphemistically called the Three Hard Years period.
Early 1960s	The government introduced a "two track" educational system, with superior schooling for talented children and lesser instruction for average students. "Keypoint" college preparatory schools were established for exceptional students. Mao Zedong attacked the new system as "revisionist."
1960	Grain output totaled 160 million metric tons, down from 200 million two years earlier.
March 17, 1960	A Communist court sentenced Gong Pinmei (KUNG P'IN-MEI; Ignatius Kung), the Roman Catholic bishop of Shanghai, to life in prison; 12 other Chinese Catholics received long prison terms.
March 18, 1960	The Communists sentenced Bishop James Walsh, the American head of the Maryknoll Catholic mission, to 20 years in prison for spying and counter-revolutionary activities.
April 6, 1960	The government announced that 73 percent of China's population (400 million people) took their meals at commune-operated public dining halls.
April 19–25, 1960	Zhou Enlai and the Indian prime minister, Jawaharlal Nehru, met in New Delhi to discuss the border dispute. The talks recessed without a resolution.
May 25, 1960	A Chinese expedition reached the summit of Mount Everest.
August–September 1960	The Soviet Union withdrew all military advisers and technicians working in China, bringing the Sino-Soviet split, developing for two years, fully into the open.
October 7, 1960	John F. Kennedy and Richard M. Nixon, in their second televised debate of the U.S. presidential campaign, clashed over the disputed islands of Quemoy and Matsu. Kennedy said they were indefensible and not worth fighting over. Nixon said principles of freedom were at issue.
December 29, 1960	The government announced that drought, floods, insect pests, and other natural calamities had seriously affected more than half of China's cultivated land. Only Tibet and Xinjiang were spared.

1961	President John F. Kennedy assured the Nationalists on Taiwan that the United States would continue to veto United Nations admission for the People's Republic of China.
1961	With the virtual elimination of private farming, hog production fell to 52 percent of the 1958 level.
1961	Artist Pan Tianshou (P'AN T'IEN-SHOU) painted *Crane and Frost Plum Together at Year's End*.
January 1961	Historian Wu Han published his play *The Dismissal of Hai Rui from Office*. The work was viewed as an implicit critique of Mao Zedong's refusal to tolerate dissent.
February 2 and 6, 1961	In separate deals, Canada and Australia agreed to sell drought-stricken China $120 million worth of grain.
May 24, 1961	China inaugurated air service between Guangzhou and Hainan Island.
June 1961	In a tour of the countryside in Hunan, Politburo member Chen Yun found chaos because of Great Leap Forward policies. He recommended restoring small private plots to peasants and reopening private rural markets.
July 1, 1961	Communist Party membership reached 17 million.
July 1, 1961	The Museum of Chinese History and the Museum of the Chinese Revolution opened in Beijing.
December 14, 1961	The government tightened control over the army with new regulations broadening the powers of political commissars assigned to individual military units.
December 21, 1961	Canada announced the sale of an additional $71 million worth of wheat and barley to China.
1962	With rapid economic development, industrial products accounted for 51 percent of Taiwan's exports, compared to only 7 percent in 1953.
January 1962	Alarmed by the fall in farm production, the government launched the Three Promises and One Guarantee program. It gave peasants permission to work small farm plots, produce handicrafts for private sale, and sell products in rural free markets. In return, peasants would meet government-set quotas—the guarantee.
February 24, 1962	China formally protested the recently established U.S. military assistance command in South Vietnam.
February 28, 1962	The Museum of Natural History, with 5,000 specimens on display, opened in Beijing.

March 28, 1962	China negotiated another $73 million worth of grain purchases from Canada.
May–June 1962	China filed a series of protests of alleged incursions of Indian troops along the border of Xinjiang.
August 1962	The People's Literary Press published the 14th and last volume of Ba Jin's *Collected Works*.
September 24, 1962	Mao Zedong launched the Socialist Education Movement calling for a renewed emphasis on class warfare. One feature: intellectuals were sent into the country to learn from the masses.
October 10, 1962	Heavy fighting broke out between Chinese and Indian troops along India's northeastern frontier.
October 20, 1962	After renewed clashes in disputed frontier areas, China unleashed a full-scale offensive along the China-India border.
October 26, 1962	India declared a state of emergency and appealed to the United States, Great Britain, France, and Canada for military assistance.
November 6, 1962	In an emergency airlift, one weapons-laden U.S. aircraft landed at Indian air bases every three hours.
November 9, 1962	China and Japan signed a long-term trade agreement.
November 20, 1962	China declared a unilateral cease-fire in the Indian frontier war and announced it would withdraw from the disputed territories it had occupied.
December 1962	China bought another $148 million worth of wheat from Canada and Australia.
1963	New oilfields at Daqing in northeastern China produced two-thirds of the country's oil, freeing China from dependence on Soviet imports.
January 7, 1963	The Soviet Union charged China and Albania with breaking "international proletarian discipline" and demanded that China cease its attacks on the Soviet Communist Party.
March 1, 1963	China announced it had completed its planned withdrawal from disputed areas along the Indian frontier.
March 8, 1963	China demanded that the Soviet Union recognize that the existing frontier between the two powers was the result of a series of unequal treaties imposed on China in the 19th and early 20th centuries.

April 1963	Jiang Qing (CHIANG CH'ING, 1914-91), Mao Zedong's wife, called for the banning of ghost plays and other traditional dramatic forms.
April 1, 1963	The government opened a new water route from Shanghai on the east coast along the Yangtze River to Chongqing in southwestern China, the country's longest inland shipping route.
May 10, 1963	Mobs looted and burned the homes and businesses of Chinese residents in Indonesia.
July 31, 1963	China denounced the nuclear test ban treaty between the United States, Great Britain, and the Soviet Union and proposed the complete prohibition of nuclear weapons. China and France refused to sign the treaty.
August 20, 1963	The Japanese government approved a private company's proposal to build a $20-million synthetic textiles plant in China.
1963–1969	Chinese and Soviet forces clashed in several thousand unpublicized skirmishes along their 4,100-mile-long border.
1963–1973	Taiwan recorded an annual economic growth rate of 9.7 percent.
January 27, 1964	China and France announced they would establish diplomatic relations; France became the first major power to recognize China since 1950.
February 1, 1964	Lin Biao inaugurated a "learn from the army" campaign featuring Lei Feng, a selfless People's Liberation Army (PLA) soldier who was killed when a truck backed over him. The posthumous "discovery" of Lei's diary was offered as a guide for all a Communist should be.
February 25, 1964	China and the Soviet Union opened new talks on their long-running border dispute.
June 5–31, 1964	The Peking Opera produced a festival of works on "contemporary themes." The government press reported packed houses.
July 7, 1964	China announced it had completed irrigation facilities for an additional 3 million hectares (close to 7.5 million acres) since the previous winter.
August 6, 1964	China protested the U.S. bombing of North Vietnam in retaliation for the Tonkin Gulf incidents, in which North Vietnamese PT boats had fired on the American destroyers *Maddox* and *C. Turner Joy* as they were patrolling in the gulf.
September 15, 1964	In an interview with Japanese socialists, Soviet Premier Nikita Krushchev compared Mao Zedong to Hitler.

October 15, 1964	China's border talks with the Soviet Union ended with no progress reported.
October 16, 1964	China detonated its first atomic bomb at a test site near Lop Nor in the Xinjiang Desert.
October 20, 1964	*The East Is Red*, a historical play with music and dancing, was staged in Beijing.
October 20, 1964	Zhou Enlai called for a world conference on nuclear disarmament.
1965	Agricultural production recovered to pre-Great Leap Forward levels.
January 25, 1965	His authority eroded, Mao Zedong told a Communist Party session he was prepared to move against his appointed successor, Liu Shaoqi.
February 8, 1965	China protested U.S. air strikes on targets in North Vietnam.
April 12, 1965	China agreed to purchase passenger and cargo vessels from the French shipbuilder Chantier de l'Atlantique.
May 1, 1965	The government opened an exhibition in Guangzhou displaying 230 rare objects found in Ming tombs northwest of Beijing.
May 14, 1965	China detonated a second nuclear explosion at Lop Nor. The United States had made 337 announced explosions as of this date, the Soviet Union 127, Great Britain 24, and France 5.
June 1, 1965	All ranks and insignia were abolished in the People's Liberation Army.
November 10, 1965	A Shanghai newspaper article denounced Wu Han's play *The Dismissal* of Hai Rui as an allegorical criticism of Mao Zedong. It would turn out to be an opening broadside in the Cultural Revolution.
November 10, 1965	Indonesian mobs attacked a Chinese consulate and the homes and businesses of Chinese settled in North Sumatra. China filed a protest with the Indonesian government.
December 30, 1965	Wu Han recanted, confessing that he had not followed Mao's theory of class struggle in *The Dismissal of Hai Rui*.
January 17, 1966	China protested continuing anti-Chinese demonstrations in Indonesia.
March 21, 1966	Nearly 200 American-China experts called on the U.S. government to drop opposition to China's admission to the U.N.

May 1966	With encouragement from Mao Zedong and his wife, Jiang Qing, radical university students in Beijing and elsewhere rose against their faculty and administration, triggering what Mao dubbed the Great Proletarian Cultural Revolution.
	The backdrop was Mao's belief in continuing revolution, his anxiety that he was losing control of the Communist Party, and his dissatisfaction with government policies that encouraged private farming, incentives in industry, and other "revisions" of Marxist-Leninist doctrine. With Lin Biao, Jiang Qing, and other radical allies, he touched off a cataclysm.
May 16, 1966	The so-called 16 May Circular established a Cultural Revolution Group to direct the revolution. Dominated by Jiang Qing and other radicals, it reported directly to Mao. The group attacked bourgeois and revisionist ideas in the party, government, army, and cultural affairs.
May 25, 1966	Radicals at Beijing University put up a big-character wall poster criticizing the university administration for following liberal policies. The critiques spread to campuses throughout China.
June 1966	As part of the Cultural Revolution, the government suspended college entrance examinations and shut down the schools for the semester.
June 1, 1966	China and France approved weekly air service between Shanghai and Paris, to begin in September.
June 1, 1966	Maoists seized control of the *People's Daily* in Beijing, a Liu Shaoqi organ, and enlisted it in the cause of the Cultural Revolution.
June–July 1966	Tens of thousands of students joined the radical student groups called the Red Guards. Jiang Qing and others incited them to criticize university, party, and government leaders. Party moderates tried unsuccessfully to control the students through "work teams" sent onto the campuses (an effort Mao dubbed "white terror") and by forming their own Red Guard units with a view to co-opting the movement.
July 11, 1966	The government suspended visas and closed China to most foreigners.
July 12, 1966	President Lyndon B. Johnson called for a policy of cooperation with China. He was the first post-revolution U.S. president to conciliate China.
July 16, 1966	Mao Zedong, 70 years old, took his famous Yangtze River swim, intended to show he had the health and political vigor needed to lead the Cultural Revolution.

Early August 1966	Packed with Red Guards, a hastily called meeting of the Central Committee adopted a resolution exhorting China's youth to criticize "those persons in authority who are taking the capitalist road." Mao named Lin Biao, the defense minister, first vice chairman of the committee, the second-ranking position in the party hierarchy.
August 18, 1966	Red Guards were mentioned by the official press for the first time, at a rally of more than 1 million people in Beijing.
August 18–November 26, 1966	A series of mass rallies in Beijing brought together 13 million Red Guards from throughout China. Mao himself, wearing a red armband, presided over some of the rallies. The Guards were urged to attack the Four Olds—old ideas, old culture, old customs, and old habits.
August 23, 1966	Thousands of Red Guards ransacked Christian churches in Beijing.
September 13, 1966	Red Guards seized Communist Party headquarters in Shanghai.
September 17, 1966	Zhou Enlai criticized Red Guard excesses and ordered the revolutionaries not to interfere with farm or industrial production.
October–December 1966	In speeches and editorials, the Cultural Revolution Group criticized the Communist Party for resisting the revolution and called for an assault on the party establishment. Red Guards were urged to target Liu Shaoqi, Deng Xiaoping, and other senior officials. Only Mao Zedong was exempt.
November 16, 1966	In an effort to curb the Red Guards, the government revoked their free transportation privileges.
December 1966	Red Guard radicals invaded China's factories.
1966–1969	Taiwan developed "export processing zones" with tax incentives and other aid to exporters of manufactured products.
1966–1969	The Red Guards campaigned against smoking, drinking, and "the bourgeois keeping of crickets, fish, cats, and dogs." Shopkeepers were coerced into adopting revolutionary names for their shops. One Red Guard group proposed that the red traffic light should henceforth signal go rather than stop. Old buildings, temples, churches, art objects, and the dwellings of "revisionists" were vandalized or destroyed. Thousands of writers and artists, as well as politicians and political and economic theorists, came under physical attack, many of them tortured and killed. The author Ding Ling spent five years in prison. Red Guards publicly humiliated Ba Jin, whose novel *Family* had been influential in the 1930s, and drove the novelist Lao She to suicide.

1967	Because of Red Guard disruptions, China's industrial output fell 15–20 percent.
1967	China published 350 million copies of the *Quotations from Chairman Mao Zedong* and 86 million sets of Mao's *Selected Works.*
1967	Cultural Revolution leaders dismantled the two-track education system and introduced egalitarian schooling for the masses.
1967	The literacy rate on Taiwan reached 97 percent.
January 6, 1967	Red Guards rallied in Shanghai. Municipal government officials were removed from office, and the radicals took over. Officials were forced to march in the streets wearing dunce caps and carrying placards detailing their crimes; many were arrested and beaten. In similar coups elsewhere, known as the January power seizures, Red Guards attempted to hijack party organizations throughout China.
January 7, 1967	Japanese news sources reported 54 dead, 900 wounded, and 6,000 arrested in three days of street fighting in Nanjing, touched off when worker mobs attacked Red Guard headquarters.
January 23, 1967	The Central Committee authorized the Shanghai seizure of power from "capitalist roaders." At the same time, Mao ordered PLA units to restore order in Shanghai and other cities. The intervention dramatically increased the army's political power and presence.
February 1967	Mao Zedong and his allies issued a set of directives known as the February Adverse Current in an effort to curb the excesses of the Cultural Revolution. Mao criticized the use of violence, even the dunce caps. When senior party leaders attacked the idea of the Cultural Revolution, Mao rescinded some of the crackdown measures.
April 30–May 10, 1967	Red Guards in Beijing touched off 133 street clashes involving 60,000 people.
May 12–15, 1967	Workers rioted in the industrial district of Kowloon; 200 were arrested.
May 21 and 22, 1967	In renewed street disturbances, thousands of Chinese rallied in central Hong Kong. Police opened fire when some in the crowd threw Molotov cocktails; another 200 rioters were arrested.
June 17, 1967	China exploded its first hydrogen bomb.
June 25–28, 1967	Communists in Hong Kong organized strikes of transport and other utility workers.

Summer 1967	Red Guards in Beijing seized Liu Shaoqi, China's head of state, and beat him in front of crowds. He died of complications from the beatings in 1969.
July 20, 1967	PLA forces restoring order in Wuhan seized two radical Red Guard leaders. In response, Jiang Qing's Cultural Revolution Group called on the Red Guards to take power from the "capitalist roaders" in the army. The so-called Wuhan Incident ushered in the most-violent phase of the Cultural Revolution.
August 1967	Deng Xiaoping faced a Red Guard public "trial." He removed his hearing aid during the harangue.
August 22, 1967	Red Guards sacked the British Mission in Beijing, burning the main building and smashing furniture in the legation residence.
September 1967	Mao Zedong announced a "strategic plan" to conclude the Cultural Revolution.
September 1, 1967	Zhou Enlai ordered the Red Guards to return to their schools.
October 17, 1967	Puyi, the last emperor, died.
1968	Life expectancy in China reached 60 years. The rise largely reflected reductions in the rate of infant mortality.
1968	After nearly two decades of land reform, owners tilled 90 percent of farmland on Taiwan; only 10 percent remained tenant-tilled.
March 6, 1968	Chinese and Japanese trade officials signed a new one-year $100 million trade agreement.
July 1968	Mao Zedong ordered an end to Red Guard violence to stave off a civil war. The People's Liberation Army gradually restored order. Purges followed. The investigation of the so-called May 16 Group (a radical plot said to be aimed at Zhou Enlai; it may never have existed) ended with many executions.
July 1968	The revolutionary opera *The Red Lantern* opened in Beijing.
July 6, 1968	The Soviet Union released figures showing trade with China had fallen to a low of $107 million in 1967, down from $2.2 billion in 1959.
July 16, 1968	The World Council of Churches, meeting in Sweden, called for the admission of the People's Republic of China to the United Nations.
November 1968	The Central Committee confirmed that Liu Shaoqi had been stripped of all party and government offices.

November 20, 1968	*The Wall Street Journal,* a U.S. newspaper, reported that China had cut the last remaining telephone cable to the United States. Linking Shanghai and Oakland, it handled only about 20 calls in its last year of operation.
December 22, 1968	Mao Zedong called for educated young people to be sent into the country to be "rusticated"—re-educated by peasants and workers.
December 29, 1968	A double-decker highway-railroad bridge over the Yangtze River opened at Nanjing.
1968-1973	Deng Xiaoping lived quietly under house arrest in Jiangxi Province.
January 16, 1969	*The New York Times* reported that 15 to 20 million Chinese had been relocated from the cities to the countryside as part of the effort to control the Cultural Revolution.
March 2, 1969	Chinese troops ambushed a Soviet force on frontier Zhenbao (Damansky) Island in the Ussuri River.
March 14–15, 1969	The Soviets retaliated with infantry and tanks against Chinese forces on Zhenbao Island, inflicting 800 casualties.
April 1969	The Communist Party Congress unanimously elected Mao Zedong chairman of the party and the Central Committee and designated Lin Biao as his successor.
May 10, 1969	Renewed border clashes were reported along the Sino-Soviet frontier in Xinjiang.
July 21, 1969	U.S. President Richard Nixon announced some easing of U.S. trade and travel restrictions on China, though a general travel ban would remain in effect.
August 1969	A 20-camel Chinese caravan crossed the Himalayas and entered Pakistan via the famous Silk Road—the first transit of the ancient route since its closing in 1949. Chinese and Pakistani merchants bartered $120,000 worth of goods.
September 11, 1969	China and the Soviet Union agreed to reject the use of force and pursue negotiations to settle border disputes.
September 19, 1969	The government announced that oilfield discoveries and increased refining capacity had made China self-sufficient in oil.
December 22, 1969	The United States partially lifted a trade embargo on the People's Republic of China.
December 26, 1969	A shipyard in Shanghai launched China's first icebreaker, the 3,200-ton *Haibing* 101.

1969–1970	China's economy reached full recovery after the dislocations of the Cultural Revolution. Most industries and agricultural enterprises climbed back to or exceeded 1966 levels.
1970	China's population reached 880 million, up from 630 million in 1957.
April 1970	A group of Japanese business leaders accepted China's Four Principles of Trade: that firms doing business with China may not trade with Taiwan or South Korea, export weapons to the United States for use in Indochina, or affiliate with U.S. companies in Japan.
April 23, 1970	The Hongqi (Red Flag) shipyard in Shanghai launched a 15,000-ton tanker built entirely of Chinese-made rolled steel.
April 24, 1970	China launched its first satellite into space. It broadcast the tune "The East Is Red" (a song praising Mao Zedong) continuously on a frequency of 20,000 megacycles.
April 30, 1970	U.S. troops crossed the border from South Vietnam into Cambodia. China-backed Prince Norodom Sihanouk prepared to form a Cambodian exile government in Beijing.
June 30, 1970	U.S. forces withdrew from Cambodia.
July 1, 1970	China opened the 600-mile Chengdu-Kunming railroad.
July 3, 1970	The government announced completion of a 65-mile flood control-irrigation canal in the Wuhan region north of the Hanjiang River.
July 10, 1970	China released James Walsh, the former bishop of Shanghai imprisoned for life in 1958.
July 21, 1970	Regular classes resumed at Qinghai University in Beijing for the first time since the Red Guard outbreak of 1966.
August 1970	The developing split between Mao Zedong and Lin Biao came into the open at a Central Committee session in Lushan. Mao moved to withdraw the designation of Lin as his successor.
September 24, 1970	The government announced that Qinghai and Beijing universities together had enrolled 4,000 students since July.
October 13, 1970	Canada established diplomatic relations with the People's Republic of China.
December 21, 1970	Japan, South Korea, and Nationalist China announced a joint development plan for oil and mineral extraction from the seabed near Taiwan.
January 4, 1971	The first highway bridge across the Yellow River in the Ningxia region opened.

January 25, 1971	U.S. President Nixon, in a State of the World Address, referred to China by its official name—the People's Republic—the first official U.S. statement to use the designation.
March 15, 1971	The United States removed all travel restrictions on Americans going to China, meaning U.S. citizens no longer needed special permission to visit the mainland.
April 10–17, 1971	A U.S. table tennis team toured China. "Ping-Pong diplomacy" led to a thaw in relations between the two countries.
April 14, 1971	The United States announced a relaxation of the direct trade embargo on China.
April 14, 1971	Direct telephone communications were open between China and Great Britain for the first time since 1949 via a radio link operating three hours a day.
July 9–11, 1971	Henry Kissinger, a senior adviser to U.S. President Richard Nixon, met secretly with Zhou Enlai to plan a Nixon visit to China.
July 15, 1971	The United States and China announced the Nixon visit.
July 25, 1971	The government announced the discovery of the oldest known manuscript of the *Analects of Confucius.*
September 13, 1971	Defense Minister Lin Biao, his alleged plans for a military coup exposed and in ruins, died in the crash of an aircraft allegedly carrying him into exile in the Soviet Union. A longtime Mao loyalist, Lin commanded victorious civil war armies and compiled the best-selling "little red book"—the *Quotations of Chairman Mao.*
September 16	The American Telephone & Telegraph Company (AT&T) announced it would restore direct telephone links between the United States and China.
October 25, 1971	The United Nations admitted the People's Republic of China to membership and expelled Taiwan.
December 1971	Thirteen thousand Chinese were at work on a 300-mile stretch of the Tanzania-Zambia railway. China agreed to supply 100 locomotives, as well as passenger and freight cars, for the new line.
1972	Artist Guan Shanyue (KUAN SHAN-YUEH) painted *Oil City in the South,* an idealized rendering of China's industrial development.
January 1, 1972	Air France, the only Western airline with service to China, said it would add a second weekly flight from Paris.

February 21–28, 1972	President Richard Nixon visited China. He and his advisers met with Mao Zedong, Zhou Enlai, and others.
February 22, 1972	President Nixon attended a special performance of the *Red Detachment of Women,* a revolutionary opera produced by Jiang Qing, Mao Zedong's wife.
February 28, 1972	The United States and China issued the Shanghai Communique. It laid out the two countries' positions on Taiwan—China affirmed it meant to recover the breakaway province—and called for normalization of U.S.-China relations.
April 19, 1972	A Moscow economics journal put Sino-Soviet trade at $153 million in 1971.
April 20, 1972	China presented two giant pandas to the Washington Zoo as a gift to the American people.
July 31, 1972	Archeologists excavated a tomb near Changsha in Hunan that contained a female corpse, wooden coffins, and burial relics from the early Western Han period.
August 16, 1972	Japan inaugurated air service between Japanese cities and Shanghai.
September 9, 1972	China agreed to purchase 10 long-range 707 jetliners from the Boeing Company.
September 25, 1972	In a first visit to China, a Japanese prime minister (Kakuei Tanaka) apologized for Japan's aggression in the 1930s and 1940s and negotiated a normalization of diplomatic and trade relations. Japan recognized the People's Republic of China as the sole legal government of China and canceled the 1952 peace treaty with the Nationalists on Taiwan.
September 29, 1972	West Germany established diplomatic relations with the People's Republic of China.
October 1, 1972	*The New York Times* reported that China had moved 500,000 high school and college graduates from the cities to the countryside since the start of the year.
October 1, 1972	The Peking Man Center opened in Zhoukoudian, Hebei Province.
November 17, 1972	The Shenyang Acrobatic Troupe left China for a tour of Canada, the United States, Peru, and Mexico.
December 1, 1972	Archeologists excavated 340 well-preserved bronzes of the early Western Zhou dynasty in Gansu Province.
1973	China purchased $1 billion worth of industrial equipment, including entire plants, from the United States.

1973	China imported nearly $1 billion worth of grain, nearly two-thirds of it from the United States.
January 1973	The United States, South Vietnam, and North Vietnam reached a cease-fire agreement in Indochina.
February 14, 1973	Shanghai's population reached 10,820,000, making it the largest city in the world.
March 1973	Zhou Enlai brought back into government Deng Xiaoping, the former "number-two capitalist roader," and other senior officials disgraced during the Cultural Revolution.
March 1973	China released a U.S. intelligence agent imprisoned for more than 20 years and two American pilots shot down over China during the Vietnam War.
March 17–27, 1973	The London Philharmonic Orchestra toured China.
April 1973	U.S. State Department officials established a liaison office in Beijing.
April 11–15, 1973	The Vienna Philharmonic Orchestra toured China.
May 14, 1973	Senior U.S. diplomat David K. E. Bruce arrived in China to take charge of the Beijing liaison office.
June 1973	The Soviet Union deployed more than 1 million troops with missiles and nuclear weapons along China's frontier. China rejected a Soviet offer of a non-aggression pact.
June 13, 1973	Chinese and British airlines agreed to establish regular air service between London and Beijing.
June 27, 1973	China tested a hydrogen bomb at the Lop Nor site in Xinjiang.
August 1973	The government launched a propaganda campaign that attacked Confucianism as reactionary and praised the first Qin emperor, long vilified as a tyrant. Disgraced officials were routinely stigmatized as "the Confuciuses of contemporary China."
August 24–28, 1973	The Tenth Party Congress in Beijing named five new party vice chairmen, suggesting a collective leadership for post-Mao China.
April 24, 1973	Zhou Enlai estimated Communist Party membership at 28 million.
September 1973	The president of France, Georges Pompidou, became the first Western European head of state to visit China.
September 6, 1973	A report showed Japan as China's leading trade partner at $1.1 billion a year, nearly 20 percent of China's total foreign trade.

September 12–22, 1973	The Philadelphia Orchestra toured China.
October 4, 1973	Two Japanese steel companies announced plans to build a $380 billion steel plant in China, with completion scheduled for 1975.
January 1974	The government reshuffled 20–25 senior regional military commanders, weakening the PLA's role in politics and removing what remained of Lin Biao's influence.
January 14, 1974	An editorial in the *People's Daily* attacked Beethoven, Schubert, and other European composers as "bourgeois."
January 19, 1974	China expelled five officials of the Soviet Embassy in Beijing for alleged spying.
January 30, 1974	China inaugurated direct commercial flights from Beijing to Moscow.
April 1974	Economists predicted U.S.-China trade would reach $1.25 billion by the end of the year, up from $800 million in 1973.
June 17, 1974	China exploded its 16th nuclear device.
August 17, 1974	Archeologists excavating an earth platform near Zhengzhou in Henan Province found a pile of slave skulls dating back 3,500 years to the Shang dynasty.
September 29, 1974	Regular passenger air service began between Tokyo and Beijing.
October 1974	Increasingly isolated, Taiwan maintained diplomatic relations with only 32 countries.
November 1974	In their turn, the Soviets rejected a Chinese offer of a non-aggression treaty.
December 27, 1974	China announced completion of a 690-mile pipeline from the Daqing oilfields to the northern China port of Qinhuangdao.
1975	The People's Republic of China signed a joint venture agreement with Rolls-Royce of Great Britain to build jet aircraft engines in China.
1975	Hu Yaobang, a protégé of Deng Xiaoping, became head of the prestigious Academy of Sciences in Beijing. He moved to shield the academy from political interference.
January 13–17, 1975	At the Fourth National People's Congress in Beijing, the rehabilitated Deng Xiaoping won appointment as first vice premier, with day-to-day responsibility for running the country. The congress approved a new constitution, replacing the 1954 version.

February 4, 1975	Linqiaxia hydroelectric station, China's largest, went into service on the upper Yellow River.
February 12, 1975	The government announced the start of work on a French-built petrochemical complex northeast of Beijing.
February 20, 1975	Archeologists in Hubei Province unearthed Shang dynasty palace foundations dating back 3,000–4,000 years.
April 5, 1975	Chiang Kai-shek died. His son Chiang Ching-kuo succeeded him as ruler of the Nationalist republic in Taiwan. Chiang would lift martial law, begin to open the political process, and permit visits to the mainland.
April 7, 1975	Swissair launched a Zurich-Geneva-Beijing-Shanghai service.
April 11, 1975	Archeologists excavated a Shang dynasty settlement in Jiangxi Province, the first Shang site found south of the Yangtze River.
July 1, 1975	The Baoji-Chengdu railway opened, China's first electric line.
December 31, 1975	A year-end New China News Agency report indicated wages of industrial workers averaged around $360 per year.
1976	With continuing Cultural Revolution instability, industrial production stagnated, rising by only 1 percent.
January 3, 1976	In an unprecedented deal, China agreed to buy land from the British Hong Kong government for construction of an oil storage depot.
January 8, 1976	Zhou Enlai died.
January 9, 1976	The government reported that 95 percent of China's primary-school-age children were enrolled, a 10 percent increase from 1966.
February 10, 1976	A wall poster campaign at Beijing University attacked Deng Xiaoping as a "capitalist roader."
March 27, 1976	Archeologists in Hubei found 1,200 bamboo slips recording laws and documents dating back 2,200 years to the Warring States–Qin dynasty period.
April 5–6, 1976	A mass act of homage to Zhou Enlai in Beijing's Tiananmen Square turned into an anti-government rally. Hundreds of the estimated 100,000 protesters were arrested.
April 6, 1976	The Beijing protests spread to Zhengzhou, Wuhan, Shanghai, Guangzhou, and other cities.
April 7, 1976	Mao Zedong again stripped Deng Xiaoping of his offices.

July 16, 1976	The government reported that 117 novels had been published in China from 1972 to 1975. Titles included *Shipbuilders, On the March, Barefoot Doctor Hongyu,* and *The Sparkling Red Star.*
July 28, 1976	A massive earthquake shattered the Hebei industrial city of Tangshan. The official death toll was 242,000, with another 164,000 injured.
August 29, 1976	The government announced the launching of the first 50,000-ton oil tanker at a Dalian shipyard. Hull construction took only 135 days, a record.
September 9, 1976	Mao Zedong died. The government declared a week-long period of mourning. Mao's successor was Hua Guofeng (HUA KUO-FENG, born 1921).
September 18, 1976	A million mourners assembled in Tiananmen Square to mark the passing of Mao.
October 5 and 6, 1976	On Hua Guofeng's orders, Mao's widow, Jiang Qing, and her radical associates Zhang Chunqiao (CHANG CH'UN-CH'IAO), Wang Hongwen (WANG HUNG-WEN), and Yao Wenyuan were arrested and jailed. Vilified as the Gang of Four, they were accused of disrupting the economy, undermining education, and sabotaging foreign trade, among other crimes.
October 1976	Hua Guofeng became chairman of the Communist Party.
December 26, 1976	A giant tractor plant began production in Yanzhou, Shendong Province.
Late 1976	Zhao Ziyang (CHAO TZU-YANG), the Communist Party leader in Sichuan, authorized an expansion of private farming to as much as 15 percent of commune land.
January 2, 1977	China's longest highway bridge, nearly 2 miles long and spanning the Yellow River at Luoyang, opened to traffic.
March 1977	The long-delayed fifth volume of the *Selected Works of Mao Zedong* was published.
March 1977	A severe spring drought, said to be the worst since 1949, threatened the northern China grain crop.
March 3, 1977	The government reported the excavation of a 2,200-year-old Qin dynasty shipbuilding site near Guangzhou.
May 1977	Foreign sources estimated China's population at 850 million.
May 20, 1977	China and India resumed trade relations after a lapse of 20 years.
July 1977	Deng Xiaoping was restored to all his offices.

October 1977	The government restored college entrance exams and the two-track schooling system as part of the dismantling of Cultural Revolution educational policy. It also dropped the requirement for middle school graduates to spend several years in manual labor before going on to college.
October 1, 1977	The government gave teachers, bureaucrats, and most workers in state enterprises a 10 percent pay raise—the first substantial increase for workers in urban areas in 20 years.
December 30, 1977	Because of drought, China reported a second consecutive short grain harvest.
1977–1979	Zhao's market reforms in industry yielded production increases of as much as 80 percent in Sichuan.
1978	Pursuing the gradual opening to the West, China sent a first group of 480 top students to study abroad.
January 1978	China won six of seven titles at the Norwich Union International Table Tennis Championships in England.
January 20, 1978	The Bank of China began issuing traveler's checks.
February–March 1978	The government announced the Four Modernizations in agriculture, industry, national defense, and science-technology. A new 10-year plan set a target of 10 percent annual growth in industry and 4 to 5 percent in agriculture.
March 1978	At a National Science Conference in Beijing, the government announced plans for new research centers and a training program for 800,000 research workers.
April 1978	The United States announced the sale of 1 million tons of wheat to China, the first such order since 1974.
May 12, 1978	The Ministry of Education announced the admission of 278,000 students of the 5.7 million who took the college entrance examinations at the end of 1977.
June 1978	The government released more than 100,000 political prisoners jailed during the Cultural Revolution.
June 11, 1978	The government announced the establishment of a Society of Traditional Chinese Medicine and the revival of the Chinese Medical Association and other professional health organizations.
June 17, 1978	Vietnam accused China of aiding Cambodia in a border war; China earlier had accused Vietnam of persecuting Chinese living in Vietnam.
October 8, 1978	U.S. officials estimated China's oil reserves at 100 billion barrels, three times the American reserves.

October 12, 1978	Regular air service began between British Hong Kong and Guangzhou.
November 2, 1978	The government reported China's continuing drought to be the most severe in more than 50 years.
November–December 1978	China's democracy movement flourished. The first "big character" posters calling for political freedom were pasted onto the Democracy Wall along the western edge of the Forbidden City in Beijing.
December 5, 1978	The electrician and dissident Wei Jingsheng (WEI CHING-SHENG, born 1949) put up a poster demanding a "fifth modernization"—democracy. Without it, he argued, Deng Xiaoping's Four Modernizations were hollow.
December 13, 1978	The U.S. soft drink company Coca Cola announced it would build a bottling plant in Shanghai.
December 16, 1978	China and the United States agreed to establish full diplomatic relations on January 1, 1979.
December 18–22, 1978	The Communist Party Central Committee endorsed the government's emphasis on economic modernization, with tentative moves toward a free market, over revolutionary politics and Maoist class warfare.
December 19, 1978	The U.S. aircraft maker Boeing announced the sale to China of three 747 jumbo jets.
1978–1980	Deng Xiaoping won a power struggle over Hua Guofeng and emerged as China's paramount leader. Deng's market-oriented economic policies triggered a boom.
1979	Taiwan's population reached 17.1 million. Three decades of rapid development made Taiwan's economy one of Asia's strongest.
1979	The government reopened China's law schools.
1979	Sichuan grain production increased 24 percent from 1966 levels, the result of party chief Zhao Ziyang's market reforms.
1979	The artist Huang Yongyu (HUANG YUNG-YU) painted *Lotus at Night*.
January 1, 1979	Publications in China using the Roman alphabet adopted the pinyin system of romanization.
January 1, 1979	The United States and the People's Republic of China established full diplomatic relations.
January 7, 1979	China denounced Vietnam for waging a "massive war of aggression" in Cambodia.

Mid-January 1979	The government began a crackdown on the Democracy Wall movement. "A few little sheets of paper and a few lines of writing, a few shouts and they're frightened out of their wits," one dissident said of the authorities.
January 28, 1979	Deng Xiaoping arrived in Washington for meetings with President Jimmy Carter.
January 28–February 4, 1979	Deng Xiaoping toured the United States, making stops in Atlanta, Houston, and Seattle.
February 1, 1979	Wu Han's *Dismissal of Hai Rui,* whose banning in 1965 touched off the Cultural Revolution, was re-staged in Beijing.
February 17, 1979	People's Liberation Army columns invaded northern Vietnam in a dispute over the border and over Vietnamese involvement in Cambodia's civil war.
February 28, 1979	The government reported that five tourist hotels were under construction in Nanjing, Zhengzhou, Xian, Nanning, and Kunming.
March 1, 1979	The United States and China exchanged ambassadors.
March 5–16, 1979	As originally planned, PLA forces withdrew from northern Vietnam.
March 17, 1979	The freighter *Letitia Lykes* arrived in Shanghai, the first U.S. merchant ship to call at a Chinese port in 30 years.
March 29, 1979	The authorities arrested Democracy Movement leader Wei Jingsheng and charged him with counter-revolutionary activities.
April 1979	The U.S. Congress passed the Taiwan Relations Act. It reaffirmed the American commitment and guaranteed a flow of defensive weaponry to Taiwan.
April 1979	China introduced market-oriented "special economic zones" around four east coast centers: Zhuhai (near Portuguese Macao), Shenzhen (opposite Hong Kong), Shantou, and Xiamen.
April 1, 1979	The government rescinded the right to hang wall posters for the purpose of expressing political opinion.
June 1979	The literary periodical *The Present* began publication.
June 7, 1979	The Bank of China opened a branch in Luxembourg, the first office to be established abroad since 1949.
September 23, 1979	The government reported that 146 million children were enrolled in 900,000 primary schools.

Autumn 1979	Hua Guofeng became the first Chinese head of state to tour Western Europe. He visited Britain, France, Germany, and Italy.
October 16, 1979	A People's Court sentenced dissident Wei Jingsheng to 15 years in prison.
December 23, 1979	The government announced that 1,200 newspapers, magazines, and journals were circulating in China.
December 26, 1979	Government figures showed that 210,000 television sets were sold in Beijing from January to November, compared to 1,000 in all of 1965.
December 31, 1979	The U.S.-Taiwan Defense Treaty expired. Washington had given notice in 1978 that it would terminate the pact.
1980	The government banned the film *Bitter Love* for its "negative" message. The film told the story of the brutalization of a painter and his family during the Cultural Revolution. The banning opened a new campaign against "spiritual pollution"— the Communist Party's term for self-expression in the arts.
January 3, 1980	The United States said it would sell nearly $300 million worth of defensive weaponry to Taiwan.
January 24, 1980	The United States said it would sell military equipment, though not weapons, to China.
February 29, 1980	The Communist Party posthumously rehabilitated Liu Shaoqi, purged during the Cultural Revolution, calling him an exemplary Marxist.
April 17, 1980	China joined the International Monetary Fund.
May 1980	China announced the successful launch of a long-range ICBM with the capability of delivering a nuclear warhead.
May 15, 1980	The World Bank admitted China to membership.
May 31, 1980	China announced it would ease central government controls on Tibet and grant increased autonomy to the region.
August 11, 1980	The Communist Party called for the removal of most public portraits and slogans of Mao Zedong, saying the practice lacked "political dignity."
September 1980	The government initiated a strict population control program. A revised marriage law raised the legal marriage age to 22 for men and 20 for women. Women were told to have only one child and were supplied with IUD contraceptives.

September 17, 1980	China and the United States signed a major trade agreement. Among other things, it established direct commercial air service and regular seaport access for the first time since 1949.
October 22, 1980	China and the United States concluded a three-year grain sales agreement worth $1 billion a year.
November 20, 1980	The trial of the Gang of Four (there were actually ten defendants) began. The gang was accused of "persecuting to death" 34,800 people during the Cultural Revolution and framing and persecuting a precisely tabulated 729,511 citizens.
Early 1980s	The Communist leadership inaugurated a push for educational advancement and permitted many more students to study abroad. A survey found that only 14 percent of the party's 40 million members were high school graduates.
1981	The World Bank approved its first loan to China.
January 7, 1981	CAAC, China's national airline, introduced Beijing–New York service.
January 25, 1981	Gang of Four sentences were handed down: Jiang Qing and Zhang Chunqiao were condemned to death but with a two-year stay during which they could recant and thus avoid the executioner. The others were given prison terms.
July 1981	The Communist Party Central Committee passed a preliminary judgment on Mao Zedong. He was praised for his wartime leadership and his intellectual contributions but blamed for much of what had gone awry in China since 1956, particularly the Great Leap Forward and the Cultural Revolution. Overall, the committee concluded that Mao was right 70 percent of the time, wrong 30 percent.
July 9–14, 1981	Floods in Sichuan claimed 700 lives and left 150,000 people homeless.
October 1, 1981	The government approved salary increases for primary and secondary school teachers.
1982	A census revealed continued widespread illiteracy, with 28 percent of the population classified as illiterate or semi-literate.
1982	Undergraduate law studies were offered at 20 universities and institutes, with 2,000 students enrolled.
1982	Private incomes accounted for nearly 40 percent of a typical farm family's income, double the proportion in 1964.
1982	An estimated 5,500 lawyers were practicing full-time in China.

July 1982	A census put China's population at more than 1 billion. For political purposes, the count included Taiwan, Hong Kong, and Macao.
1982–1992	Most of British Hong Kong's 3,200 toy factories relocated to mainland Guangdong Province, where labor costs were low and profits high.
1983	China's urban population climbed to 23.5 percent of the total. Millions of people a year flowed into the towns from the country.
1983	Direct foreign investment in China exceeded $900 billion.
1983	Eleven thousand Chinese studied in 54 countries at government expense; another 7,000 paid their own fees in schools overseas.
January 25, 1983	The death sentences of Jiang Qing and Zhang Chunqiao were commuted to life imprisonment.
October 6, 1983	China and the Soviet Union met in Beijing to discuss easing border tensions and normalizing relations.
1984	The Central Committee's Document Number 1 acknowledged the dismantling of the system of collectivized farms and established the so-called responsibility system. In return for negotiated payments to the state, farmers were permitted to grow whatever they chose and to keep what remained after fulfilling their obligations.
1984	The Central Committee extended special economic zone status to 14 additional coastal cities and Hainan Island.
1984	Life expectancy in China was 65 years.
January 12, 1984	Zhao Ziyang became the first Chinese premier to visit the United States. During the visit, the two countries agreed on trade cooperation and a new science and technology treaty.
February 10, 1984	China and the Soviet Union signed a treaty calling for a 50 percent increase in trade in 1984, to $1.2 billion.
May 7, 1984	With increasing worker mobility making it difficult for the government to keep track of its citizens, China mandated identity cards for everyone 16 and older.
July 28, 1984	China won its first-ever Olympic gold medal at Los Angeles, in a pistol shooting event.
September 1, 1984	China's first civilian nuclear power plant went into service.

September 19, 1984	Great Britain and China reached agreement for Hong Kong's reversion to Chinese sovereignty on July 1, 1997. The pact contained a guarantee of economic autonomy for the colony—the "one country, two systems" arrangement.
December 16, 1984	Archeologists working near the ancient city of Xuzhou unearthed 1,100 terra-cotta warriors from the Han dynasty.
December 31, 1984	A congress of 500 poets, novelists, and playwrights called for an end to government and Communist Party restrictions on expression.
1984–1987	China negotiated arms agreements with Iran worth $2.5 billion and with Iraq worth $1.5 billion.
Mid-1980s	A popular joke, mimicking the Maoist style, listed the "eight bigs" every Chinese must possess: a color television, a refrigerator, a stereo, a camera, a motorcycle, a suite of furniture, a washing machine, and an electric fan.
1985	With a thaw in Sino-Soviet relations, the two countries reopened consulates in Leningrad (now St. Petersburg) and Shanghai.
January 5, 1985	The government issued a new charter for the Chinese Writers Association, promising freedom of expression as long as writers followed party and Marxist-Leninist guidelines.
April–June 1985	China moved to reduce its 4.2 million–strong armed forces by 25 percent. The People's Liberation Army reintroduced insignia of rank to distinguish officers and enlisted personnel.
May 19, 1985	A riot erupted in Beijing after a Hong Kong team defeated China in a soccer match.
Summer 1985	China sold 200 military transport aircraft to private firms and provincial airlines.
Summer 1985	In a notorious corruption scandal, Hainan enterprise zone officials illegally resold $1.5 billion worth of imported motor vehicles, television sets, and video recorders.
July 3, 1985	The government freed Gong Pinmei, 83 years old, the former bishop of Shanghai, after 30 years in prison.
1986	Taiwan legalized political parties.
1986	China's official cost of living index rose 12 percent. Unofficially, the increase was much higher.
1986	The government adopted a revised Code of Civil Procedure. Around 20,000 lawyers were practicing in China.

1986	Four hundred thousand small- and medium-sized businesses produced 40 percent of China's industrial output. Most firms were collectively owned, but an increasing number were in private hands.
April 21, 1986	China mandated nine years of compulsory education in cities and other developed areas by 1990 and everywhere else by 2000.
August 3, 1986	The government reported the first bankruptcy case in the history of the People's Republic of China, a factory in Shenyang.
September 26, 1986	The Shanghai stock exchange opened for the first time since 1949.
December 5 and 9, 1986	An estimated 3,000 students at the University of Science and Technology in Hefei protested campus issues and manipulated local elections. Student protests also broke out in Wuhan and Beijing.
December 19–21, 1986	A rally in Shanghai drew 30,000 students, with as many non-student supporters. "The time has come to awaken the democratic ideas that have long been suppressed," a student broadside said. The protests spread to Kunming, Chongqing, Tianjin, and Beijing.
January 1987	Communist hard-liners launched a crackdown on the student protest movement. They blamed physicist Fang Lizhi (FANG LI-CHIH), writer Liu Binyan, and other older intellectuals for fanning the flames of student dissent. Fang and Liu were dismissed from the Communist Party; Fang was stripped of his teaching and research positions.
January 16, 1987	Hu Yaobang (HU YAO-PANG), more tolerant of dissent than other senior leaders, became the scapegoat from the student uprising; he "resigned" as secretary-general of the Communist Party.
May 1987	Forest fires consumed 2.5 million acres in Heilongjiang Province in northeast China.
October–November 1987	The Thirteenth Communist Party Congress reaffirmed Deng Xiaoping's liberal economic policies. Deng resigned from the Central Committee, though he remained China's most powerful leader. Zhao Ziyang, a supporter of Deng's market reforms, won election as party secretary-general. Four new members, including Li Peng (born 1928) were elected to the Politburo, and Li Peng became acting premier.
October 1–6, 1987	Tibetan monks and Chinese police clashed during independence rallies in Lhasa, Tibet's capital.

1988	The government released figures showing that 150,000 Communist Party members were punished in 1987 for graft or abuse of power.
1988	Scattered strikes were reported, including one in which 1,100 medical appliance factory workers stayed off the job for three months.
1988	More than 7 million children dropped out of China's schools. The State Statistical Bureau reported that 230 million Chinese were illiterate.
January 13, 1988	Taiwan's leader, Chiang Ching-kuo, died. Lee Teng-hui, a native Taiwanese, became president of Taiwan and head of the Guomindang.
Spring 1988	A popular television documentary titled *River Elegy* blamed China's troubles on ancient habits of thought such as inwardness, xenophobia, and lack of curiosity about the larger world.
April 9, 1988	The Communist Party confirmed Li Peng as premier.
May 1988	With Lee Teng-hui's lifting of all travel restrictions to the People's Republic, 10,000 Taiwanese a month were visiting relatives on the mainland.
November 6, 1988	An earthquake in Yunnan measuring 7.6 on the Richter scale killed an estimated 1,000 people.
December 22, 1988	China's first exhibit of nude paintings opened in Beijing.
March 5–7, 1989	Tibetans demonstrated for independence; protester-police clashes were said to be the worst since 1959. China imposed martial law and sent thousands of troops into Lhasa. At least 50 demonstrators were reported killed, with hundreds wounded.
April 15–22, 1989	Students massed in Beijing's Tiananmen Square to honor the recently deceased Hu Yaobang. (He died of natural causes.) Student leaders demanded the right of political participation, increases in education spending, and disclosure of government officials' income.
April 24, 1989	Students declared a boycott of classes. The government moved to bring the nonstop Tiananmen rallies under control. Deng Xiaoping labeled the protests "an episode of turmoil"—a euphemism for counter-revolution.
May 4, 1989	An estimated 100,000 students rallied in Beijing to mark the 70th anniversary of the 1919 demonstrations that launched the May Fourth Movement.
May 13, 1989	Three thousand students in Tiananmen Square began a hunger strike.

May 15, 1989	The Soviet leader Mikhail Gorbachev arrived in Beijing, marking the formal end to the 30-year Sino-Soviet split. Continuing student protests deeply embarrassed the government during Gorbachev's three-day visit.
May 17, 1989	One million pro-democracy supporters rallied in Beijing.
May 20, 1989	With Deng Xiaoping pressing for a hard line, the government proclaimed martial law in Beijing. Premier Li Peng called the protesters "counter-revolutionaries."
May 21, 1989	A million people massing in the streets of Beijing successfully blocked PLA troops trying to approach Tiananmen Square.
May 29, 1989	Student protesters put up a 37-foot-high foam plastic statue of the "goddess of liberty" near a giant portrait of Mao Zedong in Tiananmen Square.
June 3, 1989	Troops closed in on Tiananmen Square.
June 3–4, 1989	Troops and armored vehicles attacked the Tiananmen Square protesters. Estimates of the dead ranged from 1,000–10,000. Li Peng and other hard-liners pressed for the arrest and jailing of hundreds of student leaders. Fang Lizhi, Liu Binyan, and other dissidents escaped into exile abroad.
June 4, 1989	PLA units killed 300 pro-democracy protesters in Chengdu.
June 9, 1989	In a speech, Deng Xiaoping branded the protesters as rebels. He also called for renewed economic growth along free market lines.
Mid-June 1989	The United States suspended arms sales to China in protest of the massacre. The World Bank deferred action on $780 million in loan requests.
June 24, 1989	General Secretary Zhao Ziyang, a reformist, was dismissed from his Communist party posts, a further signal that China's leadership meant to follow a hard line on the pro-democracy movement.
July 1989	Floods in Sichuan cost hundreds of lives and damaged croplands. Flooding in Zhejiang destroyed 10,000 dwellings.
September 4, 1989	The leadership dismissed novelist Wang Meng, an advocate of increased literary freedom, from his post as minister of culture.
January 11, 1990	The government lifted martial law in Beijing.
January 18, 1990	Nearly 600 student leaders were freed after they "confessed and reformed."
April 24, 1990	China and the Soviet Union signed a 10-year economic and scientific agreement.

May 10, 1990	The government freed 211 dissidents arrested during the 1989 suppression of the pro-democracy movement.
Early 1990s	After more than a decade of economic liberalization, average incomes tripled. Implementation of the "responsibility system," which turned land back to individual peasant households, helped an estimated 170 million peasants climb out of extreme poverty.
May 1991	Taiwan renounced the use of force to retake the Chinese mainland.
June 4, 1991	Jiang Qing, Mao Zedong's widow, jailed with the Gang of Four for Cultural Revolution crimes, killed herself in prison.
August 10, 1991	China agreed to join the rest of the world's nuclear powers and sign the Nuclear Non-proliferation Treaty.
September 16, 1991	Pro-democracy candidates won 16 of 18 legislative seats in the British colony of Hong Kong.
October 18, 1991	In a first-ever weapons export pact, China, the United States, France, the United Kingdom, and Russia agreed to exchange information about sales of major conventional weapons systems to the Middle East and elsewhere.
December 11, 1991	Li Peng became the first Chinese prime minister to visit India since the rupture of relations over border issues in 1960.
December 18, 1991	China began trial operations at its first nuclear power station, at Qinshan in Zhejiang Province.
December 21, 1991	The Nationalist party won 71 percent of the vote in the first nationwide election in Taiwan in 40 years. The opposition Democratic Progressive party called for full independence and a Taiwan seat in the United Nations.
1992	Per capita income in Taiwan is second in Asia only to that in Japan.
February 21, 1992	The United States agreed to lift sanctions on technology transfers to China after the Chinese pledged to honor restrictions on missile sales to Middle Eastern countries.
October 23, 1992	China warned Great Britain against expanding democracy in Hong Kong and said it would roll back democratic gains there when it assumed control in 1997.
December 30, 1992	Ling-ling, the female giant panda who for 20 years symbolized normal relations between China and the United States, died in the National Zoo in Washington at age 23.
February 1993	The government released the prominent dissident Wang Dan, a leader of the Tiananmen demonstrations, from prison.

August 26, 1993	The United States imposed new sanctions on China, banning $1 billion worth of high-technology exports as penalty for the Chinese sale of missile technology to Pakistan.
October 5, 1993	China exploded a nuclear device, breaking a major power moratorium on such testing.
Late 1993	The authorities released dissident Wei Jingsheng from prison. He resumed his political activity at once and was re-arrested.
1994	Construction began on the long-planned Three Gorges Dam on the Yangtze River. Cost estimates ran to $100 billion and more for what would be the largest hydroelectric project in history, forming a 400-mile-long reservoir that would flood 160 towns and force 1.3 million people to relocate. Critics charged the dam would seriously damage the Yangtze environment.
1994	The government banned the film *The Blue Kite,* a story of family suffering during the political upheavals of the 1950s and 1960s.
March 12–14, 1994	During a visit to China, U.S. Secretary of State Warren Christopher warned China to improve its human rights record or lose trade privileges. No progress was reported in negotiations on trade and rights.
April 11, 1994	The United States imposed sanctions on Taiwan for refusing to stop the sale of tiger bones and rhinoceros horns, an unprecedented action to protect the environment.
May 1994	The Clinton Administration agreed to separate trade and human rights issues in U.S. relations with China, opening the way for renewal of China's Most Favored Nation trade status.
June 6, 1994	In China's worst air disaster, 160 people were killed in the crash of a Russian-built airliner near Xian.
January 1995	Communist Party secretary Jiang Zemin (CHIANG TSE-MIN) called for state visits, an end to hostility, and reunification of China and Taiwan.
February 26, 1995	China and the United States reached agreement on measures to protect intellectual property such as movies, CDs, and computer software from piracy.
March 1995	The Taiwanese rejected Jiang Zemin's normalization overture.
June 16, 1995	China recalled its ambassador in protest of the United States decision to grant a visa to Taiwan's president, Lee Teng-hui.
June–August 1995	China conducted missile tests near Taiwan.

August 25, 1995	A Chinese court found human rights activist Harry Wu, a U.S. citizen, guilty of spying and stealing state secrets and sentenced him to 15 years in prison. In a conciliatory gesture toward the United States, China expelled Wu instead of jailing him.
September 17, 1995	Voters in Hong Kong handed pro-Beijing candidates a decisive defeat in the last legislative elections under British rule.
December 1995	Pro-democracy activist Wei Jingsheng was found guilty of "counter-revolution" and sentenced to 14 years in prison.
1996	Colleges and universities in China enrolled 3.2 million undergraduates; 50 million students attended junior secondary schools.
February 3, 1996	An earthquake in Yunnan in southwestern China killed 200 people and destroyed thousands of homes. China appealed for international aid to speed reconstruction.
February 7, 1996	The United States accused China of secretly selling atomic-weapons technology to Pakistan.
March 1996	The National People's Congress revised China's criminal code, limiting detentions without charge to 30 days and giving defendants speedier access to lawyers. Human rights groups said the changes did not go far enough.
March 23, 1996	China conducted military exercises near Taiwan as the island turned out for its first direct presidential vote. Taiwan elected Lee Teng-hui.
June 8, 1996	China exploded a nuclear weapon, announced a second explosion for September, and said it would then join the world ban on atomic testing.
July 1996	Yangtze River flooding killed several hundred people and washed away thousands of dwellings in China's central provinces.
February 19, 1997	Deng Xiaoping, China's paramount leader, died. (He had not appeared in public since 1994.) Jiang Zemin (born 1926) became president; Li Peng retained his post as premier.
March 25, 1997	General Motors Corporation announced a $1.3 billion joint venture to produce cars in partnership with a Chinese state-run auto manufacturer.
July 1, 1997	Great Britain formally returned Hong Kong and the New Territories to China.
November 16, 1997	China released political activist Wei Jingsheng from prison and sent him into exile.

November 17, 1997	Wei arrived in Detroit, Michigan.
1998	China detained more than 200,000 people without charge and without trial in 1997, according to a human rights report from Amnesty International. The organization said it documented widespread torture in prison and police cells and unfair trials.
January 5, 1998	The government railways ministry announced plans to lay off 1.1. million workers, one-third of the total, by the year 2000. China planned to turn over 40,000 miles of state-run railway to private management.
January 18, 1998	An official newspaper, the *China Daily,* reported that businesses owned and managed by the People's Liberation Army exported goods worth $7 billion in 1997.
April 23, 1998	Semi-official representatives of Taiwan and China began meeting in Beijing to discuss "technical" matters on which the two countries might cooperate. Political issues were not to be discussed. Taiwanese increasingly regarded their island as an independent country; China continued to consider it a renegade province.
April 30, 1998	Violence erupted in Chengdu in Sichuan Province when police moved in to shut down the stalls of some 3,000 street vendors. Rights groups said 4 vendors were killed and 30 seriously injured. Police went on to demolish the stalls.
June 25, 1998	Zhao Ziyang, the Communist Party chief at the time of the 1989 Tiananmen Square suppression of the pro-democracy movement, challenged China's government to admit to moral error and political blundering in connection with the massacre. Zhao was ousted as party chief during the Tiananmen disturbances.
June 25–July 3, 1998	U.S. President Bill Clinton traveled to China to meet with Chinese President Jiang Zemen. Clinton's visit to China was the first by a U.S. president since the Tiananmen Square riots of 1989.
Summer 1998	Major flooding destroyed crops and left thousands homeless in the Yangtze valley.
April 6–14, 1999	Chinese Premier Zhu Rongji visited the United States, with stops in Los Angeles and Washington, D.C. One of the goals of the visit was to come to a major trade agreement with the United States. Zhu's trip would end without an agreement between the United States and China.
May 7, 1999	A U.S. B-2 bomber mistakenly dropped bombs on the Chinese embassy in Belgrade, Yugoslavia, killing 3 Chinese citizens and injuring another 20. The bombing, called a "tragic mis-

take" by NATO officials and U.S. President Bill Clinton, was part of NATO's efforts to end the rule of Yugoslavia's Slobodon Milosevic.

July 10, 1999

The United States defeated China to win the Women's World Cup Championship in soccer in Pasadena, California.

July 15, 1999

For the first time, China publicly acknowledged that it possessed the capabilities to build a neutron bomb. Though it was widely known to the United States and other countries that China possessed the ability, China had never before publicly stated this fact.

September 21, 1999

A major earthquake in Taiwan's Nantou county killed more than 2,000 people and injured more than 8,000.

November 15, 1999

The United States and China signed a landmark trade agreement. According to the agreement, the United States would also back China's entry into the World Trade Organization (WTO). The U.S. backing was important in influencing other countries to support China's entry into the WTO.

November 20, 1999

China launched its first unmanned spacecraft. Although China had launched satellites before, this launch was the first one with the goal of an eventual manned space flight.

March 18, 2000

Taiwanese voters elected Democratic Progressive Party (DPP) and former Taipei mayor Chen Shui-bian president, ending more than 50 years of rule by the Nationalist Party. The DPP traditionally favored declaring Taiwan independent from China. Many saw Chen's election as a sign that Taiwan was soon going to declare its independence from China.

April 18, 2000

China protested the U.S. approval of missile and radar sales to Taiwan. The U.S. sale came amidst China's increased military buildup around Taiwan.

May 19, 2000

China and the European Union (EU) agreed to terms under which the EU would support China's entry into the World Trade Organization.

September 14, 2000

Cheng Kejie, 66, the former deputy chairman of the National People's Congress, China's parliament, was executed for corruption. Cheng was the highest-ranking Chinese official executed since the beginning of Communist rule in 1949.

October 23, 2000

General Motors announced a joint venture with Shanghai Auto Industrial Corporation, one of China's largest car companies, to produce in China a compact car for Chinese consumers.

December 4, 2000

The Dalai Lama announced that he had reopened indirect talks with China through his brother, Gyalo Thondup.

January 13, 2001	China launched its first spacecraft carrying animals into space. The types of animals and the number were not identified, but all were returned to earth safely.
March 16, 2001	Four bombs exploded within an hour in Shijiazhuang, the capital of Hebei Province. The four blasts killed 108 people.
April 1–12, 2001	A Chinese fighter jet and a U.S. Navy reconnaissance aircraft collided over the South China Sea on April 1. The U.S. plane made an emergency landing at an airport in Lingshui on the island of Hainan. The 24 crewmen were detained as spies by Chinese authorities. The pilot of the Chinese plane ejected, but his body was never found. Over the next several days, both the United States and China blamed one another for the mishap. The 11-day standoff ended on April 12 with the release of the U.S. crew after the United States issued a statement saying it was "very sorry" for the incident.
April 23, 2001	For the first time, Chinese health officials acknowledged that there was a growing AIDS crisis in China. Breaking with the government's long-held silence on the issue, China's deputy health minister Yin Dakui said that China faced a growing AIDS epidemic.
July 13, 2001	The International Olympic Committee (IOC) selected Beijing as the site of the 2008 Summer Olympic Games.
July 16, 2001	Russian president Vladimir Putin and Chinese president Jiang Zemin signed a comprehensive friendship treaty.
February 21, 2002	U.S. president George W. Bush visited China and met with Chinese president Jiang Zemin.
March 14–18, 2002	A group of 25 North Koreans forced their way into Spain's embassy in Beijing and demanded political asylum and safe passage to South Korea. The 25 were permitted to leave the country for the Philippines on March 15 and arrived in Seoul, South Korea, on March 18.
May 7, 2002	A China Northern Airlines MD-82 carrying 112 people crashed into the Bo-Hai Sea near the city of Dalian. All 112 were killed.
June 26, 2002	Yao Ming, 21, became the first Chinese person ever drafted by a team in the National Basketball League (NBA) of the United States. Yao, a 7-foot-5-inch center, was selected by the Houston Rockets with the first pick in the draft. Under an agreement between the NBA and Chinese officials, Yao would still be able to fulfill his commitments to the Chinese national team.
November 8–14, 2002	China's ruling Communist Party held its 16th five-year congress in Beijing. Vice President Hu Jintao, 59, was named the party's new general secretary, replacing Jiang Zemin.
March 16, 2003	Hu Jintao becomes president of China.

KEY RESEARCH SOURCES

Gittings, John. *The Role of the Chinese Army*. New York: Oxford University Press, 1967.

Hsu, Immanuel C. Y. *Rise of Modern China*. 2d ed. New York: Oxford University Press, 1975.

Lewis, John Wilson, and Xue Litai. *China Builds the Bomb*. Stanford: Stanford University Press, 1988.

Meisner, Maurice. *The Deng Xiaoping Era*. New York: Hill and Wang, 1996.

Spence, Jonathan. *Search for Modern China*. 2d ed. New York: W.W. Norton, 1999.

Part III

China A to Z

By Michael Golay and Ron Irwin

Academia Sinica: The Academia Sinica was founded in Nanjing, China, on June 9, 1928, by the Nationalist government to conduct research into the fields of the humanities and to raise academic standards in the country. It is the highest and most respected academic institution in the Republic of China. After 1949, its name was changed to the Chinese Academy of Sciences. It continued operating more than one hundred research institutions on behalf of the State Science and Technological Commission while the Academia Sinica itself continued in Nankang, Taiwan.

The Academia Sinica is composed of 24 institutes and preparatory offices under three divisions: The Division of Mathematics and Physical Sciences, the Division of Life Sciences, and the Division of Social Sciences and Humanities. Its goals for the 21st century are to concentrate on interdisciplinary research projects and provide greater opportunities for research collaborations with foreign institutions.

Ancient Text School: The Ancient Text School of Confucian studies arose in opposition to the preponderance of the Modern Text School of the Qin (221–206 B.C.) and Han (202 B.C.–A.D. 220) periods. The latter had accepted classical Confucian texts preserved after the First Emperor of Chin in 213 B.C. had supposedly destroyed the original Confucian classics. However, toward the end of the Western Han period (206 B.C.–A.D. 8), a descendant of Confucius claimed to have discovered original Confucian texts written on the walls of his ancestral home. Despite widespread skepticism regarding the authenticity of these texts, a scholar named Liu Xin (46 B.C.–A.D. 23) sought to establish them as the cornerstone of what would become the Ancient Text School during the Xin period (A.D. 8–23). With the downfall of the Xin dynasty, the Ancient Text School declined. It was restored again toward the end of the Later Han period (A.D. 25–220) upon the appearance of several great Ancient Text scholars, including Zheng Xuan (A.D. 127–200). His work ensured that the precepts of the Ancient Text School would dominate Confucian studies into the late 19th century.

An Lushan (A.D. 703–757): A Tang general of nomadic background, he was the adopted son of the consort of the Emperor Xuanzong. With her patronage, he rose to command a powerful army along China's northeastern frontier.

An Lushan led his troops in revolt in 755, taking Luoyang and Chang'an, the twin capitals, and forcing the emperor to flee into Sichuan. His own son killed him two years later, but by then, he had already permanently weakened Tang central control.

Anti-Rightist Movement: The Anti-Rightist Movement was launched against so-called rightist elements—critics of Maoist policies—who revealed themselves after Mao's injunction to encourage the expression of the "hundred schools" of Chinese political and cultural thought during the Hundred Flowers period of 1956 to 1957. Because of the Anti-Rightist campaign, many critics of governmental policies were sent to labor camps or were forced to sign "self-reform pacts." They pledged their allegiance to the state during the so-called "socialist education movement" launched by the Maoist government in 1957.

Bagua: A Daoist form of martial arts dating back to the late 17th century but with origins stretching as far back as 1,000 years. Referred to as *Baguazhang* in martial arts circles (literally "eight trigram palm circles"), the discipline uses a basic series of eight "palm movements." Each position change in the art corresponds to one of the trigrams that combine to form the sixty-four hexagrams of the *I Ching* (p. Yijing, "Book of changes"). Baguazhang is

547

the second of the "three sisters" of Neijia, or Internal Martial Arts practice—the other two being Taiji and Xingyi.

Ba Jin (1904–): Ba Jin is the pseudonym of Li Feigan. He is a prolific Chinese writer whose most famous novel *Jia* (The family), the first of the *Jiliu* (Torrent) trilogy, attacked the traditional family system. In 1966, Ba was labeled a "counterrevolutionary" during the Cultural Revolution of 1966 to 1976 and was publicly tortured. In 1975, he was nominated for the Nobel Prize in Literature. After being "revived" in China in 1977, Ba Jin was elected a deputy to the National People's Congress in 1978; in 1981, he was elected chairman of the Chinese Writer's Association.

Bai Juyi (772–846): Bai Juyi (sometimes pronounced Bo Juyi) was perhaps the first Chinese poet to have an international reputation. During the mid-800s, his ballad "The Song of Lasting Regret" was sung in teahouses across the Chinese empire, and he was widely read in Korea and Japan. He lived during the Tang dynasty (618–907), the "golden age" of Chinese poetry which saw the ascendancy of such famous poets as Du Fu, Wang Wei, Li Bai, and Li Shangyin. Bai Juyi wrote in simple diction that appealed to educated and uneducated readers alike. His work is often compared to that of that of Yuan Zhen (779–831), with whom he often collaborated.

Ban Gu (32–92): One of China's most noteworthy historians, Ban Gu lived during the Eastern Han dynasty (A.D. 25–220) and wrote the cornerstone text *Han shu* (The history of the Han dynasty). This volume became the model for recording official histories of successive ruling houses in China. Modeled on the *Shi Ji*, the tremendous, comprehensive history of China written by Ssu-ma-Chien (d. 90 B.C.), the *Han Shu* is an exhaustive overview of the entire Han empire (206 B.C.–A.D. 220). The *Han Shu* is factual, detailed, and relatively unbiased, leading some scholars to refer to Ban as China's first historiographer. The book also has sections on law, science, geography, and literature.

Banners: The Manchu leader Nurhaci developed this system of military organization in the 17th century. It grouped soldiers and their families into divisions identified by different colors. The Manchus established eight banners altogether, using the colors red, blue, yellow, and white in four solid and four bordered banners. The banners proved useful for identification in battle and were a means of registering the civilian population.

Bannermen carried Qing power into the west of China and pacified these outlying regions for the dynasty in the later 17th and 18th centuries. As time went on, the banner soldiers gained a reputation for incompetence and cruelty. The New Qing Army abandoned the system early in the 20th century.

Baojia: Imperial China employed this system of household organization and mutual security from the Song (960–1279) through the Qing (Ching) (1644–1911) dynasties. Based on forms described in ancient texts, baojia organized 100-household units as jia, with 10 jia making up a bao.

All Chinese households were supposed to be registered in these groups. The elected leaders of individual units, chosen on a rotating basis, were responsible for maintaining order, directing public works such as dike and road repairs, and collecting taxes. The "headmen," as they were called, also commanded the local militia.

Late Qing reformers attempted, without much success, to adapt baojia to the 20th century. In the 1940s, Communist cadres imposed their own form of the baojia system.

Beijing (Peking) Opera: The Beijing (Peking) Opera developed in Beijing between 1790 and 1828 during the Qing dynasty (1644–1911). It is widely considered one of the highest expressions of Chinese culture. A comprehensive performing art that includes elements of grand opera, ballet, acrobatics, and drama, its oeuvre includes thousands of pieces that cover the entire history of China. During the Cultural Revolution (1966–1976) the established operas were banned and replaced by the Eight Model Plays, stories concerning highlights of Chinese Communist history. Reintroduced to a declining audience in 1978, traditional Beijing Opera performances have been aired on national television to find new and badly needed supporters.

Blueshirts: Formed in the 1930s, this fascist-inspired paramilitary group served as Chiang Kai-shek's secret police. Led by Whampoa Military Academy graduates loyal to Chiang, the Blueshirts gathered intelligence on Nationalist opponents and carried out assassinations of political rivals and critics.

Blueshirt leader Dai Li allegedly directed the assassination of the editor of the main Shanghai newspaper in 1934.

Book of Changes (I Ching, Yi Jing): One of the Five Classics (Wu ching) Confucius is said to have taught his students, this handbook of divination was prepared as an alternative to the consultation of oracle bones.

The book was based on the eight trigrams of whole and broken lines, which could be combined to form 64 hexagrams. The figures corresponded to characteristic human situations and patterns of change. Each hexagram had a name and an explanation that suggested its meaning. By drawing odd-even lots, one would consult a particular hexagram for an omen or advice.

Parts of the *Book of Changes* and its commentary date from the early Zhou dynasty (1122–256 B.C.); other parts might have been added later, perhaps as late as the seventh century B.C. It was specifically exempted from the Qin emperor's edict for the Burning of the Books in 213 B.C.

The book formed a part of every educated Chinese person's learning for many centuries.

Book of Rites (Record of Rites): This is one of the Five Classics of Chinese Confucian literature. The original text is said to have been compiled by Confucius himself (551–479 B.C.), although the vast majority of the book was authored by Confucian scholars during the Han dynasty (206 B.C.–A.D. 220). The other four of the five are the *Book of Documents*, the *Book of Changes*, *The Spring and Autumn Annals*, and the *Book of Songs*. The *Book of Rites* outlines moral principles in its treatment of such subjects as royal regulations, development of rites, ritual objects and sacrifices, education, music, the behavior of scholars, and the doctrine of the mean. Two chapters of the *Book of Rites*, the "Doctrine of the Mean" and "The Great Learning," are often considered as separate texts.

Borodin, Mikhail (1884–1952): The Soviets sent this senior Comintern operative to China in October 1926 to act as an adviser to Sun Yat-sen and the Guomindang (GMD). Borodin persuaded the Chinese Communist Party to ally with the GMD and, with Sun's authorization, carried out a general reorganization of the party.

Borodin introduced the Soviet notion of "democratic centralism" to the GMD, meaning any decision reached by a majority of members would be binding on all. From his base in Guangzhou (Canton), known as the "Red City," he sought to lead the GMD leftward in the mid-1920s, but conservative elements behind Chiang Kai-shek checked him.

Boxer Rebellion: This uprising aimed at westerners and Chinese Christians developed in 1898 in northern Shandong Province. The rebels, poor peasants mostly, practiced a form of marital arts, hence the Westerners called them the "Boxers."

Foreigners demanded that the Qing government crack down on the Boxers after several Christians were killed in early 1899. By June 1900, armed Boxer groups had drifted into Tianjin and Beijing. They killed a number of foreigners, tore up railroad track, and cut telegraph lines.

The Empress Dowager Cixi seemed to condone the violence and on June 21, 1900, issued a declaration of war against foreigners. The Boxers laid siege to the foreign legation quarter in Beijing and launched a series of attacks elsewhere, including a massacre of 44 men, women, and children in Shanxi.

A joint western expedition of 20,000 troops marched out of Tianjin on August 4 and entered the capital 10 days later. They broke the siege, quelled the rebellion, and forced the Empress Cixi and her court to retreat to Xi'an.

The western powers and China signed the Boxer Protocol, formally ending the conflict in September 1901.

Buck, Pearl (1892–1973): Her missionary parents raised the West Virginia–born Buck in China among Chinese children, and she lived mostly in China until she was 40. The experience yielded numerous novels, including a best seller, *The Good*

Earth, in 1931. It established her as the leading American popular interpreter of the Chinese experience.

The Good Earth did not impress literary critics but sold more than 2 million copies and won a Pulitzer Prize. Buck returned to the United States for good in 1935. She received the Nobel Prize for Literature in 1938.

Buddhism: A religion of compassion and salvation, Buddhism originated in India about the sixth century B.C. To a degree, its tenets were based on the teachings of Sakyamuni Gautama Siddhartha, "the Buddha" (c. 563–483 B.C.).

Buddhism probably reached China via central Asia during the Eastern Han dynasty (A.D. 25–220). It became influential almost at once. At times at odds with the chief indigenous Chinese systems, Confucianism and Daoism, Buddhism also absorbed and transformed elements of these indigenous Chinese philosophies.

The Buddhist message is otherworldly; Confucianism centers on relationships between human beings. In Buddhist thought, humans live in a world of illusion; the ultimate purpose of being is to achieve ultimate enlightenment and enter nirvana, which is a state of being that is beyond the mundane cycle of life and death. Daoists with their search for the unknowable were closer in spirit to Buddhists, and each borrowed liberally from the other.

Buddhism reached its greatest level of influence during the Tang dynasty (618–907). This resulted in a backlash, a widespread suppression of Buddhism that reached its peak in 845. Tang rulers confiscated large amounts of Buddhist property and forced hundreds of thousands of monks and nuns to return to lay life.

The Chan School gave Buddhism a distinctly Chinese coloration. Its main element, the notion that sudden enlightenment is possible, is absent from Indian and Central Asian forms of Buddhism with their doctrine that many years of intense meditation are required to achieve the higher plane.

Burma Road: The Allies used this 715-mile overland route connecting Lashio in the British colony of Burma with Kunming in southwestern China to supply Chiang Kai-shek's Nationalist forces fighting Japan in World War II.

The road shut down in 1942 when the Japanese occupied Burma.

Burning of the Books (213 B.C.): On the advice of his chief minister Li Si, the first emperor of the Qin dynasty (221–206 B.C.) attempted to suppress all non-Legalist literature by ordering a mass Burning of the Books. Books on technical subjects were exempt from burning.

The extent of the destruction is not clear, and many works doubtless survived. Some scholars, however, were almost certainly put to death for disobeying the emperor's command.

Cai E (1882–1916): Cai E was the leader of a small group of military commanders who helped foment revolutionary activity against the Republican government of Yuan Shihkai (1859–1916) in Yunnan Province between December 25, 1915, and June 6, 1916. Cai helped spearhead revolts in Guizhou and Guangxi, prompting Yuan to postpone and then cancel his enthronement as self-proclaimed emperor of China. By May 1916, both Sichuan and Hunan had joined in the rebellion against Yuan's rule. A month later, Yuan suddenly died of uremia, thus ending the struggle. Yuan's death left China bitterly divided and ushered in a period of so-called warlord rule.

Cai Yuanpei (1868–1940): A classically educated member of the Hanlin Academy, he served as a reforming president of Beijing University from 1916 to 1926. Cai emerged as an influential supporter of the May Fourth Movement, the period of intellectual unrest that followed student demonstrations in protest of unfair terms of the Treaty of Versailles in 1919.

Cai later held the title of minister of education for the Guomindang. In December 1927, he presided over the Chinese marriage ceremony of Chiang Kai-shek and Soong Meiling.

Calendar, Chinese: The Chinese calendar represents one of the longest unbroken sequences of time measurement in history. Based on planetary, solar, and lunar cycles, the Chinese calendar has been in existence, many believe, since 2953 B.C. The Chinese year is divided into 12 months, but there is also an alternative way of dividing the year into 24 periods of about two weeks each. The Chinese New Year, which, according to legend, was established in 2600 B.C. during the reign of Emperor Huang Di, falls on the new moon nearest the 15th degree of Aquarius, or any time from January 21 to February 15. According to the calendar, a complete lunar cycle is 60 years and is made up of five cycles of 12 years each. Each year in the 12-year cycle has a representative animal (see the table below). Many Chinese people believe that the animal under which a person is born has a marked effect on personality. Both the Western (Gregorian) and traditional lunar calendars are used publicly in today's China.

Cao Cao (155–220): Cao Cao rose to power in the central plain and the valley of the Wei during the last years of the Han dynasty (206 B.C.–A.D. 220). Between 205 and 219, he unified all of northern China, becoming one of the three rulers to emerge from the failing Han empire. The area over which he held sway is referred to as the Kingdom of Wei, which he improved through establishing a series of military/agricultural colonies known as *t'un t'ien*. A classically Legalist ruler, Cao Cao concerned himself with strengthening penal legislation while he held power. His fabled million-man army and his skillful fighting earned him a legendary place in Chinese history and folklore. After his death, his son Cao Pi forced the abdication of the last Han emperor and founded a new dynasty, the Wei, or Cao Wei (220–265/66), with its capital at Luoyang. The dynasty ruled the north and in 263 conquered southwestern China.

Cao Kun (1862–1938): Cao Kun served in the Sino-Japanese war in 1894 and played a major role in the Republican Revolution of 1911, which overthrew the Manchu (Qing) dynasty. Cao took over the Beijing government in 1923, forcing the deposition of then-president Li Yuan-hong. As contested head of the so-called Zhili Clique, which controlled most of northern China and Manchuria, Cao Kun gained official leadership of the Beijing government by bribing 500 members of parliament. A year later, the Zhili forces collapsed when their commander, Feng Yuxiang, mutinied and formed his own National People's Army, forcing Cao Kun out of office on November 2, 1924.

Cao Rulin: Cao Rulin was a Chinese cabinet minister who handled negotiations with Japan regarding the 1916 "good neighbor policy" between the two countries. He also helped negotiate the infamous "Nishihara loans" of 1917 and 1918. They were Japanese loans of 145 and 240 million yen to his avaricious associates in the Chinese government in exchange for

The Chinese Calendar

Rat	Ox	Tiger	Hare	Dragon	Snake	Horse	Sheep	Monkey	Rooster	Dog	Pig
1876	1877	1878	1879	1880	1881	1882	1883	1884	1885	1886	1887
1888	1889	1890	1891	1892	1893	1894	1895	1896	1897	1898	1899
1900	1901	1902	1903	1904	1905	1906	1907	1908	1909	1910	1911
1912	1913	1914	1915	1916	1917	1918	1919	1920	1921	1922	1923
1924	1925	1926	1927	1928	1929	1930	1931	1932	1933	1934	1935
1936	1937	1938	1939	1940	1941	1942	1943	1944	1945	1946	1947
1948	1949	1950	1951	1952	1953	1954	1955	1956	1957	1958	1959
1960	1961	1962	1963	1964	1965	1966	1967	1968	1969	1970	1971
1972	1973	1974	1975	1976	1977	1978	1979	1980	1981	1982	1983
1984	1985	1986	1987	1988	1989	1990	1991	1992	1993	1994	1995
1996	1997	1998	1999	2000	2001	2002	2003	2004	2005	2006	2007

official concessions to the Japanese in respect to railways, mining, and military cooperation. On May 4, 1919, a massive student demonstration in protest of the tenets of the 1919 Versailles Agreement erupted at Beijing University. The students attacked Cao's house, demanding his resignation from government. He was fired from his job about a month later.

Centrality and Commonality: This neo-Confucian notion posits human nature as originally received from heaven as in a state of balance or harmony with all things—the mean, or centrality. When unruly human feelings and selfish desires arise, the mean is lost. Only spiritual cultivation can restore the original mean.

The Doctrine of the Mean (also translated as *Centrality and Commonality*), which dates probably from the early Han dynasty (206 B.C.–A.D. 8), is one of the Four Books of the Confucian canon.

Chan Buddhism: This is China's unique contribution to Buddhist thought. Known to the Japanese as Zen, Chan is a short form of the Chinese translation of the Sanskrit word *dhyana*, meaning "meditation." Unknown in central Asia and India, Chan Buddhism became the most popular form in China, Korea, and Japan.

By Chan tradition, some of the Buddha's teachings were passed on to his disciples without transcription and texts because they were to be understood by intuition rather than by long and arduous study, as in other schools of Buddhism. Nor is a devotion to good deeds and the lifelong study of Buddhist texts the central part of the Chan doctrine.

A Chan Buddhist who achieves sudden enlightenment through intuitive understanding gains the ability to deal with life's concerns with perfect mental clarity, calmness and magnanimity.

With its emphasis on meditation and sudden enlightenment, Chan has similarities with Daoism. It attracted large numbers of adherents during the Tang (618–906) and Song (960–1279) dynasties.

Chen Duxiu (1879–1942): Son of a well-to-do Qing official, he returned from study in Japan in 1915 to establish the radical journal *New Youth*. As a dean at Beijing University in 1917, Chen played a major role in the May Fourth Movement.

He used the journal to attack Confucian ways of thinking and to promote radical solutions to China's problems. An early Marxist, Chen devoted a special issue of *New Youth* to Marxism on May 1, 1919, introducing Communist theory to a wide audience. With Li Dazhao, he founded the Chinese Communist Party.

Chen Guofu (1892–1951) and Chen Lifu (1900–2001): Two party bosses of the Guomindang (GMD) under Chiang Kai-shek (1887–1975), Chen Guofu and his brother Chen Lifu formed the CC Clique. It was one of the three main opposing factions of the Nationalist Nanjing government (1928–1937). The other two were the Political Science Clique and the graduates and instructors from the Whampoa Military Academy. The CC Clique, headed by the Chen brothers, gained full control of the GMD central apparatus as well as one of the regime's early intelligence services. Dedicated Confucianists, both Chen Guofu and Chen Lifu were opposed to any substantial change in the ancient structure of Chinese civilization and concentrated their attention on preventing agrarian reforms while the Nationalist government was in place.

Chen Yi (1901–1972): Chen Yi was a noted Communist military leader in the Red Army and later the Fourth New Army in the 1930s and 1940s. He became mayor of Shanghai in 1949 and a member of the ruling politburo in 1956, succeeding Zhou Enlai (1898–1976) as foreign minister in 1958. In 1966, he was subject to extreme censure during the Cultural Revolution (1966–1976). Chen was subsequently dismissed from the politburo at the Ninth Party Congress in 1969 and stripped of all his offices.

Chen Yonggui (1913–1986): A team leader of the Dazhai brigade in a commune in rural Shanxi, he became nationally known in 1964 for using elements of Mao Zedong's theories to boost agricultural output.

Dazhai again emerged as a model of socialist production in the mid-1970s, but criticism of the model in 1980 cost Chen his high government post.

Chiang Ching-kuo (p. Jiang Jingguo, 1909–1988): The Soviet-educated son of Guomindang (GMD) leader Chiang Kaishek by his first marriage, Chiang followed his father into Nationalist politics. He held administrative posts in Jiangxi Province after his return from the Soviet Union in 1937.

Chiang served as an energetic commissioner of GMD financial reforms in Shanghai in the late 1940s. Using youth groups and paramilitary organizations, he cracked down on hoarders and speculators with some success. His campaign yielded some highly publicized arrests, including the son of a Green Gang leader accused of black market activities and of Shanghai financiers for manipulating foreign exchange.

"Their wealth and foreign-style homes are built on the skeletons of the people," he wrote of Shanghai's rich. "How is their conduct different from that of armed robbers?"

Chiang's gains were only temporary. He retreated to Taiwan in 1949 and succeeded his father as president in 1978, retaining the office until his death. Taiwan's economy went through remarkable growth under his leadership. He is credited with some of the liberalizing reforms that eventually led to the democratization of Taiwan.

Chiang Kai-shek (p. Jiang Jieshi, 1887–1975): The Nationalist generalissimo and president of the Republic of China in Taiwan was born in Zhejiang Province, the son of a merchant. He attended a military school in Japan from 1908 to 1910, met Sun Yat-sen there, and joined the Republican Revolution in the autumn of 1911.

Sun sent Chiang to the Soviet Union for military training and put him in charge of the prestigious Whampoa Military Academy on his return. With Sun's death in 1925, Chiang succeeded to the military and political leadership of the Guomindang.

In July 1926, Chiang launched the Northern Expedition with the aim of crushing the warlords and unifying the country. His forces entered Beijing in June 1928, nominally completing reunification of China south of the Great Wall. During the 1930s, Chiang launched five successive campaigns against the Communists, forcing them on the Long March out of central China in 1934.

Chiang led the Nationalist government and military in the eight-year war (1937–1945) against the Japanese invasion, absorbing a series of defeats and the loss of territory. With massive American aid, he managed to carry on the conflict from Chongqing in Sichuan. Although his armies were said to have been corrupt and incompetent, they kept large Japanese forces occupied in China while the Allies advanced elsewhere.

With the Communist triumph in the Civil War of 1945–1950, Chiang and the Nationalists withdrew to the island of Taiwan and relocated the government of the Republic of China there. He held the presidency of the Republic of China until his death.

Chinese People's Volunteers: A few months after the outbreak of war in Korea in June 1950, People's Liberation Army units 400,000 strong, having sewn patches to their uniforms that read Chinese People's Volunteers (PVA), crossed the Yalu River. In a series of quick offenses, they drove the American forces across the 38th parallel, capturing Seoul in January 1951. The Americans were to drive PVA forces from Seoul in that March. The PVA, headed by Peng Dehuai (1898–1974), repeatedly engaged American forces in combat until the Chinese agreed to begin negotiations with the United States in July 1951. They concluded with the June 1953 armistice.

Christian Missionaries: Nestorians from western Asia introduced Christianity into China during the Tang dynasty (618–907). Beginning in the late 14th century, papal missionaries attempted to spread the Roman Catholic faith. Matteo Ricci established a Jesuit presence late in the 16th century, and Jesuits remained in favor at the Qing court through much of the reign of Qianlong (1736–1799).

The London Missionary Society established the first British Protestant presence in China in 1795. The earliest Chinese translations of the Bible appeared in the 1820s. With the military and commercial "opening" of China in the second half of the 19th century, Protestant missionaries poured into the country. Though they claimed thousands of converts, their greatest influence lay in education and in their efforts to raise the status of women.

Identified also with western exploitation, the missionaries often were unpopular with Chinese nationalists, and they were occasionally targets of popular wrath, as in the summer of 1870 when 10 Catholic nuns were victims of the "Tianjin massacre." Boxer rebels in 1898 and 1899 persecuted Chinese Christians, killed many converts, and threatened foreign missionaries. In Shanxi, in the most notorious atrocity of the rebellion, Qing officials, acting with the Boxers, rounded up 44 missionary men, women, and children and killed them all.

Altogether, Christian missionaries might have converted 1 percent of China's population. When the Communists came to power in 1949, the missionary era in China ended abruptly. Since the 1980s, however, the influence of Christianity seems to have grown again with the gradual opening of Chinese society.

Cixi, Dowager Empress, (1836–1908): Emperor Xianfeng's concubine, mother of Emperor Tongzhi, Cixi became regent for her son in 1861 and remained the most powerful figure in Qing government until her death. Westerners knew her as the dowager empress. During most of her years in power, she was known for her conservative stance. In 1898, she crushed the Hundred Days Reform, led by Emperor Guangxu and the scholar-official Kang Youwei.

However, in 1905, with the Qing failing, she appointed a small group to study government in Japan, the United States, and Western Europe. When the group advised a form of constitutional government for China, Cixi issued an edict promising reforms and the convening of a national assembly. The assembly gathered two years after her death and produced a draft constitution the following year.

Cohong: A Chinese merchant guild established in 1720, the Cohong (combined merchant companies) held a monopoly on trade with the West for more than a century. With the restriction of trade to Guangzhou after 1760, the Cohong operated as a Qing government agency, negotiating with foreign firms and collecting Customs duties.

The Treaty of Nanjing abolished the Cohong system in 1842.

Comintern: Lenin established the Third International of the Communist Party— the Comintern—in 1919 for the purpose of promoting socialist revolution abroad. In 1920, Lenin sent the first two Comintern agents, Grigory Voitinski and Yang Mingzhai, to China. They helped Chen Duxiu to clarify organizational and doctrinal ideas that led to the first plenary meeting of the Chinese Communist Party in Shanghai in 1921.

Mikhail Borodin, the best-known Comintern agent, reached China in October 1923 and became a "special adviser" to the Guomindang.

Communist Youth League: The junior subsidiary of the Chinese Communist Party (CCP), the Communist Youth League catered to young people of about 14 to 25. Younger children had the option of joining the Young Pioneers. The league was formed in 1957 from the existing New Democratic Youth League and had as its purpose the education of Chinese young people in preparation for future membership and leadership in the Communist Party. In 1966, it was all but replaced by the Red Guard organizations that actively mobilized Chinese youth during the Cultural Revolution of 1966 to 1976 and insinuated itself heavily into Chinese schools and universities. However, the Communist Youth League experienced a resurgence of support in the 1980s and now has a membership of well over 50 million young people. It is currently the primary means through which young people prepare themselves to apply for membership in the Communist Party after the age of eighteen.

Confucianism: This ethical system derived from the teachings of Confucius (551–479 B.C.) and his later followers. It laid down principles for rulers and ruled alike and survived as the official ideology of imperial China until the collapse of the Qing dynasty (1644–1911) in 1911.

Confucius taught that humans were in harmony with the universe when they behaved with righteousness and restraint and accepted their assigned social roles. Confucian teachings emphasized study of the classics, the veneration of ancestors, and submission to authority. They were concerned specifically with relations between persons, such as an emperor and his minister, a man and his wife, a father and his son. They gave little consideration to the spiritual world.

Mencius (372–289 B.C.), the most important follower of Confucius, added his own gloss to Confucian teachings on human nature and government. The neo-Confucians, whose ideas developed during the middle part of the Tang dynasty (c. A.D. 750), attempted a fusion of Buddhist, Daoist, and Confucian beliefs that became widely influential.

The Four Books and Five Classics were collections and interpretations of Confucian thought that formed the core of Chinese higher learning until early in the 20th century. Reformers in the 19th and 20th centuries attacked Confucianism as static and conservative and blamed many of China's problems on Confucian patterns of thought.

Confucius (latinated name of Kong Qiu, 551–479 B.C.): The most famous, most revered of all Chinese philosophers, he was born in the state of Lu (modern Shandong Province) during the Spring and Autumn era, the son of a member of the lesser gentry.

With his good education, Confucius found himself dissatisfied with his minor official post in Lu and wandered from state to state in China in quest of a position—and a ruler—worthy of his talents. Failing to find a suitable post, he turned to teaching.

Confucius argued that government should be based on ethics rather than practical politics and self-interest and that rulers exist to promote the happiness of their subjects. From his own era of tumult, he glanced back to the early Zhou period (1122–771 B.C.) of King Wen and the Duke of Zhou as a golden age.

In the Confucian ideal, a person should possess five cardinal virtues: he should be upright, righteous, conscientious, humane, and cultured. Humanity or goodness should be the leading principle of all human conduct.

Confucius's *Analects* are believed to be collections of his sayings recorded by his disciples. Confucians traditionally believe that the Five Classics were edited by Confucius (some even believe that the *Spring and Autumn Annals*, which constitutes one of these classics, was composed by him). Among modern scholars, the authorship of these Five Classics is still open to debate.

Coolie Trade: Due to the worldwide anti-slavery movement, which largely ended the international trade in African slaves by the late 1830s, unscrupulous contractors looked to China to find cheap labor. By the 1840s, Chinese laborers were being induced to work for plantations, railroads, and mines in Cuba, Peru, Hawaii, Sumatra, the United States, British Columbia, British Malaya, the Netherlands Indies, and South Africa. Between 250,000 and 500,000 Chinese emigrated to those countries between 1847 and 1874. Derogatorily referred to as "coolies" (from the Chinese word *kuli*, or "bitter laborers"), these workers were treated little better than slaves.

Cultural Revolution (1966–1976): A group of radicals launched this upheaval in the spring of 1966, partly in a bid for control of the Communist Party and partly at the instigation of Mao Zedong. He believed the revolution had lost momentum and that too many Communists were "taking the capitalist road."

Protests began in universities of China and rapidly spread into the high schools. Cultural Revolution leaders, prominent among them Mao's wife, Jiang Qing, declared the protesting students "Red Guards" in the vanguard of a new revolution against bourgeois and revisionist ideas in the party, government, army, and cultural institutions. Mao himself reviewed mass parades of Red Guards in Beijing in the summer of 1966.

Red Guard rampages escalated during the fall and winter. Authority figures came under increasing attack; there were thousands of killings and widespread destruction of temples, churches, and other symbolic buildings. The uprising peaked with the "January power seizures" of early 1967. Mao moved in February to bring the

Cultural Revolution under control, calling on the People's Liberation Army (PLA) to restore order.

After a series of violent clashes over the following eighteen months, the PLA curbed the worst of the Red Guard excesses, though the "continuing revolution" went on with varying degrees of intensity until 1976. With Mao's death, senior Communists moved against leading Cultural Revolution radicals, jailing Jiang Qing and the other members of the Gang of Four after a show trial late in 1976.

Dai Li (1897–1946): Dai Li was a Whampoa Military Academy graduate. In 1932, he became founder and head of what would become Chiang Kai-shek's Special Service in the Bureau of Investigation and Statistics (Junshi Weiyuanhui Tongji Diaocha Ju, or Juntong). It was a secret police organization devoted to ferreting out subversive forces critical of the Nationalist government. During his tenure as head of the Juntong, Dai expanded the number of operatives under his control from 145 to 1,700. He is believed to have been responsible for the deaths of many intellectuals opposed to Chiang's rule. Dai Li died in an airplane accident in 1946, triggering a breakup of the Juntong into three contending factions. The Chinese Communist government and Western press have traditionally vilified Dai, often comparing him to the Nazi Gestapo leader Heinrich Himmler.

Dalai Lama: The title of the spiritual leader of the "Yellow Sect" (Gelukpa) of Tibetan Buddhism and, from 1642 to 1959, the title of the supreme political leader of Tibet. According to Tibetan Buddhist belief, when a Dalai Lama dies, he does not really leave this world. Instead, he reincarnates as a boy. In theory, this boy will be found by an official search party consisting mainly of monks and will become the next Dalai Lama once his connection with his previous incarnation has been verified. The current Dalai Lama (b. 1935) is the 14th incarnation. The relationship between the various Dalai Lamas and the Chinese government has varied from warm friendship to outright hostility. From 1727 to 1911, the government of the Qing dynasty kept Tibet firmly within its sphere of influence (some scholars would argue that Tibet actually constituted a part of the Qing empire) and played a decisive role in the selection and verification of the new incarnations of Dalai Lama. After the collapse of the Qing government in 1911, the government of Tibet, under the leadership of the 13th Dalai Lama, was able to break away from Chinese influence and reach a kind of de facto independence.

After the founding of the People's Republic of China in 1950, the Chinese government claimed legitimate ownership over all former Qing territories, with the exception of Outer Mongolia (which by then had become the People's Republic of Mongolia), and proceeded to re-incorporate Tibet into China. In 1959, anti-Chinese protests by Tibetans escalated into armed rebellion. Faced with the overwhelming strength of the Chinese army in Tibet, the Dalai Lama fled the country and now lives in India.

Below are the dates of the first 13 incarnations of the Dalai Lama:

First Dalai Lama: 1391–1475

Second Dalai Lama: 1475–1542

Third Dalai Lama: 1543–1588

Fourth Dalai Lama: 1588–1617

Fifth Dalai Lama: 1617–1682

Sixth Dalai Lama: 1683–1706

Seventh Dalai Lama: 1708–1757

Eighth Dalai Lama: 1758–1804

Ninth Dalai Lama: 1806–1815

Tenth Dalai Lama: 1816–1837

Eleventh Dalai Lama: 1838–1856

Twelfth Dalai Lama: 1856–1875

Thirteenth Dalai Lama: 1876–1933

Daoguang (1782–1850): He became the sixth emperor of the Qing dynasty (1644–1911) in 1821. Daoguang's attempt to crack down on the opium trade in China and other conflicts with Westerners led to the Opium War (1839–1942) with Great Britain.

Daoism (philosophical): Along with Confucianism and Legalism, Daoism was one of three indigenous Chinese philosophies and, next to Confucianism, the most influential. Daoism as a philosophy probably had its origin in Laozi's *Dao de jing*, a short text that dates probably from the late Zhou dynasty.

The name is from the *dao* (the Way), the road, which Daoists regard as the source of all being and the regulator of existence. It can be read as a metaphor for nature. The central tenet is to do nothing against the Way. Daoists tend to deal with problems by laying aside ambition and seeking a return to a simpler, if perhaps idealized, past. Daoism in one sense is a doctrine of inaction.

The *Dao de jing*, written sometime between the sixth and third centuries B.C. but based on earlier thought, is a discussion of metaphysics and a vague one at that. Its ambiguity has given rise to almost limitless interpretations and, at times, it has had an enormous impact on Chinese culture, especially on the arts. One Tang emperor issued an edict requiring that every noble family obtain a copy of the book.

Daoism (religious): Daoism developed into a religion after the fall of the Han dynasty. In its religious form, Daoism emphasized harmony with nature and the search for immortality or at least a long and serene life.

The quest sometimes involved a search for the Isles of the Blest, thought to be in the sea off Shandong, as well as a regular dosing with pills and elixirs said to contain magical properties. When properly used, Daoists believed, the concoctions could confer invisibility or make possible the otherwise impossible act of levitation. Daoists are also know for their physical exercises and meditation techniques for the purpose of increasing and refining their vital energy.

Zhang Ling (fl. second century A.D.) is regarded as the historical founder of religious Daoism. Zhang introduced the Way of Five Bushels of Rice—the amount of grain he collected from his followers—and thus became known as the "Heavenly Teacher." Daoism spread rapidly in influence and won recognition as the state religion in 440.

Imperial patronage of Daoism reached its peak during the Tang dynasty. High-ranking nobles were required to study Laozi's work, Daoist temples were established throughout the empire, and Laozi and some of his followers were canonized.

Daoism, however, flourished primarily as a religion of the masses. Part of its appeal lay in its diverse and colorful pantheon, with natural objects, historical figures, and even parts of the human body as deities, and in its search for an alchemy of immortality.

Daqing Oil Field: The Daqing oil field is located in Heilongjiang Province in northeastern China. It was held up during the Chinese Cultural Revolution (1966–1976) as an example of self-reliance to be aimed at by all industry. Oil was first stuck there in 1959, but with the withdrawal of Soviet aid to the country in 1961, development of the resource relied on fledgling Chinese techniques. Chinese workers opened the field in 1963, thus allowing China's oil industry to be self-sufficient. Today the Daqing accounts for almost half of Chinese oil production, producing well over 55 million tons of crude oil yearly.

Dazhai: Dazhai is an agricultural production brigade that all others were meant to emulate during the Cultural Revolution of 1966–1976. It was established in the early 1950s as a cooperative in Shanxi Province. On the arid and rocky northern steppe, Dazhai achieved high agricultural output and crop diversification by 1964, using only local manual labor and without aid from the state. This success was achieved through terracing the hillsides, an arduous and labor-intensive process. During the 1970s, the Dazhai was held up as a triumph of the creative application of Maoist thought and the possibilities of collective endeavor. See related entry: **Chen Yonggui**.

Democracy Wall Movement: In a drive for political expression in China, activists put up pro-democracy posters on a stretch of wall along the Forbidden City in Beijing in 1978 and 1979. These wall posters, usually essays or poems, were the main medium of expression during the short life of the movement.

On December 5, 1978, a poster of Wei Jingsheng, a former Red Guard, called for democracy as the fifth modernization to accompany Deng Xiaoping's Four Modernizations—probably the best known of the Democracy Wall broadsides. Wei drew a long prison term for his efforts.

Deng Xiaoping (1904–1997): Born into a peasant family in Sichuan, he joined the Communist Party during a work-study interlude in France in the 1920s. Deng Xiaoping survived Mao Zedong's Long March and occupied a series of important posts in the Central Committee in the 1950s and 1960s.

Deng lost all his preferments during the Cultural Revolution, then returned to power in 1980, replacing Hua Guofeng as the leader of China. Although Deng was never the official head of state, he maintained his position as the most powerful man in China by selecting a younger generation of leaders, by determining the general directions of the state's policies, and by controlling the military. His Four Modernizations, including the forging of new trade ties with the West, set China on the road to spectacular economic expansion. His political and social policies were deeply conservative, however. Taking a hard line, he saw to it that the democracy protests of 1989 were put down harshly.

Documents (Shu jing), Book of: Often referred to as the *Book of History*, the *Book of Documents* contains homilies, speeches, oaths, and injunctions dating from the early Zhou period that deal mostly with the moral law of government and early Chinese ideals regarding statesmanship. Some scholars believe that a large part of the text was reconstructed in the fourth century. *The Book of Documents* begins China's 3,000-year-old chronicle of its history, a period of unbroken historical record that is unmatched in any other modern society. It has long been associated with Confucius, who supposedly selected the documents to transmit to later generations the beliefs and values of an ideal age. *The Book of Documents* is one of the Five Classics that encapsulate the principles of Confucian philosophy, cosmology, and government. The segments of the text that have been proved authentic bear a strong resemblance to bronze inscriptions from the Zhou dynasty.

Dong Zhongshu (c. 179–104 B.C.): One of the most important Confucian ("Ru") scholars in the Former Han period (206 B.C.–A.D. 9). He is often credited with convincing the Han government to adopt Confucianism as its ruling ideology. For his philosophy, see the section on Han thought in the chapter "Systems of Thought and Belief."

Donglin Academy: Early in the 17th century, a group of like-minded scholar-officials established this society, dedicated to restoring orthodox Confucian morality against the encroachments of the intuitive philosophy of Wang Yangming in the city of Wuxi in Jiangsu Province. They argued that Wang's thought led to a degeneration of social and political morality.

In everyday political terms, the Donglin allies fought to curb the power of the eunuchs at the late Ming court. Large numbers of academicians were tortured and killed or driven to suicide during the eunuch Wei Zhongxian's purge of 1625.

Door Gods: These are pictures painted on the doors of Daoist temples and on the doors of some modern private homes. Such pictures are believed to protect the occupants from evil spirits, bad luck, ill health, and attack from one's enemies. Paintings of door gods are usually vivid, full-size representations of ancient martial or scholarly figures. The practice is believed to have originated during the Tang dynasty, when the sleep of Emperor Taizong of Tang (597–649) was disturbed by dreams of ghosts and dragons. He posted court officials outside his door to guard him from these disturbances and later replaced them with painted images.

Dorgon (1612–1650): A Manchu military commander, a son of the Nurhaci, Dorgon led the first campaigns against China below the Great Wall and captured Beijing in 1644. In July 1645, he issued an edict requiring all Chinese men to shave their heads and begin to grow a queue within ten days or face death.

At the first Qing court, he held the powerful post of co-regent to his half-brother Hong Taiji's son, the boy emperor Shunzhi.

Dragon Boat Festival: Called the Duanwu Jie in Chinese, the Dragon Boat Festival is celebrated across China on the fifth day of the fifth month of the Chinese lunar calendar. On the day of the festival, people across the country carry on such traditional activities as putting moxa leaves and calamus twigs on their doors and eating the rice dish zongzi. Most important, brightly decorated Dragon Boats race against one another to commemorate the death of the poet Qu Yuan (c. 343–289 B.C.), who wrote during the Warring States period of 480–222 B.C. It has also been posited that the contentions of the Dragon Boats represent the struggle of heavenly dragons to make rain for newly transplanted rice.

Dream of the Red Chamber, The: Cao Xueqin wrote this novel, regarded as China's greatest, during the reign of Qianlong (1736-1799), the fourth emperor of the Qing (1644–1911).

The novel offers a realistic picture of Qing life and is also a tragic love story. Set in the Yangtze delta, it follows the fortunes of the hero Jia Baoyu and the woman he loves but is forbidden to marry, Lin Daiyu. It is sometimes known by its alternate title, *The Story of the Stone*.

Du Fu (712–770): Du Fu was one of China's great national poets and is usually thought of alongside his contemporary poet and friend Li Bo (701–762). In contrast to the freewheeling writings of Li Bo, Du Fu's works reflect the moralizing of a serious Confucian. His greatest influences were his friendship with Li Bo as well as his frustrated ambitions in the realm of imperial service during the Tang dynasty (618–907), acknowledged to be the golden age of Chinese poetry. The emperor during Du Fu's time was the artistically conscious Xuanzong, whom Du Fu greatly admired.

Duan Qirui (1865–1936): After studying military science in Germany, he rose to senior rank in the Qing New Army and used his service connections to achieve political prominence. Duan served as minister of war in Yuan Shikai's government beginning in 1912 and succeeded Yuan as premier in 1916.

He built his own military power, using bribes and loans from Japan. Duan's secret agreements with the Japanese during World War I were the basis of Treaty of Versailles awards of Shandong rights to Japan in 1919. Nationalist Chinese bitterly resented these arrangements.

Dunhuang: Dunhuang was a central Asian trading post during the Han dynasty. Situated near the terminus of the Great Wall, it was also the beginning of the caravan route to the west known as the Silk Road. In about 1034, a Buddhist library in the Dunhuang cave temples was sealed to protect it from marauding Tibetans. Thousands of manuscripts in Chinese, Tibetan, Uighur, and other Central Asian languages remained there undisturbed until they were found in 1900. They have provided scholars with a unique record of life between the Han and Tang dynasties. Surviving documents also include contracts, local histories, and legislative data.

Eight Immortals: The Eight Immortals are popular Chinese religious figures that supposedly live on Penglai Shan, a mythical island paradise east of China. They are said to have been born human but became immortal deities (*xian*) through the practice of Daoist ideals. They appear in folklore from the Yuan dynasty (1276–1368) and were highly popularized in the drama of that period. The story of the Eight Immortals voyaging together across the sea from Penglai Shan is a popular theme of Chinese opera. By name, they are Zhongli Quan, Zhang Guolao (also named Zhang Guo), Lü Dongbin, Cao Guojiu, Li Tieguai, Han Xiangzi, Lan Caihe, and He Xiangu.

Eight-Legged Essay: Civil service examiners assigned this highly structured form during the Ming (1368–1644) and Qing (1644–1912) eras. Mastery of it became essential for success in the exams, which in turn were the prerequisite for a career in the bureaucracy.

Reformers in the 19th century blamed some of China's weaknesses on educating officials by stressing skills in written interpretation of the Confucian classics rather than in the modern and worldly disciplines of science, technology, and foreign languages. This form of essay quickly died out after the abolition of traditional civil service exams in 1905.

Eighth Route Army: This was the designation for the bulk of the Red Army assigned to Guomindang command during the second Guomindang-Communist united front against Japan from 1937 to 1945.

The army suffered 100,000 casualties in the Hundred Regiments offensive against Japanese strong points and communications in north China in 1940. In contravention of the united front agreement, Nationalist Gen. Chiang Kai-shek in December 1940 ordered Eighth Route Army units to withdraw north of the Yangtze River.

Empress Wu (625–705): She dominated her husband, the Emperor Gaozong, during his lifetime and after his death ruled China through two puppets. She finally took the imperial title for herself in 690.

A strong ruler, a patron of Buddhism, and a supporter of the educated bureaucracy over the claims of the aristocratic elite, the Empress Wu governed capably until forced to abdicate in 705 at the age of 80. Traditional historians regarded her as a usurper.

Eunuchs: Castrated male servants. Usually the castration occurred in early boyhood, but there were also rare cases where adult men would castrate themselves to get jobs as eunuchs. Most of the eunuchs mentioned in historical texts are the ones who served the emperor. Originally employed to guard the palace harem, they gradually acquired other functions and, in many reigns, high posts and great power in the imperial household.

Eunuchs were engaged in nearly constant conflict with the governing bureaucracy. Traditional historians condemn them for misrule. The zenith of eunuch power and abuse of power came during the Ming dynasty, from 1624 to 1627, when the eunuch Wei Zhongxian carried out a reign of terror against his political opponents.

Extraterritoriality: The Treaty of Nanjing in 1843 established the system of extraterritoriality through which accused foreigners were tried under their own national laws for crimes committed on Chinese soil.

Chinese Nationalists detested the system, and Qing reformers pressed for an independent judiciary and impartial courts as a means of ending it. The United States in the late 1920s negotiated the issue with China, but extraterritoriality remained in effect until the Allies abolished it by common consent in January 1943.

Feng Yuxiang (1882–1948): This powerful Soviet-influenced warlord held sway in the 1920s from Shaanxi Province in north-west China to Beijing. Feng joined the Guomindang in the Northern Expedition of 1926 to 1928, Chiang Kai-shek's unification campaign against the warlords.

Feng's forces helped Chiang Kai-shek consolidate Nationalist power in north China in 1927 and 1928. His loyalty remained conditional, and he made war on Chiang several times.

Feng shui (Geomancy): A pseudo-science, feng shui (the Chinese words mean "wind" and "water") stipulates a set of rules for the relations of human beings with their surroundings. It gives the vital energy (*qi*) of land and water an active role in human affairs.

In practical terms, feng shui requires that the lie of the land be consulted for, say, the siting of temples, offices, and residences or the placement of graves. According to feng shui, the internal layout and decoration of offices and residences can also affect individual fortunes.

Filial Piety: Filial piety is the Confucian concept of the supreme importance of loyalty to one's parents. It was enunciated by a disciple of Confucius in the classic *Book of Filial Piety*, which was probably written toward the end of the third century B.C. Filial piety is the most admired of Confucian virtues, which include righteousness, propriety, and integrity. *The Twenty-Four Examples of Filial Piety* (also translated as *24 Stories of Filial Devotion*), written by Guo Jujing during the Yuan dynasty (1276–1368), examines this concept and provides examples of filial devotion that readers were meant to emulate.

Being a filial son meant showing complete obedience to one's parents during their lifetime. After their death, the eldest son is required to perform ritual sacrifices at their gravesite or temple. Additionally, a filial son was expected to ensure that the family line was continued. Dying without a son of one's own was considered one of the worst possible offenses against filial piety. Filial conduct for a woman meant faithfully serving her in-laws, in particular her mother-in-law. Under strict interpretation of the ideals of filial piety, a son was expected to divorce a wife who could not get along with his mother.

The ideal of filial piety inexorably ties the authoritarian family to the state and came into precedence during the Han dynasty (206 B.C.–A.D. 220). During that period, Confucian precepts gained a widespread acceptance in Chinese intellectual and political life. They remained in place until the May Fourth Movement of 1919, when Confucianism was branded decadent and reactionary due to its association with traditional imperial rule.

Filial Piety, Book of: Also known as *The Classic of Filial Piety*, *The Book of Filial Piety*, though sometimes attributed to Confucius, has never had its authorship conclusively proved. Some scholars suggest it was forged in Confucius's name during the Han period (206 B.C.–A.D. 220.); others claim it was written by a disciple of Confucius named Zeng Zi during the fifth century B.C. One of the most important works outlining Confucian thought, the book is written as a form elicitation between the author and Confucius, a format that might have preceded the Socratic method by a hundred years. In the work, Confucius puts forward the view that obeying and revering one's parents and ancestors is the basis of all virtue.

Five Agents: See **Five Elements**.

Five Classics: This group of five philosophical works formed the main canon of Confucian learning and was said to have been edited by Confucius himself. They are *Li Ji* (The book of ritual, or Book of rites), *Chun Qiu* (Spring and Autumn annals), *Shu Jing* or *Shang Shu* (The book of history), *Shi Jing* (The book of poetry), and *I Ching* (The book of changes).

Five Elements: Also translated as "Five Phases" and "Five Agents." The theory of the Five Elements (Wood, Metal, Fire, Water, and Earth) appeared during the Eastern Zhou period (771–256 B.C.), one of the most productive eras in Chinese philosophy. In this age, the first materialist views were formulated, including the theory of the Five Elements, seen as the essential mechanisms of the physical world and the key to understanding the workings of nature. The Five Elements theory is often spoken of in conjunction with the yin-yang theory, a dualistic conception of the fundamental source of all natural phenom-

ena. Both theories were combined into one by Tsou Yen (350–270 B.C.) to form the basic tenets of the Naturalist School.

Five Phases: See **Five Elements**.

Flying Tigers (American Volunteer Group): This group of around fifty U.S. Army Air Force volunteer pilots fought for China against Japan in 1941 and 1942. Led by Claire Lee Chennault (1890–1958), a former U.S. military pilot and an adviser to Chiang Kai-shek, the "Flying Tigers" in their brief existence became one of the best-known and most highly publicized air units of the war.

Foot Binding: For centuries, Chinese girls followed the painful practice of binding their feet to make them tiny, a mark of rank, elegance, and feminine beauty.

The Manchu, after conquering China in 1644, forbade Manchu women to bind their feet. Qing scholar-reformers such as Gong Zizhen attacked the custom, but it died hard. Millions of women continued the practice well into the first decades of the 20th century, though by then large feet had become a sign of emancipation.

Forbidden City: Completed in 1420 during the Ming dynasty under the Emperor Yongle, the Forbidden City stands in the center of Beijing. Occupying a rectangular area of 720,000 square meters, the Forbidden City's buildings with their 8,886 and a half rooms were home to twenty-four Ming and Qing emperors until 1911. The last emperor and his family lived there after his 1912 abdication until 1924. Formerly inaccessible to common people, the Forbidden City's awe-inspiring majesty serves as a reminder to this day of the power of the Chinese emperor. Renamed the Palace Museum, it is now open to the public.

Four Books: With the Five Classics, these works were at the center of Confucian learning in imperial China.

The *Lun yu* (Analects) were a record of the thoughts and statements of Confucius, collected by his disciples and presented in twenty chapters. Quotations of some of his leading disciples are also included. The *Mengzi* (Mencius) collected the thoughts on government and society of Mencius, a scholar of the fourth century B.C. and probably the most important thinker in the history of Confucianism after the master himself. *Zhong yong* (The doctrine of the mean, also translated as Centrality and commonality), sometimes attributed to Confucius's grandson, considered the ideas of moderation, balance, and suitability. *Da xue* (The great learning), also attributed to Confucian disciples and dating from around 200 B.C., discussed self-cultivation as a means to good government.

Neo-Confucian scholars of the Song dynasty combined the essays *The Doctrine of the Mean* and *The Great Learning* to the *Analects* and *Mencius* to form the primer of Chinese education. It was the first major course of study leading to the Five Classics. From 1313 to 1905, the Four Books were the basis of civil service examinations for posts in the imperial bureaucracy.

Four Great Inventions: The Four Great Inventions are traditionally considered to be paper, printing, gunpowder, and the magnetic compass. Paper was invented during the first century A.D. during the Han dynasty (206 B.C.–A.D. 220). Woodblock printing was invented around 770, during the Tang dynasty, and the first reference to a printed book dates as early as 835. The phenomenon of magnetic polarity was recognized in China as early as the third century. By 1119, the magnetic compass was in regular use on Chinese ships, several decades before Arab traders introduced it to Europeans. Gunpowder was invented no later than the early Tang period (A.D. 618–907). At first used for fireworks, by the 11th century gunpowder was being used in hand grenades, mines, and projectiles.

Four Olds, Smash: During the Cultural Revolution, in August 1966, Mao Zedong (1893–1976) encouraged the Red Guards to attack people, customs, and institutions that were felt to be "traditional" and outdated. He also asked them to publicly expose members of the Chinese Communist Party who were backward in their thinking and behavior. These attacks were known at the time as struggles against the Four Olds (old ideas, customs, culture, and habits of mind), and the movement quickly escalated to the commission of atrocities against private citizens and leading intellectuals of the time.

Fu Xi: Fu Xi is a legendary figure from China's prehistoric past who is reputed to have taught his people to hunt, fish with nets, rear domestic animals, and create musical instruments. He reportedly invented the eight trigrams, called *ba gua*, used in divination. He is also reputed to have devised a system of writing based on hexagrams, replacing the old method of knots and strings. Fu Xi is often associated with the legendary leader Nü Wa, who is said to have invented the institution of marriage.

Gang of Four: *The Gang of Four* was the name given by Mao Zedong to his wife, Jiang Qing, and her associates Zhang Chunqiao, Yao Wenyuan, and Wang Hongwen. After Mao's death in September 1976 and the naming of Hua Guofeng as Mao's successor early in October of that year, the Gang of Four was placed under house arrest. Jiang was under suspicion of planning a coup that would instate herself in Hua's place and her accused co-conspirators in positions of power around her. Publicly branded as counterrevolutionaries, the Gang of Four was expelled from the Communist Party and removed from all official posts. They were later formally imprisoned after a show trial that began in November 1980 and ended in January 1981.

Genghis Khan (Chinggis Khan, 1162–1227): Chinggis Khan, the most brilliant Mongol leader in history, unified the Mongol tribes at a *khuriltai* or "great meeting" of Mongol tribes on the Kerulen River in 1206, creating the most powerful military state on Earth. Between 1205 and 1215, Chinggis destroyed the Xi Xia kingdom and took over the Jin capital in northern China. Between 1219 and 1221, he took control of the Kara Khitai empire in the west and the Turkish empire of Khorezm. His empire at his death stretched from the Pacific Ocean to the Caspian Sea. He was succeeded as great khan by his third son, Ogodei.

Gongsun Long (320–250 B.C.): Gongsun was one of the best-known representatives of *Mingjia* (School of names), a sect arising out of the work of the fifth-century Chinese philosopher Mo Ti (c. 470–390 B.C.). Gongsun and his lesser-known predecessor Hui

Shi (380–300 B.C.) are often referred to as the foremost ancient Chinese Dialecticians, or Chinese Sophists (Bianzhe). Followers of the philosophical school used a rhetoric based on analogies, lengthy comparisons, and repetition to win debates and make propositions regarding abstract concepts and ideas. Chinese sophistry, unlike its Greek counterpart, did not make a deep impression upon later Chinese philosophical thinking. Gongson's *Gongson Long zi*, of which only six of the original 14 chapters survive, is the only independent work of ancient Chinese literature dealing with logic and Chinese rhetorical argument to survive to the present time.

Gongyang zhuan: The *Gongyang zhuan* is a commentary written between the fourth and third centuries B.C. on the *Springs and Autumns* or *The Spring and Autumn Annals*, a history of China said to be edited by Confucius (551–471 B.C.). The *Gongyang zhuan*, like many texts from this time, expounds upon classical Chinese theories such as the Five Elements and the yin and yang. It is often grouped with two other important contemporary commentaries on *The Spring and Autumn Annals*: The *Zuo zhuan* and the *Guliang zhuan*.

Gordon, Charles George (1833–1885): A British soldier, known as "Chinese" Gordon, he took part in the capture of Beijing and the destruction of the Summer Palace in 1860 and stayed on to command the Ever-Victorious Army. It was a mercenary unit that helped Qing imperial forces suppress the Taiping Rebellion in 1863 and 1864. His successes encouraged the Chinese to adopt western military technology.

Gordon went on to serve the khedive in Egypt. His death at the hands of the mahdi in Khartoum in January 1885 made him a popular British hero and martyr.

Grand Canal: This system of waterways connected Beijing with the rich Yangtze River Delta. Canal craft carried rice and other products from the south to the imperial capital at Beijing.

The Grand Canal served military purposes at various times. The invading Manchu used it as a highway in 1645 to reach the rich commercial city of Yangzhou. British forces blocked the canal during the Opium War of 1839 to 1842, cutting off supplies to the north and forcing the Qing to sue for peace.

Bargees and coolies employed on canal work formed a pool of recruits for rebel movements of the Qing era.

Great Leap Forward: In 1958, Mao Zedong launched this three-year program of mass mobilization to increase China's industrial and agricultural production. Features were a diversion of resources to some 1 million backyard steel furnaces and the mass collectivization of peasants into "people's communes."

The results of this revolutionary upheaval were disastrous. Industrial production fell; the backyard furnaces produced substandard steel. Harvests declined dramatically. An estimated 20 million people died during the famine years of 1959 to 1962.

Mao admitted his Great Leap Forward policies were mistaken, but he accepted no censure for them.

Great Learning, The: Song-era scholars placed *The Great Learning*, one of the Four Books of the Confucian canon, at the forefront of Confucian literature. The work, a 1,750-word essay whose title in Chinese, *Da xue*, means "education for adults" or "higher education," has been attributed to Zisi (483–402? B.C.), Confucius's grandson or to one or another of Confucius's disciples.

Self-cultivation is the main theme of *The Great Learning*, with the corollary argument that good government depends upon the proper conduct of individuals. Students took its "eight points" as a program or system for self-improvement. The essay had wide influence in Japan and Korea, as well as China.

Great Wall: This 3,750-mile fieldwork, constructed as a defensive barrier, stretches from the China coast northeast of Beijing to the Gobi Desert. It is the largest human-made structure on Earth.

The first Qin emperor (r. 221–206 B.C.) consolidated the Great Wall from earlier sections as a barrier to foreign invasion. It was later extended during the Han, Northern Wei, and Sui dynasties and was reconstructed during the 16th century.

Green Gang: This secret society controlled organized crime in Shanghai from the 1920s to the triumph of the Communists in 1949.

In the 1920s, the Guomindang and some Shanghai businesses used their Green Gang connections to control or crush strikes. Chiang Kai-shek turned to Green Gang members to suppress the Chinese Communist Party. Green Gang racketeers and Guomindang officials also controlled the opium trade in Shanghai—and divided up the profits.

Guan Yu (d. 219): Guan Yu is the Chinese god of war, a quasi-mythical figure who lived during the third century A.D. and whose exploits have romanticized him in popular lore as a warrior of impeccable moral character. Guan Yu was captured and executed by his enemies in A.D. 219, but his legend continued to grow until 1594, during the Ming dynasty (1368–1644). He was canonized as the god of war and the protector of China, prompting the erection of thousands of temples, each bearing the title Wu Miao (Warrior Temple) or Wu Sheng Miao (Temple of the Martial Sage). Because he reputedly memorized the Confucian classic *Zuozhuan*, he is considered one of the gods of literature.

Guan Zhong (seventh century B.C.): Often considered the first of the Legalist philosophers, Guan Zhong was a semi-legendary administrative expert who advised Duke Huan of Chi during the seventh century B.C. The book known as *Guanzi* (Book of master Guan) has been attributed to him. Though the date and authorship of the book are in doubt, it plays a significant role in the Legalist tradition of Chinese philosophy. Guan Zhong is believed to have centralized the Chi government and provided the country with the first state monopoly of salt and iron, advances that would be utilized to great effect by later rulers.

Guangxu (1871–1908): A nephew of the Emperor Xianfeng, Guangxu ascended as the ninth emperor of the Qing through his aunt Cixi's agency in 1875 after the death of his cousin, the Emperor Tongzhi. The dowager Cixi remained the de facto ruler of China.

Guangxu was sympathetic to the aims of the late Qing Confucian reformer Kang Youwei and his associates and helped launch the Hundred Days Reform of 1898. Cixi, an opponent of the reforms, had him imprisoned for his trouble. He and the dowager died within a day of each other in 1908.

Guliang zhuan: The *Guliang zhuan* is a commentary written between the fourth and third centuries B.C. on the *Springs and Autumns* or the *Spring and Autumn Annals*. This history of China between 722 and 481 B.C. is said to have been edited by Confucius (551 B.C.–471 B.C.). Like many texts from this time, it expounds upon classical Chinese theories such as the Five Elements and the yin and yang. It is often grouped with two other important contemporary commentaries on *The Annals of Lu*: The *Zuo zhuan* and the *Gongyang zhuan*.

Guomindang (GMD, also spelled Kuomingtang, or KMT): Sun Yat-sen and his chief lieutenant Song Jiaoren established the Nationalist Party late in 1911 out of the Revolutionary Alliance and smaller groups. The new party won a clear majority over its rivals in the national parliamentary elections of 1912.

The dictator Yuan Shikai outlawed the Nationalists in 1913, and Sun fled to Japan. Renamed the Chinese Nationalist Party (Guomindang), Sun's organization formed a Republican government in Guangzhou in 1921. With advice from the Soviet Union, Sun rebuilt the party organization along Soviet lines and admitted Communists to the party councils.

Chiang Kai-shek succeeded to Nationalist leadership after Sun's death in 1925. His Northern Expedition of 1926 to 1928 nominally reunified most of China under the Nanjing government. Chiang moved to expel the Communists from the party and, except for short experiments with a united front, remained staunchly anti-Communist through the 1930s.

Ill-trained, poorly led Nationalists armies gave ground to the invading Japanese after 1937, forcing the government to withdraw to a new capital at Chongqing in Sichuan. Despite large-scale U.S. aid, the Nationalists failed to establish stable government after World War II and, after a bitter four-year civil war, gave way to the

Communists of Mao Zedong. Chiang and his supporters retreated to the island of Taiwan in 1949 and formed a Nationalist government there. The Nationalists remained in power in Taiwan until the party was defeated in the island's first direct presidential election in 2002.

Gu Jiegang (1895–): This Chinese historian's historiographical method has served as a foundation for 20th-century historical studies on China. Gu was an associate of two important Chinese intellectual reformers of the early 20th century, Zhang Binglin (1868–1936) and Hu Shi (1891–1962).

Guo Moruo (1892–1978): Guo Moruo was a major writer in post-1949 China. He also played a significant role in the Shanghai Literary Movement of the 1920s. Greatly influenced by American poet Walt Whitman, Guo's writings reflected an abiding fascination with the spirit and strength of the living world and the character of great men throughout history. Between 1949 and 1969, he represented China at many World Peace Council Meetings. A non-practicing doctor, Guo held top positions in the Academy of Sciences, the Scientific Planning Commission, and the Federation of Literary and Art Circles.

Guo Songtao (1818–1891): Guo was a Chinese diplomat and liberal statesman who advocated a peaceful response on China's part toward a growing western presence in China. Appointed as China's first minister to Great Britain and France (1876–1878), Guo wrote the Qing government urging the Chinese to introduce such Western innovations as railways, mining technology, and telegraphy as part of the ultimately unsuccessful Self-Strengthening Movement (1861–1895). He also wrote in praise of the Western jurisprudence system, its political and educational institutions, and its economic success, urging China to emulate European modernization and thought. In 1879, outraged officials who were unprepared to abandon principles of governing that Guo castigated as completely backward ordered him back to China.

Gu Yanwu (1613–1682): A scholar of the late Ming and early Qing periods, he practiced what would become known as the *kaozheng* (evidential research) approach. It abandoned Confucian speculation in favor of facts and the rigorous evaluation of data.

Later scholars regarded Gu as an exemplar of intellectual precision. His investigations covered government, ethics, history, and geography, and he always kept a careful record of his findings.

Hai Rui (1513–1587): Hai Rui was a Ming dynasty (1368–1644) official who is remembered for relentless attacks on government corruption. In 1565, he submitted a memorandum to the throne criticizing the emperor Jiajing (1507–1567) for the corruption of his government and his participation in Taoist religious ceremonies, an action that landed Hai in prison. Released upon the death of the emperor in 1567, Hai was promoted to governor of southern Zhili, where his career was curtailed by his political opponents. He was given another political office in 1585 but died two years later. The play *Hai Rui Dismissed*, written by Wu Han in 1961, is based upon Hai's life and addresses the universal theme of the lone righteous man against the corrupt state. The fierce attacks on this play by radical journalist Yao Wenyuan in the Shanghai-based *Liberation Army Daily* are generally regarded as the beginning of the Cultural Revolution (1966–1976).

Hakka: Also called "Kejia" in Chinese. This ethnic minority inhabited the hill districts of south-central China. The Hakka, or "guest peoples," migrated from Jiangxi in the 18th and 19th centuries into the Guangdong region, where they competed with the settled population for land and jobs.

Hakka women were noteworthy soldiers for the Taiping during the rebellion of 1850 to 1864. The Taiping leader Hong Xiuquan was Hakka; so were the Soongs, a prominent Nationalist family in the early decades of the 20th century.

Han Fei (c. 280–233 B.C.): Han Fei was the leading Legalist philosopher during the Warring States period (480–222 B.C.). His ideas were set forth in the *Han Fei zi*, in which he advocated a strict system of rewards and punishments to ensure the authority of the state. These ideas challenged traditional Confucian ideals of governing, as they assumed a civil administration that had to be coerced into loyalty rather than one that obeyed the ruler as a matter of moral obligation. The state of Qin put Han Fei's principles of statecraft to great effect by completing its conquest of China in 221 B.C.

Han Gaozu (256–195 B.C.): Han Gaozu is the posthumous title of Liu Bang, the founder of the Former Han (also called the Western Han dynasty, 202 B.C.–A.D. 8). Han came to power after crushing Qin troops in the valley of the Wei and eliminating his former commander and military rival Xiang Yu (232–202 B.C.). As part of his efforts to consolidate his rule, he made a pact with the belligerent Xiongnu, a nomadic people in northern China. It is now recognized as the first official peace treaty between two independent powers in the Far East.

Han Wudi (156–87 B.C.): Han Wudi (martial emperor) expanded and consolidated the Han empire. Coming to the throne at age 16 in 140 B.C., he ruled until 87 B.C., the longest reign of the Han dynasty. He instituted a program of canal building using forced labor and embarked upon a series of foreign wars, notably against the Asian Xiongnu, extending the empire significantly to the west and south. Not a Confucian himself, Wudi made Confucianism the official ideology of his empire, though he did not use the philosophy to guide state policy.

Han Yu (A.D. 768–824): Han Yu was a prose stylist and a notorious anti-Buddhist who lived and wrote during the Tang dynasty (618–907). His work gave special prominence to the Confucian classic *Mencius* and *The Great Learning*. His practice of writing prose in the so-called antique style (*guwen*) provided the groundwork for the neo-Confucian School of the Song period (960–1279).

Hanlin Academy: Established in the middle of the eighth century by Emperor Xuanzong (A.D. 685–762, r. 712–756) of the Tang dynasty (618–907), the Hanlin Academy was a carefully selected body of scholars who studied the classics for the court and compiled edicts and proclamations. It also was charged with providing official interpretation of the Confucian classics,

which were the basis of the civil service examinations necessary for entrance into the upper levels of the official bureaucracy. The academy existed until the Republican Revolution of 1911 and the overthrow of the Qing dynasty (1644–1911). The Hanlin Academy was very influential during the Ming dynasty (1368–1644) when, in the 1420s, it held control of the eunuch school in the imperial palace. It was proclaimed the highest academic institution of China during the Qing dynasty.

Hart, Sir Robert (1835–1911): Irish-born, a veteran British consular official in China, he headed the Imperial Maritime Customs for the Qing from the 1860s until his death. Efficient and honest, he built up a bureaucracy of international officials that collected vast sums of money for the Qing and produced reliable statistics on trade and local economic conditions throughout China.

Hart also advised the Zongli Yamen, the Qing foreign ministry, on negotiations with the Japanese and others on trade and territorial issues.

Heshen (1750–1799): Hoshen was a corrupt official in the Qing court. His manipulations of the Qianlong emperor (r. 1735–1796) allowed him to embezzle vast wealth from the empire while at the same time attaining positions of great responsibility for himself and his cronies. When the Bailian jiao (White Lotus Society) orchestrated a peasant revolt in central and western China in 1796, Heshen was put in charge of suppressing the rebels. He and his minions within the government—including Fu Kang'an, Holin, and Sun Shiyi—used the opportunity to prolong the campaign and channel much of the money for the war effort into their own pockets. With the death of the Qianlong emperor in 1799, Heshen was removed from power and executed by his successor, the Jiaqing emperor (r. 1796–1820).

Hu Jintao (1942–): Originally trained as a hydraulic engineer, Hu served as the Party Secretary of Tibet Autonomous Region from 1988 to 1992. A member of the Standing Committee of the Politburo since 1992, Hu became vice president of China in 1998. In 1999, Hu took on the additional position of the vice chairman of the Central

Military Commission of the Communist Party. After November 2002, Hu became the general-secretary of the Communist Party, while retaining his positions as the vice chairman of the Central Military Commission and the vice president of China. On March 16, 2003, he took on the additional position of president of China.

Hu Shi (1891–1962): A member of an Anhui official family, educated in westernized schools in Shanghai, he took a B.A. degree from Cornell University in the United States and studied philosophy at Columbia with John Dewey.

Hu returned to China in 1917, taking a post as professor of philosophy at Beijing University. As a writer and philosopher, he became a leading figure of the May Fourth Movement.

A pragmatist and gradualist, he sought an "ever-enduring process of perfecting" rather than perfection itself. In 1919, he published an attack on the Marxist Chen Duxiu and other radicals, "Study More Problems, Talk Less of Isms," that circulated widely among China's intellectuals.

Like Chen, Hu urged China to embrace "Science and Democracy" and promoted the use of the vernacular in Chinese publications. He produced a groundbreaking analysis of *The Dream of the Red Chamber*, China's greatest novel, in the early 1920s. He also pioneered new approaches to the study of Chinese philosophy and Chan Buddhism.

Hu served as the Nationalist government's ambassador to the United States from 1938 to 1942. He was appointed the head of Academia Sinica in Taiwan in November 1957 and began serving in that capacity in April 1958. He remained in that post until his death.

Hu Yaobang (1915–1989): Hu Yaobang was the general secretary of the Chinese Communist Party from 1981 to 1987. His tenure was characterized by his efforts to move the party away from strict Maoist ideology and in favor of toleration of limited political dissent and pragmatism in the governing. He is often considered a symbol of openness and political liberalization in modern China. In an attempt to prevent future leaders of the party from exerting the all-powerful control Mao Zedong had as chairman of the Communist Party, Hu orchestrated the abolition of that post at a party congress in 1982. In 1987, he was forced to resign his post for his leniency regarding the government crackdown on students participating in pro-democracy demonstrations.

Hua Guofeng (1921–): Hua was China's premier from 1976 to 1980 and the chairman of the Chinese Communist Party from 1976 to 1981. As Mao's successor to the top party position, Hua, along with Marshall Ye Jianying, arranged for the arrest of Mao's widow, Jiang Qing, and three of her associates.

Huang Zongxi (1610–1695): Huang Zongxi was one of the foremost political philosophers in the early Qing period (1644–1911). His major contributions to Chinese political thought were a critique of the excessive authoritarianism of the Chinese political system of his day and his passionate convictions regarding the importance of education and the study of history. After refusing to serve the Manchu Qing dynasty, whose army he had fought while serving with Ming resistance leaders in Nanjing, he retired into semi-seclusion to write *Mingyi daifang lu* (Waiting for the dawn: A plan for the prince; 1662). It was a general criticism of the despotism of the late Ming period (1368–1644). His *Ming ru xue'an* (Survey of Ming Confucianists; 1676) is considered to be the first systematic history of the philosophies of the Ming period. His unfinished *Song Yuan xue'an* (Survey of song and Yuan Confucianists; posthumous, 1846), was a comprehensive study of Chinese thought during the Song (960–1279) and Yuan (1276–1368) periods.

Hui: The Hui people are found in greatest concentrations in the Ningxia Hui Autonomous Region and scattered around China proper. The Hui, believers in Islam, were either local converts to the religion, descendants of Arab soldiers who were sent to China in the eighth century to help quell the An Lushan Rebellion, or, in other cases, the descendants of Arab traders who settled in China during the Yuan (1279–1398) and Qing (1644–1911) dynasties. There are more than 8.5 million Hui people now living primarily in the Ningxia, Gansu, Qinghai and Xinjiang regions of China.

Huineng (638–713): Huineng was a Cantonese Buddhist monk who is considered the sixth great patriarch of Zen (Chan) Buddhism. In 700, he founded the Southern School, which became the dominant school of Zen both in China and in Japan. Chan Buddhists rejected long periods of arduous training in pursuit of personal enlightenment, striving instead for detachment from the physical world and the notion of self. Iconoclastic and hostile to systems, scripture, and dogma, followers of the sect were urged to seek instant illumination through meditation, shouts, and bizarre riddles called *kung-an*.

Huiyüan (334–416): Huiyuan was a celebrated early Chinese Buddhist priest. With the famous Buddhist scholar and seer Kumarajiva (344–413) in northern China, Huiyuan was largely responsible for the spread of Buddhism within China and its permeation into Chinese society in the centuries following his death. In 380, he formed a devotional society of monks at the Donglin monastery on the mountain of Lushan in the Yangtze Valley to worship the Buddha Amitabha. The society inspired the establishment in later centuries (sixth and seventh) of the Jingtu or Pure Land (Sukhavati) cult, which is today the most popular form of Buddhism in east Asia. Huiyuan devoted himself to a clear understanding of the essence of Buddhism and its differences from other religions and intellectual traditions in China.

Hundred Days Reform: During a three-month stretch in the summer of 1898, Kang Youwei and his reform allies persuaded the Emperor Guangxu to issue edicts implementing political and economic reforms.

The dowager empress Cixi engineered a coup that ended the Hundred Days Reform abruptly. The emperor was imprisoned, and six reformers, including Kang's younger brother, were put to death.

Hundred Flowers Campaign: Mao Zedong launched a brief period of liberalization in May 1957 when he called for "the blooming of a hundred flowers and the contending of a hundred schools of thought." When criticisms of the Communist Party and his rule began to pour in, Mao put a brake on the campaign.

Not long after the wilting of the Hundred Flowers at the end of June, an "Anti-Rightist" campaign targeted those who had volunteered criticisms of the regime. By year's end, 300,000 intellectuals had been stigmatized as rightists.

Islam: Islam spread to China as early as the eighth century A.D., during the Tang dynasty, via seafaring Arab and Persian merchants who settled permanently in Chinese cities, most notably in Yangzhou, Guangzhou, and later in the ports of Fujian Province. During the Yuan dynasty, the Chinese Islamic community greatly increased in number as the Mongol conquerors of China brought many Muslim soldiers into the country. The decline of the Qing dynasty brought about a short Muslim revivalist movement that threw much of the northwest and southwest of China into chaos. Muslims in China have had a tenuous relationship with the government since 1949, facing close government supervision of their religious practice during the 1950s and during the Cultural Revolution (1966–1976). Estimates place the total population of the Muslim community in China today at about 40 million. The Uighur in Xinjiang and the Hui in Ningxia enjoy autonomous status, and there are large Muslim communities today in Shaanxi, Shanxi, Gansu, Yunnan, and Sichuan.

Jesuits: The first Jesuit missionaries reached China from Europe in the late Ming. The most prominent early arrival, Father Matteo Ricci, lived in Beijing from 1583 to 1610 and became a great admirer of Chinese civilization.

The Emperor Kangxi (r. 1661–1722) favored the Jesuits at court and, in 1692, granted toleration to the Christian religion as long as the Christians allowed Chinese converts to continue to practice ancestor worship and venerate Confucius. Of the religious orders, only the Jesuits agreed to observe the emperor's stipulation, and many missionaries consequently left China.

Jesuits were responsible for much of the West's knowledge of China. Their books on Chinese government and society were the best available. Worldly Jesuits were in high favor at the court of Qianlong (r. 1736–99). He patronized Jesuit landscape painters, and Jesuit architects designed the European-style buildings in his Summer Palace Yuanming Yuan near Beijing.

Jews: The earliest evidence of Judaism in China comes from the Tang dynasty, when in A.D. 878 in Guangzhou Jews were said to have been slaughtered. Their most notable community was in Kaifeng during the Song dynasty, where Jews from Persia first settled in 1127 and built the area's first synagogue in 1163. This area flourished until the 19th century, with Jews attaining positions as court officials, army officers, and physicians during the Ming and early Qing dynasties. Their original synagogue was destroyed in the flood of 1642, and after that time, the religion fell into decline. By 1866, the Kaifeng synagogue had disappeared entirely from the community, though the Jewish character of the area remained into the late 1940s.

Other Jewish communities grew up in China from the mid-1840s on, most notably in Shanghai (and Hong Kong) and in Harbin, where, by 1917, the number of Russian Jews had grown to 10,000. Between 1933 and 1941, the Jewish community of Shanghai benefited greatly from an influx of German and Austrian refugees escaping persecution from the Nazi government. By 1939, there were more than 20,000 Jews in Shanghai, 3,000 in Harbin, and 2,000 in Tianjin. From 1949 on, there was a steady exodus of Jewish people to Israel and the United States. By 1959, the number of Jews left in China was probably no more than 300. By 1970, there was no evidence of any practicing Jews in mainland China, although a small community survived in Hong Kong.

Jiang Jieshi: See **Chiang Kai-shek**.

Jiang Qing (Chiang Ching, 1914–1991): A former Shanghai movie actress, Jiang was Mao Zedong's third wife and rose to become the most powerful woman in China and an important political force during the Cultural Revolution.

She was arrested after Mao's death in 1976 and accused, as leader of the Gang of Four, of persecuting party members and indirectly causing the deaths of millions during the Cultural Revolution. The authorities commuted her capital sentence to imprisonment for life.

Jiang Zemin (1926–): Jiang joined the Communist Party in 1946. Originally trained as an engineer, he worked as a trainee in the Stalin Automobile Works in the Soviet Union in 1955. In addition to his native language (Chinese), he also speaks English, Russian, and Romanian and has some knowledge of Japanese and French. After his return from the Soviet Union, he gradually shifted from engineering to management and politics. In 1985, he became the mayor of Shanghai. After the Chinese government suppressed the student protests in Beijing in June 1989, the paramount leader **Deng Xiaoping** (see entry) brought him into the central government, with the intention that he replace the outgoing general secretary Zhao Ziyang. Jiang subsequently became the head of the Central Military Commission of the Chinese Communist Party (which controls the Chinese military) and the general secretary of the Chinese Communist Party. In March 1993, he became the president of China. After the 16th Communist Party Congress held in November 2002, Jiang retired from his position as the general secretary of the Party. On March 16, 2003, he retired from his position as president. However, he is expected to continue to wield considerable influence from behind the scenes. It is also likely that he will remain the chairman of the Central Military Commission after his retirement from his other posts.

Journey to the West (Xiyou ji): One of the great works of Chinese fiction, this picaresque tale by Wu Chengen (c. 1500–1582) had its origin in the Tang dynasty monk Xuanzang's pilgrimage to India in search of Buddhist scriptures.

The hero of the novel is a monkey with human characteristics who accompanies the monk on his quest. *The Journey to the West* first appeared in novel form during the late Ming period and remains part of Chinese folk culture today. It has been translated into English under the titles *The Journey to the West* and *The Monkey*.

Jurchen: These Manchurian tribal groups, the ancestors of the Manchu, rose to power early in the 12th century and established the Jin dynasty. It conquered the Khitan Liao state, ruling northern China from 1127 to 1234.

The Jurchen were in turn conquered by the Mongols, who established the Yuan dynasty in 1276. The tribal name fell into disfavor in the 17th century, allegedly because of its servile connotation; the term *Manchu* replaced it.

Kang Sheng (1899–1975): Kang Sheng was a Chinese Communist official considered to have been one of the three or four most powerful individuals in the government during the Cultural Revolution (1966–1976). He was a trade union organizer in Shanghai during the 1920s and director of security in the Communist Party in the 1930s and 1940s. He served as governor of Shandong from 1949 to 1955. In 1956, he became an alternate member of the Politburo and, in 1966, an adviser to the Cultural Revolution Group. After the Cultural Revolution, he became a member of the Politburo's standing committee. In 1970, his name was listed just below that of premier of the Chinese People's Republic, Zhou Enlai (1898–1976), in official party pronouncements. In 1973, he was made third vice chairman of the Chinese Communist Party.

Kang Youwei (1858–1927): A Confucian scholar, Kang rose to become a leading figure in late Qing reform movements.

Arguing that economic and political modernization could occur within a traditional Confucian framework, he won the support of the Emperor Guangxu, whose edicts launched the Hundred Days Reform of 1898. Kang had just left Beijing and thus escaped arrest when the dowager empress Cixi moved to quell the reform movement in September 1898.

Kangxi (1654–1722): The second son of the Emperor Shunzhi, Kangxi ascended the throne as the second emperor of the Qing and reigned for 61 years.

Consolidating Manchu rule, he led several military expeditions to the northwest while his subordinate commanders pacified south China. During Kangxi's long reign, China emerged as the largest and one of the richest unified empires in the world.

Khitan: These semi-nomadic tribes, millet farmers and livestock raisers, rose to prominence in Manchuria in the ninth and 10th centuries.

The Khitan Liao state ruled Mongolia, Manchuria, and the northeastern corner of China proper from 907, just after the fall of the Tang, until 1125. Then the Jurchen, a new wave of powerful invaders from the north, destroyed the Liao.

KMT: See **Guomindang**.

Kublai Khan (1214–1294): The grandson of Genghis Khan, he became great khan in 1620 and ruled for 34 years. From his winter capital in Beijing, Kublai's armies conquered southern China, taking Hangzhou in 1276 and Guangzhou in 1279. He failed, however, in two attempts to invade Japan.

Kublai took the Chinese dynastic title of Yuan in 1271 and ruled in the Chinese style. The Venetian traveler Marco Polo claimed to have served at Kublai's court from 1275 to 1292.

Kumarajiva (344–413): Kumarajiva is recognized as one of the greatest translators of Buddhist scriptures from Sanskrit into Chinese. Largely because of his efforts and influence, Mahayana Buddhist religious and philosophical concepts were disseminated across China. After being imprisoned in 384 at Wuwei for seventeen years by the powerful Early Qin general Lü Guang, Kumarajiva was taken to Chang'an in 402 by the Later Jin ruler Yao Xing. There Kumarajiva organized a team of translators who translated 98 Buddhist scriptures into Chinese, of which 52 are still extant. The team provided Chinese versions of Buddhist sutras as well as translations of Buddhist treatises on discipline, manuals of dhyana, and metaphysical and scholastic documents. This tremendous corpus of translated Buddhist literature enabled the religion to spread more quickly throughout China during the fifth century A.D.

Kuomingtang: See **Guomindang**.

Lao She (1889–1966): A novelist and playwright, his works attacked the corruption and unfairness of Chinese society before 1949. After the founding of the People's Republic of China, Lao also wrote works showing the progress of Chinese society under socialism. An ethnic Manchu from Beijing, he successfully incorporated the everyday language of Beijing city dwellers into his writing. He is best known for his novel *Camel Xiangzi* (1936) set in the Beijing underclass of the 1930s. See "Literature" chapter.

Red Guards persecuted Lao She to death during the Cultural Revolution.

Laozi (Lao Tzu): Laozi, probably mythical, is the author of the chief work of the Daoist classic, *Dao de jing*. By tradition, Laozi, or the old master, lived before Confucius; dates often given are 604–521 B.C.

Writings attributed to Laozi taught that liberation occurred when humans were in harmony with "the Way."

Legalism: An authoritarian school of philosophy, Legalism developed during the Warring States period (480–222 B.C.). Han Fei (d. 233 B.C.) is widely regarded as the last and greatest of the Legalist philosophers. Rejecting the Confucian notion of benevolent rule, Legalists argued that humans were selfish in essence and are most effectively motivated by reward and punishment through the application of strict laws.

Legalists were practical politicians dealing with everyday problems. They laid down that absolute rulers should govern from comprehensive sets of laws rewarding behavior that benefited the military and financial strength of the state and punishing behavior that brought harm to it. Applying Legalist tenets, Qin rulers overpowered other Warring States to establish the first Chinese empire.

Lei Feng: The Communist Party used this young People's Liberation Army soldier in propaganda as a model of patriotism and selfless service. He appeared first in 1963 in Defense Minister Lin Biao's "learn from the army" campaign.

Lei Feng was killed when an army truck backed over him. His posthumously discovered "diary," actually the invention of an army propaganda unit, showed the soldier's love of country, revolutionary ardor, and devotion to Mao Zedong. He is especially known for his willingness to provide selfless help to complete strangers.

Liang Qichao (1873–1929): A student of the Confucian reformer Kang Youwei, he went into exile in Japan after the collapse of the Hundred Days Reform movement in 1898.

Liang wrote widely in support of reform and a strong China, eventually advocating a liberal republicanism at odds with his mentor's preferences for a constitutional monarchy. As a leading historian, he greatly influenced the development of historical research in China.

Liao: Khitan from Manchuria swept south into China proper to establish a state after the fall of the Tang dynasty in 907. The Khitan functioned with the advice and assistance of Chinese bureaucrats and ruled in the Chinese style, using Chinese titles, court ceremonials, and written language. The Liao ruled Mongolia, Manchuria, and the northeastern corner of China proper, including present-day Beijing.

The Liao dynasty collapsed in 1125 under pressure from a new wave of invaders from the north, the Jurchen, who pushed the Khitan west and formed a north China state of their own.

Liao Chengzhi (1908–1983): An official of the People's Republic, educated in Japan, he became active in leftwing student groups in the 1920s and joined the Chinese Communist Party in 1927. Liao was a veteran of the Long March from Jiangxi in 1934 and 1935.

After 1948, Liao was an important figure in Communist youth organizations. He also held a succession of senior Communist Party posts. He was Liao Zhongkai's son.

Liao Zhongkai (1878–1925): Liao was born in the United States and educated in Japan. An early ally of Sun Yat-sen, he managed the financial affairs of the Guomindang from 1914 to 1925 and served as Nationalist governor of Guangdong Province.

He was murdered in August 1925 in reprisal for his support for a Hong Kong–Guangzhou workers' strike launched as a protest of British actions. His killers were probably anti-leftists in the Guomindang.

Li Dazhao (1889–1927): A leading member of the May Fourth Movement, he studied in Japan and returned to China to head the library at Beijing University and co-edit the influential *New Youth* magazine.

Li was an early Marxist, a founder of the Chinese Communist Party, and an important figure during the first Guomindang-

Communist united front of 1923 to 1927. The warlord Zhang Zuolin had him arrested and executed in Beijing in 1927.

Li Guang (d. 119 B.C.): In the conflict between the Han empire and the Xiongnu nomads, Li distinguished himself as one of the most brilliant generals on the Chinese side. Li was known for his amazing archery and cavalry skills. He was once captured by the Xiongnu nomads, but was able to escape by suddening unhorsing a Xiongnu warrior and taking his horse. After the daring escape, Li earned the nickname "flying general" among the Chinese and Xiongnu alike. Li was not only a brilliant tactician, but also a father figure to his troops. After forced marches on the dry steppes in the north, he would refuse to go near water until all his soldiers had drank, and refuse food until all his soldiers had eaten. In the expedition against the Xiongnu in 119 B.C., Li's commanding officer intentionally ordered Li to take a roundabout route, so that the commanding officer's own relative could take the credit for leading the frontal assault. Sadly, Li and his troops got lost on the steppes because of the lack of local guides. To protect his subordinates from punishment, Li took full responsibility and committed suicide. It is said that when he died, his whole army cried. Even Chinese civilians who had never met him shed tears for him.

Li Hongzhang (1823–1901): One of the most powerful military-political figures of the late Qing, he rose to the fore in the 1860s as a commander of the Huai Army in the war of the Taiping Rebellion. After a long campaign, his forces quelled the Nian rebels in northern China in 1868. After the death of **Zeng Guofan** (see entry), he was undoubtedly China's most important official and diplomat.

Li became involved in railway and telegraph development and in the expansion of shipping and arms manufacturing, part of the Self-Strengthening Movement in China during the last decades of the 19th century.

He was a principal shareholder in the China Merchants Steamship Navigation Company. In the late 1870s, he directed the expansion of China's coal-mining industry in the Tianjin region. In an effort to curb textile imports, he founded a large cotton mill in Shanghai in 1878.

Li established training programs for young Chinese in the United States and Europe and established military and naval academies in China.

Li Lisan (1896–1967): Li Lisan is best known for his implementation of the "Li Lisan line," a strategy for worker uprisings across urban centers of China that he implemented as effective head of the Chinese Communist Party in 1928. However, his failure to accomplish successful Communist offensives against the cities of Changsha, Wuhan, Nanchang, and other centers caused him to be condemned by the Communist Party and to lose authority within the CCP until 1946, when he rejoined the Central Committee. In 1958, he became the vice chairman of the national Trade Union Federation and served for a time as minister of labor. During the first year of the Cultural Revolution (1966), he was attacked by Red Guards and subsequently committed suicide in 1967.

Li Peng (1929–): The son of a leading Communist, Li Peng become an orphan at the age of three. In 1939 he was adopted by **Zhou Enlai** (see entry) as a foster son. Between 1948 and 1955, Li Peng studied engineering in the Soviet Union. He was the premier of China from 1987 to 1998 and became head of the National People's Congress in 1998. On March 16, 2003, he retired from this position but is expected to continue to exert considerable influence in Chinese politics. During the student protests in the Spring of 1989, Li Peng was one of the main targets of student criticism. With a reputation as a political hardliner, he is often faulted for spearheading the military crackdown against the protestors on June 4, 1989.

Li Ruihan (1934–): Li Ruihan is the chairman of the Chinese People's Political Consultative Conference and a member of the Politburo standing committee since 1989. The former mayor of Tianjin, Li is known as a progressive-minded liberal and has spoken openly about reforms leading to the establishment of democracy in China. He also advocated an independent system of government for Hong Kong.

Li Shizhen (1518–1593): Li Shizhen compiled a giant *mataeria medica* called *Bencao gang mu* (Materia medica ordered on the basis of monographs and individual characteristics, or The great pharmacopoeia), which described more than 2,000 drugs and presented directions for preparing more than 8,000 prescriptions. Completed in 1578, the book contained 142 illustrations and descriptions of 1,074 vegetable, 443 animal, and 217 mineral substances. In it, Li described modern processes such as distillation; the uses of mercury, ephedrine, chaulmoogra oil, and iodine; and even smallpox inoculation. It contains not only the expert knowledge of Li and earlier authors on the subject of pharmacology but also critical essays on natural science and its history. No author in later centuries attempted to expand or even equal this tremendous work.

Li Si (c. 280–208 B.C.): Li Si is credited with using harsh but effective Legalist methods of government during his time to meld the Warring States of China into the Qin dynasty (221–206 B.C.). Serving from 247 until his death under the Shi Huangdi (First Sovereign Emperor) of the state of Qin, Li was responsible for massive political and cultural changes in the China ruled by the Qin after 221. He divided the empire into 36 regions and initiated construction of the Great Wall to keep out barbarians from the north. He created a unified writing system, a standard system of weights and measures, axle lengths, and coinage. To curtail the growth of subversive thought, he ordered the notorious Burning of the Books of 213. After the death of Shi Huangdi in 209 B.C., Li conspired with the eunuch Zhao Gao to replace the legimate successor to the throne with a prince they favored. After the success of their conspiracy, Zhao turned against Li and had him arrested. Under repeated torture, Li was forced to admit to trumped-up charges of treason and was executed.

Li Yuanhong (1864–1928): Li Yuanhong was the only president of the Republic of China in Beijing who served for two terms. On December 29, 1911, Li was elected vice

president of the Republic of China and held that position until the death of President Yuan Shikai (1859–1916) in June 1916. Li then assumed the presidency and held office until the brief restoration of the emperor in July 1917. Although he was asked to resume his presidency in 1922, the following year Li was forced to resign, having been unsuccessful in his efforts to reunify Republican China.

Li Zhi (1527–1602): Born into a Muslim family, Li Zhi is known to posterity as a radical Confucian philosopher. Influenced by Chan Buddhism, Li Zhi's Confucian philosophy emphasized the belief that all humans were born with the full potential to become sages. According to Li Zhi, every person was born with his/her special value to this world, and there was no reason why everyone had to agree with Confucius in everything. He also promoted women's education. In 1602, he was arrested for promoting subversive ideas. He committed suicide in prison shortly after his arrest. See also *Chan Buddhist Tendencies in Wang Yangming Idealism* in the chapter "Systems of Thought and Belief," page 115.

Li Zicheng (1605–1645): A one-time ironworker and Ming army deserter, he raised his own rebel army, marched unopposed into Beijing in April 1644, and overturned the tottering Ming dynasty. Manchu invaders in turn destroyed Li's army.

Liezi (third or fourth century B.C.): Liezi was a Daoist writer and teacher who lived during China's Warring States period (480–222 B.C.). He is remembered as one of the three philosophers responsible for the development of Daoist thought; the others were Laozi and Zhuangzi. Lie's book, *Liezi*, advises readers not to challenge the force of the Dao—the great, mysterious cosmic force that Daoists believe animates Earth—and to embrace a life of self-interest. Lie's work has been viewed as anti-Confucian and fatalistic, though many scholars believe the book's subtext of despair and cynicism might not be a true reflection of Lie's actual teachings.

Likin: The likin, "a tax of one-thousandth," was levied in the second half of the 19th century on goods transported over Customs barriers. The tax was first imposed in 1853 in the central Chinese province of Jiangsu to finance the suppression of the Taiping Rebellion (1851–1864) and the Nian Rebellion (1851–1863). By 1860, the likin had spread to almost every province in China. The likin soon became one of the major sources of revenue for the Qing dynasty's government. It was assessed at anything from 2 to 3 percent of the value of the goods transported or up to 10 percent for a consolidated tax. Under pressure from Western countries, China agreed to abolish the likin in 1928.

Lin Biao (1908–1971): Perhaps the best field commander of the Communist army, he inflicted serious defeats on the Nationalists during the civil war. After the beginning of the Korean War, Mao had wanted Lin to lead the Chinese People's Volunteers into Korea. Lin refused, using "illness" as an excuse. After some years of relative inactivity, Lin became the minister of defense in 1958. At the beginning of the Cultural Revolution (1966–1976), Mao, who needed Lin as an ally, made Lin his successor, a designation made official in 1969. Lin died under mysterious circumstances after an alleged coup attempt went awry in 1971.

Lin, Commisioner: See **Lin Zexu**.

Lin Zexu (1785–1850): The Qing appointed this scholar-official an imperial commissioner charged with ending the opium trade. Taking up his appointment in 1838, Lin launched a campaign to curb domestic use of the drug and to block imports at the same time.

In 1839, he confiscated 3 million pounds of opium from British warehouses in Guangzhou, an action that enraged British merchants and helped ignite the Opium War of 1839 to 1842.

Liu Shaoqi (1898–1969): Liu Shaoqi served as the chairman of the People's Republic of China (1959–1968) and chief theoretician for the Chinese Communist Party (CCP). His early career within the party was centered around building trade unions within China, his work earning him, in 1934, a seat on the Politburo (political bureau) of the Sixth Central Committee. In 1948, he became chairman of the All China Federation of Labor and from 1954 to 1959 was chairman of the Standing Committee of the National People's Con-

gress. Because of his heavy influence in the CCP, he was the obvious successor to Mao Zedong (1893–1976), the chairman of the Chinese Communist Party. In 1959, Liu was appointed chairman of the People's Republic of China (head of state).

Perhaps because he and Mao had clashed on internal government and party policies during the Cultural Revolution (1966), Liu was severely criticized for being a revisionist and "the leading person in authority taking the capitalist road." By 1968, he had lost all his political posts except that of chairman of the People's Republic, which was formally removed from him in 1969. By that time, he had completely disappeared from public life and died quietly in Hunan Province. In February 1980, he was posthumously "rehabilitated" by the Eleventh Central Committee of the CCP.

Liu Zongyuan (773–819): Liu Zongyuan was a poet, prose writer, and supporter of his contemporary, the anti-Buddhist poet and essayist Han Yu (768–824). Both men were instrumental in the movement to create a new literary style. Chinese literati practiced the ancient Chinese classical style of official reports and decrees called *pianwen*, the "parallel prose" style, for nearly 1,000 years before Liu's time. Liu and his contemporary authors favored a clear, sharp writing style that is evident in his famous tale *The Snake Catchers*, a savage portrayal of the rapacious treatment of peasants by Tang dynasty (618–907) tax collectors. Liu supported the short-lived reform movement of 805 against eunuch rule and other abuses of government during the early ninth century. Because of this, he was forced to spend the rest of his life in exile.

Long March: Communists retreated 6,000 miles in 1934 and 1935 in an attempt to flee the suppression campaign of Chiang Kai-shek's Nationalists.

Leaving most of the women and children behind, the column set out from Jiangxi on October 16, 1934, some eighty thousand strong. A year of epic hardship began, including a crossing of the "Great Snow" mountain ranges in which the troops suffered severely from hunger and frostbite. On October 20, 1935, a remnant of between 8,000 and 9,000 survivors reached Yan'an in the northwestern province of Shaanxi and established a new Communist base there.

The Long March became a Communist legend. "It is a manifesto, a propaganda force, a seeding machine," Mao Zedong said. "It has proclaimed to the world that the Red Army is an army of heroes, while the imperialists and their running dogs, Chiang Kai-shek and his like, are impotent."

Lotus Sutra (The "Lotus of the Good Law" or the "Lotus of the True Doctrine"): The Lotus Sutra is one of the texts that contain the essence of Mahayana Buddhist beliefs. The work is known in China as the *Miaofa lianhua jing* or *Fahua jing*. Composed largely of 29 verses, the Lotus Sutra contains many charms and mantras (sacred chants). It was first translated into Chinese in the third century A.D.

Lu Jiuyuan (also known as Lu Xiangshan, 1139–1193): Lu Jiuyuan was one of the first neo-Confucian philosophers of the Southern Song period (1127–1279) and philosophical rival of the great neo-Confucian statesman, historian, and commentator on Confucian classics Zhu Xi (1130–1200). Lu's thought heavily influenced the teachings and writings of the neo-Confucianist Wang Yangming (1472–1529) during the Ming dynasty (1368–1644.)

Lu's thinking diverged from Zhu's in that in advising his followers, he emphasized spiritual enrichment through inner reflection rather than through traditional learning and study. He posited that personal growth came through eschewing desires (wu yü) in favor of self-contemplation. Some scholars have argued that Lu's influence on neo-Confucianism represented the influence of meditative Buddhism on traditional Confucian beliefs, while Zhu's represented the influence of monastic Buddhism. Lu's various works were collected and published under the title of *Xiangshan xiansheng quanji* (Complete works of master Xiangshan) after his death. In 1530, a tablet in his honor was placed in the central Confucian temple of the Ming dynasty.

Lu Xiangshan: See **Lu Jiuyuan**.

Lu Xun (1881–1936): Penname of Zhou Shuren. Lu Xun was one of China's foremost writers and social critics during the rule of the Nationalist government between 1927 and 1937. His strength lay in his sharp, satirical short stories and the barbed *zawen n*, an essay format he used to great effect to criticize both contemporary and traditional Chinese society. His short story collections *Nahan* (Call to arms, 1923) and *Panghuang* (Hesitation, 1926) established his reputation as one of the leading Chinese writers of the early 20th century. He is best known for his short stories "Diary of a Madman" and "The True Story of Ah Q." Lu translated Nikolai Gogol, Georgi Plekhanov, Anatoli Lunacharsky, and Jules Verne, as well as Japanese, Polish, and Hungarian writers. His meticulously researched *Zhonggu xiaoshuo shilue* (Outline history of Chinese fiction) and companion compilations of classical fiction remain as relevant and useful today as they were during Lu's era. Lu founded the League of Left Wing Writers in 1930 and later declared himself a Marxist, although he never joined the Chinese Communist Party.

Ma Yinchu (1882–1982): Ma Yinchu was the president of the Beijing (Peking) University, as well as a prominent economist. He was one of the first to point out that the massive population growth of China would threaten its economic growth. In the 1970s, Mao Zedong, who thought a large population was a source of strength, denounced Ma's pessimistic views. The Chinese government began to appreciate Ma's wisdom only in the late 1970s, when overpopulation became too evident a problem to ignore.

Macao: With China's tacit consent, the Portuguese took control of this port city southwest of Guangzhou in 1557. With the imperial ban on direct Chinese trade with Japan in the 17th century, Portuguese merchants in Macao prospered as middlemen exchanging silk for silver.

This city of 400,000 remained the last foreign-controlled outpost on Chinese soil into the late 1990s. It returned to Chinese rule on December 20, 1999.

Mahayana Buddhism: Mahayana Buddhism is China's most popular Buddhist movement and has existed in the country since the beginning of the fourth century, though scholars recognize its inception in India as dating as far back as the second century. Of the 10 historical schools of Buddhism in China, seven were Mahayana and three were Theravada. The most popular Buddhist schools of today's China are the fifth-century Mahayana movements of Pure Land and Chan (Zen). The former stresses faith in Amitabha Buddha. The latter, supposedly transmitted to China through the semi-legendary Bodhidharma, emphasizes meditation as a means of realizing one's personal Buddha nature.

Manchu: The Manchu people, partly descended from the Tungus tribes, were ethnically related to the Jurchen people, the founders of the Jin empire in the 12th century. The Manchu people rose to power in the 16th century in Manchuria on the periphery of the state and culture of China, uniting their scattered tribes under the banner system devised by the powerful leader Nurhaci (d. 1626) in 1601. The Manchu gradually extended their influence through Mongolia, Korea, and parts of northern China. Their successful raids on cities of northern China prompted them to proclaim the formation of the Qing dynasty in 1636 at Mukden. The Qing quickly conquered China proper after the fall of the Ming dynasty in 1644.

Manchuria: Manchuria is originally the home of the Manchu people in northeastern China, comprising the provinces of Heilongjiang, Jilin, and Liaoning. Part of the Qing empire until 1911, it was controlled by the warlord Chang Tso-lin during the 1920s. It was taken over by the Japanese in 1931 and renamed Manchukuo by its occupiers in 1932. The Cairo Declaration of 1943 declared Manchuria part of China in 1943. In 1949, a part of western Manchuria was incorporated into the Inner Mongolian autonomous region. The principal cities of Manchuria are Shenyang, Harbin, Dalian, Fushun, and Anshan.

Manchukuo: The Japanese gave the name, which means "land of the Manchu," to the puppet regime they established after taking effective control of Manchuria in 1931 and 1932.

Japan ignored League of Nations admonitions and consolidated its hold on the region. With the "last emperor," the deposed Puyi (formerly emperor Xuantong of the Qing dynasty), installed as "chief executive" in 1932, the Japanese remained in Manchuria until the end of World War II in 1945.

Mandate of Heaven: Referred to as "Tianming" in pinyin, the "mandate of heaven" is a cornerstone of Confucian political thought that traces its beginnings to the Zhou dynasty in the 11th century B.C. It is the concept that heaven (*tian*) confers the right to rule directly upon Chinese emperors, similar to the concept of the "divine right" of kings. The continuation of this mandate was dependent upon the personal behavior of the ruler, who was expected to show righteousness (*yi*) and benevolence (*ren*). If a ruler became dissolute, it was often believed, he had lost the "mandate of heaven" and the people could remove him by revolution, if necessary.

Manicheism: Manicheism is a Persian religion named for its founder, Mani (216–276), who arrived in China in 694. The fundamental doctrine of Manicheism is a dualistic division of the universe into contending realms of good and evil: the realm of Light (spirit) and the realm of Darkness (matter), ruled by Satan. The religion flourished in China after 762 with the conversion of the powerful Uighur. In 768, a Manicheian temple was built in Chang'an, followed in 771 by temples in Jing, Yang, Nanchang, and Shaoxing. After the Uighur decline in 842 and 843, Manicheism fell into decline and was forced underground. It was proscribed in 1370. Today, most Uighurs are Muslims.

Mao Dun (1896–1982): Mao Dun, the pseudonym of Shen Yanbing, was a left-wing author who served as minister of culture of the People's Republic from 1949 to 1964.

Often considered China's greatest realist novelist in the Republican period, he is best known for his novel *Midnight* (1932), which exposed Shanghai's corrupt capitalist society of the 1930s. He also published polemics against the policies of the Nationalists under Chiang Kai-shek.

Mao Zedong (1893–1976): Born into a peasant family in Hunan, Mao became involved in Republican politics in Changsha in 1911. Trained as a teacher in Changsha, he moved on to a librarian's post at Beijing University, where he was introduced to Marxism. He helped found the Chinese Communist Party in Shanghai in 1921.

Mao held a series of party posts in the 1920s and from 1925 to 1927 worked with peasant political associations in his native Hunan, an experience that showed him the revolutionary potential of the peasant class. After the Guomindang suppression of the Communists in 1927, he withdrew to a rural base in Jiangxi, where he and his associates set up the famous Jiangxi Soviet.

Mao's notions about the revolutionary power of the peasantry were at odds with prevailing Soviet doctrine, and he did not consolidate his power in the party until the Zunyi Conference during the Long March in 1935. He established a powerful base at Yan'an during World War II, when the Communists and Nationalists formed a united front against the Japanese invasion. Although there were actual military conflicts between the Communists and Nationalists even under the "united front," the Nationalists did not attack Yan'an, thus giving Mao space to develop his strength. After the end of World War II, the troops Mao built up during World War II were used for the successful campaign against the Nationalists of Chiang Kai-shek in the civil war of 1945 to 1949.

Mao held the top post of chairman of the Communist Party from the founding of the People's Republic in 1949. With the failure of his Great Leap Forward in 1958, he yielded the power to manage everyday economic affairs but remained China's paramount leader. His notions of continuing revolution were expressed in the Cultural Revolution of 1966 to 1976, but by the early 1970s, the more practical-minded Communists were again gaining influence. With Mao's death in 1976, the conservative faction moved against the radicals.

Mao Zedong was important as a political philosopher as well as a leader, particularly for incorporating Marxist theory into the Chinese experience. His *Collected Works* run to several volumes.

Marco Polo Bridge Incident: Japanese troops attacked the Marco Polo Bridge over the Yongding River, 10 miles west of Beijing on the night of July 7, 1937, signaling the start of open warfare between China and Japan.

Fighting continued in the vicinity for around three weeks. On July 27, the Japanese suddenly seized the bridge and dug in on the far bank. The incident is sometimes considered the first battle of World War II.

Marshall Mission: In December of 1945, President Harry Truman sent General George C. Marshall, the former head of the U.S. Joint Chiefs of Staff, to mediate the civil war between the Nationalists and the Communists.

Marshall persuaded both sides to agree to a cease-fire and to negotiate their differences at a political consultative conference in January 1946. The cease-fire collapsed, however, and the talks broke down without an accord. Marshall announced the failure of his mission and left China in January 1947.

May Fourth Movement: Student demonstrations protesting unfair provisions of the Treaty of Versailles in Beijing's Tiananmen Square on May 4, 1919, gave a name to a period of political and intellectual ferment in China.

The demonstrators clashed several times with police; one student was killed and thirty-two were arrested. The ramifications were felt far beyond Tiananmen Square. The May Fourth Movement sought self-expression in the arts, promoted the use of the Chinese vernacular to reach a mass audience, and explored western political and cultural models that could be adapted to Chinese conditions.

The movement originated with faculty and students at Beijing University. Among the leaders were Cai Yuanpei, president of the university; Chen Duxiu, the university dean; and the philosophy professor Hu Shi. Cai resigned in protest of the May 4 arrests, though he later returned to his post. Chen edited the influential journal

New Youth and was an early member of the Chinese Communist Party. Hu campaigned for the widespread use of the vernacular in writing.

The tone of most May Fourth practitioners was decidedly anti-Confucian. Lu Xun, one of the more prominent writers associated with the movement, attacked the Confucian legacy in bitterly satirical short stories, particularly the influential "My Old Home" of 1921.

Student protesters celebrated the seventieth anniversary of the May Fourth Movement in Tiananmen Square in 1989.

Mei Lanfang (1894–1961): The best known of all Beijing (Peking) Opera singers, Mei Lanfang received training from the legendary performer Tan Xinpei (1847–1917). The son and grandson of noted opera singers, Mei was famous for his interpretation of *dan* (female) roles. He was especially known for his portrayal of the "Flower-shattering Diva." After the outbreak of the Sino-Japanese War, he settled in Hong Kong (1937) and withdrew from opera for five years, only returning to the theater in 1946 to work on stage and in film. Mei was one of the last female impersonators: Female roles are now usually played by female actors.

Mencius (the latinated name of Meng Ke, 372–289 B.C.): Mencius was an early Confucian philosopher whose writings and teachings earned him the title "second sage" behind Confucius himself. The book *Mencius* records his statements on the innate goodness of human nature and on the conduct of proper government. For Mencius, even more than for Confucius, government was an exercise in ethics and morality. According to Mencius, the just ruler concerned himself with the moral guidance of his subjects as well as their material prosperity. *Mencius* was included among the Four Books of the Confucian canon during the Song dynasty (960–1279).

During his lifetime, Mencius worked as a teacher and, for a brief period, served as an official in the state of Qi. The age in which Mencius lived is known in Chinese history as the period of Warring States (480–222 B.C.) during the Eastern Zhou (771–256 B.C.). It was arguably the most fertile age of Chinese philosophy despite, or perhaps because of, the instability, lawlessness,

and violence of the times. In an age of tyrannical warlords and social upheaval, Mencius advocated light taxes, free trade, conservation of natural resources, welfare measures for the old and disadvantaged, and shared wealth. It was his fundamental belief that "only when the people had a steady livelihood would they have a steady heart." Despite the failure of the major leaders of his time to abide by his teachings, Mencius stubbornly contended that only the voice of the people—or, more accurately, the voice of the upper class—could ascertain the "mandate" on who should rule China. His beliefs, though long lasting, never led to the foundation of a true democracy in China, though for centuries after his death various rebel leaders would claim the mandate of heaven.

Mongolia: Mongolia is an extensive territory in Inner Asia. It includes Inner Mongolia, located between the Gobi and the Great Wall, and Outer Mongolia, part of which is occupied by the Republic of Mongolia and part of which is in the Tuva Republic of Russia. The area has been inhabited since the 12th century by the nomadic Mongol people, whose power reached its apex in the 13th-century empire of Kublai Khan. In 1949, the Chinese Communists organized the autonomous region of Inner Mongolia, which includes the northern section of the former Charar Province and parts of western Manchuria.

Most Favored Nation Clause: The "most favored nation" clause was inserted into the "unequal treaties" of the 19th century to ensure that any trading privilege granted to one European power in China would be enjoyed by all. Great Britain instated itself as a most favored nation with China one year after the signing of the 1842 Treaty of Nanjing. The United States essentially gained most favored nation status with China under the terms of the 1844 Treaty of Wangxia. These agreements and others contributed greatly to the growth of Chinese resentment over European economic oppression. Ironically, by the time the People's Republic of China actively sought to expand its foreign trade in the late 1970s, the United States had also been granting "Most Favored Nation" status to its trading partners. By this time, a "Most Favored Nation" to the United States essentially meant that the nation enjoys normal trade status granted to most of the leading trade partners of the United States. Thus, remaining a "Most Favored Nation" to the U.S. became very important to China in the last years of the 20th century and beyond.

Mozi (personal name: Mo Di; c. 478–392 B.C.): Mozi was the founder of the Mohist school, which argued a utilitarian, altruistic philosophy that challenged Confucianism in China for several centuries. Critical of wealth and luxury, Mozi taught that only through universal love and neighborliness are peace and order imparted to a country and its people. In contrast to the importance the Confucian schools placed on order and ceremony in society, Mozi proposed that universal love of the family must be extended to all persons within society in order to reduce the friction between the individual and the state. The *Mozi* is the principal work left by Mozi and his followers and contains the essence of his political, ethical, and religious teachings. The teachings of Mozi continued to vie with Confucianism for centuries after his death, disappearing from the Chinese intellectual scene after the second century B.C.

Mukden Incident: An outbreak of fighting between Chinese and Japanese troops in Mukden on September 18, 1931, led to an escalation of tensions and the eventual Japanese occupation of Manchuria.

The Japanese command claimed Chinese troops touched off the incident with an attack on a railway line outside Mukden (Shenyang in Chinese). In the wake of the incident, Japan mobilized a large army and seized control of Manchuria.

Mustard Seed Garden Manual of Painting: The *Jiezi yuan hua zhuan* (Painting manual of the mustard seed garden) was published in China in 1679 during the Qing dynasty (1644–1911). It is a study of painting methods undertaken during the later Ming dynasty (1368–1644) by Dong Qichang (1555–1636) of a great practitioner of literati painting. Literati painters' comprehensive study of painting techniques produced many exhaustive guides to painting and art, including *Mus-*

tard Seed Garden Manual, in which techniques of painting objects were meticulously described and classified. Many art historians claim that the extreme formalism Dong and his followers advocated through rigid texts such as the *Mustard Seed Garden Manual of Painting* had a negative effect on the future of Chinese painting after the collapse of the Ming dynasty.

Nanchang Uprising: The Nanchang Uprising was a revolt organized by Chinese Communist Party members in Nanchang, the capital of Jiangxi Province, on August 1, 1927. They held the city, with the aid of peasants and workers, for three days before being besieged by Nationalist troops. On August 5, they fled to the border areas of Guangdong, Kiansi, and Fukian. Although unsuccessful, the Nanchang Uprising provided the men and means from which the Chinese Red Army (predecessor of the People's Liberation Army) would later develop. The failure of the uprising and the subsequent Autumn Harvest Insurrection and Canton Commune demonstrated that the Communist revolution could succeed only through the mobilization of the peasants.

Nanjing Massacre: Japanese troops entered the city on December 13, 1937, and launched one of the most brutal reigns of terror in modern military history. Chinese civilians and POWs were systematically slaughtered. A large number of women were raped. When the Japanese had completed their work, much of the city lay in ruins.

The event has gone down in history as "the Rape of Nanjing." Recent scholarship suggests the actual numbers of Chinese killed were far higher than once believed. Most estimates range from 100,000 to 300,000. Chinese scholars generally accept the number 300,000.

Nanzhao: Nanzhao was a southwestern kingdom located in the regions between Sichuan and Myanmar founded by the warrior king Nanzhao in 750. In the ninth century, the kingdom of Nanzhao began expanding vigorously into China during the instability of the final years of the Tang dynasty (A.D. 618–906). The invaders seized control of the Red River Basin and

Hanoi in 827 and occupied the capital of Sichuan briefly after 867. Known from 902 onward as Dali, after a city in western Yunnan Province on the western shore of Er Hai Lake, this kingdom flourished until conquered by the Mongol army under Kublai Khan in 1253.

National People's Congress: According to the Chinese constitution, the National People's Congress (NPC) is the supreme legislative organ of the Chinese state. However, actual authority resides in the Chinese Communist Party and in the State Council, which is the top executive department at the national level. Plans for convening the NPC were first drawn up in 1953. It met for the first time in September 1954, taking over from the Central People's Government Council, which had been acting as the highest organ of state since 1949.

Neo-Confucianism: Neo-Confucianism arose during the Song dynasty (960–1279). A new kind of Confucianism that had absorbed certain philosophical concepts from Buddhism and Daoism, it encompasses many different schools of philosophy. Ironically, many of these schools are actually anti-Buddhist and anti-Daoist, in spite of their unacknowledged borrowings from Buddhism and Daoism. For the convenience of analysis, some modern scholars categorize the Neo-Confucians into two branches of Neo-Confucianism. The first was epitomized by the Cheng brothers (Cheng Hao, 1032–1085, and Cheng Yi, 1033–1108) and Zhu Xi (1130–1200), and is called the Li Xue (School of Principal), which posited that all objects in nature were composed of two inherent forces: *Li*, an immaterial universal principal or law; and *chi*, physical substance. Opposed to the Li School is the Xin Xue (School of mind), the tenets for which were formulated by Lu Jiuyuan (1139–1193) and Wang Yangming (1472–1529). They advocated the unity of knowledge and practice and taught that one's chief goal was developing the "intuitive knowledge" of the mind through reflection and meditation. Many scholars during the Qing dynasty (1644–1912) advocated a turning away from both of these schools to the earlier Confucianism of the Han period (206 B.C.–A.D. 220). Whatever their philosophical differences, Neo-Confucian scholars, like most other Confucian scholars, advocated Confucian principles as political ideals. However, the Republican Revolution of 1911 and the Communist Revolution of 1949 both signified the end of institutional support for the religion and a decline in the general popularity of Confucian ideals and thinking in China.

Nestorian Christians: Nestorian Christianity originated in Asia Minor and Syria out of the condemnation of Nestorius and his teachings by the councils of Ephesus (A.D. 431) and Chalcedon (A.D. 451). Nestorian Christians arrived in China via Persia during the Tang dynasty (618–917), when the Persian bishop Aloben reached China's capital, Chang'an, in 635 and founded monasteries to spread the faith. In common with Zoroastrianism and Manichaeism, Nestorianism was proscribed in China during the 841 to 845 religious persecutions, and by the end of the Tang dynasty, the Nestorian community within Chinese borders had disappeared. However, the Khitan and Jurchen peoples along the western borders of China revived it. Many of the Uighur of the Turfan area who served Genghis Khan in the 13th century were in fact Nestorian Christians. Due to the support of the Yuan rulers of China and the influx of believers from outside China's borders, the Nestorian church was once again strong enough by 1275 for the patriarch in Baghdad to name an archbishop at Peking. Churches were erected at Chenchiang and Yangchow in the lower Yangtze area, as well as at Hangzhou. Nevertheless, the religion never was to gain significant popularity within China and had largely disintegrated by the beginning of the 14th century.

New Fourth Army: Communist guerrilla units left behind in central China after the Long March in 1934 and 1935 were reorganized during the period of the second united front against Japan as the New Fourth Army.

Veteran Communists commanded this 12,000-strong force, which fell under the nominal control of the Guomindang.

New Fourth Army Incident: The Guomindang, moving to rid central China of Communist armed forces, ordered the

New Fourth Army north of the Yangtze River late in 1940. When the Communists were slow to comply, Guomindang forces ambushed their columns in the mountains of Jiangxi.

In a series of attacks from January 7 to 13, 1941, Nationalists inflicted 3,000 battle deaths on the Communists. Others were shot after capture or taken away to prison camps. The incident, considered a propaganda victory for the Communists, exposed the hollowness of the united front.

New Text School: Also referred to as the Modern Text Movement, the New Text School was formed after the destruction of the original Confucian texts by the Legalist Ch'in emperor Shi Huangdi in 213 B.C. during the infamous Burning of the Books. The New Text scholars of the Han period (206 B.C.–A.D. 220) accepted current, reconstructed editions of classical texts as authentic teachings of Confucius (551–479 B.C.). However, at the end of the Western Han period (206 B.C.–A.D. 8), the New Text School clashed with the so-called Ancient Text School after the latter claimed to have discovered original copies of the Confucian classics. The Ancient Text School was to win precedence during the Han dynasty and onward. The controversy was renewed during the Qing dynasty (1644–1911) when the radical reformer Kang Youwei (1858–1927) lent his support to the New Text School.

Nurhaci (1559–1626): Nurhaci was chieftain of the Chien-chou Jurchen, a Manchurian tribe, and one of the founders of the Manchu, or Qing, dynasty. After uniting the smaller Manchu chieftains living near him, Nurhaci organized his tribesmen into banners with appointed officers rather than hereditary chiefs. In 1599, he ordered Chinese works to be translated and recorded in Manchu, using a modified form of the Mongolian alphabet, thus prompting the inception of written Manchu. In 1616, Nurhaci took the title of Emperor of the Later Jin (to continue the Jurchen Jin dynasty of 1122–1234) and in 1618, launched his first attack against China. After moving his capital to Shenyang (Mukden) in 1625, he attempted to defeat the Chinese forces guarding the entrance to China proper. In February 1626, he was defeated for the first time by the Chinese

at Ningyuan, and he died in September of that year of his wounds. He was succeeded by his eighth son, Abahai, and then by his 14th son, Dorgon, who would seize Beijing in 1644 to formally establish the Manchu Qing dynasty (1644–1911).

Open Door Policy: The European and Japanese scramble for special rights in China led the United States in 1898 to propose an "open door" policy that would grant all countries equal access to Chinese markets.

The policy might have had some moral effect in slowing the imperial scramble to divide China into spheres of influence, but no sanctions were attached for violators, and the United States lacked the power to enforce it.

Opium War: British outrage against imperial confiscation of British opium in Guangzhou in 1839 touched off this one-sided conflict. China, furious over an incident in which British and American soldiers murdered a Chinese, chose to resist the British rather than negotiate a settlement over the opium.

Initial military operations were confined to the Guangzhou area, with British warships attacking Chinese war junks in the Bogue, the waterway leading to the great South China port. A full British fleet arrived off Guangzhou in June 1940, detached ships to block up the port, and sailed north to attack Ningbo and Tianjin.

Chinese and British negotiators reached a cease-fire settlement in January 1841, but the emperor rejected it. British forces went on to occupy Guangzhou and Shanghai and cut the Grand Canal, the main supply line linking Beijing and the south.

The fighting ended with the Treaty of Nanjing, greatly disadvantageous to China, in August 1842.

Oracle Bones: The Oracle Bones, often called Dragon Bones, are turtle plastrons and ox scapulae with inscribed texts. They were used by the late Shang kings (1554–1045 B.C.) in a system of divination that the Shang rulers used to communicate with their deceased ancestors. Questions were inscribed on the bones, and the answers were divined by the carving of a groove after the application of intense heat, a method known as scapulimancy.

The Oracle Bones first came to modern notice in 1899 in the Beijing markets, where they were being sold for medicinal purposes. Since then, thousands of specimens have been recovered from the site of the last Shang capital near Anyang in Henan Province. The inscriptions on the bones include nearly all the names of the Shang rulers and prove conclusively that the Shang dynasty in fact existed. Through careful study of the inscriptions on the Oracle Bones, much has been learned about ancient Chinese history and the character of the Shang period (19th to 12th centuries B.C.).

***Outlaws of the Marsh*:** Also known to English readers as *All Men Are Brothers* or *The Water Margin*, this famous novel is a semi-historical work of 100 chapters that follows the exploits of a band of 108 heroes and rebels led by Song Jiang, a historical character of the Northern Song (960–1126) period. This band of renegade heroes struggles against the injustices of the Song dynasty, which is presented as a thinly veiled version of the contemporary Ming dynasty in place during the time of the book's publication. *Outlaws of the Marsh* has been attributed to Luo Guanzhong (c. 1330–1400) and Shi Nai'an (1296–1370), though some scholars have cast doubt upon Luo's part in the authorship. Luo has also traditionally been considered the author of *The Romance of the Three Kingdoms*, another immensely popular story during the late Yuan and early Ming periods. Sequels to each were produced throughout the Ming period. Both novels are written in a colloquial style and remain popular in China as classic works of historical narrative and adventure

Ouyang Xiu (1007–1072): A Song dynasty (960–1279) poet, historian, and colorful statesman, Ouyang reintroduced the simple and direct "ancient style" of writing of his literary forebear Han Yu (768–824) into Chinese literature. He sought to reform Chinese political life through classical Confucian principles. In his two most famous texts, *Xin Wudai shi* (The new history of the five dynasties) and *Xin Tang shu* (The new history of the Tang dynasty), Ouyang imitated Confucius's harsh moral judgment of important historical figures and institutions. Ouyang was a leader of the famous "Minor Reform" of 1043–1045, in which he and his reformist colleagues sought to streamline the government by cutting unnecessary positions and increasing administrative efficiency.

Overseas Chinese: The term designates people of Chinese ethnic origin (but not necessarily of Chinese citizenship) who live outside of China—the Chinese diaspora, with large communities in Southeast Asia, Australia, Europe, and America.

Large-scale emigration from China occurred in the middle decades of the 19th century, spurred by crowding (China's population reached 430 million in 1850), rebellion, and economic dislocation. Chinese communities flourished in the Dutch East Indies (Indonesia). By the mid-1870s, more than half a million migrants were settled in the Singapore area at the tip of the Malay Peninsula.

Chinese came to the western United States in growing numbers, drawn first by the California gold rush and later by opportunities for jobs in railroad construction and mining. More than 100,000 male Chinese had arrived by the 1880s. Americans, particularly laboring Americans, resented the new settlers, a resentment that eventually found expression in legislation limiting Chinese immigration.

Thousands of Chinese laborers were imported to work on sugar plantations in the Hawaiian Islands. Nearly 100,000 Chinese were settled in Peru by 1875; tens of thousands of Chinese were employed on sugar plantations in Cuba and elsewhere in the Caribbean.

Chinese overseas communities gave substantial support to the Republican and Nationalist movements at home in the late 19th and early 20th centuries. The overseas population is well in excess of 20 million today.

It is worth noting that because the term "overseas Chinese" denotes ethnicity and location of residence rather than citizenship, it is not a very useful term for the discussion of people's political identity. However, it is a term that many in China still use when discussing people's ethnicity and culture.

Peking Man: Peking Man is an extinct hominid of the species *Homo erectus*, whose fossils were found in Zhoukoudian caves near Beijing. Identified as a new fossil human being by Davidson Black in 1927 on the basis of a single tooth, the Peking Man hominid fossils date to the middle Pleistocene (about 900,000 to 130,000 years ago). Evidence from the site, which yielded fossilized remains of approximately forty individuals, suggests that Peking Man had a communal culture, used fire, and could manipulate crude stone tools. The original Peking Man fossils disappeared in 1941 before the imminent Japanese invasion of China. Renewed excavation in the caves in 1958 turned up new specimens.

Peng Dehuai (1898–1974): A top Communist general, Peng was one of the leading commanders of Mao Zedong's forces in the epic Long March from Jiangxi to Yan'an in 1934 and 1935 and commanded Chinese "volunteers" fighting the United States and the United Nations in Korea from 1950 to 1953.

Peng ran afoul of Mao when he criticized the chairman's disastrous Great Leap Forward policies at a conference at Lushan in 1959. In reprisal, Mao had him stripped of his senior party offices.

People's Communes: Introduced by the Chinese Communist Party Central Committee on August 29, 1958, the People's Communes were the basic unit of China's early socialist system. In a commune, common owners controlled multipurpose organizations for the carrying out of local government, economic and social activity. Early communes were begun through the amalgamation of agricultural collectives in Hebei, Henan, and parts of Manchuria. Rural communes took over the administrative functions of villages and operated schools, nurseries, public banks, retirement homes, cemeteries, and other public resources. By the early 1960s, there were more than 74,000 communes in China. The Cultural Revolution of 1966 to 1976 brought strict regimentation and government control to the People's Communes, and modernizing reforms after Mao Zedong's death in September 1976 gradually wiped out the traditional commune system.

People's Daily: *The People's Daily* is the official newspaper of the Central Committee of the Chinese Communist Party and the most important daily paper in China. The paper was established in 1948 and has been headquartered in Beijing since 1949. Its pages contain a high proportion of policy statements from the government as well as news of economic and political developments within China. Copies of the paper are posted in public places, radio stations broadcast selected articles, and local schools are given copies so that the paper's readership is many times its circulation. *The People's Daily* has extensive coverage of news from abroad, notably from southeast Asia and developing countries. An overseas edition has been published since 1985.

People's Liberation Army: From its beginning as a Red Army guerrilla force in the 1930s, the PLA evolved to include border and garrison troops, an air force and a navy. It was formally established in 1946 out of the Eighth Route Army, the New Fourth Army, and newly raised units in Manchuria. PLA strength approaches two and a half million.

Lin Biao and other skilled commanders led the PLA to an overwhelming victory over the Nationalists in the civil war of 1945 to 1949. Thousands of PLA troops fought as "volunteers" against United States and United Nations forces in Korea from 1950 to 1953, with mixed results. PLA forces fought brief inconclusive campaigns along the Indian frontier in 1959 and 1962 and in Vietnam in 1979.

The PLA gradually took on an increasing role in Chinese politics, especially under Lin Biao in the late 1950s. Lin placed a high priority on educating recruits in the thought of Mao Zedong; in a series of propaganda campaigns, he offered the PLA as a model for the rest of Chinese society.

The army rallied behind Mao during the Cultural Revolution of 1966 to 1976, intervening sometimes on behalf of radicals and sometimes to impose order; the army served as the local administration in many parts of the country. Senior PLA commanders were appointed to high positions in the Communist Party's Central Committee and Politburo.

In the 1980s, the PLA became increasingly involved in the economy as owner and operator of a wide range of profit-making enterprises.

Poetry, Book of: Also known as the *Book of Songs* or *Book of Odes*, the *Book of Poetry* is an anthology of verse dating from the 11th to the sixth centuries B.C. and includes a collection of 305 folk songs, love songs, political poems, and longer ritual hymns. Many were sung or chanted during ceremonies held by rulers of the Zhou dynasty (1122–256 B.C.), which had the longest reign in the history of China. Members of the dynasty's official class required thorough knowledge of the poems contained within the *Book of Poetry*. Tradition attributes the editorship of the *Book of Poetry* to Confucius (551–479 B.C.) himself, though this is highly unlikely despite his familiarity with the work and his admiration of it. The *Book of Poetry* became one of the Five Classics (Wu jing) in the third century B.C.

Polo, Marco (1254–1324): Marco Polo was a Venetian merchant, adventurer, and explorer who claimed to have journeyed from Europe to Asia from 1271 to 1295. He supposedly remained in China for seventeen of those years (1275–1292), serving Kubilai Khan. His book *Il Milione* (The million), which is known in English as *The Travels of Marco Polo*, became a geographical, autobiographical, and biographical classic. Dictated by Polo in a Genoese prison to a fellow prisoner, *The Travels of Marco Polo* was a vivid description of the Mongol empire and its technological achievements. It was much disputed by the Mediterranean merchant communities who considered southern Europe to be the center of civilization. Some modern scholars have doubted whether Marco Polo really went to China, although some of the information contained in his book seems authentic.

Pure Land Sect: The Pure Land Sect is a Buddhist movement that appeared in China during the fourth century, possibly founded by Hui Yuan (334–416), who established a Buddhist center in the present Jiangxi. The main practice of those who follow the Pure Land teachings is simply the continual calling upon of the name

Amitabha. In Pure Land Buddhism, the attainment of nirvana is not the primary goal; it is, rather, to become reborn in the Pure Land of Amitabha, a western paradise where one might live forever in a state of bliss. This sect was immensely popular with the humble believers who, because they had to make a living, did not have time to devote themselves to constant study of arcane texts, elaborate ritual, and meditation called for by other Buddhist sects. The Pure Land sect reached its apex of popularity between the sixth and eighth centuries, though Pure Land believers persisted in China into the 20th century.

Puyi ("Henry Puyi," Emperor Xuantong; 1905–1967): He ascended the throne in 1908, age three, as the 10th and last emperor of the Qing dynasty, and formally abdicated with the fall of the dynasty in 1912.

The Japanese installed Puyi as the figurehead leader of their puppet regime in Manchuria in 1932. He held that powerless post until 1945. With the advent of the People's Republic, he underwent rehabilitation in a Communist prison, made a full "confession," and spent his last years as an employee of a Beijing park.

Qiao Shi (1924–): Qiao Shi was a lifelong government official who ended his career as a member of the Political Bureau Standing Committee and chairman of the National People's Congress (NPC). He joined the Chinese Communist Party (CCP) in 1940 and between 1940 and 1963 worked in the Shanghai CCP underground before devoting himself to security and intelligence at the Anshan Iron and Steel Co. In 1963, Qiao was transferred to the CCP headquarters in Beijing, where for twenty years he worked in the International Liaison Department of the Central Committee, becoming its head in 1982. In that year, Qiao was also elected to the Central Committee. He was given a place on the Politburo in September 1985 and the Standing Committee in 1987. In 1992, he was named chairman of the National People's Congress. His tenure as head of the NPC was marked by willingness to debate policy in a limited forum and to deal forthrightly with student protest movements that were erupting around China at the time. Many observers suggested that Qiao, with his forward-thinking policies and his solid political background, was a prospective leader of China after Deng Xiaoping's death. However, after Deng's death on Feb 19, 1997, Jiang Zemin was named head of the CCP after Qiao's retirement.

Qin Hui (1090–1155): Qin Hui was chancellor to the ailing Southern Song state (1127–1279). His conciliatory dealings with the aggressive Jurchen Jin empire (1122–1234) to the north of China resulted in formation of a border between the two states at the Huai River in 1141. Tens of thousand of Chinese were left to the Jurchen invaders. Qin is best remembered for his unwillingness to do battle with this much-stronger northern enemy and his machinations within court. They brought about the murder of the talented Southern Song general Yue Fei (1104–1142), who had promoted an active policy of resistance against the Jin. Wang Fuzhi's (1619–1692) famous book *Song lun* (On Song history) vilifies Qin and glorifies Yue, lending credence to the traditional representation of Qin as a traitor and Yue as a noble hero.

Qiu Jin (1875–1907): A feminist and an anti-Qing revolutionary, she ran from an arranged marriage and her two children in 1904 to study in Japan. Returning in 1906, she set up a girls' school in her native Zhejiang Province.

With a handful of comrades, Qiu launched an uprising against the Qing in Zhejiang Province in July 1907. Government forces easily quelled the insurrection, arrested Qiu, and put her to death.

Qu Yuan (c. 340–278 B.C.): Qu Yuan was one of the greatest poets of ancient China and the first one to be known by name. He has been presented to history as a talented courtier in the southern state of Chu who was exiled by his rivals. During his travels, he is said to have written most, if not all, of the *Chu ci* (Elegies of Chu), which includes the long, somber poem "Li sao" ("The Lament"). Qu Yuan's most famous piece, "Li sao," a poem of 374 lines, is beautifully constructed and rich in imagery, reflecting the traditional culture of the Yangtze Valley, Qu's place of exile. Qu is believed to have drowned himself in the Miluo River, a tributary of the Yangtze. The famous Dragon Boat Festival, held on the fifth day of the fifth month of the Chinese lunar year, is believed to have begun as a search for Qu Yuan's body.

Red Eyebrows: The Red Eyebrows were leaders of a peasant uprising in Shantung in A.D. 18 during the rule of the Western Han (206 B.C.–A.D. 8) ruler Wang Mang (45 B.C.–A.D. 23, r. A.D. 8–23). The rebellion had its origins when, between 2 and 5 and again in 11, the Yellow River changed its course, devastating one of the most populous regions of China and causing political and economic chaos. On Oct. 4, A.D. 23, the Red Eyebrows broke through the palace gates and killed Wang Mang along with the 1,000 soldiers who made up his personal guard. The Red Eyebrows were crushed soon after this by Wang Mang's successor, Liu Xiu, who became known as Guangwu (5 B.C.–A.D. 57, r. 25–57) after he took power. The era of Chinese dynastic history referred to as the Eastern Han period (25–220) had begun.

Red Guards: Cultural Revolution radicals moved in mid-1966 to direct turmoil in China's universities and high schools by issuing arm bands to loosely organized student protest groups and calling them Red Guards. Growing in size, power, and boldness, these bands professed to carry out a revolutionary cleansing on Mao Zedong's behalf.

In their assault on "feudal" and "reactionary" individuals and institutions, the Red Guards launched a reign of terror in China. In August 1966, Mao himself reviewed masses of parading Red Guards from atop the Tiananmen gate. Red Guard rampages in the fall and winter caused widespread damage and loss of life. Urged on by Jiang Qing (Mao's wife) and other Cultural Revolution leaders, the Red Guards attacked the "Four Olds"—old customs, old habits, old culture, and old thinking.

Spreading chaos finally induced China's top leadership to quell the Red Guards. In a series of clashes in 1967 and 1968, the People's Liberation Army brought the Red Guard revolutionary era to a violent close.

Red Turbans: The Red Turbans was a group of peasant revolutionaries seeking the reinstatement of the Song dynasty (960–1279). They revolted against the

Mongol Yuan dynasty (1276–1368) in the province of Hunan in 1351. The revolt, spearheaded by more than 100,000 soldiers and peasants sent to repair the dikes of the Yellow River after it flooded its banks that year, spread quickly to the neighboring provinces of Hubei, Shandong, and Anhui. From 1357 to 1359, the Red Turbans launched a series of raids into northern China, at one point approaching Beijing itself. The movement was finally suppressed in 1363.

Ricci, Matteo (1552–1610): Born in Ancona, Italy, Ricci worked as a Jesuit missionary in Ming China from 1582 until his death, living in Beijing from 1583. High imperial officials welcomed Father Ricci for his knowledge of western science and instrumentation, particularly clocks and optical devices.

Ricci defended the case for permitting Chinese converts to practice Confucian rites, such as ancestor worship, arguing that these were civil rather than religious in nature. Nearly a century after his death, this view led to the rites controversy and a major setback for Christianity in China.

Rites Controversy: This conflict between the Roman Catholic Church and the Qing emperor Kangxi (r. 1661–1722) involved the practice of ancient Chinese rites of ancestor worship and homage to Confucius.

The emperor and the Jesuits at his court, following the precedent of Matteo Ricci during the Ming, argued that the rites were civil rather than religious, and that Catholic missionaries should allow Chinese Catholic converts to observe them.

The Vatican strongly objected. After lengthy discussions with the imperial court in 1705 and 1706, the envoy of Pope Clement XI issued instructions barring missionaries from following Kangxi's edict on rites. In retaliation, the emperor expelled most Catholic missionaries from China. Only the Jesuits were allowed to remain in the capacity of court astronomers and mathematicians.

The controversy choked the growth of Christianity in China and effectively prevented the spread of Western teaching, especially in science.

Romance of the Three Kingdoms: One of the best-known Chinese works of literature, *The Romance of the Three Kingdoms* has been traditionally attributed to Luo Guanzhong (c. 1330–1400?). A novel of 120 chapters, *The Romance of the Three Kingdoms* is an epic story of struggle, heroism, and friendship set during the period of the Three Kingdoms (A.D. 220–265). It was the interregnum after the collapse of the Han dynasty (206 B.C.–A.D. 220) and a time of perpetual feudal war in China. It depicts Zhuge Liang (181–234), the great political strategist of the period, as immensely clever and skilled while vilifying the notorious Han general Cao Cao (155–220).

Ru: The Chinese term for the school of philosophy that Westerners often call "Confucianism."

Russo-Japanese War (1904–1905): The Russo-Japanese War was a military dispute between Japan and Russia for dominance in Manchuria and Korea. Japan's victory was the first Asian defeat of a European power in the modern era and led to a treaty signed at Portsmouth, New Hampshire, in September 1905, after American mediation. The Treaty of Portsmouth gave Japan control of the Liaodong Peninsula (and Port Arthur), the South Manchurian Railroad, and half of Sakhalin Island. In addition, Russia agreed to recognize Japan's control of Korea. The war was a humiliating event for the Chinese, as Manchuria was Chinese territory, and Korea used to pay tribute to China before 1895. The Chinese feeling of humiliation incited a tremendous Chinese nationalist movement that helped bring about the demise of Qing rule.

Second Revolution: The Second Revolution was an unsuccessful 1913 rebellion of seven southern provinces against the leadership of Yuan Shikai, a former military leader in the Qing army and first president of the Republic of China (1912–1916). The Second Revolution followed the Nationalist success in the parliamentary elections of 1912 and Yuan's attempt to crush them through the assassination of the Guomindang Kuomintang Nationalist Party (GMD) leader Song Jiaoren. Yuan used the Second Revolution as an excuse to dissolve parliament on January 10, 1914, and consolidate his power with the aim of forming a constitutional monarchy with himself at the head.

Shang Yang (d. 338 B.C.): Shang Yang was a great statesman of the state of Qin. He assisted in bringing all the feudal territories of the Qin state under the control of a central administration and, in 350, dividing these into sub-units called prefectures under a central administrator called a prefect. These reforms helped make possible the rise of the Qin state and the eventual formation of the Qin empire, the first empire of China. *The Book of Lord Shang*, an outline of his Legalist theories, has often been attributed to him, though it was probably written much later.

Shanghai Communiqué: China and the United States issued this document on February 28, 1972, at the conclusion of President Richard Nixon's historic visit to China. The communiqué summarized the two countries' positions on world affairs without making an effort to reconcile them.

The U.S. part of the communiqué reaffirmed a commitment to individual freedom, defended the American intervention in Vietnam, and proclaimed continued support for South Korea. The Chinese part called for the withdrawal of "all foreign troops to their own country" and proposed the unification of Korea along Communist North Korean lines.

On the most critical long-term point of dispute, China claimed to be the sole legal government of Taiwan and called its "liberation" an internal affair. The United States said it did not challenge the claim that "there is but one China and that Taiwan is part of China."

A major diplomatic breakthrough, the Shanghai Communiqué laid the groundwork for the normalization of Sino-American relations.

Shaolin Temple: Located in Henan, the Shaolin Temple was built in A.D. 495 for the Buddhist monk Batuo (later known as "Fu Tuo" or "Grand Monk"). In 537, another Buddhist teacher, named Bodhidharma, supposedly settled there and created the Chan (Zen) sect of Buddhism, as well as bare-handed combat techniques to strengthen his followers. The 30,000-square-meter (10,000-square-acre) site is composed of seven rows of buildings, including the Hall of the Heavenly King, Dharma Pavilion, Thousand-Buddha Hall, White-Robe Bodhisattva Hall, and the Hall of Ksitigarbba (Guardian of the Earth). The famous murals of the Eastern Hall depict monks practicing martial arts.

Shi Dakai (1831–1863): Shi Dakai was one of the principal military commanders of the Taiping Rebellion (1851–1864). It was the most important of the many rebellions that plagued the tumultuous last century of the Qing dynasty (1644–1911) and arguably the most important "peasant" rebellion in Chinese history. In 1856, an internal purge among the Taiping rebels caused Shi to lose his trust for Hong Xiuquan, the leader of the Taipings. In 1857, Shi left the Taiping capital of Nanjing with over 200,000 of his troops. After this, Shi continued to claim to be a part of the Taiping Rebellion, although in reality he acted independently of Hong's commands. His army engaged in mobile warfare against the Qing until 1863, when the last remnants of his troops were trapped on the southern bank of the Dadu River in Sichuan province. When his troops ran out of supplies, Shi offered his own life to the Qing commander in exchange for having his soldiers spared. The Qing commander pretended to agree, but executed all of Shi's soldiers anyway after Shi gave himself up. Shi himself was brought to Chengdu, the provincial capital of Sichuan, and executed.

Shi Huangdi (259–210 B.C.): Shi Huangdi is the sovereign title of Ying Zheng, which he adopted in 221 B.C. after his consolidation of the Warring States. He was the first emperor of the Qin dynasty (221–206 B.C.) and therefore the first emperor of China. His Legalist chancellor Li Si largely influenced his despotic rule. Credited with the linking of a series of fortresses to form the Great Wall, Shi Huangdi concentrated on fighting foreign enemies such as the Xiongnu, quelling dissension, centralizing his administration, and studying the occult. Deprived of his leadership, the Qin dynasty collapsed a mere four years after his death.

Shun (23rd Century B.C.): Shun is considered one of the Three Sages—legendary emperors from prehistoric times. The other two were Shun's predecessor, Yao, and his successor, Yu. Shun has been remembered as a man of virtue and faultless integrity. He is reported to have performed various sacrifices, to have introduced a uniform system of weights and measures, to have traveled widely, to have fought successfully against barbarian hordes, and to have regulated some of China's waterways. Like his predecessor Yao, Shun did not selfishly pass on his throne to his own son. Instead, he selected Yu, the most qualified man in the empire, to be his successor.

Silk: The creation of silk in China dates traditionally to about 2700 B.C. when early Chinese discovered the art of reeling and weaving silk from the mulberry silk moth cocoon. Its production has been conclusively traced to the Shang period of about 1554–1045 B.C. Chinese silk production became widespread during the Zhou (1045–256 B.C.) and Han (206 B.C.–A.D. 220) dynasties but did not spread to other countries until the late sixth century. The Yangtze estuary in Zhejiang and Jiangsu, the Pearl River Delta in Kwangtung, and Sichuan are China's main silk producing areas. Silk became an important export to the West from Han times onward.

Silk Road: Also called the Silk Route, the Silk Road was an ancient trade route linking China to imperial Rome. It came into widespread use about 100 B.C. after Han emperor Wu-Ti consolidated the Chinese empire, making foreign trade viable. Silk came westward, while wool, gold, and silver went east. China also received Nestorian Christianity and Buddhism (from India) via the road. Approximately 6,000 kilometers (4,000 miles) long, the Silk Road traversed some of the harshest terrain in the world. It wound from the Chinese capital Changan (now Xi'an), across the north China plain, through the Pamirs and the Karakorum Range to Samarkand and Bactria, to Damascus, Edessa, and the Mediterranean ports of Alexandria and Antioch. The Silk Road fell into disuse when the Roman Empire disintegrated in the fifth century and could be used only sporadically during times of stability.

Marco Polo traveled down it over a period of three years in the 13th century during the Yuan dynasty. During the 16th century, silk was exchanged with the Russians for furs and, later, tea was traded for manufactured goods. The road now partially exists in the form of a paved highway connecting Pakistan and Xinjiang Uighur autonomous region, China. The remnants of the Silk Road have prompted a United Nations plan for a trans-Asian highway.

Sima Guang (1019–1086): Sima Guang was a scholar, statesman, and historian who, between 1072 and 1084, compiled the highly influential *Zizhi tongjian* (Comprehensive mirror for aid in government). A general chronicle of Chinese history from 403 B.C. to A.D. 959, it is considered one of the finest single historical works in Chinese. The main text of the chronicle consists of 294 chapters and covers more than 9,600 pages in its standard modern edition. In addition, Sima Guang wrote 30 chapters of *Kaoyi* ("examination of divergences in sources"), in which he examined the disagreements among the various historical sources he cited, and explained how he chose the correct historical accounts.

Sima Guang was also known as a great statesman in his time. During the so-called Major Reform (c.f. entry on **Wang Anshi**) of 1069–1085, Sima Guang was the leader of the conservatives who strongly opposed the reform policies. Although emperor Shenzong (r. 1067–1085) supported the reform programs, he also respected Sima Guang for the latter's integrity. After the death of Shenzong, Sima Guang became the most powerful civil official in China, and was able to reverse many of the reform programs.

Sima Qian (145–85 B.C.): Sima Qian was an astronomer, a calendar expert, and one of China's greatest historians. He was noted for his authorship of the *Shi ji* (Records of the grand historian), a history of China from its earliest times to early decades of the Han dynasty (206 B.C.–A.D. 220). The *Shi ji* is considered the most important history of China down to the end of the second century. In this work, Sima paints for the first time a picture of the entire historical Chinese world, thanks to a variety of meticulously researched oral traditions, texts, archives, and contemporary witnesses. In 99 B.C. Sima fell afoul of the Han emperor Wudi (156–187, r. 141–187) when he defended a disgraced general. Because Sima could not afford to pay the hefty fine required of him, he was left with the choice of castration or execution. Sima chose the disgrace of castration so that he could live to finish his historical work.

Sino-Japanese War (1894–1895): The Sino-Japanese war broke out between China and Japan over their respective influence in Korea, which was at that time a Chinese tributary and buffer state. The Tonghak insurrection in Korea provided Japan with the opportunity to send troops to the area, where they clashed with Chinese forces on August 1, 1894. China suffered a humiliating defeat that culminated in the Treaty of Shimonoseki of April 1895, which required that China recognize the independence of Korea and cede land to Japan. The war signaled the emergence of Japan as a world power and proved the ineffectiveness of Chinese modernization attempts in the second half of the 19th century. The Chinese defeat in the war set the stage for Japan's conquest of Korea in 1905, and also signaled the beginning of Japanese expansion into Manchuria.

Sixth Patriarch's Platform Sutra: The "Sixth Patriarch's Platform Sutra" is traditionally considered the transcript of a sermon given by Huineng (638–713), the sixth great patriarch of Chan (Zen) Buddhism and founder of the Southern School of Chan. Huineng preaches that through inner reflection one may achieve enlightenment through a sudden spiritual awakening. The idea opposed the teachings of the great Chan master Shenxiu (605–706) and most of the other Buddhist thinkers who preceded Huineng. They taught that enlightenment could come only through a gradual process of meditation and study. Huineng also taught that every person already had "Buddha nature" (i.e. the potential to become a Buddha) in him or her.

Snow, Edgar (1905–1972): A Missouri-born American journalist, Snow covered China as a reporter from 1928 to 1940 and made a later career of writing on Chinese affairs.

Snow filed the first foreign news accounts from Mao Zedong's stronghold of Yan'an in the mid-1930s. He later reworked his dispatches into an influential book, *Red Star over China* (1937), that presented the Communists in a sympathetic light and suggested they would eventually prevail over the Nationalists.

In the 1950s and 1960s, Snow enjoyed the privilege, rarely granted to Western journalists, of direct access to Mao and Zhou Enlai.

Socialist Education Movement (1962–1965): The Socialist Education Movement was a mass movement ordered by Mao Zedong (1893–1976) in 1962 to propagate the Yan'an model of society and to stress the importance of class struggle in China. Officials and intellectuals were sent to the countryside to learn from the masses, and writers were mandated to produce books, articles, and journals that encouraged the complete Socialist transformation of Chinese society.

Song Yingxing (c. 1598–1660?): Song Yingxing was the author of the *Tiangong kaiwu* (Creations of heaven and human labor), which was published in 1637 toward the end of the Ming dynasty (1368–1644). The book stands as one of the most important single works on Chinese historical technology, examining in great detail such things as agricultural techniques, weaving, ceramics, iron and steel, river transport, armaments, inks, and the making of paper. Song also wrote a book on phonology and a collection of critical essays. After the collapse of the Ming dynasty, he retired into seclusion with his elder brother Yingsheng.

Soong, Charles Jones (1866–1918): Charles Jones Soong, also called Charlie Soong, was educated and trained in the United States by the Methodists for missionary work among the Chinese. However, he is best remembered as a shrewd businessman and the patriarch of what has often been called the "Soong dynasty." The ironic term referred to the influence of his children on Nationalist policies and banking during the 1920s and 1930s, both in the United States and China. In 1906, Soong was officially appointed treasurer of the Revolutionary Alliance and was responsible for financing the Nationalist Party (Guomindang) revolution. His second daughter Mei-ling (1897–) was the wife of Chiang K'ai-shek, and his oldest daughter, Ch'ing-ling (p. Qingling, 1892–1981), married Sun Yat-sen and served as vice chairperson of the Central People's Government Council in 1949. Soong's eldest son, T. V. (1894–1971), was the minister of finance, premier, and foreign minister of China under his brother-in-law Chiang K'ai-shek. He also served as governor of the Central Bank of China before moving to the United States in 1949.

Soong, Ch'ing-ling (p. Song Qinglin, 1892–1981): The oldest of three sisters married to prominent Nationalists, she became revolutionary leader Sun Yat-sen's wife in 1914. After her husband's death in 1925, she backed the alliance of the Guomindang left wing and the Chinese Communist Party.

Soong stayed on in the mainland after the triumph of the People's Republic in 1949 and held several more-or-less honorary positions in the Communist government.

Soong, Mei-ling (p. Song Meiling, 1897–): Mei-ling Soong is the second wife of Chiang K'ai-shek and sister of Ch'ingling Soong, widow of Sun Yat-sen and T. V. Soong, prominent industrialist and official to the Nationalist Chinese government. Educated in the United States from 1908 to 1917, she helped advance Chiang Kai-shek's cause to the West after their marriage in 1927. She wrote prolifically about China during World War II and in 1943 became the first Chinese citizen and the second woman to address a joint session of the U.S. Congress. She has written a number of books and articles, including *This Is Our China* (1940), *The Sure Victory* (1955), and two volumes of her own speeches. She currently lives in the United States.

Soong, T. V. (1894–1971): A Harvard-educated economist, brother of the Soong sisters, and brother-in-law of Chiang Kaishek, he helped Chiang finance the Northern Expedition of 1926 to 1928 as head of the Canton Central Bank.

Soong lobbied the United States for military aid against the Japanese in 1940, presented a $500 million loan request to the Americans in 1941, and served as minister of finance in Chiang's Guomindang government.

Stilwell, Joseph (1883–1946): Joseph Warren Stilwell, nicknamed "Vinegar Joe," was appointed commanding general of the U.S. Army forces in the China-Burma-India theater in 1942, chief of staff to Chiang Kai-shek, and supervisor of U.S. Lend-Lease aid to China. Having served in China throughout the 1920s, he greatly admired Chinese culture and could speak the language fluently. He prepared Chinese soldiers to mount a joint campaign with the British army to open the Burma Road into Chongqing. In 1944, he was relieved of his post after becoming highly critical of Chiang Kai-shek's refusal to permit him unrestricted command of Chinese Communist troops.

Su Shi (1036–1101): Also known as Su Dongpo or Su Tung-p'o, Su Shi was a Song dynasty (960–1279) lyric poet, prose stylist, calligrapher, and statesman. Su was a leader of Song-dynasty poets attempting to loosen contemporary poetic conventions, particularly in the song form known as *ci*. Su wrote in the *guwen* ("ancient prose") style that had renewed popularity among the literati of his time. He spent much of his life in service to the government, organizing the ordinary channels of the state examination and serving as governor of Hangzhou. Su Shi was also a noted art critic and essayist.

Summer Palace: Qianlong, the fourth emperor of the Qing (r. 1736–1799), commissioned architects and designers (including some Jesuit priests) to create the magnificent Summer Palace, the Yuanming Yuan, in a lakeside park near Beijing.

To enforce treaty terms, the British and French in 1860 sent a punitive expedition to Beijing. On the expedition commander Lord Elgin's orders, British and French troops burned the Yuanming Yuan to the ground on October 18, 1860.

The current "Summer Palace" on the outskirts of Beijing is a much smaller (though still very large in absolute terms) palace named Yihe Yuan. This reconstructed version of the Summer Palace was built in 1886 for the enjoyment of Empress Dowager Cixi (1835–1908).

Sun Bin (c. fourth to fifth centuries B.C.): Sun Bin was a military strategist and tactician who lived approximately a hundred years after his more famous ancestor Sun Tzu (p. Sunzi, or Sun Wu), whose *The Art of War* was transcribed in the fourth century B.C. Sun Bin, supposedly a lineal descendent of Sun Tzu, wrote his own treatise on warfare that is often referred to as *The Lost Art of War*. He served as the military consultant to general Tian Ji of the state of Qi during the Warring States period of 480–222 B.C. Sun Bin is often referred to as Sun Tzu II.

Sun Yat-sen (p. Sun Zhongshan, 1866–1925): The guiding figure of the Chinese Republican Revolution, Sun was born into a poor country family in the Guangzhou region. He joined a brother in Hawaii in the 1880s and attended mission schools there, absorbing ideas about democracy and republican government and learning the tenets of Christianity.

Sun studied medicine in British Hong Kong, then returned to Hawaii in 1894 to found the Revive China Society, a secret (and illegal) organization dedicated to the overthrow of the Manchu Qing dynasty and the establishment of a Chinese republic. He continued his revolutionary work in Hong Kong, the United States, and Japan from 1895.

Sun's Revolutionary Alliance achieved the overthrow of the Qing in 1911 and 1912, and he served temporarily as provisional president of the People's Republic. In late 1912, the alliance, now renamed the Guomindang (National People's Party), won a clear victory in elections for a new National Assembly.

Sun struggled for the rest of his life to overcome warlord rule and unify China under his Three People's Principles—nationalism, democracy, and the people's livelihood. Accepting political and material assistance from the Soviet Union, he agreed to a united front alliance with the Chinese Communist Party in 1923. The right wing of the Guomindang repudiated the alliance after Sun's death from cancer in Beijing at age fifty-nine.

Sun Zi (Sun Tzu): A scholar of the fourth century B.C., he authored the classic *The Art of War*, one of the earliest extant treatises on war and strategy.

Little is known about Sun's life, but his emphasis on the political aspects of war influenced modern military strategists. *The Art of War* was translated into French in 1782, and Napoléon Bonaparte was said to have read and admired it.

Taijiquan: Also spelled Tai Chi Chuan. Taijiquan ("Supreme Ultimate Fist") is an ancient form of Chinese exercise for self-defense, health, relaxation, meditation, and self-cultivation. It draws from the principles of Taiji (Supreme Ultimate), an ancient philosophical concept that calls for the harmonizing of the yin and yang sides of one's vital energy. It combines a graceful combination of rhythmic, deliberate movements with careful attention to different stances and positions. The origin of Taijiquan is a controversial topic. Some scholars trace its origin to ancient Daoist practices, while others claim that it was invented by a martial artist named Chen Wangting in the 17th century.

Taiping Rebellion: The largest, most destructive, and most important of the insurgencies of the late Qing, it grew out of a backdrop of peasant agony resulting from overcrowding and a series of floods and droughts. The rebellion's leader, Hong Xiuquan (1813–1864), a member of the southern China Hakka minority, invented a new religion based on his reading of Christian pamphlets and claimed that he was the younger brother of Jesus.

Hong organized a small army of peasants, miners, charcoal-burners, and bargees and ignited a rebellion in Guangxi Province during the great famine of 1849 and 1850. On January 11, 1851, he declared himself emperor of "The Heavenly Kingdom of Great Peace"—Taiping Tianguo. Hong led his forces gradually northward against fragmented Qing opposition, taking Wuhan and occupying the old capital of Nanjing in 1853. He ruled from Nanjing for 11 years.

The Taiping Rebellion collapsed in 1864, partly because of internal dissension and partly under pressure from revitalized Qing forces. Hong committed suicide in June 1864 as Zeng Guofan's Hunan provincial army besieged Hong's capital. Zeng entered Nanjing in July and crushed the last life out of the insurgency.

An estimated 20 million Chinese died as a direct or indirect consequence of the 13-year rebellion. The Taiping rebels' anti-Manchu attitude and land reform ideas influenced later nationalist and revolutionary groups.

Talas, Battle of (A.D. 751): The Battle of Talas was the culmination of close to a century of conflict between Arab and Chinese forces on the Chinese border between Mesopotamia and Lake Balkhash, and the result of the Tang empire's (618–907) largely unsuccessful policy of enemy containment in this area. The Battle of Talas itself was the climax of a Chinese counteroffensive in response to Arab advances in Khorezm, Ferghana, and Kashgar. It marked an end to Chinese ambitions in the Transoxiania and Kashgar regions.

It is believed that Chinese soldiers taken prisoner at the Battle of Talas transmitted the secret of paper manufacturing to their Arab foes, a secret China had kept to itself since the first century A.D. The process of paper making quickly spread from Talas to nearby Samarkand, then to Baghdad and Damascus. From there, it spread to Egypt, to Muslim-held Spain by the 10th and 11th centuries, and on to the rest of Europe. Some modern scholars have pointed out that Chinese influences made themselves felt in Persia long before the middle of the eighth century, and the secret of paper manufacture was already on its way to Europe by the time the Battle of Talas was fought.

Tan Sitong (1865–1898): Tan Sitong was a leading intellectual and political activist during the Qing dynasty (1644–1911). He published his ideas in a local provincial newspaper, *The New Hunan Study Journal*, and in a book titled *A Study of Benevolence*. In these and other publications, Tan attacked the conservative ruling class of the Qing dynasty and argued for a republican regime. He argued for the need for political reform of China and the rights of the individual. Tan played a crucial role in the Hundred Days Reform movement of 1898 and was executed with five other key

reformers after the movement's suppression by Yuan Shikai (1859–1916) and the empress dowager Cixi (1835–1908).

Tang, King of Shang: Also referred to as "Tang the Victorious," Tang was the first emperor of the Shang dynasty (c. 1554–1045 B.C.). Some modern scholars place the Shang dynasty from the mid-16th to the mid-11th centuries B.C. According to legend, Tang was the descendant of the mythical Yellow Emperor. His overthrow of Jie, the evil last ruler of the quasi-mythical Xia dynasty, is said to have been foretold on a tortoiseshell. History has painted Tang as a wise and generous ruler. He is often represented as a nine-foot-tall, white-faced, whiskered man with a pointed head, six jointed arms, and a lopsided body.

Tangshan Earthquake: The Tangshan earthquake was a massive earthquake measuring 8.2 on the Richter scale that devastated the mining city of Tangshan in Hebei Province on July 28, 1976. The death toll exceeded 240,000, and approximately half a million people were injured. The tremendous casualty rate was partly due to the collapse of the city's many un-reinforced masonry homes, in which most victims were sleeping at the time of the quake. The catastrophe has been widely remembered as an omen for the death of the revered Communist leader and founder of the People's Republic of China, Mao Zedong (1893–1976), who died on September 9 of that year.

Tantric Buddhism: Also known as Vajrayana Buddhism, Tantric Buddhism is an esoteric branch of Buddhism that concentrates on one's realizing the highest state of being through yogic and ritualistic practices. It has long been associated with alchemy and even magic. It flourished in India and many neighboring countries, including China, Ceylon, countries in Southeast Asia and, most notably, Tibet from the sixth to the 11th centuries. Tantric Buddhism was introduced to China during the Tang period (618–907), and Chinese translations of Tantric texts multiplied during the eighth century. The religion's most famous master and translator, Amoghavajra (Bukong Jingang, 704–744), was a favorite of the Tang court.

Taoism. See **Daoism.**

Tea: Legend places the discovery of tea in 2737 B.C. by the second mythical Chinese emperor, Shennong ("Divine Peasant"), who is remembered as a skilled ruler, herbalist, and agriculturalist. It was most likely introduced into China from Southeast Asia during the Six Dynasties period (222–589), and historical records relate its being drunk from the third century onward. By the sixth century, it had become a common beverage in China. By the eighth century, the Tang government had imposed a tax on it. In 780, Lu You wrote the first book on tea, titled *Cha jing*. The Dutch East India Company carried the first consignment of Chinese tea to Europe in 1610. In 1669, the English East India Company introduced Chinese tea to London. By the late 19th century, it was a commodity of great importance to both European and Chinese markets, though by the end of the century England had begun to depend upon cheaper and stronger Indian and Ceylon teas. Many of the most popular varieties of Chinese tea today, including Longjing (green tea), Oolong, Pekoe, Jasmine and a variety of compressed teas come from traditional growing areas in Fujian, Anhui, Zhejiang, and Jiangxi. The modern term *tea* comes from the Chinese dialect words *tchai*, *cha*, and *tay*, used both to describe the beverage and the leaf of the tea plant (*Camellia sinensis*).

Theravada Buddhism: Theravada Buddhism (*Theravada* means "the Way of the Elders") claims strict adherence to the teachings of the Buddha. One of the two major branches of Buddhism (the other is Mahayana Buddhism), Theravada Buddhism recognizes as saints (*arhats*) those who have attained nirvana (the state of bliss) and therefore salvation from *samsara* (the compulsory circle of rebirth) by their own efforts. Theravada Buddhists believe the Buddha to be the perfect master but differentiate themselves from Mahayana Buddhists in that they do not pay homage to buddhas and bodhisattvas in Mahayana temples. Theravada Buddhism came into existence during the third century A.D. in India, traveling first to Sri Lanka and then eastward, becoming dominant in Myanmar, Cambodia, and Laos by the 13th and 14th centuries. Buddhism, in

a slightly different form that resembles Mayhayana Buddhism more than Theravada, arrived in China during the Han dynasty (206 B.C.–A.D. 220), reaching its apex during the Sui dynasty (581–618). Although Chinese Buddhism assimilated many beliefs from both Taoism and Confucianism, it was never able to approach either in popularity. In 845, the emperor Wuzong began a major persecution of Buddhists in China. However, the persecution was short-lived, and Buddhism remains a major religion in China today. Buddhist beliefs have exerted a considerable influence in the arts and culture of China to the present day.

Thirteen Classics: The Thirteen Classics are a collection of traditional Confucian writings. They include the *Book of Songs*, the *Book of Documents*, the *Book of Changes*, the *Record of Rituals*, and the *Spring and Autumn Annals*, which also make up the Five Classics. The *Spring and Autumn Annals* count as three of the 13 because of the three commentaries, *Gongyang zhuan* (Tradition of Gongyang), *Guliang zhuan* (Tradition of Guliang), and *Zuo zhuan* (Tradition of Zuo), that go with the main text. The remaining six are *Zhou li* (The rituals of Zhou), the *Yi li* (Ceremonies and rituals), the *Analects*, *Mencius*, the *Book of Filial Piety*, and the *Er ya*, which is sometimes considered China's first dictionary.

Tiantai Buddhism: This sect developed as a branch of Mahayana Buddhism in China and later reached Japan, where it is called the "Tendai." Using the Lotus Sutra as its main text, it was taught in northern China during the fifth century, when the founder of the school, Zhiyi, settled on Mount Tiantai and established a famous monastery. Tiantai has been able to absorb many Confucian and Daoist principles in its many centuries of existence. It propounds a threefold belief system and an elaborate cosmology of 3,000 realms. Central to followers of this school is the importance of meditation and enlightenment.

Tibet (Tibet Autonomous Region): Tibet is bounded by the Chinese provinces of Sichuan to the east and Qinghai to the northeast, Kashmir and India to the west, and India and Nepal to the south. With an average elevation of more than 4,875 meters (1,486 feet), Tibet has the highest elevation of any large region on Earth. It is also one of the most isolated, bounded on three sides by the tremendous mountain systems of the Himalayas, the Karakorum Range, and the Kunlun Mountains. Tibet has a total area of just under half a million square miles, about 804,500 square kilometers, and its capital is Lhasa. With only 2.2 million people, Tibet has the lowest population density of any region of China. The majority of Tibet's residents are Tibetan, though Chinese form a large minority. Tibetan is the principal language. The principal religion of the country was Tibetan Buddhism before the Chinese made Tibet part of China and put severe restrictions on local religious practices.

In the seventh century, Tibet was first unified by a great chief named Songsten Gampo (c. 620–649). Songsten Gampo married the Tang dynasty princess Wencheng in 641 and thus formed a formal relationship with the Chinese empire. By the eighth century, Tibet had become strong enough militarily to become a major threat to China under the Tang dynasty. However, the centralized authority in Tibet did not survive long. By the time Chinggis Khan incorporated the area into his empire in 1206, it was merely a number of petty principalities. In 1270, political power was given to a form of government that was heavily dominated by the Buddhist clergy, making the Dalai Lama both the political and the spiritual leader of the country. The Chinese declared sovereignty over the area in the 17th century, though their hold on the country was relatively weak. After the Chinese Republican Revolution of 1911 and the demise of the Manchu Qing dynasty, the Chinese were expelled from Tibet. However, in 1950, Communist Chinese troops invaded Tibet and forced the capitulation of the 14th Dalai Lama, who fled to India in 1959. During the 1950s, the Chinese made a concerted effort to modernize Tibet and suppress the widespread and pervasive practice of Buddhism within the country. Tibetan resentment at this attempt to remake society erupted in a popular uprising in 1959 that was quickly and forcibly suppressed. In 1965, Tibet was established as an autonomous region of the People's Republic of China. Relations

between China and Tibet have become more relaxed in recent years, though as of this writing the Dalai Lama is still in exile from his country. The Chinese government has repeatedly urged the Dalai Lama to return to China, but the two sides have not been able to agree on the terms of his return.

Tongzhi Restoration: The Tongzhi Restoration was a series of reforms that occurred during the regency of the Qing dynasty (1644–1911) emperor Tongzhi (1856–1875, r. 1861–1875). The restoration followed the many invasions and rebellions of the 19th century and served to restore the authority of the Qing monarchy. After suppressions of such uprisings as the Taiping Rebellion (1850–1864) in the south of China and the Nian Rebellion (1853–1868) in northern China, local administrations were rebuilt and the economy was revised through support of agricultural and handicraft interests in China. During the Tongzhi Restoration, the military was rearranged under the auspices of the Self Strengthening Movement (1861–1895). An ambassadorial bureau, known as the Zongli Yamen (Office of General Management), was put into place and led to the treaties of Tianjin (1858) and Beijing (1860) with the West. Efforts were also made to send Chinese students and officials abroad for education. The Tongzhi Restoration is traditionally considered a failure because it could not enable China—and the Qing rulers—to effectively contend with internal divisions and external threats to the country. The restoration's failure has also been blamed on the inability of those who implemented it to eschew their traditionalist Confucian ideology and embrace more progressive ideas regarding industrialization and the organization of a modern society.

Treaty Ports: These designated areas for foreign contact with China developed as the result of European military and diplomatic pressure on the Qing imperial government to relax trade and other restrictions.

The Treaty of Nanjing of 1842, which ended the Opium War, set up the modern treaty port system. Areas were set aside for foreign settlement. Foreign troops and police were present, and foreign laws were in force, even for crimes committed against Chinese.

The original five treaty ports were Guangzhou, Fuzhou, Xiamen, Shanghai, and Ningbo. Others were added later in the 19th century.

Triads: The origins of these secret societies are very obscure. Probably originating in Taiwan and Fujian during the latter part of the 19th century, triads were groups of organized criminals with a tendency to sometimes violent opposition to the imperial government. Triads also went by the name of Heaven and Earth Society.

Their close ties with corrupt local officials and military commanders made the triads a powerful force in southern China. Some members of Triad members claim that the Triads were originally founded by Ming loyalists who aspired to overthrow the Manchu Qing dynasty to restore the Ming dynasty. Modern scholars, however, generally do not accept this claim as historically correct.

Tribute System: A system for the premodern Chinese empire to manage its relationship with some of the smaller states near its border. The last period in which this system flourished was from the founding of the Ming dynasty (1368–1644) to the early part of the 19th century. A smaller state that entered into this system with China would incur the following obligations. First, it must acknowledge China's political and cultural superiority. Second, it must periodically pay tribute to the Chinese emperor. The tribute paid often consisted of specialty products of this smaller state. In return, the Chinese emperor would repay the head of the smaller state with a gift, which was usually worth much more than the tribute he received. Thus, both sides of this system gained something: The Chinese emperor gained "honor," while the head of the small state gained in money and goods. Sometimes the tribute system also morally obliged China to defend the smaller state in a military crisis. For example, when the Japanese warriors under Toyotomi Hideyoshi invaded Korea in the 1590s, the government of the Ming dynasty in China sent troops to help

Korea defend itself, in spite of the fact the Ming government was already suffering from financial difficulties.

Twenty-one Demands: In January 1915, Japan sent China a list of demands calling for special rights in Manchuria and elsewhere in China. The Japanese also wanted the right to interfere with Chinese financial, political, and police affairs.

After Japan's ultimatum in May 1915, the government of Yuan Shikai approved the demands over widespread popular protest.

Uighur (Uyghur): The Uighur are a Turkic-speaking people of interior Asia who live primarily in the Xinjiang Uighur autonomous region. They first appear in Chinese records from the third century A.D. The Uighur established a kingdom on the Orhon River in today's north-central Mongolia in 744. They were forced out by the Kyrgyz in 840 to form an independent kingdom in the Turfan region. It was in turn overthrown by the expanding Mongols in the 13th century, though the Uighur have retained a presence in this area ever since. There were more than 7,700,000 Uighur in China in the late 20th century, most of them in Xinjiang; there were also some 300,000 in Uzbekistan, Kazakhstan, and Kyrgyzstan. The Xinjiang Uighur are Sunnite Muslims.

Unequal Treaties: The Unequal Treaties were negotiated during the 19th and early-20th centuries between China and foreign powers, particularly Great Britain, France, Germany, the United States, Russia, and Japan. Signed by the Chinese government under foreign pressure, the treaties forced China to concede many of its territorial and sovereignty rights as well as to grant foreign powers access to important ports in China and various commercial and diplomatic privileges. The most important of the many Unequal Treaties signed during this period were the Treaty of Nanjing (1842), which ended the so-called Opium War between China and Great Britain; the Treaty of Wangxia (Wanghia) (1844), with the United States; the Treaty of Whampoa (1844), with France; the Treaty of Tianjin (1858), with Great Britain, which ended the "Second Opium War" (also known as the "Arrow War" of 1860); and the Treaty of Aigun (May 16, 1858), with Russia, which gave that country navigation rights to the Amur, Ussuri, and Songhuajiang Rivers. Another significant Unequal Treaty was the Convention of Beijing (1860), which forced China to ratify the Nanjing and Tianjin agreements. Between 1928 and 1931, the Guomindang government negotiated the return of tariff autonomy to China, but extraterritorial privileges were not relinquished by Great Britain, France, and the United States until 1946.

Versailles Treaty (1919): The Treaty of Versailles, negotiated principally by the European states and the United States after the end of World War I (1914–1918), had a profound effect on China. The treaty affected China's relations with the West and with its belligerent neighbor Japan. It also created political discord in China itself. The Chinese delegation to the Paris Peace Conference arrived with the primary goal of gaining back the port of Jiaozhou and the large parts of Shandong Province that had been in Germany's possession before Japan took them over at the beginning of World War I. Though the Beijing and Tokyo governments had secretly agreed to a Chinese concession regarding these possessions in September 1918, before the convening of the Paris Peace Conference (and unbeknownst to the Chinese delegation sent to Versailles), the Chinese unsuccessfully contended the occupation. The Western powers at the Conference acceded to Japan's position, in part to ensure that it joined the League of Nations. News of the delegation's failure and humiliation set off a wave of irate nationalism on May 4, 1919, in China. The Chinese public could not understand why, given the fact that China was on the winning side of World War I, it could not take back its territories that were formerly occupied by Germany. The May Fourth Movement was fueled in part by resentment against the ineffectual Beijing government and its inability to defend China's interests.

Wang Anshi (1021–1086): Wang Anshi was a highly controversial governmental reformer and a respected polemicist and writer who implemented his "New Laws," or "New Policies" between 1069 and 1076.

With his appointment in 1069 as second privy councilor to the Song dynasty (960–1279) emperor Shenzong (1048–1085, r. 1067–1085), Wang launched a reform program. He focused on improving conditions of the peasants and raising agricultural production to strengthen the country's economy and defensive capability. Wang centralized the financial affairs of the empire by stabilizing commodity exchange and fixing prices, loaning money at a favorable rate to peasants, reassessing land taxes, and commuting unpaid labor. Wang also reorganized the Hanlin Academy and restructured the civil service examinations. Moreover, he revived a system of collective policing in the countryside called the *baojia* and found innovative ways to build up the Song militia. Wang's far reaching and momentous reforms remained intact until the emperor's death in 1085, though Wang himself faced great opposition to his forward thinking policies from political and financial interests. He was pressured into resigning his post in 1076. His excellent, penetrating prose led him to be named one of the Eight Great Masters of the Tang and Song dynasties, and his poetry has also been noted by historians of the period. After the death of the emperor Shenzong in 1085, Wang's own reforms were reversed by conservative officials, although institutional reforms designed by Shenzong himself remained largely intact.

Wang Fuzhi (1619–1692): Wang Fuzhi was a Chinese Nationalist philosopher, historian and poet in the early years of the Qing dynasty (1644–1911). After a short stint with resistance fighters loyal to the Ming dynasty (1368–1644) against the Manchu Qing dynasty (1644–1911), which took power in 1644, Wang realized the futility of his cause. He gave up his life to study, writing works on history, philosophy, and literature. His best-known studies are the *Du Tongjian lun* (Commentary on reading the comprehensive mirror; the "comprehensive mirror" refers to Sima Guang's *Zizhi tongjian*. See entry to **Sima Guang**) and the *Song lun* (Commentary on the Song dynasty). Wang, an ardent Confucianist, was outspoken in his belief that the central purpose of the state was to serve the people. He was a staunch defender of Chinese culture and an unrepentant opponent of past or present alien rule of China, a view that no doubt was partly formed by his hatred of the Qing. Wang also posited a theory of historical evolution that depended on differing stages of social development dependent on a myriad of historical forces. His ideas became very popular in the late 19th century and early 20th century.

Wang Jingwei (1883–1943): An ally of Sun Yat-sen, he helped establish the Revolutionary Alliance (Tongmeng hui) in Japan in 1905.

In the 1920s, Wang co-authored a Guomindang manifesto that attacked the unequal distribution of property and made common cause with international revolutionaries; he was said to have drafted Sun's pro-Soviet last will and testament. He occupied senior posts during the first Communist Guomindang alliance of 1923 to 1927.

Wang was later generally regarded as a centrist. Though a one-time opponent of Chiang Kai-shek, he held office in the Nationalist Nanjing government from 1928 to 1937, rising briefly to the post of Chiang's second in command.

Wang consented in March 1940 to be the figurehead leader of a Japanese collaborationist government in central China, with its capital at Nanjing. Only the Japanese accorded recognition to this puppet regime.

Wang Jinxi (d. 1970): Known as "Iron Man Wang," Wang became famous during the 1960s, leading a team opening the Daqing oil field. Along with the Dazhai agricultural production brigade, it was the model for self-reliance for all industry in Communist China. Upon its completion, the Daqing oil field became the most important source for the country's oil production, despite its development in the barren Heilongjiang Province, which has extreme weather conditions. In 1968, Wang was appointed vice chairman of the Daqing Oil Field Revolutionary Committee and to the Chinese Communist Party Central Committee.

Wang Mang (45 B.C.–A.D. 23): Wang Mang was the founder of the short-lived Xin dynasty (A.D. 9–25). The nephew of an empress of the ruling Early Han dynasty

(206 B.C.–A.D. 8), he schemed his way to power. In 9, he ascended the throne and proclaimed the foundation of the Hsin dynasty, claiming the "mandate of heaven" to rule. He embarked on a series of unremarkable land redistribution initiatives and programs aimed at strengthening the government and its economic interests. His reforms were met with strong resistence from the bureaucrats and wealthy families, while his inept management style caused his government to operate with great inefficiency. The Yellow River flooded in A.D. 11—following disastrous floods in 2 and 5—adding to the difficulties of his reign. The floods were followed by massive peasant unrest. Roaming bands of insurrectionists, including a group called the Red Eyebrows, formed. By 18, the Red Eyebrows were strong enough to defeat Wang's armies. In 23, the rebels broke through one of the city gates on the east wall of the capital and joined in battle with Wang and about one thousand of his supports. In the ensuing fray, Wang and his men were killed. After a period of brutal civil war, Liu Xiu, a descendant of the Han imperial house, emerged as the new ruler of China. Liu Xiu is also known as Emperor Guangwu, the founder of the Eastern Han dynasty (25–220).

Wang Yangming (a.k.a. Wang Shouren, 1472–1529): A philosopher-soldier-official of the early Ming dynasty. Although Wang studied the Confucian classics like all Confucian philosophers, he emphasized that all persons, whether literate or not, could become perfect moral beings by awakening the original goodness in their human nature. Wang thus offered a vision in which anyone, peasant or scholar, could find the way to wisdom.

Even in his own time, the authorities found Wang's thought subversive and sought to suppress it, sometimes even closing down academies in which it was taught. Some later scholars charged him with promoting individualism and thus undermining Confucian moral standards, developments that weakened the Ming and eventually helped bring about its downfall.

However, Wang's teaching remained influential after his time. Chiang Kai-shek, the great Nationalist leader, claims to have been much inspired by Wang's teachings and even named a mountain in Taiwan after Wang Yangming.

Ward, Fredrick Townsend (1831–1862): Fredrick Townsend Ward, an American, assembled and commanded the Ever-Victorious Army, a body of Western-trained troops. The Ever-Victorious Army aided the Qing dynasty (1644–1911) in suppressing the Taiping Rebellion, a tremendous religious and political upheaval in southern China that occurred between 1850 and 1864. Using Chinese troops and Western arms, Ward managed to win numerous victories against the Taiping. He died on September 21, 1862, in battle; the British Major Charles "Chinese" Gordon took over Ward's command.

Warlords: These independent, regional military rulers cropped up in the turbulent years between the establishment of the Republican government in 1911 and the Communist takeover of China in 1949. Among the better-known warlords of the early 20th century were Yan Xishan, Feng Yuxiang, and Zhang Zuolin. Warlords rose to power across the country after the death of Yuan Shikai (1859–1916). He had served as the first president of the Republic of China from 1912 to 1916. In 1921, Sun Yat-sen established an independent revolutionary regime under the control of his Nationalist Party (Guomindang), which bound many of the southern warlords under one flag. The year after Sun's death in 1925, Nationalist forces under Chiang Kai-shek swept northward and in 1928 theoretically reunified China. However, local warlords continued to be a factor in Chinese politics until the Communist government was established in 1949.

Wei Yuan (1794–1856): This historian and geographer of the Qing dynasty (1644–1911/12) published the *Huangchao jingshi wenbian* (Collected essays on statecraft under the reigning dynasty) in 1826. He followed this study of political and economic issues with the *Haiguo tuzhi* (Illustrated treatise on overseas countries) in 1844. In this volume on the geography and material conditions of foreign nations, Wei proposed that the Chinese learn the superior technology of the West so as to set rapacious foreign nations against one

another. The concept was called *Yi yi zhi yi*, or "overcoming the barbarians by the barbarians." Wei's ideas were among the sources of inspiration for the modernization efforts of the Qing government in the 1860s and 1870s.

Wei Zhongxian (1568–1627): Wei Zhongxian was a eunuch leader who completely dominated the Ming dynasty's government (1368–1644) between 1624 and 1627. In 1624, Wei induced the imbecilic emperor Tianqi (1605–1627, r. 1620–1627) to permit him to take control of state affairs. The corruption and terror Wei quickly imposed on the population prompted members of the Donglin Party, a group of Confucian scholar-officials, to briefly and unsuccessfully oppose his rule. Wei responded with a ferocious persecution of Donglin adherents in 1625 and 1626 that ended with the execution of a considerable number of prominent officials. When the emperor died in 1627 and his successor Chongzhen rose to power (1611–1644, r. 1627–1644), Wei hung himself, leaving behind a bankrupt state. It would be unable to contend with the Manchu challenge for power and a rebellious peasantry, both of which would cause upheaval throughout the remaining two decades of Ming rule.

Well-field System: According to Mencius and the Zhou text *Zuo zhuan* (Tradition of Zuo, probably fourth century B.C.), this system of communal land organization was in effect throughout China early in the Zhou dynasty (1045–256 B.C.). Mencius reports that each unit of the well-field system was divided among eight peasant families, with each having its own outlying field with a central shared field. All the families jointly worked a ninth central plot for their lord. The name for the system is derived from the Chinese character for "well," which provides a graphic representation of the central shared field surrounded by eight outlying fields. All community members were subject to labor service, or *corvée*. The service each peasant owed to his lord seemed to vary. Some scholars have doubted the historical existence of the well-field system as described by Mencius. Other scholars have pointed out that the well-field system, while creating virtual serfdoms and a high degree of peasant dependence on the nobility, is proof that the Zhou did not practice agricultural slavery. They apparently did use slaves for domestic service and the manufacture of handicrafts, however. Some historians have argued that the well-field system justifies the classification of the Zhou era as an early stage of Chinese feudalism.

Wellington Koo (p. Gu Weijun, 1888–1985): After attaining an American education at Cook Academy and Columbia University, Koo graduated with a Ph.D. from the latter in 1912. He went on to become China's premier diplomat in the early 20th century, serving as ambassador to England, France, the United States, the League of Nations, and the United Nations. He played an important role in the negotiations leading up to the Treaty of Versailles but declined to sign the final treaty because it granted Germany's treaty rights in China to Japan. In 1931, Koo became minister of foreign affairs in the Nanjing government and in 1932 China's representative to the League of Nations, where he denounced Japan's seizure of Manchuria. In 1945, Koo was named to the United Nations Preparatory Commission and in 1946, he became ambassador to the United States, attempting to garner U.S. aid for the Nationalist cause against Chinese Communist forces. After serving on the International Court of Justice for 10 years, in 1967 he moved to New York, where he lived until his death.

Wen Jiabao (1942–): Trained as a geologist and engineer, Wen Jiabao has been the vice premier of China since 1998. He is widely regarded as a protégé of the Chinese premier Zhu Rongji, who has pushed through sweeping reforms in the Chinese economy since the 1990s. On March 16, 2003, Mr. Wen succeeded Zhu Rongji as China's premier.

Whampoa Military Academy: Sun Yat-sen established this officer training school on an island downstream from Guangzhou in 1924 and appointed Chiang Kai-shek its first director, with the Communist Zhou Enlai as head of the political department.

Large numbers of Whampoa's first graduating classes were fiercely loyal to Chiang, giving him a political and military power base he used to advantage later in the 1920s.

White Lotus Society: The White Lotus was a secret society based in northern China. The real origin of the White Lotus Society is controversial. According to one account, it was founded by Mao Ziyuan of Suzhou a little before 1133 under the Southern Song dynasty, though it indirectly traces its origins as an offshoot of the Tiantai Buddhist sect as far back as the fourth century A.D. Drawing believers mainly from the ranks of poor peasants, the White Lotus placed great importance on imparting principles of mutual aid and cooperation and believed that the Buddha would return to end worldly suffering.

Between 1796 and 1804, the White Lotus orchestrated a guerrilla rebellion in the central mountainous region of China against the Manchu rulers of the Qing dynasty (1644–1911) in the vain hope of restoring the Ming dynasty (1368–1644). The Qing government was never fully able to squash the White Lotus, and intermittent fighting orchestrated by White Lotus militias erupted between Lotus members and the government into the 20th century after the initial rebellion was defused.

Working Unit (Danwei): The term denotes a place of work in the People's Republic of China since 1949. A *danwei* is an organization or employer; it sometimes also provides housing and social services for employees, whose numbers can range into the many thousands. Since the beginning of the economic reforms in the late 1970s, however, the social services and job security provided by the *danwei* have been gradually eroded.

World War I (1914–1918): World War I broke out just as the young Chinese republic was in the process of seeking unification within its borders as well as fending off an overtly hostile Japan. At the beginning of the war, Japan sided with the Allies and immediately took the opportunity to seize German-held ports around Jiaozhou Bay and German-held railways in Shandong. On January 16, 1915, the Japanese secretly presented to Yuan Shikai, the president of the Republic, the infamous Twenty-one Demands, which made China a Japanese dependency. Yuan, meanwhile, attempted to restore the monarchy to China and have himself enthroned. This sparked a revolt in Yunnan and a general declaration of independence on the part of military leaders in Guizhouo, Jiangxi, and parts of Guangdong. Yuan fell ill and died shortly thereafter on June 6, 1916.

General Li Yuanhong succeeded Yuan, and General Duan Qirui continued as premier. In February of 1917, Li faced his first crisis as president of the Republic: The United States severed diplomatic relations with Germany and invited all neutral countries, such as China, to do the same. As Li considered his options, he was forced to quell another revolt in Beijing, headed by General Zhang Xun who tried to restore the Qing dynasty. Finally, China declared war on Germany on August 4, 1917. Because of its domestic concerns, however, China could take no part in the fighting, though it did permit the recruitment of tens of thousands of Chinese laborers to serve behind the lines in Great Britain, France, Africa, and Mesopotamia.

Subsequently Sun Yat-sen formed a rival government at Guangzhou, in southern China. The southern government declared war on Germany on August 26 and unsuccessfully strove for Allied recognition as the legitimate Chinese government. Duan turned his attention to halting the northward advance of Sun's troops, finally driving them from Hunan by April 18, 1918, and prompting Sun's flight back to Shanghai in defeat, leaving a divided China behind him.

China enjoyed some benefits from its experience in World War I, including winning some German and Austrian concessions and the cancellation of portions of the Boxer indemnities. They were debts amounting to up to 450 million taels, approximately $100 million U.S., stipulated in the Boxer Protocol of 1901 in reparation for attacks on foreigners during the Boxer Rebellion at the end of the century. The Republican government, however, was facing a massive internal division by the time the Versailles Treaty was signed and faced the post-war world in a semi-chaotic state, with the Beijing government only marginally in control of a severely faction-alized country. Japan, moreover, arranged with the Allies to take over railways in Shandong, Mongolia, and Manchuria and induced the Beijing government to recognize claims to former German ports that Japan had seized at the beginning of the war. This led to two decades of smoldering hostility between Japan and China, which would flare up again by the outbreak of the second Sino-Japanese War (1937–1945).

World War II (1939–1945): Throughout the 1930s, Japan followed a policy of relentless annexation of parts of northern China, which had been weakened by fighting between Communist and Nationalist (Guomindang) factions. By 1931, the Japanese had seized control of Manchuria, transforming its three provinces into the state of Manchukuo, and had forced China to cede northeastern Hebei. Chinese Communist and Nationalist leaders were unable to take a united stand against Japanese aggression until 1937, when Chiang Kai-shek, leader of the Nationalist government in China, moderated his anti-Communist stand. That enabled China to present a united Guomindang-Communist front against the Japanese. On July 7, 1937, Japanese forces invaded China without a formal declaration of war, beginning what is known as the second Sino-Japanese War (1937–1945). By that fall, the Japanese had overrun most of northern China. By November of that same year, Shanghai and the Yangtze Valley had fallen as well. Nanjing, Hankou and Guangzhou fell in 1938. For the duration of the war, Japan controlled all the main cities in eastern China as well as most of the country's infrastructure.

When World War II broke out in Europe, the Nationalist government already faced severe setbacks and financial hardship. The Communists, headquartered in Yan'an, expanded their influence, bases, and membership. The Nationalist government was forced to retreat to Chongqing and began to weaken and factionalize in the face of financial difficulties caused by the loss of northern China.

The Communist forces, on the other hand, mobilized guerrilla units, which resisted the Japanese invasion with greater success from their bases in the North. Using a vigorous campaign of propaganda and thought reform, the Communists mobilized and armed a significant portion of the Chinese peasantry. Their effectiveness earned the Communists wide support within China and enabled them to emerge from World War II a stronger and better-disciplined force than before.

Shortly after the Japanese surrender in 1945, a full-scale civil war broke out between the weakened Nationalists and Communist troops over the reoccupation of Manchuria. By 1949, the Nationalist government, bankrupt and rent by internal division, collapsed completely, fleeing to the island of Taiwan. Consequently, the Communist People's Republic of China, with Mao Zedong as the head of state, was officially proclaimed on October 1, 1949.

Xi Xia: The Tangut founded this kingdom in northwestern China in 1038. In 1038, their leader, Li Yuanhao, assumed the title of emperor, broke his tributary relationship with the Song empire, and began to attack Song territories. In 1044, the Tangut were fended off by Song dynasty (960–1279) armies and were compelled to make a treaty with the Chinese government and the Liao dynasty (907–1125) to the north. The Song sent gifts to Xi Xia and actively engaged in trade to ensure peaceful relations. They bartered tea, silks, and other goods for fine Tangut horses. Though the Xi Xia government was modeled on the Song exemplar, it still followed most of the traditional Tangut customs. Between 1205 and 1209, the Xi Xia government fell under the control of the great Mongol ruler Chinggis Khan (1167–1227). When the Tangut revolted against his rule in 1224 and in 1227, Chinggis Khan responded with overwhelming force.

Xi'an (Sian) Incident: Warlord Zhang Xueliang abducted Chiang Kai-shek in this northern China city on December 12, 1936. He wanted to force Chiang into a united front against the Japanese, who had driven Zhang from his power base in Manchuria in 1931.

After two weeks of intense negotiations between the Guomindang and the Chinese Communist Party, Zhang released his captive on Christmas Day. The Nationalists later court-martialed Zhang for insubordination. However, Chiang also fulfilled his promise of declaring a united front with the Communists against the Japanese invasion.

Xiang Yu (232–202 B.C.): Xiang Yu was an aristocratic Chinese general and leader of one of the rebel forces that overthrew the Qin dynasty (221–206 B.C.). He vied for control of China with Liu Bang, who went on to become the founder of the Han dynasty (206 B.C.–A.D. 220). Xiang was a member of a prominent family from the state of Chu, which had been absorbed by the Qin empire, and his death marked the end of feudal, aristocratic rule in China. In 207 B.C. Xiang Yu's forces burned and looted the Qin capital and killed the last Qin emperor and his family before dividing the country among the various rebel leaders. Xiang took the state of Chu for himself. Almost immediately, rival leaders, including Liu Bang, who had become the king of Han after the fall of the Qin, began to contest Xiang's power. In 202, after almost five years of constant struggle, Xiang Yu's forces were overwhelmed by Liu's, and Xiang chose suicide rather than capture. His chivalrous heroism has been celebrated in Chinese lore for centuries.

Xingyi: Xingyi is one of the three main schools of "internal style" martial arts, the others being Bagua and Taijit. Developed within China, Xingyi and its related disciplines are considered to be essentially Daoist disciplines. Xingyi is most often attributed to General Yue Fei (1103–1142) of the Song dynasty (960–1279) who supposedly promoted the art among his troops, though some martial arts scholars believe Xingyi was actually invented much later. The Xingyi system is based upon five basic movements or "fists," as well as a series of more complicated techniques based on the imitation of the movements of animals that include the "dragon," "monkey," "tiger," "bear," and "horse."

Xiongnu: The Xiongnu were a nomadic, tribal people from Inner Asia. According to Chinese historical records, they first appeared in China during the fifth century as marauders from the north, prompting the northern Chinese kingdoms to erect fortifications that would later become the Great Wall. After the third century B.C., the Xiongnu founded an empire that ruled over a territory extending from western Manchuria to the Pamirs and covering much of present Siberia and Mongolia. The Early Han dynasty (206 B.C.–A.D. 220) rulers had constant problems with the Xiongnu. The emperor Wudi (r. 141–87 B.C.) sent army after army against them in a war of attrition that gradually reduced the power of the Xiongnu by 119 B.C. By A.D. 58, their empire had collapsed due to internal dissension, and the Xiongnu never again were an urgent threat to China. In 304, some Xiongnu tribes settled in northern China. Although Xiongnu raids continued periodically throughout the next hundred years or so, all references to the tribe disappeared after the fifth century. Some scholars have affiliated the Xiongnu with the Turks and the legendary Huns who invaded the Roman Empire in the fifth century, though conclusive proof of either of these associations has not been made.

Xuanzang (602–664): This Buddhist monk and Chinese pilgrim traveled to India between 629 and 654, returning to China with sacred scriptures of Buddhism, which he spent the rest of his life translating from Sanskrit into Chinese. Xuanzang's *Record of the Western Regions* (648) is an account of his travels, and the Ming dynasty (1368–1644) novel *Journey to the West* is based on his pilgrimage. Xuanzang's main interest centered on the philosophy of the Yogacara (Vijnanavada) school. He and his disciple Kuiji (632–682) were responsible for the formation of the related, highly philosophical Weishi (Consciousness-Only School), which declined shortly after its two founders died.

Xunzi (personal name: Xun Kuang, 300–230 B.C.): Xunzi was a Warring States (480–222 B.C.) philosopher and teacher. Along with Mencius (372–288 B.C.) and Confucius (551–479 B.C.), Xunzi is considered one of the three great Confucian philosophers in history. Xunzi's major work, known today as the *Xunzi*, argued that a person is by nature evil and that only culture and society make one good. Xunzi's avocation of traditionalism, discipline, and the study of the classics greatly influenced the Legalist theoretician Han Fei (280–233 B.C.) and the Legalist statesman Li Si (280–208 B.C.).

Yan Xishan (1883–1960): A powerful anti-Communist warlord, Yan was the most powerful man in his native Shanxi Province from 1917 until the founding of the People's Republic in 1949. Before the Japanese army occupied much of the Shanxi province from 1937 to 1945, Yan succeeded in controlling the Shanxi almost like his independent kingdom. He once boasted that his regime combined the best features of militarism, nationalism, anarchy, democracy, capitalism, communism, and paternalism.

An ally of Chiang Kai-shek in the war against the Communists, Yan carefully studied Marxist theories so that he could fight the Communists not only on the military front, but also on the ideological front. When Communist forces took over Shanxi, many of his followers died in a last stand in the provincial capital Taiyuan in April 1949; Yan fled with his life.

Ye Jianying (1897–1986): Ye Jianying was a Communist military officer, administrator, and statesman. He had an outstanding military career in which he served as chief of staff in the (Communist) Eighth Route Army during much of World War II. Ye was made a member of the ruling Politburo of the Chinese Communist Party (CCP) in 1966 and was named to the powerful Standing Committee of the Politburo in 1973. He opposed the Gang of Four and supported Hua Guofeng, Mao Zedong's (1893–1976) successor as chairman of the CCP, after Mao's death in 1976. Ye served as defense minister from 1975 to 1978 and in 1978 was made chairman of the Standing Committee of the National People's Congress, the highest legislative body in China aside from the CCP and its Central Committee. Ye retired from his principal posts, including his membership in the Politburo, in 1985.

Yellow Emperor (28th to 27th Centuries B.C.): Known as Huang Di, the Yellow Emperor is one of the most important mythological emperors of China of the pre-Xia period (27th to 23rd centuries B.C.). Huang Di is reputed to have been born in 2704 B.C. and to have begun his role as emperor in 2697 B.C. He is credited with a tremendous victory against unspecified "barbarians" in a battle near today's Shanxi. The victory won him leadership of tribes throughout the Huanghe (Yellow River) plain. He is most often presented as a wise leader who sought to teach the virtues of peace and law to his subjects. Many legends hold that upon his death he became immortal.

Yellow Turbans: The Yellow Turbans were a Chinese secret society whose uprising, the Yellow Turban Rebellion (A.D. 184–204), contributed to the upheaval during the final decades of the Han dynasty (206 B.C.–A.D. 220). The rebels, led by Zhang Jue (sometimes pronounced Zhang Jiao), a Daoist diviner and founder of the Road to Universal Peace sect (Taiping Dao), was dissatisfied with the government of the Han and secretly plotted rebellion. Zhang Jue was killed in 184, but the rebellion and the subsequent outbreaks of violence on the part of renegade Yellow Turban leaders were partly responsible for the eventual demise of the Han dynasty and the following period of instability known as the Three Kingdoms (220–265).

Yin Dynasty: Another name for Shang dynasty (c.1554–1045).

Yongzheng (1678–1735): The fourth son of Kangxi and the third emperor of the Qing dynasty, he reigned from 1723 to 1735.

A vigorous ruler, Yongzheng reformed the Qing tax system and bypassed the slow-acting bureaucracy to establish a cabinet of grand secretaries he used to manage imperial military campaigns along the northwest frontier. His son, the emperor Qianlong, institutionalized this small, responsive agency as the Grand Council.

Yuan Shikai (Yuan Shih-k'ai, 1859–1916): As commander of the imperial North China Army, Yuan helped bring down the Qing dynasty in 1911 and 1912 after professing initial loyalty to the dowager empress Cixi. On Sun Yat-sen's invitation, he became the first president of the republic in 1912.

Yuan choked off democratic expression, dissolved the elected parliament, and set himself up as dictator. In 1915, he announced his own ascension as emperor but backed off in the face of a firestorm of opposition.

Zeng Guofan (1811–1872): This Confucian soldier-official created and commanded the Hunan provincial army—the Xiang Army, named for the river that runs through the region—that captured Nanjing in July 1864, bringing the 13-year Taiping Rebellion to a close.

Zeng later played an important role in the Qing Self-Strengthening Movement, particularly in military affairs. He vigorously promoted the spread of modern weapons technology, using his protégé Yung Wing, the first Chinese graduate of an American university (Yale, 1854), to purchase machine tools and arms in the United States.

As a means to progress, he called for the rebuilding of schools and the re-establishment of a strict Confucian curriculum. He himself exemplified Confucian ideals of discipline and loyalty to the end of his life.

Zhang Chunqiao (1917–1991): He headed the Communist Party in Shanghai and became a close ally of Jiang Qing, Mao Zedong's wife, during the Cultural Revolution.

Brought to trial as a member of the Gang of Four in 1980, accused of bringing about the deaths of thousands, Zhang was convicted and sentenced to death on January 25, 1981. He was later reprieved and held in prison.

Zhang Zhidong (1837–1909): A soldier and official, governor of several provinces, he played an important role in the Self-Strengthening Movement of the late Qing as a developer of textile mills, arsenals, and railroads.

Zhang introduced the catchphrase "Chinese learning for the essentials, Western learning for practical applications"—usually abbreviated as the *ti-yong* idea from the Chinese words for "essence" and "practical use."

Zhao Ziyang (1919–): A protégé of Deng Xiaoping, a secretary of the Chinese Communist Party in Guangdong in the 1960s, he rose to become China's premier and then party secretary-general in the mid-1980s.

Known as a supporter of economic reform and expanded contacts with the West, Zhao was stripped of his posts in 1989. He had supported mass student demonstrations in Beijing in April 1989, the run-up to the violent climax in Tiananmen Square in June, and lost his job as secretary-general as a result.

Zheng He (1371–1435): Zheng was a Muslim court eunuch from Yunnan who was selected by the Ming emperor Yongle to be commander in chief of a series of missions to the "Western Oceans." He first set sail in 1405 in charge of sixty-two ships and 27,800 men. The fleet visited Southeast Asia and India over the course of a two-year journey, returning to China in 1407. Zheng set sail to India again that same year and once more in 1409 before journeying to Aden and the Persian Gulf in 1413 and 1417. A sixth voyage took place in 1421 to Southeast Asia, India, Arabia, and Africa. During the course of his last voyage in 1431, seven Chinese visited Mecca. Zheng returned from his last trip in 1433 and died in 1435.

The Ming empire never capitalized on these journeys commercially, and many scholars believe them to be merely exercises in vanity for Zheng's royal supporter, Yongle. However, some historians argue that Zheng's explorations encouraged many other Chinese to emigrate and therefore indirectly contributed to the growth of Chinese immigrant communities of Southeast Asia and to the accompanying trade benefits, which lasted until the 19th century.

Zhou, King of Shang (1154–1111 B.C.): According to traditional accounts, the last king of the Shang dynasty, Zhou lost his empire due to his immense cruelty and debauched sexual relationship with Daji, his favored concubine. His ostentatious Deer Palace was built through levying harsh taxes upon his people. History records that when King Wu, ruler of Zhou, a principality in the valley of the Wei, overthrew his empire, Zhou set fire to his palace and threw himself into the flames. Other sources, however, report that Wu had Zhou beheaded in approximately 1045 B.C. after the battle of Muye, north of the Yellow River, to found the Zhou dynasty of c.1045–256 B.C.

Zhou, King Wen of (12th or 11th century B.C.): Wen was ruler of Zhou, a tribal state on the frontier of China. By King Wen's time, the state of Zhou had begun to threaten the Shang dynasty (c. 1554–1045 B.C.). As a result, he was imprisoned by Zhou, the last Shang ruler for some years. (Please note that the name for the state of Zhou and the king Zhou of Shang are written differently in Chinese but are spelled in exactly the same way in the standard Pinyin romanization system.) During this time, Wen is said to have written the Confucian classic the *Yijing* (*I Ching*, or Book of changes). Wen was freed in exchange for a beautiful girl, a fine horse, and four chariots. His son, Wu, overthrew the Shang and the debauched King Zhou about 1045 B.C. and founded the Zhou dynasty (1045–256 B.C.). Because of his writings and his lifelong avocation of peace and justice, Confucian historians present Wen as a model king.

Zhou, King Wu of (12th century B.C.): Founder of the Zhou dynasty (1045–256 B.C.) and son of sage King Wen of the state of Zhou, Wu crushed the last Shang ruler, King Zhou of Shang and thus brought an end to the Shang dynasty (c. 1554–1045 B.C.). After establishing his own dynasty, Wu consolidated his empire into a feudal system. He ruled with the assistance of the Duke of Zhou, traditionally thought to be his brother. Like his father, Wu was presented as a model king by Confucius.

Zhou Enlai (1899–1976): One of the most important leaders of the Chinese Communist Party, Zhou became premier of China in 1954 and directed China's foreign policy for thirty years.

Zhou led student protesters in Tianjin in the May Fourth Movement, studied in France, and returned to China a member of the Communist Party. He coordinated the withdrawal strategy from the Jiangxi Soviet in 1934 and participated in the Long March to Yan'an the following year.

Zhou negotiated skillfully for China on Southeast Asian matters in Geneva after World War II. He won praise as a flexible negotiator at the Bandung Conference of non-aligned nations in 1955. He helped arrange U.S. President Nixon's visit to

China in 1972, which opened the door for a normalization of relations between the two countries.

Ordinary Chinese widely credited Zhou with exerting a moderating influence during the tumult of the Cultural Revolution.

Zhu Rongji (1928–): Zhu Rongji began serving as the premier of the State Council of China March 17, 1998. He is a lifelong Communist official whose expertise lies in economic development and planning. Known in the western press as China's "economic czar," Zhu played an instrumental role throughout the last decade of the 20th century in shaping China's fiscal polices.

After joining the Chinese Communist Party in 1949, Zhu served as deputy head of the production planning office of the Northeast China Ministry of Industries. He then worked for the State Planning Commission (1951–1975) and the State Economic Commission (1979–1987). From 1988 to 1991, he served as mayor of Shanghai. In 1991, Zhu was named vice premier of the State Council and in 1993 governor of the People's Bank of China, a post he filled for two years. In 1997, he was named to the Standing Committee of the Politburo before being named premier a year later. In this new capacity, Zhu instituted sweeping reforms that actively promoted economic growth in the country by cutting down China's bloated official bureaucracy, revamping money-losing state enterprises, and initiating a massive cut in the number of state employees. As of November 2002, Zhu Rongji ranked third in power in China after president and Communist Party secretary-general Jiang Zemin (1926–) and retired premier Li Peng (1928–). After November 2002, however, Jiang had handed the position of secretary-general to Hu Jintao (1942–). Since secretary-general is a more powerful position than premier, one could argue that Zhu is now fourth in power. However, since seniority is very important in the amount of influence one can wield in Chinese politics, it is not clear whether Hu really is more powerful than Zhu. Moreover, as of this writing, Zhu Rongji is expected to retire from his position as premier after the National People's Congress meets in March 2003. This presents another level of uncertainty over the future of his political influence in China.

Zhu Xi (1130–1200): Zhu Xi unified and canonized neo-Confucian thought during the Song dynasty (960–1279). His philosophical work and his commentaries on the primary works outlining the teachings of Confucius (551–449 B.C.) reverberated for hundreds of years in both China and Japan.

In 1077, Zhu wrote commentaries in response to two Confucian classics, *Analects* and *Mencius*. He also wrote a series of historical books and political commentaries during this time. Between 1179 and 1181, he restored the White Deer Grotto Academy, which would become a center for neo-Confucianist thinking for the next eight centuries. In 1189, Zhu finished his first commentaries on the Confucian classics *Da xue* (Great learning) and *Zhong yong* (Doctrine of the mean). Zhu's work thus elevated *Da xue, Zhong yong, Mencius*, and the *Analects* to canonical status within China and the made them a cornerstone of the Chinese educational curriculum.

The neo-Confucianist philosophy emphasized logic, consistency, and the observance of philosophical principles set forth by Confucius and his follower Mencius (372–288 B.C.). Zhu held to a dualistic universe of *qi* (matter) and *li* (universal principles). He stressed the importance of ethical conduct and advised his followers to study the Confucian classics with the purpose of living a life guided by rational thought and empirical study of the world. By 1313, his commentaries on the classic Confucian texts had become prescribed for state examinations, and the principles he defined would enable neo-Confucianism to remain the dominant philosophy in China until the 20th century.

Zuo Zongtang (1812–1885): He led his own militia against the insurgents in the Taiping Rebellion of 1851 to 1864 and commanded the Qing imperial armies that quelled Muslim revolts in northwestern China from 1862 to 1873.

Zuo established an arsenal and shipyard in Fuzhou in Fujian Province and held other important governmental posts during the late Qing.

Zuo is also the namesake of the famous Chinese dish "General Tso's Chicken" ("Tso Tsung-t'ang" being the Wade-Giles romanization of his name).

Part IV

Traveling to China

By Victoria Harlow

1. PLANNING A TRIP

Passports and Visas

Foreign visitors are required to have a valid passport and tourist visa before entering China. As this is written, citizens of the United States, Canada, New Zealand, Australia, and the European Economic Community are not required to have a visa if staying in Macao for fewer than twenty days. Otherwise, visas may be obtained from China embassies or consulates and by some China International Travel Service offices (CITS) or the China Travel Service. Visas are usually issued for a three-month stay, which may be extended by applying to the Public Safety Bureau in China.

Air Travel to and from China

The most popular way of traveling to China is by plane. The international airports most frequently used are in Beijing, Guangzhou, and Shanghai. Other international facilities are in Hong Kong, on Lantau Island, and on the island of Macao. Traveling to airports from major cities is easy with limousine or shuttle bus service. Be prepared to pay a departure tax at the airport.

Major Airlines Flying to China from North America:

1. United: 1-800-241-6522
2. Cathay Pacific: 1-800-233-2742
3. Northwest/KLM: 1-800-441-1818
4. Japan Airline: 1-800-525-3663
5. Korean Air: 1-800-438-5000
6. British Air: 1-800-247-9297
7. Air France: 1-800-237-6639
8. Air Canada: 1-800-422-7533

Cathay Pacific offers the "Passport to Asia" fare in their off season (January 15–May 7), which runs under $1,000 for flights from Boston or New York to Hong Kong. This fare includes inter-country air hops as long as Hong Kong remains the hub. Northwest offers the quickest direct flight to Beijing, from the United States. Leaving from Detroit, the flight takes 13 hours and 40 minutes.

Ship and Train Travel to China

Some people arrive in China by boat from Japan or South Korea. Ferry service is available to the mainland from Hong Kong and Macao.

Arrival by train into China is usually on the Hong-Kong–Guangzhou express. Traveling across Russia into China may be done on the Trans-Siberian express.

Student Travel

There are many opportunities for young people and students who are looking for reduced costs. It takes time to plan well and search all avenues for the most inexpensive transport and accommodations packages.

Travel Insurance

Travelers are encouraged to sign up for some inclusive travel insurance before traveling to China. This coverage is readily available through most travel agencies.

Pharmaceutical Drugs

Travelers should take Western medicines with them because some may not be readily available in Chinese drugstores. Prescription medications and painkillers that require a doctor's consent should be brought from home. Some nonprescription drugs are available in large hotels.

Customs

There is a duty-free limit of 2 liters of alcohol, 600 cigarettes, and 0.5 liters of perfume. There is a limit of 1,000 meters of video and 72 rolls of still film. No limit is set on how much foreign currency may be brought into China. However, if the amount exceeds $5,000 U.S., it must be declared. Travelers should save any foreign exchange receipts should they wish to leave with the currency at the end of the trip. Chinese currency may not be taken out of the country.

It is ill advised to become involved with illegal narcotics or pornographic materials. Government officials also frown on bringing in anti-government literature or large amounts of religious reading matter. Punishment for offenders can be severe.

2. ESSENTIAL INFORMATION FOR TRAVELERS WHILE IN CHINA

Currency/Money Matters

One yuan, the main unit of currency, is made up of 10 jiao. One jiao is composed of 10 fen. All of these are called renminbi (RMB), which means "the people's money." Notes come in denominations of 100, 50, 10, 5, 2, and 1 yuan; 1, 2, and 5 jiao. Coins are 1 yuan and 5, 2, and 1 jiao. Prices for items are listed in foreign currencies; however, you are required to pay in renminbis.

Foreign exchange rates fluctuate. Local banks, the Bank of China, hotels, and the *China Daily* newspaper can provide current rates. Cash is exchanged at a slightly lower rate than travelers' checks.

U.S. dollars are widely accepted in China. Many other currencies are accepted as well: from Australia, Austria, Belgium, United Kingdom, Canada, Denmark, France, Germany, Hong Kong, Japan, Malaysia, the Netherlands, Norway, Singapore, Sweden, and Switzerland.

Major credit cards are accepted throughout China at hotels, restaurants, and many stores. However, a cash advance will cost about 4 percent more, and the transaction may take several hours. Five banking days are required to cable money to China. Correct information is vital (passport numbers, etc.), or the transaction could take longer. There are a limited number of ATM machines that accept international credit cards in major cities. The service charge may be steep.

Electricity

Electricity is supplied by 220 volts, 50 cycles AC. Visitors should bring an adapter plug, as various socket sizes are in use.

Emergency Telephone Numbers

Accidents/Ambulance—120

Police—110

Hospitals:

Beijing—Capital Hospital, Dongdanbei Avenue, phone: (010) 651-3226

Canton—No # 1 People's Hospital, 602 Renmin Bei Lu, phone: (020) 83359670

Shanghai—Shanghai #1 People's Hospital, 190 Suzhou Bei Lu, phone: 021-6-324-1000

Mail

The postal service in China is run by the government, and most branches are open from 8 A.M. to 6 P.M. Because this service is understaffed and overused, going through your hotel to mail out material is a better choice. Usually, it takes seven to ten days for mail to reach the United States from China. An express mail service enables mail to reach the United States in three days. Telexes, as well as faxes, are widely used and may be sent or received through a hotel or business center.

Media

The *International Herald Tribune*, the *Wall Street Journal Asia*, *Time*, *Newsweek*, and *Business Week* are available at most hotels in Beijing, Shanghai, and Guangzhou. The English-language newspaper the *China Daily* concentrates heavily on local news within the country. Most hotels offer shows from CNN and BBC World Service television.

Police

Officers of the Public Security Bureau (PSB) dress in green uniforms and are usually helpful to foreigners. If language presents a problem, the local PSB office has English-speaking staff who can help tourists.

Public Health

Visitors to China should have up-to-date vaccinations (especially typhoid and hepatitis) before traveling to China. Visitors should take precautions when consuming food and water, making sure that all food is prepared (washed and cooked) properly and drinking bottled water if unsure of the water source.

Religious Establishments

There are various churches and cathedrals scattered throughout Beijing, Guangzhou, and Shanghai that host Christian services. However, most are in the Chinese language.

Telephones and Telecommunications

China's country code is 86. When calling China from abroad, do not dial the first 0 in the area code.

Areas Codes for Cities:

Beijing—010

Chengde—0314

Chengdu—028

Chongqing—0811

Guangzhou—020

Guilin—0773

Harbin—0451

Hong Kong—5

Kowloon—3

Lhasa—0891

Nanjing—025

Shanghai—021

Suzhou—0512

Ürümqi—0991

Xi'an—029

To dial abroad from China, dial 00 + the country and area codes, and the number.

Country Codes:

Australia—61

New Zealand—64

United Kingdom—44

United States and Canada—1

Operator—114 (local) and 113 (long distance)

More than 500 cities have International Direct Dial (IDD) that will save time making calls abroad. Most major hotels and business complexes have telex, fax, and telegram services available. Tourists should note that the government has the right to monitor telecommunication systems (telephone, fax, and e-mail).

Public telephones may present a problem, depending on what type of coins are used. Telephones located in hotels, restaurants, or business centers are more reliable. Operator-assisted and collect calls cost a bit more.

Time

The time zone is standardized throughout China, which is on Greenwich mean time plus eight hours, and eastern daylight time plus 13 hours. China is 13 hours ahead of New York time, eight hours ahead of London time, and two hours behind Melbourne (Australia) time.

Tipping

Tipping is not widely accepted in most of China. It is accepted more readily in Macao and Hong Kong.

Toilets

The best public toilets are found in Hong Kong and Macao, where Western standards prevail. Throughout most of China, however, toilets are unclean and emit unpleasant odors. Toilet paper is a rare commodity, except in hotels and restaurants.

Transportation Within China

Visitors to China for only a short time will not want to drive. Roads are poorly designed and maintained, and cities have horrendous traffic. Rental cars are available on a very limited basis only in Beijing and Shanghai. It's much easier and safer to rent a car with a driver or to use public transportation. Most hotels and tourist offices have information on either of those options.

Public transportation options include taxis, the metro system, buses, trains, or planes. Street taxis are cheaper than hotel taxis, and dishonest taxi drivers quote unreasonable fares.

Shanghai and Hong Kong have good but limited metro systems. However, lines do not stretch very far into outlying areas. Buses are readily available and reasonably priced but are usually crowded, especially at peak periods. For visitors traveling long distances throughout the country, trains may be the best choice, although they are not known for speed. Accommodations are usually decent (with sleepers and restaurant cars) but vary greatly depending on the particular train. Reservations are suggested and may be made through hotels. Air service in China has improved, with a network of routes throughout the country. Because of the demand, reservations are a must and may be arranged through hotels or local tourist offices.

3. INFORMATION SOURCES FOR VISITORS

United States

U.S. State Department
Washington, D.C.
Phone: 202-647-5225
Fax: 202-647-3000

Chinese Embassy:

Embassy of the People's Republic of China
Room 110
2201 Wisconsin Ave, NW
Washington, DC 20007
Phone: 202-338-6688
Fax: 202-265-9809
www.china-embassy.org

Consulate General (CG) Offices:

Consulate General, People's Republic of
    China
104 South Michigan Avenue, Suite 1200

Chicago, IL 60603
Phone: 312-803-0095
Fax: 312/803-0122

Consulate General, People's Republic of
    China
3400 Montrose Blvd.
Houston, TX 77006
Phone: 713-524-4311
Fax: 713-524-8466

Consulate General, People's Republic of
    China
443 Shatto Place, Ste.
Los Angeles, CA 90020
Phone: 213-807-8088
Fax: 213-380-1961

Consulate General, People's Republic of
    China
520 Twelfth Avenue
New York, NY 10036
Phone: 212-330-7410

Fax: 212-502-0245

Consulate General, People's Republic of
    China
1450 Laguna Street
San Francisco, CA 94115
Phone: 415-674-2900
Fax: 415-563-0494

Chinese Embassies/
Consulates Located
Abroad

Australia:

Embassy of the People's Republic of China
15 Coronation Drive
Yarralumla, ACT 2600
Australia
Phone: (02) 6273-4780 (or 6373-4781)
Consulates: Melbourne, Perth, and Sydney

Canada:

Embassy of the People's Republic of China
515 St. Patrick Street, Ottawa
Ontario KIN 5H3
Canada
Phone: 613-789-3434
Fax: 613-789-1414

Consulate General, People's Republic of
    China
240 St. George Street
Toronto
Ontario M5R 2P4
Canada
Phone: 416-324-6466
Fax: 416-324-6468

Consulate General, People's Republic of
    China
3380 Granville Street
Vancouver
British ColumbiaV6H 3K3
Canada
Phone: 604-736-3910
Fax: 604-734-0704

New Zealand:

Embassy of the People's Republic of China
2-6 Glenmore Street, Kelburr
Wellington
New Zealand
Phone: 011 644 472 1382
Fax: 011 644 499 0419

Consulate: Auckland

United Kingdom:

Embassy of the People's Republic of China
31 Portland Place,
WIN 5AG, London
England
Phone: (020) 79369756

Foreign Embassies in
China

Foreign embassies in China are located
in two areas of Beijing: Jianguomenwai
Compound, east of the Forbidden City, and
the Sanlitun Compound, located northeast
of the Forbidden City.

Embassies located in Jianguomenwai:

Embassy of New Zealand
1 Ritan Dong
2-Jie
Beijing 100600
China
Phone: (86) 010 6532-2731
Fax: (86) 010 6532-4317

Embassy of the United Kingdom
11 Guanghau Lu
Jianguo Men Wai
Beijing 100600
China
Phone: (86) 010 6532-1961
Fax: (86) 010 6532-1937
Consulate: Shanghai

Embassy of the United States
3 Xiu Shui Bei Jie 3
Beijing 100600
China
Phone: (86) 010 6532-3831
Fax: (86) 010 6532-6422

Consulate General (CG) Offices:

Chengdu (CG)
4 Lingshiguan Road
Chengdu 610041
China
Phone: (86) 28 558-3992
Fax: (86) 28 558-3520

Guangzhou
No #1 Shamian Street South
Guangzhou 510133
China

Phone: (86) 20 8188-9811
Fax: (86) 20 8186-2341

Shanghai (CG)
1469 Huai Hai Zhong Lu
Shanghai 200031
China
Phone: (86) 21 6433-6880
Fax (86) 21 6433-4122

Shenyang (CG)
52, Shisi Wei Road
Heping District
Shenyang 110003
China
Phone: (86) 24 322-1198
Fax: (86) 24 282-0074

Embassies Located in Sanlitun:

Embassy of Australia
21 Dongzhimenwai Dajie
Beijing 100600
China
Phone: (86) 010 6532-2331
Fax: (86) 010 6532-6957

Embassy of Canada
19 Dongzhimenwai Dajie
Beijing 100600
China
Phone: (86) 010 6532-3536
Fax: (86) 010 6532-4072

U.S. Chamber of Commerce Offices Located in China

Main Office in Beijing:

China Resources Building, Suite 1903
Building 8
Jianguomen Beijie,
Beijing 10005
China
Phone: (86) 010 8519 1920
Fax: (86) 010 6501-8273

Main Office in Shanghai:

1376 Nanjing Xi Lu
Shanghai Centre-Room 435
Shanghai 200040
China

China National Tourist Offices (CNTO)

To handle complaints from visitors, the China National Tourist Offices (CNTO) are located throughout the country. Within China, the CNTO is also known as the China International Travel Service (CITS). The main branch is in Beijing:

Beijing Tourism Group (formerly CITS)
The Beijing Tourist Building
28 Jianguamenwai
Dajie
Beijing
Phone: 010-6515-8562
Fax: 010-6515-8603

Languages: Chinese, Japanese, and English

There is an English-speaking 24-hour phone line to help tourists with questions or complaints: (010) 6513-0828.

Australia:

China National Tourist Office, Sydney
19th Floor, 44 Market Street
Sydney, N.S.W. 2000 Australia
Phone: (2) 299-4057

Canada:

China National Tourist Office, Toronto
480 University Avenue
80628013, Toronto
Canada M5G1V2
Phone: 416/599-6636
Fax: 416/599-6382

United Kingdom:

China National Tourist Office, London
4 Glentworth Street
London NW1, U.K.
Phone: 020-79359427
020-79359787

United States:

China National Tourist Office, Los Angeles
333 West Broadway, Suite #201
Glendale, CA 91204
Phone: 818-545-7504, 7505
Fax: 818-545-7506

China National Tourist Office, New York

350 Fifth Avenue, Suite 6413
Empire State Building
New York, NY 10018
Phone: 212-760-8218
Fax: 212-760-8809

New Zealand:

There is no China National Tourist Office located in New Zealand.

4. Recommended Travel Guides to China

Business Guide to Modern China, Jon P. Alston and Stephen Yongxin He. East Lansing: Michigan State University Press, 1997.

China, Robert Storey (with Nicko Goncharoff, Damian Harper, Marie Cambon, Thomas Huhti, Caroline Liou, Alexander English). Oakland, Calif.: Lonely Planet Publications, July 1998.

China Guide: Your Passport to Great Travel (Ninth Edition), Ruth Lor Malloy. New York: Open Road Publishing 1996.

Insider's Guide to China, Derek Maitland. Edison, N.J.: Hunter Publishing Inc. 1987.

Passport's Illustrated Travel Guide to China, George McDonald. Basingstoke, England: Passport Books in conjunction with AA Publishing and the Thomas Cook Group Ltd., 1996.

Treasures and Pleasures of China (Best of the Best), Ron and Caryl Krannich. Manassas Park, Va.: Impact Publications 1999.

5. Tourist Sites and Attractions

China has an extraordinary number of tourist attractions. The following list covers just the major sites.

Beijing

Beijing has been the capital of China for more than 500 years. As the nation's political and cultural center, Beijing has a long history, with its earliest section constructed during the Zhou dynasty around 1000 B.C. At the beginning of the 10th century, it became the provincial capital of the Liao dynasty (916–1125). Subsequently, the Jin (1125–1271), Yuan (1271–1368), Ming (1368–1644), and Qing (1644–1911) dynasties all made that city their capital. The diligence and creative ingenuity of the Chinese people through the centuries have resulted in a splendid culture. Numerous sites of historical interest attract visitors from all over the world. The Forbidden City, Tiananmen Square, Temple of Heavenly Peace, the Summer Palace, the Ming Tombs, and the Great Wall are just a few remarkable examples of the traditional art and unique style of Chinese architecture.

Places to Visit

Forbidden City (*Zljin Cheng*)

The Forbidden City (or Imperial Palace) is also called the Palace Museum (*gugong*) by Beijing officials and may be toured daily from 8:30 A.M. to 5:00 P.M. It is located on the north side of Tiananmen Square. For more than 500 years, it was "forbidden," or off limits, for the common people to visit.

Formerly the imperial palace of the Ming and Qing dynasties, it was built between 1406 and 1420 during the reign of Emperor Yong Le of the Ming dynasty. Today, it remains the largest and most complete among the ancient Chinese architectural groups still in existence. The palace occupies an area of 720,000 square meters (7,747,200 square feet) and has more than

9,000 rooms. A 52-meter (172-foot) wide moat and 10-meter (33-foot) high walls surround the entire palace.

The palace consists of two main sections: the outer palace in the south and the inner palace in the north. There are three principal halls in the outer palace: the Hall of Supreme Harmony, the Hall of Middle Harmony, and the Hall of Preserving Harmony. The emperors issued decrees and held other important ceremonies in the halls. The Hall of Supreme Harmony, also known as the Hall of the Gold Imperial Throne, is the highest building in the palace and is where the emperors held their coronations and issued important decrees.

The inner palace encompasses the palace of Heavenly Purity, the Hall of Union, and the Palace of Earthly Tranquillity, as well as a number of eastern and western palaces. The inner palace was for emperors to live in and conduct their daily activities of government and for empresses to keep their bedchambers. Among the numerous palaces, emperors lived in the Palace of Heavenly Purity and had weddings in the eastern chamber of the Palace of Earthly Tranquillity. The Ming and Qing empresses lived in the Palace of Gathering Excellence. They were crowned and celebrated their birthdays in the Hall of Union.

There are four entrances to the palace. The main one facing south is the Wu Men, or Meridian Gate. Wu Men has three gateways; the one in the middle was exclusively for the emperor, and those on the sides were for the court officials and members of the royal family.

In addition to the fine characteristics and unique style of ancient Chinese architecture, the Palace Museum displays many national treasures.

Tiananmen Square

Located in the center of Beijing, Tiananmen Square is the creation of former Communist Party chairman Mao Zedong (1893–1976). During the 1970s, millions of people paraded through the square during the Cultural Revolution. Today, it is used mainly for public ceremonies and as a place for people to meet. The flag-raising ceremony at sunrise (and/or) sunset is impressive as People's Liberation Army (PLA) soldiers march at exactly 108 paces

per minute, with crowds of people watching the drill. It was also, of course, the site of the pro-democracy demonstrations of 1989, which were crushed by the military in June of that year.

Tiananmen Gate (*Tian Anmen*)

Also called the Heavenly Peace Gate, this is a national symbol for China and was built in the 15th century. Mao Zedong announced his People's Republic on October 1, 1949, from this gate, and a huge portrait is displayed of him there today. People visiting the Forbidden City will pass through the gate, and going upstairs affords a commanding view of the entire square.

The Great Hall of the People (*Renmin Dahui Tang*)

This site is commonly called the National People's Congress and is open to the public when the congress is not in session. A banquet room seats 5,000 and an auditorium holds 10,000 people. This Great Hall, located on the western side of Tiananmen Square, is quite impressive.

Summer Palace (*Yuanmingyuan*)

Qianlong, the fourth emperor of the Qing (r. 1736–1799), commissioned architects and designers (including some Jesuit priests) to create the magnificent Summer Palace, the Yuanming Yuan, in a lakeside park near Beijing.

To enforce treaty terms, the British and French in 1860 sent a punitive expedition to Beijing. On the expedition commander Lord Elgin's orders, British and French troops burned the Yuanming Yuan to the ground on October 18, 1860.

The current "Summer Palace" on the outskirts of Beijing is a much smaller (though still very large in absolute terms) palace named Yihe Yuan. This reconstructed version of the Summer Palace was built in 1886 for the enjoyment of Empress Dowager Cixi (1835–1908).

Ming Tombs (*Shisan Ling*)

Located about 50 kilometers (30 miles) northwest of Beijing, this is a site of 13 (of 16) Ming emperors. Dingling, the tomb of

Emperor Wanli (1573–1620), was the first of the tombs to be excavated and renovated for the public to view. Two other tombs, Changling and Zhaoling, have recently been opened to the public. A museum nearby displays artifacts discovered in the tomb. Next door to this, is the Avenue of Animals, which displays huge stone-carved animals (elephants, horses, etc.) and also figures of mandarins.

To attract more tourists to the Ming Tombs site, the Chinese government has added some new facilities, including a golf course, the Dingling Museum (including a Genghis Khan wax figure), an amusement park, an aerospace museum, an aquarium, a campground, a fishing pier, a velodrome, and more. Visitors may take helicopter rides over the tombs and over the Great Wall, which is very close by.

The Great Wall (*Chang Cheng*)

The Great Wall is thought to be the only structure built by humans that is visible from space. Also called Ten-Thousand-Li Great Wall (1 kilometer equals 2 li), it stretches more than 6,300 kilometers (3,915 miles) across 16 provinces, municipalities, and autonomous regions in northern China. Starting in the West from the Jiayu Guan in the Gobi Desert, the Great Wall winds over vast deserts, grasslands, mountains, along a part of the Yellow River, and finally reaches the Yalu River in Heilongjiang Province in the east.

Building of defense walls in China began in the seventh century B.C. In the third century B.C., during the Qin dynasty (221–206 B.C.), they were joined and expanded into the Great Wall. It was rebuilt about 800 years later, in the Ming dynasty, and has stood as it is today.

The Great Wall is 8 meters high (25 feet) and 5 meters (16.5 feet) wide in most places. On the outer edge of the wall, there are 1.2-meter (4-foot) high merlons to shelter the defenders as they shot at the enemy. The inner edge has a parapet. Five soldiers on horseback can ride abreast on the wall.

Most tourists visit the best-developed section of the wall which is located 80 kilometers (128 miles) north of Beijing in Badaling, where a cable car was recently added to improve traffic flow. The Great Wall Circle Vision Theater opened in 1990, enabling tourists to view a 15-minute film projected on the wall of a 360-degree amphitheater. There is a small entrance fee, but it includes admission into the China Great Wall Museum.

Another viewing spot for the wall is a newer section (and not as crowded as Badaling) that lies 100 kilometers (60 miles) northeast of Beijing in Mutianyu. Walls in this area are steeper, and there is also a cable car to ride.

The Temple of Heaven (*Tiantan*)

Also called Tiantan Park, this massive walled complex is one of Beijing's most famous temples. Its Ming-style architecture, with blue-tiled roofs and surrounded by pavilions, makes it is a popular tourist attraction. Built in the 15th century, this lasting symbol of Beijing has been restored to its original appearance. It is open to the public on a daily basis.

Natural History Museum (*Ziran Bowuguan*)

The largest museum of its kind in China houses four main exhibition halls focusing on human evolution, flora, fauna, and ancient fauna. There is a small admission fee to the museum, which is open daily. It is located in the Tianqiao area, just north of Tiantan Park's west gate.

Chinese Revolution History Museum (*Zhongguo Geming Lishi Bowuguan*)

The largest museum in Beijing is actually two museums in one—the Museum of History and the Museum of the Revolution. Though the captions for the exhibits are only in Chinese, visitors can request an English-language translation to carry with them while visiting the museum. The museum has five areas of particular interest: the beginning of the Chinese Communist Party (CCP) (1919–1921), the first civil war (1924–1927), the second civil war (1927–37), resistance against Japan (1937–1945), and the third civil war (1945–1949). The Museum of History has artifacts and cultural relics (some copies) dated from the year zero to 1919 categorized into subject collections such as ancient weapons, inventions, and ancient Chinese musical instruments. The museum is open daily.

Lama Temple (*Yonghe Gong*)

This is the most picturesque temple in Beijing, with colorful gardens, tapestries, and fine woodwork. Outside the Tibetan region, the Lama Temple is the most important Tibetan Buddhist temple in China. In 1949, the temple was named a major historical site, and an extensive restoration was completed in 1979. Today, novices from Inner Mongolia study the Tibetan language and the practices of the Yellow Sect within the temple. It is open daily, but photography is forbidden in the inner temple buildings.

Great Bell Temple (*Dazhong Si*)

This houses the largest bell in China (at more than 46 tons). Cast in 1946, it is engraved with Buddhist sutras, totaling more than 227,000 Chinese characters. The Bell Tower was constructed in 1733. To haul the enormous bell from the foundry to the tower, a shallow canal was dug. This enabled the bell to be transported by sled when the canal froze in winter.

There are other halls and temples on the property of the monastery that are open daily and may be reached along the northwestern part of the third ring road in Beijing.

Marco Polo Bridge (*Lugouqiao*)

Made of gray marble, the Reed Moat Bridge, also known as the Marco Polo Bridge, has more than 250 marble railings supporting nearly 500 carved stone lion figures. It was first constructed in 1192 and has been modernized slightly through the years. Although the bridge was mentioned in Marco Polo's travel narrative, its fame in history dates from the Marco Polo Bridge Incident in 1937. Chinese and Japanese soldiers clashed nearby, providing Japan with the pretext to attack and take over the city of Beijing.

Yangtze River (*Chang Jiang*) and Chongqing

The Yangtze River, also known as the Water of Gold, is the longest river in China and the third longest river in the world. Starting from the Tangulashan Mountains in (southwest) Qinghai, it runs through Tibet and seven Chinese provinces before it ends at the East China Sea north of Shanghai, covering 6,300 kilometers (3,780 miles). The Yangtze River basin encompasses a quarter of available land in China, and the river supplies hydroelectric power and irrigation water. It also drains away much of the human and industrial waste created in nearby areas. Numerous commercial vessels use this main artery. There are many scenic attractions along its banks that can be viewed from tour boats leaving from the city of Chongqing.

The largest city in Sichuan Province, Chongqing is one of China's most picturesque cities. It lies on a narrow peninsula where the Jialing and Yangtze Rivers meet, amidst massive hills in the surrounding countryside. Many of the downriver boat cruises begin in Chongqing at Chaotianmen Dock, a busy riverside tourist spot. A steamer ride down the Yangtze from Chongqing to Wuhan is scenic and popular. At first, the shore is cluttered with factories, but after a short while, the green countryside comes into view. Visitors should reserve passage two to three days ahead of time from one of the tourist bureaus in China. There are a variety of accommodations available when taking a cruise on the river, from first- to fifth-class cabins. While en route, boats make frequent stops at cities and towns along the way. Passengers have time to disembark and eat at on-shore restaurants or do some sightseeing. Most cruises last two to three days.

Places to Visit in Chongqing and Along the Yangtze River

Chongqing Museum

Open daily, this museum houses relics from ship burials, Han dynasty (206 B.C.–A.D. 220) tomb remnants, and dinosaur skeletons discovered near Chongqing.

Northern Hot Springs

The waters from this thermal springs complex, located within a park, may be enjoyed in a public pool or privately. Visitors may view a Buddhist Temple founded in 1432. It is open daily.

Pipashan Park

Resting high above the Chongqing peninsula, Pipashan Park provides a commanding view of the city as well as the Yangtze River. Tourists may visit teahouses, pavilions, and a few amusement areas. The park is open daily.

Fengdu Ghost City

Pingdu Shan Mountain is commonly known as Ghost Mountain, with temples and pavilions all along its rugged hillsides. A pagoda rises on Shiboazhai Rock, on Jade Seal Hill.

Yunyang Zhang Fei Temple

Celebrated statues adorn galleries with multi-colored lamps, giving this temple a magical appearance, especially in the evening. It is usually a crowded area, with a steep approach to the temple that requires caution when going up stairways (with no railings).

Fengjie

Fengjie was the ancient capital of Kui during the Warring States era (480–222 B.C.) and is an interesting town to visit.

Baidicheng (White King Town)

This was the capital of the Western Han dynasty's White King and is a popular tourist attraction along the river.

Three Gorges

The Three Gorges is considered to be the most scenic site on the Yangtze River. From Fengjie (Sichuan Province) in the west to Yichang (Hubei Province) in the east, the 200-kilometer (124-mile) long passage is divided into three gorges: Qutang in the west, Wu in the middle, and Xiling in the east. Mountains and cliffs along the riverbanks rise as high as 1,500 meters (4,920 feet) and overlook the narrow river, which is fewer than 100 meters (328 feet) wide. There is a so-called Small Three Gorges on the Daning River, a tributary of the Yangtze and joining the main river at Wushan between the Qutang Xia and the Wu Xia gorges. The Small Three Gorges has an even narrower river surface and steeper mountains on the riverbanks.

Yangtze Dam Project

In 1919, Sun Yat-sen (1866–1925) first suggested creating a dam on the Yangtze River. Today, the expansive plan known as Three Gorges Project is scheduled for completion in 2013, with costs estimated at more than $70 billion. A 600-kilometer (360-mile) reservoir will be created, flooding the gorges along with 30,000 hectares of farmland. More than 1 million residents will be relocated from 300 towns along the route. Many residents and people around the world are concerned about the environmental impact of the dam. It promises to supply 10 percent of the electricity needed for China.

Yueyang

Some passengers leave the Yangtze River cruise at this point, where they can connect to a train at Changsha that heads farther south. Yueyang is known for the Tang dynasty (618–907) Yueyang Pavilion and the immense Dongting Lake.

Wuhan

The capital of Hubei Province, Wuhan is usually the starting or ending point for riverboat excursions. The Guiyuan Temple dates from the Ming period and is one of the 10 largest temples in all of China. Located on Cuiweiheng Road (south of the railway station), this temple houses 500 statues of Buddha in the Hall of the Five Hundred Luohan. It is open daily. Another popular attraction is the Hubei Provincial Museum. The collection includes 20,000 relics from the 2,400-year-old tomb of Marquis Yi of Zeng, in Suzhou. Excavated items include gold, bronze, jade, and lacquerware objects. The museum is located on Donghu Road and is closed on Mondays.

Sichuan Province and Chengdu

Located in west central China, Chengdu is the capital of Sichuan Province, one of the largest and most heavily populated (84 million people) provinces in China. Chengdu is also an administrative, educational, and cultural center. Tourists will see a fairly prosperous and fashionable city, with large department stores with an array of electronic goods for sale, as well as street vendors, basket makers, and cobblers adorning the busy streets. Chengdu is known as the home of China's endangered pandas.

Places to Visit

Chengdu Zoo (*Chengdu Dongwuyan*)

Located 6 kilometers (3.5 miles) northeast of the city, this zoo houses more than 200 species of animals, including golden-haired monkeys. Most people stop here to see the giant black-and-white pandas. Red pandas may also be viewed. In 1995, a Giant Panda Research Base was opened to the public. It is located about 3.5 miles north of the zoo, and about a dozen panda bears reside there for breeding purposes. The bears' most active time is when they are eating, from 8:30–10:00 A.M. Most other times, they are resting or asleep. The zoo is open daily.

People's Park (*Renmin Gongyuan*)

Although this park is located within the bustling city, it is away from the crowds and is a quiet place to relax. The People's Teahouse (*Renmin Chaguan*) is a popular lakeside spot for a bite to eat. It is open daily.

River Viewing Pavilion Park (*Wangjiang Lou*)

In honor of Tang dynasty poet Xue Tao, who loved bamboo, this park houses a pavilion displaying more than a hundred varieties of bamboo from around the globe. Located in the southeastern part of Chengdu, the park is open daily.

Sichuan Provincial Museum (*Sichuan Sheng Bowuguan*)

The history of Sichuan is depicted on murals and frescoes from ancient times through the 20th century. Highlights include calligraphy from the Ming dynasty and tiled murals of Mao Zedong's Long March through Sichuan. The museum is located at the junction with Nan Yihuan Road and is open daily.

Zhaojue Temple (*Zhaojue Si*)

Located near the zoo, this temple dates from the seventh century Tang dynasty. Modernized through the years, the temple now includes waterways and lush vegetation. However, the building fell into disrepair during the Cultural Revolution. It has since been restored, with a restaurant on the premises and a teahouse next door. The temple is open daily.

Wenshu Monastery (*Wenshu Yuan*)

Dating back to the Tang dynasty, this is the biggest and best-preserved Buddhist monastery in Chengdu. It was formerly named the Xinxiang Temple, after a Buddhist monk who resided there in the 17th century. The monastery is decorated with ornate relief carvings, and it remains a popular and active house of worship. It is open daily.

Monastery of Divine Light (*Baoguang Si*)

Various Buddhist monasteries have been located on this site over the last 1,900 years. Several have been destroyed by war. The current building, erected in 1671, contains more than 500 Buddha representations, a Tang pagoda (13 stories high) and numerous stone carvings. The monastery is open daily.

Temple of Marquis Wu (*Wuhou Ci*)

This temple is named for a marquis whose real name was Zhu Geliang, a prominent statesman of the third-century Three Kingdoms period, who is still honored each day by the monks who reside here. Also called the Wuhou Temple, it is open daily.

Leshan (*Leshan*)

Once a quiet, obscure city in Sichuan Province, Leshan has attracted more tourists in recent years.

Grand Buddha (*Dafo*)

Modeled into the face of a cliff overlooking the Dadu and Min Rivers, this is one of the largest Buddhas in the world, measuring 71m high (234 feet). A Buddhist monk, Haitong, began carving this Buddha in the year A.D. 713, hoping its presence would protect boaters on the river. Unfortunately, Haitong died before he could complete his project, which was finished in 803.

Wuyou Temple (*Wuyou Si*)

On the way to the Grand Buddha, you will pass the Wuyou Temple, a monastery dating back to the Tang dynasty. It offers superb views along with some interesting paintings and artifacts. The temple is known for its 1,000 terra-cotta soldiers, each with a different facial expression. There is also a vegetarian restaurant on the premises.

Oriental Buddha Park (*Dongfang Fodu*)

This park displays 3,000 Buddhist figures and statues collected from many Asian countries throughout the years.

Mahaoya Tomb Museum (*Mahaoyamu Bowuguan*)

This museum houses an interesting collection of tombs and relics beginning with the Eastern Han dynasty (A.D. 25–220).

Thousand Buddha Cliffs (Jiajiang Qianfoyan)

Just north of Leshan and west of the Jiajiang railroad station, more than 2,400 Buddhas that date back as early as A.D. 25 are carved into the cliffs. In spite of time and the Cultural Revolution, the carvings remain in decent shape.

Guangdong Province (Guangzhou and the South)

Located in the southern part of the country, on the delta of the Pearl River, Guangzhou is today a prosperous and important city in China. The city has a population of around 4 million people. Serving as the capital of Guangdong Province, it is also an economic development center for the Pearl River Delta that encompasses Hong Kong, Macao, and other nearby areas. Guangzhou is the ancestral home of many Chinese now living abroad, who have helped stimulate the area's political and economic growth in recent decades.

Places to Visit in Guangzhou

The Temple Tour

This begins at the market area from which you can travel north along Haizhu Zhonglu, running parallel to Renmin Road. Here you will see the Daoist temple known as the Five Genies Temple. Its history goes back 2,000 years, and it tells the story of five rams and celestial beings that appeared at Guangzhou's beginning.

Other temples include the Bright Filial Piety Temple, one of the oldest in the city of Guangzhou. There is also the Temple of the Six Banyan Trees with its nine-story Flower pagoda (the tallest in the city). The Guangdong Antique Store at the Guangxiao Temple displays and sells Tang horses, camels, and human figurines.

Guangzhou Zoo (*Guangzhou Dongwuyuan*)

One of the largest zoos in China houses more than 200 kinds of animals, including pandas. It is open daily and is located on Xianlie Road.

Conghua Hot Springs (*Conghua Wenquan*)

Located in the mountains northeast of Guangzhou, this hot springs resort is a popular and relaxing tourist attraction. You may drink or swim in the pools, located at numerous hotels in the region.

Lotus Mountain (*Lianhua Shan*)

What was previously a stone quarry is now an impressive mountain of weathered holes and granite, providing interesting walkways for hikers. Improvements through the years include lotus-filled pools and pavilions. It's best to visit during the week as it is crowded on the weekends.

Mausoleum of the 72 Martyrs (*Huanghuagang Qishi'er Lieshi Mu*)

Created in 1918 to honor Sun Yat-sen's attempt in 1911 to oust the Qing dynasty, this monument was funded by contributions from Chinese people all over the world. Their names appear on the monument today, along with a miniature replica of the Statue of Liberty, symbolizing democratic beliefs. The mausoleum is open daily and is located on Xianli Nanlu Road.

Yuexiu Park and Guangzhou (Municipal) Museum

Set amid foliage and artificial lakes, Yuexiu Park and Guangzhou (Municipal) Museum are in the Central District's Jeifang North Road. It is the largest park in Guangzhou and contains the Zhenhai Tower, a red wooden pagoda of five stories in the form of a rectangular pagoda. It is all that remains of the ancient city wall of Guangzhou. Standing on its balconies, one can see right over the city. It houses the Guangzhou City Museum, with displays of scrolls, porcelain, and other artifacts of the city from the Neolithic Age until World War II. West of the tower is the Sculpture of the Five Rams, an ornate scene depicting the legendary founders of Guangzhou (also called the City of Rams or Goat City).

Sun Yat-sen Memorial Hall

Located south of the park, this building served as Sun Yat-Sen's dwelling when he became president of the Republic of China in 1912.

The Peasant Movement Institute

This modern monument can be viewed at 42 Zhonghan Silu. It was originally a Confucian temple, but in 1926, Mao Zedong used it as a training center for followers (including Zhou Enlai [1898–1976]) who helped to carry out his Communist revolution.

Next to the Peasant Movement Institute is the Exhibition Hall of the Revolution. It houses many historical photos and materials from the Communist revolution, focusing on Guangzhou and key people involved, including Mao Zedong and Zhou Enlai.

Shamian Island

Joined by two bridges to the Pearl River waterfront, Shamian Island lies in the southern part of Guangzhou. In this quieter part of the city, some Victorian-style buildings still remain from the Opium Wars, when French and British traders as well as taipans (powerful businesspeople) built warehouses, dwellings, and business headquarters soon after the British victory. Throughout the year, crowded bazaars thrive and offer tourists a variety of products for sale, from live snakes, fish, and other creatures to fresh fruits and vegetables.

Cultural Park

Northeast of Shamian Island, the Cultural Park opened in 1956. This expansive playground of Ferris wheels, skating rinks, and arcades comes alive each evening for tourists and residents. One nightly highlight is the open-air chess tournament, which draws thousands of spectators.

Foshan

Throughout Foshan, located 27 kilometers (17 miles) southwest of Guangzhou, there are a number of notable ceramics and crafts establishments. The Foshan Folk Art Research Society displays lanterns and brick carvings, and the Shiwan

Artistic Pottery and Porcelain Factory has weavers spinning silk and potters creating ceramic miniatures. There is also an ancestral temple displaying some innovative architecture, with ceramic figures and animals carved into the crests of the roofs.

Xiamen (*Amoy*) and Fujian Province

The mountainous province of Fujian is located on the southeast coast of China. Its capital is Fuzhou. Although it is not a key tourist destination, this coastal province does offer some nice cultural attractions. It is bounded on the west by the Wuyi Mountains, which have been a Buddhist retreat since the days of the Tang dynasty. Dozens of monasteries were constructed, some of which still stand. Dahongpao tea is grown in this region, which is a leading producer of Fujian teas.

Founded as a major seaport during the Ming reign, Xiamen is an island joined to the mainland by a long causeway. It is the site of an international airport.

Places to Visit

Nanputuo Temple (*Nanputuo Si*)

A three-hour ride up the coast from the waterfront district in Xiamen brings you to the city of Quanzhou and this Tang dynasty temple. Redone by the Manchu Qing, the building houses many Buddhist figures and other deities. Next to the Nanputuo Temple is Xiamen University.

Kaiyuan Monastery

Located in Quanzhou and formerly known as the Lotus Monastery, this building was constructed in 686 during the Tang reign. There are many Buddhist images as well as bas-relief carvings resembling Egyptian pharaonic art. Behind the monastery is the Museum of Overseas Communications History with maps from great ocean voyages and relics from ocean-sailing vessels dating back to the Song dynasty (960–1279).

Gulang Yu (*Gulangyu*)

A five-minute boat or ferry trip enables visitors to reach the neighboring island of Gulangyu, where they may climb Sunlight Rock, the highest peak on the island, or visit Xiamen Seaworld, a marine attraction.

Hainan Island

China's second largest island, Hainan covers 33,990 square kilometers (13,124 square miles) with a mixture of beaches, lush vegetation, rice fields, and mountainous regions. In the commercial center of Haikou there is a popular open market district with a variety of items for sale. Near Xinglong, there is an Indonesian Village designed for tourists with singing performances, snake acts, and complimentary native Xinglong coffee. In the southern port of Sanya, there are many fine beaches.

This island is also of interest to foreign investors. In the past 10 to 15 years, it has become a targeted economic zone to attract overseas (Chinese and foreign) businesses. There are a number of naval and military bases on the west coast of the island.

Guangxi Province

Located in southern China, this province has more than 45 million residents. Guilin, located on the banks of the Li River, is a popular tourist destination. Its landscapes and scenery have been depicted on Chinese art or in poetry for centuries. Nanning is the provincial capital.

Places to Visit

Li River

This waterway connects Guilin to Yanshou, passing picturesque villages and hillside foliage. Tour boats are usually crowded as they depart from Guilin each morning from the Yu Gui Hotel for the trip down the Li River.

Solitary Beauty Peak (*Duxiu Feng*)

Commanding views of Guilin, the Li River, and the surrounding hills reward the effort made climbing to the top of this peak. There once was a palace, built by a

Ming emperor in the 14th century, at the bottom of the peak. The palace is now gone, but the original gate remains. A teacher's college is now on the site of the original palace.

Seven Star Park (*Qixing Gongyuan*)

The name of this park is derived from the configuration of the Great Bear constellation. Traveling here by boat will enable you to see many floating restaurants, waterfront hotels, bazaars, and gambling spots along the route.

Reed Flute Cave (*Ludi Yan*)

Located on Ludi Road at Yujiazhang 14 kilometers (9 miles) northwest of Guilin, this cave has many colorful rock formations and stalactites, with multicolored lighting.

Thousand Buddha Cave (*Qianfo Dong*)

Located on Fubo Hill (on the bank of the Li River, west of Duxiu), this popular attraction has many fine carvings of Buddha from the Tang and Song dynasties. Wind Cave is another interesting attraction nearby.

South Park (*Nan Gongyuan*)

Located in the southern section of Guilin, this park is supposedly named after an alleged immortal who lived in the caves.

Banyan Lake (*Rong Hu*)

Located on the western side of Guilin, this body of water is named after an 800-year-old banyan tree that still graces the shore. This lake is in an especially nice area of Guilin.

Fir Lake (*Shan Hu*)

Attractive scenery makes this a popular place for tourists, locals, and especially hikers.

Yangshuo (*Yangshou*)

This city is about an hour's ride from Guilin. Nearby, picturesque villages surrounded by rivers and hills are among the prettiest in all of China.

Yangshuo Park (*Yangshou Gongyuan*)

Located in the western part of town, this park's attractions are Man Hill (Xiling Shan), which resembles a young man bowing to a young woman, depicted by Lady Hill (Xiaogu Shan). Moon Hill is south of the Jingbao River in Yangshuo. Close by are several caves worth seeing: Black Buddha Caves, New Water Caves, and Dragon Caves. Guided tours are available for both Moon Hill and the caves. Some charge an entrance fee.

Wuzhou (*Wuzhou*)

Part of Guangxi Province, this city is on the route from Yangshuo and Guangzhou to Hong Kong. There are a few interesting sites, if you are traveling on this route.

Snake Repository (*Shecang*)

The largest collection of live snakes in the world includes species from around the globe as well as other Chinese provinces.

Sun Yat-sen Park (*Zhongshan Gongyuan*)

This is China's first memorial hall to honor the founder of the Republic of China. It was built in 1928.

Western Bamboo Temple (*Xizhu Yuan*)

Forty Buddhist nuns live in this temple, located in the northern section of Yangshuo. It offers a vegetarian restaurant, open for breakfast and lunch. Hours are irregular, so it's best to arrive early in the day.

Zhejiang Province and Hangzhou

One of the smallest provinces in southeastern China, Zhejiang has always been one of the most affluent regions. Its capital, Hangzhou, is often called the tourist capital of China; it and Guilin are China's two most popular tourist cities. This coastal province has 18,000 islands. From its inception, Hangzhou has always been a thriving city, with Marco Polo commenting in the 13th century that it was "one of the most splendid cities in the world." It suffered greatly during the Taiping Rebellion (1851–1864) when the city was reduced to ashes and half a million people died.

Places to Visit

West Lake (*Xihu*)

There are numerous scenic areas around this extraordinary freshwater lake, bordered on three sides by hills. The eastern shore is highly developed for tourism; the western side is fairly quiet and peaceful. The banks are filled with temples and festive gardens.

Grand Canal (*Da Yunhe*)

There are two boats each day that offer a leisurely sail on the Grand Canal from Hangzhou and Suzhou. The 1,800-kilometer (1,080-mile) canal stretches along the northern and eastern sections of Hangzhou, along Huancheng Bei Road and Huancheng Dong Road. In earlier times, the canal offered the only practical means of transportation in this region for common people, as well as emperors.

Zhejiang Provincial Museum (*Zhejiang Bowuguan*)

This museum is situated on the largest island on West Lake, Solitary Hill Island (Gushan). The structures were originally part of Emperor Qianlong's eighteenth-century holiday palace. Today the collection focuses on natural history, including whale and dinosaur skeletons.

Six Harmonies Pagoda

Named after the six codes of Buddhism, this 60-meter (198-foot) high octagonal pagoda was once a lighthouse said to possess mythical powers that controlled the fierce tides on the Quintang River each September. Today, it's a pleasant attraction with terraces adorned with sculptures and shrines.

Temple of Spiritual Retreat (*Lingin Si*)

This temple dates back to A.D. 326 but has been renovated many times since then. Premier Zhou Enlai protected it during the Cultural Revolution. A 24-meter (79-foot) sculpted Buddha is on display in the Great Hall. Located on Lingyin Road, the temple is open daily.

Hong Kong Island and Macao

A British colony from the mid-19th century, the island of Hong Kong was returned to Chinese sovereignty in July 1997. Hong Kong is a thriving financial center, offering a great deal to tourists and businesspeople. The island itself varies greatly; the north is far more urban than the south. The central region is very mountainous with a large country park.

Macao lies 60 kilometers (36 miles) west of Hong Kong. The 16-square-kilometer (6-square-mile) territory includes two islands (Taipa and Colôane) and a peninsula joined to the mainland by a causeway and two bridges. To reach Macao from Hong Kong, visitors can choose from various kinds of boats and high-speed ferries that operate 24 hours a day. The trip takes one to one-and-a-half hours, depending on the boat.

The Portuguese originally settled here in the mid-1550s, but Macao became part of China in 1999. Nearly all (95 percent) of Macao's residents are Chinese, with the remaining either Portuguese or foreigners. The Portuguese promoted Roman Catholicism among the people of the territory, so Chinese nuns are a common sight.

The highly publicized casinos also attract quite a few tourists. Nearly one-third of Macao's revenues are attributed to gambling run by a government franchise (and local business groups) that oversee eight casinos. Dog racing is held at the Canidrome and horse racing on Taipa Island.

Star Ferry to Kowloon Public Pier and Central-Jordan Road Ferry

The best sea route to and from Hong Kong begins with the busy green-and-white ferries that transport tourists to Kowloon at the Star Ferry Pier in Hong Kong, offering close-up views of the Victoria Harbor waterfront. Along the Kowloon waterfront is a walkway with museums (described below), hotels, and more. It leads to a bus terminal and the Kowloon Public Pier, where boats arrive from Hong Kong.

The Central-Jordan Road Ferry transports visitors to Hong Kong from the mainland on vessels not quite as pretty as the green-and-white ferries people take from Hong Kong. However, they are reliable and the harbor views are still remarkable.

Places to Visit in Kowloon (on the Southern Tip of Mainland China, Facing Hong Kong)

Hong Kong Cultural Centre/Museum of Modern Art

Situated next door to one another on the waterfront at the Kowloon Public Pier are these two interesting attractions, offering a variety of exhibits on China. (They are closed on Mondays.)

Space Museum

This building is next door to the Museum of Modern Art. It has several exhibition halls and a planetarium, with the Space Theatre offering seven shows daily (except Mondays).

Kowloon Park

This popular site, located on Nathan Road, adds more amusements each year and includes a huge swimming pool, complete with waterfalls. It is open daily.

Museum of History

Near the Haiphong Road entrance, this museum houses a collection of relics and photographs on Hong Kong from prehistoric times to the current day. It is open from Tuesday through Saturday. Admission charge.

The Science Museum

Located on the corner of Chatham and Granville Roads, this building displays more than 500 exhibits. Hours vary each day; the museum is closed on Mondays.

Wong Tai Sin Temple

Located in northern Kowloon, this is one of the largest Daoist temples in the area. Built in 1973, it is quite busy and is open daily.

Song Dynasty Village

Although a Disney-like atmosphere prevails here, Chinese life and traditions from the Song dynasty (960–1279) are depicted through various ceremonies, displays, martial arts demonstrations, and a medley of arts and crafts. Performers wear traditional costumes for this attraction, which is open daily and has an admission.

Places to Visit on Hong Kong Island

Victoria Peak/ Victoria Peak Garden

The Peak Tram railway operating on Garden Road takes travelers to the top of the 553-meter (608-yard) high Victoria Peak, located in the northern section of Hong Kong. The view of the city is spectacular, especially at night. There are fountains and a shopping gallery to attract visitors.

Hong Kong Park

This park offers fountains, pools, lush greenery, an aviary, greenhouse, a visual arts center, and an amphitheater. Tai chi exercises are conducted each morning. Situated within the park is the Museum of Tea Ware. The park is located on Supreme Court Road and is open daily.

Tiger Balm Gardens

Located near Happy Valley, on Tai Hang Road, this theme park is also called Aw Boon Haw Gardens. It is filled with pagodas, grottoes, and scenes from Chinese legends. Aw Boon Haw is noted in history as the inventor of the tiger balm medication that was a cure-all cream throughout Asia. The park is open daily, and admission is free.

Fung Ping Shan Museum

Located at the University of Hong Kong, this museum houses a collection of noted Chinese art, arranged in chronological order. There are bronzes, ceramics, and some interesting paintings.

Arts Centre

In Wanchai on Harbour Road, this center focuses on contemporary art, with local and international exhibits displayed throughout the year.

Police Museum

Located on Coombe Road, this museum displays items dealing with the history of the Royal Hong Kong Police Force. Hours vary, and it is closed on Monday. Admission is free.

Hong Kong Convention and Exhibition Center

This colossal building features a seven-story window (the largest in the world). Riding the escalator to the seventh floor offers visitors spectacular views of Hong Kong's harbor. In this building on June 30, 1997, control of Hong Kong was transferred to China.

Museum of Chinese Historical Relics

Located at 28 Harbour Road (first floor) in Wanchai, this museum houses exhibits on Chinese relics and treasures from various archaeological digs. It is open daily, but hours vary so it's best to phone ahead (2827-4692).

Aberdeen

Located on the southern side of Hong Kong, this harbor area is bustling with fishing boats and sampans operated by locals who are happy to take tourists aboard for a floating excursion. There are many interesting sites, several good restaurants, and the Jumbo Floating Restaurant, which provides its own shuttle bus to and from the establishment.

Ocean Park

This extravagant attraction encompasses the world's biggest aquarium, along with various amusement rides. Included in the admission fee to the park is entrance to Middle Kingdom, an amusement area, done in an ancient motif, similar to Ocean Park. To get to Ocean Park, visitors should go to the Star Ferry Terminal on the waterfront in central Hong Kong.

Water World

Located next door to Ocean Park, Water World offers swimming pools, water slides, diving boards, etc. It is open daily during the warm months, but the hours vary.

Shek O

Located on the southeastern coast, this is one of the Hong Kong's finest beaches. Public transportation (trams or buses) is available from various spots in Hong Kong.

Places to visit on Macao

Ruins of St. Paul's

All that is left of this old church are the front and the grand staircase, as the remainder was destroyed in a fire during a devastating typhoon in 1853. Originally designed by a Jesuit priest in 1602, the church was built by Japanese refugees after they were driven from Nagasaki because of their Christian beliefs. Some relics remain and may be viewed at the small museum toward the back of the site.

Monte Fort

Built by Jesuits in the 1600s, this fort sits high on a hill in the center of the island offering a grand view of Macao and also of St. Paul's ruins.

Kum Iam Temple

This Ming-dynasty Buddhist temple, the largest and most historic temple (nearly 400 years old) on Macao, is dedicated to the Queen of Heaven and the Goddess of Mercy. Of the many statues there, one is of Buddha. Another, sitting among 18 wise men, supposedly is Marco Polo.

Camoes Grotto and Gardens

A bust of Luis de Camoes, a 16th-century Portuguese poet, rests in colorful gardens where many Chinese come to play checkers.

Guia Fortress

Resting high atop Guia Hill, within the cannon-lined walls of the fortress, is a small 17th-century church and the oldest lighthouse on the China coast. The fortress dates from the early 1600s and the lighthouse from 1865. This is the highest spot on Macao and offers a commanding view of the scenery below.

A-Ma Temple

The name *Macao* is derived from A-Ma-Gau (the Bay of A-Ma), and means *City of God*. The A-Ma Temple dates back to the Ming dynasty and is located at the southern end of the island. Legend has it that A-Ma, the goddess of sailors, was aboard a ship sailing for Guangzhou and saved it from sinking in a storm. Many other ships that did not allow her to sail with them were lost in the storm. Each year boat people from Macao visit the temple in her memory.

Macao Maritime Museum

A number of interesting boats are exhibited here. They include a *lorcha*, a vessel which used to sail on the Pearl River. Also offered are short boat cruises and a small aquarium.

Grand Prix Museum and Wine Museum

These museums operate on the same site, across from the Kingsway Hotel. On exhibit are several autos that have raced in the Macao Grand Prix, which began in 1954. The Wine Museum offers Portuguese wine history and a taste of the wines themselves.

Taipa House Museum

This fairly new building is housed in Taipa Village, one of the oldest colonial Portuguese villages on Macao. Various items documenting Portuguese culture in the region are on display.

Places to Visit in the New Territories

Taking a guided tour or using public transportation, tourists can view some interesting attractions in this region, located between Kowloon and the Chinese border. On the northwestern coast, the Mai Po Marshes attract birdwatchers. In Tsuen Wan, there are the Yuen Yuen Institute, multiple Daoist temples, and the (Buddhist) Western Monastery. In the hills north of Tsuen Wan, there is another large monastery, Chuk Lam Sim Yuen. Taking a bus from the Tsuen Wan station to the west will bring visitors to Tai Mo Shan, the highest mountain peak in Hong Kong. Heading on to Yuen Long will bring visitors to Kam Tin, where there are interesting little villages with individual entrances dating back to the 16th century. At one village in particular, Kat Hing Wai, elderly Hakka women in local costumes will (for a small fee) pose for photographers.

In the busy city of Shatin is the Temple of the Ten Thousand Buddhas (in reality more than 12,000). The Sai Kung Peninsula remains one of the most unspoiled regions on Hong Kong, and it also has one of the best beaches, at Clearwater Bay.

Place to Visit in the Outlying Islands

Lantau

Although nearly twice the size of Hong Kong, this island has a population of only about 30,000. There are some fine beaches and uncrowded hiking trails. On the western side of the island is Ngong Ping. Here visitors will see the Po Lin Monastery, a fascinating and fairly new building. The biggest outdoor bronze Buddha stands outside the monastery; a vegetarian restaurant is on the premises. On the northern side of Lantau is Tung Chung Fort, housing various relics and cannons from the

1800s. On the northern part of Lantau is the up-beat Discovery Bay, with shopping malls, a golf course, and more. From here, visitors may hike (for about an hour) to Trappist Haven Monastery, an interesting attraction. Most people arrive by ferry at Mui Wo (Silvermine Bay).

Lamma

The second largest outlying island of Lamma offers some excellent beaches, good restaurants, and a busy nightlife.

Cheung Chau

Western residents inhabit much of the island and enjoy its slow pace, small fishing villages, and remote beaches that can only be reached by foot. At the southern end of Cheung Chau, there is a secluded cave, supposedly once the home of the scandalous pirate Cheung Po Tsai.

Shandong (*Shandong*) Province and the Huang He (Yellow River)

Shandong Province lies across the Yellow Sea from Korea. China's second longest river, the Yellow River begins with small tributaries in Qinghai and ends its journey in Shandong as its waters empty into the Bo Hai Sea. Its yellow color comes from silt, which also makes the river difficult to navigate. Named "China's Sorrow," due to the many floods it has suffered throughout the centuries, Shandong has experienced famines, innumerable droughts, and rebellions.

South of the capital city, Jinan, is Qufu, the birthplace of social philosopher Confucius (551–479 B.C.).

Places to Visit

Jinan

Also called the City of Springs, this city was founded in the eighth century B.C. and grew to be a successful commercial center during the Tang dynasty. More than a hundred active springs once lured tourists here, but years of drought have diminished water flow, except during the rainy season in August. The most popular springs are

listed below. Jinan's location makes it a transportation hub within Shandong Province.

Springs

The four main springs are Black Tiger Spring (*Heihuquan*), Pearl Spring (*Zhuquan*), Five Dragon Pond (*Wulongtan*), and Gushing-from-the-Ground Spring (*Baotuquan*). All are open daily and located within walking distance of each other, south of Daming Hu in the center of Jinan.

Daming Lake (*Daming Hu*)

Also called the Lake of Great Brightness, this pleasant spot has willow trees, playgrounds, pavilions, teahouses, and colorful gardens. Located on Daming Hu Road, it is open daily and has an admission charge.

Shandong Provincial Museum (*Shandong Sheng Bowuguan*)

A collection of artifacts from various archaeological digs is housed here. There are Buddhist sculptures, musical instruments, and tomb ornaments; a 4,000-year-old collection of Longshan black pottery; and a treatise on the art of war, created on strips of bamboo, said to be 2,000 years old. The museum, once in the center of Jinan, is now on Qianfoshan Road. The museum is closed on Mondays.

Thousand Buddha Mountain (*Qianfoshan*)

Located next to the Shandong Provincial Museum, this mountain is named for the Buddhist carvings created on the cliffs. The Temple of the Flourishing State (*Xingguo*) at the top of the steep mountain contains more than 50 images of Buddha, ranging from 20 centimeters (1.25 inches) to more than 3 meters (nearly 10 feet) in height.

Tai Shan Holy Mountain (*Taishan*)

Located 50 kilometers (30 miles) south of Jinan in Shandong Province, Tai Shan is known as the mountain of mountains and is the most revered of the five sacred mountains in China. In ancient times many emperors came here to pay homage to Heaven and Earth. The main hall, Tian-shao (Sky Burning) Palace, is one of the three greatest palaces (the other two are Taihe Palace in the Forbidden City and the Dacheng Palace in the Confucian Temple) in China. Many notable figures in Chinese history travelled here to contribute various treasures.

Gansu Province

Another province along the Yellow River is Gansu, located in northern central China. It is a territory of mountains and deserts and has a few interesting sites but is generally not popular with tourists. The capital is Lanzhou.

Places to Visit:

Five Springs Park (*Wuquan Gongyuan*)

A cable car transports visitors to the top of 2,000-meter (6,600-foot) high Lanshan Mountain for some scenic views. At the base of the mountain, an attractive park features temples and waterfalls amid rugged terrain. Located on Jiuquan Road, the park is open every day.

Gansu Provincial Museum

Exhibited here are some fine examples of Neolithic pottery, including the noted Galloping Horse of Gansu, dating back to the Eastern Han dynasty. Located on Xijin Road, near the West Railway Station, the museum is closed on Mondays.

Dunhuang Mogao Grottoes

Dunhuang, in the west of Gansu Province, was the gateway to the Silk Road during the Western Han dynasty (202 B.C.–A.D. 8). The west-east trade brought about the development of Buddhist art in the area around Dunhuang. The Mogao Grottoes, commonly known as Thousand Buddha Cave, are located southeast of Dunhuang. Starting in 366 A.D., the caves were under constant construction over the next 1,000 years. A high level of artistic excellence was achieved in such fields as architecture, sculpture, and painting. The caves have three or four layers and stretch more than 1,600 meters (5,248 feet). Today, 492 grottoes remain, with about 2,100 statues painted in different colors.

Henan Province (Luoyang and Environs)

Henan is one of China's smallest provinces, and the Yellow River intersects its northern tip. Its origins are traced back to the very beginning of Chinese civilization, 3,500 years ago. One city, Luoyang, was founded in 1200 B.C. and is thought to be the eastern terminus of the Silk Road. This province is densely populated and characterized by old-world charm.

Places to Visit:

Longmen Grottoes (*Longmen Shiku*)

The Buddhist cave carvings here are remarkable, with more than 1,352 grottoes and one hundred thousand Buddhist figures. Dating back to the Wei dynasty (494), most of the major carvings are in the Binyang Caves (*Binyang Dong*) and Ten Thousand Buddha Cave (*Wanfo Dong*). Located south of Luoyang, the attraction is open daily, and admission is charged.

Luoyang Municipal Museum (*Luoyang Bowuguan*)

Historical maps and relics, most discovered in tombs, can be found in this museum located on Zhongzhou Road. The museum charges admission and is closed Mondays.

White Horse Temple (*Baima Si*)

Although this building has been renovated many times, the original temple was founded on this site in A.D. 68 by monks who traveled here from India. It is the first known Buddhist temple in China. The temple structures have all been re-created, mainly during the Ming dynasty, and display gateways carved with statues of monks on horses.

Yunnan Province (Kunming and the Environs)

Yunnan, located in the south near the borders of Vietnam, Laos, and Burma, is one of the most popular travel destinations in China. The climate is very tropical. Its capital city, Kunming, has been called City of Eternal Spring. This province is known for its fauna and flora, with more than 2,500 kinds of plants and wildflowers. The province is also home for most of China's minorities.

Places to Visit in and Around Kunming

Bamboo Temple (*Qiongzhu*)

There are 500 Buddhist sculptures here, dating back to the 1880s. Each figure has its own facial expression and performs a different job. Located northwest of the city, the temple is open daily and charges admission.

Golden Temple (*Jindian*)

This Daoist temple, dating back to the Ming dynasty, rests high on a hill 7 kilometers (4.25 miles) northeast of Kunming. Made of copper, the temple is 6.5 meters (21.5 feet) high, and weighs 300 tons. It is open daily, and admission is charged.

Yuantong Temple (*Yuantong Si*)

This thousand-year-old structure is the largest Buddhist temple in Kunming and has been through many renovations. Decorated with flowers and potted plants, the courtyard has a square pond with surrounding walkways and an octagonal pavilion. There is also a vegetarian restaurant near the temple. Open daily, it is located northeast of the Green Lake Hotel, and admission is charged.

Anning Hot Springs (*Anning Wenquan*)

Many tourists visit the hotels and guesthouses to enjoy theses hot spring waters. Buses provide transportation to the springs region, located 44 kilometers (26.5 miles) southwest of Kunming. Some establishments do not allow couples to use the rooms (together), so it's best to call ahead for information.

Lake Dian (*Dian Chi*)

China's sixth largest lake (330 square kilometers [127 square miles]) begins in Kunming's southern countryside and winds its way for 40 kilometers (24 miles), south of the city. On the western shores, there are rugged hillsides adorned with temple structures, and the east has rice paddies and low-lying settlements. There are many attractions around this lake, including Daguan Park (*Daguan Gonguan*), also known as Grand View Park, dating back to the late 1600s. There are boat rides, children's play areas, and the Daguan Tower (*Daguan Lou*), which offers superb views of the lake. Haigeng Park and Yunnan Nationalities Village (*Haigeng Gongyuan/Yunnan Minzucan*) displays sample models of all 26 of Yunnan minority villages. There are many activities, such as song and dance performances throughout the day. Though the attraction illuminates the architecture and customs of the people, the admission is high by Chinese standards.

Stone Forest (*Shilin*)

Located 120 kilometers (72 miles) southeast of the city, the Stone Forest is one of the chief attractions of a visit to Kunming. It is a huge collection of limestone pillars eroded through decades of wind and rain into various shapes. The discovery of marine fossils in the surrounding area indicates this region was once under water. Along the pathways, some of the rock formations have titles such as Baby Elephant, Moon-Gazing Rhino, and Sword Pond. It is open daily, and there is an admission fee for foreigners.

Places to Visit in or Around Xiaguan

Dali

The historical and cultural atmosphere lures tourists to this small, picturesque city, located on the western shores of Er Hai Lake. It is a restful haven away from the crowds; its cobblestone streets and stone buildings are enjoyable, especially on a walking tour. The Dali Museum (*Dali Bowuguan*) houses a small collection of archaeological items and a permanent art exhibition for many noted Yunnan artists. The museum is open daily and charges an admission fee. The Three Pagodas (*Santasi*) rest on a hillside just northwest of Dali. They are some of the oldest buildings still standing in southwestern China, dating back to the mid-ninth century. The buildings are open daily and charge an admission fee.

Places to Visit in and Around Lijiang

Hei Long Tan Park (*Heilongtan Gongyuan*)

Also known as Black Dragon Pool, this park is in the northern section of Lijiang, about 11 kilometers (6.5 miles) north of Kunming. There are groups of Daoist pavilions, colorful walkways, gardens, and a pool filled from the springs in Kunming. There is also a small but interesting botanical garden with camellias, rhododendrons, and more. Open daily, the park charges an admission fee.

Tiger Leaping Gorge (*Hutiao Xia*)

The Yangtze River gushes 16 kilometers (9.5 miles) through the Haba Mountains and the Jade Dragon Snow Mountain through one of the deepest gorges in the world. There are several sensational cliffs and waterfalls here. This site is especially interesting to hikers, who can usually walk the entire area in two days.

Places to Visit in and Around the Xishuangbanna (Banna) Region

Tropical Plant Research Center (*Redai Zuowu Yanjiusuo*)

Located in Jinghong (*Jinghong*), the capital of Xishuangbanna Prefecture, this institute is a popular tourist site. There are more than a thousand types of plant life on display from Yunnan's tropical forests.

National Minorities Park (*Minzu Fengqing Yuan*)

Various exhibits and minority dances are held each Friday and Saturday evening from 7:00–11:00 P.M.

Sanchahe Nature Preserve (*Sanchahe*)

Just north of Jinghong, this is one of four massive forest preserves totaling 1.5 million hectares (3.7 million acres) in the south of Yunnan Province. It's best to ask for a tour guide or a local resident to walk you through the dense jungle.

Manfeilong Pagoda (*Manfeilong Ta*)

Built in 1204, this attraction is located in Damenglong. It features the hallowed footprint left by (the legendary) Sakyamuni, who was supposed to have visited the site that the temple was built on. Each year the Tan Ta Festival is held here (October or November) and attended by large crowds.

Jiangsu (*Jiangsu*) Province (Nanjing, Suzhou, and Wuxi)

Bordering the Yellow Sea in eastern China, this province is often called "the land of fish and rice," for its agricultural abundance. A mixture of towns and cities produce one of the highest levels of industrial output in China. The population is just over 71 million people.

Founded in 900 B.C., Nanjing is a charming capital city with an abundance of maple trees and colorful mums during the autumn months. Nanjing served as the capital of China on two occasions: first, early in the Ming dynasty and, second, for the People's Republic of China early in the 20th century. Still growing, Nanjing is one of China's major cities.

Another popular region is the city of Suzhou, known for its silk production. One of the oldest towns in the Yangtze Basin, Suzhou was once on a major trading route. Named the "Venice of the East" by Marco Polo, it is a city rich in culture, filled with an abundance of colorful gardens and canals.

The Grand Canal runs right through the town of Wuxi with a history dating back 3,000 years, Today it is a busy industrial settlement, but some outlying attractions, especially Lake Tai Hu, are pleasant.

Places to Visit in and Around Nanjing

Ming City Wall

Between 1366 and 1386, 200,000 workers built this defensive wall. Today, two-thirds of the wall is still standing. It is about 12 meters (40 feet) high and 7 meters (23 feet) wide at the top. Each brick used in constructing the wall was stamped with the brick maker's name on it. Bricks came from five different provinces in China. Some of the original 13 Ming City Gates are still in existence, including the Zhonghua Gate (*Zhonghua Men*) in the south.

Ming Palace Ruins (*Minggugong*)

The Forbidden City in Beijing was supposed to have been modeled after this palace, most of which is now gone. The Manchu invasion and the Taiping Rebellion helped destroy the building. All that is left are the Five Dragon Bridges, a gate, and some huge columns from the base of the palace. Open daily, this attraction is on Zhongshan Road. Admission is charged.

Chaotian Palace (*Chaotion Gong*)

Originally built during the Ming dynasty to educate children of Chinese noblemen, it was totally rebuilt in 1866 to add a Confucian temple. The palace, the Flying Cloud Pavilion, and the Imperial Stele Pavilion (both at the same site) together form a center for religious devotion. Also called the Worshipping Heaven Palace, it is used today for a number of activities, including a pottery center. Located on Mochou Road, it is open daily, and admission is charged.

Confucius Temple (*Kong Fuzi Si*)

This temple is located in Fuzimiao, in the southern region of the city. Known as a busy amusement area, this peaceful site is a reminder of China's historical past. Recently renovated, waterside dwellings line the canal, just outside the gate to the temple. Open daily, this attraction is on Gongyuan Road. Admission is charged.

Drum Tower (*Gulou*)

Perched on a traffic circle on Beijing Xi Road, this drum tower was built in 1382. At that time, drums were used to warn of danger or to change night watches. There is only one drum left today. Open daily, the tower charges admission.

Nanjing Museum (*Nanjing Bowuguan*)

Built in 1933, this museum houses artifacts and objects from the Stone Age to the Communist period (1919). There are items from various archaeological digs, porcelain, bricks from the Ming City Wall, and objects from the Taiping Rebellion. The museum, closed on Mondays, is located on Zhongshan Road. Admission is charged.

Sun Yat-sen Mausoleum (*Zhongshan Ling*)

This spectacular 8-hectare (20-acre) site honors the first president of the Republic of China, Sun Yat-sen. His tomb is located at the top of a massive stone stairway, which is 323 meters (1,066 feet) long and 70 meters (231 feet) wide. With white Fujian marble walls and blue-tiled roof, the Ming-style mausoleum displays a combination of colors that symbolizes the (Nationalist) Kuomintang flag (white sun against a blue sky). Located on Zhongshan Guangchang Road, the mausoleum is open daily and charges admission.

Xuanwu Park (*Xuanwu Gongyuan*)

This park centers on a lake. There are boat and barge tours available, along with a children's amusement area, temples, pavilions, and pagodas. The park has some historical significance, as the Ming and Qing dynasty emperors enjoyed this spot for recreation. The main entrance gate is off of Zhongyang Road. It is open daily, and there is an entrance fee.

Nanjing Yangtze River Bridge (*Nanjing Changjiang Daqiao*)

Opened on December 23, 1968, this double-decker road and rail bridge is one of the longest in China—4,500 meters (1,350 feet). Originally, the bridge was to be built with the Soviets. After the Soviets left in 1960 (taking the plans with them), the Chinese had to finish the construction themselves. Until it was built, there was no rail connection from Beijing to Shanghai. The bridge is located in the northwest section of Nanjing, off Daqiao Nan Road.

Places to Visit in and Around Suzhou

Garden of the Master of Nets (*Wangshi Yuan*)

Although this is the smallest of Suzhou's gardens, the detailed elegance throughout the courtyards and pavilions is breathtaking. Observation points such as Pine Viewing and the Moon and Wind Pavilion memorialize the taste of the former owners. Folk dancers and musicians entertain guests during the evening hours as lanterns illuminate the gardens. Many of the gardens in Suzhou have been modeled after this one. Located in the southeastern corner of the old city and open every day, the garden charges admission.

Humble Administrator's Garden (*Zhuozheng Yuan*)

This garden, the second favorite of tourists (after the Garden of the Master of Nets), is located in the northeast corner of the old city. A "humble administrator" laid out this garden in 1522, and then his gambling son lost it. Graceful bridges and stone causeways guide visitors from one display to another through 5 hectares (12.5 acres) of streams, ponds, and islands of bamboo. The garden is open daily and charges admission.

Blue Wave Pavilion (*Canglangting*)

This is one of the oldest gardens in Suzhou, with winding creeks and lush greenery set in rugged terrain. Structures date back to the 11th century, although many have been rebuilt through the years. Originally owned by a prince, it was turned over to Su Zimei, a scholar, who officially named it the Blue Wave Pavilion.

North Temple Pagoda (*Beisi Ta*)

The temple complex dates back to the 10th century. Rebuilt many times, the wooden pagoda is nine stories high and offers a spectacular view of the city and farmlands below. It is the tallest pagoda south of the Yangtze. There is also a teahouse and small garden on the back property. Open daily, it is located in the northern section of the old city on Renmin Road. Admission is charged.

Lingering Garden

Spread out over 3 hectares (7.5 acres), this is one of the largest gardens in Suzhou, with distinctive pavilions, rockeries, and walkways. A 700-meter (2,310-foot) hallway connects the scenic attractions. Hundreds of latticed windows are decorated in various floral patterns, enabling visitors to peer out at colorful plants, water, and rock formations. This garden is located in the northwestern suburbs, on Liuyuan Road, and is open daily. Admission is charged.

Suzhou Silk Museum

The silk industry is centuries old in this region, and this small but educational museum displays the historical and cultural aspects of silk cultivation and its impact on the province. It is located on Renmin Road (near the Humble Administrator's Garden) and is open daily. The museum charges admission.

Tiger Hill

According to legend, a white tiger emerged on this site at the burial of Emperor He Lu in the fifth century. Today, musicians perform at the Tiger Hill Pagoda, which leans from its weight and now must be propped up. Located northwest of Suzhou, it is open daily. Admission is charged.

Places to Visit in and Around Wuxi

Lake Tai Hu

This is one of the largest lakes in China at 2,235 kilometers (1,341 feet) across. Some 90 islands lie within it, and the fishing industry is quite active. The lake supports about 30 kinds of freshwater fish. Various cruises glide visitors over this clear body of water with views of rugged hillsides and colorful fishing boats, junks, and pleasure cruisers. Turtle Head Isle (really a peninsula), on the end of Chongshan Peninsula offers a mirage of attractions and may be reached by monorail.

Li Garden (*Liyuan*)

Practically in Lake Tai Hu, the Lake-Gazing Pavilion looks out directly onto the water. Built in the 1930s, it was refurbished in 1949. The garden is open daily and is located east of the Baojie Bridge.

Plum Garden (*Meiyuan*)

In the spring, the blossoming plum trees here are quite beautiful, but this park is not as elegant as the Li Garden. Kingfishers are seen frequently around the main pool. It is open daily and located near the Taihu Hotel. Admission is charged.

Grand Canal (*Dayunhe*)

This is the longest human-made waterway in the world at 1,800 kilometers (1,125 miles). It starts in Hangzhou, goes through Beijing, and runs through Suzhou and Wuxi. Construction began in the fifth century B.C., and the canal was finally completed early in the seventh century A.D., providing a major waterway connection between north and south China. Unfortunately, pollution and silting have damaged this waterway over the years. Wuxi is one of the best places to view the Grand Canal, especially from the bridges on Renmin Xilu and Liangxi Lu.

Shanghai (*Shanghai*)

Starting out nearly 6,000 years ago as a small fishing village, Shanghai is now the second largest city in the world and the largest city in China. Its key location near the Yangtze and Huangpu Rivers has enabled Shanghai to be one of the country's major ports, trading in opium, silk, and tea. A busy industrial city, Shanghai is also known for its shopping and has emerged as a major financial center during the past two decades of economic liberalization. A strong focus on economic development began in 1990 with plans to improve Pudong, along the Huangpu River. Shanghai is a modern, thriving city, and neither Beijing nor Guangzhou can keep pace with its fast-growing economy. Shanghai itself is extensive (6,200 square kilometers [2,400 square miles]) but the inner city is moderate in size. The island of Chongming, the second-largest island in China (third, if you count Taiwan) is included within the city area. There are two main areas in Shanghai: Pudong, which lies east of the Huangpu River; and Puxi, which is west of the river. Most of the tourist attractions are in Puxi, where visitors will find hotels, shopping areas, and the Bund.

Places to Visit Around the Bund

The Bund (*Waitan*) and Nanjing Road (*Nanjing Lu*)

The Bund (an Anglo-Indian word meaning "embankment") is a fancy riverside boardwalk and an important symbol of Shanghai's bygone colonial era. After the British seized China in 1842, Shanghai's doors were soon opened to foreign trade. Many foreigners chose to settle in this area, building commercial buildings, homes, and churches with western style and appeal. On Zhongshan Dong Road, many buildings from the 1920s and 30s still remain, used for a variety of commercial ventures. Huangpu Park stands at the northern end of this impressive quay. Formerly the Municipal Gardens and built by the British, the park once displayed this notorious sign: "No Dogs and Chinese Allowed." Today, everyone is welcome from 5:00 A.M. to 10:00 P.M. daily. Other areas of interest on the Bund are the Bank of China and the Shanghai Municipal Museum.

Nanjing Road is busy with tourists shopping in numerous stores, from designer-label outlets to electronic showrooms. An escape from all the frenzy of Shanghai's busy streets can be found in Renmin (People's) Park (*Renmin Gongyuan*). Its lush greenery and tranquil ponds are enjoyed by Shanghai residents and tourists alike. Next to the park is Renmin Square (Renmin Guangchang), a massive structure of concrete built in 1951, basically for Communist parades. Today, people use it as a meeting place or for kite flying. Located in Renmin Square is the Shanghai Museum, (*Shanghai Bowuguan*) which houses an interesting collection of historical artifacts and dioramas. Some objects on display include paintings, porcelain, costumes, and tomb relics dating back to the prehistoric era.

Places to Visit in and Around Shanghai

Hongkou Park

Taking the Sichuan Bei Road out of the city, visitors can reach Shanghai's largest park, where tai chi exercises are conducted most mornings. The heart of the park is a lake, and grounds are filled with pavilions, gardens, and bridges, as well as two noted monuments honoring Lu Xun, a Chinese writer. The park is open daily and charges admission.

Lu Xun Museum and Lu Xun Tomb (*Lu Xun Bowuguan and Lu Xun Ling*)

An important Chinese writer, Lu Xun's (1881–1936) ideas were democratic and modern. He is honored in a museum, and his tomb is open to the public. Although they are part of Hongkou Park, visiting hours vary for the tomb and museum.

Jade Buddha Temple (*Yufu Si*)

Once located on the southern edge of the city, this temple has a 1.9-meter (6-foot) high jade Buddha located on the second floor of the main pavilion. It was sculpted from one piece of white jade, brought from Burma to China in 1882, and finally moved to its present location in 1918. Located off Anyuan Road, the temple complex is open daily and charges admission.

Longhua Temple and Pagoda (*Longhua Si and Longhua Ta*)

Built by the Emperor Sun Quan, this seven-story tower was built in A.D. 247 in honor of the emperor's mother. Reconstructed in 977, this monument is one of the best of its type in China. Located in the southern area of the suburbs, off Longhua Road, it is open daily. Admission is charged.

Shanghai Zoo (*Shanghai Dongwuyuan*)

This well-kept zoo has more than 280 different kinds of animals to view. It is located on Hongqiao Road near the Shanghai Airport. The zoo is closed on Tuesdays, and admission is charged.

Site of the First National Congress of the Communist Party of China (*Zhonggong Yidahuizhi*)

In July 1921, the Communist Party of China was inaugurated in this house, with Mao Zedong as one of the 12 representatives. The site's schedule varies, so visitors should call ahead (021-328-1177). Admission is charged.

Sun Yat-sen's Residence (*Sun Zhongshan Guju*)

Chinese-Canadians bought this house for Sun Yat-sen, where he lived from 1921 to 1924. Mementos are displayed throughout the residence, which is still furnished in 1920s decor. Located on Xiangshan Road, it is closed on Sundays. Admission is charged.

Frenchtown (*Faguo Zujei*)

The area that was once the French concession is now located near Huaihi Lu and the Jinjiang Hotel. Colorful flower boxes line the streets, bordered with all types of stores and boutiques. South off Yan'an Lu, visitors can see period architecture at its best and what Frenchtown was like in old Shanghai.

Shanghai Exhibition Center

Local industrial products and some heavy machinery are displayed here amid rough, unpolished architecture, in Bolshevik style.

Huangpu River Trip (*Huangpu Jiang Youlan Chuan*)

Shanghai is one of the world's major ports, and tour boats along the Huangpu River pass many freighters, sampans, junks, and navy vessels. Unfortunately, the river has become quite polluted over the years, but the views and the liveliness of the waterfront are still fascinating, and the three-and-a-half–hour trip begins from a dock on the Bund near Huangpu Park. The trip provides good opportunity for photographs, but it is forbidden to photograph Chinese navy vessels.

Yuyuan Gardens and Bazaar (*Yuyuan Shangsha*)

Also known as Mandarin Gardens and Bazaar, there are two sections to this popular attraction in Shanghai. The elegant Yuyuan Gardens date back to 1577, when Ming dynasty officials founded them. Rebellions and wars caused serious damage to them throughout the years, but the gardens have been carefully restored. They are filled with a number of colorful pavilions and pools, along with bridges, rock gardens, and more.

The Bazaar is a shopper's paradise but very crowded. The Huxington Teahouse, located on the lake can be reached only by a very crooked bridge (a legend says that evil spirits travel on only straight paths). Open daily, these attractions are best visited during the week to avoid weekend crowds. Located on Yuyuan Road, the sites charge admission.

Shaanxi and Xi'an

Xi'an is the capital of Shaanxi Province in northwestern China. Xi'an served as the capital for 73 emperors of 11 dynasties for more than 1,000 years. Xi'an is noted for its wealth of antiquities, cultural relics, and art treasures. The army of terra-cotta warriors in Xi'an has been called "the Eighth Wonder of the World." Among the other treasures in Xi'an are the Big Wild Goose Pagoda, the Small Wild Goose Pagoda, the forest of Steles, the Bell Tower, and the Drum Tower, to name a few.

Places to Visit in and Around Shaanxi

Army of Terry-Cotta Warriors/Qin Terra-Cotta Army Museum (*Qin Bingmayong Bowuguan*)

Built between 247 B.C. and 211 B.C., the tomb of the first emperor of the Qin dynasty (Qin Shi Huang Di) is located in Lintong County near Xi'an. This fascinating archaeological discovery was unearthed in 1974 when peasants digging for a well uncovered an underground vault full of terra-cotta soldiers. East of the Tomb, three soldier-and-horse digs have been discovered since 1974, and opened to the public since October 1, 1979. Among the three digs, Dig 1 occupies an area of 14,260 square meters (153,437 square ft) and has about 6,000 life-size terra-cotta warriors and horses arranged regularly into rows and columns. They make up a neat formation with a grand air as if on a march, representing the powerful army of China's first emperor.

The warriors and horses were made of clay and then went through a burning process. The human figures represent generals, low-ranking officers, and soldiers of the infantry and cavalry. The facial features of the soldiers display divergence of character: some brave and staunch, some simple and honest, some clever and witty, others cheerful and good-humored. Together, they make up one of the world's finest groups of sculpted figures unparalleled both for scale and excellence of workmanship. Located about 40 kilometers (25 miles) northeast of Xi'an, the museum is open daily and charges admission.

Big Wild Goose Pagoda (*Da Yan Ta*)

Dating back to the seventh century, this pagoda is interesting to climb. Originally built by Emperor Gaozong in memory of his mother, it stands 64 meters (211 feet) high and provides good views of Xi'an from the top.

Small Wild Goose Pagoda (*Xiao Yan Ta*)

A smaller version of the pagoda described above, this monument lost two stories in an earthquake during the 1500s and now stands 43 meters (142 feet) high. Open daily, it is located south of Nanmen Gate, off Youyi Road. Admission is charged.

Shaanxi Historical Museum (*Shanxi Lishi Bowuguan*)

In a fairly modern building, this museum houses various artifacts from Shaanxi's history, particularly around Xi'an. One of the best museums in China, its collection dates back to China's prehistory, beginning with the Palaeolithic Langtian man. Open daily, it is located near the Big Wild Goose Pagoda, off Xiaozhai Road. Admission is charged.

Shaanxi Provincial Museum (*Shanxi Sheng Bowuguan*)

Formerly the temple of Confucius, this museum displays objects focusing on the history of the Silk Road. Also exhibited here is The Forest of Steles, a collection of 2,300 tablets, said to be the heaviest books in the world, some dating back to the Han dynasty. Tablets include the 114 Stone Classics of Kaichen, recording historical accounts of the Tang dynasty. Many of the prominent displays have English labels. Open daily, there is an admission charge for foreigners.

Drum Tower (*Gu Lou*)

Located in the center of Xi'an's old Muslim quarter, this historical monument was used to announce the opening and closing of the city gates.

Bell Tower (*Zhong Lu*)

Just south of the Drum Tower, this massive structure was originally built in the late fourteenth century and rebuilt and moved to its present location in 1739. The bell was used to announce the time of day.

City Walls (*Chengqiang*)

The city walls in Xi'an are among the few remaining in all of China. These walls were constructed on the foundation of the Tang Forbidden City walls during the Ming dynasty. Some sections of the walls have vanished, but others have been restored or rebuilt. One of the main entrance gates is South Gate (Nanmen), near the Provincial Museum. Admission is charged.

Great Mosque (*Da Qingzhensi*)

One of the biggest mosques in China, the present building dates back to the 1700s. Located northwest of the Drum Tower, this is an active house of worship, with prayer services daily. There is an admission fee to see the courtyard, but only Muslims may enter the mosque. There is a total of 15 mosques in Xi'an for the city's Muslim minority, totaling about 60,000. Much of the Muslim quarter has retained its original flavor. Its back streets are lined with mud-brick homes, and it's common to see older bearded men wearing white skull-caps.

Distant China (Lhasa, Tibet, and Inner Mongolia)

Tibet is known as the "Roof of the World," with snow-capped mountains and some of the highest plateaus on the globe. Its mountain scenery and unique culture make Lhasa, the capital of Tibet, an exotic place to visit. Tibet has been part of China since the 1950s and it has an extreme climate, especially during the winter when sudden storms bring on snows, and temperatures drop to -40 degrees Fahrenheit.

Inner Mongolia (*Nei Menggu*) is an autonomous area of China. Most of the Mongolian horsemen of the grasslands are now a thing of the past, except when they perform for tourists. The capital of Inner Mongolia is Hohhot, and organized tours are available to see the grasslands.

Places to Visit in Tibet

Lhasa and the Potala Palace

Lhasa is located 3,650 meters (11,972 feet) above sea level on the Tibetan plateau. The sacred city has a history dating back more than 1,400 years. The Potala Palace (*Budala Gong*) occupies 41 hectares (101 acres) on a mountainside and is the largest and most notable architectural monument in the region. The palace was built more than 1,300 years ago for Princess Wencheng of Tang, who married Prince Songzanganbu. The 1,000-room palace was named Potala, a holy place of Buddhism. The palace that visitors see today was reconstructed by the fifth Dalai in 1645. Since then, it has served as the holy residence of the successive Dalai Lamas.

The Jokhank Temple (*Juglaking*)

This is the most significant Buddhist temple in Tibet, where visitors will see many pilgrims stretched out in devotion. Photos may be taken. The Great Prayer Festival is held here each year from the third to the twenty-fifth in the first month of the Tibetan calendar.

Sera Monastery

Located in the northern suburbs, this place of worship was built in 1419. It is one of the four main monasteries in Tibet and housed 10,000 lamas and monks at one point. Today, about 500 monks live here. There is an interesting gold statue of the Goddess of Mercy located on the grounds.

Drepung Monastery (*Daipung*)

About 600 monks live here today, but the building once housed 10,000 monks and lamas. A white conch and a gilded Buddha are on display in this monastery, one of the four main ones in Tibet.

Norbulingka Park

Once a summer home of the Dalai Lamas, this 370-room mansion has a 100-acre garden for tourists to view. The first building, Kalsang Podang, was built in 1755, and its rooms contain many murals and statues.

Royal Tibetan Tombs

Located in Lhoka (Shannan) prefecture, about 180 kilometers (108 miles) southeast of Lhasa, these tombs date from the seventh century.

Treks

Many travel/tour agencies offer excursions through the mountains of Tibet. The best months to do so are either June–July or September–October. Heavy rains and possible landslides occur in August.

Places to Visit in Inner Mongolia

An interesting attraction in Hohhot is the Inner Mongolia Museum (*Nei Menggu Bowuguan*) which houses a collection of objects depicting the traditional culture of the Mongolian people. Also of interest is the Great Mosque, (*Qingzhen Da Si*) located within the city, which dates back to the Ming dynasty. Near it is the Five Pagoda Temple (*Wuta Si*). A fairly new building, the Genghis Khan Mausoleum (*Chengji Sihan Lingyuan*) is near Dongsheng and contains some elegant pavilions.

6. Schedule of Major Holidays, Festivals, and Annual Cultural Events

Month	Location	Event name and date	Description	Special comments
January	Throughout China	New Years Day, January 1	Official holiday	
January	Hangzhou, Zhejiang Province	Striking Bells to Welcome the New Year, January 1	On January 1, bells are rung to welcome in the New Year. Other festivities include dragon and lion dances and colorful boats sailing on West Lake, one of China's most popular tourist attractions.	
January	Beijing	Beijing Longqing Gorge Ice and Snow Festivities	Colorful ice lanterns, fireworks and ice fishing.	
January	Jilin	Jilin Rime Festival, held in early January	People come out each January to decorate lanterns, play in various ice and snow games, enjoy fireworks, and watch a parade of boats and Korean and Manchu dances.	
January	Kaili, Guizhou Province, and Danxi	Lusheng Festival, usually occurs in January, from the 11th through the 18th day of the first lunar month	About 30,000 people attend this affair to celebrate the reed instrument used by the Miao people, named the lusheng. Many participants play the instrument and dance, but bull fighting and horse racing are also part of the event.	In Kaili, there are more than 100 small festivals each year.

Month	Location	Event name and date	Description	Special comments
January	Xiahe County, Gansu Province	Buddhist Assembly in the Labrang Monastery, from the fourth to the seventeenth on the first lunar month (also from the 29th day of the sixth lunar month to the 15th day of the seventh lunar month)	The Labrang Monastery is one of the six main monasteries of the Gelug sect of Tibetan Buddhism. Each year seven large Buddhist assemblies are held in this monastery. Activities include displays of images of Buddha, religious dances, prayer, chants of scriptures, etc. A month-long Tibetan Travel Festival is also held here.	
January/ February	Macao	Chinese Lunar New Year, in January or early February	This three-day event is considered a public holiday in some provinces.	
January/ February	Harbin, Heilongjiang Province	Harbin Ice and Snow Festival	People celebrate by carving huge ice sculptures and decorating them with festive lanterns. These creations stand in the city square and along the river, where people enjoy winter swimming, hockey, skiing, and folk ceremonies performed on ice. A film festival is also held.	
January/ February	Macao	Lantern Festival	Residents make, decorate, and display colorful lanterns that they parade through the streets after dark.	

Month	Location	Event name and date	Description	Special comments
January/ February	Throughout China	Spring Festival (also called Chinese New Year), usually in February, but the holiday always occurs on the first day of the first lunar month.	Official holiday. Festivities last for three days, but residents as well as visitors may carry out the celebration for a week.	
January/ February	Guangzhou, Guangdong Province	Spring Festival Flower Fair, on the 28th to the 30th of the 12th lunar month.	The Flower Fair is held during the Spring Festival. This is a traditional cultural activity unique to Guangzhou citizens. Massive amounts of fresh flowers are displayed along the city's main streets. Flowers are for viewing and are also available for sale.	
February	Throughout many Chinese provinces	Lantern Festival (yuánxiao jie), on the 15th day of the first moon.	During this colorful celebration, people parade through the streets at night with an array of lanterns made of paper, silk, and bamboo, as well as porcelain dragons and glass peacocks.	
February	Xishuang-banna region of Yunnan	Tanpa Festival	Young boys visit local temples for the initiation of young monks.	
February/ March	Xishuang-banna region of Yunnan	Tan Jing Festival	A Dai festival honors Buddhist writings housed in local temples.	

Month	Location	Event name and date	Description	Special comments
February/ March	Zigong, Sichuan Province	Lantern Festival	Dating back to the Tang dynasty, this festival displays samples of several thousand festive Chinese lanterns, in addition to more than 100 collections. Dragons made of porcelain, dinner sets, and peacocks made of glass, bamboo, silk, or paper are also on display. Trade fairs and commodity exhibitions are also held during this event.	
March	Throughout China	International Working Women's Day, March 8	Official holiday	
March	Shanghai	Shanghai Marathon Cup	This race is one of the most popular sporting events in China. Runners compete from many parts of the world.	
March/ April	Throughout China	Guanyin's birthday, celebrated on the 19th day of the second moon.	Many residents and tourists visit Daoist temples as this festival falls on the birthday of the bodhisattva Guanyin, often loosely referred to as "the Buddhist goddess of mercy."	
April	Island of Hainan	Hainan International Coconut Festival, occurs in early April	Lantern festivals, dragon boat races, and martial arts contests, in addition to Miao and Li ceremonies.	

Month	Location	Event name and date	Description	Special comments
April	Island of Hainan	Third Day of the Third Lunar Month. Depending on the lunar cycle, this festival is usually celebrated in early April.	Li people compete in archery contests. There are also singing performances and bamboo dancing.	
April	Dali, southern Yunnan Province	Third Moon Fair (sanyue jie). The festivities begin on the 15th day of the third lunar month (most likely in April), and end on the 21st day.	To honor the bodhisattva Guanyin, often loosely called "the Buddhist goddess of mercy," residents from Yunnan crowd the streets to buy, sell, and celebrate on the occasion.	
April	Qintong and Yangzhou, Jiangsu Province	Dragon Boat Festival (duanwu jie), celebrated in early April	To protest corruption in government, a statesman named Qu Yuan killed himself by drowning in the Milo River (in Hunan) in 295 B.C. As a remembrance, people enjoy boat races, operas, and colorful lion and dragon dances.	
April	Guangzhou, Guangdong Province	International Trade Fair or Chinese Export Fair, lasts for 20 days during the months of April and October	More than 35 million business visitors walk through crowded streets during this two-week, semi-annual event. An invitation is required to attend the affair, highlighting Chinese export products.	The entire region is very hectic during April and October, with traffic jams, crowded restaurants, etc. If visitors plan an overnight stay, it is wise to reserve a hotel room several months in advance.
April	Qianxi and Dafang Counties, Guizhou Province	Guizhou Azalea Festival, the month of April	People celebrate with bonfires and minority folk dances. Many tourists visit the Huangguoshu Waterfall (the highest falls in China).	

Month	Location	Event name and date	Description	Special comments
April	Yunnan Province	Three Temples Festival (raosanling)	Tourists and residents visit three temples over a three-day period. The walk begins from Dali's South Gate and goes to the Xizhou Shenguan Temple at the base of Mt. Wutai. After dancing and singing throughout the night, the participants move to the Jingui Temple on the shores of Er Hai Lake as dawn arrives. On the last day, walkers head back to Dali and pass by the Majiuyi Temple.	
April	Throughout China	Tomb Sweep Day (qing ming jie) April 5 in most years, April 4 in a leap year.	To honor ancestors, people visit grave sites of departed loved ones to clean the area and place flowers at the sites. Some burn "ghost money" while worshiping the dead.	
April	Xishuangbanna region, Yunnan Province	Water-Splashing Festival (po shui jie), in mid-April	At the end of a three-day celebration, participants cleanse their souls to remove demons and sorrow from the previous year. The first day features a giant market with items for sale; the second day has dragon-boat races and rocket launchings. On the third day, there is water splashing that promises to bring good luck to those drenched in wetness.	

Month	Location	Event name and date	Description	Special comments
April	Luoyang	Peony Fair, lasts throughout the entire month	More than 350 varieties of peonies are exhibited in honor of the first flower grown in China 1,400 years ago. In addition to live flowers, lanterns, paintings, calligraphy, and photographs of the peony are also on display.	
April	Xi'an	Chang'an Annual International Calligraphy Meeting, occurs at the end of April	Local and international calligraphers exhibit their work, speak about four treasures, and visit historic carved stones.	
April	Weifang, Shandong Province	Weifang International Kite Festival, end of April	Participants enjoy tours of the Kite Museum, kite contests, and demonstrations.	
April	Shanghai	Shanghai International Tea Festival, end of April	Different varieties of teas are exhibited and are offered for sale.	
April	Nanning or Liuzhou, Guangxi Province	Guangxi International Folk Song Festival, throughout the month	This festival includes folk songs, contests, and a large fair.	
April/May	Daoist temples in coastal areas throughout China	Mazu's birthday (mazu shengri) occurs on the twenty-third day of the third moon	People celebrate Mazu's birthday, goddess of the sea. In Guangdong Province, Mazu's name is Tianhou, and in Hong Kong, it's "Tin Hau."	
May	Throughout China	International Labor Day, May 1	Official holiday. This is celebrated as a worldwide Communist holiday.	

Month	Location	Event name and date	Description	Special comments
May	Throughout China	Youth Day, May 4	Official holiday. This is a remembrance of student demonstrations in Beijing on May 4, 1919, when the Allies in Versailles handed over Germany's rights to the Japanese in Shandong.	
May	Dalian, Liaoning Province	Dalian Chinese Locust Blossom Festival, toward the end of May	Colorful flowers, folk performances, and a variety of sports are part of this celebration.	
May	Shanghai	Shanghai Music Festival	Various groups perform during this music celebration.	
June	Throughout China	International Children's Day, June 1	Official holiday	
June	Macao	Macao Dragon Boat Festival, early June	In Macao, this is considered a public holiday, celebrated with lively boat races.	
June	Nanning, Guangxi-Zhuang Province of Canton	Dragon Boat Festival, fifth day of the fifth lunar month	To protest corruption in government, a statesman named Chu Yuan killed himself by drowning in the Milo River (in Hunan) in 295 B.C. Dragon boat races on South Lake are held in his memory each year, with crews competing from around the world.	This is a very popular and colorful tourist event.
June/July	Beijing, Guangzhou, Shanghai, Shenzhen, and Zhuhai	Carnivals	Nearly 20 holiday resorts sponsor carnivals during these two summer months, hosting dances, operas, and acrobatic events.	

Month	Location	Event name and date	Description	Special comments
June/July	Daxing, Beijing	Daxing County Watermelon Festival	Festivities include watermelon tasting, folk performances, and visits to local farmers' houses.	
July	Throughout China	Founding of the Chinese Communist Party in Shanghai on July 1, 1921	Official holiday	
July	Yunnan	Torch Festival (huoba jie), usually falls in July but always occurs on the twenty-fourth day of the sixth lunar month	People carry lighted torches through homes and fields. Fireworks and dragon-boat racing may also be part of the celebration.	
July	Shicun and Chuxiong	Torch Festival of Yi Minority, on the twenty-fourth day of the sixth lunar month	Activities include archery competitions, horse races, bull fights, wrestling, bonfires, and dragon-boat racing.	
July	Harbin, Heilongjiang Province	Music Festival, lasts for 12 days	Many types of music are performed at this event.	
July	Xining, Qinghai Province	Double Six Folk Song Fair, early July	Thousands of ethnic musical groups meet to perform a variety of folk songs.	
July	Shanghai	Shanghai Beer Festival, toward the end of the month	A beer-tasting festival.	
July/ August	Taibuai, part of Wutai County, Shanxi Province	Mt. Wutai International Tourist Month, July 25– August 25	Participants enjoy a mule and horse fair, folk entertainment, and various Buddhist activities.	
July/ August	Jiayuguan Pass, Gansu Province	Jiayuguan Pass International Hang Glider Festival	Hang gliders soar over the Great Wall and the Gobi Desert.	

Month	Location	Event name and date	Description	Special comments
July/ August	Inner Mongolia	Nadam Grassland Tourist Festival, July 15–August 30	Mongolian games, horse races, archery, and wedding ceremonies are all part of the festivities. Another option is to visit the Genghis Khan Mausoleum.	
July/ August	Throughout China	Ghost Month (gui yue), seventh lunar month	Those who have strong religious beliefs feel that this time of the year is very unsettling and unsafe; people should not travel, marry, move, etc. If someone passes away, the body is embalmed and the burial delayed until the following month.	The Chinese government does not approve of this month-long event, discouraging residents as well as tourists from participating.
July/ August	Zunyi's Shizhang Caves, Guizhou Province	China Guizhou Famous Liquor and Wine Festival	Activities include touring the museum of wine and the Maotai brewery. Visitors may also visit caves and numerous waterfalls located in the area.	
August	Throughout China	Anniversary of the Founding of the People's Liberation Army (PLA), August 1	This official holiday recognizes the founding of the PLA, beginning at Nanchang, Jiangxi, in August 1927.	
August	Turfan, Xinjiang	Xinjiang Grape Festival, late August	Uighur minority ceremonies and dances, hami melon contests, and tours of the vineyards are part of this festival.	
August	Nagqu, Tibet	Tibetan Horse Race Festival, late August	Horse races, mounted archery, and horsemanship are all part of this annual event.	
August	Changchun, Jilin Province	China Changchun International Film Festival, late August	Chinese as well as foreign films are shown and critiqued.	

Month	Location	Event name and date	Description	Special comments
August	Qingdao, Shandong Province	Qingdao International Beer Festival, mid-August	Visitors enjoy a beer-tasting fair, with fireworks, fashion shows, and sports contests.	
August	Jinhua, Anhui Province	Temple Fair, mid-August	This fair includes Buddhist ceremonies and a symposium, along with a produce fair.	
August	Lhasa, Tibet	Tibetan Shoton Festival	Various Buddhist images are on display. People perform in operas and participate in yogurt banquets.	
August–October	Beijing, Shanghai, and Guangzhou	Shopping festivals	Local, as well as foreign, orchestras perform symphony concerts. They are held in the Forbidden City, Temple of Heaven, the Summer Palace, and on the Great Wall.	
September	Xi'an, Shaanxi Province	Xi'an Ancient Culture Art Festival	Numerous exhibitions, folk performances, and a large trade fair are part of this cultural fair.	
September	Yangguan, Hangzhou, Zhejiang Province	International Qiantang River Tide-Observing Festival	Residents and tourists watch water reverse and move swiftly upriver.	
September	Zhengzhou, Henan Province	Zhengzhou International Shaolin Martial Arts Festival	This festival includes martial arts demonstrations and contests, along with folk art displays.	
September	Dalian, Liaoning Province	Dalian International Fashion Festival	Fashion shows, a design competition, various exhibits, and a trade fair are part of this festival.	

Month	Location	Event name and date	Description	Special comments
September	Zhangiajie, Hunan Province	Zhangjiajie International Forest Festival, mid-September	This celebration includes white-water rafting, rock climbing, and nature trail walks.	
September	Chengdu, Sichuan Province	Chengdu International Panda Festival, late September	A symposium on panda conservation includes trips to the nearby Wolong Nature Reserve.	
September	Shandong Province	Birthday of Confucius (kongzi shengri), September 28 each year (different date in leap year)	In honor of the Chinese philosopher, the birthplace of Confucius, Shandong hosts an annual ceremony at the temple beginning at 4 P.M.	Making accommodations in advance is highly recommended, as most hotels in the area are solidly booked for this event.
September	Suzhou, Jiangsu Province	Suzhou Silk Tournament Festival, late September	Various silk exhibitions and trade talks are included in this festival.	
September	Shanghai	Shanghai Tourist Festival, late September	Residents of Shanghai welcome tourists with a parade of floats, open-air concerts, symposiums, and a tea cure exchange. They also sponsor "Shanghai Citizen for a Day."	If an overnight stay is planned, it is wise to reserve a hotel room ahead of time.
September/October	Throughout China	Mid-Autumn Festival (zhongqiu jie), also known as the Moon Festival, 15th day of the eighth moon	This is an especially popular holiday for lovers, who stare at the moon, eat moon cakes, and light fireworks.	In Macao, this is considered a public holiday.
September/ October	Shandong Province	Qufu International Confucius Cultural Festival, throughout September and October	Residents and tourists celebrate the birthday of Confucius with ancient music, exhibitions, seminars, and tours of Confucian tombs.	

Month	Location	Event name and date	Description	Special comments
September/October	Guangzhou, Guangdong Province	Chinese Tourist Festival, throughout September and October	This city festival has dancing and stage performances, contests, and shopping tours.	
September/October	Yichang, Hubei Province	Hubei Three Gorges Festival, throughout September and October	Visitors participate in tours conducted through the Three Gorges, cultural exhibitions, and a trade fair.	
September/October	Tianjin	Chinese Beijing Opera Art Festival, every two years in September/October	Foreign and local opera artists perform on stage. The nearby Street of Ancient Culture and Nanshi Food Court are worth visiting.	
October	Throughout China	National Day, October 1	This official holiday commemorates the founding of the People's Republic of China (PRC), in Beijing, October 1949.	
October	Coastal areas throughout China	Fujian Mazu Festival, or Mazu's birthday, early October. The birthday occurs on the twenty-third day of the third moon.	People celebrate Mazu's birthday, goddess of the sea, at Daoist temples in coastal areas throughout China.	
October	Hangzhou, Zhejiang Province	West Lake International Tour Boat Festival, early October	People dress up in traditional costumes and decorate boats docked at West Lake.	
October	Jingdezhen, Jiangxi Province	Jingdezhen International Pottery and Porcelain Festival, mid-October	Browsers see a World Pottery Techniques Competition, pottery and porcelain-making exhibits, contests, and various demonstrations. Many fine crafts are offered for sale.	This is one of China's most popular tourist events.

Month	Location	Event name and date	Description	Special comments
October	Throughout China	Cheung Yeung Festival	This is considered a public holiday in Macao and Hong Kong.	
October	Huangshan, Anhui Province	Huangshan Mountain International Tourist Festival	A lantern festival, tour of the mountains, folk performances, and a trade fair are part of this festival.	
October	Banding, Hubei Province	Banding Health Building Festival for Seniors	Senior citizens join in a number of festivities, including Tai Jii exercises in different parks, visits to Qigong Hospital, the Martial Arts Hall, and Medicine King Temple. A sampling of traditional health foods is also offered.	
October	Guangzhou, Guangdong Province	International Trade Fair or Chinese Export Fair, lasts for 20 days during the months of April and October.	More than 35 million business visitors walk through crowded streets during this two-week, semi-annual event. An invitation is required to attend the affair, highlighting Chinese export products.	The entire region is very hectic during April and October, with traffic jams, crowded restaurants, etc. If visitors plan an overnight stay, it is wise to reserve a hotel room several months in advance.
October/ November	Xishuang-banna region of Yunnan Province	The Tan Ta Festival, late October or early November	Ceremonies are held in various temples, with rocket launchings and hot-air balloons. Amulets within the rockets are released by explosions, and those who find them are assured good luck.	

Month	Location	Event name and date	Description	Special comments
November	Guilin, Guangxi Province	Guilin Scenery Festival	A lantern festival on the Li River, with a bonfire party and traditional songs and dances are the highlights of this festival.	
November	Macao	Macao Grand Prix, two days on the third weekend in November	When this racing event occurs, town streets become the roadway and remain this way for two days.	On short notice, finding accommodations is very difficult. Book well in advance.
December	Macao	Winter Solstice	Although this is not a public holiday in Macao, it is still considered an important time of the year, equal to the Chinese Lunar New Year. There are numerous feasts, and many temples are crowded with worshippers.	

7. USEFUL INFORMATION FOR BUSINESS TRAVELERS

Most Western business ventures in China are located in three cities—Beijing, Guangzhou, and Shanghai. However, throughout the year, some 17 cities host more than 200 trade fairs, congresses, and conventions to promote the purchase and sale of merchandise, from toys to aerospace equipment. Contacting established Chinese banks or business-oriented organizations is usually advisable when seeking information on economic opportunities in this country. Two key organizations are the China Council for the Promotion of International Trade (CCPIT) and the China Chamber of International Commerce (CCOIC). The former is a national non-government economic and trade organization, established more than 45 years ago. It has local branches throughout China and 16 representative offices overseas. Their Web site is *www.ccpit.org*.

The China National Tourism Administration (CNTA) works under the State Council, China's cabinet. The administration controls tourism throughout China by monitoring the quality and prices of accommodations, eating establishments, and some travel agencies. Tourists may contact the administration with complaints about travel accommodations made abroad:

CNTA
9A, Jianguomenei Ave
Beijing 100740
China
Phone: (86) 10-6513-8866
Fax: (86) 10-6512-2096
www.cnta.com

Joint business ventures with China are handled through the Ministry of Foreign Trade and Economic Cooperation

(MOFTEC). There are an increasing number of opportunities available for private companies. The ministry can be reached at:

MOFTEC
2 Dong Chang'anjie
Beijing, 100731
China
Phone: (86) 010-512-6644
Fax: (86) 010-512-9214/9327
www.moftec.gov.cn

Two useful guides for businesspeople are *China Business Guide* and a yearly *Guide to Fairs and Promotions in China*. Another helpful information source is *Trade Promotion*—a business newsletter written in English that reports current news items on China's foreign trade and economy. Read in more than 80 countries, it was established in 1987 and is published every two weeks. All of these are available via mail from the following address:

Head Office, Bank of China
Account #50180652
410 Fuchengmennei Street, Xicheng District
Beijing 100818
China
Account Unit: China Council for the Promotion of International Trade
Phone: (86) 010-6601-6688
Fax: (86) 010-6601-6869

Another useful guide for business tourists is the annual *Directory of China's Foreign Trade*, with more than 9,000 entries that include foreign trade import and export companies, self-employment operations, and export commodities manufacturers. Cost is about $90 U.S. (varies from year to year) and may be ordered through:

CCPIT Building
Directory of China's Foreign Trade
Attention: Ms. Yang Haiqing
1 Fuxingmenwai Street
Beijing 100860
China
Phone: (86) 010-685-13344 ext. 8625
Fax (86) 010-68510201

Other useful names and addresses include the following:

In Beijing

China Investment Bank
Fuxing Road
Beijing 100818
China
Phone: (86) 010-851-5868

Head Office, Bank of China
410 Fuchengmennei Street, Xicheng District
Beijing 100818
China
Phone: (86) 010-6601-6688
Fax: (86) 010-6601-6869

China Economic Development Corporation
93 Beiheyan Avenue
Beijing 100818
China
Phone: (86) 010-554-231

China International Trust & Investment Corporation (CITIC)
19 Jiangguomen Wai Avenue
Beijing 100818
China
Phone: (86) 010-500-2255

China Council for the Promotion of International Trade (CCPIT)
No #1 Fuxingmenwai Street
Beijing
China 100860
Phone: (86) 010-68013344
Fax: (86) 010-68030747
E-mail: *ccpitweb@public.bta.net.cn*

In Guangzhou

Bank of China
120 Liu Hua Road
Guangzhou 510133
China
Phone: (86) 020-666-9900; ext. 1161

External Economic Information Consultancy & Service
120 Liu Hua Road
Guangzhou 510133
China
Phone: (86) 020-666-9900 ext. 1112

Guangzhou Administrative Bureau for Industry and Commerce
120 Liu Hua Road
Guangzhou 510133
China

Phone: (86) 020-666-9900 ext. 1112

Guangzhou Economic & Technical Development Office
120 Liu Hua Road
Guangzhou 510133
China
Phone: (86) 020-666-9900 ext. 1123

Guangzhou Foreign Trade Corporation
120 Liu Hua Road
Guangzhou 510133
China
Phone: (86) 020-666-9900 ext. 1123

In Shanghai

China Council for the Promotion of International Trade (CCPIT)
27 Zhongshan Dong Road
Shanghai 200031
China
Phone: (86) 021-210-7221

Shanghai International Trade Information and Exhibition Corporation
33 Zhongshan Dongyi Road
Shanghai 200031
China
Phone: (86) 021-233-480

U.S. Chamber of Commerce Offices located in China

Main Office in Beijing:
Great Wall Sheraton Hotel
Room 444
North Donghuan Avenue
Beijing 100026
China
Phone: (86) 010 6500-5566 ext. 2271
Fax: (86) 010 6501-8273

Main Office in Shanghai:
1376 Nanjing Xi Lu
Shanghai Centre-Room 435
Shanghai 200040
China

Overseas Representatives (Banks/Organizations) Outside China

United States:

Bank of China

410 Madison Avenue
New York, NY 10017
Phone: 212-935-3101
Fax: 212-593-1831
www.bocusa.com

CCPIT and CCOIC Representative Office in the United States
Suite 136, 4301 Connecticut Avenue, NW
Washington, D.C. 20008
Phone: 202-244-3244
Fax: 202-244-0478
E-mail: *ccpitus@aol.com*

Australia:

CCPIT and CCOIC Representative Office in Australia
Suite 102, 40 Yeo Street
Neutral Bay
N.S.W. 2089 Sydney
Australia
Phone: 61-2-99530677
Fax: 61-2-99530458
E-mail: *ccpitaus@loom.net.au*

Canada:

CCPIT and CCOIC Representative Office in Canada
150 York Street, Suite 908
Toronto, Ontario
Canada M5H3S5
Phone: 416-363-8561/363-0599
Fax: 416-363-0152
E-mail: *ccpit@pathcom.com*

United Kingdom:

CCPIT and CCOIC Representative Office in United Kingdom
40/41 Pall Wall
London SWIY 5JQ
United Kingdom
Phone: 44-171-321044
Fax: 44-171-3212055

Business Etiquette in China

Language barriers may hinder good relationships in any business venture. Few foreigners are fluent in the Chinese languages. Mandarin (or putonghua) is spoken by business leaders and professionals in most parts of China, but 55 other languages and dialects are spoken in

China. Making an attempt to learn the language will impress the Chinese, so business tourists should try to remember certain words and phrases. It will also make visitors' stays much easier.

When meeting possible business acquaintances, first impressions are important. Western habits and styles sometimes seem brash or rude to the Chinese. Westerners should be sensitive to how people react to their style and avoid over-familiarity upon first meeting. Although Chinese people are becoming used to foreign dress and culture, clothing is still conservative, with businesspeople wearing appropriate clothing. Americans often have a very firm handshake, and that should be relaxed a little. Chinese people do not bow when meeting people. A nod or brief handshake is appropriate. People in China frown on touching (poking or slapping someone on the shoulder).

Learning to control feelings, especially anger, is vital. If two parties cannot reach an agreement on a matter, discussion is important. Sometimes, different ethnic backgrounds or a language barrier hinders the solution, and both parties should work together to solve the problem. Getting angry easily about insignificant matters is just not appropriate for a business tourist. Patience is also a key issue, and having a personal touch through words and actions will impress Chinese businesspeople. A courteous demeanor with respectful body language (a friendly smile, correct posture) will make a good impression. Showing superiority or arrogance offends Chinese people's deep-seated cultural pride.

Accepting or giving an apology is important in China. In China, apologizing has nothing to do with who is at fault; it's just good manners and happens frequently. Apologizing for a minor infraction is considered a courteous gesture; keeping a peaceful demeanor portrays good character.

Westerners are known for their humorous anecdotes, but some jokes are difficult to comprehend because of language differences. It's best to avoid telling jokes because the interpretation might turn a funny tale into an offensive story.

If a Western business is required to give a gift to a Chinese company, one useful, practical present for the group is preferred to several small ones to individuals. Personal attention should go into choosing a gift. For example, giving an item of Chinese art or design (a painting, or framed print) shows that a foreign businessperson has some appreciation of Chinese culture. Artwork, books, calculators, or alcoholic beverages are usually acceptable gifts. Never present Chinese people with clocks or shoes, as clock and death are pronounced the same way in Chinese as are shoes and evil. It might be a bad omen to give such gifts. Never present a gift of a sexual nature (including artwork or calendars); most Chinese people might consider such a gift an insult.

Chinese businesspeople appreciate bilingual business cards, with English on one side and Chinese on the other. Correct business titles and pronunciations of names should be noted. Such business cards may be made in China and by reputable printers in the United States and Hong Kong. Western businesspeople should hand out cards to everyone at a group meeting to avoid offending anyone.

Smoking is widespread throughout China; there is no such thing as a "no-smoking zone." In fact, it is inconsiderate to ask someone not to smoke.

Entertaining business acquaintances is common in China. Because private homes may not be large enough to accommodate large groups, banquets are often held for visitors. It is courteous for guests to arrive on time with all members of the party. Banquets are usually several (six to eight) courses, beginning with cold dishes. It's polite for guests to try them all, commenting on each one. Drinking alcohol prior to the start of the banquet is rarely done. When the meal begins and the host offers a toast, it is safe to consume alcoholic beverages. When a visitor is asked to give a toast, one promoting friendship or future success is a safe choice. A good-luck toast may be made to an individual or to the entire party. More than one toast may occur during the meal; it's acceptable to ask for a soft drink or juice to replace an alcoholic beverage. The host or his organization is expected to pay for the entire banquet and may even pay for guests' transportation back to the hotel.

Appendix

CONVERTING FROM PINYIN TO WADE-GILES

Pinyin	Wade-Giles	Pinyin	Wade-Giles	Pinyin	Wade-Giles
a	a	chuang	ch'uang	fo	fo
ai	ai	chui	ch'ui	fou	fou
an	an	chun	ch'un	fu	fu
ang	ang	chuo	ch'o	ga	ka
ao	ao	ci	tz'u	gai	kai
ba	pa	cong	ts'ung	gan	kan
bai	pai	cou	ts'ou	gang	kang
ban	pan	cu	ts'u	gao	kao
bang	pang	cuan	ts'uan	ge	ke, ko
bao	pao	cui	ts'ui	gei	kei
bei	pei	cun	ts'un	gen	ken
ben	pen	cuo	ts'o	geng	keng
beng	peng	da	ta	gong	kung
bi	pi	dai	tai	gou	kuo
bian	pien	dan	tan	gu	ku
biao	piao	dang	tang	gua	kua
bie	pieh	dao	tao	guai	kuai
bin	pin	de	te	guan	kuan
bing	ping	dei	tei	guang	kuang
bo	po	deng	teng	gui	kuei
bou	pou	di	ti	gun	kun
bu	pu	dian	tien	guo	kuo
ca	ts'a	diao	tiao	ha	ha
cai	ts'ai	die	tieh	hai	hai
can	ts'an	ding	ting	han	han
cang	ts'ang	diu	tiu	hang	hang
cao	ts'ao	dong	tung	hao	hao
ce	ts'e	dou	tou	he	he, ho
cen	ts'en	du	tu	hei	hei
ceng	ts'eng	duan	tuan	hen	hen
cha	ch'a	dui	tui	heng	heng
chai	ch'ai	dun	tun	hong	hung
chan	ch'an	duo	to	hou	hou
chang	ch'ang	e	e, o	hu	hu
chao	ch'ao	ei	ei	hua	hua
che	ch'e	en	en	huai	huai
chen	ch'en	eng	eng	huan	huan
cheng	ch'eng	er	erh	huang	huang
chi	ch'ih	fa	fa	hui	hui
chong	ch'ung	fan	fan	hun	hun
chou	ch'ou	fang	fang	huo	huo
chu	ch'u	fei	fei	ji	chi
chuai	ch'uai	fen	fen	jia	chia
chuan	ch'uan	feng	feng	jian	chien

661

Pinyin	Wade-Giles	Pinyin	Wade-Giles	Pinyin	Wade-Giles
jiang	chiang	liu	liu	niu	niu
jiao	chiao	long	lung	nong	nung
jie	chieh	lou	lou	nou	nou
jin	chin	lu	lu	nu	nu
jing	ching	luan	luan	nuan	nuan
jiong	chiung	lun	lun	nun	nun
jiu	chiu	luo	lo	nuo	no
ju	chü	lü	lü	nü	nü
juan	chüan	lüan	lüan	nüe	nüeh
jue	chüeh	lüe	lüeh	ou	ou
jun	chün	ma	ma	pa	p'a
ka	k'a	mai	mai	pai	p'ai
kai	k'ai	man	man	pan	p'an
kan	k'an	mang	mang	pang	p'ang
kang	k'ang	mao	mao	pao	p'ao
kao	k'ao	mei	mei	pei	p'ei
ke	k'o	men	men	pen	p'en
ken	k'en	meng	meng	peng	p'eng
keng	k'eng	mi	mi	pi	p'i
kong	k'ung	mian	mien	pien	p'ien
kou	k'ou	miao	miao	piao	p'iao
ku	k'u	mie	mieh	pie	p'ieh
kua	k'ua	min	min	pin	p'in
kuai	k'uai	ming	ming	ping	p'ing
kuan	k'uan	miu	miu	po	p'o
kuang	k'uang	mo	mo	pou	p'ou
kui	k'uei	mou	mou	pu	p'u
kun	k'un	mu	mu	qi	ch'i
kuo	k'ua	na	na	qia	ch'ia
la	la	nai	nai	qian	ch'ien
lai	lai	nan	nan	qiang	ch'iang
lan	lan	nang	nang	qiao	ch'iao
lang	lang	nao	nao	qie	ch'ieh
lao	lao	ne	ne	qin	ch'in
le	le	nei	nei	qing	ch'ing
lei	lei	nen	nen	qiong	ch'iung
leng	leng	neng	neng	qiu	ch'iu
li	li	ni	ni	qu	ch'ü
lian	lien	nian	nien	quan	ch'üan
liang	liang	niang	niang	que	ch'üeh
liao	liao	niao	niao	qun	ch'ün
lie	lieh	nie	nieh	ran	ran
lin	lin	nin	nin	rang	jang
ling	ling	ning	ning	rao	jao

Pinyin	Wade-Giles	Pinyin	Wade-Giles	Pinyin	Wade-Giles
re	je	sun	sun	xiu	hsiu
ren	jen	suo	so	xu	hsü
reng	jeng	ta	t'a	xuan	hsuan
ri	jih	tai	t'ai	xue	hsüeh
rong	jung	tan	t'an	xun	hsun
rou	jou	tang	t'ang	ya	ya
ru	ju	tao	t'ao	yai	yai
ruan	juan	te	t'e	yan	yen
rui	jui	teng	t'eng	yang	yang
run	jun	ti	t'i	yao	yao
ruo	jo	tian	t'ien	ye	yeh
sa	sa	tiao	t'iao	yi	i
sai	sai	tie	t'ieh	yin	yin
san	san	ting	t'ing	ying	ying
sang	sang	tong	t'ung	yong	yung
sao	sao	tou	t'ou	you	yu
se	se	tu	t'u	yu	yü
sen	sen	tuan	t'uan	yuan	yüan
seng	seng	tui	t'ui	yue	yüeh
sha	sha	tun	t'un	yun	yün
shai	shai	tuo	t'o	za	tsa
shan	shan	tu	t'u	zai	tsai
shang	shang	tuan	t'uan	zan	tsan
shao	shao	tui	t'ui	zang	tsang
she	she	tun	t'un	zao	tsao
shei	shei	tuo	t'o	ze	tse
shen	shen	wa	wa	zei	tsei
sheng	sheng	wai	wai	zen	tsen
shi	shih	wan	wan	zeng	tseng
shou	shou	wang	wang	zha	cha
shu	shu	wei	wei	zhai	chai
shua	shua	wen	wen	zhan	chan
shuai	shuai	weng	weng	zhang	chang
shuan	shuan	wo	wo	zhao	chao
shuang	shuang	wu	wu	zhe	che
shui	shui	xi	hsi	zhei	chei
shun	shun	xia	hsia	zhen	chen
shuo	shuo	xian	hsien	zheng	cheng
si	szu/ssu	xiang	hsiang	zhi	chih
song	sung	xiao	hsiao	zhong	chung
sou	sou	xie	hsieh	zhou	chou
su	su	xin	hsin	zhu	chu
suan	suan	xing	hsing	zhua	chua
sui	sui	xiong	hsiung	zhuai	chuai

Pinyin	Wade-Giles
zhuan	chuan
zhuang	chuang
zhui	chui
zhun	chun
zhuo	cho
zi	tzu
zong	tsung
zou	tsou
zu	tsu
zuan	tsuan
zui	tsui
zun	tsun
zuo	tso

Modern

and Its Neighboring

RUSSIAN

Astana •

KAZAKHSTAN

Caspian Sea

Alma Ata ○

AZERBAIJAN **UZBEKISTAN** Tashkent • Bishkek • **KYRGYZSTAN**

• Baku

TURKMENISTAN **TAJIKISTAN**

Ashgabat • Dushanbe •

ARMENIA • Tehrān Jammu and Kashmir **C H I**

ISLAMIC REPUBLIC OF IRAN **AFGHANISTAN** Kābul • Kathmandu

Islāmābād **NEPAL** Thimphu

PAKISTAN New Delhi • **BHUTAN**

Persian Gulf Karāchi **BANGLADESH** Dhaka •

Gulf of Oman

INDIA **MYANMAR**

Mumbai ○ ○ Hyderabad Yangon •

Bay of Bengal **Bangkok**

Arabian Sea

Sri Jayawardhanapura-Kotte **SRI LANKA**
MALDIVES

China

Countries

Index